Religious Belief and Philosophical Thought

WILLIAM P. ALSTON

University of Michigan

RELIGIOUS BELIEF AND PHILOSOPHICAL THOUGHT

Readings in the Philosophy of Religion

HARCOURT, BRACE & WORLD, INC.
New York / Burlingame

© 1963 BY HARCOURT, BRACE & WORLD, INC.

Library of Congress Catalog Card Number: 63-13110

Printed in the United States of America

FOR MY MOTHER

PREFACE

This volume is designed for use in courses in the philosophy of religion. There should be ample material here for assigned reading in a one-semester course. The selections are on the average somewhat longer than is customary in books of readings. I have tried to make them of sufficient length to enable the student to form from a single reading a fairly adequate idea of a given position on a given topic. I believe that all of the selections in this volume can be read with profit by a student with no previous preparation in philosophy. Some of them are difficult, and none has been chosen solely on the grounds that it presented certain points in a simple manner. There is no point at which it is easy to begin to study philosophy, but it seems to me that the readings here presented offer a good introduction to the subject. On the other hand, the readings are sufficiently meaty to offer more than enough challenge to students in a course which presupposes several courses in philosophy.

The topics dealt with in this book are those that seem to me to be most significant for a person in our society who is trying to think seriously about religious issues. The section headings do not fall into any neat classificatory scheme, but I am convinced that any attempt to force the material into such a scheme would necessitate either serious deletions of important material or unrealistic labeling, which would give the appearance of symmetry without the substance. The order in which the topics are presented seems natural to me, but I am sure that equally good courses can be given with the topics arranged in other ways. Each of the eight sections is preceded by an introduction that is designed to set forth the complex of problems treated in that section and to indicate how each of the selections contributes to the discussion of those problems, as well as to give some background for the selections and their authors.

The readings have been selected in such a way as to give the clearest and most incisive statement of several positions on each of the topics. No other criteria were consciously employed. In particular, there has been no attempt to cover the history of the philosophy of religion. There has not even been any attempt to give an adequate representation of the most important periods in the history of the subject, though in fact the range in this respect is fairly wide. In general, although there are several selections from well-known earlier philosophical works, preference has been given to relatively recent authors, because I think that, with certain exceptions, they present the issues in terms which are more meaningful to contemporary students.

Within most of the sections, the spread of readings reflects the opposition between theism and naturalism, which I take to be the basic philosophical alternatives confronting anyone thinking about religion today. (Section 6, on Faith, where naturalism is not represented, and Section 8, which is solely devoted to alternatives to theism, are exceptions.) Thus Section 1 presents theistic arguments for the existence of God and (more or less) naturalistic criticisms of these arguments; Section 2 presents theistic claims for the cognitive status of religious experience and naturalistic criticisms of these claims, and so on. It would be difficult to set some readings on either side of this divide; for example, in the selections from Kierkegaard and Tillich we find pro-Christian positions that are very different from traditional theism. But the theism-naturalism opposition provides a basic ground-plan.

The general introduction discusses the conception of the philosophy of religion which underlies this volume and the way in which the various sections of the book are designed to fit into that conception.

I should like to express gratitude to William A. Christian of Yale University, John Hick of the Princeton Theological Seminary, and Alvin Plantinga of Wayne State University for their helpful suggestions and criticisms with respect to the choice of readings. My grasp of the issues in the philosophy of religion has been greatly strengthened by discussions over many years with a number of people, among whom I should especially like to mention Henry Aiken, Virgil Aldrich, Roderick Firth, John Hick, George Nakhnikian, Nelson Pike, Alvin Plantinga, and Paul Ziff. Finally, I wish to thank my students over the years at the University of Michigan for reacting in various ways to my teaching of the philosophy of religion, and thus helping me to see what such a course might usefully be.

WILLIAM P. ALSTON

Ann Arbor, Michigan
February 1963

CONTENTS

2.

RELIGIOUS EXPERIENCE   117

3.

4.

5.

REVELATION   389

6.

FAITH   429

INTRODUCTION:

RELIGION AND THE PHILOSOPHY OF RELIGION

In view of the enormous variety of topics and problems to be found in works on the philosophy of religion, the only safe way to characterize this subject is to say that it is what philosophers do when they think about religion. But this is to purchase safety at too high a price. Something should be said which will be illuminating to those not already familiar with what philosophers do at such times.

There are a great many branches of philosophy which are termed "philosophy of ———": of science, of history, of education, of art, of mind, even of intercollegiate athletics and of investment. When the philosopher, as contrasted with other specialists, turns his attention to one of these areas, what he does can be usefully summarized under four headings: formulation, clarification, integration, and evaluation. These classifications can be briefly explained as follows: Formulation and clarification are really inseparable aspects of the same enterprise. The philosopher typically seeks to make explicit the basic concepts, assumptions, and modes of reasoning of whatever area he is dealing with (formulation), and in doing so he attempts to give as clear and precise a formulation as possible,

1

thus removing certain confusions and perplexities with which thinking in and about the area is often plagued (clarification). Thus the philosopher of science will seek to set out as clearly as possible some of the basic concepts employed in science, such as explanation, law of nature, evidence, confirmation, and some of the basic principles which seem to be ingredient in the scientific enterprise, such as the principle that every event is causally determined. As for integration, one of the most common goads to philosophical thinking is the tension engendered by conflicting, or apparently conflicting, beliefs held in different areas of our thought and experience. When this sort of tension develops, it is for philosophy, which here can be simply equated with reflective thought not bound to any particular subject matter, to bring about some sort of unification. This may be brought about by handing down a judgment for one or the other side, by effecting some sort of compromise, or by showing that the conflict is apparent rather than real. The problem of free will is perhaps the best-known example: the problem arises because of what seems to be a conflict between our common-sense belief that we are often able to choose any one of a number of alternatives in a given situation and the scientific assumption that everything that happens, including human choices and human actions, is uniquely determined to happen in just that way by causal factors.

Finally, philosophy has always been an evaluative activity. Philosophers have always asked questions concerning the worth, validity, or justifiability of whatever they were considering—whether moral standards, common-sense knowledge of physical objects, scientific knowledge, or religious faith. There are those (from the camp of so-called analytical philosophers, but hardly representative of that group) who seem to want to limit philosophy to the first three tasks and to abjure the evaluative enterprise. But it is doubtful that this is more than a verbal (or academic administrative) issue, for presumably reflective men will always feel a need to raise fundamental questions of justification and validity with respect to various sorts of claims to knowledge, standards, and so on, and there seems to be no reason not to call such activity "philosophy."

Before we can fully grasp the form these activities take when they are directed onto religion, we shall have to sharpen our understanding of the nature of religion itself. For what the philosopher of religion is going to be doing depends, at least in part, on what religion is. And this means that we must begin by formulating and clarifying the concept of religion.

A survey of various attempts to state the nature of religion reveals a confused picture. Consider the following examples.

1. Religion is the belief in an ever living God, that is, in a Divine Mind and Will ruling the Universe and holding moral relations with mankind.
   —JAMES MARTINEAU

2. By religion, then, I understand a propitiation or conciliation of powers superior to man which are believed to direct and control the course of Nature and of human life.
   —J. G. FRAZER

3. Religion is rather the attempt to express the complete reality of goodness through every aspect of our being.
   —F. H. BRADLEY

4. Religion is ethics heightened, enkindled, lit up by feeling.
—MATTHEW ARNOLD

5. Religion is, in truth, that pure and reverential disposition or frame of mind which we call piety.
—C. P. TIELE

6. The essence of religion consists in the feeling of an absolute dependence.
—FRIEDRICH SCHLEIERMACHER

7. A man's religion is the expression of his ultimate attitude to the universe, the summed-up meaning and purport of his whole consciousness of things.
—EDWARD CAIRD

These examples give us a fair idea of the range of attempts to define religion. Now it is not difficult to subject all these formulations to devastating criticism. As for the first, there are, of course, many religions in which no such belief figures. No polytheism recognizes a single Divine Mind and Will ruling the Universe; and in some forms of Buddhism there is no recognition of a personal deity of any kind. With respect to the third and fourth examples, we can cite certain primitive communities in which there is no significant connection between the system of rites directed to the gods, which would normally be called the religion of the culture, and the moral code. The latter simply rests on tribal precedent and is not thought of as either originating with the gods or sanctioned by them. This is an unusual, but not impossible, state of affairs. And at the other end of the scale we have extreme mystical sects in which the aim for an immediate union with God crowds out any real concern for morality. As for the fifth and sixth, it seems impossible to find any particular feeling which is characteristic of religion and only of religion. If, for example, we take "absolute dependence" strictly it would seem to be present only in something like a strict monotheism. And if we do not insist on *absolute* dependence, we can find weaker forms of dependence in non-religious contexts. A man might feel considerable dependence on his boss, his wife, or the weather.

There are other difficulties. The formulations we have been considering can be viewed as stressing the doctrinal, the ethical, and the emotional aspects of religion, respectively. And it may well be doubted that any definition in terms of only one of these can give us an adequate idea of the nature of so complex a form of human activity and experience. This incompleteness is manifested in various ways. On the one hand, as the last paragraph indicated, it will be difficult to find any particular belief, feeling, or moral stance which is found in all religons. On the other hand, so long as we require only a certain kind of belief, moral attitude, or emotion, there is no guarantee that it exists within a religion rather than in some other sort of setting. A belief in a Divine Mind and Will ruling the universe might be held purely as a speculative hypothesis; it will not be a *religious* belief unless it makes contact with the believer's feeling, attitudes, and action in a characteristically religious way. And similarly it seems that the quest for goodness might occur in a religious or in a nonreligious context. The seventh example is not subject to these criticisms; it escapes partiality by featuring a global term, *ultimate attitude,* which embraces belief, feeling, and moral endeavor. But one may still wonder whether all ultimate attitudes are necessarily religious, or whether there is not some further feature which makes religious attitudes religious. As James suggests in *The Varieties of Religious Experience,* it is doubtful whether a frivolous attitude toward life deserves to be called religious, even if it is the basic attitude of the person in question.]

At this point the reader may well feel quite puzzled. None of these definitions is fully satisfactory. And yet surely after going through such a list we have a deeper understanding of the nature of religion than we did before. How can this be? How can the consideration of several inadequate definitions help us to realize what religion is like?

Perhaps our trouble arises from being dominated by an oversimple model of definition. In each case the objection was that one could find cases of religion to which the definition did not apply, or that the definition would apply to things that were not religions. Each formulation was seen to be either too narrow or too broad, or both. Now this is an objection only if one expects a definition of religion to provide a characteristic, or set of characteristics, which something has whenever it is a religion and only when it is a religion. That is, we expect the definition to provide both a necessary condition of religion (satisfied by every religion) and a sufficient condition (satisfied only by religion). We get this ideal from mathematics, a very atypical sphere of thought which, unfortunately, provides the logician with most of his examples. In geometry, for example, we can define a circle as a closed curve, each point on the circumference of which is equidistant from a fixed point called the center. Anything which satisfies these conditions is a circle, and anything which does not satisfy them is not a circle.

This sort of definition is possible not only in mathematics, though the neatest and most unmistakable examples of it occur there; we define, for example, a thermometer as an instrument for measuring temperature, or an oculist as a doctor specializing in the treatment of the eye. But there are other places where difficulties are encountered, most noticeably when we try to define terms which have to do with important segments or products of human culture. Consider for a moment the term *poem*.[1] What is the defining characteristic of a poem? Rhyme? What about blank verse? Meter? What about free verse? Other possible defining features which suggest themselves are an emphasis on the sound of words as such, the use of metaphors and other figures of speech, a pre-occupation with imaginative and emotional material—all are often found in prose, for example, the novels of Thomas Wolfe. Many poems (particularly those called didactic) deal with quite prosaic and unimaginative themes. Wordsworth's poetry makes little use of figures of speech.

And yet the presence of these features certainly has something to do with making a literary composition a poem. None of them is irrelevant to the question of whether or not a piece of writing is a poem. We could call them "poem-making characteristics." The problem is to conceive the precise relation they have to being a poem. They cannot go to make up a definition in the mathematical sense, because neither individually nor collectively do they constitute a neces-

---

[1] This discussion of "poem" is mostly taken from C. L. Stevenson, "On 'What is a Poem?'" *Philosophical Review,* LXVI (1957), 329–62.

sary condition for being a poem. As we have just seen no one of these features has to be present to make something a poem, nor is it necessary that a poem include them all. It may be that the presence of all these features would be a sufficient condition for "poemhood," but the fact that this congeries of characteristics is not also a necessary condition prevents it from forming a definition in the usual sense. Perhaps to get a necessary condition we need something in between some one feature and all the features. Let us say we cannot have a poem unless we have a sufficient number of these features realized, and to a sufficient extent. But how many does it take to make a "sufficient" number? There is no definite answer to that question. First, the features are weighted unequally. Meter goes a longer way toward making something a poem than do imaginative themes or figures of speech. Yet it is not possible to say how much more weight it has. Second, how many features are required will depend on the extent to which each is realized—how definite is the meter, how vividly the content stimulates the imagination, how frequent are the figures of speech. And these gradations are likewise insusceptible to any exact measure. It seems that the best we can do by way of a definition is to say that a poem is a literary composition which contains a substantial number of these features to a substantial degree, and then rely on a series of examples to give our pupil a sense of what constitutes a substantial amount.

Something like this is true for religion. The definitions we have been considering, or most of them, have real value, just because they present characteristic features of religion—"religion-making characteristics." Perhaps the most that can be done by way of a definition of religion is to list such characteristic features. Here is such a list, which embodies the features stressed by one or another of the definitions we have been considering.

1. Beliefs in supernatural beings (gods).
2. A distinction between sacred and profane objects.
3. Ritual acts focused around sacred objects.
4. A moral code believed to be sanctioned by the gods.
5. Characteristically religious feelings (awe, sense of mystery, sense of guilt, adoration, etc.), which tend to be aroused in the presence of sacred objects and during the practice of ritual, and which are associated with the gods.
6. Prayer and other forms of communication with gods.
7. A world view. (By a world view I mean a general picture of the world as a whole and the place of the individual therein, this picture containing some specification of an over-all purpose or point, and an indication of how the individual fits into this whole.)
8. A more or less total organization of one's life based on the world view.
9. A social group bound together by the first eight factors.

It is important to realize that these various factors do not just happen to be thrown together in religion; they are intimately interfused in a variety of ways. Some of these connections have already been indicated in the way the items were specified, but there are many others as well. For example, the distinction between sacred and profane objects is primarily based on other items in this list. It is not some intrinsic feature of a thing that gives it the role of a sacred object in a religion, for things of every conceivable sort have occupied this position—animals, plants, topographical features like mountains, rivers, and springs, persons, heavenly bodies, articles of furniture, and so on. What leads the adherents of a religion to mark out certain objects as sacred is that those objects fill them with awe, dread, and a sense of mystery, and they tend to respond to them with ritual acts. This is a quasi-operational definition of "sacred." Again, the emotional reaction to sacred objects is typically rationalized by conceiving the object to be the dwelling place or manifestation of a supernatural personal being. That is, the beliefs about gods serve to explain the emotional reactions. The awe aroused by the wild bull leads to its identification with the god of wine and intoxication, Dionysus. And the awe aroused by a volcanic mountain may be translated into conceptual terms by speaking of the mountain as the habitation of a fierce god. The unique impression which Jesus of Nazareth made on certain of his contemporaries was expressed by their calling him the Son of God. This sounds as if the emotional reaction to objects comes first and is then explained by positing gods as its cause. But we cannot take the priority of any one of these items as a general rule. The acceptance of beliefs about the gods and about their earthly habitations can arouse, or help arouse, awe and other religious feelings in the presence of certain objects. Indeed the members of a religious community are taught to hold certain objects in awe, feel various emotions at certain times and places, by being taught various doctrines about the gods. Thus Christians are taught to regard the Cross and the consecrated bread and wine with reverence by being told of the Crucifixion and the Last Supper. Jews are taught to feel a certain way about unleavened bread by being told of the Exodus.

A similar reciprocal relationship holds between ritual and doctrine. On the one hand, a doctrine can supervene on an already established ritual, as its justification. Thus the story of Proserpine being carried off to the underworld and remaining there half the year seems to have been introduced as an explanation of a pre-existing magical fertility cult, in which an ear of grain, perhaps called the corn-maiden, is buried in the fall, and raised sprouting in the spring. Apparently there was first a wild ceremony in which a live bull was torn to pieces, and the raw flesh eaten, perhaps in order to incorporate the mysterious potency believed to reside therein; and then this rite was interpreted as a re-enactment of the occasion on which Dionysus (who has been identified with the bull) was torn to pieces by Titans, and the aim of the rite is reinterpreted as the attainment of union with the god. Similarly the Christian doctrine of transubstantiation arose out of the great significance which Christians already attached to the common memorial meal.

On the other hand, changes in doctrine can engender, modify, or abolish rituals. It seems likely that a growing conviction of the benevolence of God has played a part in the cessation of human sacrifice; intellectual difficulties in the doctrine of transubstantiation have been a factor in the de-emphasis or discontinuance of the sacrament of Holy Communion in many Christian sects; and the Christmas festival originated, at least in part, from the belief in the divinity of Jesus Christ (only in part, because it is a continuation of pagan festivals held at the winter solstice).

The only way we can adequately reflect our actual use of *religion* is to say that the word is applied whenever enough of these conditions are satisfied. But how much is enough? Let us not oversimplify by pretending that the application of the term requires any five out of seven, or a certain three plus any two of the others, or anything else of the sort. In fact we will never obtain an adequate idea of the working of the term *religion* until we abandon the clear-cut dichotomy between a term applying or not applying to something in favor of the more complex concept of the *extent* to which a term applies. We shall have to think of religion applying in some cases clearly, unequivocally (Christianity, Islam, Hinduism), but in other cases more or less questionably, tentatively (Communism, complete devotion to science).

At one end of the scale we have the ideally clear cases, the sort that one would cite if asked to give examples of religion: Roman Catholicism, Orthodox Judaism, Orphism. Here we have all the religion-making characteristics present in a clear way, and to a marked degree. In Roman Catholicism, for example, there is an elaborate cultus centering around sacred objects (priest, cross, altar, consecrated bread and wine); there are beliefs about God, to Whom these cultic acts are directed, Whose nature and doings form the rationale of the cultus; when the individual is participating in the rites, when he is in the presence of sacred objects, or when he is thinking of God, characteristically religious feelings are aroused in him, not always or invariably, but often enough to give a strong emotional coloration to the whole. There is a moral code believed to have been ordained and enforced by God. And all this provides the individual with a general picture of the cosmos and human history, and with an indication of his place therein.

Note that in singling out this type of religion as a paradigm case I am not suggesting that it is the best or truest kind of religion. The only sense in which it is best is a logical or semantic one. It is an ideally clear and unquestionable example of the application of the term *religion.* We should beware of supposing that in defining the term *religion,* we are trying to delineate the religious ideal or to determine what the most perfect sort of religion would be. In defining religion we are trying to make explicit the criteria we use for applying the term to anything, be it good or bad. The evaluative question, "What is the best religion?" in its very wording presupposes that the term *religion* applies to cases other than the best. Hence the elucidation of the nonevaluative use of the term must precede the evaluative job of determining the religious ideal.

Since the paradigm case is defined by a number of different features, there can be cases which deviate from it in a number of different ways, that is, by one or the other of these features becoming less prominent or dropping out altogether.

⚹ Ritual can be sharply de-emphasized, and with it the demarcation of certain objects as sacred. This de-emphasis has occurred in Protestantism and in Islam. It can even drop out altogether, as with the Quakers and other groups, who are mainly concerned with the cultivation of mystical experience.

Morality can have no connection with the other elements. (Cf. our discussion, page 3, of the third and fourth definitions.)

Beliefs in supernatural beings can be whittled away to nothing. We have seen a development of this sort in Western culture over the last few hundred years. The deity has been successively relieved of his spatial habitation in heaven and of his temporal priority to the world. With the extension of natural knowledge, one range of phenomena after another has been removed from his direct and immediate control—the motions of heavenly bodies, the ebb and flow of disease, earthquake, tempest, and flood, the adaptation of living organisms to their environment, the course of history, even the stream of human conscious experience. When this tendency to kick God upstairs is given full reign, what is left is a remote and bodiless abstraction, which some religious groups have proceeded to ignore altogether. Thus in some Unitarian groups, and in Humanism, we have a religiously toned orientation around certain ideals, like social equality, and a moral code based thereon, but without the ardor being directed in any way toward a supernatural being, and without any cultus in which this ardor is expressed. One branch of Buddhism, the Hinayana, practiced in southeastern Asia also ignores supernatural beings, at least officially. Here the emphasis is on the cultivation of a moral and meditative discipline which will enable one to attain a state in which all craving has ceased (craving being considered the root of all evil in human life).

The social group which has the religion can be reduced to one member; that is, a person can develop his own private religious scheme. Spinoza, for example, worked out his own religion, which was based on a calm and joyful acceptance of everything that happened as necessarily flowing from the nature of the universe. The whole of nature, conceived as a unity, was the object of worship; and the worship consisted of, in Spinoza's phrase, an "intellectual love," that is, a joyful recognition that everything necessarily is as it is.

Finally, the typically religious emotions may be attenuated. It is doubtful that any group continues to realize the other religious elements unless a large proportion of its members entertain strong feelings. But it is possible for a particular individual to carry on with religious rituals, observe moral codes, even assent to the creed in a perfunctory way, without all this making any real and vital contact with his emotional life.

The important point is that as we come to examples which leave out more of the religion-making characteristics, and/or in which the characteristics are exemplified less strongly, we feel less secure about applying the term. It seems more doubtful that they really are religions, and we will find less unanimity in the language community with respect to the application of the word. No one would doubt that Roman Catholicism, or Orthodox Judaism, or Orphism is a religion. If someone did doubt it, we should take that to indicate he did not know how to use the word *religion*. But one can doubt that Hinayana Buddhism, or

Humanism, or Communism, or Spinoza's intellectual love of the universe, is a religion, without thereby giving grounds for doubt that he knows how to use the term.

Not all deviations from the paradigm equally give rise to doubt. We live in a nonritualistic society. Rites and symbols have very little meaning for us. Graduation exercises and initiation ceremonies are likely to make us uncomfortable or just bored. Therefore we do not tend to think of ritual as essential to religion; it is, we think, merely an outward trapping which can be sloughed off, leaving the inner reality undiminished. Hence we do not feel uncomfortable in calling the Quakers a religious group, although they have completely abjured ritual. But we do tend to put great store by belief in a god or gods. When there is a deviation from the paradigm in this respect, as in Communism or Hinayana Buddhism, we feel more reluctance in classing it as a religion.

This differential weighting of elements will vary from group to group, and even from person to person, which is equivalent to saying that not everyone has exactly the same concept of religion. And it is easy to understand why. According to the present analysis, a concept of religion consists of a paradigm case (or class of paradigm cases) analyzed into significant features, with different weights attached to these features. It seems that this is just the way in which the meaning of a term like *religion* is learned. Normally one starts by becoming familiar with some one religion, the one in which he is raised. This will become his paradigm case. But not yet. He does not acquire a concept of religion until he learns of other religions and compares them with his own. (It is noteworthy that there is no word corresponding to our word *religion* in the languages of cultures which have not made contact with a wide variety of other cultures.) As he becomes aware of more and more cultural phenomena, he will apply the word *religion* to those which do not differ too widely in fundamental respects from the paradigm. Thus the concepts of religion held by two persons will vary with variations in the paradigm case, in the weighting of various factors in the paradigm case, and in the tolerance of deviations (logical, not religious, tolerance). A Presbyterian will feel less compunction in applying *religion* to a nonritual group like the Quakers than will a Catholic. And one Catholic will feel less compunction than another if the first places less weight on ritual relative to other features of their common paradigm than does the other. And a Quaker will be more ready to call a highly mystical set of beliefs like Theosophy a religion than a Calvinist will, with his emphasis on creed and morality.

This analysis can be further confirmed by considering what happens when an anthropologist goes into a strange culture and sets about the job of describing it. Among the facets of this culture he will investigate will be its religion. But how is he to locate the religion and distinguish it from the morality, the art, and the government? Or, more concretely, how is he to tell when the inhabitants are engaging in religious activities, and when their activities are secular?

When we look into this problem, we can see that no single criterion will work. Suppose the criterion is E. B. Tylor's: a belief in spiritual beings. The anthropologist may find no such beliefs. Will that lead him to deny that this culture has a religion? Suppose he makes the following discoveries: The inhabitants believe in some vague, impersonal, highly potent force for good or ill, which is found in certain things and persons; these things and persons evoke characteristically religious emotions; there are elaborate ritual procedures for getting in touch with this force and controlling it to some extent; these beliefs, practices, and feelings color the whole life of the people, and set up a framework in which their other activities are carried on. He certainly would not withhold the term *religion* from this complex just because there are no beliefs in spiritual beings involved. On the other hand he may find beliefs in spiritual beings which have no vital connection with the system of rites and the generation of awe and dread. Something like this is true of the Australian aborigines, whose ritual system is concerned with the totem of the group and not with spirits, which are treated differently. What do we say here? We might say that there are two different religions, relatively independent of each other. But we could equally well reserve the term *religion* for the ritual system, and relegate the belief in spirits to the category of idle speculation.

Or suppose the criterion is Matthew Arnold's: ethics enkindled by feeling. And suppose that in the culture under investigation the moral rules are accepted solely on the basis of the custom and tradition of the group; they are observed because that is the way things are done, or because they have been handed down from time immemorial. No attempt is made to attribute them to the gods, even though there is a flourishing system of rites which is designed to influence the gods, who are held in great awe. Moreover, far from embodying the moral code, these gods are credited with acts like incest which directly violate it. Many primitive communities approximate this description. In this case, Arnold notwithstanding, the anthropologist would describe the ritual system under the heading of religion and say that the morality is dissociated from the religion.

And lest we think that ritual is becoming a common feature, let us finally envisage a society in which we find beliefs in remote and lofty "high gods," which are credited with the creation of the world and with all sorts of moral virtues, which are addressed in rather formal prayers, but which are not thought to have any influence over day-to-day affairs. No rites are directed to them, and no objects are peculiarly sacred to them. However, there are stereotyped practices designed to influence the course of events, but without any notion of gods being involved; the idea seems to be that the rites directly influence the physical processes. Here our investigator would no doubt mark out the former complex as the religion, and say that ritual practices in this culture are of a magical rather than a religious nature.

What all this shows is that our model anthropologist is operating with a set of multiple criteria, and that he will apply the term *religion* to whatever congeries of activities in the culture satisfies a preponderance of these. Sometimes this will be one set, sometimes another. And it is unlikely that any one feature will be characteristic of every such congeries. If this account of anthropological procedure is accurate, it shows that the concept of religion employed there has the kind of structure I have been setting out.

This analysis will illuminate, if not resolve, the sorts of disputes which typically lead to attempts to define religion. So long as we simply range absolute definitions alongside each other, we shall never resolve, or even throw any light on, the perennial disputes over, for example, whether a man's religion can be business or whether Communism is a religion. For each party to the dispute, if he is clever and consistent, will employ a definition which is suited to the position he is defending. *A,* who claims that Communism is a religion, will define religion as, for example, "that set of objects, habits, and convictions, whatever it might prove to be, which he would die for rather than abandon, or at least would feel himself excommunicated from humanity if he did abandon." Whereas *B,* who denies that Communism is a religion, will define religion as, for example, "the belief in an ever living God, that is, in a Divine Mind and Will ruling the Universe and holding moral relations with mankind." Obviously each man is correct on the basis of his definition. Hence it would seem that the only way to settle the dispute is to determine which is the correct definition. But we have seen that this gets us nowhere. No such definition reflects with complete accuracy the ordinary use of the term. At this point there is a temptation to say: "Anyone can mean what he pleases by a word. If *A* wants to use *religion* in the way he does, then of course in that sense Communism is a religion. And if *B* wants to use *religion* in the way he does, then of course in that sense Communism is not a religion. The whole dispute is verbal. Let *A* and *B* get together and agree to use different words for their two meanings, and the dispute will vanish."

But this is a superficial view of the matter. There is more in common between *A* and *B* than this reaction would suggest. In fact, their two "definitions" represent two contrasting emphases within a common framework. Let us suppose that *A* and *B* start out with the same paradigm, or at least closely similar paradigms, taken from within the main stream of the Judaeo-Christian tradition. However, *A* places more emphasis on the moral-orientation-emotion elements in this paradigm. As long as anything strongly manifests these elements, so long as it serves as a system of life-orientation for the individual, who is bound to it by strong emotional ties, he will call it a religion. Whereas *B* takes up a similar attitude toward the belief in a personal God and the complex of emotions, ritual, and devotional acts, and so on, which are bound up with that. Although basically their conception of religion is the same, they will diverge in their applications at certain points on the periphery. Once we understand this, we can restate the problem in a form in which it can fruitfully be attacked. Instead of working uncritically with the term *religion* and a myriad of absolute definitions, we can enumerate the religion-making characteristics, determine which of these Communism has, and in what degree. Then we will be in a position to locate the real nub of the dispute: the relative importance of these characteristics. Insofar as there is a real issue between *A* and *B* once both are in possession of all the relevant facts, it is over whether Communism is similar to clear cases of religion in important respects; that is, the dispute is over whether the respects in which it is like Catholicism are more important than those in which it is different.

Again, a man who uses *religion* in such a way that one man is said to have money for his religion, another success, and so on, is obviously focusing on life-orientation, or even one aspect of this: namely, patterning activity around some dominant goal, and regarding all the rest—ritual, belief in the supernatural, moral code—as peripheral. I think we may safely take this as a rather extreme trend. But of course once we understand what such a person is doing, there can be no question of his being mistaken.

Thus once we see that we apply the term *religion* not in accordance with any rigid set of necessary and sufficient conditions, but on the basis of some vaguely specified permissible degree of deviation from a paradigm case, we can understand why we fall into perplexities and disputes over the application of the term, and also how these perplexities and disputes can be cleared up.

Armed with these insights into the nature of religion we can return to a consideration of what the philosopher does when he thinks about religion. Taking the list of features on page 5 as indicating what sort of thing religion is, we can think of the philosopher carrying on his activities with respect to any of these features. Thus a philosopher might try to get clear about the sorts of rituals to be found in religion and raise questions about their validity or value. And he might devote a great deal of attention to the feelings that persistently crop up in religion and try to determine the extent of their contribution to the good life. A good example of the latter would be William James's *The Varieties of Religious Experience,* though many fruitless debates could be held over whether James is here functioning as a philosopher or as a psychologist. But, in fact, philosophers have almost exclusively concentrated on the cognitive, belief, or doctrinal side of religion. It is the fundamental beliefs of religion, such as the existence of God, the providence of God, the demands God makes on men, and the immortality of man—and the concepts that figure prominently therein: God, omnipotence, creation, miracle, revelation, immortality, and so on—that they have primarily sought to formulate and clarify; and it is on the validity, justifiability, or truth of such *beliefs,* rather than on rites or feelings, that they have focused their critical powers. There are, no doubt, many reasons for this selectivity. I would suppose that the main justification for it lies in the fact that the ultimate interest of the philosopher is in questions of justification and that the justification of any other element in religion ultimately rests on the justification of some belief or beliefs. If, for example, one asks a devout Roman Catholic why he goes to Mass, or what the point or value of so doing is, he would, if he knew what he was about, appeal in answer to certain basic beliefs of his religion: that the physical universe and all its constituents, including man, owe their existence to God, a supreme personal being; that God took on human form in the person of Jesus of Nazareth and suffered death in order to save man from his sinfulness; that as part of a program designed to enable men to benefit from this, God has ordained that they should participate in this rite, in which, in some mysterious way, they actually incorporate the body and blood of Jesus and so partake of His saving activity, and so forth. The ritual, as conceived by its participants, is a reasonable thing to do if and only if these beliefs can be justified. Thus in concentrating on the belief side of religion, philosophers are not really so one-sided as one might at first suppose. They are, at least indirectly, dealing with all sides of religion.

In fact, we can narrow things down more than this. Not all the beliefs of a given religion, not even all the beliefs considered crucial by that religion, receive equal attention from philosophers concerned with that religion. Thus in works on the philosophy of religion which have primarily grown out of a concern with Christianity one finds little discussion of the doctrines of the virgin birth of Jesus, the divine mission of the church, or the special status of the priesthood, however important these may be for Christianity. These are somehow felt to be too special, too particular. Instead attention is focused primarily on what might be called the metaphysical background of the system of doctrine, or what in my list of features I called the world view: the view as to the general nature of the universe, of man, of man's place in the universe. In a religion like Christianity this means concentrating on the existence and nature of God, the divine purpose(s) for the universe in general and man in particular, and the nature and destiny of man. There are, again, various reasons for this preferential treatment. I suppose that it is partly due to a desire to make the discussion relevant to more than one particular religion, partly due to a feeling that philosophical reflection will yield definite results, if at all, only on the more general aspects of a religious outlook. It might also be argued, and I should be prepared to do so, that if we abstract from any commitment to any particular religion, the world-view aspect of religion is the most undeniably significant one and hence the one which should be in the center of the picture in any general philosophical treatment of religion. For without having established, or accepted, some particular religious beliefs, it would be difficult to show that beliefs in supernatural beings, or the treating of some objects as sacred, or the participation in rites are essential parts of a fully human life. But it can be argued persuasively, on the basis of general considerations about the nature of man and the conditions of human life, that human beings have a deep-seated need to form some general view of the total universe in which they live in order to be able to relate their own particular lives and their own fragmentary activities to the universe as a whole in a way which can be seen to be meaningful, and that a life in which this is not carried through is a life which is impoverished in a most significant respect. This would seem to be an aspect of religion which would be important under any conditions, and in the last section of the book we shall see that naturalistic philosophers, who have made a decisive break with the supernatural, often still feel a need to find something which will perform this sort of function.

Before turning to a consideration of the way in which the various sections of this book exemplify the philosophy of religion as so conceived, one more point needs to be made. I have been writing much of the time as if the philosophy of religion were a response to religion in general, but of course that is not the case. There is no such thing as religion in general. Each human being, and philosophers are human beings too, is confronted with a particular religion, or at least a particular sort of religion, which is a live option for him; and if he philosophizes about religion, his philosophizing will be primarily directed toward the beliefs found in that kind of religion. Even if he is one of those rare persons who knows a great deal about many different religious traditions, he is not likely to take seriously more than one as a live possibility for his own adherence. Fruitful thinking about religious problems arises not from idle curiosity about the religions of the world or from the attempt to "choose a religion," like shopping for a refrigerator, but from a vital concern for some religion with which the thinker feels a necessity to come to terms.

One important implication of this fact is that the content of a philosophy of religion will be partly determined by the sort of religion the philosophizing is about. The problems treated as central will vary with variations in the beliefs which are central in the religion under consideration. Philosophical arguments for and against the existence of a supreme personal deity loom large in the works of European, but not in the works of Indian, philosophers of religion. Again, the question of whether a belief in miracles is compatible with the acceptance of natural law is one which worries philosophers from a Christian, but not those from a Buddhist, background.

The selections in this volume are taken almost exclusively from philosophers whose problems were set for them by some facet of the Judaeo-Christian religious tradition. The reasons for this restriction are two. First, in order really to appreciate any piece of philosophizing about religion one must have some understanding of the religious ideas and beliefs out of which it springs; and it is only of the Judaeo-Christian tradition that such understanding can be presupposed for readers of this book. Second, the study of the philosophy of religion should not only involve becoming acquainted with various specimens of philosophizing, but should also stimulate the student's own thinking about religious problems and provide him with better tools for that enterprise. Hence it is important that the philosophers here represented be concerned with issues which are live ones, religiously, for the student; and for most students in our society this would require that these be issues which have grown out of the Judaeo-Christian tradition.

Basically this volume is concerned with the issues involved in a consideration of theism, the world view which is involved in Judaism, Christianity, and Islam. The most fundamental tenets of theism are as follows:

1. The physical universe owes its existence to the creative activity of God, Who is an infinite immaterial personal being.
2. God created the universe for the realization of some purpose and is presiding over its career in the interests of that purpose. There are many different views as to what this purpose is but it is generally supposed that it has something to do with the development of man as a moral agent.
3. Man, who plays an important role in the divine scheme, has a destiny which transcends his brief embodied life on earth.

Of course, this bare outline is filled in differently in different theistic religions. Each has its special version of just what God's purposes are, what He has done in the course of history in working for them, and what demands He makes on men. But, as pointed out above, it is the less specific principles which have seemed more amenable to philosophical discussion.

It is clear that the belief in the existence of a supreme immaterial personal being is the necessary foundation of this entire scheme of thought, and discussions of this belief have occupied a large part of the literature of our subject. The first three sections of the book are primarily devoted to this topic. Section 1 presents the main arguments for this thesis, together with some criticisms of these arguments. Section 2 discusses the possibility that people can, and do, come to know God directly through religious experience. Section 3 criticizes the theistic concept of God and offers some attempts to meet these criticisms.

Section 4 discusses another fundamental tenet of theism, the immortality of man. Sections 5 and 6 are concerned with the problems of the status and validity of religious belief in general. Section 5 explores the concept of revelation and the view that certain religious beliefs are to be accepted because they have been revealed to man by God. Section 6 considers the nature of religious *faith* as a special mode of belief, and, in particular, the possibility that there is something about religious faith that makes demands for justification, of the sort we have in other areas, inappropriate.

Each of these first six sections represents a blend of formulation, clarification, and evaluation of certain basic religious beliefs and of certain kinds of claims made for religious belief. In Section 7 the emphasis is on integration. This section is concerned with the tension which has most intimately affected religious thought in the last few centuries, the so-called conflict between religion and science. Section 8 presents several attempts to delineate for our culture a religious orientation which will be an alternative to the theistic. All of these, except the one based on Zen, derive from naturalistic philosophies, and even Zen might conceivably be interpreted in this way.

There are, no doubt, many other problems which could profitably be covered in a volume of this sort and many other sources which could usefully be tapped. There is no suggestion that this is the only way to compile a volume of readings in the philosophy of religion. But this set has been compiled in the conviction that the topics chosen and the selections included are those which are most significant for a thoughtful contemporary member of our society who is trying to think about religious issues in the light of whatever considerations are most relevant.

1.

ARGUMENTS FOR THE EXISTENCE OF GOD

If we wish to provide a rational basis for the fundamental beliefs of theistic religion, the obvious place to begin is the belief in the existence of a theistic God, for this belief is the necessary presupposition of all the rest. This involves starting with something which, it is supposed, any reasonable man would accept if he considered it carefully, and then trying to show that this implies, or at least provides a strong reason for affirming, the existence of a theistic God. Most of these arguments start with some familiar feature of the world about us—motion, order, moral obligation, and so on—and then argue that this feature can only be adequately explained in terms of a theistic deity. The first argument presented in this section, the "ontological" argument, is an exception to this generalization. Here the claim is not that we have to bring in God in order to *explain* something, but rather than if we reflect on the concept of God we will realize that one cannot deny that such a being exists without falling into contradiction. For to deny that an absolutely perfect being exists is to deny that an absolutely perfect being is absolutely perfect (for existence is a perfection, that is, to exist is more perfect than not to exist), and that is a contradiction. Thus this argument is more purely *a priori* (independent of experience) than the others, for it includes no facts of experience within its premises.

A. N. Whitehead once said that the greatest philosophical accomplishment is to be refuted afresh in every century. If this is so then highest honors go to Anselm, along with the Zeno who formulated the famous paradoxes, for philosophers have been busy with the refutation of his argument ever since a contemporary of his, Gaunilon, published an answer, "In Behalf of the Fool." Most people feel on encountering the argument that there must be something wrong with it; such an important conclusion could not be established that easily. But practically no one is completely satisfied with what others have done to show exactly what is wrong with it. And so the discussion goes on. Among the important critics in the discussion have been Aquinas, Kant, and Russell, and among the defenders have been Descartes, Leibniz, and Hegel. In this country today, after a period during which it was almost universally assumed without question that the argument is worthless, two defenders have recently appeared on the scene: Charles Hartshorne and Norman Malcolm. Most of the criticisms have been variations and/or refinements of the thesis enunciated by Kant in the selection included here that existence is not a property, since we must suppose that a thing exists before we can even raise the question whether or not it has a given property, and therefore that we can never establish the existence of something simply by analyzing a concept to determine what properties are involved in it. The ontological argument is philosophically so significant largely because of the fact that in trying to deal with it philosophers have been forced to clarify such concepts as existence, perfection, and predication, and have been forced to distinguish more sharply between subject-predicate propositions and existential propositions; just as, in attempting to deal with Zeno's paradoxes, philosophers have been forced to get much clearer about the status of space and time. In the essay by J. J. C. Smart we have a good contemporary statement of the difficulties in the ontological argument.

The first three arguments of the famous "Five Ways" of Aquinas are all versions of the "cosmological" argument, which takes its start from very general considerations about the physical universe and proceeds to argue that we can only explain the existence of the universe by positing a divine creator. As both F. C. Copleston and A. E. Taylor note, these arguments in their Thomistic formulations are too bound up with medieval physics to carry much conviction with contemporary readers. For example, as Copleston points out, although it appears at first that Aquinas, in maintaining that an infinite regress of causes is impossible, is arguing for the impossibility of a temporally infinite universe, in fact he does not want to claim that a temporally infinite universe can be proved to be impossible (though he believes on what he takes to be the authority of the Bible that the universe had a beginning in time). The series of causes he has in mind is a series of entities of higher and higher levels of being, all operative at the same time in keeping a given change going. This idea is so foreign to our ways of thinking about the physical universe that Copleston has difficulty in providing a plausible illustration of Aquinas' point. If we are going to exhibit the philosophical heart of his argument without getting entangled in outmoded physics, I think we shall have to follow the route suggested, but not spelled out in detail, by Taylor and raise our questions not about some particular motion or particular thing and the series it generates, but rather about the universe as a whole. I mean by this the universe in its entire extent, both spatial and temporal. It is obvious that this could not stand in spatial or temporal relations with anything else. We might formulate the argument along the following lines:

The physical universe is temporally either finite or infinite.

If it is finite, the beginning of its existence must have been due to some cause.

Even if it is temporally infinite, there must be some cause the action of which is responsible for the fact that this (temporally infinite) universe exists rather than some other or none at all.

Even if this cause owes its existence to some other cause in a similar manner, an infinite regress of such causes is impossible.

Therefore, the entire system ultimately owes its existence to an uncaused first cause.

This statement reveals that, as Taylor points out, the essential claim in these Thomistic arguments is that the physical universe, either as a whole or in any of its parts, is not ultimately self-explanatory, that we can only fully explain its existence if we attribute its existence to a being which is radically different in that it is self-explanatory, a cause which does not itself require a cause.

In Hume's *Dialogues Concerning Natural Religion* (Part IX) Cleanthes objects to this argument by saying that the notion of a cause of a temporally infinite universe is an absurd notion since the notion of causality requires a temporal priority of the cause to the effect. This objection has seemed a powerful one to many people. And yet it seems to be based on prejudice. There are, no doubt, many cases of such causality: taking a sulfa drug caused the patient's fever to go down; melting snows in the mountains caused the river to flood downstream. But there are also many cases in which there is no such temporal succession: the cause of wood floating in water is that its density is less than that of water; my sitting on a cushion at this moment is the cause of its being depressed at this moment. If we try to think of someone having sat on a pillow from all eternity we can form a distant analogue of the notion of a beginningless entity depending throughout all eternity for its existence on some other entity.

As Taylor notes, one might ask why, since we have to admit a self-explanatory being at some point anyway, we should not regard the physical universe as self-explanatory. Is it not as good a candidate as any? If we are thinking in terms of a temporally infinite universe, we cannot make the same point here that Aquinas makes with respect to particular material substances: that we know they are contingent because they come into being and pass out of being. The only possible answer would be that we can envisage the possibility that the physical universe which we actually have should not have existed (there is nothing about its nature which requires its existence) and that therefore we need to find some other entity which is responsible for the fact that this universe exists rather than some other or none at all. But this means that we are refusing to rest in our search for a final explanation until we have arrived at a being which is logically necessary, one the nonexistence of which is inconceivable. As Smart observes, this is the point at which the cosmological argument makes contact with the ontological argument. Paradoxically enough, although Thomas is clearly making use of the notion of a logically necessary being, he not only rejects Anselm's ontological argument but even argues that it is impossible to prove God's existence merely from His nature. He does indeed say that it is possible in principle to do this but impossible for us, due to the fact that we cannot form an adequate enough concept of the divine essence. But then, as Smart points out, Aquinas is in difficulty over the *meaningfulness* of the notion of a logically necessary being. Note, too, that the fact that the notion of a necessary being is essential to the first two arguments shows the essential unity of the first three arguments.

Thus the crucial issue on which the cosmological argument hinges is an issue concerning the requirements for an adequate explanation. He who resists the argument will say something like this: So long as we explain a mother's overprotecting her daughter by pointing out her repressed hostility to the daughter and explain that in terms of her unconscious sense that her daughter is a threat to her, and so on, it is true that at each stage what we bring in to do the explaining stands in need of explanation of exactly the same sort, and that unless we can get back to something that is logically necessary we can never exhaust the task. But that is just one of the things we have to learn to face in life, and it is unreasonable to *demand* that things be tidier than this. From this standpoint Aquinas is making an unreasonable metaphysical demand on the universe by insisting that it must be such that a final completion of this process is possible in principle. (Aquinas is under no obligation to hold that we can ever actually carry through such an explanation in practice.) A Thomist will reply that this insistence is just part of the general assumption of the rationality of the universe which everyone makes whether or not he realizes it. But to this it will be replied that there are various grades and modes of rationality and that we can hold the universe to be rational in some ways, for example, ordered causally, without making such extreme demands as this. It would seem that at this point we have come up against one of those rock-bottom philosophical oppositions about which nothing further can be said.

At the end of each of his arguments Aquinas appends a phrase like "and this everyone understands to be God," or "This all men speak of as God." The reader might well wonder about the basis for this, especially in the first three arguments. Why should we suppose that a necessary being, which requires no cause outside itself, would have the personal attributes contained in the notion of God? Why should a first cause not be an impersonal force of some sort, or, if a personal being, why should it not be evil rather than good? Notice that this problem does not arise for the ontological argument. (Nor does it arise so severely for the others we shall be considering, which arrive at God as a cosmic designer or as the source or locus of moral principles.) If that argument proves anything it proves the existence of an absolutely perfect being. Aquinas attempts to fill the gap between necessary being and perfect being in the first twelve questions of the *Summa Theologica*. The line of argument is too complex to be summarized here; the interested reader may consult the original.

The "teleological" argument begins from less abstract considerations about the world and makes a bid to reach a less abstract conception of the creator. In its classic formulation by Cleanthes in David Hume's *Dialogues* it takes the form of an argument from analogy: the world is like a machine and therefore the cause of the world is probably like the cause of a machine. In F. R. Tennant's exposition, and in many others', the argument looks quite different, however. There the contention is that certain sorts of "design" or "adaptation" can only be explained if we suppose that they were produced by some mind, and the argument does not seem to be proceeding by analogy at all. But actually the two forms are not very different. In the Humean form the world is said to be like a machine, in exhibiting adaptation; and in the other form if we ask why we should suppose that the presence of design can be explained only in terms of mind, the only answer would be that in the cases where we have fullest insight into what is responsible for the presence of design, namely, human artifacts like watches, ships, and houses, it is a designing mind that is responsible.

Since none of our selections go to any lengths to elucidate the crucial terms *design* and *adaptation,* something should be said in explanation. Consider the examples that are commonly given: the outer ears which land animals, but not water animals, possess are nicely fitted to focus sound waves which are much weaker in air than in water; the hooves of horses enable them to attain great speed in flight from carnivorous pursuers on grassy plains; some insects instinctively lay their eggs on certain trees at such a time that the hatching of the eggs coincides with the budding of leaves in the spring. It is clear that the sort of design exemplified here is something more than mere causal regularity; the fact that leaves move when the wind blows would not be an example of design. On the other hand, we do not want to include in the meaning of these terms conscious planning by some mind; that would prevent us from assembling the data for the argument before we had already arrived at the conclusion. What we have to say is that we have a case of design or adaptation wherever the situation is such that things regularly come out for the benefit of the individuals involved even though there has been no conscious planning on the part of any of those individuals, or alternatively, where things come out as if they had been consciously planned even though no such planning is empirically discoverable.

There is no doubt that many examples of design in this sense can be found. The only question is as to what implications can be drawn from this fact. One way of challenging this argument is to claim that these facts can be better explained in other ways. Philo makes some rather bizarre suggestions along these lines in the *Dialogues*. A more serious candidate is the Darwinian theory of evolution, which was developed after Hume's time. On this theory we would regard, for example, the fact that the hooves of the wild horse are well adapted to his need to escape from enemies by flight as due to the fact that in the course of the continuous appearance of variations among the ancestors of the present-day horse, those who had hooves instead of toes, or at least who were tending in that direction, thereby gained an advantage over the others, were more likely to survive attacks and to reproduce like progeny, and that by a long series of such developments the modern horse finally emerged. It certainly looks as if this is an alternative to the theistic explanation that God designed the horse to be well adapted to his environment. According to Darwin all sorts of organisms appear in the world and only those that are well adapted survive and reproduce their kind. We only see the "successes"; the "failures" are no longer around. And this explanation seems to be superior in that it introduces only factors the existence of which has been empirically attested. It is true, of course, that the Darwinian theory only explains the development of relatively simple organisms into relatively complex organisms and has nothing to say about the origin of life. But this is more a comment on the division of science into various fields and theories than a comment on the problem before us. Scientists are currently making progress in the program of explaining the origin of life in chemical terms, and, although they have not completely succeeded to date, it would be rash, as Tennant points out, for a theist to pin his hopes on the continued existence of certain cracks in the scientific edifice. A more reasonable position for the theist to take is that what theism is setting out to explain in the teleogical argument is not this or that example of design, but rather the grand fact that the universe as a whole is such as to include design at various points (and not just in the structure and functions of living organisms). This is basically Tennant's position. And if this is what theism is trying to do, science, by its very nature, can offer no competition, for reasons which are made explicit in the introduction to Section 7.

But even if we agree that an explanation in terms of a supernatural designer is a proper *sort* of explanation for design, it may still be doubted whether the world exhibits clear enough traces of design to require such an explanation. Philo's criticisms in the *Dialogues* are largely given over to such doubts. Some of them seem to miss the mark, for example, the difference in size between the universe and a ship. Compare the analogy, on some physical theories, between the solar system and an atom. But some of his other criticisms are more pertinent. The basic problem would seem to be this: If we are going to argue from the fact of adaptation to anything like a theistic God, we cannot base the argument on particular cases of adaptation; for the most we could infer from such a case would be the existence of some sort of designer behind the scenes who is responsible for that particular adaptation. We need to start from the fact, if it is a fact, that the physical universe as a whole is adapted to the realization of some end which a rational being could regard as supremely worthwhile. This is an application of the general principle that we attribute something to intelligent design only if we suppose that that thing as a whole is adapted to the realization of some end. Consider, for example, an archeologist who in the course of an excavation comes upon some curiously shaped stones. If he discovers that their peculiar shape makes them specially fitted for grinding flour or moulding pottery, or serving as religious symbols for the culture prevailing at that time and place, then he will conclude that they were consciously designed by human beings to serve that purpose. But he would not conclude that the whole area he was exploring—for example, a valley—was produced by human design simply because he found some stones scattered through it which exhibited adaptive features. Moreover, if we want to conclude that the world designer is omnipotent, or even very skillful, we shall have to strengthen the premise by specifying that each part of the universe makes a contribution to the achievement of the overall end. Again, this is a generally accepted principle. If in a strange land I come across a wooden structure which as a whole is clearly adapted for human habitation, but which contains many parts which do not subserve this function (pipes with no outlets, gaps in the roof, doors which lead nowhere), I will suppose that it was constructed by a conscious designer, but a singularly inept one. Finally, if we are to show that the world designer is perfectly good, rather than evil or indifferent, we must first show that this end to the realization of which the whole universe is adapted is of supreme value. Hence the pertinence of Philo's doubts that we know enough about the universe as a whole to be able to say anything of this sort.

Concerning this complex assumption two questions must be raised.

Can we think of any end which would meet these specifications?

Is it a fact that the world process as a whole and in all its parts is directed to this goal?

The most usual answer to the first question is *man*—or to be less parochial, the existence of self-conscious, morally responsible personalities, whatever their form. There have been many other answers given: the glorification of God, the production of an ideal object of God's aesthetic contemplation, the existence of every possible sort of being, considered as an end in itself. But they are less widely accepted today.

Serious problems can be raised about the answer mentioned first.

. . . is what has happened hitherto evidence of the good intentions of the universe? The alleged ground for believing this, as we have seen, is that the universe has produced US. I cannot deny it. But are we really so splendid as to justify such a long prologue? Why . . . this glorification of Man? How about lions and tigers? They destroy fewer animal or human lives than we do, and they are much more beautiful than we are. How about ants? They manage the Corporate State much better than any Fascist. Would not a world of nightingales and larks and deer be better than our human world of cruelty and injustice and war? The believers in Cosmic Purpose make much of our supposed intelligence, but their writings make one doubt it. If I were granted omnipotence, and millions of years to experiment in, I should not think Man much to boast of as the final result of all my efforts.[1]

Note that in this passage Russell concentrates on man's actual record to date. A defender of the position he is attacking would concentrate on man's essential nature, or at least the highest potentialities of that nature. The contention would be that a self-conscious moral agent has an intrinsic value, indeed an incom-

---

[1] Bertrand Russell, *Religion and Science*, London: Oxford Univ. Press (1935), pp. 221–22.

mensurable value, and that he has that value just by being a responsible moral agent, no matter how ungodly a mess he actually makes of things. Moreover, Russell seems to be assuming some sort of utilitarianism, according to which the measure of value is the total quantity of pleasure, happiness, or satisfaction produced. Judged by this standard, the human race would be a disappointing result for the cosmic process. But perhaps the important thing is not to make as many people as comfortable as possible, but to provide maximum opportunities for the free exercise of moral choice, thus giving men the chance to develop moral characters. From this point of view, it would be quite in order for God to take as the goal of his creative activity a situation in which self-conscious personalities were turned loose and given a chance to perfect their natures, even if in fact most of them never got beyond booze, bullying, and business as usual. A vale of soul-making, however strenuous and however strewn with casualties, would be a fit product of divine omnipotence.

What can be said in answer to the second question? Men are here, and that shows that the world process did bring them about. But more than this is needed. First, unless we stay around indefinitely we can hardly claim to be the final goal. And it may be doubted that we will be here that long. Apart from some of the recent developments in military equipment, there are the gloomy predictions made from time to time by astronomers concerning the burning out of the sun and even the running down of the whole universe. Of course, human beings may all enjoy a disembodied form of existence, of one sort or another, before all that happens. But then again they may not.

Second, we still have to show, or at least show reason to believe, that everything in the universe contributes to the realization of the development of moral personalities. And in the present state of scientific knowledge, there seems to be no way of showing this. What goes on in remote parts of the universe is, so far as we can see, not causally relevant to the emergence and maintenance of human beings. It seems that human life on earth would be just what it is even if distant galaxies were very different from what they are. If scientists could not make this assumption, if they had to take into account what is going on in remote stars every time they tried to explain animal or human behavior, they would never get started. Of course, if there were self-conscious moral agents scattered all over the universe, that would change the picture, but are there? And for that matter we cannot see that everything which has happened on earth contributes to the realization of this end. There have been many blind alleys in animal evolution: for example, the dinosaurs, which could have been completely short-circuited without affecting the development of intelligent beings.

Tennant tries to avoid the necessity of showing that the universe as a whole is instrumental to the attainment of some one end or system of ends by basing his argument on the premise that the universe is such as to display various sorts of adaptation. But it would seem that if he is to reach anything like a theistic conclusion he will at least have to give reasons for supposing that everything in the universe contributes in some way to some sort of adaptation.

It was Immanuel Kant who, after claiming to have refuted arguments we have been considering, formulated an argument based on moral considerations. Kant did not regard this argument as proving the existence of God but only as showing that it is a necessary presupposition of morality; but those who have further developed this line of thought have not always drawn that distinction. In Kant's version the argument runs as follows: It is a necessary presupposition of moral endeavor that the morally virtuous will eventually attain happiness. For only in the union of moral virtue and happiness do we have the supreme good; it is a fundamental moral obligation that we should strive to realize the supreme good, and this could be an obligation only if it were possible to attain it. But we cannot have any assurance that virtue and happiness will be united unless the universe is under the control of a morally good personal being. Therefore it is a necessary presupposition of morality that this is the case. Apart from the unwarranted jump from the *possibility* of attaining the supreme good to its actuality or the assurance of its actuality, it has seemed to most who have examined this argument that we do not have enough basis for assuming that the good will get the goods to warrant bringing in something as fundamental as the existence of God in order to shore up that assumption.

The argument as presented by Hastings Rashdall is quite different. In opposition to all theories which would treat moral distinctions as matters of individual taste, feeling, or attitude, or of social agreement, Rashdall insists that moral judgments are objectively either true or false, that there is some objective reality to which we either fail or succeed in conforming when we say of some action, or of some kind of action, that it is right or wrong. (This opposition gives rise to some of the most crucial issues in moral philosophy, and Rashdall does a good job of defending his point of view.) If the moral law exists outside man there must be a superhuman mind in which it exists. God is required as a locus for the moral law. So runs the argument. But it is not at all clear in what sense a moral law has to exist some*where*. Why could it not just be an ultimate fact about the universe that kindness is good and cruelty is bad. This seems to have been Plato's view. Rashdall contrasts physical laws, which have physical objects "in" which to exist, with the homeless status of the moral law. But this contrast is misleading. The objective reality of the law of gravitation, for example, requires that physical objects actually act in accordance with it, but this is due to the fact that a physical law is a statement about the way in which physical things actually do behave. A moral law, by contrast, is not a statement about the way in which persons do in fact behave but about the way in which they *ought* to behave. There is therefore no reason to expect the moral law to be "embodied" in the same sort of way as physical laws.

How does locating the moral law in the mind of God make it *objectively* valid? Is it not still just as subjective as before except for the size of the subject? Are we not simply replacing my or your attitudes with God's? Of course the theist will say that this "simple" difference is in fact the crucial difference. No doubt a theistic God is very different from human beings, but in virtue of what difference does the fact that God recognizes a moral principle make it objective? There are two kinds of answers which can be, and have been, given to this question, and whichever one is given we run into difficulties. A favorite question for dispute in the Middle Ages was: Does God will what is right because it is right, or is what is right right because God wills it? The possible answers to our question include a similar alternative. It may be said that God's endorsement confers objectivity because He is supremely good. But presumably to say that He is supremely good is to say that He consistently does what is right. This presupposes that the distinction between right and wrong has some status antecedent (logically) to God. And we are still left wondering what that status could be. The other answer is that it is God's power, or the fact that everything owes its existence to Him, that gives Him this authority. But, as Rashdall points out, this leaves us with the uncomfortable implication that anything that God decided to approve, even cruelty, would thereby become right; and this seems to be at variance with the moral convictions from which we set out. Rashdall clearly indicates that he wants to give the first of these answers. Presumably he would reply to the above objection by saying that it is the fact that God recognizes a given moral law to be valid that gives it its objective status, and that this status is prior to any *action* on God's part in conformity to it. Whether such an answer would be acceptable would depend on whether or not it makes sense to speak of one recognizing something which is constituted what it is in the act of recognition. This is one of the ancient disputes between idealism (which would maintain that it does make sense) and realism (which would deny it).

SAINT ANSELM

The Ontological Argument

St. Anselm (1033–1109), Archbishop of Canterbury and the most important philosopher of the eleventh century, is best known today as the inventor of the Ontological Argument. The Proslogium *was written about 1077–1078.*

CHAPTER II

Truly there is a God, although the fool hath said in his heart, There is no God.

And so, Lord, do thou, who dost give understanding to faith, give me, so far as thou knowest it to be profitable, to understand that thou art as we believe; and that thou art that which we believe.

And, indeed, we believe that thou art a being than which nothing greater can

From St. Anselm, *Proslogium, Monologium, An Appendix in Behalf of the Fool by Gaunilon; and Cur Deus Homo,* tr. by S. N. Deane (1903), Chs. II–V. Reprinted by permission of The Open Court Publishing Company (1961 edition; introd. by Charles Hartshorne).

be conceived. Or is there no such nature, since the fool hath said in his heart, there is no God? (Psalms xiv. 1). But, at any rate, this very fool, when he hears of this being of which I speak—a being than which nothing greater can be conceived—understands what he hears, and what he understands is in his understanding; although he does not understand it to exist.

For, it is one thing for an object to be in the understanding, and another to understand that the object exists. When a painter first conceives of what he will afterwards perform, he has it in his understanding, but he does not yet understand it to be, because he has not yet performed it. But after he has made the painting, he both has it in his understanding, and he understands that it exists, because he has made it.

Hence, even the fool is convinced that something exists in the understanding, at least, than which nothing greater can be conceived. For, when he hears of this, he understands it. And whatever is understood, exists in the understanding. And assuredly that, than which nothing greater can be conceived, cannot exist in the understanding alone. For, suppose it exists in the understanding alone: then it can be conceived to exist in reality; which is greater.

Therefore, if that, than which nothing greater can be conceived, exists in the understanding alone, the very being, than which nothing greater can be conceived, is one, than which a greater can be conceived. But obviously this is impossible. Hence, there is no doubt that there exists a being, than which nothing greater can be conceived, and it exists both in the understanding and in reality.

CHAPTER III

God cannot be conceived not to exist.—God is that, than which nothing greater can be conceived.—That which can be conceived not to exist is not God.

And it assuredly exists so truly, that it cannot be conceived not to exist. For, it is possible to conceive of a being which cannot be conceived not to exist; and this is greater than one which can be conceived not to exist. Hence, if that, than which nothing greater can be conceived, can be conceived not to exist, it is not that, than which nothing greater can be conceived. But this is an irreconcilable contradiction. There is, then, so truly a being than which nothing greater can be conceived to exist, that it cannot even be conceived not to exist; and this being thou art, O Lord, our God.

So truly, therefore, dost thou exist, O Lord, my God, that thou canst not be conceived not to exist; and rightly. For, if a mind could conceive of a being better than thee, the creature would rise above the Creator; and this is most absurd. And, indeed, whatever else there is, except thee alone, can be conceived not to exist. To thee alone, therefore, it belongs to exist more truly than all other beings, and hence in a higher degree than all others. For, whatever else exists does not exist so truly, and hence in a less degree it belongs to it to exist. Why, then, has the fool said in his heart, there is no God (Psalms xiv. 1), since it is so evident, to a rational mind, that thou dost exist in the highest degree of all? Why, except that he is dull and a fool?

CHAPTER IV

How the fool has said in his heart what cannot be conceived.—A thing may be conceived in two ways: (1) when the word signifying it is conceived; (2) when the thing itself is understood. As far as the word goes, God can be conceived not to exist; in reality he cannot.

But how has the fool said in his heart what he could not conceive; or how is it that he could not conceive what he said in his heart? since it is the same to say in the heart, and to conceive.

But, if really, nay, since really, he

both conceived, because he said in his heart; and did not say in his heart, because he could not conceive; there is more than one way in which a thing is said in the heart or conceived. For, in one sense, an object is conceived, when the word signifying it is conceived; and in another, when the very entity, which the object is, is understood.

In the former sense, then, God can be conceived not to exist; but in the latter, not at all. For no one who understands what fire and water are can conceive fire to be water, in accordance with the nature of the facts themselves, although this is possible according to the words. So, then, no one who understands what God is can conceive that God does not exist; although he says these words in his heart, either without any, or with some foreign, signification. For, God is that than which a greater cannot be conceived. And he who thoroughly understands this, assuredly understands that this being so truly exists, that not even in concept can it be non-existent. Therefore, he who understands that God so exists, cannot conceive that he does not exist.

I thank thee, gracious Lord, I thank thee; because what I formerly believed by thy bounty, I now so understand by thine illumination, that if I were unwilling to believe that thou dost exist, I should not be able not to understand this to be true.

CHAPTER V

God is whatever it is better to be than not to be; and he, as the only self-existent being, creates all things from nothing.

What art thou, then, Lord God, than whom nothing greater can be conceived? But what art thou, except that which, as the highest of all beings, alone exists through itself, and creates all other things from nothing? For, whatever is not this is less than a thing which can be conceived of. But this cannot be conceived of thee. What good, therefore, does the supreme Good lack, through which every good is? Therefore, thou art just, truthful, blessed, and whatever it is better to be than not to be. For it is better to be just than not just; better to be blessed than not blessed.

SAINT THOMAS AQUINAS

Five Arguments for the Existence of God

St. Thomas Aquinas (1225–1274) is the most famous of the medieval Christian philosophers. His great intellectual achievement was the expression of a Christian philosophy and theology in Aristotelian terms, Aristotle having been previously regarded as a threat to the Christian faith. In the ensuing centuries Aquinas has become something like the official philosopher of the Roman Catholic Church.

. . .

The existence of God can be proved in five ways.

The first and more manifest way is the argument from motion. It is certain, and evident to our senses, that in the world some things are in motion. Now whatever is moved is moved by another, for nothing can be moved except it is in potentiality to that towards which it is moved; whereas a thing moves inasmuch as it is in act. For motion is nothing else than the reduction of something from potentiality to actuality. But nothing can be reduced from potentiality to actuality, except by something in a state of actuality. Thus that which is actually hot, as fire, makes wood, which is potentially hot, to be actually hot, and thereby moves and changes it. Now it is not possible that the same thing should be at once in actuality and potentiality in the same respect, but only in different respects. For what is actually hot cannot simultaneously be potentially hot; but it is simultaneously potentially cold. It is therefore impossible that in the same respect and in the same way a thing should be both mover and moved, *i.e.,* that it should move itself. Therefore, whatever is moved must be moved by another. If that by which it is moved be itself moved, then this also must needs be moved by another, and that by another again. But this cannot go on to infinity, because then there would be no first mover, and, consequently, no other mover, seeing that subsequent movers move only inasmuch as they are moved by the first mover; as the staff moves only because it is moved by the hand. Therefore it is necessary to arrive at a first mover, moved by no other; and this everyone understands to be God.

The second way is from the nature of efficient cause. In the world of sensible things we find there is an order of efficient causes. There is no case known (neither is it, indeed, possible) in which a thing is found to be the efficient cause

From St. Thomas Aquinas, *Summa Theologica,* in *The Basic Writings of St. Thomas Aquinas* (1945), ed. by A. C. Pegis, Pt. I, Q. 2, Art. 3. Reprinted by permission of Random House, Inc., and Burns & Oates Ltd.

of itself; for so it would be prior to itself, which is impossible. Now in efficient causes it is not possible to go on to infinity, because in all efficient causes following in order, the first is the cause of the intermediate cause, and the intermediate is the cause of the ultimate cause, whether the intermediate cause be several, or one only. Now to take away the cause is to take away the effect. Therefore, if there be no first cause among efficient causes, there will be no ultimate, nor any intermediate, cause. But if in efficient causes it is possible to go on to infinity, there will be no first efficient cause, neither will there be an ultimate effect, nor any intermediate efficient causes; all of which is plainly false. Therefore it is necessary to admit a first efficient cause, to which everyone gives the name of God.

The third way is taken from possibility and necessity, and runs thus. We find in nature things that are possible to be and not to be, since they are found to be generated, and to be corrupted, and consequently, it is possible for them to be and not to be. But it is impossible for these always to exist, for that which can not-be at some time is not. Therefore, if everything can not-be, then at one time there was nothing in existence. Now if this were true, even now there would be nothing in existence, because that which does not exist begins to exist only through something already existing. Therefore, if at one time nothing was in existence, it would have been impossible for anything to have begun to exist; and thus even now nothing would be in existence —which is absurd. Therefore, not all beings are merely possible, but there must exist something the existence of which is necessary. But every necessary thing either has its necessity caused by another, or not. Now it is impossible to go on to infinity in necessary things which have their necessity caused by another, as has been already proved in regard to efficient causes. Therefore we cannot but admit the existence of some being having of itself its own necessity, and not receiving it from another, but rather causing in others their necessity. This all men speak of as God.

The fourth way is taken from the gradation to be found in things. Among beings there are some more and some less good, true, noble, and the like. But *more* and *less* are predicated of different things according as they resemble in their different ways something which is the maximum, as a thing is said to be hotter according as it more nearly resembles that which is hottest; so that there is something which is truest, something best, something noblest, and, consequently, something which is most being, for those things that are greatest in truth are greatest in being, as it is written in *Metaph.* ii.[1] Now the maximum in any genus is the cause of all in that genus, as fire, which is the maximum of heat, is the cause of all hot things, as is said in the same book.[2] Therefore there must also be something which is to all beings the cause of their being, goodness, and every other perfection; and this we call God.

The fifth way is taken from the governance of the world. We see that things which lack knowledge, such as natural bodies, act for an end, and this is evident from their acting always, or nearly always, in the same way, so as to obtain the best result. Hence it is plain that they achieve their end, not fortuitously, but designedly. Now whatever lacks knowledge cannot move towards an end, unless it be directed by some being endowed with knowledge and intelligence; as the arrow is directed by the archer. Therefore some intelligent being exists by whom all natural things are directed to their end; and this being we call God.

. . .

[1] *Metaph.* Ia, 1 (993b 30).
[2] *Ibid.* (993b 25).

F. C. COPLESTON

A Commentary on Aquinas'
Five Arguments

F. C. Copleston (1907–   ), a member of the Jesuit order, is best known for his multi-volume History of Philosophy, *which is fast becoming the standard work in English. He has been very active in forming links between Thomism and other areas of contemporary thought.*

. . .

Aquinas did not, of course, deny that people can come to know that God exists by other ways than by philosophic reflection. Nor did he ever assert that the belief of most people who accept the proposition that God exists is the result of their having elaborated metaphysical arguments for themselves or of their having thought through the metaphysical arguments developed by others. Nor did he confuse a purely intellectual assent to the conclusion of such a metaphysical argument with a living Christian faith in and love of God. But he did think that reflection on quite familiar features of the world affords ample evidence of God's existence. The reflection itself, sustained and developed at the metaphysical level, is difficult, and he explicitly recognized and acknowledged its difficulty: he certainly did not consider that everyone is capable of sustained metaphysical reflection. At the same time the empirical

From F. C. Copleston, *Aquinas* (1955), Ch. III. Reprinted by permission of Penguin Books Ltd.

facts on which this reflection is based were for him quite familiar facts. In order to see the relation of finite things to the being on which they depend we are not required to pursue scientific research, discovering hitherto unknown empirical facts. Nor does the metaphysician discover God in a manner analogous to the explorer who suddenly comes upon a hitherto unknown island or flower. It is attention and reflection which are required rather than research or exploration.

What, then, are the familiar facts which for Aquinas imply the existence of God? Mention of them can be found in the famous 'five ways' of proving God's existence, which are outlined in the *Summa theologica* (Ia, 2, 3). In the first way Aquinas begins by saying that 'it is certain, and it is clear from sense-experience, that some things in this world are moved.' It must be remembered that he, like Aristotle, understands the term 'motion' in the broad sense of change, reduction from a state of potentiality to one of act; he does not refer exclusively to local motion. In the second way he starts with the remark that 'we find in material things an order of efficient causes.' In other words, in our experience of things and of their relations to one another we are aware of efficient causality. Thus while in the first way he begins with the fact that some things are acted upon and changed by other things, the second way is based upon the fact that some things act upon other things, as efficient causes. In the third way he starts by stating that 'we find among things some which are capable of existing or not existing, since we find that some things come into being and pass away.' In other words, we perceive that some things are corruptible or perishable. In the fourth proof he observes that 'we find in things that some are more or less good and true and noble and so on (than others).' Finally in the fifth way he says: 'we see that some things which lack knowledge, namely natural bodies, act for an end, which is clear from the fact that they always or in most cases act in the same way, in order to attain what is best.'

There is, I think, little difficulty in accepting as empirical facts the starting-points of the first three ways. For nobody really doubts that some things are acted upon and changed or 'moved,' that some things act on others, and that some things are perishable. Each of us is aware, for example, that he is acted upon and changed, that he sometimes acts as an efficient cause, and that he is perishable. Even if anyone were to cavil at the assertion that he is aware that he himself was born and will die, he knows very well that some other people were born and have died. But the starting-points of the two final arguments may cause some difficulty. The proposition that there are different grades of perfections in things stands in need of a much more thorough analysis than Aquinas accords it in his brief outline of the fourth way. For the schematic outlining of the five proofs

was designed, not to satisfy the critical minds of mature philosophers, but as introductory material for 'novices' in the study of theology. And in any case Aquinas could naturally take for granted in the thirteenth century ideas which were familiar to his contemporaries and which had not yet been subjected to the radical criticism to which they were later subjected. At the same time there is not very much difficulty in understanding the sort of thing which was meant. We are all accustomed to think and speak as though, for example, there were different degrees of intelligence and intellectual capacity. In order to estimate the different degrees we need, it is true, standards or fixed points of reference; but, given these points of reference, we are all accustomed to make statements which imply different grades of perfections. And though these statements stand in need of close analysis, they refer to something which falls within ordinary experience and finds expression in ordinary language. As for the fifth way, the modern reader may find great difficulty in seeing what is meant if he confines his attention to the relevant passage in the *Summa theologica*. But if he looks at the *Summa contra Gentiles* (1, 13) he will find Aquinas saying that we see things of different natures co-operating in the production and maintenance of a relatively stable order or system. When Aquinas says that we see purely material things acting for an end, he does not mean to say that they act in a manner analogous to that in which human beings consciously act for definite purposes. Indeed, the point of the argument is that they do not do so. He means that different kinds of things, like fire and water, the behaviour of which is determined by their several 'forms,' co-operate, not consciously but as a matter of fact, in such a way that there is a relatively stable order or system. And here again, though much more would need to be said in a full discussion of the matter, the basic idea is nothing particularly extraordinary nor is it contrary to our ordinary experience and expectations.

It is to be noted also that Aquinas speaks with considerable restraint: he avoids sweeping generalizations. Thus in the first argument he does not say that all material things are 'moved' but that we see that some things in this world are moved or changed. In the third argument he does not state that all finite things are contingent but that we are aware that some things come into being and pass away. And in the fifth argument he does not say that there is an invariable world-order or system but that we see natural bodies acting always or in most cases in the same ways. The difficulty, therefore, which may be experienced in regard to Aquinas' proofs of God's existence concerns not so much the empirical facts or alleged empirical facts with which he starts as in seeing that these facts imply God's existence.

Perhaps a word should be said at once about this idea of 'implication.' As a matter of fact Aquinas does not use the word when talking about the five ways: he speaks of 'proof' and of 'demonstration.' And by 'demonstration' he means in this context what he calls *demonstratio quia* (S.T., Ia, 2, 2), namely a causal proof of God's existence, proceeding from the affirmation of some empirical fact, for example that there are things which change, to the affirmation of a transcendent cause. It is, indeed, his second proof which is strictly the causal argument, in the sense that it deals explicitly with the order of efficient causality; but in every proof the idea of ontological dependence on a transcendent cause appears in some form or other. Aquinas' conviction was that a full understanding of the empirical facts which are selected for consideration in the five ways involves seeing the dependence of these facts on a transcendent cause. The existence of things which change, for instance, is, in his opinion, not self-explanatory: it can be rendered intelligible only if seen as dependent on a transcendent cause, a cause, that is to say, which does not itself belong to the order of changing things.

This may suggest to the modern reader that Aquinas was concerned with causal explanation in the sense that he was concerned with framing an empirical hypothesis to explain certain facts. But he did not regard the proposition affirming God's existence as a causal hypothesis in the sense of being in principle revisable, as a hypothesis, that is to say, which might conceivably have to be revised in the light of fresh empirical data or which might be supplanted by a more economical hypothesis. This point can perhaps be seen most clearly in the case of his third argument, which is based on the fact that there are things which come into being and pass away. In Aquinas' opinion no fresh scientific knowledge about the physical constitution of such things could affect the validity of the argument. He did not look on a 'demonstration' of God's existence as an empirical hypothesis in the sense in which the electronic theory, for example, is said to be an empirical hypothesis. It is, of course, open to anyone to say that in his own opinion cosmological arguments in favour of God's existence are in fact analogous to the empirical hypotheses of the sciences and that they have a predictive function; but it does not follow that this interpretation can legitimately be ascribed to Aquinas. We should not be misled by the illustrations which he sometimes offers from contemporary scientific theory. For these are mere illustrations to elucidate a point in terms easily understandable by his readers: they are not meant to indicate that the proofs of God's existence were for him empirical hypotheses in the modern sense of the term.

Does this mean, therefore, that Aquinas regarded the existence of God as being logically entailed by facts such as change or coming into being and passing away? He did not, of course, regard the proposition 'there are things which come into being and pass away' as logically entailing the proposition 'there is an absolutely necessary or independent being' in the sense that affirmation of the one proposition and denial of the other involves one in a verbal or formal linguistic contradiction. But he thought that metaphysical analysis of what it objectively means to be a thing which comes into being and passes away shows that such a thing must depend existentially on an absolutely necessary being. And he thought that metaphysical analysis of what it objectively means to be a changing thing shows that such a thing depends on a supreme unmoved mover. It follows that for Aquinas one is involved in a contradiction if one affirms the propositions 'there are things which come into being and pass away' and 'there are things which change' and at the same time denies the propositions 'there is an absolutely necessary being' and 'there is a supreme unmoved mover.' But the contradiction can be made apparent only by means of metaphysical analysis. And the entailment in question is fundamentally an ontological or causal entailment.

Not a few philosophers (certainly all 'empiricists') would presumably comment that if this represents Aquinas' real mind it is clear that he confused the causal relation with logical entailment. But it should be remembered that though Aquinas was convinced that the proposition stating that everything which begins to exist has *a* cause is absolutely certain he did not think that the existence of any finite thing entails the existence of any other finite thing in the sense that the existence of any finite thing can be said to entail the existence of God. In

theological language, if we once admit that there is an omnipotent Creator, we can say that He could create and maintain in existence any finite thing without the existence of any other finite thing. But it does not follow that there can be any finite thing without God. In other words, Aquinas is not bound to produce other instances of the ontological entailment which he asserts between the existence of finite things and God. Though the relation of creatures to God is analogous in some way to the relation of causal dependence of one finite thing on another, the former relation is, if we consider it as such, unique. Aquinas was not confusing causal relations in general with logical entailments: he was asserting a unique relation between finite things and the transfinite transcendent cause on which they depend.

It is worth emphasizing perhaps that it does not necessarily follow from Aquinas' view that a metaphysical approach to God's existence is an easy matter. It is true that he was confident of the power of the human reason to attain knowledge of God's existence; and he did not regard his arguments as standing in need of support from rhetoric or emotional appeal. And in the *Summa theologica,* where he is writing for 'novices' in theology, he states the arguments in a bald and perhaps disconcertingly impersonal manner. But we cannot legitimately conclude that he thought it easy for a man to come to the knowledge of God's existence by philosophic reflection alone. Indeed, he makes an explicit statement to the opposite effect. He was well aware that in human life other factors besides metaphysical reflection exercise a great influence. Moreover, he would obviously agree that it is always possible to stop the process of reflection at a particular point. For Aquinas every being, in so far as it is or has being, is intelligible. But we can consider things from different points of view or under different aspects. For example, I might consider coming-into-being and passing-away simply in regard to definite instances and from a subjective point of view. It grieves me to think that someone I love will probably die before me and leave, as we say, a gap in my life. Or it grieves me to think that I shall die and be unable to complete the work which I have undertaken. Or I might consider coming-into-being and passing-away from some scientific point of view. What are the finite phenomenal causes of organic decay or of the generation of an organism? But I can also consider coming-into-being and passing-away purely as such and objectively, adopting a metaphysical point of view and directing my attention to the sort of being, considered as such, which is capable of coming into being and passing away. Nobody can compel me to adopt this point of view. If I am determined to remain on the level of, say, some particular science, I remain there; and that is that. Metaphysical reflections will have no meaning for me. But the metaphysical point of view is a possible point of view, and metaphysical reflection belongs to a full understanding of things so far as this is possible for a finite mind. And if I do adopt this point of view and maintain it in sustained reflection, an existential relation of dependence, Aquinas was convinced, should become clear to me which will not become clear to me if I remain on a different level of reflection. But just as extraneous factors (such as the influence of the general outlook promoted by a technical civilization) may help to produce my decision to remain on a non-metaphysical level of reflection, so also can extraneous factors influence my reflections on the metaphysical level. It seems to me quite wrong to suggest that Aquinas did not regard metaphysical reflection as a possible way of becoming aware of God's existence and that he looked on it, as some writers have suggested, as being simply a rational justification of an assurance which is necessarily attained in some other way. For if it constitutes a rational justification at all, it must, I think, be a possible way of becoming aware of God's existence. But it does not necessarily follow, of course, that it is an easy way or a common way.

After these general remarks I turn to Aquinas' five proofs of the existence of God. In the first proof he argues that 'motion' or change means the reduction of a thing from a state of potentiality to one of act, and that a thing cannot be reduced from potentiality to act except under the influence of an agent already in act. In this sense 'everything which is moved must be moved by another.' He argues finally that in order to avoid an infinite regress in the chain of movers, the existence of a first unmoved mover must be admitted. 'And all understand that this is God.'

A statement like 'all understand that this is God' or 'all call this (being) God' occurs at the end of each proof, and I postpone consideration of it for the moment. As for the ruling out of an infinite regress, I shall explain what Aquinas means to reject after outlining the second proof, which is similar in structure to the first.

Whereas in the first proof Aquinas considers things as being acted upon, as being changed or 'moved,' in the second he considers them as active agents, as efficient causes. He argues that there is a hierarchy of efficient causes, a subordinate cause being dependent on the cause above it in the hierarchy. He then proceeds, after excluding the hypothesis of an infinite regress, to draw the conclusion that there must be a first efficient cause, 'which all call God.'

Now, it is obviously impossible to discuss these arguments profitably unless they are first understood. And misunderstanding of them is only too easy, since the terms and phrases used are either unfamiliar or liable to be taken in a sense other than the sense intended. In the first place it is essential to understand that in the first argument Aquinas supposes that movement or change is dependent on a 'mover' acting here and now, and that in the second argument he supposes that there are efficient causes in the world which even in their causal activity are here and now dependent on the causal activity of other causes. That is why I have spoken of a 'hierarchy' rather than of a 'series.' What he is thinking of can be illustrated in this way. A son is dependent on his father, in the sense that he would not have existed except for the causal activity of his father. But when the son acts for himself, he is not dependent here and now on his father. But he is dependent here and now on other factors. Without the activity of the air, for instance, he could not himself act, and the life-preserving activity of the air is itself dependent here and now on other factors, and they in turn on other factors. I do not say that this illustration is in all respects adequate for the purpose; but it at least illustrates the fact that when Aquinas talks about an 'order' of efficient causes he is not thinking of a series stretching back into the past, but of a hierarchy of causes, in which a subordinate member is here and now dependent on the causal activity of a higher member. If I wind up my watch at night, it then proceeds to work without further interference on my part. But the activity of the pen tracing these words on the page is here and now dependent on the activity of my hand, which in turn is here and now dependent on other factors.

The meaning of the rejection of an infinite regress should now be clear. Aquinas is not rejecting the possiblity of an infinite series as such. We have already seen that he did not think that anyone had ever succeeded in showing the impossibility of an infinite series of events stretching back into the past. Therefore he does not mean to rule out the possibility of an infinite series of causes and effects, in which a given member depended on the preceding member, say X on Y, but does not, once it exists, depend here and now on the present causal acitivity of the preceding member. We have to imagine, not a lineal or horizontal series, so to speak, but a vertical hierarchy, in which a lower member depends here and now on the present causal activity of the member above it. It is the latter type of series, if prolonged to infinity, which Aquinas rejects. And he rejects it on the ground that unless there is a 'first' member, a mover which is not itself moved or a cause which does not itself depend on the causal activity of a higher cause, it is not possible to explain the 'motion' or the causal activity of the lowest member. His point of view is this. Suppress the first unmoved mover and there is no motion or change here and now. Suppress the first efficient cause and there is no causal activity here and now. If therefore we find that some things in the world are changed, there must be a first unmoved mover. And if there are efficient causes in the world, there must be a first efficient, and completely non-dependent cause. The word 'first' does not mean first in the temporal order, but supreme or first in the ontological order.

A remark on the word 'cause' is here in place. What precisely Aquinas would have said to the David Humes either of the fourteenth century or of the modern era it is obviously impossible to say. But it is clear that he believed in real causal efficacy and real causal relations. He was aware, of course, that causal efficacy is not the object of vision in the sense in which patches of colours are objects of vision; but the human being, he considered, is aware of real causal relations and if we understand 'perception' as involving the co-operation of sense and intellect, we can be said to 'perceive' causality. And presumably he would have said that the sufficiency of a phenomenalistic interpretation of causality for purposes of physical science proves nothing against the validity of a metaphysical notion of causality. It is obviously possible to dispute whether his analyses of change or 'motion' and of efficient causality are valid or invalid and whether there is such a thing as a hierarchy of causes. And our opinion about the validity or invalidity of his arguments for the existence of God will depend very largely on our answers to these questions. But mention of the mathematical infinite series is irrelevant to a discussion of his arguments. And it is this point which I have been trying to make clear.

In the third proof Aquinas starts from the fact that some things come into being and perish, and he concludes from this that it is possible for them to exist or not to exist: they do not exist 'necessarily.' He then argues that it is impossible for things which are of this kind to exist always; for 'that which is capable of not existing, at some time does not exist.' If all things were of this kind, at some time there would be nothing. Aquinas is clearly supposing for the sake of argument the hypothesis of infinite time, and his proof is designed to cover this hypothesis. He does not say that infinite time is impossible: what he says is that if time is infinite and if all things are capable of not existing, this potentiality would inevitably be fulfilled in infinite time. There would then be nothing. And if there had ever been nothing, nothing would now exist. For no thing can bring itself into existence. But it is clear as a matter of fact that there are things. Therefore it can never have been true to say that there was literally no thing. Therefore it is impossible that all things should be capable of existing or not existing. There must, then, be some necessary being. But perhaps it is neces-

sary in the sense that it must exist if something else exists; that is to say, its necessity may be hypothetical. We cannot, however, proceed to infinity in the series or hierarchy of necessary beings. If we do so, we do not explain the presence here and now of beings capable of existing or not existing. Therefore we must affirm the existence of a being which is absolutely necessary (*per se necessarium*) and completely independent. 'And all call this being *God*.'

This argument may appear to be quite unnecessarily complicated and obscure. But it has to be seen in its historical context. As already mentioned, Aquinas designed his argument in such a way as to be independent of the question whether or not the world existed from eternity. He wanted to show that on either hypothesis there must be a necessary being. As for the introduction of hypothetical necessary beings, he wanted to show that even if there are such beings, perhaps within the universe, which are not corruptible in the sense in which a flower is corruptible, there must still be an absolutely independent being. Finally, in regard to terminology, Aquinas uses the common medieval expression 'necessary being.' He does not actually use the term 'contingent being' in the argument and talks instead about 'possible' beings; but it comes to the same thing. And though the words 'contingent' and 'necessary' are now applied to propositions rather than to beings, I have retained Aquinas' mode of speaking. Whether one accepts the argument or not, I do not think that there is any insuperable difficulty in understanding the line of thought. The fourth argument is admittedly difficult to grasp. Aquinas argues that there are degrees of perfections in things. Different kinds of finite things possess different perfections in diverse limited degrees. He then argues not only that if there are different degrees of a perfection like goodness there is a supreme good to which other good things approximate but also that all limited degrees of goodness are caused by the supreme good. And since goodness is a convertible term with being, a thing being good in so far as it has being, the supreme good is the supreme being and the cause of being in all other things. 'Therefore there is something which is the cause of the being and goodness and of every perfection in all other things; and this we call *God*.'

Aquinas refers to some remarks of Aristotle in the *Metaphysics;* but this argument puts one in mind at once of Plato's *Symposium* and *Republic*. And the Platonic doctrine of participation seems to be involved. Aquinas was not immediately acquainted with either work, but the Platonic line of thought was familiar to him from other writers. And it has not disappeared from philosophy. Indeed, some of those theists who reject or doubt the validity of the 'cosmological' arguments seem to feel a marked attraction for some variety of the fourth way, arguing that in the recognition of objective values we implicitly recognize God as the supreme value. But if the line of thought represented by the fourth way is to mean anything to the average modern reader, it has to be presented in a rather different manner from that in which it is expressed by Aquinas who was able to assume in his readers ideas and points of view which can no longer be presupposed.

Finally, the fifth proof, if we take its statement in the *Summa theologica* together with that in the *Summa contra Gentiles,* can be expressed more or less as follows. The activity and behaviour of each thing is determined by its form. But we observe material things of very different types co-operating in such a way as to produce and maintain a relatively stable world-order or system. They achieve an 'end,' the production and maintenance of a cosmic order. But non-intelligent material things certainly do not co-operate consciously in view of a purpose. If it is said that they co-operate in the realization of an end or purpose, this does not mean that they intend the realization of this order in a manner analogous to that in which a man can act consciously with a view to the achievement of a purpose. Nor, when Aquinas talks about operating 'for an end' in this connexion, is he thinking of the utility of certain things to the human race. He is not saying, for example, that grass grows to feed the sheep and that sheep exist in order that human beings should have food and clothing. It is of the unconscious co-operation of different kinds of material things in the production and maintenance of a relatively stable cosmic system that he is thinking, not of the benefits accruing to us from our use of certain objects. And his argument is that this co-operation on the part of heterogeneous material things clearly points to the existence of an extrinsic intelligent author of this co-operation, who operates with an end in view. If Aquinas had lived in the days of the evolutionary hypothesis, he would doubtless have argued that this hypothesis supports rather than invalidates the conclusion of the argument.

No one of these arguments was entirely new, as Aquinas himself was very well aware. But he developed them and arranged them to form a coherent whole. I do not mean that he regarded the validity of one particular argument as necessarily depending on the validity of the other four. He doubtless thought that each argument was valid in its own right. But, as I have already remarked, they conform to a certain pattern, and they are mutually complementary in the sense that in each argument things are considered from a different point of view or under a different aspect. There are so many different approaches to God.

. . .

A. E. TAYLOR

A Contemporary Restatement of Traditional Arguments for the Existence of God

A. E. Taylor (1869–1945) was Professor of Moral Philosophy in the University of Edinburgh. He was well known both as an interpreter of Plato and as an original philosopher.

I FROM NATURE TO GOD

(1) The argument "from Nature up to Nature's God" can be presented in very different forms and with very different degrees of persuasiveness, corresponding with the more or less definite and accurate knowledge of different ages about the detailed facts of Nature and the greater or less degree of articulation attained by Logic. But the main thought underlying these very different variations is throughout the same, that the incomplete points to the complete, the dependent to the independent, the temporal to the eternal. Nature, in the sense of the complex of "objects presented to our notice," the bodies animate and inanimate around us, and our own bodies which interact with them and each other, is, in the first place, always something incomplete; it has no limits or bounds; the horizon in space and time endlessly recedes as we carry our adventure of exploration further; "still beyond the sea,

From A. E. Taylor, "The Vindication of Religion," in *Essays Catholic and Critical* (1926), ed. by E. G. Selwyn. Reprinted by permission of The Society for Promoting Christian Knowledge.

there is more sea." What is more, Nature is always dependent; no part of it contains its complete explanation in itself; to explain why any part is what it is, we have always to take into account the relations of that part with some other, which in turn requires for explanation its relation to a third, and so on without end. And the fuller and richer our knowledge of the content of Nature becomes, the more, not the less, imperative do we find the necessity of explaining everything by reference to other things which, in their turn, call for explanation in the same way. Again, mutability is stamped on the face of every part of Nature. "All things pass and nothing abides." What was here in the past is now here no more, and what is here now will some day no longer be here. "There stood the rock where rolls the sea." Even what looks at first like permanence turns out on closer examination to be only slower birth and decay. Even the Christian Middle Ages thought of the "heavens" as persisting unchanged from the day of their creation to that of their coming dissolution in fiery heat and new creation; modern astronomy tells us of the gradual production and dissolution of whole "stellar systems." Thoughts like these suggested to the Greek mind from the very infancy of science the conclusion that Nature is no self-contained system which is its own *raison d'être*. Behind all temporality and change there must be something unchanging and eternal which is the source of all things mutable and the explanation why they are as they are. In the first instance this sense of mutability gave rise only to a desire to know what is the permanent stuff of which what we call "things" are only passing phases; is it water, or vapour, or fire, or perhaps something different from them all? The one question which was primary for the earliest men of science was just this question about the stuff of which everything is made. To us it seems a very different thing to say "all things are water," or to say "I believe in God," but at bottom the quest after the stuff of which things are made is a first uncertain and half-blind step in the same direction as Aristotle's famous argument, adopted by St. Thomas, for the existence of an "unmoved Mover" (who, remaining *immotus in se*, is the source of all the movement and life of this lower world), and as all the since familiar *a posteriori* proofs of the existence of God.

(2) It is but a further step in the same direction, which was soon taken by the early founders of science, when it is perceived that the persistence of an unchanged "stuff" is no complete explanation of the apparent facts of Nature, and that we have further to ask where the "motion" which is the life of all natural processes comes from. This is the form in which the problem presented itself to Aristotle and his great follower St. Thomas. They believed that "Nature is uniform" in the sense that all the apparently irregular and lawless movements and changes with which life makes us familiar in the world around us issue from, and are the effects of, other movements (those of the "heavens"), which

are absolutely regular and uniform. On this view, the supreme dominant uniform movement in Nature is naturally identified with the apparently absolutely regular diurnal revolution of the whole stellar heavens round the earth. But Aristotle could not be content to accept the mere fact of this supposed revolution as an ultimate fact needing no further explanation. No motion explains itself, and we have therefore to ask the "cause" or reason why the heavens should display this uniform continuous movement. That reason Aristotle and his followers could only explain in the language of imaginative myth. Since nothing can set itself going, the movement which pervades the whole universe of Nature must be set going by something which is not itself set going by anything else; not mutable and changeable therefore, but eternally selfsame and perfect, because it already is all that it can be, and so neither needs nor permits of development of any kind. "From such a principle depends the whole heaven." [1] And it follows from certain other presuppositions of Aristotle's philosophy that this "principle" must be thought of as a perfect and living intelligence. Thus in Aristotle's formulation of the principles of natural science we reach the explicit result that Nature is in its inmost structure only explicable as something which depends on a perfect and eternal source of life, and this source is not itself Nature nor any part of Nature; the "transcendence of God" has at last been explicitly affirmed as a truth suggested (Aristotle and St. Thomas would say demonstrated) by the rational analysis of Nature herself. In principle their argument is that of every later form of the "cosmological proof."

. . .

Let us look back at this line of thought, out of which the familiar "proofs of the existence of God" brought forward in

[1] Aristotle, *Metaphysics*, 1072*b*, 14.

popular works on Natural Theology have been developed, and ask ourselves what permanent value it retains for us to-day and how far it goes towards suggesting the real existence of a God whom a religious man can worship "in spirit and in truth." We must not suppose that the thought itself is necessarily antiquated because the language in which it is clothed strikes us as old-fashioned, or because those who gave it its first expression held certain views about the details of Nature's structure (notably the geocentric conception in astronomy) which are now obsolete. It may very well be that the substituion of contemporary for antiquated views about the structure of the "stellar universe" or the fixity of animal species will leave the force of the argument, whatever that force may be, unaffected. There are two criticisms in particular which it is as well to dispose of at once, since both sound plausible, and both, unless I am badly mistaken, go wide of the mark.

The point of the argument about the necessity of an "unmoving source of motion" must not be missed. We shall grasp it better if we remember that "motion" in the vocabulary of Aristotle means change of every kind, so that what is being asserted is that there must be an unchanging cause or source of change. Also, we must not fancy that we have disposed of the argument by saying that there is no scientific presumption that the series of changes which make up the life of Nature may not have been without a beginning and destined to have no end. St. Thomas, whose famous five proofs of the existence of God are all of them variations on the argument from "motion," or, as we might say, the appeal to the principle of causality, was also the philosopher who created a sensation among the Christian thinkers of his day by insisting stiffly that, apart from the revelation given in Scripture, no reasons can be produced for holding that the world had a beginning or need have an end, as indeed Aristotle maintained that it has neither. The dependence meant in the argument has nothing to do with succession in time. What is really meant is that our knowledge of any event in Nature is not complete until we know the full reason for the event. So long as you only know that A is so because B is so, but cannot tell why B is so, your knowledge is incomplete. It only becomes complete when you are in a postion to say that ultimately A is so because Z is so, Z being something which is its own *raison d'être,* and therefore such that it would be senseless to ask *why* Z is so. This at once leads to the conclusion that since we always have the right to ask about any event in Nature why that event is so, what are its conditions, the Z which is its own *raison d'être* cannot itself belong to Nature. The point of the reasoning is precisely that it is an argument from the fact that there is a "Nature" to the reality of a "Supernature," and this point is unaffected by the question whether there ever was a beginning of time, or a time when there were no "events."

Again, we must not be led off the track by the plausible but shallow remark that the whole problem about the "cause of motion" arose from the unnecessary assumption that things were once at rest and afterwards began to move, so that you have only to start, as the modern physicist does, with a plurality of moving particles, or atoms, or electrons to get rid of the whole question. Nor would it be relevant to remark that modern physics knows of no such absolutely uniform motions as those which Aristotle ascribes to "the heavens," but only of more or less stable motions. If you start, for example, with a system of "particles" all in uniform motion, you have still to account for the rise of "differential" motions. If you start, as Epicurus tried to do, with a rain of particles all moving in the same direction and with the same relative velocities, you cannot explain why these particles ever came together to form complexes. If you prefer, with Herbert Spencer, to start with a strictly "homogeneous" nebula, you have to explain, as Spencer does not, how "heterogeneity" ever got in. You must have individual variety, as well as "uniformity," in whatever you choose to take as your postulated original data if you are to get out of the data a world like ours, which, as Mill truly says, is not only uniform but also infinitely various. *Ex nihilo, nihil fit,* and equally out of blank uniformity nothing *fit* but a uniformity equally blank. Even if, *per impossibile,* you could exclude all individual variety from the initial data of a system of natural science, you might properly be asked to account for this singular absence of variety, and a naturalistic account of it could only take the form of deriving it from some more ultimate state of things which was not marked by absolute "uniformity." Neither uniformity nor variety is self-explanatory; whichever you start with, you are faced by the old dilemma. Either the initial data must simply be taken as brute "fact," for which there is no reason at all, or if there is a reason, it must be found outside Nature, in the "supernatural."

. . .

We may, for example, consider how the old-fashioned argument from "motion" to the "unmoving" source of motion, when stated in its most general form, might still be urged even to-day. As we have seen, the argument is simply from the temporal, conditioned and mutable to something eternal, unconditioned and immutable as its source. The nerve of the whole reasoning is that every explanation of given facts or events involves bringing in reference to further unexplained facts; a complete explanation of anything, if we could obtain one, would therefore require that we should trace the fact explained back to something which contains its own explanation within itself, a something which is and is what it is in its own right; such a something plainly is not an event or mere fact and therefore not included in "Nature," the complex of all events and facts, but "above" Nature. Any man has a right to say, if he pleases, that he personally does not care to spend his time in exercising this mode of thinking, but would rather occupy himself in discovering fresh facts or fresh and hitherto unsuspected relations between facts. We need not blame him for that; but we are entitled to ask those who are alive to the meaning of the old problem how they propose to deal with it, if they reject the inference from the unfinished and conditioned to the perfect and unconditioned. For my own part I can see only two alternatives.

(i) One is to say, as Hume [2] did in his "Dialogues on Natural Religion," that, though every "part" of Nature may be dependent on other parts for its explanation, the *whole* system of facts or events which we call Nature may as a whole be self-explanatory; the "world" itself may be that "necessary being" of which philosophers and divines have spoken. In other words, a complex system in which every member, taken singly, is temporal, may as a complex be eternal; every member may be incomplete, but the whole may be complete; every member mutable, but the whole unchanging. Thus, as many philosophers of yesterday and to-day have said, the "eternal" would just be the temporal fully understood; there would be no contrast between Nature and "supernature," but only between "Nature apprehended as a whole" and Nature as we have to apprehend her fragmentarily. The thought is a pretty one, but I cannot believe that it will stand criticism.

---

[2] Or rather, the sceptical critic in the *Dialogues.* We cannot be sure of Hume's own agreement with the suggestion.

The very first question suggested by the sort of formula I have just quoted is whether it is not actually self-contradictory to call Nature a "whole" at all; if it is, there can clearly be no apprehending of Nature as something which she is not. And I think it quite clear that Nature, in the sense of the complex of events, is, in virtue of her very structure, something incomplete and not a true whole. I can explain the point best, perhaps, by an absurdly simplified example. Let us suppose that Nature consists of just four constituents, A, B, C, D. We are supposed to "explain" the behaviour of A by the structure of B, C, and D, and the interaction of B, C, and D with A, and similarly with each of the other three constituents. Obviously enough, with a set of "general laws" of some kind we can "explain" why A behaves as it does, if we know all about its structure and the structures of B, C, and D. But it still remains entirely unexplained why A should be there at all, or why, if it is there, it should have B, C, and D as its neighbours rather than others with a totally different structure of their own. That this is so has to be accepted as a "brute" fact which is not explained nor yet self-explanatory. Thus no amount of knowledge of "natural laws" will explain the present actual state of Nature unless we also assume it as a brute fact that the distribution of "matter" and "energy" (or whatever else we take as the ultimates of our system of physics) a hundred millions of years ago was such and such. With the same "laws" and a different "initial" distribution the actual state of the world to-day would be very different. "Collocations," to use Mill's terminology, as well as "laws of causation" have to enter into all our scientific explanations. And though it is true that as our knowledge grows, we are continually learning to assign causes for particular "collocations" originally accepted as bare facts, we only succeed in doing so by falling back on other anterior "collocations" which we have equally to take as unexplained bare facts. As M. Meyerson puts it, we only get rid of the "inexplicable" at one point at the price of introducing it again somewhere else. Now any attempt to treat the complex of facts we call Nature as something which will be found to be more nearly self-explanatory the more of them we know, and would become quite self-explanatory if we only knew them all, amounts to an attempt to eliminate "bare fact" altogether, and reduce Nature simply to a complex of "laws." In other words, it is an attempt to manufacture particular existents out of mere universals, and therefore must end in failure. And the actual progress of science bears witness to this. The more we advance to the reduction of the visible face of Nature to "law," the more, not the less, complex and baffling become the mass of characters which we have to attribute as bare unexplained fact to our ultimate constituents. An electron is a much stiffer dose of "brute" fact than one of Newton's hard impenetrable corpuscles.

Thus we may fairly say that to surrender ourselves to the suggestion that Nature, if we only knew enough, would be seen to be a self-explanatory whole is to follow a will-of-the-wisp. The duality of "law" and "fact" cannot be eliminated from natural science, and this means that in the end either Nature is not explicable at all, or, if she is, the explanation has to be sought in something "outside" on which Nature depends.

(ii) Hence it is not surprising that both among men of science and among philosophers there is just now a strong tendency to give up the attempt to "explain" Nature completely and to fall back on an "ultimate pluralism." This means that we resign ourselves to the admission of the duality of "law" and "fact." We assume that there are a plurality of ultimately different constituents of Nature, each with its own specific character and way of behaving, and our business in explanation is simply to show how to account for the world as we find it by the fewest and simplest laws of interaction between these different constituents. In other words we give up altogether the attempt to "explain Nature"; we are content to "explain" lesser "parts" of Nature in terms of their specific character and their relations to other "parts." This is clearly a completely justified mode of procedure for a man of science who is aiming at the solution of some particular problem such as, *e.g.,* the discovery of the conditions under which a permanent new "species" originates and maintains itself. But it is quite another question whether "ultimate pluralism" can be the last word of a "philosophy of Nature." If you take it so, it really means that in the end you have no reason to assign why there should be just so many ultimate constituents of "Nature" as you say there are, or why they should have the particular characters you say they have, except that "it happens to be the case." You are acquiescing in unexplained brute fact, not because in the present state of knowledge you do not see your way to do better, but on the plea that there is and can be no explanation. You are putting unintelligible mystery at the very heart of reality.

Perhaps it may be rejoined, "And why should we not acknowledge this, seeing that, whether we like it or not, we must come to this in the end?" Well, at least it may be retorted that to acquiesce in such a "final inexplicability" as final means that you have denied the validity of the very assumption on which all science is built. All through the history of scientific advance it has been taken for granted that we are not to acquiesce in inexplicable brute fact; whenever we come across what, with our present light, has to be accepted as merely fact, we

have a right to ask for further explanation, and should be false to the spirit of science if we did not. Thus we inevitably reach the conclusion that either the very principles which inspire and guide scientific inquiry itself are an illusion, or Nature itself must be dependent on some reality which is self-explanatory, and therefore not Nature nor any part of Nature, but, in the strict sense of the words, "supernatural" or "transcendent" —transcendent, that is, in the sense that in it there is overcome that duality of "law" and "fact" which is characteristic of Nature and every part of Nature. It is not "brute" fact, and yet it is not an abstract universal law or complex of such laws, but a really existing self-luminous Being, such that you could see, if you only apprehended its true character, that to have that character and to be are the same thing. This is the way in which Nature, as it seems to me, inevitably points beyond itself as the temporal and mutable to an "other" which is eternal and immutable.

. . .

II   FROM MAN TO GOD

With the line of thought we have now to consider we can deal more briefly. If meditation on the creatures in general leads us by a circuitous route and an obscure light to the thought of their Maker, meditation on the moral being of man suggests God more directly and much less obscurely. For we are now starting a fresh stage of the "ascent" from a higher level, and it is with the road to God as with Dante's purgatorial mountain: the higher you have mounted, the easier it is to rise higher still. In Nature we at best see God under a disguise so heavy that it allows us to discern little more than that someone is there; within our own moral life we see Him with the mask, so to say, half fallen off.

Once more the general character of the ascent is the same; we begin with the temporal, and in a certain sense the natural, to end in the eternal and supernatural. But the line of thought, though kindred to the first, is independent, so that Nature and Man are like two witnesses who have had no opportunity of collusion. The clearer and more emphatic testimony of the latter to what was testified less unambiguously by the former affords a further confirmation of our hope that we have read the suggestions of Nature, so ambiguous in their purport, aright.

A single sentence will be enough to show both the analogy of the argument from Man to God with the argument from Nature and the real independence of the two lines of testimony. Nature, we have urged, on inspection points to the "supernatural" beyond itself as its own presupposition; if we look within ourselves we shall see that in man "Nature" and "supernature" meet; he has both within his own heart, and is a denizen at once of the temporal and of the eternal. He has not, like the animals, so far as we can judge of their inner life, one "environment" to which he must adapt himself but two, a secular and an eternal. Because he is designed ultimately to be at home with God in the eternal, he can never be really at home in this world, but at best is, like Abraham, a pilgrim to a promised but unseen land; at worst, like Cain, an aimless fugitive and wanderer on the face of the earth. The very "image" of his Maker which has been stamped on him is not only a sign of his rightful domination over the creatures; it is also "the mark of Cain" from which all creatures shrink. Hence among all the creatures, many of whom are comic enough, man is alone in being tragic. His life, at the very best, is a tragi-comedy; at the worst, it is stark tragedy. And naturally enough this is so; for, if man has only the "environment" which is common to him with the beasts of the field, his whole life is no more than a perpetual attempt to find a rational solution of an equation all whose roots are surds. He can only achieve adjustment to one of his two "environments" by sacrifices of adjustment to the other; he can no more be equally in tune with the eternal and the secular at once than a piano can be exactly in tune for all keys. In practice we know how the difficulty is apparently solved in the best human lives; it is solved by cultivating our earthly attachments and yet also practising a high detachment, not "setting our hearts" too much on the best of temporal goods, since "the best in this kind are but shadows," "using" the creatures, but always in the remembrance that the time will come when we can use them no more, loving them but loving them *ordinate,* with care not to lose our hearts to any of them. Wise men do not need to be reminded that the deliberate voluntary refusal of real good things is necessary, as a protection against the over-valuation of the secular, in any life they count worth living. And yet wise men know also that the renunciation of real good which they recommend is not recommended for the mere sake of being without "good." Good is always renounced for the sake of some "better good." But the "better good" plainly cannot be any of the good things of this secular existence. For there is none of them whatever which it may not be a duty to renounce for some man and at some time.

I do not mean merely that occasions demand the sacrifice of the sort of thing the "average sensual man" calls good— comfort, wealth, influence, rank and the like. For no serious moralist would dream of regarding any of these as more, at best, than very inferior goods. I mean that the same thing holds true of the very things to which men of nobler mould are ready to sacrifice these obvious and secondary goods. For example, there are few, if any, earthly goods to compare with our personal affections. Yet a man must be prepared to sacrifice all his personal affections in the service of his country, or for what he honestly believes to be the one Church of God. But there are things to which the greatest lover of his country or his Church must be prepared in turn to sacrifice what lies so near his heart. I may die for my country, I may, as so many a fighting man does, leave wife and young children to run the extreme hazards of fortune, but I must not purchase peace and safety for this country I love so much by procuring the privy murder of a dangerous and remorseless enemy. I may give my body to be burned for my faith, I may leave my little ones to beg their bread for its sake, but I must not help it in its need by a fraud or a forgery. It may be argued that for the good of the human race I ought to be prepared to sacrifice the very independence of my native land, but for no advantage to the whole body of mankind may I insult justice by knowingly giving sentence or verdict against the innocent. If these things are not true, the whole foundation of our morality is dissolved; if they are true, the greatest good, to which I must at need be prepared to sacrifice everything else, must be something which cannot even be appraised in the terms of a secular arithmetic, something incommensurable with the "welfare" of Church and State or even of the whole human race. If it is to be had in fruition at all, it must be had where the secular environment has finally and for ever fallen away, "yonder" as the Neo-Platonist would say, "in heaven" as the ordinary Christian says. If this world of time and passage were really our home and our only home, I own I should find it impossible to justify such a complete surrender of all temporal good as that I have spoken of; yet it is certain that the sacrifice is no more than what is de-

manded, when the need arises, by the most familiar principles of morality. Whoever says "ought," meaning "ought," is in the act bearing witness to the supernatural and supra-temporal as the destined home of man. No doubt we should all admit that there are very many rules of our conventional morality which are not of unconditional and universal obligation; we "ought" to conform to them under certain specified and understood conditions. I ought to be generous only when I have first satisfied the just claims of my creditors, just as I ought to abstain from redressing grievances with the high hand when society supplies me with the machinery for getting them redressed by the law. But whoever says "ought" at all, must mean that at least *when* the requisite conditions are fulfilled the obligation is absolute. There may be occasions when it is not binding on me to speak the truth to a questioner, but if there is one single occasion on which I ought to speak the truth, I ought to speak it then, "though the sky should fall."

Now, if there ever is a single occasion on which we ought to speak the truth, or to do anything else, "at all costs" as we say, what is the good in the name of which this unconditional demand is made of me? It cannot be any secular good that can be named, my own health or prosperity or life, nor even the prosperity and pleasurable existence of mankind. For I can never, since the consequences of my act are endless and unforeseeable, be sure that I may not be endangering these very goods by my act, and yet I am sure that the act is one which I ought to do. No doubt, you may fall back upon probability as the guide of life and say, "I ought to do this act because it seems to me most likely to conduce to the temporal well-being of myself, my family, my nation, or my kind." And in practice these are, no doubt, the sort of considerations by which we are constantly influenced. But it should be clear that they cannot be the ultimate grounds of obligation, unless all morality is to be reduced to the status of a convenient illusion. To say that the ultimate ground of an obligation is the mere fact that a man thinks he would further such a concrete tangible end by his act involves the consequence that no man is bound to do any act unless he thinks it will have these results, and that he may do anything he pleases so long as he thinks it will have them. At heart, I believe, even the writers who go furthest in professing to accept these conclusions do themselves a moral injustice. I am convinced that there is not one of them, whatever he may hold in theory, who would not in practice "draw the line" somewhere and say, "This thing I will not do, whatever the cost may be to myself or to anyone else or to everyone." Now an obligation wholly independent of all temporal "consequences" clearly cannot have its justification in the temporal, nor oblige any creature constructed to find his good wholly in the temporal. Only to a being who has in his structure the adaptation to the eternal can you significantly say "You ought." [3]

It will be seen that the thought on which we have dwelt in the last paragraph is one of the underlying fundamental themes of Kant's principal ethical treatise, the "Critique of Practical Reason." It is characteristic of Kant that, wrongly as I think, he wholly distrusted the suggestions of the "supernatural" to be derived from the contemplation of Nature itself, and that, from an exaggerated dread of unregulated fanaticism and superstition, characteristic of his century, he was all but blind to the third source of suggestion of which we have yet to speak. Hence with him it is our knowledge of our own moral being, as creatures who have unconditional obligations, which has to bear the whole weight of the argument. Here, I own, he seems to me to be definitely wrong. The full force of the vindication of religion cannot be felt unless we recognise that its weight is supported not by one strand only but by a cord of three intertwined strands; we need to integrate Bonaventura and Thomas and Butler with Kant to appreciate the real strength of the believer's position. Yet Kant seems to me unquestionably right as far as this. Even were there nothing else to suggest to us that we are denizens at once of a natural and temporal and of a supernatural and eternal world, the revelation of our own inner division against ourselves afforded by Conscience, duly meditated, is enough to bear the strain. Or, to make my point rather differently, I would urge that of all the philosophical thinkers who have concerned themselves with the life of man as a moral being, the two who stand out, even in the estimation of those who dissent from them, as the great undying moralists of literature, Plato and Kant, are just the two who have insisted most vigorously on what the secularly-minded call, by way of depreciation, the "dualism" of "this world" and the "other world," or, in Kantian language, of "man as (natural) phenomenon" and "man as (supernatural) reality." To deny the reality of this antithesis is to eviscerate morality.

We see this at once if we compare Kant, for example, with Hume, or Plato with Aristotle. It is so obvious that Plato and Kant really "care" about moral practice and Aristotle and Hume do not care, or do not care as much as they ought. In Hume's hands moral goodness is put so completely on a level with mere respectability that our approval of virtue and disapproval of vice is said in so many words to be at bottom one in kind with our preference of a well-dressed man to a badly-dressed. Aristotle cares

[3] I owe the expression to a report of a recent utterance of some Roman Catholic divine. I regret that I cannot give the precise reference.

A. E. TAYLOR   47

more than this. He reduces moral goodness to the discharge of the duties of a good citizen, family man, and neighbour in this secular life, and is careful to insist that these obligations are not to be shirked. But when he comes to speak of the true happiness of man and the kind of life which he lives "as a being with something divine in him," we find that the life of this "divine" part means nothing more than the promotion of science. To live near to God means to him not justice, mercy, and humility, as it does to Plato and the Hebrew prophets, but to be a metaphysician, a physicist, and an astronomer. Justice, mercy, and humility are to be practised, but only for a secular purpose, in order that the man of science may have an orderly and quiet social "environment" and so be free, as he would not be if he had to contend with disorderly passions in himself or his neighbours, to give the maximum of time and interest to the things which really matter. We cannot say of Hume, nor of Aristotle, nor indeed of any moralist who makes morality merely a matter of right social adjustments in this temporal world, what you can say of Plato or Kant, *beati qui esuriunt et sitiunt justitiam.* "Otherworldliness" is as characteristic of the greatest theoretical moralists as it is of all the noblest livers, whatever their professed theories may be.

. . .

DAVID HUME

The Argument from Design

David Hume (1711–1766) was perhaps the greatest of the line of British empiricists. After publishing at the age of 28 the revolutionary Treatise of Human Nature, *he largely turned his attention to other matters, such as history. His most important work on religion, the* Dialogues, *was published posthumously. It is still a matter of controversy as to the extent to which the various participants in the* Dialogues *represent Hume's views, but he is usually identified with Philo.*

PART II

. . .

Not to lose any time in circumlocutions, said Cleanthes, addressing himself to Demea, much less in replying to the pious declamations of Philo, I shall

From David Hume, *Dialogues Concerning Natural Religion*, Pts. II–VII.

briefly explain how I conceive this matter. Look round the world, contemplate the whole and every part of it: you will find it to be nothing but one great machine, subdivided into an infinite number of lesser machines, which again admit of subdivisions to a degree beyond what human senses and faculties can trace and explain. All these various machines, and even their most minute parts, are adjusted to each other with an accuracy which ravishes into admiration all men who have ever contemplated them. The curious adapting of means to ends, throughout all nature, resembles exactly, though it much exceeds, the productions of human contrivance—of human design, thought, wisdom, and intelligence. Since therefore the effects resemble each other, we are led to infer, by all the rules of analogy, that the causes also resemble, and that the Author of nature is somewhat similar to the mind of man, though possessed of much larger faculties, proportioned to the grandeur of the work which he has executed. By this argument *a posteriori*, and by this argument alone, do we prove at once the existence of a Deity and his similarity to human mind and intelligence.

I shall be so free, Cleanthes, said Demea, as to tell you that from the beginning I could not approve of your conclusion concerning the similarity of the Deity to men, still less can I approve of the mediums by which you endeavour to establish it. What! No demonstration of the Being of God! No abstract arguments! No proofs *a priori!* Are these which have hitherto been so much insisted on by philosophers all fallacy, all sophism? Can we reach no farther in this subject than experience and probability? I will not say that this is betraying the cause of a Deity; but surely, by this affected candour, you give advantages to atheists which they never could obtain by the mere dint of argument and reasoning.

What I chiefly scruple in this subject, said Philo, is not so much that all religious arguments are by Cleanthes reduced to experience, as that they appear not to be even the most certain and irrefragable of that inferior kind. That a stone will fall, that fire will burn, that the earth has solidity, we have observed a thousand and a thousand times; and when any new instance of this nature is presented, we draw without hesitation the accustomed inference. The exact similarity of the cases gives us a perfect assurance of a similar event, and a stronger evidence is never desired nor sought after. But wherever you depart, in the least, from the similarity of the cases, you diminish proportionably the evidence, and may at last bring it to a very weak *analogy,* which is confessedly liable to error and uncertainty. After having experienced the circulation of the blood in human creatures, we make no doubt that it takes place in Titius and Maevius; but from its circulation in frogs and fishes it is only a presumption, though a strong one, from analogy that it takes place in men and other animals. The analogical reasoning is much weaker when we infer the circulation of the sap in vegetables from our experience that the blood circulates in animals; and those who hastily followed that imperfect analogy are found, by more accurate experiments, to have been mistaken.

If we see a house, Cleanthes, we conclude, with the greatest certainty, that it had an architect or builder because this is precisely that species of effect which we have experienced to proceed from that species of cause. But surely you will not affirm that the universe bears such a resemblance to a house that we can with the same certainty infer a similar cause, or that the analogy is here entire and perfect. The dissimilitude is so striking that the utmost you can here pretend to is a guess, a conjecture, a presumption concerning a similar cause; and how that pretension will be received in the world, I leave you to consider.

It would surely be very ill received, replied Cleanthes; and I should be deservedly blamed and detested did I allow that the proofs of a Deity amounted to no more than a guess or conjecture. But is the whole adjustment of means to ends in a house and in the universe so slight a resemblance? the economy of final causes? the order, proportion, and arrangement of every part? Steps of a stair are plainly contrived that human legs may use them in mounting; and this inference is certain and infallible. Human legs are also contrived for walking and mounting; and this inference, I allow, is not altogether so certain because of the dissimilarity which you remark; but does it, therefore, deserve the name only of presumption or conjecture?

Good God! cried Demea, interrupting him, where are we? Zealous defenders of religion allow that the proofs of a Deity fall short of perfect evidence! And you, Philo, on whose assistance I depended in proving the adorable mysteriousness of the Divine Nature, do you assent to all these extravagant opinions of Cleanthes? For what other name can I give them? or, why spare my censure when such principles are advanced, supported by such an authority, before so young a man as Pamphilus?

You seem not to apprehend, replied Philo, that I argue with Cleanthes in his own way, and, by showing him the dangerous consequences of his tenets, hope at last to reduce him to our opinion. But what sticks most with you, I observe, is the representation which Cleanthes has made of the argument *a posteriori;* and, finding that that argument is likely to escape your hold and vanish into air, you think it so disguised that you can scarcely believe it to be set in its true light. Now, however much I may dissent, in other respects, from the dangerous principle of Cleanthes, I must allow that he has fairly represented that argument, and I shall endeavour so to state the matter to you that you will entertain no further scruples with regard to it.

Were a man to abstract from everything which he knows or has seen, he would be altogether incapable, merely from his own ideas, to determine what kind of scene the universe must be, or to give the preference to one state or situation of things above another. For as nothing which he clearly conceives could be esteemed impossible or implying a contradiction, every chimera of his fancy would be upon an equal footing; nor could he assign any just reason why he adheres to one idea or system, and rejects the others which are equally possible.

Again, after he opens his eyes and contemplates the world as it really is, it would be impossible for him at first to assign the cause of any one event, much less of the whole of things, or of the universe. He might set his fancy a rambling, and she might bring him in an infinite variety of reports and representations. These would all be possible, but, being all equally possible, he would never of himself give a satisfactory account for his preferring one of them to the rest. Experience alone can point out to him the true cause of any phenomenon.

Now, according to this method of reasoning, Demea, it follows (and is, indeed, tacitly allowed by Cleanthes himself) that order, arrangement, or the adjustment of final causes, is not of itself any proof of design, but only so far as it has been experienced to proceed from that principle. For aught we can know *a priori,* matter may contain the source or spring of order originally within itself, as well as mind does; and there is no more difficulty in conceiving that the several elements, from an internal unknown cause, may fall into the most exquisite arrangement, than to conceive that their ideas, in the great universal mind, from a like internal unknown cause, fall into that arrangement. The equal possibility of both these suppositions is allowed. But, by experience, we find (according to Cleanthes) that there is a difference between them. Throw several pieces of steel together, without shape or form, they will never arrange themselves so as to compose a watch. Stone and mortar and wood, without an architect, never erect a house. But the ideas in a human mind, we see, by an unknown, inexplicable economy, arrange themselves so as to form the plan of a watch or house. Experience, therefore, proves that there is an original principle of order in mind, not in matter. From similar effects we infer similar causes. The adjustment of means to ends is alike in the universe, as in a machine of human contrivance. The causes, therefore, must be resembling.

I was from the beginning scandalized, I must own, with this resemblance which is asserted between the Deity and human creatures, and must conceive it to imply such a degradation of the Supreme Being as no sound theist could endure. With your assistance, therefore, Demea, I shall endeavour to defend what you justly call the adorable mysteriousness of the Divine Nature, and shall refute this reasoning of Cleanthes, provided he allows that I have made a fair representation of it.

When Cleanthes had assented, Philo, after a short pause, proceeded in the following manner.

That all inferences, Cleanthes, concerning fact are founded on experience, and that all experimental reasonings are founded on the supposition that similar causes prove similar effects, and similar effects similar causes, I shall not at present much dispute with you. But observe, I entreat you, with what extreme caution all just reasoners proceed in the transferring of experiments to similar cases. Unless the cases be exactly similar, they repose no perfect confidence in applying their past observation to any particular phenomenon. Every alteration of circumstances occasions a doubt concerning the event; and it requires new experiments to prove certainly that the new circumstances are of no moment or importance. A change in bulk, situation, arrangement, age, disposition of the air, or surrounding bodies—any of these particulars may be attended with the most unexpected consequences. And unless the objects be quite familiar to us, it is the highest temerity to expect with assurance, after any of these changes, an event similar to that which before fell under our observation. The slow and deliberate steps of philosophers here, if anywhere, are distinguished from the precipitate march of the vulgar, who, hurried on by the smallest similitude, are incapable of all discernment or consideration.

But can you think, Cleanthes, that your usual phlegm and philosophy have been preserved in so wide a step as you have taken when you compared to the universe houses, ships, furniture, machines, and, from their similarity in some circumstances, inferred a similarity in their causes? Thought, design, intelligence, such as we discover in men and other animals, is no more than one of the springs and principles of the universe, as well as heat or cold, attraction or repulsion, and a hundred others which fall under daily observation. It is an active cause by which some particular parts of nature, we find, produce alterations on other parts. But can a conclusion, with any propriety, be transferred from parts to the whole? Does not the great disproportion bar all comparison and inference? From observing the growth of a hair, can we learn anything concerning the generation of a man? Would the manner of a leaf's blowing, even through perfectly known, afford us any instruction concerning the vegetation of a tree?

But allowing that we were to take the *operations* of one part of nature upon another for the foundation of our judgment concerning the *origin* of the whole (which never can be admitted), yet why select so minute, so weak, so bounded a principle as the reason and design of animals is found to be upon this planet? What peculiar privilege has this little agitation of the brain which we call *thought,* that we must thus make it the model of the whole universe? Our partiality in our own favour does indeed present it on all occasions, but sound philosophy ought carefully to guard against so natural an illusion.

So far from admitting, continued Philo, that the operations of a part can afford us any just conclusion concerning the origin of the whole, I will not allow any one part to form a rule for another part if the latter be very remote from the former. Is there any reasonable ground to conclude that the inhabitants of other planets possess thought, intelligence, reason, or anything similar to these faculties in men? When nature has so extremely diversified her manner of operation in this small globe, can we imagine that she incessantly copies herself throughout so immense a universe? And if thought, as we may well suppose, be confined merely to this narrow corner and has even there so limited a sphere of action, with what propriety can we assign it for the original cause of all things? The narrow views of a peasant who makes his domestic economy the rule for the government of kingdoms is in comparison a pardonable sophism.

But were we ever so much assured that a thought and reason resembling the human were to be found throughout the whole universe, and were its activity elsewhere vastly greater and more commanding than it appears in this globe, yet I cannot see why the operations of a world constituted, arranged, adjusted, can with any propriety be extended to a world which is in its embryo state, and is advancing towards that constitution and arrangement. By observation we know somewhat of the economy, action, and nourishment of a finished animal, but we must transfer with great caution that observation to the growth of a

foetus in the womb, and still more to the formation of an animalcule in the loins of its male parent. Nature, we find, even from our limited experience, possesses an infinite number of springs and principles which incessantly discover themselves on very change of her position and situation. And what new and unknown principles would actuate her in so new and unknown a situation as that of the formation of a universe, we cannot, without the utmost temerity, pretend to determine.

A very small part of this great system, during a very short time, is very imperfectly discovered to us; and do we thence pronounce decisively concerning the origin of the whole?

Admirable conclusion! Stone, wood, brick, iron, brass, have not, at this time, in this minute globe of earth, an order or arrangement without human art and contrivance; therefore, the universe could not originally attain its order and arrangement without something similar to human art. But is a part of nature a rule for another part very wide of the former? Is it a rule for the whole? Is a very small part a rule for the universe? Is nature in one situation a certain rule for nature in another situation vastly different from the former?

And can you blame me, Cleanthes, if I here imitate the prudent reserve of Simonides, who, according to the noted story, being asked by Hiero, *What God was?* desired a day to think of it, and then two days more; and after that manner continually prolonged the term, without ever bringing in his definition or description? Could you even blame me if I had answered, at first, *that I did not know,* and was sensible that this subject lay vastly beyond the reach of my faculties? You might cry out sceptic and rallier, as much as you pleased; but, having found in so many other subjects much more familiar the imperfections and even contradictions of human reason, I never should expect any success from its feeble conjectures in a subject so sublime and so remote from the sphere of our observation. When two *species* of objects have always been observed to be conjoined together, I can *infer,* by custom, the existence of one wherever I *see* the existence of the other; and this I call an argument from experience. But how this argument can have place where the objects, as in the present case, are single, individual, without parallel or specific resemblance, may be difficult to explain. And will any man tell me with a serious countenance that an orderly universe must arise from some thought and art like the human because we have experience of it? To ascertain this reasoning it were requisite that we had experience of the origin of worlds; and it is not sufficient, surely, that we have seen ships and cities arise from human art and contrivance.

Philo was proceeding in this vehement manner, somewhat between jest and earnest, as it appeared to me, when he observed some signs of impatience in Cleanthes, and then immediately stopped short. What I had to suggest, said Cleanthes, is only that you would not abuse terms, or make use of popular expressions to subvert philosophical reasonings. You know that the vulgar often distinguish reason from experience, even where the question relates only to matter of fact and existence, though it is found, where that *reason* is properly analyzed, that it is nothing but a species of experience. To prove by experience the origin of the universe from mind is not more contrary to common speech than to prove the motion of the earth from the same principle. And a caviller might raise all the same objections to the Copernican system which you have urged against my reasonings. Have you other earths, might he say, which you have seen to move? Have . . .

Yes! cried Philo, interrupting him, we have other earths. Is not the moon another earth, which we see to turn round its centre? Is not Venus another earth, where we observe the same phenomenon? Are not the revolutions of the sun also a confirmation, from analogy, of the same theory? All the planets, are they not earths which revolve about the sun? Are not the satellites moons, which move round Jupiter and Saturn, and along with these primary planets round the sun? These analogies and resemblances, with others which I have not mentioned, are the sole proofs of the Copernican system; and to you it belongs to consider whether you have any analogies of the same kind to support your theory.

In reality, Cleanthes, continued he, the modern system of astronomy is now so much received by all inquirers, and has become so essential a part even of our earliest education, that we are not commonly very scrupulous in examining the reasons upon which it is founded. It is now become a matter of mere curiosity to study the first writers on that subject who had the full force of prejudice to encounter, and were obliged to turn their arguments on every side in order to render them popular and convincing. But if we peruse Galileo's famous *Dialogues* concerning the system of the world, we shall find that that great genius, one of the sublimest that ever existed, first bent all his endeavours to prove that there was no foundation for the distinction commonly made between elementary and celestial substances. The schools, proceeding from the illusions of sense, had carried this distinction very far; and had established the latter substances to be ingenerable, incorruptible, unalterable, impassible; and had assigned all the opposite qualities to the former. But Galileo, beginning with the moon, proved its similarity in every particular to the earth: its convex figure, its natural darkness when not illuminated, its density, its distinction into solid and liquid, the variations of its phases, the mutual illuminations of the earth and moon, their mutual eclipses, the inequalities of the lunar surface, etc. After many instances of this kind, with regard to all the planets, men plainly saw that these bodies became proper objects of experience, and that the similarity of their nature enabled us to extend the same arguments and phenomena from one to the other.

In this cautious proceeding of the astronomers you may read your own condemnation, Cleanthes, or rather may see that the subject in which you are engaged exceeds all human reason and inquiry. Can you pretend to show any such similarity between the fabric of a house and the generation of a universe? Have you ever seen nature in any such situation as resembles the first arrangement of the elements? Have worlds ever been formed under your eye, and have you had leisure to observe the whole progress of the phenomenon, from the first appearance of order to its final consummation? If you have, then cite your experience and deliver your theory.

PART III

How the most absurd argument, replied Cleanthes, in the hands of a man of ingenuity and invention, may acquire an air of probability! Are you not aware, Philo, that it became necessary for Copernicus and his first disciples to prove the similarity of the terrestrial and celestial matter because several philosophers, blinded by old systems and supported by some sensible appearances, had denied this similarity? But that it is by no means necessary that theists should prove the similarity of the works of *nature* to those of *art* because this similarity is self-evident and undeniable? The same matter, a like form; what more is requisite to show an analogy between their causes, and to ascertain the origin of all things

from a divine purpose and intention? Your objections, I must freely tell you, are no better than the abstruse cavils of those philosophers who denied motion, and ought to be refuted in the same manner—by illustrations, examples, and instances rather than by serious argument and philosophy.

Suppose, therefore, that an articulate voice were heard in the clouds, much louder and more melodious than any which human art could ever reach; suppose that this voice were extended in the same instant over all nations and spoke to each nation in its own language and dialect; suppose that the words delivered not only contain a just sense and meaning, but convey some instruction altogether worthy of a benevolent Being superior to mankind—could you possibly hesitate a moment concerning the cause of this voice, and must you not instantly ascribe it to some design or purpose? Yet I cannot see but all the same objections (if they merit that appellation) which lie against the system of theism may also be produced against this inference.

Might you not say that all conclusions concerning fact were founded on experience; that, when we hear an articulate voice in the dark and thence infer a man, it is only the resemblance of the effects which leads us to conclude that there is a like resemblance in the cause; but that this extraordinary voice, by its loudness, extent, and flexibility to all languages, bears so little analogy to any human voice that we have no reason to suppose any analogy in their causes; and, consequently, that a rational, wise, coherent speech proceeded, you know not whence, from some accidental whistling of the winds, not from any divine reason or intelligence? You see clearly your own objections in these cavils, and I hope too you see clearly that they cannot possibly have more force in the one case than in the other.

But to bring the case still nearer the

present one of the universe, I shall make two suppositions which imply not any absurdity or impossibility. Suppose that there is a natural, universal, invariable language, common to every individual of human race, and that books are natural productions which perpetuate themselves in the same manner with animals and vegetables, by descent and propagation. Several expressions of our passions contain a universal language: all brute animals have a natural speech, which, however limited, is very intelligible to their own species. And as there are infinitely fewer parts and less contrivance in the finest composition of eloquence than in the coarsest organized body, the propagation of an *Iliad* or *Æneid* is an easier supposition than that of any plant or animal.

Suppose, therefore, that you enter into your library thus peopled by natural volumes containing the most refined reason and most exquisite beauty; could you possibly open one of them and doubt that its original cause bore the strongest analogy to mind and intelligence? When it reasons and discourses; when it expostulates, argues, and enforces its views and topics; when it applies sometimes to the pure intellect, sometimes to the affections; when it collects, disposes, and adorns every consideration suited to the subject; could you persist in asserting that all this, at the bottom, had really no meaning, and that the first formation of this volume in the loins of its original parent proceeded not from thought and design? Your obstinacy, I know, reaches not that degree of firmness; even your sceptical play and wantonness would be abashed at so glaring an absurdity.

But if there be any difference, Philo, between this supposed case and the real one of the universe, it is all to the advantage of the latter. The anatomy of an animal affords many stronger instances of design then the perusal of Livy or Tacitus; and any objection which you start in the former case, by carrying me back to so unusual and extraordinary a scene as the first formation of worlds, the same objection has place on the supposition of our vegetating library. Choose, then, your party, Philo, without ambiguity or evasion; assert either that a rational volume is no proof of a rational cause or admit of a similar cause to all the works of nature.

Let me here observe, too, continued Cleanthes, that this religious argument, instead of being weakened by that scepticism so much affected by you, rather acquires force from it and becomes more firm and undisputed. To exclude all argument or reasoning of every kind is either affectation or madness. The declared profession of every reasonable sceptic is only to reject abstruse, remote, and refined arguments; to adhere to common sense and the plain instincts of nature; and to assent, wherever any reasons strike him with so full a force that he cannot, without the greatest violence, prevent it. Now the arguments for natural religion are plainly of this kind; and nothing but the most perverse, obstinate metaphysics can reject them. Consider, anatomize the eye, survey its structure and contrivance, and tell me, from your own feeling, if the idea of a contriver does not immediately flow in upon you with a force like that of sensation. The most obvious conclusion, surely, is in favour of design; and it requires time, reflection, and study, to summon up those frivolous though abstruse objections which can support infidelity. Who can behold the male and female of each species, the correspondence of their parts and instincts, their passions and whole course of life before and after generation, but must be sensible that the propagation of the species is intended by nature? Millions and millions of such instances present themselves through every part of the universe, and no language can convey a more intelligible irresistible meaning than the curious adjustment of final causes. To what degree, therefore, of blind dogmatism must one have attained to reject such natural and such convincing arguments?

Some beauties in writing we may meet with which seem contrary to rules, and which gain the affections and animate the imagination in opposition to all the precepts of criticism and to the authority of the established masters of art. And if the argument for theism be, as you pretend, contradictory to the principles of logic, its universal, its irresistible influence proves clearly that there may be arguments of a like irregular nature. Whatever cavils may be urged, an orderly world, as well as a coherent, articulate speech, will still be received as an incontestable proof of design and intention.

It sometimes happens, I own, that the religious arguments have not their due influence on an ignorant savage and barbarian, not because they are obscure and difficult, but because he never asks himself any question with regard to them. Whence arises the curious structure of an animal? From the copulation of its parents. And these whence? From *their* parents? A few removes set the objects at such a distance that to him they are lost in darkness and confusion; nor is he actuated by any curiosity to trace them farther. But this is neither dogmatism nor scepticism, but stupidity: a state of mind very different from your sifting, inquisitive disposition, my ingenious friend. You can trace causes from effects; you can compare the most distant and remote objects; and your greatest errors proceed not from barrenness of thought and invention, but from too luxuriant a fertility which suppresses your natural good sense by a profusion of unnecessary scruples and objections.

Here I could observe, Hermippus, that Philo was a little embarrassed and confounded; but, while he hesitated in delivering an answer, luckily for him, Demea broke in upon the discourse and saved his countenance.

Your instance, Cleanthes, said he, drawn from books and language, being familiar, has, I confess, so much more force on that account; but is there not some danger, too, in this very circumstance, and may it not render us presumptuous, by making us imagine we comprehend the Deity and have some adequate idea of his nature and attributes? When I read a volume, I enter into the mind and intention of the author; I become him, in a manner, for the instant, and have an immediate feeling and conception of those ideas which revolved in his imagination while employed in that composition. But so near an approach we never surely can make to the Deity. His ways are not our ways. His attributes are perfect but incomprehensible. And this volume of nature contains a great and inexplicable riddle, more than any intelligible discourse or reasoning.

The ancient Platonists, you know, were the most religious and devout of all the pagan philosophers, yet many of them, particularly Plotinus, expressly declare that intellect or understanding is not to be ascribed to the Deity, and that our most perfect worship of him consists, not in acts of veneration, reverence, gratitude, or love, but in a certain mysterious self-annihilation or total extinction of all our faculties. These ideas are, perhaps, too far stretched, but still it must be acknowledged that, by representing the Deity as so intelligible and comprehensible, and so similar to a human mind, we are guilty of the grossest and most narrow partiality, and make ourselves the model of the whole universe.

All the *sentiments* of the human mind, gratitude, resentment, love, friendship, approbation, blame, pity, emulation, envy, have a plain reference to the state and situation of man, and are calculated for preserving the existence and promoting the activity of such a being in such circumstances. It seems, therefore, unreasonable to transfer such sentiments to a supreme existence or to suppose him actuated by them; and the phenomena, besides, of the universe will not support us in such a theory. All our *ideas* derived from the senses are confessedly false and illusive, and cannot therefore be supposed to have place in a supreme intelligence. And as the ideas of internal sentiment, added to those of the external senses, compose the whole furniture of human understanding, we may conclude that none of the *materials* of thought are in any respect similar in the human and in the divine intelligence. Now, as to the *manner* of thinking, how can we make any comparison between them or suppose them anywise resembling? Our thought is fluctuating, uncertain, fleeting, successive, and compounded; and were we to remove these circumstances, we absolutely annihilate its essence, and it would in such a case be an abuse of terms to apply to it the name of thought or reason. At least, if it appear more pious and respectful (as it really is) still to retain these terms when we mention the Supreme Being, we ought to acknowledge that their meaning, in that case, is totally incomprehensible, and that the infirmities of our nature do not permit us to reach any ideas which in the least correspond to the ineffable sublimity of the Divine attributes.

PART IV

It seems strange to me, said Cleanthes, that you, Demea, who are so sincere in the cause of religion, should still maintain the mysterious, incomprehensible nature of the Deity, and should insist so strenuously that he has no manner of likeness or resemblance to human creatures. The Deity, I can readily allow, possesses many powers and attributes of which we can have no comprehension; but, if our ideas, so far as they go, be not just and adequate and correspondent to his real nature, I know not what there is in this subject worth insisting on. Is the name, without any meaning, of such mighty importance? Or how do you mystics, who maintain the absolute incomprehensibility of the Deity, differ from sceptics or atheists, who assert that the first cause of all is unknown and unintelligible? Their temerity must be very great if, after rejecting the production by a mind—I mean a mind resembling the human (for I know of no other)—they pretend to assign, with certainty, any other specific intelligible cause; and their conscience must be very scrupulous, indeed, if they refuse to call the universal unknown cause a God or Deity, and to bestow on him as many sublime eulogies and unmeaning epithets as you shall please to require of them.

Who could imagine, replied Demea, that Cleanthes, the calm philosophical Cleanthes, would attempt to refute his antagonists by affixing a nickname to them, and, like the common bigots and inquisitors of the age, have recourse to invective and declamation instead of reasoning? Or does he not perceive that these topics are easily retorted, and that *anthropomorphite* is an appellation as invidious, and implies as dangerous consequences, as the epithet of *mystic* with which he has honoured us? In reality, Cleanthes, consider what it is you assert when you represent the Deity as similar to a human mind and understanding. What is the soul of man? A composition of various faculties, passions, sentiments, ideas—united, indeed, into one self or person, but still distinct from each other. When it reasons, the ideas which are the parts of its discourse arrange themselves in a certain form or order which is not preserved entire for a moment, but immediately gives place to another arrangement. New opinions, new passions, new affections, new feelings arise which continually diversify the mental scene and produce in it the greatest variety and most rapid succession imaginable. How is this compatible with that perfect immutability and simplicity which all true theists ascribe to the Deity? By the same act, say they, he sees past, present, and future; his love and hatred, his mercy and justice, are one individual operation; he is entire in every point of space, and complete in every instant of duration. No succession, no change, no acquisition, no diminution. What he is implies not in it any shadow of distinction or diversity. And what he is this moment he ever has been and ever will be, without any new judgment, sentiment, or operation. He stands fixed in one simple, perfect state; nor can you ever say, with any propriety, that this act of his is different from that other, or that this judgment or idea has been lately formed and will give place, by succession, to any different judgment or idea.

I can readily allow, said Cleanthes, that those who maintain the perfect simplicity of the Supreme Being, to the extent in which you have explained it, are complete mystics, and chargeable with all the consequences which I have drawn from their opinion. They are, in a word, atheists, without knowing it. For though it be allowed that the Deity possesses attributes of which we have no comprehension, yet ought we never to ascribe to him any attributes which are absolutely incompatible with that intelligent nature essential to him. A mind whose acts and sentiments and ideas are not distinct and successive, one that is wholly simple and totally immutable, is a mind which has no thought, no reason, no will, no sentiment, no love, no hatred; or, in a word, is no mind at all. It is an abuse of terms to give it that appellation, and we may as well speak of limited extension without figure, or of number without composition.

Pray consider, said Philo, whom you are at present inveighing against. You are honouring with the appellation of *atheist* all the sound, orthodox divines, almost, who have treated of this subject; and you will at last be, yourself, found, according to your reckoning, the only sound theist in the world. But if idolaters be atheists, as, I think, may justly be asserted, and Christian theologians the same, what becomes of the argument, so much celebrated, derived from the universal consent of mankind?

But, because I know you are not much swayed by names and authorities, I shall endeavour to show you, a little more distinctly, the inconveniences of that anthropomorphism which you have embraced, and shall prove that there is no ground to suppose a plan of the world to be formed in the Divine mind, consisting of distinct ideas, differently arranged, in the same manner as an architect forms in his head the plan of a house which he intends to execute.

It is not easy, I own, to see what is gained by this supposition, whether we judge of the matter by *reason* or by *experience*. We are still obliged to mount higher in order to find the cause of this cause which you had assigned as satisfactory and conclusive.

If *reason* (I mean abstract reason derived from inquiries *a priori*) be not alike mute with regard to all questions concerning cause and effect, this sentence at least it will venture to pronounce: that a mental world or universe of ideas requires a cause as much as does a material world or universe of objects, and, if similar in its arrangement, must require a similar cause. For what is there in this subject which should occasion a different conclusion or inference? In an abstract view, they are entirely alike; and no difficulty attends the one supposition which is not common to both of them.

Again, when we will needs force *experience* to pronounce some sentence, even on these subjects which lie beyond her sphere, neither can she perceive any material difference in this particular between these two kinds of worlds, but finds them to be governed by similar principles, and to depend upon an equal variety of causes in their operations. We have specimens in miniature of both of them. Our own mind resembles the one; a vegetable or animal body the other. Let experience, therefore, judge from these samples. Nothing seems more delicate, with regard to its causes, than thought; and as these causes never operate in two persons after the same manner, so we never find two persons who think exactly alike. Nor indeed does the same person think exactly alike at any two different periods of time. A difference of age, of the disposition of his body, of weather, of food, of company, of books, of passions—any of these particulars, or others more minute, are sufficient to alter the curious machinery of thought and communicate to it very different movements and operations. As far as we can judge, vegetables and animal bodies are not more delicate in their motions, nor depend upon a greater variety or more curious adjustment of springs and principles.

How, therefore, shall we satisfy ourselves concerning the cause of that Being whom you suppose the Author of nature, or, according to your system of anthropomorphism, the ideal world into which you trace the material? Have we not the same reason to trace that ideal world into another ideal world or new intelligent principle? But if we stop and go no farther, why go so far? why not stop at the material world? How can we satisfy ourselves without going on *in infinitum?* And, after all, what satisfaction is there in that infinite progression? Let us remember the story of the Indian philosopher and his elephant. It was never more applicable than to the present subject. If the material world rests upon a similar ideal world, this ideal world must rest upon some other, and so on without end. It were better, therefore, never to look beyond the present material world. By supposing it to contain the principle of its order within itself, we really assert it to be God; and the sooner we arrive at that Divine Being, so much the better. When you go one step beyond the mundane system, you only excite an inquisitive humour which it is impossible ever to satisfy.

To say that the different ideas which compose the reason of the Supreme Being fall into order of themselves and by their own nature is really to talk without any precise meaning. If it has a meaning, I would fain know why it is not as good sense to say that the parts of the material world fall into order of themselves and by their own nature. Can the one opinion be intelligible, while the other is not so?

We have, indeed, experience of ideas which fall into order of themselves and without any *known* cause. But, I am sure, we have a much larger experience of matter which does the same, as in all instances of generation and vegetation where the accurate analysis of the cause exceeds all human comprehension. We have also experience of particular systems of thought and of matter which have no order; of the first in madness, of the second in corruption. Why, then, should we think that order is more essential to one than the other? And if it requires a cause in both, what do we gain by your system, in tracing the universe of objects into a similar universe of ideas? The first step which we make leads us on for ever. It were, therefore, wise in us to limit all our inquiries to the present world, without looking farther. No satisfaction can ever be attained by these speculations which so far exceed the narrow bounds of human understanding.

It was usual with the Peripatetics, you

know, Cleanthes, when the cause of any phenomenon was demanded, to have recourse to their *faculties* or *occult qualities,* and to say, for instance, that bread nourished by its nutritive faculty, and senna purged by its purgative. But it has been discovered that this subterfuge was nothing but the disguise of ignorance, and that these philosophers, though less ingenuous, really said the same thing with the sceptics or the vulgar who fairly confessed that they knew not the cause of these phenomena. In like manner, when it is asked, what cause produces order in the ideas of the Supreme Being, can any other reason be assigned by you, anthropomorphites, than that it is a *rational* faculty, and that such is the nature of the Deity? But why a similar answer will not be equally satisfactory in accounting for the order of the world, without having recourse to any such intelligent creator as you insist on, may be difficult to determine. It is only to say that *such* is the nature of material objects, and that they are all originally possessed of a *faculty* of order and proportion. These are only more learned and elaborate ways of confessing our ignorance; nor has the one hypothesis any real advantage above the other, except in its greater conformity to vulgar prejudices.

You have displayed this argument with great emphasis, replied Cleanthes: You seem not sensible how easy it is to answer it. Even in common life, if I assign a cause for any event, is it any objection, Philo, that I cannot assign the cause of that cause, and answer every new question which may incessantly be started? And what philosophers could possibly submit to so rigid a rule?—philosophers who confess ultimate causes to be totally unknown, and are sensible that the most refined principles into which they trace the phenomena are still to them as inexplicable as these phenomena themselves are to the vulgar. The order and arrangement of nature, the curious adjustment of final causes, the plain use and intention of every part and organ —all these bespeak in the clearest language an intelligent cause or author. The heavens and the earth join in the same testimony: The whole chorus of nature raises one hymn to the praises of its Creator. You alone, or almost alone, disturb this general harmony. You start abstruse doubts, cavils, and objections; you ask me what is the cause of this cause? I know not; I care not; that concerns not me. I have found a Deity; and here I stop my inquiry. Let those go farther who are wiser or more enterprising.

I pretend to be neither, replied Philo; and for that very reason I should never, perhaps, have attempted to go so far, especially when I am sensible that I must at last be contented to sit down with the same answer which, without further trouble, might have satisfied me from the beginning. If I am still to remain in utter ignorance of causes and can absolutely give an explication of nothing, I shall never esteem it any advantage to shove off for a moment a difficulty which you acknowledge must immediately, in its full force, recur upon me. Naturalists indeed very justly explain particular effects by more general causes, though these general causes themselves should remain in the end totally inexplicable, but they never surely thought it satisfactory to explain a particular effect by a particular cause which was no more to be accounted for than the effect itself. An ideal system, arranged of itself, without a precedent design, is not a whit more explicable than a material one which attains its order in a like manner; nor is there any more difficulty in the latter supposition than in the former.

PART V

But to show you still more inconveniences, continued Philo, in your anthropomorphism, please to take a new survey of your principles. *Like effects prove like causes*. This is the experimental argument; and this, you say too, is the sole theological argument. Now it is certain that the liker the effects are which are seen and the liker the causes which are inferred, the stronger is the argument. Every departure on either side diminishes the probability and renders the experiment less conclusive. You cannot doubt of the principle; neither ought you to reject its consequences.

All the new discoveries in astronomy which prove the immense grandeur and magnificence of the works of nature are so many additional arguments for a Deity, according to the true system of theism; but, according to your hypothesis of experimental theism, they become so many objections, by removing the effect still farther from all resemblance to the effects of human art and contrivance.

. . .

The discoveries by microscopes, as they open a new universe in miniature, are still objections, according to you, arguments, according to me. The further we push our researches of this kind, we are still led to infer the universal cause of all to be vastly different from mankind, or from any object of human experience and observation.

And what say you to the discoveries in anatomy, chemistry, botany? . . . These surely are no objections, replied Cleanthes; they only discover new instances of art and contrivance. It is still the image of mind reflected on us from innumerable objects. Add a mind *like the human,* said Philo. I know of no other, replied Cleanthes. And the liker, the better, insisted Philo. To be sure, said Cleanthes. Now, Cleanthes, said Philo, with an air of alacrity and triumph, mark the consequences. *First,* by this method of reasoning you renounce all claim to infinity in any of the attributes of the Deity. For, as the cause ought only to be proportioned to the effect, and the effect, so far as it falls under our cognizance, is not infinite, what pretensions have we, upon your suppositions, to ascribe that attribute to the Divine Being? You will still insist that, by removing him so much from all similarity to human creatures, we give in to the most arbitrary hypothesis, and at the same time weaken all proofs of his existence.

Secondly, you have no reason, on your theory, for ascribing perfection to the Deity, even in his finite capacity, or for supposing him free from every error, mistake, or incoherence, in his undertakings. There are many inexplicable difficulties in the works of nature which, if we allow a perfect author to be proved *a priori,* are easily solved, and become only seeming difficulties from the narrow capacity of man, who cannot trace infinite relations. But according to your method of reasoning, these difficulties become all real, and, perhaps, will be insisted on as new instances of likeness to human art and contrivance. At least, you must acknowledge that it is impossible for us to tell, from our limited views, whether this system contains any great faults or deserves any considerable praise if compared to other possible and even real systems. Could a peasant, if the *Æneid* were read to him, pronounce that poem to be absolutely faultless, or even assign to it its proper rank among the productions of human wit, he who had never seen any other production?

But were this world ever so perfect a production, it must still remain uncertain whether all the excellences of the work can justly be ascribed to the workman. If we survey a ship, what an exalted idea must we form of the ingenuity of the carpenter who framed so complicated, useful, and beautiful a machine? And what surprise must we feel when we find him a stupid mechanic who imitated others, and copied an art which, through a long succession of ages, after multiplied trials, mistakes, corrections, deliberations, and controversies, had been gradually improving? Many worlds might have been botched and bungled, throughout an eternity, ere this system was struck out; much labour lost, many fruitless trials made, and a slow but continued improvement carried on during infinite ages in the art of world-making. In such subjects, who can determine where the truth, nay, who can conjecture where the probability lies, amidst a great number of hypotheses which may be proposed, and a still greater which may be imagined?

And what shadow of an argument, continued Philo, can you produce from your hypothesis to prove the unity of the Deity? A great number of men join in building a house or ship, in rearing a city, in framing a commonwealth; why may not several deities combine in contriving and framing a world? This is only so much greater similarity to human affairs. By sharing the work among several, we may so much further limit the attributes of each, and get rid of that extensive power and knowledge which must be supposed in one deity, and which, according to you, can only serve to weaken the proof of his existence. And if such foolish, such vicious creatures as man can yet often unite in framing and executing one plan, how much more those deities or demons, whom we may suppose several degrees more perfect!

To multiply causes without necessity is indeed contrary to true philosophy, but this principle applies not to the present case. Were one deity antecedently proved by your theory who were possessed of every attribute requisite to the production of the universe, it would be needless, I own, (though not absurd) to suppose any other deity existent. But while it is still a question whether all these attributes are united in one subject or dispersed among several independent beings, by what phenomena in nature can we pretend to decide the controversy? Where we see a body raised in a scale, we are sure that there is in the opposite scale, however concealed from sight, some counterpoising weight equal to it; but it is still allowed to doubt whether that weight be an aggregate of several distinct bodies or one uniform united mass. And if the weight requisite very much exceeds anything which we have ever seen conjoined in any single body, the former supposition becomes still more probable and natural. An intelligent being of such vast power and capacity as is necessary to produce the universe, or, to speak in the language of ancient philosophy, so prodigious an animal exceeds all analogy and even comprehension.]

But further, Cleanthes: Men are mortal, and renew their species by generation; and this is common to all living creatures. The two great sexes of male and female, says Milton, animate the world. Why must this circumstance, so universal, so essential, be excluded from those numerous and limited deities? Behold, then, the theogeny of ancient times brought back upon us.

And why not become a perfect anthropomorphite? Why not assert the deity or deities to be corporeal, and to have eyes, a nose, mouth, ears, etc.? Epicurus maintained that no man had ever seen reason but in a human figure; therefore, the gods must have a human figure. And this argument, which is deservedly so much ridiculed by Cicero, becomes, according to you, solid and philosophical. In a word, Cleanthes, a man who follows your hypothesis is able, perhaps, to assert or conjecture that the universe sometime arose from something like design; but beyond that position he cannot ascertain one single circumstance, and is left afterwards to fix every point of his theology by the utmost license of fancy and hypothesis. This world, for aught he knows, is very faulty and imperfect, compared to a superior standard, and was only the first rude essay of some infant deity who afterwards abandoned it, ashamed of his lame performance; it is the work only of some dependent, inferior deity, and is the object of derision to his superiors; it is the production of old age and dotage in some superannuated deity, and ever since his death has run on at adventures, from the first impulse and active force which it received from him. You justly give signs of horror, Demea, at these strange suppositions; but these, and a thousand more of the same kind, are Cleanthes' suppositions, not mine. From the moment the attributes of the Deity are supposed finite, all these have place. And I cannot, for my part, think that so wild and unsettled a system of theology is, in any respect, preferable to none at all.

These suppositions I absolutely disown, cried Cleanthes: they strike me, however, with no horror, especially when proposed in that rambling way in which they drop from you. On the contrary, they give me pleasure when I see that, by the utmost indulgence of your imagination, you never get rid of the hypothesis of design in the universe, but are obliged at every turn to have recourse to it. To this concession I adhere steadily; and this I regard as a sufficient foundation for religion.

PART VI

It must be a slight fabric, indeed, said Demea, which can be erected on so tottering a foundation. While we are uncertain whether there is one deity or many, whether the deity or deities, to whom we owe our existence, be perfect or imperfect, subordinate or supreme, dead or alive, what trust or confidence can we repose in them? What devotion or worship address to them? What veneration or obedience pay them? To all the purposes of life the theory of religion becomes altogether useless; and even with regard to speculative consequences its uncertainty, according to you, must render it totally precarious and unsatisfactory.

To render it still more unsatisfactory, said Philo, there occurs to me another hypothesis which must acquire an air of probability from the method of reasoning so much insisted on by Cleanthes. That like effects arise from like causes —this principle he supposes the foundation of all religion. But there is another principle of the same kind, no less certain and derived from the same source of experience, that, where several known circumstances are observed to be similar, the unknown will also be found similar. Thus, if we see the limbs of a human body, we conclude that it is also attended with a human head, though hid from us. Thus, if we see, through a chink in a wall, a small part of the sun, we conclude that were the wall removed we should see the whole body. In short, this method of reasoning is so obvious and familiar that no scruple can ever be made with regard to its solidity.

Now, if we survey the universe, so far as it falls under our knowledge, it bears a great resemblance to an animal or organized body, and seems actuated with a like principle of life and motion. A continual circulation of matter in it produces no disorder; a continual waste in every part is incessantly repaired; the closest sympathy is perceived throughout the entire system; and each part or member, in performing its proper offices, operates both to its own preservation and to that of the whole. The world, therefore, I infer, is an animal; and the Deity is the *soul* of the world, actuating it, and actuated by it.

You have too much learning, Cleanthes, to be at all surprised at this opinion which, you know, was maintained by almost all the theists of antiquity, and chiefly prevails in their discourses and reasonings. For though, sometimes, the ancient philosophers reason from final causes, as if they thought the world the workmanship of God, yet it appears rather their favourite notion to consider it as his body whose organization renders it subservient to him. And it must be confessed that, as the universe resembles more a human body than it does the works of human art and contrivance, if our limited analogy could ever, with any propriety, be extended to the whole of nature, the inference seems juster in favour of the ancient than the modern theory.

There are many other advantages, too, in the former theory which recommended it to the ancient theologians. Nothing more repugnant to all their notions because nothing more repugnant to common experience than mind without body, a mere spiritual substance which fell not under their senses nor comprehension, and of which they had not observed one single instance throughout all nature. Mind and body they knew because they felt both; an order, arrangement, organization, or internal machinery, in both they likewise knew, after the same manner; and it could not but seem reasonable to transfer this experience to the universe, and to suppose the divine mind and body to be also coeval and to have, both of them, order and arrangement naturally inherent in them and inseparable from them.

Here, therefore, is a new species of *anthropomorphism,* Cleanthes, on which you may deliberate, and a theory which seems not liable to any considerable difficulties. You are too much superior, surely, to *systematical prejudices* to find any more difficulty in supposing an animal body to be, originally, of itself or from unknown causes, possessed of order and organization, than in supposing a similar order to belong to mind. But the *vulgar prejudice* that body and mind ought always to accompany each other ought not, one should think, to be entirely neglected; since it is founded on *vulgar experience,* the only guide which you profess to follow in all these theological inquiries. And if you assert that our limited experience is an unequal standard by which to judge of the unlimited extent of nature, you entirely abandon your own hypothesis, and must thenceforward adopt our mysticism, as you call it, and admit of the absolute incomprehensibility of the Divine Nature.

. . .

PART VII

But here, continued Philo, in examining the ancient system of the soul of the world there strikes me, all on a sudden, a new idea which, if just, must go near to subvert all your reasoning, and destroy even your first inferences on which you repose such confidence. If the universe bears a greater likeness to animal bodies and to vegetables than to the works of human art, it is more probable that its cause resembles the cause of the former than that of the latter, and its origin ought rather to be ascribed to generation or vegetation than to reason or design. Your conclusion, even according to your own principles, is therefore lame and defective.

Pray open up this argument a little further, said Demea, for I do not rightly apprehend it in that concise manner in which you have expressed it.

Our friend Cleanthes, replied Philo, as you have heard, asserts that, since no question of fact can be proved otherwise than by experience, the existence of a Deity admits not of proof from any other medium. The world, says he, resembles the works of human contrivance; therefore its cause must also resemble that of the other. Here we may remark that the operation of one very small part of nature, to wit, man, upon another very small part, to wit, that inanimate matter lying within his reach, is the rule by which Cleanthes judges of the origin of the whole; and he measures objects, so widely disproportioned, by the same individual standard. But to waive all objections drawn from this topic, I affirm that there are other parts of the universe (besides the machines of human invention) which bear still a greater resemblance to the fabric of the world, and which, therefore, afford a better conjecture concerning the universal origin of this system. These parts are animals and vegetables. The world plainly resembles more an animal or a vegetable than it does a watch or a knitting-loom. Its cause, therefore, it is more probable, resembles the cause of the former. The cause of the former is generation or vegetation. The cause, therefore, of the world we may infer to be something similar or analogous to generation or vegetation.

But how is it conceivable, said Demea, that the world can arise from anything similar to vegetation or generation?

Very easily, replied Philo. In like manner as a tree sheds its seed into the neighbouring fields and produces other trees, so the great vegetable, the world, or this planetary system, produces within itself certain seeds which, being scattered into the surrounding chaos, vegetate into new worlds. A comet, for instance, is the seed of a world; and after it has been fully ripened, by passing from sun to sun, and star to star, it is, at last, tossed into the unformed elements which everywhere surround this universe, and immediately sprouts up into a new system.

Or if, for the sake of variety (for I see no other advantage), we should suppose this world to be an animal: a comet is the egg of this animal; and in like manner as an ostrich lays its egg in the sand, which, without any further care, hatches the egg and produces a new animal, so .

. . . I understand you, says Demea. But what wild, arbitrary suppositions are these! What *data* have you for such extraordinary conclusions? And is the slight, imaginary resemblance of the world to a vegetable or an animal sufficient to establish the same inference with regard to both? Objects which are in general so widely different ought they to be a standard for each other?

Right, cries Philo: This is the topic on which I have all along insisted. I have still asserted that we have no *data* to establish any system of cosmogony. Our experience, so imperfect in itself and so limited both in extent and duration, can afford us no probable conjecture concerning the whole of things. But if we must needs fix on some hypothesis, by what rule, pray, ought we to determine our choice? Is there any other rule than the greater similarity of the objects compared? And does not a plant or an animal, which springs from vegetation or generation, bear a stronger resemblance to the world than does any artificial machine, which arises from reason and design?

But what is this vegetation and generation of which you talk? said Demea. Can you explain their operations, and anatomize that fine internal structure on which they depend?

As much, at least, replied Philo, as Cleanthes can explain the operations of reason, or anatomize that internal structure on which it depends. But without any such elaborate disquisitions, when I see an animal, I infer that it sprang from generation; and that with as great certainty as you conclude a house to have been reared by design. These words *generation, reason* mark only certain powers and energies in nature whose effects are known, but whose essence is incomprehensible; and one of these principles, more than the other, has no privilege for being made a standard to the whole of nature.

In reality, Demea, it may reasonably be expected that the larger the views are which we take of things, the better will they conduct us in our conclusions concerning such extraordinary and such magnificent subjects. In this little corner of the world alone, there are four principles, *reason, instinct, generation, vegetation,* which are similar to each other, and are the causes of similar effects. What a number of other principles may we naturally suppose in the immense extent and variety of the universe could we travel from planet to planet, and from system to system, in order to examine each part of this mighty fabric? Any one of these four principles above mentioned (and a hundred others which lie open to our conjecture) may afford us a theory by which to judge of the origin of the world; and it is a palpable and egregious partiality to confine our view entirely to that principle by which our own minds operate. Were this principle more intelligible on that account, such a partiality might be somewhat excusable; but reason, in its internal fabric and structure, is really as little known to us as instinct or vegetation; and, perhaps, even that vague, undeterminate word *nature* to which the vulgar refer everything is not at the bottom more inexplicable. The effects of these principles are all known to us from experience; but the principles themselves and their manner of operation are totally unknown; nor is it less intelligible or less conformable to experience to say that the world arose by vegetation, from a seed shed by another world, than to say that it arose from a divine reason or contrivance, according to the sense in which Cleanthes understands it.

But methinks, said Demea, if the world had a vegetative quality and could sow the seeds of new worlds into the infinite chaos, this power would be still an additional argument for design in its author. For whence could arise so wonderful a faculty but from design? Or how can order spring from anything which perceives not that order which it bestows?

You need only look around you, replied Philo, to satisfy yourself with regard to this question. A tree bestows order and organization on that tree which springs from it, without knowing the order; an animal in the same manner on its offspring; a bird on its nest; and instances of this kind are even more frequent in the world than those of order which arise from reason and contrivance. To say that all this order in animals and vegetables proceeds ultimately from design is begging the question; nor can that great point be ascertained otherwise than by proving, *a priori,* both that order is, from its nature, inseparably attached to thought and that it can never of itself or from original unknown principles belong to matter.

But further, Demea, this objection which you urge can never be made use of by Cleanthes, without renouncing a defence which he has already made against one of my objections. When I inquired concerning the cause of that supreme reason and intelligence into which he resolves everything, he told me that the impossibility of satisfying such inquiries could never be admitted as an objection in any species of philosophy. *We must stop somewhere,* says he; *nor is it ever within the reach of human capacity to explain ultimate causes or show the last connections of any objects. It is sufficient if any steps, so far as we go, are supported by experience and observation.* Now that vegetation and generation, as well as reason, are experienced to be principles of order in nature is undeniable. If I rest my system of cosmogony on the former, preferably to the latter, it is at my choice. The matter seems entirely arbitrary. And when Cleanthes asks me what is the cause of my great vegetative or generative faculty, I am equally entitled to ask him the cause of his great reasoning principle. These questions we have agreed to forebear on both sides; and it is chiefly his interest on the present occasion to stick to this agreement. Judging by our limited and imperfect experience, generation has some privileges above reason; for we see every day the latter arise from the former, never the former from the latter.

Compare, I beseech you, the consequences on both sides. The world, say I, resembles an animal; therefore it is an animal, therefore it arose from generation. The steps, I confess, are wide, yet there is some small appearance of analogy in each step. The world, says Cleanthes, resembles a machine; therefore it is a machine, therefore it arose from design. The steps are here equally wide, and the analogy less striking. And if he pretends to carry on *my* hypothesis a step further, and to infer design or reason from the great principle of generation on which I insist, I may, with better authority, use the same freedom to push further *his* hypothesis, and infer a divine generation or theogony from his principle of reason. I have at least some faint shadow of experience, which is the utmost that can ever be attained in the present subject. Reason, in innumerable instances, is observed to arise from the principle of generation, and never to arise from any other principle.

Hesiod and all the ancient mythologists were so struck with this analogy that they universally explained the origin of nature from an animal birth, and copulation. Plato, too, so far as he is intelligible, seems to have adopted some such notion in his *Timæus*.

The Brahmins assert that the world arose from an infinite spider, who spun this whole complicated mass from his bowels, and annihilates afterwards the whole or any part of it, by absorbing it again and resolving it into his own essence. Here is a species of cosmogony which appears to us ridiculous because a spider is a little contemptible animal whose operations we are never likely to take for a model of the whole universe. But still here is a new species of analogy, even in our globe. And were there a planet wholly inhabited by spiders (which is very possible), this inference would there appear as natural and irrefragable as that which in our planet ascribes the origin of all things to design and intelligence, as explained by Cleanthes. Why an orderly system may not be spun from the belly as well as from the brain, it will be difficult for him to give a satisfactory reason.

·   ·   ·

F. R. TENNANT

Cosmic Teleology

F. R. Tennant (1866–1957) was a lecturer in the Philosophy of Religion at Cambridge University. He is one of the clearest thinkers among the theologians of this century.

The classical proofs of the being of God sought to demonstrate that there is a Real counterpart to a preconceived idea of God, such as was moulded in the course of the developement of religion, or constructed by speculative philosophy aloof from religious experience and from avowedly anthropic interpretation, or obtained by both these methods combined. The empirically-minded theologian adopts a different procedure. He asks how the world, inclusive of man, is to be explained. He would let the Actual world tell its own story and offer its own suggestions: not silence it while abstractive speculation, setting out with presuppositions possibly irrelevant to Actuality, weaves a system of thought which may prove to conflict with facts. The *explicanda* which he investigates, and the results of his investigation, alone will determine the content or essence of the explicative idea of God to which he is led, as well as the grounds for belief that such an essence exists. He will thus entertain, at the outset, no such presuppositions as that the Supreme Being, to which the world may point as its

From F. R. Tennant, *Philosophical Theology* (1930), Vol. II, Ch. IV. Reprinted by permission of Cambridge University Press (New York and London).

principle of explanation, is infinite, perfect, immutable, suprapersonal, unqualifiedly omnipotent or omniscient. The attributes to be ascribed to God will be such as empirical facts and their sufficient explanation indicate or require. And if the empiricist deems the alleged religious 'instinct' and the *lumen naturale* proved to be non-existent, and, previously to the inferential establishment of theism, he must consider the mystic's claims to be untrustworthy, all that he can expect to emerge from his inquiry is grounds for reasonable belief rather than rational and coercive demonstration. Should this seem a mean ambition for the theologian, we need but recall that other selves, as to whose existence each of us has an unshakable conviction, and whose works we can understand or explain only by using teleological categories, are neither directly apprehended nor provable otherwise than by cumulative pragmatic verification.

It has already been submitted that revealed religion, such as the Christian Faith, logically presupposes natural religion, in so far as a distinction between the two is to be drawn, and that religion presupposes some theological notion, crude or refined according to stage of developement, suggested by observation of man and the world. And now it may further be remarked that natural theology is not to be identified with rational theology, though one name has often covered both of them. Rational and *a priori* theology stands or falls with the ontological argument; and if that argument—or some substitute for it, alleged to express its intent—still seems self-evidently cogent to a philosopher here and there, its fallaciousnes is self-evident to all the rest. Natural theology, on the other hand, sets out from facts and inductions; its premisses are as firmly established and as universally acknowledged as any of the stable generalisations of science. Here there is at least common ground, as distinct from private certitude, from which argumentation may proceed. Coercive demonstration being confessedly unattainable, it is to be inquired what kind of justification for reasonable belief natural theology can afford. And the first step is to set forth the facts and generalisations which collectively constitute our data or premisses.

The forcibleness of Nature's suggestion that she is the outcome of intelligent design lies not in particular cases of adaptedness in the world, nor even in the multiplicity of them. It is conceivable that every such instance may individually admit of explanation in terms of proximate causes or, in the first instance, of explanation other than in terms of cosmic or 'external' teleology. And if it also admits of teleological interpretation, that fact will not of itself constitute a rigorous certification of external design. The forcibleness of the world's appeal consists rather in the conspiration of innumerable causes to produce, by their united and reciprocal action, and to maintain, a general order of Nature. Narrower kinds of teleological argument, based on surveys of restricted spheres of fact, are much more precarious than that for which the name of 'the wider teleology' may be appropriated in that the comprehensive design-argument is the outcome of synopsis or conspection of the knowable world.

The knowable world, however, is not identical with the universe as to which, as a whole, we have no knowledge. It may be objected, therefore, that to use the phrase 'the world' to denote both of these things seems to beg a vital question. Of course, if trustworthy evidence of design in the limited portion of the universe that we know were forthcoming, a world-designer would be 'proved,' and our ignorance as to other parts would be irrelevant. But it is a graver objection—perhaps the gravest that the teleologist has to encounter—that rich suggestions of design in the known world yield no proof of design in the universe, since our ordered fragment may be but a temporary and casual episode in the history of the universe, an oasis in a desert of 'chaos,' a chance product of mindless agency in a universe which has had opportunity to produce all sorts of local and ephemeral worlds within A World. To this objection it may be replied that teleology does not profess to base itself on the principle of 'the inconceivability of the opposite,' while interpretations of the known cannot be refuted, even if they can be made to appear more precarious, by considerations as to possibilities within the unknowable. Certainly a mechanical theory of the universe must not be tacitly assumed to which our known world gives the lie. More specifically it may be said that the ordered oasis is not an isolable fragment. It and the supposed desert or 'chaos' are interdependent. It is because the desert is what it is that the oasis is what it is; and the one has orderedness only by permission, so to say, of the other. The force of the objection, indeed, seems to be derived from the assumption that our ordered world is due to some evolutionary process within the whole universe analogous to that secured within organic

Nature by natural selection out of random variations. This is but conjecture or appeal to the unknown, and, confronted with the second law of thermodynamics, is overwhelmingly improbable. And if it includes the supposition that even unlimited re-shufflings of matter by mechanical forces can produce minds and personalities in a corner of the universe, it conflicts with knowledge. Further, if the nerve of the teleological argument be that design issues in the realisation of ethical values, the spatio-temporal immensities of the universe become less significant than the petty oasis. Teleology, after all, is a value-concept; and magnitude and worth are incommensurable.

Nevertheless the inquiry that is here first to be undertaken, whether the knowable world, or Nature, has been devised by intelligence, is to be distinguished, though it cannot be separated, from the further inquiry, what the ultimate purpose or goal of the world-process is. The latter question may admit of no complete answer by man: reasonable belief as to the former involves but the application of mother-wit to forthcoming facts. A machine can evince intelligent contrivance or design to a man ignorant of engineering and unable to tell precisely what the machine is for. Once more, by way of making relevant distinctions, a teleological interpretation of Nature does not require that every detail in Nature was purposed or fore-ordained. Processes may inevitably produce by-products which, as such, were not purposed, but are the necessary outcome of processes by which a purpose is fulfilled.

The main fields of fact in which adaptation is conspicuous, and which have severally afforded data for particular arguments of the teleological kind and of restricted scope, are those of the knowability or intelligibility of the world (or the adaptation of thought to things), the internal adaptedness of organic beings, the fitness of the inorganic to minister to life, the aesthetic value of Nature, the world's instrumentality in the realisation of moral ends, and the progressiveness in the evolutionary process culminating in the emergence of man with his rational and moral status. A brief examination of these fields in turn will not only enable us to estimate the respective strengths of the more or less independent arguments derived from them severally, but also to appreciate the interconnexions within the world, and the comprehensive teleology which such interconnectedness suggests.

(i) We may begin with the mutual adaptation of thought and things, Nature and Knowledge. The correspondence between human thought and the external world, rendering science possible, has evoked what may be called epistemological arguments for the being of God. Descartes accounted for the marvel, as it seemed to him, of this correspondence by invoking, as its necessary cause, the veracious Deity, whose existence he sought to prove—almost superfluously, on his own presuppositions—by other lines of reasoning. If a subject's 'ideas' were as disparate from percepts and from external Objects as Descartes supposed, each class forming a closed system independent of the other, there might be something to be said for the invocation of divine agency to explain the elaborate correspondence between the two systems. But if our primary ideas of objects are but images of such objects defecated to pure transparency, or are but elements of the objective matter of perceptual experience isolated for thought by selective and restricted attention, then that they apply to the objects from which they have but been abstracted is no wonder to be supernaturally accounted for. And if, as in science, general ideas and the constituents of developed thought are determined and controlled by things external to thought, and so enjoy validity, there is no cause for amazement even at the predictiveness of theoretical physics. The mysterious element in knowledge does not lie where Descartes would place it: it lies deeper. Similarly, Shelley's apostrophe,

O thou immortal Deity
Whose throne is in the depths of human thought,

supposing it to have any relevance to the present context, errs as to the location of the "throne." It is in the world, as allowing itself to be thought about, rather than in our thinking, if anywhere, that considerations as to the penetrability of things by thought may lead teleology to enthrone its Deity. Reason might soliloquize: world or no world, I must think thus and thus, in order to think at all. Pure reason may have power to decree *how* thoughts must be linked in order to yield Thought, and certainly can without limit form ideas—as in the pure sciences —to which there is no knowable counterpart in Actuality; but it is powerless to prescribe to things *what* they shall be, and that they shall satisfy the demands of any pure science. The world might answer: you must think me thus and thus, as to my 'what,' and not otherwise, if you would know me. Nature will open to the right pass-word; but she has chosen it, not we. To revert to plain speech: the primary epistemological contribution to teleological reasoning consists in the fact that the world is more or less intelligible, in that it happens to be more or less a cosmos, when conceivably it might have been a self-subsistent and determinate 'chaos' in which similar events never occurred, none recurred, universals had no place, relations no fixity, things no nexus of determination, and 'real' categories no foothold. But whether such logico-mathematical order as has been found to obtain in our world bespeaks 'chance' [1] in self-

subsistent entities, or purposiveness in a designer or a creator, there is of course no logical method of deciding: the probability-calculus can gain no purchase. We know that similar ordering is sometimes due to human design; that it always is due to design we have no means of knowing. Again, the amenability of things to the more interpretative kind of knowledge, constituted by the 'real' or the anthropic categories, shews that things, or their ontal counterparts, have so much of affinity with us as to be assimilable and to be understood, or alogically interpreted, as well as to be ordered by number, etc.: it does not of itself testify that the adaptedness is teleological.

It is in that Nature evokes thought of richer kind than is involved in scientific knowledge, and responds to thinking such as is neither logically necessary nor biologically needful, thus suggesting a Beyond, that considerations as to the relation between thought and things assume their chief significance for the teleologist. These considerations, however, belong to another context; and those, the logical coerciveness of which has been denied, will later be discussed again when criticism of demonstrative proofs will give place to construction of a cumulative argument for a reasonable, if indemonstrable, teleological interpretation.

(ii) The adaptiveness that is so abundantly evinced in the organic world has

---

[1] By 'chance' is here meant absence of a sufficient ground. The word, as commonly used, carries several meanings; and which of them is to the fore in any context where the term subsequently appears will perhaps not need to be stated. Among its senses the following may be mentioned. It may signify an event not as yet included by known law, or one which, in that it is unique, is absolutely non-subsumable under a general law; or one that is determined by causes as to which we have but imperfect, or perhaps no relevant, knowledge. It may simply exclude final causation, and then denote the non-purposed. It may even suggest the supposed indeterminateness, which can never actually subsist, *e.g.*, of a configuration.

already been discussed from the point of view of science and proximate causation. We have seen that if the behaviour of matter be regarded as completely describable in terms of least action, shortest path, dissipation of kinetic energy, and so forth, matter must be regarded also as unable, of itself, to fall into such systems as organisms. There is indeed some tendency to-day in scientific circles to seek an organic conception of the physical atom, etc., rather than a mechanical conception of the organism. But as for the organic at the molar and phenomenal level of description, its formative principle, irreducible to rigid mechanism, is provided by mentality wherever we have reason to infer psychic behaviour; there we can account for the facts of function and structure, heredity and progressive adaptation. Where, as in plants, there is no macroscopic evidence of psychic behaviour, the formative principle, as yet mysterious to science, is further to seek. It may be that only in metaphysics such as spiritualistic monadism, or hylozoism of the microscopic order, is a natural explanation to be found. But in proportion as psychological or other explanation is forthcoming in the organic realm as a whole, resort to external or cosmic teleology, in order to account for adaptations within the organism, becomes superfluous for the special sciences. So long as organisms were believed to have originated, in their present forms and with all their specialised organs 'ready made,' the argument that adaptation of part to whole, of whole to environment, and of organ to function, implied design, was forcible. But its premiss became untenable when Darwin shewed that every organic structure had come to be what it now is through a long series of successive and gradual modifications. Gradualness of construction is in itself no proof of the absence of external design: it is not at this point that Darwinism delivered its alleged death-blow to tele-

ology. The sting of Darwinism rather lay in the suggestion that proximate and 'mechanical' causes were sufficient to produce the adaptations from which the teleology of the eighteenth century had argued to God. Assignable proximate causes, whether mechanical or not, are sufficient to dispose of the particular kind of teleological proof supplied by Paley. But the fact of organic evolution, even when the maximum of instrumentality is accredited to what is figuratively called natural selection, is not incompatible with teleology on a grander scale: as exponents of Darwinism were perhaps the first to recognise and to proclaim. Subversive of Paley's argument, it does not invalidate his theistic conclusion, nor even his view that every organism and organ is an end as well as a means. Indeed the science of evolution was the primary source of the wider teleology current for the last half century, as well as the main incentive to the recovery of the closely connected doctrine of divine immanence. This kind of teleology does not set out from the particular adaptations in individual organisms or species so much as from considerations as to the progressiveness of the evolutionary process and as to the organic realm as a whole; but its connexion with the former class of facts belongs to the subject-matter of the present section.

The survival of the fittest presupposes the arrival of the fit, and throws no light thereupon. Darwin did not account for the origin of variations; their forthcomingness was simply a datum for him. It is of no great significance for the wider teleology that variations are not in all cases so indefinite or random, nor so infinitesimal and gradual, as was generally assumed in *The Origin of Species*. But it may be observed that, in the absence either of a mechanical or of an 'internal' explanation of variation, room is left for the possibility that variation is externally predetermined or guided, so that not only the general trend of the organic process, but also its every detail, may be pre-ordained or divinely controlled. Even this observation is pointless save for those who regard a nexus of traceable proximate causes and a theistic interpretation as incompatibilities. Theism such as has over-emphasised the idea of God's immanence denies proximate causes as distinct from acts of God; and advocates of anti-theistic mechanism sometimes appear to think that the traceability of proximate causes bespeaks the superfluity, to philosophy as well as to science, of the idea of God. Thus, in connexion with the topic now before us, Weismann wrote: "It is certainly the absence of a theoretical definition of variability which leaves open the door for smuggling in a teleological power. A mechanical explanation of variability must form the basis of this side of natural selection." But theism, such as is sufficiently leavened with deism to distinguish itself from pantheism, and the world from a deified mechanism, is indifferent to the banishment of the Paleyan type of teleology which relied on particular organic adaptations, any one of which was deemed sufficient to prove a divine artificer; and at the same time it has no need of going to the extreme of asserting that God is "either everywhere or nowhere," or that He is nothing if not all. The discovery of organic evolution has caused the teleologist to shift his ground from special design in the products to directivity in the process, and plan in the primary collocations. It has also served to suggest that the organic realm supplies no better basis for teleological argument of the narrower type than does inorganic Nature. Indeed it suggests that, since the adaptiveness of an organism is non-teleological, the adaptiveness of the whole world may perhaps similarly be *Zweckmässigkeit ohne Zweck*. But this suggestion calls for examination later.

(iii) Although teleologists in the past have generally set out from adaptations in organisms, it has occurred now and again to a theistic apologist, *e.g.* to Aquinas, that adaptation in inorganic Nature, where there cannot be a formative principle such as non-intelligent organisms evince, should more unequivocally bespeak external design. The teleologist of to-day, however, would rather call attention to the continuity of apparent purposiveness between the two realms, or to the dependence of adaptation in the one on adaptiveness in the other. Since Darwin, we have realised that organisms can only be understood in connexion with their environment. And more recently it has been argued, as by Mr Henderson, that the inorganic environment is as plainly adapted to life as living creatures are to their environment. The vast complexity of the physico-chemical conditions of life on the earth suggests to common sense that the inorganic world may retrospectively receive a biocentric explanation, which, if 'unconscious purpose' do but restate the facts rather than account for them, and ungrounded coincidence be as humanly incredible as it is logically unassailable, becomes a teleological explanation. Waiving, as here irrelevant, the metaphysical possibility that what we call inorganic matter is an appearance of relatively unorganised spirit, we may say that if science is to be trusted when it regards the organic realm as later in time than the inorganic world, and when it asserts that the processes, which made the emergence and persistence of life possible, would have been precisely the same had life not emerged at all, then there would seem to be a developement of this fitness for life, involving convergence of innumerable events towards a result, as if that result were an end to which the inorganic processes were means. The fitness of our world to be the home of living beings depends upon certain primary conditions, astronomical, thermal, chemical, etc., and on the coincidence of qualities apparently not causally connected with one another, the number of which would doubtless surprise anyone wholly unlearned in the sciences; and these primary conditions, in their turn, involve many of secondary order. Unique assemblages of unique properties on so vast a scale being thus essential to the maintenance of life, their forthcomingness makes the inorganic world seem in some respects comparable with an organism. It is suggestive of a formative principle. But, if there be such a principle, it is not conceivable after analogy with the life and mind of organisms, and cannot be said to be intrinsic or internal; because the inorganic—at the molar and phenomenal level of explanation—is devoid of life, and—at any level of explanation—is devoid of intelligence and foresight. Unless cosmic teleology is invoked, the intricate adaptations that have been mentioned must be referred by the dualist to a mechanically controlled concourse of atoms, and by the pluralistic spiritualist to conative monads that are no more capable of conspiration than are inert particles.

Such is the teleological appeal of this field of facts to commonsense reasonableness, or mother-wit, which regards the 'probability,' that the apparent preparedness of the world to be a theatre of life is due to 'chance,' as infinitesimally small. It remains to ask whether either science or logic is able to abate the forcibleness of this appeal.

Science does not seem to lessen the convincingness of the argument now before us when it suggests that (as if organic chemistry were irrelevant), had the conditions upon which life, as we know it, depends been wholly or partly different, other forms of organism might equally well have emerged, adapted to the altered environment: silicon perhaps replacing carbon in another kind of protoplasm, and iron replacing calcium phosphate in skeletons. For the point is that, for the existence of any forms of life that we may conceive, the necessary environment, whatever its nature, must be complex and dependent on a multiplicity of coincident conditions, such as are not reasonably attributable to blind forces or to pure mechanism. Nor, again, can science explain the adaptation of the inorganic environment to life after the manner in which Darwinism, its sufficiency being assumed, explains progressive adaptations in organisms without resort to design. Of a struggle for existence between rival worlds, out of which ours has survived as the fittest, we have no knowledge upon which to draw. Natural selection cannot here be invoked; and if the term 'evolution' be applicable at all to the whole world-process, it must have a different meaning from that which it bears in Darwinian biology. Presumably the world is comparable with a single throw of dice. And common sense is not foolish in suspecting the dice to have been loaded.

But here the logician intervenes. He will first point out that the remarkableness, or surprisingness, of manifold coincidences, evoking our teleological explanation of them, is but a fact pertaining to human psychology, unless 'remarkable' means what he calls antecedently improbable. He will then remind us that a remarkable world might result from 'one throw' in spite of there being indefinitely large chances against it, just as double sixes may be cast in one's first toss of two unloaded dice, although the adverse odds are 35 to 1. But his most harmful observation will be that, if the world be the sole instance of its kind, or be analogous to a single throw, there can be no talk of chances or of antecedent probability in connexion with our question. Sound as this caution is, it does not affect the teleologist; for, when he calls coincidence on the vast scale improbable, he has in mind not mathematical probability, or a logical relation, but the alogical probability which is the guide of life and which has been found to be the ultimate basis of all scientific induction. If teleology here strays from the path of logical rectitude into one marked by logicians with a warning-post, it does so in the light-hearted company of common sense and inductive science. Science has been so continuously successful in its venturesomeness that the wise-head, logic, now lets it pass without remonstrance; but theology, though arm in arm with science, receives a reprimand. The teleologist is told that there is no antecedent probability, as to the existence of the intelligent Being invoked to explain adaptation suggestive of intelligent activity, after observation of the facts in question, unless there was an appreciable probability, before observation of them, that such a Being exists. Robinson Crusoe can be said to have inferred Friday from footprints legitimately, because he already knew that men existed and that they could reach his island; but the teleologist does not know beforehand that any superhuman being exists, and therefore cannot legitimately reason from what apparently are Mind-prints to their divine causation. But some favouritism would seem to be shewn to science in this illustration; for when we inquire how Crusoe originally got his knowledge as to the existence of fellow-men who can not only make footprints but also supply service and friendship, we find that it seems to have been mediated in much the same way as is the teleologist's belief in God. It is true that in the former case there is a psychologically stronger compulsion, a nearer analogy, and a more immediate and constantly reiterated verification-process than in the latter; but the origination of our belief in fellow-subjects, like remarkableness of coincidences, is ultimately an affair of human psychology and life, of teleology and not of logic or of direct apprehension of soul-substance. Moreover, though we have no 'knowledge' of a spirit above man in the hierarchy of spirits that we 'know,' neither have we knowledge that there is no such being. Knowledge leaves room for the faith which teleology involves; and the faith-venture is similar *in kind* to that on which all scientific knowledge relies. Previously to verification of his faith the teleologist need ask of science no further recognition than this. He would but insist that, in so far as relations with logic are concerned, it is not true that science rests on reason while, in a corresponding sense, teleology rests on unreason.

(iv) Besides possessing a structure that happens to render it habitable by living creatures and intelligible to some of them, the world is a bearer of values, thus evincing affinity with beings such as can appreciate as well as understand. The beauty and sublimity of Nature have been made the basis of a special teleological argument; and if, as standing by itself, this argument falls short of cogency, the facts from which it sets out may be said to form a link in the chain of evidence which comprehensive teleology presents. The few considerations that lend themselves to either of these uses do not call for lengthy or subtle disputation; and fortunately it is not necessary to enter the scientifically trackless domain of aesthetics in order to ascertain their bearing on theism. Whether the adaptation to our faculties, involved in aesthetic estimation, be, as Kant thought, formal and the same for all, though subjective; whether it be subjectively constituted and not the same for all; whether beauty be wholly Objective and literally intrinsic to Nature: these controversial questions are here immaterial. For the doctrine that aesthetic value is constituted by feeling does not imply that the feeling is not objectively evoked, as if we could see beauty when and where we chose.

It has a parallel in the phenomenalist theory of knowledge: that is to say, beauty is not created by minds out of nothing, but is subjectively made out of *rapport* with the ontal. Thus diverse theories as to the constitution of beauty may be said to have in common the implication that the ontal world is ultimately responsible for the evocation of aesthetic thrills and sentiments, though the value-judgments evoked by the same 'perceptual' Objects are different in different percipients. Theories differ but as to what exactly is intrinsic, whether that is intrinsic to Nature as ontal or as phenomenal, and how much is subjectively contributed. And whatever be our proportioning of the shares of the human mind and external Reality in constituting aesthetic value, the dependence or non-dependence of beauty on design will not be affected by it. There is a point in Toby Veck's remark as to the chimes: "If I hear 'em, what does it matter whether they speak it or not?" Yet "We receive but what we give," [2] in this connexion, is a partial truth because it suppresses the fact that our giving is solicited by a prior and different gift to us. If we minimise phenomenal Nature's gift by denying that her beauty is intrinsic, as is form or colour, we must allow to ontal Nature an intrinsic constitution such that minds can make beauty as well as nomic order out of it. And the more we magnify man's part in this making, phenomenalising, and appreciating, the more motivation have we to believe that Nature comes to herself in man, has a significance for man that exists not for herself, and without man is a broken circle. Theologically expressed, this is the belief that Nature is meaningless and valueless without God behind it and man

in front; and that is what teleology in its comprehensiveness, and the aesthetic argument in its particularity, endeavour to establish.

The latter argument, at least in its more popular forms, treats the beauty of Nature as Paley treated organic adaptations. That it discusses the beauty of the world, as we now contemplate it, as if it were a 'special creation' with no past history or developement, may not signify. The weak spot in what purports to be a special proof of theism lies rather in the assumption that, since in human art a beautiful or sublime production is the outcome of human design, similar effects must everywhere be due to design. This generalisation is all too precarious; it can hardly be maintained that arrangements of matter, accounted beautiful, humanly caused but not contrived or selectively constructed with a view to exciting aesthetic admiration, *never* occur. Prescience or purpose is involved in art; but art is not necessarily the sole source of beauty. We may deem some of Kant's criticisms of the teleological explanation of the beautiful and the sublime to be captious, and such explanation to be natural and reasonable; but it is hardly necessitated by the considerations on which this would-be coercive argument relies.

The aesthetic argument for theism becomes more persuasive when it renounces all claim to proof and appeals to alogical probability. And it becomes stronger when it takes as the most significant fact not the forthcomingness of beautiful phenomena but what may be called, with almost negligible need of qualification, the saturation of Nature with beauty. On the telescopic and on the microscopic scale, from the starry heaven to the siliceous skeleton of the diatom, in her inward parts (if scientific imagination be veridical) as well as on the surface, in flowers that "blush unseen" and gems that the "unfathomed caves of ocean bear," Nature is sublime or beautiful, and the

---

[2] . . . We receive but what we give,
And in our life alone does Nature live:
Ours is her wedding-garment, ours her shroud!
  S. T. Coleridge, *Dejection: An Ode*.

exceptions do but prove the rule. However various be the taste for beauty, and however diverse the levels of its education or the degrees of its refinement, Nature elicits aesthetic sentiment from men severally and collectively; and the more fastidious becomes this taste, the more poignantly and the more lavishly does she gratify it. Indeed, from contemplation of Nature, whose "every prospect pleases," the atheist might be led to conclude that processes only need *not* to be fraught with aesthetic design in order to excite, almost without fail, aesthetic admiration. But this generalisation would become untenable as soon as he bethought himself of similar causal *nexa* into which human agency, seeking any end save beauty, enters. In general, man's productions (other than professed works of art), and almost only they, are aesthetically vile. An automobile, with its noises, stench, etc., can disgust all our senses simultaneously, and is not wholly untypical; while human output of larger scale is often not only unsightly and otherwise offensive in itself, but mars the fair face of Nature. Here, then, are two kinds of agency, *ex hypothesi* proceeding with indifference to the realisation of aesthetic values: we might almost say the one never achieves, while the other never misses, the beautiful. And the same contrast subsists between their processes as between their products. Compare, *e.g.*, "the rattling looms and the hammering noise of human workshops" with Nature's silent or musical constructiveness; or the devastating stinks of chemical works with Nature's fragrant distillations. "In the very act of labouring as a machine [Nature] also sleeps as a picture." [3]

If "God made the country" whereas man made the town—and the black country—we have a possible explanation of these things; but if the theism contained in this saying be rejected, explanation does not seem to be forthcoming. The universality of Nature's beauty,—to speak as if beauty were the same for all and were intrinsic—is a generalisation roughly comparable with the uniformity of natural law. That natural Objects evoke aesthetic sentiment is as much a fact about them as that they obey the laws of motion or that they have such and such chemical composition. And this potency is not coextensive with 'mechanicalness,' or absence of aesthetic design, as man's utilitarian productions shew. Nor can Nature's mechanism be regarded as a sufficient cause of the adaptiveness to our subjectivity in which beauty consists; for we may still ask why *Nature's* mechanism affects us in such wise that we deem her sublime and beautiful, since mere mechanism, as such, is under no universal necessity to do so, and what we may call human mechanisms usually fail to do so. Yet this potency, describable as the Objective factor in beauty, belongs to Nature's very texture. And our scientific knowledge that the world-elements are ordered by number brings us no nearer to understanding why Nature is comparable with elaborately polyphonic music, or a harmony of many combined melodies.

It may further be observed that, in so far as the mechanical stability and the analytic intelligibility of the inorganic world are concerned, beauty is a superfluity. Also that in the organic world aesthetic pleasingness of colour, etc., seems to possess survival-value on but a limited scale, and then is not to be identified with the complex and intellectualised aesthetic sentiments of humanity, which apparently have no survival-value. From the point of view of science, beauty proper is, in both its subjective and its objective factors, but a by-product, an epiphenomenon, a biologically superfluous accompaniment of the cosmic

---

[3] J. B. Mozley, *University Sermons,* 6th ed., p. 123.

process. Once more then lucky accidents and coincidences bewilderingly accumulate until the idea of purposiveness, already lying to hand as indispensable within the sphere of human conduct, is applied to effect the substitution of reasonable, if alogical, probability for groundless contingency. If we do apply this category of design to the whole time-process, the beauty of Nature may not only be assigned a cause but also a meaning, or a revelational function. It may then be regarded as no mere by-product, like physical evil, in a teleologically ordered world whose *raison d'être* is the realisation of other values —the moral and the religious. Indeed Nature's potency to evoke aesthetic sentiment, however otiose in the cosmic process studied by science, is efficient in the world's *rapport* with man. From its very origination religious experience seems to have been conditioned by the impressiveness or the awesomeness of natural phenomena, suggestive of an invisible and mysterious presence. Aesthetic values are closely associated, and often are inextricably interwoven, with ethico-religious values. God reveals Himself, to such as have differentiated these valuations, in many ways; and some men enter His Temple by the Gate Beautiful. Values alone can provide guidance as to the world's meaning, structure being unable to suggest more than intelligent power. And beauty may well be *a* meaning. That is the element of sense contained in the romanticist's paradox, beauty is truth, or truth is beauty.

It may be remarked by the way that if sensuous beauty be accounted a world-meaning, so far will the anthropocentric factor in interpretation of the world become accentuated. For as to the ontal counterpart to sensory beauty, or what Nature's beauty is for the Creator Himself, we cannot speculate. If Nature's beauty embody a purpose *of* God, it would seem to be a purpose *for* man, and to bespeak that God is "mindful of him." Theistically regarded, Nature's beauty is of a piece with the world's intelligibility and with its being a theatre for moral life; and thus far the case for theism is strengthened by aesthetic considerations.

.   .   .

In an exposition of the significance of the moral order for theistic philosophy, the first step is to point out that man belongs to Nature, and is an essential part of it, in such a sense that the world cannot be described or explained as a whole without taking him and his moral values into account. Prof. Pringle-Pattison, especially, has elaborated the doctrine that, as he expresses it, "man is organic to the world." What precisely this, or the similar phrase "man is the child of Nature," should mean, if either is to be more than a half-truth, needs to be made clear. In so far as man's soul, *i.e.* man as *noümenon,* or (in the language of spiritualistic pluralism) the dominant monad in the empirical self, is concerned, we are not authorised by known facts to regard man as organic to Nature, or as the child of Nature, in the sense that he is an emergent product of cosmic evolution. We are rather forbidden by psychology to entertain any such notion. But, this proviso being observed—it must qualify all that is further said in the present connexion—we can affirm that man's body, with all its conditioning of his mentality, his sociality, knowledge and morality, is 'of a piece' with Nature; and that, in so far as he is a phenomenal being, man is organic to Nature, or a product of the world. And this fact is as significant for our estimation of Nature as for our anthropology. If man is Nature's child, Nature is the wonderful mother of such a child. Any account of her which ignores the fact of her maternity is scientifically partial and philosophically insignificant. Her capacity to produce man must be reckoned among her potencies, explain it how we may. And man is no monstrous birth out of due time, no freak or sport. In respect of his body and the bodily conditioning of his mentality, man is like, and has genetic continuity with, Nature's humbler and earlier-born children. In the fulness of time Nature found self-utterance in a son possessed of the intelligent and moral status. Maybe she was pregnant with him from the beginning, and the world-ages are the period of her gestation. As to this anthropocentric view of the world-process, and its co-extensiveness with teleological interpretation, more will presently be said. But in the light of man's continuity with the rest of the world we can at once dismiss the view that Nature suddenly "stumbled" or "darkly blundered" on man, while "churning the universe with mindless motion." The world-process is a *praeparatio anthropologica,* whether designedly or not, and man is the culmination, up to the present stage of the knowable history of Nature, of a gradual ascent. We cannot explain man in terms of physical Nature; conceivably Nature may be found explicable —in another sense of the word—in terms of man, and can be called 'the threshold of spirit.' Judging the genealogical tree by its roots, naturalism once preached that Darwin had put an end to the assumption that man occupies an exceptional position on our planet; apparently implying that there is no difference of status between man and the primordial slime because stages between the two are traceable. But if we judge the tree by its fruits, Darwin may rather be said to have restored man to the position from which Copernicus seemed to have ousted him, in making it possible to read the humanising of Nature in the

naturalising of man, and to regard man as not only the last term and the crown of Nature's long upward effort, but also as its end or goal.[4]

The phrase 'organic to Nature,' as applied to man, may serve to sum up other relations between humanity and the world besides that of parentage or blood-affinity. It implies also a denial of the assertion that man is an excrescence upon Nature in the sense of being an alien in a world that is indifferent to his moral aims, or hostile to his ideals. The most forcible presentation of this view, that the cosmic process and human morality are antithetical, is perhaps that contained in Huxley's *Romanes Lecture.* It is therefore here selected for examination. Huxley's first point was that the world, as involving struggle for existence and extermination of the less fit, is no "school of virtue." If that statement merely meant that it is not from Nature that we are to imbibe our ethical maxims, no one would wish to dispute it. But it would then overlook the fact that in other senses Nature may fairly be called a school of virtue. In the first place, Nature is largely a cosmos ruled by uniformity or law; and if Nature's uniformity and impartiality are a main source of the trouble to which man is born, they are also a precondition of all intelligent, and therefore of all moral, life. In this respect Nature is the power that makes it possible for noümenal man to be, as phenomenal man, a moral being. Further, it is partly through his being "the plaything of hazard and the prey of hardship" that man's moral virtues are acquired. The world is thus instrumental to the emergence, maintenance, and progressiveness, of morality. The second charge which Huxley preferred against the cosmos is that the physical world

---

[4]A. Seth Pringle-Pattison, *The Idea of God,* 1917, pp. 82 f.

works upon man solely through his lower nature, his ingrained appetites, etc., and against his higher ethical interests. Nature is thus the cause of his 'original sin,' and is diabolically provocative of his diverse immoralities. This also is true; but again it presents but one aspect of the facts. For, apart from man's bodily appetites and impulses it is inconceivable that ethical principles should gain purchase on him. Hunger and sex are the bed-rock of human morality; and the self-determination which human morality presupposes is hardly possible without the conflict between moral reason and non-moral impulse. Morality cannot be made without raw material; and in providing this raw material Nature is once more instrumental to man's acquisition of the moral status. Morality thus has its roots in Nature, however indispensable be the innate and non-inherited potentialities of the pure ego or soul. The non-moral cosmos, personified into a morally evil world by pessimistic poets for the purpose of giving it, as Mr Chesterton has said of one of them, a piece of their mind, has nevertheless subserved the moralisation of human souls, even when soliciting to carnality. And it is an exaggeration to say that Nature fosters only tendencies that issue in vice. We have seen before that there is such a thing as 'natural virtue,' or 'original rectitude,' as 'instinctive' as is self-seeking; and Nature plainly appraises health and vigour, thus inciting to temperance and self-control. Lastly, Huxley maintained that the world is indifferent to man's moral aspirations, in that they along with him are destined to be extinguished before the break-up of the solar system. Here he became unwarrantably dogmatical: for, apart from the fact that science's predictions are not unconditional, speculations as to the ruin of a fragment of the universe, based on partial knowledge of a larger fragment of what, for all we know, may be

possessed of a power to make all things new, are too precarious to be considered exhaustive of the possibilities even as to our terrestrial home, let alone those as to a future life.

Nature, then, has produced moral beings, is instrumental to moral life and therefore amenable to 'instrumental' moral valuation, and is relatively modifiable by operative moral ideas—or, rather, by moral agents pursuing ideals. Nature and moral man are not at strife, but are organically one. The whole process of Nature is capable of being regarded as instrumental to the developement of intelligent and moral creatures. Acquisition of the moral status is in line with the other stages of the long 'ascent of man,' and is its climax—unless we reserve that name for the morality which, tinged with sentiment transcending reverence for duty, passes into religion.

(vi) The more or less separable fields of fact which have now been surveyed may each be said to admit of teleological explanation even if explanation of the causal or the descriptive type be forthcoming in every case. None of them calls for resort to final causes merely because other kinds of causality, or linkage according to law, are not assignable. Theism no longer plants its God in the gaps between the explanatory achievements of natural science, which are apt to get scientifically closed up. Causal explanation and teleological explanation are not mutually exclusive alternatives; and neither can perform the function of the other. It is rather when these several fields of fact are no longer considered one by one, but as parts of a whole or terms of a continuous series, and when for their dovetailing and interconnectedness a sufficient ground is sought, such as mechanical and proximate causation no longer seems to supply, that divine design is forcibly suggested. Paley's watch is no analogue of the human eye; but it may none the less be an approximate analogue of Nature as a whole. Thus the wider teleological argument is not comparable with a chain whose strength is precisely that of its weakest link; it is comparable rather with a piece of chain-armour. And this can the better be seen if the relevant facts be presented again so as to display especially their connexions and their gradually increasing suggestiveness.

There is no intrinsic necessity that a world, or an assemblage of existents and happenings, indefinably and unaccountably 'standing out' as against nothingness, be a cosmos, even to the extent of any one existent being comparable with another or behaving in the same way twice. Reality, or the aggregate of those determinate beings, might conceivably be a 'chaos' of disparates and inconsistencies such that if any of its members possessed consciousness or awareness and the potentiality of intelligence, they would find the world presented to them utterly unintelligible. Our world is, however, a cosmos, at least in the humblest sense of the word, and the original determinateness of its terms or *posita* is such as to make it intelligible. This, of course, constitutes a teleological proof of theism no more than does the existence of the world afford a causal or cosmological proof. The mystery of mysteries is that something exists; and if the one underived or uncaused existent be God, the creator of all things else, God is "the last irrationality," and creation is the next to the last inexplicability. To replace absolute pluralism by theism is to reduce an indefinite number of separate inexplicabilities to these two alone; and so far economy, and therefore explicability of a kind, is secured. It is of no important kind, however: for there is no more wonder about a self-subsistent plurality than about a self-subsistent individual. But when the intelligibility of a cosmos, rather than the mere existence of a world of any sort, is the fact to be

considered, teleological theism evinces more conspicuously its advantage, in other respects than that of economy, over absolute pluralism. For over and above the forthcomingness, conceived as self-subsistence, of the many existents, is their adaptiveness, inherent in their primary determinateness and their relations, to the requirements of intelligibility. This further particularises their determinateness and so bespeaks more of coincidence in the 'fortuitous.' For cosmos-quality, or intelligibility, in our world, which conceivably might have been but a determinate 'chaos,' non-theistic philosophy can assign no reason. If the world 'made itself,' so to say, or is the self-subsistent Absolute, its adaptiveness to understanding has simply happened, and is part and parcel of the pluralist's last irrationality. It gives him more to explain or to refuse to explain: for why should the many arrange themselves to form an intelligible and an organic whole? If, on the other hand, this be due to an intelligent Creator designing the world to be a theatre for rational life, mystery is minimised, and a possible and sufficient reason is assigned. More than this cannot be extracted out of the initial fact that the world is intelligible, in the sense that has as yet solely been in question; but if it be merely a hint that Nature's dice may be loaded, it is to be observed that the hint becomes broader as Nature is further examined, and as the knowledge-process is analysed. For instance, the particular species of intelligibility, in which the knowledge of common sense and science consists, is mediated by the 'real' categories; and they depend for their forthcomingness on the contingency that the dominant monad in man is embodied, or associated with monads such as also constitute Nature but which, in virtue of some mysterious affinity, are not merely bits of Nature to the soul but also its windows and telephonic exchange-office mediating to it all its knowledge whatsoever, even its self-knowledge. Thus, as step by step the machinery which produces intelligibility is scientifically explored and made manifest, the richer in specialised determinateness are some of the world's constituents found to be; and therefore the more suggestive is the intricate adaptiveness, involved in knowledge of the world by man, of pre-established harmony or immanent guidance, or both, and the less reasonable or credible becomes the alternative theory of cumulative groundless coincidence. The doctrine that man is organic to Nature can now be broadened out so as to embrace the fact that it is only in so far as he is part and parcel of Nature that he can ejectively make the knowledge-venture, and only in virtue of Nature's affinity with him that his postulatory categories receive pragmatic verification, and his assimilation-drafts are honoured. When the impossible Cartesian rationalism is exchanged for the humanism or anthropism which, implicit in Kant, is explicitly demanded by more modern empirical knowledge of the human mind, the epistemological argument for theism begins to acquire a forcibleness that was lacking to the arbitrary, if not circular, reasoning of Descartes. It is, however, but a fragment of the epistemological argument to establish the anthropocentric theory of knowledge, which is ultimately based on the fact that between the soul and the world, in so far as knowledge of the one by the other is concerned, stands the body; and the epistemological line or mesh-work is but a fragment of the teleological argument as a whole.

Turning now from Nature's knowability to her structure and history, we may revert first to the fact of adaptiveness in the organic realm, which, so far, has only been found not to yield teleological proof of the narrower kind. Here adaptiveness, unhappily described as internal teleology, is not teleological at all in so far as it is internal to the organism. There is no end present to the agent. It is from the (ps) standpoint of the biologist, not from the (ψ) standpoint of the organism, that reference to the future is involved in organic adaptedness. Again, neither the occurrence nor the progressiveness of organic adaptations, taken *singillatim,* calls for other than natural, if non-mechanical, causation. It is true that the course of living Nature is not mere change, but change that admits of valuation, of one kind or another; of valuation not only in terms of fitness for survival but also in terms of differentiation or complexity of structure and function, and of subservience to further developement culminating, in man, in rationality and morality. Despite cases of stagnancy and of degeneration, which equally with progress may ensure biological fitness, the plasticity, formative power, or *élan* in organic Nature secures not only self-conservation but also progress, morphological and ultimately mental, so that within the main line of developement there has been a steady advance from amoeba to man. But each step and special adaptation, each case of emergence of something new and higher, in this long process, can be sufficiently accounted for in terms of natural, non-teleological causation. So far as the foregoing facts are concerned there is no need to resort to external teleology. It is not *necessary* to invoke design in order to find a guarantee for the stability, in face of the ever-present possibility of deletion of the 'higher' by the 'fitter,' of the long and gradual ascent, remarkable as that is. It is rather when the essential part played by the environment, physical and organic, in the progressive developement of the organic world, is appreciated, that non-teleological explanation ceases to be plausible in this sphere, and, conspiration being precluded, external design begins to be indicated or strongly suggested. It is the environment that is the selector, though 'selection' is a figurative expression when applied to non-intelligent Nature. Subjective selection, or the Lamarckean factor, may decide what shall arise; but the environment decides what shall stand. And before discussing the alternatives of theistic teleology and naturalistic Pyrrhonism (if the doctrine of fortuitousness or ungrounded coincidence may so be called), it may be submitted that the fact just mentioned restricts our choice to the one or the other of them, in that, when taken into account, it deprives the only other forthcoming alternative, viz. the theory of 'unconscious purpose,' of such plausibility as, *prima facie,* it may seem to possess.

. . .

The empirical approach to theism being essentially teleological, it is now necessary to raise the question, what an end or purpose, as attributable to the Deity, consists in. The idea of purpose is derived from the sphere of human activity; and such meaning as is imported into it from that context has necessary relevance only so long as that context is not transcended: such is the empirical doctrine as to the scope and validity of ideas or ideational propositions. But when applied to God, whose activities, by definition or *ex hypothesi,* include some that are unique, and whose intelligence is necessarily different in some respects from ours, the idea may become non-significant. Theism that would use the idea, it has sometimes been urged, must be unduly anthropomorphic. That need not be so, however, if such constituents of the complex idea of purpose as involve intrinsic limitations of human mentality and activity can be eliminated from it, while others, essential to the conception of purposiveness but separable from their human manifestation, can be isolated for legitimate transference to the sphere of divine activity. What elements require to be eliminated, modified, or newly related, in such recasting of the idea, has been differently decided by different exponents of theism; and perhaps it is premature to undertake the analysis and re-synthesis until an exposition has been given of one's conception of the nature and attributes of the Deity. In the absence of such preliminary discussion it may suffice to indicate possible divergences of view, as occasion calls.

In the conception of human purpose we may distinguish the following constituent elements: (1) the pre-conceived idea of a situation to be reached, (2) desire for that situation because of its value to the agent, (3) the use—in general—of means for the attainment of it, (4) the actualisation—generally by stages —of what was contemplated in thought and striven for. Into the first of these, and indeed into all of them, the idea of temporal succession enters: idea of the goal is previous to attainment of goal, desire to fruition, and so on. And whether the temporal form, characterising human experience, is to be carried over into the conception of God's activity and experience is a disputed question; that it has been variously answered is the chief source of divergence of view as to what exactly purpose, ascribed to the Deity, is. This question is not to be discussed for the present. It need only be remarked here that *if* it be possible to conceive of purposive activity as not necessarily involving the temporal stages which have been indicated, so that separation of ideated end and accomplished end be non-essential, and if concomitance of plan with actualised volition be as useful a notion as that of succession of the one upon the other, then the purposiveness of the world will consist in its being an organic system, or one in which the natures and interconnexions of the parts are determined by the whole, and in its being an expression of intelligence but not an actualisation of a *pre*-existent plan. According to this attenuated conception of purpose the relation of means to end, generally involved in human purposefulness, also vanishes.

The element of value, of desire and satisfaction, is not eliminable from the idea of purpose. Without it the category of end would lose its distinctiveness and become identical with some other, such as cause or ground, mechanism, or non-contradiction. The tendency to minimise or cancel valuation, in this connexion, and to speak of satisfactoriness as something of logical nature, conceivable in abstraction from satisfaction, is evinced by absolute monists rather than by theists. In whatever sense the world may be said to embody divine purpose, the least that can be meant is that the world contains what is of worth to the Supreme Being.

The third factor in human purposing, adaptation of means to end, is again one which some theists have been reluctant to admit into the conception of divine purpose: partly because of its temporal implication; partly because it is thought to bespeak limited power and need to overcome difficulties; and sometimes on the ground that the divine end is the world-process, not some perfected outcome of it, and that everything that we would regard as but a stage or a means toward something else is, for God, itself an end. This last issue may be considered immediately; but whether the relation of a determinate God to a determinate world, other than Himself, admits of being conceived without ascription to Him of some kinds of limitation such as do not render the distinction between means or stages and end obviously superfluous in the case of divine activity, is a question that will receive later the discussion for which it calls. The fourth of the factors into which the idea of purpose has been resolved presents no especial problem other than that already indicated when the first was touched upon.

It has been remarked before that Na-ture and man, empirically studied, may strongly suggest that the world is an outcome of intelligence and purpose, while *the* purpose or divine end which the universe and the world-process subserve may remain unknowable to us. But, as we have also seen, speculation on the latter subject must be allowed to influence views as to the nature of the purposiveness that is involved in the former assertion. The forthcoming alternative views, between which facts scarcely enable us to decide, may be briefly mentioned. The divine purposing may be conceived as pre-ordination, in which every detail is foreseen. An analogy is presented in Mozart's (alleged) method of composition, who is said to have imaged a movement—its themes, developement, embroidery, counterpoint and orchestration—in all its detail and as a simultaneous whole, before he wrote it. If God's composition of the cosmos be regarded as similar to this, all its purposiveness will be expressed in the initial collocations, and evolution will be preformation. On the other hand, God's activity might be conceived as fluent, or even as "increasing," rather than as wholly static, purpose. It might then be compared, in relevant respects, with the work of a dramatist or a novelist such, perhaps, as Thackeray, who seems to have moulded his characters and plot, to some extent, as he wrote. And it would appear that the divine purposiveness must be partly thus conceived if conative creaturely activity may either co-operate or clash with the Creator's, so that providential control and adaptation to the emergent must enter into the realisation of the divine plan.

Again, though the divine end is usually construed eschatologically, there is an alternative interpretation. It may be that there is no "far off divine event" toward which creation was predestined to move: the process itself may constitute the end. Certainly progress has a unique value, incapable of the absorption or transmutation which some values undergo; and the conception of the divine end as a perfected society of ethical individuals, and a philosophy of history such as is based on that presupposition, are not free from difficulties. At any rate the securing of the consummation will need to be so conceived as not to involve sacrifice of the ethical dignity of the individual person as an end for himself, and no mere instrument to the future perfecting of others. The social good may but be good in that it ministers to the goodness of individuals, each of whom —as the Christian conception of the Fatherhood of God implies—is singly an end for God. Position in the time-series, or the progress-series of social developement towards perfection, may be of no moment as compared with the individual's use of his opportunities, such as they may be: timelessness, in the sense of indifference to axiological rank as temporally circumstanced, may characterise the valuation he receives from God, who seeth not as man seeth, and may read the heart rather than 'Objectively' estimate the actual output of the will. If so, asymptotic attainment of ethical perfection, and the ideal consummation, may be contingent or conditional aspects of the divine end, while progressive becoming, throughout all reaches and domains of the universe, may be its ultimate essence. These alternative conceivabilities are here merely mentioned; their relative tenability is not to be investigated. But it may further be observed that if evolution is itself an end and not a means to an end, the hard dualism of means and end must vanish. Childhood, for instance, will not be merely a stage in the making of a man; nor will groping past generations have worked merely to provide their posterity with better opportunities for making further advance. As a rosebud has a beauty or perfection different from but equal to that of the full-blown rose, so may each stage in the life of the individual or the race have, along with its appropriate work, an intrinsic value, or be an end in itself as well as a means to something beyond. The only conclusion now to be elicited from the foregoing remarks is that teleology and theism may admit of statement in terms of other than the static concepts, and the abstractions such as perfection that is of no *kind,* which dominated thought until a century or so ago, and which, within the spheres of philosophy and theology, still impose themselves on some evolutionists.

The teleological approach to theism, with which this chapter has been concerned, has been made from the fact that conformity to law is intrinsic to the world, and from the conclusion that such order belongs to the world as ontal. It has already been found not to be blocked by science or by mechanistic philosophy of Nature and its law-abidingness. Besides being a cosmos explicable, in one general sense, in terms of its structure and scientific intelligibility, the world is a bearer and a producer of values in that in our *rapport* with it we are affected by it. The world is not completely described if this aspect of it is left out: less than all the data would but then be taken account of. The Actual or historical world-process, from which mechanism is an abstraction, is characterised by irreversibility, epigenesis, progressiveness of developement, and by manifold adaptations which adaptedly interlace. It evokes explanation, consequently, of a different type from that pursued by physical science; and it accords pragmatic verification to use of the category of design for this new kind of explanation, as well as to use of the causal category for scientific explanation. If reason stand to formal rationality in a relation similar to that in which philosophy stands to mechanical science, philosophical reasonableness cannot be a mere extension of scientific, or of logico-mathematical, rationality; and if existential 'knowledge' is allowed its postulates, it seems but partial to disallow to 'knowledge' concerning the value-aspect of Actuality the postulate that is similarly needful to it. *Homo* who provides the *mensura* for all and every kind of intelligibility needs not to blind himself to the fact that he is more than a logical thinker, or to the fact that he stands in other relations with the universe than that of knowing about its structure. He cannot but have other problems besides that of the relation of being to thought. Philosophy, in other words, is an affair of living as well as a mode of thinking. All causal knowledge is, in the last resort, but reasonable and postulatory: teleology is therefore a developement from science along its own lines, or a continuation, by extrapolation, of the plotted curve which comprehensively describes its knowledge. And this is the *apologia* of theism such as professes to be reasonable belief for the guidance of life, when arraigned by science and logic—or by more pretentious theology.

HASTINGS RASHDALL

God and the Moral Consciousness

Hastings Rashdall (1858–1924) was a leader of the liberal school in Anglican theology. He taught at Oxford University during most of his career.

A course of purely metaphysical reasoning has led us up to the idea of God— that is to say, of a conscious and rational Mind and Will for which the world exists and by which that world and all other spirits are caused to exist. I have passed over a host of difficulties—the relation of God to time, the question whether or in what sense the world may be supposed to have a beginning and an end, the question of the relation in which God, the universal Mind, stands to other minds, the question of Freewill. These are difficulties which would involve elaborate metaphysical discussions: I shall return to some of them in a later lecture. It must suffice for the present to say that more than one answer to many of these questions might conceivably be given consistently with the view of the divine nature which I have contended for. All that I need insist on for my present purpose is—

(1) That God is personal in the sense that He is a self-conscious, thinking, willing, feeling Being, distinguishable from each and all less perfect minds.

(2) That all other minds are in some sense brought into being by the divine Mind, while at the same time they have such a resemblance to, or community of nature with, their source that they may be regarded as not *mere* creations but as

From Hastings Rashdall, *Philosophy and Religion* (1909), Lect. III. Reprinted by permission of Gerald Duckworth & Co. Ltd.

in some sense reproductions, more or less imperfect, of that source, approximating in various degrees to that ideal of Personality which is realised perfectly in God alone. In proportion as they approximate to that ideal, they are causes of their own actions, and can claim for themselves the kind of causality which we attribute in its perfection to God. I content myself now with claiming for the developed, rational human self a measure of freedom to the extent which I have just defined—that it is the real cause of its own actions. It is capable of self-determination. The man's actions are determined by his character. That is quite consistent with the admission that God is the ultimate cause of a self of such and such a character coming into existence at such and such a time.

(3) I will not say that the conception of those who regard the human mind as literally a part of the divine, so that the human consciousness is in no sense outside of the divine, is necessarily, for those who hold it, inconsistent with the conception of personality both in God and man: I will only say that I do not myself understand such an assertion. I regard the human mind as derived from God, but not as being part of God. Further discussion of this question I reserve for my next lecture.

We have led up to the idea of God's existence. But so far we have discovered nothing at all about His character or purposes. And it is clear that without some such knowledge the belief in God could be of little or no value from any religious or moral point of view. How are we to learn anything about the character of God? I imagine that at the present day few people will attempt to prove the goodness or benevolence of God from an empirical examination of the facts of Nature or of History. There is, no doubt, much in History and in Nature to suggest the idea of Benevolence, but there is much to suggest a directly opposite conclusion. Few of us at the present day are likely to be much impressed by the argument which Paley bases upon the existence of the little apparatus in the throat by which it is benevolently arranged that, though constantly on the point of being choked by our food, we hardly ever are choked. I cannot help reminding you of the characteristic passage: 'Consider a city-feast,' he exclaims, 'what manducation, what deglutition, and yet not one Alderman choked in a century!' Such arguments look at the matter from the point of view of the Alderman: the point of view of the turtle and the turkey is entirely forgotten. I would not for a moment speak disrespectfully of the argument from design. Darwinsim has changed its form, but anybody who reads Edouard von Hartmann's *Philosophy of the Unconscious* is not likely to rise from its perusal with the idea that the evidences of design have been destroyed by Darwinism, whatever he may think of Hartmann's strange conclusion that the design can be explained by the operation of an *unconscious* Mind or Will. The philosophical argument of Mr. R. B. Haldane in *The Pathway to Reality*,[1] and the purely biological argument of Dr. John Haldane in his two lectures on *Life and Mechanism,* and still more recently the brilliant and very important work of M. Bergson, *L'Évolution Créatrice* have, as it seems to me, abundantly shown that it is as impossible as ever it was to explain even the growth of a plant without supposing that in it and all organic Nature there is a striving towards an end. But the argument from design, though it testifies to purpose in the Universe, tells us nothing about the nature of that purpose. Purpose is one thing; benevolent purpose is another. Nobody's estimate of the comparative amount of happiness and misery in the world is worth much; but for my

---

[1] See especially Book II. Lect iii.

own part, if I trusted simply to empirical evidence, I should not be disposed to do more than slightly attenuate the pessimism of the Pessimists. At all events, Nature is far too 'red in tooth and claw' to permit of our basing an argument for a benevolent deity upon a contemplation of the facts of animal and human life. There is but one source from which such an idea can possibly be derived—from the evidence of our own moral consciousness.

Our moral ideals are the work of Reason. That the happiness of many ought to be preferred to the happiness of one, that pleasure is better than pain, that goodness is of more value than pleasure, that some pleasures are better than others—such judgements are as much the work of our own Reason, they are as much self-evident truths, as the truth that two and two make four, or that A cannot be both B and not B at the same time, or that two straight lines cannot enclose a space. We have every right to assume that such truths hold good for God as well as for man. If such Idealism as I have endeavoured to lead you to is well founded, the mind which knows comes from God, and therefore the knowledge which that mind possesses must also be taken as an imperfect or fragmentary reproduction of God's knowledge. And the Theist who rejects Idealism but admits the existence of self-evident truths will be equally justified in assuming that, for God as well as for man, two and two must make four. We have just as much right to assume that our moral ideas—our ideas of value—must come from God too. For God too, as for us, there must exist the idea, the ultimate category of the good; and our judgements of value—judgements that such and such an end is good or worth striving for—in so far as they are true judgements, must be supposed to represent His judgements. We are conscious, in proportion as we are rational, of pursuing ends which we judge to be good. If such judgements reveal God's judgements, God must be supposed to aim likewise at an ideal of good—the same ideal which is revealed to us by our moral judgements. In these judgements then we have a revelation, the only possible revelation, of the character of God. The argument which I have suggested is simply a somewhat exacter statement of the popular idea that Conscience is the voice of God.

Further to vindicate the idea of the existence, authority, objective validity of Conscience would lead us too far away into the region of Moral Philosophy for our present subject. I will only attempt very briefly to guard against some possible misunderstandings, and to meet some obvious objections:

(1) It need hardly be pointed out that the assertion of the existence of the Moral Consciousness is not in the slightest degree inconsistent with recognising its gradual growth and development. The moral faculty, like every other faculty or aspect or activity of the human soul, has grown gradually. No rational man doubts the validity—no Idealist doubts the *a priori* character—of our mathematical judgements because probably monkeys and possibly primitive men cannot count, and certainly cannot perform more than the very simplest arithmetical operations. Still less do we doubt the validity of mathematical reasoning because not only children and savages, but sometimes even distinguished classical scholars—a Macaulay, a Matthew Arnold, a T. S. Evans,—were wholly incapable of understanding very simple mathematical arguments. Equally little do we deny a real difference between harmony and discord because people may be found who see no difference between 'God save the King' and 'Pop goes the Weasel.' Self-evident truth does not mean truth which is evident to everybody.

(2) It is not doubted that the gradual evolution of our actual moral ideas—our actual ideas about what is right or wrong in particular cases—has been largely influenced by education, environment, association, social pressure, superstition, perhaps natural selection—in short, all the agencies by which naturalistic Moralists try to account for the existence of Morality. Even Euclid, or whatever his modern substitute may be, has to be taught; but that does not show that Geometry is an arbitrary system invented by the ingenious and interested devices of those who want to get money by teaching it. Arithmetic was invented largely as an instrument of commerce; but it could not have been invented if there were really no such things as number and quantity, or if the human mind had no original capacity for recognizing them. Our scientific ideas, our political ideas, our ideas upon a thousand subjects have been partly developed, partly thwarted and distorted in their growth, by similar influences. But, however great the difficulty of getting rid of these distorting influences and facing such questions in a perfectly dry light, nobody suggests that objective truth on such matters is non-existent or for ever unattainable. A claim for objective validity for the moral judgement does not mean a claim for infallibility on behalf of any individual Conscience. We may make mistakes in Morals just as we may make mistakes in Science, or even in pure Mathematics. If a class of forty small boys are asked to do a sum, they will probably not all bring out the same answer: but nobody doubts that one answer alone is right, though arithmetical capacity is a variable quantity. What is meant is merely that, if I am right in affirming that this is good, you cannot be likewise right in saying that it is bad: and that we have some capacity—though doubtless a variable capacity—of judging which is the true view. Hence our moral judgements, in so far as they are true judgements, must be taken to be reproductions in us of the thought of God. To show that an idea has been gradually developed, tells us nothing as to its truth or falsehood—one way or the other.

(3) In comparing the self-evidence of moral to that of mathematical judgements, it is not suggested that our moral judgements in detail are as certain, as clear and sharply defined, as mathematical judgements, or that they can claim so universal a consensus among the competent. What is meant is merely (a) that the notion of good in general is an ultimate category of thought; that it contains a meaning intelligible not perhaps to every individual human soul, but to the normal, developed, human consciousness; and (b) that the ultimate truth of morals, if it is seen at all, must be seen immediately. An ultimate moral truth cannot be deduced from, or proved by, any other truth. You cannot prove that pleasure is better than pain, or that virtue is better than pleasure, to any one who judges differently. It does not follow that all men have an equally clear and delicate moral consciousness. The power of discriminating moral values differs as widely as the power of distinguishing musical sounds, or of appreciating what is excellent in music. Some men may be almost or altogether without such a power of moral discrimination, just as some men are wholly destitute of an ear for music; while the higher degrees of moral appreciation are the possession of the few rather than of the many. Moral insight is not possessed by all men in equal measure. Moral genius is as rare as any other kind of genius.

(4) When we attribute Morality to God, it is not meant that the conduct which is right for men in detail ought to be or could possibly in all cases be practised by God. It is a childish objection (though it is sometimes made by modern

philosophers who should know better) to allege with Aristotle that God cannot be supposed to make or keep contracts. And in the same way, when we claim universal validity for our moral judgements, we do not mean that the rules suitable for human conduct would be the same for beings differently organized and constituted. Our rules of sexual Morality are clearly applicable only to sexually constituted beings. What is meant in asserting that these rules are universally and objectively valid is that these are the rules which every rational intelligence, in proportion as it is rational, will recognize as being suitable, or conducive to the ideal life, in beings constituted as we are. The truth that permanent monogamous marriage represents the true type of sexual relations for human beings will be none the less an objectively valid ethical truth, because the lower animals are below it, while superior beings, it may be, are above it. Universal love is none the less the absolute moral ideal because it would be absurd to say that beasts of prey do wrong in devouring other creatures, or because war is sometimes necessary as a means to the end of love at our present imperfect stage of social and intellectual development. The means to the highest good vary with circumstances; the amount of good that is attainable in such and such circumstances varies also; consequently the right course of conduct will be different for beings differently constituted or placed under different circumstances: but the principles which, in the view of a perfect intelligence, would determine what is the right course for different beings in different circumstances will be always the same. The ultimate principles of our moral judgement, *e.g.* that love is better than hate, are just as applicable to God as they are to us. Our conception of the highest good may be inadequate; but we certainly shall not attain to greater adequacy, or a nearer

approach to ultimate truth, by flatly contradicting our own moral judgements. It would be just as reasonable to argue that because the law of gravitation might be proved, from the point of view of the highest knowledge, to be an inadequate statement of the truth, and all inadequacy involves some error, therefore we had better assume that from the point of view of God there is no difference whatever between attraction and repulsion. All arguments for what is called a 'super-moral' Deity or a 'super-moral' Absolute are open to this fatal objection: moral judgements cannot possibly rest upon anything but the moral consciousness, and yet these doctrines contradict the moral consciousness. The idea of good is derived from the moral consciousness. When a man declares that from the point of view of the Universe all things are very good, he gets the idea of good from his own moral consciousness, and is assuming the objective validity of its dictates. His judgement is an ethical judgement as much as mine when I say that to me some things in this world appear very bad. If he is not entitled to assume the validity of his ethical judgements, his proposition is false or meaningless. If he is entitled to assume their validity, why should he distrust that same moral consciousness when it affirms (as it undoubtedly does) that pain and sin are for ever bad, and not (as our 'super-moral' Religionists suggest) additional artistic touches which only add to the æsthetic effect of the whole?

I shall now proceed to develop some of the consequences which (as it appears to me) flow from the doctrine that our belief in the goodness of God is an inference from our own moral consciousness:

(1) It throws light on the relations between Religion and Morality. The champions of ethical education as a substitute for Religion and of ethical societies as a substitute for Churches are fond of

assuming that Religion is not only unnecessary to, but actually destructive of, the intrinsic authority of the moral law. If we supposed with a few theologians in the most degenerate periods of Theology (with William of Occam, some extreme Calvinists, and a few eighteenth-century divines like Archdeacon Paley) that actions are right or wrong merely because willed by God—meaning by God simply a powerful being without goodness or moral character, then undoubtedly the Secularists would be right. If a religious Morality implies that Virtue means merely (in Paley's words) 'the doing good to mankind in obedience to the will of God and for the sake of everlasting happiness' (so that if God were to will murder and adultery, those practices would forthwith become meritorious), then undoubtedly it would be better to teach Morality without Religion than with it. But that is a caricature of the true teaching of Christ or of any considerable Christian theologian. Undoubtedly we must assert what is called the 'independence' of the moral judgement. The judgement 'to love is better than to hate' has a meaning complete in itself, which contains no reference whatever to any theological presupposition. It is a judgement which is, and which can intelligibly be, made by people of all religions or of none. But we may still raise the question whether the validity of that judgement can be defended without theological implications. And I am prepared most distinctly to maintain that it cannot. These moral judgements claim objective validity. When we say 'this is right,' we do not mean merely 'I approve this course of conduct,' 'this conduct gives me a thrill of satisfaction, a "feeling of approbation," a pleasure of the moral sense.' If that were all that was meant, it would be perfectly possible that another person might feel an equally satisfactory glow of approbation at conduct of a precisely opposite character

without either of them being wrong. A bull-fight fills most Spaniards with feelings of lively approbation, and most Englishmen with feelings of acute disapprobation. If such moral judgements were mere feelings, neither of them would be wrong. There could be no question of objective rightness or wrongness. Mustard is not objectively nice or objectively nasty: it is simply nice to some people and nasty to others. The mustard-lover has no right to condemn the mustard-hater, or the mustard-hater the mustard-lover. If Morality were merely a matter of feeling or emotion, actions would not be objectively right or objectively wrong; but simply right to some people, wrong to others. Hume would be right in holding the morality of an action to consist simply in the pleasure it gives to the person who contemplates it. Rightness thus becomes simply a name for the fact of social approbation.[2] And yet surely the very heart of the affirmation which the moral consciousness makes in each of us is that right and wrong are not matters of mere subjective feeling. When I assert 'this is right,' I do not claim personal infallibility. I may, indeed, be wrong, as I may be wrong in my political or scientific theories. But I do mean that I think I am right; and that, if I am right, you cannot also be right when you affirm that this same action is wrong. This objective validity is the very core and centre of the idea of Duty or moral obligation. That

---

[2] 'We do not infer a character to be virtuous, because it pleases: but in feeling that it pleases after such a particular manner, we in effect feel that it is virtuous.' (*Treatise*, Part I. § ii, ed. Green and Grose, vol. ii. p. 247.) 'The distinction of moral good and evil is founded in the pleasure or pain, which results from the view of any sentiment, or character; and as that pleasure or pain cannot be unknown to the person who feels it, it follows that there is just so much virtue in any character as every one places in it, and that 'tis impossible in this particular we can ever be mistaken.' (*Ibid.* vol. ii. p. 311.)

is why it is so important to assert that moral judgements are the work of Reason, not of a supposed moral sense or any other kind of feeling. Feelings may vary in different men without any of them being in the wrong; red really is the same as green to a colour-blind person. What we mean when we talk about the existence of Duty is that things are right or wrong, no matter what you or I think about them—that the laws of Morality are quite as much independent of my personal likings and dislikings as the physical laws of Nature. That is what is meant by the 'objectivity' of the moral law.

Now, the question arises—'Can such an objectivity be asserted by those who take a purely materialistic or naturalistic view of the Universe?' Whatever our metaphysical theories about the nature of Reality may be, we can in practice have no difficulty in the region of Physical Science about recognizing an objective reality of some kind which is other than my mere thinking about it. That fire will burn whether I think so or not is practically recognized by persons of all metaphysical persuasions. If I say 'I can cloy the hungry edge of appetite by bare imagination of a feast,' I try the experiment, and I fail. I imagine the feast, but I am hungry still: and if I persist in the experiment, I die. But what do we mean when we say that things are right or wrong whether I think them so or not, that the Moral Law exists outside me and independently of my thinking about it? Where and how does this moral law exist? The physical laws of Nature may be supposed by the Materialist or the Realist somehow to exist *in* matter: to the Metaphysician there may be difficulties in such a view, but the difficulties are not obvious to common-sense. But surely (whatever may be thought about physical laws) the moral law, which expresses not any matter of physical fact but what *ought* to be thought of acts, cannot be supposed to exist in a purely material Universe. An 'ought' can exist only in and for a mind. In what mind, then, does the moral law exist? As a matter of fact, different people's moral judgements contradict one another. And the consciousness of no living man can well be supposed to be a flawless reflection of the absolute moral ideal. On a non-theistic view of the Universe, then, the moral law cannot well be thought of as having any actual existence. The objective validity of the moral law can indeed be and no doubt is *asserted,* believed in, acted upon without reference to any theological creed; but it cannot be defended or fully justified without the presupposition of Theism. What we mean by an objective law is that the moral law is a part of the ultimate nature of things, on a level with the laws of physical nature, and it cannot be *that,* unless we assume that law to be an expression of the same mind in which physical laws originate. The idea of duty, when analysed, implies the idea of God. Whatever else Plato meant by the 'idea of the good,' this at least was one of his meanings—that the moral law has its source in the source of all Reality.

And therefore at bottom popular feeling is right in holding that religious belief is necessary to Morality. Of course I do not mean to say that, were religious belief to disappear from the world, Morality would disappear too. But I do think Morality would become quite a different thing from what it has been for the higher levels of religious thought and feeling. The best men would no doubt go on acting up to their own highest ideal just as if it did possess objective validity, no matter how unable they might be to reconcile their practical with their speculative beliefs. But it would not be so for the many—or perhaps even for the few in their moments of weakness and temptation, when once the consequences of purely naturalistic Ethics were thoroughly admitted and realized. The only kind of objective valdity which can be recognized on a purely naturalistic view of Ethics is conformity to public opinion. The tendency of all naturalistic Ethics is to make a God of public opinion. And if no other deity were recognized, such a God would assuredly not be without worshippers. And yet the strongest temptation to most of us is the temptation to follow a debased public opinion—the opinion of our age, our class, our party. Apart from faith in a perfectly righteous God whose commands are, however imperfectly, revealed in the individual Conscience, we can find no really valid reason why the individual should act on his own sense of what is intrinsically right, even when he finds himself an 'Athanasius contra mundum,' and when his own personal likings and inclinations and interests are on the side of the world. Kant was at bottom right, though perhaps he did not give the strongest reasons for his position, in making the idea of God a postulate of Morality.

From a more directly practical point of view I need hardly point out how much easier it is to feel towards the moral law the reverence that we ought to feel when we believe that that law is embodied in a personal Will. Not only is religious Morality not opposed to the idea of duty for duty's sake: it is speculatively the only reasonable basis of it; practically and emotionally the great safeguard of it. And whatever may be thought of the possibility of a speculative defence of such an idea without Theism, the practical difficulty of teaching it—especially to children, uneducated and unreflective persons—seems to be quite insuperable.[3] In more than one country in which religious education has been banished from the primary schools, grave observers complain that the idea of Duty seems to be suffering an eclipse in the minds of the rising generation; some of them add that in those lands crime is steadily on the increase. Catechisms of civil duty and the like have not hitherto proved very satisfactory substitutes for the old teaching about the fear of God. Would that it were more frequently remembered on both sides of our educational squabbles that the supreme object of all religious education should be to instil into children's minds in the closest possible connexion the twin ideas of God and of Duty!

. . .

[3] There are no doubt ways of making Morality the law of the Universe without what most of us understand by Theism, though not without Religion, and a Religion of a highly metaphysical character; but because such non-theistic modes of religious thought exist in Buddhism, for instance, it does not follow that they are reasonable, and, at all events, they are hardly intelligible to most Western minds. Such non-theistic Religions imply a Metaphysic quite as much as Christianity or Buddhism. There have been Religions without the idea of a personal God, but never without Metaphysic, i.e. a theory about the ultimate nature of things.

IMMANUEL KANT

The Impossibility of a Theoretical Proof of a Supreme Being

Immanuel Kant (1724–1804) is one of the towering figures in the history of Western philosophy. Though he never during his eighty years left the environs of his native Konigsberg, where he was a Professor in the University, his influence on subsequent thought has been enormous. His criticisms of the traditional arguments for the existence of God have often been taken to be decisive, though Kant himself tried to develop in moral considerations an alternative rational basis for theistic religion.

SECTION III

Of the Arguments of Speculative Reason in Proof of the Existence of a Supreme Being

. . .

There are only three kinds of proofs of the existence of God from speculative reason.

All the paths that can be followed to this end begin either from definite experience and the peculiar nature of the world of sense, known to us through experience, and ascend from it, according to the laws of causality, to the highest cause, existing outside the world; or they rest on indefinite experience only, that is, on any existence which is empirically given; or lastly, they leave all experience out of account, and conclude, entirely *a priori* from mere concepts, the existence of a supreme cause. The first proof is the *physico-theological,* the second the *cosmological,* the third the *ontological* proof. There are no more, and there can be no more.

I shall show that neither on the one path, the empirical, nor on the other, the transcendental, can reason achieve anything, and that it stretches its wings in vain, if it tries to soar beyond the world of sense by the mere power of speculation. With regard to the order in which these three arguments should be examined, it will be the opposite of that, followed by reason in its gradual development, in which we placed them also at first ourselves. For we shall be able to show that, although experience gives the first impulse, it is the transcendental concept only which guides reason in its endeavours, and fixes the last goal which reason wishes to retain. I shall therefore begin with the examination of the transcendental proof, and see afterwards how far it may be strengthened by the addition of empirical elements.

From Immanuel Kant, *Critique of Pure Reason,* tr. by F. M. Muller (1896), Bk. II, Ch. III, Secs. III–VII.

Of the Impossibility of an Ontological Proof of the Existence of God

It is easily perceived, from what has been said before, that the concept of an absolutely necessary Being is a concept of pure reason, that is, a mere idea, the objective reality of which is by no means proved by the fact that reason requires it. That idea does no more than point to a certain but unattainable completeness, and serves rather to limit the understanding, than to extend its sphere. It seems strange and absurd, however, that a conclusion of an absolutely necessary existence from a given existence in general should seem urgent and correct, and that yet all the conditions under which the understanding can form a concept of such a necessity should be entirely against us.

People have at all times been talking of an *absolutely necessary* Being, but they have tried, not so much to understand whether and how a thing of that kind could even be conceived, as rather to prove its existence. No doubt a verbal definition of that concept is quite easy, if we say that it is something the nonexistence of which is impossible. This, however, does not make us much wiser with reference to the conditions that make it necessary [1] to consider the nonexistence of a thing as absolutely inconceivable. It is these conditions which we want to know, and whether by that concept we are thinking anything or not. For to use the word *unconditioned*, in order to get rid of all the conditions which the understanding always requires, when wishing to conceive something as necessary, does not render it clear to us in the least whether, after that, we are still thinking anything or perhaps nothing, by the concept of the unconditionally necessary.

Nay, more than this, people have imagined that by a number of examples they had explained this concept, at first risked at haphazard, and afterwards become quite familiar, and that therefore all further inquiry regarding its intelligibility were unnecessary. It was said that every proposition of geometry, such as, for instance, that a triangle has three angles, is absolutely necessary, and people began to talk of an object entirely outside the sphere of our understanding, as if they understood perfectly well what, by that concept, they wished to predicate of it.

But all these pretended examples are taken without exception from *judgments* only, not from *things,* and their existence. Now the unconditioned necessity of judgments is not the same thing as an absolute necessity of things. The absolute necessity of a judgment is only a conditioned necessity of the thing, or of the predicate in the judgment. The above proposition did not say that three angles were absolutely necessary, but that under the condition of the existence of a triangle, three angles are given (in it) by necessity. Nevertheless, this pure logical necessity has exerted so powerful an illusion, that, after having formed of a thing a concept *a priori* so constituted that it seemed to include existence in its sphere, people thought they could conclude with certainty that, because existence necessarily belongs to the object of that concept, provided always that I accept the thing as given (existing), its existence also must necessarily be accepted (according to the rule of identity), and that the Being therefore must itself be absolutely necessary, because its existence is implied in a concept, which is accepted voluntarily only, and always under the condition that I accept the object of it as given.

If in an identical judgment I reject

---

[1] Read *nothwendig* instead of *unmöglich.* Noiré.

the predicate and retain the subject, there arises a contradiction, and hence, I say, that the former belongs to the latter necessarily. But if I reject the subject as well as the predicate, there is no contradiction, because there is nothing left that can be contradicted. To accept a triangle and yet to reject its three angles is contradictory, but there is no contradiction at all in admitting the non-existence of the triangle and of its three angles. The same applies to the concept of an absolutely necessary Being. Remove its existence, and you remove the thing itself, with all its predicates, so that a contradiction becomes impossible. There is nothing external to which the contradiction could apply, because the thing is not meant to be externally necessary; nor is there anything internal that could be contradicted, for in removing the thing out of existence, you have removed at the same time all its internal qualities. If you say, God is almighty, that is a necessary judgment, because almightiness cannot be removed, if you accept a deity, that is, an infinite Being, with the concept of which that other concept is identical. But if you say, God is not, then neither his almightiness, nor any other of his predicates is given; they are all, together with the subject, removed out of existence, and therefore there is not the slightest contradiction in that sentence.

We have seen therefore that, if I remove the predicate of a judgment together with its subject, there can never be an internal contradiction, whatever the predicate may be. The only way of evading this conclusion would be to say that there are subjects which cannot be removed out of existence, but must always remain. But this would be the same as to say that there exist absolutely necessary subjects, an assumption the correctness of which I have called in question, and the possibility of which you had undertaken to prove. For I cannot form to myself the smallest concept of a thing which, if it had been removed together with all its predicates, should leave behind a contradiction; and except contradiction, I have no other test of impossibility by pure concepts a priori. Against all these general arguments (which no one can object to) you challenge me with a case, which you represent as a proof by a fact, namely, that there is one, and this one concept only, in which the non-existence or the removal of its object would be self-contradictory, namely, the concept of the most real Being (ens realissimum). You say that it possesses all reality, and you are no doubt justified in accepting such a Being as possible. This for the present I may admit, though the absence of self-contradictoriness in a concept is far from proving the possibility of its object.[2] Now reality comprehends existence, and therefore existence is contained in the concept of a thing possible. If that thing is removed, the internal possibility of the thing would be removed, and this is self-contradictory.

I answer:—Even in introducing into the concept of a thing, which you wish to think in its possibility only, the concept of its existence, under whatever disguise it may be, you have been guilty of a contradiction. If you were allowed to do this, you would apparently have carried your point but in reality you have achieved nothing, but have only committed a tautology. I simply ask you,

---

[2] A concept is always possible, if it is not self-contradictory. This is the logical characteristic of possibility, and by it the object of the concept is distinguished from the *nihil negativum*. But it may nevertheless be an empty concept, unless the objective reality of the synthesis, by which the concept is generated, has been distinctly shown. This, however, as shown above, must always rest on principles of possible experience, and not on the principle of analysis (the principle of contradiction). This is a warning against inferring at once from the possibility of concepts (logical) the possibility of things (real).

whether the proposition, that *this or that thing* (which, whatever it may be, I grant you as possible) *exists*, is an analytical or a synthetical proposition? If the former, then by its existence you add nothing to your thought of the thing; but in that case, either the thought within you would be the thing itself, or you have presupposed existence, as belonging to possibility, and have according to your own showing deduced existence from internal possibility, which is nothing but a miserable tautology. The mere word *reality*, which in the concept of a thing sounds different from existence in the concept of the predicate, can make no difference. For if you call all accepting or positing (without determining what it is) reality, you have placed a thing, with all its predicates, within the concept of the subject, and accepted it as real, and you do nothing but repeat it in the predicate. If, on the contrary, you admit, as every sensible man must do, that every proposition involving existence is synthetical, how can you say that the predicate of existence does not admit of removal without contradiction, a distinguishing property which is peculiar to analytical propositions only, the very character of which depends on it?

I might have hoped to put an end to this subtle argumentation, without many words, and simply by an accurate definition of the concept of existence, if I had not seen that the illusion, in mistaking a logical predicate for a real one (that is the predicate which determines a thing), resists all correction. Everything can become a *logical predicate*, even the subject itself may be predicated of itself, because logic takes no account of any contents of concepts. *Determination*, however, is a predicate, added to the concept of the subject, and enlarging it, and it must not therefore be contained in it.

Being is evidently not a real predicate, or a concept of something that can be added to the concept of a thing. It is merely the admission of a thing, and of certain determinations in it. Logically, it is merely the copula of a judgment. The proposition, *God is almighty*, contains two concepts, each having its object, namely, God and almightiness. The small word *is*, is not an additional predicate, but only serves to put the predicate *in relation* to the subject. If, then, I take the subject (God) with all its predicates (including that of almightiness), and say, *God is*, or there is a God, I do not put a new predicate to the concept of God, but I only put the subject by itself, with all its predicates, in relation to my concept, as its object. Both must contain exactly the same kind of thing, and nothing can have been added to the concept, which expresses possibility only, by my thinking its object as simply given and saying, it is. And thus the real does not contain more than the possible. A hundred real dollars do not contain a penny more than a hundred possible dollars. For as the latter signify the concept, the former the object and its position by itself, it is clear that, in case the former contained more than the latter, my concept would not express the whole object, and would not therefore be its adequate concept. In my financial position no doubt there exists more by one hundred real dollars, than by their concept only (that is their possibility), because in reality the object is not only contained analytically in my concept, but is added to my concept (which is a determination of my state), synthetically; but the conceived hundred dollars are not in the least increased through the existence which is outside my concept.

By whatever and by however many predicates I may think a thing (even in completely determining it), nothing is really added to it, if I add that the thing exists. Otherwise, it would not be the same that exists, but something more than was contained in the concept, and

I could not say that the exact object of my concept existed. Nay, even if I were to think in a thing all reality, except one, that one missing reality would not be supplied by my saying that so defective a thing exists, but it would exist with the same defect with which I thought it; or what exists would be different from what I thought. If, then, I try to conceive a being, as the highest reality (without any defect), the question still remains, whether it exists or not. For though in my concept there may be wanting nothing of the possible real content of a thing in general, something is wanting in its relation to my whole state of thinking, namely, that the knowledge of that object should be possible *a posteriori* also. And here we perceive the cause of our difficulty. If we were concerned with an object of our senses, I could not mistake the existence of a thing for the mere concept of it; for by the concept the object is thought as only in harmony with the general conditions of a possible empirical knowledge, while by its existence it is thought as contained in the whole content of experience. Through this connection with the content of the whole experience, the concept of an object is not in the least increased; our thought has only received through it one more possible perception. If, however, we are thinking existence through the pure category alone, we need not wonder that we cannot find any characteristic to distinguish it from mere possibility.

. . .

SECTION V

Of the Impossibility of a Cosmological Proof of the Existence of God

It was something quite unnatural, and a mere innovation of scholastic wisdom, to attempt to pick out of an entirely arbitrary idea the existence of the object corresponding to it. Such an attempt would never have been made, if there had not existed beforehand a need of our reason of admitting for existence in general something necessary, to which we may ascend and in which we may rest; and if, as that necessity must be unconditioned and *a priori* certain, reason had not been forced to seek a concept which, if possible, should satisfy such a demand and give us a knowledge of an existence entirely *a priori.* Such a concept was supposed to exist in the idea of an *ens realissimum,* and that idea was therefore used for a more definite knowledge of that, the existence of which one had admitted or been persuaded of independently, namely, of the necessary Being. This very natural procedure of reason was carefully concealed, and instead of ending with that concept, an attempt was made to begin with it, and thus to derive from it the necessity of existence, which it was only meant to supplement. Hence arose that unfortunate ontological proof, which satisfies neither the demands of our natural and healthy understanding, nor the requirements of the schools.

The *cosmological proof,* which we have now to examine, retains the connection of absolute necessity with the highest reality, but instead of concluding, like the former, from the highest reality necessity in existence, it concludes from the given unconditioned necessity of any being, its unlimited reality. It thus brings everything at least into the groove of a natural, though I know not whether of a really or only apparently rational syllogism, which carries the greatest conviction, not only for the common, but also for the speculative understanding, and has evidently drawn the first outline of all proofs of natural theology, which have been followed at all times, and will be followed in future also, however much they may be hidden and disguised. We shall now proceed to exhibit and to examine this cosmological proof which Leibniz calls also the proof *a contingentia mundi.*

It runs as follows: If there exists anything, there must exist an absolutely necessary Being also. Now I, at least, exist; therefore there exists an absolutely necessary Being. The minor contains an experience, the major the conclusion from experience in general to the existence of the necessary.[3] This proof therefore begins with experience, and is not entirely *a priori,* or ontological; and, as the object of all possible experience is called the world, this proof is called the *cosmological proof.* As it takes no account of any peculiar property of the objects of experience, by which this world of ours may differ from any other possible world, it is distinguished, in its name also, from the physico-theological proof, which employs as arguments, observations of the peculiar property of this our world of sense.

The proof then proceeds as follows: The necessary Being can be determined in one way only, that is, by one only of all possible opposite predicates; it must therefore be determined completely by its own concept. Now, there is only one concept of a thing possible, which *a priori* completely determines it, namely, that of the *ens realissimum.* It follows, therefore, that the concept of the *ens realissimum* is the only one by which a necessary Being can be thought, and therefore it is concluded that a highest Being exists by necessity.

There are so many sophistical propositions in this cosmological argument, that it really seems as if speculative rea-

[3] This conclusion is too well known to require detailed exposition. It rests on the apparently transcendental law of causality in nature, that everything *contingent* has its cause, which, if contingent again, must likewise have a cause, till the series of subordinate causes ends in an absolutely necessary cause, without which it could not be complete.

son had spent all her dialectical skill in order to produce the greatest possible transcendental illusion. Before examining it, we shall draw up a list of them, by which reason has put forward an old argument disguised as a new one, in order to appeal to the agreement of two witnesses, one supplied by pure reason, the other by experience, while in reality there is only one, namely, the first, who changes his dress and voice in order to be taken for a second. In order to have a secure foundation, this proof takes its stand on experience, and pretends to be different from the ontological proof, which places its whole confidence in pure concepts *a priori* only. The cosmological proof, however, uses that experience only in order to make one step, namely, to the existence of a necessary Being in general. What properties that Being may have, can never be learnt from the empirical argument, and for that purpose reason takes leave of it altogether, and tries to find out, from among concepts only, what properties an absolutely necessary Being ought to possess, i.e. which among all possible things contains in itself the requisite conditions (*requisita*) of absolute necessity. This requisite is believed by reason to exist in the concept of an *ens realissimum* only, and reason concludes at once that this must be the absolutely necessary Being. In this conclusion it is simply assumed that the concept of a being of the highest reality is perfectly adequate to the concept of absolute necessity in existence; so that the latter might be concluded from the former. This is the same proposition as that maintained in the ontological argument, and is simply taken over into the cosmological proof, nay, made its foundation, although the intention was to avoid it. For it is clear that absolute necessity is an existence from mere concepts. If, then, I say that the concept of the *ens realissimum* is such a concept, and is the only concept adequate to necessary existence, I am bound to admit that the latter may be deduced from the former. The whole conclusive strength of the so-called cosmological proof rests therefore in reality on the ontological proof from mere concepts, while the appeal to experience is quite superfluous, and, though it may lead us on to the concept of absolute necessity, it cannot demonstrate it with any definite object. For as soon as we intend to do this, we must at once abandon all experience, and try to find out which among the pure concepts may contain the conditions of the possibility of an absolutely necessary Being. But if in this way the possibility of such a Being has been perceived, its existence also has been proved: for what we are really saying is this, that under all possible things there is one which carries with it absolute necessity, or that this Being exists with absolute necessity.

Sophisms in arguments are most easily discovered, if they are put forward in a correct scholastic form. This we shall now proceed to do.

If the proposition is right, that every absolutely necessary Being is, at the same time, the most real Being (and this is the *nervus probandi* of the cosmological proof), it must, like all affirmative judgments, be capable of conversion, at least *per accidens*. This would give us the proposition that some *entia realissima* are at the same time absolutely necessary beings. One *ens realissimum,* however, does not differ from any other on any point, and what applies to one, applies also to all. In this case, therefore, I may employ absolute conversion, and say, that every *ens realissimum* is a necessary Being. As this proposition is determined by its concepts *a priori* only, it follows that the mere concept of the *ens realissimum* must carry with it its absolute necessity; and this, which was maintained by the ontological proof, and not recognised by the cosmological, forms really the foundation of the conclusions of the latter, though in a disguised from.

We thus see that the second road taken by speculative reason, in order to prove the existence of the highest Being, is not only as illusory as the first, but commits in addition an *ignoratio elenchi,* promising to lead us by a new path, but after a short circuit bringing us back to the old one, which we had abandoned for its sake.

• • •

Discovery and Explanation of the Dialectical Illusion in All Transcendental Proofs of the Existence of a Necessary Being

Both proofs, hitherto attempted, were transcendental, that is, independent of empirical principles. For although the cosmological proof assumes for its foundation an experience in general, it does not rest on any particular quality of it, but on pure principles of reason, with reference to an existence given by the empirical consciousness in general, and abandons even that guidance in order to derive its support from pure concepts only. What then in these transcendental proofs is the cause of the dialectical, but natural, illusion which connects the concepts of necessity and of the highest reality, and realises and hypostasises that which can only be an idea? What is the cause that renders it inevitable to admit something as necessary in itself among existing things, and yet makes us shrink back from the existence of such a Being as from an abyss? What is to be done that reason should understand itself on this point, and, escaping from the wavering state of hesitatingly approving or disapproving, acquire a calm insight into the matter?

It is surely extremely strange that, as soon as we suppose that something exists, we cannot avoid the conclusion that something exists necessarily. On this quite natural, though by no means, therefore, certain conclusion, rests the whole cosmological argument. On the other side, I may take any concept of anything, and I find that its existence has never to be represented by me as absolutely necessary, nay, that nothing prevents me, whatever may exist, from thinking its non-existence. I may, therefore, have to admit something necessary as the condition of existing things in general, but I need not think any single thing as necessary in itself. In other words I can never *complete* the regressus to the conditions of existence without admitting a necessary Being, but I can never *begin* with such a Being.

If, therefore, I am obliged to think something necessary for all existing things, and at the same time am not justified in thinking of anything as in itself necessary, the conclusion is inevitable: that necessity and contingency do not concern things themselves, for otherwise there would be a contradiction, and that therefore neither of the two principles can be objective; but that they may possibly be subjective principles of reason only, according to which, on one side, we have to find for all that is given as existing, something that is necessary, and thus never to stop except when we have reached an *a priori* complete explanation; while on the other we must never hope for that completion, that is, never admit anything empirical as unconditioned, and thus dispense with its further derivation. In that sense both principles as purely heuristic and *regulative,* and affecting the formal interests of reason only, may well stand side by side. For the one tells us that we ought to philosophise on nature as if there was a necessary first cause for everything that exists, if only in order to introduce systematical unity into our knowledge, by always looking for such an idea as an imagined highest cause. The other warns us against mistaking any single determination concerning the existence of things for such a highest cause, i.e. for something absolutely necessary, and bids us to keep the way always open for further derivation, and to treat it always as conditioned. If, then, everything that is perceived in things has to be considered by us as only conditionally necessary, nothing that is empirically given can ever be considered as absolutely necessary.

It follows from this that the absolutely necessary must be accepted as *outside the world,* because it is only meant to serve as a principle of the greatest possible unity of phenomena, of which it is the highest cause, and that it can never be reached *in the world,* because the second rule bids you always to consider all empirical causes of that unity as derived.

. . .

SECTION VI

Of the Impossibility of the Physico-Theological Proof

The principal points of the physico-theological proof are the following. 1st. There are everywhere in the world clear indications of an intentional arrangement carried out with great wisdom, and forming a whole indescribably varied in its contents and infinite in extent.

2ndly. The fitness of this arrangement is entirely foreign to the things existing in the world, and belongs to them contingently only; that is, the nature of different things could never spontaneously, by the combination of so many means, co-operate towards definite aims, if these means had not been selected and arranged on purpose by a rational disposing principle, according to certain fundamental ideas.

3rdly. There exists, therefore, a sublime and wise cause (or many), which must be the cause of the world, not only as a blind and all-powerful nature, by means of unconscious *fecundity,* but as an intelligence, by *freedom.*

4thly. The unity of that cause may be inferred with certainty from the unity of the reciprocal relation of the parts of the world, as portions of a skilful edifice, so far as our experience reaches, and beyond it, with plausibility, according to the principles of analogy.

Without wishing to argue, for the sake of argument only, with natural reason, as to its conclusion in inferring from the analogy of certain products of nature with the works of human art, in which man does violence to nature, and forces it not to follow its own aims, but to adapt itself to ours (that is, from the similarity of certain products of nature with houses, ships, and watches), in inferring from this, I say, that a similar causality, namely, understanding and will, must be at the bottom of nature, and in deriving the internal possibility of a freely acting nature (which, it may be, renders all human art and even human reason possible) from another though superhuman art— a kind of reasoning, which probably could not stand the severest test of transcendental criticism; we are willing to admit, nevertheless, that if we have to name such a cause, we cannot do better than to follow the analogy of such products of human design, which are the only ones of which we know completely both cause and effect. There would be no excuse, if reason were to surrender a causality which it knows, and have recourse to obscure and indemonstrable principles of explanation, which it does not know.

According to this argument, the fitness and harmony existing in so many works of nature might prove the contingency of the form, but not of the matter, that is, the substance in the world, because, for the latter purpose, it would be necessary to prove in addition, that the things of the world were in themselves incapable of such order and harmony, according to general laws, unless there existed, even in their *substance,* the product of a supreme wisdom. For this purpose, very different arguments would be required from those derived from the analogy of human art. The utmost, therefore, that could be established by such a proof would be an *architect of the world,* always very much hampered by the quality of the material with which he has to work, not a *creator,* to whose idea everything is subject. This would by no means suffice for the purposed aim of proving an all-sufficient original Being. If we wished to prove the contingency of matter itself, we must have recourse to a transcendental argument, and this is the very thing which was to be avoided.

The inference, therefore, really proceeds from the order and design that can everywhere be observed in the world, as an entirely contingent arrangement, to the existence of a cause, *proportionate to it.* The concept of that cause must therefore teach us something quite *definite* about it, and can therefore be no other concept but that of a Being which possesses all might, wisdom, etc., in one word, all perfection of an all-sufficient Being. The predicates of a *very great,* of an astounding, of an immeasurable might and virtue give us no definite concept, and never tell us really what the thing is by itself. They are only relative representations of the magnitude of an object, which the observer (of the world) compares with himself and his own power of comprehension, and which would be equally grand, whether we magnify the object, or reduce the observing subject to smaller proportions in reference to it. Where we are concerned with the magnitude (of the perfection) of a thing in general, there exists no definite concept, except that which comprehends all possible perfection, and only the all (*omnitudo*) of reality is thoroughly determined in the concept.

Now I hope that no one would dare to comprehend the relation of that part of the world which he has observed (in its extent as well as in its contents) to omnipotence, the relation of the order of the world to the highest wisdom, and the relation of the unity of the world to the absolute unity of its author, etc. Physico-theology, therefore, can never give a definite concept of the highest cause of the world, and is insufficient, therefore, as a principle of theology, which is itself to form the basis of religion.

The step leading to absolute totality is entirely impossible on the empirical road. Nevertheless, that step is taken in the physico-theological proof. How then has this broad abyss been bridged over?

The fact is that, after having reached the stage of admiration of the greatness, the wisdom, the power, etc. of the Author of the world, and seeing no further advance possible, one suddenly leaves the argument carried on by empirical proofs, and lays hold of that contingency which, from the very first, was inferred from the order and design of the world. The next step from that contingency leads, by means of transcendental concepts only, to the existence of something absolutely necessary, and another step from the absolute necessity of the first cause to its completely determined or determining concept, namely, that of an all-embracing reality. Thus we see that the physico-theological proof, baffled in its own undertaking, takes suddenly refuge in the cosmological proof, and as this is only the ontological proof in disguise, it really carries out its original intention by means of pure reason only; though it so strongly disclaimed in the beginning all connection with it, and professed to base everything on clear proofs from experience.

Those who adopt the physico-theolog-ical argument have no reason to be so very coy towards the transcendental mode of argument, and with the conceit of enlightened observers of nature to look down upon them as the cobwebs of dark speculators. If they would only examine themselves, they would find that, after they had advanced a good way on the soil of nature and experience, and found themselves nevertheless as much removed as ever from the object revealed to their reason, they suddenly leave that soil, to enter into the realm of pure possibilities, where on the wings of ideas they hope to reach that which had withdrawn itself from all their empirical investigations. Imagining themselves to be on firm ground after that desperate leap, they now proceed to expand the definite concept which they have acquired, they do not know how, over the whole field of creation; and they explain the ideal, which was merely a product of pure reason, by experience, though in a very poor way, and totally beneath the dignity of the object, refusing all the while to admit that they have arrived at that knowledge or supposition by a very different road from that of experience.

Thus we have seen that the physico-theological proof rests on the cosmological, and the cosmological on the ontological proof of the existence of one original Being as the Supreme Being; and, as besides these three, there is no other path open to speculative reason, the ontological proof, based exclusively on pure concepts of reason, is the only possible one, always supposing that any proof of a proposition, so far transcending the empirical use of the understanding, is possible at all.

SECTION VII

Criticism of All Theology Based on Speculative Principles of Reason

Although then reason, in its purely speculative application, is utterly insufficient for this great undertaking, namely, to prove the existence of a Supreme Being, it has nevertheless this great advantage of being able to *correct* our knowledge of it, if it can be acquired from elsewhere, to make it consistent with itself and every intelligible view, and to purify it from everything incompatible with the concept of an original Being, and from all admixture of empirical limitations.

In spite of its insufficiency, therefore, transcendental theology has a very important negative use, as a constant test of our reason, when occupied with pure ideas only, which, as such, admit of a transcendental standard only. For suppose that on practical grounds the *admission* of a highest and all-sufficient Being, as the highest intelligence, were to maintain its validity without contradiction, it would be of the greatest importance that we should be able to determine that concept accurately on its transcendental side, as the concept of a necessary and most real Being, to remove from it what is contradictory to that highest reality and purely phenomenal (anthropomorphic in the widest sense), and at the same time to put an end to all opposite assertions, whether *atheistic, deistic,* or *anthropomorphistic.* Such a critical treatment would not be difficult, because the same arguments by which the insufficiency of human reason in asserting the existence of such a Being has been proved, must be sufficient also to prove the invalidity of opposite asser-

tions. For whence can anybody, through pure speculation of reason, derive his knowledge that there is no Supreme Being, as the cause of all that exists, or that it can claim none of those qualities which we, to judge from their effects, represent to ourselves as compatible with the dynamical realities of a thinking Being, or that, in the latter case, they would be subject to all those limitations which sensibility imposes inevitably on all the intelligences known to us by experience?

For the purely speculative use of reason, therefore, the Supreme Being remains, no doubt, an ideal only, but an ideal *without a flaw,* a concept which finishes and crowns the whole of human knowledge, and the objective reality of which, though it cannot be proved, can neither be disproved in that way. If then there should be an Ethico-theology to supply that deficiency, transcendental theology, which before was problematical only, would prove itself indispensable in determining its concept, and in constantly testing reason, which is so often deceived by sensibility, and not even always in harmony with its own ideas. Necessity, infinity, unity, extra-mundane existence (not as a world-soul), eternity, free from conditions of time, omnipresence, free from conditions of space, omnipotence, etc., all these are transcendental predicates, and their purified concepts, which are so much required for every theology, can therefore be derived from transcendental theology only.

J. J. C. SMART

A Contemporary Critique of Traditional Arguments for the Existence of God

J. J. C. Smart (1920–   ) is Professor of Philosophy in the University of Adelaide, Australia. The present essay is an eminently clear presentation of objections to traditional theistic arguments from the standpoint of contemporary analytical philosophy.

This lecture is not to discuss whether God exists. It is to discuss reasons which philosophers have given for saying that God exists. That is, to discuss certain arguments.

First of all it may be as well to say what we may hope to get out of this. Of course, if we found that any of the traditional arguments for the existence of God were sound, we should get out of our one hour this Sunday afternoon something of inestimable value, such as one never got out of any hour's work in our lives before. For we should have got out of one hour's work the answer to that question about which, above all, we want to know the answer. (This is assuming for the moment that the question 'Does God exist?' is a proper question. The fact that a question is all right as far as the rules of ordinary grammar are concerned does not ensure that it has a sense. For example, 'Does virtue run faster than length?' is certainly all right as far as ordinary grammar is concerned, but it is

obviously not a meaningful question. Again, 'How fast does time flow?' is all right as far as ordinary grammar is concerned, but it has no clear meaning. Now some philosophers would ask whether the question 'Does God exist?' is a proper question. The greatest danger to theism at the present moment does not come from people who deny the validity of the arguments for the existence of God, for many Christian theologians do not believe that the existence of God can be proved, and certainly nowhere in the Old or New Testaments do we find any evidence of people's religion having a metaphysical basis. The main danger to theism today comes from people who want to say that 'God exists' and 'God does not exist' are equally absurd. The concept of God, they would say, is a nonsensical one. Now I myself shall later give grounds for thinking that the question 'Does God exist?' is not, in the full sense, a proper question, but I shall also give grounds for believing that to admit this is not necessarily to endanger theology.)

However, let us assume for the moment that the question 'Does God exist?' is a proper question. We now ask: Can a

From J. J. C. Smart, "The Existence of God" (1955), a public lecture given at the University of Adelaide in 1951. Reprinted by permission of J. J. C. Smart.

study of the traditional proofs of the existence of God enable us to give an affirmative answer to this question? I contend that it can not. I shall point out what seem to me to be fallacies in the main traditional arguments for the existence of God. Does proving that the arguments are invalid prove that God does not exist? Not at all. For to say that an argument is invalid is by no means the same thing as to say that its conclusion is false. Still, if we do find that the arguments we consider are all fallacious, what do we *gain* out of our investigation? Well, one thing we gain is a juster (if more austere) view of what philosophical argument can do for us. But, more important, we get a deeper insight into the logical nature of certain concepts, in particular, of course, the concepts of deity and existence. Furthermore we shall get some hints as to whether philosophy can be of any service to theologians, and if it can be of service, some hints as to how it can be of service. I think that it can be, but I must warn you that many, indeed perhaps the majority, of philosophers today would not entirely agree with me here. . . .

One very noteworthy feature which must strike anyone who first looks at the usual arguments for the existence of God is the extreme brevity of these arguments. They range from a few lines to a few pages. St. Thomas Aquinas presents five arguments in three pages! Would it not be rather extraordinary if such a great conclusion should be got so easily? Before going on to discuss any of the traditional arguments in detail I want to give general grounds for suspecting anyone who claims to settle a controversial question by means of a short snappy argument.

My reason for doubting whether a short snappy argument can ever settle any controversial question is as follows: *any argument can be reversed.* Let me explain this. A question of elementary logic is involved. Let us consider an argument from two premisses, *p, q,* to a conclusion *r*:

$$p$$
$$q$$
$$r$$

If the argument is valid, that is, if *r* really does follow from *p* and *q*, the argument will lead to agreement about *r* provided that there already is agreement about *p* and *q*. For example, if we have the premisses

p All A, B and C grade cricketers are entitled to a free pass to the Adelaide Oval for Test matches, Sheffield Shield matches, etc. (quite uncontroversial, it can be got from the rules of the South Australian Cricket Association.)

q John Wilkin is an A, B or C grade cricketer. (Quite uncontroversial, everyone knows it.)

we may conclude

r John Wilkin is entitled to a free pass to the Adelaide Oval for Test matches, Sheffield Shield matches, etc.

But we now consider this argument: [1]

p Nothing can come into existence except through the activity of some previously existing thing or being.

q The world had a beginning in time.

therefore

r The world came into existence through the activity of some previously existing thing or being.

If this argument is valid (as it certainly is) then it is equally the case that

(not-*r*) The world did not come into existence through the activity of some previously existing thing or being

---

[1] I owe this illustration, and the whole application to the idea of 'reversing the argument,' to Prof. D. A. T. Gasking of Melbourne.

implies that either

> (not-p) Something *can* come into existence otherwise than through the activity of a previously existing thing or being

or

> (not-q) The world had no beginning in time.

That is, if $\begin{array}{c}p\\ \hline q\\ \hline r\end{array}$ is valid $\begin{array}{c}\text{not-}r\\ \hline q\\ \hline \text{not-}p\end{array}$ and $\begin{array}{c}\text{not-}r\\ \hline p\\ \hline \text{not-}q\end{array}$

must be equally valid.

Now it is possible that a person might think that we have *fewer* reasons for believing r than we have for believing (not-p) or (not-q). In which case the argument $\begin{array}{c}p\\ \hline q\\ \hline r\end{array}$ though perfectly valid will not convince him. For he will be inclined to argue in the opposite direction, that is, from the falsity of r to the falsity of either p or q.

This last example is perhaps itself a —not very good—argument for the existence of God, but I have given it purely as an example to show *one* of the things to look out for when criticizing more serious arguments. The other thing to look out for, of course, is whether the argument is *valid*. It is my belief that in the case of any metaphysical argument it will be found that if the premises are uncontroversial the argument is unfortunately not valid, and that if the argument is valid the premises will unfortunately be just as doubtful as the conclusion they are meant to support.

With these warnings in mind let us proceed to the discussion of the three most famous arguments for the existence of God. These are:

(1) The Ontological Argument.
(2) The Cosmological Argument.
(3) The Teleological Argument.

The first argument—the ontological argument—really has no premises at all. It tries to show that there would be a contradiction in denying that God exists. It was first formulated by St. Anselm and was later used by Descartes. It is not a convincing argument to modern ears, and St. Thomas Aquinas gave essentially the right reasons for rejecting it. However, it is important to discuss it, as an understanding of what is wrong with it is necessary for evaluating the second argument, that is, the cosmological argument. This argument does have a premiss, but not at all a controversial one. It is that something exists. We should all, I think, agree to that. The teleological argument is less austere in manner than the other two. It tries to argue to the existence of God not purely *a priori* and not from the mere fact of *something* existing, but from actual features we observe in nature, namely those which seem to be evidence of design or purpose.

We shall discuss these three arguments in order. I do not say that they are the only arguments which have been propounded for the existence of God, but they are, I think, the most important ones. For example, of St. Thomas Aquinas' celebrated 'Five Ways' the first three are variants of the cosmological argument, and the fifth is a form of the teleological argument.

The Ontological Argument. This as I remarked, contains no factual premiss. It is a *reductio-ad-absurdum* of the supposition that God does not exist. Now *reductio-ad-absurdum* proofs are to be suspected whenever there is doubt as to whether the statement to be proved is *significant*. For example, it is quite easy, as anyone who is familiar with the so-called Logical Paradoxes will know, to produce a not *obviously* nonsensical statement, such that both it *and* its denial imply a contradiction. So unless we are sure of the significance of a statement we cannot regard a *reductio-ad-absurdum* of its contradictory as proving its truth. This point of view is well known to those versed in the philosophy of mathematics; there is a well-known school of mathematicians, led by Brouwer, who in certain circumstances refuse to employ *reductio-ad-adsurdum* proofs. However, I shall not press this criticism of the ontological argument, for this criticism is somewhat abstruse (though it has been foreshadowed by Catholic philosophers, who object to the ontological argument by saying that it does not first show that the concept of an infinitely perfect being is a *possible* one). We are at present assuming that 'Does God exist?' is a proper question, and if it is a proper question there is no objection so far to answering it by means of a *reductio-ad-absurdum* proof. We shall content ourselves with the more usual criticisms of the ontological argument.

The ontological argument was made famous by Descartes. It is to be found at the beginning of his Fifth Meditation. As I remarked earlier it was originally put forward by Anselm, though I am sorry to say that to read Descartes you would never suspect that fact! Descartes points out that in mathematics we can deduce various things purely *a priori,* 'as for example,' he says, 'when I imagine a triangle, although there is not and perhaps never was in any place . . . one such figure, it remains true nevertheless that this figure possesses a certain determinate nature, form, or essence, which is . . . not framed by me, nor in any degree dependent on my thought; as appears from the circumstance, that diverse properties of the triangle may be demonstrated, for example that its three angles are equal to two right, that its greatest side is subtended by its greatest angle, and the like.' Descartes now goes on to suggest that just as having the sum of its angles equal to two right angles is involved in the idea of a triangle, so *ex*-

istence is involved in the very idea of an infinitely perfect being, and that it would therefore be as much of a contradiction to assert that an infinitely perfect being does not exist as it is to assert that the three angles of a triangle do not add up to two right angles or that two of its sides are not together greater than the third side. We may then, says Descartes, assert that an infinitely perfect being *necessarily* exists, just as we may say that two sides of a triangle are together *necessarily* greater than the third side.

This argument is highly fallacious. To say that a so-and-so exists is not in the least like saying that a so-and-so has such-and-such a property. It is not to amplify a concept but to say that a concept applies to something, and whether or not a concept applies to something can not be seen from an examination of the concept itself. Existence is not a property. 'Growling' is a property of tigers, and to say that 'tame tigers growl' is to say something about tame tigers, but to say 'tame tigers exist' is not to say something about tame tigers but to say that there are tame tigers. Prof. G. E. Moore once brought out the difference between existence and a property such as that of being tame, or being a tiger, or being a growler, by reminding us that though the sentence 'some tame tigers do not *growl*' makes perfect sense, the sentence 'some tame tigers do not *exist*' has no clear meaning. The fundamental mistake in the ontological argument, then, is that it treats 'exists' in 'an infinitely perfect being exists' as if it ascribed a property existence to an infinitely perfect being, just as 'is loving' in 'an infinitely perfect being is loving' ascribes a property, or as 'growl' in 'tame tigers growl' ascribes a property: the verb 'to exist' in 'an infinitely perfect being exists' does not ascribe a property to something already conceived of as existing but says that the concept of an infinitely perfect being applies to something. The verb 'to exist' here takes us right out of the purely conceptual world. This being so, there can never be any *logical contradiction* in denying that God exists. It is worth mentioning that we are less likely to make the sort of mistake that the ontological argument makes if we use the expression 'there is a so-and-so' instead of the more misleading form of words 'a so-and-so exists.'

I should like to mention another interesting, though less crucial, objection to Descartes' argument. He talks as though you can deduce further properties of, say, a triangle, by considering its definition. It is worth pointing out that from the definition of a triangle as a figure bounded by three straight lines you can only deduce trivialities, such as that it is bounded by more than one straight line, for example. It is not at all a contradiction to say that the two sides of a triangle are together not greater than the third side, or that its angles do not add up to two right angles. To get a contradiction you have to bring in the specific axioms of Euclidean geometry. (Remember school geometry, how you used to prove that the angles of a triangle add up to two right angles. Through the vertex *C* of the triangle *ABC* you drew a line parallel to *BA,* and so you assumed the axiom of parallels for a start.) Definitions, by themselves, are not deductively potent. Descartes, though a very great mathematician himself, was profoundly mistaken as to the nature of mathematics. However, we can interpret him as saying that from the definition of a triangle, *together with the axioms of Euclidean geometry,* you can deduce various things, such as that the angles of a triangle add up to two right angles. But this just shows how pure mathematics is a sort of game with symbols; you start with a set of axioms, and operate on them in accordance with certain rules of inference. All the mathematician requires is that the axiom set should be *consistent.* Whether or not it has application to reality lies outside pure

mathematics. Geometry is no fit model for a proof of real existence.

We now turn to the *Cosmological Argument.* This argument does at least seem more promising than the ontological argument. It does start with a factual premiss, namely that something exists. The premiss that something exists is indeed a very abstract one, but nevertheless it *is* factual, it does give us a foothold in the real world of things, it does go beyond the consideration of mere concepts. The argument has been put forward in various forms, but for present purposes it may be put as follows:

Everything in the world around us is *contingent.* That is, with regard to any particular thing, it is quite conceivable that it might not have existed. For example, if you were asked why you existed, you could say that it was because of your parents, and if asked why they existed you could go still further back, but however far you go back you have not, so it is argued, made the fact of your existence really intelligible. For however far back you go in such a series you only get back to something which itself might not have existed. For a really satisfying explanation of why anything contingent (such as you or me or this table) exists you must eventually begin with something which is not itself contingent, that is, with something of which we cannot say that it might not have existed, that is we must begin with a necessary being. So the first part of the argument boils down to this. *If anything exists an absolutely necessary being must exist. Something exists. Therefore an absolutely necessary being must exist.*

The second part of the argument is to prove that a necessarily existing being must be an infinitely perfect being, that is, God. Kant [2] contended that this second stage of the argument is just the ontological argument over again, and of course

------

[2] *Critique of Pure Reason,* A 603.

if this were so the cosmological argument would plainly be a fraud; it begins happily enough with an existential premiss ('something exists') but this would only be a cover for the subsequent employment of the ontological argument. This criticism of Kant's has been generally accepted but I think that certain Thomist philosophers have been right in attributing to Kant's own criticism a mistake in elementary logic. Let us look at Kant's criticism. Kant says, correctly enough, that the conclusion of the second stage of the cosmological argument is 'All necessarily existing beings are infinitely perfect beings.' This, he says, implies that 'Some infinitely perfect beings are necessarily existing beings.' Since, however, there could be only one infinitely perfect, unlimited, being, we may replace the proposition 'Some infinitely perfect beings are necessarily existing beings' by the proposition 'All infinitely perfect beings are necessarily existing beings.' (To make this last point clearer let me take an analogous example. If it is true that some men who are Prime Minister of Australia are Liberals and if it is also true that there is only one Prime Minister of Australia, then we can equally well say that all men who are Prime Minister of Australia are Liberals. For 'some' means 'at least one,' and if there is only one Prime Minister, then 'at least one' is equivalent to 'one,' which in this case is 'all.') So the conclusion of the second stage of the cosmological argument is that 'all infinitely perfect beings are necessarily existing beings.' This, however, is the principle of the ontological argument, which we have already criticized, and which, for that matter, proponents of the cosmological argument like Thomas Aquinas themselves reject.

Kant has, however, made a very simple mistake. He has forgotten that the existence of a necessary being has already been proved (or thought to have been proved) in the first part of the argument.

He changes 'All necessary beings are infinitely perfect beings' round to 'Some infinitely perfect beings are necessary beings.' If this change round is to be valid the existence of a necessary being is already presupposed. Kant has been misled by an ambiguity in 'all.' 'All X's are Y's' may take it for granted that there are some X's or it may not. For example if I say, 'All the people in this room are interested in Philosophy,' it is already agreed that there are some people in this room. So we can infer that 'Some of the people interested in Philosophy are people in this room.' So 'All the people in this room are interested in Philosophy' says more than 'If anyone were in this room he would be interested in Philosophy,' for this would be true even if there were in fact no people in this room. (As I wrote this lecture I was quite sure that if anyone came he would be interested in Philosophy, and I could have been quite sure of this even if I had doubted whether anyone would come.) Now sometimes 'All X's are Y's' does mean only 'If anything is an X it is a Y.' Take the sentence 'All trespassers will be prosecuted.' This does not imply that some prosecuted people will be trespassers, for it does not imply that there are or will be any trespassers. Indeed the object of putting it on a notice is to make it more likely that there won't be any trespassers. All that 'All trespassers will be prosecuted' says is, 'If anyone is a trespasser then he will be prosecuted.' So Kant's criticism won't do. He has taken himself and other people in by using 'all' sometimes in the one way and sometimes in the other.

While agreeing thus far with Thomist critics of Kant [3] I still want to assert that the cosmological argument is radically un-

[3] See, for example, Fr. T. A. Johnston, *Australasian Journal of Philosophy*, Vol. XXI, pp. 14–15, or D. J. B. Hawkins, *Essentials of Theism*, pp. 67–70, and the review of Fr. Hawkins' book by A. Donagan, *Australasian Journal of Philosophy*, Vol. XXVIII, especially p. 129.

sound. The trouble comes much earlier than where Kant locates it. The trouble comes in the *first* stage of the argument. For the first stage of the argument purports to argue to the existence of a necessary being. And by 'a necessary being' the cosmological argument means 'a *logically* necessary being,' i.e. 'a being whose non-existence is inconceivable in the sort of way that a triangle's having four sides is inconceivable.' The trouble is, however, that the concept of a logically necessary being is a self-contradictory concept, like the concept of a round square. For in the first place 'necessary' is a predicate of *propositions,* not of things. That is, we can contrast *necessary* propositions such as '3 + 2 = 5,' 'a thing cannot be red and green all over,' 'either it is raining or it is not raining,' with *contingent* propositions, such as 'Mr. Menzies is Prime Minister of Australia,' 'the earth is slightly flattened at the poles,' and 'sugar is soluble in water.' The propositions in the first class are guaranteed solely by the rules for the use of the symbols they contain. In the case of the propositions of the second class a genuine possibility of agreeing or not agreeing with reality is left open; whether they are true or false depends not on the conventions of our language but on reality. (Compare the contrast between 'the equator is 90 degrees from the pole,' which tells us nothing about geography but only about our map-making conventions, and 'Adelaide is 55 degrees from the pole,' which does tell us a geographical fact.) So no informative proposition can be logically necessary. Now since 'necessary' is a word which applies primarily to propositions, we shall have to interpret 'God is a necessary being' as 'The proposition "God exists" is logically necessary.' But this *is* the principle of the ontological argument, and there is no way of getting round it this time in the way that we got out of Kant's criticism. No existential proposition can be logically necessary, for we saw that the truth of a logically necessary proposition depends only on our symbolism, or to put the same thing in another way, on the relationship of concepts. We saw, however, in discussing the ontological argument, that an existential proposition does not say that one concept is involved in another, but that a concept applies to something. An existential proposition must be very different from any logically necessary one, such as a mathematical one, for example, for the conventions of our symbolism clearly leave it open for us either to affirm or deny an existential proposition; it is not our symbolism but reality which decides whether or not we must affirm it or deny it.

The demand that the existence of God should be *logically* necessary is thus a self-contradictory one. When we see this and go back to look at the first stage of the cosmological argument it no longer seems compelling, indeed it now seems to contain an absurdity. If we cast our minds back, we recall that the argument was as follows: that if we explain why something exists and is what it is, we must explain it by reference to something else, and we must explain that thing's being what it is by reference to yet another thing, and so on, back and back. It is then suggested that unless we can go back to a logically necessary first cause we shall remain intellectually unsatisfied. We should otherwise only get back to something which might have been otherwise, and with reference to which the same questions can again be asked. This is the argument, but we now see that in asking for a logically necessary first cause we are doing something worse than asking for the moon. It is only *physically* impossible for us to get the moon; if I were a few million times bigger I could reach out for it and give it to you. That is, I know what it would be *like* to give you the moon, though I cannot *in fact* do it. A logically necessary first cause, however, is not impossible in the way that giving you the moon is impossible; no, it is *logically* impossible. 'Logically necessary being' is a self-contradictory expression like 'round square.' It is not any good saying that we would only be intellectually satisfied with a logically necessary cause, that nothing else would do. We can easily have an absurd wish. We should all like to be able to eat our cake and have it, but that does not alter the fact that our wish is an absurd and self-contradictory one. We reject the cosmological argument, then, because it rests on a thorough absurdity.

. . .

The cosmological argument, we saw, failed because it made use of the absurd conception of a *logically* necessary being. We now pass to the third argument which I propose to consider. This is the *Teleological Argument*. It is also called 'the Argument from Design.' It would be better called the argument *to* design, as Kemp Smith does call it, for clearly that the universe has been designed by a great architect is to assume a great part of the conclusion to be proved. Or we could call it 'the argument from apparent design.' The argument is very fully discussed in Hume's *Dialogues concerning Natural Religion,* to which I should like to draw your attention. In these dialogues the argument is presented as follows: 'Look round the world: Contemplate the whole and every part of it: You will find it to be nothing but one great machine, subdivided into an infinite number of lesser machines. . . . The curious adapting of means to ends, throughout all nature, resembles exactly, though it much exceeds, the productions of human contrivance. . . . Since therefore the effects resemble each other, we are led to infer, by all the rules of analogy, that the causes also resemble; and that the Author of nature is somewhat similar to the mind of man; though possessed of much larger faculties, proportioned to the grandeur of the work which he has executed.'

This argument may at once be criticized in two ways: (1) We may question whether the analogy between the universe and artificial things like houses, ships, furniture, and machines (which admittedly are designed) is very close. Now in any ordinary sense of language, it is true to say that plants and animals have *not* been designed. If we press the analogy of the universe to a plant, instead of to a machine, we get to a very different conclusion. And why should the one analogy be regarded as any better or worse than the other? (2) Even if the analogy were close, it would only go to suggest that the universe was designed by a *very great* (not infinite) architect, and note, an *architect,* not a *creator.* For if we take the analogy seriously we must notice that we do not create the materials from which we make houses, machines and so on, but only *arrange* the materials.

This, in bare outline, is the general objection to the argument from design, and will apply to any form of it. In the form in which the argument was put forward by such theologians as Paley, the argument is, of course, still more open to objection. For Paley laid special stress on such things as the eye of an animal, which he thought must have been contrived by a wise Creator for the special benefit of the animal. It seemed to him inconceivable how otherwise such a complex organ, so well suited to the needs of the animal, should have arisen. Or listen to Henry More: 'For why have we three joints in our legs and arms, as also in our fingers, but that it was much better than having two or four? And why are our fore-teeth sharp like chisels to cut, but our inward teeth broad to grind, [instead of] the fore-teeth broad and the other sharp? But we might have made a hard shift to have lived through in that worser condition. Again, why are the teeth so luckily placed, or rather, why are there not teeth in other bones as well as in the jaw-bones? for they might have been as capable as these. But the reason is, nothing is done foolishly or in vain; that is, there is a divine Providence that orders all things.' This type of argument has lost its persuasiveness, for the theory of Evolution explains why our teeth are so luckily placed in our jaw-bones, why we have the most convenient number of joints in our fingers, and so on. Species which did not possess advantageous features would not survive in competition with those which did.

The sort of argument Paley and Henry More used is thus quite unconvincing. Let us return to the broader conception, that of the universe as a whole, which seems to show the mark of a benevolent and intelligent Designer. Bacon expressed this belief forcibly: 'I had rather beleeve all the Fables in the Legend and the Talmud and the Alcoran than that this Universal Frame is without a Minde.' So, in some moods, does the universe strike us. But sometimes, when we are in other moods, we see it very differently. To quote Hume's dialogues again: 'Look around this Universe. What an immense profusion of beings, animated and organized, sensible and active! You admire this prodigious variety and fecundity. But inspect a little more narrowly these living existences, the only beings worth regarding. How hostile and destructive to each other! How insufficient all of them for their own happiness! . . . the whole presents nothing but the idea of a blind Nature, impregnated by a great vivifying principle, and pouring forth from her lap, without discernment or parental care, her maimed and abortive children!' There is indeed a great deal of suffering, some part of which is no doubt attributable to the moral choices of men, and to save us from which would conflict with what many people would regard as the greater good of moral freedom, but there is still an immense residue of apparently needless suffering, that is, needless in the sense

that it could be prevented by an omnipotent being. The difficulty is that of reconciling the presence of evil and suffering with the assertion that God is both omnipotent and benevolent. If we *already* believe in an omnipotent and benevolent God, then some attempt may be made to solve the problem of evil by arguing that the values in the world form a sort of organic unity, and that making any *part* of the world better would perhaps nevertheless reduce the value of the whole. Paradoxical though this thesis may appear at first sight, it is perhaps not theoretically absurd. If, however, evil presents a *difficulty* to the believing mind, it presents an *insuperable* difficulty to one who wishes to argue rationally from the world as we find it to the existence of an omnipotent and benevolent God. As Hume puts it: 'Is the world considered in general, and as it appears to us in this life, different from what a man . . . would *beforehand* expect from a very powerful, wise and benevolent Deity? It must be a strange prejudice to assert the contrary. And from thence I conclude, that, however consistent the world may be, allowing certain suppositions and conjectures, with the idea of such a Deity, it can never afford us an inference concerning his existence.'

The teleological argument is thus extremely shaky, and in any case, even if it were sound, it would only go to prove the existence of a very great architect, not of an omnipotent and benevolent Creator.

Nevertheless, the argument has a fascination for us that reason can not easily dispel. Hume, in his twelfth dialogue, and after pulling the argument from design to pieces in the previous eleven dialogues, nevertheless speaks as follows: 'A purpose, an intention, a design strikes everywhere the most careless, the most stupid thinker; and no man can be so hardened in absurd systems as at all times to reject it . . . all the sciences almost lead us insensibly to acknowledge a first Author.'

Similarly Kant, before going on to exhibit the fallaciousness of the argument, nevertheless says of it: 'This proof always deserves to be mentioned with respect. It is the oldest, the clearest and the most accordant with the common reason of mankind. It enlivens the study of nature, just as it itself derives its existence and gains ever new vigour from that source. It suggests ends and purposes, where our observation would not have detected them by itself, and extends our knowledge of nature by means of the guiding-concept of a special unity, the principle of which is outside nature. This knowledge . . . so strengthens the belief in a supreme Author of nature that the belief acquires the force of an irresistible conviction.' It is somewhat of a paradox that an invalid argument should command so much respect even from those who have demonstrated its invalidity. The solution of the paradox is perhaps somewhat as follows: [4] The argument from design is no good as an argument. But in those who have the seeds of a genuinely religious attitude already within them the facts to which the argument from design draws attention, facts showing the grandeur and majesty of the universe, facts that are evident to anyone who looks upwards on a starry night, and which are enormously multiplied for us by the advance of theoretical science, these facts have a powerful effect. But they only have this effect on the already religious mind, on the mind which has the capability of feeling the religious type of awe. That is, the argument from design is in reality no argument, or if it is regarded as an argument it is feeble, but it is a potent instrument in heightening religious emotions.

Something similar might even be said of the cosmological argument. As an argument it cannot pass muster at all; indeed it is completely absurd, as employing the notion of a logically necessary being. Nevertheless it does appeal to something deep seated in our natures. It takes its stand on the fact that the existence of you or me or this table is not logically necessary. Logic tells us that this fact is not a fact at all, but is a truism, like the 'fact' that a circle is not a square. Again, the cosmological argument tries to base the existence of you or me or this table on the existence of a logically necessary being, and hence commits a rank absurdity, the notion of a logically necessary being being self-contradictory. So the only rational thing to say if someone asks 'Why does this table exist?' is some such thing as that such and such a carpenter made it. We can go back and back in such a series, but we must not entertain the absurd idea of getting back to something logically necessary. However, now let us ask, 'Why should anything exist at all?' Logic seems to tell us that the only answer which is not absurd is to say, 'Why shouldn't it?' Nevertheless, though I know how any answer on the lines of the cosmological argument can be pulled to pieces by a correct logic, I still feel I want to go on asking the question. Indeed, though logic has taught me to look at such a question with the gravest suspicion, my mind often seems to reel under the immense significance it seems to have for me. That anything should exist at all does seem to me a matter for the deepest awe. But whether other people feel this sort of awe, and whether they or I ought to is another question. I think we ought to. If so, the question arises: If 'Why should anything exist at all?' cannot be interpreted after the manner of the cosmological argument, that is, as an absurd request for the nonsensical postulation of a logically necessary being, what sort of question is it? What sort of question is this question 'Why should anything exist at all?' All I can say is, that I do not yet know.

---

[4] See also N. Kemp Smith's Henrietta Hertz Lecture, 'Is Divine Existence Credible?', *Proceedings of the British Academy,* 1931.

SUGGESTIONS FOR FURTHER READING

Important presentations of various traditional arguments for the existence of God are to be found in René Descartes, *Meditations;* G. W. Leibniz, *Monadology;* George Berkeley, *Dialogues;* and Josiah Royce, *The Conception of God* (New York: Macmillan, 1898).

Contemporary presentations of the Thomistic arguments include G. H. Joyce, *The Principles of Natural Theology* (New York: Longmans, Green, 1951); Réginald Garrigou-Lagrange, *God, His Existence and His Nature* (St. Louis: Herter Book Co., 1934–36); E. L. Mascall, *He Who Is* (New York: Longmans, Green, 1948); and D. J. B. Hawkins, *The Essentials of Theism* (New York: Sheed and Ward, 1949).

Recent articles on the ontological argument include Norman Malcolm, "Anselm's Ontological Arguments," *Philosophical Review* (1960); and W. P. Alston, "The Ontological Argument Revisited," *Philosophical Review* (1960). The January 1961 issue of the *Philosophical Review* contains a number of criticisms of Malcolm's article. Charles Hartshorne's *The Logic of Perfection,* on the same subject, is forthcoming from The Open Court Publishing Company.

The teleological argument receives a full presentation in *Evidences of the Existence and Attributes of the Deity,* by the eighteenth-century thinker William Paley. A good contemporary presentation is in A. E. Taylor, *Does God Exist?* (New York: Macmillan, 1947).

Important statements of the moral argument are contained in Immanuel Kant, *Critique of Practical Reason;* W. R. Sorley, *Moral Values and the Idea of God* (New York: Cambridge Univ. Press, 1919); and A. E. Taylor, *Does God Exist?*

Belief in a nonabsolute personal deity is defended by J. S. Mill, *Three Essays on Religion;* A. N. Whitehead, *Process and Reality* (New York: Macmillan, 1929); and W. P. Montague, *Belief Unbound* (New Haven: Yale Univ. Press, 1930).

Important criticisms of the arguments are to be found in J. M. E. McTaggart, *Some Dogmas of Religion* (London: Arnold, 1906); John Laird, *Theism and Cosmology* (London: Allen and Unwin, 1940), and *Mind and Deity* (London: Allen and Unwin, 1941); and Bertrand Russell, *Why I Am Not a Christian and Other Essays* (New York: Simon and Schuster, 1957).

Distinctively different versions of the traditional arguments are contained in Austen Farrar, *Finite and Infinite* (Westminster: Dacre Press, 1943); and Jacques Maritain, *Approaches to God,* Peter O'Reilly, tr. (New York: Harper, 1954).

2.

RELIGIOUS
EXPERIENCE

If, one winter morning, I discover some footprints in the snow leading up to my kitchen window, I can, by reasoning from effect to cause, come to realize that during the night someone came and peered into the house. But if during the night I had happened to look out my bedroom window at the time the intruder was approaching, I could have discovered his presence in a direct fashion, without the necessity of such inferences. The various arguments for the existence of God which were presented in the previous section purported to reveal God to us in the former, indirect sort of way. But there have been many religious men who have believed that they were able to discover that God exists in a more direct fashion, by experiencing His presence in as direct a way as that in which one experiences the presence of trees, buildings, and other human beings. This section is primarily devoted to discussions of the possibility that certain types of experience constitute a direct awareness of God, and thus provide us with the best possible reason for believing in His existence. It is true that religious people have not prized religious experience solely, or even primarily, for its evidential value. It is sought because it is regarded as a state of being which is, in itself, incomparably superior to any other, and because vitalizing, ennobling, transforming consequences are thought to derive from it. Intimate communion with God, like human love, is not thought of primarily as a research technique. Nevertheless, it is often invoked as the most conclusive reason for believing that a god does exist, and it is with this aspect that we shall be chiefly concerned.

Some preliminary indication of the sort of experience in which we are interested would be in order. There are many states of experience which are typically involved in religious activity, and not all of these are of interest for this discussion. We are not, for example, concerned with the awe one feels when kneeling before the Cross, the sense of mystery which is often aroused by elaborate ceremonial, the feeling of abasement which can accompany public or private confession, the feeling of relief experienced when absolution of one's sins is pronounced, the sense of new significance which sometimes accompanies the rereading of a Bible passage, or the peace which one sometimes feels in the course of prayer. That is, we are not dealing with religious emotions as such. We are interested in experiences which, in James's words, involve a "noetic" aspect— that is, which seem to the experiencer to bring knowledge of something beyond his own immediate state of consciousness. Such experiences are usually bound up with emotions of the sorts enumerated above, but it is their "noetic" quality that makes them of interest in the present inquiry. Incidentally, the defining criteria set forth by James for a "mystical state of consciousness"—ineffability, noetic quality, transiency, and passivity—determine, as James notes, a very wide class of experiences, which is by no means restricted to what would ordinarily be regarded as religious. It will include, for example, very deep responses to music in which it seems for the moment as if through the music one is somehow seeing into the heart of things, even though this is not taken to have any religious significance. With respect to the problems under consideration in this chapter it would be better further to restrict the term *mystical experience* by requiring a mystical experience to be such that the experiencer takes it to be an awareness of some object of religious worship. And since we are concerned primarily with theistic religion, we are most interested in those experiences which are taken to involve direct awareness of a supernatural supreme personal being.

Our central question is: Are experiences of this sort, always or sometimes, really direct apprehensions of an objectively existing personal deity, or are they purely subjective states of feeling which have no reference to anything beyond the subject? It is clear that if I *have* directly experienced a personal deity (as opposed to merely having supposed that I have done so) then I have the strongest possible basis for believing that such a being exists; just as I have the strongest possible basis for believing that yaks exist if I really have seen one. It is important to realize that this claim goes beyond merely saying that such *experiences* occur. If we define mystical experiences purely in terms of the individual's feelings and what he is inclined to believe about them, as James does, then we can recognize that there are experiences as so defined, while leaving completely open the question as to whether such experiences do, in fact, put us in touch with an objectively existing deity. As C. B. Martin insists, the occurrence of a certain experience never in itself carries any guarantee as to the existence of anything apart from the experience.

There are two rather different ways of tackling this problem. We may regard the mystic's claim to have directly experienced the presence of God as analogous to someone's claim to have seen an airplane or a waterfall or a flying saucer, and then try to apply to the mystic the same, or analogous, tests as those we use in assessing claims of the latter sort. Or we can treat the mystic's experience as a datum to be explained and we can ask what factors have to be considered in order to obtain an adequate explanation. Both these approaches are represented in our readings. Let us look at both, beginning with the second.

This second approach is usually made in connection with the claim that one can adequately explain the occurrence of mystical experiences in terms of purely natural factors, usually psychological or physiological: nervous disorders, repressed desires, auto-suggestion, and so on. Let us take some examples of the kinds of explanations that might be offered. Consider the following passage from St. Teresa: [1]

> Often when the soul least expects it, our Lord calls her suddenly. She hears very distinctly that her God calls her, and it gives her such a start, especially at the beginning, that she trembles and utters plaints. She feels that an *ineffable wound* has been dealt her and that the wound is so precious in her sight that she would like it never to heal. She knows that her divine Spouse is near her, although He does not let her enjoy His adorable presence, and she cannot help complaining to Him in words of love. The voice of the Well-Beloved causes in the soul such transports that she is consumed by desire, and yet does not know what to ask, because she sees clearly that her Lord is with her. What pains could she have? And for what greater happiness could she wish? To this I do not know what to answer; but that of which I am certain, is that the pain penetrates down to the very bottom of the bowels, and that it seems that they are being torn away when the heavenly Spouse withdraws the arrow with which he has transpierced them. As long as that pain lasts, it is always on the increase or on the decrease, it never remains at the same intensity. It is for that reason that the soul is never entirely on fire; the spark goes out and the soul feels a desire stronger than ever to endure again the love-pain she has just experienced.

When one finds such experiences reported by not over-aged females who have long been under vows of chastity, it is not at all implausible to suggest an explanation along the following lines: Natural desires for sexual love had not only been inhibited but also repressed (excluded from consciousness). But these desires were, nevertheless, active and pressed for some sort of fulfillment. Though they could receive neither expression nor fulfillment in a direct way, they could achieve some sort of partial satisfaction through a hallucinatory experience of the intimate presence of a male deity.

Of course not all mystical experiences provide such easy targets for the psychologist. But something similar might be done with more rarefied experiences. One prominent feature of many mystical experiences is a sense of losing

---

[1] *The Interior Castle.* The translation is from J. H. Leuba, *The Psychology of Religious Mysticism,* New York: Harcourt, Brace & World (1925), pp. 150–51.

one's own individuality, of merging with some all-inclusive whole, together with a profound peace and ineffable joy (for examples, see pages 131–36). This might be explained along Freudian lines as follows: The primary model for such experiences is to be found in the experience of the infant, who has not yet made any distinction between himself and the external world and whose experience, therefore, is one undifferentiated sea of feeling; and more especially in the experience of the fed, satisfied infant just before he relapses into slumber. When the adult encounters various difficulties in his life, there is a natural tendency to "regress" to earlier modes of organization in which the problems currently encountered did not have to be dealt with. Such regression, if severe, might involve, along with various more or less infantile modes of behavior, hallucinatory experiences of being in something like the infantile state just described.[2]

Various questions can be raised as to the cogency of such explanations. It must not be forgotten that at this stage of the development of psychology they are purely speculative in character. Theorists have taken principles which have been more or less established in other contexts and have tried to apply them to mystical experience. Eventually these applications will have to receive a more direct test. Of course, it is difficult to lure mystics into the psychological laboratory, or even to get comprehensive case histories of nonpsychotic individuals who have mystical experiences. But in any event a discussion of the adequacy of such explanations, as psychological explanations, lies outside the purview of this volume. The crucial philosophical question is: If some such explanations are adequate, what bearing does that have on the status of the mystic's claim to have directly experienced God?

James's discussion is relevant at this point. It is noteworthy that although James suggests, and it is only a suggestion without any attempt to work out details, that mystical experiences can be explained as "invasions from the subconscious region," he does not take this as ruling out the possibility that through his unconscious mind the individual is in contact with some supernatural reality. In fact, James goes on to affirm his "overbelief" that this is the case, though he does not purport to be able to establish it. But is this a reasonable position to take? Would not the success of such a psychological explanation prove that the experience is purely subjective? This question leads us into fundamental epistemological issues which can only be touched on here. The mystic might argue that attempts to explain the occurrence of mystical experience are quite irrelevant to the validity of his claim to have directly experienced God, on the grounds that his claim was not that one would have to *postulate* a supernatural personal being in order to *explain* his experience. On the contrary, he is not interested in explanation at all, and the fact that he has been directly aware of God obviates any need to bring God in as a term in an explanation. Clearly he has a point. When I claim to see a maple tree just outside my window, I am certainly not saying that I believe that a maple tree will have to be postulated or hypothesized in order to explain the fact that I am now having the visual

---

[2] For a discussion along these lines see M. Ostow and B. Scharfstein, *The Need to Believe,* New York: International Universities Press (1954), Ch. VII.

experience I am having. Here, too, I feel that I know that the maple tree exists in a more secure way than if I could get to know it only by seeing that it must be assumed in order to explain something else. But this does not show that questions of explanation are completely irrelevant to the mystic's claim. Although I am not setting out to explain my visual experience every time I say that I saw something, it still seems to be the case that our general conviction that our visual experience gives us accurate information about external objects is intimately tied up with our conviction that in general such external objects are among the causes which produce that experience. And in a case in which questions are raised as to whether one did really see what he supposed himself to have seen, as when I claimed to have seen John and Mary together in the garden, if it can be shown that the external objects in question could not possibly have been among the factors responsible for the production of my visual experience (as would be the case if there were a tall stone wall between those two and me at the time), then that would suffice to discredit my claim to have seen them. By analogy, we might argue that if one can show that a complete account of the causal factors which produce mystical experience can be given without having to mention any supernatural personal being, this would serve to discredit the claim that in such experiences one is directly aware of such a being. But the mystic might reply that the two cases are so different as not to be amenable to the same treatment, or that God figures in a kind of explanation of mystical experience which is different from causal explanation. And it is difficult to know what to say at this point.

Of course, it is very important to consider the *kind* of explanation offered. For what is usually suggested, as in the examples given above, is that mystical experiences are due to abnormal or pathological states. And this means that apart from the above considerations, which have to do with any explanation, we have the additional suggestion that since mystical experience springs from an abnormal condition one cannot reasonably suppose that it gives us any accurate information about the external world. This point has been stated most trenchantly by Bertrand Russell: [3]

> From a scientific point of view, we can make no distinction between the man who eats little and sees heaven and the man who drinks much and sees snakes. Each is in an abnormal physical condition, and therefore has abnormal perceptions. Normal perceptions, since they have to be useful in the struggle for life, must have some correspondence with fact; but in abnormal perceptions there is no reason to expect such correspondence, and their testimony, therefore, cannot outweigh that of normal perception.

This contention raises some important issues. But first we must carefully note a distinction between the claim that mystical experiences spring from abnormal states and the much weaker claim that experiences similar to mystical experiences are known to occur in abnormal states. Nothing really crucial for our problem follows from the latter, although it is sometimes supposed that it does. It is a well-known fact that inmates of mental institutions often have

---

[3] *Religion and Science*, London: Oxford Univ. Press (1935), p. 188.

experiences, for example, of being in touch with some vaguely described higher being, that are strikingly similar to the reported experiences of famous religious mystics. But this in itself does nothing to show that the latter experiences are delusory, any more than the fact that persons suffering from delirium tremens have experiences similar to those involved in the ordinary seeing of snakes proves that experiences of the latter sort are delusory or that there are no such things as snakes. We must get below phenomenological similarity to similarity in the actual determining conditions if we are to have a criticism that is even initially plausible.

Let us ignore the consideration that no one has yet shown that mystical experience does, universally or even for the most part, spring from abnormal conditions, and confine ourselves to asking what implications this claim would have if true. It is clear that "abnormal" here does not simply mean "unusual," for in that case the ideas of the genius would be deemed less likely to be correct than those of more ordinary people. It is clear that in the passage from Russell "abnormal" means something like "in a condition which is relatively unconducive to efficiency of interaction with one's environment, or which is such that it hampers one's attempts to achieve one's aims." If this is approximately what is meant, then it is almost true by definition that experiences which are essentially determined by abnormal states will not give us accurate information about the world around us; for if such experiences did give us accurate information, they would be aiding us in our attempts to deal with the environment and that would be a strong reason for refusing to call the states "abnormal." But one should be suspicious of conclusions which are true by definition. In this case we may well suspect that the states in question have been labeled abnormal by reference to an environment, and types of dealings with the environment, restricted in such a way as to rule out some of those recognized by the mystic. To be more specific, let us suppose that mystical experiences only occur (apart from deliberate inducement by drugs) when the individual is in one of several neurotic conditions. There is no doubt that neurotic conditions, again by definition, hamper a person in his ordinary dealings with his physical and social environment. And from this Russell draws his conclusion. But let us remember, as C. D. Broad points out, that the realities the mystic thinks his experience puts him in touch with are enormously different from those that make up our physical and social environment. Therefore we may be quite unwarranted in supposing that the conditions which are conducive to accurate perception of, and effective dealing with, the two sorts of entities are the same. If one lives in the Arizona desert, a pair of sun glasses may be an aid to accurate observation, but they may well diminish observational acuity in the Aleutians. A theistic God, if He exists, is much more different from the natural world than the Aleutians from Arizona. In other words, if "abnormal" means "making for ineffective dealing with the environment," then we should not suppose that a condition is abnormal relative to environment B, if all we have shown is that it makes for ineffective dealings with environment A, and A is very different from B. "If there were such a thing as inspiration from a higher realm, it might well be that the neurotic temperament would furnish the chief condition of the requisite receptivity." [4] Of course, it might seem strange for God to so order things that neuroticism would be a condition of apprehending Him. But a theist will have to recognize that many things in the world are arranged in a way which seems strange to us.

Let us turn now to the first of the ways of dealing with our problem: trying to determine the extent to which a mystic experience is confirmed or disconfirmed by the experiences of others. It is sometimes maintained, as in the James selection (though rather halfheartedly there), that we have an argument in support of the mystic's claims in the fact that many men in widely scattered times and places have had similar experiences and have made similar claims. Now the similarity of the claims made from these experiences has often been exaggerated. James himself, after calling attention to a "pretty distinct theoretic drift," confesses that he was able to give that impression only by a rigid selection of cases which belong to "classic religious mysticism." He goes on to point out that, for example, sometimes people think they are in contact with a supreme personal being, sometimes with an all-inclusive impersonal whole; sometimes the being is experienced as loving, sometimes as indifferent to such matters, and so on. And these differences are well illustrated by the cases James cites. But there is a more serious difficulty with the argument from widespread occurrence. Even if the interpretations of the experiences were much more nearly uniform than is in fact the case, it would still be true, as Broad points out, that the facts could be accounted for either by supposing that there is a supernatural reality with which they are all in touch or by supposing that they are all under the influence of the same psychological forces. Broad suggests that we should accept the former hypothesis unless there are strong reasons for supposing such experiences to be delusive.

But there is another tack one might take, which is represented by the selection from Martin. If someone claims to have seen a waterfall 10,000 feet high in the Andes last summer, we do not decide the matter simply by looking around the world to determine how many people in the course of history have had waterfall experiences. We try to determine whether people who have been in a certain place have seen the waterfall, or we set out ourselves to have a look. Of course in this example, unlike the mystical experience case, the supposed object is located in a certain place, but we can generalize the point so as to avoid dependence on that particular feature. In order to test the accuracy of a statement made on the basis of sense perception, we need some indication of what we have to do, or the conditions we have to satisfy, in order that our sense experiences will count for or against what is being claimed. And if the person is unable to give us any such indication, we do not take his claim seriously. If we ask the person who said he saw a waterfall 10,000 feet high how we can verify what he says and he replies that we should go somewhere or other and then we may or may not see something similar, we would not know what to make of his assertion. Now it does seem to be the case, as Martin suggests, that

---

[4] William James, *Varieties of Religious Experience,* New York: New American Library (1958), p. 37.

nothing of this sort is forthcoming in the case of the mystic. Of course mystics do specify various things one can do if one wants to attain the vision of God: purify oneself morally, detach oneself from affairs of the world, acquire the ability to concentrate the mind rigidly on a single point, and so on. But these are never intended to be testing procedures. If one does all these things and still has not experienced God, this would not generally be taken as even partially disconfirming the principle that God exists, in the way that a persistent failure of people to have waterfall experiences in a certain place would generally be taken as disconfirming the existence of a waterfall in that place. The belief is not subject to disconfirmation by the experiences of others. And, as James sees clearly, this means that it is not subject to confirmation by the experiences of others. One cannot have the advantages of confirmation without running the risk of disconfirmation. As James puts it, no one else can challenge the mystic's right to interpret his own experience, but conversely he cannot suppose that his experience has any authority for others.

It would seem to follow from this that it is hopeless to try to evaluate the mystic's claim by using anything like the procedures of corroboration by other observers which we use in sense perception. And at the end of the selection from James he tells us, in effect, that we will have a chance of determining whether the mystic's reports are veridical only if we can find some independent (of mystical experience) way of testing them—by determining what consequences would follow for the *common* experience of men if the realities the mystic supposes himself to have experienced are, indeed, realities; we could then, in principle, test the claims by determining whether these consequences do occur in our experience. (Unfortunately James does very little toward indicating what such consequences would be. But we should not be overly critical of James here. It is very difficult to find any empirically testable consequences which unquestionably follow from the theistic hypothesis. See the selection by Antony Flew *et al.* in Section 3.) But Martin draws a much stronger conclusion from these considerations, namely, that if no public testing procedures are possible, we cannot suppose that the mystic is making any claim (even a false one) of the *objective* existence of anything, and hence that his utterances will have to be understood as more like reports or expressions of his state of mind. Martin's basic principle is that we can only distinguish objective from subjective reference by the presence or absence of ways in which others can determine whether what one claims to have found is really there. (Again see Antony Flew in Section 3 for a discussion of this issue.) Martin's position is subject to the following serious objection. If a God of the theistic sort does exist, we could not expect to have knowledge of any regularities governing His behavior; the creator of nature would not be bound by the laws of nature. This means that His appearances in the experience of men either follow no regularities or we have no way of finding out what these regularities are. And this in turn means that it would be unreasonable to expect to be able to lay down conditions the satisfaction of which would guarantee the experience of God if God exists. After all, the only reason that we feel confident in not taking a waterfall report seriously unless such conditions are specified is that we suppose ourselves to be in firm possession of some basic regularities governing the behavior of waterfalls. They do not, for example, pop into and out of existence every few minutes, or suddenly change their location. We are less ready to demand such conditions, even in the sphere of sense perception, when we are less sure of the regularities the reported objects follow, as in the case of flying saucers. This means that the conditions Martin lays down for taking seriously claims to objective existence could not be satisfied in this case even if God does exist. To proceed in this way seems unreasonable unless we have additional reasons to hold that the notion of the objective existence of such a being is somehow confused. Such reasons are advanced in the selection from Baron d'Holbach in Section 3.

The selections from Rudolf Otto and John Hick stand outside the discussion of the problem just considered. The Otto material is valuable as an analysis of a certain type of religious experience which Otto, perhaps rightly, considers central to religion. This analysis has been enormously influential in twentieth-century religious thought and at the very least it throws some important aspects of religious experience into sharp relief. Moreover, Otto has some illuminating points to make about the way in which we characterize religious experience by way of various sorts of analogy with more ordinary experiences. The selection from Hick represents a mode of thought, which is becoming increasingly prominent, according to which it is a mistake to think of experience of God as a distinct kind of perception, which might conceivably exist by itself and occupy the whole of consciousness, uncontaminated by the "other senses." Instead, we should think of the awareness of God as something which is always more or less present, but is always mediated through our awareness of objects in our physical and social environment. It is obvious that this position gives rise to problems very different from those posed by the more usual view that at very special and relatively unusual moments one perceives God in an immediate fashion, not through the perception of something else. Hick, unlike some who hold this position, does not claim that this experience *establishes* the existence of God. He considers the religious man to be experiencing the world about him as having a certain kind of "significance," but he recognizes that a sense of significance can be delusory, that one can "apprehend" a significance that is not really there. And so he recognizes that the credentials of such experience must be established in some other way. On this point he is in agreement with James.

WILLIAM JAMES

The Significance of Mysticism

William James (1842–1910), a member of a distinguished family, which included Henry James, the novelist, was equally renowned as a psychologist and as a philosopher. In the latter capacity he is best known as one of the leaders of the pragmatic movement. His Varieties of Religious Experience *remains a classic in the psychology of religion.*

LECTURES XVI AND XVII

MYSTICISM

Over and over again in these lectures I have raised points and left them open and unfinished until we should have come to the subject of Mysticism. Some of you, I fear, may have smiled as you noted my reiterated postponements. But now the hour has come when mysticism must be faced in good earnest, and those broken threads wound up together. One may say truly, I think, that personal religious experience has its root and centre in mystical states of consciousness; so for us, who in these lectures are treating personal experience as the exclusive subject of our study, such states of consciousness ought to form the vital chapter from which the other chapters get their light. Whether my treatment of mystical states will shed more light or darkness, I do not know, for my own constitution shuts me out from their enjoyment almost entirely, and I can speak of them only at second hand. But though forced to look upon the subject so externally, I will be as objective and receptive as I can; and I think I shall at least succeed in convincing you of the reality of the states in question, and of the paramount importance of their function.

First of all, then, I ask, What does the expression 'mystical states of consciousness' mean? How do we part off mystical states from other states?

The words 'mysticism' and 'mystical' are often used as terms of mere reproach, to throw at any opinion which we regard as vague and vast and sentimental, and without a base in either facts or logic. For some writers a 'mystic' is any person who believes in thought-transference, or spirit-return. Employed in this way the word has little value: there are too many less ambiguous synonyms. So, to keep it useful by restricting it, I will do what I did in the case of the word 'religion,' and simply propose to you four marks which, when an experience has them, may justify us in calling it mystical for the purpose of the present lectures. In this way we shall save verbal disputation, and the recriminations that generally go therewith.

From William James, *The Varieties of Religious Experience* (1902), Lects. XVI, XVII, and XX. Permission to reprint granted by Paul R. Reynolds & Son.

1. *Ineffability.*—The handiest of the marks by which I classify a state of mind as mystical is negative. The subject of it immediately says that it defies expression, that no adequate report of its contents can be given in words. It follows from this that its quality must be directly experienced; it cannot be imparted or transferred to others. In this peculiarity mystical states are more like states of feeling than like states of intellect. No one can make clear to another who has never had a certain feeling, in what the quality or worth of it consists. One must have musical ears to know the value of a symphony; one must have been in love one's self to understand a lover's state of mind. Lacking the heart or ear, we cannot interpret the musician or the lover justly, and are even likely to consider him weak-minded or absurd. The mystic finds that most of us accord to his experiences an equally imcompetent treatment.

2. *Noetic quality.*—Although so similar to states of feeling, mystical states seem to those who experience them to be also states of knowledge. They are states of insight into depths of truth unplumbed by the discursive intellect. They are illuminations, revelations, full of significance and importance, all inarticulate though they remain; and as a rule they carry with them a curious sense of authority for after-time.

These two characters will entitle any state to be called mystical, in the sense in which I use the word. Two other qualities are less sharply marked, but are usually found. These are:—

3. *Transiency.*—Mystical states cannot be sustained for long. Except in rare instances, half an hour, or at most an hour or two, seems to be the limit beyond which they fade into the light of common day. Often, when faded, their quality can but imperfectly be reproduced in memory; but when they recur it is recognized; and from one recurrence to another it is susceptible of continuous development in what is felt as inner richness and importance.

4. *Passivity.*—Although the oncoming of mystical states may be facilitated by preliminary voluntary operations, as by fixing the attention, or going through certain bodily performances, or in other ways which manuals of mysticism prescribe; yet when the characteristic sort of consciousness once has set in, the mystic feels as if his own will were in abeyance, and indeed sometimes as if he were grasped and held by a superior power. This latter peculiarity connects mystical states with certain definite phenomena of secondary or alternative personality, such as prophetic speech, automatic writing, or the mediumistic trance. When these latter conditions are well pronounced, however, there may be no recollection whatever of the phenomenon, and it may have no significance for the subject's usual inner life, to which, as it were, it makes a mere interruption. Mystical states, strictly so called, are never merely interruptive. Some memory of their content always remains, and a profound sense of their importance. They modify the inner life of the subject between the times of their recurrence. Sharp divisions in this region are, however, difficult to make, and we find all sorts of gradations and mixtures.

These four characteristics are sufficient to mark out a group of states of consciousness peculiar enough to deserve a special name and to call for careful study. Let it then be called the mystical group.

Our next step should be to gain acquaintance with some typical examples. Professional mystics at the height of their development have often elaborately organized experiences and a philosophy based thereupon. But you remember what I said in my first lecture: phenomena are best understood when placed within their series, studied in their germ and in their over-ripe decay, and compared with their exaggerated and degenerated kindred. The range of mystical experience is very wide, much too wide for us to cover in the time at our disposal. Yet the method of serial study is so essential for interpretation that if we really wish to reach conclusions we must use it. I will begin, therefore, with phenomena which claim no special religious significance, and end with those of which the religious pretensions are extreme.

The simplest rudiment of mystical experience would seem to be that deepened sense of the significance of a maxim or formula which occasionally sweeps over one. "I've heard that said all my life," we exclaim, "but I never realized its full meaning until now." "When a fellow-monk," said Luther, "one day repeated the words of the Creed: 'I believe in the forgiveness of sins,' I saw the Scripture in an entirely new light; and straightway I felt as if I were born anew. It was as if I had found the door of paradise thrown wide open." [1] This sense of deeper significance is not confined to rational propositions. Single words,[2] and conjunctions of words, effects of light on land and sea, odors and musical sounds, all bring it when the mind is tuned aright. Most of us can remember the strangely moving power of passages in certain poems read when we were young, irrational doorways as they were through which the mystery of fact, the wildness and the pang of life, stole into our hearts and thrilled them.

The words have now perhaps become mere polished surfaces for us; but lyric poetry and music are alive and significant only in proportion as they fetch these vague vistas of a life continuous with our own, beckoning and inviting, yet ever eluding our pursuit. We are alive or dead to the eternal inner message of the arts according as we have kept or lost this mystical susceptibility.

A more pronounced step forward on the mystical ladder is found in an extremely frequent phenomenon, that sudden feeling, namely, which sometimes sweeps over us, of having 'been here before,' as if at some indefinite past time, in just this place, with just these people, we were already saying just these things. As Tennyson writes:

> Moreover, something is or seems,
> That touches me with mystic gleams,
> Like glimpses of forgotten dreams—
>
> Of something felt, like something here;
> Of something done, I know not where;
> Such as no language may declare.[3]

---

[1] Newman's *Securus judicat orbis terrarum* is another instance.

[2] 'Mesopotamia' is the stock comic instance.—An excellent old German lady, who had done some traveling in her day, used to describe to me her *Sehnsucht* that she might yet visit 'Phīladelphīā,' whose wondrous name had always haunted her imagination. Of John Foster it is said that "single words (as *chalcedony*), or the names of ancient heroes, had a mighty fascination over him. 'At any time the word *hermit* was enough to transport him.' The words *woods* and *forests* would produce the most powerful emotion." Foster's Life, by RYLAND, New York, 1846, p. 3.

[3] The Two Voices. In a letter to Mr. B. P. Blood, Tennyson reports of himself as follows:—

"I have never had any revelations through anaesthetics, but a kind of waking trance—this for lack of a better word—I have frequently had, quite up from boyhood, when I have been all alone. This has come upon me through repeating my own name to myself silently, till all at once, as it were out of the intensity of the consciousness of individuality, individuality itself seemed to dissolve and fade away into boundless being, and this not a confused state but the clearest, the surest of the surest, utterly beyond words—where death was an almost laughable impossibility—the loss of personality (if so it were) seeming no extinction, but the only true life. I am ashamed of my feeble description. Have I not said the state is utterly beyond words?"

Professor Tyndall, in a letter, recalls Tennyson saying of this condition: "By God Almighty! there is no delusion in the matter! It is no nebulous ecstasy, but a state of transcendent wonder, associated with absolute clearness of mind." Memoirs of Alfred Tennyson, ii. 473.

Sir James Crichton-Browne has given the technical name of 'dreamy states' to these sudden invasions of vaguely reminiscent consciousness.[4] They bring a sense of mystery and of the metaphysical duality of things, and the feeling of an enlargement of perception which seems imminent but which never completes itself. In Dr. Crichton-Browne's opinion they connect themselves with the perplexed and scared disturbances of self-consciousness which occasionally precede epileptic attacks. I think that this learned alienist takes a rather absurdly alarmist view of an intrinsically insignificant phenomenon. He follows it along the downward ladder, to insanity; our path pursues the upward ladder chiefly. The divergence shows how important it is to neglect no part of a phenomenon's connections, for we make it appear admirable or dreadful according to the context by which we set it off.

Somewhat deeper plunges into mystical consciousness are met with in yet other dreamy states. Such feelings as these which Charles Kingsley describes are surely far from being uncommon, especially in youth:—

When I walk the fields, I am oppressed now and then with an innate feeling that everything I see has a meaning, if I could but understand it. And this feeling of being surrounded with truths which I cannot grasp amounts to indescribable awe sometimes. . . . Have you not felt that your real soul was imperceptible to your mental vision, except in a few hallowed moments?[5]

A much more extreme state of mystical consciousness is described by J. A. Symonds; and probably more persons than we suspect could give parallels to it from their own experience.

"Suddenly," writes Symonds, "at church, or in company, or when I was reading, and always, I think, when my muscles were at rest, I felt the approach of the mood. Irresistibly it took possession of my mind and will, lasted what seemed an eternity, and disappeared in a series of rapid sensations which resembled the awakening from anæsthetic influence. One reason why I disliked this kind of trance was that I could not describe it to myself. I cannot even now find words to render it intelligible. It consisted in a gradual but swiftly progressive obliteration of space, time, sensation, and the multitudinous factors of experience which seem to qualify what we are pleased to call our Self. In proportion as these conditions of ordinary consciousness were subtracted, the sense of an underlying or essential consciousness acquired intensity. At last nothing remained but a pure, absolute, abstract Self. The universe became without form and void of content. But Self persisted, formidable in its vivid keenness, feeling the most poignant doubt about reality, ready, as it seemed, to find existence break as breaks a bubble round about it. And what then? The apprehension of a coming dissolution, the grim conviction that this state was the last state of the conscious Self, the sense that I had followed the last thread of being to the verge of the abyss, and had arrived at demonstration of eternal Maya or illusion, stirred or seemed to stir me up again. The return to ordinary conditions of sentient existence began by my first recovering the power of touch, and then by the gradual though rapid influx of familiar impressions and diurnal interests. At last I felt myself once more a human being; and though the riddle of what is meant by life remained unsolved, I was thankful for this return from the abyss—this deliverance from so awful an initiation into the mysteries of skepticism.

[4] The Lancet, July 6 and 13, 1895, reprinted as the Cavendish Lecture, on Dreamy Mental States, London, Baillière, 1895. They have been a good deal discussed of late by psychologists. See, for example, BERNARD-LEROY: L'Illusion de Fausse Reconnaissance, Paris, 1898.
[5] Charles Kingsley's Life, i. 55, quoted by INGE: Christian Mysticism, London, 1899, p. 341.

"This trance recurred with diminishing frequency until I reached the age of twenty-eight. It served to impress upon my growing nature the phantasmal unreality of all the circumstances which contribute to a merely phenomenal consciousness. Often have I asked myself with anguish, on waking from that formless state of denuded, keenly sentient being, Which is the unreality? —the trance of fiery, vacant, apprehensive, skeptical Self from which I issue, or these surrounding phenomena and habits which veil that inner Self and build a self of flesh-and-blood conventionality? Again, are men the factors of some dream, the dream-like unsubstantiality of which they comprehend at such eventful moments? What would happen if the final stage of the trance were reached?" [6]

In a recital like this there is certainly something suggestive of pathology.[7] The next step into mystical states carries us into a realm that public opinion and ethical philosophy have long since branded as pathological, though private practice and certain lyric strains of poetry seem still to bear witness to its ideality. I refer to the consciousness produced by intoxicants and anæsthetics, especially by alcohol. The sway of alcohol over mankind is unquestionably due to its power to stimulate the mystical faculties of human nature, usually crushed to earth by the cold facts and dry criticisms of the sober hour. Sobriety diminishes, discriminates, and says no; drunkenness expands, unites,

and says yes. It is in fact the great exciter of the *Yes* function in man. It brings its votary from the chill periphery of things to the radiant core. It makes him for the moment one with truth. Not through mere perversity do men run after it. To the poor and the unlettered it stands in the place of symphony concerts and of literature; and it is part of the deeper mystery and tragedy of life that whiffs and gleams of something that we immediately recognize as excellent should be vouchsafed to so many of us only in the fleeting earlier phases of what in its totality is so degrading a poisoning. The drunken consciousness is one bit of the mystic consciousness, and our total opinion of it must find its place in our opinion of that larger whole.

Nitrous oxide and ether, especially nitrous oxide, when sufficiently diluted with air, stimulate the mystical consciousness in an extraordinary degree. Depth beyond depth of truth seems revealed to the inhaler. This truth fades out, however, or escapes, at the moment of coming to; and if any words remain over in which it seemed to clothe itself, they prove to be the veriest nonsense. Nevertheless, the sense of a profound meaning having been there persists; and I know more than one person who is persuaded that in the nitrous oxide trance we have a genuine metaphysical revelation.

Some years ago I myself made some observations on this aspect of nitrous oxide intoxication, and reported them in print. One conclusion was forced upon my mind at that time, and my impression of its truth has ever since remained unshaken. It is that our normal waking consciousness, rational consciousness as we call it, is but one special type of consciousness, whilst all about it, parted from it by the filmiest of screens, there lie potential forms of consciousness entirely different. We may go through life without suspecting their existence; but apply the requisite stimulus, and at a touch

---

[6] H. F. BROWN: J. A. Symonds, a Biography, London, 1895, pp. 29–31, abridged.
[7] Crichton-Browne expressly says that Symonds's "highest nerve centres were in some degree enfeebled or damaged by these dreamy mental states which afflicted him so grievously." Symonds was, however, a perfect monster of many-sided cerebral efficiency, and his critic gives no objective grounds whatever for his strange opinion, save that Symonds complained occasionally, as all susceptible and ambitious men complain, of lassitude and uncertainty as to his life's mission.

they are there in all their completeness, definite types of mentality which probably somewhere have their field of application and adaptation. No account of the universe in its totality can be final which leaves these other forms of consciousness quite disregarded. How to regard them is the question,—for they are so discontinuous with ordinary consciousness. Yet they may determine attitudes though they cannot furnish formulas, and open a region though they fail to give a map. At any rate, they forbid a premature closing of our accounts with reality. Looking back on my own experiences, they all converge towards a kind of insight to which I cannot help ascribing some metaphysical significance. The keynote of it is invariably a reconciliation. It is as if the opposites of the world, whose contradictoriness and conflict make all our difficulties and troubles, were melted into unity. Not only do they, as contrasted species, belong to one and the same genus, but *one of the species,* the nobler and better one, *is itself the genus, and so soaks up and absorbs its opposite into itself.* This is a dark saying, I know, when thus expressed in terms of common logic, but I cannot wholly escape from its authority. I feel as if it must mean something, something like what the Hegelian philosophy means, if one could only lay hold of it more clearly. Those who have ears to hear, let them hear; to me the living sense of its reality only comes in the artificial mystic state of mind.[8]

I just now spoke of friends who believe in the anæsthetic revelation. For them too it is a monistic insight, in which

the *other* in its various forms appears absorbed into the One.

"Into this pervading genius," writes one of them, "we pass, forgetting and forgotten, and thenceforth each is all, in God. There is no higher, no deeper, no other, than the life in which we are founded. 'The One remains, the many change and pass;' and each and every one of us *is* the One that remains. . . . This is the ultimatum. . . . As sure as being—whence is all our care —so sure is content, beyond duplexity, antithesis, or trouble, where I have triumphed in a solitude that God is not above."

This has the genuine religious mystic ring! I just now quoted J. A. Symonds. He also records a mystical experience with chloroform, as follows:—

After the choking and stifling had passed away, I seemed at first in a state of utter blankness; then came flashes of intense light, alternating with blackness, and with a keen vision of what was going on in the room around me, but no sensation of touch. I thought that I was near death; when, suddenly, my soul became aware of God, who was manifestly dealing with me, handling me, so to speak, in an intense personal present reality. I felt him streaming in like light upon me. . . . I cannot describe the ecstasy I felt. Then, as I gradually awoke from the influence of the anæsthetics, the old sense of my relation to the world began to return, the new sense of my relation to God began to fade. I suddenly leapt to my feet on the chair where I was sitting, and shrieked out, 'It is too horrible, it is too horrible, it is too horrible,' meaning that I could not bear this disillusionment. Then I flung myself on the ground, and at last awoke covered with blood, calling to the two surgeons (who were frightened), 'Why did you not kill me? Why would you not let me die?' Only think of it. To have felt for that long dateless ecstasy of vision the very God, in

---

[8] What reader of Hegel can doubt that that sense of a perfected Being with all its otherness soaked up into itself, which dominates his whole philosophy, must have come from the prominence in his consciousness of mystical moods like this, in most persons kept subliminal? The notion is thoroughly characteristic of the mystical level, and the *Aufgabe* of making it articulate was surely set to Hegel's intellect by mystical feeling.

all purity and tenderness and truth and absolute love, and then to find that I had after all had no revelation, but that I had been tricked by the abnormal excitement of my brain.

Yet, this question remains, Is it possible that the inner sense of reality which succeeded, when my flesh was dead to impressions from without, to the ordinary sense of physical relations, was not a delusion but an actual experience? Is it possible that I, in that moment, felt what some of the saints have said they always felt, the undemonstrable but irrefragable certainty of God? [9]

---

[9] Op. cit., pp. 78–80, abridged. I subjoin, also abridging it, another interesting anaesthetic revelation communicated to me in manuscript by a friend in England. The subject, a gifted woman, was taking ether for a surgical operation.

"I wondered if I was in a prison being tortured, and why I remembered having heard it said that people 'learn through suffering,' and in view of what I was seeing, the inadequacy of this saying struck me so much that I said, aloud, 'to suffer *is* to learn.'

"With that I became unconscious again, and my last dream immediately preceded my real coming to. It only lasted a few seconds, and was most vivid and real to me, though it may not be clear in words.

"A great Being or Power was traveling through the sky, his foot was on a kind of lightning as a wheel is on a rail, it was his pathway. The lightning was made entirely of the spirits of innumerable people close to one another, and I was one of them. He moved in a straight line, and each part of the streak or flash came into its short conscious existence only that he might travel. I seemed to be directly under the foot of God, and I thought he was grinding his own life up out of my pain. Then I saw that what he had been trying with all his might to do was to *change his course,* to *bend* the line of lightning to which he was tied, in the direction in which he wanted to go. I felt my flexibility and helplessness, and knew that he would succeed. He bended me, turning his corner by means of my hurt, hurting me more than I had ever been hurt in my life, and at the acutest point of this, as he passed, I *saw.* I understood for a moment things that I have now forgotten, things that no one could remember while retaining sanity. The

With this we make connection with religious mysticism pure and simple. Symonds's question takes us back to those examples which you will remember my quoting in the lecture on the Reality of the Unseen, of sudden realization of the immediate presence of God. The phenomenon in one shape or another is not uncommon.

"I know," writes Mr. Trine, "an officer on our police force who has told me that many times when off duty, and on his way home in the evening, there comes to him such a vivid and vital realization of his oneness with

---

angle was an obtuse angle, and I remember thinking as I woke that had he made it a right or acute angle, I should have both suffered and 'seen' still more, and should probably have died.

"He went on and I came to. In that moment the whole of my life passed before me, including each little meaningless piece of distress, and I *understood* them. *This* was what it had all meant, *this* was the piece of work it had all been contributing to do. I did not see God's purpose, I only saw his intentness and his entire relentlessness towards his means. He thought no more of me than a man thinks of hurting a cork when he is opening wine, or hurting a cartridge when he is firing. And yet, on waking, my first feeling was, and it came with tears, 'Domine non sum digna,' for I had been lifted into a position for which I was too small. I realized that in that half hour under ether I had served God more distinctly and purely than I had ever done in my life before, or than I am capable of desiring to do. I was the means of his achieving and revealing something, I know not what or to whom, and that, to the exact extent of my capacity for suffering.

"While regaining consciousness, I wondered why, since I had gone so deep, I had seen nothing of what the saints call the *love* of God, nothing but his relentlessness. And then I heard an answer, which I could only just catch, saying, 'Knowledge and Love are One, and the *measure* is suffering'—I give the words as they came to me. With that I came finally to (into what seemed a dream world compared with the reality of what I was leaving), and I saw that what would be called the 'cause' of my experience was a slight operation under insufficient ether, in a

this Infinite Power, and this Spirit of Infinite Peace so takes hold of and so fills him, that it seems as if his feet could hardly keep to the pavement, so buoyant and so exhilarated does he become by reason of this inflowing tide." [10]

Certain aspects of nature seem to have a peculiar power of awakening such mystical moods.[11] Most of the striking cases which I have collected have occurred out of doors. Literature has commemorated this fact in many passages of great beauty —this extract, for example, from Amiel's Journal Intime:—

Shall I ever again have any of those prodigious reveries which sometimes came to me in former days? One day, in youth, at sunrise, sitting in the ruins of the castle of Faucigny; and again in the mountains, under the noonday sun, above Lavey, lying at the foot of a tree and visited by three butterflies; once more at night upon the shingly shore of the Northern Ocean, my back upon the sand and my vision ranging through the milky way;—such grand and spacious, immortal, cosmogonic reveries, when one reaches to the stars, when one owns the infinite! Moments divine, ecstatic hours; in which our thought flies from world to world, pierces the great enigma, breathes with a respiration broad, tranquil, and deep as the

---

bed pushed up against a window, a common city window in a common city street. If I had to formulate a few of the things I then caught a glimpse of, they would run somewhat as follows:—

"The eternal necessity of suffering and its eternal vicariousness. The veiled and incommunicable nature of the worst sufferings;— the passivity of genius, how it is essentially instrumental and defenseless, moved, not moving, it must do what it does;—the impossibility of discovery without its price;— finally, the excess of what the suffering 'seer' or genius pays over what his generation gains. (He seems like one who sweats his life out to earn enough to save a district from famine, and just as he staggers back, dying and satisfied, bringing a lac of rupees to buy grain with, God lifts the lac away, dropping *one* rupee, and says, 'That you may give them. That you have earned for them. The rest is for ME.') I perceived also in a way never to be forgotten, the excess of what we see over what we can demonstrate.

"And so on!—these things may seem to you delusions, or truisms; but for me they are dark truths, and the power to put them into even such words as these has been given me by an ether dream."

[10] In Tune with the Infinite, p. 137.

[11] The larger God may then swallow up the smaller one. I take this from Starbuck's manuscript collection:—

"I never lost the consciousness of the presence of God until I stood at the foot of the Horseshoe Falls, Niagara. Then I lost him in the immensity of what I saw. I also lost myself, feeling that I was an atom too small for the notice of Almighty God."

I subjoin another similar case from Starbuck's collection:—

"In that time the consciousness of God's nearness came to me sometimes. I say God, to describe what is indescribable. A presence, I might say, yet that is too suggestive of personality, and the moments of which I speak did not hold the consciousness of a personality, but something in myself made me feel myself a part of something bigger than I, that was controlling. I felt myself one with the grass, the trees, birds, insects, everything in Nature. I exulted in the mere fact of existence, of being a part of it all—the drizzling rain, the shadows of the clouds, the tree-trunks, and so on. In the years following, such moments continued to come, but I wanted them constantly. I knew so well the satisfaction of losing self in a perception of supreme power and love, that I was unhappy because that perception was not constant." The cases quoted in my third lecture, pp. 67, 68, 70, are still better ones of this type. In her essay, The Loss of Personality, in The Atlantic Monthly (vol. lxxxv. p. 195), Miss Ethel D. Puffer explains that the vanishing of the sense of self, and the feeling of immediate unity with the object, is due to the disappearance, in these rapturous experiences, of the motor adjustments which habitually intermediate between the constant background of consciousness (which is the Self) and the object in the foreground, whatever it may be. I must refer the reader to the highly instructive article, which seems to me to throw light upon the psychological conditions, though it fails to account for the rapture or the revelation-value of the experience in the Subject's eyes.

respiration of the ocean, serene and limitless as the blue firmament; . . . instants of irresistible intuition in which one feels one's self great as the universe, and calm as a god. . . . What hours, what memories! The vestiges they leave behind are enough to fill us with belief and enthusiasm, as if they were visits of the Holy Ghost.[12]

Here is a similar record from the memoirs of that interesting German idealist, Malwida von Maysenbug:—

I was alone upon the seashore as all these thoughts flowed over me, liberating and reconciling; and now again, as once before in distant days in the Alps of Dauphiné, I was impelled to kneel down, this time before the illimitable ocean, symbol of the Infinite. I felt that I prayed as I had never prayed before, and knew now what prayer really is: to return from the solitude of individuation into the consciousness of unity with all that is, to kneel down as one that passes away, and to rise up as one imperishable. Earth, heaven, and sea resounded as in one vast world-encircling harmony. It was as if the chorus of all the great who had ever lived were about me. I felt myself one with them, and it appeared as if I heard their greeting: 'Thou too belongest to the company of those who overcome.'[13]

The well-known passage from Walt Whitman is a classical expression of this sporadic type of mystical experience.

I believe in you, my Soul . . .
Loaf with me on the grass, loose the
     stop from your throat; . . .
Only the lull I like, the hum of your
     valved voice.
I mind how once we lay, such a trans-
     parent summer morning.
Swiftly arose and spread around me
     the peace and knowledge that pass
     all the argument of the earth,

And I know that the hand of God is
     the promise of my own,
And I know that the spirit of God is
     the brother of my own,
And that all the men ever born are
     also my brothers and the women
     my sisters and lovers,
And that a kelson of the creation is
     love.[14]

I could easily give more instances, but one will suffice. I take it from the Autobiography of J. Trevor.[15]

One brilliant Sunday morning, my wife and boys went to the Unitarian Chapel in Macclesfield. I felt it impossible to accompany them—as though to leave the sunshine on the hills, and go down there to the chapel, would be for the time an act of spiritual suicide. And I felt such need for new inspiration and expansion in my life. So, very reluctantly and sadly, I left my wife and boys to go down into the town, while I went further up into the hills with my stick and my dog. In the loveliness of the morning, and the beauty of the hills and valleys, I soon lost my sense of sadness and regret. For nearly an hour I walked along the road to the

---

[12] Op. cit., i. 43–44.
[13] Memoiren einer Idealistin, 5te Auflage, 1900, iii. 166. For years she had been unable to pray, owing to materialistic belief.

[14] Whitman in another place expresses in a quieter way what was probably with him a chronic mystical perception: "There is," he writes, "apart from mere intellect, in the make-up of every superior human identity, a wondrous something that realizes without argument, frequently without what is called education (though I think it the goal and apex of all education deserving the name), an intuition of the absolute balance, in time and space, of the whole of this multifariousness, this revel of fools, and incredible make-believe and general unsettledness, we call *the world;* a soul-sight of that divine clue and unseen thread which holds the whole congeries of things, all history and time, and all events, however trivial, however momentous, like a leashed dog in the hand of the hunter. [Of] such soul-sight and root-centre for the mind mere optimism explains only the surface." Whitman charges it against Carlyle that he lacked this perception. Specimen Days and Collect, Philadelphia, 1882, p. 174.
[15] My Quest for God, London, 1897, pp. 268, 269, abridged.

'Cat and Fiddle,' and then returned. On the way back, suddenly, without warning, I felt that I was in Heaven —an inward state of peace and joy and assurance indescribably intense, accompanied with a sense of being bathed in a warm glow of light, as though the external condition had brought about the internal effect— a feeling of having passed beyond the body, though the scene around me stood out more clearly and as if nearer to me than before, by reason of the illumination in the midst of which I seemed to be placed. This deep emotion lasted, though with decreasing strength, until I reached home, and for some time after, only gradually passing away.

The writer adds that having had further experiences of a similar sort, he now knows them well.

"The spiritual life," he writes, "justifies itself to those who live it; but what can we say to those who do not understand? This, at least, we can say, that it is a life whose experiences are proved real to their possessor, because they remain with him when brought closest into contact with the objective realities of life. Dreams cannot stand this test. We wake from them to find that they are but dreams. Wanderings of an overwrought brain do not stand this test. These highest experiences that I have had of God's presence have been rare and brief—flashes of consciousness which have compelled me to exclaim with surprise—God is *here!*—or conditions of exaltation and insight, less intense, and only gradually passing away. I have severely questioned the worth of these moments. To no soul have I named them, lest I should be building my life and work on mere phantasies of the brain. But I find that, after every questioning and test, they stand out to-day as the most real experiences of my life, and experiences which have explained and justified and unified all past experiences and all past growth. Indeed, their reality and their

far-reaching significance are ever becoming more clear and evident. When they came, I was living the fullest, strongest, sanest, deepest life. I was not seeking them. What I was seeking, with resolute determination, was to live more intensely my own life, as against what I knew would be the adverse judgment of the world. It was in the most real seasons that the Real Presence came, and I was aware that I was immersed in the infinite ocean of God." [16]

Even the least mystical of you must by this time be convinced of the existence of mystical moments as states of consciousness of an entirely specific quality, and of the deep impression which they make on those who have them. A Canadian psychiatrist, Dr. R. M. Bucke, gives to the more distinctly characterized of these phenomena the name of cosmic consciousness. "Cosmic consciousness in its more striking instances is not," Dr. Bucke says, "simply an expansion or extension of the self-conscious mind with which we are all familiar, but the super-addition of a function as distinct from any possessed by the average man as *self*-consciousness is distinct from any function possessed by one of the higher animals."

The prime characteristic of cosmic consciousness is a consciousness of the cosmos, that is, of the life and order of the universe. Along with the consciousness of the cosmos there occurs an intellectual enlightenment which alone would place the individual on a new plane of existence—would make him almost a member of a new species. To this is added a state of moral exaltation, an indescribable feeling of elevation, elation, and joyousness, and a quickening of the moral sense, which is fully as striking, and more important than is the enhanced intellectual power. With these come what may be called a sense of immortality, a con-

[16] Op. cit., pp. 256, 257, abridged.

sciousness of eternal life, not a conviction that he shall have this, but the consciousness that he has it already.[17]

It was Dr. Bucke's own experience of a typical onset of cosmic consciousness in his own person which led him to investigate it in others. He has printed his conclusions in a highly interesting volume, from which I take the following account of what occurred to him:—

I had spent the evening in a great city, with two friends, reading and discussing poetry and philosophy. We parted at midnight. I had a long drive in a hansom to my lodging. My mind, deeply under the influence of the ideas, images, and emotions called up by the reading and talk, was calm and peaceful. I was in a state of quiet, almost passive enjoyment, not actually thinking, but letting ideas, images, and emotions flow of themselves, as it were, through my mind. All at once, without warning of any kind, I found myself wrapped in a flame-colored cloud. For an instant I thought of fire, an immense conflagration somewhere close by in that great city; the next, I knew that the fire was within myself. Directly afterward there came upon me a sense of exultation, of immense joyousness accompanied or immediately followed by an intellectual illumination impossible to describe. Among other things, I did not merely come to believe, but I saw that the universe is not composed of dead matter, but is, on the contrary, a living Presence; I became conscious in myself of eternal life. It was not a conviction that I would have eternal life, but a consciousness that I possessed eternal life then; I saw that all men are immortal; that the cosmic order is such that without any peradventure all things work together for the good of each and all; that the foundation principle of the world, of all the worlds, is what we call love, and that the hap-

piness of each and all is in the long run absolutely certain. The vision lasted a few seconds and was gone; but the memory of it and the sense of the reality of what it taught has remained during the quarter of a century which has since elapsed. I knew that what the vision showed was true. I had attained to a point of view from which I saw that it must be true. That view, that conviction, I may say that consciousness, has never, even during periods of the deepest depression, been lost.[18]

We have now seen enough of this cosmic or mystic consciousness, as it comes sporadically. We must next pass to its methodical cultivation as an element of the religious life. Hindus, Buddhists, Mohammedans, and Christians all have cultivated it methodically. YOGA

In India, training in mystical insight has been known from time immemorial under the name of yoga. Yoga means the experimental union of the individual with the divine. It is based on persevering exercise; and the diet, posture, breathing, intellectual concentration, and moral discipline vary slightly in the different systems which teach it. The yogi, or disciple, who has by these means overcome the obscurations of his lower nature sufficiently, enters into the condition termed *samâdhi,* "comes face to face with facts which no instinct or reason can ever know." He learns—

That the mind itself has a higher state of existence, beyond reason, a superconscious state, and that when the mind gets to that higher state, then this knowledge beyond reasoning comes. . . . All the different steps in yoga are intended to bring us scientifically to the superconscious state or samâdhi. . . . Just as unconscious work is beneath consciousness, so there is an-

---

[17] Cosmic Consciousness: a study in the evolution of the human Mind, Philadelphia, 1901, p. 2.

[18] Loc. cit., pp. 7, 8. My quotation follows the privately printed pamphlet which preceded Dr. Bucke's larger work, and differs verbally a little from the text of the latter.

other work which is above consciousness, and which, also, is not accompanied with the feeling of egoism. . . . There is no feeling of *I*, and yet the mind works, desireless, free from restlessness, objectless, bodiless. Then the Truth shines in its full effulgence, and we know ourselves—for Samâdhi lies potential in us all—for what we truly are, free, immortal, omnipotent, loosed from the finite, and its contrasts of good and evil altogether, and identical with the Atman or Universal Soul.[19]

The Vedantists say that one may stumble into superconsciousness sporadically, without the previous discipline, but it is then impure. Their test of its purity, like our test of religion's value, is empirical: its fruits must be good for life. When a man comes out of Samâdhi, they assure us that he remains "enlightened, a sage, a prophet, a saint, his whole character changed, his life changed, illumined." [20]

The Buddhists use the word 'samâdhi' as well as the Hindus; but 'dhyâna' is their special word for higher states of contemplation. There seem to be four stages recognized in dhyâna. The first stage comes through concentration of the mind upon one point. It excludes desire, but not discernment or judgment: it is still intellectual. In the second stage the intellectual functions drop off, and the satisfied sense of unity remains. In the third stage the satisfaction departs, and indifference begins, along with memory and self-consciousness. In the fourth stage the indifference, memory, and self-consciousness are perfected. [Just what 'memory' and 'self-consciousness' mean in this connection is doubtful. They cannot be the faculties familiar to us in the lower life.] Higher stages still of contemplation are mentioned—a region where there exists nothing, and where the meditator says: "There exists absolutely nothing," and stops. Then he reaches another region where he says: "There are neither ideas nor absence of ideas," and stops again. Then another region where, "having reached the end of both idea and perception, he stops finally." This would seem to be, not yet Nirvâna, but as close an approach to it as this life affords.[21]

In the Mohammedan world the Sufi sect and various dervish bodies are the possessors of the mystical tradition. The Sufis have existed in Persia from the earliest times, and as their pantheism is so at variance with the hot and rigid monotheism of the Arab mind, it has been suggested that Sufism must have been inoculated into Islam by Hindu influences. We Christians know little of Sufism, for its secrets are disclosed only to those initiated. To give its existence a certain liveliness in your minds, I will quote a Moslem document, and pass away from the subject.

Al-Ghazzali, a Persian philosopher and theologian, who flourished in the eleventh century, and ranks as one of the greatest doctors of the Moslem church, has left us one of the few autobiographies to be found outside of Christian literature. Strange that a species of book so abundant

---

[19] My quotations are from VIVEKANANDA, Raja Yoga, London, 1896. The completest source of information on Yoga is the work translated by VIHARI LALA MITRA: Yoga Vasishta Maha Ramayana, 4 vols., Calcutta, 1891–99.

[20] A European witness, after carefully comparing the results of Yoga with those of the hypnotic or dreamy states artificially producible by us, says: "It makes of its true disciples good, healthy, and happy men. . . . Through the mastery which the yogi attains over his thoughts and his body, he grows into a 'character.' By the subjection of his impulses and propensities to his will, and the fixing of the latter upon the ideal of goodness, he becomes a 'personality' hard to influence by others, and thus almost the opposite of what we usually imagine a 'medium' so-called, or 'psychic subject' to be." KARL KELLNER: Yoga: Eline Skizze, München, 1896, p. 21.

[21] I follow the account in C. F. KOEPPEN: Die Religion des Buddha, Berlin, 1857, i. 585 ff.

among ourselves should be so little represented elsewhere—the absence of strictly personal confessions is the chief difficulty to the purely literary student who would like to become acquainted with the inwardness of religions other than the Christian.

M. Schmölders has translated a part of Al-Ghazzali's autobiography into French: [22]—

"The Science of the Sufis," says the Moslem author, "aims at detaching the heart from all that is not God, and at giving to it for sole occupation the meditation of the divine being. Theory being more easy for me than practice, I read [certain books] until I understood all that can be learned by study and hearsay. Then I recognized that what pertains most exclusively to their method is just what no study can grasp, but only transport, ecstasy, and the transformation of the soul. How great, for example, is the difference between knowing the definitions of health, of satiety, with their causes and conditions, and being really healthy or filled. How different to know in what drunkenness consists,—as being a state occasioned by a vapor that rises from the stomach,—and *being* drunk effectively. Without doubt, the drunken man knows neither the definition of drunkenness nor what makes it interesting for science. Being drunk, he knows nothing; whilst the physician, although not drunk, knows well in what drunkenness consists, and what are its predisposing conditions. Similarly there is a difference between knowing the nature of abstinence, and *being* abstinent or having one's soul detached from the world.—Thus I had learned what words could teach of Sufism, but what was left could be learned neither by study nor through the ears, but solely by giving one's

self up to ecstasy and leading a pious life.

"Reflecting on my situation, I found myself tied down by a multitude of bonds—temptations on every side. Considering my teaching, I found it was impure before God. I saw myself struggling with all my might to achieve glory and to spread my name. [Here follows an account of his six months' hesitation to break away from the conditions of his life at Bagdad, at the end of which he fell ill with a paralysis of the tongue.] Then, feeling my own weakness, and having entirely given up my own will, I repaired to God like a man in distress who has no more resources. He answered, as he answers the wretch who invokes him. My heart no longer felt any difficulty in renouncing glory, wealth, and my children. So I quitted Bagdad, and reserving from my fortune only what was indispensable for my subsistence, I distributed the rest. I went to Syria, where I remained about two years, with no other occupation than living in retreat and solitude, conquering my desires, combating my passions, training myself to purify my soul, to make my character perfect, to prepare my heart for meditating on God— all according to the methods of the Sufis, as I had read of them.

"This retreat only increased my desire to live in solitude, and to complete the purification of my heart and fit it for meditation. But the vicissitudes of the times, the affairs of the family, the need of subsistence, changed in some respects my primitive resolve, and interfered with my plans for a purely solitary life. I had never yet found myself completely in ecstasy, save in a few single hours; nevertheless, I kept the hope of attaining this state. Every time that the accidents led me astray, I sought to return; and in this situation I spent ten years. During this solitary state things were revealed to me which it is impossible either to describe or to point out. I recognized for certain that the Sufis are assuredly walking in the

---

[22] For a full account of him, see D. B. MACDONALD: The Life of Al-Ghazzali, in the Journal of the American Oriental Society, 1899, vol. xx. p. 71.

path of God. Both in their acts and in their inaction, whether internal or external, they are illumined by the light which proceeds from the prophetic source. The first condition for a Sufi is to purge his heart entirely of all that is not God. The next key of the contemplative life consists in the humble prayers which escape from the fervent soul, and in the meditations on God in which the heart is swallowed up entirely. But in reality this is only the beginning of the Sufi life, the end of Sufism being total absorption in God. The intuitions and all that precede are, so to speak, only the threshold for those who enter. From the beginning, revelations take place in so flagrant a shape that the Sufis see before them, whilst wide awake, the angels and the souls of the prophets. They hear their voices and obtain their favors. Then the transport rises from the perception of forms and figures to a degree which escapes all expression, and which no man may seek to give an account of without his words involving sin.

"Whoever has had no experience of the transport knows of the true nature of prophetism nothing but the name. He may meanwhile be sure of its existence, both by experience and by what he hears the Sufis say. As there are men endowed only with the sensitive faculty who reject what is offered them in the way of objects of the pure understanding, so there are intellectual men who reject and avoid the things perceived by the prophetic faculty. A blind man can understand nothing of colors save what he has learned by narration and hearsay. Yet God has brought prophetism near to men in giving them all a state analogous to it in its principal characters. This state is sleep. If you were to tell a man who was himself without experience of such a phenomenon that there are people who at times swoon away so as to resemble dead men, and who [in dreams] yet perceive things that are hidden, he would deny it [and give his reasons]. Nevertheless, his arguments would be refuted by actual experience. Wherefore, just as the understanding is a stage of human life in which an eye opens to discern various intellectual objects uncomprehended by sensation; just so in the prophetic the sight is illumined by a light which uncovers hidden things and objects which the intellect fails to reach. The chief properties of prophetism are perceptible only during the transport, by those who embrace the Sufi life. The prophet is endowed with qualities to which you possess nothing analogous, and which consequently you cannot possibly understand. How should you know their true nature, since one knows only what one can comprehend? But the transport which one attains by the method of the Sufis is like an immediate perception, as if one touched the objects with one's hand." [23]

This incommunicableness of the transport is the keynote of all mysticism. Mystical truth exists for the individual who has the transport, but for no one else. In this, as I have said, it resembles the knowledge given to us in sensations more than that given by conceptual thought. Thought, with its remoteness and abstractness, has often enough in the history of philosophy been contrasted unfavorably with sensation. It is a commonplace of metaphysics that God's knowledge cannot be discursive but must be intuitive, that is, must be constructed more after the pattern of what in ourselves is called immediate feeling, than after that of proposition and judgment. But *our* immediate feelings have no content but what the five senses supply; and we have seen and shall see again that mystics may emphatically deny that the senses play any part in the very highest type of knowledge which their transports yield.

In the Christian church there have always been mystics. Although many of them have been viewed with suspicion,

[23] A. SCHMÖLDERS: Essai sur les écoles philosophiques chez les Arabes, Paris, 1842, pp. 54–68, abridged.

some have gained favor in the eyes of the authorities. The experiences of these have been treated as precedents, and a codified system of mystical theology has been based upon them, in which everything legitimate finds its place.[24] The basis of the system is 'orison' or meditation, the methodical elevation of the soul towards God. Through the practice of orison the higher levels of mystical experience may be attained. It is odd that Protestantism, especially evengelical Protestantism, should seemingly have abandoned everything methodical in this line. Apart from what prayer may lead to, Protestant mystical experience appears to have been almost exclusively sporadic. It has been left to our mind-curers to reintroduce methodical meditation into our religious life.

The first thing to be aimed at in orison is the mind's detachment from outer sensations, for these interfere with its concentration upon ideal things. Such manuals as Saint Ignatius's Spiritual Exercises recommend the disciple to expel sensation by a graduated series of efforts to imagine holy scenes. The acme of this kind of discipline would be a semi-hallucinatory mono-ideism—an imaginary figure of Christ, for example, coming fully to occupy the mind. Sensorial images of this sort, whether literal or symbolic, play an enormous part in mysticism.[25] But in certain cases imagery may fall away entirely, and in the very highest raptures it tends to do so. The state of consciousness becomes then insusceptible of any verbal description. Mystical teachers are unanimous as to this. Saint John of the Cross, for instance, one of the best of them, thus describes the condition called the 'union of love,' which, he says, is reached by 'dark contemplation.' In this the Deity compenetrates the soul, but in such a hidden way that the soul—

finds no terms, no means, no comparison whereby to render the sublimity of the wisdom and the delicacy of the spiritual feeling with which she is filled. . . . We receive this mystical knowledge of God clothed in none of the kinds of images, in none of the sensible representations, which our mind makes use of in other circumstances. Accordingly in this knowledge, since the senses and the imagination are not employed, we get neither form nor impression, nor can we give any account or furnish any likeness, although the mysterious and sweet-tasting wisdom comes home so clearly to the inmost parts of our soul. Fancy a man seeing a certain kind of thing for the first time in his life. He can understand it, use and enjoy it, but he cannot apply a name to it, nor communicate any idea of it, even though all the while it be a mere thing of sense. How much greater will be his powerlessness when it goes beyond the senses! This is the peculiarity of the divine language. The more infused, intimate, spiritual, and supersensible it is, the more does it exceed the senses, both inner and outer, and impose silence upon them. . . . The soul then feels as if placed in a vast and profound solitude, to which no created thing has access, in an immense and boundless desert, desert the more delicious the more solitary it is. There, in this abyss of wisdom, the soul grows by what it drinks in from the wellsprings of the comprehension of love, . . . and recognizes, however sublime and learned may be the terms we employ, how utterly vile, insignificant, and improper they are, when we seek

---

[24] Görres's Christliche Mystik gives a full account of the facts. So does Ribet's Mystique Divine, 2 vols., Paris, 1890. A still more methodical modern work is the Mystica Theologia of Vallgornera, 2 vols., Turin, 1890.

[25] M. Récéjac, in a recent volume, makes them essential. Mysticism he defines as "the tendency to draw near to the Absolute morally, *and by the aid of Symbols.*" See his Fondements de la Connaissance mystique, Paris, 1897, p. 66. But there are unquestionably mystical conditions in which sensible symbols play no part.

to discourse of divine things by their means.[26]

I cannot pretend to detail to you the sundry stages of the Christian mystical life.[27] Our time would not suffice, for one thing; and moreover, I confess that the subdivisions and names which we find in the Catholic books seem to me to represent nothing objectively distinct. So many men, so many minds: I imagine that these experiences can be as infinitely varied as are the idiosyncrasies of individuals.

The cognitive aspects of them, their value in the way of revelation, is what we are directly concerned with, and it is easy to show by citation how strong an impression they leave of being revelations of new depths of truth. Saint Teresa is the expert of experts in describing such conditions, so I will turn immediately to what she says of one of the highest of them, the 'orison of union.'

"In the orison of union," says Saint Teresa, "the soul is fully awake as regards God, but wholly asleep as regards things of this world and in respect of herself. During the short time the union lasts, she is as it were deprived of every feeling, and even if she would, she could not think of any single thing. Thus she needs to employ no artifice in order to arrest the use of her understanding: it remains so

[26] Saint John of the Cross: The Dark Night of the Soul, book ii. ch. xvii., in Vie et Œuvres, 3me édition, Paris, 1893, iii. 428–432. Chapter xi. of book ii. of Saint John's Ascent of Carmel is devoted to showing the harmfulness for the mystical life of the use of sensible imagery.
[27] In particular I omit mention of visual and auditory hallucinations, verbal and graphic automatisms, and such marvels as 'levitation,' stigmatization, and the healing of disease. These phenomena, which mystics have often presented (or are believed to have presented), have no essential mystical significance, for they occur with no consciousness of illumination whatever, when they occur, as they often do, in persons of non-mystical mind. Consciousness of illumination is for us the essential mark of 'mystical' states.

stricken with inactivity that she neither knows what she loves, nor in what manner she loves, nor what she wills. In short, she is utterly dead to the things of the world and lives solely in God. . . . I do not even know whether in this state she has enough life left to breathe. It seems to me she has not; or at least that if she does breathe, she is unaware of it. Her intellect would fain understand something of what is going on within her, but it has so little force now that it can act in no way whatsoever. So a person who falls into a deep faint appears as if dead. . . .

"Thus does God, when he raises a soul to union with himself, suspend the natural action of all her faculties. She neither sees, hears, nor understands, so long as she is united with God. But this time is always short, and it seems even shorter than it is. God establishes himself in the interior of this soul in such a way, that when she returns to herself, it is wholly impossible for her to doubt that she has been in God, and God in her. This truth remains so strongly impressed on her that, even though many years should pass without the condition returning, she can neither forget the favor she received, nor doubt of its reality. If you, nevertheless, ask how it is possible that the soul can see and understand that she has been in God, since during the union she has neither sight nor understanding, I reply that she does not see it then, but that she sees it clearly later, after she has returned to herself, not by any vision, but by a certitude which abides with her and which God alone can give her. I knew a person who was ignorant of the truth that God's mode of being in everything must be either by presence, by power, or by essence, but who, after having received the grace of which I am speaking, believed this truth in the most unshakable manner. So much so that, having consulted a half-learned man who was as ignorant on this point as she had been before she was enlightened, when he replied that God is in us only by 'grace,' she disbelieved his reply, so sure she was of the true answer; and when she came to ask wiser doctors, they confirmed her in her belief, which much consoled her. . . .

"But how, you will repeat, *can* one have such certainty in respect to what one does not see? This question, I am powerless to answer. These are secrets of God's omnipotence which it does not appertain to me to penetrate. All that I know is that I tell the truth; and I shall never believe that any soul who does not possess this certainty has ever been really united to God." [28]

The kinds of truth communicable in mystical ways, whether these be sensible or supersensible, are various. Some of them relate to this world,—visions of the future, the reading of hearts, the sudden understanding of texts, the knowledge of distant events, for example; but the most important revelations are theological or metaphysical.

Saint Ignatius confessed one day to Father Laynez that a single hour of meditation at Manresa had taught him more truths about heavenly things than all the teachings of all the doctors put together could have taught him. . . . One day in orison, on the steps of the choir of the Dominican church, he saw in a distinct manner the plan of divine wisdom in the creation of the world. On another occasion, during a procession, his spirit was ravished in God, and it was given him to contemplate, in a form and images fitted to the weak understanding of a dweller on the earth, the deep mystery of the holy Trinity. This last vision flooded his heart with such sweetness, that the mere memory of it in after times made him shed abundant tears.[29]

Similarly with Saint Teresa. "One day, being in orison," she writes, "it was granted me to perceive in one instant how all things are seen and contained in God. I did not perceive them in their proper form, and nevertheless the view I had of them was of a sovereign clearness, and has remained vividly impressed upon my soul. It is one of the most signal of all

and replenished with the heavenly knowledge; insomuch as going abroad into the fields to a green, at Görlitz, he there sat down, and viewing the herbs and grass of the field, in his inward light he saw into their essences, use, and properties, which was discovered to him by their lineaments, figures, and signatures." Of a later period of experience he writes: "In one quarter of an hour I saw and knew more than if I had been many years together at an university. For I saw and knew the being of all things, the Byss and the Abyss, and the eternal generation of the holy Trinity, the descent and original of the world and of all creatures through the divine wisdom. I knew and saw in myself all the three worlds, the external and visible world being of a procreation or extern birth from both the internal and spiritual worlds; and I saw and knew the whole working essence, in the evil and in the good, and the mutual original and existence; and likewise how the fruitful bearing womb of eternity brought forth. So that I did not only greatly wonder at it, but did also exceedingly rejoice, albeit I could very hardly apprehend the same in my external man and set it down with the pen. For I had a thorough view of the universe as in a chaos, wherein all things are couched and wrapt up, but it was impossible for me to explicate the same." Jacob Behmen's Theosophic Philosophy, etc., by EDWARD TAYLOR, London, 1691, pp. 425, 427, abridged. So George Fox: "I was come up to the state of Adam in which he was before he fell. The creation was opened to me; and it was showed me, how all things had their names given to them, according to their nature and virtue. I was at a stand in my mind, whether I should practice physic for the good of mankind, seeing the nature and virtues of the creatures were so opened to me by the Lord." Journal, Philadelphia, no date, p. 69. Contemporary 'Clairvoyance' abounds in similar revelations. Andrew Jackson Davis's cosmogonies, for example, or certain experiences related in the delectable 'Reminiscences and Memories of Henry Thomas Butterworth,' Lebanon, Ohio, 1886.

---

[28] The Interior Castle, Fifth Abode, ch. i., in Œuvres, translated by BOUIX, iii. 421–424.

[29] BARTOLI-MICHEL: Vie de Saint Ignace de Loyola, i. 34–36. Others have had illuminations about the created world, Jacob Boehme, for instance. At the age of twenty-five he was "surrounded by the divine light,

the graces which the Lord has granted me. . . . The view was so subtle and delicate that the understanding cannot grasp it." [30]

She goes on to tell how it was as if the Deity were an enormous and sovereignly limpid diamond, in which all our actions were contained in such a way that their full sinfulness appeared evident as never before. On another day, she relates, while she was reciting the Athanasian Creed,—

> Our Lord made me comprehend in what way it is that one God can be in three Persons. He made me see it so clearly that I remained as extremely surprised as I was comforted, . . . and now, when I think of the holy Trinity, or hear It spoken of, I understand how the three adorable Persons form only one God and I experience an unspeakable happiness.

On still another occasion, it was given to Saint Teresa to see and understand in what wise the Mother of God had been assumed into her place in Heaven.[31]

The deliciousness of some of these states seems to be beyond anything known in ordinary consciousness. It evidently involves organic sensibilities, for it is spoken of as something too extreme to be borne, and as verging on bodily pain.[32] But it is too subtle and piercing a delight for ordinary words to denote. God's touches, the wounds of his spear, references to ebriety and to nuptial union have to figure in the phraseology by which it is shadowed forth. Intellect and senses both swoon away in these highest states of ecstasy. "If our understanding comprehends," says Saint Teresa, "it is in a mode which remains unknown to it, and it can understand nothing of what it comprehends. For my own part, I do not believe that it does comprehend, because, as I said, it does not understand itself to do so. I confess that it is all a mystery in which I am lost." [33] In the condition called *raptus* or ravishment by theologians, breathing and circulation are so depressed that it is a question among the doctors whether the soul be or be not temporarily dissevered from the body. One must read Saint Teresa's descriptions and the very exact distinctions which she makes, to persuade one's self that one is dealing, not with imaginary experiences, but with phenomena which, however rare, follow perfectly definite psychological types.

To the medical mind these ecstasies signify nothing but suggested and imitated hypnoid states, on an intellectual basis of superstition, and a corporeal one of degeneration and hysteria. Undoubtedly these pathological conditions have existed in many and possibly in all the cases, but that fact tells us nothing about the value for knowledge of the consciousness which they induce. To pass a spiritual judgment upon these states, we must not content ourselves with superficial medical talk, but inquire into their fruits for life.

Their fruits appear to have been various. Stupefaction, for one thing, seems not to have been altogether absent as a result. You may remember the helplessness in the kitchen and schoolroom of poor Margaret Mary Alacoque. Many other ecstatics would have perished but for the care taken of them by admiring followers. The 'otherworldliness' encouraged by the mystical consciousness makes this over-abstraction from practical life

---

[30] Vie, pp. 581, 582.

[31] Loc. cit., p. 574.

[32] Saint Teresa discriminates between pain in which the body has a part and pure spiritual pain (Interior Castle, 6th Abode, ch. xi.). As for the bodily part in these celestial joys, she speaks of it as "penetrating to the marrow of the bones, whilst earthly pleasures affect only the surface of the senses. I think," she adds, "that this is a just description, and I cannot make it better." Ibid., 5th Abode, ch. i.

[33] Vie, p. 198.

peculiarly liable to befall mystics in whom the character is naturally passive and the intellect feeble; but in natively strong minds and characters we find quite opposite results. The great Spanish mystics, who carried the habit of ecstasy as far as it has often been carried, appear for the most part to have shown indomitable spirit and energy, and all the more so for the trances in which they indulged.

Saint Ignatius was a mystic, but his mysticism made him assuredly one of the most powerfully practical human engines that ever lived. Saint John of the Cross, writing of the intuitions and 'touches' by which God reaches the substance of the soul, tells us that—

> They enrich it marvelously. A single one of them may be sufficient to abolish at a stroke certain imperfections of which the soul during its whole life had vainly tried to rid itself, and to leave it adorned with virtues and loaded with supernatural gifts. A single one of these intoxicating consolations may reward it for all the labors undergone in its life—even were they numberless. Invested with an invincible courage, filled with an impassioned desire to suffer for its God, the soul then is seized with a strange torment—that of not being allowed to suffer enough.[34]

Saint Teresa is as emphatic, and much more detailed. You may perhaps remember a passage I quoted from her in my first lecture.[35] There are many similar pages in her autobiography. Where in literature is a more evidently veracious account of the formation of a new centre of spiritual energy than is given in her description of the effects of certain ecstasies which in departing leave the soul upon a higher level of emotional excitement?

> Often, infirm and wrought upon with dreadful pains before the ecstasy, the soul emerges from it full of health and

admirably disposed for action . . . as if God had willed that the body itself, already obedient to the soul's desires, should share in the soul's happiness. . . . The soul after such a favor is animated with a degree of courage so great that if at that moment its body should be torn to pieces for the cause of God, it would feel nothing but the liveliest comfort. Then it is that promises and heroic resolutions spring up in profusion in us, soaring desires, horror of the world, and the clear perception of our proper nothingness. . . . What empire is comparable to that of a soul who, from this sublime summit to which God has raised her, sees all the things of earth beneath her feet, and is captivated by no one of them? How ashamed she is of her former attachments! How amazed at her blindness! What lively pity she feels for those whom she recognizes still shrouded in the darkness! . . . She groans at having ever been sensitive to points of honor, at the illusion that made her ever see as honor what the world calls by that name. Now she sees in this name nothing more than an immense lie of which the world remains a victim. She discovers, in the new light from above, that in genuine honor there is nothing spurious, that to be faithful to this honor is to give our respect to what deserves to be respected really, and to consider as nothing, or as less than nothing, whatsoever perishes and is not agreeable to God. . . . She laughs when she sees grave persons, persons of orison, caring for points of honor for which she now feels profoundest contempt. It is suitable to the dignity of their rank to act thus, they pretend, and it makes them more useful to others. But she knows that in despising the dignity of their rank for the pure love of God they would do more good in a single day than they would effect in ten years by preserving it. . . . She laughs at herself that there should ever have been a time in her life when she made any case of money, when she ever desired it. . . . Oh! if human beings might only agree together to re-

---

[34] Œuvres, ii. 320.
[35] Above, p. 34 [1902 edition].

gard it as so much useless mud, what harmony would then reign in the world! With what friendship we would all treat each other if our interest in honor and in money could but disappear from earth! For my own part, I feel as if it would be a remedy for all our ills.[36]

Mystical conditions may, therefore, render the soul more energetic in the lines which their inspiration favors. But this could be reckoned an advantage only in case the inspiration were a true one. If the inspiration were erroneous, the energy would be all the more mistaken and misbegotten. So we stand once more before that problem of truth which confronted us at the end of the lectures on saintliness. You will remember that we turned to mysticism precisely to get some light on truth. Do mystical states establish the truth of those theological affections in which the saintly life has its root?

In spite of their repudiation of articulate self-description, mystical states in general assert a pretty distinct theoretic drift. It is possible to give the outcome of the majority of them in terms that point in definite philosophical directions. One of these directions is optimism, and the other is monism. We pass into mystical states from out of ordinary consciousness as from a less into a more, as from a smallness into a vastness, and at the same time as from an unrest to a rest. We feel them as reconciling, unifying states. They appeal to the yes-function more than to the no-function in us. In them the unlimited absorbs the limits and peacefully closes the account. Their very denial of every adjective you may propose as applicable to the ultimate truth,—He, the Self, the Atman, is to be described by 'No! no!' only, say the Upanishads,[37]—though it seems on the surface to be a no-function, is a denial made on behalf of a deeper yes. Whoso calls the Absolute anything in particular, or says that it is *this,* seems implicitly to shut it off from being *that*—it is as if he lessened it. So we deny the 'this,' negating the negation which it seems to us to imply, in the interests of the higher affirmative attitude by which we are possessed. The fountainhead of Christian mysticism is Dionysius the Areopagite. He describes the absolute truth by negatives exclusively.

"The cause of all things is neither soul nor intellect; nor has it imagination, opinion, or reason, or intelligence; nor is it reason or intelligence; nor is it spoken or thought. It is neither number, nor order, nor magnitude, nor littleness, nor equality, nor inequality, nor similarity, nor dissimilarity. It neither stands, nor moves, nor rests. . . . It is neither essence, nor eternity, nor time. Even intellectual contact does not belong to it. It is neither science nor truth. It is not even royalty or wisdom; not one; not unity; not divinity or goodness; nor even spirit as we know it," etc., *ad libitum.*[38]

But these qualifications are denied by Dionysius, not because the truth falls short of them, but because it so infinitely excels them. It is above them. It is *super*-lucent, *super*-splendent, *super*-essential, *super*-sublime, *super* everything that can be named. Like Hegel in his logic, mystics journey towards the positive pole of truth only by the 'Methode der Absoluten Negativität.'[39]

Thus come the paradoxical expressions that so abound in mystical writings. As when Eckhart tells of the still desert of the Godhead, "where never was seen difference, neither Father, Son, nor Holy Ghost, where there is no one at home,

---

[36] Vie, pp. 200, 229, 231–233, 243.
[37] MÜLLER's translation, part ii. p. 180.

[38] T. DAVIDSON's translation, in Journal of Speculative Philosophy, 1893, vol. xxii. p. 399.
[39] "Deus propter excellentiam non immerito Nihil vocatur." Scotus Erigena, quoted by ANDREW SETH: Two Lectures on Theism, New York, 1897, p. 55.

yet where the spark of the soul is more at peace than in itself."[40] As when Boehme writes of the Primal Love, that "it may fitly be compared to Nothing, for it is deeper than any Thing, and is as nothing with respect to all things, forasmuch as it is not comprehensible by any of them. And because it is nothing respectively, it is therefore free from all things, and is that only good, which a man cannot express or utter what it is, there being nothing to which it may be compared, to express it by."[41] Or as when Angelus Silesius sings:—

> Gott ist ein lauter Nichts, ihn rührt
> kein Nun noch Hier;
> Je mehr du nach ihm greiffst, je mehr
> entwind er dir.[42]

To this dialectical use, by the intellect, of negation as a mode of passage towards a higher kind of affirmation, there is correlated the subtlest of moral counterparts in the sphere of the personal will. Since denial of the finite self and its wants, since asceticism of some sort, is found in religious experience to be the only doorway to the larger and more blessed life, this moral mystery intertwines and combines with the intellectual mystery in all mystical writings.

> "Love," continues Behmen, is Nothing, for "when thou art gone forth wholly from the Creature and from that which is visible, and art become Nothing to all that is Nature and Creature, then thou art in that eternal One, which is God himself, and then thou shalt feel within thee the highest virtue of Love. . . . The treasure of treasures for the soul is where she goeth out of the Somewhat into that Nothing out of which all things may be made. The soul here

saith, *I have nothing,* for I am utterly stripped and naked; *I can do nothing,* for I have no manner of power, but am as water poured out; *I am nothing,* for all that I am is no more than an image of Being, and only God is to me I AM; and so, sitting down in my own Nothingness, I give glory to the eternal Being, and *will nothing* of myself, that so God may will all in me, being unto me my God and all things."[43]

In Paul's language, I live, yet not I, but Christ liveth in me. Only when I become as nothing can God enter in and no difference between his life and mine remain outstanding.[44]

---

[43] Op. cit., pp. 42, 74, abridged.
[44] From a French book I take this mystical expression of happiness in God's indwelling presence:—

"Jesus has come to take up his abode in my heart. It is not so much a habitation, as association, as a sort of fusion. Oh, new and blessed life! life which becomes each day more luminous. . . . The wall before me, dark a few moments since, is splendid at this hour because the sun shines on it. Wherever its rays fall they light up a conflagration of glory; the smallest speck of glass sparkles, each grain of sand emits fire; even so there is a royal song of triumph in my heart because the Lord is there. My days succeed each other; yesterday a blue sky; to-day a clouded sun; a night filled with strange dreams; but as soon as the eyes open, and I regain consciousness and seem to begin life again, it is always the same figure before me, always the same presence filling my heart. . . . Formerly the day was dulled by the absence of the Lord. I used to wake invaded by all sorts of sad impressions, and I did not find him on my path. To-day he is with me; and the light cloudiness which covers things is not an obstacle to my communion with him. I feel the pressure of his hand, I feel something else which fills me with a serene joy; shall I dare to speak it out? Yes, for it is the true expression of what I experience. The Holy Spirit is not merely making me a visit; it is no mere dazzling apparition which may from one moment to another spread its wings and leave me in my night, it is a permanent habitation. He can depart only if he takes me with him. More than that; he is not other than myself: he is one with me. It is not a juxtaposition, it is

---

[40] J. ROYCE: Studies in Good and Evil, p. 282.
[41] Jacob Behmen's Dialogues on the Supersensual Life, translated by BERNARD HOLLAND, London, 1901, p. 48.
[42] Cherubinischer Wandersmann, Strophe 25.

This overcoming of all the usual barriers between the individual and the Absolute is the great mystic achievement. In mystic states we both become one with the Absolute and we become aware of our oneness. This is the everlasting and triumphant mystical tradition, hardly altered by differences of clime or creed. In Hinduism, in Neoplatonism, in Sufism, in Christian mysticism, in Whitmanism, we find the same recurring note, so that there is about mystical utterances an eternal unanimity which ought to make a critic stop and think, and which brings it about that the mystical classics have, as has been said, neither birthday nor native land. Perpetually telling of the unity of man with God, their speech antedates languages, and they do not grow old.[45]

'That art Thou!' say the Upanishads, and the Vedantists add: 'Not a part, not a mode of That, but identically That, that absolute Spirit of the World.' "As pure water poured into pure water remains the same, thus, O Gautama, is the Self of a thinker who knows. Water in water, fire in fire, ether in ether, no one can distinguish them; likewise a man whose mind has entered into the Self." [46] " 'Every man,' says the Sufi Gulshan-Râz, 'whose heart is no longer shaken by any doubt, knows with certainty that there is no being save only One. . . . In his divine majesty the *me*, the *we*, the *thou*, are not found, for in the One there can be no distinction. Every being who is annulled and entirely separated from himself, hears resound outside of him this voice and this echo: *I am God:* he

has an eternal way of existing, and is no longer subject to death.' " [47] In the vision of God, says Plotinus, "what sees is not our reason, but something prior and superior to our reason. . . . He who thus sees does not properly see, does not distinguish or imagine two things. He changes, he ceases to be himself, preserves nothing of himself. Absorbed in God, he makes but one with him, like a centre of a circle coinciding with another centre." [48] "Here," writes Suso, "the spirit dies, and yet is all alive in the marvels of the Godhead . . . and is lost in the stillness of the glorious dazzling obscurity and of the naked simple unity. It is in this modeless *where* that the highest bliss is to be found." [49] "Ich bin so gross als Gott," sings Angelus Silesius again, "Er ist als ich so klein; Er kann nicht über mich, ich unter ihm nicht sein." [50]

In mystical literature such self-contradictory phrases as 'dazzling obscurity,' 'whispering silence,' 'teeming desert,' are continually met with. They prove that not conceptual speech, but music rather, is the element through which we are best spoken to by mystical truth. Many mystical scriptures are indeed little more than musical compositions.

He who would hear the voice of Nada, 'the Soundless Sound,' and comprehend it, he has to learn the nature of Dhâranâ. . . . When to himself his form appears unreal, as do on waking all the forms he sees in dreams; when he has ceased to hear the many, he may discern the ONE—the inner sound which kills the outer. . . . For then the soul will hear, and will remember. And then to the inner ear will speak THE VOICE OF THE SILENCE. . . . And now thy *Self* is lost in SELF, *thyself*

---

a penetration, a profound modification of my nature, a new manner of my being." Quoted from the MS. 'of an old man' by WILFRED MONOD: Il Vit: six méditations sur le mystère chrétien, pp. 280–283.

[45] Compare M. MAETERLINCK: L'Ornement des Noces spirituelles de Ruysbroeck, Bruxelles, 1891, Introduction, p. xix.

[46] Upanishads, M. MÜLLER's translation, ii. 17, 334.

[47] SCHMÖLDERS: Op. cit., p. 210.

[48] Enneads, BOUILLIER's translation, Paris, 1861, iii. 561. Compare pp. 473–477, and vol. i. p. 27.

[49] Autobiography, pp. 309, 310.

[50] Op. cit., Strophe 10.

unto THYSELF, merged in that SELF from which thou first didst radiate. . . . Behold! thou hast become the Light, thou hast become the Sound, thou art thy Master and thy God. Thou art THYSELF the object of thy search: the VOICE unbroken, that resounds throughout eternities, exempt from change, from sin exempt, the seven sounds in one, the VOICE OF THE SILENCE. *Om tat Sat.*[51]

These words, if they do not awaken laughter as you receive them, probably stir chords within you which music and language touch in common. Music gives us ontological messages which non-musical criticism is unable to contradict, though it may laugh at our foolishness in minding them. There is a verge of the mind which these things haunt; and whispers therefrom mingle with the operations of our understanding, even as the waters of the infinite ocean send their waves to break among the pebbles that lie upon our shores.

> Here begins the sea that ends not till
>   the world's end. Where we stand,
> Could we know the next high sea-mark
>   set beyond these waves that gleam,
> We should know what never man hath
>   known, nor eye of man hath
>   scanned. . . .
> Ah, but here man's heart leaps, yearn-
>   ing towards the gloom with ven-
>   turous glee,
> From the shore that hath no shore
>   beyond it, set in all the sea.[52]

That doctrine, for example, that eternity is timeless, that our 'immortality,' if we live in the eternal, is not so much future as already now and here, which we find so often expressed to-day in certain philosophic circles, finds its support in a 'hear, hear!' or an 'amen,' which floats up from that mysteriously deeper level.[53] We recognize the passwords to the mystical region as we hear them, but we cannot use them ourselves; it alone has the keeping of 'the password primeval.' [54]

I have now sketched with extreme brevity and insufficiency, but as fairly as I am able in the time allowed, the general traits of the mystic range of consciousness. *It is on the whole pantheistic and optimistic, or at least the opposite of pessimistic. It is anti-naturalistic, and harmonizes best with twice-bornness and so-called otherworldly states of mind.*

My next task is to inquire whether we can invoke it as authoritative. Does it furnish any *warrant for the truth* of the twice-bornness and supernaturality and pantheism which it favors? I must give my answer to this question as concisely as I can.

In brief my answer is this,—and I will divide it into three parts:—

(1) Mystical states, when well developed, usually are, and have the right to be, absolutely authoritative over the individuals to whom they come.

(2) No authority emanates from them which should make it a duty for those who stand outside of them to accept their revelations uncritically.

(3) They break down the authority of the non-mystical or rationalistic consciousness, based upon the understanding and the senses alone. They show it to be only one kind of consciousness. They open out the possibility of other orders of truth, in which, so far as anything in us vitally responds to them, we may freely continue to have faith.

I will take up these points one by one.

---

[51] H. P. BLAVATSKY: The Voice of the Silence.

[52] SWINBURNE: On the Verge, in 'A Midsummer Vacation.'

[53] Compare the extracts from Dr. Bucke, quoted on p. 136.

[54] As serious an attempt as I know to mediate between the mystical region and the discursive life is contained in an article on Aristotle's Unmoved Mover, by F. C. S. SCHILLER, in Mind, vol. ix., 1900.

I

As a matter of psychological fact, mystical states of a well-pronounced and emphatic sort *are* usually authoritative over those who have them.[55] They have been 'there,' and know. It is vain for rationalism to grumble about this. If the mystical truth that comes to a man proves to be a force that he can live by, what mandate have we of the majority to order him to live in another way? We can throw him into prison or a madhouse, but we cannot change his mind—we commonly attach it only the more stubbornly to its beliefs.[56] It mocks our utmost efforts, as a matter of fact, and in point of logic it absolutely escapes our jurisdiction. Our own more 'rational' beliefs are based on evidence exactly similar in nature to that which mystics quote for theirs. Our senses, namely, have assured us of certain states of fact; but mystical experiences are as direct perceptions of fact for those who have them as any sensations ever were for us. The records show that even though the five senses be in abeyance in them, they are absolutely sensational in their epistemological quality, if I may be pardoned the barbarous expression,—that is, they are face to face presentations of what seems immediately to exist.

The mystic is, in short, *invulnerable,* and must be left, whether we relish it or not, in undisturbed enjoyment of his creed. Faith, says Tolstoy, is that by which men live. And faith-state and mystic state are practically convertible terms.

II

But I now proceed to add that mystics have no right to claim that we ought to accept the deliverance of their peculiar experiences, if we are ourselves outsiders and feel no private call thereto. The utmost they can ever ask of us in this life is to admit that they establish a presumption. They form a consensus and have an unequivocal outcome; and it would be odd, mystics might say, if such a unanimous type of experience should prove to be altogether wrong. At bottom, however, this would only be an appeal to numbers, like the appeal of rationalism the other way; and the appeal to numbers has no logical force. If we acknowledge it, it is for 'suggestive,' not for logical reasons: we follow the majority because to do so suits our life.

But even this presumption from the unanimity of mystics is far from being strong. In characterizing mystic states as pantheistic, optimistic, etc., I am afraid I over-simplified the truth. I did so for expository reasons, and to keep the closer to the classic mystical tradition. The classic religious mysticism, it now must be confessed, is only a 'privileged case.' It is an *extract,* kept true to type by the selection of the fittest specimens and their preservation in 'schools.' It is carved out from a much larger mass; and if we take the larger mass as seriously as religious mysticism has historically taken itself, we find that the supposed unanimity largely disappears. To begin with, even religious mysticism itself, the kind that accumulates traditions and makes schools, is much less unanimous than I have al-

---

[55] I abstract from weaker states, and from those cases of which the books are full, where the director (but usually not the subject) remains in doubt whether the experience may not have proceeded from the demon.

[56] Example: Mr. John Nelson writes of his imprisonment for preaching Methodism: "My soul was as a watered garden, and I could sing praises to God all day long; for he turned my captivity into joy, and gave me to rest as well on the boards, as if I had been on a bed of down. Now could I say, 'God's service is perfect freedom,' and I was carried out much in prayer that my enemies might drink of the same river of peace which my God gave so largely to me." Journal, London, no date, p. 172.

lowed. It has been both ascetic and antinomianly self-indulgent within the Christian church.[57] It is dualistic in Sankhya, and monistic in Vedanta philosophy. I called it pantheistic; but the great Spanish mystics are anything but pantheists. They are with few exceptions non-metaphysical minds, for whom 'the category of personality' is absolute. The 'union' of man with God is for them much more like an occasional miracle than like an original identity.[58] How different again, apart from the happiness common to all, is the mysticism of Walt Whitman, Edward Carpenter, Richard Jefferies, and other naturalistic pantheists, from the more distinctively Christian sort.[59] The fact is that the mystical feeling of enlargement, union, and emancipation has no specific intellectual content whatever of its own. It is capable of forming matrimonial alliances with material furnished by the most diverse philosophies and theologies, provided only they can find a place in their framework for its peculiar emotional mood. We have no right, therefore, to invoke its prestige as distinctively in favor of any special belief, such as that in absolute idealism, or in the absolute monistic identity, or in the absolute goodness, of the world. It is only relatively in favor of all these things— it passes out of common human consciousness in the direction in which they lie.

So much for religious mysticism proper. But more remains to be told, for religious mysticism is only one half of mysticism. The other half has no accumulated traditions except those which the text-books on insanity supply. Open any one of these, and you will find abundant cases in which 'mystical ideas' are cited as characteristic symptoms of enfeebled or deluded states of mind. In delusional insanity, paranoia, as they sometimes call it, we may have a *diabolical* mysticism, a sort of religious mysticism turned upside down. The same sense of ineffable importance in the smallest events, the same texts and words coming with new meanings, the same voices and visions and leadings and missions, the same controlling by extraneous powers; only this time the emotion is pessimistic: instead of consolations we have desolations; the meanings are dreadful; and the powers are enemies to life. It is evident that from the point of view of their psychological mechanism, the classic mysticism and these lower mysticisms spring from the same mental level, from that great subliminal or transmarginal region of which science is beginning to admit the existence, but of which so little is really known. That region contains every kind of matter: 'seraph and snake' abide there side by side. To come from thence is no infallible credential. What comes must be sifted and tested, and run the gauntlet of confrontation with the total context of experience, just like what comes from the outer world of sense. Its value must be ascertained by empirical methods, so long as we are not mystics ourselves.

Once more, then, I repeat that non-mystics are under no obligation to acknowledge in mystical states a superior authority conferred on them by their intrinsic nature.[60]

[57] RUYSBROECK, in the work which Maeterlinck has translated, has a chapter against the antinomianism of disciples. H. DELACROIX's book (Essai sur le mysticisme spéculatif en Allemagne au XIVme Siècle, Paris, 1900) is full of antinomian material. Compare also A. JUNDT: Les Amis de Dieu au XIVme Siècle, Thèse de Strasbourg, 1879.

[58] Compare PAUL ROUSSELOT: Les Mystiques Espagnols, Paris, 1869, ch. xii.

[59] See CARPENTER's Towards Democracy, especially the latter parts, and JEFFERIES's wonderful and splendid mystic rhapsody, The Story of my Heart.

[60] In chapter i. of book ii. of his work Degeneration, 'MAX NORDAU' seeks to undermine all mysticism by exposing the weakness of the lower kinds. Mysticism for him means any sudden perception of hidden significance in things. He explains such perception by the abundant uncompleted associations which experiences may arouse in a degenerate

III

Yet, I repeat once more, the existence of mystical states absolutely overthrows the pretension of non-mystical states to be the sole and ultimate dictators of what we may believe. As a rule, mystical states merely add a supersensuous meaning to the ordinary outward data of consciousness. They are excitements like the emotions of love or ambition, gifts to our spirit by means of which facts already objectively before us fall into a new expressiveness and make a new connection with our active life. They do not contradict these facts as such, or deny anything that our senses have immediately seized.[61] It is the rationalistic critic rather who plays the part of denier in the controversy, and his denials have no strength, for there never can be a state of facts to which new meaning may not truthfully be added, provided the mind ascend to a more enveloping point of view. It must always remain an open question whether mystical states may not possibly be such superior points of view, windows through which the mind looks out upon a more extensive and inclusive world. The difference of the views seen from the different mystical windows need not prevent us from entertaining this supposition. The wider world would in that case prove to have a mixed constitution like that of this world, that is all. It would have its celestial and its infernal regions, its tempting and its saving moments, its valid experiences and its counterfeit ones, just as our world has them; but it would be a wider world all the same. We should have to use its experiences by selecting and subordinating and substituting just as is our custom in this ordinary naturalistic world; we should be liable to error just as we are now; yet the counting in of that wider world of meanings, and the serious dealing with it, might, in spite of all the perplexity, be indispensable stages in our approach to the final fullness of the truth.

In this shape, I think, we have to leave the subject. Mystical states indeed wield no authority due simply to their being mystical states. But the higher ones among them point in directions to which the religious sentiments even of non-mystical men incline. They tell of the supremacy of the ideal, of vastness, of union, of safety, and of rest. They offer us *hypotheses,* hypotheses which we may voluntarily ignore, but which as thinkers we cannot possibly upset. The supernaturalism and optimism to which they would persuade us may, interpreted in one way or another, be after all the truest of insights into the meaning of this life.

"Oh, the little more, and how much it is; and the little less, and what worlds away!" It may be that possibility and permission of this sort are all that the religious consciousness requires to live on. In my last lecture I shall have to try to persuade you that this is the case. Meanwhile, however, I am sure that for many of my readers this diet is too slender. If supernaturalism and inner union with the divine are true, you think, then not so much permission, as compulsion to believe, ought to be found. Philosophy has always professed to prove religious truth by coercive argument; and the con-

---

brain. These give to him who has the experience a vague and vast sense of its leading further, yet they awaken no definite or useful consequent in his thought. The explanation is a plausible one for certain sorts of feeling of significance; and other alienists (WERNICKE, for example, in his Grundriss der Psychiatrie, Theil ii., Leipzig, 1896) have explained 'paranoiac' conditions by a laming of the association-organ. But the higher mystical flights, with their positiveness and abruptness, are surely products of no such merely negative condition. It seems far more reasonable to ascribe them to inroads from the subconscious life, of the cerebral activity correlative to which we as yet know nothing.

[61] They sometimes add subjective *audita et visa* to the facts, but as these are usually interpreted as transmundane, they oblige no alteration in the facts of sense.

struction of philosophies of this kind has always been one favorite function of the religious life, if we use this term in the large historic sense. But religious philosophy is an enormous subject, and in my next lecture I can only give that brief glance at it which my limits will allow.

LECTURE XX

CONCLUSIONS

. . .

Let us agree, then, that Religion, occupying herself with personal destinies and keeping thus in contact with the only absolute realities which we know, must necessarily play an eternal part in human history. The next thing to decide is what she reveals about those destinies, or whether indeed she reveals anything distinct enough to be considered a general message to mankind. We have done as you see, with our preliminaries, and our final summing up can now begin.

I am well aware that after all the palpitating documents which I have quoted, and all the perspectives of emotion-inspiring institution and belief that my previous lectures have opened, the dry analysis to which I now advance may appear to many of you like an anticlimax, a tapering-off and flattening out of the subject, instead of a crescendo of interest and result. I said awhile ago that the religious attitude of Protestants appears poverty-stricken to the Catholic imagination. Still more poverty-stricken, I fear, may my final summing up of the subject appear at first to some of you. On which account I pray you now to bear this point in mind, that in the present part of it I am expressly trying to reduce religion to its lowest admissible terms, to that minimum, free from individualistic excrescences, which all religions contain as their nucleus, and on which it may be hoped that all religious persons may agree. That

established, we should have a result which might be small, but would at least be solid; and on it and round it the ruddier additional beliefs on which the different individuals make their venture might be grafted, and flourish as richly as you please. I shall add my own over-belief (which will be, I confess, of a somewhat pallid kind, as befits a critical philosopher), and you will, I hope, also add your over-beliefs, and we shall soon be in the varied world of concrete religious constructions once more. For the moment, let me dryly pursue the analytic part of the task.

Both thought and feeling are determinants of conduct, and the same conduct may be determined either by feeling or by thought. When we survey the whole field of religion, we find a great variety in the thoughts that have prevailed there; but the feelings on the one hand and the conduct on the other are almost always the same, for Stoic, Christian, and Buddhist saints are practically indistinguishable in their lives. The theories which Religion generates, being thus variable, are secondary; and if you wish to grasp her essence, you must look to the feelings and the conduct as being the more constant elements. It is between these two elements that the short circuit exists on which she carries on her principal business, while the ideas and symbols and other institutions form loop-lines which may be perfections and improvements, and may even some day all be united into one harmonious system, but which are not to be regarded as organs with an indispensable function, necessary at all times for religious life to go on. This seems to me the first conclusion which we are entitled to draw from the phenomena we have passed in review.

The next step is to characterize the feelings. To what psychological order do they belong?

The resultant outcome of them is in any case what Kant calls a 'sthenic' affection, an excitement of the cheerful, expansive, 'dynamogenic' order which, like any tonic, freshens our vital powers. In almost every lecture, but especially in the lectures on Conversion and on Saintliness, we have seen how this emotion overcomes temperamental melancholy and imparts endurance to the Subject, or a zest, or a meaning, or an enchantment and glory to the common objects of life.[1] The name of 'faith-state,' by which Professor Leuba designates it, is a good one.[2] It is a biological as well as a psychological condition, and Tolstoy is absolutely accurate in classing faith among the forces *by which men live*.[3] The total absence of it, anhedonia,[4] means collapse.

The faith-state may hold a very minimum of intellectual content. We saw examples of this in those sudden raptures of the divine presence, or in such mystical seizures as Dr. Bucke described.[5] It may be a mere vague enthusiasm, half spiritual, half vital, a courage, and a feeling that great and wondrous things are in the air.[6]

When, however, a positive intellectual content is associated with a faith-state, it gets invincibly stamped in upon belief,[7] and this explains the passionate loyalty of religious persons everywhere to the minutest details of their so widely differing creeds. Taking creeds and faith-state together, as forming 'religions,' and treating these as purely subjective phenomena, without regard to the question of their 'truth,' we are obliged, on account of their extraordinary influence upon action and endurance, to class them amongst the most important biological functions of mankind. Their stimulant and anæsthetic effect is so great that Professor Leuba, in a recent article,[8] goes so far as to say that so long as men can *use* their God, they care very little who he is, or even whether he is at all. "The truth of the matter can be put," says Leuba, "in this way: *God is not known, he is not understood; he is used*—sometimes as meat-purveyor, sometimes as moral support, sometimes as friend, sometimes as an object of love. If he proves himself useful, the religious consciousness asks for no

---

[1] Compare, for instance, pages 166, 178, 181, 183, 199 to 204, 218 to 220 [1902 edition].

[2] American Journal of Psychology, vii. 345.

[3] Above, p. 153 [1902 edition].

[4] Above, p. 124 [1902 edition].

[5] Above, p. 136.

[6] Example: Henri Perreyve writes to Gratry: "I do not know how to deal with the happiness which you aroused in me this morning. It overwhelms me; I want to *do* something, yet I can do nothing and am fit for nothing. . . . I would fain do *great things*." Again, after an inspiring interview, he writes: "I went homewards, intoxicated with joy, hope, and strength. I wanted to feed upon my happiness in solitude, far from all men. It was late; but, unheeding that, I took a mountain path and went on like a madman, looking at the heavens, regardless of earth. Suddenly an instinct made me draw hastily back—I was on the very edge of a precipice, one step more and I must have fallen. I took fright and gave up my nocturnal promenade." A. GRATRY: Henri Perreyve, London, 1872, pp. 92, 89.

This primacy, in the faith-state, of vague expansive impulse over direction is well expressed in Walt Whitman's lines (Leaves of Grass, 1872, p. 190):—

"O to confront night, storms, hunger, ridicule, accidents, rebuffs, as the trees and animals do. . . .
Dear Camerado! I confess I have urged you onward with me, and still urge you, without the least idea what is our destination,
Or whether we shall be victorious, or utterly quell'd and defeated."

This readiness for great things, and this sense that the world by its importance, wonderfulness, etc., is apt for their production, would seem to be the undifferentiated germ of all the higher faiths. Trust in our own dreams of ambition, or in our country's expansive destinies, and faith in the providence of God, all have their source in that onrush of our sanguine impulses, and in that sense of the exceedingness of the possible over the real.

[7] Compare LEUBA: Loc. cit., pp. 346–349.

[8] The Contents of Religious Consciousness, in The Monist, xi. 536, July, 1901.

more than that. Does God really exist? How does he exist? What is he? are so many irrelevant questions. Not God, but life, more life, a larger, richer, more satisfying life is, in the last analysis, the end of religion. The love of life, at any and every level of development, is the religious impulse." [9]

At this purely subjective rating, therefore, Religion must be considered vindicated in a certain way from the attacks of her critics. It would seem that she cannot be a mere anachronism and survival, but must exert a permanent function, whether she be with or without intellectual content, and whether, if she have any, it be true or false.

We must next pass beyond the point of view of merely subjective utility, and make inquiry into the intellectual content itself.

(1) First, is there, under all the discrepancies of the creeds, a common nucleus to which they bear their testimony unanimously? *Yes*

(2) And second, ought we to consider the testimony true?

I will take up the first question first, and answer it immediately in the affirmative. The warring gods and formulas of the various religions do indeed cancel each other, but there is a certain uniform deliverance in which religions all appear to meet. It consists of two parts:—

1. An uneasiness; and
2. Its solution.

1. The uneasiness, reduced to its simplest terms, is a sense that there is *something wrong about us* as we naturally stand.

2. The solution is a sense that *we are saved from the wrongness* by making proper connection with the higher powers.

In those more developed minds which alone we are studying, the wrongness takes a moral character, and the salvation takes a mystical tinge. I think we shall keep well within the limits of what is common to all such minds if we formulate the essence of their religious experience in terms like these:—

The individual, so far as he suffers from his wrongness and criticises it, is to that extent consciously beyond it, and in at least possible touch with something higher, if anything higher exist. Along with the wrong part there is thus a better part of him, even though it may be but a most helpless germ. With which part he should identify his real being is by no means obvious at this stage; but when stage 2 (the stage of solution or salvation) arrives,[10] the man identifies his real being with the germinal higher part of himself; and does so in the following way. *He becomes conscious that this higher part is conterminous and continuous with a* MORE *of the same quality, which is operative in the universe outside of him, and which he can keep in working touch with, and in a fashion get on board of and save himself when all his lower being has gone to pieces in the wreck.*

It seems to me that all the phenomena

---

[9] Loc. cit., pp. 571, 572, abridged. See, also, this writer's extraordinarily true criticism of the notion that religion primarily seeks to solve the intellectual mystery of the world. Compare what W. BENDER says (in his Wesen der Religion, Bonn, 1888, pp. 85, 38): "Not the question about God, and not the inquiry into the origin and purpose of the world is religion, but the question about Man. All religious views of life are anthropocentric." "Religion is that activity of the human impulse towards self-preservation by means of which Man seeks to carry his essential vital purposes through against the adverse pressure of the world by raising himself freely towards the world's ordering and governing powers when the limits of his own strength are reached." The whole book is little more than a development of these words.

[10] Remember that for some men it arrives suddenly, for others gradually, whilst others again practically enjoy it all their life.

are accurately describable in these very simple general terms.[11] They allow for the divided self and the struggle; they involve the change of personal centre and the surrender of the lower self; they express the appearance of exteriority of the helping power and yet account for our sense of union with it;[12] and they fully justify our feelings of security and joy. There is probably no autobiographic document, among all those which I have quoted, to which the description will not well apply. One need only add such specific details as will adapt it to various theologies and various personal temperaments, and one will then have the various experiences reconstructed in their individual forms.

So far, however, as this analysis goes, the experiences are only psychological phenomena. They possess, it is true, enormous biological worth. Spiritual strength really increases in the subject when he has them, a new life opens for him, and they seem to him a place of conflux where the forces of two universes meet; and yet this may be nothing but his subjective way of feeling things, a mood of his own fancy, in spite of the effects produced. I now turn to my second question: What is the objective 'truth' of their content?[13]

The part of the content concerning which the question of truth most perti-nently arises is that 'MORE of the same quality' with which our own higher self appears in the experience to come into harmonious working relation. Is such a 'more' merely our own notion, or does it really exist? If so, in what shape does it exist? Does it act, as well as exist? And in what form should we conceive of that 'union' with it of which religious geniuses are so convinced?

It is in answering these questions that the various theologies perform their theoretic work, and that their divergencies most come to light. They all agree that the 'more' really exists; though some of them hold it to exist in the shape of a personal god or gods, while others are satisfied to conceive it as a stream of ideal tendency embedded in the eternal structure of the world. They all agree, moreover, that it acts as well as exists, and that something really is effected for the better when you throw your life into its hands. It is when they treat of the experience of 'union' with it that their speculative differences appear most clearly. Over this point pantheism and theism, nature and second birth, works and grace and karma, immortality and reincarnation, rationalism and mysticism, carry on inveterate disputes.

At the end of my lecture on Philosophy I held out the notion that an impartial science of religions might sift out from the midst of their discrepancies a common body of doctrine which she might also formulate in terms to which physical science need not object. This, I said, she might adopt as her own reconciling hypothesis, and recommend it for general belief. I also said that in my last lecture I should have to try my own hand at framing such an hypothesis.

The time has now come for this attempt. Who says 'hypothesis' renounces the ambition to be coercive in his arguments. The most I can do is, accordingly, to offer something that may fit the facts so easily that your scientific logic will

---

[11] The practical difficulties are: 1, to 're-alize the reality' of one's higher part; 2, to identify one's self with it exclusively; and 3, to identify it with all the rest of ideal being.

[12] "When mystical activity is at its height, we find consciousness possessed by the sense of a being at once *excessive* and *identical* with the self: great enough to be God; interior enough to be *me*. The 'objectivity' of it ought in that case to be called *excessivity*, rather, or exceedingness." RÉCÉJAC: Essai sur les fondements de la conscience mystique, 1897, p. 46.

[13] The word 'truth' is here taken to mean something additional to bare value for life, although the natural propensity of man is to believe that whatever has great value for life is thereby certified as true.

find no plausible pretext for vetoing your impulse to welcome it as true.

The 'more,' as we called it, and the meaning of our 'union' with it, form the nucleus of our inquiry. Into what definite description can these words be translated, and for what definite facts do they stand? It would never do for us to place ourselves offhand at the position of a particular theology, the Christian theology, for example, and proceed immediately to define the 'more' as Jehovah, and the 'union' as his imputation to us of the righteousness of Christ. That would be unfair to other religions, and, from our present standpoint at least, would be an over-belief.

We must begin by using less particularized terms; and, since one of the duties of the science of religions is to keep religion in connection with the rest of science, we shall do well to seek first of all a way of describing the 'more,' which psychologists may also recognize as real. The *subconscious self* is nowadays a well-accredited psychological entity; and I believe that in it we have exactly the mediating term required. Apart from all religious considerations, there is actually and literally more life in our total soul than we are at any time aware of. The exploration of the transmarginal field has hardly yet been seriously undertaken, but what Mr. Myers said in 1892 in his essay on the Subliminal Consciousness [14] is as true as when it was first written: "Each of us is in reality an abiding psychical entity far more extensive than he knows—an individuality which can never express itself completely through any corporeal manifestation. The Self manifests through the organism; but there is always some part of the Self unmanifested; and always, as it seems, some power of organic expression in abeyance or reserve." [15] Much of the content of this larger background against which our conscious being stands out in relief is insignificant. Imperfect memories, silly jingles, inhibitive timidities, 'dissolutive' phenomena of various sorts, as Myers calls them, enter into it for a large part. But in it many of the performances of genius seem also to have their origin; and in our study of conversion, of mystical experiences, and of prayer, we have seen how striking a part invasions from this region play in the religious life.

Let me then propose, as an hypothesis, that whatever it may be on its *farther* side, the 'more' with which in religious experience we feel ourselves connected is on its *hither* side the subconscious continuation of our conscious life. Starting thus with a recognized psychological fact as our basis, we seem to preserve a contact with 'science' which the ordinary theologian lacks. At the same time the theologian's contention that the religious man is moved by an external power is vindicated, for it is one of the peculiarities of invasions from the subconscious region to take on objective appearances, and to suggest to the Subject an external control. In the religious life the control is felt as

[14] Proceedings of the Society for Psychical Research, vol. vii. p. 305. For a full statement of Mr. Myers's views, I may refer to his posthumous work, 'Human Personality in the Light of Recent Research,' which is already announced by Messrs. Longmans, Green & Co. as being in press. Mr. Myers for the first time proposed as a general psychological problem the exploration of the subliminal region of consciousness throughout its whole extent, and made the first methodical steps in its topography by treating as a natural series a mass of subliminal facts hitherto considered only as curious isolated facts, and subjecting them to a systematized nomenclature. How important this exploration will prove, future work upon the path which Myers has opened can alone show. Compare my paper: 'Frederic Myers's Services to Psychology,' in the said Proceedings, part xlii., May, 1901.

[15] Compare the inventory given above on pp. 365–366, and also what is said of the subconscious self on pp. 188–190, 193–195 [1902 edition].

'higher'; but since on our hypothesis it is primarily the higher faculties of our own hidden mind which are controlling, the sense of union with the power beyond us is a sense of something, not merely apparently, but literally true.

This doorway into the subject seems to me the best one for a science of religions, for it mediates between a number of different points of view. Yet it is only a doorway, and difficulties present themselves as soon as we step through it, and ask how far our transmarginal consciousness carries us if we follow it on its remoter side. Here the over-beliefs begin: here mysticism and the conversion-rapture and Vedantism and transcendental idealism bring in their monistic interpretations [16] and tell us that the finite self rejoins the absolute self, for it was always one with God and identical with the soul of the world.[17] Here the prophets of all the different religions come with their visions, voices, raptures, and other openings, supposed by each to authenticate his own peculiar faith.

Those of us who are not personally favored with such specific revelations must stand outside of them altogether and, for the present at least, decide that, since they corroborate incompatible theological doctrines, they neutralize one another and leave no fixed result. If we follow any one of them, or if we follow philosophical theory and embrace monistic pantheism on non-mystical grounds, we do so in the exercise of our individual freedom, and build out our religion in the way most congruous with our personal susceptibilities. Among these susceptibilities intellectual ones play a decisive part. Although the religious question is primarily a question of life, of living or not living in the higher union which opens itself to us as a gift, yet the spiritual excitement in which the gift appears a real one will often fail to be aroused in an individual until certain particular intellectual beliefs or ideas which, as we say, come home to him, are touched.[18] These ideas will thus

---

[16] Compare above, pp. 147 ff.

[17] One more expression of this belief, to increase the reader's familiarity with the notion of it:—

"If this room is full of darkness for thousands of years, and you come in and begin to weep and wail, 'Oh, the darkness,' will the darkness vanish? Bring the light in, strike a match, and light comes in a moment. So what good will it do you to think all your lives, 'Oh, I have done evil, I have made many mistakes'? It requires no ghost to tell us that. Bring in the light, and the evil goes in a moment. Strengthen the real nature, build up yourselves, the effulgent, the resplendent, the ever pure, call that up in every one whom you see. I wish that every one of us had come to such a state that even when we see the vilest of human beings we can see the God within, and instead of condemning, say, 'Rise, thou effulgent One, rise thou who art always pure, rise thou birthless and deathless, rise almighty, and manifest your nature.' . . . This is the highest prayer that the Advaita teaches. This is the one prayer: remembering our nature." . . . "Why does man go out to look for a God? . . . It is your own heart beating, and you did not know, you were mistaking it for something external. He, nearest of the near, my own self, the reality of my own life, my body and my soul.—I am Thee and Thou art Me. That is your own nature. Assert it, manifest it. Not to become pure, you are pure already. You are not to be perfect, you are that already. Every good thought which you think or act upon is simply tearing the veil, as it were, and the purity, the Infinity, the God behind, manifests itself—the eternal Subject of everything, the eternal Witness in this universe, your own Self. Knowledge is, as it were, a lower step, a degradation. We are It already; how to know It?" SWAMI VIVEKANANDA: Addresses, No. XII., Practical Vedanta, part iv. pp. 172, 174, London, 1897; and Lectures, The Real and the Apparent Man, p. 24, abridged.

[18] For instance, here is a case where a person exposed from her birth to Christian ideas had to wait till they came to her clad in spiritistic formulas before the saving experience set in:—

"For myself I can say that spiritualism has saved me. It was revealed to me at a critical moment of my life, and without it I don't know what I should have done. It has taught me to detach myself from worldly

be essential to that individual's religion; —which is as much as to say that over-beliefs in various directions are absolutely indispensable, and that we should treat them with tenderness and tolerance so long as they are not intolerant themselves. As I have elsewhere written, the most interesting and valuable things about a man are usually his over-beliefs.

Disregarding the over-beliefs, and confining ourselves to what is common and generic, we have in *the fact that the conscious person is continuous with a wider self through which saving experiences come,*[19] a positive content of religious experience which, it seems to me, *is literally and objectively true as far as it goes.* If I now proceed to state my own hypothesis about the farther limits of this extension of our personality, I shall be offering my own over-belief—though I know it will appear a sorry under-belief to some of you—for which I can only bespeak the same indulgence which in a converse case I should accord to yours.

The further limits of our being plunge, it seems to me, into an altogether other

dimension of existence from the sensible and merely 'understandable' world. Name it the mystical region, or the supernatural region, whichever you choose. So far as our ideal impulses originate in this region (and most of them do originate in it, for we find them possessing us in a way for which we cannot articulately account), we belong to it in a more intimate sense than that in which we belong to the visible world, for we belong in the most intimate sense wherever our ideals belong. Yet the unseen region in question is not merely ideal, for it produces effects in this world. When we commune with it, work is actually done upon our finite personality, for we are turned into new men, and consequences in the way of conduct follow in the natural world upon our regenerative change.[20] But that which produces effects within another reality must be termed a reality itself, so I feel as if we

---

[20] That the transaction of opening ourselves, otherwise called prayer, is a perfectly definite one for certain persons, appears abundantly in the preceding lectures. I append another concrete example to reinforce the impression on the reader's mind:—

"Man can learn to transcend these limitations [of finite thought] and draw power and wisdom at will. . . . The divine presence is known through experience. The turning to a higher plane is a distinct act of consciousness. It is not a vague, twilight or semiconscious experience. It is not an ecstasy; it is not a trance. It is not super-consciousness in the Vedantic sense. It is not due to self-hypnotization. It is a perfectly calm, sane, sound, rational, common-sense shifting of consciousness from the phenomena of sense-perception to the phenomena of seership, from the thought of self to a distinctively higher realm. . . . For example, if the lower self be nervous, anxious, tense, one can in a few moments compel it to be calm. This is not done by a word simply. Again I say, it is not hypnotism. It is by the exercise of power. One feels the spirit of peace as definitely as heat is perceived on a hot summer day. The power can be as surely used as the sun's rays can be focused and made to do work, to set fire to wood." The Higher Law, vol. iv. pp. 4, 6, Boston, August, 1901.

---

things and to place my hope in things to come. Through it I have learned to see in all men, even in those most criminal, even in those from whom I have most suffered, undeveloped brothers to whom I owed assistance, love, and forgiveness. I have learned that I must lose my temper over nothing, despise no one, and pray for all. Most of all I have learned to pray! And although I have still much to learn in this domain, prayer ever brings me more strength, consolation, and comfort. I feel more than ever that I have only made a few steps on the long road of progress; but I look at its length without dismay, for I have confidence that the day will come when all my efforts shall be rewarded. So Spiritualism has a great place in my life, indeed it holds the first place there." Flournoy Collection.

[19] "The influence of the Holy Spirit, exquisitely call the Comforter, is a matter of actual experience, as solid a reality as that of electromagnetism." W. C. BROWNELL, Scribner's Magazine, vol. xxx. p. 112.

had no philosophic excuse for calling the unseen or mystical world unreal.

God is the natural appellation, for us Christians at least, for the supreme reality, so I will call this higher part of the universe by the name of God.[21] We and God have business with each other; and in opening ourselves to his influence our deepest destiny is fulfilled. The universe, at those parts of it which our personal being constitutes, takes a turn genuinely for the worse or for the better in proportion as each one of us fulfills or evades God's demands. As far as this goes I probably have you with me, for I only translate into schematic language what I may call the instinctive belief of mankind: God is real since he produces real effects.

The real effects in question, so far as I have as yet admitted them, are exerted on the personal centres of energy of the various subjects, but the spontaneous faith of most of the subjects is that they embrace a wider sphere than this. Most religious men believe (or 'know,' if they be mystical) that not only they themselves, but the whole universe of beings to whom the God is present, are secure in his parental hands. There is a sense, a dimension, they are sure, in which we are *all* saved, in spite of the gates of hell and all adverse terrestrial appearances. God's existence is the guarantee of an ideal order that shall be permanently preserved. This world may indeed, as science assures us, some day burn up or freeze; but if it is part of his order, the old ideals are sure to be brought elsewhere to fruition, so that where God is, tragedy is only provisional and partial, and shipwreck and dissolution are not the absolutely final things. Only when this farther step of

faith concerning God is taken, and remote objective consequences are predicted, does religion, as it seems to me, get wholly free from the first immediate subjective experience, and bring a *real hypothesis* into play. A good hypothesis in science must have other properties than those of the phenomenon it is immediately invoked to explain, otherwise it is not prolific enough. God, meaning only what enters into the religious man's experience of union, falls short of being an hypothesis of this more useful order. He needs to enter into wider cosmic relations in order to justify the subject's absolute confidence and peace.

That the God with whom, starting from the hither side of our own extra-marginal self, we come at its remoter margin into commerce should be the absolute world-ruler, is of course a very considerable over-belief. Over-belief as it is, though, it is an article of almost every one's religion. Most of us pretend in some way to prop it up upon our philosophy, but the philosophy itself is really propped upon this faith. What is this but to say that Religion, in her fullest exercise of function, is not a mere illumination of facts already elsewhere given, not a mere passion, like love, which views things in a rosier light. It is indeed that, as we have seen abundantly. But it is something more, namely, a postulator of new *facts* as well. The world interpreted religiously is not the materialistic world over again, with an altered expression; it must have, over and above the altered expression, *a natural constitution* different at some point from that which a materialistic world would have. It must be such that different events can be expected in it, different conduct must be required.

This thoroughly 'pragmatic' view of religion has usually been taken as a matter of course by common men. They have interpolated divine miracles into the field of nature, they have built a heaven out beyond the grave. It is only transcenden-

---

[21] Transcendentalists are fond of the term 'Over-soul,' but as a rule they use it in an intellectualist sense, as meaning only a medium of communion. 'God' is a causal agent as well as a medium of communion, and that is the aspect which I wish to emphasize.

talist metaphysicians who think that, without adding any concrete details to Nature, or subtracting any, but by simply calling it the expression of absolute spirit, you make it more divine just as it stands. I believe the pragmatic way of taking religion to be the deeper way. It gives it body as well as soul, it makes it claim, as everything real must claim, some characteristic realm of fact as its very own. What the more characteristically divine facts are, apart from the actual inflow of energy in the faith-state and the prayer-state, I know not. But the over-belief on which I am ready to make my personal venture is that they exist. The whole drift of my education goes to persuade me that the world of our present consciousness is only one out of many worlds of consciousness that exist, and that those other worlds must contain experiences which have a meaning for our life also; and that although in the main their experiences and those of this world keep discrete, yet the two become continuous at certain points, and higher energies filter in. By being faithful in my poor measure to this over-belief, I seem to myself to keep more sane and true. I *can,* of course, put myself into the sectarian scientist's attitude, and imagine vividly that the world of sensations and of scientific laws and objects may be all. But whenever I do this, I hear that inward monitor of which W. K. Clifford once wrote, whispering the word 'bosh!' Humbug is humbug, even though it bear the scientific name, and the total expression of human experience, as I view it objectively, invincibly urges me beyond the narrow 'scientific' bounds. Assuredly, the real world is of a different temperament,— more intricately built than physical science allows. So my objective and my subjective conscience both hold me to the over-belief which I express. Who knows whether the faithfulness of individuals here below to their own poor over-beliefs may not actually help God in turn to be more effectively faithful to his own greater tasks?

POSTSCRIPT

In writing my concluding lecture I had to aim so much at simplification that I fear that my general philosophic position received so scant a statement as hardly to be intelligible to some of my readers. I therefore add this epilogue, which must also be so brief as possibly to remedy but little the defect. In a later work I may be enabled to state my position more amply and consequently more clearly.

Originality cannot be expected in a field like this, where all the attitudes and tempers that are possible have been exhibited in literature long ago, and where any new writer can immediately be classed under a familiar head. If one should make a division of all thinkers into naturalists and supernaturalists, I should undoubtedly have to go, along with most philosophers, into the supernaturalist branch. But there is a crasser and a more refined supernaturalism, and it is to the refined division that most philosophers at the present day belong. If not regular transcendental idealists, they at least obey the Kantian direction enough to bar out ideal entities from interfering causally in the course of phenomenal events. Refined supernaturalism is universalistic supernaturalism; for the 'crasser' variety 'piecemeal' supernaturalism would perhaps be the better name. It went with that older theology which to-day is supposed to reign only among uneducated people, or to be found among the few belated professors of the dualisms which Kant is thought to have displaced. It admits miracles and providential leadings, and finds no intellectual difficulty in mixing the ideal and the real worlds together by interpolating influences from the ideal region among the forces that causally determine the real world's details. In this the refined supernaturalists think that it muddles disparate dimensions of existence. For them the world of the ideal has no efficient causality, and never bursts into the world of phenomena at particular points. The ideal world, for them, is not a world of facts, but only of the meaning of facts; it is a point of view for judging facts. It appertains to a different '-ology,' and inhabits a different dimension of being altogether from that in which existential propositions obtain. It cannot get down upon the flat level of experience and interpolate itself piecemeal between distinct portions of nature, as those who believe, for example, in divine aid coming in response to prayer are bound to think it must.

Notwithstanding my own inability to accept either popular Christianity or scholastic theism, I suppose that my belief that in communion with the Ideal new force comes into the world, and new departures are made here below, subjects me to being classed among the supernaturalists of the piecemeal or crasser type. Universalistic supernaturalism surrenders, it seems to me, too easily to naturalism. It takes the facts of physical science at their face-value, and leaves the laws of life just as naturalism finds them, with no hope of remedy, in case their fruits are bad. It confines itself to sentiments about life as a whole, sentiments which may be admiring and adoring, but which need not be so, as the existence of systematic pessimism proves. In this universalistic way of taking the ideal world, the essence of practical religion seems to me to evaporate. Both instinctively and for logical reasons, I find it hard to believe that principles can exist which make no difference in facts.[1] But all facts are particular facts,

and the whole interest of the question of God's existence seems to me to lie in the consequences for particulars which that existence may be expected to entail. That no concrete particular of experience should alter its complexion in consequence of a God being there seems to me an incredible proposition, and yet it is the thesis to which (implicitly at any rate) refined supernaturalism seems to cling. It is only with experience *en bloc,* it says, that the Absolute maintains relations. It condescends to no transactions of detail.

I am ignorant of Buddhism and speak under correction, and merely in order the better to describe my general point of view; but as I apprehend the Buddhistic doctrine of Karma, I agree in principle with that. All supernaturalists admit that facts are under the judgment of higher law; but for Buddhism as I interpret it, and for religion generally so far as it remains unweakened by transcendentalistic metaphysics, the word 'judgment' here means no such bare academic verdict or platonic appreciation as it means in Vedantic or modern absolutist systems; it carries, on the contrary, *execution* with it, is *in rebus* as well as *post rem,* and operates 'causally' as partial factor in the total fact. The universe becomes a gnosticism [2] pure and simple on any other terms. But this view that judgment and

our finite minds work for the better ought to be done within this world, setting in at single points. Our difficulties and our ideals are all piecemeal affairs, but the Absolute can do no piecework for us; so that all the interests which our poor souls compass raise their heads too late. We should have spoken earlier, prayed for another world absolutely, before this world was born. It is strange, I have heard a friend say, to see this blind corner into which Christian thought has worked itself at last, with its God who can raise no particular weight whatever, who can help us with no private burden, and who is on the side of our enemies as much as he is on our own. Odd evolution from the God of David's psalms!

[2] See my Will to Believe and other Essays in Popular Philosophy, 1897, p. 165.

---

[1] Transcendental idealism, of course, insists that its ideal world makes *this* difference, that facts *exist.* We owe it to the Absolute that we have a world of fact at all. 'A world' of fact!—that exactly is the trouble. An entire world is the smallest unit with which the Absolute can work, whereas to

execution go together is that of the crasser supernaturalist way of thinking, so the present volume must on the whole be classed with the other expressions of that creed.

I state the matter thus bluntly, because the current of thought in academic circles runs against me, and I feel like a man who must set his back against an open door quickly if he does not wish to see it closed and locked. In spite of its being so shocking to the reigning intellectual tastes, I believe that a candid consideration of piecemeal supernaturalism and a complete discussion of all its metaphysical bearings will show it to be the hypothesis by which the largest number of legitimate requirements are met. That of course would be a program for other books than this; what I now say sufficiently indicates to the philosophic reader the place where I belong.

If asked just where the differences in fact which are due to God's existence come in, I should have to say that in general I have no hypothesis to offer beyond what the phenomenon of 'prayerful communion,' especially when certain kinds of incursion from the subconscious region take part in it, immediately suggests. The appearance is that in this phenomenon something ideal, which in one sense is part of ourselves and in another sense is not ourselves, actually exerts an influence, raises our centre of personal energy, and produces regenerative effects unattainable in other ways. If, then, there be a wider world of being than that of our everyday consciousness, if in it there be forces whose effects on us are intermittent, if one facilitating condition of the effects be the openness of the 'subliminal' door, we have the elements of a theory to which the phenomena of religious life lend plausibility. I am so impressed by the importance of these phenomena that I adopt the hypothesis which they so naturally suggest. At these places at least, I say, it would seem as though transmun-

dane energies, God, if you will, produced immediate effects within the natural world to which the rest of our experience belongs.

The difference in natural 'fact' which most of us would assign as the first difference which the existence of a God ought to make would, I imagine, be personal immortality. Religion, in fact, for the great majority of our own race *means* immortality, and nothing else. God is the producer of immortality; and whoever has doubts of immortality is written down as an atheist without farther trial. I have said nothing in my lectures about immortality or the belief therein, for to me it seems a secondary point. If our ideals are only cared for in 'eternity,' I do not see why we might not be willing to resign their care to other hands than ours. Yet I sympathize with the urgent impulse to be present ourselves, and in the conflict of impulses, both of them so vague yet both of them noble, I know not how to decide. It seems to me that it is eminently a case for facts to testify. Facts, I think, are yet lacking to prove 'spirit-return,' though I have the highest respect for the patient labors of Messrs. Myers, Hodgson, and Hyslop, and am somewhat impressed by their favorable conclusions. I consequently leave the matter open, with this brief word to save the reader from a possible perplexity as to why immortality got no mention in the body of this book.

The ideal power with which we feel ourselves in connection, the 'God' of ordinary men, is, both by ordinary men and by philosophers, endowed with certain of those metaphysical attributes which in the lecture on philosophy I treated with such disrespect. He is assumed as a matter of course to be 'one and only' and to be 'infinite'; and the notion of many finite gods is one which hardly any one thinks it worth while to consider, and still less to uphold. Nevertheless, in the interests of intellectual clearness, I feel bound to say that religious experience, as we have studied it, cannot be cited as unequivocally supporting the infinitist belief. The only thing that it unequivocally testifies to is that we can experience union with *something* larger than ourselves and in that union find our greatest peace. Philosophy, with its passion for unity, and mysticism with its monoideistic bent, both 'pass to the limit' and identify the something with a unique God who is the all-inclusive soul of the world. Popular opinion, respectful to their authority, follows the example which they set.

Meanwhile the practical needs and experiences of religion seem to me sufficiently met by the belief that beyond each man and in a fashion continuous with him there exists a larger power which is friendly to him and to his ideals. All that the facts require is that the power should be both other and larger than our conscious selves. Anything larger will do, if only it be large enough to trust for the next step. It need not be infinite, it need not be solitary. It might conceivably even be only a larger and more godlike self, of which the present self would then be but the mutilated expression, and the universe might conceivably be a collection of such selves, of different degrees of inclusiveness, with no absolute unity realized in it at all.[3] Thus would a sort of polytheism return upon us—a polytheism which I do not on this occasion defend, for my only aim at present is to keep the testimony of religious experience clearly within its proper bounds. (Compare p. 115 above [1902 edition].)

Upholders of the monistic view will say to such a polytheism (which, by the way, has always been the real religion of common people, and is so still to-day) that unless there be one all-inclusive God, our guarantee of security is left imperfect. In the Absolute, and in the Absolute only, *all* is saved. If there be different gods, each caring for his part, some portion of some of us might not be covered with divine protection, and our religious consolation would thus fail to be complete. It goes back to what was said on pages 115–116 [1902 edition], about the possibility of there being portions of the universe that may irretrievably be lost. Common sense is less sweeping in its demands than philosophy or mysticism have been wont to be, and can suffer the notion of this world being partly saved and partly lost. The ordinary moralistic state of mind makes the salvation of the world conditional upon the success with which each unit does its part. Partial and conditional salvation is in fact a most familiar notion when taken in the abstract, the only difficulty being to determine the details. Some men are even disinterested enough to be willing to be in the unsaved remnant as far as their persons go, if only they can be persuaded that their cause will prevail—all of us are willing, whenever our activity-excitement rises sufficiently high. I think, in fact, that a final philosophy of religion will have to consider the pluralistic hypothesis more seriously than it has hitherto been willing to consider it. For practical life at any rate, the *chance* of salvation is enough. No fact in human nature is more characteristic than its willingness to live on a chance. The existence of the chance makes the difference, as Edmund Gurney says, between a life of which the keynote is resignation and a life of which the keynote is hope.[4] But all these statements are unsatisfactory from their brevity, and I can only say that I hope to return to the same questions in another book.

---

[3] Such a notion is suggested in my Ingersoll Lecture on Human Immortality, Boston and London, 1899.

[4] Tertium Quid, 1887, p. 99. See also pp. 148, 149.

C. D. BROAD

The Argument from Religious Experience

C. D. Broad (1887–   ) was Knightbridge Professor of Moral Philosophy at Cambridge University. His main contribution to philosophy has been by way of making careful distinctions between concepts and the careful sorting out of problems.

. . .

I shall confine myself to specifically religious experience and the argument for the existence of God which has been based on it.

This argument differs in the following important respect from the other two empirical types of argument. The Argument from Design and the arguments from ethical premises start from facts which are common to every one. But some people seem to be almost wholly devoid of any specifically religious experience; and among those who have it the differences of kind and degree are enormous. Founders of religions and saints, e.g., often claim to have been in direct contact with God, to have seen and spoken with Him, and so on. An ordinary religious man would certainly not make any such claim, though he might say that he had had experiences which assured him of the existence and presence of God. So the first thing that we have to notice is that capacity for religious experience is in certain respects like an ear for music.

From C. D. Broad, *Religion, Philosophy and Psychical Research* (1953). Reprinted by permission of Routledge & Kegan Paul Ltd., and Humanities Press Inc.

There are a few people who are unable to recognize and distinguish the simplest tune. But they are in a minority, like the people who have absolutely no kind of religious experience. Most people have some slight appreciation of music. But the differences of degree in this respect are enormous, and those who have not much gift for music have to take the statements of accomplished musicians very largely on trust. Let us, then, compare tone-deaf persons to those who have no recognizable religious experience at all; the ordinary followers of a religion to men who have some taste for music but can neither appreciate the more difficult kinds nor compose; highly religious men and saints to persons with an exceptionally fine ear for music who may yet be unable to compose it; and the founders of religions to great musical composers, such as Bach and Beethoven.

This analogy is, of course, incomplete in certain important respects. Religious experience raises three problems, which are different though closely interconnected. (i) What is the *psychological analysis* of religious experience? Does it contain factors which are present also in certain experiences which are not religious? Does it contain any factor which never occurs in any other kind of experience? If it contains no such factor, but is a blend of elements each of which can occur separately or in non-religious experiences, its psychological peculiarity must consist in the characteristic way in which these elements are blended in it. Can this peculiar structural feature of religious experience be indicated and described? (ii) What are the *genetic and causal conditions* of the existence of religious experience? Can we trace the origin and development of the disposition to have religious experiences (*a*) in the human race, and (*b*) in each individual? Granted that the disposition is present in nearly all individuals at the present time, can we discover and state the variable conditions which call it into activity on certain occasions and leave it in abeyance on others? (iii) Part of the content of religious experience is alleged knowledge or well-founded belief about the nature of reality, e.g., that we are dependent on a being who loves us and whom we ought to worship, that values are somehow conserved in spite of the chances and changes of the material world at the mercy of which they seem *prima facie* to be, and so on. Therefore there is a third problem. Granted that religious experience exists, that it has such-and-such a history and conditions, that it seems vitally important to those who have it, and that it produces all kinds of effects which would not otherwise happen, is it *veridical?* Are the claims to knowledge or well-founded belief about the nature of reality, which are an integral part of the experience, *true or probable?* Now, in the case of musical experience, there are analogies to the psychological problem and to the genetic or causal problem, but there is no analogy to the epistemological problem of validity. For, so far as I am aware, no part of the content of musical experience is alleged knowledge about the nature of reality; and therefore no question of its being veridical or delusive can arise.

Since both musical experience and religious experience certainly exist, any theory of the universe which was incompatible with their existence would be false, and any theory which failed to show the connexion between their existence and the other facts about reality would be inadequate. So far the two kinds of experience are in exactly the same position. But a theory which answers to the condition that it allows of the *existence* of religious experience and indicates the *connexion* between its existence and other facts about reality may leave the question as to its *validity* quite unanswered. Or, alternatively, it may throw grave doubt on its cognitive claims, or else it may tend to support them. Suppose, e.g., that it could be shown that religious experience contains no elements which are not factors in other kinds of experience. Suppose further it could be shown that this particular combination of factors tends to originate and to be activated only under certain conditions which are known to be very commonly productive of false beliefs held with strong conviction. Then a satisfactory answer to the questions of psychological analysis and causal antecedents would have tended to answer the epistemological question of validity in the negative. On the other hand, it might be that the only theory which would satisfactorily account for the origin of the religious disposition and for the occurrence of actual religious experiences under certain conditions was a theory which allowed some of the cognitive claims made by religious experience to be true or probable. Thus the three problems, though entirely distinct from each other, may be very closely connected; and it is the existence of the third problem in connexion with religious experience which puts it, for the present purpose, in a different category from musical experience.

In spite of this essential difference the analogy is not to be despised, for it brings out at least one important point. If a man who had no ear for music were to give himself airs on that account, and were to talk *de haut en bas* about those who can appreciate music and think it highly important, we should regard him, not as an advanced thinker, but as a self-satisfied Philistine. And, even if he did not do this but only propounded theories about the nature and causation of musical experience, we might think it reasonable to feel very doubtful whether his theories would be adequate or correct. In the same way, when persons without religious experience regard themselves as being *on that ground* superior to those who have it, their attitude must be treated as merely silly and offensive. Similarly, any theories about religious experience constructed by persons who have little or none of their own should be regarded with grave suspicion. (For that reason it would be unwise to attach very much weight to anything that the present writer may say on this subject.)

On the other hand, we must remember that the possession of a great capacity for religious experience, like the possession of a great capacity for musical appreciation and composition, is no guarantee of high general intelligence. A man may be a saint or a magnificent musician and yet have very little common sense, very little power of accurate introspection or of seeing causal connexions, and scarcely any capacity for logical criticism. He may also be almost as ignorant about other aspects of reality as the non-musical or non-religious man is about musical or religious experience. If such a man starts to theorize about music or religion, his theories may be quite as absurd, though in a different way, as those made by persons who are devoid of musical or religious experience. Fortunately it happens that some religious mystics of a high order have been extremely good at introspecting and describing their own experiences. And some highly religious persons have had very great critical and philosophical

abilities. St. Teresa is an example of the first, and St. Thomas Aquinas of the second.

Now I think it must be admitted that, if we compare and contrast the statements made by religious mystics of various times, races, and religions, we find a common nucleus combined with very great differences of detail. Of course the interpretations which they have put on their experiences are much more varied than the experiences themselves. It is obvious that the interpretations will depend in a large measure on the traditional religious beliefs in which various mystics have been brought up. I think that such traditions probably act in two different ways.

(i) The tradition no doubt affects the theoretical interpretation of experiences which would have taken place even if the mystic had been brought up in a different tradition. A feeling of unity with the rest of the universe will be interpreted very differently by a Christian who has been brought up to believe in a personal God and by a Hindu mystic who has been trained in a quite different metaphysical tradition.

(ii) The traditional beliefs, on the other hand, probably determine many of the details of the experience itself. A Roman Catholic mystic may have visions of the Virgin and the saints, whilst a Protestant mystic pretty certainly will not.

Thus the relations between the experiences and the traditional beliefs are highly complex. Presumably the outlines of the belief are determined by the experience. Then the details of the belief are fixed for a certain place and period by the special peculiarities of the experiences had by the founder of a certain religion. These beliefs then become traditional in that religion. Thenceforth they in part determine the details of the experiences had by subsequent mystics of that religion, and still more do they determine the interpretations which these mystics will put upon their experiences. Therefore, when a set of religious beliefs has once been established, it no doubt tends to produce experiences which can plausibly be taken as evidence for it. If it is a tradition in a certain religion that one can communicate with saints, mystics of that religion will seem to see and to talk with saints in their mystical visions; and this fact will be taken as further evidence for the belief that one can communicate with saints.

Much the same double process of causation takes place in sense-perception. On the one hand, the beliefs and expectations which we have at any moment largely determine what *interpretation* we shall put on a certain sensation which we should in any case have had then. On the other hand, our beliefs and expectations do to some extent determine and modify some of the sensible characteristics of the *sensa themselves*. When I am thinking only of diagrams a certain visual stimulus may produce a sensation of a sensibly flat sensum; but a precisely similar stimulus may produce a sensation of a sensibly solid sensum when I am thinking of solid objects.

Such explanations, however, plainly do not account for the first origin of religious beliefs, or for the features which are common to the religious experiences of persons of widely different times, races, and traditions.

Now, when we find that there are certain experiences which, though never very frequent in a high degree of intensity, have happened in a high degree among a few men at all times and places; and when we find that, in spite of differences in detail which we can explain, they involve certain fundamental conditions which are common and peculiar to them; two alternatives are open to us. (i) We may suppose that these men are in contact with an aspect of reality which is not revealed to ordinary persons in their everyday experience. And we may suppose that the characteristics which they agree in ascribing to reality on the basis

of these experiences probably do belong to it. Or (ii) we may suppose that they are all subject to a delusion from which other men are free. In order to illustrate these alternatives it will be useful to consider three partly analogous cases, two of which are real and the third imaginary.

(*a*) Most of the detailed facts which biologists tell us about the minute structure and changes in cells can be perceived only by persons who have had a long training in the use of the microscope. In this case we believe that the agreement among trained microscopists really does correspond to facts which untrained persons cannot perceive. (*b*) Persons of all races who habitually drink alcohol to excess eventually have perceptual experiences in which they seem to themselves to see snakes or rats crawling about their rooms or beds. In this case we believe that this agreement among drunkards is merely a uniform hallucination. (*c*) Let us now imagine a race of beings who can walk about and touch things but cannot see. Suppose that eventually a few of them developed the power of sight. All that they might tell their still blind friends about colour would be wholly unintelligible to and unverifiable by the latter. But they would also be able to tell their blind friends a great deal about what the latter would feel if they were to walk in certain directions. These statements would be verified. This would not, of course, *prove* to the blind ones that the unintelligible statements about colour correspond to certain aspects of the world which they cannot perceive. But it would show that the seeing persons had a source of additional information about matters which the blind ones could understand and test for themselves. It would not be unreasonable then for the blind ones to believe that probably the seeing ones are also able to perceive other aspects of reality which they are describing correctly when they make their unintelligible statements containing colour-names. The question then is whether it is reasonable to regard the agreement between the experiences of religious mystics as more like the agreement among trained microscopists about the minute structure of cells, or as more like the agreement among habitual drunkards about the infestation of their rooms by pink rats or snakes, or as more like the agreement about colours which the seeing men would express in their statements to the blind men.

Why do we commonly believe that habitual excess of alcohol is a cause of a uniform delusion and not a source of additional information? The main reason is as follows. The things which drunkards claim to perceive are not fundamentally different in kind from the things that other people perceive. We have all seen rats and snakes, though the rats have generally been grey or brown and not pink. Moreover the drunkard claims that the rats and snakes which he sees are literally present in his room and on his bed, in the same sense in which his bed is in his room and his quilt is on his bed. Now we may fairly argue as follows. Since these are the sort of things which we could see if they were there, the fact that we cannot see them makes it highly probable that they are not there. Again, we know what kinds of perceptible effect would generally follow from the presence in a room of such things as rats or snakes. We should expect fox-terriers or mongooses to show traces of excitement, and cheese to be nibbled, corn to disappear from bins, and so on. We find that no such effects are observed in the bedrooms of persons suffering from *delirium tremens*. It therefore seems reasonable to conclude that the agreement among drunkards is a sign, not of a revelation, but of a delusion.

Now the assertions in which religious mystics agree are not such that they conflict with what we can perceive with our senses. They are about the structure and organization of the world as a whole and about the relations of men to the rest of it. And they have so little in common with the facts of daily life that there is not much chance of direct collision. I think that there is only one important point on which there is conflict. Nearly all mystics seem to be agreed that time and change and unchanging duration are unreal or extremely superficial, whilst these seem to plain men to be the most fundamental features of the world. But we must admit, on the one hand, that these temporal characteristics present very great philosophical difficulties and puzzles when we reflect upon them. On the other hand, we may well suppose that the mystic finds it impossible to state clearly in ordinary language what it is that he experiences about the facts which underlie the appearance of time and change and duration. Therefore it is not difficult to allow that what we experience as the temporal aspect of reality corresponds in some sense to certain facts, and yet that these facts appear to us in so distorted a form in our ordinary experience that a person who sees them more accurately and directly might refuse to apply temporal names to them.

Let us next consider why we feel fairly certain that the agreement among trained microscopists about the minute structure of cells expresses an objective fact, although we cannot get similar experiences. One reason is that we have learned enough, from simpler cases of visual perception, about the laws of optics to know that the arrangement of lenses in a microscope is such that it will reveal minute structure, which is otherwise invisible, and will not simply create optical delusions. Another reason is that we know of other cases in which trained persons can detect things which untrained people will overlook, and that in many cases the existence of these things can be verified by indirect methods. Probably most of us have experienced such results of training in our own lives.

Now religious experience is not in nearly such a strong position as this. We do not know much about the laws which govern its occurrence and determine its variations. No doubt there are certain standard methods of training and meditation which tend to produce mystical experiences. These have been elaborated to some extent by certain Western mystics and to a very much greater extent by Eastern Yogis. But I do not think that we can see here, as we can in the case of microscopes and the training which is required to make the best use of them, any conclusive reason why these methods should produce veridical rather than delusive experiences. Uniform methods of training and meditation would be likely to produce more or less similar experiences, whether these experiences were largely veridical or wholly delusive.

Is there any analogy between the facts about religious experience and the fable about the blind men some of whom gained the power of sight? It might be said that many ideals of conduct and ways of life, which we can all recognize now to be good and useful, have been introduced into human history by the founders of religions. These persons have made actual ethical discoveries which others can afterwards recognize to be true. It might be said that this is at least roughly analogous to the case of the seeing men telling the still blind men of facts which the latter could and did verify for themselves. And it might be said that this makes it reasonable for us to attach some weight to what founders of religions tell us about things which we cannot understand or verify for ourselves; just as it would have been reasonable for the blind men to attach some weight to the unintelligible statements which the seeing men made to them about colours.

I think that this argument deserves a certain amount of respect, though I should find it hard to estimate how much

weight to attach to it. I should be inclined to sum up as follows. When there is a nucleus of agreement between the experiences of men in different places, times, and traditions, and when they all tend to put much the same kind of interpretation on the cognitive content of these experiences, it is reasonable to ascribe this agreement to their all being in contact with a certain objective aspect of reality *unless* there be some positive reason to think otherwise. The practical postulate which we go upon everywhere else is to treat cognitive claims as veridical unless there be some positive reason to think them delusive. This, after all, is our only guarantee for believing that ordinary sense-perception is veridical. We cannot *prove* that what people agree in perceiving really exists independently of them; but we do always assume that ordinary waking sense-perception is veridical unless we can produce some positive ground for thinking that it is delusive in any given case. I think it would be inconsistent to treat the experiences of religious mystics on different principles. So far as they agree they should be provisionally accepted as veridical unless there be some positive ground for thinking that they are not. So the next question is whether there is any positive ground for holding that they are delusive.

There are two circumstances which have been commonly held to cast doubt on the cognitive claims of religious and mystical experience. (i) It is alleged that founders of religions and saints have nearly always had certain neuropathic symptoms or certain bodily weaknesses, and that these would be likely to produce delusions. Even if we accept the premisses, I do not think that this is a very strong argument. (*a*) It is equally true that many founders of religions and saints have exhibited great endurance and great power of organization and business capacity which would have made them extremely successful and competent in secular affairs. There are very few offices in the cabinet or in the highest branches of the civil service which St. Thomas Aquinas could not have held with conspicuous success. I do not, of course, regard this as a positive reason *for* accepting the metaphysical doctrines which saints and founders of religions have based on their experiences; but it is relevant as a *rebuttal* of the argument which we are considering. (*b*) Probably very few people of extreme genius in science or art are perfectly normal mentally or physically, and some of them are very crazy and eccentric indeed. Therefore it would be rather surprising if persons of religious genius were completely normal, whether their experiences be veridical or delusive. (*c*) Suppose, for the sake of argument, that there is an aspect of the world which remains altogether outside the ken of ordinary persons in their daily life. Then it seems very likely that some degree of mental and physical abnormality would be a necessary condition for getting sufficiently loosened from the objects of ordinary sense-perception to come into cognitive contact with this aspect of reality. Therefore the fact that those persons who claim to have this peculiar kind of cognition generally exhibit certain mental and physical abnormalities is rather what might be anticipated if their claims were true. One might need to be slightly 'cracked' in order to have some peep-holes into the supersensible world. (*d*) If mystical experience were veridical, it seems quite likely that it would *produce* abnormalities of behaviour in those who had it strongly. Let us suppose, for the sake of argument, that those who have religious experience are in frequent contact with an aspect of reality of which most men get only rare and faint glimpses. Then such persons are, as it were, living in two worlds, while the ordinary man is living in only one of them. Or, again, they might be compared to a man who has to conduct his

life with one ordinary eye and another of a telescopic kind. Their behaviour may be appropriate to the aspect of reality which they alone perceive and think all-important; but, for that very reason, it may be inappropriate to those other aspects of reality which are all that most men perceive or judge to be important and on which all our social institutions and conventions are built.

(ii) A second reason which is commonly alleged for doubt about the claims of religious experience is the following. It is said that such experience always originates from and remains mixed with certain other factors, e.g., sexual emotion, which are such that experiences and beliefs that arise from them are very likely to be delusive. I think that there are a good many confusions on this point, and it will be worth while to begin by indicating some of them.

When people say that B 'originated from' A, they are liable to confuse at least three different kinds of connexion between A and B. (i) It might be that A is a necessary but insufficient condition of the existence of B. (ii) It might be that A is a necessary and sufficient condition of the existence of B. Or (iii) it might be that B simply *is* A in a more complex and disguised form. Now, when there is in fact evidence only for the first kind of connexion, people are very liable to jump to the conclusion that there is the third kind of connexion. It may well be the case, e.g., that no one who was incapable of strong sexual desires and emotions could have anything worth calling religious experience. But it is plain that the possession of a strong capacity for sexual experience is not a *sufficient* condition of having religious experience; for we know that the former quite often exists in persons who show hardly any trace of the latter. But, even if it could be shown that a strong capacity for sexual desire and emotion is *both* necessary and sufficient to produce religious experience, it would not follow that the latter is just the former in disguise. In the first place, it is not at all easy to discover the exact meaning of this metaphorical phrase when it is applied to psychological topics. And, if we make use of physical analogies, we are not much helped. A mixture of oxygen and hydrogen in presence of a spark is necessary and sufficient to produce water accompanied by an explosion. But water accompanied by an explosion is not a mixture of oxygen and hydrogen and a spark 'in a disguised form,' whatever that may mean.

Now I think that the present rather vaguely formulated objection to the validity of the claims of religious experience might be stated somewhat as follows. 'In the individual religious experience originates from, and always remains mixed with, sexual desires and emotions. The other generative factor of it is the religious tradition of the society in which he lives, the teachings of his parents, nurses, schoolmasters, etc. In the race religious experience originated from a mixture of false beliefs about nature and man, irrational fears, sexual and other impulses, and so on. Thus the religious tradition arose from beliefs which we now recognize to have been false and from emotions which we now recognize to have been irrelevant and misleading. It is now drilled into children by those who are in authority over them at a time of life when they are intellectually and emotionally at much the same stage as the primitive savages among whom it originated. It is, therefore, readily accepted, and it determines beliefs and emotional dispositions which persist long after the child has grown up and acquired more adequate knowledge of nature and of himself.'

Persons who use this argument might admit that it does not definitely *prove* that religious beliefs are false and groundless. False beliefs and irrational fears in our remote ancestors might conceivably be the origin of true beliefs and of an ap-

propriate feeling of awe and reverence in ourselves. And, if sexual desires and emotions be an essential condition and constituent of religious experience, the experience *may* nevertheless be veridical in important respects. We might merely have to rewrite one of the beatitudes and say 'Blessed are the *im*pure in heart, for they shall see God.' But, although it is logically possible that such causes should produce such effects, it would be said that they are most unlikely to do so. They seem much more likely to produce false beliefs and misplaced emotions.

It is plain that this argument has considerable plausibility. But it is worth while to remember that modern science has almost as humble an ancestry as contemporary religion. If the primitive witch-smeller is the spiritual progenitor of the Archbishop of Canterbury, the primitive rain-maker is equally the spiritual progenitor of the Cavendish Professor of Physics. There has obviously been a gradual refinement and purification of religious beliefs and concepts in the course of history, just as there has been in the beliefs and concepts of science. Certain persons of religious genius, such as some of the Hebrew prophets and the founders of Christianity and of Buddhism, do seem to have introduced new ethico-religious concepts and beliefs which have won wide acceptance, just as certain men of scientific genius, such as Galileo, Newton, and Einstein, have done in the sphere of science. It seems somewhat arbitrary to count this process as a continual approximation to true knowledge of the material aspect of the world in the case of science; and to refuse to regard it as at all similar in the case of religion. Lastly, we must remember that all of us have accepted the current common-sense and scientific view of the material world on the authority of our parents, nurses, masters, and companions at a time when we had neither the power nor the inclination to criticize it. And most of us accept, without even understanding, the more recondite doctrines of contemporary physics simply on the authority of those whom we have been taught to regard as experts.

On the whole, then, I do not think that what we know of the conditions under which religious beliefs and emotions have arisen in the life of the individual and the race makes it reasonable to think that they are *specially* likely to be delusive or misdirected. At any rate any argument which starts from that basis and claims to reach such a conclusion will need to be very carefully handled if its destructive effects are to be confined within the range contemplated by its users. It is reasonable to think that the concepts and beliefs of even the most perfect religions known to us are extremely inadequate to the facts which they express, that they are highly confused and are mixed up with a great deal of positive error and sheer nonsense; and that, if the human race goes on and continues to have religious experiences and to reflect on them, they will be altered and improved almost out of recognition. But all this could be said, *mutatis mutandis,* of scientific concepts and theories. The claim of any particular religion or sect to have complete or final truth on these subjects seems to me to be too ridiculous to be worth a moment's consideration. But the opposite extreme of holding that the whole religious experience of mankind is a gigantic system of pure delusion seems to me to be almost (though not quite) as far-fetched.

C. B. MARTIN

"Seeing" God

C. B. Martin (1924–   ) was born in the United States but carried on most of his philosophical studies in England, primarily with John Wisdom. He is now Senior Lecturer in Philosophy at the University of Adelaide, Australia.

Religious people may feel impatient with the harshness of argument in the last chapter. They may feel confident that they have something that nonreligious people lack, namely, a direct experience or apprehension of God. They may claim that such religious experience is a way of

From C. B. Martin, *Religious Belief* (1959), Ch. V. Reprinted by permission of Cornell University Press.

knowing God's existence. This claim must now be examined.

We shall first consider accounts of religious experience that seem to sacrifice an existential claim for the security of the feeling of the moment. There is an influential and subtle group of religious thinkers who would not insist upon any existential claim. My remarks are largely irrelevant to this group. It would be hasty to describe their religious belief as "subjective" or to employ any other such general descriptive term. For example, the "call," in even the most liberal and "subjective" Quaker sects, could not be reduced to statements about feelings. The "call," among other things, implies a mission or intricate pattern of behavior. The nonsubjective element of the "call" is evident, because insofar as one failed to live in accordance with a mission just so far would the genuineness of the "call" be questioned. It will be seen that this verification procedure is necessarily not available in the religious way of knowing to be examined.

In the second part of the chapter we shall consider accounts of religious experience that are not so easily reduced to mere subjectivity.

I

We are rejecting logical argument of any kind as the first chapter of our theology or as representing the process by which God comes to be known. We are holding that our knowledge of God rests rather on the revelation of His personal Presence as Father, Son, and Holy Spirit. . . . Of such a Presence it must be true that to those who have never been confronted with it argument is useless, while to those who have it is superfluous.[1]

It is not as the result of an inference of any kind, whether explicit or implicit, whether laboriously excogitated or swiftly intuited, that the knowledge of God's reality comes to us. It comes rather through our direct, personal encounter with Him in the Person of Jesus Christ His Son our Lord.[2]

It will not be possible to describe the compelling touch of God otherwise than as the compelling touch of God.

To anyone who has no such awareness of God, leading as it does to the typically religious attitudes of obeisance and worship, it will be quite impossible to indicate what is meant; one can only hope to evoke it, on the assumption that the capacity to become aware of God is part of normal human nature like the capacity to see light or to hear sound.[3]

The arguments of the theologians quoted have been taken out of context. The quotations by themselves do not give a faithful or complete impression of their total argument. The following quotations from Professor Farmer indicate two further lines of argument which cannot be discussed here.

For what we have now in mind is no demonstrative proofs from the world, but rather confirmatory considerations which present themselves to us when we bring belief in God with us to the world. It is a matter of the coherence of the belief with other facts. If we find that the religious intuition which has arisen from other sources provides the mind with a thought in terms of which much else can without forcing be construed, then that is an intellectual satisfaction, and a legitimate confirmation of belief, which it would be absurd to despise.[4]

We shall first speak in general terms of what may be called the human situation and need, and thereafter we shall try to show how belief in God, as particularized in its Christian form (though still broadly set forth), fits on to this situation and need.[5]

The alleged theological way of knowing may be described as follows: I have direct experience (knowledge, acquaintance, apprehension) of God; therefore

---

[1] John Baillie, *Our Knowledge of God* (London: Oxford University Press, 1949), p. 132.
[2] *Ibid.,* p. 143.

[3] H. H. Farmer, *Towards Belief in God* (London: S. C. M. Press, 1942), Pt. II, p. 40.
[4] *Ibid.,* p. 113.
[5] *Ibid.,* p. 62.

I have valid reason to believe that God exists. By this it may be meant that the statement "I have had direct experience of God, but God does not exist" is contradictory. If so, the assertion that "I have had direct experience of God" commits one to the assertion that God exists. From this it follows that "I have had direct experience of God" is more than a psychological statement, because it claims more than the fact that I have certain experiences—it claims that God exists. On this interpretation the argument is deductively valid. The assertion "I have direct experience of God" includes the assertion "God exists." Thus, the conclusion "Therefore, God exists" follows tautologically.

Unfortunately, this deduction is useless. If the deduction were to be useful, the addition of the existential claim "God exists" to the psychological claim of having religious experiences would have to be shown to be warrantable, and this cannot be done.

Consider the following propositions: (1) I feel as if an unseen person were interested in (willed) my welfare. (2) I feel an elation quite unlike any I have ever felt before. (3) I have feelings of guilt and shame at my sinfulness. (4) I feel as if I were committed to bending all my efforts to living in a certain way. These propositions state only that I have certain complex feelings and experiences. Nothing else follows deductively. The only thing that I can establish beyond possible correction on the basis of having certain feelings and experiences is that I have these feelings and sensations. No matter how unique people may think their experience to be, it cannot do the impossible.

Neither is the addition of the existential claim "God exists" to the psychological claim made good by any inductive argument. There are no tests agreed upon to establish genuine experience of God and distinguish it decisively from the nongenuine.[6] Indeed, many theologians deny the possibility of any such test or set of tests.

The believer may persuade us that something extraordinary has happened by saying, "I am a changed man since 6:37 P.M., May 6, 1939." This is a straightforward empirical statement. We can test it by noticing whether or not he has given up his bad habits. We may allow the truth of the statement even if he has not given up his bad habits, because we may find evidence of bad conscience, self-searchings and remorse that had not been present before that date.

However, if the believer says, "I had a direct experience of God at 6:37 P.M., May 6, 1939," this is not an empirical statement in the way that the other statement is. How could we check its truth? No matter how much or how little his subsequent behavior, such as giving up bad habits and so on, is affected, it could never prove or disprove his statement.

An important point to note is that theologians tend to discourage any detailed description of the required experience ("apprehension of God").[7] The more naturalistic and detailed the description of the required experience becomes, the easier would it become to deny the existential claim. One could say, "Yes, I had those very experiences, but they certainly did not convince me of God's existence." The only sure defense here would be for the theologian to make the claim analytic: "You couldn't have those experiences and at the same time sincerely deny God's existence."

The way in which many theologians talk would seem to show that they think of knowing God as something requiring a kind of sixth sense. The Divine Light is not of a color usually visible only to eagles, and the Voice of God is not of a

---

[6] This will be qualified in the second part of this chapter.
[7] The detailed descriptions of the Catholic mystics will be discussed later.

pitch usually audible only to dogs. No matter how much more keen our senses became, we should be no better off than before. The sixth sense, therefore, must be very different from the other five.

This supposed religious sense has no vocabulary of its own but depends upon metaphors drawn from the other senses. There are no terms which apply to it and it alone. There is a vocabulary for what is sensed but not for the sense. We "see" the Holy, the Numinous, the Divine. In a similar way we often speak of "hearing" the voice of conscience and "seeing" logical connections. By using this metaphor we emphasize the fact that often we come to understand the point of an argument or problem in logic suddenly. We mark this occurrence by such phrases as "the light dawned," "understood it in a flash." Such events are usually described in terms of a complete assurance that one's interpretation is correct and a confidence that one will tend to be able to reproduce or recognize the argument or problem in various contexts in the future. But a vitally important distinction between this "seeing" and the religious "seeing" is that there is a checking procedure for the former but not for the latter. If, while doing a problem in geometry you "see" that one angle is equal to another and then on checking over your proof find that they are not equal after all, you say "I didn't really 'see,' I only thought I did."

The religious way of knowing is described as being unique. No one can deny the existence of feelings and experiences which the believer calls "religious," and no one can deny their power. Because of this and because the way of knowing by direct experience is neither inductive nor deductive, theologians have tried to give this way of knowing a special status. One way of doing this is to claim that religious experience is unique and incommunicable.

Professor Baillie, in likening our knowledge of God to our knowledge of other minds, says that it is "like our knowledge of tridimensional space and all other primary modes of knowledge, something that cannot be imagined by one who does not already possess it, since it cannot be described to him in terms of anything else than itself." [8] This kind of comparison is stated in the two sentences following, and we shall now examine the similarities and dissimilarities between them. (1) You don't know what the experience of God is until you have had it. (2) You don't know what the color blue is until you have seen it. Farmer says, "All the basic elements in our experience are incommunicable. Who could describe light and colour to one who has known nothing but darkness?" [9] All that Farmer proves is that a description of one group of sensations A in terms of another set of sensations B is never sufficient for knowing group A. According to this definition of "know," in order to know one must have those sensations. Thus, all that is proved is that, in order to know what religious experience is, one must have a religious experience. This helps in no way at all to prove that such experience is direct apprehension of God and helps in no way to support the existential claim "God exists."

Farmer makes the point that describing the experience of God to an unbeliever is like describing color to a man blind from birth. So it is, in the sense that the believer has usually had experiences which the unbeliever has not. However, it is also very much unlike. The analogy breaks down at some vital points.

The blind man may have genuine, though incomplete knowledge of color. He may have an instrument for detecting wave lengths, and the like. Indeed, he may even increase our knowledge of color. More important still, the blind man

---

[8] Baillie, *Our Knowledge of God,* p. 217.
[9] Farmer, *Towards Belief in God,* p. 41.

may realize the differences in powers of prediction between himself and the man of normal eyesight. He is well aware of the fact that, unlike himself, the man of normal eyesight does not have to wait to hear the rush of the bull in order to be warned.

The point concerning differences in powers of prediction is connected with the problem of how we are to know when someone has the direct experience of God or even when we ourselves have the direct experience of God. It was shown above how the situation is easier in the case of the blind man knowing about color. It is only when one comes to such a case as knowing God that the society of tests and checkup procedures, which surround other instances of knowing, completely vanishes. What is put in the place of these tests and checking procedures is an immediacy of knowledge that is supposed to carry its own guarantee. This feature will be examined later.

It is true that the man of normal vision has a way of knowing color which the blind man does not have, that is, he can see colored objects. However, as we have seen, it would be wrong to insist that this is the only way of knowing color and that the blind man has *no* way of knowing color. Perhaps Farmer has this in mind when he tries to make an analogy between the incommunicability of the believer's direct knowledge of God to the unbeliever and the incommunicability of the normal man's knowledge of color to the blind man. The analogy is justified if "knowing color" is made synonymous with "having color sensations." On this account, no matter how good his hearing, reliable his color-detecting instruments, and so on, the blind man could not know color, and the man of normal vision could not communicate to him just what this knowledge would be like.

The believer has had certain unusual experiences, which, presumably, the un-believer has not had. If "having direct experience of God" is made synonymous with "having certain religious experiences," and the believer has had these and the unbeliever has not, then we may say that the believer's knowledge is incommunicable to the unbeliever in that it has already been legislated that in order to know what the direct experience of God is one must have had certain religious experiences. "To anyone who has no such awareness of God, leading as it does to the typically religious attitudes of obeisance and worship, it will be quite impossible to indicate what is meant; one can only hope to evoke it." [10] Reading theological textbooks and watching the behavior of believers is not sufficient.

The theologian has made the analogy above hold at the cost of endangering the existential claim about God which he hoped to establish. If "knowing color" is made synonymous with "having color sensations" and "having direct experience of God" is made synonymous with "having certain religious experiences," then it is certainly true that a blind man cannot "know color" and that a nonreligious man cannot "have direct experience of God." By definition, also, it is true that the blind man and the nonreligious man cannot know the meaning of the phrases "knowing color" and "having direct experience of God," because it has been previously legislated that one cannot know their meaning without having the relevant experiences.

If this analogy is kept, the phrases "knowing color" and "having direct experience of God" seem to make no claim beyond the psychological claims about one's color sensations and religious feelings.

If this analogy is not kept, there is no sense in the comparison of the incommunicability between the man of normal

---

[10] *Ibid.*, p. 40.

vision and the blind man with the incommunicability between the believer and the unbeliever.

If "knowing color" is to be shaken loose from its purely psychological implications and made to have an existential reference concerning features of the world, then a whole society of tests and checkup procedures, which would be wholly irrelevant to the support of the psychological claim about one's own color sensations, become relevant. For example, what other people see, the existence of light waves, and the description of their characteristics, which needs the testimony of research workers and scientific instruments, all must be taken into account.

Because "having direct experience of God" does not admit the relevance of a society of tests and checking procedures, it tends to place itself in the company of the other ways of knowing which preserve their self-sufficiency, "uniqueness," and "incommunicability" by making a psychological and not an existential claim. For example, "I seem to see a piece of blue paper," [11] requires no further test or checking procedure in order to be considered true. Indeed, if Jones says, "I seem to see a piece of blue paper," he not only needs no further corroboration but cannot be shown to have been mistaken. If Smith says to Jones, "It does not seem to me as if I were seeing a piece of blue paper," this cannot rightly raise any doubts in Jones's mind, though it may express Smith's doubts. That is, Smith may feel that Jones is lying. However, if Jones had said, "I see a piece of blue paper," and Smith, in the same place and at the same time, had replied, "I do not see a piece of blue paper," or, "It does not seem to me as if I were now seeing a piece of blue paper," then Smith's remarks can rightly raise doubts in Jones's

mind. Further investigation will then be proper, and if no piece of paper can be felt and other investigators cannot see or feel the paper and photographs reveal nothing, then Jones's statement will be shown to have been false. Jones's only refuge will be to say, "Well, I certainly seem to see a piece of blue paper." This is a perfect refuge, because no one can prove him wrong, but its unassailability has been bought at the price of making no claim about the world beyond the claim about his own experience of the moment.

The closeness of the religious statement to the psychological statement can be brought out in another way, as follows. When one wishes to support the assertion that a certain physical object exists, the tests and checking procedures made by Jones himself are not the only things relevant to the truth of his assertion. Testimony of what others see, hear, and so on is also relevant. That is, if Jones wanted to know whether it was really a star that he saw, he could not only take photographs, look through a telescope, and the like but also ask others if they saw the star. If a large proportion of a large number of people denied seeing the star, Jones's claim about the star's existence would be weakened. Of course, he might still trust his telescope. However, let us now imagine that Jones does not make use of the tests and checking procedures (photographs and telescopes) but is left with the testimony of what he sees and the testimony of others concerning what they see. In this case, it is so much to the point if a large number of people deny seeing the star that Jones will be considered irrational or mad if he goes on asserting its existence. His only irrefutable position is to reduce his physical object claim to an announcement concerning his own sensations. Then the testimony of men and angels cannot disturb his certitude. These sensations of the moment he knows directly

[11] I shall call such statements "low-claim assertions."

and immediately, and the indirect and nonimmediate testimony of men and angels is irrelevant. Absolute confidence and absolute indifference to the majority judgment is bought at the price of reducing the existential to the nonexistential.

The religious claim is similar to, though not identical with, the case above in certain important features. We have seen that there are no tests or checking procedures open to the believer to support his existential claim about God. Thus, he is left with the testimony of his own experience and the similar testimony of the experience of others. And, of course, he is not left wanting for such testimony, for religious communities seem to serve just this sort of function.

Let us imagine a case comparable to the one concerning the existence of a physical object. In this case Brown is a professor of divinity, and he believes that he has come to know of the existence of God through direct experience of God. In order to understand the intricate character of what Professor Brown is asserting we must imagine a highly unusual situation. The other members of the faculty and the members of Professor Brown's religious community suddenly begin sincerely to deny his, and what has been their own, assertion. Perhaps they still attend church services and pray as often as they used to do, and perhaps they claim to have the same sort of experiences as they had when they were believers, but they refuse to accept the conclusion that God exists. Whether they give a Freudian explanation or some other explanation or no explanation of their experiences, they are agreed in refusing to accept the existential claim (about God) made by Professor Brown. How does this affect Professor Brown and his claim? It may affect Professor Brown very deeply—indeed, he may die of broken-hearted disappointment at the loss of his fellow believers. However, the loss of fellow believers may not weaken his confidence in the truth of his assertion or in the testimony of his experience. In this matter his experience may be all that ultimately counts for him in establishing his confidence in the truth of his claim about the existence of God. It has been said that religious experience carries its own guarantee, and perhaps the account above describes what is meant by this.

It is quite obvious from these examples that the religious statement "I have direct experience of God" is of a different status from the physical object statement "I see a star" and shows a distressing similarity to the low-claim assertion "I seem to see a star." The bulk of this chapter has so far been devoted to showing some of the many forms this similarity takes. Does this mean then that the religious statement and its existential claim concerning God amount to no more than a reference to the complex feelings and experiences of the believer?

Perhaps the best way to answer this question is to take a typical low-claim assertion and see if there is anything which must be said of it and all other low-claim assertions which cannot be said of the religious statement. One way of differentiating a physical object statement from a low-claim assertion is by means of prefixing the phrase "I seem." [12] For instance, the statement "I see a star" may be transformed into a statement concerning my sensations by translating it into the form "I seem to see a star." The first statement involves a claim about the existence of an object as well as an announcement concerning my sensations and therefore subjects itself to the risk of being

---

[12] This, clearly, is a superficial and mechanical move, for the prefixing of this phrase ordinarily would result in a qualified and hedging physical object statement. I shall just have to plead that the possibility that such a prefixing should result in a low-claim assertion is here realized.

wrong concerning that further claim. Whether one is wrong in this case is determined by a society of tests and checking procedures such as taking photographs and looking through telescopes and by the testimony of others that they see or do not see a star. The second statement involves no claim about the existence of an object and so requires no such tests and no testimony of others; indeed, the final judge of the truth of the statement is the person making it. If no existential claim is lost by the addition of this phrase to a statement then the assertion is low-claim. For instance, the statement "I feel pain" loses nothing by the addition "I seem to feel pain."

In the case of the religious statement "I have direct experience of God" the addition of the phrase is fatal to all that the believer wants to assert. "I seem to be having direct experience of God" is a statement concerning my feelings and sensations of the moment, and as such it makes no claim about the existence of God. Thus, the original statement "I have direct experience of God" is not a low-claim assertion. This should not surprise us. We should have known it all along, for is it not an assertion that one comes to know something, namely God, by means of one's feelings and sensations and this something is not reducible to them? The statement is not a low-claim one just because it is used to assert the existence of something. Whether this assertion is warranted and what exactly it amounts to is quite another question.

We are tempted to think that the religious statement must be of one sort or another. The truth is that *per impossible* it is both at once. The theologian must use it in both ways, and which way he is to emphasize at a particular time depends upon the circumstances of its use and most particularly the direction of our probings.

The statement "I seem to be having direct experience of God" is an eccentric one. It is eccentric not only because introspective announcements are unusual and because statements about God have a peculiar obscurity but for a further and more important reason. This eccentricity may be brought out by comparing this statement with others having the same form. A first formulation of this may be put in the following way. In reference to things other than our sensations of the moment knowledge is prior to seeming as if.

The statement "I seem to be looking directly at a chair" has a meaning only insofar as I already *know* what it is like to look directly at a chair. The statement "I seem to be listening to a choir," has a meaning only insofar as I already *know* what it is like to be listening to a choir. The assumption of knowledge in both these cases is one which all normal people are expected to be able to make and do in fact make.

The statement "I seem to be having direct experience of God" does not lend itself so easily to the criterion for meaning exemplified above, because if this statement has meaning only insofar as one already *knows* what it is like to have direct experience of God, the assumption of such knowledge is certainly not one which all normal people may be expected to be able to make or do in fact make. However, it may be said that the assumption of such knowledge as knowledge of what it is like to see a gorgon may not be made of all normal people and, therefore, the case of religious knowledge is in no peculiar position. This objection can be answered when we ask the question "How do we come to learn what it would be like to look directly at a chair, hear a choir, see a gorgon, have direct experience of God?"

It is not that there are no answers to the question concerning how we come to learn what it would be like to have direct experience of God. We are not left completely in the dark. Instead, the point is that the answers to this question are quite different from the answers to the questions concerning how we come to learn what it would be like to look directly at a chair, hear a choir, and see a gorgon. No one in our society has seen a gorgon, yet there are people who, by means of their specialized knowledge of mythical literature, may claim in a perfectly meaningful way that it now seems to them as if they were seeing a gorgon.

Let us imagine a society in which there are no chairs and no one knows anything at all about chairs. If we were to try to teach one of the members of this society what it would be like to see a chair and if we were not allowed to construct a chair, what might we do? We might look around at the furniture and say, "A chair is a kind of narrow settee. It is used to sit on." This would be a beginning. Then we might compare different settees as to which are more chairlike. We might draw pictures of chairs, make gestures with our hands showing the general shape and size of different sorts of chairs. If, on the following day, the person being instructed said, "I had a most unusual dream last night—I seemed to be looking directly at a chair," we should admit that his statement was closer in meaning to a similar one which we who have seen chairs might make than it would be to a similar one which another member might make who had no information or instruction or experience of chairs. We would insist that we had better knowledge of what it is to see a chair than has the instructed member of society who has still actually to see a chair. However, to know pictures of chairs is to know about chairs in a legitimate sense.

But let us now imagine a utopian society in which none of the members has ever been in the least sad or unhappy. If we were to try to teach one of the members of this society what it would be like to feel sad, how would we go about it?

It can be said that giving definitions, no matter how ingenious, would be no help; drawing pictures of unhappy faces, no matter how well drawn, would be no help, so long as these measures failed to evoke a feeling of sadness in this person. Comparing the emotion of sadness with other emotions would be no help, because no matter how like other emotions (weariness and the like) are to sadness they fail just because they are not sadness. No, sadness is unique and incomparable.

To anyone who has no such awareness of sadness, leading, as it does, to the typically unhappy behavior of tears and drawn faces, it will be quite impossible to indicate what is meant. One can only hope to evoke it on the assumption that the capacity to become aware of sadness is part of normal human nature like the capacity to see light or to hear sound.

This last paragraph is a play upon a quotation given at the very beginning of this chapter. The following is the original version.

> To anyone who has no such awareness of God, leading as it does to the typically religious attitudes of obeisance and worship, it will be quite impossible to indicate what is meant; one can only hope to evoke it, on the assumption that the capacity to become aware of God is part of normal human nature like the capacity to see light or to hear sound.[13]

Consider the following statements:

1. We are rejecting logical argument of any kind as the first chapter of our epistemology of aesthetics, or as representing the process by which beauty comes to be known.

2. It is not as the result of an inference of any kind, whether explicit or implicit, whether laboriously excogitated or swiftly intuited, that the knowledge of beauty comes to us.

---

[13] Farmer, *Towards Belief in God*, p. 40.

3. To those who have never been confronted with the experience of seeing the beauty of something, argument is useless. As these statements stand, they are plainly false. Professors of aesthetics and professional art critics often do help us to come to "knowledge of beauty" by all kinds of inference and arguments. They may, and often do, help us to come to a finer appreciation of beautiful things. Knowledge of the rules of perspective and understanding of an artist's departure from them is relevant to an aesthetic appreciation of his work.

However, it is possible to interpret these statements as true, and this is more important for our purpose. There is sense in saying that an art critic, who has vastly increased our aesthetic sensitivity and whose books of art criticism are the very best, may never have known beauty. If there are no signs of this critic ever having been stirred by any work of art, then no matter how subtle his analyses, there is sense in claiming that he has never been confronted with the experience of seeing the beauty of something. This sense just is that we may be determined not to say that a person has seen the beauty of something or has knowledge of beauty if he does not at some time have certain complex emotions and feelings which are typically associated with looking at paintings, hearing music, and reading poetry. To "know beauty" or to "see the beauty of something" here means, among other things, to have certain sorts or emotions and feelings.

The statements on aesthetics given above are a play on a quotation given at the beginning of this chapter. The following is the original version with the appropriate omissions and transpositions.

We are rejecting logical argument of any kind as the first chapter of our theology or as representing the process by which God comes to be known. . . .

It is not as the result of an inference of any kind, whether explicit or implicit, whether laboriously excogitated or swiftly intuited, that the knowledge of God's reality comes to us.

. . . To those who have never been confronted with it [direct, personal encounter with God] argument is useless.[14]

As these statements stand they are plainly false. Professors of divinity and clergymen are expected to do what Baillie claims cannot be done.

However, it is possible to interpret these statements as true, and this is more important for our purpose. There is sense in saying that a theologian (who has vastly increased our religious sensitivity and whose books of theology are the very best) may never have known God. If there are no signs of this theologian's ever having been stirred by a religious ritual or act of worship, then, no matter how subtle his analyses, there is sense in claiming that he has never been confronted with God's personal Presence. This sense just is that we are determined not to say that a person has knowledge of God if he does not at some time have certain complex emotions and feelings which are associated with attending religious services, praying, and reading the Bible. To "know God" or to be confronted with God's "personal Presence" means, of necessity, having certain sorts of emotions and feelings.

In this section the analogy between seeing blue and experiencing God has been examined and found to be misleading. I shall not deal in this chapter with the connexion between what the believer expects from immortality and his religious belief. This peculiar kind of test or verification has special difficulties which will be treated in another chapter.

So far I have tried to indicate how statements concerning a certain alleged religious way of knowing betray a logic

---

[14] Baillie, *Our Knowledge of God*, pp. 132, 143.

extraordinarily like that of statements concerning introspective and subjective ways of knowing. It is not my wish to go from a correct suggestion that the logic is *very, very* like to an incorrect suggestion that their logic is *just* like that of introspective and subjective statements, for, after all, such statements are logically in order.

I have argued that one cannot read off the existence of God from the existence of religious experience. Now, I must insist, in all charity, that *neither* can one read off the *non*-existence of God from the existence of religious experience.

In criticizing some of the foregoing argument, Mr. W. D. Glasgow claims,

It is essential here for the defender of the religious way of knowing to assert that there are cases where a man *knows* himself to be experiencing an objective Deity, just as there are cases where he knows himself to be experiencing a subjective pain. Unless it is insisted that there is such a thing as *cognitive experience* in religion, Martin's assimilation of all religious existential statements to psychological statements (or what ought to be called psychological statements) becomes highly plausible. Indeed, even the phrase *"may be objective"* has no meaning, probably, for Martin, unless theoretically at least it is possible to find out or test whether religious experience *is* objective. The position is only saved, again, if we say that in some cases the agent himself anyhow *does* know.[15]

Glasgow cannot mean "a man *knows* himself to be experiencing an objective Deity" *in just the same way as* "he knows himself to be experiencing a subjective pain." One's pain is not a thing that exists

independently of one's experience. I do not establish the existence of my pain on the basis of experience. There is nothing to establish beyond the experience. Presumably there is something to establish on the basis of religious experience, namely, the presence of God. When Glasgow says "there is such a thing as *cognitive experience* in religion" and "in some cases the agent himself anyhow *does* know," he must be read as saying that the presence of God is known on the basis of religious experience. That is, the presence of God is something over and above the experience itself. The model that Glasgow implies is that a cognitive experience is rather like a photograph of a friend: one can read off from the photograph that it is of that friend: and though this is a misleading model, there is something in it. If I am sitting at my desk and someone asks me if there is an ash tray on my desk, *all* that I have to do is have a look and say "Yes" or "No." But whether or not I know there is an ash tray on my desk is not to be read off simply from what my eyes at that moment told me. For if my eyes can tell me the truth they can tell me a lie, and the difference here would not be decided by what they tell. For me really to have seen and known there was an ash tray, other people must have been able to have seen it if they had looked. If I have only the testimony of my eyes and discount all else, then that testimony is mute concerning the existence of what is external. My eyes can tell me (in an hallucination) of the presence of an ash tray when there is no ash tray.

When someone uses the sentence "I see an ash tray" in such a way that he counts as relevant to its truth *only* his visual experience at the time, he is talking *only* about that experience, though the sentence has the form of making a statement about an ash tray. It does not help if he calls it a "cognitive experience" or if he says that he "anyhow *does* know"

[15] W. D. Glasgow, "Knowledge of God," *Philosophy*, XXXII (1957), 236. This article is a criticism of my article "A Religious Way of Knowing," printed in Flew and MacIntyre, *New Essays in Philosophical Theology* (London: S. C. M. Press, 1955), pp. 76–95.

or if he says that his experience is "self-authenticating" or is a "direct encounter." We cannot allow a speaker any final authority in the account of how he is using his sentences. If such special dispensation were allowable, conceptual confusion would be rare indeed.

Similarly, I have argued, when someone uses the sentence "I have or have had direct experience of God" in such a way that he counts as relevant to its truth *only* his experience at the time, he is talking *only* about that experience, though the sentence has the form of making a statement about the presence of God, and neither does it help if he calls it a "cognitive experience."

From the fact that someone uses the sentence "I see an ash tray" so that he is talking *only* about his visual experience, nothing at all follows about whether or not he is actually seeing an ash tray in front of him. His *statement* may be only about his visual experience itself, and his actual *situation* may be that of seeing the ash tray. Also, from the fact that someone uses the sentence "I have or have had direct experience of God" in such a way that he is talking *only* about his experience at the time, nothing at all follows about whether or not he is actually experiencing the presence of a supernatural being. His *statement* may be only about his experience itself, and his actual *situation* may be that of experiencing the presence of a supernatural being.

The religious person will want, in what he says, to be able to distinguish between a "delusive" and a "veridical" experience of God. The experience should be due to the actual presence of God and not due only to a drug or to self-deception or to the action of Satan. Therefore he must use his sentence to refer to more than an experience that is, in principle, compatible with these and other similar causes.

What makes a form of experience a way of knowing? It is often suggested that the mystic who "sees" God is like a man (in a society of blind men) who sees colors. It is claimed that each has a form of experience and a way of knowing that others lack. Let us now work out this analogy. A society of blind men is told by one of its members that he has come to have a form of experience and a way of knowing by means of which he has been able to discover the existence of things not discoverable by ordinary experience. He says that these things have a *kind* of size (not just like size as it is felt by the blind) and a *kind* of shape (not just like shape as it is felt by the blind); he further says that these things are somehow "everywhere" and that they cannot expect to understand what these things are like and what he means by experiencing them unless they themselves have these experiences. He then tells them of a procedure by which they will be able to discover for themselves the existence of these things. He warns them that these things do not always reveal themselves when the procedure is carried out, but, if a person is sufficiently diligent and believes strongly enough in their existence, he will probably come to know by means of unique and incomparable experiences of the existence of these things.

Some people, with faith and diligence, submit themselves to the required procedure, and some of these are rewarded by a kind of experience they have not known before. Color shapes float before them—things that they cannot touch or feel and that are beyond the reach of their senses, and things that may be present to one of their group and not experienced by the others, things that may as well be everywhere as anywhere, since they are locatable only in the sense of being "before" each observer to whom they appear. These people cannot correlate this new form of experience with the rest of experience, they cannot touch or smell these "things." Indeed, they "see" visions, not things. Or rather these people have no way of *knowing* the existence of the things that may or may not exist over and above the momentary experiences. May these experiences all the same be "cognitive?" Yes and no. Yes, there may be something, they know not what, responsible for their having these experiences. No, their experiences are not a way of *knowing* about this something. For the experience of a colored shape that needs no corroboration by the experience of others similarly placed, and that is not related to one's other senses, is not in itself a way of knowing what in the world is responsible for this experience even if there is something beyond the condition of the "observer" that is so responsible. So far, even the people concerned have no *way of knowing* what more is involved than the fact of their experiencing momentary "visions."

I have not denied that the religious mystic may have experiences that others do not. Neither have I denied that there might be some external agency responsible for these experiences. What I have denied is that the mystic's possession of these experiences is in itself a way of knowing the existence or nature of such an agency.

The argument of this chapter lies in an area in which confusion is common. I shall consider two cases of such confusion especially relevant to what I have been saying.

You are acquainted with the distinction between feeling and emotion. Feeling, such as pleasure or pain, is in itself a purely subjective experience; emotion implies an objective situation within which there is something which arouses the emotion, and towards which the emotion is directed. The Divine is, it would seem, first experienced in such a situation; and is initially apprehended solely and exclusively as that which arouses certain types of emotion. If the emotion be awe, then the Divine is so far apprehended as the awesome, what Otto has so helpfully entitled the numinous.[16]

There are two questionable assumptions here: first, that whether or not an experience refers to an objective state of affairs can be read off from the experience itself; second, that emotions *must* do so.

The second claim that an emotion as such implies an objective situation can be refuted very simply. My feeling of pleasure while watching a game of football is related to something in my environment, but my feeling of pleasure at a tune running through my head is not. My emotion of awe in the presence of a particularly magnificent race horse is related to something in my environment, but my emotion of awe during a dream of a coronation service is not. Some people have aesthetic emotions aroused by the contemplation of mathematical proofs and theorems, and others have the emotion of fear toward ghosts and goblins.

In a criticism of the argument of the first part of this chapter (as originally published in "A Religious Way of Knowing," in *Mind*, October, 1952) Professor H. D. Lewis seems to be making the first claim, that a reference to an objective state of affairs can be read off from the experience itself.

He [Martin] seems to think that the only claim to objectivity which an experience may have is that which is established by tests and checking procedures. A man's statement that he "seems to see a blue piece of paper" is thus said to be unassailable only because it is a "claim about his own state of mind." This I would doubt, for the colour expanse which we only seem to see is neither a mere appearance nor a state of mind. It is "out there before me"

---

[16] N. Kemp Smith, *Is Divine Existence Credible?*, British Academy Lecture (London: British Academy, 1931), p. 23.

and real enough while I seem to see it, however many problems may be involved in distinguishing between it and physical entities. . . . "Having been stirred" by a religious ritual or act of worship, or having "certain sorts of emotions and feelings," is not the essential thing in religious experience; it is what we apprehend that comes first.[17]

However, "what we apprehend," if anything, is the whole problem and cannot "come first." Certainly, people have had special sorts of experience which incline them to claim with the greatest confidence that their experiences are of God. But whether the experiences are or are not of God is not to be decided by describing or having those experiences. For whether anything or nothing is apprehended by experiences is not to be read off from the experiences themselves. The presence of a piece of blue paper is not to be read off from my experience as of a piece of blue paper. Other things are relevant: What would a photograph reveal? Can I touch it? What do others see? It is only when I admit the relevance of such checking procedures that I can lay claim to apprehending the paper, and, indeed, the admission of the relevance of such procedures is what gives meaning to the assertion that I am apprehending the paper. *What I apprehend is the sort of thing that can be photographed, touched, and seen by others.*

It does not help when Lewis says,

The colour expanse which we only seem to see is neither a mere appearance nor a state of mind. It is "out there before me" and real enough while I seem to see it, however many problems may be involved in distinguishing between it and physical entities.

Think now of a man who claims to see a blue piece of paper, and when we com-plain that we cannot, he replies, "Oh, it isn't the sort of thing that can be photographed, touched, or seen by others, but all the same, it is out there before me." Are we to think that he has come upon a special sort of object that is nevertheless "out there" as are desks and tables and the rest of the furniture of the world? No, ontological reference is something to be earned. We earn the designation "out there" of a thing by allowing its presence to be determined by the procedures we all know. We cannot just *say* "out there" of it, and we cannot just *say* "apprehended" of God.

It can be objected, "But God is different, and we never meant that our experiences of God should be checked by procedures relevant to physical objects." Of course not, but what *sort* of checks are there then, so that we are left with more than the mere experiences whose existence even the atheist need not deny?

II

Yet checking procedures are not on all accounts in all ways irrelevant. As in all theological discourse concerning the status of religious experience there are many, many voices, and so far we have listened to too few.

A religious experience is not just an ineffable, indescribable something that comes and goes unbidden and amenable to no criteria of identity. At least, the mystics seldom describe it in this way. There are certain steps one can take to bring about such experiences, and the experiences are describable within limits, and they leave certain kinds of identifiable afteraffects.

Alvarez de Paz and other mystics have emphasized the importance of practicing austerities, conquering the flesh, and mortifying the body.

Of course, this training of the body is not sufficient. The mind must be trained as well. To have a vision of the Holy

---

[17] H. D. Lewis, "Philosophical Surveys X, The Philosophy of Religion, 1945–1952," *Philosophical Quarterly*, IV (July, 1954), p. 263.

Virgin one must be acquainted with the basic facts of "Christ's birth and life and death." To have the highest mystical apprehension of the Trinity, as did St. Teresa, one must have some elementary theological training.

Nor is bodily and intellectual training enough, for there must be moral and emotional training as well. The commandment to love one another was given not only to lead us to peace and brotherhood on earth but also to change our hearts so that we might see God.

Yet all of these may not be enough, for it is possible one should train oneself most assiduously in all of these ways and still not have truly religious experience. This possibility is characterized by saying that finally the favor and grace of God are required.

The paradoxical and negative ways in which mystics most often describe their experiences may seem, at first, unsatisfactory. But it helps to consider how similar sorts of descriptions are employed outside the religious context. One might say of one's emotion at a particular time that one felt both love and hate toward someone. This would be understood as a description of a complex emotion that most of us have experienced. And the paradoxical expression is not reducible to "in some ways love, in other ways hate," because it refers not only to different patterns of behaving and feeling but also to a particular feeling at a particular moment.

Alvarez de Paz gives a particularly sharp description that must strike even the most sceptical reader as in no way obscure or evasive.

One perceives no representation of the face or the body, yet one knows with greater certainty than if one saw it with one's eyes that the person (Jesus Christ or the Blessed Virgin) is present on one's right hand or in one's heart. . . . It is as if, in darkness, one should feel at once that someone is at one's side, knowing that he has goodwill and not enmity towards you; while one remains absolutely ignorant whether it is a man or a woman, young or old, handsome or ugly, standing or seated.[18]

It would be wrong for us to legislate against the mystic's claim that his experience is not sensory. For in a nonreligious context there may be a parallel. Many of us have felt or experienced the presence of some loved one dead or living but distant. (Of course, we do not tend to think that the person is in any way *actually* present unless the person is dead.) Certainly in such cases we do not see or hear the person. It is not even *as if* we heard or saw the person. Making the parallel even closer to the mystical, we do not even have to have any kind of mental image of the loved one. Neither is the presence felt as being in any specific place. The very subtle feelings and emotions typically directed to this one person and no other are now aroused as once they were by this person alone. The unique love and regard this person showed us, we, as it were, receive again. And we can feel ashamed at having done things of which the loved one would disapprove. And so we can feel guided where there is no guide and loved where the lover is dead. The emotion is in shadow felt but is no less real for that.

A child may read of a fairy-story giant who eats the children who do not think he is real and even some who do. He is described in detail (perhaps there is even a picture), and his hatred of children is made too clear. The child may have a bad dream about the giant. Or he may, as in the case above, just feel the giant's presence in no very localized place yet somewhere near. That is, the child reads the story, comes to feel a kind of fear toward the giant, and hates him in a way

_____
[18] Quoted in Joseph Marechal, *Studies in the Psychology of the Mystics* (London: Burns Oates & Washbourne, 1927), p. 110.

that others do not. Then the child, hearing and seeing nothing, may, in the dark, feel that fear and sense that hate so strongly that he will claim, even when the light is turned on and in spite of the most tender parental reassurance, that the giant had been in the room. That is, the experience of the child is such that he is left with a certitude which he considers the giant alone could give.

In order to have such an experience, then, with all of the sense of reality and conviction that it carries, it is not necessary that the being whose presence is so felt should ever have existed.

As children we are taught to love Christ in a very special way, and we are taught of Christ's very special love for us. Christ, as a person, is made extremely real to us. That we cannot see or hear him takes very little from his reality. He was once seen and heard, and we are told so much of his life and actions and visible love that we are apt to feel that we know him more clearly than we do any other historical person. As children (or, indeed, as adults) we are encouraged in this feeling by being told that he is somehow, if not actually somewhere, alive. We are told that God loves us as Christ loves us, and we learn that Christ and God are somehow One. So we know roughly how we *should* feel in God's presence. We have as reference countless stories of how others have felt. These experiences are very different, but they form a kind of family. At one extreme there is a visible vision, and at the other extreme there is almost a kind of unconscious trance.

Let us now speak of the sign which proves the prayer of union to have been genuine. As you have seen, God then deprives the soul of all its senses that he may the better imprint in it true wisdom; it neither sees, hears, nor understands anything while this state lasts. . . . God visits the soul in a manner which prevents its doubting, on re-

turning to itself, that it dwelt in him and that he was within it. . . . But, you may ask, how can a person who is incapable of sight and hearing see or know these things? I do not say that she saw it at the time, but that she perceives it clearly afterwards, not by any vision but by a certitude which remains in the heart which God alone could give. . . . If we did not see it, how can we feel so sure of it? That I do not know: it is the work of the Almighty and I am certain that what I say is the fact. I maintain that a soul which does not feel this assurance has not been united to God entirely, but only by one of its powers, or has received one of the many other favours God is accustomed to bestow on men.[19]

Yet, with all of this, it could be argued that all that has been accomplished is a description of a class of experiences and of methods of obtaining and recognizing them. Their ontological reference has still to be established. It could be dogmatically asserted that these experiences by definition come only through the grace of God, but this would be no more than a way of stamping one's foot and insisting on, rather than arguing for, that reference. St. Teresa once again is of help. She was plagued during her lifetime not by doubts about the character of her experiences but about their source. Was she perhaps being subtly deceived by Satan? She was not at a loss to provide a kind of settlement procedure.

I could not believe that Satan, if he wished to deceive me, could have recourse to means so adverse to his purpose as this, of rooting out my faults and implanting virtues and spiritual strength: for I saw clearly that I had become another person by means of these visions. . . . Neither the imagination nor the evil one could represent what leaves such peace, calm, and good fruits in the soul, and particularly

---

[19] St. Teresa, *Interior Castle* (London: Thomas Baker, 1930), pp. 91–93.

the following three graces of a very high order. The first of these is a perception of the greatness of God, which becomes clearer to us as we witness more of it. Secondly, we gain self-knowledge and humility as we see how creatures so base as ourselves in comparison with the Creator of such wonders, have dared to offend Him in the past or venture to gaze on Him now. The third grace is a contempt of all earthly things unless they are consecrated to the service of so great a God.[20]

But now, what more has really been accomplished by this? To say that the source of these experiences is God and not Satan in the absence of further criteria reduces to saying that these experiences have certain sorts of profound effects upon one's character, attitudes, and behavior. And why should an atheist deny any of this? If there is more that cannot be so reduced and if it is inconsistent with the claims of an atheist, it still remains to be said.

[20] *Ibid.*, p. 171.

Unlike the first section of this chapter, this section has been concerned with views (those of the great Catholic mystics) in which statements about religious experience are not employed as in any way arguments for, or evidence of, the existence of God. The mystics are convinced on other grounds of the existence of God. Religious experience, then, is conceived by them as a way of coming to know better the object of their worship, whose existence is proved or assumed independent of that experience.

This conservative estimate of the status of religious experience in theology is not, however, necessarily safe from censure. The conceptual weight is shifted from the experience to the previously established or assumed notion of the object of the experience. In the previous chapter difficulties were found in typical notions of the qualities of God. No Catholic theologian and few Protestant theologians would claim that religious experience could resolve problems of this conceptual sort.

RUDOLF OTTO

The Essence of Religious Experience

*The German Protestant theologian Rudolf Otto (1869–1937)
developed a Neo-Kantian interpretation of religion, but his greatest
impact on contemporary religious thought has been through his
analysis of religious experience, the heart of which is presented here.*

CHAPTER III

THE ELEMENTS IN THE 'NUMINOUS'

Creature-Feeling

The reader is invited to direct his mind to a moment of deeply-felt religious experience, as little as possible qualified by other forms of consciousness. Whoever cannot do this, whoever knows no such moments in his experience, is requested to read no farther; for it is not easy to discuss questions of religious psychology with one who can recollect the emotions of his adolescence, the discomforts of indigestion, or, say, social feelings, but cannot recall any intrinsically religious feelings. We do not blame such an one, when he tries for himself to advance as far as he can with the help of such principles of explanation as he knows, interpreting 'aesthetics' in terms of sensuous pleasure, and 'religion' as a function of the gregarious instinct and social standards, or as something more primitive still. But the artist, who for his part has an intimate personal knowledge of the distinctive element in the aesthetic experience, will decline his theories with thanks, and the religious man will reject them even more uncompromisingly.

Next, in the probing and analysis of such states of the soul as that of solemn worship, it will be well if regard be paid to what is unique in them rather than to what they have in common with other similar states. To be *rapt* in worship is one thing; to be morally *uplifted* by the contemplation of a good deed is another; and it is not to their common features, but to those elements of emotional content peculiar to the first that we would have attention directed as precisely as possible. As Christians we undoubtedly here first meet with feelings familiar enough in a weaker form in other departments of experience, such as feelings of gratitude, trust, love, reliance, humble submission, and dedication. But this does not by any means exhaust the content of religious worship. Not in any of these have we got the special features of the quite unique and incomparable experience of solemn worship. In what does this consist?

Schleiermacher has the credit of isolating a very important element in such

From Rudolf Otto, *The Idea of the Holy*, tr. by J. W. Harvey (1923), Chs. III–VI. Reprinted by permission of Oxford University Press.

an experience. This is the 'feeling of dependence.' But this important discovery of Schleiermacher is open to criticism in more than one respect.

In the first place, the feeling or emotion which he really has in mind in this phrase is in its specific quality not a 'feeling of dependence' in the 'natural' sense of the word. As such, other domains of life and other regions of experience than the religious occasion the feeling, as a sense of personal insufficiency and impotence, a consciousness of being determined by circumstances and environment. The feeling of which Schleiermacher wrote has an undeniable analogy with these states of mind: they serve as an indication to it, and its nature may be elucidated by them, so that, by following the direction in which they point, the feeling itself may be spontaneously felt. But the feeling is at the same time also qualitatively different from such analogous states of mind. Schleiermacher himself, in a way, recognizes this by distinguishing the feeling of pious or religious dependence from all other feelings of dependence. His mistake is in making the distinction merely that between 'absolute' and 'relative' dependence, and therefore a difference of degree and not of intrinsic quality. What he overlooks is that, in giving the feeling the name 'feeling of dependence' at all, we are really employing what is no more than a very close analogy. Anyone who compares and contrasts the two states of mind introspectively will find out, I think, what I mean. It cannot be expressed by means of anything else, just because it is so primary and elementary a datum in our psychical life, and therefore only definable through itself. It may perhaps help him if I cite a well-known example, in which the precise 'moment' or element of religious feeling of which we are speaking is most actively present. When Abraham ventures to plead with God for the men of Sodom, he says (Gen. xviii. 27):

'Behold now, I have taken upon me to speak unto the Lord, which am but dust and ashes.' There you have a self-confessed 'feeling of dependence,' which is yet at the same time far more than, and something other than, *merely* a feeling of dependence. Desiring to give it a name of its own, I propose to call it 'creature-consciousness' or creature-feeling. It is the emotion of a creature, submerged and overwhelmed by its own nothingness in contrast to that which is supreme above all creatures.

It is easily seen that, once again, this phrase, whatever it is, is not a *conceptual* explanation of the matter. All that this new term, 'creature-feeling,' can express, is the note of submergence into nothingness before an overpowering, absolute might of some kind; whereas everything turns upon the *character* of this overpowering might, a character which cannot be expressed verbally, and can only be suggested indirectly through the tone and content of a man's feeling-response to it. And this response must be directly experienced in oneself to be understood.

We have now to note a second defect in the formulation of Schleiermacher's principle. The religious category discovered by him, by whose means he professes to determine the real content of the religious emotion, is merely a category of *self*-valuation, in the sense of self-depreciation. According to him the religious emotion would be directly and primarily a sort of *self*-consciousness, a feeling concerning oneself in a special, determined relation, viz. one's dependence. Thus, according to Schleiermacher, I can only come upon the very fact of God as the result of an inference, that is, by reasoning to a cause beyond myself to account for my 'feeling of dependence.' But this is entirely opposed to the psychological facts of the case. Rather, the 'creature-feeling' is itself a first subjective concomitant and effect of another feeling-element, which casts it like a shadow, but which in itself indubitably has immediate and primary reference to an object outside the self.[1]

Now this object is just what we have already spoken of as 'the numinous.' For the 'creature-feeling' and the sense of dependence to arise in the mind the 'numen' must be experienced as present, a *numen praesens,* as is in the case of Abraham. There must be felt a something 'numinous,' something bearing the character of a 'numen,' to which the mind turns spontaneously; or (which is the same thing in other words) these feelings can only arise in the mind as accompanying emotions when the category of 'the numinous' is called into play.

The numinous is thus felt as objective

---

[1] This is so manifestly borne out by experience that it must be about the first thing to force itself upon the notice of psychologists analysing the facts of religion. There is a certain naïveté in the following passage from William James's *Varieties of Religious Experience* (p. 58), where, alluding to the origin of the Grecian representations of the gods, he says: 'As regards the origin of the Greek gods, we need not at present seek an opinion. But the whole array of our instances leads to a conclusion something like this: It is as if there were in the human consciousness *a sense of reality, a feeling of objective presence,* a *perception* of what we may call *"something there,"* more deep and more general than any of the special and particular "senses" by which the current psychology supposes existent realities to be originally revealed.' (The italics are James's own.) James is debarred by his empiricist and pragmatist standpoint from coming to a recognition of faculties of knowledge and potentialities of thought in the spirit itself, and he is therefore obliged to have recourse to somewhat singular and mysterious hypotheses to explain this fact. But he grasps the fact itself clearly enough and is sufficient of a realist not to explain it away. But this 'feeling of reality', the feeling of a 'numinous' *object* objectively given, must be posited as a primary immediate datum of consciousness, and the 'feeling of dependence' is then a consequence, following very closely upon it, viz. a depreciation of the *subject* in his own eyes. The latter presupposes the former.

and outside the self. We have now to inquire more closely into its nature and the modes of its manifestation.

CHAPTER IV

'MYSTERIUM TREMENDUM'

The Analysis of 'Tremendum'

We said above that the nature of the numinous can only be suggested by means of the special way in which it is reflected in the mind in terms of feeling. 'Its nature is such that it grips or stirs the human mind with this and that determinate affective state.' We have now to attempt to give a further indication of these determinate states. We must once again endeavour, by adducing feelings akin to them for the purpose of analogy or contrast, and by the use of metaphor and symbolic expressions, to make the states of mind we are investigating ring out, as it were, of themselves.

Let us consider the deepest and most fundamental element in all strong and sincerely felt religious emotion. Faith unto salvation, trust, love—all these are there. But over and above these is an element which may also on occasion, quite apart from them, profoundly affect us and occupy the mind with a wellnigh bewildering strength. Let us follow it up with every effort of sympathy and imaginative intuition wherever it is to be found, in the lives of those around us, in sudden, strong ebullitions of personal piety and the frames of mind such ebullitions evince, in the fixed and ordered solemnities of rites and liturgies, and again in the atmosphere that clings to old religious monuments and buildings, to temples and to churches. If we do so we shall find we are dealing with something for which there is only one appropriate expression, *'mysterium tremendum.'* The feeling of it may at times come sweeping like a gentle tide, pervading the mind with a tranquil mood of deepest worship. It may pass over into a more set and lasting attitude of the soul, continuing, as it were, thrillingly vibrant and resonant, until at last it dies away and the soul resumes its 'profane,' non-religious mood of everyday experience. It may burst in sudden eruption up from the depths of the soul with spasms and convulsions, or lead to the strangest excitements, to intoxicated frenzy, to transport, and to ecstasy. It has its wild and demonic forms and can sink to an almost grisly horror and shuddering. It has its crude, barbaric antecedents and early manifestations, and again it may be developed into something beautiful and pure and glorious. It may become the hushed, trembling, and speechless humility of the creature in the presence of—whom or what? In the presence of that which is a *mystery* inexpressible and above all creatures.

It is again evident at once that here too our attempted formulation by means of a concept is once more a merely negative one. Conceptually *mysterium* denotes merely that which is hidden and esoteric, that which is beyond conception or understanding, extraordinary and unfamiliar. The term does not define the object more positively in its qualitative character. But though what is enunciated in the word is negative, what is meant is something absolutely and intensely positive. This pure positive we can experience in feelings, feelings which our discussion can help to make clear to us, in so far as it arouses them actually in our hearts.

1. *The Element of Awefulness*

To get light upon the positive *'quale'* of the object of these feelings, we must analyse more closely our phrase *mysterium tremendum,* and we will begin first with the adjective.

Tremor is in itself merely the perfectly familiar and 'natural' emotion of *fear*. But here the term is taken, aptly enough

but still only by analogy, to denote a quite specific kind of emotional response, wholly distinct from that of being afraid, though it so far resembles it that the analogy of fear may be used to throw light upon its nature. There are in some languages special expressions which denote, either exclusively or in the first instance, this 'fear' that is more than fear proper. The Hebrew *hiqdīsh* (hallow) is an example. To 'keep a thing holy in the heart' means to mark it off by a feeling of peculiar dread, not to be mistaken for any ordinary dread, that is, to appraise it by the category of the numinous. But the Old Testament throughout is rich in parallel expressions for this feeling. Specially noticeable is the *'ēmāh* of Yahweh ('fear of God'), which Yahweh can pour forth, dispatching almost like a daemon, and which seizes upon a man with paralysing effect. It is closely related to the δεῖμα πανικόν of the Greeks. Compare Exod. xxiii. 27: 'I will send my fear before thee, and will destroy all the people to whom thou shalt come . . .'; also Job ix. 34; xiii. 21 ('let not his fear terrify me'; 'let not thy dread make me afraid'). Here we have a terror fraught with an inward shuddering such as not even the most menacing and overpowering created thing can instil. It has something spectral in it.

In the Greek language we have a corresponding term in σεβαστός. The early Christians could clearly feel that the title σεβαστός (*augustus*) was one that could not fittingly be given to any creature, not even to the emperor. They felt that to call a man σεβαστός was to give a human being a name proper only to the *numen*, to rank him by the category proper only to the *numen,* and that it therefore amounted to a kind of idolatry. Of modern languages English has the words 'awe,' 'aweful,' which in their deeper and most special sense approximate closely to our meaning. The phrase, 'he stood aghast,' is also suggestive in this connexion. On the other hand, German has no native-grown expression of its own for the higher and riper form of the emotion we are considering, unless it be in a word like *erschauern,* which does suggest it fairly well. It is far otherwise with its cruder and more debased phases, where such terms as *grausen* and *Schauer,* and the more popular and telling *gruseln* ('grue'), *gräsen,* and *grässlich* ('grisly'), very clearly designate the numinous element. In my examination of Wundt's Animism I suggested the term *Scheu* (dread); but the special 'numinous' quality (making it 'awe' rather than 'dread' in the ordinary sense) would then, of course, have to be denoted by inverted commas. 'Religious dread' (or 'awe') would perhaps be a better designation. Its antecedent stage is 'daemonic dread' (cf. the horror of Pan) with its queer perversion, a sort of abortive offshoot, the 'dread of ghosts.' It first begins to stir in the feeling of 'something uncanny,' 'eerie,' or 'weird.' It is this feeling which, emerging in the mind of primeval man, forms the starting-point for the entire religious development in history. 'Daemons' and 'gods' alike spring from this root, and all the products of 'mythological apperception' or 'fantasy' are nothing but different modes in which it has been objectified. And all ostensible explanations of the origin of religion in terms of animism or magic or folk-psychology are doomed from the outset to wander astray and miss the real goal of their inquiry, unless they recognize this fact of our nature—primary, unique, underivable from anything else—to be the basic factor and the basic impulse underlying the entire process of religious evolution.[1]

[1] Cf. my papers in *Theologische Rundschau,* 1910, vol. i, on 'Myth and Religion in Wundt's *Völkerpsychologie,*' and in *Deutsche Literaturzeitung,* 1910, No. 38. I find in more recent investigations, especially those of R. R. Marett and N. Söderblom, a

Not only is the saying of Luther, that the natural man cannot fear God perfectly, correct from the standpoint of psychology, but we ought to go farther and add that the natural man is quite unable even to 'shudder' (*grauen*) or feel horror in the real sense of the word. For 'shuddering' is something more than 'natural,' ordinary fear. It implies that the mysterious is already beginning to loom before the mind, to touch the feelings. It implies the first application of a category of valuation which has no place in the everyday natural world of ordinary experience, and is only possible to a being in whom has been awakened a mental predisposition, unique in kind and different in a definite way from any 'natural' faculty. And this newly-revealed capacity, even in the crude and violent manifestations which are all it at first evinces, bears witness to a completely new function of experience and standard of valuation, only belonging to the spirit of man.

Before going on to consider the elements which unfold as the '*tremendum*' develops, let us give a little further consideration to the first crude, primitive forms in which this 'numinous dread' or *awe* shows itself. It is the mark which really characterizes the so-called 'religion of primitive man,' and there it appears as 'daemonic dread.' This crudely naïve and primordial emotional disturbance, and the fantastic images to which it gives rise, are later overborne and ousted by more highly developed forms of the nu-

very welcome confirmation of the positions I there maintained. It is true that neither of them calls attention quite as precisely as, in this matter, psychologists need to do, to the unique character of the religious 'awe' and its qualitative distinction from all 'natural' feelings. But Marett more particularly comes within a hair's breadth of what I take to be the truth about the matter. Cf. his *Threshold of Religion* (London, 1909), and N. Söderblom's *Das Werden des Gottesglaubens* (Leipzig, 1915), also my review of the latter in *Theol. Literaturzeitung,* Jan. 1915.

minous emotion, with all its mysteriously impelling power. But even when this has long attained its higher and purer mode of expression it is possible for the primitive types of excitation that were formerly a part of it to break out in the soul in all their original naïveté and so to be experienced afresh. That this is so is shown by the potent attraction again and again exercised by the element of horror and 'shudder' in ghost stories, even among persons of high all-round education. It is a remarkable fact that the physical reaction to which this unique 'dread' of the uncanny gives rise is also unique, and is not found in the case of any 'natural' fear or terror. We say: 'my blood ran icy cold,' and 'my flesh crept.' The 'cold blood' feeling may be a symptom of ordinary, natural fear, but there is something non-natural or supernatural about the symptom of 'creeping flesh.' And any one who is capable of more precise introspection must recognize that the distinction between such a 'dread' and natural fear is not simply one of degree and intensity. The awe or 'dread' *may* indeed be so overwhelmingly great that it seems to penetrate to the very marrow, making the man's hair bristle and his limbs quake. But it may also steal upon him almost unobserved as the gentlest of agitations, a mere fleeting shadow passing across his mood. It has therefore nothing to do with intensity, and no natural fear passes over into it merely by being intensified. I may be beyond all measure afraid and terrified without there being even a trace of the feeling of uncanniness in my emotion.

We should see the facts more clearly if psychology in general would make a more decisive endeavour to examine and classify the feelings and emotions according to their qualitative differences. But the far too rough division of elementary feelings in general into pleasures and pains is still an obstacle to this. In point of fact 'pleasures' no more than other feelings are differentiated merely by degrees of intensity: they show very definite and specific differences. It makes a specific difference to the condition of mind whether the soul is merely in a state of pleasure, or joy, or aesthetic rapture, or moral exaltation, or finally in the religious bliss that may come in worship. Such states certainly show resemblances one to another, and on that account can legitimately be brought under a common class-concept ('pleasure'), which serves to cut them off from other psychical functions, generically different. But this class-concept, so far from turning the various subordinate species into merely different degrees of the same thing, can do nothing at all to throw light upon the essence of each several state of mind which it includes.

Though the numinous emotion in its completest development shows a world of difference from the mere 'daemonic dread,' yet not even at the highest level does it belie its pedigree or kindred. Even when the worship of 'daemons' has long since reached the higher level of worship of 'gods,' these gods still retain as *numina* something of the 'ghost' in the impress they make on the feelings of the worshipper, viz. the peculiar quality of the 'uncanny' and 'aweful,' which survives with the quality of exaltedness and sublimity or is symbolized by means of it. And this element, softened though it is, does not disappear even on the highest level of all, where the worship of God is at its purest. Its disappearance would be indeed an essential loss. The 'shudder' reappears in a form ennobled beyond measure where the soul, held speechless, trembles inwardly to the farthest fibre of its being. It invades the mind mightily in Christian worship with the words: 'Holy, holy, holy'; it breaks forth from the hymn of Tersteegen:

God Himself is present:
Heart, be stilled before Him:
Prostrate inwardly adore Him.

The 'shudder' has here lost its crazy and bewildering note, but not the ineffable something that holds the mind. It has become a mystical awe, and sets free as its accompaniment, reflected in self-consciousness, that 'creature-feeling' that has already been described as the feeling of personal nothingness and submergence before the awe-inspiring object directly experienced.

The referring of this feeling numinous *tremor* to its object in the numen brings into relief a property of the latter which plays an important part in our Holy Scriptures, and which has been the occasion of many difficulties, both to commentators and to theologians, from its puzzling and baffling nature. This is the ὀργή (*orgé*), the Wrath of Yahweh, which recurs in the New Testament as ὀργή θεοῦ, and which is clearly analogous to the idea occurring in many religions of a mysterious *ira deorum*. To pass through the Indian Pantheon of gods is to find deities who seem to be made up altogether out of such an ὀργή; and even the higher Indian gods of grace and pardon have frequently, beside their merciful, their 'wrath' form. But as regards the 'wrath of Yahweh,' the strange features about it have for long been a matter for constant remark. In the first place, it is patent from many passages of the Old Testament that this 'wrath' has no concern whatever with moral qualities. There is something very baffling in the way in which it 'is kindled' and manifested. It is, as has been well said, 'like a hidden force of nature,' like stored-up electricity, discharging itself upon anyone who comes too near. It is 'incalculable' and 'arbitrary.' Anyone who is accustomed to think of deity only by its rational attributes must see in this 'wrath' mere caprice and wilful passion. But such a view would have been emphatically rejected by the religious men of the Old Covenant, for to them the Wrath of God, so far from being a diminution of His Godhead, appears as a natural expression of it, an element of 'holiness' itself, and a quite indispensable one. And in this they are entirely right. This ὀργή is nothing but the *tremendum* itself, apprehended and expressed by the aid of a naïve analogy from the domain of natural experience, in this case from the ordinary passional life of men. But naïve as it may be, the analogy is most disconcertingly apt and striking; so much so that it will always retain its value and for us no less than for the men of old be an inevitable way of expressing one element in the religious emotion. It cannot be doubted that, despite the protest of Schleiermacher and Ritschl, Christianity also has something to teach of the 'wrath of God.'

It will be again at once apparent that in the use of this word we are not concerned with a genuine intellectual 'concept,' but only with a sort of illustrative substitute for a concept. 'Wrath' here is the 'ideogram' of a unique emotional moment in religious experience, a moment whose singularly *daunting* and awe-inspiring character must be gravely disturbing to those persons who will recognize nothing in the divine nature but goodness, gentleness, love, and a sort of confidential intimacy, in a word, only those aspects of God which turn towards the world of men.

This ὀργή is thus quite wrongly spoken of as 'natural' wrath: rather it is an entirely non- or super-natural, i.e. numinous, quality. The rationalization process takes place when it begins to be filled in with elements derived from the moral reason: righteousness in requital, and punishment for moral transgression. But it should be noted that the idea of the wrath of God in the Bible is always a synthesis, in which the original is combined with the later meaning that has come to fill it in. Something supra-rational throbs and gleams, palpable and visible, in the 'wrath of God,' prompting to a sense of 'terror' that no 'natural' anger can arouse.

Beside the 'wrath' or 'anger' of Yahweh stands the related expression 'jealousy of Yahweh.' The state of mind denoted by the phrase 'being jealous *for* Yahweh' is also a numinous state of mind, in which features of the *tremendum* pass over into the man who has experience of it.

2. *The element of 'Overpoweringness' ('majestas')*

We have been attempting to unfold the implications of that aspect of the *mysterium tremendum* indicated by the adjective, and the result so far may be summarized in two words, constituting, as before, what may be called an 'ideogram,' rather than a concept prover, viz. 'absolute unapproachability.'

It will be felt at once that there is yet a further element which must be added, that, namely, of 'might,' 'power,' 'absolute overpoweringness.' We will take to represent this the term *majestas,* majesty—the more readily because anyone with a feeling for language must detect a last faint trace of the numinous still clinging to the word. The *tremendum* may then be rendered more adequately *tremenda majestas,* or 'aweful majesty.' This second element of majesty may continue to be vividly preserved, where the first, that of unapproachability, recedes and dies away, as may be seen, for example, in mysticism. It is especially in relation to this element of majesty or absolute over-poweringness that the creature-consciousness, of which we have already spoken, comes upon the scene, as a sort of shadow or subjective reflection of it. Thus, in contrast to 'the overpowering' of which we are conscious as an object over against the self, there is the feeling of one's own submergence, of being but 'dust and ashes' and nothingness. And this forms the numinous raw material for the feeling of religious humility.[2]

Here we must revert once again to Schleiermacher's expression for what we call 'creature-feeling,' viz. the 'feeling of dependence.' We found fault with this phrase before on the ground that Schleiermacher thereby takes as basis and point of departure what is merely a secondary effect; that he sets out to teach a consciousness of the religious *object* only by way of an inference from the shadow it casts upon *self*-consciousness. We have now a further criticism to bring against it, and it is this. By 'feeling of dependence' Schleiermacher means consciousness of *being conditioned* (as effect by cause), and so he develops the implications of this logically enough in his sections upon Creation and Preservation. On the side of the deity the correlate to 'dependence' would thus be 'causality,' i.e. God's character as all-causing and all-conditioning. But a sense of this does not enter at all into that immediate and first-hand religious emotion which we have in the moment of worship, and which we can recover in a measure for analysis; it belongs on the contrary decidedly to the *rational* side of the idea of God; its implications admit of precise conceptual determination; and it springs from quite a distinct source. The difference between the 'feeling of dependence' of Schleiermacher and that which finds typical utterance in the words of Abraham already cited might be expressed as that between the consciousness of *createdness*[3] and the consciousness of *creaturehood*.[4] In the one case you have the creature as the work of the divine creative act; in the other, impotence and general nothingness as against overpowering might, dust and ashes as against 'majesty.' In the one case you have the fact of having been created; in the other, the status of the creature. And as soon as speculative thought has come to concern itself with this latter

---

[2] Cf. R. R. Marett, 'The Birth of Humility,' in *The Threshold of Religion*, 2nd ed., 1914. [Tr.]

[3] *Geschaffenheit.*
[4] *Geschöpflichkeit.*

type of consciousness—as soon as it has come to analyse this 'majesty'—we are introduced to a set of ideas quite different from those of creation or preservation. We come upon the ideas, first, of the annihilation of self, and then, as its complement, of the transcendent as the sole and entire reality. These are the characteristic notes of mysticism in all its forms, however otherwise various in content. For one of the chiefest and most general features of mysticism is just this *self-depreciation* (so plainly parallel to the case of Abraham), the estimation of the self, of the personal 'I,' as something not perfectly or essentially real, or even as mere nullity, a self-depreciation which comes to demand its own fulfilment in practice in rejecting the delusion of selfhood, and so makes for the annihilation of the self. And on the other hand mysticism leads to a valuation of the transcendent object of its reference as that which through plenitude of being stands supreme and absolute, so that the finite self contrasted with it becomes conscious even in its nullity that 'I am naught, Thou art all.' There is no thought in this of any causal relation between God, the creator, and the self, the creature. The point from which speculation starts is not a 'consciousness of absolute dependence'—of myself as result and effect of a divine cause—for that would in point of fact lead to insistence upon the reality of the self; it starts from a consciousness of the absolute superiority or supremacy of a power other than myself, and it is only as it falls back upon ontological terms to achieve its end—terms generally borrowed from natural science—that that element of the *tremendum*, originally apprehended as 'plenitude of power,' becomes transmuted into 'plenitude of being.'

This leads again to the mention of mysticism. No mere inquiry into the genesis of a thing can throw any light upon its essential nature, and it is hence immaterial to us how mysticism historically arose. But essentially mysticism is the stressing to a very high degree, indeed the overstressing, of the non-rational or supra-rational elements in religion; and it is only intelligible when so understood. The various phases and factors of the non-rational may receive varying emphasis, and the type of mysticism will differ according as some or others fall into the background. What we have been analysing, however, is a feature that recurs in all forms of mysticism everywhere, and it is nothing but the 'creature-consciousness' stressed to the utmost and to excess, the expression meaning, if we may repeat the contrast already made, not 'feeling of our createdness' but 'feeling of our creaturehood,' that is, the consciousness of the littleness of every creature in face of that which is above all creatures.

A characteristic common to all types of mysticism is the *Identification*, in different degrees of completeness, of the personal self with the transcendent Reality. This identification has a source of its own, with which we are not here concerned, and springs from 'moments' of religious experience which would require separate treatment. 'Identification' alone, however, is not enough for mysticism; it must be Identification with the Something that is at once absolutely supreme in power and reality and wholly non-rational. And it is among the mystics that we most encounter this element of religious consciousness. Récéjac has noticed this in his *Essai sur les fondements de la connaissance mystique* (Paris, 1897). He writes (p. 90):

Le mysticisme commence par la crainte, par le sentiment d'une *domination* universelle, *invincible,* et devient plus tard un désir d'union avec ce qui domine ainsi.

And some very clear examples of this taken from the religious experience of the present day are to be found in W. James (*op. cit.,* p. 66):

The perfect stillness of the night was thrilled by a more solemn silence. The darkness held a presence that was all the more felt because it was not seen. I could not any more have doubted that *He* was there than that I was. Indeed, I felt myself to be, if possible, the less real of the two.

This example is particularly instructive as to the relation of mysticism to the 'feelings of identification,' for the experience here recounted was on the point of passing into it.

3. *The Element of 'Energy' or Urgency*

There is, finally, a third element comprised in those of *tremendum* and *majestas*, awefulness and majesty, and this I venture to call the 'urgency' or 'energy' of the numinous object. It is particularly vividly perceptible in the ὀργή or 'wrath'; and it everywhere clothes itself in symbolic expressions—vitality, passion, emotional temper, will, force, movement,[5] excitement, activity, impetus. These features are typical and recur again and again from the daemonic level up to the idea of the 'living' God. We have here the factor that has everywhere more than any other prompted the fiercest opposition to the 'philosophic' God of mere rational speculation, who can be put into a definition. And for their part of the philosophers have condemned these expressions of the energy of the numen, whenever they are brought on to the scene, as sheer anthropomorphism. In so far as their opponents have for the most part themselves failed to recognize that the terms they have borrowed from the sphere of human conative and affective life have merely value as analogies, the philosophers are right to condemn them. But they are wrong, in so far as, this error notwithstanding, these terms stood for a genuine aspect of the divine nature—its non-rational aspect—a due consciousness

[5] The 'mobilitas Dei' of Lactantius.

of which served to protect religion itself from being 'rationalized' away.

For wherever men have been contending for the 'living' God or for voluntarism, there we may be sure, have been non-rationalists fighting rationalists and rationalism. It was so with Luther in his controversy with Erasmus; and Luther's *omnipotentia Dei* in his *De Servo Arbitrio* is nothing but the union of 'majesty'—in the sense of absolute supremacy—with this 'energy,' in the sense of a force that knows not stint nor stay, which is urgent, active, compelling, and alive. In mysticism, too, this element of 'energy' is a very living and vigorous factor, at any rate in the 'voluntaristic' mysticism, the mysticism of love, where it is very forcibly seen in that 'consuming fire' of love whose burning strength the mystic can hardly bear, but begs that the heat that has scorched him may be mitigated, lest he be himself destroyed by it. And in this urgency and pressure the mystic's 'love' claims a perceptible kinship with the ὀργή itself, the scorching and consuming wrath of God; it is the same 'energy,' only differently directed. 'Love,' says one of the mystics, 'is nothing else than quenched wrath.'

The element of 'energy' reappears in Fichte's speculations on the Absolute as the gigantic, never-resting, active world-stress, and in Schopenhauer's daemonic 'Will.' At the same time both these writers are guilty of the same error that is already found in myth; they transfer 'natural' attributes, which ought only to be used as 'ideograms' for what is itself properly beyond utterance, to the non-rational as real qualifications of it, and they mistake symbolic expressions of feelings for adequate concepts upon which a 'scientific' structure of knowledge may be based.

In Goethe, as we shall see later, the same element of energy is emphasized in a quite unique way in his strange descriptions of the experience he calls 'daemonic.'

CHAPTER V

THE ANALYSIS
OF 'MYSTERIUM'

Ein begriffener Gott ist kein Gott.
'A God comprehended is no God.'
(TERSTEEGEN)

We gave to the object to which the numinous consciousness is directed the name *mysterium tremendum,* and we then set ourselves first to determine the meaning of the adjective *tremendum*—which we found to be itself only justified by analogy—because it is more easily analysed than the substantive idea *mysterium.* We have now to turn to this, and try, as best we may, by hint and suggestion, to get to a clearer apprehension of what it implies.

4. *The 'Wholly Other'*

It might be thought that the adjective itself gives an explanation of the substantive; but this is not so. It is not merely analytical; it is a synthetic attribute to it; i.e. *tremendum* adds something not necessarily inherent in *mysterium.* It is true that the reactions in consciousness that correspond to the one readily and spontaneously overflow into those that correspond to the other; in fact, anyone sensitive to the use of words would commonly feel that the idea of 'mystery' (*mysterium*) is so closely bound up with its synthetic qualifying attribute 'aweful' (*tremendum*) that one can hardly say the former without catching an echo of the latter, 'mystery' almost of itself becoming 'aweful mystery' to us. But the passage from the one idea to the other need not by any means be always so easy. The elements of meaning implied in 'awefulness' and 'mysteriousness' are in themselves definitely different. The latter may so far preponderate in the religious consciousness, may stand out so vividly, that in comparison with it the former almost

sinks out of sight; a case which again could be clearly exemplified from some forms of mysticism. Occasionally, on the other hand, the reverse happens, and the *tremendum* may in turn occupy the mind without the *mysterium.*

This latter, then, needs special consideration on its own account. We need an expression for the mental reaction peculiar to it; and here, too, only one word seems appropriate, though, as it is strictly applicable only to a 'natural' state of mind, it has here meaning only by analogy: it is the word 'stupor.' *Stupor* is plainly a different thing from *tremor;* it signifies blank wonder, an astonishment that strikes us dumb, amazement absolute.[1] Taken, indeed, in its purely natural sense, *mysterium* would first mean merely a secret or a mystery in the sense of that which is alien to us, uncomprehended and unexplained; and so far *mysterium* is itself merely an ideogram, an analogical notion taken from the natural sphere, illustrating, but incapable of exhaustively rendering, our real meaning. Taken in the religious sense, that which is 'mysterious' is—to give it perhaps the most striking expression—the 'wholly other' ($\theta\acute{\alpha}\tau\epsilon\rho o\nu$, *anyad, alienum*), that which is quite beyond the sphere of the usual, the intelligible, and the familiar, which therefore falls quite outside the limits of the 'canny,' and is

---

[1] Compare also *obstupefacere.* Still more exact equivalents are the Greek $\theta\acute{\alpha}\mu\beta o\varsigma$ and $\theta\alpha\mu\beta\epsilon\hat{\imath}\nu.$ The sound $\theta\ \alpha\ \mu\ \beta$ (*thamb*) excellently depicts this state of mind of blank, staring wonder. And the difference between the moments of *stupor* and *tremor* is very finely suggested by the passage, Mark x. 32 (cf. *infra,* p. 158). On the other hand, what was said above of the facility and rapidity with which the two moments merge and blend is also markedly true of $\theta\acute{\alpha}\mu\beta o\varsigma$, which then becomes a classical term for the (ennobled) awe of the numinous in general. So Mark xvi. 5 is rightly translated by Luther 'und sie entsetzten sich,' and by the English Authorized Version 'and they were affrighted.'

contrasted with it, filling the mind with blank wonder and astonishment.

This is already to be observed on the lowest and earliest level of the religion of primitive man, where the numinous consciousness is but an inchoate stirring of the feelings. What is really characteristic of this stage is *not*—as the theory of Animism would have us believe—that men are here concerned with curious entities, called 'souls' or 'spirits,' which happen to be invisible. Representations of spirits and similar conceptions are rather one and all early modes of 'rationalizing' a precedent experience, to which they are subsidiary. They are attempts in some way or other, it little matters how, to guess the riddle it propounds, and their effect is at the same time always to weaken and deaden the experience itself. They are the source from which springs, not religion, but the rationalization of religion, which often ends by constructing such a massive structure of theory and such a plausible fabric of interpretation, that the 'mystery' is frankly excluded.[2] Both imaginative 'myth,' when developed into a system, and intellectualist Scholasticism, when worked out to its completion, are methods by which the fundamental fact of religious experience is, as it were, simply rolled out so thin and flat as to be finally eliminated altogether.

Even on the lowest level of religious development the essential characteristic is therefore to be sought elsewhere than in the appearance of 'spirit' representations. It lies rather, we repeat, in a peculiar 'moment' of consciousness, to wit, the *stupor* before something 'wholly other,' whether such an other be named 'spirit' or 'daemon' or 'deva,' or be left

without any name. Nor does it make any difference in this respect whether, to interpret and preserve their apprehension of this 'other,' men coin original imagery or their own or adapt imaginations drawn from the world of legend, the fabrications of fancy apart from and prior to any stirrings of daemonic dread.

In accordance with laws of which we shall have to speak again later, this feeling or consciousness of the 'wholly other' will attach itself to, or sometimes be indirectly aroused by means of, objects which are already puzzling upon the 'natural' plane, or are of a surprising or astounding character; such as extraordinary phenomena or astonishing occurrences or things in inanimate nature, in the animal world, or among men. But here once more we are dealing with a case of association between things specifically different—the 'numinous' and the 'natural' moments of consciousness —and not merely with the gradual enhancement of one of them—the 'natural' —till it becomes the other. As in the case of 'natural fear' and 'daemonic dread' already considered, so here the transition from natural to daemonic amazement is not a mere matter of degree. But it is only with the latter that the complementary expression *mysterium* perfectly harmonizes, as will be felt perhaps more clearly in the case of the adjectival form 'mysterious.' No one says, strictly and in earnest, of a piece of clockwork that is beyond his grasp, or of a science that he cannot understand: 'That is "mysterious" to me.'

It might be objected that the mysterious is something which is and remains absolutely and invariably beyond our understanding, whereas that which merely eludes our understanding for a time but is perfectly intelligible in principle should be called, not a 'mystery,' but merely a 'problem.' But this is by no means an adequate account of the matter.

[2] A spirit or soul that has been conceived and comprehended no longer prompts to 'shuddering,' as is proved by Spiritualism. But it thereby ceases to be of interest for the psychology of religion.

The truly 'mysterious' object is beyond our apprehension and comprehension, not only because our knowledge has certain irremovable limits, but because in it we come upon something inherently 'wholly other,' whose kind and character are incommensurable with our own, and before which we therefore recoil in a wonder that strikes us chill and numb.[3]

This may be made still clearer by a consideration of that degraded offshoot and travesty of the genuine 'numinous' dread or awe, the fear of ghosts. Let us try to analyse this experience. We have already specified the peculiar feeling-element of 'dread' aroused by the ghost as that of 'grue,' grisly horror.[4] Now this 'grue' obviously contributes something to the attraction which ghost-stories exercise, in so far, namely, as the relaxation of tension ensuing upon our release from it relieves the mind in a pleasant and agreeable way. So far, however, it is not really the ghost itself that gives us pleasure, but the fact that we are rid of it. But obviously this is quite insufficient to explain the ensnaring attraction of the ghost-story. The ghost's real attraction rather consists in this, that of itself and in an uncommon degree it entices the imagination, awakening strong interest and curiosity; it is the weird thing itself that allures the fancy. But it does this,

not because it is 'something long and white' (as someone once defined a ghost), nor yet through any of the positive and conceptual attributes which fancies about ghosts have invented, but because it is a thing that 'doesn't really exist at all,' the 'wholly other,' something which has no place in our scheme of reality but belongs to an absolutely different one, and which at the same time arouses an irrepressible interest in the mind.

But that which is perceptibly true in the fear of ghosts, which is, after all, only a caricature of the genuine thing, is in a far stronger sense true of the 'daemonic' experience itself, of which the fear of ghosts is a mere off-shoot. And while, following this main line of development, this element in the numinous consciousness, the feeling of the 'wholly other,' is heightened and clarified, its higher modes of manifestation come into being, which set the numinous object in contrast not only to everything wonted and familiar (i.e. in the end, to nature in general), thereby turning it into the 'supernatural,' but finally to the world itself, and thereby exalt it to the 'supramundane,' that which is above the whole world-order.

In mysticism we have in the 'beyond' (ἐπέκεινα) again the strongest stressing and over-stressing of those non-rational elements which are already inherent in all religion. Mysticism continues to its extreme point this contrasting of the numinous object (the numen), as the 'wholly other,' with ordinary experience. Not content with contrasting it with all that is of nature or this world, mysticism concludes by contrasting it with Being itself and all that 'is,' and finally actually calls it 'that which is nothing.' By this 'nothing' is meant not only that of which nothing can be predicated, but that which is absolutely and intrinsically other than and opposite of everything that is and can be thought. But while exaggerating to the point of paradox this *negation* and con-

---

[3] In *Confessions*, ii. 9. 1, Augustine very strikingly suggests this stiffening, benumbing element of the 'wholly other' and its contrast to the rational aspect of the numen; the *dissimile* and the *simile*:

'Quid est illud, quod interlucet mihi et percutit cor meum sine laesione? Et inhorresco et inardesco. Inhorresco, in quantum *dissimilis* ei sum. Inardesco, in quantum *similis* ei sum.'

('What is that which gleams through me and smites my heart without wounding it? I am both a-shudder and a-glow. A-shudder, in so far as I am unlike it, a-glow in so far as I am like it.')

[4] *gruseln, gräsen.*

trast—the only means open to conceptual thought to apprehend the *mysterium*—mysticism at the same time retains the *positive quality* of the 'wholly other' as a very living factor in its over-brimming religious emotion.

But what is true of the strange 'nothingness' of our mystics holds good equally of the *sūnyam* and the *sūnyatā*, the 'void' and 'emptiness' of the Buddhist mystics. This aspiration for the 'void' and for becoming void, no less than the aspiration of our western mystics for 'nothing' and for becoming nothing, must seem a kind of lunacy to anyone who has no inner sympathy for the esoteric language and ideograms of mysticism, and lacks the matrix from which these come necessarily to birth. To such an one Buddhism itself will be simply a morbid sort of pessimism. But in fact the 'void' of the eastern, like the 'nothing' of the western, mystic is a numinous ideogram of the 'wholly other.'

These terms 'supernatural' and 'transcendent' [5] give the appearance of positive attributes, and, as applied to the mysterious, they appear to divest the *mysterium* of its originally negative meaning and to turn it into an affirmation. On the side of conceptual thought this is nothing more than appearance, for it is obvious that the two terms in question are merely negative and exclusive attributes with reference to 'nature' and the world or cosmos respectively. But on the side of the feeling-content it is otherwise; that *is* in very truth positive in the highest degree, though here too, as before, it cannot be rendered explicit in conceptual terms. It is through this positive feeling-content that the concepts of the 'transcendent' and 'supernatural' become forthwith designations for a unique 'wholly other' reality and quality, something of whose special character we can *feel*, without being able to give it clear conceptual expression.

---

[5] Literally, supramundane: *überweltlich.*

CHAPTER VI

5. THE ELEMENT OF FASCINATION

The qualitative *content* of the numinous experience, to which 'the mysterious' stands as *form,* is in one of its aspects the element of daunting 'awefulness' and 'majesty,' which has already been dealt with in detail; but it is clear that it has at the same time another aspect, in which it shows itself as something uniquely attractive and *fascinating*.

These two qualities, the daunting and the fascinating, now combine in a strange harmony of contrasts, and the resultant dual character of the numinous consciousness, to which the entire religious development bears witness, at any rate from the level of the 'daemonic dread' onwards, is at once the strangest and most noteworthy phenomenon in the whole history of religion. The daemonic-divine object may appear to the mind an object of horror and dread, but at the same time it is no less something that allures with a potent charm, and the creature, who trembles before it, utterly cowed and cast down, has always at the same time the impulse to turn to it, nay even to make it somehow his own. The 'mystery' is for him not merely something to be wondered at but something that entrances him; and beside that in it which bewilders and confounds, he feels a something that captivates and transports him with a strange ravishment, rising often enough to the pitch of dizzy intoxication; it is the Dionysiac-element in the numen.

The ideas and concepts which are the parallels or 'schemata' on the rational side of this non-rational element of 'fascination' are love, mercy, pity, comfort; these are all 'natural' elements of the common psychical life, only they are here thought as absolute and in completeness. But important as these are for the experience of religious bliss or felicity, they do not by any means exhaust it. It is just the same as with the opposite experience of religious infelicity—the experience of the ὀργή or 'wrath' of God:—both alike contain fundamentally non-rational elements. Bliss or beatitude is more, far more, than the mere natural feeling of being comforted, of reliance, of the joy of love, however these may be heightened and enhanced. Just as 'wrath,' taken in a purely rational or a purely ethical sense, does not exhaust that profound element of *awefulness* which is locked in the mystery of deity, so neither does 'graciousness' exhaust the profound element of *wonderfulness* and rapture which lies in the mysterious beatific experience of deity. The term 'grace' may indeed be taken as its aptest designation, but then only in the sense in which it is really applied in the language of the mystics, and in which not only the 'gracious intent' but 'something more' is meant by the word. This 'something more' has its antecedent phases very far back in the history of religions.

It may well be possible, it is even probable, that in the first stage of its development the religious consciousness started with only one of its poles—the 'daunting' aspect of the numen—and so at first took shape only as 'daemonic dread.' But if this did not point to something beyond itself, if it were not but one 'moment' of a completer experience, pressing up gradually into consciousness, then no transition would be possible to the feelings of positive self-surrender to the numen. The only type of worship that could result from this 'dread' alone would be that of ἀπαιτεῖσθαι and ἀποτρέπειν, taking the form of expiation and propitiation, the averting or the appeasement of the 'wrath' of the numen. It can never explain how it is that 'the numinous' is the object of search and desire and yearning, and that too for its own sake and not only for the sake of the aid and backing that men ex-

pect from it in the natural sphere. It can never explain how this takes place, not only in the forms of 'rational' religious worship, but in those queer 'sacramental' observances and rituals and procedures of communion in which the human being seeks to get the numen into his possession.

Religious practice may manifest itself in those normal and easily intelligible forms which occupy so prominent a place in the history of religion, such forms as propitiation, petition, sacrifice, thanksgiving, &c. But besides these there is a series of strange proceedings which are constantly attracting greater and greater attention, and in which it is claimed that we may recognize, besides mere religion in general, the particular roots of mysticism. I refer to those numerous curious modes of behaviour and fantastic forms of mediation, by means of which the primitive religious man attempts to master 'the mysterious,' and to fill himself and even to identify himself with it. These modes of behaviour fall apart into two classes. On the one hand the 'magical' identification of the self with the numen proceeds by means of various transactions, at once magical and devotional in character— by formula, ordination, adjuration, consecration, exorcism, &c.: on the other hand are the 'shamanistic' ways of procedure, possession, indwelling, self-fulfilment in exaltation and ecstasy. All these have, indeed, their starting-points simply in magic, and their intention at first was certainly simply to appropriate the prodigious force of the numen for the natural ends of man. But the process does not rest there. Possession of and by the numen becomes an end in itself; it begins to be sought for its own sake; and the wildest and most artificial methods of asceticism are put into practice to attain it. In a word, the *vita religiosa* begins; and to remain in these strange and bizarre states of numinous possession becomes a good in itself, even a way of salvation, wholly different from the profane goods pursued by means of magic. Here, too, commences the process of development by which the experience is matured and purified, till finally it reaches its consummation in the sublimest and purest states of the 'life within the Spirit' and in the noblest mysticism. Widely various as these states are in themselves, yet they have this element in common, that in them the *mysterium* is experienced in its essential, positive, and specific character, as something that bestows upon man a beatitude beyond compare, but one whose real nature he can neither proclaim in speech nor conceive in thought, but may know only by a direct and living experience. It is a bliss which embraces all those blessings that are indicated or suggested in positive fashion by any 'doctrine of salvation,' and it quickens all of them through and through; but these do not exhaust it. Rather by its all-pervading, penetrating glow it makes of these very blessings more than the intellect can conceive in them or affirm of them. It gives the peace that passes understanding, and of which the tongue can only stammer brokenly. Only from afar, by metaphors and analogies, do we come to apprehend what it is in itself, and even so our notion is but inadequate and confused.

'Eye hath not seen, nor ear heard, neither have entered into the heart of man, the things which God hath prepared for them that love him.' Who does not feel the exalted sound of these words and the 'Dionysiac' element of transport and fervour in them? It is instructive that in such phrases as these, in which consciousness would fain put its highest consummation into words, 'all images fall away' and the mind turns from them to grasp expressions that are purely negative. And it is still more instructive that in reading and hearing such words their merely negative character simply is not noticed; that we can let whole chains of

such negations enrapture, even intoxicate us, and that entire hymns—and deeply impressive hymns—have been composed, in which there is really nothing positive at all! All this teaches us the independence of the positive content of this experience from the implications of its overt conceptual expression, and how it can be firmly grasped, thoroughly understood, and profoundly appreciated, purely in, with, and from the feeling itself.

Mere love, mere trust, for all the glory and happiness they bring, do not explain to us that moment of rapture that breathes in our tenderest and most heartfelt hymns of salvation, as also in such eschatological hymns of longing as that Rhyme of St. Bernard in which the very verses seem to dance.

Urbs Sion unica, mansio mystica, condita coelo,
Nunc tibi gaudeo, nunc tibi lugeo, tristor, anhelo,
Te, quia corpore non queo, pectore saepe penetro;
Sed caro terrea, terraque carnea, mox cado retro.
Nemo retexere, nemoque promere sustinet ore,
Quo tua moenia, quo capitolia plena nitore.
Id queo dicere, quo modo tangere pollice coelum,
Ut mare currere, sicut in aere figere telum.
Opprimit omne cor ille tuus decor, O Sion, O Pax.
Urbs sine tempore, nulla potest fore laus tibi mendax.
O nova mansio, te pia concio, gens pia munit,
Provehit, excitat, auget, identitat, efficit, unit.[1]

---

[1] 'O Sion, thou city sole and single, mystic mansion hidden away in the heavens, now I rejoice in thee, now I moan for thee and mourn and yearn for thee; thee often I pass through in the heart, as I cannot in the body, but being but earthly flesh and fleshly earth soon I fall back. None can disclose or utter in speech what plenary radiance fills thy

This is where the living 'something more' of the *fascinans*, the element of fascination, is to be found. It lives no less in those tense extollings of the blessing of salvation, which recur in all religions of salvation, and stand in such remarkable contrast to the relatively meagre and frequently childish import of that which is revealed in them by concept or by image. Everywhere salvation is something whose meaning is often very little apparent, is even wholly obscure, to the 'natural' man; on the contrary, *so far as he understands it*, he tends to find it highly tedious and uninteresting, sometimes downright distasteful and repugnant to his nature, as he would, for instance, find the beatific vision of God in our own doctrine of salvation, or the *henōsis* of 'God all in all' among the mystics. 'So far as he understands,' be it noted; but then he does not understand it in the least. Because he lacks the inward teaching of the Spirit, he must needs confound what is offered him as an expression for the experience of salvation —a mere ideogram of what is felt, whose import it hints at by analogy—with 'natural' concepts, as though it were itself just such an one. And so he 'wanders ever farther from the goal.'

It is not only in the religious feeling of longing that the moment of fascination is a living factor. It is already alive and present in the moment of 'solemnity,' both in the gathered concentration and humble submergence of private devotion, when the mind is exalted to the holy, and in the common worship of the congregation, where this is practised with earnest-ness and deep sincerity, as, it is to be feared, is with us a thing rather desired than realized. It is this and nothing else that in the solemn moment can fill the soul so full and keep it so inexpressibly tranquil. Schleiermacher's assertion [2] is perhaps true of it, as of the numinous consciousness in general, viz. that it cannot really occur alone on its own account, or except combined and penetrated with rational elements. But, if this be admitted, it is upon other grounds than those adduced by Schleiermacher; while, on the other hand, it may occupy a more or less predominant place and lead to states of calm ($\dot{\eta}\sigma\upsilon\chi\dot{\iota}\alpha$) as well as of transport, in which it *almost* of itself wholly fills the soul. But in all the manifold forms in which it is aroused in us, whether in eschatological promise of the coming kingdom of God and the transcendent bliss of Paradise, or in the guise of an entry into that beatific reality that is 'above the world'; whether it come first in expectancy or pre-intimation or in a present experience ('When I but *have* Thee, I ask no question of heaven and earth'); in all these forms, outwardly diverse but inwardly akin, it appears as a strange and mighty propulsion towards an ideal good known only to religion and in its nature fundamentally non-rational, which the mind knows of in yearning and presentiment, recognizing it for what it is behind the obscure and inadequate symbols which are its only expression. And this shows that above and beyond our rational being lies hidden the ultimate and highest part of our nature, which can find no satisfaction in the mere allaying of the needs of our sensuous, psychical, or intellectual impulses and cravings. The mystics called it the basis or ground of the soul.

We saw that in the case of the element of the mysterious the 'wholly other' led on to the supernatural and transcendent

---

walls and thy citadels. I can as little tell of it as I can touch the skies with my finger, or run upon the sea or make a dart stand still in the air. This thy splendour overwhelms every heart, O Sion, O Peace! O timeless City, no praise can belie thee. O new dwelling-place, thee the concourse and people of the faithful erects and exalts, inspires and increases, joins to itself, and makes complete and one.'

[2] *Glaubenslehre*, § 5.

RUDOLF OTTO   205

and that above these appeared the 'beyond' (ἐπέκεινα) of mysticism, through the non-rational side of religion being raised to its highest power and stressed to excess. It is the same in the case of the element of 'fascination'; here, too, is possible a transition into mysticism. At its highest point of stress the fascinating becomes the 'overabounding,' 'exuberant,' [3] the mystical 'moment' which exactly corresponds upon this line to the ἐπέκεινα upon the other line of approach, and which is to be understood accordingly. But while this feeling of the 'overabounding' is specially characteristic of mysticism, a trace of it survives in all truly felt states of religious beatitude, however restrained and kept within measure by other factors. This is seen most clearly from the psychology of those great experiences—of grace, conversion, second birth—in which the religious experience appears in its pure intrinsic nature and in heightened activity, so as to be more clearly grasped than in the less typical form of piety instilled by education. The hard core of such experiences in their Christian form consists of the redemption from guilt and bondage to sin, and we shall have presently to see that this also does not occur without a participation of non-rational elements. But leaving this out of account, what we have here to point out is the unutterableness of what has been yet genuinely experienced, and how such an experience may pass into blissful excitement, rapture, and exaltation verging often on the bizarre and the abnormal.[4] This is vouched for

by the autobiographical testimony of the 'converted' from St. Paul onward. William James has collected a great number of these, without, however, himself noticing the non-rational element that thrills in them.

Thus, one writes

> . . . For the moment nothing but an ineffable joy and exaltation remained. It is impossible fully to describe the experience. It was like the effect of some great orchestra, when all the separate notes have melted into one swelling harmony, that leaves the listener conscious of nothing save that his soul is being wafted upwards and almost bursting with its own emotion. (*Varieties of Religious Experience*, p. 66.)

And another:

> . . . The more I seek words to express this intimate intercourse, the more I feel the impossibility of describing the thing by any of our usual images. (Ibid., p. 68.)

And almost with the precision of dogma, a third (Jonathan Edwards) indicates the qualitative difference of the experience of beatitude from other 'rational' joy:

> The conceptions which the saints have of the loveliness of God and that kind of delight which they experience in it are quite peculiar and entirely different from anything which a natural man can possess or of which he can form any proper notion. (Ibid., p. 229.)

Cf. also pp. 192, 225; and the testimony of Jacob Boehme given on p. 417. Also this of Boehme:

> But I can neither write nor tell of what sort of Exaltation the triumphing in the Spirit is. It can be compared with nought, but that when in the midst of

---

[3] *das Überschwengliche.*

[4] This may be found fatal to the attempt to construct a 'religion within the limits of pure reason,' or 'of humanity'; but, none the less, the matter is as we have described it, as far as concerns the psychological inquiry into religion, which asks, not what it is within the aforementioned limits, but what it is in its own essential nature. And for that matter this proceeding of constructing a 'humanity' prior to and apart from the most

central and potent of human capacities is like nothing so much as the attempt to frame a standard idea of the human body after having previously cut off the head.

death life is born, and it is like the resurrection of the dead.

With the mystics these experiences pass up wholly into the 'over-abounding.' 'O that I could tell you what the heart feels, how it burns and is consumed inwardly! Only, I find no words to express it. I can but say: Might but one little drop of what I feel fall into Hell, Hell would be transformed into a Paradise.' So says St. Catherine of Genoa; and all the multitude of her spiritual kindred testify to the same effect.

What we Christians know as the experiences of grace and the second birth have their parallels also in the religions of high spiritual rank beyond the borders of Christianity. Such are the breaking out of the saving 'Bodhi,' the opening of the 'heavenly eye,' the *Fñāna*, by *Išvaras prasāda*, which is victorious over the darkness of nescience and shines out in an experience with which no other can be measured. And in all these the entirely non-rational and specific element in the beatific experience is immediately noticeable. The qualitative character of it varies widely in all these cases, and is again in them all very different from its parallels in Christianity; still in all it is very similar in intensity, and in all it is a 'salvation' and an absolute 'fascination,' which in contrast to all that admits of 'natural' expression or comparison is deeply imbued with the 'over-abounding' ('exuberant') nature of the numen.

And this is also entirely true of the rapture of Nirvana, which is only in appearance a cold and negative state. It is only conceptually that 'Nirvana' is a negation; it is felt in consciousness as in the strongest degree positive; it exercises a 'fascination' by which its votaries are as much carried away as are the Hindu or the Christian by the corresponding objects of their worship. I recall vividly a conversation I had with a Buddhist monk. He had been putting before me method-

ically and pertinaciously the arguments for the Buddhist 'theology of negation,' the doctrine of Anātman and 'entire emptiness.' When he had made an end, I asked him, what then Nirvana itself is; and after a long pause came at last the single answer, low and restrained: 'Bliss —unspeakable.' And the hushed restraint of that answer, the solemnity of his voice, demeanour, and gesture, made more clear what was meant than the words themselves.

And so we maintain, on the one hand, following the *via eminentiae et causalitatis*, that the divine is indeed the highest, strongest, best, loveliest, and dearest that man can think of; but we assert on the other, following the *via negationis*, that God is not *merely* the ground and superlative of all that can be thought; He is in Himself a subject on His own account and in Himself.

In the adjective δεινός the Greek language possesses a word peculiarly difficult to translate, and standing for an idea peculiarly difficult to grasp in all its strange variations. And if we ask whence this difficulty arises, the answer is plain; it is because δεινός is simply the numinous (mostly of course at a lower level, in an arrested form, attenuated by rhetorical or poetic usage). Consequently δεινός is the equivalent of *dirus* and *tremendus*. It may mean evil or imposing, potent and strange, queer and marvellous, horrifying and fascinating, divine and daemonic, and a source of 'energy.' Sophocles means to awaken the feeling of 'numinous awe' through the whole gamut of its phases at the contemplation of man, the creature of marvel, in the choric song of the *Antigone*:

πολλὰ τὰ δεινά, κοὐδὲν ἀνθρώπου δεινότερον πέλει.

This line defies translation, just because our language has no term that can isolate distinctly and gather into one word the total numinous impression a thing may make on the mind. The nearest that German can get to it is in the expression *des Ungeheuere* (monstrous), while in English 'weird' is perhaps the closest rendering possible. The mood and attitude represented in the foregoing verse might then be fairly well rendered by such a translation as:

> Much there is that is weird; but nought is weirder than man.

The German *ungeheuer* is not by derivation simply 'huge,' in quantity or quality; —this, its common meaning, is in fact a rationalizing interpretation of the real idea; it is that which is not *geheuer*, i.e. approximately, the *uncanny*—in a word, the numinous. And it is just this element of the uncanny in man that Sophocles has in mind. If this, its fundamental meaning, be really and thoroughly felt in consciousness, then the word could be taken as a fairly exact expression for the numinous in its aspects of mystery, awefulness, majesty, augustness, and 'energy'; nay, even the aspect of fascination is dimly felt in it.

The variations of meaning in the German word *ungeheuer* can be well illustrated from Goethe.[5] He, too, uses the word first to denote the huge in size— what is too vast for our faculty of space-perception, such as the immeasurable vault of the night sky. In other passages the word retains its original non-rational colour more markedly; it comes to mean the uncanny, the fearful, the dauntingly 'other' and incomprehensible, that which arouses in us *stupor* and θάμβος; and finally, in the wonderful words of Faust which I have put at the beginning of this book, it becomes an almost exact synonym for our 'numinous' under all its aspects.

> Das Schaudern ist der Menschheit bestes Teil.
> Wie auch die Welt ihm das Gefühl verteuere,
> Ergriffen fühlt er tief das Ungeheuere.[6]

---

[5] Cf. *Wilhelm Meisters Wanderjahre,* Bk. I, ch. 10; *Wahlverwandtschaften,* 2. 15; *Dichtung und Wahrheit,* 2. 9: 4. 20.

[6] Awe is the best of man: howe'er the world's
   Misprizing of the feeling would prevent us,
   Deeply we feel, once gripped, the weird Portentous.
                     (GOETHE, *Faust,* Second Part,
                                       Act 1, Sc. v.)

JOHN HICK

Man's Awareness of God

John Hick (1922–   ) is now Stuart Professor of Christian Philosophy at Princeton Theological Seminary. His distinctive contributions have been made through examining and defending the Christian faith from the standpoint of analytical philosophy.

We come now to our main problem. What manner of cognition is the religious man's awareness of God, and how is it related to his other cognitions?

We have already taken stock in a general way of our situation as cognizing beings. We become conscious of the existence of other objects in the universe, whether things or persons, either by experiencing them for ourselves or by inferring their existence from evidences within our experience. We have also noted that the awareness of God reported by the ordinary religious believer is of the former kind. He professes, not to have inferred that there is a God, but that God as a living being has entered into his own experience. He claims to enjoy something which he describes as an experience of God.

The ordinary believer does not, however, report an awareness of God as existing in isolation from all other objects of experience. His consciousness of the divine does not involve a cessation of his consciousness of a material and social environment. It is not a vision of God in solitary glory, filling the believer's entire mind and blotting out his normal field of perception. Whether such phrases correctly describe the mystic's goal, the ultimate Beatific Vision which figures in Christian doctrine, is a question for a later chapter. But at any rate the ordinary person's religious awareness here on earth is not of that kind. He claims instead an apprehension of God meeting him in and through his material and social environments. He finds that in his dealings with the world of men and things he is somehow having to do with God, and God with him. The moments of ordinary life possess, or may possess, for him in varying degrees a religious significance. As has been well said, religious experience is "the whole experience of religious persons." [1] The believer meets God not only in moments of worship, but also when through the urgings of conscience he feels the pressure of the divine demand upon his life; when through the gracious actions of his friends he apprehends the divine grace; when through the marvels and beauties of nature he traces the hand of the Creator; and he has increasing

From John Hick, *Faith and Knowledge* (1957), Ch. VI. Reprinted by permission of Cornell University Press.

[1] William Temple, *Nature, Man and God* (London, 1934), p. 334.

knowledge of the divine purpose as he responds to its behests in his own life. In short, it is not apart from the course of mundane life, but in it and through it, that the ordinary religious believer claims to experience, however imperfectly and fragmentarily, the divine presence and activity.

This at any rate, among the variety of claims to religious awareness which have been and might be made, is the claim whose epistemological credentials we are to examine. Can God be known through his dealings with us in the world which he has made? The question concerns human experience, and the possibility of an awareness of the divine being mediated through awareness of the world, the supernatural through the natural.

In answer to this query I shall try to show in the present chapter that "mediated" knowledge, such as is postulated by this religious claim, is already a common and accepted feature of our cognitive experience. To this end we must study a basic characteristic of human experience, which I shall call "significance," together with the correlative mental activity by which it is apprehended, which I shall call "interpretation." We shall find that interpretation takes place in relation to each of the three main types of existence, or orders of significance, recognized by human thought—the natural, the human, and the divine; and that in order to relate ourselves appropriately to each, a primary and unevidenceable act of interpretation is required which, when directed toward God, has traditionally been termed "faith." Thus I shall try to show that while the object of religious knowledge is unique, its basic epistemological pattern is that of all our knowing.

This is not to say that the logic of theistic belief has no peculiarities. It does indeed display certain unique features; and these (I shall try to show) are such as follow from the unique nature of its object, and are precisely the peculiarities which we should expect if that object is real. In the present chapter, then, we shall take note of the common epistemological pattern in which religious knowledge partakes, and in the following chapter we shall examine some special peculiarities of religious knowing.

. . .

By significance I mean that fundamental and all-pervasive characteristic of our conscious experience which *de facto* constitutes it for us the experience of a "world" and not of a mere empty void or churning chaos. We find ourselves in a relatively stable and ordered environment in which we have come to feel, so to say, "at home." The world has become intelligible to us, in the sense that it is a familiar place in which we have learned to act and react in appropriate ways. Our experience is not just an unpredictable kaleidoscope of which we are bewildered spectators, but reveals to us a familiar, settled cosmos in which we live and act, a world in which we can adopt purposes and adapt means to ends. It is in virtue of this homely, familiar, intelligible character of experience—its possession of significance—that we are able to inhabit and cope with our environment.

If this use of "significance" be allowed it will, I think, readily be granted that our consciousness is essentially consciousness of significance. Mind could neither emerge nor persist in an environment which was totally nonsignificant to it. For this reason it is not possible to define "significance" ostensively by pointing to contrasting examples of significant and nonsignificant experience. In its most general form at least, we must accept the Kantian thesis that we can be aware only of that which enters into a certain framework of basic relations which is correlated with the structure of our own consciousness. These basic relations represent the minimal conditions of significance for the human mind. The totally nonsignificant is thus debarred from entering into our experience. A completely undifferentiated field, or a sheer "buzzing, booming confusion," would be incapable of sustaining consciousness. For our consciousness is (to repeat) essentially consciousness of significance. Except perhaps in very early infancy or in states of radical breakdown, the human mind is always aware of its environment as having this quality of fundamental familiarity or intelligibility. Significance, then, is simply the most general characteristic of our experience.

. . .

Although the locus of significance is primarily our environment as a whole, we can in thought divide this into smaller units of significance. We may accordingly draw a provisional distinction between two species of significance, object-significance and situational significance, and note the characteristics of significance first in terms of the former.

Every general name, such as "hat," "book," "fire," "house," names a type of object-significance. For these are isolable aspects of our experience which (in suitable contexts) render appropriate distinctive patterns of behavior. The word "hat," for example, does not name a rigidly delimited class of objects but a particular *use* to which things can be put, namely, as a covering for the head. Objects are specially manufactured for this use; but if necessary many other items can be made to fulfill the function of hat. This particular way of treating things, as headgear, is the behavioral correlate of the type of object-significance which we call "being a hat." Indeed the boundaries of each distinguishable class of objects are defined by the two *foci* of (1) physical structure and (2) function in relation to human interests. Our names

are always in part names for functions or uses or kinds of significance as apprehended from the standpoint of the agent.

Significance, then, is a relational concept. A universe devoid of consciousness would be neither significant nor nonsignificant. An object or a sense-field is significant *for* or *to* a mind. We are only concerned here with significance for the human mind, but it is well to remember that the lower animals also are aware of their environment as being significant, this awareness being expressed not in words or concepts but in actions and readinesses for action.

There is, I hope, no suggestion of anything occult about this fundamental feature of our experience which I am calling "significance." The difficulty in discussing it is not novelty but, on the contrary, overfamiliarity. It is so completely obvious that we can easily overlook its importance, or even its existence. There is also the related difficulty that we do not apprehend significance as such, but only each distinguishable aspect of our experience as having its own particular type of significance. For significance is a genus which exists only in its species. Just as we perceive the various colors, but never color in general, so we perceive this and that kind of significance, but never significance *simpliciter*.

After this preliminary characterization of the nature of significance, we may take note of the mental activity of interpretation which is its subjective correlate. The word "interpretation" suggests the possibility of differing judgments; we tend to call a conclusion an interpretation when we recognize that there may be other and variant accounts of the same subject matter. It is precisely because of this suggestion of ambiguity in the given, and of alternative modes of construing data, that "interpretation" is a suitable correlate term for "significance."

Two uses of "interpretation" are to be distinguished. In one of its senses, an interpretation is a (true or false) *explanation,* answering the question, Why? We speak, for example, of a metaphysician's interpretation of the universe. In its other sense, an interpretation is a (correct or incorrect) *recognition,*[2] or attribution of significance, answering the question, What? ("What is that, a dog or a fox?") These two meanings are closely connected. For all explanation operates ultimately in terms of recognition. We explain a puzzling phenomenon by disclosing its context, revealing it as part of a wider whole which does not, for us, stand in need of explanation. We render the unfamiliar intellectually acceptable by relating it to the already recognizable, indicating a connection or continuity between the old and the new. But in the unique case of the universe as a whole the distinction between explanation and recognition fails to arise. For the universe has no wider context in terms of which it might be explained; an explanation of it can therefore only consist in a perception of its significance. In this case, therefore, interpretation is both recognition and explanation. Hence the theistic recognition, or significance-attribution, is also a metaphysical explanation or theory. However, although the explanatory and the recognition aspects of theistic faith are inseparable, they may usefully be distinguished for purposes of exposition. In the present chapter we shall be examining interpretation, including the religious interpretation, as a recognition, or perception of significance; and in the following chapter, as an explanation.

An act of recognition, or of significance-attribution, is a complex occurrence dealing with two different types

of ambiguity in the given. There are, on the one hand, interpretations which are mutually exclusive (e.g., "That is a fox" and "That is a dog," referring to the same object), and on the other hand interpretations which are mutually compatible (e.g., "That is an animal" and "That is a dog"; or "He died by asphyxiation" and "He was murdered"). Of two logically alternative interpretations only one (at most) can be the correct interpretation. But two compatible interpretations may both be correct. We shall be concerned henceforth with this latter kind of difference, in which several levels or layers or orders of significance are found in the same field of data.

The following are some simple examples of different levels or orders of object-significance.

(a) I see a rectangular red object on the floor in the corner. So far I have interpreted it as a "thing" (or "substance"), as something occupying space and time. On looking more closely, however, I see that it is a red-covered book. I have now made a new interpretation which includes my previous one, but goes beyond it.

(b) There is a piece of paper covered with writing. An illiterate savage can perhaps interpret it as something made by man. A literate person, who does not know the particular language in which it is written, can interpret it as being a document. But someone who understands the language can find in it the expression of specific thoughts. Each is answering the question, "What is it?" correctly, but answering it at different levels. And each more adequate attribution of significance presupposes the less adequate ones.

This relationship between types of significance, one type being superimposed upon and interpenetrating another, is a pattern which we shall find again in larger and more important spheres.

We have already noted that significance is essentially related to action. The

---

[2] This is a slightly off-dictionary sense of "recognition," equating it, not with the identification of the appearances of an object at different times as appearances of the same object, but with the apprehension of what has been discussed above as the "significance" of objects.

significance of an object to an individual consists in the practical difference which that object makes to him, the ways in which it affects either his immediate reactions or his more long-term plans and policies. There is also a reciprocal influence of action upon our interpretations. For it is only when we have begun to act upon our interpretations, and have thereby verified that our environment is capable of being successfully inhabited in terms of them, that they become fully "real" modes of experience. Interpretations which take the dispositional form of readinesses for action, instead of immediate overt activity, borrow this feeling of "reality" from cognate interpretations which are being or have already been confirmed in action. (For example, when I see an apple on the sideboard, but do not immediately eat it, I nevertheless perceive it as entirely "real" because I have in the past verified similar interpretations of similar apple-like appearances.) It is by acting upon our interpretations that we build up an apprehension of the world around us; and in this process interpretations, once confirmed, suggest and support further interpretations. The necessity of acting-in-terms-of to "clinch" or confirm an interpretation has its importance, as we shall note later, in relation to the specifically religious recognition which we call theistic faith.

We have been speaking so far only of object-significance. But, as already indicated, object-significance as contrasted with situational significance is an expository fiction. An object absolutely per se and devoid of context would have no significance for us. It can be intelligible only as part of our familiar world. What significance would remain, for example, to a book without the physical circumstance of sight, the conventions of language and writing, the acquired art of reading, and even the literature of which the book is a part and the civilization within which it occurs? An object owes its significance as much to its context as to itself; it is what it is largely because of its place in a wider scheme of things. We are indeed hardly ever conscious of anything in complete isolation. Our normal consciousness is of groups of objects standing in recognizable patterns of relations to one another. And it is the resulting situation taken as a whole that carries significance for us, rendering some ranges of action and reaction appropriate and others inappropriate. We live and plan and act all the time in terms of the situational significance of our environment; although of course our interest may focus at any given moment upon a particular component object within the current situation.

We do not, it is true, as plain men generally think of the familiar situations which constitute our experience from moment to moment as having "significance" and of our actions as being guided thereby. But in the fundamental sense in which we are using the term, our ordinary consciousness of the world is undoubtedly a continuous consciousness of significance. It is normally consciousness of a routine or humdrum significance which is so familiar that we take it entirely for granted. The significance for me, for example, of my situation at the present moment is such that I go on quietly working; this is the response rendered appropriate by my interpretation of my contemporary experience. No fresh response is required, for my routine reactions are already adjusted to the prevailing context of significance. But this significance is none the less real for being undramatic. The component elements of situational significance are not only physical objects —tables, mountains, stars, houses, hats, and so on—but also such nonmaterial entities as sounds and lights and odors and, no less important, such psychological events and circumstances as other peoples' thoughts, emotions, and attitudes. Thus the kinds of situational significance in terms of which we act and react are enormously complex. Indeed the philosopher who would trace the morphology of situational significance must be a dramatist and poet as well as analyst. Attempts at significance-mapping have been undertaken by some of the existentialist writers: what they refer to as the "existential" character of experience is the fact that we are ourselves by definition *within* any relational system which constitutes a situation for us. However, these writers have usually been concerned to bring out the more strained and hectic aspects of human experience, presenting it often as a vivid nightmare of metaphysical anxieties and perils. They are undoubtedly painting from real life, particularly in this frightened age, but I venture to think that they are depicting it in a partial and one-sided manner.

A "situation" may be defined, then, as a state of affairs which, when selected for attention by an act of interpretation, carries its own distinctive practical significance for us. We may be involved in many different situations at the same time and may move by swift or slow transitions of interpretation from one to another. There may thus occur an indefinitely complex interpenetration of situations. For example I am, let us say, sitting in a room playing a game of chess with a friend. The game, isolated by the brackets of imagination, is a situation in itself in which I have a part to play as one of the two competing intelligences presiding over the chess board. Here is an artificial situation with its conventional boundaries, structure, and rules of procedure. But from time to time my attention moves from the board to the friend with whom I am playing, and I exchange some conversation with him. Now I am living in another situation which contains the game of chess as a sub-situation. Then suddenly a fire breaks out in the building, and the attention of both of us

shifts at once to our wider physical situation; and so on. There are the wider and wider spatial situations of the block, the city, the state, continent, globe, Milky Way, and finally, as the massive permanent background situation inclusive of all else, the physical universe. And there are also the widening circles of family, class, nation, civilization, and all the other groupings within the inclusive group of the human species as a whole. The complex web of interplays within and between these two expanding series gives rise to the infinite variety of situations of which our human life is composed. Finally, enfolding and interpenetrating this interlocking mass of finite situations there is also, according to the insistent witness of theistic religion, the all-encompassing situation of being in the presence of God and within the sphere of an ongoing divine purpose. Our main concern, after these prolonged but unavoidable preliminaries, is to be with this alleged ultimate and inclusive significance and its relation to the more limited and temporary significances through which it is mediated.

Our inventory, then, shows three main orders of situational significance, corresponding to the threefold division of the universe, long entertained by human thought, into nature, man, and God. The significance for us of the physical world, nature, is that of an objective environment whose character and "laws" we must learn, and toward which we have continually to relate ourselves aright if we are to survive. The significance for us of the human world, man, is that of a realm of relationships in which we are responsible agents, subject to moral obligation. This world of moral significance is, so to speak, superimposed upon the natural world, so that relating ourselves to the moral world is not distinct from the business of relating ourselves to the natural world but is rather a particular manner of so doing. And likewise the more ultimately fateful and momentous matter of relating ourselves to the divine, to God, is not distinct from the task of directing ourselves within the natural and ethical spheres; on the contrary, it entails (without being reducible to) a way of so directing ourselves.

In the case of each of these three realms, the natural, the human, and the divine, a basic act of interpretation is required which discloses to us the existence of the sphere in question, thus providing the ground for our multifarious detailed interpretations within that sphere.

Consider first the level of natural significance. This is the significance which our environment has for us as animal organisms seeking pleasure and survival and shunning pain and death. In building houses, cooking food, avoiding dangerous precipices, whirlpools, and volcanoes, and generally conducting ourselves prudently in relation to the material world, we are all the time taking account of what I am calling (for want of a better name) the *natural* significance of our environment.

We have already noted some instances of natural significance when discussing the recognition of objects and situations. It is a familiar philosophical tenet, and one which may perhaps today be taken as granted, that all conscious experience of the physical world contains an element of interpretation. There are combined in each moment of experience a presented field of data and an interpretative activity of the subject. The perceiving mind is thus always in some degree a selecting, relating and synthesizing agent, and experiencing our environment involves a continuous activity of interpretation. "Interpretation" here is of course an unconscious and habitual process, the process by which a sense-field is perceived, for example, as a three-dimensional room, or a particular configuration of colored patches within that field as a book lying upon a table. Interpretation in this sense

is generally recognized as a factor in the genesis of sense perception. We have now to note, however, the further and more basic act of interpretation which reveals to us the very existence of a material world, a world which we explore and inhabit as our given environment. In attending to this primary interpretative act we are noting the judgment which carries us beyond the solipsist predicament into an objective world of enduring, causally interacting objects, which we share with other people. Given the initial rejection of solipsism (or rather given the interpretative bias of human nature, which has prevented all but the most enthusiastic of philosophers from falling into solipsism) we can, I think, find corroborations of an analogical kind to support our belief in the unobserved continuance of physical objects and the reality of other minds. But the all-important first step, or assumption, is unevidenced and unevidenceable—except for permissive evidence, in that one's phenomenal experience is "there" to be interpreted either solipsistically or otherwise. But there is no event within our phenomenal experience the occurrence or nonoccurrence of which is relevant to the truth or falsity of the solipsist hypothesis. That hypothesis represents one possible interpretation of our experience as a whole, and the contrary belief in a plurality of minds existing in a common world represents an alternative and rival interpretation.

· · ·

But the ordering of our lives in relation to an objective material environment thus revealed to us by a basic act of interpretation is not the most distinctively human level of experience. It is characteristic of mankind to live not only in terms of the natural significance of his world but also in the dimension of personality and responsibility. And so we find that presupposing consciousness of the physical world, and supervening upon it, is the kind of situational significance which we call "being responsible" or "being under obligation." The sense of moral obligation, or of "oughtness," is the basic datum of ethics. It is manifested whenever someone, in circumstances requiring practical decision, feels "obligated" to act, or to refrain from acting, in some particular way. When this occurs, the natural significance of his environment is interpenetrated by another, ethical significance. A traveler on an unfrequented road, for example, comes upon a stranger who has met with an accident and who is lying injured and in need of help. At the level of natural significance this is just an empirical state of affairs, a particular configuration of stone and earth and flesh. But an act or reflex of interpretation at the moral level reveals to the traveler a situation in which he is under obligation to render aid. He feels a categorical imperative laid upon him, demanding that he help the injured man. The situation takes on for him a peremptory ethical significance, and he finds himself in a situation of inescapable personal responsibility.

As has often been remarked, it is characteristic of situations exhibiting moral significance that they involve, directly or indirectly, more than one person. The other or others may stand either in an immediate personal relationship to the moral agent or, as in large-scale social issues, in a more remote causal relationship. (The sphere of politics has been defined as that of the *im*personal relationships between persons.) Ethical significance, as the distinctive significance of situations in which persons are components, includes both of these realms. To feel moral obligation is to perceive (or misperceive) the practical significance for oneself of a situation in which one stands in a responsible relationship to another person or to other people. That the perception of significance in personal situations sets up (in Kant's terms) a categorical imperative, while natural situations give rise only to hypothetical imperatives, conditional upon our own desires, is a defining characteristic of the personal world.

Clearly, moral significance presupposes natural significance. For in order that we may be conscious of moral obligations, and exercise moral intelligence, we must first be aware of a stable environment in which actions have foreseeable results, and in which we can learn the likely consequences of our deeds. It is thus a precondition of ethical situations that there should be a stable medium, the world, with its own causal laws, in which people meet and in terms of which they act. Indeed the two spheres of significance, the moral and the physical, entirely interpenetrate. For all occasions of obligation have reference, either immediately or ultimately, to overt action. Relating oneself to the ethical sphere is thus a particular manner of relating oneself to the natural sphere: ethical significance is mediated to us in and through the natural world. As in the case of natural situational significance, we can enter the sphere of ethical significance only by our own act of interpretation. But at this level the interpretation is a more truly voluntary one. That is to say, it is not forced upon us from outside, but depends upon an inner capacity and tendency to interpret in this way, a tendency which we are free to oppose and even to overrule. If a man chooses to be a moral solipsist, or absolute egoist, recognizing no responsibility toward other people, no one can prove to him that he has any such responsibilities. The man who, when confronted with some standard situation having ethical significance, such as a bully wantonly injuring a child, fails to see it as morally significant, could only be classified as suffering from a defect of his nature analogous to physical blindness. He can of course be compelled by threats of punishment to conform to a stated code of behavior; but he cannot be compelled to feel moral obligation. He must see and accept for himself his own situation as a responsible being and its obverse of ethical accountability.

Has this epistemological paradigm—of one order of significance superimposed upon and mediated through another—any further application? The contention of this essay is that it has. As ethical significance interpenetrates natural significance, so religious significance interpenetrates both ethical and natural. The divine is the highest and ultimate order of significance, mediating neither of the others and yet being mediated through both of them.

But what do we mean by religious significance? What is it that, for the ethical monotheist, possesses this significance, and in what does the significance consist?

The primary locus of religious significance is the believer's experience as a whole. The basic act of interpretation which reveals to him the religious significance of life is a uniquely "total interpretation," whose logic will be studied in the next chapter. But we must at this point indicate what is intended by the phrase "total interpretation," and offer some preliminary characterization of its specifically theistic form.

Consider the following imagined situation. I enter a room in a strange building and find that a militant secret society appears to be meeting there. Most of the members are armed, and as they take me for a fellow member I judge it expedient to acquiesce in the role. Subtle and bloodthirsty plans are discussed for a violent overthrow of the constitution. The whole situation is alarming in the extreme. Then I suddenly notice behind me a gallery in which there are batteries of arc lights and silently whirring cameras, and I realize that I have walked by accident onto the set of a film. This realization consists in a change of interpretation of my immediate environment. Until now I had automatically interpreted it as being "real life," as a dangerous situation demanding considerable circumspection on my part. Now I interpret it as having practical significance of a quite different kind. But there is no corresponding change in the observable course of events. The meeting of the "secret society" proceeds as before, although now I believe the state of affairs to be quite other than I had previously supposed it to be. The same phenomena are interpreted as constituting an entirely different practical situation. And yet not quite the same phenomena, for I have noticed important new items, namely, the cameras and arc lights. But let us now in imagination expand the room into the world, and indeed expand it to include the entire physical universe. This is the strange room into which we walk at birth. There is no space left for a photographers' gallery, no direction in which we can turn in search of new clues which might reveal the significance of our situation. Our interpretation must be a *total* interpretation, in which we assert that the world as a whole (as experienced by ourselves) is of this or that kind, that is to say, affects our plans and our policies in such and such ways.

The monotheist's faith-apprehension of God as the unseen Person dealing with him in and through his experience of the world is from the point of view of epistemology an interpretation of this kind, an interpretation of the world as a whole as mediating a divine presence and purpose. He sees in his situation as a human being a significance to which the appropriate response is a religious trust and obedience. His interpretative leap carries him into a world which exists through the will of a holy, righteous, and loving Being who is the creator and sustainer of all that is. Behind the world—to use an almost inevitable spatial metaphor—there is apprehended to be an omnipotent, personal Will whose purpose toward mankind guarantees men's highest good and blessedness. The believer finds that he is at all times in the presence of this holy Will. Again and again he realizes, either at the time or in retrospect, that in his dealings with the circumstances of his own life he is also having to do with a transcendent Creator who is the determiner of his destiny and the source of all good.

Thus the primary religious perception, or basic act of religious interpretation, is not to be described as either a reasoned conclusion or an unreasoned hunch that there is a God. It is, putatively, an apprehension of the divine presence within the believer's human experience. It is not an inference to a general truth, but a "divine-human encounter," a mediated meeting with the living God.

As ethical significance presupposes natural, so religious significance presupposes both ethical and natural. Entering into conscious relation with God consists in large part in adopting a particular style and manner of acting towards our natural and social environments. For God summons men to serve him *in* the world, and in terms of the life of the world. Religion is not only a way of cognizing but also, and no less vitally, a way of living. To see the world as being ruled by a divine love which sets infinite value upon each individual and includes all men in its scope, and yet to live as though the world were a realm of chance in which each must fight for his own interests against the rest, argues a very dim and wavering vision of God's rule. So far as that vision is clear it issues naturally in a trust in the divine purpose and obedience to the divine will.

. . .

In one respect this theistic interpretation is more akin to the natural than to the ethical interpretation. For while only *some* situations have moral significance, *all* situations have for embodied beings a continuous natural significance. In like manner the sphere of the basic religious interpretation is not merely this or that isolable situation, but the uniquely total situation constituted by our experience as a whole and in all its aspects, up to the present moment.

But on the other hand the theistic interpretation is more akin to the ethical than to the natural significance-attribution in that it is clearly focused in some situations and imperceptible in others. Not all the moments of life mediate equally the presence of God to the ordinary believer. He is not continuously conscious of God's presence (although possibly the saint is), but conscious rather of the divine Will as a reality in the background of his life, a reality which may at any time emerge to confront him in absolute and inescapable demand. We have already observed how one situation may interpenetrate another, and how some sudden pressure or intrusion can cause a shift of interpretation and attention so that the mind moves from one interlocking context to another. Often a more important kind of significance will summon us from a relatively trivial kind. A woman may be playing a game of bridge when she hears her child crying in pain in another room; and at once her consciousness moves from the artificial world of the game to the real world in which she is the mother of the child. Or an officer in the army reserve may be living heedless of the international situation until sudden mobilization recalls him to his military responsibility. The interrupting call of duty may summon us from trivial or relatively unimportant occupations to take part in momentous events. Greater and more ultimate purposes may without warning supervene upon lesser ones and direct our lives into a new channel. But the final significance, which takes precedence over all others as supremely important and overriding, is (according to theism) that of our situation as being in the presence of God. At any time a man may be confronted by some momentous decision, some far-reaching moral choice either of means or of ends, in which his responsibility as a servant of God intrudes upon and conflicts with the requirements of his earthly "station and its duties," so that the latter pales into unimportance and he acts in relation to a more ultimate environment whose significance magisterially overrules his customary way of life. When the call of God is clearly heard other calls become inaudible, and the prophet or saint, martyr or missionary, the man of conscience or of illumined mind may ignore all considerations of worldly prudence in responding to a claim with which nothing else whatever may be put in the balance.

To recapitulate and conclude this stage of the discussion, the epistemological point which I have sought to make is this. There is in cognition of every kind an unresolved mystery. The knower-known relationship is in the last analysis *sui generis:* the mystery of cognition persists at the end of every inquiry—though its persistence does not prevent us from cognizing. We cannot explain, for example, how we are conscious of sensory phenomena as constituting an objective physical environment; we just find ourselves interpreting the data of our experience in this way. We are aware that we live in a real world, though we cannot prove by any logical formula that it *is* a real world. Likewise we cannot explain how we know ourselves to be responsible beings subject to moral obligations; we just find ourselves interpreting our social experience in this way. We find ourselves inhabiting an ethically significant universe, though

we cannot prove that it *is* ethically significant by any process of logic. In each case we discover and live in terms of a particular aspect of our environment through an appropriate act of interpretation; and having come to live in terms of it we neither require nor can conceive any further validation of its reality. The same is true of the apprehension of God. The theistic believer cannot explain *how* he knows the divine presence to be mediated through his human experience. He just finds himself interpreting his experience in this way. He lives in the presence of God, though he is unable to prove by any dialectical process that God exists.

To say this is not of course to demonstrate that God *does* exist. The outcome of the discussion thus far is rather to bring out the similarity of epistemological structure and status between men's basic convictions in relation to the world, moral responsibility, and divine existence. If our line of thought in Chapter 1 has been sound, these three parallel convictions all qualify, as instances of rational certainty, for the title of knowledge. The aim of the present chapter has thus been to show how, if there be a God, he is known to mankind, and how such knowledge is related to other kinds of human knowing. I hope that at least the outline of a possible answer to these questions has now been offered. The answer, however, at once raises further questions, especially with regard to the experimental verification of the theistic interpretation, and these questions will be taken up in the next chapter.

SUGGESTIONS FOR FURTHER READING

For a sympathetic presentation of the nature and history of mysticism see Evelyn Underhill, *Mysticism* (London: Macmillan, 1930); W. R. Inge, *Mysticism in Religion* (Chicago: Univ. of Chicago Press, 1948); R. M. Jones, *Studies in Mystical Religion* (London: Macmillan, 1936); and J. B. Pratt, *The Religious Consciousness* (New York: Macmillan, 1945).

J. H. Leuba, *The Psychology of Religious Mysticism* (New York: Harcourt, Brace & World, 1925), is an outstanding example of an attack on mysticism from a psychological point of view. Also critical is R. C. Zaehner, *Mysticism, Sacred and Profane* (New York: Oxford Univ. Press, 1957). Aldous Huxley, *The Perennial Philosophy* (New York: Harper, 1945), is a rich sourcebook. Henri Bergson, *The Two Sources of Morality and Religion,* R. A. Audra and Cloudesley Brereton, trs. (New York: Holt, 1935), attempts to weave mystical experience into the Bergsonian philosophy.

In the recent works by W. T. Stace, *Time and Eternity* (Princeton: Princeton Univ. Press, 1952), and *Mysticism and Philosophy* (Philadelphia: Lippincott, 1960), we find an interesting combination of analytical acuity and a disposition to take Oriental mysticism seriously. Stace's *Teachings of the Mystics* (New York: New American Library, 1960) is an excellent sourcebook.

The use of mystical experience as evidence for the existence of God is discussed in C. A. Bennett, *A Philosophical Study of Mysticism* (New Haven: Yale Univ. Press, 1923); and H. J. Paton, *The Modern Predicament* (New York: Macmillan, 1955).

The view that religious experience is a pervasive part of all experience is well presented by John Baillie, *Our Knowledge of God* (New York: Scribner's, 1939); and Martin Buber, *I and Thou,* R. G. Smith, tr. (Edinburg: T. and T. Clark, 1937).

Logical difficulties in the mystic's position are discussed in Paul Henle, "Mysticism and Semantics," *Philosophy and Phenomenological Research* (1949), and W. P. Alston, "Ineffability," *Philosophical Review* (1956).

3.

CRITICISMS
OF
THEISM

This section contains a wide variety of criticisms of the theistic position. The most ancient of these, and perhaps the most telling, is the one based on the problem of evil—a problem which has been troubling men for centuries. Given the fact that there is evil in the world, how can we maintain that the world owes its existence to a personal being that is both all-powerful and perfectly good? To resolve this problem a theist would have to show that even with the wickedness and suffering the world does contain, it could have been created by an omnipotent and perfectly good deity; or, since to *prove* this would require superhuman powers, let us say that he would have to show that it is not unreasonable to accept it. (The phrase "the best of all possible worlds" used by Leibniz, for example, might suggest that it is up to the theist to show that the world we have is the *only* sort that a theistic God would create. But this requirement would make his task unnecessarily difficult.) I think that F. R. Tennant in the selection included here does as much as it is possible to do along this line, and even he would admit, I am sure, that he has not quite succeeded. We must remember that even if the theist does not succeed in fully meeting the criticism, he is not thereby committed to giving up his position on pain of irrationality. Consider the following analogy: The director of a research organization hires a young chemist who is recommended by eminently reputable authorities as a creative genius. But during his first year with the organization he accomplishes nothing, except the breakage of expensive equipment. Whenever he is observed by his superiors he is staring dreamily out the window, and he never submits any reports. The director is unable to see *how* the facts of his experience are compatible with the hypothesis that the man is a genius. But he can envisage ways in which they might be compatible with that hypothesis (for example, the man works out everything very carefully in his mind before either experimenting or communicating with others), and so long as he has strong testimony in support of the hypothesis he will be justified, for a time, in continuing to accept it, in continuing to believe that somehow it is compatible with the facts at his disposal, even though he cannot see how it is. Similarly, provided the theist has strong reasons to support the principle that the world was created by an omnipotent and perfectly good deity, reasons which have to do with something other than the distribution of good and evil in the world, then he would be justified in supposing that the evil in the world is somehow compatible with theism, though he cannot fully see how. But this holds only if he has strong reasons for his position.

The selection from Baron d'Holbach contains at least a mention of almost every important complaint ever levied against theism. A passionate atheist, Holbach has neglected no opportunity for discrediting the theistic position, and he is not at all concerned to represent theism in the strongest possible form. Despite this he brings forward some points which are worth serious attention. We should distinguish between two objections that are brought out in this chapter: they are claims that theism is not borne out by certain facts, and claims that there are internal inconsistencies in the theistic concept of God. Most of the objections of the former sort can be regarded as various forms of the problem of evil, some of which are not often encountered elsewhere—for example, the suggestion that the supposed revelation of God in the Bible is not carried out as effectively and fairly as would be expected from an omnipotent and perfectly good deity. Among objections of the second sort we can distinguish between those which can be disposed of fairly readily either by showing that they rest on confusions or by making fairly simple revisions in the theistic concept, and those which cannot be avoided so simply. In the first group we have the many supposed inconsistencies involving moral attributes of God. Thus Holbach maintains that the attribution of justice to God is inconsistent with the principle that He owes us nothing, since justice consists in rendering to each that which is due him. But this is a confusion. When a judge settles a financial dispute justly, he is rendering to each party what is due him, but this does not mean he is rendering what he (the judge) owes them; he may owe them nothing. Again, it is claimed that since mercy is either a violation of justice or an exemption from a law which is too severe, we cannot suppose that God is merciful, assuming that

He is perfectly just and that His laws are never too severe. But this ignores the point that there may be an intrinsic value in a merciful suspension of a perfectly just punishment and that this value may be so great as to outweigh the value of the doing of justice. The argument that it is inconceivable that an omnipotent being should work for His own glory or that we should contribute to His glory would seem to require some revisions in the traditional conception. If we think of God as limited in certain ways, as in the selection from Charles Hartshorne, it would make sense to speak of increasing His glory.

Other difficulties are not so easily met. Holbach alludes to the difficulty of conceiving an immaterial being acting in the various ways in which God is supposed to act: creating, speaking, commanding, punishing, forgiving, guiding, comforting, and so on. And if we think of God as immutable (in an absolute sense which excludes any sort of change whatsoever) or as absolutely simple, it is even more difficult to think of Him as acting. Surely any action—whether making something, issuing a command, or pardoning someone—takes time for its performance, involves a temporal succession of stages. And for an agent to engage in various kinds of actions, it must be possible to distinguish one of these actions from the others in a way which would be rendered impossible by absolute simplicity, in a sense of that term which would rule out any differentiation of parts or aspects. But, as Hartshorne argues, it is doubtful whether these attributions have any real basis in the actual thoughts, actions, attitudes, and feelings of religious people. It would seem that insistence on absolute immutability and absolute simplicity has been foisted on the Judaeo-Christian tradition by a coalition of mystics and speculative philosophers for purposes of their own. But even if we restrict ourselves to the notion that God is immaterial, there are serious difficulties. It seems that as we ordinarily use action words like "speaks," "makes," "punishes," "guides," the occurrence of bodily behavior is essential for their attribution. It seems that it is an essential part of what we mean in saying that X punished Y that X moved parts of his body in one way or another. Of course no particular sort of bodily movement is required. It may have been spanking, signing a document, or just "tongue-lashing." But there must have been some motion. Purely private thinking about Y on the part of X is not enough.

Theists usually try to handle this and similar difficulties in terms of some form of the doctrine of analogy. Although terms are not applied in quite the same sense to men and to God, still there is enough carry-over between the two applications to enable us to derive from the ordinary sense a related sense which can be used in speaking about God. But the difficulty is that either we confess ourselves unable to say just what is common to the two senses, in which case we are admitting that we do not know what we mean when we talk about God, or, if we try to state in detail the derived theological sense, we find ourselves, as I. M. Crombie suggests in his contribution to the "Theology and Falsification" symposium, saddled with something that is obviously too meager to serve religious purposes. Thus if we take away from our action terms all publicly observable bodily behavior, it would seem that all we have left are private thoughts, feelings, attitudes, and so on. Thus, "God has forgiven X's sins" would mean something like "God has thought to Himself 'I forgive X's sins,' God feels compassion toward X, and God does not feel grudges or resentments against X." But this clearly will not do. If divine acts like forgiving are to serve a religious function they must involve some sort of actual contact with the human being involved. God's private feelings and soliloquies are not enough. And Crombie's alternative view—that words are used in the same sense when speaking of God, but that they are used with this common sense in a "parable" which is referred as a whole to God in a way that we cannot really understand—seems simply to transfer us back to the first horn of the dilemma in a slightly different form. For if we do not know how the parable of the forgiving of the prodigal son applies to God, then we do not know just what it means to speak of God as forgiving. Crombie says that we simply take it on authority that the parable does somehow apply. But one reason for not stopping here is that it does seem that in our religious practice, and in taking one sort of feeling or attitude toward God rather than another, we do suppose that we have more of an understanding of what is meant when these terms are applied to God than would be allowed by Crombie's position, and it would seem to be the task of the philosopher to make this explicit.

The challenge to theism on the grounds of verifiability, which is the peg on which the "Theology and Falsification" symposium is hung, is not so different from the above difficulties as might appear at first sight. Antony Flew's question, "What would have to occur or to have occurred to constitute for you a disproof of the love of, or of the existence of, God?" stems from the preoccupation with a verifiability criterion of meaningfulness in the movement known as Logical Positivism. This movement originated in the so-called Vienna Circle in the 1920's and has numbered among its adherents such men as Moritz Schlick, Rudolph Carnap, and A. J. Ayer. In attempting to sweep away what they took to be futile and profitless philosophical speculations and disputes, these men enunciated the verifiability criterion of meaningfulness, according to which an utterance is meaningful if and only if there is some conceivable way in which it could be put to an empirical test, some conceivable way in which sense observations would count for or against its truth. Later, having recognized that there are many utterances such as "Shut the door" or "Splendid" for which one could hardly specify any empirical test but which could definitely not be called meaningless, the criterion was more narrowly specified as a criterion for "cognitive" or "factual" meaningfulness; that is, it was laid down as a necessary condition for an utterance being a statement of fact, a claim as to what objectively exists (cf. Martin's essay " 'Seeing' God" in Section 2). The positivists used this criterion to argue that metaphysical utterances like "Everything is an appearance of a single non-temporal reality," or "Every happening presupposes a substance which undergoes the happening" could not, in spite of their grammatical form, be taken to be statements as to what the world is objectively like, for it is impossible to specify any sense observations which would count for or against them. Similarly, Flew argues that since the religious believer will continue to believe (in the face of any happenings whatsoever) that God loves His creatures, he is not, contrary to appearances, really making an assertion as to what there is in the world. (Flew does not explicitly put his challenge in this form; he does not explicitly speak of *empirical* tests. But if we do not give it that interpretation it is not a serious challenge, for otherwise his question is easily answered. One thing that would constitute a disproof of the love of God would be the existence—in the mind of God—of a continuous attitude of hatred toward men. If we ask why *this* reply would not be considered satisfactory by Flew the only possible answer seems to be that the existence of such hatred would be as hard to verify empirically as the original supposition that God loves us.)

There are a number of ways in which the theist might attempt to meet Flew's challenge. He might argue, as do Basil Mitchell and I. M. Crombie in this symposium, and William James at the end of our selection from *The Varieties of Religious Experience,* that we can think of things we might conceivably observe, or establish by observation, which, if so established, would count decisively against theism. Mitchell says that apparently unmerited suffering does count against the hypothesis that God loves us, but that the believer would not take anything as counting decisively against it; perhaps we can join with Flew in doubting that such "counting against" has much significance. Crombie is more satisfactory on this point. In answer to the question, "Could anything count decisively against it?" he replies, "Yes, suffering which was utterly, eternally and irredeemably pointless." He admits that we are not in a position actually to determine whether any given piece of suffering is utterly, eternally, and irredeemably pointless because "we can never see all of the picture." But the positivists have always distinguished testability in practice from testability in principle and have recognized that the latter is the most they can require if they are to avoid seriously crippling science.

I think it is important to realize that the sort of religious belief for which it is this difficult to find any conceivable empirical test represents an extreme case, and that even if this is the sort of religious belief prevalent among the more educated religious people in our society, we would be seriously misled if we took this as typical of the way religious beliefs have generally been held in human culture. In most primitive religions beliefs about the gods are taken to imply all sorts of (at least apparently) empirically testable implications, for example, the agricultural and military effects of engaging in certain rites. And on a more sophisticated level beliefs about God in the Judaeo-Christian tradition have been taken to imply such things as the eventual political dominance of Israel and the eventual triumph of the Christian Church on earth, and these would seem to be empirically verifiable in principle. Let us not forget the contest between Elijah and the priests of Baal on Mount Carmel, in which the dispute between their respective theologies was put to the test of which of the supposed deities did in fact fulfill requests. And this calls to mind the statement attributed to Jesus in Matthew 21:22: "And all things whatsoever ye shall ask in prayer, believing, ye shall receive." That sounds empirically easy to test. Of course it must be admitted that in all these cases the carrying out of an empirical test is not so easy as it may sound. There are always more or less elaborate built-in protective devices to cushion the belief, up to a point at least, against empirical disproof. If the rites do not produce good crops or victory in battle, they must have been improperly performed. If I do not receive what I asked for in prayer, I must not have true faith. And no date is set for the final victory of the church on earth. The degree to which the belief is thus cushioned varies greatly and we might look on the present situation, on which Flew is focusing, as one in which the beliefs are very well cushioned indeed. But it is difficult to draw a line across this continuum beyond which we are to deny that one is really making an assertion. In this connection it might be salutary to reflect on the extent to which "She loves me" is sometimes protected from empirical disproof.

Another response to the positivist challenge is the one represented by R. M. Hare. What Hare is saying is that beliefs about God have a status which does not require empirical testability. There are many versions of this sort of position. Some philosophers want to interpret religious utterances as expressions of feelings or attitudes (for a discussion of this see the introduction to Section 8), and in this case no demand for a mode of verification would be in order; but, of course, this would really be to admit the positivist contention. What Hare does is to insist that the things we say about God are assertions (it seems to me that Flew and Mitchell are mistaken in supposing that Hare denies that they are assertions, though since philosophers so seldom make explicit the technical sense they give to this term it is difficult to be sure), but are very special kinds of assertion, "bliks," which are not susceptible to empirical test. They constitute fundamental presuppositions which may underlie the possibility of empirical test for more special assertions but are not themselves so testable. There is some similarity between this and the position taken by Hick in the selection in Section 2, according to which theistic belief has the status of a fundamental kind of interpretation of our experience, though Hick does not want to rule out the possibility of an empirical test of a sort. This means that Hare is really challenging the positivist criterion; he is suggesting that one can make statements (of a certain special sort) about the world without being able to specify any empirical verification procedure. And it has often been pointed out that the positivists have never given very cogent grounds for accepting their restrictions as to what is to count as "factually meaningful."

A third tack, not clearly represented in our selections, would be to maintain that Flew's demand for something that would count *decisively* against the love of God is too strong. It does seem that if we count an utterance as factually meaningful only if one can envisage empirical data which decisively prove or disprove it, we shall have to discard a great many scientific hypotheses along with metaphysics and theology. And, in fact, positivists have had a great deal of difficulty in formulating their criterion so that it excludes what they want to get rid of while including what they want to preserve.

The positivist attack ties in with the difficulty about the meaning of terms in their application to God in the following way: If we want to show what sense the term *love,* for example, takes on when applied to God, we might indicate how a statement like "God loves His creatures" would be empirically tested, showing what implications it has for our experience. This would be a very effective way of delimiting the theological sense of the term. In fact, the positivist position might be stated as the claim that this is the only way of exhibiting a sense of a term (in "factual" discourse). But of course many thinkers would maintain that there are ways of elucidating the theological sense of such terms without specifying possible empirical tests, for example, the "whittling-away" procedure criticized by Crombie.

The selections from Sigmund Freud and Maurice Cornforth represent a different kind of attack on theism. The previous selections contained relatively direct criticisms of the theistic position, either on the grounds that it could not take account of certain facts or that the position was internally contradictory or unclear. Freud and Cornforth are much more indirect; they attempt to explain the existence of religious belief in terms of psychological and/or sociological factors. Such explanations could not come into direct conflict with the beliefs themselves, for the beliefs are not about their own explanations. (More generally, the fundamental beliefs of religion are not about religion, any more than most poems are about poetry, but about God, His nature and activities, His relation to men, and so on.) But they may serve indirectly to discredit the beliefs. For one thing, if the occurrence of these beliefs can be explained in terms of purely psychological and sociological mechanisms, it will not be necessary to attribute their origin to a divine revelation. For another, the mechanism responsible for their production may be such that they could not possibly be taken seriously. This topic is in many ways parallel to the attempts to explain mystical experience psychologically, and the reader should consult the discussion of that topic in the introduction to Section 2.

The Freudian theory of religion falls into two sections: a historical theory of the development of religion in society and a more purely psychological theory of the factors within the individual which give him his strong inclination to accept religious beliefs without adequate evidence. Since the first theory has been well discredited, and since it is the second which is the more interesting for our purpose, I shall concentrate on it. In a very condensed form it runs as follows: Normally, in the process of growing up the individual has to repress various needs for love, protection, and direction from his father (to stick to the one parent for the sake of simplicity), as well as fears of and hostility toward his father. Society will not tolerate a direct expression of desires for infantile dependence after a certain age, and a direct expression of the hostile impulses would be dangerous. For these and other reasons consciousness of these needs and feelings is so painful that they are more or less permanently prevented from becoming conscious, but they do continue to exist and exert pressure for some sort of fulfillment. When an adult encounters difficulties, frustrations, terrors, which he does frequently, he tends to regress to earlier modes of psychical organization and these repressed infantile desires are strengthened. The individual then finds ready at hand in his culture a system of religious beliefs and practices which will give him an imaginary fulfillment of these needs, which will put him into something like the relation of a small child to a father who will love, protect, and guide him—and is also to be feared and approached with awe and reverence. Men have so strong a tendency to accept all of this because of the extent to which it affords a partial satisfaction of these infantile needs.

That is an oversimplified presentation of the Freudian account, which in its full form is very complex. The Marxist theory, presented in the selection from Cornforth, is much simpler. The chief determinant of all "ideology," including religion, is the economic structure of society. The details of a theology are simply etherealizations of the economic relations among various parts of the society in which the theology was developed. These abstract ideas arise automatically out of the economic system without any awareness on the part of the participants as to what is going on. Thus medieval Christian theology was a reflection of the feudal system. Other social scientists have developed this approach without restricting the base to economic relations as rigorously as did Marx.[1]

Of course, there are very serious questions as to the adequacy of these explanations. Marxists, like Cornforth in this selection, generally set forth the theory as received dogma without any real attempt to marshal evidence in its support. Freud and his followers are much more sensitive to the need for empirical testing, but little has actually been done. If we could get a reliable measure of the extent to which a person has repressed material of the sort in question, and then determine whether readiness to accept theistic religious belief varies in proportion to the extent of repressed desires, we would be making progress. But at present the theory simply has the status of a series of fascinating extrapolations to religious phenomena of ideas gained from the study of neurosis. But again, as in the case of explanations of mystical experience, our main job is to determine what bearing the explanations, if successful, would have on the truth or acceptability of the beliefs being explained. Marxists like Cornforth tend to suppose uncritically that their account discredits the beliefs. Freud is more cautious. He says, "It does not lie within the scope of this enquiry to estimate the value of religious doctrines as truth," and he is careful to distinguish the concept of an illusion from the concept of an error. (An illusion may or may not be an error.) Nevertheless he goes on to say that, given this explanation of the occurrence of religious beliefs, it would be very odd if these beliefs turned out to be correct. The fact that on this account the strength of religious belief is traced to the operation of unconscious infantile needs, just as neuroses are (Freud terms religion the "universal obsessional neurosis of humanity"), makes this account inherently hostile to any attempt to take these ideas as serious candidates for belief, even if accepting the account is not strictly incompatible with accepting the beliefs. If we contrast Freud's discussion of religion with that of Carl Jung, we can see that whereas it seems to be implied by Freud's theory that a perfectly healthy individual (no repressed fears, hostilities, needs, or desires) would have no inclination to be religious, Jung considers religion to be a normal and necessary psychic function. It is clear that the one theory is antithetical to religious belief in a way in which the other is not.

The selection from Hartshorne represents a serious attempt to reconceive

---

[1] For a recent careful and brilliant study see G. E. Swanson, *The Birth of the Gods,* Ann Arbor: Univ. of Michigan Press, 1960.

the theistic concept of God so as to avoid some of the objections brought against it. This reconception primarily involves loosening up the traditional absolutes—omniscience, omnipotence, etc.—so as to allow their application to a being that moves through time, undergoes change, can continually attain higher and higher levels of perfection, and encounters some limits to His will. It is clear that if we conceive of God as limited to some extent in carrying out His intentions, the problem of evil is no longer insoluble. And many of the contradictions pointed out by Holbach seem to disappear in Hartshorne's view. It is not at all clear, however, that Hartshorne has anything to say to the positivist demand that we specify some possible mode of empirical verification (despite his references to positivism) or to the destructive explanations proffered by Freud and Marx, if indeed these challenges need to be answered.

DAVID HUME

Evil and the First Cause of the Universe

PART X

It is my opinion, I own, replied Demea, that each man feels, in a manner, the truth of religion within his own breast, and, from a consciousness of his imbecility and misery rather than from any reasoning, is led to seek protection from that Being on whom he and all nature is dependent. So anxious or so tedious are even the best scenes of life that futurity is still the object of all our hopes and fears. We incessantly look forward and endeavour, by prayers, adoration, and sacrifice, to appease those unknown powers whom we find, by experience, so able to afflict and oppress us. Wretched creatures that we are! What resource for us amidst the innumerable ills of life did not religion suggest some methods of atonement, and appease those terrors with

From David Hume, *Dialogues Concerning Natural Religion*, Pts. X–XI.

which we are incessantly agitated and tormented?

I am indeed persuaded, said Philo, that the best and indeed the only method of bringing everyone to a due sense of religion is by just representations of the misery and wickedness of men. And for that purpose a talent of eloquence and strong imagery is more requisite than that of reasoning and argument. For is it necessary to prove what everyone feels within himself? It is only necessary to make us feel it, if possible, more intimately and sensibly.

The people, indeed, replied Demea, are sufficiently convinced of this great and melancholy truth. The miseries of life, the unhappiness of man, the general corruptions of our nature, the unsatisfactory enjoyment of pleasures, riches, honours —these phrases have become almost proverbial in all languages. And who can doubt of what all men declare from their own immediate feeling and experience?

In this point, said Philo, the learned are perfectly agreed with the vulgar; and in all letters, *sacred* and *profane,* the topic of human misery has been insisted on with the most pathetic eloquence that sorrow and melancholy could inspire. The poets, who speak from sentiment, without a system, and whose testimony has therefore the more authority, abound in images of this nature. From Homer down to Dr. Young, the whole inspired tribe have ever been sensible that no other representation of things would suit the feeling and observation of each individual.

As to authorities, replied Demea, you need not seek them. Look round this library of Cleanthes. I shall venture to affirm that, except authors of particular sciences, such as chemistry or botany, who have no occasion to treat of human life, there is scarce one of those innumerable writers from whom the sense of human misery has not, in some passage or other, extorted a complaint and confession of it. At least, the chance is entirely on that side; and no one author has ever, so far as I can recollect, been so extravagant as to deny it.

There you must excuse me, said Philo: Leibniz has denied it, and is perhaps the first [1] who ventured upon so bold and paradoxical an opinion; at least, the first who made it essential to his philosophical system.

And by being the first, replied Demea, might he not have been sensible of his error? For is this a subject in which philosophers can propose to make discoveries especially in so late an age? And can any man hope by a simple denial (for the subject scarcely admits of reasoning) to bear down the united testimony of mankind, founded on sense and consciousness?

And why should man, added he, pre-tend to an exemption from the lot of all other animals? The whole earth, believe me, Philo, is cursed and polluted. A perpetual war is kindled amongst all living creatures. Necessity, hunger, want stimulate the strong and courageous; fear, anxiety, terror agitate the weak and infirm. The first entrance into life gives anguish to the new-born infant and to its wretched parent; weakness, impotence, distress attend each stage of that life, and it is, at last, finished in agony and horror.

Observe, too, says Philo, the curious artifices of nature in order to embitter the life of every living being. The stronger prey upon the weaker and keep them in perpetual terror and anxiety. The weaker, too, in their turn, often prey upon the stronger, and vex and molest them without relaxation. Consider that innumerable race of insects, which either are bred on the body of each animal or, flying about, infix their stings in him. These insects have others still less than themselves which torment them. And thus on each hand, before and behind, above and below, every animal is surrounded with enemies which incessantly seek his misery and destruction.

Man alone, said Demea, seems to be, in part, an exception to this rule. For by combination in society he can easily master lions, tigers, and bears, whose greater strength and agility naturally enable them to prey upon him.

On the contrary, it is here chiefly, cried Philo, that the uniform and equal maxims of nature are most apparent. Man, it is true, can, by combination, surmount all his *real* enemies and become master of the whole animal creation; but does he not immediately raise up to himself *imaginary* enemies, the demons of his fancy, who haunt him with superstitious terrors and blast every enjoyment of life? His pleasure, as he imagines, becomes in their eyes a crime; his food and repose give them umbrage and offence; his very sleep and dreams furnish new materials to anx-

---

[1] That sentiment had been maintained by Dr. King and some few others before Leibniz, though by none of so great fame as that German philosopher.

ious fear; and even death, his refuge from every other ill, presents only the dread of endless and innumerable woes. Nor does the wolf molest more the timid flock than superstition does the anxious breast of wretched mortals.

Besides, consider, Demea: This very society by which we surmount those wild beasts, our natural enemies, what new enemies does it not raise to us? What woe and misery does it not occasion? Man is the greatest enemy of man. Oppression, injustice, contempt, contumely, violence, sedition, war, calumny, treachery, fraud —by these they mutually torment each other, and they would soon dissolve that society which they had formed were it not for the dread of still greater ills which must attend their separation.

But though these external insults, said Demea, from animals, from men, from all the elements, which assault us from a frightful catalogue of woes, they are nothing in comparison of those which arise within ourselves, from the distempered condition of our mind and body. How many lie under the lingering torment of diseases? Hear the pathetic enumeration of the great poet.

Intestine stone and ulcer, colic-pangs,
Demoniac frenzy, moping melancholy,
And moon-struck madness, pining atrophy,
Marasmus, and wide-wasting pestilence.
Dire was the tossing, deep the groans: *Despair*
Tended the sick, busiest from couch to couch.
And over them triumphant *Death* his dart
Shook: but delay'd to strike, though oft invok'd
With vows, as their chief good and final hope.

The disorders of the mind, continued Demea, though more secret, are not perhaps less dismal and vexatious. Remorse, shame, anguish, rage, disappointment, anxiety, fear, dejection, despair—who has ever passed through life without cruel inroads from these tormentors? How many have scarcely ever felt any better sensations? Labour and poverty, so abhorred by everyone, are the certain lot of the far greater number; and those few privileged persons who enjoy ease and opulence never reach contentment or true felicity. All the goods of life united would not make a very happy man, but all the ills united would make a wretch indeed; and any one of them almost (and who can be free from every one?), nay, often the absence of one good (and who can possess all?) is sufficient to render life ineligible.

Were a stranger to drop on a sudden into this world, I would show him, as a specimen of its ills, an hospital full of diseases, a prison crowded with malefactors and debtors, a field of battle strewed with carcases, a fleet foundering in the ocean, a nation languishing under tyranny, famine, or pestilence. To turn the gay side of life to him and give him a notion of its pleasures—whether should I conduct him? To a ball, to an opera, to court? He might justly think that I was only showing him a diversity of distress and sorrow.

There is no evading such striking instances, said Philo, but by apologies which still further aggravate the charge. Why have all men, I ask, in all ages, complained incessantly of the miseries of life? . . . They have no just reason, says one: these complaints proceed only from their discontented, repining, anxious disposition. . . . And can there possibly, I reply, be a more certain foundation of misery than such a wretched temper?

But if they were really as unhappy as they pretend, says my antagonist, why do they remain in life? . . .

Not satisfied with life, afraid of death—this is the secret chain, say I, that holds us. We are terrified, not bribed to the continuance of our existence.

It is only a false delicacy, he may insist, which a few refined spirits indulge, and which has spread these complaints among the whole race of mankind. . . . And what is this delicacy, I ask, which you blame? Is it anything but a greater sensibility to all the pleasures and pains of life? And if the man of a delicate, refined temper, by being so much more alive than the rest of the world, is only so much more unhappy, what judgment must we form in general of human life?

Let men remain at rest, says our adversary, and they will be easy. They are willing artificers of their own misery. . . . No! reply I: an anxious languor follows their repose; disappointment, vexation, trouble, their activity and ambition.

I can observe something like what you mention in some others, replied Cleanthes, but I confess I feel little or nothing of it in myself, and hope that it is not so common as you represent it.

If you feel not human misery yourself, cried Demea, I congratulate you on so happy a singularity. Others, seemingly the most prosperous, have not been ashamed to vent their complaints in the most melancholy strains. Let us attend to the great, the fortunate emperor, Charles V, when, tired with human grandeur, he resigned all his extensive dominions into the hands of his son. In the last harangue which he made on that memorable occasion, he publicly avowed *that the greatest prosperities which he had ever enjoyed had been mixed with so many adversities that he might truly say he had never enjoyed any satisfaction or contentment.* But did the retired life in which he sought for shelter afford him any greater happiness? If we may credit his son's account, his repentance commenced the very day of his resignation.

Cicero's fortune, from small beginnings, rose to the greatest lustre and renown; yet what pathetic complaints of the ills of life do his familiar letters, as well as philosophical discourses, contain?

And suitably to his own experience, he introduces Cato, the great, the fortunate Cato protesting in his old age that had he a new life in his offer he would reject the present.

Ask yourself, ask any of your acquaintance, whether they would live over again the last ten or twenty years of their life. No! but the next twenty, they say, will be better:

And from the dregs of life, hope to
    receive
What the first sprightly running could
    not give.

Thus, at last, they find (such is the greatness of human misery, it reconciles even contradictions) that they complain at once of the shortness of life and of its vanity and sorrow.

And is it possible, Cleanthes, said Philo, that after all these reflections, and infinitely more which might be suggested, you can still persevere in your anthropomorphism, and assert the moral attributes of the Deity, his justice, benevolence, mercy, and rectitude, to be of the same nature with these virtues in human creatures? His power, we allow, is infinite; whatever he wills is executed; but neither man nor any other animal is happy; therefore, he does not will their happiness. His wisdom is infinite; he is never mistaken in choosing the means to any end; but the course of nature tends not to human or animal felicity; therefore, it is not established for that purpose. Through the whole compass of human knowledge there are no inferences more certain and infallible than these. In what respect, then, do his benevolence and mercy resemble the benevolence and mercy of men?

Epicurus' old questions are yet unanswered.

Is he willing to prevent evil, but not able? then is he impotent. Is he able, but not willing? then is he malevolent. Is he both able and willing? whence then is evil?

You ascribe, Cleanthes, (and I believe justly) a purpose and intention to nature. But what, I beseech you, is the object of that curious artifice and machinery which she has displayed in all animals—the preservation alone of individuals, and propagation of the species? It seems enough for her purpose, if such a rank be barely upheld in the universe, without any care or concern for the happiness of the members that compose it. No resource for this purpose: no machinery in order merely to give pleasure or ease; no fund of pure joy and contentment; no indulgence without some want or necessity accompanying it. At least, the few phenomena of this nature are overbalanced by opposite phenomena of still greater importance.

Our sense of music, harmony, and indeed beauty of all kinds, gives satisfaction, without being absolutely necessary to the preservation and propagation of the species. But what racking pains, on the other hand, arise from gouts, gravels, megrims, toothaches, rheumatisms, where the injury to the animal machinery is either small or incurable? Mirth, laughter, play, frolic seem gratuitous satisfactions which have no further tendency; spleen, melancholy, discontent, superstition are pains of the same nature. How then does the Divine benevolence display itself, in the sense of you anthropomorphites? None but we mystics, as you were pleased to call us, can account for this strange mixture of phenomena, by deriving it from attributes infinitely perfect but incomprehensible.

And have you, at last, said Cleanthes smiling, betrayed your intentions, Philo? Your long agreement with Demea did indeed a little surprise me, but I find you were all the while erecting a concealed battery against me. And I must confess that you have now fallen upon a subject worthy of your noble spirit of opposition and controversy. If you can make out the present point, and prove mankind to be unhappy or corrupted, there is an end at once of all religion. For to what purpose establish the natural attributes of the Deity, while the moral are still doubtful and uncertain?

You take umbrage very easily, replied Demea, at opinions the most innocent and the most generally received, even amongst the religious and devout themselves; and nothing can be more surprising than to find a topic like this—concerning the wickedness and misery of man—charged with no less than atheism and profaneness. Have not all pious divines and preachers who have indulged their rhetoric on so fertile a subject, have they not easily, I say, given a solution of any difficulties which may attend it? This world is but a point in comparison of the universe; this life but a moment in comparison of eternity. The present evil phenomena, therefore, are rectified in other regions, and in some future period of existence. And the eyes of men, being then opened to larger views of things, see the whole connection of general laws, and trace, with adoration, the benevolence and rectitude of the Deity through all the mazes and intricacies of his providence.

No! replied Cleanthes, no! These arbitrary suppositions can never be admitted, contrary to matter of fact, visible and uncontroverted. Whence can any cause be known but from its known effects? Whence can any hypothesis be proved but from the apparent phenomena? To establish one hypothesis upon another is building entirely in the air; and the utmost we ever attain by these conjectures and fictions is to ascertain the bare possibility of our opinion, but never can we, upon such terms, establish its reality.

The only method of supporting Divine benevolence—and it is what I willingly embrace—is to deny absolutely the misery and wickedness of man. Your representations are exaggerated; your melancholy views mostly fictitious; your inferences contrary to fact and experience. Health is more common than sickness; pleasure than pain; happiness than misery. And for one vexation which we meet with, we attain, upon computation, a hundred enjoyments.

Admitting your position, replied Philo, which yet is extremely doubtful, you must at the same time allow that, if pain be less frequent than pleasure, it is infinitely more violent and durable. One hour of it is often able to outweigh a day, a week, a month of our common insipid enjoyments; and how many days, weeks, and months are passed by several in the most acute torments? Pleasure, scarcely in one instance, is ever able to reach ecstasy and rapture; and in no one instance can it continue for any time at its highest pitch and altitude. The spirits evaporate, the nerves relax, the fabric is disordered, and the enjoyment quickly degenerates into fatigue and uneasiness. But pain often, good God, how often! rises to torture and agony; and the longer it continues, it becomes still more genuine agony and torture. Patience is exhausted, courage languishes, melancholy seizes us, and nothing terminates our misery but the removal of its cause or another event which is the sole cure of all evil, but which, from our natural folly, we regard with still greater horror and consternation.

But not to insist upon these topics, continued Philo, though most obvious, certain, and important, I must use the freedom to admonish you, Cleanthes, that you have put the controversy upon a most dangerous issue, and are unawares introducing a total scepticism into the most essential articles of natural and revealed theology. What! no method of fixing a just foundation for religion unless we allow the happiness of human life, and maintain a continued existence even in this world, with all our present pains, infirmities, vexations, and follies, to be eligible and desirable! But this is contrary to everyone's feeling and experience; it is contrary to an authority so established as nothing can subvert. No decisive proofs can ever be produced against this authority; nor is it possible for you to compute, estimate, and compare all the pains and all the pleasures in the lives of all men and of all animals; and thus, by your resting the whole system of religion on a point which, from its very nature, must for ever be uncertain, you tacitly confess that that system is equally uncertain.

But allowing you what never will be believed, at least, what you never possibly can prove, that animal or, at least, human happiness in this life exceeds its misery, you have yet done nothing; for this is not, by any means, what we expect from infinite power, infinite wisdom, and infinite goodness. Why is there any misery at all in the world? Not by chance, surely. From some cause then. Is it from the intention of the Deity? But he is perfectly benevolent. Is it contrary to his intention? But he is almighty. Nothing can shake the solidity of this reasoning, so short, so clear, so decisive, except we assert that these subjects exceed all human capacity, and that our common measures of truth and falsehood are not applicable to them—a topic which I have all along insisted on, but which you have, from the beginning, rejected with scorn and indignation.

But I will be contented to retire still from this intrenchment, for I deny that you can ever force me in it. I will allow that pain or misery in man is *compatible* with infinite power and goodness in the Deity, even in your sense of these attributes: what are you advanced by all these concessions? A mere possible compatibility is not sufficient. You must *prove* these pure, unmixt, and uncontrollable attributes from the present mixed and confused phenomena, and from these alone. A hopeful undertaking! Were the phenomena ever so pure and unmixed, yet, being finite, they would be insufficient for that purpose. How much more, where they are also so jarring and discordant!

Here, Cleanthes, I find myself at ease in my argument. Here I triumph. Formerly, when we argued concerning the natural attributes of intelligence and design, I needed all my sceptical and metaphysical subtilty to elude your grasp. In many views of the universe and of its parts, particularly the latter, the beauty and fitness of final causes strike us with such irresistible force that all objections appear (what I believe they really are) mere cavils and sophisms; nor can we then imagine how it was ever possible for us to repose any weight on them. But there is no view of human life or of the condition of mankind from which, without the greatest violence, we can infer the moral attributes or learn that infinite benevolence, conjoined with infinite power and infinite wisdom, which we must discover by the eyes of faith alone. It is your turn now to tug the labouring oar, and to support your philosophical subtilties against the dictates of plain reason and experience.

PART XI

I scruple not to allow, said Cleanthes, that I have been apt to suspect the frequent repetition of the word *infinite,* which we meet with in all theological writers, to savour more of panegyric than of philosophy, and that any purposes of reasoning, and even of religion, would be better served were we to rest contented with more accurate and more moderate expressions. The terms *admirable, excellent, superlatively great, wise,* and *holy* —these sufficiently fill the imaginations of men, and anything beyond, besides that it leads into absurdities, has no influence on the affections or sentiments. Thus, in the present subject, if we abandon all human analogy, as seems your

intention, Demea, I am afraid we abandon all religion and retain no conception of the great object of our adoration. If we preserve human analogy, we must forever find it impossible to reconcile any mixture of evil in the universe with infinite attributes; much less can we ever prove the latter from the former. But supposing the Author of nature to be finitely perfect, though far exceeding mankind, a satisfactory account may then be given of natural and moral evil, and every untoward phenomenon be explained and adjusted. A less evil may then be chosen in order to avoid a greater; inconveniences be submitted to in order to reach a desirable end; and, in a word, benevolence, regulated by wisdom and limited by necessity, may produce just such a world as the present. You, Philo, who are so prompt at starting views and reflections and analogies, I would gladly hear, at length, without interruption, your opinion of this new theory; and if it deserve our attention, we may afterwards, at more leisure, reduce it into form.

My sentiments, replied Philo, are not worth being made a mystery of; and, therefore, without any ceremony, I shall deliver what occurs to me with regard to the present subject. It must, I think, be allowed that, if a very limited intelligence whom we shall suppose utterly unacquainted with the universe were assured that it were the production of a very good, wise, and powerful Being, however finite, he would, from his conjectures, form *beforehand* a different notion of it from what we find it to be by experience; nor would he ever imagine, merely from these attributes of the cause of which he is informed, that the effect could be so full of vice and misery and disorder, as it appears in this life. Supposing now that this person were brought into the world, still assured that it was the workmanship of such a sublime and benevolent Being, he might, perhaps, be surprised at the disappointment, but would never retract his former belief if founded on any very solid argument, since such a limited intelligence must be sensible of his own blindness and ignorance, and must allow that there may be many solutions of those phenomena which will for ever escape his comprehension. But supposing, which is the real case with regard to man, that this creature is not antecedently convinced of a supreme intelligence, benevolent, and powerful, but is left to gather such a belief from the appearances of things—this entirely alters the case, nor will he ever find any reason for such a conclusion. He may be fully convinced of the narrow limits of his understanding, but this will not help him in forming an inference concerning the goodness of superior powers, since he must form that inference from what he knows, not from what he is ignorant of. The more you exaggerate his weakness and ignorance, the more diffident you render him, and give him the greater suspicion that such subjects are beyond the reach of his faculties. You are obliged, therefore, to reason with him merely from the known phenomena, and to drop every arbitrary supposition or conjecture.

Did I show you a house or palace where there was not one apartment convenient or agreeable, where the windows, doors, fires, passages, stairs, and the whole economy of the building were the source of noise, confusion, fatigue, darkness, and the extremes of heat and cold, you would certainly blame the contrivance, without any further examination. The architect would in vain display his subtilty, and prove to you that, if this door or that window were altered, greater ills would ensue. What he says may be strictly true: the alteration of one particular, while the other parts of the building remain, may only augment the inconveniences. But still you would assert in general that, if the architect had had skill and good intentions, he might have formed such a plan of the whole, and might have adjusted the parts in such a manner as would have remedied all or most of these inconveniences. His ignorance, or even your own ignorance of such a plan, will never convince you of the impossibility of it. If you find any inconveniences and deformities in the building, you will always, without entering into any detail, condemn the architect.

In short, I repeat the question: Is the world, considered in general and as it appears to us in this life, different from what a man or such a limited being would, *beforehand,* expect from a very powerful, wise, and benevolent Deity? It must be strange prejudice to assert the contrary. And from thence I conclude that, however consistent the world may be, allowing certain suppositions and conjectures with the idea of such a Deity, it can never afford us an inference concerning his existence. The consistency is not absolutely denied, only the inference. Conjectures, especially where infinity is excluded from the Divine attributes, may perhaps be sufficient to prove a consistency, but can never be foundations for any inference.

There seem to be *four* circumstances on which depend all or the greatest part of the ills that molest sensible creatures; and it is not impossible but all these circumstances may be necessary and unavoidable. We know so little beyond common life, or even of common life, that, with regard to the economy of a universe, there is no conjecture, however wild, which may not be just, nor any one, however plausible, which may not be erroneous. All that belongs to human understanding, in this deep ignorance and obscurity, is to be sceptical or at least cautious, and not to admit of any hypothesis whatever, much less of any which is supported by no appearance of probability. Now this I assert to be the case with regard to all the causes of evil and the circumstances on which it depends. None of them appear to human reason in the least degree necessary or unavoidable, nor can we suppose them such, without the utmost license of imagination.

The *first* circumstance which introduces evil is that contrivance or economy of the animal creation by which pains, as well as pleasures, are employed to excite all creatures to action, and make them vigilant in the great work of self-preservation. Now pleasure alone, in its various degrees, seems to human understanding sufficient for this purpose. All animals might be constantly in a state of enjoyment; but when urged by any of the necessities of nature, such as thirst, hunger, weariness, instead of pain, they might feel a diminution of pleasure by which they might be prompted to seek that object which is necessary to their subsistence. Men pursue pleasure as eagerly as they avoid pain; at least, they might have been so constituted. It seems, therefore, plainly possible to carry on the business of life without any pain. Why then is any animal ever rendered susceptible of such a sensation? If animals can be free from it an hour, they might enjoy a perpetual exemption from it, and it required as particular a contrivance of their organs to produce that feeling as to endow them with sight, hearing, or any of the senses. Shall we conjecture that such a contrivance was necessary, without any appearance of reason, and shall we build on that conjecture as on the most certain truth?

But a capacity of pain would not alone produce pain were it not for the *second* circumstance, viz., the conducting of the world by general laws; and this seems nowise necessary to a very perfect Being. It is true, if everything were conducted by particular volitions, the course of nature would be perpetually broken, and no man could employ his reason in the conduct of life. But might not other particular volitions remedy this inconvenience? In short, might not the Deity exterminate all ill, wherever it were to be found, and produce all good, without any preparation or long progress of causes and effects?

Besides, we must consider that, according to the present economy of the world, the course of nature, though supposed exactly regular, yet to us appears not so, and many events are uncertain, and many disappoint our expectations. Health and sickness, calm and tempest, with an infinite number of other accidents whose causes are unknown and variable, have a great influence both on the fortunes of particular persons and on the prosperity of public societies; and indeed all human life, in a manner, depends on such accidents. A being, therefore, who knows the secret springs of the universe might easily, by particular volitions, turn all these accidents to the good of mankind and render the whole world happy, without discovering himself in any operation. A fleet whose purposes were salutary to society might always meet with a fair wind. Good princes enjoy sound health and long life. Persons born to power and authority be framed with good tempers and virtuous dispositions. A few such events as these, regularly and wisely conducted, would change the face of the world, and yet would no more seem to disturb the course of nature or confound human conduct than the present economy of things where the causes are secret and variable and compounded. Some small touches given to Caligula's brain in his infancy might have converted him into a Trajan. One wave, a little higher than the rest, by burying Caesar and his fortune in the bottom of the ocean, might have restored liberty to a considerable part of mankind. There may, for aught we know, be good reasons why Providence interposes not in this manner, but they are unknown to us; and, though the mere supposition that such reasons exist may be sufficient to *save* the conclusion concerning the Divine attributes, yet surely it can never be sufficient to *establish* that conclusion.

If everything in the universe be conducted by general laws, and if animals be rendered susceptible of pain, it scarcely seems possible but some ill must arise in the various shocks of matter and the various concurrence and opposition of general laws; but this ill would be very rare were it not for the *third* circumstance which I proposed to mention, viz., the great frugality with which all powers and faculties are distributed to every particular being. So well adjusted are the organs and capacities of all animals, and so well fitted to their preservation, that, as far as history or tradition reaches, there appears not to be any single species which has yet been extinguished in the universe. Every animal has the requisite endowments, but these endowments are bestowed with so scrupulous an economy that any considerable diminution must entirely destroy the creature. Wherever one power is increased, there is a proportional abatement in the others. Animals which excel in swiftness are commonly defective in force. Those which possess both are either imperfect in some of their senses or are oppressed with the most craving wants. The human species, whose chief excellence is reason and sagacity, is of all others the most necessitous, and the most deficient in bodily advantages, without clothes, without arms, without food, without lodging, without any convenience of life, except what they owe to their own skill and industry. In short, nature seems to have formed an exact calculation of the necessities of her creatures, and, like a *rigid master,* has afforded them little more powers or endowments than what are strictly sufficient to supply those necessities. An *indulgent parent* would have bestowed a large stock in order to guard against accidents, and secure the happiness and welfare of the creature in the most unfortunate concurrence of circumstances. Every course of life would not have been so surrounded with precipices that the least departure from the true path, by mistake or necessity, must involve us in misery and ruin. Some reserve, some fund, would have been provided to ensure happiness, nor would the powers and the necessities have been adjusted with so rigid an economy. The Author of nature is inconceivably powerful; his force is supposed great, if not altogether inexhaustible, nor is there any reason, as far as we can judge, to make him observe this strict frugality in his dealings with his creatures. It would have been better, were his power extremely limited, to have created fewer animals, and to have endowed these with more faculties for their happiness and preservation. A builder is never esteemed prudent who undertakes a plan beyond what his stock will enable him to finish.

In order to cure most of the ills of human life, I require not that man should have the wings of the eagle, the swiftness of the stag, the force of the ox, the arms of the lion, the scales of the crocodile or rhinoceros; much less do I demand the sagacity of an angel or cherubim. I am contented to take an increase in one single power or faculty of his soul. Let him be endowed with a greater propensity to industry and labour, a more vigorous spring and activity of mind, a more constant bent to business and application. Let the whole species possess naturally an equal diligence with that which many individuals are able to attain by habit and reflection, and the most beneficial consequences, without any allay of ill, is the immediate and necessary result of this endowment. Almost all the moral as well as natural evils of human life arise from idleness; and were our species, by the original constitution of their frame, exempt from this vice or infirmity, the perfect cultivation of land, the improvement of arts and manufactures, the exact execution of every office and duty, immediately follow; and men at once may fully reach that state of society which is so imperfectly attained by the best regulated government. But as industry is a power, and the most valuable of any, nature seems determined, suitably to her usual maxims, to bestow it on men with a very sparing hand, and rather to punish him severely for his deficiency in it than to reward him for his attainments. She has so contrived his frame that nothing but the most violent necessity can oblige him to labour; and she employs all his other wants to overcome, at least in part, the want of diligence, and to endow him with some share of a faculty of which she has thought fit naturally to bereave him. Here our demands may be allowed very humble, and therefore the more reasonable. If we required the endowments of superior penetration and judgment, of a more delicate taste of beauty, of a nicer sensibility to benevolence and friendship, we might be told that we impiously pretend to break the order of nature, that we want to exalt ourselves into a higher rank of being, that the presents which we require, not being suitable to our state and condition, would only be pernicious to us. But it is hard, I dare to repeat it, it is hard that, being placed in a world so full of wants and necessities, where almost every being and element is either our foe or refuses its assistance . . . we should also have our own temper to struggle with, and should be deprived of that faculty which can alone fence against these multiplied evils.

The *fourth* circumstance whence arises the misery and ill of the universe is the inaccurate workmanship of all the springs and principles of the great machine of nature. It must be acknowledged that there are few parts of the universe which seem not to serve some purpose, and whose removal would not produce a visible defect and disorder in the whole. The parts hang all together, nor can one be touched without affecting the rest, in a greater or less degree. But at the same time, it must be observed that none of these parts or principles, however useful, are so accurately adjusted as to keep precisely within those bounds in which their utility consists; but they are, all of them, apt, on every occasion, to run into the one extreme or the other. One would imagine that this grand production had not received the last hand of the maker —so little finished is every part, and so coarse are the strokes with which it is executed. Thus the winds are requisite to convey the vapours along the surface of the globe, and to assist men in navigation; but how often, rising up to tempests and hurricanes, do they become pernicious? Rains are necessary to nourish all the plants and animals of the earth; but how often are they defective? how often excessive? Heat is requisite to all life and vegetation, but is not always found in the due proportion. On the mixture and secretion of the humours and juices of the body depend the health and prosperity of the animal; but the parts perform not regularly their proper function. What more useful than all the passions of the mind, ambition, vanity, love, anger? But how often do they break their bounds and cause the greatest convulsions in society? There is nothing so advantageous in the universe but what frequently becomes pernicious, by its excess or defect; nor has nature guarded, with the requisite accuracy, against all disorder or confusion. The irregularity is never perhaps so great as to destroy any species, but is often sufficient to involve the individuals in ruin and misery.

On the concurrence, then, of these *four* circumstances does all or the greatest part of natural evil depend. Were all living creatures incapable of pain, or were the world administered by particular volitions, evil never could have found access into the universe; and were animals endowed with a large stock of powers and faculties, beyond what strict necessity requires, or were the several springs and principles of the universe so accurately framed as to preserve always the just temperament and medium, there must have been very little ill in comparison of what we feel at present. What then shall we pronounce on this occasion? Shall we say that these circumstances are not necessary, and that they might easily have been altered in the contrivance of the universe? This decision seems too presumptuous for creatures so blind and ignorant. Let us be more modest in our conclusions. Let us allow that, if the goodness of the Deity (I mean a goodness like the human) could be established on any tolerable reasons *a priori,* these phenomena, however untoward, would not be sufficient to subvert that principle, but might easily, in some unknown manner, be reconcilable to it. But let us still assert that, as this goodness is not antecedently established but must be inferred from the phenomena, there can be no grounds for such an inference while there are so many ills in the universe, and while these ills might so easily have been remedied, as far as human understanding can be allowed to judge on such a subject. I am sceptic enough to allow that the bad appearances, notwithstanding all my reasonings, may be compatible with such attributes as you suppose, but surely they can never prove these attributes. Such a conclusion cannot result from scepticism, but must arise from the phenomena, and from our confidence in the reasonings which we deduce from these phenomena.

Look round this universe. What an immense profusion of beings, animated and organized, sensible and active! You admire this prodigious variety and fecundity. But inspect a little more narrowly these living existences, the only beings worth regarding. How hostile and destructive to each other! How insufficient all of them for their own happiness! How contemptible or odious to the spectator! The whole presents nothing but the idea of a blind nature, impregnated by a great vivifying principle, and pouring forth from her lap, without discernment or parental care, her maimed and abortive children!

Here the Manichaean system occurs as a proper hypothesis to solve the difficulty; and, no doubt, in some respects it is very specious and has more probability than the common hypothesis, by giving a plausible account of the strange mixture of good and ill which appears in life. But if we consider, on the other hand, the perfect uniformity and agreement of the parts of the universe, we shall not discover in it any marks of the combat of a malevolent with a benevolent being. There is indeed an opposition of pains and pleasures in the feelings of sensible creatures; but are not all the operations of nature carried on by an opposition of principles, of hot and cold, moist and dry, light and heavy? The true conclusion is that the original Source of all things is entirely indifferent to all these principles, and has no more regard to good above ill than to heat above cold, or to drought above moisture, or to light above heavy.

There may *four* hypotheses be framed concerning the first causes of the universe: that they are endowed with perfect goodness; that they have perfect malice; that they are opposite and have both goodness and malice; that they have neither goodness nor malice. Mixed phenomena can never prove the two former unmixed principles; and the uniformity and steadiness of general laws seem to oppose the third. The fourth, therefore, seems by far the most probable.

What I have said concerning natural evil will apply to moral with little or no variation; and we have no more reason to infer that the rectitude of the Supreme Being resembles human rectitude than that his benevolence resembles the human. Nay, it will be thought that we have still greater cause to exclude from him moral sentiments, such as we feel them, since moral evil, in the opinion of many, is much more predominant above moral good than natural evil above natural good.

. . .

F. R. TENNANT
The Problem of Evil

Theism has been found to provide a sufficient explanation of the intelligibility, the adaptiveness, and the progressiveness of the course of Nature, and to offer the most reasonable and satisfying interpretation of certain wide ranges of fact and of their interconnexions. It now remains to be inquired whether, like some alternative theories as to the world-ground, it sets up any new difficulties, and whether it is consistent with all the facts as well as with most of them. The outstanding fact, or group of facts, with which a teleologically grounded world-view may seem to be incompatible, is the abundant forthcomingness of the apparently dysteleological in a world-order alleged to embody the moral purpose of a benevolent creator. And before theistic faith, however sanguinely it may be entertained by individual believers, can be redeemed from subjectivity and be pronounced to be reasonable from the point of view of common or Objective 'knowledge,' a solution of the problem of evil must be found. It is as incumbent upon empirically reached theism as upon theology of the *a priori* kind to provide a theodicy, or to afford grounds for a belief equivalent to the rationalistically derived assertion that

From F. R. Tennant, *Philosophical Theology* (1930), Vol. II, Ch. VII. Reprinted by permission of Cambridge University Press (New York and London).

this is the best possible world. It is commonly held, however, that the problem of evil is the *crux* of theism, and that though it does not exist for theism alone amongst theories as to the world-ground, this problem is graver for that than for any other world-view, in that theism regards the rationality of the world as including more than its intelligibility to the analytic understanding, to wit the ethical purposiveness of a creative will which is wholly good. For materialism and mechanistic naturalism, for spiritualistic pluralism, and for singularism which conceives The Absolute as above, or indifferent to, the distinction between good and evil, no such problem exists, be the world as replete with evil as a pessimist could wish; and upholders of one or another of these antitheistic theories have declared the question, how the evil in the world of a good God is to be accounted for, to be one which has received many replies but no answer. Indeed there have been convinced theists, *e.g.* Lotze, who have professed ignorance as to the lines along which a solution of this problem is to be sought. On the other hand, more recent exponents of theism have argued that the problem of evil, as such, is not thus hopelessly insoluble, but that the existence of both physical and moral evil may reasonably be accounted for if the *raison d'être* of the world be, as theism maintains, the realisation of moral values. Even the remoter question, why the world is evolutionary rather than statically perfect, is not left wholly unanswerable if theism be true. And Prof. Sorley has emboldened theists to go even further than this and to declare what has been called the *crux* of theism to be its glory. So far is theism from being the one philosophy to which the existence of evil presents an insuperable difficulty that it alone assigns evil a meaning—whereas singularism accounts it to be illusion—and a place within that order which non-theistic pluralism, etc., must be content to regard as an accident of luck.

Such are the various views as to the possibility of a theodicy, between which a decision must be reached by consideration of the relevant facts.

The fact that evil exists in the world is a primary datum for the empirical theist, knowable with much more immediacy and certainty than is the being of God. And he cannot approve of either of the chief ways in which pantheists and theists respectively have sought in the past to explain the reality of evil away. He finds no comfort in the supposition that evil is an illusion of finite and temporal experience, an inadequate idea, or an appearance which would dissolve away if only we saw *sub specie aeternitatis*. For, if evil is illusion, the illusion is an evil; and if no evil would confront timeless vision, it is an evil that we see *sub specie temporis*. The problem of evil is raised by the world as we find it, and is not to be solved by diverting attention to otherworldly cognition of a world-order other than the phenomenal and temporal.

Nor, again, can the theist of to-day resort to the view that evil is unreal or "non-existent" in the sense of being mere deficiency or negation, having and needing no efficient cause: he possesses psychological knowledge to the contrary. The privation-theory of evil owed its plausibility to the ease with which abstractions can be verbally manipulated.

It abstracts moral evil from moral agents, and, because the resulting concept no longer includes subjective activity, asserts that it denotes nothing actual or active, substantial or causative. Of course if good were similarly regarded in abstraction from its agents it would likewise be reduced to the unsubstantial. Evil in the abstract is indeed nothing existent, and cannot be said to resist the good; but evil wills none the less resist good wills. S. Augustine, in teaching that the evil will or act has no efficient cause, stated that it is due to *not* setting the will upon God; but he overlooked the fact that evil volition also consists in actually setting the will upon something other than God. Thus the positive element in moral evil was suppressed by substituting an abstraction for a concrete fact, and by adopting a negative form of words where a positive form is equally called for. Even the will is an abstraction: the only actuality is an agent willing; and he is the efficient cause which the deficiency-theory failed to find because, by a mere verbal device, it had left him out. When S. Augustine [1] and other defenders of the privation-theory have sought to present it in such a form as to escape the force of these considerations, they have relied on the special assumptions that only the immutable really exists, and that goodness and existence are the same. But, as has been observed in previous contexts, the former assumption is baseless, and the latter is derived from wordplay. Lastly, when the theory identifies moral evil with so-called metaphysical evil, which is but morally neutral finiteness, it obliterates the morality of the evil. For these reasons all forms of the theory in question must be discarded as useless for the purpose of theodicy. The error in the theory is nowhere more vicious than in such reasoning as that evil is non-existent, *therefore* God cannot be its cause, or in

---

[1] *The Confessions,* Book VII.

the ingenious argument (said to emanate from Boëthius): there is nothing that the omnipotent God cannot do; He cannot do evil; therefore evil is nothing. At best the privation-theory is a misstatement of such truths as that evil is never an end in itself, nor a power or 'principle' co-ordinate with goodness and absolutely antithetic to it, since moral evil is always choice of a lower good, while physical evil may be instrumental to ethical good-ness, and may be inevitable in a world which is to be a theatre of moral life. Such facts, it may be observed by the way, preclude the possibility, logically open so long as Actuality is not con-sulted, that the good in the world is but a necessary condition of the maximum of evil in a worst possible world.

What is meant by the assertion that this world, in spite of its evil, is the best possible, needs to be explained, else it may seem to state an absurdity. And explanation may begin with clearing away certain gratuitous errors which have been historically associated with the dictum. It is not necessary to analyse the divine creativity into the actualisation of one best world subsequently to the choosing of it, and choice of it subsequently to contemplation of an infinite number of unrealised, purely ideal or possible, sys-tems presented to God's thought or imagination. It is not only unnecessary, but also inconsistent in several ways with the requirements of thought and knowl-edge, so to represent the origination of God's world. God without a world is a superfluous abstraction, and a God who might have 'chosen' a different seminal world from this, or different 'primary col-locations,' would be a different God. The supposed possibilities with which the Creator is alleged to have been confronted are not to be conceived as eternally inde-pendent of Him; nor are ideas, properly so called, prior to actualities, but are de-rived from them. Possibility, in the sense that is here relevant, presupposes actu-ality; and to speak of possible worlds as prior to an actual world is but to indulge in the reification of abstractions that are meaningless apart from relation to *some* actuality. When possibility rules out not only, *e.g.*, the round square, but also non-compossibility with other possibles within one system and with the determinate na-ture of God, apart from which He is nothing, the supposed infinity of possible worlds vanishes: unrealised possibilities become impossibilities. What is possible for God is not determined by a *prius* of eternal laws, for there can be no such thing, but primarily by His nature and secondarily by that of His one world. As Lotze has shewn, empty images or ideas of other possible actualities can only be said to arise with the actual world and its logical and other kinds of order. God and his world are the ground and cause of the distinction between the possible and the impossible, and between the pos-sible and the actual. Having derived the notion of the possible from the actual, the human mind has been apt to invert the order, and to regard the actual as but one case of illimitable possibilities, 'existentially' and logically prior to it. Similarly, when it has not regarded the true and the good as arbitrarily deter-mined by the divine will, it has tended to conceive them as a *prius* which the Cre-ator must recognise, as if He had once been an indeterminate being for whom truth and goodness were not as yet valid. But, once more to quote Lotze, as there is no motion without velocity and direc-tion, on which they can be afterwards imposed, so is there no power that has not some mode of procedure, and no empty capacity which somehow hits upon definite modes of activity. Determinate-ness excludes what are called possibilities, or other subsequently conceivable modes of action; choice between them, as if none were ruled out by the determinate nature of the Deity, is thus a superfluous suppo-sition. The world is what it is because

God is what He is.

That God might have 'chosen' another world than this out of the unlimited sphere of the possible, and one in which there was less evil or none at all, has sometimes been urged as an objection to ethical theism. To suggest this as a bare possibility is easy. Imaginatively to construct such a possible world is less easy, as is also a demonstration of the alleged possibility. Such initial attempts as are forthcoming are trivial, and have been described as specifications for a fool's paradise. Thus it has been surmised that the physical world might have been framed with a view to safeguarding man's physical well-being at every turn. It is a question, however, whether this happy state of things is compatible with the world being a cosmos, and a further question whether the world would then be instrumental to the realisation of moral worth. The particular incompatibilities involved in particular suggestions as to how the elimination of physical and moral evil from a world such as ours might have been effected will be exhibited in due course. At this stage it may but be observed that a world characterised by static perfection is incompatible with a world characterised by evolutionary process, and that ours is of the latter type. This brings us to a remoter problem, of which the problem of evil is an outgrowth, and to the alleged ultimate insolubility of which that of the narrower problem is due. Why God created a world at all is a superfluous question if by 'God' we primarily mean the world-ground; but why His world is evolutionary rather than already perfected is a question that is perhaps not quite futile, nor so wholly beyond a reasonable answer, in the light of the fundamental tenets of ethical theism, as some would pronounce it to be. A world, as a sphere of existence objective to God, must be composed of finite beings: God cannot create Gods, because 'God,' in the theistic sense of the term, connotes unoriginateness. And if the world is to realise the good, that being its *raison d'être,* it would seem that it then must be characterised by development or epigenesis. For moral goodness cannot be created as such; it cannot be implanted in any moral agent by an 'almighty' Other. It is the outcome of freedom, and has to be acquired or achieved by creatures. We cannot imagine a living world, in which truly ethical values are to be actualised, save as an evolutionary cosmos in which free agents live and learn, make choices and build characters. If there be theists who think otherwise, they must be content to regard the evolutionary character of the world as but part of the ultimate nature of things, and as inexplicable because ultimate. At any rate philosophy must start from what simply is; and it deserves no blame if it modestly withholds inquiry as to how and why things came to be. Theism would only go so far further as to apply its doctrine that God is love which seeks reciprocation.

Apart from all variable and incidental qualities which may belong to love as possessed by mankind, and from such enrichment of the conception of divine love as is supplied by religion, it may be said that love must everywhere and always involve self-imparting and seeking the highest welfare of the beings on whom it is bestowed. In God it must also involve self-limitation in respect of power. Love, in this sense, has always been assigned by theology as what we can only speak of as the 'motive' of God in His volitional creativity. Taking this cardinal doctrine and also the reality of the world's evil for granted, the theist needs to shew that in and behind this evil there is a soul of good, or at least to afford reasons for disbelieving that the world, in so far as it is due to God's making and not to man's mismaking, contains absolute and superfluous evils. If he can do so, he will not need to seek refuge from an intellectual difficulty by merely assuming a wholly incomprehensible divine love, or by faintly trusting the larger hope: his faith will remain reasonable, supported by what passes for knowledge—knowledge which, however, itself ultimately rests on other faith.

Since theism teaches that the world-ground is an ethical Spirit, or that God is love, it must also teach that, in some sense, the world is the 'best possible' of its kind. And it may now be submitted that this implication is defensible, so long as we are consistent and in earnest in the use of both the words 'best' and 'possible.'

There is no sense in calling a world a best world unless we specify the *kind* of goodness or worth which that world is said to manifest in the fullest measure. Different values may not be actually compossible, especially if each of them is to be present in its superlative degree; so the notion of a world as an *omnitudo* of values may be as 'impossible' as is the notion of God as the *omnitudo* of all positive attributes. What the theist means by 'best,' in this connexion, is best in respect of moral worth, or of instrumentality thereto. But those who have allowed themselves to "charge God foolishly" have substituted for this meaning that of happiest, or sensuously pleasantest. Certainly our world is not, in this sense, the best that we can imagine. Equally certainly, the theist maintains, it was not meant to be. If it were, it would not be truly the best; for we cannot go behind our judgment, rational or non-rational, that the highest value in the hierarchy of values is moral worth, or—what is the ultimate essence of all morality—personal love. The hedonistic theory that pleasure is what gives worth to life, the ultimate good to be striven for, is generally acknowledged to be untenable: at any rate it is out of court for the theist. Happiness may be a constituent element in the highest complex good that we can conceive, and may accompany the attainment of a higher good; but the ultimate standard for the valuation of human life it cannot be. The 'best possible' world, then, or the world that is worthiest of God and man, must be a moral order, a theatre of moral life and love. Moral character and moral progress must be its purpose, as the best things which any world can realise. To dispense with them would be, for the Creator, to prefer a worse world. Unalloyed pleasure is condemned by man himself as unworthy to be his "life's crown." No pain or want, no effort; no effort, no progress; no progress, no attainment. *Necessity* is the mother of invention; experience is the "becoming expert *by experiment*": mere happiness would entail stagnation.

Thus we cannot have it both ways: the best world cannot be the most pleasurable; and it cannot lack its crown in moral agents.

The word 'cannot' leads on to a discussion of our second leading term, 'possible': on this occasion in connexion with the notion of divine omnipotence. It has already been found vain to speak of a *prius* of possibilities independent of actualities. It may now be added that, possibilities and impossibilities being once constituted by an actual order, omnipotence cannot be conceived as power or control over the possible and the impossible alike, as if both were the same to God. That leads to absurdity. Yet when theism has been rejected on the ground that the evil in the world furnishes an argument against the goodness, or even the existence, of God, it would seem to have been generally assumed that such a being must, by arbitrary exercise of will, be the author of possibility as well as of actuality.

That whatever power may be called omnipotence must be limited by the impossible has been maintained in at least two ways. One of these is to assert that the laws of thought, *i.e.* the laws of identity, contradiction, etc., are valid independently of God as well as of the world, and impose themselves upon Him as well as upon ourselves with necessity. If this be so, we at once reach a distinction between the possible and the impossible which must be eternally binding upon the Supreme Being. Such a doctrine will not be unacceptable to common sense, but it does not commend itself to all philosophers. It has several times been insisted in this work that the valid, abstracted from that of which it is valid, is a mental figment, not an 'existent' *prius*. And it may be argued that this is so even in the case of the fundamental laws of thought, as well as in that of the empirical laws of Nature. The sum of eternal truths cannot exist, so to say, *in vacuo,* prior both to the things in which they are embodied and to the thinker in whose mind they are ideas, etc. When we speak of God as recognising truths independent of Him, or as establishing truth or validity by fiat, and when we try to conceive of God as able to obliterate the difference between the logically possible and impossible, or to set up that difference as if it once did not exist, we are endeavouring to think of Him as a being for whom truth is not as yet truth, and therefore as an indeterminate being eventually indistinguishable from nothing.

On the other hand, if the thinker of the eternal truths is determinate, self-consistent, and so forth, with a definite nature and mode of activity, other modes of being and conceivable or possible activities are *ipso facto* precluded. Hence the sum of eternal truths becomes the mode of God's being and activity, and is neither their *prius* nor their product. And this is the better answer to the supposition that the possible is an arbitrary creation of God, and that the possible and the impossible are alike to omnipotence. In that God is love, He is not hate: in that He wills a developing moral order He is not the creator of a paradise of angels. Pos-

sibilities are thus determined by what God is; and God is limited by His very determinateness, not an indeterminate Absolute in whom all differences are lost. Theism has no concern with such an Absolute, and the puzzles set up by the adoption of such a notion constitute no difficulties for theism. Nor is determinateness, or the kind of finiteness which it implies, any derogation from such 'almightiness' as theology can predicate of the Deity without self-stultification.

But, granted that God is a determinate being, restricted to consistency and compatibility in His action, and granted that His world is to be a developing moral order—the highest ideal of a world that we can conceive—then it must follow that there be a possibility and a risk of moral evil in that world. There cannot be moral goodness in a creature such as man without the possibility of his sinning. Without freedom to choose the evil, or the lower good, a man might be a well-behaved puppet or a sentient automaton, but not a moral agent. But the best possible world implies the existence of moral agents; its crown cannot be the puppet or the automaton. Were our conduct determined like the movements of the machinery of a clock, our world might manifest a pre-established harmony and fulfil the purpose of a clock-maker. But it could not fulfil any ideal of its own, and could not have one. Nor could it realise the purpose of a God willing a best possible world. In both these respects a world from which the possibility of moral evil was excluded would be other than a moral order. It is idle, then, wistfully to contemplate the happiness which the world might have known had its creator made us capable only of what is right; to profess, like Huxley, our readiness to close with an offer to remove our capacity to do wrong and cause misery; or to indulge the wish that we had been made good at the expense of freedom. There is no moral goodness in a clock, however perfectly it may keep time. Freedom to do good alone, except after suppression of lower motives by moral conflict, is not freedom. Such regrets as these, to which the ablest of men have occasionally allowed themselves to give expression, do but shew how hard it is to avoid playing fast and loose with plain words when we would apply logic to a question which excites emotion.

The best world, then, must include free agents, creatures that are in turn 'creators' in the sense that their 'utterances' are not God's positings but their own. And freewill introduces contingencies, new causal series, and new possibilities. God stands "a hand-breadth off" to give His creatures room to act and grow: and here another limitation is involved—the self-limitation of love. The Actual world, including human society and human achievements, is due to man as well as to God. We are fellow-workers together with God in the actualisation of a moral order: otherwise the world were not a moral order at all. For the possibility of moral evil entering into this moral order, God, who foreknew it, is responsible: He permits, so to say, the evil in order that there may be the good. But for the actual emergence of man's moral evil we cannot say that He is responsible: our sin, when 'sin' is strictly and correctly defined, is not God's act but the product of our volition, or devolved freedom. Conceivably moral evil *might* not have emerged, though the basic motivations to it, themselves morally neutral or non-moral, are inevitable consequences of the evolutionary process through which phenomenal man came to be. This vindication of the goodness of God is indeed sometimes alleged to be worthless, on the ground that in creating human wills God created all their volitional issues. But this objection involves the crude notion that a will is a concrete thing, like a machine, instead of a name for an activity, or a trend of activity, of a substantial subject which

has nothing in common with a machine. Although, according to theism, God assigned to each soul its specific nature or individuality, determinative of its original responses (when it should become embodied) to primary presentations, and prescribed the scope of certain of its capacities and faculties, this was not to foreordain, as a chain of quasi-mechanical effects, all its future actions, and so to be responsible for its misdeeds. Freewill consists in subjective activities of a plastic person, in directivity of assigned capacities, etc., in choice and transvaluation, in selective distribution of attention such as determines the strengths of motives, and so on: doings which are not quasi-mechanical issues of a preformed 'will,' on the one hand, nor creative acts of God, on the other hand. Whatever be the beginnings of a man's natural history, his moral history begins with himself. And it begins not in the affective response evoked willy-nilly in a subject of determinate nature, but in the governable responses which a more or less rational being makes to more or less rationally synthesised value-complexes.

Such freewill is the human being's burden at the same time that it is a condition of "the glorious liberty of the children of God." And the demand that it should be the one of these things, and not the other, is but the child's cry for the impossible or self-contradictory. Morality, in an evolved creature such as man, involves the possibility of moral evil, and entails conflict and warfare. The objection raised against theism on the score of the prevalence of moral evil is that there is too much of contingency in the world. It will presently appear that the objection raised on the score of the prevalence of physical evil is that there is too much of rigid regularity. As they stand, these objections cancel one another; and the theist's reply to them is that neither the contingency in the human realm nor the uniformity in the physical realm is a superfluity, but both are essential conditions of moral life. Conceivably Nature's regularity and man's waywardness might be tempered by divine intervention; and it is sometimes urged that such intervention ought to be forthcoming if God be both benevolent and omnipotent. Moral evil alone being for the present under consideration, it suffices here to repeat that though safeguards which would make us immune from temptation might secure Objective rightness or correctness in conduct, such right-doing would possess no moral worth. They would not secure the morality which, in the last resort, is love—the only real fulfilling of the law—and would not conduce to moral character. Character is made, not born nor given ready-made. The developement of morality is naturally not continuous or uninterruptedly progressive; but to coerce it to be so would be to destroy its morality. Suppression of freedom might reduce human suffering, but it would mean surrender of the ideal which the world embodies; and the omnipotence invoked would be inconsistency or indeterminateness such as the idea of God excludes. A world "in leading-strings" may realise *an* ideal, but can have no ideal that is its own or is moral. To preclude moral evil would be to preclude moral goodness, to do evil, to prefer a worse to a better world.

Thus the difficulties raised by the existence of sin are of an insuperable kind only on one or both of the suppositions, (1) that to God there must be no difference between the possible and the impossible, and (2) that the best possible world must be the happiest world and not a moral order. But theism repudiates omnipotence, in this sense, in its characterisation of the Deity; and it asserts that the instrumentality of the world to the production of a moral order is an expression or revelation of the nature of God, the empirically suggested world-ground. And if the moral ideal be the best or the highest that a world conceivably can fulfil,

the process by which alone it is attainable is also good, despite the evil incidental to it. Theism *requires* that the world be an imperfect or mixed world, in that it takes the purpose of the world to consist in the realisation of the highest values by finite and developing creatures, with which an omnipotent establishment of non-moral or static perfection would have nothing in common.

If we suppose the ethical status of man to be less than the whole of the divine purpose, and but a stage to something higher but transcending our power to conceive, the further elements in the world-purpose may condition the evils with which we men are confronted, in respects that are beyond our ken. But, however this may be—and it is practically useless, if theoretically wholesome, to invoke the limitations of our knowledge and the inscrutability of the divine purpose in its fulness—theism is not unable to find a place and a meaning for moral evil in the world of an all-good God, in so far as the world is knowable and its purpose can reasonably be assigned.

Thus far God's purpose has alone been contemplated. And the theodicy which has as yet been constructed in part would not be satisfactory unless man, in struggling through many sins and miseries, could account himself to be striving for his own ideal, as well as fulfilling a divine end. This, however, mankind acknowledges through those who represent it at its best. Indictments of God based on the facts of human sin and suffering seldom imply a denial of the claim of moral values to be the highest in human judgement. We deem the prize worth the cost, and life without moral strife and attainment to be not worth while. If there is no "peace in ever climbing up the climbing wave," there is zest in warring with evil, and the supreme joys of life are found in love such as is not mere passion. Confronted with the choice between the happy and innocent life of the brute, without thought before and after and pining for what is not, on the one hand, and the life of moral endeavour and spiritual progress, on the other hand, human beings would be practically unanimous in deciding that it is better to have risen above the non-moral level and to have tasted of the tree of knowledge:

> What were life
> Did soul stand still therein, forgo her
> strife
> Through the ambiguous Present to the
> goal
> Of some all-reconciling Future?

If the best things we can conceive are bound up with moral character, or rather with personality which includes much more than morality in the barer sense of the word, the best possible world we can conceive is a world which affords opportunity for their attainment. The worser man generally recognises the supremacy of goodness, while the morally advancing man, from the standpoint he has gained, condemns any other sort of life than that of moral growth as incapable of satisfying his soul's needs, and as unworthy of him as he now is. Had mankind never appeared, had Nature stopped short of her crowning in a rational and moral species, the world's falling short of being a moral order would have remained both unregretted and unapproved. The moral race which has emerged, though born to suffer through its freedom, nevertheless rejoices in living, approves it creator's ideal, accepts the chance of the prize of learning love: at least so long as it can believe the cost to be inevitable and the possibility of moral evil to be not superfluous.

To these qualifying conditions, which have been found to be satisfied, another will be added by those who would regard the divine purpose as finding fulfilment, not in the world-process, but in the far off consummation toward which they believe all creation moves. Reasons have been given for rejecting the notion that evil is absolutely and exclusively evil, ministering to nothing but further evil, never subservient or instrumental to good, and not necessarily or contingently incidental to the actualisation of moral good. But some will also require theodicy to supply reasons for believing that moral evil is not ultimately insuperable, that it will eventually give place to the good, or at least that it is not destined to become supreme over the good so that the world, though a moral order in one sense, would mock our highest moral aspirations. When self-limitation is ascribed to God in place of that omnipotence which is but inconsistency or indeterminateness, such possibilities as these, it is urged, present themselves to be reckoned with. They therefore need to be considered.

Looked at in the abstract, freedom in antithesis to external coercion, and contingency in antithesis to external necessitation, imply the possibility that universal goodness will not be finally realised, and even that moral evil may ever assert and reassert itself until it culminates in moral anarchy. But bare possibilities, like sheer impossibilities, need not be taken too seriously. Probabilities reasonably grounded on experience are another matter; and it is a question whether the theist may not claim that, in so far as the defeat of the divine purpose by man's delegated freedom is concerned, probability favours the view which theism would prefer. Moral advance, in spite of relapses, has undoubtedly marked mankind's history, on the whole, hitherto; and though it cannot be argued from that fact that progress will continue throughout future ages, neither are we at liberty to regard humanity's past progress as a mere accident, or as a state of things which is likely to be permanently reversed. We may reject the view that the contingencies of history are somehow ruled by a dialectic process of which the world-process is a manifestation; we may renounce the Victorian notion of progress as intrinsic and necessarily involved in the world as a whole including man, and regard such optimism as the outcome of a false analogy between spiritual and physical evolution, ignoring human freedom and over-emphasising the influence of environment; we may refuse to appeal to God's supposed power to subdue all things, including freewill, to Himself, so as to conserve the good and exterminate the morally evil; we may deem an inductive inference from the fragment of history up to date to the far future to be absurd; and we may reasonably assume that, in so far as this world is concerned, and while human nature remains essentially what it now is, motivation to evil will never be lacking and sinlessness may never be universal: yet there is good reason to disbelieve in the possibility of evil becoming supreme over good in the world. Man is not merely an organism, and moral evolution is by no means wholly determined by natural heredity and environment. Moreover the environment, in the present case, is partly moral, as is also adaptation to it. What is called social heredity is an important factor in moral evolution. And when we contemplate this latter determinant we find that there is something in goodness which promotes its own conservation, and something in evil that promises disruption— if not self-extinction, at least impotence to become supreme. And this is so, contingency and freewill notwithstanding. The wicked are like the troubled sea which cannot rest: the double-minded man is unstable in all his ways. Accordingly, the encroachments of moral evil upon the established good do not become consolidated. Apparent gains are apt to prove vanity, even loss. And it is plain that no universal conspiracy in evil is possible, such as would produce a hell on earth. If that be what is meant by defeat of God's purpose through human freedom, it seems to be precluded by the intrinsic nature of both human goodness and human badness. Evil desires and evil purposes conflict with one another, so that evil as well as goodness resists and thwarts conspiration in evil. On the other hand, conquests in moral goodness and truth, despite their temporary obscuration, when once made are made for ever. The world always has knowledge that it is the better for them. There is a unity of aim, a co-operation in purpose, a solidarity of interest, a growing consensus, amongst men of goodwill. The moral law, in spite of its continual violation, survives and increases its dominion: the good is self-conservative.

Again, moral evil does not come out of moral goodness, but good does come out of evil and error. Error exposes itself, to the further elucidation and definition of the truth: evil, in its very acquisition, reveals itself to the lesser good, and learns by bitter experience that it is evil. Nor does each new generation, or each fresh individual, advance *wholly* by first hand experience, though experimenting for self is a right that never will be renounced, in whatever disasters it may issue. For in human society the social inheritance, or stored experience, counts for much. The higher the moral tone of the many, the more difficult to realise and to entertain become the evil inclinations of the few.

For these reasons, then, it is no flimsy and sentimental optimism, but a reasoned and reasonable expectation, that, as history establishes the fact of moral progress up to date, that progress is not an accident, but will maintain itself. In future ages it may proceed with accelerated speed: for the gains of the good over the evil would seem to be cumulative, although evil may ever take new forms. The tendencies inherent in goodness and badness, as such, preclude the possibility that the purpose of a self-limited God, supposing it to include the final victory of goodness over evil, should be defeated by the freedom of His creatures. There is no more reason to believe that moral evil is destined to become supreme than to believe that its possibility, or even its actuality, is incompatible with a moral order such as the 'best possible' world must be.

It is another question whether moral evil is destined, here or hereafter, to become extinct through the response of free-will to fuller light: conceivably, evil may continue everlastingly while unable to become universal and supreme. But this question is not vital for the theodicy of theism such as confesses to limitations besetting its knowledge or probable belief. If natural theology is able to supply reasons for belief in a future life, it is utterly unable to imagine the conditions of such a life or of knowledge accessible to souls that are disembodied or embodied otherwise than they are in this life. It is impossible to foreknow individually, or non-statistically, the issues of the free-will of moral agents in any imaginable circumstances. And theism, while able to adduce reasonable grounds for believing the cosmic process and human history to reveal the purpose of establishing a moral order, in the sense of a theatre for the life of persons possessed of freedom and the moral status, cannot supply similar reasonable grounds for the conjecture that cosmic and human history are but a means, or a stage, towards a future and final consummation in which nothing evil will remain. This is not a necessary corollary of the doctrine that God is a lover of free persons. It is a belief motivated by religious yearning for the fleeing away of all sorrow and sighing, and by the ancient predilection for the static and perfected, or for the conception of God as, figuratively or literally, all in all. Natural theology, however, cannot make use of either cravings or predilections, and possesses no data for the construction of an eschatology. Theism is not pledged to the doctrine of uni-versal hope, or of the perfecting of every soul, nor to that of the annihilation of the hardened unrighteous, if any such there will be. The possibility of endless warfare against spiritual wickedness in the world to come presents no greater difficulty to theism than does the forthcomingness of moral evil in this present world.

Indeed some theists have gone to the other extreme and have argued that the divine love must ever involve sacrifice and victory, and that the presence of evil is necessary for the continued exercise of the highest love. Just as God is not God without His world, so, it is said, divine love is not divine love without sinning recipients for Him to seek and to save. According to this view there is no rest remaining for all the people of God, and no tranquil blessedness for God Himself: evil will for ever be in process of being overcome. It is implied that a statically perfect world would be less noble than process towards it, or that progress is not necessarily approach to a realisable goal. Just as we may find satisfaction in conflict and tension, so God may ever rejoice in His own sorrows and find peace in the victory over evil: "the eternal world contains Gethsemane." So some have speculated: but in recoil from the old ideas of impassibility and static perfection they have retained somewhat of the rigidity which belonged to ancient thought. It is not necessary to believe that, because the highest kind of good that we know is only realisable in our world through the possibility, if not the actuality, of evil, therefore the continuous presence of evil is essential to the conservation of goodness. Human experience suggests the contrary. There is such a thing as has been called 'the saint's rest'—the relative freedom from moral conflict and from temptation, earned by self-discipline and struggle; and it may have a joy of its own and an interest which does not need the zest of militancy for its maintenance. All morality is not the same morality: there is one goodness of the happy warrior, and another goodness of him who has fought the good fight. And all these kinds of moral state, or of goodness and blessedness, cannot be fully actualised potentialities at once, because some are incompatible with others. It is therefore forbidden to us to postulate that the divine love must ever manifest itself in every specific type; and it is unnecessary to suppose that ethical life is precluded to the Supreme Spirit unless there be for Him the possibility of ever sorrowing and striving with sinful souls, or that the existence of evil is an essential condition of the continuing love of God. But, apart from the baselessness of both the kinds of *a priori* speculation that have been considered, the question of the continuance or the self-extinction of moral evil is irrelevant to theodicy.

The problem of evil has thus far been discussed with almost exclusive reference to evil of the moral kind. And the solution that has been presented consists in shewing the tenability of the belief that in our developing world all things work together, as a whole, for the highest conceivable good. The possibility of moral evil and the actuality of its consequences are inevitable concomitants of the 'best possible' evolutionary world. It is not maintained that everything is good, or that "whatever is, is right," or that partial evil is not evil because it is a condition of universal good. Nor is it implied that every particular evil is directly essential to the emergence of some particular good, or that it has its necessary place, like a dissonance in music, in the harmony of the world-process. When it is asserted that all things work together for good, by 'all things' is not meant each and every single thing, but the sum of things regarded as one whole or complex, the universe as a coherent order.

It is by adhering to this general view that the theist can best face the problem presented by the existence of that form of evil for which human freedom is not necessarily, and generally not at all, responsible: the physical evil, or the pain and suffering occasioned by the course of Nature in sentient beings. Indeed any other position than that which has just been summarised seems obviously inadequate as a basis for the explanation of the forthcomingness of physical ills. In order to reconcile the suffering inflicted by the material world upon mankind and other sentient creatures with the goodness and power of the Creator it is both superfluous and insufficient to seek to shew that in every particular case pain is essential to some special end, or that in each single instance suffering may fulfil some particular providential purpose. To attempt a theodicy on these lines is as hopeless as it would be to-day to develop a teleological argument from particular instances of adaptedness, after the manner of Paley. But, as there is a wider teleology than Paley's so is there a wider theodicy than that which consists in pleading that human and animal pain are sometimes prophylactic—a warning against danger, or that human suffering is sometimes punitive or purgatorial, and thus subservient to benign ends. These assertions are undoubtedly true, and there is no need to belittle their import. But by themselves they will not carry us far towards a theodicy. They but touch the fringe of the problem: or, to change the metaphor, they do not go to the root of the matter. It is useless, again, to minimise the pain of the sentient world, or even to reduce our possibly extravagant and unscientific estimate of its intensity, except for the purpose of arguing that, in spite of pain, animal life is probably happy on the whole: otherwise a single pang of useless or superfluous pain is enough to raise our problem. It involves faulty psychology to assert that pain is the necessary background to pleasure; for a lesser pleasure would seem to yield a sufficient contrast to render the enjoyment of intenser pleasure possible. And if pain be sometimes stimulating, educational, preventative, or remedial, as well as sometimes stunting, crushing, and provocative of moral evil, this fact is only significant for an estimation of the worth-whileness of sentient life. The knife may be necessary to cure the disease, but why the necessity of the disease? The escape from mortal danger may require the painful warning, but why the mortal danger? Or, speaking generally, what are we to make of the remoter evil which renders the nearer evil necessary or salutary? The real problem obviously lies further back than these particular and partial solutions reach. It must be shewn that pain is either a necessary by-produce of an order of things requisite for the emergence of the higher goods, or an essential instrument to organic evolution, or both. Short of this, we cannot refute the charge that the world is a clumsy arrangement or an imperfectly adjusted mechanism.

It can be argued, however, that the former of the foregoing alternatives is applicable in the case of human suffering, while the latter of them can be invoked to meet especially the case of animal pain. The suffering of the lower animals is not merely an accidental superfluity emerging out of the evolutionary process, but is essentially instrumental to organic progress. It renders unnecessary a large amount of inheritance of specialised structure and function, and so prevents the suppression of plasticity; and, as the 'sensitive edge' turned towards danger, or as prophylactic, it is of value for organic progressiveness. Although evil, it is also good for something. Much of human suffering, and many of the outrages of this present life upon our rational prudences and our most sacred affections, on the other hand, seem to be good for nothing, or to be non-essential for the realisation of goodness. If a man already has it in him to meet pain with fortitude and pa-

tience, he is not necessarily one whit the better man after actually enduring excruciating tortures; and if an all-powerful being 'appointed' him such tortures, merely in order that his fortitude might pass from potentiality to actuality, such a being would be but a super-brute. However, it can be argued that the forthcomingness of our suffering is inevitably incidential to a moral order in a developing world. It issues ultimately out of what is inappropriately called metaphysical evil, or is a necessary outcome of a determinate cosmos of the particular kind that can sustain rational and moral life. The problem which it raises will therefore be solved if it can be maintained that no suffering such as we experience is superfluous to the cosmos as a coherent system and a moral order, however excessive pain often may be as a means to the accomplishment of specific ends such as are attainable by discipline and chastening.

It cannot be too strongly insisted that a world which is to be a moral order must be a physical order characterised by law or regularity. The routine of Nature may be differently described by the spiritualist, the dualist, etc.; but the diversity of these ultimate explanations of law does not affect the present problem. The theist is only concerned to invoke the fact that law-abidingness, on the scale which science is able to assert its subsistence in Nature as already *naturata,* is an essential condition of the world being a theatre of moral life. Without such regularity in physical phenomena there could be no probability to guide us: no prediction, no prudence, no accumulation of ordered experience, no pursuit of premeditated ends, no formation of habit, no possibility of character or of culture. Our intellectual faculties could not have developed. And, had they been innate, they would have wasted themselves, as Comte observed, in wild extravagances and sunk rapidly into incurable sloth; while our nobler feelings would have been unable to prevent the ascendancy of the lower instincts, and our active powers would have abandoned themselves to purposeless agitation. All this is obvious; but it has often been ignored in discussion of the problem of physical evil. Nevertheless, Nature's regularity is the key to this problem. Once let it be admitted that, in order to be a theatre for moral life, the world must be largely characterised by uniformity or constancy, and most significant consequences will be seen to follow. It becomes idle to complain, as some writers have done, that the orderliness of the world is too dear at the cost of the suffering and hardship which it entails, and might more or less be dispensed with for the benefit of the sentient and rational beings which people the world. As Hume admitted, if the "conducting of the world by general laws" were superseded by particular volitions, no man could employ his reason in the conduct of his life. And without rationality, morality is impossible: so, if the moral status of man be the goal of the evolutionary process, the reign of law is a *sine quâ non*. It is a condition of the forthcomingness of the highest good, in spite of the fact that it is not an unmixed good but a source of suffering. We cannot have the advantages of a determinate order of things without its logically or its causally necessary disadvantages. Nor can we be evaluating subjects without capacity to feel. The disadvantages, viz. particular ills, need not be regarded, however, as directly willed by God as ends in themselves or as particular means, among other equally possible but painless means, to particular ends. To make use of an ancient distinction, we may say that God wills them consequently, not antecedently. That is to say, they are not desired as such, or in themselves, but are only willed because the moral order, which is willed absolutely or antecedently by God, cannot be had without them. Now to will

a moral order is to will the best possible world; and it also involves adoption of what we necessarily, if somewhat anthropomorphically, must call a determinate world-plan. Such a determinate method of procedure to realise a definite end in an evolutionary world, however, rules out once and for all any other possible goals and methods. As Dr Martineau has put it, the cosmical equation being defined, only such results as are compatible with the values of its roots can be worked out, and these must be worked out. All determination is negation. If two consequences follow from a system of propositions, or two physical properties are involved in a configuration of particles, we cannot have the one without the other, though the one may be pleasing or beneficial to man and the other may be painful, or in its immediate effects hurtful. And such a result by no means implies lack of benevolence or of power on the part of the Creator, so long as power does not include inconsistency or indeterminateness. It simply bespeaks the inexorableness of logic, the compatibility of things, and the self-consistency of the Supreme Being. That painful events occur in the causal chain is a fact; but, that there could be a determinate evolutionary world of unalloyed comfort, yet adapted by its law-abidingness to the developement of rationality and morality, is a proposition the burden of proving which must be allotted to the opponent of theism. One can only add that, in so far as experience in this world enables us to judge, such proof seems impossible. To illustrate what is here meant: if water is to have the various properties in virtue of which it plays its beneficial part in the economy of the physical world and the life of mankind, it cannot at the same time lack its obnoxious capacity to drown us. The specific gravity of water is as much a necessary outcome of its ultimate constitution as its freezing-point, or its thirst-quenching and cleansing functions. There cannot be assigned to any substance an arbitrarily selected group of qualities, from which all that ever may prove unfortunate to any sentient organism can be eliminated, especially if one organism's meat is to be another's poison, and yet the world, of which that substance forms a part, be a calculable cosmos. Mere determinateness and fixity of nature involve such and such concatenations of qualities, and rule out others. Thus physical ills follow with the same necessity as physical goods from the determinate 'world-plan' which secures that the world be a suitable stage for intelligent and ethical life.

And if this be so, the disadvantages which accrue from the determinateness and regularity of the physical world cannot be regarded either as absolute or as superfluous evils. They are not absolute evils because they are parts of an order which subserves the highest good in providing opportunity for moral developement. And they are not superfluous ills because they are the necessary outcome of that order. They are collateral effects of what, in itself or as a whole, is good because instrumental to the highest good. They are not good, when good is hedonically defined; but they are good for good, when good is otherwise defined, rather than good for nothing.

As in the case of moral evil, so also in the case of physical evil, appeal has sometimes been made from necessary linkages and conditionings to a supposed possibility of their being over-ridden by divine omnipotence. And as it was found absurd to suppose that God could make developing beings at the same time morally free and temptationless, so it involves absurdity to suppose that the world could be a moral order without being a physical cosmos. To save mankind from the painful consequences which flow from a determinate world-order, such as the earthquake and the pestilence, would involve renunciation of a world-order, and therefore a moral order, and the substitution of a chaos of incalculable miracle. Doubtless some directive agency, or the introduction of new streams of causation into the course of Nature, is conceivable without subversion of such regularity as is requisite for human prudence and without the stultification of our science. But the general suspension of painful events, requisite on the vast scale presupposed in the elimination of physical ills, would abolish order and convert a cosmos into an unintelligible chaos in which anything might succeed upon anything. We should have to "renounce reason" if we would thus be "saved from tears," as Martineau says.

Physical evil, then, must necessarily be. And the goodness of God is vindicated if there be no reason to believe that the world-process involves more misery than Nature's uniformity entails. It is not incumbent on the theist to prove that particular evils are never greater than we judge to be necessary for the production of particular salutary effects: that difficult task confronts only the particular kind of theism which is concerned to dispense with proximate causes and a more or less autonomous world, and regards God as the sole and immediate cause of every natural event, and of every incident in a personal life. According to the theodicy which has here been sketched, it is not necessary to suppose that every specific form of suffering that man undergoes—e.g. the agony of tetanus or of cancer—is antecedently willed by God as a means to some particular end. It can be admitted that excruciating pains are more severe than they need be for evoking virtues such as patience and fortitude, and that to assign them to God's antecedent will would be to attribute devilishness to the Deity. Moreover, the fact that some human beings are born as abortions, as imbecile or insane, seems to be inexplicable on the view that every form of suffering is a particular providence, or an antecedently willed dispensation for educating and spiritually perfecting the person on whom the affliction falls; while to suppose that suffering is inflicted on one person for the spiritual edification of another is again to conceive of God as immoral. But the hardest fact of all for human equanimity, in presence of physical and mental evil, is that the apportionment of suffering among individuals is entirely irreconcilable by us with any divine plan of adjustment of particular afflictions to the particular needs, circumstances, and stages of moral developement, of individual sufferers. Even more distressing to human thought than the goading intensity of some kinds of pain is the seemingly chaotic distribution of human ills. If we could trace the utility of particular sufferings with their varying degrees of endurableness, or discern any adaptation of pain to the person's sensibility, moral state, and need of awakening or chastening, then philosophy might be able to agree with the simple-minded piety which assigns a special purpose to every instance of suffering, and finds therein the visitation or appointment of an all-wise and all-good God. But the wind is not tempered to the shorn lamb; the fieriest trials often overtake those who least need torments to inspire fear, to evoke repentance, or to perfect patience, and also those who, through no fault of their own, lack the mature religious faith and moral experience by which alone they could understand how affliction may be endured for their souls' good. "All things come alike to all: there is one event to the righteous and to the wicked"—to those who may be enabled, and to those who are unable, to profit by severe trial.

Disastrous as these facts are to the extremer forms of the doctrine of divine immanence in Nature, they are compatible with theism such as allows to the created world somewhat of delegated autonomy. According to the wider theodicy which has here been presented, the human afflictions arising from our relations with the physical world are not willed as such by God at all, or for any purpose. They are rather inevitable, if incidental, accompaniments or by-products of the world-order which, as a whole, and by means of its uniformity, is a pre-requisite of the actualisation of the highest good that we can conceive a world as embodying. The world is none the less God's world for its callousness to man; but its autonomy, not the particular incidence of each single ill, is what the religious should attribute to His "appointment."

Further, man himself does not deem his suffering to be an excessive price to pay for the dignity of his ethical status, once he recognises physical evil to be inevitable in a moral world. He is then not compelled to see in his suffering self a mere means either to the perfecting of the race, or to the realisation of a divine purpose, or to the manifestation of the 'glory' of God. And this is an important consideration for any theodicy. For man is an end for himself, whatever else he may be. *My* ills can only be justified to *me* if the remoter advantage of there being ills at all be *mine:* not humanity's, or even God's, alone. But in that the remoter advantage is the enjoyment of rational and ethical dignity, the individual man can acquiesce in God's purpose for the world: God's ideal may be his also. It is the assurance that God is fulfilling us individually as well as Himself, and fulfilling us for ourselves as well as for Himself, that makes human life in this bitter-sweet world endurable by the sensitively and delicately minded, the tender-hearted, believer. It is because a being of the earth, yet so God-like as man, could not be moulded into the image of God *save from within himself,* as a person or a free agent, that man can account the payment of the sometimes exorbitant price of the chance of learning love inevitable.

If the doctrine of a future life be a

corollary of theism, or an implication of the moral purposiveness and meaning which may reasonably be read into the cosmos, it can be invoked to throw further light on the problem of evil. The balance of felicity and unhappiness in an individual life cannot be struck so long as we confine our thought to experience of the present world alone, if we have reason to believe that the earth is "no goal, but starting-point for man." We may then venture to add to our knowledge the faith that "the sufferings of this present time are not worthy to be compared with the glory that shall be revealed." Pain is indeed none the less pain, nor any kind of evil the less evil, for that it shall be done away, or compensated, or because it is a necessary means or by-product. But its hideousness is somewhat transfigured if, besides being involved in the 'best possible' world, it can be seen to have been "but for a moment" in the time-span of just men made perfect. It is not the reality of evil that is here under consideration, but simply the worthwhileness of this life in which evil has a temporary and necessary place. That should not be estimated by looking only at what may now be seen; but for the idea of compensation hereafter theodicy and theistic religion have no further use. They do not ask us to tolerate the evils of the present world, and to abstain from blaming the Creator for them, because of a compensation stored up for us in another world: they rather insist that in this life, with all its evils, we may already discern the world-purpose of God to be a reign of love.

This life acquires, indeed, a new aspect if death be but translation to another mansion in the Father's house, and exchange of one kind of service for another. And it is a question whether theism, in asserting the world-ground to be a Spirit and the Father of spirits, and in ascribing to the world the rôle of ministering to rational and moral life, can stop short of adding the doctrine of a future life to its fundamental articles of belief, without stultifying its previously reached interpretation of the world and man. For it would not be a perfectly reasonable world which produced free beings, with Godward aspirations and illimitable ideals, only to cut them off in everlasting death, mocking their hopes and frustrating their purposes. Such spirits, even with their moral status, would after all be pawns, not children of God. Certainly a God who can be worshipped by moral beings must be a respecter of the persons whom He has moulded into His own image. Hence theists generally regard the Supreme Being as a God, not of the dead, but of the living.

There is one particular problem within the larger problem of evil, to which the doctrine of a future life has a special relevance: a problem of the kind indicated by the remark, made at the beginning of this chapter, that explanatory theories are apt to bear within themselves, or to set up, fresh difficulties. If the theistic gospel be the only sufficient interpretation of the intelligibility, orderliness, and progressiveness of the world as a whole, it is not unique in respect of explaining without creating new *explicanda*. It does not forthwith brightly illumine every dark recess of the mind of him who would use it as a lantern to his feet. Its very acceptance creates at least one perplexity, not forthcoming for those who reject the theistic interpretation, and necessitates a special theodicy to resolve that perplexity. For it is a difficulty besetting theistic faith that faith itself can be tried; and perhaps many will find here the sharpest edge of the wider problem of evil. God may seem to them to allow so little insight into His dealings with persons, and so little of intelligent—as distinct from purely moral—co-operation with Him in working out their individual destiny, that they scarcely dare call Him 'Father,' though ethical theism requires that they should do so. Their cosmic philosophy appears to collapse in that some of its deduced consequences do not seem to be verified in experience. Moreover, an unwavering faith, a steady and unfaltering sense of the reality of things unseen, is a condition of the peace which alone enables the believer to serve God with a quiet mind, and also of the spiritual zeal and effectiveness of his life. It is the feeling with which the believer regards that life, his alone and his for once alone, that should most strongly evidence his kinship with the Deity; and he should be able to deem the efficacy of his little life-work not indifferent to his God. Should God then try his very faith, and so render all that he might build with it precarious? Should the very spring of religious love, the source of the unique beauty and sublimity of character moulded by pure religious sentiment, be capable of being lost, though a man may yearn to retain possession of it above all things else? Duty, service, and blamelessness of life are not always easy even when faith is unclouded; but that the one bond which links the soul with God should be imperilled by the probationary influences of this life seems at first sight had to reconcile with the relations which theism asserts to subsist between the soul, the world, and God.

We can see that it is of the very nature of faith to provide from within itself for its own trial; for faith is not sight, and whatever truth may be apprehended by faith must be "deadened of its absolute blaze." We can also see that a trial of faith is necessitated from without, in that advance in knowledge and in ethical appreciation render beliefs, which in earlier times were (ψ) reasonable, no longer tenable. So the difficulty before us narrows down to the old and recurrent question, why, if there is a God whose world-purpose is communion between finite spirits and Himself, is faith rather than knowledge vouchsafed to us, or why is not revelation readable by him who runs, with infallible certainty and (ps) immediacy?

The conditions of revelation and its apprehension will be discussed later; but, in so far as they are involved in the outgrowth from the problem of evil that is now before us, there are two considerations of which theism may avail itself in meeting its difficulty.

Firstly, it may be suggested that if our wills be ours to make harmonious with the divine will, and the quest for the highest is to be veritably *our* quest and adventure, God must not be too certainly knowable to us, as well as not too active upon us. Otherwise, just as excess of motivation would defeat ethical freedom, so over-abundance of light would preclude that 'groping after God' which is the obverse of revelation to a developing and free agent such as man. The formation (as contrasted with the fruition) of character, and the winning of truth by truth-seeking (as contrasted with the passive imbibing of ready-made infallibilities), require an invisible rather than a visible or demonstrable God, a partial revelation rather than a beatific vision, a divine co-operation rather than a divine overwhelming, the possibility of failure to find rather than the security of essentially non-moral and non-personal success. There must "needs provision be For keeping the soul's prowess possible." In other words, the confinement of cognition, as to God and His dealings, or as to our whence and whither, to the form of faith, which is the free soul's venture and cannot be, as ecclesiastical theology has generally taught, an arbitrary gift of God; the consequent possibility of reasonable doubt; the necessity of each soul to fight its way to reasonable belief or conviction compatible with knowledge: these appear to be implications of the purpose of God, and conditions of religious life for creaturely and developing moral personalities. It is from religion, rather than from cosmic philosophy, that we must seek any more light on this matter. And perhaps it begins to appear that these are not discontinuous.

Further, the difficulty presented to theistic faith by the fact that faith is dangerously liable to trial, so long as it does not degenerate into supine credulity, is removed if the belief that this present life is not the whole of life be not faithlessly treated. The momentousness of failure here to achieve our life's ends then becomes relatively insignificant: especially if God cares more for what we are than for what we do. There is such a thing as success in failure. We can attach exaggerated importance, in one sense, to the actual filling of this life with finished products, just as too much importance used to be attached to the particular moral state and the particular contents of an individual's faith at the hour of his passing. It is in harmony with the world-view presented by theism to regard growth towards perfection, whether of character or of faith, rather than attainment of perfectness, as the divine purpose for our earthly life. All aspiration that is here unrealised, all tasks remaining unaccomplished when death cuts us off, all baffled search, honest doubt, and faith that has been shipwrecked while men of goodwill and pure heart have worked in half-light or shadow, may be fulfilled in the life beyond. Bereavement of faith, therefore, like bereavement of friends, is not endless separation, but rather a phase in a process which knows vicissitudes.

Thus the special problem of the temptability of personal faith is to be met in the same way as the larger problem of evil in general. It remains no less a trial to faith that faith necessarily must be tried, just as evil is none the less evil for that it is necessary or that it shall be done away. But if this life is not *all*-important, and if the world-purpose is not consistently ethical unless there is a hereafter for moral persons, the question why faith that is vital for the fullest life is not immune from trial no longer constitutes a formidable difficulty. The facts which suggest a theistic interpretation of the world also suggest that in this life our seeking rather than our finding is God's purpose for us: question and counter-question, intercourse and dialogue, rather than full light and certain knowledge. The risks attending faith are not fatal, while they are conditions of the ethico-religious status in the life that now is.

P. H. D. d'HOLBACH

The Confused and Contradictory Ideas of Theology

Baron P. H. D. d'Holbach (1725–1789) was a leading figure in the French enlightenment. He went further in the direction of materialism and opposition to supernaturalism than other members of the group.

Every thing that has been said, proves to us, that in despite of all the efforts of their imagination, men have never been able to prevent themselves from drawing together from their own peculiar nature the qualities which they have assigned to the being who governs the universe. We have already discovered the contradictions necessarily resulting from the incompatible mixture of these human qualities, which cannot be able to become suitable to the same subject, seeing that they destroy themselves the one by the other; the theologians themselves have felt the insurmountable difficulties which their divinities presented to reason: they were not able to withdraw themselves out of them but by preventing men from reasoning, by throwing their minds into confusion, by perplexing more and more those ideas, already so confused and so discordant, which they gave them of their god; by these means they enveloped him with clouds, they rendered him inaccessible, and they became the masters of explaining, according to their whim and fantasy, the ways of the enigmatical being

From P. H. D. d'Holbach, *The System of Nature,* Vol. III, tr. by W. Hodgson (1795–96), Ch. III.

which they made them adore. For this purpose, they exaggerated him more and more; neither time, nor space, nor the entire of nature could be able to contain his immensity; every thing became in him an impenetrable mystery. Although man had in the origin borrowed from himself the colours and the primitive lines of which he composed his god; although he had made him a powerful, jealous, vindictive monarch, who could be unjust without wounding his justice; in short, like unto the most perverse princes; theology, by the dint of dreaming, lost, as we have said, sight of human nature, and in order to render the divinity more different from his creatures, it assigned him, over and above, qualities so marvellous, so uncommon, so far removed from every thing of which of our mind could form a conception, that it lost sight of him itself; it persuaded itself without doubt that from thence these qualities were divine; they believed them worthy of God, because no man could be able to form to himself any one idea of them. They arrived at persuading men they must believe that which they could not be able to conceive; that they must receive with submission improbable systems and conjectures contrary to reason; that this reason was the most agreeable sacrifice they could possibly make to a fantastical master, who was not willing they should make use of his gifts. In short, they made mortals believe they were not made to comprehend the thing the most important to them.[1] On the other hand, man persuaded himself that the gigantic and truly incomprehensible attributes which they assigned to his celestial monarch, placed between him and his slaves a distance so sufficiently large, that this supreme master was not by any means offended with the comparison; he promised himself that his haughty despot would take kindly these efforts which he made to render him still greater, more marvellous, more powerful, more arbitrary, more inaccessible to the observations of his feeble subjects. Men have always entertained the idea that that which they could not be able to conceive was much more noble and more respectable than that which they were in a capacity to comprehend: they imagined that their god, like tyrants, was not willing to be examined too closely.

They are these prejudices which appear to have given birth to those marvellous, or rather those unintelligible qualities which theology pretends to grant exclusively to the sovereign of the world. The human mind, whose invincible ignorance and whose fears reduced it to despair, gave birth to those obscure and vague notions with which he has decorated his god; he believed he could not be able to displease him provided he rendered him totally incommensurable or impossible to be compared with any thing which he knew, either the most sublime, or of the

greatest magnitude. From thence that multitude of negative attributes with which ingenious dreamers have successively embellished the phantom of the divinity, to the end that they might form a being distinguished from all others, or which had nothing in common with that which the human mind had the faculty of being acquainted with.

The theological attributes or metaphysics of God are in effect nothing but pure negations of the qualities which are found in man, or in all the beings of which he has a knowledge; these attributes suppose the divinity exempted from that which he calls weakness and imperfection in himself, and in all the beings which surround him. To say that GOD IS INFINITE, is, as we have already been enabled to see, to affirm that he is not, like man, or like all the beings with which we are acquainted, circumscribed by the limits of space:[2] to say that GOD IS ETERNAL, signifies that he has not had, like us, or like every thing which exists, a beginning, and that he will never have an end: to say that GOD IS IMMUTABLE, is to pretend that he is not like us, or like every thing with which we are environed, subject to change: to say that GOD IS IMMATERIAL, is to advance that his substance, or his essence, is of a nature which we cannot conceive, but which must be

---

[1] It is evident that all religion is founded upon the absurd principle that man is obliged to believe firmly that which he is in the most complete impossibility of comprehending. According to the notions of theology, even man by his nature must be in an *invincible ignorance* relatively to God.

[2] HOBBES says, that, *"every thing which we can imagine is finite, and that therefore the word* INFINITE *cannot furnish us with any one idea or any one notion."*—See his LEVIATHAN, CHAP. III.

A theologian speaks in the same manner; "Even the word INFINITE confounds," says he, "our ideas of God, and renders the most perfect of beings totally unknown to us: because the word INFINITE is only a negation, which signifies that which has neither end, nor limits, nor extent, and, consequently, that which has no positive and determinate nature, and is therefore nothing:" he adds, "there is nothing but custom that has caused this word to be adopted, which without that would appear devoid of sense, and a contradiction."—See SHERLOCK'S VINDICATION OF THE TRINITY, 77.

from that circumstance totally different from every thing that we know.

It is from the confused collection of these negative qualities, that has resulted the theological god, this metaphysical whole, of which it will be impossible for man to form to himself any idea. In this abstract being every thing is infinity, immensity, spirituality, omniscience, order, wisdom, intelligence, omnipotence. In combining these vague words, or these modifications, they believed they made something; they extended these qualities by thought, and they believed they had made a god, whilst they only formed a chimera. They imagined that these perfections or these qualities must be suitable to this god, because they were not suitable to any thing of which we have a knowledge; they believed that an incomprehensible being must have inconceivable qualities. Here are the material of which theology makes use to compose the inexplicable phantom before which they command the human species to fall on their knees.

Nevertheless, a being so vague, so impossible to be conceived or defined, so far removed from every thing which men could be able to know or feel, is very little suited to fix their restless views; their mind wants to be arrested by qualities which they are capacitated to ascertain and to judge. Thus after it had subtilized this metaphysical god, and had rendered him in idea so different from every thing that acts upon the senses, theology found itself obliged again to assimilate him to man, from whom it had removed him so far; it again made him a man by the MORAL qualities which it assigned him; it felt that without this they would not be able to persuade mortals, there could possibly be any relation between them and this vague, ethereal, fugitive, incommensurable being, which they made them adore; they perceived that this marvellous god was only suited to exercise the imagination of some thinkers, whose brains are accustomed to labour upon chimeras, or to take words for realities: in short, it found that it was necessary for the greater number of the material children of the earth, to have a god more analagous to themselves, more sensible, more known to them. In consequence, the divinity, in despite of his ineffable or divine essence, was re-clothed with human qualities; and they never felt their incompatibility with a being whom they had made essentially different from man, and who consequently could neither have his properties, nor be modified like him. They did not see that a god who was immaterial, and destitute of corporeal organs, could neither be able to think nor to act like a material being, whose peculiar organization renders him susceptible of the qualities, the feeling, the will, the virtues which we find in him. The necessity of assimilating God to his creatures, has made it pass over these palpable contradictions; and theology always continued obstinately to attribute to him those qualities which the human mind would vainly attempt to conceive or to reconcile. According to it, a pure spirit is the motive-power or mover of the material world; an immense being can be able to fill up space, without however excluding nature; an immutable being is the cause of those continual changes which are operated in the world; an omnipotent being cannot be able to prevent that evil which displeases him; the source of order is obliged to permit confusion; in short, the marvellous qualities of the theological god, are at each moment contradicted.

We do not find less contradiction and incompatibility in the human perfections or qualities which they have believed they ought to attribute to him, to the end that man should be able to form to himself an idea of the divinity. These qualities, which they inform us god possesses EMINENTLY, contradict each other every moment. They assure us that he is good; goodness is a known quality, seeing that it is recognised in some beings of our species; we desire to find it above all in those upon whom we are in a state of dependence; they pretend that the goodness of God is visible in all his works; nevertheless we do not give the title of good except to those amongst men whose actions produce on us only those effects which we approve; the master of nature has he then this goodness? Is he not the author of all things? In this case are we not bound to attribute to him equally the pains of the gout, the burning heat of a fever; those contagions, those famines, those wars which desolate the human species? When I am a prey to the keenest sorrows; when I languish in indigence, and under infirmities; when I groan under oppression, where is the goodness of God to me? When perverse and negligent governments produce and multiply misery, sterility, depopulation, and ravages, in my country, where is the goodness of God to it? When terrible revolutions, deluges, earthquakes, overthrow a great part of the globe which I inhabit, where is the goodness of this God; where is the beautiful order which his wisdom has introduced in the universe? How shall we be able to discern his beneficent providence, when every thing appears to announce that he is sporting with the human species? Who thinks of the tenderness of a god who afflicts us, who tries experiments upon us, who pleases himself with vexing his children? Whence come these FINAL CAUSES, so falsely supposed, and which they give us as the most incontestible proofs of the existence of an omnipotent and wise god, who, notwithstanding, can only be able to preserve his work, by destroying it, and who has not been able all at once to give it that degree of perfection and consistency of which it was susceptible? They assure us that God created the universe only for man, that he was willing that under him, he should be king of nature. Feeble monarch! of whom a grain of sand, some atoms of bile, some displaced humours, destroy the existence and the reign, thou pretendest that a good god hath made every thing for thee! Thou wilt that the entire of nature should be thy domain, and thou canst not defend thyself against the slightest of its blows! Thou makest thyself a god for thyself alone, thou supposest that he watcheth for thy preservation, thou believest that he occupieth himself with thine happiness; thou imaginest that he hath created every thing for thee, and following up these presumptuous ideas, thou pretendest that he is good! Dost thou not see that every moment his goodness for thee is contradicted? Dost thou not see that those beasts which thou believest submitted to thine empire, frequently devour thy fellow-creatures; that fire consumeth them; that the ocean swalloweth them up; that those elements, of which thou admirest the order, make them the victims of their frightful confusion? Dost thou not see that this power, which thou callest thy God, which thou pretendest laboureth only for thee, which thou supposest entirely occupied with thy species, it acts necessarily? Indeed even in thine own ideas, this god is an universal cause, who must think of maintaining the great whole from which thou hast so foolishly distinguished him. This being, is he not then, according to thyself, the god of nature, the god of the seas, of the rivers, of the mountains, of this globe in which thou occupiest so very small a place, of all those other globes which thou seest flattered by thine homage, touched with thy prayers, cannot be called good, since roll in the space round the sun that enlighteneth thee? Cease then obstinately to persist in seeing nothing but thyself in nature; do not flatter thyself that the human species, which renews itself, and disappeareth like the leaves of the trees, can be able to absorb all the care and tenderness of the universal agent, which, according to thee, ruleth the destiny of all things.

What is the human race compared to the earth? What is this earth compared to the sun? What is our sun compared to those myriads of suns, which, at immense distances, fill the canopy of heaven, not for the purpose of diverting thine eyes, not for the purpose of exciting thine admiration, as thou imaginest they are, but to occupy the place which necessity hath assigned them. Man, feeble and vain! restore thyself to thy proper place; acknowledge every where the effect of necessity; recognise in thy benefits, and in thy sorrows, the different modes of acting in beings endowed with various properties, of which nature is the assemblage, and do not any longer suppose in its pretended mover an incompatible goodness or malice, human qualities, ideas, and views, which have no other existence than in thyself.

In despite of the experience which contradicts at each moment the beneficent views which men suppose in their god, they do not cease to call him good: when we complain of the disorders and of the calamities of which we are so frequently the victims and the witnesses, they assure us that these evils are only apparent; they tell us that if our limited mind was capable of fathoming the depths of the divine wisdom and the treasures of his goodness, we should always see the greatest benefits result from that which we call evil. Maugre these frivolous answers, we can never be able to find good but in those objects which affect, as in a manner favourable to our actual existence; we shall always be obliged to find confusion and evil in every thing that shall affect us, even cursorily, in a grievous manner; if God is the author of those causes which produce in us these two modes of feeling, so very opposite the one to the other, we shall be obliged to conclude from it, that he is sometimes good and sometimes wicked; at least, if they will not allow that, he is neither the one nor the other, and that he acts necessarily. A world where man experiences so much evil, cannot be submitted to a god perfectly good; a world where man experiences so many benefits, cannot be governed by a wicked god. We must then admit two principles, equally powerful, which are opposed to each other; or rather, they must agree that the same god is alternately good and wicked; or in short they must avow that this god cannot be able to act otherwise than he does; in this case would it not be useless either to pay him adoration or to pray to him? Seeing that he would then only be DESTINY, the necessity of things; or at least he would be submitted to invariable rules which he would prescribe to himself.

To justify this god from those evils which he makes the human species experience, they tell us that he is just, and that they are punishments which he inflicts for injuries he has received from man. Thus man has the power to make his god suffer. But to offend any one, we must suppose relations between us and him whom we offend; what are the relations which can be able to subsist, between feeble mortals and the infinite Being who hath created the world? To offend any one, is to diminish the sum of his happiness, it is to afflict him, it is to deprive him of something, it is to make him experience a painful sensation. How is it possible that man can be able to change the well-being of the omnipotent Sovereign of nature, whose happiness is unalterable? How can physical actions in a material being, be able to have an influence upon an immaterial substance, and make him experience incommodious sensations? How can a weak creature, who has received from God his being, his organization, his temperament, from whence result his passions, his mode of acting and of thinking, be able to act against the will of an irresistible force who never consents to confusion or to sin?

On the other hand, JUSTICE, according

to the only ideas of it that we can be able to form to ourselves, supposes a permanent disposition to render to each that which is due to him: now theology unceasingly repeats to us that God owes us nothing; that, the benefits which he bestows on us are the gratuitous effects of his goodness; and that, without wounding his EQUITY, he can be able to dispose, according to his pleasure, of the work of his hands, and even plunge it, if it should so please him, into the abyss of misery. But in this I do not see the shadow of justice; I only see in it the most frightful of tyrannies; I find in it the most revolting abuse of power. Indeed, do we not see innocence suffering, virtue in tears, crime triumphant and recompensed under the empire of this god of whose justice they boast? [3] These evils are transient, you say, they will only last for a time; very well, but then your God is unjust at least for some time. It is, you say, for their good that he chastises his friends. But if he is good, how can he consent to let them suffer even for a time. If he knows every thing, what reason has he to reprove his favourites, from whom he has nothing to fear? If he is really omnipotent, can he not be able to spare them these transitory misfortunes, and procure them at once a durable and permanent felicity? If his power is steady and not to be shaken, what reason has he to make himself uneasy at the vain conspiracies which they would form against him?

Where is the man filled with kindness

---

[3] *Dies deficiet si velim numerare quibus bonis male evenerit; nec minus si commenorem quibus malis optime.*
                    CICER. DE NAT. DEOR. LIB. III.

If a virtuous king possessed the ring of GYGES, that is to say, had the faculty of rendering himself invisible, would he not make use of it to remedy abuses, to reward the good, to prevent the conspiracies of the wicked, to make order and happiness reign throughout his states? God is an invisible and all-powerful Monarch, nevertheless his states are the theatre of crime, of confusion; he remedies nothing.

and humanity, who does not desire with all his heart to render his fellow creatures happy? If God surpasseth in goodness all the beings of the human species, why doth he not make use of his infinite power to render them all happy? Nevertheless, we see that scarcely any one hath reason to be satisfied with his condition on earth. For one mortal that enjoys, we see thousands who suffer; for one rich man who lives in the midst of abundance, there are thousands of poor who want necessaries; whole nations groan in indigence to satisfy the passions of some princes, of some nobles, whom all their vexations do not render more fortunate on that account. In short, under an omnipotent god, whose goodness hath no limits, the earth is every where bathed with the tears of the miserable. What reply do they make to all this? They tell us coolly that THE JUDGMENTS OF GOD ARE IMPENETRABLE; in this case, I demand by what right do you reason upon them? Upon what foundation do you attribute to him a virtue that you cannot penetrate? What idea do you form to yourself of a justice that never resembles that of man?

They tell us that the justice of God is tempered with his mercy, his compassion, and his goodness. But what do we understand by mercy? Is it not a derogation to the severe rules of an exact and rigorous justice, which causes us to remit to some one the punishment that he had merited? In a prince, clemency is either a violation of justice, or the exemption from a too severe; they cannot be able to foresee all good, equitable, and wise, can they then be too severe, and if they are truly immutable, can he be able to derogate from them an instant? We nevertheless approve of clemency in a sovereign, when its too great facility does not become prejudicial to society; we esteem it because it announces in him humanity, mildness, a compassionate and noble soul, qualities which we prefer in our masters to rigour, cruelty, inflexibility. Besides, human laws are defective; they are frequently too severe; they cannot be able to foresee all circumstances and all cases; the punishments which they decree are not always just and proportionate to the offences. It is not thus with the laws of a god, whom we suppose perfectly just and wise; his laws ought to be so perfect that they never can be able to admit of exceptions; the Divinity cannot in consequence ever derogate from them without wounding his immutable equity.

The future life was invented to shelter the divine justice, and to exculpate him from those evils which he so frequently causes his greatest favorites to experience in this world: it is there, they tell us, that the celestial monarch will procure for his elect that unalterable happiness, which he has refused them on earth; it is there that he will indemnify those whom he loves for that transitory injustice, those afflicting trials, which he makes them suffer here below. In the mean time, is this invention calculated to give us those clear ideas suitable to justify providence? If God oweth nothing to his creatures, upon what foundation can they expect, in a future life, an happiness more real, more constant, than that which they at present enjoy? It will be founded, say they, upon his promises contained in his revealed oracles. But are they quite certain that these oracles have emanated from him? On the other hand, the system of another life doth not justify this god for the most fleeting and transitory injustice; for does not injustice, even when it is transient, destroy that immutability which they attribute to the Divinity? In short is not that omnipotent being whom they have made the author of all things, himself the first cause or accomplice of the offences which they commit against him? Is he not the true author of evil, or of the sin which he permits, whilst he can be able to prevent it; and in this case can he be able, consistently with justice, to punish those whom he renders culpable?

We have already seen the multitude of contradictions and extravagant hypotheses, to which the attributes, which theology gives to its god, must necessarily give place. A being clothed at one time with so many discordant qualities, will be always undefinable; will only present those notions which will destroy each other, and he will in consequence remain a being of the imagination. This god hath, say they, created the heavens, the earth, and the beings who inhabit therein, to manifest his own peculiar glory: but a monarch who is superior to all beings, who hath neither rivals nor equals in nature, who cannot be compared to any of his creatures, is he susceptible of being animated with the desire of glory? Can he fear to be debased, degraded in the eyes of his fellow creatures? Hath he occasion for the esteem, the homage, the admiration of men? The love of glory is in us only the desire of giving our fellow creatures an high opinion of ourselves; this passion is laudable, when it determines us to perform great and useful actions; but more frequently it is only a weakness attached to our nature, it is only a desire in us to be distinguished from those beings with whom we compare ourselves. The god of whom they speak to us ought to be exempt from this passion; he has no fellow creatures, he has no competitors, he cannot be offended with those ideas which we form of him; his power cannot suffer any diminution, nothing can be able to disturb his eternal felicity; must we not conclude from this that he cannot be able to be either susceptible of desiring glory, or sensible to the praises and esteem of men? If this god is jealous of his prerogatives, of his titles, of his rank, of his glory, wherefore doth he suffer that so many men are capable of offending him? Why doth he permit so many others to have such unfavorable opinions of him? Why alloweth he others to have the termerity to refuse him that incense which is so flattering to his pride? How cometh he to permit that a mortal like me, should dare attack his rights, his titles, even his existence? It is in order to punish thee, you will say, for having made a bad use of his favours. But why doth he permit me to abuse his kindness? Or why are not the favours which he confers on me sufficient to make me act agreeably to his views? It is because he hath made thee free. Why hath he given me a liberty, of which he must have foreseen that I should be able to make an improper use? Is it then a present worthy of his goodness, to give me a faculty that enables me to brave his omnipotence, to detach from him his adorers, to render myself eternally miserable? Would it not have been much more advantageous for me never to have been born, or at least to have been placed in the rank of brutes or stones, than to have been in despite of myself placed amongst intelligent beings, there to exercise the fatal power of losing myself without redemption, by offending or mistaking the arbiter of my fate? Had not God much better have shewn me his omnipotent goodness on my account, and would he not have laboured much more efficaciously to his true glory if he had obliged me to render him my homage, and thereby to have merited an ineffable happiness?

The system of the liberty of man, so little founded, which we have formerly destroyed, was visibly imagined to wipe from the Author of nature the reproach which they must make him of being the author, the source, the first cause of the crimes of his creatures. In consequence of this fatal present given by a beneficent god, men, according to the sinister ideas of theology, will for the most part be eternally punished for their faults in this world. Farfetched and endless torments are by the justice of a merciful and compassionate god, reserved for fragile beings, for transitory offences, for false reasonings, for involuntary errors, for necessary passions, which depend on the temperament which this god has given them, circumstances in which he has placed them, or, if they will, the abuse of this pretended liberty, which a provident god ought never to have accorded to beings capable of abusing it. Should we call that father good, rational, just, clement, and compassionate, who should arm with a dangerous and sharp knife the hands of a petulant child, with whose imprudence he was acquainted, and who should punish him all his life, for having wounded himself with it? Should we call that prince just, merciful, and compassionate, who did not proportion the punishment to the offence, who should put no end to the torments of that subject who in a state of inebriety should have transiently wounded his vanity, without however causing him any real prejudice; above all, after having himself taken pains to intoxicate him? Should we look upon that monarch as all-powerful whose dominions should be in such a state of anarchy, that with the exception of a small number of faithful subjects, all the others should be able every instant to despise his laws, insult himself, frustrate his will? O, theologians! agree that your god is nothing but an heap of qualities which form a whole as perfectly incomprehensible to your mind as to mine; by dint of over-burthening him with incompatible qualities, ye have made him truly a chimera, which all your hypotheses cannot be able to maintain in the existence you are willing to give him.

They will nevertheless reply to these difficulties, that goodness, wisdom, justice, are, in God, qualities so eminent, or have such little similarity to ours, that they have no relation with these same qualities, when they are found in men. But I shall answer, how shall I form to myself ideas of these divine perfections, if they bear no resemblance to those of these virtues which I find in my fellow creatures, or to the dispositions which I feel in myself? If the justice of God is not that of men; if it operates in that mode which men call injustice, if his goodness, his clemency, his wisdom, do not manifest themselves by such signs, that we can be able to recognize them; if all his divine qualities are contrary to the received ideas; if in theology all the human actions are obscured or overthrown, how can mortals like myself pretend to announce them, to have a knowledge of them, to explain them to others? Would theology, give to the mind the ineffable boon of conceiving that which no man is in a capacity to comprehend? Would it procure to its agents the marvellous faculty of having precise ideas of a god composed of so many contradictory qualities? In short, the theologian would he be himself a god?

They shut our mouths by saying, that God himself hath spoken, that he hath made himself known to men. But when, where, and to whom hath this god spoken? where are the divine oracles? An hundred voices raise themselves at the same moment, an hundred hands shew them to me in absurd and discordant collections: I run them over, and through the whole I find that the GOD OF WISDOM hath spoken an obscure, insidious, and irrational language. I see that the GOD OF GOODNESS hath been cruel and sanguinary; that the GOD OF JUSTICE hath been unjust and partial, hath ordered iniquity; that the GOD OF MERCIES destines the most hideous punishments to the unhappy victims of his anger. Besides, obstacles present themselves when men attempt to verify the pretended relations of a divinity, who in two countries hath never literally holden the same language; who hath spoken in so many places, at so many times, and always so variously, that he appears every where to have shewn himself only with the determined design of throwing the human mind into the most strange perplexity.

The relations which they suppose between men and their god can only be founded upon the moral qualities of this being; if these moral qualities are not known to men, they cannot serve them for models. It were needful that these qualities were natural in a known being to be imitated; how can I imitate a god of whom the goodness and the justice do not resemble mine in any thing, or rather are directly contrary to that which I call either just or good? If God partakes of nothing of that which forms us, how can we be able, even distantly, to propose to ourselves the imitating him, the resembling him, the following a conduct necessary to please him by conforming ourselves to him? What can be, in effect, the motives of that worship, of that homage, of that obedience which we are told to render to the Supreme Being, if we do not establish them upon his goodness, upon his veracity, upon his justice, in short upon such qualities as we can be able to understand? How can we have clear ideas, if these qualities in God are no longer of the same nature as in us?

They will tell us, no doubt, there cannot be able to be any proportion between the creator and his work; that the clay has no right to demand of the potter who hath formed it, *why have you fashioned me thus?* But if there be no proportion between the workman and his work; if there be no analogy between them, what can be the relations that will subsist between them? If God is incorporeal, how doth he act upon bodies, or how can corporeal beings be able to act upon him, offend him, disturb his repose, excite in him motions of anger? If man is relatively to God only an EARTHEN VASE, this VASE owes neither prayers nor thanks to its potter for the form which he has been willing to give it. If this potter irritates himself against his VASE for having formed it badly, or for having rendered it incapable of the uses to which he had destined it, the potter, if he is not an irrational being, ought to take to himself the defects which he finds in it; he certainly has the power to break it, and the VASE cannot prevent him; it will neither have motives nor means to soften his anger, but will be obliged to submit to its destiny; and the potter would be completely deprived of reason if he were willing to punish his vase, rather than, by forming it anew, give it a figure more suitable to his designs.

We see, that according to these notions, men have no more relation with God than stones. But if God owes nothing to men, if he is not bound to shew them either justice or goodness, men on their parts cannot be able to owe any thing to him. We have no knowledge of any relations between beings which may not be reciprocal; the duties of men amongst themselves are founded upon their mutual wants; if God has not occasion for them, they cannot owe him any thing, and men cannot possibly offend him. In the mean time, the authority of God can only be founded on the good which he does to men, and the duties of these towards God, can have no other motives than the hope of that happiness which they expect from him; if he does not owe them this happiness, all their relations are annihilated, and their duties no longer exist. Thus, in whatever manner we view the theological system, IT DESTROYS ITSELF. Will theology never feel that the more it endeavours to exalt its god, to exaggerate his grandeur, the more incomprehensible it renders him to us? That the farther it removes him from man, or the more it debases this man, the more it weakens the relations which they have supposed between this god and him; if the sovereign of nature is an infinite being and totally different from our species, and if man is only in his eyes a worm or a speck of dirt, it is clear there cannot

be any MORAL RELATIONS between two beings so little analogous to each other; and again it is still more evident that the VASE which he has formed is not capable of reasoning upon him.

It is however upon the relations subsisting between man and his god that all worship is founded. Nevertheless all the religions of the world have a despotic god for their basis; but is not despotism an unjust and unreasonable power? Is it not equally to undermine his goodness, his justice, and his infinite wisdom, to attribute to the divinity the exercise of such a power? Men in seeing the evils with which they are frequently assailed in this world, without being able to guess by what means they have attracted the divine anger, will always be tempted to believe that the master of nature is a SULTAN, who owes nothing to his subjects, who is not obliged to render them any account of his actions, who is not bound to conform himself to those laws, who is not himself submitted to those rules, which he prescribes for others; who in consequence can be unjust, who hath the right to carry his vengeance beyond all bounds; in short, the theologians have pretended that God would have the right of destroying the universe, and replunging it into the chaos from whence his wisdom hath withdrawn it; whilst the same theologians, quote to us the order and marvellous arrangement of this world, as the most convincing proof of his existence.[4]

In short, theology numbers among the qualities of God the incommunicable privilege of acting contrary to all the laws of nature and of reason, whilst it is upon his reason, his justice, his wisdom, his fidelity in fulfilling his pretended engagements, that they are willing to establish

---

[4] We conceive at least, says DOCTOR GASTRILL, that God could be able to overturn the universe, and replunge it into chaos.— SEE HIS DEFENCE OF RELIGION AS WELL NATURAL AS REVEALED.

the worship which we owe him, and the duties of morality. What an ocean of contradictions! A being who can do every thing and who owes nothing to any one, who in his eternal decrees can elect or reject them, predestinate them to happiness or to misery, who hath the right of making them serve for the playthings of his caprice, and to afflict them without reason, who could go so far as even to destroy and annihilate the universe, is he not a tyrant or a demon? is there any thing more hideous than the immediate consequences that are capable of being drawn from these revolting ideas which are given us of their god by those who tell us to love him, to serve him, to imitate him, to obey his orders? Would it not be a thousand times more preferable to depend upon blind matter, upon a nature destitute of intelligence, upon chance' or upon nothing, upon a god of stone or of wood, than upon a god whom they suppose is laying snares for men, inviting them to sin, permitting them to commit those crimes which he could prevent, to the end that he may have the barbarous pleasure of punishing them without measure, without utility to himself, without correction to them, without their example serving to reclaim others? A gloomy terror must necessarily result from the idea of such a being; his power will wrest from us much servile homage; we shall call him good to flatter him or to disarm his malice; but, without overturning the essence of things, such a god will never be able to make himself beloved by us, when we shall reflect that he owes us nothing, that he hath the right of being unjust, that he hath the power to punish his creatures for making a bad use of the liberty which he grants them, or for not having had that grace which he hath been pleased to refuse to them.

Thus, in supposing that God is not bound towards us by any rules, they visibly sap the foundation of all religion. A theology which assures us that God hath been able to create men for the purpose of rendering them eternally miserable, shews us nothing but an evil and malicious genius, whose malice is an inconceivable abyss, and infinitely surpasseth the cruelty of the most depraved beings of our species. Such is nevertheless the god which they have the confidence to propose for a model to the human species! Such is the divinity which is adored even by those nations who boast of being the most enlightened in this world!

It is however upon the moral character of the divinity, that is to say, upon his goodness, his wisdom, his equity, his love of order, that they pretend to establish our morals, or the science of those duties which connect us to the beings of our species. But as his perfections and his goodness contradict themselves very frequently and give place to weakness, to injustice, to cruel severities, we are obliged to find him changeable, fickle, capricious, unequal in his conduct, in contradiction with himself, according to the various modes of action which they attribute to him. Indeed we sometimes see him favourable to, and sometimes disposed to injure the human species; sometimes the friend to reason and the happiness of society; sometimes he interdicts the use of reason, he acts as the enemy of all virtue, he is flattered with seeing society disturbed. Nevertheless, as we have seen mortals crushed by fear, hardly ever daring to avow that their god was unjust or wicked, nor to persuade themselves that he authorized them to be so; they concluded simply that every thing which they did according to his pretended orders or with the view of pleasing him, was always extremely good, however prejudicial it might otherwise appear in the eyes of reason. They supposed him the master of creating, the just and the unjust, of changing good into evil, and evil into good, truth into falsehood, and falsehood into truth: in short, they gave him the right of changing the eternal essence of things; they made this god superior to the laws of nature, of reason, and of virtue; they believed they could never do wrong in following his precepts, although the most absurd, the most contrary to morals, the most opposite to good sense, and the most prejudicial to the repose of society. With such principles do not let us be surprised at seeing those horrors which religion causes to be committed on the earth. The most atrocious religion was the most immediate consequence.[5]

In founding morals upon the character of a god, who is so little in accord with morality, who changes his conduct, man will never be able to ascertain what conduct he ought to hold, either upon that which he owes to God, upon that which he owes to himself, or upon that which he owes to others. Nothing then was more dangerous, than to persuade him, there existed a being superior to nature, before whom reason must remain silent, to whom, to be happy, he must sacrifice

every thing here below. His pretended orders, and his example must necessarily be much stronger than the precepts of human morals; the adorers of this god, cannot then listen to nature and good sense, but when by chance they accord with the caprice of their god, in whom they suppose the power of annihilating the invariable relation of beings, of changing reason into folly, justice into injustice, and even crime into virtue. By a consequence of these ideas, the religious man never examines the will and the conduct of the celestial despot, according to the ordinary rules; he will be inspired with every thing that comes from him, and those who shall pretend they are charged with interpreting his oracles, will always assume the right of rendering him irrational and criminal; his first duty will always be to obey his god without murmuring.

Such are the fatal and necessary consequences of the moral character which they give to the Divinity, and of the opinion which persuades mortals they ought to pay a blind obedience to the absolute Sovereign, whose arbitrary and fluctuating will regulates all duties. Those who first had the confidence to tell men, that in matters of religion, it was not permitted them to consult their reason, nor the interests of society, evidently proposed to themselves, to make them the sport or the instruments of their own peculiar wickedness. It is from this radical error then, that have sprung all those extravagancies, which the different religions have introduced upon the earth; that sacred fury which has deluged it in blood; those inhuman persecutions which have so frequently desolated nations; in short, all those horrid tragedies, of which the name of the Most-High was the cause and the pretext here below. Every time they have been willing to render men unsociable, they have cried that God was willing they should be so. Thus the theologians themselves have taken pains to calumniate and

---

[5] The modern religion of Europe hath visibly caused more ravages and troubles than any other known superstition; it was in that respect very accordant to its principles. They may well preach tolerance and mildness in the name of a despotic god, who alone hath a right to the homage of the earth, who is extremely jealous, who is willing that they should admit some doctrines, who punisheth cruelly for erroneous opinions, who demandeth zeal from his adorers, such a god must consequently make fanatical persecutors of all men. The theology of the present day is a subtile venom, suitable to infect all by the importance which they attach to it. By the dint of METAPHYSICS, the modern theologians have become systematically absurd and wicked: by once admitting the odious ideas which they gave of the Divinity, it was impossible to make them understand that they ought to be humane, equitable, pacific, indulgent, tolerant; they pretended and proved that these humane and social virtues, were not seasonable in the cause of religion, and would be treason and crimes in the eyes of the celestial Monarch, to whom every thing ought to be sacrificed.

to defame the phantom which they have erected upon the ruins of human reason, of a nature well known, and a thousand times preferable to a tyrannical god, whom they render odious to every honest soul, in believing they exalt him, and cover him with glory. These theologians, are the true destroyers of their own peculiar idol, by the contradictory qualities which they accumulate in him: they are the theologians, as we shall yet prove in the sequel, who render morals uncertain and fluctuating, by founding them upon a changeable and capricious god, much more frequently unjust and cruel, than filled with goodness. They are the same theologians who overturn and annihilate him, who command crime, carnage, and barbarity, in the name of the Sovereign of the universe, who interdict us the use of reason, which alone ought to regulate all our actions and ideas.

Whatever it may be, admitting, if they will, for a moment, that God possesses all the human virtues in an infinite degree of perfection, we shall presently be obliged to acknowledge, that he cannot connect them with those metaphysical, theological, and negative attributes, of which we have already spoken. If God is a spirit, how can he be able to act like man, who is a corporeal being? A pure spirit sees nothing; it neither hears our prayers nor our cries, it cannot be conceived to have compassion for our miseries, being destitute of organs, by the ministry of which the sentiments of pity can be excited in us. He is not *immutable,* if his dispositions can be able to change: he is not *infinite,* if the totality of nature, without being him, can exist conjointly with him; he is not *omnipotent,* if he permits, or if he does not prevent evil and disorder in the world: he is not *omnipresent,* if he is not in the man who sins, or if he retires at the moment in which he commits the sin. Thus, in whatever manner we consider this god, the human qualities which they assign him, necessarily destroy each

other, and these same qualities cannot, in any possible manner, combine themselves with the supernatural attributes, given him by theology.

With respect to the pretended REVELATION of the will of God, far from being a proof of his goodness, or of his commiseration for men, it would only be a proof of his malice. Indeed all revelation supposes the Divinity has been capable of leaving the human species, during a considerable time, unacquainted with truths, the most important to their happiness. This revelation, made to a small number of chosen men, would moreover announce a partiality in this being, an unjust predilection, but little compatible with the goodness of the common Father of the human race. This revelation also injures the divine immutability, since, by it, God would have permitted at one time, that men should be ignorant of his will, and be willing at another time, that they should be instructed in it. This granted, all revelation is contrary to the notions which they give us of the justice, of the goodness of a god, who they tell us is immutable, and who, without having occasion to reveal himself, or to make himself known to them by miracles, could easily instruct and convince men, inspire them with those ideas, which he desires; in short, dispose of their minds and of their hearts. What will they be, if we are willing to examine in detail all those pretended revelations, which they assure us, have been made to mortals? we shall see in them that this God only delivers out fables unworthy of a wise being; only acts in them, in a manner contrary to the natural notions of equity; only announces in them enigmas and oracles impossible to be comprehended; paints himself in them under traits incompatible with his infinite perfections; exacts puerilities which degrade him in the eyes of reason; deranges the order which he has established in nature, to convince creatures, whom he will never make to adopt those ideas, those sentiments, and that conduct, with which he would inspire them. In short, we shall find, that God has never manifested himself, but to announce inexplicable mysteries, unintelligible doctrines, ridiculous practices; to throw the human mind into fear, distrust, perplexity, and above all, to furnish a never failing source of dispute to mortals.[6]

We see, then, the ideas which theology gives us of the Divinity will always be confused and incompatible, and will necessarily finish by injuring the repose of human nature. These obscure notions, and these vague speculations, would be sufficiently indifferent, if men would not regard their reveries on this unknown being, upon whom they believe they depend, as important, and if they did not draw from them conclusions pernicious for themselves. As they never will have a common and fixed standard, whereby they can determine on this Being, to whom various and diversely modified imaginations have given birth, they will never be able either to understand each other, or to be in accord the one with the other, upon those ideas which they shall form to themselves of him. From thence, that necessary diversity, in religious opinions, which in all times, have given rise to the most irrational quarrels, which

they always look upon as materially essential, and which have consequently always interested the tranquillity of nations. A man with an heated mind, will not accommodate himself to the god of a phlegmatic and tranquil man; an infirm, bilious, discontented man, will never see this god in the same point of view with him who enjoys a temperament more sound, from whence commonly results gaiety, contentment, and peace. An equitable, good, compassionate, and tender man, will not delineate to himself the same portrait of this god, as the man who is of an harsh, inflexible, and wicked character. Each individual will always modify his god after his own peculiar manner of being, of thinking, and of feeling. A wise, honest, and rational man, will never be able to figure to himself, that a god can be cruel and unreasonable.

Nevertheless, as fear necessarily presided at the formation of these gods; as the idea of the divinity was continually associated with that of terror, his name always made mortals tremble, it awakened in their minds melancholy and afflicting ideas; sometimes it threw them into inquietude; sometimes it inflamed their imagination. The experience of all ages proves to us, that this vague name becomes, for the human species, the most important of all their affairs; diffuses every where consternation or inebriety, and produces in their minds the most frightful ravages. It is extremely difficult for an habitual fear, which is without exception the most incommodious of passions, not to become a fatal leaven, capable of exasperating and souring, in the long run, the most moderate temperament.

If a misanthrope, in hatred of the human race, had formed the project of throwing man into the greatest perplexity, could he have been able to have imagined a more efficacious means, than to occupy them, without relaxation, with a being not only unknown, but also totally

---

[6] It is evident that all revelation, which is not distinct, or which teaches MYSTERIES cannot be the work of a wise and intelligent Being: as soon as he speaks, they ought to presume, it is for the purpose of being understood by those to whom he is willing to manifest himself. To speak so as not to be understood, only announces folly or want of good faith. It is then very demonstrable, that every thing which the priesthood have called MYSTERY, are inventions, made to throw a thick veil over their own peculiar contradictions, and their own peculiar ignorance of the Divinity. They think they shall solve all difficulties by saying IT IS A MYSTERY. Besides, their interest dictates that men should know nothing of that pretended science, of which they have made themselves the depositaries.

impossible to be known, which should, however, have been announced to them as the centre of all their thoughts, as the model and the only end of all their actions, as the object of all their researches, as a thing more important than life, since their present felicity, and their future happiness must necessarily depend upon it? What would it be, if to these ideas, already so suitable to disturb their brain, he also joined that of an absolute monarch, who followed no rule in his conduct, who was not bound by any duty, who could punish, to all eternity, the offences which they committed against him in the course of time; whose fury it is extremely easy to provoke, who is irritated by the ideas and the thoughts of men, and of whom without even their knowledge they can incur the displeasure? The name of such a being, would assuredly be sufficient to carry trouble, affliction, and consternation in the souls of those, who should hear it pronounced; his idea would follow them every where, it would unceasingly afflict them, it would plunge them into despair. To what torture would not their mind put itself to discover this formidable being, to ascertain the secret of pleasing him, to imagine what would be able to disarm his anger! What fears would they not entertain of not having justly hit upon him! What disputes would they not have upon the nature, upon the qualities of a being equally unknown to all men, and seen variously by each of them! What variety in the means to which imagination would give birth, in order to find favour in his eyes or to remove his wrath!

Such is, word for word, the history of those effects which the name of God produces upon the earth. Men were always frightened at it, because they never had any fixed ideas of the being which this name represented. The qualities which some speculators, by dint of racking the brain, have believed they discovered in him, have done no more than

disturb the repose of nations and of each of the citizens who compose it, alarm them without reason, fill them with spleen and animosity, render their existence unhappy, make them lose sight of the realities necessary to their happiness. By the magical charm of this formidable word, the human species have remained as if they were benumbed and stupified, or else a blind fanaticism rendered them furious: sometimes desponding with fear, man cringed like a slave who bends under the scourge of an inexorable master, always ready to strike him; he believed he was only born to serve this master whom he never knew, and of whom they gave him the most terrible ideas; to tremble under his yoke; to labour to appease him; to dread his vengeance; to live in tears and misery. If he raised his eyes bathed in tears towards his god, it was in the excess of his grief; he nevertheless always mistrusted him, because he believed him unjust, severe, capricious, and implacable. He could neither labour for his happiness, cheer his heart, nor consult his reason, because he was always sighing, and he was never permitted to lose sight of his fears. He became the enemy of himself and of his fellow creatures, because they persuaded him that his well-being here below was interdicted. Every time there was a question of his celestial tyrant, he no longer had any judgment, he no longer reasoned, he fell into a state of infancy or of delirium, which submitted him to authority. Man was destined to this servitude as soon as he quitted the womb of his mother, and tyrannical opinion obliged him to wear his fetters during the rest of his days. A prey to the panic terrors with which they never ceased to inspire him, he appeared to have come upon the earth only to dream, to groan, to sigh, to injure himself, to deprive himself of all pleasures, to embitter his life, or disturb the felicity of others. Perpetually infected by the terrific chimeras which the delirium of the imagination presented to him without ceasing, he was abject, stupid, irrational, and he frequently became wicked, to honour the god whom they proposed to him for a model, or whom they told him to avenge.

It was thus that mortals prostrated themselves, from race to race, before the vain phantoms to which fear originally gave birth in the bosom of ignorance and the calamities of the earth. It was thus that they tremblingly adored those vain idols which they erected in the recesses of their own brain, where they have given them a sanctuary; nothing can undeceive them, nothing can make them feel that it is themselves whom they adore, that they fall on their knees before their own work, that they frighten themselves with the extravagant picture which they have themselves delineated; they obstinately persist in prostrating themselves, in perplexing themselves, in trembling; they make a crime even of the pleasure of dissipating their fears; they mistake the ridiculous production of their own folly; their conduct resembles that of children, who are afraid of themselves, when they see in a mirror their own peculiar traits which they have disfigured. Their extravagancies, so grievous to themselves, have their epoch in this world from the fatal notion of a god; they will continue them and renew them until such time as this unintelligible notion shall no longer be looked upon as important and necessary to the happiness of society. In the mean time, it is evident that the man who should arrive at the destruction of this fatal notion, or at least should diminish its terrible influence, would certainly be the friend of the human species.

ANTONY FLEW et al.

Can Theological Statements Be Tested Empirically?

The contributors to this symposium, with the exception of Antony Flew, who is a professor at the University College of North Staffordshire, are all currently teaching philosophy at Oxford. They are all identified with the style of analytical philosophy which has flourished at Oxford since World War II and which emphasizes the careful examination of the ordinary use of linguistic expressions.

A

ANTONY FLEW

Let us begin with a parable. It is a parable developed from a tale told by John Wisdom in his haunting and revelatory article

'Gods.' Once upon a time two explorers came upon a clearing in the jungle. In

From *New Essays in Philosophical Theology*, ed. by Antony Flew and Alasdair MacIntyre. Reprinted by permission of the authors and The Macmillan Company. First published in 1955 by the SCM Press Ltd.

the clearing were growing many flowers and many weeds. One explorer says, 'Some gardener must tend this plot.' The other disagrees, 'There is no gardener.' So they pitch their tents and set a watch. No gardener is ever seen. 'But perhaps he is an invisible gardener.' So they set up a barbed-wire fence. They electrify it. They patrol with bloodhounds. (For they remember how H. G. Wells's *The Invisible Man* could be both smelt and touched though he could not be seen.) But no shrieks ever suggest that some intruder has received a shock. No movements of the wire ever betray an invisible climber. The bloodhounds never give cry. Yet still the Believer is not convinced. 'But there is a gardener, invisible, intangible, insensible to electric shocks, a gardener who has no scent and makes no sound, a gardener who comes secretly to look after the garden which he loves.' At last the Sceptic despairs, 'But what remains of your original assertion? Just how does what you call an invisible, intangible, eternally elusive gardener differ from an imaginary gardener or even from no gardener at all?'

In this parable we can see how what starts as an assertion, that something exists or that there is some analogy between certain complexes of phenomena, may be reduced step by step to an altogether different status, to an expression perhaps of a 'picture preference.' [1] The Sceptic says there is no gardener. The Believer says there is a gardener (but invisible, etc.). One man talks about sexual behaviour. Another man prefers to talk of Aphrodite (but knows that there is not really a superhuman person additional to, and somehow responsible for, all sexual phenomena).[2] The process of

qualification may be checked at any point before the original assertion is completely withdrawn and something of that first assertion will remain (Tautology). Mr. Wells's invisible man could not, admittedly, be seen, but in all other respects he was a man like the rest of us. But though the process of qualification may be, and of course usually is, checked in time, it is not always judiciously so halted. Someone may dissipate his assertion completely without noticing that he has done so. A fine brash hypothesis may thus be killed by inches, the death by a thousand qualifications.

And in this, it seems to me, lies the peculiar danger, the endemic evil, of theological utterance. Take such utterances as 'God has a plan,' 'God created the world,' 'God loves us as a father loves his children.' They look at first sight very much like assertions, vast cosmological assertions. Of course, this is no sure sign that they either are, or are intended to be, assertions. But let us confine ourselves to the cases where those who utter such sentences intend them to express assertions. (Merely remarking parenthetically that those who intend or interpret such utterances as crypto-commands, expressions of wishes, disguised ejaculations, concealed ethics, or as anything else but assertions, are unlikely to succeed in making them either properly orthodox or practically effective.)

Now to assert that such and such is the case is necessarily equivalent to deny-

---

[1] Cf. J. Wisdom, 'Other Minds,' *Mind*, 1940; reprinted in his *Other Minds* (Blackwell, 1952).

[2] Cf. Lucretius, *De Rerum Natura,* II, 655–60.

Hic siquis mare Neptunum Cereremque vocare
Constituet fruges et Bacchi nomine abuti
Mavolat quam laticis proprium proferre vocamen
Concedamus ut hic terrarum dictitet orbem
Esse deum matrem dum vera re tamen ipse
Religione animum turpi contingere parcat.

ing that such and such is not the case.[3] Suppose then that we are in doubt as to what someone who gives vent to an utterance is asserting, or suppose that, more radically, we are sceptical as to whether he is really asserting anything at all, one way of trying to understand (or perhaps it will be to expose) his utterance is to attempt to find what he would regard as counting against, or as being incompatible with, its truth. For if the utterance is indeed an assertion, it will necessarily be equivalent to a denial of the negation of that assertion. And anything which would count against the assertion, or which would induce the speaker to withdraw it and to admit that it had been mistaken, must be part of (or the whole of) the meaning of the negation of that assertion. And to know the meaning of the negation of an assertion, is as near as makes no matter, to know the meaning of that assertion.[4] And if there is nothing which a putative assertion denies then there is nothing which it asserts either: and so it is not really an assertion. When the Sceptic in the parable asked the Believer, 'Just how does what you call an invisible, intangible, eternally elusive gardener differ from an imaginary gardener or even from no gardener at all?' he was suggesting that the Believer's earlier statement had been so eroded by qualification that it was no longer an assertion at all.

Now it often seems to people who are not religious as if there was no conceivable event or series of events the occurrence of which would be admitted by sophisticated religious people to be a sufficient reason for conceding 'There wasn't a God after all' or 'God does not really love us then.' Someone tells us that God loves us as a father loves his children. We are reassured. But then we see a child dying of inoperable cancer of the throat. His earthly father is driven frantic in his efforts to help, but his Heavenly Father reveals no obvious sign of concern. Some qualification is made—God's love is 'not a merely human love' or it is 'an inscrutable love,' perhaps—and we realize that such sufferings are quite compatible with the truth of the assertion that 'God loves us as a father (but, of course, ...).' We are reassured again. But then perhaps we ask: what is this assurance of God's (appropriately qualified) love worth, what is this apparent guarantee really a guarantee against? Just what would have to happen not merely (morally and wrongly) to tempt but also (logically and rightly) to entitle us to say 'God does not love us' or even 'God does not exist?' I therefore put to the succeeding symposiasts the simple central questions, 'What would have to occur or to have occurred to constitute for you a disproof of the love of, or of the existence of, God?'

University College of North Staffordshire
ENGLAND

B

R. M. HARE

I wish to make it clear that I shall not try to defend Christianity in particular, but religion in general—not because I do not believe in Christianity, but because you cannot understand what Christianity is, until you have understood what religion is.

I must begin by confessing that, on the ground marked out by Flew, he seems to me to be completely victorious. I therefore shift my ground by relating another parable. A certain lunatic is convinced that all dons want to murder him. His friends introduce him to all the mildest and most respectable dons that they

---

[3] For those who prefer symbolism: $p \equiv \sim\sim p$.

[4] For by simply negating $\sim p$ we get p: $\sim\sim p \equiv p$.

can find, and after each of them has retired, they say, 'You see, he doesn't really want to murder you; he spoke to you in a most cordial manner; surely you are convinced now?' But the lunatic replies 'Yes, but that was only his diabolical cunning; he's really plotting against me the whole time, like the rest of them; I know it I tell you.' However many kindly dons are produced, the reaction is still the same. *Uses Flew's test*

Now we say that such a person is deluded. But what is he deluded about? About the truth or falsity of an assertion? Let us apply Flew's test to him. There is no behaviour of dons that can be enacted which he will accept as counting against his theory; and therefore his theory, on this test, asserts nothing. But it does not follow that there is no difference between what he thinks about dons and what most of us think about them—otherwise we should not call him a lunatic and ourselves sane, and dons would have no reason to feel uneasy about his presence in Oxford.

Let us call that in which we differ from this lunatic, our respective *bliks*. He has an insane *blik* about dons; we have a sane one. It is important to realize that we save a sane one, not no *blik* at all; for there must be two sides to any argument —if he has a wrong *blik,* then those who are right about dons must have a right one. Flew has shown that a *blik* does not consist in an assertion or system of them; but nevertheless it is very important to have the right *blik.* *Diff. bliks*

Let us try to imagine what it would be like to have different *bliks* about other things than dons. When I am driving my car, it sometimes occurs to me to wonder whether my movements of the steering-wheel will always continue to be followed by corresponding alterations in the direction of the car. I have never had a steering failure, though I have had skids, which must be similar. Moreover, I know enough about how the steering of my car

steering of car

is made, to know the sort of thing that would have to go wrong for the steering to fail—steel joints would have to part, or steel rods break, or something—but how do I know that this won't happen? The truth is, I don't know; I just have a *blik* about steel and its properties, so that normally I trust the steering of my car; but I find it not at all difficult to imagine what it would be like to lose this *blik* and acquire the opposite one. People would say I was silly about steel; but there would be no mistaking the reality of the difference between our respective *bliks*—for example, I should never go in a motor-car. Yet I should hesitate to say that the difference between us was the difference between contradictory assertions. No amount of safe arrivals or bench-tests will remove my *blik* and restore the normal one; for my *blik* is compatible with any finite number of such tests.

It was Hume who taught us that our whole commerce with the world depends upon our *blik* about the world; and that differences between *bliks* about the world cannot be settled by observation of what happens in the world. That was why, having performed the interesting experiment of doubting the ordinary man's *blik* about the world, and showing that no proof could be given to make us adopt one *blik* rather than another, he turned to backgammon to take his mind off the problem. It seems, indeed, to be impossible even to formulate as an assertion the normal *blik* about the world which makes me put my confidence in the future reliability of steel joints, in the continued ability of the road to support my car, and not gape beneath it revealing nothing below; in the general non-homicidal tendencies of dons; in my own continued well-being (in some sense of that word that I may not now fully understand) if I continue to do what is right according to my lights; in the general likelihood of people like Hitler coming to a bad end. But perhaps a formulation less inadequate than most is to be found in the Psalms: 'The earth is weak and all the inhabiters thereof: I bear up the pillars of it.'

The mistake of the position which Flew selects for attack is to regard this kind of talk as some sort of *explanation,* as scientists are accustomed to use the word. As such, it would obviously be ludicrous. We no longer believe in God as an Atlas —*nous n'avons pas besoin de cette hypothèse.* But it is nevertheless true to say that, as Hume saw, without a *blik* there can be no explanation; for it is by our *bliks* that we decide what is and what is not an explanation. Suppose we believed that everything that happened, happened by pure chance. This would not of course be an assertion; for it is compatible with anything happening or not happening, and so, incidentally, is its contradictory. But if we had this belief, we should not be able to explain or predict or plan anything. Thus, although we should not be *asserting* anything different from those of a more normal belief, there would be a great difference between us; and this is the sort of difference that there is between those who really believe in God and those who really disbelieve in him.

The word 'really' is important, and may excite suspicion. I put it in, because when people have had a good Christian upbringing, as have most of those who now profess not to believe in any sort of religion, it is very hard to discover what they really believe. The reason why they find it so easy to think that they are not religious, is that they have never got into the frame of mind of one who suffers from the doubts to which religion is the answer. Not for them the terrors of the primitive jungle. Having abandoned some of the more picturesque fringes of religion, they think that they have abandoned the whole thing—whereas in fact they still have got, and could not live

without, a religion of a comfortably substantial, albeit highly sophisticated, kind, which differs from that of many 'religious people' in little more than this, that 'religious people' like to sing Psalms about theirs—a very natural and proper thing to do. But nevertheless there may be a big difference lying behind—the difference between two people who, though side by side, are walking in different directions. I do not know in what direction Flew is walking; perhaps he does not know either. But we have had some examples recently of various ways in which one can walk away from Christianity, and there are any number of possibilities. After all, man has not changed biologically since primitive times; it is his religion that has changed, and it can easily change again. And if you do not think that such changes make a difference, get acquainted with some Sikhs and some Mussulmans of the same Punjabi stock; you will find them quite different sorts of people.

There is an important difference between Flew's parable and my own which we have not yet noticed. The explorers do not *mind* about their garden; they discuss it with interest, but not with concern. But my lunatic, poor fellow, minds about dons; and I mind about the steering of my car; it often has people in it that I care for. It is because I mind very much about what goes on in the garden in which I find myself, that I am unable to share the explorers' detachment.

Balliol College
OXFORD

C

BASIL MITCHELL

Flew's article is searching and perceptive, but there is, I think, something odd about his conduct of the theologian's case. The theologian surely would not deny that the fact of pain counts against the assertion that God loves men. This very incompatibility generates the most intractable of theological problems—the problem of evil. So the theologian *does* recognize the fact of pain as counting against Christian doctrine. But it is true that he will not allow it—or anything—to count decisively against it; for he is committed by his faith to trust in God. His attitude is not that of the detached observer, but of the believer.

Perhaps this can be brought out by yet another parable. In time of war in an occupied country, a member of the resistance meets one night a stranger who deeply impresses him. They spend that night together in conversation. The Stranger tells the partisan that he himself is on the side of the resistance—indeed that he is in command of it, and urges the partisan to have faith in him no matter what happens. The partisan is utterly convinced at that meeting of the Stranger's sincerity and constancy and undertakes to trust him.

They never meet in conditions of intimacy again. But sometimes the Stranger is seen helping members of the resistance, and the partisan is grateful and says to his friends, 'He is on our side.'

Sometimes he is seen in the uniform of the police handing over patriots to the occupying power. On these occasions his friends murmur against him: but the partisan still says, 'He is on our side.' He still believes that, in spite of appearances, the Stranger did not deceive him. Sometimes he asks the Stranger for help and receives it. He is then thankful. Sometimes he asks and does not receive it. Then he says, 'The Stranger knows best.' Sometimes his friends, in exasperation, say 'Well, what *would* he have to do for you to admit that you were wrong and that he is not on our side?' But the partisan refuses to answer. He will not consent to put the Stranger to the test. And sometimes his friends complain, 'Well, if *that's* what you mean by his being on

our side, the sooner he goes over to the other side the better.'

The partisan of the parable does not allow anything to count decisively against the proposition 'The Stranger is on our side.' This is because he has committed himself to trust the Stranger. But he of course recognizes that the Stranger's ambiguous behaviour *does* count against what he believes about him. It is precisely this situation which constitutes the trial of his faith.

When the partisan asks for help and doesn't get it, what can he do? He can (*a*) conclude that the stranger is not on our side; or (*b*) maintain that he is on our side, but that he has reasons for withholding help.

The first he will refuse to do. How long can he uphold the second position without its becoming just silly?

I don't think one can say in advance. It will depend on the nature of the impression created by the Stranger in the first place. It will depend, too, on the manner in which he takes the Stranger's behaviour. If he blandly dismisses it as of no consequence, as having no bearing upon his belief, it will be assumed that he is thoughtless or insane. And it quite obviously won't do for him to say easily, 'Oh, when used of the Stranger the phrase "is on our side" *means* ambiguous behaviour of this sort.' In that case he would be like the religious man who says blandly of a terrible disaster 'It is God's will.' No, he will only be regarded as sane and reasonable in his belief, if he experiences in himself the full force of the conflict.

It is here that my parable differs from Hare's. The partisan admits that many things may and do count against his belief: whereas Hare's lunatic who has a *blik* about dons doesn't admit that anything counts against his *blik*. Nothing *can* count against *bliks*. Also the partisan has a reason for having in the first instance committed himself, viz. the character of the Stranger; whereas the lunatic has no reason for his *blik* about dons—because, of course, you can't have reasons for *bliks*.

This means that I agree with Flew that theological utterances must be assertions. The partisan is making an assertion when he says, 'The Stranger is on our side.'

Do I want to say that the partisan's belief about the Stranger is, in any sense, an explanation? I think I do. It explains and makes sense of the Stranger's behaviour: it helps to explain also the resistance movement in the context of which he appears. In each case it differs from the interpretation which the others put upon the same facts.

'God loves men' resembles 'the Stranger is on our side' (and many other significant statements, e.g. historical ones) in not being conclusively falsifiable. They can both be treated in at least three different ways: (1) As provisional hypotheses to be discarded if experience tells against them; (2) As significant articles of faith; (3) As vacuous formulae (expressing, perhaps, a desire for reassurance) to which experience makes no difference and which make no difference to life.

The Christian, once he has committed himself, is precluded by his faith from taking up the first attitude: 'Thou shalt not tempt the Lord thy God.' He is in constant danger, as Flew has observed, of slipping into the third. But he need not; and, if he does, it is a failure in faith as well as in logic.

Keble College
OXFORD

D

ANTONY FLEW

It has been a good discussion: and I am glad to have helped to provoke it. But now—at least in *University*—it must come to an end: and the Editors of *University* have asked me to make some concluding remarks. Since it is impossible to deal with all the issues raised or to comment separately upon each contribution, I will concentrate on Mitchell and Hare, as representative of two very different kinds of response to the challenge made in 'Theology and Falsification.'

The challenge, it will be remembered, ran like this. Some theological utterances seem to, and are intended to, provide explanations or express assertions. Now an assertion, to be an assertion at all, must claim that things stand thus and thus; *and not otherwise*. Similarly an explanation, to be an explanation at all, must explain why this particular thing occurs; *and not something else*. Those last clauses are crucial. And yet sophisticated religious people—or so it seemed to me—are apt to overlook this, and tend to refuse to allow, not merely that anything actually does occur, but that anything conceivably could occur, which would count against their theological assertions and explanations. But in so far as they do this their supposed explanations are actually bogus, and their seeming assertions are really vacuous.

Mitchell's response to this challenge is admirably direct, straightforward, and understanding. He agrees 'that theological utterances must be assertions.' He agrees that if they are to be assertions, there must be something that would count against their truth. He agrees, too, that believers are in constant danger of transforming their would-be assertions into 'vacuous formulae.' But he takes me to task for an oddity in my 'conduct of the theologian's case. The theologian surely would not deny that the fact of pain counts against the assertion that God loves men. This very incompatibility generates the most intractable of theological problems, the problem of evil.' I think he is right. I should have made a distinc-

Mitchell

tion between two very different ways of dealing with what looks like evidence against the love of God: the way I stressed was the expedient of qualifying the original assertion; the way the theologian usually takes, at first, is to admit that it looks bad but to insist that there is—there must be—some explanation which will show that, in spite of appearances, there really is a God who loves us. His difficulty, it seems to me, is that he has given God attributes which rule out all possible saving explanations. In Mitchell's parable of the Stranger it is easy for the believer to find plausible excuses for ambiguous behaviour: for the Stranger is a man. But suppose the Stranger is God. We cannot say that he would like to help but cannot: God is omnipotent. We cannot say that he would help if he only knew: God is omniscient. We cannot say that he is not responsible for the wickedness of others: God creates those others. Indeed an omnipotent, omniscient God must be an accessory before (and during) the fact to every human misdeed; as well as being responsible for every non-moral defect in the universe. So, though I entirely concede that Mitchell was absolutely right to insist against me that the theologian's first move is to look for an *explanation,* I still think that in the end, if relentlessly pursued, he will have to resort to the avoiding action of *qualification.* And there lies the danger of that death by a thousand qualifications, which would, I agree, constitute 'a failure in faith as well as in logic.'

Hare's approach is fresh and bold. He confesses that 'on the ground marked out by Flew, he seems to me to be completely victorious.' He therefore introduces the concept of *blik.* But while I think that there is room for some such concept in philosophy, and that philosophers should be grateful to Hare for his invention, I nevertheless want to insist that any attempt to analyse Christian religious utterances as expressions or affirmations of a *blik* rather than as (at least would-be) assertions about the cosmos is fundamentally misguided. *First,* because thus interpreted they would be entirely unorthodox. If Hare's religion really is a *blik,* involving no cosmological assertions about the nature and activities of a supposed personal creator, then surely he is not a Christian at all? *Second,* because thus interpreted, they could scarcely do the job they do. If they were not even intended as assertions then many religious activities would become fraudulent, or merely silly. If 'You ought *because* it is God's will' asserts no more than 'You ought,' then the person who prefers the former phraseology is not really giving a reason, but a fraudulent substitute for one, a dialectical dud cheque. If 'My soul must be immortal *because* God loves his children, etc.' asserts no more than 'My soul must be immortal,' then the man who reassures himself with theological arguments for immortality is being as silly as the man who tries to clear his overdraft by writing his bank a cheque on the same account. (Of course neither of these utterances would be distinctively Christian: but this discussion never pretended to be so confined.) Religious utterances may indeed express false or even bogus assertions: but I simply do not believe that they are not both intended and interpreted to be or at any rate to presuppose assertions, at least in the context of religious practice; whatever shifts may be demanded, in another context, by the exigencies of theological apologetic.

One final suggestion. The philosophers of religion might well draw upon George Orwell's last appalling nightmare *1984* for the concept of *doublethink.* 'Doublethink means the power of holding two contradictory beliefs simultaneously, and accepting both of them. The party intellectual knows that he is playing tricks with reality, but by the exercise of *doublethink* he also satisfies himself that reality is not violated' (*1984,* p. 220). Perhaps religious intellectuals too are sometimes driven to doublethink in order to retain their faith in a loving God in face of the reality of a heartless and indifferent world. But of this more another time, perhaps.

University College of North Staffordshire
ENGLAND

I. M. CROMBIE [5]

There are some who hold that religious statements cannot be fully meaningful, on the ground that those who use them allow nothing to count decisively against them, treat them, that is, as incapable of falsification. This paper is an attempted answer to this view; and in composing it I have had particularly in mind an article by Antony Flew (A above), and an unpublished paper read by A. M. Quinton to the Aquinas Society of Oxford. I shall offer only a very short, and doubtless tendentious, summary of my opponents' views.

Briefly, then, it is contended that there are utterances made from time to time by Christians and others, which are said by those who make them to be statements, but which are thought by our opponents to lack some of the properties which anything must have before it deserves to be called a statement. 'There is a God,' 'God loves us as a father loves his children,' 'He shall come again with glory . . .' are examples of such utterances. *Prima facie* such utterances are neither exhortations, nor questions, nor expressions of wishes; *prima facie* they appear to assert the actuality of some state of affairs; and yet (and this is the objection) they are allowed to be compatible with any and every state of af-

fairs. If they are compatible with any and every state of affairs, they cannot mark out some one state of affairs (or group of states of affairs); and if they do not mark out some one state of affairs, how can they be statements? In the case of any ordinary statement, such as 'It is raining,' there is at least one situation (the absence of falling water) which is held to be incompatible with the statement, and it is the incompatibility of the situation with the statement which gives the statement its meaning. If, then, religious 'statements' are compatible with anything and everything, how can they be statements? How can the honest inquirer find out what they mean, if nobody will tell him what they are incompatible with? Are they not much more like such exhortations as 'Keep smiling,' whose confessed purpose is to go on being in point whatever occurs? Furthermore, is it not true that they only appear to be statements to those of us who use them, because we deceive ourselves by a sort of conjuring trick, oscillating backwards and forwards between a literal interpretation of what we say when we say it, and a scornful rejection of such anthropomorphism when anybody challenges us? When we *say:* 'He shall come again with glory. . . ,' do we not picture real angels sitting on real clouds; when asked whether we really mean the clouds, we hedge; offer perhaps another picture, which again we refuse to take literally; and so on indefinitely. Whatever symbolism we offer, we always insist that only a crude man would take it literally, and yet we never offer him anything but symbolism; deceived by our imagery into supposing that we have something in mind, in fact there is nothing on which we are prepared to take our stand.

This is the position I am to try to criticize. It is, I think, less novel than its clothes; but none the less it is important. I turn to criticism.

Let us begin by dismissing from our

---

[5] This paper was composed to be read to a non-philosophical audience. In composing it I have also filched shamelessly (and shamefully no doubt distorted) some unpublished utterances of Dr. A. M. Farrer's.

inquiry the troublesome statement 'There is a God' or 'God exists.' As every student of logic knows, all statements asserting the existence of something offer difficulties of their own, with which we need not complicate our embarrassment.

That being dismissed, I shall want to say of statements about God that they consist of two parts. Call them, if you like, subject and predicate. Whatever you call them, there is that which is said, and that which it is said about—namely God. It is important to make this distinction, for different problems arise about the different parts. As a first approximation towards isolating the difference, we may notice that the predicate is normally composed of ordinary words, put to unordinary uses, whereas the subject-word is 'God,' which has no other use. In the expression 'God loves us,' the word 'God' is playing, so to speak, on its Home Ground, the phrase 'loves us' is playing Away. Now there is one set of questions which deal with the problem of why we say, and what we mean by saying, that God loves us, rather than hates us, and there is another set of questions concerned with the problem of what it is that this statement is being made about.

To approach the matter from an angle which seems to me to afford a good view of it, I shall make a few observations about the epistemological nature of religious belief. Let me caution the reader that, in doing so, I am not attempting to describe how religious belief in fact arises.

Theoretically, then, not in how it arises, but in its logical structure, religious belief has two parents; and it also has a nurse. Its logical mother is what one might call *undifferentiated theism,* its logical father is particular events or occasions interpreted as theophanic, and the extra-parental nurture is provided by religious activity.

A word, first, about the logical mother. It is in fact the case that there are elements in our experience which lead people to a certain sort of belief, which we call a belief in God. (We could, if we wished, call it rather an attitude than a belief, so long as we were careful not to call it an attitude to life; for it is of the essence of the attitude to hold that nothing whatever in life may be identified with that towards which it is taken up.) Among the elements in experience which provoke this belief or attitude, perhaps the most powerful is what I shall call a sense of contingency. Others are moral experience, and the beauty and order of nature. Others may be actual abnormal experience of the type called religious or mystical. There are those to whom conscience appears in the form of an unconditional demand; to whom the obligation to one's neighbour seems to be something imposed on him and on me by a third party who is set over us both. There are those to whom the beauty and order of nature appears as the intrusion into nature of a realm of beauty and order beyond it. There are those who believe themselves or others to be enriched by moments of direct access to the divine. Now there are two things that must be said about these various theistic interpretations of our experience. The first is that those who so interpret need not be so inexpert in logic as to suppose that there is anything of the nature of a deductive or inductive argument which leads from a premiss asserting the existence of the area of experience in question to a conclusion expressing belief in God. Nobody who takes seriously the so-called moral argument need suppose that the *prima facie* authority of conscience cannot be naturalistically explained. He can quite well acknowledge that the imperativeness which so impresses him could be a mere reflection of his jealousy of his father, or a vestigial survival of tribal taboo. The mystic can quite well acknowledge that there is nothing which logically forbids the interpretation of the experience which he enjoys in terms of the condition of his liver or the rate of his respirations. If, being acquainted with the alternative explanations, he persists in rejecting them, it need not be, though of course it sometimes is, because he is seized with a fallacious refutation of their validity. All that is necessary is that he should be honestly convinced that, in interpreting them, as he does, theistically, he is in some sense facing them more honestly, bringing out more of what they contain or involve than could be done by interpreting them in any other way. The one interpretation is preferred to the other, not because the latter is thought to be refutable on paper, but because it is judged to be unconvincing in the light of familiarity with the facts. There is a partial parallel to this in historical judgment. Where you and I differ in our interpretation of a series of events, there is nothing outside the events in question which can over-rule either of us, so that each man must accept the interpretation which seems, on fair and critical scrutiny, the most convincing to him. The parallel is only partial, however, for in historical (and literary) interpretation there is something which to some extent controls one's interpretation, and that is one's general knowledge of human nature; and in metaphysical interpretation there is nothing analogous to this. That, then, is my first comment on theistic interpretations; for all that these journeys of the mind are often recorded in quasi-argumentative form, they are not in any ordinary sense arguments, and their validity cannot be assessed by asking whether they conform to the laws either of logic or of scientific method. My second comment upon them is, that, in stating them, we find ourselves saying things which we cannot literally mean. Thus the man of conscience uses some such concept as the juridical concept of authority, and locates his authority outside nature; the man of beauty and order speaks of an intrusion from another realm; the mystic speaks of experiencing God. In every case such language lays the user open to devastating criticism, to which he can only retort by pleading that such language, while it is not to be taken strictly, seems to him to be the natural language to use.

To bring these points into a somewhat stronger light, let me say something about the sense of contingency, the conviction which people have, it may be in blinding moments, or it may be in a permanent disposition of a man's mind, that we, and the whole world in which we live, derive our being from something outside us. The first thing I want to say about this is that such a conviction is to no extent like the conclusion of an argument; the sense of dependence feels not at all like being persuaded by arguments, but like seeing, as it were, through a gap in the rolling mists of argument, which alone, one feels, could conceal the obvious truth. One is not *persuaded* to believe that one is contingent; rather one feels that it is only by persuasion that one could ever believe anything else. The second thing I want to say about this conviction of contingency is that in expressing it, as Quinton has admirably shewn, we turn the word 'contingent' to work which is not its normal employment, and which it cannot properly do.

For the distinction between necessity and contingency is not a distinction between different sorts of entities, but between different sorts of statement. A necessary statement is one whose denial involves a breach of the laws of logic, and a contingent statement is one in which this is not the case. (I do not, of course, assert that this is the only way in which these terms have been used in the history of philosophy; but I do assert that this is the only use of them which does not give rise to impossible difficulties. I have no space to demonstrate this here; and indeed I do not think that it is any longer in need of demonstration.) But in this, the only coherent, sense of 'contingent,' the existence of the world may be contingent fact, but so unfortunately is that of God. For *all* existential statements are contingent; that is to say, it is never true that we can involve ourselves in a breach of the laws of logic by merely denying of something that it exists. We cannot therefore in this sense contrast the contingent existence of the world with the necessary existence of God.

It follows that if a man persists in speaking of the contingency of the world, he must be using the term in a new or transferred sense. It must be that he is borrowing [6] a word from the logician and putting it to work which it cannot properly do. Why does he do this, and how can he make clear what precisely this new use is? For it is no good saying that when we are talking about God we do not use words in their ordinary senses unless we are prepared to say in what senses it is that we do use them. And yet how can we explain to the honest inquirer what is the new sense in which the word 'contingent' is being used when we use it of the world? For if it is proper to use it, in this sense, of everything with which we are acquainted, and improper to use it only of God, with whom we are not acquainted, how can the new use be learnt? For we normally learn the correct use of a word by noticing the differences between the situations in which it may be applied and those in which it may not; but the word 'contingent' is applicable in all the situations in which we ever find ourselves. If I said that everything but God was flexible, not of course

---

[6] It might be argued that, historically, the borrowing was the other way round. To decide that we should have to decide where the frontier between logic and metaphysics really comes in the work of those whose doctrine on the relationship between these disciplines is unsatisfactory.

in the ordinary sense, but in some other, how could you discover what the new sense was?

The answer must be that when we speak of the world as contingent, dependent, an effect or product, and so contrast it with a necessary, self-existent being, a first cause or a creator, we say something which on analysis will not do at all (for devastating criticisms can be brought against all these formulations), but which seems to us to be the fittest sort of language for our purpose. Why we find such language appropriate, and how, therefore, it is to be interpreted, is not at all an easy question; that it does in some way, it may be in some logically anomalous way, convey the meaning of those who use it, seems however to be an evident fact. How it is that the trick is worked, how it is that this sort of distortion of language enables believers to give expression to their beliefs, this it is the true business of the natural theologian to discuss. Farrer, for example, in *Finite and Infinite,* has done much to elucidate what it is that one is striving to express when one speaks of the contingency of the world, and so to enlighten the honest inquirer who wishes to know how the word 'contingent' is here being used.

What I have said about contingency and necessity applies also to obligation and its transcendent ground (or goodness and its transcendent goal), to design and its transcendent designer, to religious experience and its transcendent object. In all these cases we use language which on analysis will not do, but which seems to us to be appropriate for the expression of our beliefs; and in all these cases the question can be, and is, discussed, why such language is chosen, and how it is to be understood.

That then is the logical mother of religious belief; call her natural theism, or what you will, she is a response, not precisely logical, and yet in no sense emotional or evaluative, to certain elements in our experience, whose characteristic is that they induce us, not to make straightforward statements about the world, but to strain and distort our media of communication in order to express what we make of them. In herself she is an honest woman; and if she is sometimes bedizened in logical trappings, and put out on the streets as an inductive argument, the fault is hardly hers. Her function is, not to prove to us that God exists, but to provide us with a 'meaning' for the word 'God.' Without her we should not know whither statements concerning the word were to be referred; the subject in theological utterances would be unattached. All that we should know of them is that they were not to be referred to anything with which we are or could hope to be acquainted; that, and also that they were to be understood in terms of whatever it is that people suppose themselves to be doing when they build churches and kneel down in them. And that is not entirely satisfactory; for while there is much to be said in practice for advising the honest inquirer into the reference of the word 'God' to pursue his inquiry by familiarizing himself with the concrete activity of religion, it remains true that the range and variety of possible delusions which could induce such behaviour is theoretically boundless, and, as visitors to the Pacific coast of the United States can testify, in practice very large.

The logical father of religious belief, that which might bring us on from the condition of merely possessing the category of the divine, into the condition of active belief in God, this consists, in Christianity (and if there is nothing analogous in other religions, so much the worse for them), in the interpretation of certain objects or events as a manifestation of the divine. It is, in other words, because we find, that, in thinking of certain events in terms of the category of the divine, we can give what seems to us the most convincing account of them, that we can assure ourselves that the notion of God is not just an empty aspiration. Without the notion of God we could interpret nothing as divine, and without concrete events which we felt impelled to interpret as divine we could not know that the notion of divinity had any application to reality. Why it is that as Christians we find ourselves impelled to interpret the history of Israel, the life and death of Christ, and the experience of his Church as relevatory of God, I shall not here attempt to say; it is an oft-told tale, and I shall content myself with saying that we can hardly expect to feel such an impulsion so long as our knowledge of these matters is superficial and altogether from without. Whyever we feel such an impulsion, it is not, of course, a logical impulsion; that is, we may resist it (or fail to feel it) without thereby contravening the laws of logic, or the rules of any pragmatically accredited inductive procedure. On the anthropological level the history of Israel, Old and New, is certainly the history of a religious development from its tribal origins. We may decide, or we may not, that it is something more, something beyond the wit of man to invent, something which seems to us to be a real and coherent communication from a real and coherent, though superhuman, mind. We may decide, or we may not; neither decision breaks the rules, for in such a unique matter there are no rules to conform to or to break. The judgment is our own; and in the language of the New Testament it judges us; that is, it reveals what, up to the moment of our decision, the Spirit of God has done in us—but that, of course, is to argue in a circle.

Belief, thus begotten, is nurtured by the practice of the Christian life—by the conviction so aroused (or, of course, not aroused; but then it is starvation and not nurture) that the Christian warfare is a real warfare. Something will have to be said about this later on, but for the moment I propose to dismiss it, and to return to the consideration of the significance of religious utterances in the light of the dual parentage of religious belief.

I have argued that unless certain things seem to us to be signs of divine activity, then we may hope that there is a God, but we cannot properly believe that there is. It follows from this that religious belief must properly involve treating something as revelatory of God; and that is to say that it must involve an element of authority (for to treat something as divine revelation is to invest it with authority). That what we say about God is said on authority (and, in particular, on the authority of Christ) is of the first importance in considering the significance of these statements. In what way this is so, I shall hope to make clear as we go along.

If we remember that our statements about God rest on the authority of Christ, whom we call his Word, we can see what seems to me the essential clue to the interpretation of the logical nature of such utterances, and that is, in a word, the notion of parable. To elucidate what I mean by 'parable' (for I am using the word in an extended sense) let us consider Christ's action on Palm Sunday, when he rode into Jerusalem on an ass. This action was an act of teaching. For it had been said to Jerusalem that her king would come to her riding upon an ass. Whoever, therefore, deliberately chose this method of entry, was saying in effect: 'What you are about to witness (namely my Passion, Death and Resurrection) is the coming of the Messianic King to claim his kingdom.' The prophecy of Messiah's kingdom was to be interpreted, not in the ordinary sense, but in the sense of the royal kingship of the Crucified. To interpret in this way is to teach by violent paradox, indeed, but none the less it is to teach. Part of the

lesson is that it is only the kings of the Gentiles that lord it over their subjects; if any man will be a king in Israel (God's chosen people), he must humble himself as a servant; part of it is that the Crucifixion is to be seen as Messianic, that is as God's salvation of his chosen people. Now the logical structure which is involved here is something like this: —You are told a story (Behold, thy king cometh, meek and lowly, and riding upon an ass). You will not know just what the reality to which the story refers will be like until it happens. If you take the story at its face value (an ordinary, though humble, king, bringing an ordinary political salvation), you will get it all wrong. If you bring to bear upon its interpretation all that the Law and the Prophets have taught you about God's purposes for his people, though you will still not know just what it will be like until it happens, none the less you will not go wrong by believing it; for then you will know that Christ ought to have suffered these things, and to enter into his glory, and so you will learn what the story has to tell you of God's purposes for man, and something therefore, indirectly, of God. If you remember what Isaiah says about humility and sacrifice, you will see that what is being forecast is that God's purposes will be accomplished by a man who fulfils the Law and the Prophets in humble obedience.

This story is that one that can be fairly fully interpreted. There are others that cannot. There is, for example, Hosea's parable in which he likens himself to God, and Israel to his unfaithful wife, and expresses his grief at his wife's unfaithfulness. If, now, you ask for this to be fully interpreted, if you ask Hosea to tell you what he supposes it is like for the Holy One of Israel, of whom no similitude may be made, to be grieved, demanding to know, not what would happen in such a case to the unfaithful sinner who had provoked the divine wrath, but what was the condition of the divine mind in itself, then no doubt he would have regarded the very question as blasphemous. As an inspired prophet, he felt himself entitled to say that God was grieved, without presuming to imagine what such a situation was like, other than in its effects. What he said was said on authority; it was not his own invention, and therefore he could rely on its truth, without supposing himself to understand its full meaning. In so far as Hosea's parable is 'interpreted,' the interpretation is confined to identifying the *dramatis personae* (Hosea=God, his wife=Israel). It is noteworthy that the interpretation which is sometimes given to the parables of the New Testament is usually of the same sketchy kind (The reapers are the angels). In Plato's famous parable of prisoners in a cave, it is quite possible to describe the situation which the parable seeks to illuminate. One can describe how a man can begin by being content to establish rough laws concerning what follows what in nature, how he may proceed from such a condition to desire explanations of the regularities which are forced on his attention, rising thus to more abstract and mathematical generalizations, and then, through the study of mathematics, to completely abstract speculation. One cannot similarly describe the situation which the parable of the Prodigal Son is intended to illustrate (or rather one can only describe the human end of it); and no attempt is ever made to do so.

I make no apology for these paragraphs about the Bible; after all the Bible is the source of Christian belief, and it cannot but illuminate the logical nature of the latter to consider the communicational methods of the former. But we must turn back to more general considerations. It is, then, characteristic of a parable that the words which are used in it are used in their ordinary senses. Elsewhere this is not always so. If you speak of the

virtues of a certain sort of car, the word 'virtue,' being applied to a car, comes to mean something different from what it means in application to human beings. If you speak of hot temper, the word 'hot' does not mean what it means in the ordinary way. Now many people suppose that something of the latter sort is happening in religious utterances. When God is said to be jealous, or active in history, it is felt that the word 'jealous' or 'active' must be being used here in a transferred sense. But if it is being used in a transferred sense, some means or other must be supplied whereby the new sense can be taken. The activity of God is presumably not like the activity of men (it does not make him hot or tired); to say then that God is active must involve modifying the meaning of the word. But, if the word is undergoing modification, it is essential that we should know in what direction. In the case of ordinary transfers, how do we know what sort of modification is involved? This is a large question, but roughly, I think, the answer is, in two ways. Firstly there is normally a certain appropriateness, like the appropriateness of 'hot' in 'hot temper'; and secondly we can notice the circumstances in which the word gets used and withheld in its transferred sense. If I hear the phrase 'Baroque music,' the meaning of the word 'Baroque' in its normal architectural employment may set me looking in a certain direction; and I can clinch the matter by asking for examples, 'Bach? Buxtehude? Beethoven?' But for either of these ways to be of any use to me, I must know something about *both* ends of the transfer. I must know something about Baroque architecture, *and* I must be able to run through musical styles in my head, to look for the musical analogue of Baroque features. If I cannot stumble on your meaning without assistance, I can still do so by eliciting from you that Bach and Buxtehude are, Handel and Mozart are not, examples of the sort of music you have in mind. This is informative to me if and only if I know something of Buxtehude and Bach, Handel and Mozart.

Now we all know what it is like for a man to be active. We can quote examples, decide correctly, and so forth. But what about divine activity? Surely we cannot have it both ways. Either God can be moderately like a man, so that the word 'active,' used of him, can set us looking in the right direction; or he can be quite unlike a man, in which case it cannot. Nor can we be helped by the giving of examples, unless it is legitimate to point to examples of divine activity —to say, 'Now here God is being active, but not there.' This constitutes the force of Flew's demand that we should tell him how statements about God can be falsified. In essence Flew is saying: 'When you speak about God, the words which occur in the predicate part of your statements are not being used in the ordinary sense; you make so great a difference between God and man, that I cannot even find that the words you use set me looking in anything that might perhaps be the right direction. You speak of God as being outside time; and when I think what I mean by "activity," I find that that word, as used about a timeless being, suggests to me nothing whatsoever. There is only one resort left; give me examples of when one of your statements is, and is not, applicable. If, as no doubt you will say, that is an unfair demand, since they are always applicable (e.g. God is always active, so that there are no cases of his inactivity to be pointed to), I will not insist on actual examples; make them up if you like. But do not point to *everything* and say, "*That* is what I mean"; for *everything* is not *that,* but this and this and this and many other mutual incompatibles; and black and white and red and green and kind and cruel and coal and ink and everything else together cannot possibly elucidate to me the meaning of a word.'

As I have said, the answer must be that when we speak about God, the words we use are intended in their ordinary sense (for we cannot make a transfer, failing familiarity with both ends of it), although we do not suppose that in their ordinary interpretation they can be strictly true of him. We do not even know how much of them applies. To some extent it may be possible to take a word like 'activity' and whittle away that in it which most obviously does not apply. It is, however, an exaggeration, at the least, to suppose that this process of whittling away leaves us in the end with a kernel about which we can say that we know that it does apply. A traditional procedure is to compose a scale on which inanimate matter is at the bottom, the characteristically human activities, such as thinking and personal relationship, at the top, and to suppose that the scale is pointing towards God; and so on this assumption the first thing to do is to pare away from the notion of human activity whatever in it is common to what stands below it on the scale—for example actual physical moving about. Taking the human residue, we try to decide what in it is positive, and what is negative, mere limitation. The tenuous ghost of a concept remaining we suppose to be the essential structure of activity (that structure which is common to running and thinking) and so to be realized also in divine activity. Perhaps this is how we imagine our language to be related to the divine realities about which we use it; but such ghostly and evacuated concepts are clearly too tenuous and elusive to be called the meanings of the words we use. To think of God thus is to think of him not in our own image, but in the rarefied ghost of our own image; and so we think of him in our own image, but do not suppose that in so thinking of him we begin to do him justice. What we do, then, is in essence to think of God in parables. The things we say about God are said on the authority of the words and acts of Christ, who spoke in human language, using parable; and so we too speak of God in parable—authoritative parable, authorized parable; knowing that the truth is not literally that which our parables represent, knowing therefore that now we see in a glass darkly, but trusting, because we trust the source of the parables, that in believing them and interpreting them in the light of each other, we shall not be misled, that we shall have such knowledge as we need to possess for the foundation of the religious life.

So far so good. But it is only the predicates of theological utterances which are parabolic; it is only in what is *said about* God that words are put to other than customary employment. When we say 'God is merciful,' it is 'merciful' that is in strange company—deprived of its usual escort of human sentiments. But the word 'God' only occurs in statements about God. Our grasp of this word, therefore, cannot be derived from our grasp of it in ordinary human contexts, for it is not used in such contexts. How then is our grasp of it to be accounted for? In other words, if I have given some account of how, and in what sense, we understand the meaning of the things we say about God, I have still to give some account of how, and in what sense, we know what it is that we are saying them about.

In thus turning back from the predicate to the subject of religious utterances, we are turning from revealed theology to natural theology, from the logical father to the logical mother of religious belief. And the answer to the question: 'What grasp have we of the meaning of the word "God"?' must be dealt with along the following lines. Revelation is important to the believer not for what it is in itself (the biography of a Jew, and the history of his forerunners and followers), nor because it is revelation of nothing in particular, but because it is revelation of God. In treating it as something important, something commanding our allegiance, we are bringing to bear upon it the category of the transcendent, of the divine. Of the nature of that category I have already spoken. In other words, there must exist within a man's mind the contrast between the contingent and the necessary, the derivative and the underivative, the finite and the infinite, the perfect and the imperfect, if anything is to be for him a revelation of God. Given that contrast, we are given also that to which the parables or stories are referred. What is thus given is certainly not knowledge of the object to which they apply; it is something much more like a direction. We do not, that is, know to what to refer our parables; we know merely that we are to refer them out of experience, and out of it *in which direction*. The expression 'God' is to refer to that object, whatever it is, and if there be one, which is such that the knowledge of it would be to us knowledge of the unfamiliar term in the contrast between finite and infinite.

Statements about God, then, are in effect parables, which are referred, by means of the proper name 'God,' out of our experience in a certain direction. We may, if we like, by the process of whittling away, which I have mentioned, try to tell ourselves what part of the meaning of our statements applies reasonably well, what part outrageously badly; but the fact remains that, in one important sense, when we speak about God, we do not know what we mean (that is, we do not know what that which we are talking about is like), and do not need to know, because we accept the images, which we employ, on authority. Because our concern with God is religious and not speculative (it is contemplative in part, but that is another matter), because our need is, not to know what God is like, but to enter into relation with him, the authorized images serve our purpose. They belong to a type of discourse—parable—with which we are familiar, and therefore they have communication value, although in a sense they lack descriptive value.

If this is so, how do we stand with regard to verification and falsification? Must we, to preserve our claim to be making assertions, be prepared to say what would count against them? Let us see how far we can do so. Does anything count against the assertion that God is merciful? Yes, suffering. Does anything count decisively against it? No, we reply, because it is true. Could anything count decisively against it? Yes, suffering which was utterly, eternally and irredeemably pointless. Can we then design a crucial experiment? No, because we can never see all of the picture. Two things at least are hidden from us; what goes on in the recesses of the personality of the sufferer, and what shall happen hereafter.

Well, then, the statement that God is merciful is not testable; it is compatible with any and every tract of experience which we are in fact capable of witnessing. It cannot be verified; does this matter?

To answer this, we must make up our minds why the demand for verification or falsification is legitimate. On this large matter I shall be summary and dogmatic, as follows. (1) The demand that a statement of fact should be verifiable is a conflation of two demands (2) The *first* point is that all statements of fact must be verifiable in the sense that there must not exist a *rule of language* which precludes testing the statement. That is to say, the way the statement is to be taken must not be such that to try to test it is to show that you do not understand it. If I say that it is wrong to kill, and you challenge my statement and adduce as evidence against it that thugs and headhunters do so out of religious duty, then you have not understood my statement. My statement was not a statement of fact, but a moral judgment, and your statement that it should be tested by anthropological investigations shows that you did not understand it. But so long as there exists no *logical* (or we might say *interpretational*) ban on looking around for verification, the existence of a *factual* ban on verification does not matter. 'Caesar had mutton before he crossed the Rubicon' cannot in fact be tested, but by trying to devise ways of testing it you do not show that you have not understood it; you are merely wasting your time. (3) The *second* point is that, *for me, fully* to understand a statement, *I* must know what a test of it would be like. If I have no idea how to test whether somebody had mutton, then I do no know what 'having mutton' means. This stipulation is concerned, not with the logical nature of the expression, but with its communication value for me. (4) There are then two stipulations, and they are different. The first is a logical stipulation, and it is to the effect that nothing can be a statement of fact if it is untestable in the sense that the notion of testing it is precluded by correctly interpreting it. The second is a communicational stipulation, and it is to the effect that nobody can fully understand a statement, unless he has a fair idea how a situation about which it was true would differ from a situation about which it was false.

Now with regard to these two stipulations, how do religious utterances fare? With regard to the first, there is no language rule implicit in a correct understanding of them which precludes putting them to the test (there may be a rule of faith, but that is another matter). If a man says, 'How can God be loving, and allow pain?' he does *not* show that he has misunderstood the statement that God is loving. There *is* a *prima facie* incompatibility between the love of God, and pain and suffering. The Christian maintains that it is *prima facie* only; others maintain that it is not. They may argue about it, and the issue cannot be decided; but it cannot be decided, not because (as in the case of e.g. moral or mathematical judgments) the appeal to facts is *logically* the wrong way of trying to decide the issue, and shows that you have not understood the judgment; *but* because, since our experience is limited in the way it is, we cannot get into position to decide it, any more than we can get into position to decide what Julius Caesar had for breakfast before he crossed the Rubicon. For the Christian the operation of getting into position to decide it is called dying; and, though we can all do that, we cannot return to report what we find. By this test, then, religious utterances can be called statements of fact; that is their *logical* classification.

With regard to the second stipulation, the case is a little complicated, for here we are concerned with communication value, and there are the two levels, the one on which we remain within the parable, and the other on which we try to step outside it. Now, on the first level we know well enough how to test a statement like 'God loves us'; it is, for example, like testing 'My father loves me.' In fact, of course, since with parents and schoolmasters severity is notoriously a way of displaying affection, the decisive testing of such a statement is not easy; but there is a point beyond which it is foolish to continue to have doubts. Now, within the parable, we are supposing 'God loves us' to be a statement like 'My father loves me,' 'God' to be a subject similar to 'My father,' 'God loves us' being thus related to 'My father loves me' as the latter is related to 'Aristotle's father loved him.' We do not suppose that we can actually test 'God loves us,' for reasons already given (any more than we can test the one about Aristotle); but the communication

value of the statement whose subject is 'God' is derived from the communication value of the same statement with a different proper name as subject. If we try to step outside the parable, then we must admit that we do not know what the situation about which our parable is being told is like; we should only know if we could know God, and know even as also we have been known; see, that is, the unfolding of the divine purposes in their entirety. Such ignorance is what we ought to expect. We do not know how what we call the divine wrath differs from the divine mercy (because we do not know how they respectively resemble human wrath and mercy); but we do know how what *we mean* when we talk about the wrath of God differs from what *we mean* when we talk about his mercy, because then we are within the parable, talking within the framework of admitted ignorance, in language which we accept because we trust its source. We know what is meant *in* the parable, when the father of the Prodigal sees him coming a great way off and runs to meet him, and we can therefore think in terms of this image. We know that we are here promised that whenever we come to ourselves and return to God, he will come to meet us. This is enough to encourage us to return, and to make us alert to catch the signs of the divine response; but it does not lead us to presume to an understanding of the mind and heart of God. In talking we remain within the parable, and so our statements communicate; we do not know how the parable applies, but we believe that it does apply, and that we shall one day see how. (Some even believe, perhaps rightly, that in our earthly condition we may by direct illumination of our minds be enabled to know progressively more about the realities to which our parables apply, and in consequence about the manner of their application.)

Much of what I have said agrees very

closely with what the atheist says about religious belief, except that I have tried to make it sound better. The atheist alleges that the religious man supposes himself to know what he means by his statements only because, until challenged, he interprets them anthropomorphically; when challenged, however, he retreats rapidly backwards towards complete agnosticism. I agree with this, with two provisos. The first is that the religious man does not suppose himself to know what he means by his statements (for what religious man supposes himself to be the Holy Ghost?); he knows what his statements mean within the parable, and believes that they are the right statements to use. (Theology is not a science; it is a sort of art of enlightened ignorance.) The second proviso is that the agnosticism is not complete; for the Christian, under attack, falls back not in any direction, but in one direction; he falls back upon the person of Christ, and the concrete realities of the Christian life.

Let us consider this for a moment with regard to the divine love. I could be attacked in this sort of way:—'You have contended,' my opponent might argue, 'that when we say that God loves us the communication value of the statement is determined by the communication value of a similar statement about a human subject; and that we know the statement to be the right statement, but cannot know *how* it is the right statement, that is, what the divine love is like. But this will not do. Loving is an activity with two poles, the lover and the loved. We may not know the lover, in the case of God, but we *are,* and therefore *must know,* the loved. Now, to say that the image or parable of human love is the right image to use about God must imply that there is some similarity or analogy between human and divine love. Father's love may be superficially very unlike mother's, but, unless there is some similarity of structure between them, we cannot use the same word of both. But we cannot believe that there is any similarity between the love of God and human love, unless we can detect some similarity between being loved by God and being loved by man. But if being loved by God is what we experience all the time, then it is not like being loved by man; it is like being let down right and left. And in the face of so great a discrepancy, we cannot believe that God loves us, if that is supposed to be in any sense a statement of sober fact.'

I cannot attempt to answer this objection; it involves the whole problem of religion. But there is something I want to say about it, which is that the Christian does not attempt to evade it either by helter-skelter flight, or by impudent bluff. He has his prepared positions on to which he retreats; and he knows that if these positions are taken, then he must surrender. He does not believe that they can be taken, but that is another matter. There are three main fortresses behind which he goes. For, *first,* he looks for the resurrection of the dead, and the life of the world to come; he believes, that is, that we do not see all of the picture, and that the parts which we do not see are precisely the parts which determine the design of the whole. He admits that if this hope be vain then we are of all men the most miserable. *Second,* he claims that he sees in Christ the verification, and to some extent also the specification, of the divine love. That is to say, he finds in Christ not only convincing evidence of God's concern for us, but also what sort of love the divine love is, what sort of benefits God is concerned to give us. He sees that, on the New Testament scale of values, it is better for a man to lose the whole world if he can thereby save his soul (which means his relationship to God); and that for that hope it is reasonable to sacrifice all that he has, and to undergo the death of the body and the mortification of the spirit.

Third, he claims that in the religious life, ③ of others, if not as yet in his own, the divine love may be encountered, that the promise 'I will not fail thee nor forsake thee' is, if rightly understood, confirmed there. If, of course, this promise is interpreted as involving immunity from bodily suffering, it will be refuted; but no reader of the New Testament has any right so to interpret it. It is less glaringly, but as decisively, wrong to interpret it as involving immunity from spiritual suffering; for in the New Testament only the undergoing of death (which means the abdication of control over one's destiny) can be the beginning of life. What then does it promise? It promises that to the man who begins on the way of the Christian life, on the way that is of seeking life through death, of seeking relationship with God through the abdication of the self-sovereignty claimed by Adam, that to him the fight will be hard but not impossible, progress often indiscernible, but real, progress which is towards the paring away of self-hood, and which is therefore often given through defeat and humiliation, but a defeat and humiliation which are not final, which leave it possible to continue. This is the extra-parental nurture of religious belief of which I spoke earlier, and it is the third of the prepared positions on to which the Christian retreats, claiming that the image and reflection of the love of God may be seen not only hereafter, not only in Christ, but also, if dimly, in the concrete process of living the Christian life.

One final word. Religion has indeed its problems; but it is useless to consider them outside their religious context. Seen as a whole religion makes rough sense, though it does not make limpidity.

Wadham College
OXFORD

SIGMUND FREUD

The Psychological Basis of Religious Belief

Sigmund Freud (1856–1939) was one of the revolutionary thinkers of our times. His ideas on the underlying unconscious basis of thought, feeling, and behavior—originally developed out of the analysis of neurotic symptoms—have profoundly influenced contemporary thought in all the social sciences and humanities, including the study of religion.

CHAPTER III

In what does the peculiar value of religious ideas lie?

We have spoken of the hostility to civilization which is produced by the pressure that civilization exercises, the renunciations of instinct which it demands. If one imagines its prohibitions lifted—if, then, one may take any woman one pleases as a sexual object, if one may without hesitation kill one's rival for her love or anyone else who stands in one's way, if, too, one can carry off any of the other man's belongings without asking leave—how splendid, what a string of satisfactions one's life would be! True, one soon comes across the first difficulty: everyone else has exactly the same wishes as I have and will treat me with no more consideration than I treat him. And so

From Sigmund Freud, *The Future of an Illusion,* tr. by W. D. Robson-Scott (1961), Chs. III–VI, VIII–X. Reprinted by permission of Liveright, Publishers, New York, and The Hogarth Press Ltd.

in reality only one person could be made unrestrictedly happy by such a removal of the restrictions of civilization, and he would be a tyrant, a dictator, who had seized all the means to power. And even he would have every reason to wish that the others would observe at least one cultural commandment: 'thou shalt not kill.'

But how ungrateful, how short-sighted after all, to strive for the abolition of civilization! What would then remain would be a state of nature, and that would be far harder to bear. It is true that nature would not demand any restrictions of instinct from us, she would let us do as we liked; but she has her own particularly effective method of restricting us. She destroys us—coldly, cruelly, relentlessly, as it seems to us, and possibly through the very things that occasioned our satisfaction. It was precisely because of these dangers with which nature threatens us that we came together and created civilization, which is also, among other things, intended to make our communal life possible. For the principal task of civilization, its actual *raison d'être,* is to defend us against nature.

We all know that in many ways civilization does this fairly well already, and clearly as time goes on it will do it much better. But no one is under the illusion that nature has already been vanquished; and few dare hope that she will ever be entirely subjected to man. There are the elements, which seem to mock at all human control: the earth, which quakes and is torn apart and buries all human life and its works; water, which deluges and drowns everything in a turmoil; storms, which blow everything before them; there are diseases, which we have only recently recognized as attacks by other organisms; and finally there is the painful riddle of death, against which no medicine has yet been found, nor probably will be. With these forces nature rises up against us, majestic, cruel and inexorable; she brings to our mind once more our weakness and helplessness, which we thought to escape through the work of civilization. One of the few gratifying and exalting impressions which mankind can offer is when, in the face of an elemental catastrophe, it forgets the discordancies of its civilization and all its internal difficulties and animosities, and recalls the great common task of preserving itself against the superior power of nature.

For the individual, too, life is hard to bear, just as it is for mankind in general. The civilization in which he participates imposes some amount of privation on him, and other men bring him a measure of suffering, either in spite of the precepts of his civilization or because of its imperfections. To this are added the injuries which untamed nature—he calls it Fate—inflicts on him. One might suppose that this condition of things would result in a permanent state of anxious expectation in him and a severe injury to his natural narcissism. We know already how the individual reacts to the injuries which civilization and other men inflict on him: he develops a corresponding degree of resistance to the regulations of civilization and of hostility to it. But how does he defend himself against the superior powers of nature, of Fate, which threaten him as they threaten all the rest?

Civilization relieves him of this task; it performs it in the same way for all alike; and it is noteworthy that in this almost all civilizations act alike. Civilization does not call a halt in the task of defending man against nature, it merely pursues it by other means. The task is a manifold one. Man's self-regard, seriously menaced, calls for consolation; life and the universe must be robbed of their terors; moreover his curiosity, moved, it is true, by the strongest practical interest, demands an answer.

A great deal is already gained with the first step: the humanization of nature. Impersonal forces and destinies cannot be approached; they remain eternally remote. But if the elements have passions that rage as they do in our own souls, if death itself is not something spontaneous but the violent act of an evil Will, if everywhere in nature there are Beings around us of a kind that we know in our own society, then we can breathe freely, can feel at home in the uncanny and can deal by psychical means with our senseless anxiety. We are still defenceless, perhaps, but we are no longer helplessly paralysed; we can at least react. Perhaps, indeed, we are not even defenceless. We can apply the same methods against these violent supermen outside that we employ in our own society; we can try to adjure them, to appease them, to bribe them, and, by so influencing them, we may rob them of a part of their power. A replacement like this of natural science by psychology not only provides immediate relief, but also points the way to a further mastering of the situation.

For this situation is nothing new. It

has an infantile prototype, of which it is in fact only the continuation. For once before one has found oneself in a similar state of helplessness: as a small child, in relation to one's parents. One had reason to fear them, and especially one's father; and yet one was sure of his protection against the dangers one knew. Thus it was natural to assimilate the two situations. Here, too, wishing played its part, as it does in dream-life. The sleeper may be seized with a presentiment of death, which threatens to place him in the grave. But the dream-work knows how to select a condition that will turn even that dreaded event into a wish-fulfilment: the dreamer sees himself in an ancient Etruscan grave which he has climbed down into, happy to find his archaeological interests satisfied.[1] In the same way, a man makes the forces of nature not simply into persons with whom he can associate as he would with his equals—that would not do justice to the overpowering impression which those forces make on him—but he gives them the character of a father. He turns them into gods, following in this, as I have tried to show,[2] not only an infantile prototype but a phylogenetic one.

In the course of time the first observations were made of regularity and conformity to law in natural phenomena, and with this the forces of nature lost their human traits. But man's helplessness remains and along with it his longing for his father, and the gods. The gods retain their threefold task: they must exorcize the terrors of nature, they must reconcile men to the cruelty of Fate, particularly as it is shown in death, and they must compensate them for the sufferings and privations which a civilized life in common has imposed on them.

But within these functions there is a gradual displacement of accent. It was observed that the phenomena of nature developed automatically according to internal necessities. Without doubt the gods were the lords of nature; they had arranged it to be as it was and now they could leave it to itself. Only occasionally, in what are known as miracles, did they intervene in its course, as though to make it plain that they had relinquished nothing of their original sphere of power. As regards the apportioning of destinies, an unpleasant suspicion persisted that the perplexity and helplessness of the human race could not be remedied. It was here that the gods were most apt to fail. If they themselves created Fate, then their counsels must be deemed inscrutable. The notion dawned on the most gifted people of antiquity that Moira [Fate] stood above the gods and that the gods themselves had their own destinies. And the more autonomous nature became and the more the gods withdrew from it, the more earnestly were all expectations directed to the third function of the gods —the more did morality become their true domain. It now became the task of the gods to even out the defects and evils of civilization, to attend to the sufferings which men inflict on one another in their life together and to watch over the fulfilment of the precepts of civilization, which men obey so imperfectly. Those precepts themselves were credited with a divine origin; they were elevated beyond human society and were extended to nature and the universe.

And thus a store of ideas is created, born from man's need to make his helplessness tolerable and built up from the material of memories of the helplessness of his own childhood and the childhood of the human race. It can clearly be seen that the possession of these ideas protects him in two directions—against the

_____

[1] [This was an actual dream of Freud's, reported in Chapter VI (G) of *The Interpretation of Dreams* (1900a), Standard Ed., **5**, 454–5.]

[2] [See Section 6 of the fourth essay in *Totem and Taboo* (1912–13), Standard Ed., **13**, 146 ff.]

dangers of nature and Fate, and against the injuries that threaten him from human society itself. Here is the gist of the matter. Life in this world serves a higher purpose; no doubt it is not easy to guess what that purpose is, but it certainly signifies a perfecting of man's nature. It is probably the spiritual part of man, the soul, which in the course of time has so slowly and unwillingly detached itself from the body, that is the object of this elevation and exaltation. Everything that happens in this world is an expression of the intentions of an intelligence superior to us, which in the end, though its ways and byways are difficult to follow, orders everything for the best—that is, to make it enjoyable for us. Over each one of us there watches a benevolent Providence which is only seemingly stern and which will not suffer us to become a plaything of the over-mighty and pitiless forces of nature. Death itself is not extinction, is not a return to inorganic lifelessness, but the beginning of a new kind of existence which lies on the path of development to something higher. And, looking in the other direction, this view announces that the same moral laws which our civilizations have set up govern the whole universe as well, except that they are maintained by a supreme court of justice with incomparably more power and consistency. In the end all good is rewarded and all evil punished, if not actually in this form of life then in the later existences that begin after death. In this way all the terrors, the sufferings and the hardships of life are destined to be obliterated. Life after death, which continues life on earth just as the invisible part of the spectrum joins on to the visible part, brings us all the perfection that we may perhaps have missed here. And the superior wisdom which directs this course of things, the infinite goodness that expresses itself in it, the justice that achieves its aim in it —these are the attributes of the divine beings who also created us and the world

as a whole, or rather, of the one divine being into which, in our civilization, all the gods of antiquity have been condensed. The people which first succeeded in thus concentrating the divine attributes was not a little proud of the advance. It had laid open to view the father who had all along been hidden behind every divine figure as its nucleus. Fundamentally this was a return to the historical beginnings of the idea of God. Now that God was a single person, man's relations to him could recover the intimacy and intensity of the child's relation to his father. But if one had done so much for one's father, one wanted to have a reward, or at least to be his only beloved child, his Chosen People. Very much later, pious America laid claim to being 'God's own Country'; and, as regards one of the shapes in which men worship the deity, the claim is undoubtedly valid.

The religious ideas that have been summarized above have of course passed through a long process of development and have been adhered to in various phases by various civilizations. I have singled out one such phase, which roughly corresponds to the final form taken by our present-day white Christian civilization. It is easy to see that not all the parts of this picture tally equally well with one another, that not all the questions that press for an answer receive one, and that it is difficult to dismiss the contradiction of daily experience. Nevertheless, such as they are, those ideas—ideas which are religious in the widest sense—are prized as the most precious possession of civilization, as the most precious thing it has to offer its participants. It is far more highly prized than all the devices for winning treasures from the earth or providing men with sustenance or preventing their illnesses, and so forth. People feel that life would not be tolerable if they did not attach to these ideas the value that is claimed for them. And now the question arises: what are these ideas in the light of psychology? Whence do they derive the esteem in which they are held? And, to take a further timid step, what is their real worth?

CHAPTER IV

An enquiry which proceeds like a monologue, without interruption, is not altogether free from danger. One is too easily tempted into pushing aside thoughts which threaten to break into it, and in exchange one is left with a feeling of uncertainty which in the end one tries to keep down by over-decisiveness. I shall therefore imagine that I have an opponent who follows my arguments with mistrust, and here and there I shall allow him to interject some remarks.[1]

I hear him say: 'You have repeatedly used the expressions "civilization creates these religious ideas," "civilization places them at the disposal of its participants." There is something about this that sounds strange to me. I cannot myself say why, but it does not sound so natural as it does to say that civilization has made rules about distributing the products of labour or about rights concerning women and children.'

I think, all the same, that I am justified in expressing myself in this way. I have tried to show that religious ideas have arisen from the same need as have all the other achievements of civilization: from the necessity of defending oneself against the crushingly superior force of nature. To this a second motive was added —the urge to rectify the shortcomings of civilization which made themselves painfully felt. Moreover, it is especially apposite to say that civilization gives the individual these ideas, for he finds them

there already; they are presented to him ready-made, and he would not be able to discover them for himself. What he is entering into is the heritage of many generations, and he takes it over as he does the multiplication table, geometry, and similar things. There is indeed a difference in this, but that difference lies elsewhere and I cannot examine it yet. The feeling of strangeness that you mention may be partly due to the fact that this body of religious ideas is usually put forward as a divine revelation. But this presentation of it is itself a part of the religious system, and it entirely ignores the known historical development of these ideas and their differences in different epochs and civilizations.

'Here is another point, which seems to me to be more important. You argue that the humanization of nature is derived from the need to put an end to man's perplexity and helplessness in the face of its dreaded forces, to get into a relation with them and finally to influence them. But a motive of this kind seems superfluous. Primitive man has no choice, he has no other way of thinking. It is natural to him, something innate, as it were, to project his existence outwards into the world and to regard every event which he observes as the manifestation of beings who at bottom are like himself. It is his only method of comprehension. And it is by no means self-evident, on the contrary it is a remarkable coincidence, if by thus indulging his natural disposition he succeeds in satisfying one of his greatest needs.'

I do not find that so striking. Do you suppose that human thought has no practical motives, that it is simply the expression of a disinterested curiosity? That is surely very improbable. I believe rather that when man personifies the forces of nature he is again following an infantile model. He has learnt from the persons in his earliest environment that the way to influence them is to establish a rela-

---

[1] [Freud had adopted the same method of presentation in his recent discussion of lay analysis (1926e) and also, though in somewhat different circumstances, a quarter of a century earlier in his paper on 'Screen Memories' (1899a).]

tion with them; and so, later on, with the same end in view, he treats everything else that he comes across in the same way as he treated those persons. Thus I do not contradict your descriptive observation; it is in fact natural to man to personify everything that he wants to understand in order later to control it (psychical mastering as a preparation for physical mastering); but I provide in addition a motive and a genesis for this peculiarity of human thinking.

'And now here is yet a third point. You have dealt with the origin of religion once before, in your book *Totem and Taboo* [1912–13]. But there it appeared in a different light. Everything was the son–father relationship. God was the exalted father, and the longing for the father was the root of the need for religion. Since then, it seems, you have discovered the factor of human weakness and helplessness, to which indeed the chief role in the formation of religion is generally assigned, and now you transpose everything that was once the father complex into terms of helplessness. May I ask you to explain this transformation?'

—With pleasure. I was only waiting for this invitation. But is it really a transformation? In *Totem and Taboo* it was not my purpose to explain the origin of religions but only of totemism. Can you, from any of the views known to you, explain the fact that the first shape in which the protecting deity revealed itself to men should have been that of an animal, that there was a prohibition against killing and eating this animal and that nevertheless the solemn custom was to kill and eat it communally once a year? This is precisely what happens in totemism. And it is hardly to the purpose to argue about whether totemism ought to be called a religion. It has intimate connections with the later god-religions. The totem animals become the sacred animals of the gods; and the earliest, but most fundamental moral restrictions—the prohibitions against murder and incest—originate in totemism. Whether or not you accept the conclusions of *Totem and Taboo*, I hope you will admit that a number of very remarkable, disconnected facts are brought together in it into a consistent whole.

The question of why in the long run the animal god did not suffice, and was replaced by a human one, was hardly touched on in *Totem and Taboo*, and other problems concerning the formation of religion were not mentioned in the book at all. Do you regard a limitation of that kind as the same thing as a denial? My work is a good example of the strict isolation of the particular contribution which psycho-analytic discussion can make to the solution of the problem of religion. If I am now trying to add the other, less deeply concealed part, you should not accuse me of contradicting myself, just as before you accused me of being one-sided. It is, of course, my duty to point out the connecting links between what I said earlier and what I put forward now, between the deeper and the manifest motives, between the father-complex and man's helplessness and need for protection.

These connections are not hard to find. They consist in the relation of the child's helplessness to the helplessness of the adult which continues it. So that, as was to be expected, the motives for the formation of religion which psycho-analysis revealed now turn out to be the same as the infantile contribution to the *manifest* motives. Let us transport ourselves into the mental life of a child. You remember the choice of object according to the anaclitic [attachment] type, which psycho-analysis talks of? [2] The libido there follows the paths of narcissistic needs and attaches itself to the objects which ensure the satisfaction of those needs. In this way the mother, who satisfies the

---

[2] [See Freud's paper on narcissism (1914c), *Standard Ed.*, **14**, 87.]

child's hunger, becomes its first love-object and certainly also its first protection against all the undefined dangers which threaten it in the external world —its first protection against anxiety, we may say.

In this function [of protection] the mother is soon replaced by the stronger father, who retains that position for the rest of childhood. But the child's attitude to its father is coloured by a peculiar ambivalence. The father himself constitutes a danger for the child, perhaps because of its earlier relation to its mother. Thus it fears him no less than it longs for him and admires him. The indications of this ambivalence in the attitude to the father are deeply imprinted in every religion, as was shown in *Totem and Taboo*. When the growing individual finds that he is destined to remain a child for ever, that he can never do without protection against strange superior powers, he lends those powers the features belonging to the figure of his father; he creates for himself the gods whom he dreads, whom he seeks to propitiate, and whom he nevertheless entrusts with his own protection. Thus his longing for a father is a motive identical with his need for protection against the consequences of his human weakness. The defence against childish helplessness is what lends its characteristic features to the adult's reaction to the helplessness which *he* has to acknowledge—a reaction which is precisely the formation of religion. But it is not my intention to enquire any further into the development of the idea of God; what we are concerned with here is the finished body of religious ideas as it is transmitted by civilization to the individual.

CHAPTER V

Let us now take up the thread of our enquiry.[1] What, then, is the psychologi-

---

[1] [From end of Chapter III, pp. 299–300.]

cal significance of religious ideas and under what heading are we to classify them? The question is not at all easy to answer immediately. After rejecting a number of formulations, we will take our stand on the following one. Religious ideas are teachings and assertions about facts and conditions of external (or internal) reality which tell one something one has not discovered for oneself and which lay claim to one's belief. Since they give us information about what is most important and interesting to us in life, they are particularly highly prized. Anyone who knows nothing of them is very ignorant; and anyone who has added them to his knowledge may consider himself much the richer.

•   •   •

We must ask where the inner force of those doctrines lies and to what it is that they owe their efficacy, independent as it is of recognition by reason.

CHAPTER VI

I think we have prepared the way sufficiently for an answer to both these questions. It will be found if we turn our attention to the psychical origin of religious ideas. These, which are given out as teachings, are not precipitates of experience or end-results of thinking: they are illusions, fulfilments of the oldest, strongest and most urgent wishes of mankind. The secret of their strength lies in the strength of those wishes. As we already know, the terrifying impression of helplessness in childhood aroused the need for protection—for protection through love—which was provided by the father; and the recognition that this helplessness lasts throughout life made it necessary to cling to the existence of a father, but this time a more powerful one. Thus the benevolent rule of a divine Providence allays our fear of the dangers of life; the establishment of a moral world-order ensures the fulfilment of the demands of justice, which have so often remained unfulfilled in human civilization; and the prolongation of earthly existence in a future life provides the local and temporal framework in which these wish-fulfilments shall take place. Answers to the riddles that tempt the curiosity of man, such as how the universe began or what the relation is between body and mind, are developed in conformity with the underlying assumptions of this system. It is an enormous relief to the individual psyche if the conflicts of its childhood arising from the father-complex—conflicts which it has never wholly overcome—are removed from it and brought to a solution which is universally accepted.

When I say that these things are all illusions, I must define the meaning of the word. An illusion is not the same thing as an error; nor is it necessarily an error. Aristotle's belief that vermin are developed out of dung (a belief to which ignorant people still cling) was an error; so was the belief of a former generation of doctors that *tabes dorsalis* is the result of sexual excess. It would be incorrect to call these errors illusions. On the other hand, it was an illusion of Columbus's that he had discovered a new sea-route to the Indies. The part played by his wish in this error is very clear. One may describe as an illusion the assertion made by certain nationalists that the Indo-Germanic race is the only one capable of civilization; or the belief, which was only destroyed by psycho-analysis, that children are creatures without sexuality. What is characteristic of illusions is that they are derived from human wishes. In this respect they come near to psychiatric delusions. But they differ from them, too, apart from the more complicated structure of delusions. In the case of delusions, we emphasize as essential their being in contradiction with reality. Illusions need not necessarily be false—that is to say,

unrealizable or in contradiction to reality. For instance, a middle-class girl may have the illusion that a prince will come and marry her. This is possible; and a few such cases have occurred. That the Messiah will come and found a golden age is much less likely. Whether one classifies this belief as an illusion or as something analogous to a delusion will depend on one's personal attitude. Examples of illusions which have proved true are not easy to find, but the illusion of the alchemists that all metals can be turned into gold might be one of them. The wish to have a great deal of gold, as much gold as possible, has, it is true, been a good deal damped by our present-day knowledge of the determinants of wealth, but chemistry no longer regards the transmutation of metals into gold as impossible. Thus we call a belief an illusion when a wish-fulfilment is a prominent factor in its motivation, and in doing so we disregard its relations to reality, just as the illusion itself sets no store by verification.

Having thus taken our bearings, let us return once more to the question of religious doctrines. We can now repeat that all of them are illusions and insusceptible of proof. No one can be compelled to think them true, to believe in them. Some of them are so improbable, so incompatible with everything we have laboriously discovered about the reality of the world, that we may compare them—if we pay proper regard to the psychological differences—to delusions. Of the reality value of most of them we cannot judge; just as they cannot be proved, so they cannot be refuted. We still know too little to make a critical approach to them. The riddles of the universe reveal themselves only slowly to our investigation; there are many questions to which science to-day can give no answer. But scientific work is the only road which can lead us to a knowledge of reality outside ourselves. It is once again merely an illusion to expect anything from intuition and introspection; they can give us nothing but particulars about our own mental life, which are hard to interpret, never any information about the questions which religious doctrine finds it so easy to answer. It would be insolent to let one's own arbitrary will step into the breach and, according to one's personal estimate, declare this or that part of the religious system to be less or more acceptable. Such questions are too momentous for that; they might be called too sacred.

At this point one must expect to meet with an objection. 'Well then, if even obdurate sceptics admit that the assertions of religion cannot be refuted by reason, why should I not believe in them, since they have so much on their side—tradition, the agreement of mankind, and all the consolations they offer?' Why not, indeed? Just as no one can be forced to believe, so no one can be forced to disbelieve. But do not let us be satisfied with deceiving ourselves that arguments like these take us along the road of correct thinking. If ever there was a case of a lame excuse we have it here. Ignorance is ignorance; no right to believe anything can be derived from it. In other matters no sensible person will behave so irresponsibly or rest content with such feeble grounds for his opinions and for the line he takes. It is only in the highest and most sacred things that he allows himself to do so. In reality these are only attempts at pretending to oneself or to other people that one is still firmly attached to religion, when one has long since cut oneself loose from it. Where questions of religion are concerned, people are guilty of every possible sort of dishonesty and intellectual misdemeanour. Philosophers stretch the meaning of words until they retain scarcely anything of their original sense. They give the name of 'God' to some vague abstraction which they have created for themselves; having done so they can pose before all the world as deists, as believers in God, and they can even boast that they have recognized a higher, purer concept of God, notwithstanding that their God is now nothing more than an insubstantial shadow and no longer the mighty personality of religious doctrines. Critics persist in describing as 'deeply religious' anyone who admits to a sense of man's insignificance or impotence in the face of the universe, although what constitutes the essence of the religious attitude is not this feeling but only the next step after it, the reaction to it which seeks a remedy for it. The man who goes no further, but humbly acquiesces in the small part which human beings play in the great world—such a man is, on the contrary, irreligious in the truest sense of the word.

To assess the truth-value of religious doctrines does not lie within the scope of the present enquiry. It is enough for us that we have recognized them as being, in their psychological nature, illusions. But we do not have to conceal the fact that this discovery also strongly influences our attitude to the question which must appear to many to be the most important of all. We know approximately at what periods and by what kind of men religious doctrines were created. If in addition we discover the motives which led to this, our attitude to the problem of religion will undergo a marked displacement. We shall tell ourselves that it would be very nice if there were a God who created the world and was a benevolent Providence, and if there were a moral order in the universe and an after-life; but it is a very striking fact that all this is exactly as we are bound to wish it to be. And it would be more remarkable still if our wretched, ignorant and downtrodden ancestors had succeeded in solving all these difficult riddles of the universe.

CHAPTER VIII

. . .

When civilization laid down the commandment that a man shall not kill the neighbour whom he hates or who is in his way or whose property he covets, this was clearly done in the interest of man's communal existence, which would not otherwise be practicable. For the murderer would draw down on himself the vengeance of the murdered man's kinsmen and the secret envy of others, who within themselves feel as much inclined as he does for such acts of violence. Thus he would not enjoy his revenge or his robbery for long, but would have every prospect of soon being killed himself. Even if he protected himself against his single foes by extraordinary strength and caution, he would be bound to succumb to a combination of weaker men. If a combination of this sort did not take place, the murdering would continue endlessly and the final outcome would be that men would exterminate one another. We should arrive at the same state of affairs between individuals as still persists in Corsica between families, though elsewhere only between nations. Insecurity of life, which is an equal danger for everyone, now unites men into a society which prohibits the individual from killing and reserves to itself the right to communal killing of anyone who violates the prohibition. Here, then, we have justice and punishment.

But we do not publish this rational explanation of the prohibition against murder. We assert that the prohibition has been issued by God. Thus we take it upon ourselves to guess His intentions, and we find that He, too, is unwilling for men to exterminate one another. In behaving in this way we are investing the cultural prohibition with a quite special solemnity, but at the same time we risk making its observance dependent on belief in God. If we retrace this step—if we no longer attribute to God what is our own will and if we content ourselves with giving the social reason—then, it is true, we have renounced the transfiguration of the cultural prohibition, but we have also avoided the risk to it. But we gain something else as well. Through some kind of diffusion or infection, the character of sanctity and inviolability—of belonging to another world, one might say—has spread from a few major prohibitions on to every other cultural regulation, law and ordinance. But on these the halo often looks far from becoming: not only do they invalidate one another by giving contrary decisions at different times and places, but apart from this they show every sign of human inadequacy. It is easy to recognize in them things that can only be the product of shortsighted apprehensiveness or an expression of selfishly narrow interests or a conclusion based on insufficient premises. The criticism which we cannot fail to level at them also diminishes to an unwelcome extent our respect for other, more justifiable cultural demands. Since it is an awkward task to separate what God Himself has demanded from what can be traced to the authority of an all-powerful parliament or a high judiciary, it would be an undoubted advantage if we were to leave God out altogether and honestly admit the purely human origin of all the regulations and precepts of civilization. Along with their pretended sanctity, these commandments and laws would lose their rigidity and unchangeableness as well. People could understand that they are made, not so much to rule them as, on the contrary, to serve their interests; and they would adopt a more friendly attitude to them, and instead of aiming at their abolition, would aim only at their improvement. This would be an important advance along the road which leads to becoming reconciled to the burden of civilization.

But here our plea for ascribing purely rational reasons to the precepts of civilization—that is to say, for deriving them from social necessity—is interrupted by a sudden doubt. We have chosen as our example the origin of the prohibition against murder. But does our account of it tally with historical truth? We fear not; it appears to be nothing but a rationalistic construction. With the help of psychoanalysis, we have made a study of precisely this piece of the cultural history of mankind,[1] and, basing ourselves on it, we are bound to say that in reality things happened otherwise. Even in present-day man purely reasonable motives can effect little against passionate impulsions. How much weaker then must they have been in the human animal of primaeval times! Perhaps his descendants would even now kill one another without inhibition, if it were not that among those murderous acts there was one—the killing of the primitive father—which evoked an irresistible emotional reaction with momentous consequences. From it arose the commandment: Thou shalt not kill. Under totemism this commandment was restricted to the father-substitute; but it was later extended to other people, though even to-day it is not universally obeyed.

But, as was shown by arguments which I need not repeat here, the primal father was the original image of God, the model on which later generations have shaped the figure of God. Hence the religious explanation is right. God actually played a part in the genesis of that prohibition; it was His influence, not any insight into social necessity, which created it. And the displacement of man's will on to God is fully justified. For men knew that they had disposed of their father by violence, and in their reaction to that impious deed, they determined to respect his will thenceforward. Thus religious doctrine tells us the historical truth—though subject, it is true, to some modification and disguise —whereas our rational account disavows it.

We now observe that the store of religious ideas includes not only wish-fulfilments but important historical recollections. This concurrent influence of past and present must give religion a truly incomparable wealth of power. But perhaps with the help of an analogy yet another discovery may begin to dawn on us. Though it is not a good plan to transplant ideas far from the soil in which they grew up, yet here is a conformity which we cannot avoid pointing out. We know that a human child cannot successfully complete its development to the civilized stage without passing through a phase of neurosis sometimes of greater and sometimes of less distinctness. This is because so many instinctual demands which will later be unserviceable cannot be suppressed by the rational operation of the child's intellect but have to be tamed by acts of repression, behind which, as a rule, lies the motive of anxiety. Most of these infantile neuroses are overcome spontaneously in the course of growing up, and this is especially true of the obsessional neuroses of childhood. The remainder can be cleared up later still by psycho-analytic treatment. In just the same way, one might assume, humanity as a whole, in its development through the ages, fell into states analogous to the neuroses,[2] and for the same reasons— namely because in the times of its ignorance and intellectual weakness the instinctual renunciations indispensable for man's communal existence had only been achieved by it by means of purely

---

[1] [Cf. the fourth essay in *Totem and Taboo* (1912–13).]

[2] [Freud returned to this question at the end of his *Civilization and Its Discontents* (1930*a*), p. 144 below, and in Part I of Chapter III of *Moses and Monotheism* (1939*a*).]

affective forces. The precipitates of these processes resembling repression which took place in prehistoric times still remained attached to civilization for long periods. Religion would thus be the universal obsessional neurosis of humanity; like the obsessional neurosis of children, it arose out of the Oedipus complex, out of the relation to the father. If this view is right, it is to be supposed that a turning-away from religion is bound to occur with the fatal inevitability of a process of growth, and that we find ourselves at this very juncture in the middle of that phase of development. Our behaviour should therefore be modelled on that of a sensible teacher who does not oppose an impending new development but seeks to ease its path and mitigate the violence of its irruption. Our analogy does not, to be sure, exhaust the essential nature of religion. If, on the one hand, religion brings with it obsessional restrictions, exactly as an individual obsessional neurosis does, on the other hand it comprises a system of wishful illusions together with a disavowal [3] of reality, such as we find in an isolated form nowhere else but in amentia,[4] in a state of blissful hallucinatory confusion. But these are only analogies, by the help of which we endeavour to understand a social phenomenon; the pathology of the individual does not supply us with a fully valid counterpart.

It has been repeatedly pointed out (by myself and in particular by Theodor Reik [5]) in how great detail the analogy between religion and obsessional neurosis can be followed out, and how many of the peculiarities and vicissitudes in the formation of religion can be understood in that light. And it tallies well with this that devout believers are safeguarded in a high degree against the risk of certain neurotic illnesses; their acceptance of the universal neurosis spares them the task of constructing a personal one.[6]

Our knowledge of the historical worth of certain religious doctrines increases our respect for them, but does not invalidate our proposal that they should cease to be put forward as the reasons for the precepts of civilization. On the contrary! Those historical residues have helped us to view religious teachings, as it were, as neurotic relics, and we may now argue that the time has probably come, as it does in an analytic treatment, for replacing the effects of repression by the results of the rational operation of the intellect. We may foresee, but hardly regret, that such a process of remoulding will not stop at renouncing the solemn transfiguration of cultural precepts, but that a general revision of them will result in many of them being done away with. In this way our appointed task of reconciling men to civilization will to a great extent be achieved. We need not deplore the renunciation of historical truth when we put forward rational grounds for the precepts of civilization. The truths contained in religious doctrines are after all so distorted and systematically disguised that the mass of humanity cannot recognize them as truth. The case is similar to what happens when we tell a child that new-born babies are brought by the stork. Here, too, we are telling the truth in symbolic clothing, for we know what the large bird signifies. But the child does not know it. He hears only the distorted part of what we say, and feels that he has been deceived; and we know how often his distrust of the grown-ups and his refractoriness actually take their start from this impression. We have become convinced that it is better

---

[3] [See the paper on 'Fetishism' (1927e), p. 153 below.]

[4] ['Meynert's amentia': a state of acute hallucinatory confusion.]

[5] [Cf. Freud, 'Obsessive Actions and Religious Practices' (1907b) and Reik (1927).]

[6] [Freud had often made this point before: e.g. in a sentence added in 1919 to his study on Leonardo da Vinci (1910c), Standard Ed., 11, 123.]

to avoid such symbolic disguisings of the truth in what we tell children and not to withhold from them a knowledge of the true state of affairs commensurate with their intellectual level.[7]

. . .

CHAPTER IX

It is certainly senseless to begin by trying to do away with religion by force and at a single blow. Above all, because it would be hopeless. The believer will not let his belief be torn from him, either by arguments or by prohibitions. And even if this did succeed with some it would be cruelty. A man who has been taking sleeping draughts for tens of years is naturally unable to sleep if his sleeping draught is taken away from him. That the effect of religious consolations may be likened to that of a narcotic is well illustrated by what is happening in America. There they are now trying—obviously under the influence of petticoat government—to deprive people of all stimulants, intoxicants, and other pleasure-producing substances, an instead, by way of compensation, are surfeiting them with piety. This is another experiment as to whose outcome we need not feel curious [p. 46, 1961 edition].[1]

Thus I must contradict you when you go on to argue that men are completely unable to do without the consolation of the religious illusion, that without it they could not bear the troubles of life and the cruelties of reality. That is true, certainly, of the men into whom you have

instilled the sweet—or bitter-sweet—poison from childhood onwards. But what of the other men, who have been sensibly brought up? Perhaps those who do not suffer from the neurosis will need no intoxicant to deaden it. They will, it is true, find themselves in a difficult situation. They will have to admit to themselves the full extent of their helplessness and their insignificance in the machinery of the universe; they can no longer be the centre of creation, no longer the object of tender care on the part of a beneficent Providence. They will be in the same position as a child who has left the parental house where he was so warm and comfortable. But surely infantilism is destined to be surmounted. Men cannot remain children for ever; they must in the end go out into 'hostile life.' We may call this *education to reality.* Need I confess to you that the sole purpose of my book is to point out the necessity for this forward step?

You are afraid, probably, that they will not stand up to the hard test? Well, let us at least hope they will. It is something, at any rate, to know that one is thrown upon one's own resources. One learns then to make a proper use of them. And men are not entirely without assistance. Their scientific knowledge has taught them much since the days of the Deluge, and it will increase their power still further. And, as for the great necessities of Fate, against which there is no help, they will learn to endure them with resignation. Of what use to them is the mirage of wide acres in the moon, whose harvest no one has ever yet seen? As honest smallholders on this earth they will know how to cultivate their plot in such a way that it supports them. By withdrawing their expectations from the other world and concentrating all their liberated energies into their life on earth, they will probably succeed in achieving a state of things in which life will become tolerable for everyone and civilization no longer

---

[7] [Freud later drew a distinction between what he termed 'material' and 'historical' truth in several passages. See, in particular, Section G of Part II of Chapter III of *Moses and Monotheism* (1939a). Cf. also an Editor's footnote on the subject in Chapter XII (C) of *The Psychopathology of Everyday Life* (1901b), *Standard Ed., 6,* 256.]

[1] [This was written in the middle of the period of National Prohibition in the United States (1920–33).]

oppressive to anyone. Then, with one of our fellow-unbelievers, they will be able to say without regret:

Den Himmel überlassen wir
Den Engeln und den Spartzen.[2]

CHAPTER X

. . .

I know how difficult it is to avoid illusions; perhaps the hopes I have confessed to are of an illusory nature, too. But I hold fast to one distinction. Apart from the fact that no penalty is imposed for not sharing them, my illusions are not, like religious ones, incapable of correction. They have not the character of a delusion. If experience should show— not to me, but to others after me, who think as I do—that we have been mistaken, we will give up our expectations. Take my attempt for what it is. A psychologist who does not deceive himself about the difficulty of finding one's bearings in this world, makes an endeavour to assess the development of man, in the light of the small portion of knowledge he has gained through a study of the mental processes of individuals during their development from child to adult. In so doing, the idea forces itself upon him that religion is comparable to a childhood neurosis, and he is optimistic enough to suppose that mankind will surmount this neurotic phase, just as so many children grow out of their similar neurosis. These discoveries derived from individual psychology may be insufficient, their application to the human race unjustified, and his optimism unfounded.

I grant you all these uncertainties. But often one cannot refrain from saying what one thinks, and one excuses oneself on the ground that one is not giving it out for more than it is worth.

And there are two points that I must dwell on a little longer. Firstly, the weakness of my position does not imply any strengthening of yours. I think you are defending a lost cause. We may insist as often as we like that man's intellect is powerless in comparison with his instinctual life, and we may be right in this. Nevertheless, there is something peculiar about this weakness. The voice of the intellect is a soft one, but it does not rest till it has gained a hearing. Finally, after a countless succession of rebuffs, it succeeds. This is one of the few points on which one may be optimistic about the future of mankind, but it is in itself a point of no small importance. And from it one can derive yet other hopes. The primacy of the intellect lies, it is true, in a distant, distant future, but probably not in an *infinitely* distant one. It will presumably set itself the same aims as those whose realization you expect from your God (of course within human limits— so far as external reality, 'Aνάγκη, allows it), namely the love of man and the decrease of suffering. This being so, we may tell ourselves that our antagonism is only a temporary one and not irreconcilable. We desire the same things, but you are more impatient, more exacting, and— why should I not say it?—more self-seeking than I and those on my side. You would have the state of bliss begin directly after death; you expect the impossible from it and you will not surrender the claims of the individual. Our God, Λόγος,[1] will fulfil whichever of these wishes nature outside us allows, but he

---

[2] ['We leave Heaven to the angels and the sparrows.' From Heine's poem *Deutschland* (Caput I). The word which is here translated 'fellow-unbelievers'—in German '*Un-glaubensgenossen*'—was applied by Heine himself to Spinoza. It had been quoted by Freud as an example of a particular kind of joke-technique in his book on jokes (1905c), *Standard Ed.*, **8**, 77.]

[1] The twin gods Λόγος [*Logos*: Reason] and 'Aνάγκη [*Ananke*: Necessity] of the Dutch writer Multatuli. [Cf. an Editor's footnote to 'The Economic Problem of Masochism' (1924c), *Standard Ed.*, **19**, 168.]

will do it very gradually, only in the unforeseeable future, and for a new generation of men. He promises no compensation for us, who suffer grievously from life. On the way to this distant goal your religious doctrines will have to be discarded, no matter whether the first attempts fail, or whether the first substitutes prove to be untenable. You know why: in the long run nothing can withstand reason and experience, and the contradiction which religion offers to both is all too palpable. Even purified religious ideas cannot escape this fate, so long as they try to preserve anything of the consolation of religion. No doubt if they confine themselves to a belief in a higher spiritual being, whose qualities are indefinable and whose purposes cannot be discerned, they will be proof against the challenge of science; but then they will also lose their hold on human interest.

And secondly: observe the difference between your attitude to illusions and mine. You have to defend the religious illusion with all your might. If it becomes discredited—and indeed the threat to it is great enough—then your world collapses. There is nothing left for you but to despair of everything, of civilization and the future of mankind. From that bondage I am, we are, free. Since we are prepared to renounce a good part of our infantile wishes, we can bear it if a few of our expectations turn out to be illusions.

Education freed from the burden of religious doctrines will not, it may be, effect much change in men's psychological nature. Our god Λόγος is perhaps not a very almighty one, and he may only be able to fulfil a small part of what his predecessors have promised. If we have to acknowledge this we shall accept it with resignation. We shall not on that account lose our interest in the world and in life, for we have one sure support which you lack. We believe that it is possible for scientific work to gain some knowledge about the reality of the world, by means of which we can increase our power and in accordance with which we can arrange our life. If this belief is an illusion, then we are in the same position as you. But science has given us evidence by its numerous and important successes that it is no illusion. Science has many open enemies, and many more secret ones, among those who cannot forgive her for having weakened religious faith and for threatening to overthrow it. She is reproached for the smallness of the amount she has taught us and for the incomparably greater field she has left in obscurity. But, in this, people forget how young she is, how difficult her beginnings were and how infinitesimally small is the period of time since the human intellect has been strong enough for the tasks she sets. Are we not all at fault, in basing our judgements on periods of time that are too short? We should make the geologists our pattern. People complain of the unreliability of science—how she announces as a law to-day what the next generation recognizes as an error and replaces by a new law whose accepted validity lasts no longer. But this is unjust and in part untrue. The transformations of scientific opinion are developments, advances, not revolutions. A law which was held at first to be universally valid proves to be a special case of a more comprehensive uniformity, or is limited by another law, not discovered till later; a rough approximation to the truth is replaced by a more carefully adapted one, which in turn awaits further perfectioning. There are various fields where we have not yet surmounted a phase of research in which we make trial with hypotheses that soon have to be rejected as inadequate; but in other fields we already possess an assured and almost unalterable core of knowledge. Finally, an attempt has been made to discredit scientific endeavour in a radical way, on the ground that, being bound to the conditions of our own organization, it can yield nothing else than subjective results, whilst the real nature of things outside ourselves remains inaccessible. But this is to disregard several factors which are of decisive importance for the understanding of scientific work. In the first place, our organization—that is, our mental apparatus—has been developed precisely in the attempt to explore the external world, and it must therefore have realized in its structure some degree of expediency; in the second place, it is itself a constituent part of the world which we set out to investigate, and it readily admits of such an investigation; thirdly, the task of science is fully covered if we limit it to showing how the world must appear to us in consequence of the particular character of our organization; fourthly, the ultimate findings of science, precisely because of the way in which they are acquired, are determined not only by our organization but by the things which have affected that organization; finally, the problem of the nature of the world without regard to our percipient mental apparatus is an empty abstraction, devoid of practical interest.

No, our science is no illusion. But an illusion it would be to suppose that what science cannot give us we can get elsewhere.

MAURICE CORNFORTH

Theology as Socially Determined Ideology

Maurice Cornforth (1909–   ) is one of the outstanding expositors of the philosophy of dialectical materialism in English. He is known in England as a publisher as well as a writer.

Ideological illusions have their source in the production relations of society. But they are not consciously derived from that source, but arise unconsciously or spontaneously. Unaware of the true source of their illusory ideas, ideologists imagine they have produced them by a process of pure thought. And so there takes place a process of inversion in ideology, by which real social relations are represented as the realisation of abstract ideas. Lastly, ideological illusions constitute a class-motivated system of deception.

From Maurice Cornforth, *Dialectical Materialism: An Introductory Course,* Vol. III: *The Theory of Knowledge* (1954), Ch. VII. Reprinted by permission of Lawrence & Wishart Ltd., and International Publishers.

IDEOLOGICAL REFLECTION OF PRODUCTION RELATIONS

In this chapter we shall consider the development of ideological preconceptions or illusions, and will then turn, in the next two chapters, to the development of scientific ideas.

There are five main, characteristic features of the development of ideological illusions in class-divided society, which can be traced in every ideology up to and including bourgeois ideology.

(1) The first feature of ideological illusions is that they always arise as reflections of particular, historically con-

stituted relations of production. Their source is the production relations of society.

In the development of ideological illusions, it seems as if abstract ideas, general theories, were being spun out of people's heads—developed and controlled, to all appearances, simply by the thinking process itself. Yet how did such ideas come into people's heads? What is their source? Unless we are to believe that ideas are formed spontaneously in the mind, or that we are born already equipped with "innate ideas," then we must suppose that a source in objective reality outside the mind can be found for all our ideas, including the most abstract and illusory—a source from which they are derived and of which they are the reflection.

Consciousness is never anything but a reflection of material existence. First there is matter, objective being, and then, secondarily, there is consciousness, the reflection of matter. The mind has no inner sources of its own, from which ideas can be derived. Every idea, every element of ideology, is derived from and reflects some objective reality, some real aspect of the material world.

The source of the illusions in ideology is always the real economic structure of society. As men live, so do they think. Corresponding to the relations they enter into in producing the means of life, they produce social ideas and social theories.

Thus, for example, it is the real relations of landowners and serfs established in the feudal mode of production that are reflected in the feudal ideas of landownership, and in feudal ideology in general. Similarly, it is the capitalist relationships which are reflected in capitalist ideology. And it was the far simpler relationships within the tribe, the solidarity of the individual with the tribe, which were reflected in the "primitive" ideology of primitive communism.

Thus as society develops, the ideas which reflect the property relations of society become elaborated in the form of systems and theories concerning politics, social rights and obligations, law, and so on. All such ideology has its source in the social relations of production, and constitutes, in the last analysis, nothing but an ideological reflection of those relations.

The same is true of moral ideas. If we have ideas of absolute standards of good and bad, right and wrong, virtue and vice, these ideas are reflections not of any objective property of persons or actions but of the social relations into which people have entered and within which their personal activity takes place. No wonder, therefore, that moral judgments change with fundamental changes in social relations; and that there is only one objective standard for saying that one morality is higher than another, namely, that it reflects and serves a higher social system.

And the same is true of the ideology of the supernatural, of religious ideology. The supernatural world which men conjure up for themselves in their ideas is never, in the last analysis, anything other than a reflection of the real world of society, of the social relations within which men live their earthly lives. The world of the supernatural always serves as the guardian of the basic fabric of society. The tribal religion stands guard over the tribe and protects tribal relations, just as the ideas of Christianity today have been so adapted that heaven seems to stand guard over the bourgeois order of society. The supernatural world which guards and justifies the social order is created in the image of that social order.

These are examples of the way in which various forms of ideological illusions are developed in terms of abstract ideas whose source lies in the development of social relations, more precisely, of the relations of production. The objective reality which is reflected in such ideas is never anything else than the existing complex of social relations which spring from the production of the material means of life.

THE SPONTANEOUS CHARACTER OF IDEOLOGICAL ILLUSION

(2) The second feature of ideological illusions is that, although their source lies in the complex of real social relations, they are neither consciously derived from that source nor are they put forward as an analysis of existing social relations.

The ideas which people employ may reflect their social relations, but their ideological illusions are not created by their *consciously* reflecting on their own social relations and working out for themselves, in a scientific manner, an accurate and systematic account of the social structure which they find in existence.

The ideas of political economy, for example, as set forth in such a book as Marx's *Capital,* are derived from a conscious, methodical investigation of actually existing relations of production. Precisely for that reason they are not illusory but scientific in character. Ideological illusion, on the other hand, arises precisely as an unconscious, unintended reflection of an existing social structure, expressed in general ideas about the world. It has an unconscious, spontaneous character. That is why, if we want to discover the most essential features of some illusory ideology, we shall not discover them in the reasoned forms in which men have presented their ideas, but rather in the unreasoned assumptions, the preconceptions which they take for granted, which underlie their reasoning.

For example, in the ideology of the medieval Catholic Church, the whole world, heaven and earth, was regarded as a hierarchy in which the lower members were necessarily subordinate to the higher. In the production of this ideology there was no intention of giving an account of the feudal order; the conscious intention was to give an account of the necessary order of the whole world, and this was consciously worked out as a logical system. But yet the ideology was in fact a reflection of the existing feudal social relations, which were thus reproduced in men's ideas by a spontaneous, unintended, unconscious process. The general ideas employed were a reflection of actual social relations, but they were not consciously produced as such a reflection, but arose unconsciously and spontaneously in men's minds. These ideas then became fixed as preconceptions which were used for the purpose of interpreting and working out the theory of everything which people were interested in, whether in nature or society or the imaginary realm of heaven.

The spontaneous, unconscious character of the ideological reflection of relations of production is due to the spontaneous, unconscious character of those relations of production themselves.

Men's relations of production, wrote Marx, are "indispensable and independent of their will." This is the key to understanding the nature of the illusory ideological reflection of those relations in abstract ideas about the world and society. The given relations of production are not deliberately instituted, but they are at the same time, at the given stage of social development, indispensable. And because people never decided to institute them but at the same time cannot get on without them, they are not conscious of them as transitory social relations which have been instituted at a definite time, in definite circumstances, to answer definite but only temporary historical needs of society. Rather do they appear as part of the necessary order of things. The characteristic features of men's social relations and relationships with nature, which are in fact the historically determined result of a definite mode of production, are reflected in abstract ideas in the form of preconceptions and illusions about the nature of man and society, as ideas about God and divine providence, about right and justice, about the eternal and necessary characteristics of all being, the ultimate nature of reality, and so on.

THE ILLUSION OF PURE THOUGHT

(3) The third feature of ideological illusions is that, just because their spontaneous character precludes people's being aware of their true source, they seem to themselves to have produced them by a free process of thought, by a pure and unfettered operation of the mind.

"Ideology [1] is a process accomplished by the so-called thinker consciously, indeed, but with a false consciousness," wrote Engels. "The real motives impell-

---

[1] Marx and Engels frequently used the term "ideology" to refer exclusively to the process of ideological illusion, thus employing it in a restricted sense. When the term is used in this restricted sense, then scientific modes of thought are by definition excluded from the ideological process, and such an expression as "scientific ideology" becomes a contradiction in terms, like, say, "round square." Lenin and Stalin, on the other hand, often used the term "ideology" in a wider sense, so that they speak, for example, of "scientific solialist ideology," and characterise Marxism as such an ideology.

In this book I have employed the term throughout in the wider sense, so that the word "ideology" is used to denote the typical outlook or theory of a period or of a class, in which both illusory and truthful or scientific elements may enter, and which, with the rise of the revolutionary working class movement and of socialism, becomes primarily scientific and dispenses with the illusory modes of thought of previous ideologies.

ing him remain unknown to him, otherwise it would not be an ideological process at all. Hence he imagines false or apparent motives. Because it is a process of thought, he derives both its form and its content from pure thought, either his own or that of his predecessors. He works with mere thought material which he accepts without examination as the product of thought, and he does not investigate further for a more remote process independent of thought." [2]

And again, Engels wrote that ideology—the working out of ideological illusions—is "occupation with thoughts as with independent entities, developing independently and subject only to their own laws. That the material life conditions of the persons inside whose heads this thought process goes on in the last resort determine the course of this process, remains of necessity unknown to these persons, for otherwise there would be an end of all ideology." [3]

IDEOLOGICAL INVERSION

(4) The fourth feature of ideological illusions is that a process of inversion takes place in them, by which real social relations are represented as the realisation of abstract ideas.

In the process of ideological illusion, products of abstract thought are treated as though they were independent of the material social relations which they in fact reflect. And so it follows that reality is turned upside down in this process. The source of abstract ideas is taken to be the mind, rather than the material reality of social relations. And so the ultimate ground for the existence of those relations themselves is conceived as being the abstractions of the mind.

According to this inverted way of

---

[2] Engels, *Letter* to Mehring, July 14, 1893.
[3] Engels, *Ludwig Feuerbach*, ch. 4.

looking at things, men create their social relationships in obedience to their abstract ideas, and not the other way round.

Take, for example, abstract conceptions of right and justice, which constitute an important part of all ideology. Abstract right and justice are represented as independent of actual social relationships, and those relationships are represented as reflecting and realising—perhaps imperfectly—an abstract right and justice. According to this topsy-turvy way of looking at things, the abstract ideas of right and justice seem to determine the real relationships of men, whereas in fact it is the real relationships of men that determine their ideas of right and justice. And similarly, the social system seems to be justified by how far it corresponds to abstract ideas of right and justice, whereas in fact ideas of right and justice are justified by how far they serve the material progress of society.

"Economic, political and other reflections are just like those in the human eye," wrote Engels. "They pass through a condensing lens and therefore appear upside down, standing on their heads. Only the nervous system which would put them on their feet again for representation is lacking. . . . This inversion . . . forms what we call ideological conception." [4]

And Marx and Engels further wrote: "If in all ideology men and their circumstances appear upside down as in a camera obscura, this phenomenon arises just as much from their historical life process as the inversion of objects on the retina does from their physical life process." [5]

As a result of this ideological inversion, it follows that in every epoch people have shared the illusion that their institutions and public activities are the expression of their abstract ideas—of their religion, philosophy, political principles, and so on. Thus the slave owners of ancient Rome thought of themselves as actuated by republican principles, just as modern capitalists thought of themselves (and still try to get others to think of them) as actuated by democratic principles. The wars of the Middle Ages were fought avowedly for religious principles, just as the wars of today are fought avowedly for national or political principles.

According to this way of looking at things, wrote Marx, "each principle has had its own century in which to manifest itself. The principle of authority, for example, had the eleventh century, just as the principle of individualism had the eighteenth century . . . it was the century that belonged to the principle, and not the principle to the century. In other words, it was the principle that made the history, and not the history that made the principle." [6]

Every epoch, then, produces its characteristic illusions, which are expressed in its dominant ideology—illusions as to the real grounds and motive forces of its insititutions and acitivites.

"For instance," wrote Marx and Engels, ". . . an epoch imagines itself to be actuated by purely political or religious motives, although religion and politics are only forms of its true motives . . ." It is this which constitutes "the illusion of that epoch." In this illusion, "the idea, the conception of these conditioned men

---

[4] Engels, *Letter* to C. Schmidt, October 27, 1890.

[5] Marx and Engels, *The German Ideology*, Part I, ch. 1. They are referring to the fact that the image formed on the lens of a camera or on the retina of the eye is always upside down. In the case of the eye, this inversion is corrected in the visual parts of the brain, so that we finally become visually conscious of things the right way up—just as a similar correction is made in the process of photography.

[6] Marx, *The Poverty of Philosophy*, ch. 2, section 1, 5th observation.

about their real practice is transformed into the sole determining active force which controls and determines their practice." [7]

In ideological illusion, the products of the mind are represented as the dominating, compelling influence in human affairs. And so it also happens that these products of the mind, which are mere distorted fantasms of real conditions of existence, come to be endowed in men's imaginations with a real existence of their own. In this way are created what Marx called "the mist-enveloped regions of the religious world. In that world the productions of the human brain appear as independent beings endowed with life, and entering into relation both with one another and the human race." [8]

And so, while men imagine their whole social life and insitutions to be based on and motivated by their ideology, at the same time this ideology conjures up a fantastic world of powers and forces superior to and independent of both man and nature, to which men feel themselves subject, on which their destinies seem to depend and whose aid they seek to enlist for their enterprises.

The "religious world," as Marx said, is never anything "but the reflection of the real world." [9]

In the most primitive social organisations men are relatively helpless in the face of natural forces; they are banded together to get a living, and would be doomed to destruction without this elementary social cohesion and co-operation. This fact is reflected in their minds in the illusions of magic. Men seem to possess a special power and virtue as members of their tribe or clan, and this virtue takes the form, in their imagination, of a special magical force. All sorts of procedures are invented for exerting it—and later, with division of labour, it comes to be regarded as the possession and concern of certain individuals only, and not of the whole people. At the same time, natural objects and natural forces are assumed to be animated, and are later personified; so that the whole intercourse of man with man, and of man with nature, is represented as depending on the activity of unseen, mysterious powers.

The development and ramification of religious ideas has kept pace with and reflected the development of men's social life.

"The primitive religious notions, which in the main are common to each group of kindred peoples," wrote Engels, "develop, after the separation of the group, in a manner peculiar to each people, according to the living conditions falling to their lot." [10]

As with all ideology, religion is not created anew in each new phase of social development. On the contrary, every ideology in its development makes use of traditional materials which are taken over from previous ideology, and incorporates in itself materials borrowed from other ideologies. It is the same in religion; and so, for example, we can still recognise even in the religious doctrines and practices of Protestant Christianity today elements which have been carried over from primitive tribal magic, overlaid and transformed as they may be with new meanings.

"Religion, once formed," wrote Engels, "always contains traditional material, just as in all ideological domains tradition is a great conservative force. But the transformations which this material undergoes spring from class relations—that is to say, out of the economic relations of the persons who execute these transformations." [11]

---

[7] Marx and Engels, *The German Ideology*, Part I, ch. 1.

[8] Marx, *Capital*, Vol. I, ch. 1, section 4.
[9] *Ibid.*

[10] Engels, *Ludwig Feuerbach*, ch. 4.
[11] *Ibid.*

This characteristic of all ideological illusion—that, because it is occupation with thoughts as with independent entities, it continually develops ideas out of the material of other ideas—effectively disguises the fact that every ideology, and every element of ideology, is but a reflection of material social existence, and makes it appear as though it were really what it purports to be, an independent march of ideas.

The nature of ideology is never obvious on the surface, but comes to light only as a result of Marx's profound scientific discovery, that "the mode of production of material life conditions the social, political and intellectual life process in general." [12]

So long as men are not the masters of their own social organisation, so long are their real social relations reflected in ideological inversions which, far from rendering their real social relations intelligible, mystify them and conceal their real character, together with the real springs and laws of human social action, behind a veil of religious, political, legal, artistic and philosophical illusions.

IDEOLOGY AND CLASS INTEREST

(5) The fifth feature of ideological illusions is that, in society divided into classes, they constitute a class-motivated system of deception, a mode of disguising the real social relations in the interests of a definite class.

Illusion always reflects the real social relations in such a way as to disguise them.

For example, the religious ideology of the Middle Ages, with its conception of a heavenly hierarchy which reflected the feudal order, meant that the exploitation of the serf by the lord was disguised as a subordination of the serf to his natural superiors under the rule of God. And similarly, the naked fact that the feudal lord appropriated the produce of the serf's labour was disguised by the abstract feudal ideas of ownership, dues, rights and obligations.

Once again, the naked fact that the capitalist appropriates the values produced by the workers' unpaid labour is disguised by the abstract capitalist ideas of ownership, contract and equality of rights. This disguise is completed by capitalist forms of religion. That is why, though bourgeois ideology has often taken non-religious or anti-religious forms, it always leaves a loophole for religion and continually comes back to it, while in periods of crisis, when the system is seriously endangered, religious ideology is always brought to the fore and takes the offensive.

"For a society based upon the production of commodities," wrote Marx, "in which the producers in general enter into social relations with one another by treating their products as commodities and values, whereby they reduce their individual private labour to the standard of homogeneous human labour—for such a society, Christianity, with its cultus of abstract man, more especially in its bourgeois developments, Protestantism, Deism, etc., is the most fitting form of religion." [13]

The whole of bourgeois ideology, from its religion to its political economy, disguises the fact of capitalist exploitation.

The disguise and deception inherent in all ideological illusion is always socially motivated. In other words, it serves definite social ends, definite social interests.

In primitive societies, before the birth of classes, it serves to strengthen and consolidate the bonds of solidarity be-

---

[12] Marx, *Critique of Political Economy*, Preface.

[13] Marx, *Capital*, Vol. I, ch. 1, section 4.

tween members of the tribe, on which their survival depends. And in conditions when people are almost totally ignorant of the natural forces which environ them, magical ideas make them feel that nevertheless they can control these forces. Primitive ideology is thus motivated by the self-preservation of the whole tribe, by the interest of the whole people to preserve their social organisation and to feel strong and secure in it.

When society splits into antagonistic classes, and when, consequently, history becomes the history of class struggles, then class interest becomes the main motivation of ideology. Every ideology becomes the ideology of a class, expressing, in however roundabout a way, the conditions of existence of a definite class and serving that class in its struggle against other classes. The dominant ideology in any period is that of the ruling class. And when this ideology is challenged, that is but the expression of the fact that the existing state of class relations is being challenged by another class.

The disguise and deception of class ideology, motivated as it is by class interest, is not to be interpreted, however, as primarily a deliberate, conscious deception.

To suppose that the thinking representatives of a class deliberately invent misleading ideas with the conscious purpose of disguising from the people what they know to be the real character of the social relations is to suppose that these thinkers do in fact know what is the real character of the social relations. But the very essence of ideological illusion is that it is a false consciousness of social relations. The mystifying ideological conception of these relations takes the place of a correct, scientific conception. This false consciousness arises, as we have seen, not by a deliberate process but rather by a spontaneous, unconscious process. It is not deliberate false-

hood but—illusion. If it is deception, it is also self-deception.

Those who would interpret ideological illusions as mere deliberate deceptions, therefore, mistake the very nature of what Marx and Engels called "false consciousness." For they suppose that the class whose interests are served by the ideology possesses in fact a true consciousness of the basis of its existence —which is just what no exploiting class possesses or ever can possess. The explanation of ideologies as products of well-laid plans to deceive the people in the interests of a class is an absurd vulgarisation of Marxism. That is not how ideologies arise.

Of course, spokesmen and ideologists of ruling classes do constantly engage in conscious, deliberate deception of the people. But behind the system of deliberate deception lies always a system of self-deception.

As a case in point we may take the example of Plato, who was a representative of extreme ideological reaction in ancient Greece. He advocated that, to keep the people down, the rulers should propagate what he called "a noble lie": although they knew very well it was not true, they should proclaim that rulers and ruled were men of two different kinds, the rulers being "golden" men and the rest being men of mere "brass and iron." [14] At the same time, Plato maintained that aristocracy was the best system of society and that any departure from it meant anarchy and degeneration. This, however, he undoubtedly believed. It was one of the illusions of his class, and constituted the very basis of his outlook. From the point of view of the aristocratic slave-owners' ideology, which Plato expounded and which he did much to shape, it was quite in order to tell the people lies, and such lies were "noble."

---

[14] Plato, *Republic,* Book III.

Such has been the situation with all ruling class ideologies. Genuine false consciousness becomes involved in deliberate deception, so that the two become closely intertwined and even, at times, indistinguishable. This is especially the case in capitalist society, in which all things, including ideas, are bought and sold. Those who have ideas to sell come to regard them as commodities to be exchanged for cash, not as truths to be believed.

The class-motivated character of particular ideologies has long been recognised. When a new class is rising to power, and consequently posing a new ideology against that of the old ruling class, it generally recognises that the old ideology expresses the interests of its political opponents. It attacks this ideology, therefore, as a system of falsehoods motivated by class interest. It advances its own ideology, on the other hand, as a system of truth, corresponding to the profounder needs of the whole of society.

"Each new class which puts itself in the place of the one ruling before it," wrote Marx and Engels, "is compelled, merely in order to carry through its aim, to represent its interest as the common interest of all the members of society, put in an ideal form; it will give its ideas the form of universality, and represent them as the only rational, universally valid ones. The class making a revolution appears from the very start, merely because it is opposed to a *class,* not as a class, but as the representative of the whole of society." [15]

A newly formed ideology, therefore, generally starts with a profound impulse to development, as a universal system of ideas opening up new horizons, corresponding to deeply felt social needs, as if it were based not on the interests of a class but on the aspirations of a whole people. In the course of time, however, as the new ruling and exploiting class becomes entangled in its own contradictions, its ideology loses its revolutionary élan and becomes conservative; it begins to decay and disintegrate; until finally it stands revealed in its turn as a system of class-motivated deceptions, while its exponents degenerate from original thinkers into mere hired propagandists of the ruling class.

---

[15] Marx and Engels, *The German Ideology,* Part I, ch. 1.

CHARLES HARTSHORNE

Alternative Conceptions of God

Charles Hartshorne (1897–) is perhaps the most important follower in the United States of the metaphysics of A. N. Whitehead. He taught philosophy at the University of Chicago from 1928 to 1955, and is currently Professor of Philosophy at the University of Texas.

It seems strange to me, said Cleanthes, that you, Demea, who are so sincere in the cause of religion, should still maintain the mysterious, incomprehensible nature of the Deity, and should insist . . . that he has no manner of likeness or resemblance to human creatures. The Deity, I can readily allow, possesses many powers and attributes, of which we can have no comprehension: But if our ideas, so far as they go, be not just and adequate I know not what there is in this subject worth insisting on. . . . Those who maintain the perfect simplicity of the Supreme Being, to the extent in which you have explained it, are complete Mystics . . . in a word Atheists, without knowing it . . . A mind, whose acts and sentiments and ideas are not distinct and successive; one, that is wholly simple and totally immutable; is a mind which has no thought, no reason, no will, no sentiment, no love, no hatred; or in a word, is no mind at all. . . .

Pray consider, said Philo, whom you are at present inveighing against. You are honoring with the appellation of Atheist all the sound orthodox divines almost, who have treated of this subject. . . .

DAVID HUME, in *Dialogues Concerning Natural Religion,* Part IV

For nearly two thousand years European theology staked its fortunes upon a certain conception of divinity. In spite of the seeming variety of doctrines, one basic principle was accepted by almost all philosophical theists. Only in the last few decades has a genuinely alternative type of theology been at all widely considered—so unobtrusively, however, that many opponents of theism, even some of the most distinguished, are still fighting the older conception exclusively, convinced that if they can dispose of it the theological question will be settled. And many of those who find the idea of a godless universe incredible suppose that it is to traditional theology that they must turn. Both parties are mistaken. Today the theistic question, like many others, is a definitely new one. Many of the old controversies, in their old forms, are antiquated.

As traditional theology was a relatively well defined system, the same in certain basic respects—despite all sorts of philosophical and ecclesiastical differ-

From Charles Hartshorne, *Man's Vision of God,* Ch. I. Copyright by Harper & Row, Publishers, Inc. Used by permission.

320   SECTION 3: CRITICISMS OF THEISM

ences—in Augustine, Thomas Aquinas, Maimonides, Leibniz, Calvin, Immanuel Kant, and some schools of Hindu thought, so the new theology which may be contrasted with the old is found more or less fully and consistently represented in thinkers as far apart as William James, the American of over a generation ago, James Ward, his English contemporary, Henri Bergson, F. R. Tennant, W. R. Matthews, dean of St. Paul's, A. N. Whitehead, Berdyaev, the Orthodox Russian thinker, and in numerous others of every brand of Protestantism, besides a few (officially opposed and obstructed) Roman Catholics. I have also heard a clear statement of some aspects of it from a leading Hindu thinker, Radhakamal Mukerjee. Of course, there are interesting differences between these theologians, just as there were between Bonaventura and Calvin; and in some writers now, as of old, the logical implications are more adequately and rigorously worked out than in others. But there are some fundamental points of agreement which are rapidly becoming standard among non-Roman Catholic theologians.

To be aware of these points of convergence is essential to a liberal education today. They are as characteristic of our time as relativity physics and logical positivism are, or as medieval theology was of the thirteenth century. Ideas which until about fifty years ago were almost wholly neglected, never clearly worked out and systematized, and perhaps passed over for centuries with scarcely a mention, are now to be met in scores of theological works and in philosophical works that deal carefully with theology. The time seems at hand for attempts to state clearly the revolution of thought through which we have been passing.

What is the "new" doctrine? We shall see presently that it *must* be an expression of one of the three and only three formally possible views (including atheism and positivism as special cases of one of the three) regarding the supreme being, and that there are reasons for characterizing the new view as that one of the three which is related to the main line of the tradition as a carefully qualified assertion is to an unqualified one, and related to atheism (and certain heretical extremes of theism) as to an unqualified denial. In other words, it is related to the two other possible views as a "higher synthesis" to its "thesis" and "antithesis," as embraced and corrected in a "higher unity," or as a balanced whole truth to its two contrasting half-truths. From this standpoint traditional atheism and traditional theism are two sides of the same error, one of the most characteristic errors of human thought.

An immediate objection to the suggestion of a new idea of God will doubtless be that the term God as defined by usage properly means the God of the religious tradition. But we must distinguish, in the tradition, between religion and theology. Granting that "God" is a religious term, and that theology attempted to describe the object of religious devotion, it is one of the principal questions at issue whether or not this attempt was wholly successful. It is a belief of many today that the "new" theology is more, not less, religious than the old, at least if religion means "devoted love for a being regarded as superlatively worthy of love," which is the Christian conception and to some extent the conception of the higher religions generally.

Of course theologians do not now regard as worthless and merely wrong the entire vast structure of historic theology, any more than Einstein so regards Newton's physics—to use an analogy which could easily be pressed too far, but whose value could also be underestimated. What is now being done is to distinguish two strands in the theological tradition which were not clearly held apart in the past, and to argue that they are not only distinguishable, but so related that only one of them can be true, and so related also that which one, if either, is true can be ascertained from the logical relations between the two strands alone, since one of the strands is incompatible alike with the assertion and the denial of the other, and hence, by recognized logical principles, is incompatible with itself and necessarily false. It is somewhat—to use another imperfect analogy—like the discovery in geometry of the independence of the parallel postulate from the other assumptions of Euclid; though in the theological case it is not really independence but inconsistency which is involved. Thus it is not a question of the logical possibility, merely, of what might be called a "non-Euclidean theology," but of its logical necessity, at least if there is to be any theology at all. (Unfortunately, there is no individual name which can conveniently serve as the theological parallel to Euclid; but Philo, a Jewish scholar of the first century, might be taken as the first man to give relatively complete expression to the postulate in question, and so we might speak of the current doctrine as non-Philonian theology, in a sense in which Aquinas, Spinoza, Royce, and orthodox Hinduism are all Philonian.)

The "strand" which theologians, on the whole, still propose to retain, and which is alone self-consistent, as judged by its relations to the other strand, is the popularly familiar definition of God as everlasting, all-controlling, all-knowing, and ethically good or "holy" to the highest possible degree. It may seem that this is just traditional theology and must involve the whole time-hallowed system. The extraordinary fact is that this has been found not to be the case. None of the older theologians (unless the neglected—and persecuted—Socinians, and the neglected Jew Gersonides, in the sixteenth and fourteenth centuries respectively, be

exceptions) were content with this popular definition of God and the consequences which genuinely follow from it. They invariably adopted other conceptions as even more fundamental; and rather than attempt seriously to deduce these other conceptions from the popular definition, they treated the latter as a more or less dangerously loose or anthropomorphic equivalent of the more fundamental definition. This more fundamental definition turns upon such terms as perfection, infinity, absoluteness, self-dependence, pure actuality, immutability. God, for all the church writers, and for many others, including Spinoza, was the "absolutely infinite," the altogether maximal, supreme, or perfect, being. All his properties, including the popular religious ones so far as philosophically valid, were to be deduced from this absoluteness or perfection, as is so beautifully explained by Thomas Aquinas.

It might seem, therefore, that the only alternative must be the now somewhat fashionable conception of a "finite" God. Fortunately this is not the case. I say fortunately, because the notion of a purely finite or imperfect deity seems to have all the weaknesses that overwhelmed primitive polytheism, plus a lamentable lack of variety. Of simply imperfect deities we can hardly have too many, in order that the virtues of one may make amends for the defects of another.

It is true that the expression "finite (or 'imperfect') God" has various meanings. Some who employ it mean perhaps only this: the traditional idea of infinity (or perfection) is erroneous, and the empirical method (which such writers are likely to profess) cannot establish any sort of perfection in God. Only if these authors assert that they *know* God to be in *no respect* perfect, or that it is impossible to know that he is in any respect perfect, is there much need to quarrel with them. They are seeking the minimal conception of God, and that is a useful attempt.

If theology is capable of rejuvenation, its hope lies rather, I believe, in a re-examination of the idea of infinity or perfection. Perhaps this idea is ambiguous, perhaps there is a sense in which God should be conceived as perfect, another sense in which perfection cannot apply to God, because (it may be) this sense involves an absurdity or, in other words, is really nonsense. Perhaps God is perfect in whatever ways perfection can really be conceived; but some among the traditional theological ways of trying to conceive perfection are capable of producing only pseudo-concepts devoid of consistent meaning.

To discuss God is, by almost universal usage, to discuss some manner of "supreme" or "highest" or "best" individual (or superindividual) being. As a minimal definition, God is an entity somehow *superior* to other entities. Now such superiority may be merely with respect to other actual entities, or with respect to all entities whether actual or possible. The second or more complete superiority seems to give the appropriate meaning of "perfection," and was defined long ago by Anselm in his description of God as "that than which none greater can be conceived." This definition presupposes only the ideas of *something* ("that"), *greater* or more or better (more in value) *than*, *negation* or none, and the conceivable or *possible,* and these ideas are secular as well as religious. Indeed, no ideas are more elementary and unavoidable in philosophy; hence it is clear that religion and philosophy can and must meet on common ground, provided the Anselmian definition successfully defines the religious object. But before we can decide whether the secular terms employed can apply to the God of religion we must be clear as to what the terms mean. Astonishingly enough, the simple phrase "none greater" involves two major equivocations, not indeed as Anselm used

the phrase, but as it might reasonably be used, even though the possibility of such usage seems not to have been clearly seen by Anselm or anyone else. The neglected usages constitute, together with Anselm's usage, a complete set of possible meanings of "perfect being," choice between which meanings *is* the theistic problem, a problem not fully stated until the neglected meanings are made explicit.

"None" may mean "no entity other than *that* (the being said to be perfect) *as it actually is,*" or it may mean "no entity other than *that as it either is or else could be or become.*" According to the first meaning (which follows automatically if one assumes that the perfect can have no potential states—an assumption not deducible from the mere idea of "none greater," because of the latter's equivocal connotation) the perfect is *unsurpassable in conception or possibility even by itself;* according to the second meaning it is *unsurpassable except by itself.* The first or absolute unsurpassability may be called *absolute perfection,* the second may be called *relative perfection.* (We shall see in the appendix to this chapter, and the reader may have noted, that there is still a third possibility, though apparently it is of no great importance.)

"Greater" has as many meanings as there are dimensions or *respects* of more and less (or better and worse). But from a purely formal point of view (important because it is exact and non-controversial) there are just three possibilities, two positive and one negative. By "greater" we may mean, "in *some* (but not all) respects" (say in size or in ethical goodness); or we may mean, "in *all* respects whatever"; while the joint negative of these two, "in *no* respect," gives the third possibility.

Combining the two meanings of "none" with the three meanings of "greater" we derive seven possible cases, only one of which is the unequivocal negation of "none greater," or of "unsurpassability even by the conceivable." Thus it is proved that the question, Is there a perfect being? is six distinct questions rather than one. Has anyone a right to assure us, in advance of exploration of the other five, that the Anselmian (unconscious) selection of one among the six—as the faithful rendering either of the religious question or of the most fruitful philosophical one—is safely established by the fact that the choice has been repeated no less unconsciously by multitudes of theologians? If anyone asserts this, I must doubt his understanding of the elementary requirements of good reasoning.

The seven cases can be arranged, in several different ways, into three main groups. The following of the possible triadic arrangements seems the most useful:

GROUP	SYM-BOL	CASE	SYM-BOL	INTERPRETATION
I	(A)	1	A	Absolute perfection in *all* respects.
II	(AX)	2	AR	Absolute perfection in *some* respects, relative perfection in all others.
		3	ARI	Absolute perfection, relative perfection, and "imperfection" (neither absolute nor relative perfection), each in *some* respects.
		4	AI	Absolute perfection in *some* respects, imperfection in all others.
III	(X)	5	R	Absolute perfection in *no* respects, relative in all.
		6	RI	Absolute perfection in *no* respects, relative in some, imperfection in the others.
		7	I	Absolute perfection in *no* respects, imperfection in all.

EXPLANATION OF SYMBOLS: A stands for absolute perfection, R for relative perfection, I for the joint negative of A and R, X for the negative of A (and thus for the disjunction of R and I), and (A) or (X) for the factors occurring throughout a group.

NOTE: It will be shown in the appendix to this chapter that imperfection can be subdivided into two possible forms, making fifteen cases in all, though the additional eight seem of little importance—despite the fact that all eight express modes of unsurpassability, and so of perfection in the most general sense!

In a different mode of presentation we have:

GROUP	I	II	III	
A in	*all*	*some*	*no*	respects
	(A)	(AX)	(X)	
CASE	1	2 3	4 5 6 7	
	A	AR ARI	AI R RI I	

NOTE: It might be thought that God's "supremacy" requires not only that he cannot conceivably be surpassed, but that he cannot even be equaled. Anyone who wishes to experiment with this conception of the *unrivaled as well as unsurpassed* is of course at liberty to do so. My reason for neglecting the concept—which might be called "incomparability"—is that I agree with the usual verdict of theologians that the unsurpassable is bound to be unique, so that if superiority is out of the question, equality is also. If good reason for doubting this verdict can be found, then "incomparability" should be substituted, at least experimentally, for "unsurpassability" in the definition of perfection.

So far as I know, this is the only rigorous *formal* classification (which as formal and a mere classification is beyond intelligent controversy) of possible doctrines about God—except mere dichotomies (e.g., God is or is not eternal, one with all reality, etc.), which are never very helpful because only one of the two classes has positive content. Yet, though formal, the classification is relevant to religion, if religion believes in an unsurpassable being. And it certainly is relevant to philosophy; for the seven cases (as formal possibilities) follow automatically from concepts which philosophy is bound to use.

At least the classification serves this purpose: it shows how hopelessly ambiguous are phrases like "perfect being," "finite God," "absolute," and the like. Six of the seven cases come under the phrase, "perfect being," if perfection means unsurpassability. At least four are compatible with the description, "finite." Four are definitely included in the class of "absolute" beings. Yet within each classification the differences are at least as important as the resemblances, indeed much more so. For it can be shown that the difference between absolute perfection in all, in some, and in no respects is the crucial difference, and yet it is neglected by all the concepts mentioned and by most generally current ones. (Some exceptions are Brightman's phrase, "finite-infinite God," and similar expressions used by W. P. Montague.)

Take, for example, the term pantheism. By any usual definition of this term, it should be possible to give a plausible interpretation of *all seven* of our cases as conforming to the definition. Thus pantheism means literally almost anything you please, and so nearly nothing. That is probably the chief reason for its popularity as a label for opponents. And it ought to be clear that to say, "God is the all," means whatever one's view of the all implies, perhaps nothing definite whatever, for offhand we have no clear notion of the all.

It is impossible to think effectively about seven possibilities at once. We think best in threes. As has been shown, the seven possibilities fall logically into three groups. God, if he exists, is *absolutely* (not relatively) perfect in all, in some, or in no respects. The usual view has been the first. Atheism is a special case of the third, in which man or some wholly imperfect thing is regarded as the nearest thing to a "supreme being" that exists. So here is the primary issue: Which group contains the truth? One of them, by absolute logical requirements, must do so. (If perfection is meaningless, this only makes case seven, that is, group three, true a priori.) When we know the answer to this question, we shall at least know whether or not the usual view of God ("usual" in philosophy and theology, perhaps not really usual in religion) is sound, and whether or not atheism or something close to it is sound, or whether, finally, the truth lies in a less explored region, the second group.

It must in all this discussion be understood that certain doubtful or trivial meanings of "perfect" or "unsurpassable" are excluded (merely to save time and energy), such as that a squirrel is perfect if it has all that is demanded by the concept (whose concept?) of a squirrel, or that a nail is as good as any other could be if it holds the building together as long and as well as is wanted. Such merely subjective or merely instrumental perfection is not what is meant by the perfection of God. It is not for this or that special purpose or point of view that God is unsurpassable. Rather it is his purpose and point of view themselves which are thought to be unsurpassable and the very standard of all other purposes or perspectives. Everything is good merely *for* something except persons, or at least sentient beings, but these are good in themselves. God (if he be an individual) must be at least sentient, or he is anything but unsurpassable.

These things being understood, it follows that *one, and only one, of the following propositions must be true:*

I. There is a being in *all* respects absolutely perfect or unsurpassable, in no way and in no respect surpassable or perfectible. (THEISM OF THE FIRST TYPE; absolutism, Thomism, most European theology prior to 1880.)

II. There is no being in all respects absolutely perfect; but there is a being in *some* respect or respects thus perfect, and in some respect or respects not so, in some respects surpassable, whether by self or others being left open. Thus it is not excluded that the being may be relatively perfect in all the respects in which it is not absolutely perfect (THEISM OF THE SECOND TYPE; much contemporary Protestant theology, doctrines of a "finite-infinite" or perfect-perfectible God.)

III. There is no being in *any* respect absolutely perfect; all beings are in all respects surpassable by something conceivable, perhaps by others or perhaps by themselves in another state. (Doctrines of a merely finite God, polytheism in some forms, atheism.)

This division is exclusive and exhaustive. To prove any two of these propositions false is to establish the truth of the remaining proposition; there can be no "higher synthesis" which combines the truth of any two or of all three of them, except as this synthesis amounts to accepting some one of the three as it stands and contradicting some part of each of the other two; that is, one of the three must be the higher synthesis. One may subdivide the three cases, but one cannot evade the necessity for rejecting some two and affirming some one of them as a whole, or else giving up the theistic question, the latter option being not an additional objective possibility but mere-

ly a subjective attitude toward the three possibilities. Of course one might say that there are two Gods, one corresponding to the first proposition, the other to the second proposition without the initial negative clause. But this would merely be a special case under Proposition One, and would have importance only if Proposition One is acceptable as it stands and Proposition Two false as it stands. After we have decided, if we do so decide, that there is one God wholly, partially, or not at all absolutely perfect, it will then be time enough to ask if there is also another God with another of the three characteristics.

Would it not be satisfying if the debate between atheism and theism turned out to have been so stubborn because the truth was in neither, as traditionally conceived, but in a middle ground not by any means a weak compromise between them but a clear-cut alternative as definite and legitimate, formally regarded, as any other? Without pretending here to anything like conclusiveness, I will give some reasons for taking this possibility seriously.

First of all, what does religion (not theology) say as to the three groups? Suppose the usual religious ideas of omniscience, omnipotence, and holiness or supreme righteousness be accepted. This seems to mean that God is absolutely perfect in knowledge, power, and ethical goodness. Does it follow that he is absolutely perfect in all respects? What about happiness or bliss? Surely religion is not, at any rate, so emphatic here. Is not God displeased by sin, and so something less than purely happy in beholding it? Does he not love us and therefore sympathize with our sufferings, wish that they might be removed? Do we not wish to "serve" God, carry out his purposes, contribute to his life somehow? All this must be explained as extremely misleading, if not indefensible, if God enjoys absolute bliss in eternity. But, you say, would not perfect power, wisdom, and goodness insure perfect bliss? Not at all, I answer with all the conviction I can feel about anything. To be happy is not a mere function of these three variables. For to know all that exists is not to know all that might exist, except as potentialities, and if potentialities are as good as actualities, then let us all cease to exist and be done with it. It is not even true that the omniscient must know details of the future, unless it can be proved, against Bergson, Whitehead, Peirce, James, and many others, that the future has any details to know. (Of course it *will be detailed,* but this does not imply that it has detailed will-be's as parts of itself now.)

Thus there is no reason why perfect knowledge could not change, grow in content, provided it changed only as its objects changed, and added as new items to its knowledge only things that were not in being, not there to know, previously. Again, to have perfect power over all individuals is not to have all power in such fashion as to leave the other individuals none. For to be individuals and to have some power are two aspects of the same thing. So even the greatest possible power (and that by definition is "perfect" power) over individuals cannot leave them powerless, and hence even perfect power must leave something to others to decide. And if one loves these others, and their decisions bring conflict and suffering, how can one, as loving toward them, escape a share in this sorrow? We know nothing of the nature of benevolence in ourselves if it is not a sharing, at least imaginative, in the interests of others, so that the partial defeat of these interests becomes in a real sense a partial defeat for us. Thus, perfect goodness is not a sufficient condition of all possible bliss. Rather, the good person suffers more than the bad at the spectacle of the badness and suffering of others. The dilemma appears final:

either value is social, and then its perfection cannot be wholly within the power of any one being, even God; *or it is not social at all,* and then the saying, "God is love," is an error. It may be said, however, that I have confused love with desire. I reply, Love *is* desire for the good of others, ideally all others, or I have yet to be told what it is.

So religion does not decide clearly in favor of group one, and seems rather to support group two. God is absolutely perfect (and in so far "without shadow of turning") in those things that depend by their nature upon one's own excellence alone. There is, for instance, nothing in the idea of knowledge to imply that God could not know all that goes on in the bad man as well as in the good; but if he equally derives (or equally does not derive) bliss from the two, so much the worse for his alleged goodness!

Inspection of the table of seven cases reveals also interesting implications for philosophy. If there is a being corresponding to case one, then there is a being totally exempt from the possibility of decrease or increase in value, hence of *change* in any significant sense. In such a being time is not, or at least is not time, which implies certain well known philosophical paradoxes. If, on the other hand, there is no being corresponding to any of the cases except those in the third group, if, that is, even the highest being is in all respects without absolute unsurpassability, then there is no individual being not capable of change (at least improvement) in any and every respect whatever; and in that case there is no enduring individual whose identity through all time is assured, for self-identity is incompatible with "change in all respects whatever." This threatens the intelligibility of time from the opposite point of view, for time must have some identity as well as differences. And it threatens religion, for the service of a God whose permanence is not assured fails to add anything essential to the service of men; and, moreover, the perfection of God is the heart of religious thought and feeling.

From another point of view one may reach the same result. Absolute and relative are polar concepts and seem to require each other, yet only group two makes this polarity affect the nature of the basic substance or individual. In religious terms, God, according to group two, is not just the creator opposed to the creatures, nor is he just another creature, but he is the creator-with-the-creatures, his reality is not in all respects as it would be did the creatures not exist. In doctrines of incarnation this is in a fashion recognized, but the point to weigh is whether any concept of God is philosophically or religiously defensible that does not make logical place for such a union of absolute and relative by rejecting case one as simply an error, not at all, as tradition affirms, the rationally knowable, as distinct from the revealed (incarnate), nature of God.

As among the three cases under group two, it might appear that case three (ARI) is the most promising of all, since it alone combines all three fundamental categories (surpassability by nothing, surpassability by self only, surpassability by others than self). But the third category is in a sense derivative. God can very well embrace surpassability by others, but as his property only in so far as it is that of relative beings united to him by virtue of his relative aspect. Thus if x comes to be surpassed by y, then God in his total value, as first including the value of x and then the value of y, will surpass himself in a manner which will be the reality of the x and y relation as enjoyed by him. But if God were incapable even of self-surpassing, then no surpassing could contribute anything whatever to his value or mean anything to him, for to him there would be no more or less but just sheer value.

On the other hand, as between cases two and four (AR and AI), the apparent choice is in favor of two. For AI implies that a being consists exclusively of an absolute fixed perfection plus a purely changeable and surpassable imperfection; or in other words, in so far as the being changed at all there would be no ultimate limit of any sort to this change, and no guarantee that the being which in some respects was absolutely perfect would remain even superior to others in his non-absolute aspects. Even supposing that two such pure opposites could constitute one individual or entity, this entity seems to have little to do with anything that has been meant by God.

Thus we have some reason for suspecting that the second case, AR, the farthest removed from atheism or pure relativism, the closest to the theological tradition, is the truth of the whole question. Since it is five steps away from atheism out of a possible six, lovers of the letter of orthodoxy who might feel inclined to attack case two as little better than atheism, or as a blasphemous or at best a crudely inept doctrine, might pause, before indulging in such judgment, long enough to consider—and I am confident they will not have done so before—what the five steps really mean. They mean, in fact, that most of traditional theology is acceptable to AR theorists as a description of one aspect of God, the A aspect. Yet since, on the other hand, the single step separating case two from the older theory involves the entire difference between admitting and not admitting real change, growth, possibility of profit, suffering, true sociality, as qualities of the divine, along with radical differences (as we shall see) in the meanings ascribed to creation, the universe, human freedom, and in the arguments for the existence of God, those inclined to think that any view that is intimately connected with theological traditions must have been disposed of by this time should also beware lest they commit a *non sequitur*. And finally, those who think that the modern experiments with a "finite" God have proved abortive might take heed of the radical ambiguity of all such phrases, and of the logical independence of case two from all of the four or five doctrines which could most reasonably be meant by them.

It is not even to be assumed that case one, at the opposite extreme seemingly from atheism, is really in every sense "farther" from it than is case two. For the "line" connecting the seven cases may be self-returning, if more than one dimension be involved. And this condition is here fulfilled. Case one makes God no more superior than does case two in the dimensions covered by A in AR, and it makes him infinitely *less* perfect in the R dimensions, if any, for these are such as to imply change, self-transcendence, for their value—as, for instance, does novelty as a dimension of value. Also, as we have seen, trying to treat these R dimensions under A might destroy even the dimensions to which A is appropriate. So the God of A might really and consistently have even less perfection than the human race, or whatever the atheist regards with such reverence as he may feel. Hume's *Dialogues* (Part IV) are one of the earliest expressions of insight into this meeting of extremes.

The formal analysis of perfection makes evident the absurdity of supposing the theistic question to be a mere product of superstition or of some "complex." The notions which define perfection are logically inevitable in philosophy. Either these notions admit consistent combination as required for the definition of perfection (in one or more of the six senses) or they do not. This depends solely upon the meanings of "greater," "none," and "possible." Hence if we do not know whether or not perfection is conceivable, and in what sense or senses, we do not know what we mean by concepts than which none could be more elementary in philosophy.

. . .

It will be noted that unsurpassability is verbally a pure negative. It can be correlated with a positive idea by the notion of totality. If a being has "all" the values that exist, then it is in all respects unsurpassed by anything actual. If it has all the values that are possible, then it is unsurpassable by anything possible. But if all values are not "compossible," cannot all coexist, as seems an almost obvious truth, then a purely final or static perfection possessing all possible values is impossible. We must then conceive perfection as partly dynamic, in some such manner as follows:

A being may have a relation to all actual values which, as a relation, has all the value possible, or as much value as possible, *in view of the relata* (the values given as actual), and the being may have a relation to all possible values as such which, as a relation to possibilities, could not be superior. Such a highest possible relation to actual and possible value might consist in this: that all possible values *would,* if and when actualized, belong to the being in question, that is, the being would always be unsurpassable, except by itself as it actualized more and more of the possibilities confronting it. Yet as possessing thus at all times the highest possible abstract *type of relation* to actuality and possibility the being would, in one aspect of itself, enjoy absolute or static perfection, be not only unrivaled but even incapable of improvement. All that is necessary to reconcile this with the religious idea is to show that such absolutes as omnipotence or omniscience or perfect righteousness or loving-kindness are abstract relational absolutes in the manner just indicated, and thus not only compatible with but inseparable from a qualitative, concrete aspect of perfection which is dynamic, since it involves inexhaustible possibilities for achievement. Is it not almost obvious, again, that the religious terms mentioned are abstract and relational precisely in the manner outlined?

One might try to make perfection positive in another way, by using the notion of surpassing all things rather than of being surpassed by none. But the reader will, I think, if he experiments with this idea, find that it leads to the same result. The importance of assuring a positive content for perfection is that otherwise one cannot well deny the contention of atheism that the word God is merely a word for what is left when we deny all that we know; that is, it represents what we know when we know nothing. This "negative theology" has often been praised, on the ground that all our knowledge is so inadequate to God that we must indeed negate it to arrive at God. But why not to arrive at non-being? Some positive content to the former idea there must be to distinguish it from the latter, and why not the utmost positive content, infinite, indeed? Surely a little dose of positivity will not suffice here. And the dilemma remains even in the negative theology, that either all value is compossible— which seems certainly untrue, for values conflict—or else God must fail to possess some values which yet are possible—and how then can he be incapable of growth in value? Possibilities which to God represented no possible achievements would be the same to him as no possibilities. True, one can recognize values for others, say their joys, without fully possessing or expecting to possess these as one's own, but what one cannot do is to fail in such a case to derive at least some value from the joys through the act of recognition itself, and precisely the most perfect mind would derive most from the satisfactions of others. It is the imperfection of man that compels him to admit that some of the joy which he wishes others to possess may when it comes contribute nothing to him, since he may be absent, dead, or somehow cut off from participation in the joy. Only the perfect can participate perfectly, gain for himself the entire sum of all actual gains.

If all values are compossible, and are all actual in God, then it is meaningless to say that some values are only possible. Possibility in that case ceases to have any distinctive meaning. Even if you say that God has not the actuality of what *for us* are possible values but rather a value above all our possibilities, you are only saying that what we call possibility is nothing from the ultimate standpoint. It is at least a serious thing to make the idea of God the destruction of a category without which it is doubtful that we can think at all.

. . .

Our classification of doctrines depends only upon the four following assumptions:

p. There is a difference between actual and possible (or conceivable) things.

q. There may be a difference between actual and possible states of an individual. (Not that God is assumed to be an individual in this sense, but that it is not assumed that he is not, in the statement of the classification, whose purpose is to state, not to answer, controversial questions.)

r. It is meaningful to say that one thing is higher or better than, or superior to (or has more of some variable property not a mere deficiency than), another; but this meaning is not simply univocal, since x may be better than y in one respect, say in ethical goodness, and not better in another, say in happiness. Thus "better than" is multi-dimensional. (The doctrine of the tradition that God is not simply better than other even possible beings, but is better than goodness itself, better than "best," since he transcends the concept of goodness altogether, does not alter the necessity that he be better-than-best in some, in none, or in all dimensions of value; or negatively, that he be surpassable in all, some, or no dimensions. The tradition spoken of clearly elected the first of the three formal cases, making God unsurpassable by anything conceivable, even by potential states of himself.)

s. The notions of "all," "some," and "none" exhaust the possible divisions of a plurality, hence of a plurality of respects of higher and lower. (Logicians distinguish between "all" and "every," but this seems of no importance here.)

These assumptions (except the last, which is clearly self-evident) are not posited absolutely. It may, you may believe, turn out that actual and possible coincide, or that the different dimensions of value or superiority are really one. The point is, we must not assume this at the outset. What we certainly must assume at the outset is that the question of such distinctions requires discussion, and that therefore every type of doctrine implied as formally possible *if* the distinctions are genuine must be given full and fair hearing. If two views formally distinguished turn out to be the same (since some alleged distinction separating them proves equal to zero), then that will be the conclusion reached; but it must be a conclusion, and not in any sense a formal premise, of the argumentation. There can be no harm in setting a terminological locus for alleged distinctions, admitting that they may assume every value of significance from zero to infinity; but there is very definite harm in depriving apparent distinctions of terminological and systematic locus, since their value is then determined as zero by fiat. Now the distinctions between "superior to actuality" and "superior even to possibility," or between "superior to other possible individuals" and to "other possible states of oneself" (as an individual identical in spite of changes or alternate possible states), or again, between "superior in all," "in some," or "in no" respects of value—these distinctions are urged upon us by universal experience and common-sense modes of thought. They may be overruled in the outcome, they can never validly be overruled before the outcome, of technical procedure. And we have painfully learned (all but one or two groups of philosophers) that the way to evaluate ideas is to deduce their consequences and compare these with the relevant data of experience. So we have no rightful alternative to the systematic development of the consequences of the distinctions mentioned. The discussion of the resulting doctrinal classifications is the bottleneck through which alone we can arrive, if ever, at a rational treatment of the theistic question.

. . .

But in pure logic it is not true that there is sheer contradiction between the joint admision of divine perfection of goodness and divine perfection of power, on the one hand, and the fact of real evil on the other, for the simple reason that the greatest possible power (which by definition is "perfect" power) may not be the same as "all the power that exists united into one individual power." For such union of "all" power may be impossible. Had God "all the power there is," he must be responsible for all that happens. But why assume that all real power could *possibly* belong to one individual? If it could not—and there is ground for this negative—then even the perfect or (by definition) greatest possible power is not all-power. Omnipotence (alas, our only word for perfection of power!) is power to the highest degree possible and over all that exists, it is "all" the power that *could* be exercised by any *one* individual over "all" that is; but it remains to be shown how much power *could* be exercised in this fashion. The minimal solution of the problem of evil is to affirm the necessity of a division of powers, hence of responsibilities, as binding even upon a maximal power. But this solution seems to imply the passivity of the supreme power, and hence not to be available to first-type theists.

Undoubtedly, "ethical" needs careful defining, but roughly it means action issuing from the fullest realization available to the individual of all the interests affected by the action. It does not necessarily mean observing the rules or codes recognized in any human society, except in so far as these represent the attempt of that society to make actions express the nearest thing to full realization of affected interests which is possible to the average human being. Being ethical does not mean never injuring anyone; for the interests of others may require such injury. Still less does being ethical mean never permitting any agency to bring injury to anyone; for not permitting this might be possible—owing to the division of power—only at the cost of greater injury through interference with other powers. Being ethical means acting from love; but love means realization in oneself of the desires and experiences of others, so that one who loves can in so far inflict suffering only by undergoing this suffering himself, willingly and fully. Those who think God cannot mean well toward us because he "sends" us suffering can prove their point only by showing that there is a way to run the universe, compatible with the existence of other real powers than just the supreme power, which would be more fully in accord with the totality of interests, or by showing that God sends us the suffering while himself remaining simply outside it, in the enjoyment of sheer bliss. Theologians themselves (first type) seem generally to have made a present of the latter notion to atheists; but the former view has its plausibility for all of us. I wish only to say here that I think neither is put beyond reasonable doubt by metaphysical necessity or empirical facts. It is poor method to try to estimate facts, especially such as are hard to measure with any accuracy, without careful survey of the logical structure of the ideas we bring to bear upon these facts. Therefore the facts of evil are not sufficient to justify dismissal of theology prior to the adequate exploration of its three main formal possibilities. Facts will never render decisions between ill-conceived alternatives; and the meaning of such terms as omnipotence or goodness depends in second-type theism upon a number of conceptions which have not been clearly considered in the classic discussions (such as the marvelous one in Hume's *Dialogues*) of the relations of such terms to the facts of evil.

One way of trying to escape a decision among the three possible views concerning God as a perfect being would be to say that perfection as "that than which nothing higher or better in a given respect is conceivable" is a meaningless concept, itself inconceivable. This, however, besides seeming tolerably dogmatic, would only be to say that Proposition Three is true by necessity; for if a predicate is nonsense, then of course nothing exists having that predicate. Hence no form of positivism can provide an evasion of the decision to be made. Nor can any other doctrine do so. What we have is a non-controversial statement of what the theistic controversy is. In general, I believe, all stubborn controversies in philosophy have involved questions the very existence of which as such is itself controversial, because they have not been formulated in neutral terms, terms that avoid arbitrarily limiting the prima facie possibilities.

. . .

Our basic trichotomy of doctrines may be put in still another way, which also gives a clue as to the possible validity of the neglected second type. If we define a "closed" dimension of value as one of which there can exist a supreme or maximal case, and an "open" dimension as one of which no supreme case is possible, then one of three things is true: *all* dimensions of value are closed, *some* dimensions are closed and some are open, or *none* are closed and all are open. It is indeed not formally evident that the first proposition defines first-type theism; for we have not specified or shown that the maximal case of the different dimensions must be found in the same real individual. But at least it is clear that if, and only if, the first of the dimensional propositions is true, first-type theism *may* be true; and that if the second dimensional proposition is true, second-type theism may be true, for then there may be a real case of perfection on some dimension which will not be a case of perfection upon all, because—by the assumptions—not all admit of perfection. (If the ontological argument were shown to be valid, the "may be true" would in both cases imply "is true.")

Now, is it particularly obvious that all dimensions of value must be closed dimensions, assuming some of them are? Consider the dimensions of goodness, knowledge, power, and duration. A being may perhaps be the maximal case of goodness if he guides his action by concern for *all* the interests affected by his actions. This "all" is the universe (up to the present, at least) so far as it contains values. Or, a being may be omniscient if he knows all there is to know: that is, again, the cosmos as a totality. A being may, similarly, be the maximal possible power if he controls all that exists to the greatest extent possible, that is, to the extent which is compatible with the measure of independence, if any, constitutive of the things controlled. Finally, a being may have maximal duration by being ungenerated and immortal, by

enduring throughout all time. So far, our dimensions seem to admit of maxima as at least conceivable.

But there are other dimensions of value. What could be meant by maximal happiness, or beauty, or "intensity" of joy, or variety, "the spice of life"? A being may enjoy all that exists, but perhaps he longs for what does not exist; or perhaps some of what exists is not altogether enjoyable (such as the sufferings of other sentient beings). Oh, well, you say, but if the being has maximal power, he can produce such beings as he wishes to enjoy. But there is social enjoyment, and this by definition depends partly on the self-determinations of the beings enjoyed. This cannot possibly be wholly coerced by any one term of the social relation, hence not even by the maximal "possible" power. The only escape at this point is to take shelter in the doctrine of the Trinity, which offers to furnish a social relation between persons all of whom are perfect. But still, we may ask, what in this relation is enjoyed? Is it "unity in variety," as seems to be the case with us? Supposing that variety in God is really compatible with his alleged simplicity, we still have to ask, What is meant by maximal variety? Is it that all possibilities are actualized in one actual state? But there are mutually incompatible alternatives (or there is no such thing as logic, or aesthetics). Besides, if all potentiality is also actuality in God, then the distinction between potential and actual must really be an anthropomorphic illusion, invisible from his point of view. At any rate, enjoyment varies as to intensity, and what can be meant by "all possible intensity," or "absolute intensity"?

Of course one could argue that an open dimension involves an infinite regress, and is therefore impossible. But this is a highly technical point, not to be taken for granted at this stage, where we are stating positions to be considered, not positions to be accepted once for all. My own view is that the infinite regress in question is an example of the "non-vicious" type of regress, since it concerns possibilities, and these not (on one view of potentiality) as a definite multitude, whose number is infinite, but as a continuum, which in the words of Peirce is "beyond all multitude," as God was formerly described as being; and indeed, as we shall see, the continuum of possibilities is one aspect of God which may be truly so described. It has also been argued that the maximal case is required as the standard or measure for all cases (Plato). But it may be that the maximal case on the closed dimensions would suffice to furnish the standard for the open ones, that, e.g., perfection of knowledge and goodness is in some sense the "measure" of degrees of happiness, even though the latter cannot be absolutely but only relatively perfect (R but not A).

Let us return to our conceivably closed dimensions and ask if they are not really ambiguous, not really in one sense necessarily open as well as, in another sense, capable of upper limits. To "know all that exists" is, in one sense, to have perfect knowledge, it is literal omniscience (provided possibilities are also known as such, as a special class of existences or, at least, of realities). But perhaps some of what exists is not as well worth knowing as some other things would have been had they existed. This implies no error or ignorance on the part of the knower, but it does imply the possibility of an increase in the aesthetic satisfaction derived from his knowledge, should a more varied or more harmonious world come into existence and be known. Again, one might deal justly and mercifully with all of one's world, and still be glad should this world itself improve in some way. The justice or mercy will not be improved from the ethical standpoint, but the just and merciful one will rejoice and gain in total satisfaction should the individuals being dealt with increase in goodness or happiness. Similarly, maximal power over a good world would not be so good as maximal power over a better one, though in both cases it would be as much power as is compatible with the world to be controlled; that is, in both cases it would be maximal simply as power, though not as total value realized by the one having the power.

True, if (as we shall later see reason to question) maximal power means power to create a beginning of finite existence in time, then it would seem that God could have started with as good a world as he chose. But a "best world" may be meaningless. And besides, the very next moment he would begin to confront the results of the choices, the exercises of power, granted to the creatures, and from then on his actual state, as constituting his knowledge, goodness, and power relations, would be as we have described it.

Nor does it help to argue that since God is timeless he knows and enjoys in advance all that the world ever will become. For he cannot enjoy all that the world ever *could* become as much as he would if it actually became it; for example, he cannot enjoy all the good deeds men might have performed as much as he would have, had the good deeds been performed. At least, this must be so if any vestige is to remain of religious ethics, and even perhaps of good sense. No more does it help to suggest that God's value is wholly independent of his relations to the world, whether of knowledge or of will, for this only means that the particular characters of the objects of his knowledge, or the results of his willing, are to him totally insignificant, which is psychologically monstrous and is religiously appalling as well. (It seems against every word concerning God in the entire Bible, for example, so far as any very direct interpretation is concerned.)

Thus we have every reason to take seriously, as the tradition has plainly not done, the hypothesis (at present merely that) of open dimensions of value, even for the perfect one. Let us remember that number is incapable of a maximum, that in whatever sense God may be "beyond number," still number can hardly be in every sense without value to him—or at any rate, variety can hardly be, and there is no more reason to speak of maximal variety than of maximal number. If, however, variety is said not to be a value for God, then one asks, Why a creation at all? Why should he add to his own perfection the contrast of the purely inferior creatures, unless contrast as such is valuable? And then, how can there be a maximum of contrast? It is no use to say that God creates the creatures out of generosity or love; for if he loves the valueless, so much the worse for his love, and what but the value of contrast can the creatures add to existence? Admittedly, they do not add "unity"!

Here then is a theology that either means nothing certainly identifiable (without supernatural grace or high genius in the art of reconnecting with experience concepts carefully divested of relation to it) or else means that the world might exactly as well not have existed, or as well have existed with far more evil or less good in it than it actually presents. In short, we have the view that the world, including the theologian, is strictly valueless to God, an absolute nullity from the standpoint of ultimate truth. I submit that this is a theology to be accepted, if at all, only after all other possibilities have been carefully considered and found hopelessly untenable. If a man denies this, I only say that I scarcely believe he is thinking about what he is saying. And the writings of those who apparently do deny it show little enough evidence of thought on this aspect of the question. The very question seems, by a near-miracle of persistent looking the other way, to be passed over. Is this merely the "method of tenacity" or is there a more generous explanation?

. . .

The philosophical importance of admitting *some* non-absolute aspects of God is in the resulting applicability of such categories as change, passivity, complexity, and the like, to him, and for this purpose surpassability of God, *as he actually is,* even if only by God himself as he could or can be, is entirely sufficient. Now though the actuality of deity is, according to second-type theism, in some respects surpassable, his *individuality* as potentially inclusive of other than his actual predicates may be in no respect whatever surpassable, in all dimensions though not in all senses perfect. To say this is not to commit second-type theism to the view that God is an "individual." We are speaking of subalternatives which the second basic proposition admits, not of corollaries which it necessarily implies. All the proposition demands is that there be a God in some respect unsurpassable, in some other surpassable—whether self-surpassable and how, or surpassable by other entities not states of himself, or whether he has "states," being left perfectly open by the proposition. Exploration of the subalternatives may well lead to the conclusion that only one of them is really "conceivable" in the full sense (in the light of the experiential content of the ideas involved). But this again is a matter to be held in suspension until we have established some control of the relations between the basic propositions.

God, for both old and much new theology, is the being whose uniqueness consists in his unrivaled excellence, or whose amount of value defines a necessarily one-membered class (and so in a sense not a class). In some respects he is absolutely unexcelled, even by himself in another conceivable state; in *all other* respects he is (to state the view reached in this book) the only individual whose states or predicates are not to be excelled unless he excel them with other states or predicates of his own. To take an imperfect analogy, no one will ever be or can ever be so Wordsworthian as Wordsworth; but Wordsworth himself, if he (or someone about him) had made a different use of his free will, might perhaps have been somewhat "more himself," might have developed his individuality more than he did. And certainly, at any stage in his life, one could have said that he was the most Wordsworthian being that would ever exist, except as he himself might later become more so. God, however, is not simply more himself than any other can ever be; he and he alone is in all respects superior to any state that will ever characterize any individual unless it characterize him. He is the greatest conceivable actuality, except perhaps as he himself can be conceived as greater (in another, perhaps subsequent, state, or in a state he might have had in the past, had men, say, served him more faithfully).

There is a slight ambiguity in the expression "excelled by himself only." We may ourselves in the future enjoy values which God now lacks (because they are not in being). But according to AR he will not lack them when we enjoy them, so that our self-excelling will be also (infinitely magnified) his self-excelling. Thus R means that "in no possible state of affairs can there be anything in any fashion superior to God as he is in that same state of affairs."

It will be seen that the new doctrine requires careful and somewhat elaborate distinctions, and yet, if some of its supporters are right, the doctrine is nothing at all but the analysis of the simple idea that God is "the perfectly loving individual," in all respects possessed of the properties which this idea requires, even if non-perfection in some respects be among the requirements.

That God is less than he might be (though more than anything else might be) agrees with the religious conception of the free service of God. For if we had no choice but to serve God in the fullest measure, or if we could not serve him at all, then it might be held with some plausibility that he is all that he might be. But the possibility of being freely served seems clearly to imply the possibility of lacking something that better service than may actually be given would furnish. Philosophical orthodoxy has had to finesse this point, and indeed, as I believe, has fallen into sophistry of a rather revolting kind. Really there was to be no service of God, but only a service of men through the—to them—beneficial practices of religion. Sin did no real harm whatever in the universe, since the absolute perfection which the universe involves in its cause could never be more or less than absolute. To say that sin at least harmed *men* is beside the point; for what harm did it do to harm men, parts of a system of reality that as a whole or in its ultimate reality was incapable of loss or gain? The world plus the absolutely infinite is no more than the latter by itself. Only from a purely race-egoistic (and illusory) point of view could the harm appear as such. Thus the motivation which is the (attempted) attitude of pure atheistic humanism was the only one philosophers could approve in religion. The idea of cosmic concern, concern for the divine values, must now at last be considered on its merits.

A very simple way to settle the theistic question is the positivistic analysis, which results in the rejection of theism of the first type as meaningless, theism of the third type (finite God, such as Zeus) as meaningful but devoid of empirical evidence and so not worth discussing, and —yes, what of theism of the second type? Is it meaningless or is it merely not in accord with the evidence? Against the first of these possibilities is to be set the fact that the very arguments by which positivists endeavor to show the meaninglessness of theism of the first type have for some decades been employed by defenders of theism, type two. Hence if the latter is also meaningless it is not likely to be for the same or very similar reasons. The doctrine has been formulated with the requirements of meaning carefully in view. Against the supposition that second-type theism is without experiential support is to be set the fact that its defenders also employ that very argument against theism of the first type, and that the emergence of the second-type theory has been the result of a deliberate and cooperative effort, undertaken by some men of genius and many men of excellent scientific and logical training, to discover the experiential referent, if any, of theism. If these men believe they have succeeded in finding such a referent, then it is not philosophy but debate to assert, without investigation, that they cannot have found it.

It will be seen that the God of second-type theism is not without qualification finite, or growing, or emergent; nor, without qualification, is he the contradictory of these. The traditional distrust of simple statement, and of language as applied to the religious vision, in the new theology ceases to be an inoperative or in-consistently employed formal concession, and becomes a systematic tracing of the relativity of concepts to each other and to experience as a whole. The concepts which still function as absolute are the strictly religious and experiential ones of love and goodness. God is the Holy One, the ethical Absolute, the literally all-loving Father. In these affirmations second-type theism sees no exaggeration. It holds that the distinction between God's ethical perfection (and hence ethical immutability) and his "aesthetic" perfectibility (and hence growth) fits the later Hebrew and other high religions (most of all what some of us would mean by Christianity) far more naturally and unambiguously than does the confusion of every perfection in the unchanging *actus purus* of the Scholastics (and even of Schleiermacher). Furthermore, Whitehead and others have shown that it is precisely love which must be perfect in God—and only love and what is implied by it as perfect—if either love or perfection is to serve as an explanatory concept in cosmology. (The idea that the religious content of Whitehead's system is dragged in, and that what his system requires is some "impersonal" force or function having no essential connection with love, is in my opinion a thorough misunderstanding.)

. . .

SUGGESTIONS FOR FURTHER READING

The problem of evil is forcibly presented in J. S. Mill, *Three Essays on Religion;* J. M. E. McTaggart, *Some Dogmas of Religion* (London: Arnold, 1906); and John Mackie, "Evil and Omnipotence," *Mind,* 1955 (replies in subsequent issues). The following works contain attempts to deal with the problem within a theistic framework: G. W. Leibniz, *Theodicy;* William Temple, *Nature, Man, and God* (New York: Macmillan, 1934); Josiah Royce, *The Religious Aspect of Philosophy* (New

York: Houghton Mifflin, 1887); D. J. B. Hawkins, *The Essentials of Theism* (New York: Sheed and Ward, 1949).

For the logical positivist rejection of theism, see A. J. Ayer, *Language, Truth, and Logic,* 2nd ed. (New York: Dover, 1946). *New Essays in Philosophical Theology,* Antony Flew and Alasdair MacIntyre, eds. (New York: Macmillan, 1955), and *Faith and Logic,* Basil Mitchell, ed. (London: Allen and Unwin, 1957), contain discussions of religious problems, both pro and con, by practitioners of linguistic analysis. See also C. B. Martin, *Religious Belief* (Ithaca: Cornell Univ. Press, 1959); John Wisdom, "Gods," in Antony Flew, ed., *Essays in Logic and Language,* First Series (Oxford: Basil Blackwell, 1951); and Alasdair MacIntyre, "The Logical Status of Religious Belief," in *Metaphysical Beliefs* (London: SCM Press, 1957).

Among the important treatments of religion from a psychological point of view are Sigmund Freud, *Totem and Taboo,* A. A. Brill, tr. (New York: Dodd, Mead, 1918), and *Moses and Monotheism,* Katherine Jones, tr. (New York: Knopf, 1939); Carl Jung, *Psychology and Religion* (New Haven: Yale Univ. Press, 1938); Erich Fromm, *Psychoanalysis and Religion* (London: Victor Gollancz, 1951); and A. T. Boisen, *The Exploration of the Inner World* (New York: Harper, 1952). From a sociological point of view: Emile Durkheim, *The Elementary Forms of the Religious Life,* J. W. Swain, tr. (London: Allen and Unwin, 1915); Vilfredo Pareto, Vol. III of *The Mind and Society,* Andrew Bongiorno and Arthur Livingston, tr. (New York: Harcourt, Brace & World, 1935), 4 vols.; V. F. Calverton, *The Passing of the Gods* (New York: Scribner's, 1934); and G. E. Swanson, *The Birth of the Gods* (Ann Arbor: Univ. of Michigan Press, 1961). R. S. Lee, *Freud and Christianity* (New York: Wyn, 1949), is a penetrating discussion of the Freudian treatment of religion.

4.

IMMORTALITY

In our society the immortality of the soul stands with the existence of God in forming the twin foundations of religious belief. As the existence of God is the basic presupposition of all the more specific beliefs concerning the nature and activities of the supernatural other, so the doctrine of the immortality of the soul is thought to be the foundation of a religious conception of man. And if we look beyond our own society, we find the belief in immortality even more widespread than the belief in God, at least if we restrict the term *God* to a supernatural personal being. Although we find religions—for example, certain forms of Buddhism —in which the belief in a personal deity plays no central role, we would be hard pressed to find any religion in which the belief in immortality is not central. As James says, "Religion, in fact, for the great majority of our own race *means* immortality, and nothing else." (See below, pp. 443–55.)

However, this is true only in a wide sense of "immortality," which will include many specific variations. In particular, immortality, in this wide sense, will embrace the following specific forms:

1. Disembodied existence of the soul after the death of the body.

2. Reincarnation of the soul, that is, continued existence in some other body.

3. Absorption or merging of the soul into the divine. This involves a loss of separateness and self-identity, an identification of the individual with the divine. Usually it is not thought of as a prolongation of existence through time, but rather as a radical shift from temporal existence to a timeless mode of being.

4. Resurrection of the body. After a time the person's body is miraculously reassembled, presumably in some more rarefied form, after which he carries on a bodily existence indefinitely.

Varied as these beliefs are, they yet possess an important common feature, one which justifies us in ranging them all under a common label: They all involve the belief that in some way or other the individual person continues to exist after the dissolution of his present body, that *he* survives bodily death. At first sight this might not seem true of the third form. If the soul loses itself in God as the river merges into the sea, it would seem that the soul does not continue its existence apart from its present body. But, paradoxically enough, the mystic continues to speak of this condition as a state of the individual soul, as something the soul enjoys and delights in, something which constitutes the supreme realization of the soul's nature. The analogy of merging is not followed to its logical conclusion.

If we ask where the Judaeo-Christian conception of immortality fits into this classification, the answer cannot be a simple one. It is noteworthy that in the classic Christian creeds there is no mention of a disembodied future existence. What is mentioned is "The resurrection of the body and the life everlasting" (Apostle's Creed) and "The resurrection from the dead and the life of the world to come" (Nicene Creed). In this, Christianity was faithful to its Jewish heritage. A pure form of the doctrine of resurrection would hold that between the death of an individual and the Day of Judgment, on which all the dead will be resurrected, nothing at all of the individual survives. On that great day he will resume his existence after a complete lapse. But the doctrine has rarely been held in so pure a form, at least in Christianity. Christian thought was heavily influenced from the beginning by Platonic notions of the soul as a separate immaterial substance with a career of its own, and most Christian theologians have attempted a synthesis of the two conceptions. Thomas Aquinas, for example, held that after death the soul continues to exist without the body, but that the human person cannot exercise a fully human existence until this soul is reunited with its appropriate body. I think it is fair to say that most Christians at the present time pay scant attention to the doctrine of resurrection and think of immortality, if at all, in terms of disembodied existence.

Some of those people who have felt that immortality is unattainable in any of the full-blooded forms we have been considering have proposed that we console ourselves with various forms of quasi-survival which undoubtedly are real. The most important of these are as follows:

Biological immortality. We become immortal through our children, through the fact that something of us survives in them. This notion is given considerable elaboration by philosophers like Bergson, who picture the germ plasm, the bearer of the reproductive mechanism, as the fundamental substantial reality, of which particular organisms are mere offshoots. The germ plasm is immortal, though the forms it assumes are continually shifting. Plato in the *Symposium* (208) speaks of "that law of succession by which all mortal things are preserved, not absolutely the same, but by substitution, the old worn-out mortality leaving another new and similar existence . . . in this way the mortal body, or mortal anything partakes of immortality."

Social immortality. We are immortal through our influence, our effects on succeeding generations, through the remembrance of us that remains in the minds of men in the future. Again, from the *Symposium* (208), "Think only of the ambition of men, and you will wonder at the senselessness of their ways, unless you consider how they are stirred by the love of an immortality of fame. They are ready to run all risks . . . for the sake of leaving behind them a name which shall be eternal. . . . I am persuaded that all men do all things, and the better they are the more they do them, in hope of the glorious fame of immortal virtue; for they desire the immortal."

Ideal immortality. This is a certain mode of existence which is atemporal in its distinctive character. A person enjoys this sort of experience whenever he is engaged in time-transcending spiritual activities like meditation, mathematical reasoning, or aesthetic contemplation, that is, whenever the objects of his attention are themselves timeless. This concept is beautifully expounded by Santayana, from whom I derived the term. (See the part of the selection from Santayana in Section 8, which bears this title.)

Though not without interest, these forms of "immortality" raise no special philosophical problems, and in any event one would not put them into the forefront of discussion unless he were convinced that the genuine article were unavailable.

Let us now consider the terms in which survival of bodily death is to be formulated. A serious problem is posed by the fact that while traditionally the problem has been discussed in terms of the fate of something called "the soul," contemporary science and philosophy have, for the most part, discarded this concept. This would seem to render belief in immortality unworthy of serious attention, unless it were possible to formulate the belief without employing the soul concept. We must now consider that possibility.

The word *soul* has traditionally been used to mean a substantial psychic agent—in Descartes' terms, a thinking substance, an entity which is as much a thing in its own right as is the human body, but which differs from the body in being immaterial and nonspatial, and which is more or less loosely connected with the bodily substance to form the complete human being. The soul is thought of as the subject of the states and activities which go to make up human consciousness: feelings, sensations, desires, thoughts, decisions, and so on. It is that which feels, desires, thinks, just as the body is that which walks, breathes, digests.

It is certainly true that this concept has been totally abandoned by modern psychology, and largely abandoned by recent philosophy. Both psychologists and philosophers now tend to operate with a more organismic picture of the human being—not as a conjunction of two substances, but as a single substance which has physical, biological, and psychological aspects or dimensions. It is neither the soul, nor the body, but the complete human being, the person, who performs physical activities like walking, biological activities like digesting, and psychological activities like thinking.

But what is the significance of this new approach for our problem? Does the belief in immortality require the assumption of a soul in the traditional sense? Or can the belief in immortality be formulated in terms of this latter conceptual framework? Of course, I cannot believe that my *soul* is immortal unless I believe that I have a soul. But perhaps the core of the traditional belief could be reconceived and restated in other terms. To explore this possibility we shall have to get clear as to what it is that we hope for, or fear, when we hope for, or fear, immortality. A long line of philosophers, beginning with John Locke, in the chapter on personal identity in his *Essay Concerning Human Understanding,* have argued persuasively that the question of the continued existence of a person after death really has nothing to do with the traditional notion of a substantial soul. Locke's point in the *Essay* could be put as follows: Assuming the existence of soul substances, suppose that when I die my soul will then enter the body of an infant being born into a shepherd family in Siberia, but that this Siberian shepherd will never have any memory of any of my actions, thoughts, or feelings, will never have any consciousness of having done or suffered the things I have done or suffered. If I believed that this would happen, would I be believing that *I* would survive the death of my body? It seems not. This is not what one means by *himself* surviving death. Given these conditions it would be just as if I had died and another person had been born in Siberia. Thus it seems that survival of the same immaterial substance is not a sufficient condition of the survival of a given person. But neither is it a necessary condition. Suppose I think of my mind as a temporally extended series of conscious states of various sorts—thoughts, feelings, sensations, wishes, and so on. These conscious states are bound together into one mind in various ways, for example, by the fact that from time to time memories of earlier parts of the series occur, by the fact that there is a continuous development from one stage to a temporally contiguous stage. If I should suppose that after the death of my body conscious states would continue to occur which were connected to my conscious states in this life, and to each other, in the same ways as those in which my conscious states in this life are connected to each other—in other words, if I should suppose that the series would continue to have new members—then I would be supposing that *I* would continue to exist, as the same person, whether or not I supposed that underlying these conscious states there was some immaterial soul substance which remained the same throughout. No doubt there are difficulties in the conception of a series of conscious states occurring without any bodily substratum; some of these difficulties are brought out in the selection by Antony Flew. But at least these considerations show that the abandonment of the traditional concept of a soul substance does not in itself force an abandonment of the belief in immortality. For, leaving aside the difficulties brought out by Flew, one can formulate a concept of a person as a series of conscious states and can then mean by the indefinite survival of the same person the indefinite continuance of a given series of such states. Philosophers like C. J. Ducasse, who take the notion of immortality seriously without subscribing to a Cartesian notion of the soul, are working with something like this interpretation.

Traditionally, there have been two principal metaphysical arguments for immortality, meaning by metaphysical arguments those which are based on very general considerations concerning the nature of man, the universe, and so on. One is the argument presented by Jacques Maritain: that the soul cannot be destroyed because it is absolutely simple, that is, without parts. How would one go about removing perception from its juxtaposition to punctuality, or tear memory away from cheerfulness? Basically one cannot do this because the soul has no spatial location. Where could it be located—in the head, the feet, or perhaps hovering a few feet above the body? Since its parts, if we may use that expression, are not spread out in space, we can attach no meaning to moving them away from their spatial juxtaposition.

Note that this argument is necessarily couched in terms of a soul, an immaterial thing, which may or may not be destroyed. If we abandon this concept and think of a person as a series of conscious states, then the question "Is it destroyed?" cannot arise. A series does not have to be destroyed. It simply ceases to have new members, or, more accurately, no new members occur. Hence if we abandon the soul concept, this argument cannot even get started. But even if we admit the existence of a soul, the argument is not conclusive. It depends on the principle that a thing can be destroyed only by separating its parts. But how was that principle established? By surveying material things and noting that any way we have of destroying them involves taking them apart. Our survey cannot include other than material things, for we do not know how to destroy anything else. But then why suppose that this principle is also applicable to a spiritual thing like a soul? If the soul is as different from material things as those who believe in its existence suppose it to be, then why should it not have a mode of destruction which is quite different from the one suitable for material things? Why suppose that anything could be destroyed only in the way physical things are destroyed? Immanuel Kant, in the *Critique of Pure Reason,* suggests a mode of destruction which would be appropriate for an immaterial soul. Although a soul does not have extensive quantity—is not spread out in space—it does have intensive quantity—its consciousness is more or less intense at different times. For example, it gradually increases in intensity as a person is waking up. Now why might not a soul be destroyed by its intensity diminishing to zero, as in deep sleep, and staying that way. It would simply die out like a note of music. That would be a mode of destruction proper to a thing exhibiting intensive quantity, just as a fragmentation of parts is proper to a thing exhibiting extensive quantity.

The second argument is based on moral considerations: We see that good or ill fortune does not come to people in accordance with their righteousness or wickedness. Hence men must continue to live beyond death, so that the ledger will be balanced in the end. As A. E. Taylor [1] puts it:

> In what we see of human life from birth to the grave, it is clearly not the case that our will finds fulfillment or frustration according to its moral quality. . . . It is plain, then, that if there is a purpose for which nature is throughout subservient, and that purpose is the development of moral personality in rational beings, this purpose is not attained in what we see of human life; there must be a continuation of our personal lives into the unseen, and it must be there, not here, that the end to which nature is the means is achieved.

On the assumption that the universe is directed by a theistic God to a moral end, this argument seems cogent, although one might object that even given that assumption, we are not entitled to feel much confidence in any supposition as to what such an end, as envisaged by God, would involve, even the supposition that it would have to include an indefinite continuance of each human person. However, one must surely admit that a belief in immortality would be a reasonable one if the assumption in question is justified. But this is a large "if."

The selection from Flew presents a line of argument of a more direct kind. If human beings do survive death, should we not expect to hear of individual cases from time to time? Of course there are many claims to such indications, and a consideration of such claims must play a part in any thorough treatment of this problem. Many people will be inclined to dismiss such claims without examination. Such people might well take to heart the following passage from C. D. Broad: [2]

> I shall no doubt be blamed by certain scientists, and, I am afraid, by some philosophers, for having taken serious account of the alleged facts which are investigated by Psychical Researchers. I am wholly impenitent about this. The scientists in question seem to me to confuse the Author of Nature with the Editor of *Nature;* or at any rate to suppose that there can be no productions of the former which would not be accepted for publication by the latter. And I see no reason to believe this.

The main argument against immortality has always been the one from the dependence, or supposed dependence, of mental phenomena on the body. This line of argument is so clearly presented by R. W. Sellars and Ducasse, and so clearly criticized by the latter, that further comment on my part is not called for.

---

[1] *Does God Exist?*, New York: Macmillan (1947), p. 95.

[2] Preface, *The Mind and Its Place in Nature,* London: Routledge & Kegan Paul (1925).

JACQUES MARITAIN

A Proof of the Immortality of the Soul

Jacques Maritain (1882–   ) is perhaps the leading contemporary Thomist philosopher. He has worked in every branch of philosophy, applying Thomistic principles to contemporary problems. He left his native France in 1940 and has been a resident in the United States since that time.

THE EXISTENCE OF THE SOUL

. . .

It is of this immortality, and of the way in which the Scholastics established its rational certainty, that I should now like to speak.

We must of course realize that we have a soul before we can discuss whether it is immortal. How does St. Thomas Aquinas proceed in this matter?

He observes first that man has an activity, the activity of the intellect, which is in itself immaterial. The activity of the intellect is immaterial because the proportionate or "connatural" object of the human intellect is not, like the object of the senses, a particular and limited category of things, or rather a particular and limited category of the qualitative properties of things. The proportionate or "connatural" object of the intellect is the nature of the sense-perceivable things considered in an all-embracing manner, whatever the sense concerned may be. It

is not only—as for sight—color or the colored thing (which absorbs and reflects such or such rays of light) nor—as for hearing—sound or the sound-source; it is the whole universe and texture of sense-perceivable reality which can be known by the intellect, because the intellect does not stop at qualities, but pierces beyond, and proceeds to look at essence (that which a thing *is*). This very fact is a proof of the spirituality, or complete immateriality of our intellect; for every activity in which matter plays an intrinsic part is limited to a given category of material objects, as is the case for the senses, which perceive only those properties which are able to act upon their physical organs.

There is already, in fact, a certain immateriality in sense-knowledge; knowledge, as such, is an immaterial activity, because when I am in the act of knowing, I become, or am, the very thing that I know, a thing other than myself, insofar as it is other than myself. And how can I be, or become, other than myself, if it is not in a supra-subjective or immaterial manner? Sense-knowledge is a very poor kind of knowledge; insofar as it is knowledge, it is immaterial, but

From Jacques Maritain, *The Range of Reason* (1952), "The Immortality of the Soul." Reprinted by permission of Geoffrey Bles Ltd., and Charles Scribner's Sons.

it is an immaterial activity intrinsically conditioned by, and dependent upon, the material functioning of the sense-organs. Sense-knowledge is the immaterial achievement, the immaterial actuation and product of a living bodily organ; and its very object is also something half material, half immaterial, I mean a physical quality *intentionally* or immaterially present in the medium by which it acts on the sense-organ (something comparable to the manner in which a painter's idea is immaterially present in his paint-brush).

But with intellectual knowledge we have to do with an activity which is in itself completely immaterial. The human intellect is able to know whatever participates in being and truth; the whole universe can be inscribed in it; this means that, in order to be known, the object known by the intellect has been stripped of any existential condition of materiality. This rose, which I see, has contours; but Being, of which I am thinking, is more spacious than space. The object of the intellect is universal, for instance that universal or de-individualized object which is apprehended in the idea of man, of animal, of atom; the object of the intellect is a universal which remains what it is while being identified with an infinity of individuals. And this is only possible because things, in order to become objects of the mind, have been entirely separated from their material existence. To this it must be added that the operation of our intellect does not stop at the knowledge of the nature of sense-perceivable things; it goes further; it knows by analogy the spiritual natures; it extends to the realm of merely possible things; its field has infinite magnitude.

Thus, the objects known by the human intellect, taken not as things existing in themselves, but precisely as objects determining the intellect and united with it, are purely immaterial.

Furthermore, just as the condition of the *object* is immaterial, so is the condition of the *act* which bears upon it, and is determined or specified by it. The object of the human intellect is, as such, purely immaterial; the act of the human intellect is also purely immaterial.

And, moreover, if the act of the intellectual power is purely immaterial, that *power* itself is also purely immaterial. In man, this thinking animal, the intellect is a purely spiritual power. Doubtless it depends upon the body, upon the conditions of the brain. Its activity can be disturbed or hindered by a physical disorder, by an outburst of anger, by a drink or a narcotic. But this dependence is an *extrinsic* one. It exists because our intelligence cannot act without the joint activity of the memory and the imagination, of the internal senses and external senses, all of which are organic powers residing in some material organ, in some special part of the body. As for the intellect itself, it is not *intrinsically* dependent upon the body since its activity is immaterial; the human intellect does not reside in any special part of the body. It is not contained by the body, but rather contains it. It uses the brain, since the organs of the internal senses are in the brain; yet the brain is not an organ of the intelligence; there is no part of the organism whose act is intellectual operation. The intellect has no organ.

Finally, since intellectual power is spiritual, or purely immaterial in itself, its *first substantial root*, the subsisting principle from which this power proceeds and which acts through its instrumentality, is also spiritual.

So much for the spirituality of the intellect. Now, thought or the operation of the intellect is an act and emanation of man as a unit; and when I think, it is not only my intellect which thinks: it is *I*, my own self. And my own self is a bodily self; it involves matter; it is not a spiritual or purely immaterial subject.

The body is an essential part of man. The intellect is not the whole man.

Therefore the intellect, or rather the substantial root of the intellect, which must be as immaterial as the intellect, is only a part, albeit an essential part, of man's substance.

But man is not an aggregate, a juxtaposition of two substances; man is a natural whole, a single being, a single substance.

Consequently, we must conclude that the essence or substance of man is single, but that this single substance itself is a compound, the components of which are the body and the spiritual intellect: or rather matter, of which the body is made, and the spiritual principle, one of the powers of which is the intellect. Matter —in the Aristotelian sense of prime matter, or of that root potentiality which is the common stuff of all corporeal substance—matter, substantially united with the spiritual principle of the intellect, is ontologically molded, shaped from within and in the innermost depths of being, by this spirtual principle as by a substantial and vital impulse, in order to constitute that body of ours. In this sense, Saint Thomas, after Aristotle, says that the intellect is the form, the substantial form of the human body.

That is the Scholastic notion of the human soul. The human soul, which is the root principle of the intellectual power, is the first principle of life of the human body, and the substantial form, the *entelechy,* or that body. And the human soul is not only a substantial form or entelechy, as are the souls of plants and animals according to the biological philosophy of Aristotle; the human soul is also a spirit, a spiritual substance able to exist apart from matter, since the human soul is the root principle of a spiritual power, the act of which is intrinsically independent of matter. The human soul is both a soul and a spirit, and it is its very substantiality, subsistence and existence, which are communicated to the whole human substance, in order to make human substance be what it is, and to make it subsist and exist. Each element of the human body is human, and exists as such, by virtue of the immaterial existence of the human soul. Our body, our hands, our eyes exist by virtue of the existence of our soul.

The immaterial soul is the first substantial root not only of the intellect, but of all that which, in us, is spiritual activity; and it is also the first substantial root of all our other living activities. It would be inconceivable that a non-spiritual soul, that kind of soul which is not a spirit and cannot exist without informing matter—namely, the souls of plants or animals in Aristotelian biology— should possess a power or faculty *superior* to its own degree in being, that is, immaterial, or act through a supra-material instrumentality independent of any corporeal organ and physical structure. But when it is a question of a spirit which is a soul, or of a *spiritual soul,* as the human soul is, then it is perfectly conceivable that such a soul should have, aside from immaterial or spiritual faculties, other powers and activities which are organic and material, and which, relating to the union between soul and body, pertain to a level of being *inferior* to that of the spirit.

THE SPIRITUALITY OF THE HUMAN SOUL

Thus, the very way in which the Scholastics arrived at the existence of the human soul also established its spirituality. Just as the intellect is spiritual, that is to say intrinsically independent of matter in its operation and in its nature, so also, and for the same reason, the human soul, the substantial root of the intellect, is spiritual, that is, intrinsically independent of matter in its nature and in its existence; it does not live by the body, the body lives by it. The human soul is a spiritual substance which, by its substantial union with matter, gives existence and countenance to the body.

That is my second point. As we have seen, the Scholastics demonstrated it by a metaphysical analysis of the intellect's operation, carefully distinguished from the operation of the senses. They adduced, of course, much other evidence in support of their demonstration. In their consideration of the intellect, they observed, for instance, that the latter is capable of *perfect reflection,* that is, of coming back entirely upon itself—not in the manner of a sheet of paper, half of which can be folded on the other half, but in a complete manner, so that it can grasp its whole operation and penetrate it by knowledge, and can contain itself and its own principle, the existing self, in its own knowing activity, a perfect reflection or self-containing of which any material agent, extended in space and time, is essentially incapable. Here we are confronted with that phenomenon of self-knowledge, of *prise de conscience* or becoming aware of oneself, which is a privilege of the spirit, as Hegel (after St. Augustine) was to emphasize, and which plays so tremendous a part in the history of humanity and the development of its spiritual energies.

In the same way it is possible to show that the human will, which is rooted in the intellect, and which is able to determine itself, or to master the very motive or judgment which determines it and is made efficacious by the will itself, is spiritual in its operation and nature. Every material agent is subject to the universal determinism. Free will is the privilege, the glorious and weighty privilege, of an agent endowed with immaterial power.

We are responsible for ourselves; we choose for ourselves and decide on our own ends and our own destinies. We are capable of spiritual, supra-sensuous love, and desire and joy, which are naturally intermingled with our organic and sensuous emotions, but which are in themselves affections of the spiritual will, and are awakened through the immaterial light of intellectual insight. We delight in beauty, we desire perfection and justice, we love truth, we love God, we love all men—not only the members of our social group, or our family, our class or nation—but all men because they are human beings, and children of God. The saints, those men who are called everywhere spiritual men, experience a contemplation which establishes their souls in a peace superior to and stronger than the whole world, and they go through inner trials, crucifixions and deaths which only a life superior to and stronger than biological existence can suffer and go through—and still remain alive. And we ourselves know that we can deliberate about ourselves, judge our own actions, cling to what is good because it is good and for no other reason; all of us know more or less obscurely that we are persons, that we have rights and duties, that we preserve human dignity within ourselves. Each one of us can, at certain moments in his existence, descend into the innermost depths of the Ego, to make there some eternal pledge or gift of himself, or face some irrefutable judgment of his conscience; and each one of us, on such occasions, alone with himself, feels that he is a universe unto himself, immersed in, but not dominated by, the great star-studded universe.

Through all these convergent ways, we may realize and experience in a certain measure, and in a concrete fashion, that living reality of our spiritual roots, or of what is above time in us, which the philosophical proofs make intellectually certain, but in the abstract manner of scientific knowledge.

THE IMMORTALITY OF THE HUMAN SOUL

The third point follows immediately from the second. The immortality of the human soul is an immediate corollary of its spirituality. A soul which is spiritual in itself, intrinsically independent of matter in its nature and existence, cannot cease existing. A spirit—that is, a "form" which needs nothing other than itself (save the influx of the Prime Cause) to exercise existence—once existing cannot cease existing. A spiritual soul cannot be corrupted, since it possesses no matter; it cannot be disintegrated, since it has no substantial parts; it cannot lose its individual unity, since it is self-subsisting, nor its internal energy, since it contains within itself all the sources of its energies. The human soul cannot die. Once it exists, it cannot disappear; it will necessarily exist forever, endure without end.

Thus, philosophic reason, put to work by a great metaphysician like Thomas Aquinas, is able to prove the immortality of the human soul in a demonstrative manner. Of course, this demonstration implies a vast and articulate network of metaphysical insights, notions and principles (relating to essence and nature, substance, act and potency, matter and form, operation, etc.) the validity of which is necessarily presupposed. We can appreciate fully the strength of the Scholastic demonstration only if we realize the significance and full validity of the metaphysical notions involved. If modern times feel at a loss in the face of metaphysical knowledge, I fancy that it is not metaphysical knowledge which is to blame, but rather modern times and the weakening of reason they have experienced.

It is not surprising, on the other hand, that the philosophical demonstration I have just summarized is an abstract and a difficult one. The great and fundamental truths which are spontaneously grasped by the natural instinct of the human mind are always the most arduous for philosophic reason to establish. With regard to the immortality of the human soul, philosophic reason must use the very refined and elaborate concept of immateriality, a concept remote from the natural understanding, not only of primitive men, but of everyone who thinks with his imagination rather than with his intellect. Were not certain monks of Asia Minor, in the early Christian centuries, indignant at the idea that God is an Immaterial Being? They did not use the English language, yet they were convinced that to be *immaterial,* or deprived of matter, actually meant to be something immaterial, or nothing at all. They surely believed in the immortality of the soul, but it is doubtful whether they would have understood the strength of the argument we have used.

Primitive men did not philosophize; but, for all that, they had their own way, an instinctive, non-conceptual way, of believing in the soul's immortality. It was a belief rooted in an obscure experience of the self, and in the natural aspirations of the spirit in us to overcome death. We need not embark on an analysis of this natural and instinctive, non-philosophical belief in immortality. I should like merely to quote a passage from a book by the late scientist Pierre Lecomte du Noüy. Speaking of prehistoric man, he said: "Not only did the Neanderthal Man, who lived in Paleolithic times, bury his dead, but sometimes he buried them in a common ground. An example of this is the Grotte des Enfants near Mentone. Because of this respect he had for his dead, we have reached an anatomical knowledge of the Neanderthal Man that is more perfect than that which we have of certain races which have recently become extinct, or which still exist, such as the Tasmanians. This is no longer a question of instinct. We are dealing already with the dawn of human thought, which reveals itself in a kind of revolt against death. And revolt against death implies love for those who have gone as well as the hope that their disappearance is not final. We see these *ideas,* the first perhaps, develop progressively alongside the first artistic feelings. Flat rocks in the shape of dolmens are placed so as to protect the faces and heads of those who are buried. Later, ornaments, weapons, food, and the colors which serve to adorn the body, are placed in the tombs. The idea of finality is unbearable. The dead man will awaken, he will be hungry, he will have to defend himself, he will want to adorn himself." [1]

The same author goes on to observe that because the primordial notions, like those of good and evil, or of immortality, were spontaneously born in the most primitive human beings, those notions would deserve for that very reason to be examined and scrutinized as possessing absolute value.

I think that these views expressed by Lecomte du Noüy are true and thought-provoking. *A priori* it is probable that the great and basic ideas, the prime ideas, which are contained in the myths of primitive man, and are handed down in the common heritage of mankind, are more sound than illusory, and deserve respect more than contempt. At the same time, we are free to prefer a genuine philosophical demonstration.

THE CONDITION AND DESTINY OF THE IMMORTAL SOUL

What can philosophy tell us about the natural condition of the immortal soul after the death of its body? That is my fourth and last point. Philosophy can tell us very little indeed on this subject.

---

[1] *L'Avenir de l'Esprit,* Gallimard, Paris, 1941, p. 188.

Let us try to summarize the few indications there are. All the organic and sensuous powers of the human soul remain dormant in a separated soul, for they cannot be brought into play without the body. The separated soul is itself engulfed in a complete sleep with regard to the material world; the external senses and their perceptions have vanished; the images of memory and imagination, the impulses of instinct and passion have vanished. But this sleep is not like the sleep we know, obscure and filled with dreams; it is lucid and intelligent, alive to spiritual realities. For now light shines from within. The intellect and the spiritual powers are awake and active. From the very fact of its separation from the body, the soul now knows itself through itself; its very substance has become transparent to its intellect; it is intellectually penetrated to its innermost depths. The soul knows itself in an intuitive manner; it is dazzled by its own beauty, the beauty of a spiritual substance, and it knows other things through its own substance already known, in the measure in which other things resemble it. It knows God through that image of God which the soul itself is. And in accordance with its state of incorporeal existence, it receives from God, the sun of the spirits, certain ideas and inspirations which directly enlighten it, and help the natural light of the human intellect, of that intellect which is, as Saint Thomas Aquinas phrased it, the lowest in the hierarchy of spirits.

Saint Thomas teaches also that all that is of the intellect and the spirit, and especially the intellectual memory, which is but one with the intellect, keeps alive, in the separated soul, the whole treasure of knowledge acquired during our bodily life. The intellectual knowledge, the intellectual virtues acquired here below subsist in the separated soul. Whereas the images of the sense-memory, which had its seat in the brain, disappear, that which has penetrated into the intellectual memory is preserved. Thus, in an intellectual and spiritual manner, the separated soul ever knows those whom it loved. And it loves them spiritually. And it is able to converse with other spirits by opening to them what abides in its inner thoughts and is taken hold of by its free will.

We may thus imagine that, at the moment when it leaves the body, the soul is suddenly immersed into itself as into a shining abyss, where all that was buried within it, all its dead, rise up again in full light, insofar as all this was encompassed in the subconscious or supraconscious depths of the spiritual life of its intellect and will. Then all that is true and good in the soul becomes a blessing for it at the touch of this all-pervading revelatory light; all that is warped and evil becomes a torment for it under the effect of the very same light.

I do not believe that natural reason can go further in its understanding of the natural condition of the separated soul. What would be the life and happiness of souls if their state after death were a purely natural state? Their supreme good would consist in wisdom, untrammeled spiritual life, mutual friendship, and first and foremost in advancing constantly in their natural knowledge and love of God, Whom they would, however, never see face to face. It would be happiness in motion, never absolutely fulfilled—what Leibniz called *un chemin par des plaisirs,* "a road amidst spiritual pleasures."

But if we wish to know more, can we not go beyond philosophy? Philosophy itself will then entrust us to the guidance of a knowledge whose sources are superior to its own. Christians know that man does not live in a state of pure nature. They know that he was created in a state of grace, and that, after the first sin which wounded our race, he has been living in a state of fallen and redeemed nature; they know that he is made for supernatural blessedness. In answer to the question of the separated soul's destiny, the Scholastic doctors spoke not as philosophers, but as theologians whose knowledge rests on the data of Revelation.

Insofar as man participates in the metaphysical privileges of spirit and personality, he has aspirations which transcend human nature and its possibilities, and which consequently may be called transnatural aspirations: the longing for a state in which he would know things completely and without error, in which he would enjoy perfect communion with spirits, in which he would be free without being able to fail or to sin, in which he would inhabit a realm of unfading justice, in which he would have the intuitive knowledge of the First Cause of being.

Such a longing cannot be fulfilled by nature. It can be fulfilled by grace. The immortal soul is involved and engaged in the great drama of the Redemption. If, at the moment of its separation from the body, at the moment when its choice is immutably fixed forever, the immortal soul prefers its own will and self-love to the will and gift of God, if it prefers misery with pride to the blessing of grace, then it is granted what it has wished for. It has it, and it will never cease wanting and preferring it, for a free choice made in the condition of a *pure* spirit is an eternal choice. If the soul opens itself to the will and gift of God, Whom it loves more than its own existence, then it is granted what it has loved, it enters forever into the joy of the uncreated Being, it sees God face to face and knows Him as it is known by Him, intuitively. Thus, it becomes God by participation, as Saint John of the Cross phrased it, and, through grace, it attains that communion in divine life, that blessedness for the sake of which all things have been created. And the degree of its blessedness itself, the degree of its vision, will correspond to the degree of the inner impetus which projects it into God, in other words, to the degree of love to which it has attained in its life on earth. In the last analysis, therefore, we must say with Saint John of the Cross: It is upon our love that we shall be judged. In its state of blessedness the immortal soul will know creation in the Creator, by that kind of knowledge which Saint Augustine called "matutinal" knowledge, because it is produced in the eternal morning of Creative Ideas; the immortal soul will be equal to the angels, and will communicate freely with the whole realm of spirts; it will love God, henceforth clearly seen, with a sovereign necessity; and it will exert free will with regard to all its actions concerning creatures, but its free will shall no longer be liable to failure and sin; the soul will inhabit the realm of unfading justice, that of the three divine Persons and of the blessed spirits; it will grasp and possess the divine Essence which, infinitely clearer and more intelligible than any of our ideas, will illumine the human intellect from within and will itself be the intelligible medium, the actuating form through which it will be known. According to a line of the Psalms which Saint Thomas loved and often quoted: "In Thy light shall we see light."

Such are the teachings of Saint Thomas, both as a philosopher and as a theologian, about the condition and destiny of the human soul. Immortality is not a more or less precarious, successful or unsuccessful survival in other men, or in the ideal waves of the universe. Immortality is a nature-given, inalienable property of the human soul as a spirtual substance. And grace makes eternal life possible to all, to the most destitute as well as to the most gifted. The eternal life of the immortal soul is its transforming union with God and His intimate life, a union which is to be accomplished inchoatively here below, by love and contemplation and, after the body's death, in a definite and perfect manner, by the beatific vision. For eternal life begins here upon earth, and the soul of man lives and breathes where it loves; and love, in living faith, has strength enough to make the soul of man experience unity with God—"two natures in a single spirit and love, *dos naturalezas en un espiritu y amor de Dios.*"

I do not believe that a philosopher can discuss the immortality of the soul without taking into consideration the complementary notions which religious thought adds to the true and inadequate answers which reason and philosophy can furnish by themselves.

ROY WOOD SELLARS

The Physiological Basis of Mind and the Problem of Immortality

Roy Wood Sellars (1880–   ) taught philosophy at the University of Michigan from 1905 to 1959. He was one of the leaders of the philosophical movement that was known as Critical Realism.

The hope of immortality is an essential feature of practically all modern religions. Even those oriental religions which lack its clear presence postulate a dim kind of personal continuity. Buddhism has always been a puzzle to the optimistic Westerner who is in love with himself and does all his thinking in terms of personality and personal relations. The idea of re-birth in accordance with a rigid moral law is alien to his traditions; while the impersonalism of the whole process leaves him cold. It is not untrue to the facts to call Buddhism an atheistic religion. Yet it is a religion because it postulates the objective efficacy of moral categories. Freedom from the wheel of re-birth is gained by the Eightfold Path of right beliefs and right acts. Enough of the idea of a soul and enough of the idea of immortality exists even in this religion to make these assumptions important. But what have modern science and philosophy to say about these age-old ideas? Is the soul any longer in favor?

Here, again, an historical approach is worth while, because it gives the proper perspective. If we can understand why people in the past developed and fostered these ideas, we can judge their reasons pretty objectively, even though we realize that we have been strongly affected by the beliefs erected upon them. Destroy the roots of a tree and the foliage will wither before long. Has science dug so sharply around the roots of these old beliefs that they are bound to decay? The subject is an extremely interesting one.

A belief in some sort of an after-life is wide-spread. It is common knowledge that the American Indians spoke of a happy hunting-ground in the West, in which the soul of the warrior would rejoice in abundance of game. Other peoples thought of the abode of the dead as in the East where the sun arises. Still others taught that it was in the sun or the other heavenly bodies, or underneath the earth in a subterranean region. We are seldom able to determine the motives which led to these varying locations.

All sorts of beliefs flourished in the Mediterranean basin a few centuries before our era; but the drift of religious thought was moving rapidly toward a passionate acceptance of another life somewhere in the heavens. Immortality

From Roy Wood Sellars, *The Next Step in Religion* (1918), Ch. XI. Reprinted by permission of Roy Wood Sellars.

was taking on a more vivid coloring and was being transformed from a passive survival to an event of marked religious significance. New ethical motives were attaching themselves to an old tendency and modifying it almost beyond recognition. The sentiments and rituals built up around the ideas of sin and salvation were reflected into the next world and created the vision of a heaven and hell. What a rich field this was for the mythopeic imagination to exploit! And what an interesting sociological fact is it that the human imagination has always been more fertile in its descriptions of hell than in its descriptions of paradise!

But a few words ought to be said about the earlier conceptions of an after-life. Both the Greeks and the Hebrews thought of the other-world as a joyless reflection of the present. Death was, to all intents, the end of what really counted. Those who deny that men can live nobly without the hope of immortality forget that men like Pericles were unaffected by that phantom dream. Even the great Hebrew prophets extolled righteousness without the promise of a reward in the next world. What men have done, we can surely do again. The Greek father felt himself a member of a family whose traditions and loyalties he wished to hand on intact. For himself, he desired only the customary funeral rites so that his shade might rest in peace. In the house of Hades dwell the senseless dead, the phantoms of men outworn. The answer of Achilles to Ulysses, when that wanderer visits him in the underworld, expresses this shadowy after-life admirably: "Nay, speak not comfortably to me of death, oh great Ulysses. Rather would I live on ground as the hireling of another, with a landless man who had no great livelihood, then bear sway among all the dead that be departed." The Homeric Greeks rejoiced in life like youths whom everything pleases. The shadowy realm of Hades was felt to be a mockery of the sunlit world. The history of the belief in an after-life among the Hebrews is very similar. Yet it is surprising to notice how few remark the paucity of reference to this idea in the Old Testament. In the book of Isaiah occurs that account of Sheol to which attention was called in an earlier chapter: "Sheol from beneath is moved for thee to meet thee at this coming. . . . All they shall answer and say unto thee, Art thou become weak as we?" The passage is a tremendous one, full of the most biting irony and vindictive hatred. This conception of Sheol evidently scarcely differs from the corresponding one of the Homeric Greek. Toward the Christian era, as a result of the infiltration of the beliefs current among surrounding peoples, the idea of a future life took hold of the Jews. The Pharisees, the popular party of the day, stressed the dogma, while the Sadducees, the Aristocratic party, denied it.

Early religion was largely a state affair, for it concerned itself with the safety of the social group; but it was rapidly becoming an engrossing concern for the individual. The religious imagination was busily painting another world and connecting it with the relations of the individual to divine powers. Given the religious view of the world, what an instrument of appeal and of dread this conception of immortality was! The shadow and sunshine of another world lay athwart this one. Endless vistas of pain and pleasure stretched into the future. No wonder that the true means of salvation became the burning question! From the beginning, Christianity emphasized the fact of another world and its terrific meaning for the soul of man, adopting as an inheritance the current views with regard to a Messianic kingdom and a place of torment. Paul even goes so far as to proclaim the cynical alternative: "If the dead are not raised, let us eat and drink, for to-morrow we die."

The ideas of immortality and salvation were the central features of the great religious revival which swept over the Roman Empire about the time of the rise of Christianity. The desire for personal safety in this world and the next moved men. Fear and hope worked together; fear of the terrors awaiting the soul after death, hope of a happy existence in some paradise. That early Christianity owed much of its success to its doctrines of final things cannot be denied. It was a period of astrology, theosophy, mysticism, cults of saviors, eschatologies. Few were able to keep their heads above this tide of oracular mythology and superstition. What moorings did they have? None of that tested knowledge of the physical world which we possess, and which keeps numbers of people fairly sane to-day in spite of themselves. When we recall the terror at Salem a few centuries ago, we must admit that these Greeks, and Romans, and Jews, and Syrians did not conduct themselves so badly in the demon-ridden world in which they lived. Yet, while it would be unfair to blame those who embraced the various cults, it would be equally unfair not to give praise to those few enlightened souls who would approve none of these things.

Up to the present, the doctrine of immortality has been an essential part of Christianity. The creeds which have come down to us procalim the faith that Christ Jesus will appear again to judge the quick and the dead. To the average man, religion is absolutely committed to such a belief. It has gone hand in hand with the idea of retribution and reward until the two have grown together. It is not strange, then, that the suspicion that immortality is not justified by physiological and psychological facts is felt to have a grave bearing upon religion. To the vast majority, religion without immortality is like *Hamlet* with Hamlet left out. Remove the faith in a special providence, likewise, and the edifice around which many religious emotions and values have entwined themselves is no more than a ruin.

But the idea of a soul always accompanies the belief in immortality. The experiences which led to the one notion naturally encouraged the other. If the soul can leave the body, it is obviously independent, in large measure, of the latter's fate. Let us glance at some of the experiences whose false interpretation is at the foundation of a belief in an immortal soul inhabiting the body for a little space.

It is surprising what an influence was exercised by dreams. We have so completely outgrown this uncritical attitude toward them that it takes some effort to realize how natural it was. For the educated man of to-day, dreams are subjective experiences, that is, experiences which do not contain information about what is happening in the external world. In the jargon of psychology, they are centrally aroused ideas playing about some organic stimulus or some repressed wish. But the savage knew nothing about such distinctions. The dead appeared to the living and talked with them. Patroclus stands before Achilles and chides him. Do not the dead, then, have some sort of life? Many psychological motives combined to convince primitive man of at least a shadowy existence after death. But there was another side to the dream-life. The living went on long journeys, doing strange things, while their bodies rested in the tent. Added to these suggestions, so naturally lending themselves to a spiritistic interpretation, were still others. Certain kinds of sickness are explained by means of the idea of possession. Invisible agents are at work in the world. What can a trance be if not the temporary absence of just such an agent? "Among the Kayans of Borneo, for example, it is the custom for an elderly person learned in such matters to sit beside the corpse, where the soul is supposed to hover for some days after death, and to impart to the latter minute directions for its journey to the land of the dead." We are in the presence, here, of natural illusions, of hypotheses which inevitably arose. Man's first guesses were mistakes. The whole history of science drives this fact home.

The various opinions men have built up around the idea of a soul are instructive. How gravely men have written about such hidden things! Only very slowly have they learned to separate an experience from its interpretation, and to seek a wide range of facts before erecting even an hypothesis. To explain by means of *agents,* visible and invisible, is the plausible method to which man always resorts first. It is only when he becomes more sophisticated that he thinks in terms of *processes.* The following examples of divergent opinion upon the soul, gathered by an able French author, show the vagueness of the idea:

Origen, the Alexandrian theologian: "The soul is material and has a definite shape."

St. Augustine: "The soul is incorporeal and immortal."

A Polynesian: "The soul is a breath, and when I saw that I was on the point of expiring, I pinched my nose in order to retain my soul in my body. But I did not grasp it tightly enough—and I am dead."

Albertus Magnus: "There are thirty arguments against the immortality of the soul and thirty-six for, which is a majority of six arguments in favor of the affirmative."

Rabbi Maimonides: "It is written: 'The wicked will be destroyed and there will not rest anything of him.'"

Ecclesiastes: "Men die as the beasts and their fate is the same. They have all one breath."

The soul was at first conceived in very material ways. The idealistic movement in Greek philosophy is responsible for the concept of an *immaterial substance.* "Under the influence of mystical, religious motives the soul becomes more and more non-spatial and intangible. The words used are negative and abstract. It is generally supposed that Plotinus was the first to describe the soul as an immaterial substance. But this immaterial substance must somehow be brought into relation with the physical body." It was this situation which gave rise to the soul-body problem in philosophy, a problem which has gradually changed into the mind-body problem. This transformation of the puzzle is significant. The very terms have changed and have become more concrete and empirical. A quotation from William James—a man who had no bias against theology—will bring out the essential reasons for this significant change of terms: "Yet it is not for idle or fantastical reasons that the notion of the substantial soul, so freely used by common men and the more popular philosophies, has fallen upon such evil days, and has no prestige in the eyes of critical thinkers. It only shares the fate of other unrepresentable substances and principles. They are without exception all so barren that to sincere inquirers they appear as little more than names masquerading."

I am inclined to believe that, to most people, to-day, the soul means no more than the personality, and the conviction that this cannot be reduced to the body. It stands for consciousness and character as somehow rooted in something permanent. Plato's idea of the soul as a simple, indestructible substance awakens hardly an echo in their minds—and why should it? Something which guarantees and makes possible the continued existence of their conscious self after the death of the body is the association which is uppermost. Educated people, at least, have outgrown the ghost-soul of primitive times and have put their hope in the inability of the philosophic scientist to explain life and consciousness without appeal to agencies which are inexplicable on naturalistic terms. But it is obvious that such a basis is overhung by an ever-threatening danger. If the mind-body problem were solved in a concrete, empirical way, what then?

It has been customary to examine the question of immortality from three angles which may be called, respectively, the empirical, the ethical and the philosophical. The more recent drift of philosophy toward realism has tended to bring the first and the third methods of approach closer together. It has increasingly been felt that philosophy coöperates with the special sciences and is inseparable from them. The ethical argument in favor of immortality is oftener found in poetry than in serious books on ethics. It cannot be said to have sufficient force to swing the balance established by science and a realistic philosophy in touch with science.

The empirical status of immortality can best be brought out by a glance at the facts of abnormal psychology. In olden days, as we have seen, insanity was explained as the disturbing effect of a demon. To-day, experiment and careful observation have proven that it is due to a functional disorder of the brain. That, whenever there is a disorder of the mind, there is some corresponding anatomical or physiological flaw in the brain has become a commonplace of modern medicine and psychology. In fact, insanity is defined as a "symptom of disease of the brain inducing disordered mental symptoms." A multitude of experiences point to the very intimate connection between the brain and consciousness. Careful observation of clinical cases has, for example, shown that a lesion in the visual center of the brain, that is, the part of the brain to which the fibers of the optic nerve run, induces the disappearance of both sight and visual imagery. Psychology and physiology have been busily engaged in discovering these correlations. So extended are they that the suggestion that consciousness is inseparable from the brain forces itself home ever more obstinately. Mental capacity runs parallel with the finer development of the brain. Is not, therefore, the very meaning of mental capacity connected with the needs and activities of the organism? But the case is still stronger when we note what happens to an individual when something goes wrong with the brain. Can this poor lunatic, who dropped from the high level of educated manhood to a condition more helpless than that of an animal, just because of a relatively slight disintegration of the cortex, be expected to recover his intellect by means of its total disintegration? Can it be denied that the burden of proof rests on those who assert immortality?

The so-called ethical argument for immortality is associated with the name of Immanuel Kant. Kant's philosophy was agnostic, and it was this agnosticism which made his use of the ethical argument possible. If you can't make any assured theoretical statement about the nature of the self, you can allow demands, which you regard as ethical and primary, to dictate your ultimate beliefs. It cannot be denied that Kant's argument savors of the popular notion that the virtuous must be rewarded. At its highest, the ethical argument signifies a demand for a future life in order to carry out that development of character which the brief span of earthly life is not equal to. It is this argument which runs through Browning. What shall we say of it?

There are both factual and theoretical objections to the ethical argument for immortality. The more we know about habit, the more we realize that character is pretty well "set" by middle life. The creative period of human life ends all too soon. Character is not an abstract possession separable from human tasks and needs. It is not like a work of art which can be polished and re-polished. But, when all is said and done, ethics must abide by the facts of the case. Take character abstractly enough and apart from its human and organic setting, and the dream of continuous perfecting may have meaning; but so would the dream of continuous intellectual advance. Yet the scholar knows all too well the judgment passed by the coming generation upon the older one: "They can't adjust themselves to this new point of view." Would progress come if the generations did not pass?

The philosophical aspect of the question can be touched upon only briefly and in an untechnical way. The basic problem may be put in this way: Can human personality be included in nature in a theoretically satisfactory way? It has been customary to stress the difficulties which confront such an attempt and to be silent in regard to the problems which the separation of body and personality has always found facing it. Yet I think that few philosophers would deny that it is the very irrationality of the traditional dualism which makes a living monism of mind and body so desirable and so urgently sought after.

There is good reason to believe that the persistence of the mind-body puzzle has been due to two conditions, the lack of an adequate theory of knowledge, and an ultra-mechanical, or non-evolutionary, view of the physical world. Scientists and philosophers, alike, were possesed by an inertia which prevented them from taking the principle of evolution seriously. They refused to readjust their ideas so as to admit that organization of a high grade, such as characterizes the nervous system, has a synthetic way of acting of its own, not reducible to the mere chain-like action of externally related units. There are many signs pointing to the conclusion that a broader and more flexible naturalism is forming which will sweep away the artificial problems and stereotyped contrasts which have stood in the way of a candid inclusion of human thought and activity within nature. When that day comes, the hesitations which have encouraged the faith in immortality in the face of empirical difficulties of an ever-increasing weight will pass away. I am inclined to prophesy that psychology and physiology will reach an adjustment of their principles before many years have passed, and that consciousness and mind will take their places along with mass and energy in the scientific view of nature. The old dualism of soul and body will pass away and give place to a flexible naturalism.

The belief in immortality and the wish for it will die out very slowly. The vague appetite for another life will persist as an undercurrent of half-understood desire for a good whose nature has not been clearly thought out. What men really want is an eternal youth in an environment which gives opportunity for self-expression and pleasant companionship. It means rest to the weary, new horizons to those who wish to achieve, a release from fetters to those who have felt themselves oppressed. What a quiet charm there is in such an uncritical play of the fancy! But is it anything more than daydreaming? Can our musings become definite without revealing themselves as fancies? Alas! our souls are old and written upon, and we would no longer be the same were these marks removed. They have a meaning for us and we cannot wish them away. If, for a forgetful moment, we envy the smooth cheeks of a youth, the envy is but momentary. What we desire is his abundant energy and hopefulness with our own humorous and wiser self in command. How completely we are parts of life as it is lived upon this planet! Desires, affections, passions, ideas, habits, all, when analyzed, point to the human organism and its environment. Our personality is like a plant which draws its nourishment from what surrounds it. Remove the old peasant from his fields and plow-fellows, and he will lose interest in life. Remove the business man from the mart and counter, and he will become restless. How can we expect to revive a zest in life by cutting the grown personality loose from what it has fed upon? It is psychologically absurd and betrays that tendency to abstract thinking which is so widespread. The human personality is a function of this sub-lunar life, of this organism, of this sky, of this soil, of this restless struggle with nature. Immortality is an impossible surgery.

At certain stages of social development, false beliefs are simply inevitable. For example, the Ptolemaic view of the solar system was bound to precede the Copernican. And false beliefs do both good and harm before they are outgrown. How many of the down-trodden have looked to another world to right their wrongs! It gave them hope: but it made them passive and all too meek. Has not the idea of another life encouraged a false perspective in regard to this one? I cannot feel that the belief was ever a very healthy one for the human race. Yet, during the coming period of transition, many who have been trained to hold false expectations will experience grievous pain. People who become used to a narcotic recoil from the idea of giving it up. Their nervous system has been taught to depend upon it. Is there not something parallel to this in ethics? Religious romanticism is a spiritual narcotic which substitutes a dream world for the more humdrum world of everyday existence. It develops a taste for the meretricious and sentimental. In revenge, the enthusiast fails to achieve insight into the significance of common things. Life's real tragedies and triumphs are veiled from his untrained eye. Only a wholehearted, even joyous, immersion in the sea of struggling human life gives the imagination that iron vigor it needs. The greatest saints have talked the least of heaven.

> Born into life!—who lists
> May what is false hold dear,
> And for himself make mists
> Through which to see less clear;
> The world is what it is, for all our dust
> and din.
>
> It it so small a thing
> To have enjoy'd the sun,
> To have lived light in the spring,
> To have loved, to have thought,
> to have done;
> To have advanced true friends, and
> beat down baffling foes—

Let those who can meet life bravely and joyously. The stage has been planned by no master artist, and the actors are only amateurs compelled to improvise their parts; but the sunlight is sometimes golden and the spoken lines often surprise us with their beauty. What critic can pass assured judgment upon this continuous play?

C. J. DUCASSE

A Refutation of Arguments Against the Possibility of Survival

C. J. Ducasse (1881–   ) was born in France but his philosophical career has been in the United States, chiefly at Brown University. He has written on a wide variety of philosophical topics.

That a man's life continues in some form after the death of his body has always been believed by a large majority of mankind. Before we ask whether it is possible that this belief should be true, it will be well to ask first why it has so generally been held. But a word concerning two points of terminology is called for at the outset.

The first relates to the name by which we shall refer to the entity the possibility of whose survival is in question. It has been variously termed man's mind, personality, soul, or spirit—these words in most cases being defined either not at all or but loosely. For the present purpose there will be no need to take account of the more or less different meanings various writers have proposed for those terms; and since we have in preceding chapters reached a definite conception of the meaning implicit in the ordinary predicative usage of the term "mind," this term is the one we shall employ here. We shall assume that it includes such more special facts as the others may denote.

From C. J. Ducasse, *Nature, Mind and Death* (1951), Ch. XIX. Reprinted by permission of The Open Court Publishing Company.

The other point of terminology concerns the common practice of describing as belief in "immortality" the belief that the human mind survives the death of its body. Strictly speaking immortality implies survival forever. But I believe few persons give much if any thought to the "forever" part of the hypothesis. It is survival of *death* that people are really interested in, and assurance of survival for some substantial period—say a thousand or even a hundred years—would probably have as much or nearly as much present psychological value as would assurance of survival strictly forever. Most men would be even less troubled by the idea of extinction at so distant a time than is a healthy and happy youth by the idea that he will die in fifty or sixty years. Therefore what I shall discuss will be the possibility that the human mind survives the death of its body for some time whether finite or not, rather than that it survives it specifically forever.

1. Why Belief in Survival Is Easy and Widespread

This being understood, let us now consider what apparently are the chief psychological determinants of the belief in survival. One of them is what may be called psychological inertia—the natural tendency to assume that what we are accustomed to find present will continue to be so. Each of us having had conscious life at all times in the past which he can remember, he tacitly assumes that this will continue. As J. B. Pratt has pointed out, the child takes the continuity of life for granted. It is the fact of death that has to be taught him. But when he has learned it, and the idea of a future life is then put explicitly before his mind, it seems to him the most natural thing in the world.[1]

It is worth noting in this connection that, although we sometimes say that we were unconscious at certain times or that some person we observe is unconscious, nevertheless, as pointed out in Chapter 17, unconsciousness is nothing we ever really observe in ourselves or in anyone else. What we actually observe when we say that another person is unconscious is only the fact that his body does not then react to certain stimuli which at other times elicit perceptible responses. He is unconscious of *those stimuli*, but for all we know he may be vividly dreaming. And as regards ourselves, we of course are never conscious of being unconscious, for this is a contradiction. When we assert that we were unconscious during a certain period, what we really know is only that we have no memories relating to that period. This is no proof, and is even hardly evidence at all, that our consciousness was totally extinguished during that period; for if this followed, then the fact that we have no memories whatever of the first few years of our lives, nor of the vast majority of our days since, would equally require us to conclude that we were totally unconscious at all those times. But we have plenty of indirect evidence to the contrary.

[1] Pratt, *The Religious Consciousness*, p. 225. Cf. C. D. Broad, *The Mind and Its Place in Nature*, p. 524.

Consciousness thus is something we have had at all times we can remember; and psychological inertia therefore makes natural and easy the idea that consciousness survives the death, as it does the sleep, of the body.

Another psychological determinant of the belief in survival is the wish to survive. How subtle is this wish is shown by the fact that even persons who believe that death means complete extinction of the individual's consciousness often find comfort in various substitute conceptions of survival. They may, for instance, dwell on the continuity of the individual's germ plasm in his descendants. Or they find solace in the thought that, the past being indestructible, their individual life remains eternally an intrinsic part of the history of the world. Also—and more satisfying to one's craving for personal importance—there is the fact that since the acts of one's life have effects, and these in turn further effects, and so on, therefore what he has done goes on forever influencing remotely and sometimes greatly the course of future events. Gratifying to one's vanity, too, is the prospect that, if the achievements of one's life have been great or even only conspicuous or his benefactions or evil deeds have been notable, his name may not only be remembered by acquaintances and relatives for a little while, but may live on in recorded history. But evidently survival in any of these senses is but a consolation prize—but a thin substitute for the continuation of conscious individual life, which may not be a fact, but which most men crave nonetheless.

The roots of this craving are certain desires which death appears to frustrate. For some, the chief of these is for union with persons dearly loved. For others whose lives have been wretched, it is the desire for another chance at the happiness they have missed. For others yet, it is desire for further opportunity to grow in ability, knowledge, or character. Often there is also the desire, already mentioned, to go on counting for something in the affairs of men. And again, a future life for oneself and others is often desired in order that the redressing of the many injustices of this life shall be possible. But it goes without saying that although belief in a future life is easy and desires such as these often suffice to induce it, they constitute no evidence at all that it is a fact.

2. The Hypothesis of Survival Logically Independent of the Hypothesis That a God Exists

Wishful thinking does not wish to regard itself as being that, and it therefore often protects itself from self-recognition, even if not from recognition by others, by clothing itself in argument. The so-called moral argument for immortality is, I believe, an instance of this and is therefore to be reckoned as rationalization of a wish-induced belief in survival, rather than as a statement of any genuine reason to pronounce the belief true.

The argument is that the annihilation of the individual would be incompatible with the goodness and power of God. As a philosophical correspondent of mine puts it, "persons are intrinsic values, and a God who annihilated such a value would be no God any more." Again, "If value is metaphysically structural in the universe, and if value is real only in, of, and for persons, we have a high degree of systematic probability for immortality." Another philosopher puts it in the question, "If God is good and God is sufficiently powerful, how can such a God allow the values (potential or actual) bound up with individuals to become forever lost? . . . The world would be irrational if, after having brought into being human beings who aspire against so many almost overwhelming odds to achieve higher values, it should dash them into nothingness. . . . How solve the problem of evil unless there be a continued existence where shall obtain appropriate rewards and readjustments and further opportunities?" [2]

The argument, let it be noted, is conditional: *if* there is a God . . . *if* he is good and sufficiently powerful . . . *if* the existence of evil is reconcilable with the goodness and power of God . . . *if* value is metaphysically structural in the universe . . . etc. Much pious ingenuity has gone into attempts to prove those "ifs" or at least show them to be more probable than not. But it seems to me in spite of it that the propositions concerned still have the status only of postulates, that is—to use Charles Peirce's characterization of a postulate—the status only of propositions which we hope are true.

If there are extrahuman intelligences at all in the universe, then the most plausible hypothesis would seem to be that they are many, that they are variously limited in power and in knowledge, and that some are good and others evil in various degrees. That one of them is perfect at least in goodness, and is supreme even if not infinite in power, is a belief not based on impartial survey of the evidential facts but born rather of a longing for the remembered comfort of the young child's relationship to his father.

But further, it is a question whether annihilation at death would be an evil. Most persons, it is true, desire survival; but if there is no survival, there can be no frustration of that desire, for frustration is an experience and cannot occur if one is no longer there to have it. What death of a man's body does frustrate, whether or not his mind survives and whether there is one God or many or none, are the desires and interests of persons who survive him on earth, who valued him and his life there. If the existence of a God is somehow compatible with *this* indubitably experienced

---

[2] Vergilius Ferm, *First Chapters in Religious Philosophy*, pp. 279–80.

evil, it would be all the more compatible with nonsurvival, which, not being experienced, would not be an evil.

God, it is true, would perceive the nonsurvival of men's minds, but if *he* did not mind it, perception of it would then not be experience by him of an evil. As regards the assertion that "persons are intrinsic values" which a God could not allow to perish without ceasing to be a God, *i.e.,* to be good, it is obscure and, in such senses of it as suggest themselves, highly dubious. Does it mean that existence of a person has *positive* value, *i.e.,* is good, even if he happens to be a wholly or predominantly evil person? This seems the opposite of evident. Again, is existence of a good person— *i.e.,* of one disposed to do good—an *intrinsic* good, and if so in what sense of "good"? and who experiences the intrinsic goodness of his existence? Or is not rather the existence of a good person good only instrumentally, *i.e.,* good only in so far as he not only has the disposition to do good, but exercises it and does so successfully, not blunderingly?

The upshot of these considerations, I submit, is that no contradiction is involved in the supposition that there is a God, or several, and yet no survival; nor any contradiction in the supposition that there is no God and yet that there is survival. The supposition that a God exists has no more logical connection with the possibility of a life after death than it has with the possibility that life exists on the planet Mars. The afterdeath world, if there is one, is just another region of the universe. The belief that there is such a region has of course been employed in the service of religion, but it is no more intrinsically religious than is the belief in life on Mars.

3. The Case Against the Possibility of Survival

Although the belief in survival is easy, tempting, and widespread, critical reflection quickly brings forth a variety of *prima facie* strong reasons to regard that belief as illusory.[3]

There are first of all certain facts which definitely suggest that both the existence and the particular nature of consciousness at various times wholly depend on the presence of a functioning nervous system. Protagonists of the impossibility of survival remark, for example, that wherever consciousness is observed it is found associated with a living and functioning body. Further, when the body dies, or the head receives a heavy blow, or some anesthetic is administered, all the familiar outward evidences of consciousness terminate, permanently or temporarily. Again, we know well that drugs of various kinds—alcohol, caffein, opium, heroin, and many others—cause specific changes at the time in the nature of a person's mental states. The secretions of the endocrine glands, or deficiency of them, also affect the mind in various ways. Also, by stimulating in appropriate ways the body's sense organs, corresponding states of consciousness— namely, the various kinds of sensations —can be caused at will. On the other hand, cutting a sensory nerve immediately eliminates a whole range of sensations. Again, the contents of consciousness, perceptual capacities, linguistic skills, and various mental powers and personality traits, are altered in characteristic ways when specific regions of the brain are destroyed by disease or injury or are disconnected from the rest surgically as in prefrontal lobotomy.

That the nervous system is the indis-

---

[3] An excellent statement of them is given by Gardner Murphy in the article, "Difficulties Confronting the Survival Hypothesis," *Jour. of the Amer. Soc. for Psych. Research,* Vol. XXXIX, No. 2, April 1945, pp. 67–94. See also Corliss Lamont's *The Illusion of Immortality,* Putnam's, 1935; C. D. Broad's *The Mind and Its Place in Nature,* Harcourt Brace, 1929, Chaps. XI and XII *passim,* and especially pp. 526–33.

pensable basis of mind is further suggested by the fact that, in the evolutionary scale, the degree of intelligence of various species of animals keeps pace closely with the degree of development of their brain; and that in an individual human being a similar correlation is to be observed between the growth and decay of his brain, and that of his mind, from infantility to maturity to senility.

That continued existence of mind after death is impossible has been argued also on the basis of theoretical considerations. It has been contended, for instance, that what we call states of consciousness—or more particularly, ideas, sensations, volitions, feelings, and the like—are really nothing but the minute physical or chemical events which take place in the tissues of the brain. For, it is urged, it would be absurd to suppose that an idea or a volition, if it is not itself a material thing or process, could cause material effects such as contractions of muscles. Moreover, it is maintained that the possibility of causation of a material event by an immaterial mental cause is ruled out *a priori* by the principle of the conservation of energy; for such causation would mean that an additional quantity of energy suddenly pops into the nervous system out of nowhere.

Another conception of consciousness, which is more often met with today than the one just mentioned but which also implies that consciousness cannot survive death, is that "consciousness" is only the name we give to certain types of behavior which differentiate the higher animals from all other things in nature. According to this view, to say, for example, that an animal is conscious of a difference between two stimuli means nothing more than that it responds to each by different behavior. That is, the difference of behavior is what consciousness of difference between the stimuli consists in; and is not, as is commonly assumed, only

the behavioral sign of something mental and not public, called "consciousness" that the stimuli are different.

Or again, consciousness of the typically human sort called thought is identified with the typically human form of behavior called speech; and this, again not in the sense that speech expresses or manifests something different from itself called "thought," but in the sense that speech—whether uttered or only whispered—is thought itself. And obviously, if thought, or any mental activity, is thus but some mode of behavior of the living body, the mind cannot possibly survive death.

A number of other difficulties of a different order also confront the survival hypothesis. Broad mentions two. One is "the apparently haphazard way in which men are born and die." Common sense rebels against the idea that, for instance, an unwanted child produced in a drunken orgy and dying of neglect or by infanticide six weeks after it is born is "a permanent and indestructible part of the universe, or indeed that it survives the death of its body at all." The other difficulty Broad mentions is "the continuity between men and animals." If the minds of men survive, why not also those of cats and dogs, and indeed those of lice and earwigs?

Still another difficulty becomes evident when one imagines in some detail what survival would apparently have to include if it were to be survival in any sense important enough to warrant giving it any thought. It would, one feels, have to include persistence not alone of consciousness, but also of personality; that is, of personal character, acquired knowledge, cultural skills and interests, memories, and awareness of personal identity. But even this would not be enough, for "survival" means to *live* beyond the body's death; and to live means to meet new situations and, by exerting oneself to deal with them, to broaden and deepen one's experience and develop one's latent capacities. But it is hard to imagine this possible without a body and an environment for it, upon which to act and from which to receive impressions. And if a body and an environment were supposed, but not material and corruptible ones, then it is paradoxical to think that, under such radically different conditions, a given personality could persist. To take a crude but telling analogy, it is past belief that, if the body of any one of us were suddenly changed into that of a shark or an octopus, and placed in the ocean, his personality could, for more than a very short time if at all, survive intact so radical a change of environment and of bodily form.

Such, in brief, are the chief reasons commonly advanced for holding that survival is impossible. Scrutiny of them, however, will I think show that they are not as strong as they first seem, and far from strong enough to prove that there can be no life after death.

4. Critique of the Case Against the Possibility of Survival

Let us consider first the assertion that "thought," or "consciousness," is but another name for subvocal speech, or for some other form of behavior, or for molecular processes in the tissues of the brain. As Paulsen and others have pointed out [4] no evidence ever is or can be offered to support that assertion, because it is in fact but a disguised proposal to make the words "thought," "feeling," "sensation," "desire," and so on, denote facts quite different from those which these words are commonly employed to denote. To say that those words are but other names for certain chemical or behavioral events is as grossly arbitrary as it would be to say that "wood" is but another name for glass, or "potato" but another name for cabbage. What thought, desire, sensation, and other mental states are like, each of us can observe directly by introspection; and what introspection reveals is that they do not in the least resemble muscular contraction, or glandular secretion, or any other known bodily events. No tampering with language can alter the observable fact that thinking is one thing and muttering quite another; that the feeling called anger has no resemblance to the bodily behavior which usually goes with it; or that an act of will is not in the least like anything we find when we open the skull and examine the brain. Certain mental events are doubtless connected in some way with certain bodily events, but they are not those bodily events themselves. The connection is not identity.

This being clear, let us next consider the arguments offered to show that mental processes, although not identical with bodily processes, nevertheless totally depend on them. We are told, for instance, that some head injuries, or anesthetics, totally extinguish consciousness for the time being. As already pointed out, however, the strict fact is only that the usual bodily signs of consciousness are then absent. But they are also absent when a person is asleep; and yet, at the same time, dreams, which are states of consciousness, may be occurring.

It is true that when the person concerned awakens, he often remembers his dreams, whereas the person that has been anesthetized or injured has usually no memories relating to the period of apparent blankness. But this could mean that his consciousness was, for the time, dissociated from its ordinary channels of manifestation, as was reported of the coconscious personalities of some of the patients of Dr. Morton Prince.[5] Moreover, it sometimes occurs that a person who has been in an accident reports lack

[4] F. Paulsen, *Introduction to Philosophy* (trans. by F. Thilly, 2nd ed.), pp. 82–83.

[5] *My Life as a Dissociated Personality* (ed. by Morton Prince), Boston: Badger.

of memories not only for the period during which his body was unresponsive but also for a period of several hours before the accident, during which he had given to his associates all the ordinary external signs of being conscious as usual. As emphasized already in § 1, if absence of memories relating to a given period proved unconsciousness for that period, this would force us to conclude that we were unconscious during the first few years of our lives, and indeed have been so most of the time since; for the fact is that we have no memories whatever of most of our days. That we were alive and conscious on any long past specific date is, with only a few exceptions, not something we actually remember, but only something which we infer must have been true.

We turn now to another of the arguments we mentioned against the possibility of survival. That states of consciousness somehow entirely depend on bodily processes and therefore cannot continue when the latter have ceased is proved, it is argued, by the fact that various states of consciousness—in particular, the several kinds of sensations—can, at will, be caused by appropriate stimulation of the body.

Now, it is very true that sensations and some other mental states can be so caused; but we have just as good and abundant evidence that mental states can cause various bodily events. John Laird mentions, among others, the fact that merely willing to raise one's arm normally suffices to cause it to rise; that a hungry person's mouth is caused to water by the idea of food; that feelings of rage, fear, or excitement cause digestion to stop; that anxiety causes changes in the quantity and quality of the milk of a nursing mother; that certain thoughts cause tears, pallor, blushing, or fainting, and so on.[6]

[6] John Laird, *Our Minds and Their Bodies,* London: Oxford University Press, 1925, pp. 16–19.

The evidence we have that the relation is one of cause and effect is exactly the same here as where bodily processes cause mental states.

It is said, of course, that to suppose something nonphysical, such as a thought, to be capable of causing motion of a physical object, such as the body, is absurd. But I submit that if the heterogeneity of mind and matter makes this absurd, then it makes equally absurd the causation of mental states by stimulation of the body. Yet no absurdity is commonly found in the assertion that cutting the skin causes a feeling of pain, or that alcohol, caffein, bromides, and other drugs, cause characteristic states of consciousness. Common sense here accords with Hume's demonstration, to which we have repeatedly referred, that no logical absurdity is ever involved in supposing an event of a given kind to cause any other particular kind of event, and therefore that only experience can tell us what in fact can cause what. And as we have also seen, the so-called principle of the conservation of energy precludes neither psycho-physical nor physico-psychical causation.

As regards the fact that certain mutilations of the body rob the mind of certain of its powers, this too is a fact, just as it is a fact that destruction of one's motor car, if one can get no other, destroys, not one's capacity to drive, but at least the possibility of exercising it. But it is equally true that certain mutilations of one's mind make it permanently or temporarily impossible for the body to exercise capacities which it still physiologically possesses. Impotence, deafness, or blindness caused by some psychological trauma are examples.

What it is essential to bear in mind in connection with the type of arguments we have just been considering is this: The fact that two substances, Mind and Brain, interact entails that some events in each can cause some events in the other, and indeed that the development of each is greatly affected by such events in the other. But this is quite compatible with a considerable range of autonomy in the body, and likewise in the mind. Hence no more contradiction is involved in supposing that such activities of the mind as are autonomous, *i.e.*, psycho-psychical, still go on when the connection between it and the body is temporarily severed—or, at death, permanently—than is involved in the fact that the autonomous activities of the body—breathing, circulation of the blood, metabolism, etc.—still go on during coma, deep sleep, or anesthesia, *i.e.*, at times when psycho-physical and physico-psychical action is suspended.

A word, next, on the parallelism between the degree of development of the nervous systems of various animals and the degree of their intelligence. This is alleged to prove that the latter is the product of the former. But the facts lend themselves equally well to the supposition that, on the contrary, or at least in equal measure, an obscurely felt need for greater intelligence in the circumstances the animal faced brought about the variations which eventually resulted in a more adequate nervous organization. In the development of the individual, at all events, it seems clear, as we have pointed out, that the specific, highly complex nerve connections which become established in the brain and cerebellum of, for instance, a skilled pianist are the results of his will over many years to acquire the skill.

We must not forget in this context that there is a converse, equally consistent with the facts, for the theory, called epiphenomenalism, that mental states are related to the brain much as the halo is to the saint, that is, as effects but never themselves as causes. The converse theory, which might be called hypophenomenalism, and which is pretty well that of Schopenhauer, is that the instruments which the various mechanisms of the body constitute are the objective products of obscure cravings for corresponding powers; and, in particular, that the organization of the nervous system is the effect and material isomorph of the variety of mental functions exercised at a given level of animal or human existence. It is clear that epiphenomenalism, and likewise a hypophenomenalism that should assert psycho-physical but deny physico-psychical causation, would be not merely arbitrary, but would clash with facts which there are none but dogmatic reasons to refuse to take at their face value.

As regards the difficulty felt to arise from the haphazard way in which men are born and die, and from the continuity between men and animals, Broad, who in mentioning it says he is conscious that it affects him personally more than any others, nevertheless goes on to show with his usual admirable objectivity that these facts have no *logical* right to exert this influence. As to the first, he writes: "There is no logical transition from 'This [mind] is caused by the careless or criminal action of a human being' to: 'This [mind] is the kind of thing whose existence is transitory.'" And as to the second, he concludes a detailed critique of it with the statement: "The alleged reasons for thinking it very unlikely that earwigs are immortal either are no reasons at all or they obviously depend on characteristics in which human beings and earwigs differ profoundly."

There remains the difficulty of forming any conception of some plausible form which a survival that would now seem to us significant could take. This difficulty can be dealt with, if at all, only by bringing forth such a conception. At this place no attempt will be made to do so, but a separate section farther on will be given to a survey of some of the chief forms, whether worth having or not, which survival might, without inconsistency with any known facts, be imagined to take.

5. What Accounts for the Prima Facie Plausibility of the Arguments Against the Possibility of Survival

Our examination of the reasons commonly given for asserting the impossibility of survival has revealed that they are logically weak—far too much so even to show that survival is more unlikely than likely. The whole question will be placed in a useful perspective if we now ask why so many of the persons who advance those reasons nevertheless think them convincing.

This is, I believe, because they approach the question with a certain metaphysical bias. It derives from a particular initial assumption they tacitly make, namely, that *to be real is to be material;* and to be material, as we have seen, is to be some process or part of the perceptually public world.

Now the assumption that to be real is to be material is a useful and appropriate one for the purpose of discovering and employing the physico-physical properties of material things; and this purpose is a legitimate and very frequent one. But those persons, and most of us, do not ordinarily realize that the validity of that metaphysical assumption is strictly relative to that specific purpose; for what that assumption automatically does is to limit one's horizon to physical causes and physical effects, and thus to make the suggestion of any nonmaterial cause or effect of a material event seem incongruous—as indeed it is *under, but only under, that assumption.* Because of one's ordinary failure to realize this state of affairs, he ordinarily continues making that assumption out of habit, and it continues to rule his judgments of relevance and plausibility in matters of causation even when, as now, the purpose in view is no longer that of discovering or employing such physico-physical prop-

erties as material things have, but is a different one, for which that assumption is no longer useful or even congruous.

The point is all important here and therefore worth stressing. Its essence is that, as made clear in Chapter 6 and again in Chapter 12, the conception of the nature of reality that proposes to define the real as the material is not the expression of an observable fact to which everyone would have to bow, but is the expression only of a certain direction of interest on the part of the persons who so define reality—of interest, namely, which they have chosen to center wholly in the material, perceptually public world. This specialized interest is of course as legitimate as any other, but it automatically ignores all the facts, commonly called facts of mind, which only introspection directly reveals. And that specialized interest is what alone compels persons in its grip to employ the word "mind" to denote, instead of what it commonly does denote, something else altogether, namely, the public behavior of bodies that have minds; or makes it seem improbable or even absurd to them that any physical event could have any but a physical cause, or that anything but the material world and its processes should be self-sufficiently real. Only so long as one's judgment is swayed unawares by that special interest do the logically weak arguments against the possibility of survival, which we have examined, seem strong.

It is possible, however, and just as legitimate, as well more conducive to fair judgment as to the possibility that a mind or some parts of it survives the death of its body, to center one's interest for a time on the facts of mind as introspectively observable—ranking them for the time being as most real in the sense that they are the facts the intrinsic nature of which we most directly experience; that they are the facts which we most certainly know to exist; and moreover, that they are the facts without the experiencing of which we should not know any other facts whatever—such, for instance, as those of the material world.

The sort of perspective one gets from this point of view equilibrates that which one gets from the materialistic point of view, and is what I propose now to sketch briefly. For one thing, the material world is then seen to be but one among other objects of our consciousness. Moreover, one becomes aware of the crucially important fact that it is an object known by interpretation rather than strictly given. What this means has been stated in detail in Chapter 15, but its present bearing may be made clear by an example. Suppose that, perhaps in a restaurant we visit for the first time, an entire wall is occupied by a large mirror and we look into it without realizing it is a mirror. We then perceive, in the part of space beyond it, various material objects, notwithstanding that in fact they have no existence there at all. A certain set of the vivid color images which we call visual sensations was all that was strictly given to us, and these we construed, automatically and instantaneously but nonetheless erroneously, as signs or appearances of the existence of certain material objects at a certain place.

Again, and similarly, we perceive in our dreams various objects which at the time we take as physical but which eventually we come to believe were not so. And this eventual conclusion, let it be noted, is forced upon us not because we then detect that something called "physical substance" was lacking in those objects, but only because we notice, as we did not at the time, that their behavior was erratic—incoherent with their ordinary one. That is, their appearance was a mere appearance, deceptive in the sense that it did not then predict truly, as ordinarily it does, their later appearances. This, it is important to notice, is the only way in which we ever discover that an object we perceive was not really physical, or was not the particular sort of physical object we judged it to be.

These two examples illustrate the fact that our perception of physical objects is sometimes erroneous. But the essential point is that, even when it is veridical instead of erroneous, all that is literally and directly *given* to our minds is still only some set of sensations. These, on a given occasion, may be only color sensations; but they often include also tactual sensations, sounds, odors, and so on. It is especially interesting, however, to remark here in passing that, with respect to almost all the many thousands of persons and other "physical" objects we have perceived in a lifetime, vivid color images were the only strict data our perceiving activity had to go by; so that, if the truth should happen to have been that those objects, like ghosts or images in a mirror, were actually intangible—that is, were only color images—we should never have discovered that this was the fact. For all we directly know, it may have been the fact!

To perceive a physical object, then, instead of merely experiencing passively certain sensations (something which perhaps hardly ever occurs), is always, as we have insisted in Part III, to interpret, that is, to construe, given sensations as signs of, and appearances to us of, a postulated something other than themselves, some event in which is causing them in us; and other events in which are capable of causing in us sensations of other specific kinds. This belief commonly is only tacit and instinctive; but when reflection considers it explicitly, it is vindicated by our belief—or as I have argued in Chapter 9, our knowledge —that every event has some cause and therefore that our sensations too must have one, although we find none for them among our other mental states.

Such a postulated extramental something we call "a physical object." We say that we observe physical objects, and this is true. But it is important for the present purpose to be clear that we "observe" them never in any more direct or literal manner than is constituted by the process of interpretive postulation just described —never, for example, in the wholly direct and literal manner in which we are able to observe our sensations themselves and our other mental states.

That perception of a physical object is thus always the product of two factors —one, a set of sensations simply given to us, and the other an act of interpretation of these, performed by us—is something which easily escapes notice and has even been denied. This, however, is only because the interpretive act is almost always automatic, instantaneous, and correct—like, for instance, that of thinking of the meaning of any familiar word we hear. But that an interpretive act does occur is forced on our attention when, in a particular case, we discover that the interpretation was incorrect— that is, we discover that we misconstrued the meaning of the sensations. Or again, the interpretive act is noticeable when, because the sensations are too scant and therefore ambiguous, we catch ourselves hesitating between two or more possible interpretations of them and say that we are not sure what object it is we see.

The remarks made in the present section have been intended to make evident that explanations in terms of material causes do not have the exclusive authoritativeness which they seem to many persons to possess, and that the tacit assumption of those persons that only material things, but not minds, can have independent existence, is quite gratuitous. We have supplemented those remarks by a sketch of the view of the universe obtained when one conceives oneself essentially as a mind rather than as a body. The enlarged perspective provided makes clear that no paradox at all is really involved in the supposition that some forms of consciousness may exist independently of connection with animal or human bodies.

ANTONY FLEW

Psychical Research and the Question of Survival

CHAPTER VI

MEDIUMSHIP: MENTAL

. . .

As an example of an impressive mental medium let us take Mrs. Osborne Leonard. There are plenty of careful and well-annotated records of sittings with her. Furthermore, all investigators, irrespective of their views about her phenomena, agree about her complete personal integrity: which, after dealing with physical mediums, comes as a relief. She developed psychic interests as a child, but then these were repressed by her parents. She started to develop her powers, especially through table-tilting, immediately after her mother's death. At one of her table-lifting sessions a Communicator gave her name as "Feda." She later became Mrs. Leonard's chief Control, and her personality enlivens the records of the sittings. In the spring of 1914 "Feda" gave Mrs. Leonard repeated messages to begin work as a professional medium as soon as possible. "Something big and terrible is going to happen to the world. Feda must help many people through you." So far the account relies on her autobiography *My Life in Two*

From Antony Flew, *A New Approach to Psychical Research* (1953), Chs. VI–VII. Reprinted by permission of C. A. Watts & Co. Ltd.

Worlds (Cassell, 1931): from here the development can be followed in the *S.P.R. Proceedings,* for in 1915 Sir Oliver Lodge brought her into contact with the Society.

The first long report was a paper by Miss Radclyffe-Hall and Lady Troubridge. In August 1916 the former, remaining anonymous, had a sitting with Mrs. Leonard, at which she was given a description of a close friend (always referred to as A. V. B.) who had died some months before. Shortly after this she and Lady Troubridge arranged to have regular sittings. For five months both sat at least once a week, one being the interlocutor, while the other took notes, being careful to record everything said by the other two during the trance, and any conversation with the medium before and after it. In the course of many years they received correct statements, purporting to come from A. V. B., about many things which they thought could not have been within Mrs. Leonard's normal knowledge, such as places visited and things done by A. V. B. and Miss Radclyffe-Hall together; and the contemporary interests and affairs of the sitters. The two investigators employed a private detective agency to find out whether inquiries had recently been made at any of the obvious sources of information; but drew a blank.

One technique—which was later used

systematically by other investigators—was the *proxy sitting*. They sat as proxies for a friend "Daisy Armstrong," who was away in the Near East at the time, and were given correct statements not only about her intended movements but also about her adoptive father. The former were in conflict with their own expectations at the time, and they had known nothing about the adoptive father. The Communicator seemed to speak of him as dead; and he had died three days before, though neither the sitters nor Daisy knew this at the time. The point of the proxy sitting technique is to try to exclude two possibilities: that the correct information is drawn from the sitter normally by fishing (or even paranormally by telepathy); or that the medium has, consciously or unconsciously, done some preliminary research.

. . .

Proxy sittings have been tried often. One striking series resulted from a request made in 1936 by Professor E. R. Dodds to the Rev. C. Drayton Thomas to try to get communications from Mr. F. W. Macaulay. The latter had recently died. He had been known neither to Professor Dodds nor to Mr. Thomas, but the former knew his daughter Mrs. Lewis and her husband, Professor Lewis. Mr. Thomas presented the request at the sittings as coming from Macaulay's daughter "Emma" (Mrs. Lewis). Five of these proxy sittings were held, and the records were annotated afterwards by Mrs. Lewis. In the first four the Communicator gave—the estimate is Mr. Thomas's—ninety-four items of information. Both Professor Dodds and Mr. Thomas awarded marks to each of these statements independently, and their results were substantially the same. Mr. Thomas scored thirty-six as right, ten as good, and twenty-four as fair; adding these figures together to give a total of seventy successes (over 70 per cent). In the fifth

sitting the "communicator" was asked for information about something which had happened after Macaulay's death, namely his daughter's recent visit to Ireland. The score this time was assessed at twenty-five successes to five failures (over 83 per cent success). Three items will serve as typical of the successes: the first two come from the first four sittings: the third from the fifth.

(1) *"Feda"*: What is that? . . . Peggy . . . Peggy . . . Puggy . . . he is giving me a little name like Puggy or Peggy. Sounds like a special name, a little special nickname, and I think it is something his daughter would know. . . .
Annotation: My father sometimes called me "pug-nose" or "Puggy."

(2) *"Feda"*: This gentleman would have had pains in his limbs. I get rather a stiff feeling and aches in the limbs. Something he suffered from in later years.
Annotation: These were symptoms of his last illness.
"Feda": Also a peculiar feeling in one hand too. Will you ask his daughter if there was something about one hand that made it uneasy sometimes? Something not quite right with one hand. I feel he had done something to one hand that would make it a little different from an ordinary person's hand.
Annotation: About a year before his death he had severe blood poisoning in one hand. I believe it was always tender afterwards.

(3) *"Feda"*: At a place "B," was she interested there in a public building or public institution that he would be interested in also? He feels that she was.
Annotation: This is interesting. The son of the architect of several of the best buildings in Belfast was a great friend of my father. When I was a child these two took me to see these buildings. I, in my

turn, showed them to my husband on this visit, telling him all I could remember of my childhood's experience.

All quotation from this sort of material is unfair because it is the accumulation of hits which is impressive (always assuming that they are not diluted with too many misses) rather than any particular success taken separately, remarkable though these often appear to be. But while any quotation of manageable length is unfair, the full records of sittings tend to be very long. There is no substitute for reference to one or two of these, many of which have been published in the *S.P.R. Proceedings,* for anyone who wishes to estimate them. Mr. Thomas wanted to put a spiritualist interpretation on the results of this set of sittings. But Professor Dodds in a Note at the end of the paper points out that certain facts suggest a more economical —though still paranormal—interpretation. He concedes that "the hypotheses of fraud, rational inference from disclosed facts, telepathy from the actual sitter, and coincidence cannot either singly or in combination account for the results obtained." But, taking this "Macaulay" series together with a later series in which Professor Lewis tried under the same conditions to get into touch with his first wife, he notices that all the veridical statements attributed by "Feda" to either Macaulay or the first Mrs. Lewis were matters within the present knowledge of the second Mrs. Lewis and Professor Lewis, respectively: "Macaulay" showed knowledge of the recent movements and even thoughts of his daughter, the present Mrs. Lewis. The latter knew little or nothing about her predecessor, though Professor Lewis naturally did. The scores in the "Macaulay" series were much higher than in the "Lewis" series. Professor Lewis appeared to Professor Dodds to be a less suitable telepathic agent (transmitter as opposed to receiver

—to use the intelligible but misleading picture). All these facts taken together strongly suggest that the veridical information given by the Communicators derived—albeit paranormally—in the former case from Mrs. Lewis II and in the latter from Professor Lewis. Which is, of course, a simpler interpretation than the spiritualistic one; for on the latter you need to postulate *both* spirits *and* a paranormal capacity whereby they get to know the doings and even the thoughts of the living. As Professor Dodds remarked: "The telepathic hypothesis has at least the relative merit of postulating one miracle instead of two."

. . .

In the early years of this century several people connected in various ways with the S.P.R. began to produce automatic writing. None of these was a professional medium. Among them were Mrs. Verrall, Lecturer in Classics at Newnham College, Cambridge, and wife of Dr. A. W. Verrall; their daughter Helen, who later became Mrs. W. H. Salter; and Dame Edith Lyttelton. Later these were joined by a medium of the ordinary type, the famous Mrs. Piper, who is memorable in the annals of the subject for being the first to provide researchers with "communications" the content of which could be considered seriously, apart from any dubious support provided by questionable physical phenomena purporting to give emphatic warrant to their authenticity. The scripts produced by this "S.P.R. group of automatists" claimed to originate from various leading members of the Society, who had previously died: at first F. W. H. Myers (*d.* 1901), Edmund Gurney (*d.* 1888), and Henry Sidgwick (*d.* 1900); and later —for the series went on for many years —A. W. Verrall (*d.* 1912) and Henry Butcher (*d.* 1910). All but one of these "Communicators" had been classical scholars. Some of the later scripts were not automatic writings: for Mrs. Piper's productions were always stenographic records of trance speech; and one other member of the group developed from automatic writing to something much like ordinary mediumship—a fairly common process.

The plan for "cross-correspondences" was devised by "Myers" and his "Communicator" colleagues. The idea was to transmit one cryptic message through one automatist, and at about the same time another—equally unintelligible—through another writer; and then to give a clue, through a third person, which, though in itself meaningless, would, when taken together with the other two, show a single meaning and purpose. The cross-correspondence was to lie in this jig-saw puzzle the pieces of which came through different automatists and the subject of which would appear only when those pieces had been properly fitted together. The automatists were, of course, to be completely isolated from one another throughout.

The object of this scheme was to eliminate the possibility of dissolving away "proofs of survival" in terms of telepathy (or some such paranormal faculty) exercised by and between living people. Even had everything gone perfectly according to plan it is questionable if this object could have been achieved definitively: but the alternative account might have become very involved.

Parenthetically it is worth pointing out two parallels to this initiative by "Myers": Mrs. Leonard's "Feda" suggested making book-tests; and B III ("Sally") gave Dr. Morton Prince a much less muddled way of looking at Miss Beauchamp's various states and their interrelations than he had had before (*Dissociation of a Personality*, Longmans, 1906, cf. pp. 268 ff.).

But up to the present no perfect cross-correspondence has been found in the scripts. Several less perfect cases have been worked out: where two automatists have produced scripts which, taken separately, are meaningless, but which, put together, explain and complement one another. Besides these there are a large number of remarkable coincidences, where the same, often rather recherché, subject is mentioned by two or more automatists at about the same time. But it is even harder to give quotations which are both fair and short to illustrate these correspondences, than it is to do so to show the quality of a séance. Things are not improved by the fact that relevant parts of the scripts are full of disjointed and obscure literary allusions, mainly classical.

With this warning, consider the Euripides example. On March 4, 1907, in Mrs. Verrall's script there comes, "Hercules Furens. [*The Mad Hercules,* a play by Euripides. This is followed by a "message" to Dr. Verrall about the play. Then . . .] Ask elsewhere for the Bound Hercules. [In the play Hercules is bound to a pillar]." Then on March 25 the topic comes up again: "The Hercules story comes in there and the clue is in the Euripides play, if you would only see it. Bound to the pillar." On April 16 in Mrs. Holland's script there came "Lucus. Margaret. To fly to find Euripides. Philemon" [Mrs. Verrall's Christian name was Margaret. One of the characters in the *Hercules Furens* is called "Lukos," which would be Latinized as "Lucus." Browning translated the *Hercules Furens* in his *Aristophanes' Apology;* and one character in that was called "Philemon"]. On April 8 Mrs. Sidgwick was sitting with Mrs. Piper when "Myers" claimed that "Euripides" was one of the words he had given in cross-correspondences. Mrs. Verrall was of course familiar with Euripides in the original. Mrs. Holland knew no Greek, and denied that she had ever read the Browning poem.

Another example is the Thanatos case.

On April 17, 1907, Mrs. Piper gave "Sanatos" then "Tanatos." Mrs. Sidgwick noted on her record that "Thanatos" was probably meant. On April 23 Mrs. Piper gave "Thanatos." On April 30 it was said three times. And on May 7 "I want to say 'Thanatos.' " ["Thanatos" is the Greek word for death.] On April 16 Mrs. Holland, in India, gave "Maurice Morris Mors. And with that the shadow of death fell upon his limbs." [The first two words might be attempts at the third, which is the Latin word for death.] On April 29 Mrs. Verrall produced "Warmed both hands before the fire of life. It fades (sic) and I am ready to depart. [Then what might be a triangle or the Greek letter delta. Mrs. Verrall had always taken the latter as a sign for death.] *Manibus date lilia plenis* [This is a quotation from the *Æneid*, from a prophecy of death.] . . . Come away, come away, Pallida mors ["Come away, come away" is followed in Shakespeare's song by the word "death." *"Pallida mors"* means pale death]. . . . You have got the word plainly written all along in your own writing. Look back."

To present these two short examples is distorting, because on the whole it is the most complicated and extended correspondences which are most impressive; and because it is precisely the accumulation of a large number of them—and not any single one—which carries weight (granted always that there are not too many compensating disparities). But they are entirely representative in certain important respects: the correspondences always come in the incoherent parts of the scripts; there is always this impression of feeling for the idea; and the way the idea comes is always appropriate to the automatist—the classical quotations come in Mrs. Verrall's scripts, not in those of Mrs. Holland or from Mrs. Piper. It is also noteworthy both that the characterization of the Communicators was thought by those who had known Myers, Gurney,

Verrall, and the others to be very good; and that they nevertheless discerned differences between "Myers" as presented by the various automatists.

CHAPTER VII

THE QUESTION OF SURVIVAL

Whether we are to live in a future state, as it is the most important question which can possibly be asked, so it is the most intelligible one which can be expressed in language.
—BISHOP BUTLER, *Of Personal Identity*

In the last chapter we concluded that enough impressive mediumistic mental phenomena had been produced under sufficiently safeguarded conditions to demand, or at least to justify, the assumption that some paranormal factor has sometimes been at work in their production. To put it more precisely, what is involved is this: some mediums and automatists have given items of true information which they could not have acquired by any normal means; not even if they were gifted with hyper-acute senses, masterly powers of inference, or superlative memory capacity; nor yet with any combination of these, whether conscious or unconscious. And these pieces of information have been presented as deriving from people who have died: often they have been presented in the style, in the voice, and with the mannerisms of those people; and often again they have been things which those people certainly did know when they were alive. Now once it has been admitted—or at least supposed for the sake of argument—that this information (and the associated characterizations) cannot have been normally acquired (or provided) by the medium or automatist (and of course that it cannot be explained away as consisting only of lucky shots), it might seem that there was no option but to put some sort of spiritualist interpretation on the facts—to say that this information did indeed derive from "the spirits of the surviving dead." In this chapter we are going to criticize this interpretation on two levels: first, taking it at its face value, by arguing that even on this level it is not really as simple and as adequate to the facts as at first sight it seems to be; second, by suggesting, albeit extremely sketchily, some of the philosophical difficulties involved in this apparently pellucid notion of personal survival.

Suppose then that we accept for the moment the survivalist interpretation at its face value. It seems natural and straight-forward. Whereas the attempt —once the presence of any paranormal factor has been conceded—to describe the phenomena alternatively—in terms of the supposed telepathic and/or clairvoyant (and/or possibly even precognitive) powers of the medium or automatist and other living people—must seem strained and far-fetched. But this —as was realized early in the history of the S.P.R., and not least acutely by some of those like F. W. H. Myers who were most keen to prove survival—is a mistake. It seems natural and straightforward to accept it because it is the interpretation which those mediumistic phenomena with which we are most familiar, so to speak, put upon themselves; and because we have not come across any closely parallel phenomena which do not fit in with such an interpretation. But there have been such parallel phenomena. The survivalist account seems simple. But only at first sight: for—quite apart from difficulties of the sort we shall raise in the second half of this chapter—it involves many *extra* assumptions, mostly unsupported by independent evidence, *in addition to* those required by the alternative account, which are suggested by independent evidence. It is thus, scientifically speaking, much more elaborate:

and *frustra fit per plura quod potest fieri per pauciora* [1] (William of Ockham: *Summa totius logicae*).

In the Anglo-Saxon countries nowadays mediumistic phenomena always tend to take a spiritualistic form: information is presented as coming from the "spirits of the surviving dead"; the dramatic characterizations are of, and allegedly by, people who have lived and died "and are now living on another plane"; putatively paranormal physical phenomena are offered as signs of the presence and powers of "spirits" and as an authentication of their supposed communications. But this has certainly not been the case universally and always: and the exceptions are of great theoretical importance. The two groups of pre-nineteenth-century mediums or quasi-mediums about whom we have most information, though said to have performed many of the feats attributed to modern mediums, did not ascribe their successes to the spirits of the dead. The κάτοχοι of the later classical period perversely gave credit to nonhuman gods or dæmons; the witches of the sixteenth and seventeenth centuries rashly confessed to assistance from the devil. Incidentally, it is hard to see what bearing the occurrence of paranormal *physical* phenomena would have on the question of survival. For unless there were reason to think that death endows a "man" with powers of levitating toy trumpets and so forth, such a performance could scarcely even assist in authenticating the claim that "messages" accompanying it originated "on the other side"; any more than—*pace* the advertisers and the mass newspapers—prowess in athletics or motor-racing gives weight

---

[1] "It is futile to do with more elements what can be done with fewer": the usual version of Ockham's Razor *Entia non sunt multiplicanda praeter necessitatem* "Entities should not be multiplied unnecessarily" is not to be found in his extant works.

to a celebrity's endorsement of a hair-cream or a religion.

In France—where the Spiritualist cult is less widespread than it is in the Anglo-Saxon world—Dr. Osty tested a subject, Mme. Morel, who produced under his supervision many true items of information, both about the living and about the dead, which were comparable in range and in accuracy with the work of the best spirit mediums; and the production of which was equally inexplicable in normal terms. But she did this without benefit of any Controls or Communicators: and did not attribute her successes to spirit aid. Presumably with a different climate of opinion to mould her development she would have become an orthodox spirit medium: and in other environments perhaps a seer or a prophetess or a "wise woman." (See "Télépathie Spontanée et Transmission de Pensée Expérimentale" in *Revue Métapsychique*, 1932–3, pp. 80–3.)

Again, to parallel the proxy sittings, Osty reports that another of his subjects, Mme. Peyroutel, on being asked to describe the past life of a living person of whom he was thinking, gave very distinctive details, which were quite unknown to Osty, were not normally accessible to her, and were later confirmed as correct by intimates of the person in question. (*La Connaissance Supernormale*, pp. 148 ff.: this and the previous reference are both borrowed from Professor E. R. Dodds' "Why I Do Not Believe in Survival," *Proc. S.P.R.*, Vol. XLII, to which and to whom I owe much else besides. It is only fair to add that it does not seem to me that Osty's work, however sound his conclusions, was up to the best S.P.R. standards.)

The vivid characterization by a medium in trance of a person who was never normally known to her can also be curiously paralleled. Dr. S. G. Soal—whose statistical ESP experiments will be mentioned later—reports that at a sitting with Mrs. Blanche Cooper a Communicator calling "himself" Gordon Davis appeared. But later—much to his surprise—Soal discovered that his acquaintance Gordon Davis had not, as he had previously believed, been killed in the war: but was still alive and had, at the time of the sittings, been practising as an estate agent in Southend. The voice of "Gordon Davis" was so apparently realistic that Soal exclaimed "By Jove! and it's *like* Gordon Davis too": and the turns of speech were later agreed by both Davis and Soal to be characteristic. Most of the statements made by "Gordon Davis" were later found to fit Gordon Davis: the most remarkable fact being that a description of the internal arrangements of a house given by "him" fitted the actual arrangements of the Davis home, into which he had not moved till a year after the sittings with Mrs. Cooper. ("A Report on some Communications Received through Mrs. Blanche Cooper," *Proc. S.P.R.*, Vol. XXXV; this particular case pp. 560 ff.)

Even the features of the cross-correspondences, which "Myers" deliberately devised in order to remove—or at least to restrict—the possibility of a description in terms of the normal and paranormal capacities of the living only, have some parallels which could only be fitted into a spiritualist account very artificially. In many experiments in telepathy the "receiver" seems to be groping near and for the idea the "transmitter" has wished to convey. In one case—the Ramsden–Miles series—when Miss Miles wanted to send *Sphinx*, Miss Ramsden recorded *Luxor in Egypt*, and when she wanted to produce *Bishop*, Miss Ramsden ended *latme, Bishop Latimer, Archbishop*. In another case when a "transmitter" wanted Professor Gilbert Murray to think of *Sir Francis Drake drinking the health of Doughty the mutineer*, what he actually got was *a faint feeling of Arabia or desert:* a neat example of the sort of disguised allusion attributed to Myers.[2] In a third case—especially interesting because two of the leading figures of the cross-correspondence work were involved—Dr. A. W. Verrall wanted to infiltrate into his wife's automatic scripts the three Greek words μονόπωλον ἐς ἀῶ (rendered as *One-Horse Dawn:* which gave a name to the case). In the next six months those scripts did in fact give just such a series of groping references as would have been scored as a cross-correspondence if they had been occurring in the products of different automatists. (They also had, on different occasions, separate sentences which made sense only when put together. And they even had one of those recondite allusive passages: *Find the herb moly, that will help—it is a clue.* The allusion was later tracked down by Mrs. Verrall to another of the papers set in the Cambridge Classical Tripos in the same year as that from which her husband had culled the three enigmatic Greek words.) (See Professor A. C. Pigou in *Proc. S.P.R.,* Vol. XXIII, pp. 286 ff.)

Besides such non-spiritualistic parallels to the marvels of "spirit" mediumship and automatism, there have been some indications in the work of the best of these mediums and automatists which point in the same direction. *First,* there are cases where erroneous "communications" seem to be most plausibly described as based on telepathy from the sitter to the medium. In the paper already referred to Soal reports that a "John Ferguson" appeared at sittings with Mrs. Blanche Cooper, claiming to be a brother of a James Ferguson with whom the investigator had been at school. Soal *privately* invented various hypotheses about this putative John Ferguson. These were duly retailed to him as facts at later sittings.

But he was in the meantime able to prove that no such John Ferguson had ever existed. Again at sittings with Mrs. Piper, Hodgson one day thought about Sir Walter Scott: next day a manifestly fictitious "Sir Walter Scott" communicated. On another occasion when he had at one sitting been thinking of the notorious physical medium D. D. Home, a similarly spurious "D. D. Home" appeared next day.

Second, if we make the assumption that, other things being equal, telepathy is more likely to occur between two people when they are close together than when they are far apart, then some results reported by Mr. H. F. Saltmarsh are suggestive. (This assumption has a fair amount of support; though nothing much can be said with assurance about what conditions favour telepathy.) Saltmarsh found that in a series of sittings, fifty-three ordinary and eighty-nine proxy, with Mrs. Warren Elliott the percentage of true statements in the former class was more than double what it was in the latter; while several Communicators who did well in ordinary conditions made no score at all at proxy sittings. ("Report on the Investigation of Some Sittings with Mrs. Warren Elliott," *Proc. S.P.R.,* Vol. XXXIX.) Similar analysis has yet to be applied to the recorded work of other outstanding mediums. But even if Saltmarsh's results were confirmed and supplemented in this way, some story about "the spirits" needing the presence of sympathetic loved ones would still fit the facts.

Third, students of mediumistic communications have frequently commented on their disjointedness: bits and pieces of information come spasmodically. This is just what would be expected on the theory that the items which are not normally available to the medium are picked up paranormally, and usually unconsciously, from other living people: for in the non-spiritualistic cases of ap-

---

[2] *Arabia Deserta* was written by (another) Doughty.

parent telepathy miscellaneous scraps of information are acquired sporadically. However, in a spiritualist account all this can be ascribed to the difficulties of getting the messages through: and this difficulty is no doubt considerable; or how are we to account for the failure—often remarked by the incredulous—of the spirits to make themselves more widely known before the middle of the last century?

Fourth, no Control or Communicator —however great was the literary ability possessed by his earthly namesake—ever seems able to give a plausible and distinctive account of his present mode of existence. What is offered always looks deplorably like the tawdry product of the medium's phantasy life, moulded by the fashionable doctrines of her culture circle (French spirits are often reincarnationists—following Allan Kardec —whereas Anglo-Saxon ones know nothing of any rebirth from the "glorious Summerland").

Fifth—a similar point—the "spirits," even when their namesakes have been active and able people, never give *evidence* either of any development since death or of any private activity between séances: though more than enough is *said* about "deepening understanding," "spiritual growth," and so on, since they "crossed over to the other side."

Now, none of these parallel cases and internal indications *rule out* a spiritualistic interpretation: something could be done to allow for all of them separately. But taken together they do make such an account look a great deal less easy and less inevitable. The telepathic (ESP) alternative involves fewer assumptions: only that mediums sometimes show a paranormal faculty for the reality of which there is much other evidence; and that they show it in a degree for which there is some other evidence. The spiritualist account demands, at least, that many human personalities survive death

(whatever precisely this may mean) *in addition to* the existence of the powers postulated in the telepathic etc. (ESP) account. If—as usually is the case—the spiritualist view is extended to cover successful book-tests and object-reading,[3] as well as paranormal physical phenomena; then the telepathic alternative is equally capable of parallel extension. For the further powers which now have to be attributed to "the spirits" could be ascribed to the medium and other people: in each case there is evidence pointing to the display by people making no spiritualist claims of such a paranormal power. (See, for instance, Chapter VIII for card-guessing under "clairvoyance" conditions and for "psychokinesis" in the laboratory.) The relative position of the ESP and the spiritualist interpretations—or rather types of interpretation, for there are many possible species in each genus—will remain the same.

It is important to emphasize the word "interpretation": the rival views certainly cannot be awarded the status of explanations. To say that the paranormal element in a séance is due to telepathy etc. between the various people concerned is not at all like saying that the coordination of the elements in an armoured division is secured by radio telephony. "Telepathy" is not the name of a means of communication; whereas the mention of radio telephony does explain how certain results are achieved, by indicating the mechanisms involved. Telepathy is no more an explanation of the paranormal element in séance performances than memory is an explanation of our capacity to give our names and addresses.

In this respect talk of "the spirits" is

---

[3] "Object-reading" or "psychometry," are the names given to the alleged performance of providing true information about the history of some object, which could not be inferred by and has never been known to the psychic.

certainly no better; in spite of the explanatory pretensions with which it is often introduced. For on this view "the spirits" also have to be credited with all the still mysterious paranormal powers, which the alternative view attributes to people only; furthermore, they must possess them to a far higher degree. For, presumably, bodiless beings could not either acquire information (some spirits *have* produced information not normally available to their mediums about things that occurred *after* the deaths of "their" namesakes) or convey it; either to one another, or, crucially, to the "spirit controls" manipulating mediums: except "by ESP" (*sensory* communication is ruled out by definition).

The postulation of surviving spirits might look plausible if with the progress of research we found that the alternative ESP account would have to attribute to people ESP capacities considerably greater *both* than those for which we could find evidence outside spiritist contexts *and* than those which the spirit account needed to attribute to spirits. The first condition would not be satisfied if we could then find any reason why mediums and others should put up in spiritualist contexts exceptionally good ESP performances; but it would be if we found that our ESP account would have to attribute to the sitters ESP performances either under conditions which were independently known to be inhibitory, or of which these particular sitters were independently known to be incapable. Once it was easier than it is now to believe that the first condition would be satisfied in this way (see e.g., Hodgson's work on Mrs. Piper, used by Broad in this sense in *The Mind and its Place in Nature,* Kegan Paul, 1925, pp. 548 ff.). The second condition would lose its force if any reason could be given why "surviving spirits" should be better ESP performers than their former namesakes. (This difficulty has too often been

overlooked: presumably partly on the same worthless principle *omne ignotum pro magnifico* [4] which has misled people to think that physical mediumship could give emphatic warrant to "spirit" claims.) Before the postulation was justified a third condition would have to be satisfied: the discovery of good independent reason for saying that memory performances could occur after the dissolution of the brain of which they were normally thought to be a function. This is important, because most of the paranormally provided information in most séances (and *mutatis mutandis* the same thing applies to characteristic mannerisms, direct voices, etc.) is such as some person, as a matter of fact dead, would have been able to give from memory were he still alive and well: hence the desire to describe the séance by reference to the "spirit" of the person in question. But even supposing that the first two conditions are met, the spiritist account is still not going to be more plausible than its rival: what it gains on the ESP side, by not having to allow for huge inexplicable increases in ESP capacity in the single context of the séance, it loses elsewhere by having to postulate a special faculty of brainless memory, possessed by its postulated spirits. This third condition might be satisfied if all the efforts of the neurophysiologists and psychologists failed to account for memory in neurophysiological terms.[5] Furthermore, until and unless the concept "spirit" is made a great deal more specific than it

---

[4] Freely: "Everything unknown is a miracle."

[5] Those who for any reason hope for this may be encouraged by the confession of K. S. Lashley, one of those who have tried hardest to outline such an account: "I sometimes feel, in reviewing the evidence on the localization of the memory trace, that the necessary conclusion is that learning just is not possible." The rest of us can reflect—with Lashley—that it is early days for despair.

is at present, the spirit account cannot serve as a scientific hypothesis. To use it as such we should have to be able to deduce from it definite and testable consequences: to be able to say that, if it *were* correct, such and such tests *would* yield such and such results. We cannot, because with the spirits anything goes; nothing is definitely predictable. Or, to put it less misleadingly: the concept of spirit is hopelessly indeterminate; which is the main reason why the word "spirit" has no place in the language of science (see p. 26).

Professor C. D. Broad's "psychic factor" theory is relevant here. He has suggested, without very firm conviction, that "minds" might be "a compound of two factors, neither of which separately has the characteristic properties of a mind, just as salt is a compound of two substances neither of which by itself has the characteristic properties of salt. . . . The psychic factor would be like some chemical element which has never been isolated; and the characteristics of a mind would depend jointly on those of the psychic factor and on those of the material organism with which it is united" (*loc. cit.,* pp. 535–6). The analogy to a chemical compound would hold in so far as "chemical compounds have properties which cannot be deduced from those which their elements display in isolation or in other compounds . . . [although] . . . the properties of the compounds are wholly dependent on those of the elements, in the sense that given such elements in such relations, a compound necessarily arises with such and such properties . . . [which] . . . do not belong to the elements, but only to the compound as a whole" (p. 536). But it would break down in so far as when "two chemical elements are united to form a chemical compound no permanent change is produced in the properties of either . . . [whereas] . . . when a psychic factor is united with a bodily organism so as to give a mind both factors may be permanently affected by this union" (p. 536).

This sort of view has two signal superiorities over spiritisms. First: while the word "spirit" combines the minimum of determinate meaning with the maximum of emotive disturbance, the new term "psychic factor" can be given precisely as much and what meaning we wish, and so far is sterile emotionally. Broad was only willing to commit himself to the chemical analogy; and to insisting that "it is capable of carrying traces of past experiences and of certain personal peculiarities" (p. 659). Second: psychic factors, unlike spirits, could not be expected either to retain all the mental capacities of their mortal namesakes or to enjoy any private life and development between séances when they are not married to any bodily factor. This squares with their "singular reticence about their present life, characters, and surroundings" (p. 540).

But, after allowing for these advantages, this view is surely open to criticisms similar to those deployed against spiritisms. It is—as Broad of course saw (p. 538)—more complex than its ESP rival: for it postulates a new class of entities, psychic factors; and attributes to them that capacity of carrying memory traces which is usually considered the prerogative of the brain; while psychic factors will have to be endowed with much the same ESP capacities as the rival interpretation has to attribute to people. When Broad originally developed this view it did have compensating advantages: for he was writing before both the great advances in laboratory ESP and the publication of much further work on mediumship suggesting that psychic factors would have to be credited with considerable ESP powers *as well as* the possession of many memory traces appropriate to their dead namesakes. But the former have made it seem that we shall have in any case to credit some people with considerable ESP capacity. While the latter have indicated that even psychic factors—which, unlike spirits, do not have private lives apart from séances, and so do not have to be credited with enormous ESP powers on that account—would have to be conceded considerable ones: since the Communicators of entranced mediums sometimes produce information which was not normally available *either* to the medium *or* to their departed namesakes when alive (see above, p. 372). Broad was writing, too, before Soal's "Gordon Davis" and "John Ferguson" cases (see above, pp. 377–78).

. . .

There is a deeper level of criticism of survivalism. The gist is that it is not clear what such a theory will *mean*. Logically this question should be prior to those raised so far; but it is so surprising as to justify a roundabout approach. For surely Butler is right? Can we not understand the hopes of the warriors of Allah who expect if they die in Holy War to go straight to the arms of the black-eyed houris in Paradise? Can we not understand the fears of the slum mother kept from the contraceptive clinic by her priest's warnings of penalties for those who die in mortal sin? Or even the hopes of a Myers or a Sidgwick? Of course we can: it would be a preposterous piece of over-sophistication to fail to understand such fears and hopes, and to discount their possible power and influence.[6] But still the sceptic urges: surely something crucial is being overlooked? For this future life is supposed to continue even *after* physical dissolution: even

after the slow corruption in the cemetery, or the swift consumption in the crematorium. To suggest that we might survive this dissolution seems like suggesting that a nation might outlast the annihilation of all its members. Certainly we can understand the promises of Paradise, the threats of Hell, the brave stories of Valhalla. But to expect that after my death and dissolution such things might happen to me is to overlook that I shall not then exist, *ex hypothesi*. To expect such things, through overlooking this, is surely like accepting a fairy tale as history, through ignoring the prefatory rubric "once upon a time, in a world that never was . . . ?"

Of course the insinuations of the sceptic are as slick and crude as they are unfair. But they can serve to throw into relief two easily and often neglected but crucial points. First, that the essence of doctrines of personal survival (or immortality)—and this alone is what gives them their huge human interest—is that they should assert that we shall exist after our deaths (for ever). It is thus, and only thus, that they can provide the basis for expecting that we shall have "experiences" after death, that with death things for us will not cease, but change. For nothing can happen to us then unless there is still an us for it to happen to. Second, that person-words mean what they do mean. Words such as "you," "I," "person," "people," "woman," "man," "Flew"—though very different in their particular functions—are all used to refer in one way or another to objects (the pejorative flavour of this word should here be discounted) which you can point at, touch, hear, see, and talk to. Person-words refer to people. And how can such objects as people survive physical dissolution? This is a massive difficulty, and the need to evade or remove it has provided the conscious or unconscious driving force for many intellectual manœuvres:

First, there have been attempts to show

---

[6] Those who issued in the 1948 Italian election the monitory poster with "Stalin cannot see you: but God can" printed over a picture of a polling-booth, made no such mistake. To say nothing of Plato (*Republic,* I and X) and Aristotle (*Metaphysics* 1074B).

that person-words have at most a contingent, and not a necessary reference to objects: that is to say that people as a matter of *fact* (which might have been, and may one day be otherwise) inhabit, or are otherwise closely associated with, their bodies; but that the reference to objects is no part of the *meaning* of person-words. These attempts have usually appeared as arguments that people are—inexplicably—compounded of two elements, body and soul (the latter sufficiently elusive and insubstantial to be a plausible candidate for survival after dissolution); and that the soul is the—real or essential—person. This last equation is crucial: for unless I am my soul, the immortality (or survival) of my soul will not be my immortality; and the news of the immortality (or future survival) of my soul would be of no more concern to me than the news that my appendix would be preserved eternally in a bottle. In psychical research contexts the term "spirit" has usually done duty for the less secular "soul."

Second, it has been thought that a doctrine of "the resurrection of the body" (better perhaps reformulated as "the reconstitution of the person") avoids this difficulty. In spiritualist contexts this move has taken the form of the view that people have (or are) "spiritual" or "astral" bodies (or persons) which (or who) at death detach themselves from their "physical" or "earth-plane" bodies. But this is surely to jump from the frying-pan of logical difficulty into the fire of factual indefensibility.

Third, whether or not talk of people surviving dissolution is, according to current usage, self-contradictory (whether or not person-words refer to objects which could not significantly be said to survive physical dissolution), it has been argued that we can attach sense to talk of spirits surviving physical dissolution. We can: but the difficulty is to attach a sense such that this talk will, if true, justify us

in nourishing expectations of experiences, instead of oblivion, after our deaths. It is in their present use—with its essential reference to certain objects one can point at (viz. people)—that person-words carry their crucial implications; that personal identity is the necessary condition of both accountability and expectation. Which is only to say that it is unjust to reward or punish someone for something unless (as a minimum condition) he is the same person as did the deed; and also that it is absurd to expect experiences for Flew in 1984 unless in that year there is going to be someone who will be the same person as I. The problem is to change the meaning of person-words so radically that it becomes significant to talk of people surviving dissolution, without changing it to such an extent that the crucial implications would be lost; and without losing touch with the facts as far as we know them. To give a sense to "Flew disembodied" or "the spirit of Flew" such that the spirit of Flew will still be the same person as the writer of this book; and such, too, that there will still be some point in talking like this in a psychical research context.

This is not a clearly hopeless task, but it certainly is far harder than, and partly of a different kind from, what is often thought. It is not clearly hopeless because people—though objects—are objects of a very remarkable kind: people—unlike things—have "private experiences" —feelings, sensations, and so forth; and particular people have a large range of, so to speak, separable characteristics— knowledge of this and that, such-and-such peculiar mannerisms, and so on. And while people—the objects we can point at—cannot conceivably survive physical dissolution, private experiences might perhaps be significantly said to occur disembodied; and some of the characteristics we have been accustomed to associate with particular people could conceivably be, and in fact sometimes actually are, manifested in the absence of those people—those objects we could once have pointed at. These two peculiarities of people as objects suggest that the task is not hopeless.

But it is far harder than it might seem. For our language—and this of course applies just as much to person-words and all the other words we use in our discourse about persons, as to the words for material things—has been evolved as an instrument for dealing with the situations in which men have found themselves: for the situations of this world. When we try—as we are trying when we want to speak of people surviving death—to use it for dealing with radically different conditions it breaks down. It begins to play tricks on us in all sorts of subtle and unexpected ways. For so many words which one might think to transfer easily to descriptions of putative spirit beings involve covert but essential reference to the corporeal. This fact is concealed from us by (and is doubtless also partly the cause of) our tendency tacitly, or even explicitly, to take spirit existence to be some sort of desubstantialized replica of the world we live in. Spirit cigars and astral trousers have often been derided. It is almost impossible to realize that our supposed bodiless beings really would be bodiless, and all that this involves. My feelings are distinguished from yours by being, as it were, attached to me and not to you; but disembodied experiences could not be "grouped" and "owned" in the same way at all. And it is no use relying on the fact that any person knows very well when he has a feeling that it is his: because the whole question at issue is precisely this, whether any sense can be given to talk of disembodied people, and of their having feelings and so on.

The problem of creating suitable senses for "person" and associated terms and expressions would also be partly of an unexpected kind. For if the existence of disembodied people in the sense to be specified is to be a doctrine of survival, is to justify living people ("people" in the old sense) in expecting experiences after death, then it will have to make sense to talk of a disembodied person (new or extended sense of "person") being the same person as some former person (ordinary sense of "person"). And this will demand a change in the meaning of "same person": since a disembodied person, a spirit, cannot be the same person as an (ordinary) person, in the present sense of "same person"; for, to speak very dogmatically, the meaning and the criteria of this expression involve reference to the continuance of a particular object, the person in question; and *ex vi termini* this cannot apply to the case of a disembodied spirit. We shall have both to produce a sense of "same person" which could do the trick, and to provide a convincing quasi-legal argument for thus changing the use of that expression.

This is a difficult business: perhaps an analogy would make things clearer. Constantly courts are confronted with perplexing issues which take the form of questions; but which are not so much questions asking for answers as demands requiring decisions. "Is a flying-boat a ship?" Well, of course, it is and yet it isn't: but the court has to decide one way or the other. The problem arises because an attempt is being made to use a word in a situation with which it was never designed to cope. A law which was passed before flying-boats were thought of has been contravened (or has it?) by a flying-boat. "Is a flying-boat a ship?" does not really ask for *information* about either flying-boats or ships, nor yet even for linguistic information about the present and proper use of the words "flying-boat" and "ship": it demands a *decision* as to what the future proper legal use is to be; whether or not the term "ship" is to cover flying-boats. It would be naïve either to wonder whether a flying-boat is *really* a ship (whatever that might mean) or to be taken in by the legal fiction that the Legislature—working before flying-boats were thought of —either did or did not intend to include them when it used the word "ships." Now, person-words and their associates were developed to deal with the activities and transactions of the objects we call people. If we want to stretch them to describe the supposed activities and transactions of putative incorporeal beings, then we must not be surprised if we find things going wrong, if we discover that what used to be straight questions now turn out sometimes to be crooked: "Is this (spirit the same person as) Myers?" is not susceptible of a straightforward yes-or-no *answer;* though we could make a *decision* (and a *reasoned* decision such as the lawyers make) about the use of "same person," in terms of which a definite answer might then be given. The question "Is this (spirit the same person as) Myers?" is very much more like the question "Is it chess if you play without the king?"[7] than it is like "Is it Soal who keeps ringing me up?"

Professor H. H. Price has tried to give a suitable sense to "disembodied survival" in a fascinating exploration (*Proc. S.P.R.,* Vol. L, pp. 1 ff.). With great skill he indicates a conceivable mode of existence of possible conscious but incorporeal beings. The crux is that such beings might have a life of mental imagery, and little else. This suggestion seems to make sense, even if the occurrence of mental imagery without a "physical basis" in a brain is —as, apart possibly from the facts of psychical research, we have every reason to suppose—*as a matter of fact* impossible: because it would always be *significant,* though often silly, in the face of no

matter what behavioural [8] evidence to the contrary, to suggest that someone might or might not be in pain or might or might not be having a mental image. There would be no *contradiction* in asserting the behavioural evidence and denying its usual experiential correlate. Consider the nightmare case, borrowed from Professor John Wisdom, of the man who says to a patient being wheeled into the operating theatre: "You'll make no sound, no movement, and afterwards you will remember nothing: but, in spite of the anæsthetic, you'll feel it all." Or the reports of people after cataleptic trances saying that their experience was continuous, though they had appeared oblivious, which provoked Edgar Allan Poe's tormented tales of burial alive.

Now Price's account of his image beings avoids the cruder errors of purporting to describe disembodied existence while surreptitiously reintroducing bodies. No mean achievement: for even Plato when speaking supposedly of the life of incorporeal souls disembodied by death describes their fortunes in precisely the terms of a (corporeal) adventure; as when he sees (*sic*) souls under physical tortures, which only (corporeal) people could suffer (see *Republic,* X). But Price still assumes that simply by providing this account he has shown that conceivably *we* might become such beings after death, that death for *us* might be a metamorphosis from a substantial to an insubstantial mode of existence. Whereas —as we have argued—it is still necessary to show that it would be reasonable, if

---

[7] Wittgenstein's example was, I believe, significantly different: "Is it chess if you play without the queen?"

[8] The word "behavioural" is being used to cover not merely what he *does,* but also— what is so often and so importantly contrasted with this—what he *says.* It is the failure both of psychologists and laymen to notice how crucially different this is from the ordinary sense (which covers the former only) which has been partly but only partly responsible for the scandal of behaviourism. Here, for good measure, we also intend the word to cover neurological occurrences.

certain conditions were satisfied, to *decide* that particular incorporeal beings could be identified with, could be said to be the same persons as, particular human beings. The word *"decide"* is crucial: the present meanings of our person-words and expressions are adapted to the needs and facts of this world; and we cannot extend them to cover the radically different possibilities of another world without, tacitly or explicitly, deciding to make *drastic* alterations in their use, their meanings. This may sound a tortuous method of remaking a trivial point. But the point only sounds trivial in the context of a speculative discussion, where it is always open to us so to arrange our suppositions about possible beings that it would be obviously reasonable to extend our notions of person and personal identity to include these. But the facts of any actual other world may be such that we should not want to decide, even in the light of the fullest knowledge, that a particular insubstantial being either was or was not Myers. Price, by speaking about what it might be like *for us* to be incorporeal beings, takes these vital decisions for granted.

He seems momentarily to have overlooked that in questions about personal identity even the honest testimony of that person does not necessarily provide the last word, as it does where the issue is whether or not someone is in pain. He writes, "And surely the important question is what constitutes my personal identity *for myself"* (p. 10). But Capone either is or is not the one who led the gang: he cannot be one thing *for himself* and another *for other people;* though some (usually *but not always* including himself; memory is not infallible) may be in the secret, while others are not. It is because this is so, because it is possible to be *mistaken* as to whether one did or suffered something, whereas it makes no sense to talk of being *mistaken* as to whether one is now in pain, that one can-

not get around these points about *decision* issues by, as it were, appealing to a possible incorporeal being "himself" (or itself) to settle expertly whether or not "he" (or it) is Myers.[9] (Unless, of course, one is prepared to abdicate the decision itself to the "spirits": which is itself a *decision;* and a very poor one.)

The argument of this chapter has been of two quite different, but interrelated, kinds: first about the possible interpretations of facts, and then about the meanings of words. *First,* we indicated the lines on which apparently strong evidence for survival might be interpreted more simply in terms of telepathy etc. Among living people only: this is a type of argument long familiar, at least to psychical researchers. *Second,* we tried to show that there are serious difficulties involved in giving sense to talk of spirits and their survival: this line of argument is not yet nearly so familiar, even to those who devote themselves to this subject. The crux is not that our possible future life would be so different from anything we know that we cannot hope to describe or imagine it: but that these spirits, if we gave determinate meaning to this term, might, precisely because of their incorporeality, be so different from what we now mean by "people" that we could not identify them with people who had

---

[9] To bring out this difficult point, consider two fantastic examples: suppose a person P split like an amœba into two identical people P_1 and P_2 *both* claiming to be P and both having the "memories" appropriate to and all other characteristics of the original person before his great divide: and suppose two incorporeal beings *both* claimed to be Myers, and *both* displayed the appropriate characteristics and "memories." Here testimony, albeit honest, could not be the last word: unless we are willing to say that in this case two things which are the same as a third can be different from one another; as we might indeed *decide* to do. (See my "Locke and the Problem of Personal Identity," *Philosophy* 1951.)

once lived, even though they might possess peculiar knowledge and other characteristics reminiscent of our dead friends.

S U G G E S T I O N S   F O R   F U R T H E R   R E A D I N G

Traditional arguments for immortality can be found in Plato, *Phaedo;* St. Augustine, "On the Immortality of the Soul"; Joseph Butler, *The Analogy of Religion;* and Immanuel Kant, *Critique of Practical Reason.* Arguments for immortality from an idealist position are presented by Josiah Royce, *The Conception of Immortality* (Boston: Houghton Mifflin, 1900); and J. M. E. McTaggart, *Some Dogmas of Religion* (London: Arnold, 1906). A. E. Taylor, *The Christian Hope of Immortality* (London: Unicorn Press, 1938), and William James, *Human Immortality* (Boston: Houghton Mifflin, 1898), are sympathetic treatments. The belief is criticized in Lucretius, *On the Nature of Things;* P. H. D. d'Holbach, *System of Nature;* Corliss Lamont, *The Illusion of Immortality* (New York: Putnam, 1935); and Bertrand Russell, *Why I Am Not a Christian and Other Essays* (New York: Simon and Schuster, 1957).

The possibility that psychical research provides evidence for survival of death is discussed in C. D. Broad, *The Mind and Its Place in Nature* (London: Routledge and Kegan Paul, 1925), and *Human Personality and the Possibility of Its Survival* (Berkeley: Univ. of California Press, 1955); Gardner Murphy, "An Outline of Survival Evidence" and "Difficulties Confronting the Survival Hypothesis," *Journal of the American Society for Psychical Research* (1945).

5.

REVELATION
AND
MIRACLE

In most religions it is believed that at certain times a god will communicate certain truths to a selected individual. In primitive religion this communication usually takes the form of the god's possession of the individual, a state involving various abnormal and even violent manifestations. In more advanced religions what actually happens when an individual is thought to receive a message from God varies widely. He may fall into a trance in which he is under an involuntary compulsion to speak or write certain words, but as a civilization advances such grossly abnormal phenomena are likely to lose favor. The individual may hear an audible voice speaking certain words which he then merely transcribes. This voice may seem to come from outside or from inside himself, and it may or may not be accompanied by visual presentations (Moses and the burning bush). More subtly, he may just seem to himself to be especially inspired to speak or write as he is doing, to be guided by another—a phenomenon which is common in various degrees among creative artists. Or more subtly still, the individual may appear to others, and to himself, to be going through the normal processes of literary composition, and yet for some reason it will be thought that these processes are being supernaturally guided by God, however unconscious the individual may be of this guidance. (The letters of St. Paul may serve as examples of this last possibility.) But however these details may vary, there is a common core which justifies the application of the single term. In all these cases God is believed to be working on the individual so as to bring it about that he apprehends and enunciates certain truths, and in that way God reveals these truths to this individual.

Revelation becomes especially important in a prophetic religion where it is taken to be the chief avenue of divine-human intercourse, in contrast to the wordless intercourse of mystical experience and the not necessarily verbal participation in rites like the sacred meal. In these religions records of divine communications are collected into sacred books (the Bible, the Koran), which are accorded a unique authority as the word of God. Judaism, Christianity, and Islam, the prophetic religions par excellence, are sometimes called "religions of the book." In these religions divine revelation is the primary basis on which the cardinal doctrines are thought to rest. These doctrines are thought to have been delivered to man by God, through selected intermediaries like Moses, Paul, and Mohammed, and hence to have the authority of God behind them. Even a theologian like Aquinas, who thinks that certain cardinal truths—the existence of God and the immortality of the soul, for example—can be established by our own reasoning powers, admits that there are many other important doctrines, such as the Incarnation, the Atonement, the Trinity, which we know to be true only because God has revealed them to us.

Very serious problems can be raised concerning the appeal to revelation. First, the sacred book which is accepted as ultimately authoritative is generally compiled from quite diverse sources, many of which had undergone considerable editing before reaching their present form. And in this heterogeneous body of material one finds both contradictions between different components of the book and contradictions between statements in the book and what is known independently. This, of course, poses a serious problem for anyone who takes the Bible to be the word of God. For how could God contradict Himself or be mistaken? Theologians have struggled through the ages to resolve such difficulties, and in the course of these struggles they have resorted to allegorical interpretations, claimed corruptions in the text, and sought to qualify in various ways the direct attribution of the words of the book to God. Whether any one of these devices, or all of them together, suffice to resolve the difficulties is an enormous problem into which we cannot go.

It is an accident, so to speak, that in the writings which are in fact accepted as messages from God there are difficulties of this kind. But even if it had been otherwise, there would still be another, more essential, problem. How do we know that these writings are in fact messages from God? Even if the text were completely free of internal or external contradictions, we would still be faced with this problem. We cannot uncritically take at face value every claim to divine revelation. For one thing, such claims sometimes come into direct conflict with each other. The Koran insists on the strict unity of God, in conscious opposition to the Trinitarian assertions (or implications) in the New Testament. The Indian Vedas speak of an unbeginning and unending series of world cycles, in opposition to the account of the creation of the world at a point in time in the Old Testament. Clearly we cannot accept all these as authentic communications from God. This means that we are faced with the question: How do we know which of them come from God? Indeed, how do we know that any of them do?

Through the centuries theologians have given various reasons for supposing that, in fact, the Scriptures are messages from God. This has always involved citing certain features of the writings, their authors, the effects they have had in the world since their composition which serve as marks of their revealed status. In the selection from Aquinas three sorts of facts are mentioned: The authors of these writings performed "works surpassing the capability of the whole of nature"; the Christian church grew rapidly and spectacularly without any external worldly aid; the Biblical prophets foretold many happenings they could not have predicted by their own unaided powers. These are all miracles, meaning by "miracle" an event which happens otherwise than as it would have happened if only natural factors had been involved. The argument is that something can happen contrary to natural regularities only if those regularities have been specially set aside in this instance by a supernatural being Who has control over them. And since this is so, the fact that such happenings occurred in connection with the composition of the Scriptures and the religious movement based on them shows that God had a direct hand in these things and hence that the contents of the Scriptures can be taken as messages from God.

There are numerous problems which arise with respect to this line of argument. First, there is the question as to whether the events in question—Moses turning a rod into a serpent, Joshua stopping the sun, Jesus walking on the water, —really did happen. This is the question to which Hume addresses himself in his essay on miracles. Hume points out that any supposed miracle runs counter to our common experience, or it would not be considered a serious candidate for the miraculous, which means that judging by our experience the probability of such an occurrence would be very low. Hence employing Hume's maxim that "no testimony is sufficient to establish a miracle, unless the testimony be of such a kind, that its falsehood would be more miraculous, than the fact, which it endeavours to establish," we can see that strong testimony would be needed to establish the actual occurrence of such an event, and Hume argues persuasively that such testimony is not forthcoming. It is not Hume's official position that no testimony whatsoever would be sufficient to establish such a happening, though he wavers on this point, as when he says, in effect, that no testimony would lead him to "admit of so signal a violation of the laws of nature" as Queen Elizabeth coming alive after having been interred for a month. (This is connected with his remark that "there must . . . be a uniform experience against every miraculous event." But, of course, we cannot know that the experience against it is absolutely uniform unless we know that the supposed miracle did not occur). Hume says only that in order to establish it we would need stronger testimony than we can ever actually obtain. So far as I can see, the only way to attack this thesis would be to maintain that in calculating the likelihood of Jesus' having actually walked on the water, for example, it is relevant to take into account more than just our experience of what happens in other cases when men step into deep water. It could be argued, as A. E. Taylor does in his essay "David Hume and the Miraculous," that if we can suppose that a theistic God exists and that He would wish to communicate some facts about Himself, His plans, His demands on men, we could reasonably expect miracles to occur somewhere as signs that such a divine communication was taking place. But if so, any procedure that would give a miracle report an initial probability so low as to make it always unreasonable to accept it could not be justified. The general expectation just mentioned would raise the initial probability of reported miracles, not enough to render them all acceptable without further question, but enough to make them susceptible of proof provided we have (not impossibly) strong testimony.

But even if Jesus did walk on the water and heal the sick by touch, there is still the question of whether these are really miracles in the relevant sense, or whether, on the contrary, they could be explained in terms of natural causes. It is plain, for example, that we can now at least see the possibility of explaining "miraculous" cures like some of those attributed to Jesus in psychological terms. Contrariety to common experience is a necessary but not a sufficient condition for something being a miracle; it may be that the true regularities are more compli- cated than the ones we had accepted on the basis of past experience. Quite often science advances by way of developing more complicated laws to accommodate deviations from previously accepted laws. Eclipses of the sun violate common- sense regularities about the succession of daylight and darkness; they were once thought to be supernatural, but they have come to be understood as necessary results of regular astronomical operations. With respect to the rise of the Chris- tian church, we may well suspect that natural factors have been responsible—for example, the despair of earthly happiness prevalent in the later Roman empire.

Partly as a result of an awareness of these difficulties, and partly on the basis of other considerations, including a Kierkegaardian conception of the na- ture of faith (see Section 6), "neo-orthodox" theologians such as Karl Barth and Emil Brunner have developed a concept of revelation which is significantly differ- ent from the traditional one. The traditional conception can be called "doctrinal" or "propositional," in that it takes revelation to be primarily a communication of true propositions or doctrines from God to man. There are differences among proponents of the traditional conception as to how this communication takes place. The more conservative thinkers suppose that God transmitted to the au- thors of the books of the Bible the exact words they wrote down; this is the "verbal inspiration" or "dictation" theory. More liberal thinkers suppose that God simply caused the individuals to apprehend certain truths, which they then expressed in words of their own choosing; and some liberals even suppose that inadequacies, and even errors, can creep in at this secondary stage. But both conservatives and liberals think of what is revealed as being certain religious truths, however they may differ as to the form in which these truths are communi- cated, or the process by which they are communicated. By contrast the neo-orthodox conception, as set forth in the selection from Brunner, can be called "personal." What God primarily reveals is not a set of propositions, but Himself; He reveals Himself to an individual through a personal encounter. The word *reveal* commonly takes as its object either a fact (expressed by a "that" clause) or a concrete thing (expressed by a noun phrase). Contrast "He wrote a letter to the police, revealing that he had committed the crime," and "He stepped out of the shadows, revealing a thoroughly frightened countenance." The traditional conception exploits the first of these uses, the neo-orthodox, the second. Members of this second school do not bother to explain very fully what they mean by a "personal encounter," a "meeting with God," and so on, but presumably it is an experience which involves something like the sense of personal presence which figured in our discussions of religious experience. This encounter may involve God speaking words to the individual, but it is the personal appearance of God that most matters, not the words taken in isolation from that encounter.

This difference involves a difference as to what is called a revelation. In the traditional view, the Bible, or the body of Christian doctrine is often called God's revelation or the Christian revelation; a revelation is a book, or a set of doctrines. But in the personal conception, a revelation is always an event, an occurrence, a personal confrontation of God and man; and where no such confrontation takes place, there has been no revelation, even though the individual has read the Bible and accepted it as true. It also involves a different conception of what it is to accept revelation. In the traditional view, the acceptance of revelation (or "faith") is primarily the assent to a proposition on the authority of God; and, except for the original recipient, this implies an acceptance of the reliability of someone's claim to be transmitting the word of God. In the personal conception, to accept revelation is to recognize that one is confronted by God and to react accordingly. The emphasis here is on trust, obedience, a transformation of the total individual in the light of his relation to the God he has encountered— rather than on assent to a proposition.

It must be admitted that these differences are not quite as clear-cut as I have been representing them. They are really differences as to what is assigned priority. Traditional theologians have also taken note of the active response of the whole individual as a part of faith, at least "saving faith," but they have taken this to be based on the intellectual assent to certain propositions on the authority of God; that is, they have given priority to the assent. Nor would traditional theologians have any quarrel with the formula "God reveals Himself." But they would not limit such self-revelations to direct personal encounters. They would think of God as also revealing Himself through the indirect transmission of doctrines through the Bible (that is, cases in which an individual accepts something in the Bible without having had a personal meeting with God). On the other side, neo-orthodox theologians would not deny that God reveals truths about His nature, His plans for men, and so on. But they would insist that we get these truths from encounters with God, and that our formulations of these truths come from human attempts to record these encounters and what is revealed therein. That is, they make the encounter primary.

If the encounter is primary it would seem that any book which figures in such encounters would have basically the same status as the Bible, though perhaps to a lesser degree. And yet Brunner insists that the Bible is, in a unique sense, God's revelation. He justifies this by an appeal to the Christian conviction that the historical person Jesus Christ is pre-eminently *the* revelation of God to man; the Bible then has a unique position among books since it is the sole source of our knowledge of Jesus Christ. Note that on this approach the Bible as a collection of documents, or a set of assertions, cannot be called a revelation from God, but can be considered only as connected with actual revelatory occurrences. Hence there is no temptation to attribute infallibility to statements of the Bible, for it is not as a set of statements that the Bible is being considered. This means that many of the problems which plague the traditionalist do not arise at all.

The problem of justifying claims of revelation assumes a different form in the neo-orthodox approach. This is clear from the following consideration. In the traditional scheme God is thought of as transmitting messages directly to a few selected individuals who then have the task of passing them on to others. And the traditional arguments all present facts (or supposed facts) about the messenger or about the circumstances or effects of their proclamations which are supposed to show that the claims of these messengers to be speaking for God must be accepted. That is, the arguments try to show that the supposed messengers have proper credentials, which means that the arguments are addressed to the great mass who have to receive revelation at second hand rather than to the select few who receive it initially. But in the neo-orthodox view, no one is given the message at second hand. If I simply read a statement by Moses, Jesus, or Paul, then no revelation has taken place, even if the author was inspired by God, and even if, in addition, I accept what he says as having, in fact, come from God. For a revelation to take place it is necessary that I be personally confronted by God, and receive this message as spoken by Him to me. But if that happens, then I am in essentially the same position as the original author: I have received the divine communication as directly from God as he did. He (the human author) plays no indispensable role; his writing simply acts as a stimulus to my apprehension of the personal presence of God. Once this has happened there is no need for me to examine the credentials of the writer; and until this happens, I have not received a revelation, no matter how excellent the writer's credentials. Hence all the traditional arguments are fundamentally irrelevant to the problem.

But this does not mean that no question of justification arises here. On the contrary, one can, and must, ask with respect to a supposed "personal encounter with God" whether the individual really did encounter *God,* and hence whether any divine revelation really did take place. Thinkers like Barth and Brunner tend to side-step this question. They assume that a real encounter is self-justifying; when one has it he will know that it is the real thing. But, of course, this still leaves the possibility that in a given case, or in all cases, one will only think that he knows that it is the real thing. This is essentially the same problem as the one discussed in the section on religious experience.

SAINT THOMAS AQUINAS

The Harmony of Reason and Revelation

CHAPTER III

On the Way in Which Divine Truth Is To Be Made Known

1. The way of making truth known is not always the same, and, as the Philosopher has very well said, "it belongs to an educated man to seek such certitude in each thing as the nature of that thing allows." [1] The remark is also introduced by Boethius. [2] But, since such is the case, we must first show what way is open to us in order that we may make known the truth which is our object.

2. There is a twofold mode of truth in what we profess about God. Some truths about God exceed all the ability of the human reason. Such is the truth that God is triune. But there are some truths which the natural reason also is able to reach. Such are that God exists, that He is one, and the like. In fact, such truths about God have been proved demonstratively by the philosophers, guided by the light of the natural reason.

[1] Aristotle, *Nicomachean Ethics*, I, 3 (1094b 24).

[2] Boethius, *De Trinitate*, II (*PL*, 64, col. 1250).

From St. Thomas Aquinas, *On the Truth of the Catholic Faith*, tr. by Anton C. Pegis, Chs. III–VIII. Copyright © 1955 by Doubleday and Company, Inc. Reprinted by permission of the publisher.

3. That there are certain truths about God that totally surpass man's ability appears with the greatest evidence. Since, indeed, the principle of all knowledge that the reason perceives about some thing is the understanding of the very substance of that being (for according to Aristotle "what a thing is" is the principle of demonstration), [3] it is necessary that the way in which we understand the substance of a thing determines the way in which we know what belongs to it. Hence, if the human intellect comprehends the substance of some thing, for example, that of a stone or of a triangle, no intelligible characteristic belonging to that thing surpasses the grasp of the human reason. But this does not happen to us in the case of God. For the human intellect is not able to reach a comprehension of the divine substance through its natural power. For, according to its manner of knowing in the present life, the intellect depends on the sense for the origin of knowledge; and so those things that do not fall under the senses cannot be grasped by the human intellect except in so far as the knowledge of them is gathered from sensible things. Now, sensible things cannot lead the human intellect to the point of seeing in them the nature of the divine substance; for

[3] Aristotle, *Posterior Analytics*, II, 3 (90b 31).

sensible things are effects that fall short of the power of their cause. Yet, beginning with sensible things, our intellect is led to the point of knowing about God that He exists, and other such characteristics that must be attributed to the First Principle. There are, consequently, some intelligible truths about God that are open to the human reason; but there are others that absolutely surpass its power.

4. We may easily see the same point from the gradation of intellects. Consider the case of two persons of whom one has a more penetrating grasp of a thing by his intellect than does the other. He who has the superior intellect understands many things that the other cannot grasp at all. Such is the case with a very simple person who cannot at all grasp the subtle speculations of philosophy. But the intellect of an angel surpasses the human intellect much more than the intellect of the greatest philosopher surpasses the intellect of the most uncultivated simple person; for the distance between the best philosopher and a simple person is contained within the limits of the human species, which the angelic intellect surpasses. For the angel knows God on the basis of a more noble effect than does man; and this by as much as the substance of an angel, through which the angel in his natural knowledge is led to the knowledge of God, is nobler than sensible things and even than the soul itself, through which the human intellect mounts to the knowledge of God. The divine intellect surpasses the angelic intellect much more than the angelic surpasses the human. For the divine intellect is in its capacity equal to its substance, and therefore it understands fully what it is, including all its intelligible attributes. But by his natural knowledge the angel does not know what God is, since the substance itself of the angel, through which he is led to the knowledge of God, is an effect that is not equal to the power

of its cause. Hence, the angel is not able, by means of his natural knowledge, to grasp all the things that God understands in Himself; nor is the human reason sufficient to grasp all the things that the angel understands through his own natural power. Just as, therefore, it would be the height of folly for a simple person to assert that what a philosopher proposes is false on the ground that he himself cannot understand it, so (and even more so) it is the acme of stupidity for a man to suspect as false what is divinely revealed through the ministry of the angels simply because it cannot be investigated by reason.

5. The same thing, moreover, appears quite clearly from the defect that we experience every day in our knowledge of things. We do not know a great many of the properties of sensible things, and in most cases we are not able to discover fully the natures of those properties that we apprehend by the sense. Much more is it the case, therefore, that the human reason is not equal to the task of investigating all the intelligible characteristics of that most excellent substance.

6. The remark of Aristotle likewise agrees with this conclusion. He says that "our intellect is related to the prime beings, which are most evident in their nature, as the eye of an owl is related to the sun." [4]

7. Sacred Scripture also gives testimony to this truth. We read in Job: "Peradventure thou wilt comprehend the steps of God, and wilt find out the Almighty perfectly?" (11:7). And again: "Behold, God is great, exceeding our knowledge" (Job 36:26). And St. Paul: "We know in part" (I Cor. 13:9).

8. We should not, therefore, immediately reject as false, following the opinion of the Manicheans and many unbelievers, everything that is said about God even

[4] Aristotle, *Metaphysics,* Ia, 1 (993b 9).

though it cannot be investigated by reason.

That the Truth About God to Which the Natural Reason Reaches Is Fittingly Proposed to Men for Belief

1. Since, therefore, there exists a two-fold truth concerning the divine being, one to which the inquiry of the reason can reach, the other which surpasses the whole ability of the human reason, it is fitting that both of these truths be proposed to man divinely for belief. This point must first be shown concerning the truth that is open to the inquiry of the reason; otherwise, it might perhaps seem to someone that, since such a truth can be known by the reason, it was uselessly given to men through a supernatural inspiration as an object of belief.

2. Yet, if this truth were left solely as a matter of inquiry for the human reason, three awkward consequences would follow.

3. The first is that few men would possess the knowledge of God. For there are three reasons why most men are cut off from the fruit of diligent inquiry which is the discovery of truth. Some do not have the physical disposition for such work. As a result, there are many who are naturally not fitted to pursue knowledge; and so, however much they tried, they would be unable to reach the highest level of human knowledge which consists in knowing God. Others are cut off from pursuing this truth by the necessities imposed upon them by their daily lives. For some men must devote themselves to taking care of temporal matters. Such men would not be able to give so much time to the leisure of contemplative inquiry as to reach the highest peak at which human investigation can arrive, namely, the knowledge of God. Finally,

there are some who are cut off by indolence. In order to know the things that the reason can investigate concerning God, a knowledge of many things must already be possessed. For almost all of philosophy is directed towards the knowledge of God, and that is why metaphysics, which deals with divine things, is the last part of philosophy to be learned. This means that we are able to arrive at the inquiry concerning the aforementioned truth only on the basis of a great deal of labor spent in study. Now, those who wish to undergo such a labor for the mere love of knowledge are few, even though God has inserted into the minds of men a natural appetite for knowledge.

4. The second awkward effect is that those who would come to discover the abovementioned truth would barely reach it after a great deal of time. The reasons are several. There is the profundity of this truth, which the human intellect is made capable of grasping by natural inquiry only after a long training. Then, there are many things that must be pre-supposed, as we have said. There is also the fact that, in youth, when the soul is swayed by the various movements of the passions, it is not in a suitable state for the knowledge of such lofty truth. On the contrary, "one becomes wise and knowing in repose," as it is said in the *Physics*.[1] The result is this. If the only way open to us for the knowledge of God were solely that of the reason, the human race would remain in the blackest shadows of ignorance. For then the knowledge of God, which especially renders men perfect and good, would come to be possessed only by a few, and these few would require a great deal of time in order to reach it.

5. The third awkward effect is this. The investigation of the human reason for the most part has falsity present within it, and this is due partly to the weakness

---

[1] Aristotle, *Physics*, VII, 3 (247b 9).

of our intellect in judgment, and partly to the admixture of images. The result is that many, remaining ignorant of the power of demonstration, would hold in doubt those things that have been most truly demonstrated. This would be particularly the case since they see that, among those who are reputed to be wise men, each one teaches his own brand of doctrine. Furthermore, with the many truths that are demonstrated, there sometimes is mingled something that is false, which is not demonstrated but rather asserted on the basis of some probable or sophistical argument, which yet has the credit of being a demonstration. That is why it was necessary that the unshakeable certitude and pure truth concerning divine things should be presented to men by way of faith.[2]

6. Beneficially, therefore, did the divine Mercy provide that it should instruct us to hold by faith even those truths that the human reason is able to investigate. In this way, all men would easily be able to have a share in the knowledge of God, and this without uncertainty and error.

7. Hence it is written: "Henceforward you walk not as also the Gentiles walk in the vanity of their mind, having their understanding darkened" (Eph. 4:17–18). And again: "All thy children shall be taught of the Lord" (Isa. 54:13).

---

[2] Although St. Thomas does not name Maimonides or his *Guide for the Perplexed* (*Dux neutrorum*), there are evident points of contact between the Catholic and the Jewish theologian. On the reasons for revelation given here, on our knowledge of God, on creation and the eternity of the world, and on Aristotelianism in general, St. Thomas has Maimonides in mind both to agree and to disagree with him. By way of background for *SCG*, I, the reader can usefully consult the references to Maimonides in E. Gilson, *History of Christian Philosophy in the Middle Ages* (New York, 1955), pp. 649–651.

CHAPTER V

That the Truths the Human Reason Is Not Able To Investigate Are Fittingly Proposed to Men for Belief

1. Now, perhaps some will think that men should not be asked to believe what the reason is not adequate to investigate, since the divine Wisdom provides in the case of each thing according to the mode of its nature. We must therefore prove that it is necessary for man to receive from God as objects of belief even those truths that are above the human reason.

2. No one tends with desire and zeal towards something that is not already known to him. But, as we shall examine later on in this work, men are ordained by the divine Providence towards a higher good than human fragility can experience in the present life. That is why it was necessary for the human mind to be called to something higher than the human reason here and now can reach, so that it would thus learn to desire something and with zeal tend towards something that surpasses the whole state of the present life. This belongs especially to the Christian religion, which in a unique way promises spiritual and eternal goods. And so there are many things proposed to men in it that transcend human sense. The Old Law, on the other hand, whose promises were of a temporal character, contained very few proposals that transcended the inquiry of the human reason. Following this same direction, the philosophers themselves, in order that they might lead men from the pleasure of sensible things to virtue, were concerned to show that there were in existence other goods of a higher nature than these things of sense, and that those who gave themselves to the active or contemplative virtues would find much sweeter enjoyment in the taste of these higher goods.

3. It is also necessary that such truth be proposed to men for belief so that they may have a truer knowledge of God. For then only do we know God truly when we believe Him to be above everything that it is possible for man to think about Him; for, as we have shown,[1] the divine substance surpasses the natural knowledge of which man is capable. Hence, by the fact that some things about God are proposed to man that surpass his reason, there is strengthened in man the view that God is something above what he can think.

4. Another benefit that comes from the revelation to men of truths that exceed the reason is the curbing of presumption, which is the mother of error. For there are some who have such a presumptuous opinion of their own ability that they deem themselves able to measure the nature of everything; I mean to say that, in their estimation, everything is true that seems to them so, and everything is false that does not. So that the human mind, therefore, might be freed from this presumption and come to a humble inquiry after truth, it was necessary that some things should be proposed to man by God that would completely surpass his intellect.

5. A still further benefit may also be seen in what Aristotle says in the *Ethics*.[2] There was a certain Simonides who exhorted people to put aside the knowledge of divine things and to apply their talents to human occupations. He said that "he who is a man should know human things, and he who is mortal, things that are mortal." Against Simonides Aristotle says that "man should draw himself towards what is immortal and divine as much as he can." And so he says in the *De animalibus* that, although what we know

of the higher substances is very little, yet that little is loved and desired more than all the knowledge that we have about less noble substances.[3] He also says in the *De caelo et mundo* that when questions about the heavenly bodies can be given even a modest and merely plausible solution, he who hears this experiences intense joy.[4] From all these considerations it is clear that even the most imperfect knowledge about the most noble realities brings the greatest perfection to the soul. Therefore, although the human reason cannot grasp fully the truths that are above it, yet, if it somehow holds these truths at least by faith, it acquires great perfection for itself.

6. Therefore it is written: "For many things are shown to thee above the understanding of men" (Ecclus. 3:25). Again: "So the things that are of God no man knoweth but the Spirit of God. But to us God hath revealed them by His Spirit" (I Cor. 2:11, 10).

CHAPTER VI

That to Give Assent to the Truths of Faith Is Not Foolishness Even Though They Are Above Reason

1. Those who place their faith in this truth, however, "for which the human reason offers no experimental evidence," [1] do not believe foolishly, as though "following artificial fables" (II Peter 1:16). For these "secrets of divine Wisdom (Job 11:6) the divine Wisdom itself, which knows all things to the full, has deigned to reveal to men. It reveals its own presence, as well as the truth of its teaching and inspiration, by fitting

---

[1] See above, ch. 3.

[2] Aristotle, *Nicomachean Ethics*, X, 7 (1177b 31).

[3] Aristotle, *De partibus animalium,* I, 5 (644b 32).

[4] Aristotle, *De caelo et mundo,* II 12 (291b 26).

[1] St. Gregory, *Homiliae in evangelia,* II, hom. 26, i (*PL,* 76, col. 1197).

arguments; and in order to confirm those truths that exceed natural knowledge, it gives visible manifestation to works that surpass the ability of all nature. Thus, there are the wonderful cures of illnesses, there is the raising of the dead, and the wonderful immutation in the heavenly bodies; and what is more wonderful, there is the inspiration given to human minds, so that simple and untutored persons, filled with the gift of the Holy Spirit, come to possess instantaneously the highest wisdom and the readiest eloquence. When these arguments were examined, through the efficacy of the abovementioned proof, and not the violent assault of arms or the promise of pleasures, and (what is most wonderful of all) in the midst of the tyranny of the persecutors, an innumerable throng of people, both simple and most learned, flocked to the Christian faith. In this faith there are truths preached that surpass every human intellect; the pleasures of the flesh are curbed; it is taught that the things of the world should be spurned. Now, for the minds of mortal men to assent to these things is the greatest of miracles, just as it is a manifest work of divine inspiration that, spurning visible things, men should seek only what is invisible. Now, that this has happened neither without preparation nor by chance, but as a result of the disposition of God, is clear from the fact that through many pronouncements of the ancient prophets God had foretold that He would do this. The books of these prophets are held in veneration among us Christians, since they give witness to our faith.

2. The manner of this confirmation is touched on by St. Paul: "Which," that is, human salvation, "having begun to be declared by the Lord, was confirmed unto us by them that hear Him: God also bearing them witness of signs, and wonders, and divers miracles, and distributions of the Holy Ghost" (Heb. 2:3–4).

3. This wonderful conversion of the world to the Christian faith is the clearest witness of the signs given in the past; so that it is not necessary that they should be further repeated, since they appear most clearly in their effect. For it would be truly more wonderful than all signs if the world had been led by simple and humble men to believe such lofty truths, to accomplish such difficult actions, and to have such high hopes. Yet it is also a fact that, even in our own time, God does not cease to work miracles through His saints for the confirmation of the faith.

4. On the other hand, those who founded sects committed to erroneous doctrines proceeded in a way that is opposite to this. The point is clear in the case of Mohammed. He seduced the people by promises of carnal pleasure to which the concupiscence of the flesh goads us. His teaching also contained precepts that were in conformity with his promises, and he gave free rein to carnal pleasure. In all this, as is not unexpected, he was obeyed by carnal men. As for proofs of the truth of his doctrine, he brought forward only such as could be grasped by the natural ability of anyone with a very modest wisdom. Indeed, the truths that he taught he mingled with many fables and with doctrines of the greatest falsity. He did not bring forth any signs produced in a supernatural way, which alone fittingly gives witness to divine inspiration; for a visible action that can be only divine reveals an invisibly inspired teacher of truth. On the contrary, Mohammed said that he was sent in the power of his arms —which are signs not lacking even to robbers and tyrants. What is more, no wise men, men trained in things divine and human, believed in him from the beginning. Those who believed in him were brutal men and desert wanderers, utterly ignorant of all divine teaching, through whose numbers Mohammed forced others to become his followers

by the violence of his arms. Nor do divine pronouncements on the part of preceding prophets offer him any witness. On the contrary, he perverts almost all the testimonies of the Old and New Testaments by making them into fabrications of his own, as can be seen by anyone who examines his law. It was, therefore, a shrewd decision on his part to forbid his followers to read the Old and New Testaments, lest these books convict him of falsity. It is thus clear that those who place any faith in his words believe foolishly.

CHAPTER VII

That the Truth of Reason Is Not Opposed to the Truth of the Christian Faith

1. Now, although the truth of the Christian faith which we have discussed surpasses the capacity of the reason, nevertheless that truth that the human reason is naturally endowed to know cannot be opposed to the truth of the Christian faith. For that with which the human reason is naturally endowed is clearly most true; so much so, that it is impossible for us to think of such truths as false. Nor is it permissible to believe as false that which we hold by faith, since this is confirmed in a way that is so clearly divine. Since, therefore, only the false is opposed to the true, as is clearly evident from an examination of their definitions, it is impossible that the truth of faith should be opposed to those principles that the human reason knows naturally.

2. Furthermore, that which is introduced into the soul of the student by the teacher is contained in the knowledge of the teacher—unless his teaching is fictitious, which it is improper to say of God. Now, the knowledge of the principles that are known to us naturally has been implanted in us by God; for God is the Author of our nature. These principles, therefore, are also contained by the divine Wisdom. Hence, whatever is opposed to them is opposed to the divine Wisdom, and, therefore, cannot come from God. That which we hold by faith as divinely revealed, therefore, cannot be contrary to our natural knowledge.

3. Again. In the presence of contrary arguments our intellect is chained, so that it cannot proceed to the knowledge of the truth. If, therefore, contrary knowledges were implanted in us by God, our intellect would be hindered from knowing truth by this very fact. Now, such an effect cannot come from God.

4. And again. What is natural cannot change as long as nature does not. Now, it is impossible that contrary opinions should exist in the same knowing subject at the same time. No opinion or belief, therefore, is implanted in man by God which is contrary to man's natural knowledge.

5. Therefore, the Apostle says: "The word is nigh thee, even in thy mouth and in thy heart. This is the word of faith, which we preach" (Rom. 10:8). But because it overcomes reason, there are some who think that it is opposed to it: which is impossible.

6. The authority of St. Augustine also agrees with this. He writes as follows: "That which truth will reveal cannot in any way be opposed to the sacred books of the Old and the New Testament." [1]

7. From this we evidently gather the following conclusion: whatever arguments are brought forward against the doctrines of faith are conclusions incorrectly derived from the first and self-evident principles imbedded in nature. Such conclusions do not have the force of demonstration; they are arguments that

---

[1] St. Augustine, *De genesi ad litteram*, II, c. 18 (*PL*, 34, col. 280).

are either probable or sophistical. And so, there exists the possibility to answer them.

CHAPTER VIII

How the Human Reason Is Related to the Truth of Faith

1. There is also a further consideration. Sensible things, from which the human reason takes the origin of its knowledge, retain within themselves some sort of trace of a likeness to God. This is so imperfect, however, that it is absolutely inadequate to manifest the substance of God. For effects bear within themselves, in their own way, the likeness of their causes, since an agent produces its like; yet an effect does not always reach to the full likeness of its cause. Now, the human reason is related to the knowledge of the truth of faith (a truth which can be most evident only to those who see the divine substance) in such a way that it can gather certain likenesses of it, which are yet not sufficient so that the truth of faith may be comprehended as being understood demonstratively or through itself. Yet it is useful for the human reason to exercise itself in such arguments, however weak they may be, provided only that there be present no presumption to comprehend or to demonstrate. For to be able to see something of the loftiest realities, however thin and weak the sight may be, is, as our previous remarks indicate, a cause of the greatest joy.

2. The testimony of Hilary agrees with this. Speaking of this same truth, he writes as follows in his *De Trinitate:* "Enter these truths by believing, press forward, persevere. And though I may know that you will not arrive at an end, yet I will congratulate you in your progress. For, though he who pursues the infinite with reverence will never finally reach the end, yet he will always progress by pressing onward. But do not intrude yourself into the divine secret, do not, presuming to comprehend the sum total of intelligence, plunge yourself into the mystery of the unending nativity; rather, understand that these things are incomprehensible." [2]

---

[2] St. Hilary, *De Trinitate,* II, 10, ii (*PL,* 10, col. 58–59).

JOHN LOCKE

The Distinct Provinces of Faith and Reason

John Locke (1632–1704) was the fountainhead of the British empiricist movement, which maintained, in various forms, that all our knowledge comes from perception. Locke's influence during the eighteenth century, both philosophical and political, was enormous. He was the patron saint of the French enlightenment and of the various liberal movements during that century.

1. It has been above shown, 1. That we are of necessity ignorant, and want knowledge of all sorts, where we want ideas. 2. That we are ignorant, and want rational knowledge, where we want proofs. 3. That we want certain knowledge and certainty, as far as we want clear and determined specific ideas. 4. That we want probability to direct our assent in matters where we have neither knowledge of our own, nor testimony of other men, to bottom our reason upon.

From these things thus premised, I think we may come to lay down the measures and boundaries between faith and reason; the want whereof many possibly have been the cause, if not of great disorders, yet at least of great disputes, and perhaps mistakes in the world. For till it be resolved how far we are to be guided by reason, and how far by faith, we shall in vain dispute, and endeavour to convince one another in matters of religion.

2. I find every sect, as far as reason will help them, make use of it gladly:

From John Locke, *An Essay Concerning Understanding*, Bk. IV, Ch. XVIII.

and where it fails them they cry out, it is matter of faith, and above reason. And I do not see how they can argue with any one, or ever convince a gainsayer who makes use of the same plea, without setting down strict boundaries between faith and reason; which ought to be the first point established in all questions where faith has any thing to do.

Reason therefore here, as contradistinguished to faith, I take to be the discovery of the certainty or probability of such propositions or truths, which the mind arrives at by deduction made from such ideas which it has got by the use of its natural faculties, viz. by sensation or reflection.

Faith, on the other side, is the assent to any proposition, not thus made out by the deductions of reason; but upon the credit of the proposer, as coming from God, in some extraordinary way of communication. This way of discovering truths to men we call revelation.

3. First then I say, that no man inspired by God can by any revelation communicate to others any new simple ideas, which they had not before from sensation or reflection. For whatsoever impressions

he himself may have from the immediate hand of God, this revelation, if it be of new simple ideas, cannot be conveyed to another, either by words or any other signs. Because words, by their immediate operation on us, cause no other ideas but of their natural sounds; and it is by the custom of using them for signs, that they excite and revive in our minds latent ideas; but yet only such ideas as were there before. For words seen or heard recall to our thoughts those ideas only which to us they have been wont to be signs of; but cannot introduce any perfectly new, and formerly unknown simple ideas. The same holds in all other signs, which cannot signify to us things of which we have before never had any idea at all.

Thus whatever things were discovered to St. Paul, when he was rapt up into the third heaven, whatever new ideas his mind there received, all the description he can make to others of that place is only this, that there are such things, "as eye hath not seen, nor ear heard, nor hath it entered into the heart of man to conceive." And supposing God should discover to any one, supernaturally, a species of creatures inhabiting, for example, Jupiter or Saturn, (for that it is possible there may be such nobody can deny) which had six senses; and imprint on his mind the ideas conveyed to theirs by that sixth sense; he could no more, by words, produce in the minds of other men those ideas, imprinted by that sixth sense, than one of us could convey the idea of any colour by the sounds of words into a man, who, having the other four senses perfect, had always totally wanted the fifth of seeing. For our simple ideas then, which are the foundation and sole matter of all our notions and knowledge, we must depend wholly on our reason, I mean our natural faculties; and can by no means receive them, or any of them, from traditional revelation; I say, traditional revelation, in distinction to original revelation. By the one, I mean that first impression, which is made immediately by God, on the mind of any man, to which we cannot set any bounds; and by the other, those impressions delivered over to others in words, and the ordinary ways of conveying our conceptions one to another.

4. Secondly, I say, that the same truths may be discovered, and conveyed down from revelation, which are discoverable to us by reason, and by those ideas we naturally may have. So God might, by revelation, discover the truth of any proposition in Euclid; as well as men, by the natural use of their faculties, come to make the discovery themselves. In all things of this kind, there is little need or use of revelation, God having furnished us with natural and surer means to arrive at the knowledge of them. For whatsoever truth we come to the clear discovery of, from the knowledge and contemplation of our own ideas, will always be certainer to us than those which are conveyed to us by traditional revelation. For the knowledge we have, that this revelation came at first from God, can never be so sure, as the knowledge we have from the clear and distinct perception of the agreement or disagreement of our own ideas; v. g. if it were revealed some ages since, that the three angles of a triangle were equal to two right ones, I might assent to the truth of that propostion, upon the credit of the tradition, that it was revealed; but that would never amount to so great a certainty as the knowledge of it, upon the comparing and measuring my own ideas of two right angles, and the three angles of a triangle. The like holds in matter of fact, knowable by our senses; v. g. the history of the deluge is conveyed to us by writings which had their original from revelation: and yet nobody, I think, will say he has as certain and clear a knowledge of the flood as Noah that saw it; or that he himself would have had, had

he then been alive and seen it. For he has no greater assurance than that of his senses that it is writ in the book supposed writ by Moses inspired; but he has not so great an assurance that Moses writ that book as if he had seen Moses write it. So that the assurance of its being a revelation is less still than the assurance of his senses.

5. In propositions then, whose certainty is built upon the clear perception of the agreement or disagreement of our ideas, attained either by immediate intuition, as in self-evident propositions, or by evident deductions of reason in demonstrations, we need not the assistance of revelation, as necessary to gain our assent, and introduce them into our minds. Because the natural ways of knowledge could settle them there, or had done it already; which is the greatest assurance we can possibly have of any thing, unless where God immediately reveals it to us: and there too our assurance can be no greater than our knowledge is, that it is a revelation from God. But yet nothing, I think, can, under that title, shake or over-rule plain knowledge; or rationally prevail with any man to admit it for true, in a direct contradiction to the clear evidence of his own understanding. For since no evidence of our faculties, by which we receive such revelations, can exceed, if equal, the certainty of our intuitive knowledge, we can never receive for a truth any thing that is directly contrary to our clear and distinct knowledge: v. g. the ideas of one body, and one place, do so clearly agree, and the mind has so evident a perception of their agreement, that we can never assent to a proposition, that affirms the same body to be in two distant places at once, however it should pretend to the authority of a divine revelation: since the evidence, first, that we deceive not ourselves, in ascribing it to God; secondly, that we understand it right; can never be so great as the evidence of our own intuitive

knowledge, whereby we discern it impossible for the same body to be in two places at once. And therefore no proposition can be received for divine revelation, or obtain the assent due to all such, if it be contradictory to our clear intuitive knowledge. Because this would be to subvert the principles and foundations of all knowledge, evidence, and assent whatsoever: and there would be left no difference between truth and falsehood, no measures of credible and incredible in the world, if doubtful propositions shall take place before self-evident, and what we certainly know give way to what we may possibly be mistaken in. In propositions therefore contrary to the clear perception of the agreement or disagreement of any of our ideas, it will be in vain to urge them as matters of faith. They cannot move our assent, under that or any other title whatsoever. For faith can never convince us of any thing that contradicts our knowledge. Because though faith be founded on the testimony of God (who cannot lie) revealing any proposition to us; yet we cannot have an assurance of the truth of its being a divine revelation greater than our own knowledge: since the whole strength of the certainty depends upon our knowledge that God revealed it; which in this case, where the proposition supposed revealed contradicts our knowledge or reason, will always have this objection hanging to it, viz. that we cannot tell how to conceive that to come from God, the bountiful Author of our being, which, if received for true, must overturn all the principles and foundations of knowledge he has given us; render all our faculties useless; wholly destroy the most excellent part of his workmanship, our understandings; and put a man in a condition, wherein he will have less light, less conduct, than the beast that perisheth. For if the mind of man can never have a clearer (and perhaps not so clear) evidence of any thing to be a divine revelation, as it has of the principles of its own reason, it can never have a ground to quit the clear evidence of its reason, to give a place to a proposition, whose revelation has not a greater evidence than those principles have.

6. Thus far a man has use of reason, and ought to hearken to it, even in immediate and original revelation, where it is supposed to be made to himself: but to all those who pretend not to immediate revelation, but are required to pay obedience, and to receive the truths revealed to others, which by the tradition of writings, or word of mouth, are conveyed down to them; reason has a great deal more to do, and is that only which can induce us to receive them. For matter of faith being only divine revelation, and nothing else; faith, as we use the word, (called commonly divine faith) has to do with no propositions but those which are supposed to be divinely revealed. So that I do not see how those who make revelation alone the sole object of faith, can say, that it is a matter of faith, and not of reason, to believe that such or such a proposition, to be found in such or such a book, is of divine inspiration; unless it be revealed, that that proposition, or all in that book, was communicated by divine inspiration. Without such a revelation, the believing or not believing that proposition or book to be of divine authority can never be matter of faith, but matter of reason; and such as I must come to an assent to only by the use of my reason, which can never require or enable me to believe that which is contrary to itself: it being impossible for reason ever to procure any assent to that, which to itself appears unreasonable.

In all things, therefore, where we have clear evidence from our ideas, and those principles of knowledge I have above-mentioned, reason is the proper judge; and revelation, though it may in consenting with it confirm its dictates, yet cannot in such cases invalidate its decrees:

nor can we be obliged, where we have the clear and evident sentence of reason, to quit it for the contrary opinion, under a pretence that it is matter of faith; which can have no authority against the plain and clear dictates of reason.

7. But, thirdly, there being many things, wherein we have very imperfect notions, or none at all; and other things, of whose parts, present, or future existence, by the natural use of our faculties, we can have no knowledge at all; these, as being beyond the discovery of our natural faculties, and above reason, are, when revealed, the proper matter of faith. Thus, that part of the angels rebelled against God, and thereby lost their first happy state; and that the dead shall rise, and live again: these, and the like, being beyond the discovery of reason, are purely matters of faith with which reason has directly nothing to do.

8. But since God in giving us the light of reason has not thereby tied up his own hands from affording us, when he thinks fit, the light of revelation in any of those matters wherein our natural faculties are able to give a probable determination; revelation, where God has been pleased to give it, must carry it against the probable conjectures of reason. Because the mind not being certain of the truth of that it does not evidently know, but only yielding to the probability that appears in it, is bound to give up its assent to such a testimony; which, it is satisfied, comes from one who cannot err; and will not deceive. But yet it still belongs to reason to judge of the truth of its being a revelation, and of the signification of the words wherein it is delivered. Indeed, if any thing shall be thought revelation which is contrary to the plain principles of reason, and the evident knowledge the mind has of its own clear and distinct ideas; there reason must be hearkened to, as to a matter within its province: since a man can never have so certain a knowledge, that a proposition, which contra-

dicts the clear principles and evidence of his own knowledge, was divinely revealed, or that he understands the words rightly wherein it is delivered; as he has, that the contrary is true: and so is bound to consider and judge of it as a matter of reason, and not swallow it, without examination, as a matter of faith.

9. First, whatever proposition is revealed, of whose truth our mind, by its natural faculties and notions, cannot judge; that is purely matter of faith, and above reason.

Secondly, all propositions, whereof the mind, by the use of its natural faculties, can come to determine and judge from naturally acquired ideas, are matter of reason; with this difference still, that in those concerning which it has but an uncertain evidence, and so is persuaded of their truth only upon probable grounds, which still admit a possibility of the contrary to be true, without doing violence to the certain evidence of its own knowledge, and overturning the principles of its own reason; in such probable propositions, I say, an evident revelation ought to determine our assent even against probability. For where the principles of reason have not evidenced a proposition to be certainly true or false, there clear revelation, as another principle of truth, and ground of assent, may determine: and so it may be matter of faith, and be also above reason. Because reason, in that particular matter, being able to reach no higher than probability, faith gave the determination, where reason came short; and revelation discovered on which side the truth lay.

10. Thus far the dominion of faith reaches, and that without any violence or hindrance to reason; which is not injured or disturbed, but assisted and improved, by new discoveries of truth coming from the eternal fountain of all knowledge. Whatever God hath revealed, is certainly true; no doubt can be made of it. This is the proper object of faith; but whether it be a divine revelation or no, reason must judge; which can never permit the mind to reject a greater evidence to embrace what is less evident, nor allow it to entertain probability in opposition to knowledge and certainty. There can be no evidence that any traditional revelation is of divine original, in the words we receive it, and in the sense we understand it, so clear and so certain as that of the principles of reason: and therefore nothing that is contrary to, and inconsistent with, the clear and self-evident dictates of reason, has a right to be urged or assented to as a matter of faith, wherein reason hath nothing to do. Whatsoever is divine revelation ought to over-rule all our opinions, prejudices, and interest, and hath a right to be received with full assent. Such a submission as this, of our reason to faith, takes not away the landmarks of knowledge; this shakes not the foundations of reason, but leaves us that use of our faculties for which they were given us.

11. If the provinces of faith and reason are not kept distinct by these boundaries, there will, in matters of religion, be no room for reason at all; and those extravagant opinions and ceremonies that are to be found in the several religions of the world will not deserve to be blamed. For to this crying up of faith, in opposition to reason, we may, I think, in good measure ascribe those absurdities that fill almost all the religions which possess and divide mankind. For men having been principled with an opinion, that they must not consult reason in the things of religion, however apparently contradictory to common sense, and the very principles of all their knowledge, have let loose their fancies and natural superstition; and have been by them led into so strange opinions, and extravagant practices in religion, that a considerate man cannot but stand amazed at their follies, and judge them so far from being acceptable to the great and wise God,

that he cannot avoid thinking them ridiculous, and offensive to a sober good man. So that, in effect, religion, which should most distinguish us from beasts, and ought most peculiarly to elevate us, as rational creatures, above brutes, is that wherein men often appear most irrational and more senseless than beasts themselves. "Credo, quia impossibile est"; I believe, because it is impossible, might in a good man pass for a sally of zeal; but would prove a very ill rule for men to choose their opinions or religion by.

DAVID HUME

Can We Ever Have Rational Grounds for Belief in Miracles?

PART I

There is, in Dr. Tillotson's writings, an argument against the *real presence,* which is as concise, and elegant, and strong as any argument can possibly be supposed against a doctrine, so little worthy of a serious refutation. It is acknowledged on all hands, says that learned prelate, that the authority, either of the scripture or of tradition, is founded merely in the testimony of the apostles, who were eyewitnesses to those miracles of our Saviour, by which he proved his divine mission. Our evidence, then, for the truth of the *Christian* religion is less than the evidence for the truth of our senses; because, even in the first authors of our religion, it was no greater; and it is evident it must diminish in passing from them to their disciples; nor can any one rest such confidence in their testimony, as in the immediate object of his senses. But a weaker evidence can never destroy a stronger; and therefore, were the doctrine of the real presence ever so clearly revealed in scripture, it were directly contrary to the rules of just reasoning to give our assent to it. It contradicts sense, though both the scripture and tradition, on which it is supposed to be built, carry not such evidence with them as sense; when they are considered merely as external evidences, and are not brought home to every one's breast, by the immediate operation of the Holy Spirit.

Nothing is so convenient as a decisive argument of this kind, which must at least *silence* the most arrogant bigotry and superstition, and free us from their impertinent solicitations. I flatter myself, that I have discovered an argument of a like nature, which, if just, will, with the wise and learned, be an everlasting check to all kinds of superstitious delusion, and consequently, will be useful as long as the world endures. For so long, I presume, will the accounts of miracles and prodigies be found in all history, sacred and profane.

Though experience be our only guide in reasoning concerning matters of fact; it must be acknowledged, that this guide

From David Hume, *An Enquiry Concerning Human Understanding* (1907), Sec. X, Pts. I–II.

is not altogether infallible, but in some cases is apt to lead us into errors. One, who in our climate, should expect better weather in any week of June than in one of December, would reason justly, and conformably to experience; but it is certain, that he may happen, in the event, to find himself mistaken. However, we may observe, that, in such a case, he would have no cause to complain of experience; because it commonly informs us beforehand of the uncertainty, by that contrariety of events, which we may learn from a diligent observation. All effects follow not with like certainty from their supposed causes. Some events are found, in all countries and all ages, to have been constantly conjoined together: Others are found to have been more variable, and sometimes to disappoint our expectations; so that, in our reasonings concerning matter of fact, there are all imaginable degrees of assurance, from the highest certainty to the lowest species of moral evidence.

A wise man, therefore, proportions his belief to the evidence. In such conclusions as are founded on an infallible experience, he expects the event with the last degree of assurance, and regards his past experience as a full *proof* of the future existence of that event. In other cases, he proceeds with more caution: He weighs the opposite experiments: He considers which side is supported by the greater number of experiments: to that side he inclines, with doubt and hesitation; and when at last he fixes his judgement, the evidence exceeds not what we properly call *probability*. All probability, then, supposes an opposition of experiments and observations, where the one side is found to overbalance the other, and to produce a degree of evidence, proportioned to the superiority. A hundred instances or experiments on one side, and fifty on another, afford a doubtful expectation of any event; though a hundred uniform experiments, with

only one that is contradictory, reasonably begets a pretty strong degree of assurance. In all cases, we must balance the opposite experiments, where they are opposite, and deduct the smaller number from the greater, in order to know the exact force of the superior evidence.

To apply these principles to a particular instance; we may observe, that there is no species of reasoning more common, more useful, and even necessary to human life, than that which is derived from the testimony of men, and the reports of eye-witnesses and spectators. This species of reasoning, perhaps, one may deny to be founded on the relation of cause and effect. I shall not dispute about a word. It will be sufficient to observe that our assurance in any argument of this kind is derived from no other principle than our observation of the veracity of human testimony, and of the usual conformity of facts to the reports of witnesses. It being a general maxim, that no objects have any discoverable connexion together, and that all the inferences, which we can draw from one to another, are founded merely on our experience of their constant and regular conjunction; it is evident, that we ought not to make an exception to this maxim in favour of human testimony, whose connexion with any event seems, in itself, as little necessary as any other. Were not the memory tenacious to a certain degree; had not men commonly an inclination to truth and a principle of probity, were they not sensible to shame, when detected in a falsehood: Were not these, I say, discovered by *experience* to be qualities, inherent in human nature, we should never repose the least confidence in human testimony. A man delirious, or noted for falsehood and villainy, has no manner of authority with us.

And as the evidence, derived from witnesses and human testimony, is founded on past experience, so it varies with the experience, and is regarded either as *proof* or a *probability,* according as the conjunction between any particular kind of report and any kind of object has been found to be constant or variable. There are a number of circumstances to be taken into consideration in all judgements of this kind; and the ultimate standard, by which we determine all disputes, that may arise concerning them, is always derived from experience and observation. Where this experience is not entirely uniform on any side, it is attended with an unavoidable contrariety in our judgements, and with the same opposition and mutual destruction of argument as in every other kind of evidence. We frequently hesitate concerning the reports of others. We balance the opposite circumstances, which cause any doubt or uncertainty; and when we discover a superiority on one side, we incline to it; but still with a diminution of assurance, in proportion to the force of its antagonist.

This contrariety of evidence, in the present case, may be derived from several different causes; from the opposition of contrary testimony; from the character or number of the witnesses; from the manner of their delivering their testimony; or from the union of all these circumstances. We entertain a suspicion concerning any matter of fact, when the witnesses contradict each other; when they are but few, or of a doubtful character; when they have an interest in what they affirm; when they deliver their testimony with hesitation, or on the contrary, with too violent asseverations. There are many other particulars of the same kind, which may diminish or destroy the force of any argument, derived from human testimony.

Suppose, for instance, that the fact, which the testimony endeavours to establish, partakes of the extraordinary and the marvellous; in that case, the evidence, resulting from the testimony, admits of a diminution, greater or less, in proportion as the fact is more or less unusual. The reason why we place any credit in witnesses and historians, is not derived from any *connexion,* which we perceive *a priori,* between testimony and reality, but because we are accustomed to find a conformity between them. But when the fact attested is such a one as has seldom fallen under our observation, here is a contest of two opposite experiences; of which the one destroys the other, as far as its force goes, and the superior can only operate on the mind by the force, which remains. The very same principle of experience, which gives us a certain degree of assurance in the testimony of witnesses, gives us also, in this case, another degree of assurance against the fact, which they endeavour to establish; from which contradiction there necessarily arises a counterpoise, and mutual destruction of belief and authority.

I should not believe such a story were it told me by Cato, was a proverbial saying in Rome, even during the lifetime of that philosophical patriot.[1] The incredibility of a fact, it was allowed, might invalidate so great an authority.

The Indian prince, who refused to believe the first relations concerning the effects of frost, reasoned justly; and it naturally required very strong testimony to engage his assent to facts, that arose from a state of nature, with which he was unacquainted, and which bore so little analogy to those events, of which he had had constant and uniform experience. Though they were not contrary to his experience, they were not conformable to it.[2]

-----

[1] Plutarch, in vita Catonis.

[2] No Indian, it is evident, could have experience that water did not freeze in cold climates. This is placing nature in a situation quite unknown to him; and it is impossible for him to tell *a priori* what will result from it. It is making a new experiment, the consequence of which is always uncertain. One may sometimes conjecture from analogy

But in order to encrease the probability against the testimony of witnesses, let us suppose, that the fact, which they affirm, instead of being only marvellous, is really miraculous; and suppose also, that the testimony considered apart and in itself, amounts to an entire proof; in that case, there is proof against proof, of which the strongest must prevail, but still with a diminution of its force, in proportion to that of its antagonist.

A miracle is a violation of the laws of nature; and as a firm and unalterable experience has established these laws, the proof against a miracle, from the very nature of the fact, is as entire as any argument from experience can possibly be imagined. Why is it more than probable, that all men must die; that lead cannot, of itself, remain suspended in the air; that fire consumes wood, and is extinguished by water; unless it be, that these events are found agreeable to the laws of nature, and there is required a violation of these laws, or in other words, a miracle to prevent them? Nothing is esteemed a miracle, if it ever happen in the common course of nature. It is no miracle that a man, seemingly in good health, should die on a sudden: because such a kind of death, though more unusual than any other, has yet been frequently observed to happen. But it is a miracle, that a dead man should come to life; because that has never been observed in any age or country. There must, therefore, be a uniform experience against every miraculous event, otherwise the event would not merit that appellation. And as a uniform experience amounts to a proof, there is here a direct and full *proof,* from the nature of the fact, against the existence of any miracle; nor can such a proof be destroyed, or the miracle rendered credible, but by an opposite proof, which is superior.[3]

The plain consequence is (and it is a general maxim worthy of our attention), 'That no testimony is sufficient to establish a miracle, unless the testimony be

---

what will follow; but still this is but conjecture. And it must be confessed, that, in the present case of freezing, the event follows contrary to the rules of analogy, and is such as a rational Indian would not look for. The operations of cold upon water are not gradual, according to the degrees of cold; but whenever it comes to the freezing point, the water passes in a moment, from the utmost liquidity to perfect hardness. Such an event, therefore, may be denominated *extraordinary,* and requires a pretty strong testimony, to render it credible to people in a warm climate: But still it is not *miraculous,* nor contrary to uniform experience of the course of nature in cases where all the circumstances are the same. The inhabitants of Sumatra have always seen water fluid in their own climate, and the freezing of their rivers ought to be deemed a prodigy: But they never saw water in Muscovy during the winter; and therefore they cannot reasonably be positive what would there be the consequence.

[3] Sometimes an event may not, *in itself, seem* to be contrary to the laws of nature, and yet, if it were real, it might, by reason of some circumstances, be denominated a miracle; because, *in fact,* it is contrary to these laws. Thus if a person, claiming a divine authority, should command a sick person to be well, a healthful man to fall down dead, the clouds to pour rain, the winds to blow, in short, should order many natural events, which immediately follow upon his command; these might justly be esteemed miracles, because they are really, in this case, contrary to the laws of nature. For if any suspicion remain, that the event and command concurred by accident, there is no miracle and no transgression of the laws of nature. If this suspicion be removed, there is evidently a miracle, and a transgression of these laws; because nothing can be more contrary to nature than that the voice or command of a man should have such an influence. A miracle may be accurately defined, *a transgression of a law of nature by a particular volition of the Deity, or by the interposition of some invisible agent.* A miracle may either be discoverable by men or not. This alters not its nature and essence. The raising of a house or ship into the air is a visible miracle. The raising of a feather, when the wind wants ever so little of a force requisite for that purpose, is as real a miracle, though not so sensible with regard to us.

of such a kind, that its falsehood would be more miraculous, than the fact, which it endeavours to establish; and even in that case there is a mutual destruction of arguments, and the superior only gives us an assurance suitable to that degree of force, which remains, after deducting the inferior.' When anyone tells me, that he saw a dead man restored to life, I immediately consider with myself, whether it be more probable, that this person should either deceive or be deceived, or that the fact, which he relates, should really have happened. I weigh the one miracle against the other; and according to the superiority, which I discover, I pronounce my decision, and always reject the greater miracle. If the falsehood of his testimony would be more miraculous, than the event which he relates; then, and not till then, can he pretend to command my belief or opinion.

PART II

In the foregoing reasoning we have supposed, that the testimony, upon which a miracle is founded, may possibly amount to an entire proof, and that the falsehood of that testimony would be a real prodigy: But it is easy to shew, that we have been a great deal too liberal in our concession, and that there never was a miraculous event established on so full an evidence.

For *first,* there is not to be found, in all history, any miracle attested by a sufficient number of men, of such unquestioned good-sense, education, and learning, as to secure us against all delusion in themselves; of such undoubted integrity, as to place them beyond all suspicion of any design to deceive others; of such credit and reputation in the eyes of mankind, as to have a great deal to lose in case of their being detected in any falsehood; and at the same time, attesting facts performed in such a public manner and in so celebrated a part of the world, as to render the detection unavoidable: All which circumstances are requisite to give us a full assurance in the testimony of men.

Secondly. We may observe in human nature a principle which, if strictly examined, will be found to diminish extremely the assurance, which we might, from human testimony, have, in any kind of prodigy. The maxim, by which we commonly conduct ourselves in our reasonings, is, that the objects, of which we have no experience, resemble those, of which we have; that what we have found to be most usual is always most probable; and that where there is an opposition of arguments, we ought to give the preference to such as are founded on the greatest number of past observations. But though, in proceeding by this rule, we readily reject any fact which is unusual and incredible in an ordinary degree; yet in advancing farther, the mind observes not always the same rule; but when anything is affirmed utterly absurd and miraculous, it rather the more readily admits of such a fact, upon account of that very circumstance, which ought to destroy all its authority. The passion of *surprise* and *wonder,* arising from miracles, being an agreeable emotion, gives a sensible tendency towards the belief of those events, from which it is derived. And this goes so far, that even those who cannot enjoy this pleasure immediately, nor can believe those miraculous events, of which they are informed, yet love to partake of the satisfaction at secondhand or by rebound, and place a pride and delight in exciting the admiration of others.

With what greediness are the miraculous accounts of travellers received, their descriptions of sea and land monsters, their relations of wonderful adventures, strange men, and uncouth manners? But if the spirit of religion join itself to the love of wonder, there is an end of common sense; and human testimony, in these circumstances, loses all pretensions to authority. A religionist may be an enthusiast, and imagine he sees what has no reality: he may know his narrative to be false, and yet persevere in it, with the best intentions in the world, for the sake of promoting so holy a cause: or even where this delusion has not place, vanity, excited by so strong a temptation, operates on him more powerfully than on the rest of mankind in any other circumstances; and self-interest with equal force. His auditors may not have, and commonly have not, sufficient judgement to canvass his evidence: what judgement they have, they renounce by principle, in these sublime and mysterious subjects: or if they were ever so willing to employ it, passion and a heated imagination disturb the regularity of its operations. Their credulity increases his impudence: and his impudence overpowers their credulity.

Eloquence, when at its highest pitch, leaves little room for reason or reflection; but addressing itself entirely to the fancy or the affections, captivates the willing hearers, and subdues their understanding. Happily, this pitch it seldom attains. But what a Tully or a Demosthenes could scarcely effect over a Roman or Athenian audience, every *Capuchin,* every itinerant or stationary teacher can perform over the generality of mankind, and in a higher degree, by touching such gross and vulgar passions.

The many instances of forged miracles, and prophecies, and supernatural events, which, in all ages, have either been detected by contrary evidence, or which detect themselves by their absurdity, prove sufficiently the strong propensity of mankind to the extraordinary and the marvellous, and ought reasonably to beget a suspicion against all relations of this kind. This is our natural way of thinking, even with regard to the most common and most credible events. For instance: There is no kind of report which rises so easily, and spreads so quickly, especially in country places and provincial towns, as those concerning marriages; insomuch that two young persons of equal condition never see each other twice, but the whole neighbourhood immediately join them together. The pleasure of telling a piece of news so interesting, of propagating it, and of being the first reporters of it, spreads the intelligence. And this is so well known, that no man of sense gives attention to these reports, till he find them confirmed by some greater evidence. Do not the same passions, and others still stronger, incline the generality of mankind to believe and report, with the greatest vehemence and assurance, all religious miracles?

Thirdly. It forms a strong presumption against all supernatural and miraculous relations, that they are observed chiefly to abound among ignorant and barbarous nations; or if a civilized people has ever given admission to any of them, that people will be found to have received them from ignorant and barbarous ancestors, who transmitted them with that inviolable sanction and authority, which always attend received opinions. When we peruse the first histories of all nations, we are apt to imagine ourselves transported into some new world; where the whole frame of nature is disjointed, and every element performs its operations in a different manner, from what it does at present. Battles, revolutions, pestilence, famine and death, are never the effect of those natural causes, which we experience. Prodigies, omens, oracles, judgements, quite obscure the few natural events, that are intermingled with them. But as the former grow thinner every page, in proportion as we advance nearer the enlightened ages, we soon learn, that there is nothing mysterious or supernatural in the case, but that all proceeds from the usual propensity of mankind towards the marvellous, and that, though this inclination may at intervals receive a check from sense and learning, it can never be thoroughly extirpated from human nature.

It is strange, a judicious reader is apt to say, upon the perusal of these wonderful historians, *that such prodigious events never happen in our days.* But it is nothing strange, I hope, that men should lie in all ages. You must surely have seen instances enough of that frailty. You have yourself heard many such marvellous relations started, which, being treated with scorn by all the wise and judicious, have at last been abandoned even by the vulgar. Be assured, that those renowned lies, which have spread and flourished to such a monstrous height, arose from like beginnings; but being sown in a more proper soil, shot up at last into prodigies almost equal to those which they relate.

It was a wise policy in that false prophet, Alexander, who though now forgotten, was once so famous, to lay the first scene of his impostures in Paphlagonia, where, as Lucian tells us, the people were extremely ignorant and stupid, and ready to swallow even the grossest delusion. People at a distance, who are weak enough to think the matter at all worth enquiry, have no opportunity of receiving better information. The stories come magnified to them by a hundred circumstances. Fools are industrious in propagating the imposture; while the wise and learned are contented, in general, to deride its absurdity, without informing themselves of the particular facts, by which it may be distinctly refuted. And thus the impostor above mentioned was enabled to proceed, from his ignorant Paphlagonians, to the enlisting of votaries, even among the Grecian philosophers, and men of the most eminent rank and distinction in Rome: nay, could engage the attention of that sage emperor Marcus Aurelius; so far as to make him trust the success of a military expedition to his delusive prophecies.

The advantages are so great, of starting an imposture among an ignorant people, that, even though the delusion should be too gross to impose on the generality of them (*which, though seldom, is sometimes the case*) it has a much better chance for succeeding in remote countries, than if the first scene had been laid in a city renowned for arts and knowledge. The most ignorant and barbarous of these barbarians carry the report abroad. None of their countrymen have a large correspondence, or sufficient credit and authority to contradict and beat down the delusion. Men's inclination to the marvellous has full opportunity to display itself. And thus a story, which is universally exploded in the place where it was first started, shall pass for certain at a thousand miles distance. But had Alexander fixed his residence at Athens, the philosophers of that renowned mart of learning had immediately spread, throughout the whole Roman empire, their sense of the matter; which, being supported by so great authority, and displayed by all the force of reason and eloquence, had entirely opened the eyes of mankind. It is true; Lucian, passing by chance through Paphlagonia, had an opportunity of performing this good office. But, though much to be wished, it does not always happen, that every Alexander meets with a Lucian, ready to expose and detect his impostures.

I may add as a *fourth* reason, which diminishes the authority of prodigies, that there is no testimony for any, even those which have not been expressly detected, that is not opposed by an infinite number of witnesses; so that not only the miracle destroys the credit of testimony, but the testimony destroys itself. To make this the better understood, let us consider, that, in matters of religion, whatever is different is contrary; and that it is impossible the religions of ancient Rome, of Turkey, of Siam, and of China should, all of them, be established on any solid foundation. Every miracle, therefore, pretended to have been wrought in any of these religions (and all of them abound in miracles), as its direct scope is to establish the particular system to which it is attributed; so has it the same force, though more indirectly, to overthrow every other system. In destroying a rival system, it likewise destroys the credit of those miracles, on which that system was established; so that all the prodigies of different religions are to be regarded as contrary facts, and the evidences of these prodigies, whether weak or strong, as opposite to each other. According to this method of reasoning, when we believe any miracle of Mahomet or his successors, we have for our warrant the testimony of a few barbarous Arabians: And on the other hand, we are to regard the authority of Titus Livius, Plutarch, Tacitus, and, in short, of all the authors and witnesses, Grecian, Chinese, and Roman Catholic, who have related any miracle in their particular religion; I say, we are to regard their testimony in the same light as if they had mentioned that Mahometan miracle, and had in express terms contradicted it, with the same certainty as they have for the miracle they relate. This argument may appear over subtile and refined; but is not in reality different from the reasoning of a judge, who supposes, that the credit of two witnesses, maintaining a crime against any one, is destroyed by the testimony of two others, who affirm him to have been two hundred leagues distant, at the same instant when the crime is said to have been committed.

One of the best attested miracles in all profane history, is that which Tacitus reports of Vespasian, who cured a blind man in Alexandria, by means of his spittle, and a lame man by the mere touch of his foot; in obedience to a vision of the god Serapis, who had enjoined them to have recourse to the Emperor, for these miraculous cures. The story may be seen in that fine historian;[4] where every circumstance seems to add weight to the testimony, and might be displayed at large with all the force of argument and eloquence, if any one were now concerned to enforce the evidence of that exploded and idolatrous superstition. The gravity, solidity, age, and probity of so great an emperor, who, through the whole course of his life, conversed in a familiar manner with his friends and courtiers, and never affected those extraordinary airs of divinity assumed by Alexander and Demetrius. The historian, a contemporary writer, noted for candour and veracity, and withal, the greatest and most penetrating genius, perhaps, of all antiquity; and so free from any tendency to credulity, that he even lies under the contrary imputation, of atheism and profaneness: The persons, from whose authority he related the miracle, of established character for judgement and veracity, as we may well presume; eyewitnesses of the fact, and confirming their testimony, after the Flavian family was despoiled of the empire, and could no longer give any reward, as the price of a lie. *Utrumque, qui interfuere, nunc quoque memorant, postquam nullum mendacio pretium.* To which if we add the public nature of the facts, as related, it will appear, that no evidence can well be supposed stronger for so gross and so palpable a falsehood.

There is also a memorable story related by Cardinal de Retz, which may well deserve our consideration. When that intriguing politician fled into Spain, to avoid the persecution of his enemies, he passed through Saragossa, the capital of Aragon, where he was shewn, in the cathedral, a man, who had served seven years as a doorkeeper, and was well known to every body in town, that had

---

[4] Hist. lib. v. cap. 8. Suetonius gives nearly the same account *in vita Vesp.*

ever paid his devotions at that church. He had been seen, for so long a time, wanting a leg; but recovered that limb by the rubbing of holy oil upon the stump; and the cardinal assures us that he saw him with two legs. This miracle was vouched by all the canons of the church; and the whole company in town were appealed to for a confirmation of the fact; whom the cardinal found, by their zealous devotion, to be thorough believers of the miracle. Here the relater was also cotemporary to the supposed prodigy, of an incredulous and libertine character, as well as of great genius; the miracle of so *singular* a nature as could scarcely admit of a counterfeit, and the witnesses very numerous, and all of them, in a manner, spectators of the fact, to which they gave their testimony. And what adds mightily to the force of the evidence, and may double our surprise on this occasion, is, that the cardinal himself, who relates the story, seems not to give any credit to it, and consequently cannot be suspected of any concurrence in the holy fraud. He considered justly, that it was not requisite, in order to reject a fact of this nature, to be able accurately to disprove the testimony, and to trace its falsehood, through all the circumstances of knavery and credulity which produced it. He knew, that, as this was commonly altogether impossible at any small distance of time and place; so was it extremely difficult, even where one was immediately present, by reason of the bigotry, ignorance, cunning, and roguery of a great part of mankind. He therefore concluded, like a just reasoner, that such an evidence carried falsehood upon the very face of it, and that a miracle, supported by any human testimony, was more properly a subject of derision than of argument.

There surely never was a greater number of miracles ascribed to one person, than those, which were lately said to have been wrought in France upon the tomb of Abbé Paris, the famous Jansenist, with whose sanctity the people were so long deluded. The curing of the sick, giving hearing to the deaf, and sight to the blind, were everywhere talked of as the usual effects of that holy sepulchre. But what is more extraordinary; many of the miracles were immediately proved upon the spot, before judges of unquestioned integrity, attested by witnesses of credit and distinction, in a learned age, and on the most eminent theatre that is now in the world. Nor is this all: a relation of them was published and dispersed everywhere; nor were the *Jesuits,* though a learned body, supported by the civil magistrate, and determined enemies to those opinions, in whose favour the miracles were said to have been wrought, ever able distinctly to refute or detect them. Where shall we find such a number of circumstances, agreeing to the corroboration of one fact? And what have we to oppose to such a cloud of witnesses, but the absolute impossibility or miraculous nature of the events, which they relate? And this surely, in the eyes of all reasonable people, will alone be regarded as a sufficient refutation.

Is the consequence just, because some human testimony has the utmost force and authority in some cases, when it relates the battle of Philippi or Pharsalia for instance; that therefore all kinds of testimony must, in all cases, have equal force and authority? Suppose that the Cæsarean and Pompeian factions had, each of them, claimed the victory in these battles, and that the historians of each party had uniformly ascribed the advantage to their own side; how could mankind, at this distance, have been able to determine between them? The contrariety is equally strong between the miracles related by Herodotus or Plutarch, and those delivered by Mariana, Bede, or any monkish historian.

The wise lend a very academic faith to every report which favours the passion of the reporter; whether it magnifies his country, his family, or himself, or in any other way strikes in with his natural inclinations and propensities. But what greater temptation than to appear a missionary, a prophet, an ambassador from heaven? Who would not encounter many dangers and difficulties, in order to attain so sublime a character? Or if, by the help of vanity and a heated imagination, a man has first made a convert of himself, and entered seriously into the delusion; who ever scruples to make use of pious frauds, in support of so holy and meritorious a cause?

The smallest spark may here kindle into the greatest flame; because the materials are always prepared for it. The *avidum genus auricularum,*[5] the gazing populace, received greedily, without examination, whatever soothes superstition, and promotes wonder.

How many stories of this nature have, in all ages, been detected and exploded in their infancy? How many more have been celebrated for a time, and have afterwards sunk into neglect and oblivion? Where such reports, therefore, fly about, the solution of the phenomenon is obvious; and we judge in conformity to regular experience and observation, when we account for it by the known and natural principles of credulity and delusion. And shall we, rather than have a recourse to so natural a solution, allow of a miraculous violation of the most established laws of nature?

I need not mention the difficulty of detecting a falsehood in any private or even public history, at the place, where it is said to happen; much more when the scene is removed to ever so small a distance. Even a court of judicature, with all the authority, accuracy, and judgement, which they can employ, find themselves often at a loss to distinguish between truth and falsehood in the most

recent actions. But the matter never comes to any issue, if trusted to the common method of altercation and debate and flying rumours; especially when men's passions have taken part on either side.

In the infancy of new religions, the wise and learned commonly esteem the matter too inconsiderable to deserve their attention or regard. And when afterwards they would willingly detect the cheat, in order to undeceive the deluded multitude, the season is now past, and the records and witnesses, which might clear up the matter, have perished beyond recovery.

No means of detection remain, but those which must be drawn from the very testimony itself of the reporters: and these, though always sufficient with the judicious and knowing, are commonly too fine to fall under the comprehension of the vulgar.

Upon the whole, then, it appears, that no testimony for any kind of miracle has ever amounted to a probability, much less to a proof; and that, even supposing it amounted to a proof, it would be opposed by another proof; derived from the very nature of the fact, which it would endeavour to establish. It is experience only, which gives authority to human testimony; and it is the same experience, which assures us of the laws of nature. When, therefore, these two kinds of experience are contrary, we have nothing to do but subtract the one from the other, and embrace an opinion, either on one side or the other, with that assurance which arises from the remainder. But according to the principle here explained, this subtraction, with regard to all popular religions, amounts to an entire annihilation; and therefore we may establish it as a maxim, that no human testimony can have such force as to prove a miracle, and make it a just foundation for any such system of religion.

I beg the limitations here made may

_____
[5] Lucret.

be remarked, when I say, that a miracle can never be proved, so as to be the foundation of a system of religion. For I own, that otherwise, there may possibly be miracles, or violations of the usual course of nature, of such a kind as to admit of proof from human testimony, though, perhaps, it will be impossible to find any such in all the records of history. Thus, suppose, all authors, in all languages, agree, that, from the first of January 1600, there was a total darkness over the whole earth for eight days: suppose that the tradition of this extraordinary event is still strong and lively among the people: that all travellers, who return from foreign countries, bring us accounts of the same tradition, without the least variation or contradiction: it is evident, that our present philosophers, instead of doubting the fact, ought to receive it as certain, and ought to search for the causes whence it might be derived. The decay, corruption, and dissolution of nature, is an event rendered probable by so many analogies, that any phenomenon, which seems to have a tendency towards that catastrophe, comes within the reach of human testimony, if that testimony be very extensive and uniform.

But suppose, that all the historians who treat of England, should agree, that, on the first of January 1600, Queen Elizabeth died; that both before and after her death she was seen by her physicians and the whole court, as is usual with persons of her rank; that her successor was acknowledged and proclaimed by the parliament; and that, after being interred a month, she again appeared, resumed the throne, and governed England for three years: I must confess that I should be surprised at the concurrence of so many odd circumstances, but should not have the least inclination to believe so miraculous an event. I should not doubt of her pretended death, and of those other public circumstances that followed it: I should only assert it to have been pretended, and that it neither was, nor possibly could be real. You would in vain object to me the difficulty, and almost impossibility of deceiving the world in an affair of such consequence; the wisdom and solid judgement of that renowned queen; with the little or no advantage which she could reap from so poor an artifice: All this might astonish me; but I would still reply, that the knavery and folly of men are such common phenomena, that I should rather believe the most extraordinary events to arise from their concurrence, than admit of so signal a violation of the laws of nature.

But should this miracle be ascribed to any new system of religion; men, in all ages, have been so much imposed on by ridiculous stories of that kind, that this very circumstance would be a full proof of a cheat, and sufficient, with all men of sense, not only to make them reject the fact, but even reject it without farther examination. Though the Being to whom the miracle is ascribed, be, in this case, Almighty, it does not, upon that account, become a whit more probable; since it is impossible for us to know the attributes or actions of such a Being, otherwise than from the experience which we have of his productions, in the usual course of nature. This still reduces us to past observation, and obliges us to compare the instances of the violation of truth in the testimony of men, with those of the violation of the laws of nature by miracles, in order to judge which of them is most likely and probable. As the violations of truth are more common in the testimony concerning religious miracles, than in that concerning any other matter of fact; this must diminish very much the authority of the former testimony, and make us form a general resolution, never to lend any attention to it, with whatever specious pretence it may be covered.

Lord Bacon seems to have embraced the same principles of reasoning. 'We ought,' says he, 'to make a collection or particular history of all monsters and prodigious births or productions, and in a word of every thing new, rare, and extraordinary in nature. But this must be done with the most severe scrutiny, lest we depart from truth. Above all, every relation must be considered as suspicious, which depends in any degree upon religion, as the prodigies of Livy: And no less so, every thing that is to be found in the writers of natural magic or alchimy, or such authors, who seem, all of them, to have an unconquerable appetite for falsehood and fable.' [6]

I am the better pleased with the method of reasoning here delivered, as I think it may serve to confound those dangerous friends or disguised enemies to the *Christian Religion*, who have undertaken to defend it by the principles of human reason. Our most holy religion is founded on *Faith*, not on reason; and it is a sure method of exposing it to put it to such a trial as it is, by no means, fitted to endure. To make this more evident, let us examine those miracles, related in scripture; and not to lose ourselves in too wide a field, let us confine ourselves to such as we find in the *Pentateuch*, which we shall examine, according to the principles of these pretended Christians, not as the word or testimony of God himself, but as the production of a mere human writer and historian. Here then we are first to consider a book, presented to us by a barbarous and ignorant people, written in an age when they were still more barbarous, and in all probability long after the facts which it relates, corroborated by no concurring testimony, and resembling those fabulous accounts, which every nation gives of its origin. Upon reading this book, we find it full of prodigies and miracles. It gives an account of a state of the world and of human nature entirely different from the present: Of our fall from that state: Of the age of man, extended to near a thousand years: Of the destruction of the world by a deluge: Of the arbitrary choice of one people, as the favourites of heaven; and that people the countrymen of the author: Of their deliverance from bondage by prodigies the most astonishing imaginable: I desire any one to lay his hand upon his heart, and after a serious consideration declare, whether he thinks that the falsehood of such a book, supported by such a testimony, would be more extraordinary and miraculous than all the miracles it relates; which is, however, necessary to make it be received, according to the measures of probability above established.

What we have said of miracles may be applied, without any variation, to prophecies; and indeed, all prophecies are real miracles, and as such only, can be admitted as proofs of any revelation. If it did not exceed the capacity of human nature to foretell future events, it would be absurd to employ any prophecy as an argument for a divine mission or authority from heaven. So that, upon the whole, we may conclude, that the *Christain Religion* not only was at first attended with miracles, but even at this day cannot be believed by any reasonable person without one. Mere reason is insufficient to convince us of its veracity: And whoever is moved by *Faith* to assent to it, is conscious of a continued miracle in his own person, which subverts all the principles of his understanding, and gives him a determination to believe what is most contrary to custom and experience.

---

[6] Nov. Org. lib. ii. aph. 29.

EMIL BRUNNER

Philosophy and Biblical Revelation

Emil Brunner (1889–   ), a Swiss Protestant theologian, is, along with Karl Barth, one of the leaders of the "Neo-Orthodox" movement in contemporary theology.

CHAPTER I

THE MEANING OF PHILOSOPHY OF RELIGION FOR PROTESTANTISM

Philosophy consists in reflection on the connection between all particular facts, and the means it employs to this end is thought investigating the way in which the facts are intellectually founded. But we shall need first to supply the ground for the inquiry into connection by showing that the latter has intelligible meaning. Hence we must define the problem of philosophy more closely and say that it inquires how far a mental ground is discoverable for the connection between particular facts. By this means we shall become convinced of the necessity, and therefore of the justification, of the inquiry in itself irrespective of its subject matter. Such an inquiry, again, will include that into the meaning of all science, all civilization and indeed human life in general. But when any school of philoso-

phy surveys the more significant expressions of human life, it will discover among them a form of life which on the one hand is in the closest connection with the set of problems peculiar to philosophy, while on the other it has characteristic differences from every school of philosophy, or is even actually opposed to philosophy. This form of life is religion. The kinship between the two rests on the fact that religion as well as philosophy has in view the whole of existence and life; the opposition between them consists in the fact that religion itself claims to supply an answer to the crucial question about reality. It gives this answer in the shape of revelation, and not as the result of the methodical reflection of the intellect, i.e. of an activity within the bounds of reason. Thus philosophy is brought face to face with a most difficult problem, that of showing the meaning and justification of religion within the mental ground known to philosophy. In this way philosophy of religion arises as a part, and perhaps indeed as the culminating point, of philosophy in general.

Provided, however, that the philosopher is serious in his concern about the truth of religion, he cannot avoid listening in the first place to the affirmations

From Emil Brunner, *The Philosophy of Religion from the Standpoint of Protestant Theology,* tr. by A. J. D. Farrer and B. L. Woolf (1958), Pt. I, Chs. I and VIII. Reprinted by permission of James Clarke & Co. Ltd.

of religion about itself—and this always means the affirmations of some specific form of religion. It might of course be the case that religion will have to reject altogether any such classification under philosophy on the plea that it would involve a misinterpretation of religion. In that case the relation between the two would have to be determined conversely, i.e. by starting from religion. Then religion would not have its basis assigned within the bounds of philosophy, but conversely, viz. philosophy, being a special department of man's activity as a reasonable creature, would take its place within the bounds of revealed truth. If such an assertion is not meant to forego every connection with the mind of science, civilization, and philosophy, we must of course make several requirements: that religion should find in her own presuppositions the grounds for thus inverting the relationship between ground and consequence; that it should also report on its mode of supplying these grounds; and once more, that, on the second presupposition, it should make plain the possibility of science, civilization, and philosophy. That would be the way in which, starting from the side of religion, the discussion would have to be carried on with a philosophy originating in the general cultural consciousness. But such an undertaking could be called philosophy of religion only in a secondary sense, and the name as just defined could merely serve to designate the sphere of the discussion.

The state of the case only becomes really clear when, as is incumbent upon us, we look from the stand-point of general possibilities at the special situation that faces us. There are two reasons why we can speak only in a secondary sense of a Christian, and more particularly of a Protestant, philosophy of religion. First, Christian faith, especially in the particular form given to it in Protestant theology, is a fundamentally different thing from every philosophy. To philosophize is to reflect on the mental grounds, with the assumption that ultimate validity belongs to the complex of grounds and consequences developed by natural reason. Christian faith on the other hand involves recognizing that this complex has been broken into by revelation. It is on this revelation that the affirmations of Christian faith are grounded. Theology, which is Christian faith in scientific form, could only lay claim to a scientific character provided it gave clear and exact expression to the fact that its complex of grounds and consequences differs from that of all other sciences as to the final authority it recognizes; provided further that it developed all its affirmations purely out of its own presuppositions and thus founded them on that complex; and provided finally, that on this basis it investigated the relations, whether positive or negative, between revealed faith and rational knowledge. Thus theology is on common ground with philosophy in showing the existence of an intelligible connection embracing all things; but this is not, as it is for philosophy, the logos of the natural reasoning process, but the logos of revelation. Hence Christian theology can never be required to make faith rational by giving it scientific form; on the contrary, it has to keep revelation and religion duly apart by means of clearly defined concepts.

It would be to weaken, or rather to do away with, the opposition were we to equate the relation between reason and revelation with that between rational and irrational. Revelation in the Christian sense stands in the same two-fold relation to the irrational as it does to the rational. The irrational (feeling, intuition, etc.) has not more but, on the contrary, less to do with the paradox of revelation than has the logos of reason. In the modern irrationalist philosophies of religion, the irrational is in every case grafted on a rational system (e.g. in the case of Otto and Scholz on an idealistic, and in that of James, on a naturalistic rationalism).

Neither can there be philosophy of religion in the strict sense of the term in the realm of Christian theology, for the further reason that theology has to do not with religion but with revelation. Whatever else religion may be, it is a mode of human life, whereas revelation is a self-disclosure of God. While the philosopher of religion is concerned with historical phenomena, i.e. with the historical religions and their "nature," the theologian is concerned with the ground of all phenomena.

To the philosopher as to the theologian, religion is not the ultimate fact but something that roots in the ultimate. In the former case it is reason that supplies the ultimate ground, while in the latter it is revelation. The aim of theology is thus something quite different from religion, and at bottom is no more closely related to religion than it is to any other department of human life. This conclusion, moreover, follows directly from the fundamental presupposition of theology: its ground, its content, and its standard alike are found not in any consciousness of man's, but in God's self-disclosure.

Christian faith, to which theology gives the form of scientific conceptions, is the knowledge and acknowledgment of God's self-revelation in Jesus Christ. He, the incarnate logos, is the ground, content, and standard of all the affirmations of faith. That is where faith differs from every religion as well as from every philosophy. By Christian faith is meant, not some universal truth, nor yet some universal religious experience, but a definite fact which as such is opposed to every universal, be it religion or philosophy. Not that it denies the existence of a certain universal knowledge of God,

religious as well as philosophical: rather it presupposes this. But it does deny that the personal and living God can be generally known from possibilities that lie either in the world or in man's spirit as such. It contends that the living and personal God can be known only by a personal meeting, through His personal word, through that special event to which the Bible, and the Bible alone, bears witness, and the content of which is Jesus Christ. Hence this definite fact is not to be understood merely as an illustration, or an embodiment, or even a symbol; where such language is used concerning this matter it is not Christian faith with which we have to do. On the contrary, the definite fact of revelation takes the place of what is universal, of truth in general, or of the final criterion of valid assertions; the incarnate logos here occupies the position otherwise held by the logos of reason, the essential idea of truth. This is the case because the personal God, who is the ground of all truth, cannot be known as personal by means of idea, but only by personal, concrete revelation; only when He no longer hides Himself, but issues forth and discloses Himself as the ground of all being, all values, and all thought.

This particular fact, this miracle of divine revelation, which by its very particularity is a stumbling block to thinking in universals, is the presupposition of Christian theology. Christian faith consists precisely in taking this peculiar view of ultimate truth. It would cease to be faith, it would indeed give the lie to its own affirmation, if it wanted to ground the truth of this affirmation on a universal truth. Either revelation supplies its own grounds or else it is not revelation. The only man who can look for some other foundation beside the *Deus dixit* is the man who withholds belief from the *Deus dixit* and wants secretly to replace revelation by symbol. Hence theology cannot substantiate its scientific character by such a change in the class of ground and consequent as falsifies faith, but on the contrary, only by giving a logically exact expression to this special, nonuniversal quality in all its uniqueness. But this means that theology is not a free science void of presuppositions, but one that is closely tied. It is tied to the definite fact of the revelation of God in Jesus Christ. How tied it is appears most clearly in the fact that theology is only possible within the borders of the Christian community or church, and has its definite content and its definite standard in the Bible. Only by perceiving in Scripture the utterance of God does a man become a believer; and only as such, i.e. as a member of the community of believers, is the thinker in a position to think theologically. Theology is in place only in the church, just as in the same way its ground and content are to be found only in the Scriptural revelation.

This again is the starting point for a Protestant philosophy of religion, using this term now in the modified or secondary sense. Such a philosophy must come from theology and, further back still, from faith. It is not the case that it leads towards faith. It is a part of Christian theology as such, i.e. that part in which it carries on the discussion with the common consciousness of truth, i.e. with philosophy; it is that chapter of Christian theology whose business is to start from definitely Christian presuppositions, and give a well-founded description of the relations between revelation and rational knowledge on the one hand, and between revelation and religion on the other. Hence it is not a universal science, of which Christian theology would form a subdivision as being the doctrine of a particular religion. This erroneous view was largely followed in the nineteenth century. The very nature of revealed faith involves reversing the classification of universal and special in this case, because here a particular, viz. revelation, is regarded as ranking above every universal.

Despite the fact then that for us philosophy of religion can be only a branch of theology in general, we have good reason for separating it as a special science from theology; the reason lies in the need of the times, which demands very special attention to this problem; and the need of the times always has determined and always should determine the perspective of theology. Unlike the rest of theology, philosophy of religion is concerned with the formal and general problems of Christian faith, i.e. specifically with the complex of grounds and consequences set forth in the affirmations of faith as distinct from all other affirmations, in other words, with the problem of revelation. Nowhere, however, is it less possible than here to keep form and content apart: what is to be the Christian conception of revelation can only be made clear in connection with the content of that revelation. But it is at least possible to distinguish between form and content. On this distinction will depend the possibility of discussing the problems of philosophy of religion apart from those of theology proper. Such separation involves the further condition that, to a greater extent than in theology as such, philosophy of religion must have its being in the realm of abstract concepts, despite the fact that the conceptions have here just the same wholly concrete and personal basis as they have in the simplest confession of faith ever made by an unlettered man. At bottom, the philosopher of religion knows no more than any plain Christian: he merely knows it in the more exact form of abstract conceptions and in connection with the rational knowledge of his age. The reverse side of this advantage is that the abstract nature of his knowledge imperils the personal character of his faith —which ought to penetrate the said knowledge—even more than does the abstract nature of theology in general.

There is no fundamental difference between a theological and a non-theological expression of Christian faith. All utterance about God, no matter how much of personal earnestness it may have, has always the abstractness of theology. Even the parables of Jesus are theology. And conversely, the very earnestness of a personal, vital faith may lead it in certain circumstances, e.g. in its discussion and contention with the thought of one's age, to avail itself of the most abstract forms conceivable. Yet the primary interest of Christianity is not systematic knowledge, but the relation of a personal faith to revelation. Hence of course faith is constantly directed towards overcoming abstract concepts as completely as possible; and therefore the philosophy of religion must be judged as lying at best on the edge of Christian doctrine and never at its centre.

Revelation meets and fits human consciousness. It is not a matter of indifference that this consciousness should be defined as human, although on the other hand it is not essential to know in what more specific way it is so defined. Faith is indeed bound up with humanity but not with any particular grade of humanity. Of course it presupposes man as man, but not a particular type of humanity, nor yet any particular feature in man. It takes man in his totality, not in some special locus that can be fixed by psychology. The locus in which revelation and the spirit of man meet each other cannot be assigned positively but only negatively: it consists in receptivity. If in place of this we would rather put a particular form of consciousness, we might say that it is "inquiry" when this

has assumed the form of a vital need. But although this is a presupposition for faith, it does not designate a particular psychological quality, but, on the contrary, what is universally human. In fact, we can indicate the locus yet more definitely without thereby abandoning what is universally human: the negative point of contact is a consciousness of vital need which is at the same time a consciousness of guilt. Therefore we might fittingly express our meaning as follows: any account of the faith evoked by revelation should be preceded by another account giving the results of man's investigation of universal mental characteristics, which investigation would lead up to the aforementioned point of contact. Lack of space obliges us to omit such an account. Ultimately, however, this makes no difference because in every case faith appropriate to revelation must be understood entirely by itself and not by means of any common consciousness of man's. Faith appropriate to revelation can be understood only by revelation, just in the same way as any rational thought can only be understood by its ground in reason, or a sensation of light only by the light-stimulus. Therefore it is necessary to start from revelation as known to faith; in doing so we have only to bear in mind that revelation is always the answer to a question on man's part. But whether man's question, and indeed humanity itself, have their ground in revelation, and only in it can attain their proper meaning; and therefore whether man's question has not its *prius* in God's address to him—these are matters that can be discussed only in connection with the knowledge appropriate to revelation. At all events faith is certain that revelation alone enables us rightly to apprehend that need, that vital incapacity, which is the presupposition of faith; and that thereby revelation itself begets its own presupposition in the crucial sense.

CHAPTER VIII

THE ELEMENT OF TRUTH IN ORTHODOXY: THE BIBLE AS THE WORD OF GOD

Bible and Revelation

Christian faith is Bible faith. When a Christian speaks without qualification of God's revelation, what he means is Holy Scripture. That is the truth contained in the Scriptural orthodoxy of Protestantism. Thereby it holds firmly to the principle that distinguishes Christian faith from all rationalism (philosophical doctrines of God and revelation), from subjectivism (revelation through mystical experience of God), and from historicism (identification of revelation with history, particularly history of religion). It is because Christian theology is consciously bound up with this unique and concrete datum that it cannot submit to be ranked in or subordinated to any general philosophy of religion. Its main thesis runs: the knowledge of God is to be drawn from Scripture. But the knowledge of God is not a special form of knowledge belonging as a class to some more inclusive conception of knowledge. It is rather the knowledge of the basis of all truth, it is the ultimate significance behind every kind of knowledge. It follows that all knowledge finds its standard and criterion here no matter whether the knower is aware of this or not. We do not measure God's word in Scripture by the standard of reason: we measure reason and indeed all knowledge by God's word in Scripture.

Orthodoxy maintains this general thesis as the fundamental thesis of Christain faith, and rightly so. But in her interpretation of the thesis she deviates from true Christian faith as widely as the other three schools. The immense difference between these two apparently so similar conceptions of the authority of the Bible has only been clearly realized through the disintegration which orthodoxy has suffered as a consequence of the impact of modern science. This is not to say that the distinction has only existed since the advent of modern science. It has always been latent in the Christian church: we have a clear theological formulation of it already in the Reformers' principle of Scripture, although in the case of the Reformers both principles, orthodox and "reformed," are often active side by side. It is only the development of science since the Enlightenment that has made a final and unmistakable distinction between them vitally necessary for Christian faith.

The crucial opposition between the orthodox and reformed doctrine of Scripture has been previously set forth in the historical part of this work. For orthodoxy, the Bible as a book is the divinely revealed truth. It is thus a revealed thing or object. For unperverted Christian faith, however, Scripture is only revelation when conjoined with God's spirit in the present. The *testimonium spiritus sancti* and the clarity of God's word are one and the same thing. The Scripture-principle is therefore a paradoxical unity of autonomy and authority, of what is given and what is not given. Faith is contact with the absolute, hidden God, who reveals Himself to us personally as real, i.e. in something real. The real thing is Scripture to the extent that it is the witness to the revelation of God in Jesus Christ. "Scripture is the cradle in which Christ lies" (Luther). Just as a sentence consists of many words but has only one meaning, so the revelation of God in Scripture in the Old and New Testaments, in law and Gospel, has only one meaning, Jesus Christ. *Christus rex et dominus scripturae* ("The king and lord of Scripture is Christ"—Luther). "Search the Scriptures, because . . . these are they that testify of me" (John v, 39). It is this content that makes them the word of God: for Christ is the Word. They are not in themselves the revelation, but only so far as and because they have this meaning, just as the words that constitute a sentence are not true by themselves, but in virtue of their single common meaning in the sentence. Hence the Christian does not speak of the words, but the word, of God. But just as it takes many words to make a meaning clear to us, so it takes the varied material which is spread out before us in Holy Scripture effectively to convey to us the meaning of the one Word, Jesus Christ. It requires the Old Testament as well as the New, the epistles as well as the gospels, the "unauthentic" gospel of John as well as the "authentic" synoptic gospels. The knowledge that this unity runs through all Scripture, is the knowledge that faith gives us. It is not the unity of an idea, even an idea of Christ, but the unity signified by the revelation of the eternal divine Word in time, i.e. in Jesus Christ who was crucified and rose again. An *idea* can be detached from its original source. It is timeless, universally and always true. Christian faith on the other hand is concerned with the truth which we perceive as true for us, not in itself, in virtue of the bare idea, but only because God actually utters it: we are concerned with revelation where everything depends on its having happened. The meaning throughout is the man, Jesus of Nazareth, in his historical "contingency," in his "servant-form," the man born of woman and subject to the law, obedient even to death on the cross. Everything in Scripture points to this as the fulfilment of all preparatory, predictive revelation, i.e. it points to the Mediator at the "central point" of history. All the books of the Bible spell out this name; whether helplessly or forcibly, stammeringly or clearly, they instruct us about this acted meaning, some pointing forward, others backward.

With the object of coming closer to modern feeling, the antithesis has been put forward that God's word is not Scripture itself, but is contained in Scripture. This proposition could conceivably be correct: but as almost always understood it is false. For the aim that lies behind it is to discriminate revelation from what is not revelation in Scripture by an *a priori* principle of selection, by a content that can be defined beforehand. But this simply cuts the nerve of the Christian belief in revelation. Here everything turns on the character of revelation as fact, a "contingent" fact not capable of being inferred or controlled by us in any way. The important thing is not merely what is written, but the fact that it is written, and that always means that it is given in an "accidental" form and in "accidental" association with other material, at an "accidental" point in space and time, and in an "accidental," limited, and finite form. It depends on the credibility of the introductory formula: Thus saith the Lord, whether the word of the prophets really has something to say to us; i.e. whether it merely expresses a commonplace of morality, or the pious, heartfelt wish of a hopeful fancy, or whether it is an authoritative communication and revelation of mystery. To faith a word that is found in the Bible, and just because it is found there, is different from a similar word in (say) Laotse or Plato. For to faith it is not the idea only that is important, but of equal importance is the fact that the idea has been given; or rather faith is concerned not with the idea, but with the concrete happening of revelation, with an actual conversation of God with man.

Our attitude to Scripture then, so far as it is God's word to us, is not like our attitude to other books however religious, true, wise, or worthy of respect they may be—even though in these books some things may be said more beautifully or even more truly. The reason is that faith is not concerned with "many things," but always with the one, and, in order that this one may exist, it necessarily appears in this "accidental" volume known as the Bible. Thereby, it is *eo ipso* different from the "similar" and better said thing.

In saying this, we have also implied that our attitude to the individual words and facts of Scripture is entirely different from that of the orthodox view. "The cradle in which Christ lies" is not the same thing as Christ Himself. The words of Scripture, which serve to witness Christ to us, are not Christ Himself, despite the fact that we only know Him through these words. Taken by themselves they are human words. The Bible is human testimony about God, but through this human factor God bears witness to Himself. The crucifixion of Jesus may have been judicial murder: that does not prevent it from being the world's salvation. It resulted from the assertions of false witnesses, but in spite of this or rather just thereby it becomes for faith the truth above all other truth. And so with the Bible as a whole. It is full of errors, contradictions, and misleading views of various circumstances relating to man, nature, and history. It contains many contradictions in its report of the life of Jesus; it is over-grown with legend, even in the New Testament. Some parts of it are written in very helpless, colloquial, and even faulty language, while others again rise to the level of the greatest works of literature. The former fact no more destroys than the latter increases the authority which Scripture exercises over faith. The word of God is able to sound out most clearly from the worst Greek—perhaps the language of John might be mentioned by way of example.

The distinction of a human from a divine side of Scripture is not only permissible—"if nothing else will do"—but without it faith in the Bible is impure and mixed with bibliolatry. It is just on its freedom to distinguish the human from the divine side (but never to separate them) that the peculiarity of Christian faith in the Bible depends, in contrast to all veneration of holy scriptures in other religions. All other holy scriptures are at the same time fetishes, books of magic—too often indeed even the Bible is thus misused—and this belongs to their essential character. It is a property of Christian faith that the Bible should not be so regarded. It is neither a book of oracles, nor a divine encyclopædia of infallible instruction on all possible and impossible subjects. When so used, it is alienated from its proper meaning and abused. As with the whole Biblical revelation of God incarnate, the saying, *finitum non est capax infiniti* (the finite cannot grasp the infinite) is in place here. We are conscious of a lack of congruity between the means and the content of revelation. The characteristic "style" of God's revelation is to avail itself of the form of a servant, to humilate itself deeply and suffer descent into earthly frailties, not to thrust itself on men's view with the pomp of heathen theophanies, but even in the act of revelation to let itself be sought for as something hidden. It is in keeping with God's choice of a small, insignificant, and uncouth people, and with His revelation of His profoundest mystery on the cross at Golgatha, that He gave us His word in a literary document which will give the critics, in the legitimate exercise of their task, enough to do for generations to come. Faith in the Bible does not exclude, but includes, criticism of the Bible.

• • •

SUGGESTIONS FOR FURTHER READING

Traditional positions on revelation are presented in Etienne Gilson, *Reason and Revelation in the Middle Ages* (New York: Scribner's, 1938); C. H. Dodd, *The Authority of the Bible* (New York: Harper, 1929); A. E. Taylor, Vol. II, Ch. II, of *The Faith of a Moralist* (New York: Macmillan, 1930), 2 vols.; William Temple, Ch. XII of *Nature, Man, and God* (New York: Macmillan, 1934); and John Baillie, Pt. II, Ch. X, of *The Interpretation of Religion* (New York: Scribner's, 1928).

The neo-orthodox conception, and allied conceptions, are set forth in Karl Barth, *The Doctrine of the Word of God,* G. T. Thomson, tr. (Edinburgh: T. and T. Clark, 1936); Emil Brunner, *Revelation and Reason* (Philadelphia: Westminster Press, 1946); Reinhold Niebuhr, Bk. I, Ch. V, of *The Nature and Destiny of Man* (New York: Scribner's, 1951); Paul Tillich, Vol. I, Ch. V, of *Systematic Theology* (Chicago: Univ. of Chicago Press, 1951–   ), 2 vols.

Penetrating discussions of the question of the possibility of miracles can be found in F. R. Tennant, *Miracle and Its Philosophical Presuppositions* (London: Cambridge Univ. Press, 1940); A. E. Taylor, *David Hume and the Miraculous* (Cambridge: Cambridge Univ. Press, 1927); and C. S. Lewis, *Miracles* (London: G. Bles, 1947).

6.

FAITH

Up to this point our authors have been proceeding, for the most part, on the assumption that religious belief is to be treated—as regards its justification—in basically the same way as any other belief. In the present section we will encounter several thinkers who challenge this assumption. James, Kierkegaard, and Tillich, in very different ways, maintain that religious faith is different from other kinds of belief in such a way as to render illegitimate the demands for evidence, proof, and so on, that are appropriate in other areas. The issue between these philosophers and men like Aquinas, Locke, and Kant is crucial, for the whole course of our thinking about religion is profoundly affected by what we think are the right questions to raise.

The selection from L. A. Reid presents a more traditional position. According to Reid faith is distinguished from other forms of belief in not being based on such strong grounds as to deserve the name of knowledge, and in involving the readiness to act and take risks. Religious faith differs from other sorts of faith only in its object. According to this view religious faith, if sound, should be well grounded rationally in basically the same way as beliefs about the physical world and other people. The only differences among philosophers who construe faith in this way would be in the degree of rational justification required for acceptability. But all these philosophers hold that a religious belief for which we do not have considerable rational support should not be accepted.

James's essay "The Will to Believe" is largely directed against this thesis. James makes many points that are not always clearly differentiated, but his most important point is that the option between believing that God exists and believing that God does not exist is a forced option—that is, one between which there is no middle ground—and that therefore one is, in effect, going to take a position on this issue even if he does not have adequate rational grounds to decide it. A philosopher like C. D. Broad, or W. K. Clifford, whom James is attacking, would hold that if there are not sufficient rational grounds to settle the issue one way or the other the only rational thing to do is to suspend judgment, to remain agnostic. But James argues that in this case to suspend judgment is, in effect, impossible. For the so-called agnostic, for virtually all practical purposes, is indistinguishable from the atheist (who explicitly denies that God exists). The agnostic, as much as the atheist, will conduct his life without any reference to God, will settle his moral problems without any attempt to discover God's will, will not turn to God for aid and comfort in times of distress, will not try to fit his lifework into God's purposes as he sees them. The only difference is that in answer to a certain question the one will say "no," and the other will say "I don't know"; and this by itself is hardly a crucial difference. Thus in practice everyone takes a stand on this question, and the supposedly neutral agnostic position is an illusion. The general principle, of which this is a particular application, is that there are beliefs which have such pervasive practical implications for human life that in all or most of our activities we will be acting as if we either accepted or rejected them; in practice it is impossible to remain neutral. These include, in addition to the existence of God, the validity of memory, causal order in nature, and the existence of other people. With respect to memory, for example, it seems that we could not conduct the simplest of our affairs without assuming that our memories and/or those of other people are generally reliable. James's point is that in all these cases if we think that we are suspending judgment we are just deceiving ourselves; our practice belies us.

Of course, this is an argument for the justifiability of taking one side *or the other* on the question of the existence of God, even without adequate evidence (and in this essay James is assuming that we cannot rationally establish either the existence or the nonexistence of God).[1] It is justifiable because we simply have no alternative. This, which I have taken to be James's central argument, must be distinguished both from other arguments for this thesis—for example,

---

[1] The reader may note that this seems to contradict what James says at the end of the selection from *The Varieties of Religious Experience* in Section 2: that the question can, in principle, be settled by empirical evidence. We can reconcile these points of view by construing the position in "The Will to Believe" to be one to be taken *pro tem* until enough empirical evidence has been amassed.

that it is better to run the risk of being mistaken than to run the risk of missing the truth—and from some tentatively presented arguments for the much stronger thesis—that in the absence of conclusive evidence either way a belief in God is more justifiable than no belief in God. James's objections to "Pascal's wager" would seem to have equal force against the latter arguments. James is on soundest ground when he is arguing that the believer in God need not be shamefaced over lack of adequate rational grounds, provided there are no adequate rational grounds for the opposite position. As James himself notes, the essay would better have been titled "The Right to Believe."

Kierkegaard's challenge to the assumption that religious faith is to be treated like any other belief is a much more radical one. For James it is just an unfortunate fact that we do not have enough evidence to settle the question of the existence of God. It is not inconceivable that we should have and it would be much better if we did. Only so long as the evidence happens to be lacking are we justified in taking up a position in the absence of evidence. But for Kierkegaard religious faith is such that it is totally irrelevant even to raise a question as to evidence or rational grounds. Because of Kierkegaard's importance, both intrinsically as the most trenchant proponent of this position and as a powerful influence on contemporary religious thought, and because his ironical style (he once referred to himself as a religious humorist) makes it difficult to extract the philosophical substance of his position, it will be worth our while to examine his position in some detail.

Kierkegaard defines faith as "an objective uncertainty held fast in an appropriation-process of the most passionate inwardness." A great deal is wrapped up in this formula. First note that there is an objective pole and a subjective pole. On the objective side, there is an object of faith, something which is believed. Let us take as our example the existence of God. On the subjective side, there is the belief, the acceptance of this object; it is held fast, appropriated. According to this definition, certain conditions must be satisfied on both sides if we are to have faith. On the side of the object, there is uncertainty; that is, there is *objective* uncertainty, which simply means that as far as any objective evidence or reasoning goes, it is uncertain whether the object really exists. But on the side of the subject there is no uncertainty. He does not accept the belief tentatively, hypothetically, or until further notice, but he accepts it wholeheartedly, without reservation. Moreover, this acceptance is characterized by passionate inwardness. *Inwardness* and its near synonym *subjectivity* are the most important terms in Kierkegaard. Inwardness, at least when Kierkegaard is using it in a religious context, does not mean *any* sort of inner experiences, feelings, desires, thoughts, and so on. He means by it something much more specific. A state of inwardness is one in which a person is preoccupied with concern for himself, his individuality, his destiny, his "eternal happiness," the shape he is going to give to his life. Christianity, says Kierkegaard, "desires that the subject should be infinitely concerned about himself." [2] Kierkegaard distin-

---

[2] *Concluding Unscientific Postscript,* tr. Swenson and Lowrie, Princeton: Princeton Univ. Press (1944), p. 116.

guishes three basic modes of existence: the aesthetic, the ethical, and the religious. This concern for one's own existence is what distinguishes the religious attitude from the aesthetic, which concentrates on maximizing the pleasure of the moment. But it does not suffice to distinguish it from the ethical mode of existence, in which there is also this concentration on one's own existence. To make this second distinction, we need the second major component of inwardness, a concern for the mode of one's relationship to another: "The believer differs from the ethicist in being infinitely interested in the reality of another." [3] Specifically religious inwardness includes a drive to relate one's own life in a satisfactory and appropriate way to the life of another or others.

Let us put these pieces together. In the state of faith, the believer has no objective grounds for believing in the existence of God. But in his "passionate inwardness," in the intensity of his need to find a center around which to orient his existence, to relate himself satisfactorily to another, he accepts the existence of God and strives to relate his life properly to God's laws, forgiveness, and so on, in spite of the lack of rational support. The intensity of his inner need is sufficient to carry the belief without any rational reinforcement.

The subjective pole of this definition would be widely accepted by religious thinkers today. There is general agreement that religious faith is not just a matter of accepting a doctrine, however religious that doctrine. In addition, there must be an active commitment, a total involvement. The individual cannot just take the reality of God for a fact; this fact must make a difference in the way he lives his life. Otherwise he does not really have religious faith, but only a theological position. The only question would be as to the exact characterization Kierkegaard gives of this "something more." Some will feel that Kierkegaard has put too much stress on the "infinite passion," and others may feel that he has unduly slighted other elements, for example, social action and mystical experience. But there would be broad agreement. In fact, this consensus is in no small part due to the influence of Kierkegaard's writings. He must be given a great deal of credit for forcing these subjective elements of religious faith on the attention of religious thinkers. We can see this if we contrast his definition of faith with that of St. Thomas Aquinas: "Faith signifies the assent of the intellect to that which is believed." This statement says nothing about passionate inwardness. And note the way in which Reid insists that if there is emotion in faith it is derivative from the cognitive aspect.

The other part of the definition, objective uncertainty, is regarded by Kierkegaard as no less essential, and this is more controversial. Why must we be objectively uncertain about the existence of God in order to have faith? Even if we are, as a matter of fact, objectively uncertain, would it not be better if we could reach certainty? Should we not *try* to decide the question objectively, and then if we succeed regulate our "inwardness" accordingly?

A careful reading of the *Postscript* will reveal that Kierkegaard really takes passionate inwardness to be the heart of his conception, and tries to justify the

---

[3] *Postscript*, p. 288.

objective uncertainty on the basis of it. Although he is antipathetic to systematic argumentation, one can dig out the following arguments for the thesis that passionate inwardness requires objective uncertainty:

1. The search for objective certainty diverts attention from subjective concern. The man who has true inwardness finds it impossible to take up the detached attitude which is required for objective investigation. For him it is a life-and-death matter. "He can scarcely regard God as something to be taken along if convenient." He cannot wait until all the evidence is in since "every moment is wasted in which he does not have God." [4]

2. Even if we could have objective certainty without having to search for it (God might have made His existence immediately obvious to everyone), still the very possession of that certainty would weaken or destroy the subjective concern. "The more objective security, the less inwardness, and the less objective security, the more profound the possible inwardness." [5] When facts are obvious to us, like the physical objects in our surroundings, we tend to take them for granted; we are not likely to focus our entire inner life—our hopes, fears, and needs—upon it. Familiarity breeds contempt. This seems to be what Kierkegaard has in mind when he says, "And why is God elusive? Precisely because He is the truth, and by being elusive desires to keep men from error?" [6] By keeping the issue in doubt, God keeps the fires of inward passion alive.

3. Religious faith essentially involves a decision on the part of the individual. The situation must be such that the individual is free either to accept God or not accept God. But if God were an objective certainty, there would be no place for a decision. I am not called on to decide whether there are people in the room in which I am sitting. Hence even to seek an objective determination of the question is "a sign that the subject seeks to shirk something of the pain and crisis of the decision." [7]

This contention is open to serious objections. It would seem that Kierkegaard reads objective thinking out of religion in much too cavalier a fashion. Basically, the argument is: Since the heart and soul of religion is inwardness, there is no place in religion for the search for objective evidence. But it may be doubted that Kierkegaard has really shown that subjective concern and objective reasoning are incompatible. There is some truth in his principle that objective security and inward passion are inversely related, but it is at best a rough approximation which fails to hold universally. Whether it holds in a particular case depends on the presence or absence of other factors. Many matters about which we are objectively uncertain will generate much less inward passion than other matters about which we are objectively certain (for example, the total precipitation in southeastern Michigan on October 10, 1947, versus Russia's possession of a hydrogen bomb). Perhaps in general, objective uncertainty about the existence of God or the incarnation will intensify concern (though I suspect

---

[4] *Concluding Unscientific Postscript,* p. 179.
[5] *Postscript,* p. 188.
[6] *Postscript,* p. 218.
[7] *Postscript,* p. 115.

that even this will vary with different temperaments); but this is because in these cases the facts are of immense interest to us anyway. The uncertainty is not the main source of the interest. It seems incredible that a person who knew with certainty that there existed an omnipotent being who made certain demands on him and laid down a certain scheme of salvation, would casually take this as another matter of fact like the annual rainfall.

But even if objective certainty and subjective concern were much more antithetical than I have just suggested, there are still values of objective certainty for religion which Kierkegaard ignores, and which might be worth a considerable sacrifice of inward voltage. Kierkegaard talks as if it does not matter religiously whether the object of faith really exists, so long as the individual's subjectivity takes on the proper shape. It is the "how" that is crucial. But again, it seems that he has inflated the most important factor into the only important factor. We certainly do not make use of his principle in other spheres. We ordinarily suppose that when a belief has important applications to our lives, it is important to find out whether or not it is (objectively) true, and the more important its applications, the more important it is to make sure that it is true before acting on it. For the more significant its implications for the way we live, the more disastrous it would be to accept it and act on it if it were false. The danger of the native hue of resolution being sicklied o'er with the pale cast of thought must be balanced against the opposite and equally real danger of blind action breaking itself on external facts which are none the less stubborn for being unheeded. Which belief we act on is as important as that we act on some belief in a thoroughgoing way. Take for example the belief that human misery is generally due to the repression of basic desires. If we thoroughly accepted this belief, the way we live our lives would be drastically changed. It is a matter of the utmost subjective concern. But people do not give this as a reason for refusing to try to determine whether it is objectively true. Quite the contrary. Just because it does have such far-reaching implications for the way we live, it is all the more important to become as certain as possible as to whether it is true to the facts. Why should it not be equally important to try to ascertain whether Christianity is objectively true?

Thus far the presentation has been predominantly negative. Kierkegaard denies that objective considerations are relevant to the acceptance or rejection of religious beliefs. Then what is relevant? Subjective consideration obviously. But this needs further explanation. Kierkegaard does not mean to give a blank check to any sort of personal preference, taste, whim, or predilection in the adoption of religious beliefs. We need a more detailed statement of the reflections or procedures Kierkegaard thinks appropriate for a man trying to decide whether to accept or reject a religion. To do so we must focus the discussion more narrowly. Up to this point we have been talking as if Kierkegaard were interested in analyzing religious faith in general, but this is not strictly accurate. His announced intention was to make clear what it is to become a Christian, and his discussion is carried on within that framework. In fact, he would reject any attempt to deal with religion in general as an evasion of that existential concern with one's own destiny which he regarded as central. Much of what Kierkegaard says about Christian faith is applicable to faith in general but to give an adequate presentation of the Kierkegaardian concept of the subjective approach to religious questions, we shall have to focus on Christianity.

What an individual does when he approaches Christianity in a Kierkegaardian spirit is this: First, he must be infinitely concerned about himself and his destiny. And in order to do this effectively he must drop the many disguises he customarily employs and resolutely face his situation as it really is—his weakness in the face of the cosmos, his inability to achieve the ideals (moral and otherwise) he has set for himself, his ignorance about the matters which concern him most, for example, his ultimate origin and ultimate destiny. If he really takes account of all this he will inevitably fall into despair—into what Kierkegaard calls "the sickness unto death." And not the least component of this despair is the consciousness of sin, the realization that he has performed, and is performing, acts for which he is guilty, and that he can do nothing effective to stop. All his attempts to extricate himself by his own efforts (scientific, moral, political, and so on) inevitably fail, and with each failure the despair returns in an intensified form. Meanwhile the guilt intensifies, and the individual feels that the weight of it is so great that nothing he can do will atone for it. In this condition of utter desperation he hears the Christian message: that God has himself become man and suffered death to make the atonement for men's sins that they are unable to make themselves, and thereby has made it possible for them to escape from guilt-ridden despair into eternal blessedness. The individual seizes hungrily on this. But how does he know that this really happened? It is uncertain. It is worse than uncertain; it is rationally absurd. How could any sensible man believe that a man could be God? It is repellent to the understanding. And so the individual is tossed back and forth between the rationally unacceptable solution and the even more insistent need for salvation. The absurdity of the message repels him and throws him back onto himself, but then the hopelessness of his situation forces him back into the search for a solution. And in this oscillation the passion of inwardness becomes excruciatingly intensified. Here we should remember that faith for Kierkegaard is not just a concatenation of objective absurdity and passionate inwardness; they do not simply exist side by side. Faith is the tension or the contradiction between them. When the breaking point is reached, something happens to effect a decisive transformation. Of course, it is not necessary that what happens is the acceptance of Christianity. There can be no guarantee of this. Some of the later existentialists like Sartre describe very different outcomes of the same sort of initially desperate situation. The Christian outcome can be described in different ways. If one were describing the occurrence from outside Christianity, he would say that the individual had made the leap of faith; things had finally become so desperate that he was able to overcome his rational scruples and accept the salvation offered him in the Christian message, and live accordingly. But if one is describing the transaction from within Christianity, as Kierkegaard does part of the time, one says that at this point God has intervened and bestowed the grace of faith on the individual, has given the individual the ability to believe in Christ and commit himself to Him, something the individual could not manage on his own.

If we take this subjective approach to religious belief, the problems will take on a quite different form. Instead of asking how I can know whether Christ is God, or what reason there is to suppose that Christ is God, I will ask what my real situation in life is, what my deepest needs, hopes, and fears are, if I can bring myself to accept the salvation offered in Christ, if there is any other hope for me, and so on. Instead of turning outward in the search for evidence, I will turn inward in quest of self-knowledge, and seek to pose in the sharpest way possible the alternative possibilities for the shaping of my existence.

This depiction of the subjective approach to religious belief has an importance which is not dependent on the cogency of Kierkegaard's attack on the *relevance* of objective considerations. For if we take the much more plausible position of James—that objective grounds though relevant are unavailable—we will just as surely be forced back to a subjective approach. And Kierkegaard has certainly given a penetrating account of one, though not the only, such approach.

Paul Tillich's way of assigning religious faith a special status is different from that of either James or Kierkegaard. It is based on his conception of faith as "ultimate concern." Ultimate concern, as Tillich conceives it, includes the following:

1. An unconditional surrender to something: x, the willingness to recognize x as holding absolute authority over one's life.
2. An expectation that one will somehow receive a supreme fulfillment through one's encounter and commerce with x.
3. Finding in x a center of meaningfulness. That is, everything in one's life and one's world takes on significance insofar as it is related in some way to x.
4. Experiencing x as holy.

According to Tillich, every human being has an ultimate concern, though the x's toward which such concern is directed vary enormously—supernatural beings, human beings (Jesus Christ, Caesar, Buddha), nations, social classes, political movements, cultural forms like science or music. One may doubt that ultimate concern, as described in Tillich's somewhat extravagant terms, can be found in every man. Tillich seems not to have taken account of wide differences in the extent to which individuals have oriented themselves around a single object. Total integration seems to be a rare achievement. Moreover, Tillich seems to overlook some crucial differences between concern with an existent object (or one believed to be existent) and concern with (or for) the realization of a goal like financial success. For example, how can a goal *promise* anything? But it cannot be denied that Tillich has given a penetrating analysis of religiosity, an analysis that reveals its important affinities with modes of personal organization such as nationalistic fervor and devotion to scientific inquiry, which lie outside what is usually called religion.

Tillich maintains that on the basis of this account we can see that it is only through an "intellectualistic distortion" of the nature of faith that one looks for evidential support for religious beliefs in the way one does for scientific theories. But even if Tillich is right in insisting that faith is a "centered act" of the whole personality and cannot be limited to the cognitive, it would still seem that it does involve the cognitive side of the personality along with others, and that this would render it liable to the problems from which Tillich wants to exempt it. How can I be ultimately concerned with something unless I believe that it exists, that it will provide certain fulfillments, and so on? And why is a demand for a justification of these beliefs not legitimate? Tillich tries to answer by saying that what seem to be beliefs about the objects of ultimate concern are to be taken symbolically and not as the literal statements of fact they appear to be. It might seem that this move would align Tillich with subjectivistic or naturalistic theories like that of Santayana,[8] but Tillich wants to resist that. He wants to maintain that ultimate concern carries a reference to a reality outside human attitudes and feelings. But how can he do this while keeping religious beliefs free from liability to demands for evidence? What he does is to hold that the concrete objects of ultimate concern, from success to a supernatural personal deity, are functioning as symbols of an ultimate reality, "being-itself," which is so ultimate that nothing can be said about it in literal terms, except that it is ultimate. Thus one is not concerned with these objects in themselves, but as symbols of being-itself; hence their actual existence or nonexistence is not of essential religious concern.

The main support for this claim comes from Tillich's contention that somehow ultimate concern must be concern with what is ultimate. "The unconditional concern which is faith is the concern about the unconditional. . . . The ultimate concern is concern about what is experienced as ultimate." When the position is flatly asserted in this way it seems that Tillich has fallen into a verbal trap. From the fact that a concern is ultimate (in the sense of being dominant in the individual's personality structure) it does not follow that the object of the concern is ultimate, in the metaphysical sense of being that on which all else depends for its being. However, elsewhere Tillich tries to justify this claim by saying: "Nothing can be of ultimate concern for us which does not have the power of threatening and saving our being . . . the term 'being' means the whole of human reality, the structure, the meaning, and the aim of existence. . . . Man is ultimately concerned about that which determines his ultimate destiny beyond all preliminary necessities and accidents." [9] Here Tillich seems to be saying that one can only be *properly* or *advisedly* ultimately concerned about what is metaphysically ultimate, rather than that one in fact is always so concerned. But from this it is a short step to saying that in ultimate concern one is always *really* concerned with being-itself, whether one realizes it or not.

One is then led to accommodate the concrete objects of concern by saying that they are being reacted to as symbols of being-itself.

The main difficulty with this complex and ingenious scheme is that Tillich nowhere gives an intelligible account of what it is for a nation or a supernatural god to symbolize or "point to" being-itself. Normally to say that *x* is a symbol

---

[8] See Section 8.

[9] *Systematic Theology,* London: Nisbet & Co. (1953), Vol. I, p. 17.

of y means, roughly, that x tends to evoke feelings, attitudes, and behavior appropriate to y, and that the person for whom x is a symbol of y could, on demand, identify y as that which is symbolized. If we try to apply this analysis here we will run into difficulty on both counts. If we ask what feelings, attitudes, and so on, would be appropriately directed to the ultimate itself, we would not know how to answer, and justifiably. Since the ultimate cannot be characterized as one thing rather than another, there can be no reason for considering one attitude or feeling more appropriate to it than another. As for the second point, it would seem that one would specify being-itself as what it is that religious symbols symbolize only if one were a metaphysician of a certain persuasion. But the conclusion to which we would then be driven—that only certain types of metaphysicians could have faith—would be as repugnant to Tillich as to anyone else.

Thus despite the brilliance of Tillich's portrayal of faith as a form of human existence one is left wondering whether he has given a satisfactory account of the status of religious belief.

L. A. REID

Credulity, Belief, and Faith

Louis A. Reid (1895–   ) has been Professor of the Philosophy of Education at London University since 1947.

Religion, it is always supposed, demands faith or belief of the kind called religious. The belief which the Church of England expects its members to utter when they worship is a *Credo* in a set of doctrines formulated by the traditional authority of the Church. I have suggested in what I have written that it is impossible for many reasonable people to accept much which the Church formulates. By implication, an artificially induced 'faith' in these things is unsound and in the end impossible. It becomes very necessary, therefore, to enquire (in this short chapter) what may be meant by 'faith,' and thereafter (in the next) to ask what things there are in which we may have faith.

Faith must be distinguished from knowledge, from belief in general and from credulity.

Of *knowledge* I need not say very much, except that in the very strictest sense of the word 'knowledge,' there is much less of it than we suppose. In common-sense language we employ, quite legitimately for common-sense purposes, the term knowledge for that which is not, strictly speaking, knowledge. I may say that I 'know' that I was in London yesterday, or that my friend is sitting in

From L. A. Reid, *A Preface to Faith* (1939), Ch. X. Reprinted by permission of George Allen & Unwin Ltd.

a chair opposite me, or that the sun will rise to-morrow. Philosophically speaking it would possibly be more correct (though this could be disputed) to say that I had *beliefs* about these things which are very probably true, which no one in his senses except a philosopher ever doubts. But since the claim of knowledge is a claim not only of subjective certitude but of objective certainty, and as in any serious discussion this objective certainty may be difficult or impossible to establish, it seems wiser to speak of belief, and to agree that beliefs may be more, or may be less, securely grounded, and that countless beliefs are so securely grounded as to justify their being called 'true beliefs' or, in the popular use of the term, 'knowledge.'

This sentence at once suggests the connexion between belief and *credulity*. Credulity may be said to be belief in propositions which are not sufficiently well grounded to justify belief in them. This credulity may be psychologically caused in a good many different ways; it may be due, for example, merely to a weak or an erring sense of evidence, or to a natural ignorance and readiness to accept the dictates of authority or prestige. And in the mentally weak or slack or in the ignorant, or even in more highly developed types of mind, credulity may be influenced by a strong submissive instinct, or a strong innate tendency to enjoy the wonderful or the strange. Or again, in a different kind of situation, the suggestibility of a nervous fear may lead one to imagine things:

> . . . Or in the dark, imagining some fear,
> How often is a bush suppos'd a bear.

Generally speaking, the credulous person may begin to believe because the act of believing is the outcome of uncritical instinct, and he may go on to cultivate this belief by a kind of mental self-indulgence, an intellectual sentimentality,

facts being manipulated to fit fancy. A good deal of religious belief is certainly to be labelled 'credulity,' and it may arise in any of these ways or in other ways.

Credulity, then, is a species of belief, but belief not sufficiently grounded in objective fact. What I will call *rational belief* is another species of belief which is quite distinct from credulous belief. Rational or grounded belief is belief which links on to and is coherent with a system of tested experience. Scientific beliefs are of such a kind. I say 'system of . . . experience,' and not 'immediate experience' because, though immediate experience is indispensable in knowledge, yet immediate experience which is not related to some *system* of beliefs is not (as yet, at any rate) rational belief. If I think I have met the postman, or a personal devil, or a ghost, or pink rats suspended in the air, these are (loosely speaking) immediate experiences; but it is not rational to believe that what I am thus immediately experiencing exists as 'real' unless it can be related to the context of the common experience which we call 'real.' Dreams, again, induce beliefs; but to believe in the 'reality' of dream-experiences is not rational because dreams have their own life which comes to an end when we awake. Finally, when the scientist is brought up against an apparent fact which conflicts with the existing system of his beliefs, his rational course is either to attempt to discover some explanation in terms of the existing beliefs, or to modify that system so as to include the new fact. If either seems impossible he must go back to re-examine the alleged fact.

All these statements about belief apply to the several objects of belief. We may believe in a 'thing' (e.g. a bridge and its stability) or in an idea (e.g. the ideal of the social reformer or the idea of an inventor) or in a theory. Belief in the Trinity is up to a point belief in a theory, although it is in another sense belief in a Person or Persons. But in each and every case a test of the rationality of belief is the degree in which the belief is objectively grounded.

The idea of *faith* is more complex. Faith is a more comprehensive attitude of mind which includes belief, but in which stress is laid upon the *conative* effects of belief, upon the disposition to put into practice, the readiness to act upon belief, to stake something, to take risks if necessary. The reference to potential action is always implied when we speak of faith. Faith is belief regarded not simply as awareness of something, but as ready for action.

There is some flexibility in the usage of the terms 'belief' and 'faith.' Belief, whether it is credulous or rational, always involves at least some tendency to action where any action is called for; yet, since in many situations the call to action is remote or indirect or even nonexistent, it becomes unnatural to speak of it as faith. The belief that an atom contains electron and proton, or that planetary orbits are elliptical, could not ordinarily be called 'faith' though faith may be indirectly involved. I, being an ignoramus, take the statements 'upon faith,' and this means that I am ready to trust the physicists or the astronomers, to do what they tell me, if the occasion should arise for them to lead me. But it would probably be a misuse of language to say that I have 'faith' in the propositions, because belief in them involves no considerable action or risk. Again, where a belief is practically so certain that there can be no considerable doubt about it at all, it seems rhetorical to speak of it as 'faith.' I believe that $2 + 2 = 4$, but because in any ordinary sense of the word I *know* that $2 + 2 = 4$, it would be misleading to insist that faith is an outstanding character of my attitude to this proposition. Certainly when I am adding up my bank book, I am acting upon the belief that $2 + 2 = 4$, but since the notion of faith seems to contain the idea of a venture, and there is nothing that could properly be called a venture in this, the word 'faith' is inappropriate, though it might be used. To sum up: faith is only used significantly when belief involves significant action, and where that action at least involves some risk because it is only based on belief (which might be wrong) and not on knowledge.

As we may have credulous, or rational belief, and as faith is belief with its conative side stressed, so we may have a credulous, or a rational faith. But since the two sides, the cognitive and the conative, are, though so intimately related, yet distinct, it is possible to have four different types of faith according as these two factors vary. (1) We may have belief with very little ground, credulous belief, together with a strong disposition to act upon it; this is strong but blind or unintelligent faith. Much mob emotion is of this kind, and so is much national faith, either in time of war, or when manipulated by a clever demagogue. And certainly there is a great deal of strong, but blind, religious faith. (2) Credulousness, on the other hand, may be accompanied by a feeble tendency to act upon belief. There are people who are ready to believe without reason what is told them, but are unreliable in an emergency when it comes to putting belief into action. (3) Or we may have a rational belief which is yet not willing to risk much; it is the tendency of the too theoretic or the too sophisticated man. Some of our present troubles arise from this: there are many intelligent and well-informed people whose beliefs on moral, political and even religious questions are quite sound and rational, yet who are not to be relied upon when action is needed. This may be because the civilization which has made it possible for them to be contemplative has at the same time devitalized their desires and their emotions, or it may be that their very capacity for seeing all sides of a question inhibits them from that practical partisanship which seems necessary if the world is to go on. These are weaknesses which seem to arise straight out of the virtues of those who possess what is sometimes called the 'academic' mind. But the distinction between the grounds of belief and the tendency to act upon the belief must be kept clear, otherwise we misjudge such persons. Their beliefs may be very surely grounded, but either they remain purely theoretical beliefs, or they are too complex to give clear practical guidance. This disease, if disease it be, looks like, but is not necessarily identical with, feebleness of will. (4) Finally, we have the combination of well-grounded rational belief (in matters which have a practical implication) with a strong disposition to act, to venture forth and to take a risk if necessary on the basis of the belief. This is faith in the best sense. Religious belief, if it is to be sound, should conform to this type.

In my analysis I have not said much about emotion. Both faith and belief might be said by some people to be emotions. I prefer to avoid this description, since it is apt to imply that belief and faith, being 'mere emotions,' are not rational. The nature of emotion is a matter for psychology, and I will content myself by saying here that whilst it seems to me wrong to call faith an emotion if by emotion is merely meant a feeling, yet strong faith may involve strong emotion and feeling, though this varies much with temperament. But if the strong belief which is faith involves strong emotion, the reason is partly that the contemplation of the object of belief both stirs into activity deep impulses and sentiments of our nature, and sets going a good deal of bodily excitement. The feeling of these cognitively aroused excitements *is* the emotion. Again, in addition to the stimulus of the object of belief itself, there is the stimulus and the resulting emotions of risk and adventure. But, it should be noted, emotion is an effect, an accompaniment, a consequence, of belief and faith—at least in the case of rational faith and belief. It is, I think, not only politic, but essential, that this order should be maintained. If it is not, the ground and rationality and meaning of belief and faith are apt to disappear, and with it all the significance of the act of faith which is involved. There *may* be faith which arises out of mere emotional feeling. But it is unstable and unreliable.

WILLIAM JAMES

When It Is Justifiable to Believe Without Adequate Evidence

In the recently published Life by Leslie Stephen of his brother, Fitz-James, there is an account of a school to which the latter went when he was a boy. The teacher, a certain Mr. Guest, used to converse with his pupils in this wise: "Gurney, what is the difference between justification and sanctification? —Stephen, prove the omnipotence of God!" etc. In the midst of our Harvard freethinking and indifference we are prone to imagine that here at your good old orthodox College conversation continues to be somewhat upon this order; and to show you that we at Harvard have not lost all interest in these vital subjects, I have brought with me tonight something like a sermon on justification by faith to read to you—I mean an essay in justification *of* faith, a defence of our right to adopt a believing attitude in religious matters, in spite of the fact that our merely logical intellect may not have been coerced. "The Will to Believe," accordingly, is the title of my paper.

I have long defended to my own students the lawfulness of voluntarily adopted faith; but as soon as they have got well imbued with the logical spirit, they have as a rule refused to admit my contention to be lawful philosophically,

even though in point of fact they were personally all the time chock-full of some faith or other themselves. I am all the while, however, so profoundly convinced that my own position is correct, that your invitation has seemed to me a good occasion to make my statements more clear. Perhaps your minds will be more open than those with which I have hitherto had to deal. I will be as little technical as I can, though I must begin by setting up some technical distinctions that will help us in the end.

I

Let us give the name of *hypothesis* to anything that may be proposed to our belief; and just as the electricians speak of live and dead wires, let us speak of any hypothesis as either *live* or *dead*. A live hypothesis is one which appeals as a real possibility to him to whom it is proposed. If I ask you to believe in the Mahdi, the notion makes no electric connection with your nature—it refuses to scintillate with any credibility at all. As an hypothesis it is completely dead. To an Arab, however (even if he be not one of the Mahdi's followers), the hypothesis is among the mind's possibilities: it is alive. This shows that deadness and liveness in an hypothesis are not intrinsic properties, but relations to the individual thinker. They are measured by his will-

From William James, *Essays in Pragmatism* (1948), an Address to the Philosophical Clubs of Yale and Brown Universities. Published in the *New World*, June, 1896.

ingness to act. The maximum of liveness in an hypothesis means willingness to act irrevocably. Practically, that means belief; but there is some believing tendency wherever there is willingness to act at all.

Next, let us call the decision between two hypotheses an *option*. Options may be of several kinds. They may be—first, *living* or *dead;* secondly, *forced* or *avoidable;* thirdly, *momentous* or *trivial;* and for our purposes we may call an option a *genuine* option when it is of the forced, living, and momentous kind.

1. A living option is one in which both hypotheses are live ones. If I say to you: "Be a theosophist or be a Mohammedan," it is probably a dead option, because for you neither hypothesis is likely to be alive. But if I say: "Be an agnostic or be a Christian," it is otherwise: trained as you are, each hypothesis makes some appeal, however small, to your belief.

2. Next, if I say to you: "Choose between going out with your umbrella or without it," I do not offer you a genuine option, for it is not forced. You can easily avoid it by not going out at all. Similarly, if I say, "Either love me or hate me," "Either call my theory true or call it false," your option is avoidable. You may remain indifferent to me, neither loving nor hating, and you may decline to offer any judgment as to my theory. But if I say, "Either accept this truth or go without it," I put on you a forced option, for there is no standing place outside of the alternative. Every dilemma based on a complete logical disjunction, with no possibility of not choosing, is an option of this forced kind.

3. Finally, if I were Dr. Nansen and proposed to you to join my North Pole expedition, your option would be momentous; for this would probably be your only similar opportunity, and your choice now would either exclude you from the North Pole sort of immortality altogether or put at least the chance of it into your hands. He who refuses to embrace a unique opportunity loses the prize as surely as if he tried and failed. *Per contra,* the option is trival when the opportunity is not unique, when the stake is insignificant, or when the decision is reversible if it later prove unwise. Such trivial options abound in the scientific life. A chemist finds an hypothesis live enough to spend a year in its verification: he believes in it to that extent. But if his experiments prove inconclusive either way, he is quit for his loss of time, no vital harm being done.

It will facilitate our discussion if we keep all these distinctions well in mind.

II

The next matter to consider is the actual psychology of human opinion. When we look at certain facts, it seems as if our passional and volitional nature lay at the root of all our convictions. When we look at others, it seems as if they could do nothing when the intellect had once said its say. Let us take the latter facts up first.

Does it not seem preposterous on the very face of it to talk of our opinions being modifiable at will? Can our will either help or hinder our intellect in its perceptions of truth? Can we, by just willing it, believe that Abraham Lincoln's existence is a myth, and that the portraits of him in *McClure's Magazine* are all of some one else? Can we, by any effort of our will, or by any strength of wish that it were true, believe ourselves well and about when we are roaring with rheumatism in bed, or feel certain that the sum of the two one-dollar bills in our pocket must be a hundred dollars? We can *say* any of these things, but we are absolutely impotent to believe them; and of just such things is the whole fabric of the truths that we do believe in made up— matters of fact, immediate or remote, as Hume said, and relations between ideas, which are either there or not there for us if we see them so, and which if not there cannot be put there by any action of our own.

In Pascal's *Thoughts* there is a celebrated passage known in literature as Pascal's wager. In it he tries to force us into Christianity by reasoning as if our concern with truth resembled our concern with the stakes in a game of chance. Translated freely his words are these: You must either believe or not believe that God is—which will you do? Your human reason cannot say. A game is going on between you and the nature of things which at the day of judgment will bring out either heads or tails. Weigh what your gains and your losses would be if you should stake all you have on heads, or God's existence: if you win in such case, you gain eternal beatitude; if you lose, you lose nothing at all. If there were an infinity of chances, and only one for God in this wager, still you ought to stake your all on God; for though you surely risk a finite loss by this procedure, any finite loss is reasonable, even a certain one is reasonable, if there is but the possibility of infinite gain. Go, then, and take holy water, and have masses said; belief will come and stupefy your scruples —*Cela vous fera croire et vous abêtira.* Why should you not? At bottom, what have you to lose?

You probably feel that when religious faith expresses itself thus, in the language of the gaming-table, it is put to its last trumps. Surely Pascal's own personal belief in masses and holy water had far other springs; and this celebrated page of his is but an argument for others, a last desperate snatch at a weapon against the hardness of the unbelieving heart. We feel that a faith in masses and holy water adopted wilfully after such a mechanical calculation would lack the inner soul of faith's reality; and if we were ourselves in the place of the Deity, we should probably take particular pleasure in cutting off believers of this pattern from

their infinite reward. It is evident that unless there be some pre-existing tendency to believe in masses and holy water, the option offered to the will by Pascal is not a living option. Certainly no Turk ever took to masses and holy water on its account; and even to us Protestants these means of salvation seem such foregone impossibilities that Pascal's logic, invoked for them specifically, leaves us unmoved. As well might the Mahdi write to us, saying, "I am the Expected One whom God has created in his effulgence. You shall be infinitely happy if you confess me; otherwise you shall be cut off from the light of the sun. Weigh, then, your infinite gain if I am genuine against your finite sacrifice if I am not!" His logic would be that of Pascal; but he would vainly use it on us, for the hypothesis he offers us is dead. No tendency to act on it exists in us to any degree.

The talk of believing by our volition seems, then, from one point of view, simply silly. From another point of view it is worse than silly, it is vile. When one turns to the magnificent edifice of the physical sciences, and sees how it was reared; what thousands of disinterested moral lives of men lie buried in its mere foundations; what patience and postponement, what choking down of preference, what submission to the icy laws of outer fact are wrought into its very stones and mortar; how absolutely impersonal it stands in its vast augustness —then how besotted and contemptible seems every little sentimentalist who comes blowing his voluntary smoke-wreaths, and pretending to decide things from out of his private dream! Can we wonder if those bred in the rugged and manly school of science should feel like spewing such subjectivism out of their mouths? The whole system of loyalties which grow up in the schools of science go dead against its toleration; so that it is only natural that those who have caught the scientific fever should pass over to the opposite extreme, and write sometimes as if the incorruptibly truthful intellect ought positively to prefer bitterness and unacceptableness to the heart in its cup.

It fortifies my soul to know
That though I perish, Truth is so—

sings Clough, while Huxley exclaims: "My only consolation lies in the reflection that, however bad our posterity may become, so far as they hold by the plain rule of not pretending to believe what they have no reason to believe, because it may be to their advantage so to pretend [the word 'pretend' is surely here redundant], they will not have reached the lowest depth of immorality." And that delicious *enfant terrible* Clifford writes: "Belief is desecrated when given to unproved and unquestioned statements for the solace and private pleasure of the believer. . . . Whoso would deserve well of his fellows in this matter will guard the purity of his belief with a very fanaticism of jealous care, lest at any time it should rest on an unworthy object, and catch a stain which can never be wiped away. . . . If [a] belief has been accepted on insufficient evidence [even though the belief be true, as Clifford on the same page explains] the pleasure is a stolen one. . . . It is sinful because it is stolen in defiance of our duty to mankind. That duty is to guard ourselves from such beliefs as from a pestilence which may shortly master our own body and then spread to the rest of the town. . . . It is wrong always, everywhere, and for every one, to believe anything upon insufficient evidence."

III

All this strikes one as healthy, even when expressed, as by Clifford, with somewhat too much of robustious pathos in the voice. Free will and simple wishing do seem, in the matter of our credences,

to be only fifth wheels to the coach. Yet if any one should thereupon assume that intellectual insight is what remains after wish and will and sentimental preference have taken wing, or that pure reason is what then settles our opinions, he would fly quite as directly in the teeth of the facts.

It is only our already dead hypotheses that our willing nature is unable to bring to life again. But what has made them dead for us is for the most part a previous action of our willing nature of an antagonistic kind. When I say "willing nature," I do not mean only such deliberate volitions as may have set up habits of belief that we cannot now escape from—I mean all such factors of belief as fear and hope, prejudice and passion, imitation and partisanship, the circumpressure of our caste and set. As a matter of fact we find ourselves believing, we hardly know how or why. Mr. Balfour gives the name of "authority" to all those influences, born of the intellectual climate, that make hypotheses possible or impossible for us, alive or dead. Here in this room, we all of us believe in molecules and the conservation of energy, in democracy and necessary progress, in Protestant Christianity and the duty of fighting for "the doctrine of the immortal Monroe," all for no reasons worthy of the name. We see into these matters with no more inner clearness, and probably with much less, than any disbeliever in them might possess. His unconventionality would probably have some grounds to show for its conclusions; but for us, not insight, but the *prestige* of the opinions, is what makes the spark shoot from them and light up our sleeping magazines of faith. Our reason is quite satisfied, in nine hundred and ninety-nine cases out of every thousand of us, if it can find a few arguments that will do to recite in case our credulity is criticized by some one else. Our faith is faith in some one else's faith, and in the greatest matters this is most the case.

Our belief in truth itself, for instance, that there is a truth, and that our minds and it are made for each other—what is it but a passionate affirmation of desire, in which our social system backs us up? We want to have a truth; we want to believe that our experiments and studies and discussions must put us in a continually better and better position towards it; and on this line we agree to fight out our thinking lives. But if a Pyrrhonistic sceptic asks us *how we know* all this, can our logic find a reply? No! certainly it cannot. It is just one volition against another—we willing to go in for life upon a trust or assumption which he, for his part, does not care to make.[1]

As a rule we disbelieve all facts and theories for which we have no use. Clifford's cosmic emotions find no use for Christian feelings. Huxley belabors the bishops because there is no use for sacerdotalism in his scheme of life. Newman, on the contrary, goes over to Romanism, and finds all sorts of reasons good for staying there, because a priestly system is for him an organic need and delight. Why do so few "scientists" even look at the evidence for telepathy, so called? Because they think, as a leading biologist, now dead, once said to me, that even if such a thing were true, scientists ought to band together to keep it suppressed and concealed. It would undo the uniformity of Nature and all sorts of other things without which scientists cannot carry on their pursuits. But if this very man had been shown something which as a scientist he might *do* with telepathy, he might not only have examined the evidence, but even have found it good enough. This very law which the logicians would impose upon us—if I may give the name of logicians to those who would rule out our willing nature here—is based on nothing but their own natural wish

to exclude all elements for which they, in their professional quality of logicians, can find no use.

Evidently, then, our non-intellectual nature does influence our convictions. There are passional tendencies and volitions which run before and others which come after belief, and it is only the latter that are too late for the fair; and they are not too late when the previous passional work has been already in their own direction. Pascal's argument, instead of being powerless, then seems a regular clincher, and is the last stroke needed to make our faith in masses and holy water complete. The state of things is evidently far from simple; and pure insight and logic, whatever they might do ideally, are not the only things that really do produce our creeds.

IV

Our next duty, having recognized this mixed-up state of affairs, is to ask whether it be simply reprehensible and pathological, or whether, on the contrary, we must treat it as a normal element in making up our minds. The thesis I defend is, briefly stated, this: *Our passional nature not only lawfully may, but must, decide an option between propositions, whenever it is a genuine option that cannot by its nature be decided on intellectual grounds; for to say, under such circumstances, "Do not decide, but leave the question open," is itself a passional decision—just like deciding yes or no— and is attended with the same risk of losing the truth.* The thesis thus abstractly expressed will, I trust, soon become quite clear. But I must first indulge in a bit more of preliminary work.

V

It will be observed that for the purposes of this discussion we are on "dogmatic" ground—ground, I mean, which

---

[1] Compare the admirable page 310 in S. H. Hodgson's *Time and Space,* London, 1865.

leaves systematic philosophical scepticism altogether out of account. The postulate that there is truth, and that it is the destiny of our minds to attain it, we are deliberately resolving to make, though the sceptic will not make it. We part company with him, therefore, absolutely, at this point. But the faith that truth exists, and that our minds can find it, may be held in two ways. We may talk of the *empiricist* way and of the *absolutist* way of believing in truth. The absolutists in this matter say that we not only can attain to knowing truth, but we can *know when* we have attained to knowing it; while the empiricists think that although we may attain it, we cannot infallibly know when. To *know* is one thing, and to know for certain *that* we know is another. One may hold to the first being possible without the second; hence the empiricists and the absolutists, although neither of them is a sceptic in the usual philosophic sense of the term, show very different degrees of dogmatism in their lives.

If we look at the history of opinions, we see that the empiricist tendency has largely prevailed in science, while in philosophy the absolutist tendency has had everything its own way. The characteristic sort of happiness, indeed, which philosophies yield has mainly consisted in the conviction felt by each successive school or system that by it bottom-certitude had been attained. "Other philosophies are collections of opinions, mostly false; *my* philosophy gives standing-ground forever"—who does not recognize in this the key-note of every system worthy of the name? A system, to be a system at all, must come as a *closed* system, reversible in this or that detail, perchance, but in its essential features never! Scholastic orthodoxy, to which one must always go when one wishes to find perfectly clear statement, has beautifully elaborated this absolutist conviction in a doctrine which it calls that of "objective evidence." If, for example, I am unable to doubt that I now exist before you, that two is less than three, or that if all men are mortal then I am mortal too, it is because these things illumine my intellect irresistibly. The final ground of this objective evidence possessed by certain propositions is the *adæquatio intellectûs nostri cum rê.* The certitude it brings involves an *aptitudinem ad extorquendum certum assensum* on the part of the truth envisaged, and on the side of the subject a *quietem in cognitione,* when once the object is mentally received, that leaves no possibility of doubt behind; and in the whole transaction nothing operates but the *entitas ipsa* of the object and the *entitas ipsa* of the mind. We slouchy modern thinkers dislike to talk in Latin,—indeed, we dislike to talk in set terms at all; but at bottom our own state of mind is very much like this whenever we uncritically abandon ourselves: You believe in objective evidence, and I do. Of some things we feel that we are certain: we know, and we know that we do know. There is something that gives a click inside of us, a bell that strikes twelve, when the hands of our mental clock have swept the dial and meet over the meridian hour. The greatest empiricists among us are only empiricists on reflection: when left to their instincts, they dogmatize like infallible popes. When the Cliffords tell us how sinful it is to be Christians on such "insufficient evidence," insufficiency is really the last thing they have in mind. For them the evidence is absolutely sufficient, only it makes the other way. They believe so completely in an anti-Christian order of the universe that there is no living option: Christianity is a dead hypothesis from the start.

VI

But now, since we are all such absolutists by instinct, what in our quality of students of philosophy ought we to do about the fact? Shall we espouse and indorse it? Or shall we treat it as a weakness of our nature from which we must free ourselves, if we can?

I sincerely believe that the latter course is the only one we can follow as reflective men. Objective evidence and certitude are doubtless very fine ideals to play with, but where on this moonlit and dream-visited planet are they found? I am, therefore, myself a complete empiricist so far as my theory of human knowledge goes. I live, to be sure, by the practical faith that we must go on experiencing and thinking over our experience, for only thus can our opinions grow more true; but to hold any one of them—I absolutely do not care which—as if it never could be reinterpretable or corrigible, I believe to be a tremendously mistaken attitude, and I think that the whole history of philosophy will bear me out. There is but one indefectibly certain truth, and that is the truth that Pyrrhonistic scepticism itself leaves standing—the truth that the present phenomenon of consciousness exists. That, however, is the bare starting-point of knowledge, the mere admission of a stuff to be philosophized about. The various philosophies are but so many attempts at expressing what this stuff really is. And if we repair to our libraries what disagreement do we discover! Where is a certainly true answer found? Apart from abstract propositions of comparison (such as two and two are the same as four), propositions which tell us nothing by themselves about concrete reality, we find no proposition ever regarded by any one as evidently certain that has not either been called a falsehood, or at least had its truth sincerely questioned by some one else. The transcending of the axioms of geometry, not in play but in earnest, by certain of our contemporaries (as Zöllner and Charles H. Hinton), and the rejection of the whole Aristotelian logic by the Hegelians, are striking instances in point.

No concrete test of what is really true has ever been agreed upon. Some make the criterion external to the moment of perception, putting it either in revelation, the *consensus gentium,* the instincts of the heart, or the systematized experience of the race. Others make the perceptive moment its own test—Descartes, for instance, with his clear and distinct ideas guaranteed by the veracity of God; Reid with his "common-sense"; and Kant with his forms of synthetic judgment *a priori.* The inconceivability of the opposite; the capacity to be verified by sense; the possession of complete organic unity or self-relation, realized when a thing is its own other—are standards which, in turn, have been used. The much lauded objective evidence is never triumphantly there; it is a mere aspiration or *Grenzbegriff,* marking the infinitely remote ideal of our thinking life. To claim that certain truths now possess it, is simply to say that when you think them true and they *are* true, then their evidence is objective, otherwise it is not. But practically one's conviction that the evidence one goes by is of the real objective brand, is only one more subjective opinion added to the lot. For what a contradictory array of opinions have objective evidence and absolute certitude been claimed! The world is rational through and through—its existence is an ultimate brute fact; there is a personal God—a personal God is inconceivable; there is an extra-mental physical world immediately known—the mind can only know its own ideas; a moral imperative exists—obligation is only the resultant of desires; a permanent spiritual principle is in every one—there are only shifting states of mind; there is an endless chain of causes—there is an absolute first cause; and eternal necessity—a freedom; a purpose—no purpose; a primal One—a primal Many; a universal continuity—an essential discontinuity in things; an infinity—no infinity. There is this—there is that; there is indeed nothing which some one has not thought absolutely true, while his neighbor deemed it absolutely false; and not an absolutist among them seems ever to have considered that the trouble may all the time be essential, and that the intellect, even with truth directly in its grasp, may have no infallible signal for knowing whether it be truth or no. When, indeed, one remembers that the most striking practical application to life of the doctrine of objective certitude has been the conscientious labors of the Holy Office of the Inquisition, one feels less tempted than ever to lend the doctrine a respectful ear.

But please observe, now, that when as empiricists we give up the doctrine of objective certitude, we do not thereby give up the quest or hope of truth itself. We still pin our faith on its existence, and still believe that we gain an ever better position towards it by systematically continuing to roll up experiences and think. Our great difference from the scholastic lies in the way we face. The strength of his system lies in the principles, the origin, the *terminus a quo* of his thought; for us the strength is in the outcome, the upshot, the *terminus ad quem*. Not where it comes from but what it leads to is to decide. It matters not to an empiricist from what quarter an hypothesis may come to him: he may have acquired it by fair means or by foul; passion may have whispered or accident suggested it; but if the total drift of thinking continues to confirm it, that is what he means by its being true.

VII

One more point, small but important, and our preliminaries are done. There are two ways of looking at our duty in the matter of opinion—ways entirely different, and yet ways about whose difference the theory of knowledge seems

hitherto to have shown very little concern. *We must know the truth;* and *we must avoid error*—these are our first and great commandments as would-be knowers; but they are not two ways of stating an identical commandment, they are two separable laws. Although it may indeed happen that when we believe the truth *A,* we escape as an incidental consequence from believing the falsehood *B,* it hardly ever happens that by merely disbelieving *B* we necessarily believe *A.* We may in escaping *B* fall into believing other falsehoods, *C* or *D,* just as bad as *B;* or we may escape *B* by not believing anything at all, not even *A.*

Believe truth! Shun error!—these, we see, are two materially different laws; and by choosing between them we may end by coloring differently our whole intellectual life. We may regard the chase for truth as paramount, and the avoidance of error as secondary; or we may, on the other hand, treat the avoidance of error as more imperative, and let truth take its chance. Clifford, in the instructive passage which I have quoted, exhorts us to the latter course. Believe nothing, he tells us, keep your mind in suspense forever, rather than by closing it on insufficient evidence incur the awful risk of believing lies. You, on the other hand, may think that the risk of being in error is a very small matter when compared with the blessings of real knowledge, and be ready to be duped many times in your investigation rather than postpone indefinitely the chance of guessing true. I myself find it impossible to go with Clifford. We must remember that these feelings of our duty about either truth or error are in any case only expressions of our passional life. Biologically considered, our minds are as ready to grind out falsehood as veracity, and he who says, "Better go without belief forever than believe a lie!" merely shows his own preponderant private horror of becoming a dupe. He may be critical of many of his desires and fears, but this fear he slavishly obeys. He cannot imagine any one questioning its binding force. For my own part, I have also a horror of being duped; but I can believe that worse things than being duped may happen to a man in this world: so Clifford's exhortation has to my ears a thoroughly fantastic sound. It is like a general informing his soldiers that it is better to keep out of battle forever than to risk a single wound. Not so are victories either over enemies or over nature gained. Our errors are surely not such awfully solemn things. In a world where we are so certain to incur them in spite of all our caution, a certain lightness of heart seems healthier than this excessive nervousness on their behalf. At any rate, it seems the fittest thing for the empiricist philosopher.

VIII

And now, after all this introduction, let us go straight at our question. I have said, and now repeat it, that not only as a matter of fact do we find our passional nature influencing us in our opinions, but that there are some options between opinions in which this influence must be regarded both as an inevitable and as a lawful determinant of our choice.

I fear here that some of you my hearers will begin to scent danger, and lend an inhospitable ear. Two first steps of passion you have indeed had to admit as necessary—we must think so as to avoid dupery, and we must think so as to gain truth; but the surest path to those ideal consummations, you will probably consider, is from now onwards to take no further passional step.

Well, of course, I agree as far as the facts will allow. Wherever the option between losing truth and gaining it is not momentous, we can throw the chance of *gaining truth* away, and at any rate save ourselves from any chance of *believing falsehood*, by not making up our minds at all till objective evidence has come. In scientific questions, this is almost always the case; and even in human affairs in general, the need of acting is seldom so urgent that a false belief to act on is better than no belief at all. Law courts, indeed, have to decide on the best evidence attainable for the moment, because a judge's duty is to make law as well as to ascertain it, and (as a learned judge once said to me) few cases are worth spending much time over: the great thing is to have them decided on *any* acceptable principle, and got out of the way. But in our dealings with objective nature we obviously are recorders, not makers, of the truth; and decisions for the mere sake of deciding promptly and getting on to the next business would be wholly out of place. Throughout the breadth of physical nature facts are what they are quite independently of us, and seldom is there any such hurry about them that the risks of being duped by believing a premature theory need be faced. The questions here are always trivial options, the hypotheses are hardly living (at any rate not living for us spectators), the choice between believing truth or falsehood is seldom forced. The attitude of sceptical balance is therefore the absolutely wise one if we would escape mistakes. What difference, indeed, does it make to most of us whether we have or have not a theory of the Röntgen rays, whether we believe or not in mind-stuff, or have a conviction about the causality of conscious states? It makes no difference. Such options are not forced on us. On every account it is better not to make them, but still keep weighing reasons *pro et contra* with an indifferent hand.

I speak, of course, here of the purely judging mind. For purposes of discovery such indifference is to be less highly recommended, and science would be far less advanced than she is if the passionate desires of individuals to get their own faiths confirmed had been kept out of the game. See for example the sagacity which Spencer and Weismann now display. On the other hand, if you want an absolute duffer in an investigation, you must, after all, take the man who has no interest whatever in its results: he is the warranted incapable, the positive fool. The most useful investigator, because the most sensitive observer, is always he whose eager interest in one side of the question is balanced by an equally keen nervousness lest he become deceived.[2] Science has organized this nervousness into a regular *technique,* her so-called method of verification; and she has fallen so deeply in love with the method that one may even say she has ceased to care for truth by itself at all. It is only truth as technically verified that interests her. The truth of truths might come in merely affirmative form, and she would decline to touch it. Such truth as that, she might repeat with Clifford, would be stolen in defiance of her duty to mankind. Human passions, however, are stronger than technical rules. *"Le cœur a ses raisons,"* as Pascal says, *"que la raison ne connaît pas";* and however indifferent to all but the bare rules of the game the umpire, the abstract intellect, may be, the concrete players who furnish him the materials to judge of are usually, each one of them, in love with some pet "live hypothesis" of his own. Let us agree, however, that wherever there is no forced option, the dispassionately judicial intellect with no pet hypothesis, saving us, as it does, from dupery at any rate, ought to be our ideal.

The question next arises: Are there not somewhere forced options in our speculative questions, and can we (as men who may be interested at least as much in positively gaining truth as in merely es-

[2] Compare Wilfrid Ward's Essay, "The Wish to Believe," in his *Witnesses to the Unseen,* Macmillan & Co., 1893.

caping dupery) always wait with impunity till the coercive evidence shall have arrived? It seems *a priori* improbable that the truth should be so nicely adjusted to our needs and powers as that. In the great boarding-house of nature, the cakes and the butter and the syrup seldom come out so even and leave the plates so clean. Indeed, we should view them with scientific suspicion if they did.

IX

Moral questions immediately present themselves as questions whose solution cannot wait for sensible proof. A moral question is a question not of what sensibly exists, but of what is good, or would be good if it did exist. Science can tell us what exists; but to compare the *worths,* both of what exists and of what does not exist, we must consult not science, but what Pascal calls our heart. Science herself consults her heart when she lays it down that the infinite ascertainment of fact and correction of false belief are the supreme goods for man. Challenge the statement, and science can only repeat it oracularly, or else prove it by showing that such ascertainment and correction bring man all sorts of other goods which man's heart in turn declares. The question of having moral beliefs at all or not having them is decided by our will. Are our moral preferences true or false, or are they only odd biological phenomena, making things good or bad for *us,* but in themselves indifferent? How can your pure intellect decide? If your heart does not *want* a world of moral reality, your head will assuredly never make you believe in one. Mephistophelian scepticism, indeed, will satisfy the head's play-instincts much better than any rigorous idealism can. Some men (even at the student age) are so naturally cool-hearted that the moralistic hypothesis never has for them any pungent life, and in their supercilious presence the hot young moralist always feels strangely ill at ease. The appearance of knowingness is on their side, of *naïveté* and gullibility on his. Yet, in the inarticulate heart of him, he clings to it that he is not a dupe, and that there is a realm in which (as Emerson says) all their wit and intellectual superiority is no better than the cunning of a fox. Moral scepticism can no more be refuted or proved by logic than intellectual scepticism can. When we stick to it that there *is* truth (be it of either kind), we do so with our whole nature, and resolve to stand or fall by the results. The sceptic with his whole nature adopts the doubting attitude; but which of us is the wiser, Omniscience only knows.

Turn now from these wide questions of good to a certain class of questions of fact, questions concerning personal relations, states of mind between one man and another. *Do you like me or not?*—for example. Whether you do or not depends, in countless instances, on whether I meet you half-way, am willing to assume that you must like me, and show you trust and expectation. The previous faith on my part in your liking's existence is in such cases what makes your liking come. But if I stand aloof, and refuse to budge an inch until I have objective evidence, until you shall have done something apt, as the absolutists say, *ad extorquendum assensum meum,* ten to one your liking never comes. How many women's hearts are vanquished by the mere sanguine insistence of some man that they *must* love him! he will not consent to the hypothesis that they cannot. The desire for a certain kind of truth here brings about that special truth's existence; and so it is in innumerable cases of other sorts. Who gains promotions, boons, appointments, but the man in whose life they are seen to play the part of live hypotheses, who discounts them, sacrifices other things for their sake before they have come, and takes risks for them in advance? His faith acts on the powers above him as a claim, and creates its own verification.

A social organism of any sort whatever, large or small, is what it is because each member proceeds to his own duty with a trust that the other members will simultaneously do theirs. Wherever a desired result is achieved by the co-operation of many independent persons, its existence as a fact is a pure consequence of the precursive faith in one another of those immediately concerned. A government, an army, a commercial system, a ship, a college, an athletic team, all exist on this condition, without which not only is nothing achieved, but nothing is even attempted. A whole train of passengers (individually brave enough) will be looted by a few highwaymen, simply because the latter can count on one another, while each passenger fears that if he makes a movement of resistance, he will be shot before any one else backs him up. If we believed that the whole car-full would rise at once with us, we should each severally rise, and train-robbing would never even be attempted. There are, then, cases where a fact cannot come at all unless a preliminary faith exists in its coming. *And where faith in a fact can help create the fact,* that would be an insane logic which should say that faith running ahead of scientific evidence is the "lowest kind of immorality" into which a thinking being can fall. Yet such is the logic by which our scientific absolutists pretend to regulate our lives!

X

In truths dependent on our personal action, then, faith based on desire is certainly a lawful and possibly an indispensable thing.

But now, it will be said, these are all childish human cases, and have nothing to do with great cosmical matters, like the question of religious faith. Let us then pass on to that. Religions differ so much in their accidents that in discussing the religious question we must make it very generic and broad. What then do we now mean by the religious hypothesis? Science says things are; morality says some things are better than other things; and religion says essentially two things.

First, she says that the best things are the more eternal things, the overlapping things, the things in the universe that throw the last stone, so to speak, and say the final word. "Perfection is eternal"—this phrase of Charles Secrétan seems a good way of putting this first affirmation of religion, an affirmation which obviously cannot yet be verified scientifically at all.

The second affirmation of religion is that we are better off even now if we believe her first affirmation to be true.

Now, let us consider what the logical elements of this situation are *in case the religious hypothesis in both its branches be really true*. (Of course, we must admit that possibility at the outset. If we are to discuss the question at all, it must involve a living option. If for any of you religion be a hypothesis that cannot, by any living possibility, be true, then you need go no farther. I speak to the "saving remnant" alone.) So proceeding, we see, first, that religion offers itself as a *momentous* option. We are supposed to gain, even now, by our belief, and to lose by our non-belief, a certain vital good. Secondly, religion is a *forced* option, so far as that good goes. We cannot escape the issue by remaining sceptical and waiting for more light, because, although we do avoid error in that way *if religion be untrue*, we lose the good, *if it be true*, just as certainly as if we positively chose to disbelieve. It is as if a man should hesitate indefinitely to ask a certain woman to marry him because he was not perfectly sure that she would prove an angel after he brought her home. Would he not cut himself off from that particular angel-possibility as decisively as if

he went and married some one else? Scepticism, then, is not avoidance of option; it is option of a certain particular kind of risk. *Better risk loss of truth than chance of error*—that is your faith-vetoer's exact position. He is actively playing his stake as much as the believer is; he is backing the field against the religious hypothesis, just as the believer is backing the religious hypothesis against the field. To preach scepticism to us as a duty until "sufficient evidence" for religion be found, is tantamount therefore to telling us, when in presence of the religious hypothesis, that to yield to our fear of its being error is wiser and better than to yield to our hope that it may be true. It is not intellect against all passions, then; it is only intellect with one passion laying down its law. And by what, forsooth, is the supreme wisdom of this passion warranted? Dupery for dupery, what proof is there that dupery through hope is so much worse than dupery through fear? I, for one, can see no proof; and I simply refuse obedience to the scientist's command to imitate his kind of option, in a case where my own stake is important enough to give me the right to choose my own form of risk. If religion be true and the evidence for it be still insufficient, I do not wish, by putting your extinguisher upon my nature (which feels to me as if it had after all some business in this matter), to forfeit my sole chance in life of getting upon the winning side—that chance depending, of course, on my willingness to run the risk of acting as if my passional need of taking the world religiously might be prophetic and right.

All this is on the supposition that it really may be prophetic and right, and that, even to us who are discussing the matter, religion is a live hypothesis which may be true. Now, to most of us religion comes in a still further way that makes a veto on our active faith even more illogical. The more perfect and more eternal aspect of the universe is represented in our religions as having personal form. The universe is no longer a mere *It* to us, but a *Thou,* if we are religious; and any relation that may be possible from person to person might be possible here. For instance, although in one sense we are passive portions of the universe, in another we show a curious autonomy, as if we were small active centres on our own account. We feel, too, as if the appeal of religion to us were made to our own active good-will, as if evidence might be forever withheld from us unless we met the hypothesis half-way. To take a trivial illustration: just as a man who in a company of gentlemen made no advances, asked a warrant for every concession, and believed no one's word without proof, would cut himself off by such churlishness from all the social rewards that a more trusting spirit would earn—so here, one who should shut himself up in snarling logicality and try to make the gods extort his recognition willy-nilly, or not get it at all, might cut himself off forever from his only opportunity of making the gods' acquaintance. This feeling, forced on us we know not whence, that by obstinately believing that there are gods (although not to do so would be so easy both for our logic and our life) we are doing the universe the deepest service we can, seems part of the living essence of the religious hypothesis. If the hypothesis *were* true in all its parts, including this one, then pure intellectualism, with its veto on our making willing advances, would be an absurdity; and some participation of our sympathetic nature would be logically required. I, therefore, for one, cannot see my way to accepting the agnostic rules for truth-seeking, or wilfully agree to keep my willing nature out of the game. I cannot do so for this plain reason, that *a rule of thinking which would absolutely prevent me from acknowledging certain kinds of truth if*

those kinds of truth were really there, would be an irrational rule. That for me is the long and short of the formal logic of the situation, no matter what the kinds of truth might materially be.

I confess I do not see how this logic can be escaped. But sad experience makes me fear that some of you may still shrink from radically saying with me, *in abstracto,* that we have the right to believe at our own risk any hypothesis that is live enough to tempt our will. I suspect, however, that if this is so, it is because you have got away from the abstract logical point of view altogether, and are thinking (perhaps without realizing it) of some particular religious hypothesis which for you is dead. The freedom to "believe what we will" you apply to the case of some patent superstition; and the faith you think of is the faith defined by the schoolboy when he said, "Faith is when you believe something that you know ain't true." I can only repeat that this is misapprehension. *In concreto,* the freedom to believe can only cover living options which the intellect of the individual cannot by itself resolve; and living options never seem absurdities to him who has them to consider. When I look at the religious question as it really puts itself to concrete men, and when I think of all the possibilities which both practically and theoretically it involves, then this command that we shall put a stopper on our heart, instincts, and courage, and *wait*—acting of course meanwhile more or less as if religion were *not* true [3]—till

---

[3] Since belief is measured by action, he who forbids us to believe religion to be true, necessarily also forbids us to act as we should if we did believe it to be true. The whole defence of religious faith hinges upon action. If the action required or inspired by the religious hypothesis is in no way different from that dictated by the naturalistic hypothesis, then religious faith is a pure superfluity, better pruned away, and controversy about its legitimacy is a piece of idle trifling,

doomsday, or till such time as our intellect and senses working together may have raked in evidence enough—this command, I say, seems to me the queerest idol ever manufactured in the philosophic cave. Were we scholastic absolutists, there might be more excuse. If we had an infallible intellect with its objective certitudes, we might feel ourselves disloyal to such a perfect organ of knowledge in not trusting to it exclusively, in not waiting for its releasing word. But if we are empiricists, if we believe that no bell in us tolls to let us know for certain when truth is in our grasp, then it seems a piece of idle fantasticality to preach so solemnly our duty of waiting for the bell. Indeed we *may* wait if we will—I hope you do not think that I am denying that —but if we do so, we do so at our peril as much as if we believed. In either case we *act,* taking our life in our hands. No one of us ought to issue vetoes to the other, nor should we bandy words of abuse. We ought, on the contrary, delicately and profoundly to respect one another's mental freedom: then only shall we bring about the intellectual republic; then only shall we have that spirit of inner tolerance without which all our outer tolerance is soulless, and which is empiricism's glory; then only shall we

---

unworthy of serious minds. I myself believe, of course, that the religious hypothesis gives to the world an expression which specifically determines our reactions, and makes them in a large part unlike what they might be on a purely naturalistic scheme of belief.

live and let live, in speculative as well as in practical things.

I began by a reference to Fitz-James Stephen; let me end by a quotation from him. "What do you think of yourself? What do you think of the world? . . . These are questions with which all must deal as it seems good to them. They are riddles of the Sphinx, and in some way or other we must deal with them. . . . In all important transactions of life we have to take a leap in the dark. . . . If we decide to leave the riddles unanswered, that is a choice; if we waver in our answer, that, too, is a choice: but whatever choice we make, we make it at our peril. If a man chooses to turn his back altogether on God and the future, no one can prevent him; no one can show beyond reasonable doubt that he is mistaken. If a man thinks otherwise and acts as he thinks, I do not see that any one can prove that *he* is mistaken. Each must act as he thinks best; and if he is wrong, so much the worse for him. We stand on a mountain pass in the midst of whirling snow and blinding mist, through which we get glimpses now and then of paths which may be deceptive. If we stand still we shall be frozen to death. If we take the wrong road we shall be dashed to pieces. We do not certainly know whether there is any right one. What must we do? 'Be strong and of a good courage.' Act for the best, hope for the best, and take what comes. . . . If death ends all, we cannot meet death better." [4]

[4] *Liberty, Equality, Fraternity,* p. 353, 2d edition. London, 1874.

SOREN KIERKEGAARD

Religious Truth and Subjectivity

Soren Kierkegaard (1813–1855), the father of existentialism and one of the major influences on contemporary religious thought, devoted his short life to literary activity designed to renew what he regarded as the degenerate state of Christianity in his time.

CHAPTER I

THE TASK OF BECOMING SUBJECTIVE

THE CONCLUSION THAT WOULD BE FORCED UPON ETHICS IF THE ATTAINMENT OF SUBJECTIVITY WERE NOT THE HIGHEST TASK CONFRONTING A HUMAN BEING—CONSIDERATIONS LEFT OUT OF ACCOUNT IN CONNECTION WITH THE CLOSER UNDERSTANDING OF THIS—EXAMPLES OF THINKING DIRECTED TOWARDS BECOMING SUBJECTIVE

Objectively we consider only the matter at issue, subjectively we have regard to the subject and his subjectivity; and behold, precisely this subjectivity is the matter at issue. This must constantly be borne in mind, namely, that the subjective problem is not something about an objective issue, but is the subjectivity itself. For since the problem in question poses a decision, and since all decisiveness, as shown above, inheres in subjectivity, it is essential that every trace of an objective issue should be elimi-

From Soren Kierkegaard, *Concluding Unscientific Postscript,* tr. by D. F. Swenson and W. Lowrie (1944), Bk. II, Pt. II, Chs. I–II. Reprinted by permission of Princeton University Press.

nated. If any such trace remains, it is at once a sign that the subject seeks to shirk something of the pain and crisis of the decision; that is, he seeks to make the problem to some degree objective. If the Introduction still awaits the appearance of another work before bringing the matter up for judgment, if the System still lacks a paragraph, if the speaker has still another argument up his sleeve, it follows that the decision is postponed. Hence we do not here raise the question of the truth of Christianity in the sense that when this has been determined, the subject is assumed ready and willing to accept it. No, the question is as to the mode of the subject's acceptance; and it must be regarded as an illusion rooted in the demoralization which remains ignorant of the subjective nature of the decision, or as an evasion springing from the disingenuousness which seeks to shirk the decision by an objective mode of approach, wherein there can in all eternity be no decision, to assume that the transition from something objective to the subjective acceptance is a direct transition, following upon the objective deliberation as a matter of course. On the contrary, the subjective acceptance is precisely the decisive factor; and an objective acceptance of Christianity (*sit venia verbo*) is paganism or thoughtlessness.

Christianity proposes to endow the individual with an eternal happiness, a good which is not distributed wholesale, but only to one individual at a time. Though Christianity assumes that there inheres in the subjectivity of the individual, as being the potentiality of the appropriation of this good, the possibility for its acceptance, it does not assume that the subjectivity is immediately ready for such acceptance, or even has, without further ado, a real conception of the significance of such a good. The development or transformation of the individual's subjectivity, its infinite concentration in itself over against the conception of an eternal happiness, that highest good of the infinite—this constitutes the developed potentiality of the primary potentiality which subjectivity as such presents. In this way Christianity protests every form of objectivity; it desires that the subject should be infinitely concerned about himself. It is subjectivity that Christianity is concerned with, and it is only in subjectivity that its truth exists, if it exists at all; objectively, Christianity has absolutely no existence. If its truth happens to be in only a single subject, it exists in him alone; and there is greater Christian joy in heaven over this one individual than over universal history and the System, which as objective entities are incommensurable for that which is Christian.

It is commonly assumed that no art or skill is required in order to be subjective. To be sure, every human being is a bit of a subject, in a sense. But now to strive to become what one already is: who would take the pains to waste his time on such a task, involving the greatest imaginable degree of resignation? Quite so. But for this very reason alone it is a very difficult task, the most difficult of all tasks in fact, precisely because

every human being has a strong natural bent and passion to become something more and different. And so it is with all such apparently insignificant tasks, precisely their seeming insignificance makes them infinitely difficult. In such cases the task itself is not directly alluring, so as to support the aspiring individual; instead, it works against him, and it needs an infinite effort on his part merely to discover that his task lies here, that this is his task—an effort from which he is otherwise relieved. To think about the simple things of life, about what the plain man also knows after a fashion, is extremely forbidding; for the differential distinction attainable even through the utmost possible exertion is by no means obvious to the sensual man. No indeed, thinking about the highfalutin is very much more attractive and glorious.

When one overlooks this little distinction, humoristic from the Socratic standpoint and infinitely anxious from the Christian, between being something like a subject so called, and being a subject, or becoming one, or being what one is through having become what one is: then it becomes wisdom, the admired wisdom of our own age, that it is the task of the subject increasingly to divest himself of his subjectivity in order to become more and more objective. It is easy to see what this guidance understands by being a subject of a sort. It understands by it quite rightly the accidental, the angular, the selfish, the eccentric, and so forth, all of which every human being can have enough of. Nor does Christianity deny that such things should be gotten rid of; it has never been a friend of loutishness. But the difference is, that philosophy teaches that the way is to become objective, while Christianity teaches that the way is to become subjective, i.e. to become a subject in truth. Lest this should seem a mere dispute about words, let me say that Christianity wishes to intensify passion to its highest pitch; but passion is subjectivity, and does not exist objectively.

. . .

For example, the problem of *what it means to die*. I know concerning this what people in general know about it; I know that I shall die if I take a dose of sulphuric acid, and also if I drown myself, or go to sleep in an atmosphere of coal gas, and so forth. I know that Napoleon always went about with poison ready to hand, and that Juliet in Shakespeare poisoned herself. I know that the Stoics regarded suicide as a courageous deed, and that others consider it a cowardly act. I know that death may result from so ridiculous and trivial a circumstance that even the most serious-minded of men cannot help laughing at death; I know that it is possible to escape what appears to be certain death, and so forth. I know that the tragic hero dies in the fifth act of the drama, and that death here has an infinite significance in pathos; but that when a bartender dies, death does not have this significance. I know that the poet can interpret death in a diversity of moods, even to the limit of the comical; I pledge myself to produce the same diversity of effects in prose. I know furthermore what the clergy are accustomed to say on this subject, and I am familiar with the general run of themes treated at funerals. If nothing else stands in the way of my passing over to world-history, I am ready; I need only purchase black cloth for a ministerial gown, and I shall engage to preach funeral sermons as well as any ordinary clergyman. I freely admit that those who wear a velvet inset in their gowns do it more elegantly; but this distinction is not essential any more than the difference between five dollars and ten dollars for the hearse.

Nevertheless, in spite of this almost extraordinary knowledge or facility in knowledge, I can by no means regard death as something I have understood. Before I pass over to universal history—of which I must always say: "God knows whether it is any concern of yours"—it seems to me that I had better think about this, lest existence mock me, because I had become so learned and high-falutin that I had forgotten to understand what will some time happen to me as to every human being—sometime, nay, what am I saying: suppose death were so treacherous as to come tomorrow! Merely this one uncertainty, when it is to be understood and held fast by an existing individual, and hence enter into every thought, precisely because it is an uncertainty entering into my beginning upon universal history even, so that I make it clear to myself whether if death comes tomorrow, I am beginning upon something that is worth beginning—merely this one uncertainty generates inconceivable difficulties, difficulties that not even the speaker who treats of death is always aware of, in that he thinks that he apprehends the uncertainty of death, while nevertheless forgetting to think it into what he says about it, so that he speaks movingly and with emotion about the uncertainty of death, and yet ends by encouraging his hearers to make a resolution for the whole of life. This is essentially to forget the uncertainty of death, since otherwise the enthusiastic resolve for the whole of life must be made commensurable with the uncertainty of death. To think about it once for all, or once a year at matins on New Year's morning, is of course nonsense, and is the same as not thinking about it at all. If someone who thinks the thought in this manner also assumes to explain universal history, then it may well be that what he says about universal history is glorious, but what he says about death is stupid. If death is always uncertain, if I am a mortal creature, then it is impossible to understand this uncertainty in terms of a mere generality unless indeed I, too, happen to be merely a human being in general. But this is surely not the case, and it is only the absent-minded, like Soldin the bookseller for example, who are merely human beings in general. And if initially my human nature is merely an abstract something, it is at any rate the task which life sets me to become subjective; and in the same degree that I become subjective, the uncertainty of death comes more and more to interpenetrate my subjectivity dialectically. It thus becomes more and more important for me to think it in connection with every factor and phase of my life; for since the uncertainty is there in every moment, it can be overcome only by overcoming it in every moment.

If, on the other hand, the uncertainty of death is merely something in general, then my own death is itself only something in general. Perhaps this is also the case for systematic philosophers, for absent-minded people. For the late Herr Soldin, his own death is supposed to have been such a something in general: "when he was about to get up in the morning he was not aware that he was dead." But the fact of my own death is not for me by any means such a something in general, although for others, the fact of my death may indeed be something of that sort. Nor am *I* for myself such a something in general, although perhaps for others I may be a mere generality. But if the task of life is to become subjective, then every subject will *for himself* become the very opposite of such a something in general. And it would seem to be a somewhat embarrassing thing to be so significant for universal history, and then at home, in company with oneself, to be merely a something in general. It is already embarrassing enough for a man who is an extraordinarily important figure in the public assembly to come home to his wife, and then to be for her only such a something in general; or to be a world-historical

Diedrich Menschenschreck, and then at home to be—aye, I do not care to say anything more. But it is still more embarrassing to have so low a standing with oneself, and it is most embarrassing of all to remain unaware of the fact that this is so.

The lofty thinker who concerns himself with universal history can scarcely refuse me a reply to the question of what it means to die, and the instant he makes answer the dialectical process begins. Let him cite whatever reason he likes for not wishing to dwell at length upon such thoughts, it will not help him; for this reason will again be subjected to a dialectical inquiry to determine what it essentially means. I would thus have to ask whether it is in general possible to have an idea of death, whether death can be apprehended and experienced in an anticipatory conception, or whether its only being is its actual being. And since the actual being of death is a non-being, I should have to ask whether it follows as a consequence that death is only when it is not; or whether, in other words, the ideality of thought can overcome death by thinking it, or whether the material is victor in death, so that a human being dies like a dog, death being capable of being conquered only by the dying individual's apprehension of it in the very moment of death.

This difficulty can also be expressed as follows: Is it the case that the living individual is absolutely excluded from the possibility of approaching death in any sense whatever, since he cannot experimentally come near enough without comically sacrificing himself upon the altar of his own experiment, and since he cannot experientially restrain the experiment, and so learns nothing from it, being incapable of taking himself out of the experience so as to profit from it subsequently, but sticks fast in the experience. If the answer is given that one cannot apprehend death by means of any conception of it, the case is by no means closed. A negative answer is dialectically just as much in need of development and further determination as a positive answer, and only children and naïve people are satisfied with a *"dass weiss man nicht."* The thinker demands to know more, not indeed positively about what by supposition can be answered only negatively; but he demands to have it made dialectically clear that the answer must be negative; and this dialectical clarification sets this negative answer into relationship with all other existential problems, so that there will be difficulties no end.

If the answer to our question is affirmative, the question then arises as to what death is, and especially as to what it is for the living individual. We wish to know how the conception of death will transform a man's entire life, when in order to think its uncertainty he has to think it in every moment, so as to prepare himself for it. We wish to know what it means to prepare for death, since here again one must distinguish between its actual presence and the thought of it. This distinction appears to make all my preparation insignificant, if that which really comes is not that for which I prepared myself; and if it is the same, then my preparation is in its perfection identical with death itself. And I must take into account the fact that death may come in the very moment that I begin my preparation. The question must be raised of the possibility of finding an ethical expression for the significance of death, and a religious expression for the victory over death; one needs a solving word which explains its mystery, and a binding word by which the living individual defends himself against the ever recurrent conception; for surely we dare scarcely recommend mere thoughtlessness and forgetfulness as wisdom.

And furthermore, it is evident that when the subject thinks his own death,

this is a deed. For a man in general, for an absent-minded individual like Soldin or a systematic philosopher, to think death in general is indeed no act or deed; it is only a something in general, and what such a something in general really is, is at bottom a very difficult thing to say. But if the task of life is to become subjective, then the thought of death is not, for the individual subject, something in general, but is verily a deed. For the development of the subject consists precisely in his active interpenetration of himself by reaction concerning his own existence, so that he really thinks what he thinks through making a reality of it. He does not for example think, for the space of a passing moment: "Now you must attend to this thought every moment"; but he really does attend to it every moment. Here then everything becomes more and more subjective, as is quite natural when the task is to develop the subjectivity of the individual. In so far it might seem as if communication between man and man were abandoned to an unhampered freedom in lying and deception, if anyone so desires; for one need only say: "I have done so and so," and we can get no further with him. Well, what of it? But suppose he has not really done it? What business is that of mine? Such a deception would be worst for himself. When we speak about something objective it is easier to exercise a control over what is said; when, for example, a man says that Frederick the Sixth was an Emperor of China, we answer that this is a lie. But when a man speaks about death, and of how he has thought it and conceived its uncertainty, and so forth, it does not follow that he has really done it. Quite so. But there is a more artistic way of finding out whether he lies or not. Merely let him speak: if he is a deceiver, he will contradict himself precisely when he is engaged in offering the most solemn assurances. The contradiction will not be a direct one, but consists in the failure of the speech to include a consciousness of what the speech professes directly to assert. Objectively the assertion may be quite straight-forward; the man's only fault is that he speaks by rote.[1] That he also perspires and pounds the table with his fists, is not proof that he does not merely patter; it only goes to show that he is very stupid, or else that he has a secret consciousness that he is guilty of ranting. For it is exceedingly stupid to think that reciting something by rote could properly stir the emotions; since the emotional is the internal, while ranting is something external, like making water. And to imagine it possible to conceal the lack of inwardness by pounding the table, is a very mediocre notion of deception.

When death thus becomes something to be related to the entire life of the subject, I must confess I am very far indeed from having understood it, even if it were to cost me my life to make this confession. Still less have I realized the task existentially. And yet I have thought about this subject again and again; I have sought for guidance in books—and I have found none.[2]

---

[1] The reduplicated presence of the thought in every word, in every parenthetical expression, in the moment of digression, in the unguarded moment of unfolding a simile or portraying an image: this is what must be watched for if anyone wishes to take the trouble to find out whether a man is lying or not—provided one first watches oneself. For the ability to observe in this manner is the by-product of exercising a watchful restraint upon oneself; in that case, one receives as a free gift the capacity to notice such things, and will not in general be very eager to use it against others.
[2] Although I have said this often, I wish here again to repeat it: What is developed in these pages does not concern the simple-minded, who bear feelingly the burdens of life, and whom God wishes to preserve in their lovable simplicity, which feels no great need of any other sort of understanding. Or in so far as such need is felt, it tends to re-

For example, what does it mean to be immortal? In this respect, I know what people generally know. I know that some hold a belief in immortality, that others say they do not hold it; whether they actually do not hold it I know not; it does not occur to me therefore to want to combat them, for such an undertaking is so dialectically difficult that I should need a year and a day before it could become dialectically clear to me whether there is any reality in such a contest; whether the dialectic of communication, when it is properly understood, would approve of such a proceeding or transform it into a mere beating of the air; whether the consciousness of immortality is a doctrinal topic which is appropriate as a subject for instruction, and how the dialectic of instruction must be determined with relation to the learner's presuppositions; whether these presuppositions are not so essential that the instruction becomes a deception in case one is not at once aware of them, and in that event the instruction is transformed into non-instruction. Moreover, I know that some have found immortality in Hegel, others have not; I know that I have not found it in the System, where indeed it is also unreasonable to seek it; for, in a fantastic sense, all systematic thinking is *sub specie aeterni,* and to that extent immortality is there in the sense of eternity, but this immortality is not at all the one about

---

duce itself to a sigh over the ills of life, the sigh humbly finding solace in the thought that the real happiness of life does not consist in having knowledge. On the other hand it does concern those who deem themselves possessed of leisure and talent for a deeper inquiry. And it concerns such an one in the following manner: it seeks to estop him from thoughtlessly taking on universal history, without first considering in self-reflection that being an existing human individual is so strenuous and yet so natural a task for everyone, that one tends first as a matter of courage to apply himself to this task, and reasonably finds in the exertion thereto requisite, a sufficiency for his entire life.

which the question is asked, since the question is about the immortality of a mortal, which is not answered by showing that the eternal is immortal, and the immortality of the eternal is a tautology and a misuse of words. I have read Professor Heiberg's *Soul after Death,* indeed I have read it with the commentary of Dean Tryde. Would I had not done so; for one rejoices aesthetically in a poetic word and does not require the utmost dialectical precision which is appropriate in the case of a learner who would direct his life in accordance with such guidance. If a commentator compels me to seek for something of that sort in the poem, he has done no service to the poem. From the commentator I could perhaps hope to learn what I have not learnt from the commentary, if Dean Tryde with catechetical instruction were to take pity on me and show how one constructs a lifeview upon the profundities he has propounded by paraphrasing the poem. For honor be to Dean Tryde—merely from that little article it would surely be possible to construct several different lifeviews—but I cannot make *one* out of it, and that, alas, is precisely the misfortune, for it is one I need, no more, since I am not a learned man. I know, moreover, that the late Professor Poul Møller, who was well acquainted after all with the newest philosophy, became aware only in his latest period, of the infinite difficulty of the question of immortality, when the question is simply put, when one does not ask about a new proof and about the opinions of Tom, Dick and Harry strung upon a thread. I know also that in a treatise he sought to explain himself, and that this treatise clearly bears the mark of his aversion to speculation. The difficulty of the question arises precisely when it is simply put, not as the well-trained *Privatdocent* enquires about the immortality of man, the abstractly understood man in general, man being understood fantastically as

the race, and so about the immortality of the human race. Such a well-trained *Privatdocent* raises and answers the question in such a way as the well-trained reader conceives that it ought to be done. A poor untrained reader is only made a fool of by such reflections, like one who overhears an examination in which the questions and answers have been agreed upon beforehand, or like one who enters a family circle which has its own language, using words of the mother tongue, but understanding something different by them. It follows from this, generally speaking, that the answer is very easy, owing to the fact that they have altered the question, wherefore one cannot deny that they answer the question, but one can indeed affirm that the question is not what it seems to be. When, in an examination, the teacher is to test the knowledge of Danish history, and, seeing that the pupil can make nothing of it, gives the examination a different turn, as by asking about the relationship of another country to Denmark, and thereupon asking about the history of this other land —can one say that there was an examination on the history of Denmark? When school children write a word in their books with a reference to p. 101 and p. 101, see p. 216 and p. 216, see p. 314, and then finally, April Fool—can one justly say that one profits by this guidance . . . to be made a fool of? A book raises the question of the immortality of the soul. The contents of the book constitute the answer. But the contents of the book, as the reader can convince himself by reading it through, are the opinions of the wisest and best men about immortality, all neatly strung on a thread. Oh! thou great Chinese god! Is this immortality? So then the question about immortality is a learned question. All honor to learning! All honor to him who can handle learnedly the learned question of immortality! But the question of immortality is essentially not a learned question, rather it is a question of inwardness, which the subject by becoming subjective must put to himself. Objectively the question cannot be answered, because objectively it cannot be put, since immortality precisely is the potentiation and highest development of the developed subjectivity. Only by really willing to become subjective can the question properly emerge, therefore how could it be answered objectively? The question cannot be answered in social terms, for in social terms it cannot be expressed, inasmuch as only the subject who wills to become subjective can conceive the question and ask rightly, "Do *I* become immortal, or am *I* immortal?" Of course, people can combine for many things; thus several families can combine for a box at the theater, and three single gentlemen can combine for a riding horse, so that each of them rides every third day. But it is not so with immortality; the consciousness of my immortality belongs to me alone, precisely at the moment when I am conscious of my immortality I am absolutely subjective, and I cannot become immortal in partnership with three single gentlemen in turn. People who go about with a paper soliciting the endorsement of numerous men and women, who feel a need in general to become immortal, get no reward for their pains, for immortality is not a possession which can be extorted by a list of endorsements. Systematically, immortality cannot be proved at all. The fault does not lie in the proofs, but in the fact that people will not understand that viewed systematically the whole question is nonsense, so that instead of seeking outward proofs, one had better seek to become a little subjective. Immortality is the most passionate interest of subjectivity; precisely in the interest lies the proof. When for the sake of objectivity (quite consistently from the systematic point of view), one systematically ignores the interest, God only knows in this case what immortality is, or even what is the sense of wishing to prove it, or how one could get into one's head the fixed idea of bothering about it. If one were systematically to hang up immortality on the wall, like Gessler's hat, before which we take off our hats as we pass by, that would not be equivalent to being immortal or to being conscious of one's immortality. The incredible pains the System takes to prove immortality is labor lost and a ludicrous contradiction—to want to answer systematically a question which possesses the remarkable trait that systematically it cannot be put. This is like wanting to paint Mars in the armor which rendered him invisible. The very point lies in the invisibility; and in the case of immortality, the point lies in the subjectivity and in the subjective development of the subjectivity.

Quite simply therefore the existing subject asks, not about immortality in general, for such a phantom has no existence, but about his immortality, about what it means to become immortal, whether he is able to contribute anything to the accomplishment of this end, or whether he becomes immortal as a matter of course, or whether he is that and can become it. In the first case, he asks what significance it may have, if any, that he has let time pass unutilized, whether there is perhaps a greater and a lesser immortality. In the second case, he asks what significance it may have for the whole of his human existence that the highest thing in life becomes something like a prank, so that the passion of freedom within him is relegated to lower tasks but has nothing to do with the highest, not even negatively, for a negative employment with relation to the highest thing would in a way be the most extenuating—when one wanted to do everything enthusiastically with all one's might, and then to ascertain that the utmost one can do is to maintain a receptive attitude towards that thing which one would more than gladly do everything to earn. The question is raised, how he is to comport himself in talking about his immortality, how he can at one and the same time talk from the standpoint of infinity and of finiteness and think these two together in one single instant, so that he does not say now the one and now the other; how language and all modes of communication are related thereto, when all depends upon being consistent in every word, lest the little heedless supplementary word, the chatty subordinate phrase, might intervene and mock the whole thing; where may be the place, so to speak, for talking about immortality, where such a place exists, since he well knows how many pulpits there are in Copenhagen, and that there are two chairs of philosophy, but where the place is which is the unity of infinitude and finiteness, where he, who is at one and the same time infinite and finite, can talk in one breath of his infinitude and his finiteness, whether it is possible to find a place so dialectically difficult, which nevertheless is so necessary to find. The question is raised, how he, while he exists, can hold fast his consciousness of immortality, lest the metaphysical conception of immortality proceed to confuse the ethical and reduce it to an illusion; for ethically, everything culminates in immortality, without which the ethical is merely use and wont, and metaphysically, immortality swallows up existence, yea, the seventy years of existence, as a thing of naught, and yet ethically this naught must be of infinite importance. The question is raised, how immortality practically transforms his life; in what sense he must have the consciousness of it always present to him, or whether perhaps it is enough to think this thought once for all, whether it is not true that, if the answer is to this effect, the answer shows that the problem has not been stated, inasmuch as to such a consciousness of immortality once for all

there would correspond the notion of being a subject as it were in general, whereby the question about immortality is made fantastically ludicrous, just as the converse is ludicrous, when people who have fantastically made a mess of everything and have been every possible sort of thing, one day ask the clergyman with deep concern whether in the beyond they will then really be the same—after never having been able in their lifetime to be the same for a fortnight, and hence have undergone all sorts of transformations. Thus immortality would be indeed an extraordinary metamorphosis if it could transform such an inhuman centipede into an eternal identity with itself, which this "being the same" amounts to. He asks about whether it is now definitely determined that he is immortal, about what this determinateness of immortality is; whether this determinateness, when he lets it pass for something once for all determined (employing his life to attend to his fields, to take to himself a wife, to arrange world-history) is not precisely indeterminateness, so that in spite of all determinateness he has not got any further, because the problem is not even conceived, but since he has not employed his life to become subjective, his subjectivity has become some sort of an indeterminate something in general, and that abstract determinateness has become therefore precisely indeterminateness; whether this determinateness (if he employs his life to become subjective) is not rendered so dialectically difficult, by the constant effort to adapt himself to the alternation which is characteristic of existence, that it becomes indeterminateness; whether, if this is the highest he attains to (namely, that the determinateness becomes indeterminateness), it were not better to give the whole thing up; or whether he is to fix his whole passion upon the indeterminateness, and with infinite passionateness embrace the indeterminateness of the determinate; and whether this might be the only way by which he can attain knowledge of his immortality so long as he is existing, because as exister he is marvelously compounded, so that the determinateness of immortality can only be possessed determinately by the Eternal, but by an exister can be possessed only in indeterminateness.

And the fact of asking about his immortality is at the same time for the existing subject who raises the question a deed—as it is not, to be sure, for absent-minded people who once in a while ask about the matter of being immortal quite in general, as if immortality were something one has once in a while, and the question were some sort of thing in general. So he asks how he is to behave in order to express in existence his immortality, whether he is really expressing it; and for the time being, he is satisfied with this task, which surely must be enough to last a man a lifetime since it is to last for an eternity. And then? Well, then, when he has completed this task, then comes the turn for world-history. In these days, to be sure, it is just the other way round: now people apply themselves first to world-history, and therefore there comes out of this the ludicrous result (as another author has remarked), that while people are proving and proving immortality quite in general, faith in immortality is more and more diminishing.

. . .

CHAPTER II

THE SUBJECTIVE TRUTH,
INWARDNESS: TRUTH IS
SUBJECTIVITY

. . .

In an attempt to make clear the difference of way that exists between an objective and a subjective reflection, I shall now proceed to show how a subjective reflection makes its way inwardly in inwardness. Inwardness in an existing subject culminates in passion; corresponding to passion in the subject the truth becomes a paradox; and the fact that the truth becomes a paradox is rooted precisely in its having a relationship to an existing subject. Thus the one corresponds to the other. By forgetting that one is an existing subject, passion goes by the board and the truth is no longer a paradox; the knowing subject becomes a fantastic entity rather than a human being, and the truth becomes a fantastic object for the knowledge of this fantastic entity.

When the question of truth is raised in an objective manner, reflection is directed objectively to the truth, as an object to which the knower is related. Reflection is not focussed upon the relationship, however, but upon the question of whether it is the truth to which the knower is related. If only the object to which he is related is the truth, the subject is accounted to be in the truth. When the question of the truth is raised subjectively, reflection is directed subjectively to the nature of the individual's relationship; if only the mode of this relationship is in the truth, the individual is in the truth even if he should happen to be thus related to what is not true.[1] Let us take as an example the knowledge of God. Objectively, reflection is directed to the problem of whether this object is the true God; subjectively, reflection is directed to the question whether the individual is related to a something *in such a manner* that his relationship is in truth a God-relationship. On which side is the truth now to be found? Ah, may we not

---

[1] The reader will observe that the question here is about essential truth, or about the truth which is essentially related to existence, and that it is precisely for the sake of clarifying it as inwardness or as subjectivity that this contrast is drawn.

here resort to a mediation, and say: It is on neither side, but in the mediation of both? Excellently well said, provided we might have it explained how an existing individual manages to be in a state of mediation. For to be in a state of mediation is to be finished, while to exist is to become. Nor can an existing individual be in two places at the same time—he cannot be an identity of subject and object. When he is nearest to being in two places at the same time he is in passion; but passion is momentary, and passion is also the highest expression of subjectivity.

The existing individual who chooses to pursue the objective way enters upon the entire approximation-process by which it is proposed to bring God to light objectively. But this is in all eternity impossible, because God is a subject, and therefore exists only for subjectivity in inwardness. The existing individual who chooses the subjective way apprehends instantly the entire dialectical difficulty involved in having to use some time, perhaps a long time, in finding God objectively; and he feels this dialectical difficulty in all its painfulness, because every moment is wasted in which he does not have God.[2] That very instant he has God, not by virtue of any objective deliberation, but by virtue of the infinite passion of inwardness. The objective inquirer, on the other hand, is not embarrassed by such dialectical difficulties as are involved in devoting an

entire period of investigation to finding God—since it is possible that the inquirer may die tomorrow; and if he lives he can scarcely regard God as something to be taken along if convenient, since God is precisely that which one takes *a tout prix,* which in the understanding of passion constitutes the true inward relationship to God.

It is at this point, so difficult dialectically, that the way swings off for everyone who knows what it means to think, and to think existentially; which is something very different from sitting at a desk and writing about what one has never done, something very different from writing *de omnibus dubitandum* and at the same time being as credulous existentially as the most sensuous of men. Here is where the way swings off, and the change is marked by the fact that while objective knowledge rambles comfortably on by way of the long road of approximation without being impelled by the urge of passion, subjective knowledge counts every delay a deadly peril, and the decision so infinitely important and so instantly pressing that it is as if the opportunity had already passed.

Now when the problem is to reckon up on which side there is most truth, whether on the side of one who seeks the true God objectively, and pursues the approximate truth of the God-idea; or on the side of one who, driven by the infinite passion of his need of God, feels an infinite concern for his own relationship to God in truth (and to be at one and the same time on both sides equally, is as we have noted not possible for an existing individual, but is merely the happy delusion of an imaginary I-am-I): the answer cannot be in doubt for anyone who has not been demoralized with the aid of science. If one who lives in the midst of Christendom goes up to the house of God, the house of the true God, with the true conception of God in his knowledge, and prays, but prays

---

[2] In this manner God certainly becomes a postulate, but not in the otiose manner in which this word is commonly understood. It becomes clear rather that the only way in which an existing individual comes into relation with God, is when the dialectical contradiction brings his passion to the point of despair, and helps him to embrace God with the "category of despair" (faith). Then the postulate is so far from being arbitrary that it is precisely a life-necessity. It is then not so much that God is a postulate, as that the existing individual's postulation of God is a necessity.

in a false spirit; and one who lives in an idolatrous community prays with the entire passion of the infinite, although his eyes rest upon the image of an idol: where is there most truth? The one prays in truth to God though he worships an idol; the other prays falsely to the true God, and hence worships in fact an idol.

When one man investigates objectively the problem of immortality, and another embraces an uncertainty with the passion of the infinite: where is there most truth, and who has the greater certainty? The one has entered upon a never-ending approximation, for the certainty of immortality lies precisely in the subjectivity of the individual; the other is immortal, and fights for his immortality by struggling with the uncertainty. Let us consider Socrates. Nowadays everyone dabbles in a few proofs; some have several such proofs, others fewer. But Socrates! He puts the question objectively in a problematic manner: *if* there is an immortality. He must therefore be accounted a doubter in comparison with one of our modern thinkers with the three proofs? By no means. On this "if" he risks his entire life, he has the courage to meet death, and he has with the passion of the infinite so determined the pattern of his life that it must be found acceptable—*if* there is an immortality. Is any better proof capable of being given for the immortality of the soul? But those who have the three proofs do not at all determine their lives in conformity therewith; if there is an immortality it must feel disgust over their manner of life: can any better refutation be given of the three proofs? The bit of uncertainty that Socrates had, helped him because he himself contributed the passion of the infinite; the three proofs that the others have do not profit them at all, because they are dead to spirit and enthusiasm, and their three proofs, in lieu of proving anything else, prove just this. A young girl may enjoy all the sweetness of love on the basis of what is merely a weak hope that she is beloved, because she rests everything on this weak hope; but many a wedded matron more than once subjected to the strongest expressions of love, has in so far indeed had proofs, but strangely enough has not enjoyed *quod erat demonstrandum*. The Socratic ignorance, which Socrates held fast with the entire passion of his inwardness, was thus an expression for the principle that the eternal truth is related to an existing individual, and that this truth must therefore be a paradox for him as long as he exists; and yet it is possible that there was more truth in the Socratic ignorance as it was in him, than in the entire objective truth of the System, which flirts with what the times demand and accommodates itself to *Privatdocents*.

The objective accent falls on WHAT is said, the subjective accent on HOW it is said. This distinction holds even in the aesthetic realm, and receives definite expression in the principle that what is in itself true may in the mouth of such and such a person become untrue. In these times this distinction is particularly worthy of notice, for if we wish to express in a single sentence the difference between ancient times and our own, we should doubtless have to say: "In ancient times only an individual here and there knew the truth; now all know it, except that the inwardness of its appropriation stands in an inverse relationship to the extent of its dissemination.[3] Aesthetically

---

[3] *Stages on Life's Way,* Note on p. 426. Though ordinarily not wishing an expression of opinion on the part of reviewers, I might at this point almost desire it, provided such opinions, so far from flattering me, amounted to an assertion of the daring truth that what I say is something that everybody knows, even every child, and that the cultured know infinitely much better. If it only stands fast that everyone knows it, my standpoint is in order, and I shall doubtless make shift to manage with the unity of the comic and the tragic. If there were anyone who did not

the contradiction that truth becomes untruth in this or that person's mouth, is best construed comically: In the ethicoreligious sphere, accent is again on the "how." But this is not to be understood as referring to demeanor, expression, or the like; rather it refers to the relationship sustained by the existing individual, in his own existence, to the content of his utterance. Objectively the interest is focussed merely on the thought-content, subjectively on the inwardness. At its maximum this inward "how" is the passion of the infinite, and the passion of the infinite is the truth. But the passion of the infinite is precisely subjectivity, and thus subjectivity becomes the truth. Objectively there is no infinite decisiveness, and hence it is objectively in order to annul the difference between good and evil, together with the principle of contradiction, and therewith also the infinite difference between the true and the false. Only in subjectivity is there decisiveness, to seek objectivity is to be in error. It is the passion of the infinite that is the decisive factor and not its content, for its content is precisely itself. In this manner subjectivity and the subjective "how" constitute the truth.

But the "how" which is thus subjectively accentuated precisely because the subject is an existing individual, is also subject to a dialectic with respect to time. In the passionate moment of decision,

where the road swings away from objective knowledge, it seems as if the infinite decision were thereby realized. But in the same moment the existing individual finds himself in the temporal order, and the subjective "how" is transformed into a striving, a striving which receives indeed its impulse and a repeated renewal from the decisive passion of the infinite, but is nevertheless a striving.

When subjectivity is the truth, the conceptual determination of the truth must include an expression for the antithesis to objectivity, a memento of the fork in the road where the way swings off; this expression will at the same time serve as an indication of the tension of the subjective inwardness. Here is such a definition of truth: *An objective uncertainty held fast in an appropriation-process of the most passionate inwardness is the truth,* the highest truth attainable for an *existing* individual. At the point where the way swings off (and where this is cannot be specified objectively, since it is a matter of subjectivity), there objective knowledge is placed in abeyance. Thus the subject merely has, objectively, the uncertainty; but it is this which precisely increases the tension of that infinite passion which constitutes his inwardness. The truth is precisely the venture which chooses an objective uncertainty with the passion of the infinite. I contemplate the order of nature in the hope of finding God, and I see omnipotence and wisdom; but I also see much else that disturbs my mind and excites anxiety. The sum of all this is an objective uncertainty. But it is for this very reason that the inwardness becomes as intense as it is, for it embraces this objective uncertainty with the entire passion of the infinite. In the case of a mathematical proposition the objectivity is given, but for this reason the truth of such a proposition is also an indifferent truth.

But the above definition of truth is

___

know it I might perhaps be in danger of being dislodged from my position of equilibrium by the thought that I might be in a position to communicate to someone the needful preliminary knowledge. It is just this which engages my interest so much, this that the cultured are accustomed to say: that everyone knows what the highest is. This was not the case in paganism, nor in Judaism, nor in the seventeen centuries of Christianity. Hail to the nineteenth century! Everyone knows it. What progress has been made since the time when only a few knew it. To make up for this, perhaps, we must assume that no one nowadays does it.

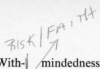
RISK/FAITH

an equivalent expression for faith. Without risk there is no faith. Faith is precisely the contradiction between the infinite passion of the individual's inwardness and the objective uncertainty. If I am capable of grasping God objectively, I do not believe, but precisely because I cannot do this I must believe. If I wish to preserve myself in faith I must constantly be intent upon holding fast the objective uncertainty, so as to remain out upon the deep, over seventy thousand fathoms of water, still preserving my faith.

In the principle that subjectivity, inwardness, is the truth, there is comprehended the Socratic wisdom, whose everlasting merit it was to have become aware of the essential significance of existence, of the fact that the knower is an existing individual. For this reason Socrates was in the truth by virtue of his ignorance, in the highest sense in which this was possible within paganism. To attain to an understanding of this, to comprehend that the misfortune of speculative philosophy is again and again to have forgotten that the knower is an existing individual, is in our objective age difficult enough. "But to have made an advance upon Socrates without even having understood what he understood, is at any rate not 'Socratic.' "

. . .

When Socrates believed that there was a God, he held fast to the objective uncertainty with the whole passion of his inwardness, and it is precisely in this contradiction and in this risk, that faith is rooted. Now it is otherwise. Instead of the objective uncertainty, there is here a certainty, namely, that objectively it is absurd; and this absurdity, held fast in the passion of inwardness, is faith. The Socratic ignorance is as a witty jest in comparison with the earnestness of facing the absurd; and the Socratic existential inwardness is as Greek light-mindedness in comparison with the grave strenuosity of faith.

What now is the absurd? The absurd is—that the eternal truth has come into being in time, that God has come into being, has been born, has grown up, and so forth, precisely like any other individual human being, quite indistinguishable from other individuals. For every assumption of immediate recognizability is pre-Socratic paganism, and from the Jewish point of view, idolatry; and every determination of what really makes an advance beyond the Socratic must essentially bear the stamp of having a relationship to God's having come into being; for faith *sensu strictissimo,* as was developed in the *Fragments,* refers to becoming. When Socrates believed that there was a God, he saw very well that where the way swings off there is also an objective way of approximation, for example by the contemplation of nature and human history, and so forth. His merit was precisely to shun this way, where the quantitative siren song enchants the mind and deceives the existing individual.

In relation to the absurd, the objective approximation-process is like the comedy, *Misunderstanding upon Misunderstanding,* which is generally played by *Privatdocents,* and speculative philosophers. The absurd is precisely by its objective repulsion the measure of the intensity of faith in inwardness. Suppose a man who wishes to acquire faith; let the comedy begin. He wishes to have faith, but he wishes also to safeguard himself by means of an objective inquiry and its approximation-process. What happens? With the help of the approximation-process the absurd becomes something different; it becomes probable, it becomes increasingly probable, it becomes extremely and emphatically probable. Now he is ready to believe it, and he ventures to claim for himself that he does not believe as shoemakers and tailors and

THE ABSURD

simple folk believe, but only after long deliberation. Now he is ready to believe it; and lo, now it has become precisely impossible to believe it. Anything that is almost probable, or probable, or extremely and emphatically probable, is something he can almost know, or as good as know, or extremely and emphatically almost *know*—but it is impossible to *believe*. For the absurd is the object of faith, and the only object that can be believed.

Or suppose a man who says that he has faith, but desires to make his faith clear to himself, so as to understand himself in his faith. Now the comedy again begins. The object of faith becomes almost probable, as good as probable, extremely and emphatically probable. He has completed his investigations, and he ventures to claim for himself that he does not believe as shoemakers and tailors and other simple folk believe, but that he has also understood himself in his believing. Strange understanding! On the contrary, he has in fact learned something else about faith than when he believed; and he has learned that he no longer believes, since he almost knows, or as good as knows, or extremely and emphatically almost knows.

In so far as the absurd comprehends within itself the factor of becoming, one way of approximation will be that which confuses the absurd fact of such a becoming (which is the object of faith) with a simple historical fact, and hence seeks historical certainty for that which is absurd, because it involves the contradiction that something which can become historical only in direct opposition to all human reason, has become historical. It is this contradiction which constitutes the absurd, and which can only be believed. If historical certainty with respect to it is assumed, the certainty attained is merely that the something which is thus assumed as certain is not the thing in question. A witness can testify that he

has believed it, and hence that so far from being an historical certainty it is directly contrary to his own reason; but such a witness thrusts the individual away in precisely the same sense that the absurd itself does. And a witness who does not so repel is *eo ipso* a deceiver, or a man who talks about something quite different, and can help only to obtain certainty about something quite different. A hundred thousand individual witnesses, who are individual witnesses precisely on account of the peculiar character of their testimony (that they have believed the absurd), cannot *en masse* become anything else, so as to make the absurd less absurd—and why less absurd? Because a hundred thousand human beings have separately, each one for himself, believed that it was absurd? On the contrary, these hundred thousand witnesses again exercise a repellent influence in nearly the same way that the absurd itself exercises it.

But this I need not here expound in greater detail. In the *Fragments* (especially where the distinction between the disciple at first-hand and at second-hand is shown to be illusory), and in the first part of this book, I have already carefully enough expounded the thesis that all approximation is useless, since on the contrary it behooves us to get rid of introductory guarantees of security, proofs from consequences, and the whole mob of public pawnbrokers and guarantors, so as to permit the absurd to stand out in all its clarity—in order that the individual may believe if he wills it; I merely say that it must be strenuous in the highest degree so to believe.

If speculative philosophy wishes to take cognizance of this, and say as always, that there is no paradox when the matter is viewed eternally, divinely, theocentrically—then I admit that I am not in a position to determine whether the speculative philosopher is right, for I am only a poor existing human being, not competent to contemplate the eternal either eternally or divinely or theocentrically, but compelled to content myself with existing. So much is certain, however, that speculative philosophy carries everything back, back past the Socratic position, which at least comprehended that for an existing individual existence is essential; to say nothing of the failure of speculative philosophy to take time to grasp what it means to be so critically situated in existence as the existing individual in the experiment.

The difference between the Socratic position as here described and the position which goes beyond it is clear enough, and essentially the same as in the *Fragments*. For nothing is altered in the latter, and the former is made only a little more difficult, though not more difficult than it is. The difficulty has also been a little increased by the fact that while in the *Fragments* I merely brought out the thought-determinations of the paradox experimentally, I have here at the same time subjoined an attempt latently to make the necessity of the paradox evident. Even if this attempt is somewhat weak, it is at any rate rather different from the speculative annulment of the paradox.

Christianity has declared itself to be the eternal essential truth which has come into being in time. It has proclaimed itself as the *Paradox,* and it has required of the individual the inwardness of faith in relation to that which stamps itself as an offense to the Jews and a folly to the Greeks—and an absurdity to the understanding. It is impossible more strongly to express the fact that subjectivity is truth, and that the objectivity is repellent, repellent even by virtue of its absurdity. And indeed it would seem very strange that Christianity should have come into the world merely to receive an explanation; as if it had been somewhat bewildered about itself, and hence entered the world to consult that wise man, the speculative philosopher, who can come to its assistance by furnishing the explanation. It is impossible to express with more intensive inwardness the principle that subjectivity is truth, than when subjectivity is in the first instance untruth, and yet subjectivity is the truth.

Suppose Christianity to be a mystery and intentionally so, a genuine and not a theatrical mystery, which is revealed in the fifth act of the drama, while a clever spectator sees through it in the course of the exposition. Suppose that a revelation *sensu strictissimo* must be a mystery, and that its sole and sufficient mark is precisely that it is a mystery; while a revelation *sensu laxiori,* the withdrawal by way of recollection into the eternal, is a revelation in the direct sense. Suppose that the degree of intellectual talent in relation to the misunderstanding was marked by the varying ability of the individual to make it seem more and more deceptively plausible that he had understood the mystery. Suppose it were after all a blessed thing, critically situated in the extreme press of existence, to sustain a relation to this mystery without understanding it, merely as a believer. Suppose Christianity never intended to be understood; suppose that, in order to express this, and to prevent anyone from misguidedly entering upon the objective way, it has declared itself to be the paradox. Suppose it wished to have significance only for existing individuals, and essentially for existing individuals in inwardness, in the inwardness of faith; which cannot be expressed more definitely than in the proposition that Christianity is the absurd, held fast in the passion of the infinite. Suppose it refuses to be understood, and that the maximum of understanding which could come in question is to understand that is cannot be understood. Suppose it therefore accentuates existence so decisively that the individual becomes a sinner, Christianity the paradox, existence the period of decision. Suppose that speculation were a temptation, the most dubious of all. Suppose that the speculative philosopher is, not indeed the prodigal son, for so the anxious divinity would characterize only the offended individual whom he nevertheless continues to love, but is the naughty child who refuses to remain where existing individuals belong, namely, in the existential training school where one becomes mature only through inwardness in existing, but instead demands a place in the divine council chamber, constantly shouting that viewed eternally, divinely, theocentrically, there is no paradox. Suppose the speculative philosopher were the restless tenant, who though it is notorious that he is merely a tenant, in view of the abstract truth that all property is from the standpoint of the eternal and the divine, in common, insists on playing the owner, so that there is nothing else to do than to send for an officer to say to him what the policemen said to Geert Westphaler: "It hurts us to have to come on such an errand."

Has the thing of being human now become somewhat different from what it was in older times, are the conditions not still the same, namely, to be a particular existing being, for whom existing is essential as long as he continues in existence? But men have now so much more knowledge than formerly. Quite true, but suppose Christianity is not a matter of knowledge, so that the increased knowledge is of no avail, except to make it easier to fall into the confusion of considering Christianity as a matter of knowledge. And if men do have more knowledge, and we are not speaking about the knowledge of railroads, machines, and kaleidoscopes, but knowledge about the religious, how have they acquired it? Surely with the aid of Christianity. So this is the way men show their gratitude. They learn something from Christianity,

misunderstand it, and by way of additional misunderstanding use it against Christianity. If in olden times the fearful thing was that one might be offended, now the fearful thing is that there is nothing fearful any more, that in a trice, before the individual has time to look around, he becomes a philosopher who speculates over faith. And over what faith does he speculate? Is it over the faith that he has, and especially over whether he has it or not? Ah, no, such a subject is too trifling for an objective speculative philosopher. What he speculates about is the objective faith. The objective faith, what does that mean? It means a sum of doctrinal propositions. But suppose Christianity were nothing of the kind; suppose on the contrary it were inwardness, and hence also the paradox, so as to thrust the individual away objectively, in order to obtain significance for the existing individual in the inwardness of his existence, in order to place him as decisively as no judge can place an accused person, between time and eternity in time, between heaven and hell in the time of salvation. The objective faith—it is as if Christianity also had been promulgated as a little system, if not quite so good as the Hegelian; it is as if Christ—aye, I speak without offense —it is as if Christ were a professor, and as if the Apostles had formed a little scientific society. Verily, if it was once difficult to become a Christian, now I believe it becomes increasingly difficult year by year, because it has now become so easy that the only ambition which stirs any competition is that of becoming a speculative philosopher. And yet the speculative philosopher is perhaps at the farthest possible remove from Christianity, and it is perhaps far preferable to be an offended individual who nevertheless sustains a relation to Christianity than a speculative philosopher who assumes to have understood it. In so far there is hope that there will be some resemblance left between a Christian now and in the earliest days, so that it will again be regarded as folly for anyone to entertain the notion of becoming a Christian. In the earliest days the Christian was a fool in the eyes of the world, and to Jews and pagans alike it seemed folly for anyone to seek to become one. Now we are Christians as a matter of course, but if anyone desires to be a Christian with infinite passion he is judged to be a fool, just as it is always folly to put forth an infinite passionate exertion for the sake of becoming what one already is; as if a man were to sacrifice all his wealth to buy a jewel—which he already owned. Formerly a Christian was a fool in the eyes of the world, and now that all men are Christians he nevertheless becomes a fool—in the eyes of Christians.

. . .

What does it mean in general to explain anything? Does it consist in showing that the obscure something in question is not this but something else? This would be a strange sort of an explanation; I thought it was the function of an explanation to render it evident that the something in question was this definite thing, so that the explanation took the obscurity away but not the object. Otherwise the explanation would not be an explanation, but something quite different, namely, a correction. An explanation of the paradox makes it clear what the paradox is, removing any obscurity remaining; a correction takes the paradox away, and makes it clear that there is no paradox. But if the paradox arises from putting the eternal and an existing particular human being into relation with one another, when the speculative explanation takes the paradox away, does the explanation also take existence away from the existing individual? And when an existing individual, with or without assistance from another, has arrived at or been brought to the point where it

seems to him as nearly as possible that he does not exist, what is he then? Why, then he is absent-minded. So that the explanation of the absolute paradox which concludes that there is no paradox except to a certain degree, which means that there are only relative paradoxes, is an explanation not for existing individuals, but for absent-minded persons. Thus everything is in order. The explanation is that the paradox is the paradox only to a certain degree, and it is quite in order that such an explanation should be valid for an existing individual who is an existing individual only to a certain degree, since he forgets it every other moment. Such an existing individual is precisely a person who suffers from absent-mindedness.

When one ventures to speak of the absolute paradox, characterizing it as a stumblingblock to the Jews, foolishness to the Greeks, and an absurdity to the understanding, and in this connection addresses himself to speculative philosophy, philosophy is not so impolite as to tell him directly that he is a fool. But it offers him an explanation which contains a correction, thus indirectly giving him to understand that he is in error; so a humane and superior mind always deals with an individual of more limited intelligence. The procedure is strictly Socratic; the only thing that might be un-Socratic in this connection would be if the speaker were after all much nearer the truth than the speculative explanation, in which case the difference would be that while Socrates politely and indirectly took away an error from the learner and gave him the truth, speculative philosophy takes the truth away politely and indirectly, and presents the learner with an error. But the politeness remains as the common feature. And when Christianity itself declares that it is a paradox, the speculative explanation is not an explanation but a correction, a polite and indirect correction to be sure, as befits a superior intelligence over against a more limited understanding.

To *explain* the paradox: is that tantamount to reducing the term paradox to a *rhetorical expression,* to something which the worshipful speculative philosopher asserts to have indeed a certain validity—but then again also not to have validity? In that case it remains true after all *summa summarum* that there is no paradox. All honor to the Herr Professor! It is not to take his honor away from him that I say this, as if I, too, could revoke the paradox—by no means. But when the professor has abrogated the paradox it is of course abrogated, and so I may venture to say that it is abrogated —unless the abrogation concerned the professor more than the paradox, so that he, instead of abrogating the paradox, himself became a sort of dubious fantastic abrogation. In other cases it is assumed that explaining something means to make it clear in its significance, that it is this and not something else. To explain the paradox would then mean to understand more and more profoundly what a paradox is, and that the paradox is the paradox.

God is a highest conception, not to be explained in terms of other things, but explainable only by exploring more and more profoundly the conception itself. The highest principles for all thought can be demonstrated only indirectly (negatively). Suppose then that the paradox were the limit for an existing individual's relationship to an eternal essential truth; in that case the paradox would also not be explainable in terms of anything else, when the explanation is to be an explanation for existing individuals. But in the speculative interpretation even the absolute paradox (for speculative philosophy is not afraid to use decisive expressions, the only thing it is afraid of is thinking anything decisive in connection with them) expresses only the relative difference between more and less gifted and cultured men. In this manner the face of the world will gradually be changed. When Christianity came into the world there were no professors and *Privatdocents* at all; then it was a paradox for everyone. In the present generation it may be assumed that one out of every ten is a *Privatdocent;* hence Christianity is a paradox for nine out of ten. And when finally the fullness of time arrives, that extraordinary future when an entire generation of male and female *Privatdocents* peoples the earth, then Christianity will have ceased to be a paradox.

Whoever, on the other hand, takes it upon himself to explain the paradox, under the supposition that he knows his own mind in the matter, will precisely concentrate his energies upon making it clear that it must be a paradox. To explain an unutterable joy, for example, what does that mean? Does it mean to explain that it is this or that? In that case the predicate "unutterable" becomes merely a rhetorical predicate, a strong expression, and the like. The explaining prestidigitator has everything in readiness for the performance, and now it begins. He dupes the hearer, he calls the joy unutterable—and then comes the surprise, a truly surprising surprise: he gives it utterance! But suppose the inexpressible joy had its ground in the contradiction that an existing human being is a synthesis of the infinite and the finite situated in time, so that the joy of the eternal in him becomes inexpressible because he is an existing individual, becomes a highest breath of the spirit which is nevertheless incapable of finding embodiment, because the existing individual exists: then the explanation would be that it is unutterable, that it cannot be otherwise; no nonsense please. But when a man of profundity first condemns one or another for denying that there is an inexpressible you, and then goes on to say: "No, I assume the existence of an inexpressible joy, and then goes on to I go further and express it,"—he merely turns himself into a fool, and differs from the other whom he condemns only in so far that the other is more honest and straightforward, and says what the man of profundity also says, since both say essentially the same thing.

. . .

Let us take the paradox of the forgiveness of sins. Forgiveness is a paradox in the Socratic sense, in so far as it involves a relationship between the eternal truth and an existing individual; it is paradox *sensu strictiori,* because the existing individual is stamped as a sinner, by which existence is accentuated a second time, and because it purports to be an eternal decision in time with retroactive power to annul the past, and because it is linked with the existence of God in time. The individual existing human being must feel himself a sinner; not objectively, which is nonsense, but subjectively, which is the most profound suffering. With all the strength of his mind, to the last thought (and if one human being has a little more intelligence than another it makes no essential difference; to appeal to the greatness of one's intelligence is to betray the defectiveness of one's inwardness, for otherwise the understanding will doubtless be tested beyond its strength), he must try to understand the forgiveness of sins, and then despair of the understanding. With the understanding directly opposed to it, the inwardness of faith must lay hold of the paradox; and precisely this struggle on the part of faith, fighting as the Romans once fought, dazzled by the fierce light of the sun, constitutes the tension of its inwardness.[4] If ever any other sort

of understanding threatens to come to power within him, the believer perceives that he is in the way of losing his faith; just as a young woman, when she discovers after the wedding that it is easy to understand how she became her husband's choice, ought to be able to understand that this is because she no longer loves.

But the speculative philosopher takes up the matter differently. He makes his appearance before a distinguished public and says: "Ladies and gentlemen, for so I must address you; before a community

the Romans demonstrated at Zama. And now the warfare of faith! Is this struggle perhaps a foolish little trick, a mock combat of gallantry, this strife that is more persistent than a thirty years' war, because the task is not merely to acquire but still more hotly to preserve, where every day the heat is as burning as the one day of the battle of Zama! While the understanding despairs, faith presses on to victory in the passion of its inwardness. But when the believer uses all his understanding, every last desperate resource of thought, merely to discover the difficulty that the paradox presents, then there is indeed no part of his understanding left with which to explain the paradox—but for all that, there may still be a rich faith-content in the passion of his inwardness. Sitting quietly in a ship while the weather is calm is not a picture of faith; but when the ship has sprung a leak, enthusiastically to keep the ship afloat by pumping while yet not seeking the harbor: this is the picture. And if the picture involves an impossibility in the long run, that is but the imperfection of the picture; faith persists. While the understanding, like a despairing passenger, stretches out its arms toward the shore, but in vain, faith works with all its energy in the depths of the soul: glad and victorious it saves the soul against the understanding. Has anyone done this, is there anyone who is engaged in doing it? What business is that of mine, provided this is what it means to believe. And though I am still far from having fully understood the difficulty of Christianity (and an explanation which renders the difficulty easy must be regarded as an evil temptation), I can none the less understand that the struggle of faith is not a subject for vaudeville poets, and that its strenuosity is not a diversion for *Privatdocents.*

---

[4] That it is possible to fight thus, dazzled by the sun, and yet see to fight, the Romans demonstrated at Zama; that it is possible to fight thus dazzled, and yet see to conquer,

of believers the paradox may be proclaimed only by a believer, but before a distinguished public the truth may be expounded by a speculative philosopher. The forgiveness of sins," he goes on to say, "is a paradox (general tension in the audience); the pantheistic tendency is an error which speculative philosophy refutes. But speculative philosophy does not remain at the standpoint of the paradox, it explains it and abrogates it." It appears from this that the very honorable speculative philosopher did not make use of all his understanding in the effort to understand, at the same time when he despaired of the understanding; his despair was despair only to a certain degree, a feigned movement; he retained a part of his understanding—for the explanation. This is certainly to make a profit out of one's understanding. The believer has absolutely no profit from his, he loses it all in his despair; but the speculative philosopher knows how to stretch his out to make it suffice. He makes use of half of it with which to despair (as if it were not nonsense to despair by half), and uses the other half to achieve the insight that there was no reason for the understanding to despair. Aye, that makes it all quite different, and where is the error? Why, naturally in the fact that the first movement was illusory, and hence not so much in his failure to remain at the standpoint of faith, as rather in his having reached this standpoint. Suppose the paradox of forgiveness of sins had its ground in the circumstances that the poor existing human individual is in existence, that he is half God-forsaken even when he strives victoriously against the understanding in the inwardness of faith; suppose that only eternity can give an eternal certainty, while existence must rest content with militant certainty, a certainty not achieved by the struggle becoming weaker, and in fact illusory, but only by its becoming stronger. In that

case the explanation is that it is and remains a paradox; and only when it becomes understood that there is no paradox, or that the paradox is only paradoxical to a certain degree, only then is all lost. "But," says perhaps a respectable public, "if this is what the forgiveness of sins is, how then can anyone believe it?" The answer is: "If this is not what the forgiveness of sins is, how could it be *believed?"*

Whether Christianity is right is another question; here we merely ask how the explanation of speculative philosophy is related to the Christianity which it explains. But if Christianity is possibly wrong, so much at least is certain: that speculative philosophy is definitely and decidedly wrong. For the only consistent position outside Christianity is that of pantheism, the taking of oneself out of existence by way of recollection into the eternal, whereby all existential decisions become a mere shadow-play beside what is eternally decided from behind. The fictitious decisiveness of speculative philosophy is, like all *fictitious* decisiveness, a piece of nonsense; for decisiveness is precisely the eternal protest against all fictions. The pantheist is eternally set at rest from behind; the moment of existence, the seventy years, is a vanishing entity. The speculative philosopher, however, desires to be an existing individual; but he wants to be an existing individual who is not subjective, who is not in passion, aye, who exists *sub specie aeterni;* in short, he is absent-minded. But what is explained in absent-mindedness is not absolutely to be depended on—such an explanation, and at this point I am at one with speculative philosophy, such an explanation is only to a certain degree.

If the speculative philosopher explains the paradox so as to remove it, and now in his knowledge knows that it is removed, that the paradox is not the essential relationship that the eternal essential truth bears to an existing individual in the extremity of his existence, but only an accidental relative-relationship to those of limited intelligence: in that case there is established an essential difference between the speculative philosopher and the plain man, which confounds existence from the foundations. God is affronted by getting a group of hangers-on, an intermediary staff of clever brains; and humanity is affronted because the relationship to God is not identical for all men. The godly formula set up above for the difference between the plain man's knowledge of the simple, and the simple wise man's knowledge of the same, that the difference consists in the insignificant trifle that the wise man knows that he knows, or knows that he does not know, what the plain man knows—this formula is by no means respected by speculative philosophy, nor does it respect the likeness involved in this distinction between the plain man and the wise man, namely, that both know the same thing. For the speculative philosopher and the plain man do not by any means know the same thing, when the plain man believes the paradox, and the speculative philosopher knows it to be abrogated. According to the above-mentioned formula, however, which honors God and loves men, the difference is that the wise man also knows that it must be a paradox, this paradox that he himself believes. Hence they both know essentially the same thing; the wise man does not know everything else about the paradox, but knows that he knows this about the paradox. The simple wise man will thus seek to apprehend the paradox more and more profoundly as a paradox, and will not engage in the business of explaining the paradox by understanding that there is none.

Thus when a simple wise man talks with a simple man about the forgiveness of sins, the simple man will doubtless say: "But I cannot understand the divine mercy which is able to forgive sins; the more vividly I believe it, the less am I able to understand it." (So it does not seem to be the case that the probability increases as faith is intensified in inwardness; rather the reverse.) But the simple wise man will say: "Such is also my experience; you know that I have had the opportunity to devote much time to investigation and reflection, and yet the sum total of all my researches amounts at most to this, that I understand that it cannot be otherwise, that it must be impossible to understand. This distinction can scarcely grieve you, or make you think sadly of your own toilsome life, and your perhaps humbler talents, as if I had any advantage over you. My advantage is something both to laugh at and to weep over, considered as the fruit of a period of study. And yet, you must not hold this study in contempt, just as I do not myself regret it; on the contrary, it pleases me most of all when I smile at it, and then again enthusiastically take hold of the strenuous labor of thought."

Such an admission is in all sincerity, and is not present merely once in a while, but essentially present in the wise man every time he engages in the task of thought. Once a year to consider that one ought always to give thanks to God, is scarcely a right understanding of the words; so also once in a while, on an extraordinary occasion, to be moved to reflect that before God all men are essentially equal, is not in truth to understand this equality, especially if one's daily work and striving tends in more than one way to bring it into forgetfulness. But precisely when most strongly entrenched in one's difference, then strongly to apprehend the equality, that is the simple wise man's noble piety.

There has been said much that is strange, much that is deplorable, much that is revolting about Christianity; but the most stupid thing ever said about it is, that it is to a certain degree true. There has been said much that is strange, much that is deplorable, much that is revolting about enthusiasm; but the most stupid thing ever said about it is, that it is to a certain degree. There has been said much that is strange, much that is deplorable, much that is revolting about love, but the most stupid thing ever said about it is, that it is to a certain degree. And when a man has prostituted himself by speaking in this manner about enthusiasm and love, he has betrayed his stupidity, which in this case is not in the direction of intelligence, however, since it has its ground rather in the fact that the understanding has become too large, in the same sense as when a disease of the liver is caused by an enlargement of the liver, and hence, as another author has remarked, "is the flatness that salt takes on when it loses its savor": then there is still one phenomenon left, Christianity. If the sight of enthusiasm has not sufficed to help him break with the understanding, if love has not been able to emancipate him from his slavery: then let him consider Christianity. Let him be offended, he is still human; let him despair of ever himself becoming a Christian, he is yet perhaps nearer than he believes; let him fight to the last drop of blood for the extermination of Christianity, he is still human— but if he is able here to say: it is true to a certain degree, then he is stupid.

Perhaps someone will think that I tremble to say this, that I must be prepared for a terrible castigation at the hands of speculative philosophy. By no means. The speculative philosopher will here again be quite consistent with himself, and say: "There is a certain degree of truth in what the man says, only we cannot stop there, but must advance beyond it." It would also be strange if my insignificance should succeed where even Christianity had failed, namely, in bringing the speculative philosopher to the point of passion; if so, then my little fragment of philosophy would suddenly take on a significance I had least of all dreamed of.

But whoever is neither cold nor hot is nauseating; and just as the hunter is ill-served by a weapon that misses fire at the crucial moment, so God is ill-served by misfiring individuals. Had not Pilate asked objectively what truth is, he would never have condemned Christ to be crucified. Had he asked subjectively, the passion of his inwardness respecting what in the decision facing him he had *in truth to do,* would have prevented him from doing wrong. It would then not have been merely his wife who was made anxious by the dreadful dream, but Pilate himself would have become sleepless. But when a man has something so infinitely great before his eyes as the objective truth, he can afford to set at naught his little bit of subjectivity, and what he as subject has to do. And the approximation-process of the objective truth is figuratively expressed in washing the hands, for objectively there is no decision, and the subjective decision shows that one was in error nevertheless, through not understanding that the decision inheres precisely in subjectivity.

Suppose, on the other hand, that subjectivity is the truth, and that subjectivity is an existing subjectivity, then, if I may so express myself, Christianity fits perfectly into the picture. Subjectivity culminates in passion, Christianity is the paradox, paradox and passion are a mutual fit, and the paradox is altogether suited to one whose situation is, to be in the extremity of existence. Aye, never in all the world could there be found two lovers so wholly suited to one another as paradox and passion, and the strife between them is like the strife between lovers, when the dispute is about whether he first aroused her passion, or she his. And so it is here; the existing individual has by means of the paradox itself come to be placed in the extremity of existence.

And what can be more splendid for lovers than that they are permitted a long time together without any alteration in the relationship between them, except that it becomes more intensive in inwardness? And this is indeed granted to the highly unspeculative understanding between passion and the paradox, since the whole of life in time is vouchsafed, and the change comes first in eternity.

But the speculative philosopher is of another kidney, he believes only to a certain degree; he sets his hand to the plow, and looks about him to find something to know. From the Christian point of view it can scarcely be said that it is anything good he finds to know. Even if it were not the case, as a simple wise man who seeks to apprehend the paradox would strive to show, that it cannot be otherwise; even if the paradox held a little remanant of divine arbitrariness within it, God might seem justified in laying some stress upon His person, scarcely needing to lower the price of the God-relationship on account of the dullness prevailing in the religious market (and this expression seems even more suitable here than in connection with the stock-market). And even if God could be imagined willing, no man with passion in his heart could desire it. To a maiden genuinely in love it could never occur that she bought her happiness too dear, but rather that she had not bought it dear enough. And just as the passion of the infinite was itself the truth, so in the case of the highest value it holds true that the price is the value, that a low price means a poor value; while even the highest possible price in relation to God has in it no meritoriousness, since the highest price is to be willing to do everything and still to know that this is nothing (for if it is something, the price is lower), and nevertheless to will it. Since I am not wholly unacquainted with what has been said and written about Chris-

tianity, I might also say one or two things. But here I do not choose to do so; I merely repeat that there is one thing I shall take care not to say about it: that it is to a certain degree true. It is just possible that Christianity is the truth; it is possible that there will sometime come a judgment, where the separation will turn on the relationship of inwardness to Christianity. Suppose then there came a man who had to say: "I have not indeed believed, but so much have I honored Christianity that I have employed every hour of my life in pondering it." Or suppose there came one of whom the accuser had to say: "He has persecuted the Christians," and the accused replied: "Aye, I admit it; Christianity has set my soul aflame, and I have had no other ambition than to root it from the earth, precisely because I perceived its tremendous power." Or suppose there came another, of whom the accuser would have to say: "He has abjured Christianity," and the accused replied: "Aye, it is true; for I saw that Christianity was such a power that if I gave it a little finger it would take the whole man, and I felt that I could not belong to it wholly." But then suppose there finally came a dapper *Privatdocent* with light and nimble steps, who spoke as follows: "I am not like these three; I have not only believed, but I have even explained Christianity, and shown that it was expounded by the Apostles and appropriated in the early centuries it was only to a certain degree true; but that now, through the interpretation of speculative philosophy it has become the true truth, whence I must ask for a suitable reward on account of my services to Christianity." Which of these four must be regarded as in the most terrible position? It is just possible that Christianity is the truth; suppose that now when its ungrateful children desire to have it declared incompetent, and placed under the guardianship of speculative philosophy, like the Greek poet whose children also demanded that the aged parent be placed under a guardian, but who astonished the judges and the people by writing one of his most beautiful tragedies as a sign that he was still in the full possession of his faculties—suppose that Christianity thus arose with renewed vigor: there would be no one else whose position would become as embarrassing as the position of the *Privatdocents*.

I do not deny that it is a lordly thing to stand so high above Christianity. I do not deny that it is comfortable to be a Christian, and at the same time be exempted from the martyrdom which is always present, even if no persecution menaces from without, even if the Christian is as unnoticed in life as if he had not lived, and is spared the martyrdom of believing against the understanding, the peril of lying upon the deep, the seventy thousand fathoms, in order there to find God. The wader feels his way with his foot, lest he get beyond his depth; and so the shrewd and prudent man feels his way with the understanding in the realm of the probable, and finds God where the probabilities are favorable, and gives thanks on the great holidays of probability, when he has acquired a good livelihood, and there is probability besides for an early advancement; when he has got himself a pretty and attractive wife, and even Councillor Marcussen says that it will be a happy marriage, and that the young woman is of the type of beauty that will in all probability last a long time, and that her physique is such that she will in all probability give birth to strong and healthy children. To believe against the understanding is something different, and to believe with the understanding cannot be done at all; for he who believes with the understanding speaks only of livelihood and wife and fields and oxen and the like, which things are not the object

of faith. Faith *always* gives thanks, is *always* in peril of life, in this collision of finite and infinite which is precisely a mortal danger for him who is a composite of both. The probable is therefore so little to the taste of a believer that he fears it most of all, since he well knows that when he clings to probabilities it is because he is beginning to lose his faith.

Faith has in fact two tasks: to take care in every moment to discover the improbable, the paradox; and then to hold it fast with the passion of inwardness. The common conception is that the improbable, the paradoxical, is something to which faith is related only passively; it must provisionally be content with this relationship, but little by little things will become better, as indeed seems probable. O miraculous creation of confusions in speaking about faith! One is to begin believing, in reliance upon the probability that things will soon become better. In this way probability is after all smuggled in, and one is prevented from believing; so that it is easy to understand that the fruit of having been for a long time a believer is, that one no longer believes, instead of, as one might think, that the fruit is a more intensive inwardness in faith. No, faith is self-active in its relation to the improbable and the paradoxical, self-active in the discovery, and self-active in every moment holding it fast—in order to believe. Merely to lay hold of the improbable requires all the passion of the infinite and its concentration in itself; for the improbable and the paradoxical are not to be reached by the understanding's quantitative calculation of the more and more difficult. Where the understanding despairs, faith is already present in order to make the despair properly decisive, in order that the movement of faith may not become a mere exchange within the bargaining sphere of the understanding. But to believe against the understanding is martyrdom; to begin to get the understanding a little in one's favor, is temptation and retrogression. This martyrdom is something that the speculative philosopher is free from. That he must pursue his studies, and especially that he must read many modern books, I admit is burdensome; but the martyrdom of faith is not the same thing. What I therefore fear and shrink from, more than I fear to die and to lose my sweetheart, is to say about Christianity that it is to a certain degree true. If I lived to be seventy years old, if I shortened the night's sleep and increased the day's work from year to year, inquiring into Chris-

tianity—how insignificant such a little period of study, viewed as entitling me to judge in so lofty a fashion about Christianity! For to be so embittered against Christianity after a casual acquaintance with it, that I declared it to be false: that would be far more pardonable, far more human. But this lordly superiority seems to me the true corruption, making every saving relationship impossible—and it may possibly be the case, that Christianity is the truth.

. . .

PAUL TILLICH

Faith as Ultimate Concern

Paul Tillich (1886–   ), one of the most influential Christian thinkers of our time, lived and worked in his native Germany until Hitler's accession to power. Since that time he has been in the United States at Union Theological Seminary and Harvard University. Tillich is noteworthy for his attempts to combine existentialist insights into the human condition with more traditional theological ideas.

CHAPTER I

WHAT FAITH IS

1. Faith as Ultimate Concern

Faith is the state of being ultimately concerned: the dynamics of faith are the dynamics of man's ultimate concern. Man, like every living being, is concerned about many things, above all about those which condition his very ex-

From Paul Tillich, *Dynamics of Faith*, Chs. I and III. Copyright © 1957 by Paul Tillich. Reprinted by permission of Harper & Row, Publishers, and George Allen & Unwin Ltd.

istence, such as food and shelter. But man, in contrast to other living beings, has spiritual concerns—cognitive, aesthetic, social, political. Some of them are urgent, often extremely urgent, and each of them as well as the vital concerns can claim ultimacy for a human life or the life of a social group. If it claims ultimacy it demands the total surrender of him who accepts this claim, and it promises total fulfillment even if all other claims have to be subjected to it or rejected in its name. If a national group makes the life and growth of the nation its ultimate concern, it demands that all other concerns, economic well-being, health and life, family, aesthetic and cognitive truth, justice and humanity, be sacrificed. The extreme nationalisms of our century are laboratories for the study of what ultimate concern means in all aspects of human existence, including the smallest concern of one's daily life. Everything is centered in the only god, the nation—a god who certainly proves to be a demon, but who shows clearly the unconditional character of an ultimate concern.

But it is not only the unconditional demand made by that which is one's ultimate concern, it is also the promise of ultimate fulfillment which is accepted in the act of faith. The content of this promise is not necessarily defined. It can be expressed in indefinite symbols or in concrete symbols which cannot be taken literally, like the "greatness" of one's nation in which one participates even if one has died for it, or the conquest of mankind by the "saving race," etc. In each of these cases it is "ultimate fulfillment" that is promised, and it is exclusion from such fulfillment which is threatened if the unconditional demand is not obeyed.

An example—and more than an example—is the faith manifest in the religion of the Old Testament. It also has the character of ultimate concern in demand, threat and promise. The content of this concern is not the nation—although Jewish nationalism has sometimes tried to distort it into that—but the content is the God of justice, who, because he represents justice for everybody and every nation, is called the universal God, the God of the universe. He is the ultimate concern of every pious Jew, and therefore in his name the great commandment is given: "You shall love the Lord your God with all your heart, and with all your soul, and with all your might" (Deut. 6:5). This is what ultimate concern means and from these words the term "ultimate concern" is derived. They state unambiguously the character of

genuine faith, the demand of total surrender to the subject of ultimate concern. The Old Testament is full of commands which make the nature of this surrender concrete, and it is full of promises and threats in relation to it. Here also are the promises of symbolic indefiniteness, although they center around fulfillment of the national and individual life, and the threat is the exclusion from such fulfillment through national extinction and individual catastrophe. Faith, for the men of the Old Testament, is the state of being ultimately and unconditionally concerned about Jahweh and about what he represents in demand, threat and promise.

Another example—almost a counterexample, yet nevertheless equally revealing—is the ultimate concern with "success" and with social standing and economic power. It is the god of many people in the highly competitive Western culture and it does what every ultimate concern must do: it demands unconditional surrender to its laws even if the price is the sacrifice of genuine human relations, personal conviction, and creative *eros*. Its threat is social and economic defeat, and its promise—indefinite as all such promises—the fulfillment of one's being. It is the breakdown of this kind of faith which characterizes and makes religiously important most contemporary literature. Not false calculations but a misplaced faith is revealed in novels like *Point of No Return*. When fulfilled, the promise of this faith proves to be empty.

Faith is the state of being ultimately concerned. The content matters infinitely for the life of the believer, but it does not matter for the formal definition of faith. And this is the first step we have to make in order to understand the dynamics of faith.

2. Faith as a Centered Act

Faith as ultimate concern is an act of the total personality. It happens in the center of the personal life and includes all its elements. Faith is the most centered act of the human mind. It is not a movement of a special section or a special function of man's total being. They all are united in the act of faith. But faith is not the sum total of their impacts. It transcends every special impact as well as the totality of them and it has itself a decisive impact on each of them.

Since faith is an act of the personality as a whole, it participates in the dynamics of personal life. These dynamics have been described in many ways, especially in the recent developments of analytic psychology. Thinking in polarities, their tensions and their possible conflicts, is a common characteristic of most of them. This makes the psychology of personality highly dynamic and requires a dynamic theory of faith as the most personal of all personal acts. The first and decisive polarity in analytic psychology is that between the so-called unconscious and the conscious. Faith as an act of the total personality is not imaginable without the participation of the unconscious elements in the personality structure. They are always present and decide largely about the content of faith. But, on the other hand, faith is a conscious act and the unconscious elements participate in the creation of faith only if they are taken into the personal center which transcends each of them. If this does not happen, if unconscious forces determine the mental status without a centered act, faith does not occur, and compulsions take its place. For faith is a matter of freedom. Freedom is nothing more than the possibility of centered personal acts. The frequent discussion in which faith and freedom are contrasted could be helped by the insight that faith is a free, namely, centered act of the personality. In this respect freedom and faith are identical.

Also important for the understanding of faith is the polarity between what Freud and his school call ego and superego. The concept of the superego is quite ambiguous. On the one hand, it is the basis of all cultural life because it restricts the uninhibited actualization of the always-driving libido; on the other hand, it cuts off man's vital forces, and produces disgust about the whole system of cultural restrictions, and brings about a neurotic state of mind. From this point of view, the symbols of faith are considered to be expressions of the superego or, more concretely, to be an expression of the father image which gives content to the superego. Responsible for this inadequate theory of the superego is Freud's naturalistic negation of norms and principles. If the superego is not established through valid principles, it becomes a suppressive tyrant. But real faith, even if it uses the father image for its expression, transforms this image into a principle of truth and justice to be defended even against the "father." Faith and culture can be affirmed only if the superego represents the norms and principles of reality.

This leads to the question of how faith as a personal, centered act is related to the rational structure of man's personality which is manifest in his meaningful language, in his ability to know the true and to do the good, in his sense of beauty and justice. All this, and not only his possibility to analyze, to calculate and to argue, makes him a rational being. But in spite of this larger concept of reason we must deny that man's essential nature is identical with the rational character of his mind. Man is able to decide for or against reason, he is able to create beyond reason or to destroy below reason. This power is the power of his self, the center of self-relatedness in which all elements of his being are united. Faith is not an act of any of his rational functions, as it is not an act of the unconscious, but it is an act in which both the rational and the nonrational elements of his being are transcended.

Faith as the embracing and centered act of the personality is "ecstatic." It transcends both the drives of the nonrational unconscious and the structures of the rational conscious. It transcends them, but it does not destroy them. The ecstatic character of faith does not exclude its rational character although it is not identical with it, and it includes nonrational strivings without being identical with them. In the ecstasy of faith there is an awareness of truth and of ethical value; there are also past loves and hates, conflicts and reunions, individual and collective influences. "Ecstasy" means "standing outside of oneself"—without ceasing to be oneself—with all the elements which are united in the personal center.

A further polarity in these elements, relevant for the understanding of faith, is the tension between the cognitive function of man's personal life, on the one hand, and emotion and will, on the other hand. In a later discussion I will try to show that many distortions of the meaning of faith are rooted in the attempt to subsume faith to the one or the other of these functions. At this point it must be stated as sharply and insistently as possible that in every act of faith there is cognitive affirmation, not as the result of an independent process of inquiry but as an inseparable element in a total act of acceptance and surrender. This also excludes the idea that faith is the result of an independent act of "will to believe." There is certainly affirmation by the will of what concerns one ultimately, but faith is not a creation of the will. In the ecstasy of faith the will to accept and to surrender is an element, but not the cause. And this is true also of feeling. Faith is not an emotional outburst: this is not the meaning of ecstasy. Certainly, emotion is in it, as in every act of man's spiritual life. But emotion does not produce faith. Faith has a cognitive content and is an act of the will. It is the unity of every element in the centered self. Of course, the unity of all elements in the act of faith does not prevent one or the other element from dominating in a special form of faith. It dominates the character of faith but it does not create the act of faith.

This also answers the question of a possible psychology of faith. Everything that happens in man's personal being can become an object of psychology. And it is rather important for both the philosopher of religion and the practical minister to know how the act of faith is embedded in the totality of psychological processes. But in contrast to this justified and desirable form of a psychology of faith there is another one which tries to derive faith from something that is not faith but is most frequently fear. The presupposition of this method is that fear or something else from which faith is derived is more original and basic than faith. But this presupposition cannot be proved. On the contrary, one can prove that in the scientific method which leads to such consequences faith is already effective. Faith precedes all attempts to derive it from something else, because these attempts are themselves based on faith.

3. The Source of Faith

We have described the act of faith and its relation to the dynamics of personality. Faith is a total and centered act of the personal self, the act of unconditional, infinite and ultimate concern. The question now arises: what is the source of this all-embracing and all-transcending concern? The word "concern" points to two sides of a relationship, the relation between the one who is concerned and his concern. In both respects we have to imagine man's situation in itself and in his world. The reality of man's ultimate concern reveals something about his being, namely, that he is able to transcend the flux of relative and transitory experiences of his ordinary life. Man's experiences, feelings, thoughts are conditioned and finite. They not only come and go, but their content is of finite and conditional concern—unless they are elevated to unconditional validity. But this presupposes the general possibility of doing so; it presupposes the element of infinity in man. Man is able to understand in an immediate personal and central act the meaning of the ultimate, the unconditional, the absolute, the infinite. This alone makes faith a human potentiality.

Human potentialities are powers that drive toward actualization. Man is driven toward faith by his awareness of the infinite to which he belongs, but which he does not own like a possession. This is in abstract terms what concretely appears as the "restlessness of the heart" within the flux of life.

The unconditional concern which is faith is the concern about the unconditional. The infinite passion, as faith has been described, is the passion for the infinite. Or, to use our first term, the ultimate concern is concern about what is experienced as ultimate. In this way we have turned from the subjective meaning of faith as a centered act of the personality to its objective meaning, to what is meant in the act of faith. It would not help at this point of our analysis to call that which is meant in the act of faith "God" or "a god." For at this step we ask: What in the idea of God constitutes divinity? The answer is: It is the element of the unconditional and of ultimacy. This carries the quality of divinity. If this is seen, one can understand why almost every thing "in heaven and on earth" has received ultimacy in the history of human religion. But we also can understand that a critical principle was and is at work in man's religious consciousness, namely, that which is really ultimate over against what claims to be ultimate but is only preliminary, transitory, finite.

The term "ultimate concern" unites the subjective and the objective side of the act of faith—the *fides qua creditur* (the Faith through which one believes) and the *fides quae creditur* (the faith which is believed). The first is the classical term for the centered act of the personality, the ultimate concern. The second is the classical term for that toward which this act is directed, the ultimate itself, expressed in symbols of the divine. This distinction is very important, but not ultimately so, for the one side cannot be without the other. There is no faith without out a content toward which it is directed. There is always something meant in the act of faith. And there is no way of having the content of faith except in the act of faith. All speaking about divine matters which is not done in the state of ultimate concern is meaningless. Because that which is meant in the act of faith cannot be approached in any other way than through an act of faith.

In terms like ultimate, unconditional, infinite, absolute, the difference between subjectivity and objectivity is overcome. The ultimate of the act of faith and the ultimate that is meant in the act of faith are one and the same. This is symbolically expressed by the mystics when they say that their knowledge of God is the knowledge God has of himself; and it is expressed by Paul when he says (I Cor. 13) that he will know as he is known, namely, by God. God never can be object without being at the same time subject. Even a successful prayer is, according to Paul (Rom. 8), not possible without God as Spirit praying within us. The same experience expressed in abstract language is the disappearance of the ordinary subject-object scheme in the experience of the ultimate, the unconditional. In the act of faith that which is the source of this act is present beyond the cleavage of subject and object. It is present as both and beyond both.

This character of faith gives an additional criterion for distinguishing true and false ultimacy. The finite which claims infinity without having it (as, e.g., a nation or success) is not able to transcend the subject-object scheme. It remains an object which the believer looks at as a subject. He can approach it with ordinary knowledge and subject it to ordinary handling. There are, of course, many degrees in the endless realm of false ultimacies. The nation is nearer to true ultimacy than is success. Nationalistic ecstasy can produce a state in which the subject is almost swallowed by the object. But after a period the subject emerges again, disappointed radically and totally, and by looking at the nation in a skeptical and calculating way does injustice even to its justified claims. The more idolatrous a faith the less it is able to overcome the cleavage between subject and object. For that is the difference between true and idolatrous faith. In true faith the ultimate concern is a concern about the truly ultimate; while in idolatrous faith preliminary, finite realities are elevated to the rank of ultimacy. The inescapable consequence of idolatrous faith is "existential disappointment," a disappointment which penetrates into the very existence of man! This is the dynamics of idolatrous faith: that it is faith, and as such, the centered act of a personality; that the centering point is something which is more or less on to the periphery; and that, therefore, the act of faith leads to a loss of the center and to a disruption of the personality. The ecstatic character of even an idolatrous faith can hide this consequence only for a certain time. But finally it breaks into the open.

· · ·

CHAPTER III

SYMBOLS OF FAITH

1. The Meaning of Symbol

Man's ultimate concern must be expressed symbolically, because symbolic language alone is able to express the ultimate. This statement demands explanation in several respects. In spite of the manifold research about the meaning and function of symbols which is going on in contemporary philosophy, every writer who uses the term "symbol" must explain his understanding of it.

Symbols have one characteristic in common with signs; they point beyond themselves to something else. The red sign at the street corner points to the order to stop the movements of cars at certain intervals. A red light and the stopping of cars have essentially no relation to each other, but conventionally they are united as long as the convention lasts. The same is true of letters and numbers and partly even words. They point beyond themselves to sounds and meanings. They are given this special function by convention within a nation or by international conventions, as the mathematical signs. Sometimes such signs are called symbols; but this is unfortunate because it makes the distinction between signs and symbols more difficult. Decisive is the fact that signs do not participate in the reality of that to which they point, while symbols do. Therefore, signs can be replaced for reasons of expediency or convention, while symbols cannot.

This leads to the second characteristic of the symbol: It participates in that to which it points: the flag participates in the power and dignity of the nation for which it stands. Therefore, it cannot be replaced except after an historic catastrophe that changes the reality of the nation which it symbolizes. An attack on the flag is felt as an attack on the majesty of the group in which it is acknowledged. Such an attack is considered blasphemy.

The third characteristic of a symbol is that it opens up levels of reality which otherwise are closed for us. All arts create symbols for a level of reality which cannot be reached in any other way. A picture and a poem reveal elements of reality which cannot be approached scientifically. In the creative work of art we encounter reality in a dimension which is closed for us without such works. The symbol's fourth characteristic not only opens up dimensions and elements of reality which otherwise would remain unapproachable but also unlocks dimensions and elements of our soul which correspond to the dimensions and elements of reality. A great play gives us not only a new vision of the human scene, but it opens up hidden depths of our own being. Thus we are able to receive what the play reveals to us in reality. There are within us dimensions of which we cannot become aware except through symbols, as melodies and rhythms in music.

Symbols cannot be produced intentionally—this is the fifth characteristic. They grow out of the individual or collective unconscious and cannot function without being accepted by the unconscious dimension of our being. Symbols which have an especially social function, as political and religious symbols, are created or at least accepted by the collective unconscious of the group in which they appear.

The sixth and last characteristics of the symbol is a consequence of the fact that symbols cannot be invented. Like living beings, they grow and they die. They grow when the situation is ripe for them, and they die when the situation changes. The symbol of the "king" grew in a special period of history, and it died in most parts of the world in our period. Symbols do not grow because people are longing for them, and they do not die because of scientific or practical criticism. They die because they can no longer produce response in the group where they originally found expression.

These are the main characteristics of every symbol. Genuine symbols are created in several spheres of man's cultural creativity. We have mentioned already the political and the artistic realm. We could add history and, above all, religion, whose symbols will be our particular concern.

2. Religious Symbols

We have discussed the meaning of symbols generally because, as we said, man's ultimate concern must be expressed symbolically! One may ask: Why can it not be expressed directly and properly? If money, success or the nation is someone's ultimate concern, can this not be said in a direct way without symbolic language? Is it not only in those cases in which the content of the ultimate concern is called "God" that we are in the realm of symbols? The answer is that everything which is a matter of unconditional concern is made into a god. If the nation is someone's ultimate concern, the name of the nation becomes a sacred name and the nation receives divine qualities which far surpass the reality of the being and functioning of the nation. The nation then stands for and symbolizes the true ultimate, but in an idolatrous way. Success as ultimate concern is not the national desire of actualizing potentialities, but is readiness to sacrifice all other values of life for the sake of a position of power and social predominance. The anxiety about not being a success is an idolatrous form of the anxiety about divine condemnation. Success is grace; lack of success, ultimate judgment. In this way concepts designating ordinary realities become idolatrous symbols of ultimate concern.

The reason for this transformation of concepts into symbols is the character of ultimacy and the nature of faith. That which is the true ultimate transcends the realm of finite reality infinitely. Therefore, no finite reality can express it directly and properly. Religiously speaking, God transcends his own name. This is why the use of his name easily becomes an abuse or a blasphemy. Whatever we say about that which concerns us ultimately, whether or not we call it God, has a symbolic meaning. It points beyond itself while participating in that to which it points. In no other way can faith express itself adequately. The language of faith is the language of symbols. If faith were what we have shown that it is not, such an assertion could not be made. But faith, understood as the state of being ultimately concerned, has no language other than symbols. When saying this I always expect the question: Only a symbol? He who asks this question shows that he has not understood the difference between signs and symbols nor the power of symbolic language, which surpasses in quality and strength the power of any nonsymbolic language. One should never say "only a symbol," but one should say "not less than a symbol." With this in mind we can now describe the different kinds of symbols of faith.

The fundamental symbol of our ultimate concern is God. It is always present in any act of faith, even if the act of faith includes the denial of God. Where there is ultimate concern, God can be denied only in the name of God. One God can deny the other one. Ultimate concern cannot deny its own character as ultimate. Therefore, it affirms what is meant by the word "God." Atheism, consequently, can only mean the attempt to remove any ultimate concern—to remain unconcerned about the meaning of one's existence. Indifference toward the ultimate question is the only imaginable form of atheism. Whether it is possible is a problem which must remain unsolved at this point. In any case, he who denies God as a matter of ultimate concern affirms God, because he affirms ultimacy in his concern. God is the fundamental symbol for what concerns us ultimately. Again it would be completely wrong to ask: So God is nothing but a symbol? Because the next question has to be: A symbol for what? And then the answer would be: For God! God is symbol for

God. This means that in the notion of God we must distinguish two elements: the element of ultimacy, which is a matter of immediate experience and not symbolic in itself, and the element of concreteness, which is taken from our ordinary experience and symbolically applied to God. The man whose ultimate concern is a sacred tree has both the ultimacy of concern and the concreteness of the tree which symbolizes his relation to the ultimate. The man who adores Apollo is ultimately concerned, but not in an abstract way. His ultimate concern is symbolized in the divine figure of Apollo. The man who glorifies Jahweh, the God of the Old Testament, has both an ultimate concern and a concrete image of what concerns him ultimately. This is the meaning of the seemingly cryptic statement that God is the symbol of God. In this qualified sense God is the fundamental and universal content of faith.

It is obvious that such an understanding of the meaning of God makes the discussions about the existence or nonexistence of God meaningless. It is meaningless to question the ultimacy of an ulitmate concern. This element in the idea of God is in itself certain. The symbolic expression of this element varies endlessly through the whole history of mankind. Here again it would be meaningless to ask whether one or another of the figures in which an ultimate concern is symbolized does "exist." If "existence" refers to something which can be found within the whole of reality, no divine being exists. The question is not this, but: which of the innumerable symbols of faith is most adequate to the meaning of faith? In other words, which symbol of ultimacy expresses the ultimate without idolatrous elements? This is the problem, and not the so-called "existence of God"—which is in itself an impossible combination of words. God as the ultimate in man's ultimate concern is more certain than any other certainty, even that of oneself. God as symbolized in a divine figure is a matter of daring faith, of courage and risk.

God is the basic symbol of faith, but not the only one. All the qualities we attribute to him, power, love, justice, are taken from finite experiences and applied symbolically to that which is beyond finitude and infinity. If faith calls God "almighty," it uses the human experience of power in order to symbolize the content of its infinite concern, but it does not describe a highest being who can do as he pleases. So it is with all the other qualities and with all the actions, past, present and future, which men attribute to God. They are symbols taken from our daily experience, and not information about what God did once upon a time or will do sometime in the future. Faith is not the belief in such stories, but it is the acceptance of symbols that express our ultimate concern in terms of divine actions.

Another group of symbols of faith are manifestations of the divine in things and events, in persons and communities, in words and documents. This whole realm of sacred objects is a treasure of symbols. Holy things are not holy in themselves, but they point beyond themselves to the source of all holiness, that which is of ultimate concern.

3. Symbols and Myths

The symbols of faith do not appear in isolation. They are united in "stories of the gods," which is the meaning of the Greek word "mythos"—myth. The gods are individualized figures, analogous to human personalities, sexually differentiated, descending from each other, related to each other in love and struggle, producing world and man, acting in time and space. They participate in human greatness and misery, in creative and destructive works. They give to man cultural and religious traditions, and defend these sacred rites. They help and threaten the human race, especially some families, tribes or nations. They appear in epiphanies and incarnations, establish sacred places, rites and persons, and thus create a cult. But they themselves are under the command and threat of a fate which is beyond everything that is. This is mythology as developed most impressively in ancient Greece. But many of these characteristics can be found in every mythology. Usually the mythological gods are not equals. There is a hierarchy, at the top of which is a ruling god, as in Greece; or a trinity of them, as in India; or a duality of them, as in Persia. There are savior-gods who mediate between the highest gods and man, sometimes sharing the suffering and death of man in spite of their essential immortality. This is the world of the myth, great and strange, always changing but fundamentally the same: man's ultimate concern symbolized in divine figures and actions. Myths are symbols of faith combined in stories about divine-human encounters.

Myths are always present in every act of faith, because the language of faith is the symbol. They are also attacked, criticized and transcended in each of the great religions of mankind. The reason for this criticism is the very nature of the myth. It uses material from our ordinary experience. It puts the stories of the gods into the framework of time and space although it belongs to the nature of the ultimate to be beyond time and space. Above all, it divides the divine into several figures, removing ultimacy from each of them without removing their claim to ultimacy. This inescapably leads to conflicts of ultimate claims, able to destroy life, society, and consciousness.

The criticism of the myth first rejects the division of the divine and goes beyond it to one God, although in different ways according to the different types of religion. Even one God is an object of mythological language, and if spoken about is drawn into the frame work of time and space. Even he loses his ultimacy if made to be the content of concrete concern. Consequently, the criticism of the myth does not end with the rejection of the polytheistic mythology.

Monotheism also falls under the criticism of the myth. It needs, as one says today, "demythologization." This word has been used in connection with the elaboration of the mythical elements in stories and symbols of the Bible, both of the Old and the New Testaments—stories like those of the Paradise, of the fall of Adam, of the great Flood, of the Exodus from Egypt, of the virgin birth of the Messiah, of many of his miracles, of his resurrection and ascension, of his expected return as the judge of the universe. In short, all the stories in which divine-human interactions are told are considered as mythological in character, and objects of demythologization. What does this negative and artificial term mean? It must be accepted and supported if it points to the necessity of recognizing a symbol as a symbol and a myth as a myth. It must be attacked and rejected if it means the removal of symbols and myths altogether. Such an attempt is the third step in the criticism of the myth. It is an attempt which never can be successful, because symbol and myth are forms of the human consciousness which are always present. One can replace one myth by another, but one cannot remove the myth from man's spiritual life. For the myth is the combination of symbols of our ultimate concern.

A myth which is understood as a myth, but not removed or replaced, can be called a "broken myth." Christianity denies by its very nature any unbroken myth, because its presupposition is the first commandment: the affirmation of the ultimate as ultimate and the rejection of any kind of idolatry. All mythological elements in the Bible, and doctrine and liturgy should be recognized as mythologi-

cal, but they should be maintained in their symbolic form and not be replaced by scientific substitutes. For there is no substitute for the use of symbols and myths: they are the language of faith.

The radical criticism of the myth is due to the fact that the primitive mythological consciousness resists the attempt to interpret the myth of myth. It is afraid of every act of demythologization. It believes that the broken myth is deprived of its truth and of its convincing power. Those who live in an unbroken mythological world feel safe and certain. They resist, often fanatically, any attempt to introduce an element of uncertainty by "breaking the myth," namely, by making conscious its symbolic character. Such resistance is supported by authoritarian systems, religious or political, in order to give security to the people under their control and unchallenged power to those who exercise the control. The resistance against demythologization expresses itself in "literalism." The symbols and myths are understood in their immediate meaning. The material, taken from nature and history, is used in its proper sense. The character of the symbol to point beyond itself to something else is disregarded. Creation is taken as a magic act which happened once upon a time. The fall of Adam is localized on a special geographical point and attributed to a human individual. The virgin birth of the Messiah is understood in biological terms, resurrection and ascension as physical events, the second coming of the Christ as a telluric, or cosmic, catastrophe. The presupposition of such literalism is that God is a being, acting in time and space, dwelling in a special place, affecting the course of events and being affected by them like any other being in the universe. Literalism deprives God of his ultimacy and, religiously speaking, of his majesty. It draws him down to the level of that which is not ultimate, the finite and conditional. In the last analysis it is not rational criticism of the myth which is decisive but the inner religious criticism. Faith, if it takes its symbols literally, becomes idolatrous! It calls something ultimate which is less than ultimate. Faith, conscious of the symbolic character of its symbols, gives God the honor which is due him.

One should distinguish two stages of literalism, the natural and the reactive. The natural stage of literalism is that in which the mythical and the literal are indistinguishable. The primitive period of individuals and groups consists in the inability to separate the creations of symbolic imagination from the facts which can be verified through observation and experiment. This stage has a full right of its own and should not be disturbed, either in individuals or in groups, up to the moment when man's questioning mind breaks the natural acceptance of the mythological visions as literal. If, however, this moment has come, two ways are possible. The one is to replace the unbroken by the broken myth. It is the objectively demanded way, although it is impossible for many people who prefer the repression of their questions to the uncertainty which appears with the breaking of the myth. They are forced into the second stage of literalism, the conscious one, which is aware of the questions but represses them, half consciously, half unconsciously. The tool of repression is usually an acknowledged authority with sacred qualities like the Church or the Bible, to which one owes unconditional surrender. This stage is still justifiable, if the questioning power is very weak and can easily be answered. It is unjustifiable if a mature mind is broken in its personal center by political or psychological methods, split in his unity, and hurt in his integrity. The enemy of a critical theology is not natural literalism but conscious literalism with repression of and aggression toward autonomous thought.

Symbols of faith cannot be replaced by other symbols, such as artistic ones, and they cannot be removed by scientific criticism. They have a genuine standing in the human mind, just as science and art have. Their symbolic character is their truth and their power. Nothing less than symbols and myths can express our ultimate concern.

One more question arises, namely, whether myths are able to express every kind of ultimate concern. For example, Christian theologians argue that the word "myth" should be reserved for natural myths in which repetitive natural processes, such as the seasons, are understood in their ultimate meaning. They believe that if the world is seen as a historical process with beginning, end and center, as in Christianity and Judaism, the term "myth" should not be used. This would radically reduce the realm in which the term would be applicable. Myth could not be understood as the language of our ultimate concern, but only as a discarded idiom of this language. Yet history proves that there are not only natural myths but also historical myths. If the earth is seen as the battleground of two divine powers, as in ancient Persia, this is an historical myth. If the God of creation selects and guides a nation through history toward an end which transcends all history, this is an historical myth. If the Christ—a transcendent, divine being—appears in the fullness of time, lives, dies and is resurrected, this is an historical myth. Christianity is superior to those religions which are bound to a natural myth. But Christianity speaks the mythological language like every other religion. It is a broken myth, but it is a myth; otherwise Christianity would not be an expression of ultimate concern.

SUGGESTIONS FOR FURTHER READING

Traditional conceptions of the nature and status of faith are set forth in J. H. Newman, *A Grammar of Assent* (New York: Longmans, Green, 1947); J. G. Machen, *What Is Faith?* (Grand Rapids: W. B. Eerdmans, 1946); and John Baillie, *The Interpretation of Religion* (New York: Scribner's, 1928).

Help in understanding Kierkegaard, and guidance in further reading, can be found in D. F. Swenson, *Something About Kierkegaard*, 2nd ed. (Minneapolis: Augsburg Publishing House, 1945); and Reidar Thomte, *Kierkegaard's Philosophy of Religion* (Princeton: Princeton Univ. Press, 1948). Other existentialist interpretations of faith can be found in Martin Buber, *I and Thou*, R. G. Smith, tr. (Edinburgh: T. and T. Clark, 1937), and *The Eclipse of God* (New York: Harper, 1952); and Gabriel Marcel, *The Mystery of Being*, René Hague, tr. (London: Harvill Press, 1950–51), 2 vols. Tillich's views are further elaborated in *The Courage To Be* (New Haven: Yale Univ. Press, 1952), and the still incomplete *Systematic Theology* (Chicago: Univ. of Chicago Press, 1951–), 2 vols.

For other interesting discussions not so easily classified see Martin Buber, *Two Types of Faith*, N. P. Goldmark, tr. (London: Routledge and Kegan Paul, 1951); and Richard Kroner, *The Primacy of Faith* (New York: Macmillan, 1943).

7.

RELIGION AND SCIENCE

A large portion of the religious thought in our society over the past few centuries has been devoted to the relations between religion and the various sciences which have been assuming a more and more dominant position in our intellectual life. Although there has been some dispassionate reflection on the interconnections, or lack thereof, between the two, most of the discussion has been sparked by the existence of real or apparent conflicts. Some have attacked scientific theories for being inconsistent with religious doctrine; some have attacked religion for being out of step with the advance of science; and some have tried to reconcile in one way or another the warring parties. These debates do not make such a noise in the world today as they did in the nineteenth century, but the discussion continues, and will continue so long as both science and religion continue to develop and so long as our philosophical understanding of the nature of each continues to grow.

As a matter of fact, very different kinds of opposition have been grouped together under the heading "the conflict of science and religion." [1] Consider the following passage from Julian Huxley [2] (in this discussion we are restricting our attention to conflicts between science and *theistic* religion):

> The supernatural hypothesis, taken as involving both the god hypothesis and the spirit hypothesis and the various consequences drawn from them, appears to have reached the limits of its usefulness as an interpretation of the universe and of human destiny, and as a satisfactory basis for religion. It is no longer adequate to deal with the phenomena, as disclosed by the advance of knowledge and discovery.

> This is the crux of the so-called conflict between science and religion, which should more properly be described as a conflict between the progress of established knowledge and a particular type of religious hypothesis.

> It would be interesting to discuss the history of this conflict, and to show how, for instance, the advance of knowledge, both in the natural and the human sciences, has led to modifications in the god hypothesis—how the Newtonian and the Darwinian revolutions combined to push the deity ever further into the background, until his only role in cosmic affairs appears as that of initial creator of a self-running machine; how, with our knowledge of the orderly working of nature, the idea of miraculous intervention has grown progressively less and less tenable, until it has now become repugnant and indeed intellectually immoral to a growing body of those educated in the scientific tradition; how theistically minded astronomers and philosophers have been reduced to presenting god in the unsatisfying role of a cosmic mathematician, or the nebulous guise of an absolute principle.

> But I have no space for this, and can merely state the plain fact that the advance of knowledge is making supernaturalism in general, and the god hypothesis in particular, untenable for an increasing number of people.

The kind of conflict emphasized by Huxley in the first of these passages is that between particular scientific theories and particular religious beliefs. The two most violent conflicts of this sort in modern times have been those over the Copernican theory of the solar system and the Darwinian theory of evolution. In the sixteenth century Copernicus advanced the theory that the earth and all the other planets revolved around the sun. Why should there be any theological opposition to this piece of pure astronomy? For two reasons. First, it was supposed that Holy Scripture had asserted ("The world also is established, that it cannot be moved") and implied (Joshua commanded the sun to stand still, and not the earth) that the sun revolves around the earth. As Calvin said, "Who will venture to place the authority of Copernicus above that of the Holy Spirit?" Second, the new system, by taking the earth away from its traditional place in the center of the universe, made it seem less plausible that man should be as important in the divine plan as Christianity supposes, or that God should bother to become incarnate on a second-rate planet moving around a third-rate sun off

---

[1] One not mentioned, and not treated in this section, is that stemming from explanations of religion developed in the social sciences. (See the introduction to Section 3 and the selections from Freud and Cornforth in that section.)

[2] *Religion Without Revelation*, New York: New American Library (1958), pp. 185.

in some corner. The opposition to Darwin came from the same sources. The thesis that organic species have gradually evolved over a period of many millions of years was thought to contradict statements which are either made or implied by Scripture: that each of the species was separately created at the time of the creation of the universe, that the creation of the universe took place in 4004 B.C., that no animals preyed on each other until after Adam's fall, that the earth was repopulated from the ark after the flood. Again, the picture of man evolving gradually from the lower animals seemed not to fit in with the theological doctrine that man, unlike the lower animals, possessed an immortal soul. If there was a gradual period of evolution, at precisely what point was an immortal soul infused?

From present-day perspectives these disputes do not seem very significant. It does not seem to most religious thinkers today that anything of crucial importance to religion was at issue here. As to the first difficulty, there is now very wide agreement (though not universal) that it is not essential to Christianity to maintain that every statement in the Bible is true on a literal interpretation. Even if, as most Christian thinkers as well as thinkers in other prophetic religions would maintain, the notion of divine revelation is essential, this revelation is not necessarily embodied in a set of infallible statements. The Bible may represent the attempt of human beings to respond as best they can to encounters with God, and so be subject to all the errors to which mortal man is heir, and still none the less be a genuine revelation from God. As to the second kind of difficulty, it seems to rest on bad reasoning. The relative position of the earth in the universe need have nothing to do with God's concern for men. Why should we suppose that God would distribute His attention in proportion to proximity to the center of the universe, as if He only had a certain amount and had to ration it out? This is anthropomorphism with a vengeance. Nor does the evolution of man from lower animals really make it any less likely that he has an immortal soul. After all, man differs from the other animals in various ways; why not in this way too? Again, why suppose that God could not, or would not, endow beings with souls at a certain point in the evolutionary process?

Can we generalize these results and say that there can be no conflicts between particular scientific theories and essential beliefs of theistic religion? We could if we were to adopt the policy of declaring a belief inessential whenever it comes into conflict with a scientific theory. Some uncharitable commentators charge that this is what theologians have been doing for the past few centuries. But it would be an oversimplification to suppose that religion has given up its pretensions in the fields of astronomy, biology, psychology, and so on, solely because it could not meet the competition from empirical science in these areas. Quite apart from pressure from science, there are sound reasons, drawn from the nature of religion itself, for distinguishing between properly religious doctrines which play a role in the essential business of religion and other doctrines with which the former get associated for more or less adventitious reasons. If, as it was suggested in the general introduction to this volume, we think of religion as concerned with providing an over-all world view, a picture of the ultimate origin, nature, and purpose of the cosmos, and man's place therein, we can see a reason for holding that it is not the business of religion to propound answers to the sorts of questions science tries to answer, and therefore that there can be no fundamental conflicts between the two. Put in its most general terms, what science tries to do is to discover correlations between various things or factors within the spatio-temporal universe, whether these be between the pressure and volume of a gas, between population and food supply, or between motivation and performance. It is, by its very nature, limited to tracing out the details of the internal economy of the universe, the ways in which its various components are regularly interconnected. If this account of the nature of religion and science is accurate, it would follow that, so long as each sticks to its proper business, there can be no fundamental *direct* conflict between the two. When such conflicts apparently arise, it is because one or the other side goes beyond its proper task, as when Christian doctrine becomes so wedded to a certain astronomy that even so sophisticated a thinker as C. D. Broad cannot take it seriously in any other setting (see the selection from Broad below), or as when biologists insert pronouncements on the ultimate purpose of the universe, or lack thereof, into their empirically grounded conclusions on the course of biological evolution and the mechanisms responsible for it.

This is basically the kind of position taken by J. A. Thomson, A. S. Eddington, and C. D. Broad, though only Thomson sets it forth in anything like these terms. Huxley's position however is quite different. He considers "god hypotheses" to be in competition with scientific hypotheses, and he feels that the success of the latter has fatally weakened the former. This is because, unlike the other thinkers represented in this section, he thinks of religious beliefs primarily as attempts to explain natural phenomena in basically the same sense as that in which science tries to explain them: "Gods, like scientific hypotheses, are attempts to understand the cosmos and explain or at least interpret the facts of experience." Huxley goes on to point out various differences between the two, but since he regards them as basically trying to perform the same task, he can hold that they come into direct conflict. We shall have more to say about this issue later.

When Huxley, in the passage quoted at the beginning of this introduction, speaks of "how, with our increasing knowledge of the orderly working of nature, the idea of miraculous intervention has grown progressively less and less tenable . . . ," he is alluding to a very different sort of conflict. The considerations I have been presenting certainly do not show that this conflict is not a real one. Nor could it be maintained that the belief in miraculous intervention is not a fundamental one for a theistic religion. For the God of theistic religion is an active God, one Who actively guides the course of events and makes dynamic, personal contact with His worshippers, not simply an artificer Who constructs the universe and then leaves it to run under its own power. But this does not constitute a counterexample to the thesis that there can be no fundamental conflict between science and religion, for this is not that sort of conflict. The belief that nature works in an orderly manner is not a particular scientific theory; we will never find any experiments or surveys designed to establish it. It is a component of a world view which is a rival to the theistic world view, and so it is not surprising that genuine conflict should arise here.

This particular conflict is one of many conflicts between elements of the theistic world view and elements of the world view which is closely associated with the rise of modern science, often called "naturalism." It is difficult to say anything concise about this matter which would be completely accurate, for naturalists differ among themselves as much as the adherents of any broad philosophical movement do, but at the cost of considerable oversimplification we may list the following as basic components of naturalism.

Materialism. The fundamental reality is matter. We can distinguish a more hard-boiled form of materialism which denies that anything exists other than material things, and a more soft-boiled form which admits the existence of nonmaterial things but insists that they are completely dependent on matter for their existence.

Determinism. Everything that happens is uniquely determined to happen by causes within the natural world; "uniquely" in that, given those causes, no other outcome is possible. If one knew all the causal factors which exist at a certain moment and knew all the laws according to which things occur, he would know with certainty what is going to happen next.

Mechanism. The laws according to which things happen are mechanistic laws. Without trying to explain exactly what *mechanistic* means I will point out one negative implication of this doctrine. Natural laws never take purpose into account. We can never say that things happen as they do in order that certain ends should be realized.

It should be apparent that each of these principles comes into direct conflict with a fundamental doctrine of theism. Materialism is incompatible with the existence of God. To say that matter is primary is to deny the possibility that the material universe owes its existence to the creative activity of a purely spiritual being. Indeed it rules out the very existence of a purely spiritual being, considered not to be dependent on the physical universe for its existence. We have already noted that determinism contradicts the belief in God's miraculous interventions in the course of events. Mechanism comes into conflict with the doctrine that everything which happens in the world is directed to the realization of some purpose or purposes. If the universe is created by a personal being, then it will have a teleological structure; everything in it will have a role in the carrying out of a purpose. But according to mechanism, purposes have nothing to do with the way things happen; in trying to understand the course of events we can safely ignore purpose altogether.

It should be clear that this conflict between two rival world views is not itself a conflict between religion and science. For if the above characterization of science is accurate, it is not the business of science to establish any conclusions, whether naturalistic or otherwise, as to the ultimate nature of reality as a whole. Nevertheless, science might be involved in this conflict in a more indirect way. Indeed, naturalists generally invoke the authority and prestige of science in support of their position and talk as if the success of modern science has rendered all alternative world views untenable. So far as I can see, the most plausible line of this sort the naturalist can take is to maintain that the basic principles of naturalism are necessarily *presupposed* by the scientific enterprise, and that by pursuing his task in the way he does the scientist is committed to a naturalistic world view whether he realizes it or not. Let us see how this might be argued for two of the principles, beginning with determinism. Science assumes that everything that happens is determined to happen by natural causes in accordance with regularly repeated patterns; it assumes this, and must assume it, for the simple reason that it looks for such patterns, and in the very act of looking for something one assumes that there is something there to be found. The physicist asks why uranium emits radiation; the biologist asks why certain traits are inherited in certain ways; the psychologist asks why certain people learn more quickly than others or why certain people have an irrational compulsion to wash their hands after every contact. In all these cases the scientist is looking for certain natural factors which are connected in some regular way with the phenomena he is trying to explain.

The same point can be made with respect to materialism. By and large the contemporary scientist assumes that the subject matter he is investigating is basically material or physical in character (provided we understand these terms in a rather broad sense); that is, he supposes that their fundamental characteristics are physical characteristics, that the characteristics in terms of which they are to be understood and explained are physical features like mass, velocity, shape, and intensity. The basic evidence for this is the same as in the last case: it is these characteristics that the scientist looks for and pays attention to; he simply does not consider any other properties that things may have. In other words, his practice shows that he considers the material characteristics to be fundamental, to constitute the fundamental reality of things. This is most obvious in the physical sciences. A physicist who tried to understand the motions of a body in terms of its beauty, or its desires, would not be taken seriously, and even the social and biological sciences have been increasingly moving in this direction in the last fifty years. One of the major revolutions in psychology in this century came about when many psychologists ceased trying to understand human behavior in terms of mentalistic concepts like desire, feeling, and thought, and turned instead to physical, publicly observable features like the time elapsing between a stimulus and response, the strength of a response, the strength and frequency of reward and punishment, and so on. In biology we have a similar movement away from nonmaterial concepts like vital principle toward concentration on chemical reactions and the mechanics of the movements of organisms.

If these principles are necessary presuppositions of science, then in effect there is a fundamental conflict between science and (theistic) religion, because this would mean that one could not accept the scientific enterprise as a valid way of finding out how things in the universe are interrelated without accepting a naturalistic world view; and that would mean abandoning theistic religion. But even if we confine our attention to the physical sciences where these principles play the strongest role, there are strong reasons for denying that science and naturalism are related that closely. What we have just seen is that generally scientists assume that these principles hold for what they are investigating. But naturalism consists in applying these principles unrestrictedly, maintaining that they hold for everything whatsoever. All that the physicist assumes is that the physical bodies he investigates are basically material in character and that they behave in accordance with fixed natural law. He does not also assume that everything whatsoever is basically material, and so on. It is hard to see what it would contribute to the physicist's investigation of thermal systems, electric currents, and atomic nuclei to assume that there is nothing which cannot be understood in the terms he is using. It would not hamper his investigations in the least to admit the possibility, or even the actuality, of things—for example, angels and gods—to which physical categories do not apply at all and which are not subject to investigation by scientific method. Such an admission might be a painful check to his pride, but it certainly would not interfere with his actual scientific work, so long as there is enough subject matter available for which these principles do hold. Thus a scientist like Thomson can accept a theistic religion without in any way contradicting his scientific assumptions; he must recognize that there are things with which science is not, and cannot be, concerned.

There is an assumption which would justify the naturalistic extension of these principles, namely, the assumption that scientific method is the only avenue to knowledge, that it is the only way of finding out what there is. For to admit this is to admit that there is nothing in existence other than what can be discovered scientifically. At least it is to admit that we can never know of the existence of anything outside the subject matter of science, and if this is not quite the same as saying that there is nothing other than the subject matter of science, it comes to the same thing in practice.

This brings us to a third kind of opposition: that between the method(s) of science and the methods traditionally used to support religious doctrine (appeal to authority, mystical experience, metaphysical argumentation). Again, this is not directly a conflict between *science* and religion. If science attacks its problems using one method and religion attacks its problems using another, then, provided that the problems are different in principle, there is so far no conflict but only a difference. This in itself no more gives rise to conflict than does the fact that the musician uses sounds and the painter uses colors. There is a conflict only when the naturalistic philosopher claims, as Huxley does, that scientific method is the only legitimate way of justifying beliefs. But this claim goes beyond science itself in exactly the same way as do the metaphysical principles of naturalism. In order to get on with his work the scientist does not have to assume that *all* questions are to be investigated by scientific method; he only has to assume that the sorts of questions he is interested in as a scientist are to be so investigated.

It could be argued that this claim for scientific method is the deepest root of the naturalistic opposition to theistic religion. We have already noted that this claim has to be granted if we are to have any chance of showing that a naturalistic metaphysics is supported by science. And I think we can see that this same principle underlies Huxley's penchant, noted earlier, for regarding religious beliefs as attempts to explain natural phenomena and hence in direct competition with scientific attempts to do the same thing. Suppose it were pointed out to Huxley that religious beliefs serve many functions other than providing explanations of rain, disease, the rise and fall of empires, and the motions of the heavenly bodies; for example, they provide a basis for ritual practices, give an articulation of various sorts of religious experience, exhibit a basis for morality, provide a metaphysical explanation of the existence of the world *à la* Aquinas. I suspect that Huxley would reply that none of this provides any justification for such beliefs, and that such justification could come only through their success in explaining natural phenomena in the way scientific theories do. This reply would reveal that he treats scientific theories in this way because of his conviction that any belief can be justified only by the methods employed in science.

But, though very fundamental, or perhaps because it is so fundamental, it is extremely difficult to imagine any way in which this principle itself could be put to a test. Of course, it can be pointed out that scientific method has been successful in yielding results on which investigators can agree and in giving us control over nature in a way that alternative methods—for example, authority or self-evidence—have not. But apart from problems that might be raised about using agreement and control over nature as our basic criteria for the validity of a method, there is the disquieting point that we are using scientific method to establish the facts on which this argument is based, namely, that scientific method gives more agreement and more control than other methods. And it is an interesting fact that *any* method can be justified if we are willing to use that method itself in the justification. The method of papal authority, for example, can be justified if we use the method itself in its own justification, that is, by asking the Pope whether he is reliable. Perhaps in the last analysis the claim that scientific method is the only way to attain knowledge is itself the expression of a fundamental, quasi-religious orientation.

JULIAN HUXLEY

Science and God

Julian Huxley (1887–   ), a grandson of T. H. Huxley, is a distinguished biologist who has been active in a wide variety of fields, and was for a time Director-General of UNESCO.

Gods are among the empirical facts of cultural history. Like other empirical facts, they can be investigated by the method of science—dispassionate observation and analysis, leading to the formulation of hypotheses which can then be tested by further observation and analysis, followed by synthesis and the framing of broad interpretative concepts.

Thanks to the labours of social anthropologists, historians, archæologists, and students of comparative religion, the facts about gods are now so abundant that their comparative and evolutionary study can readily be pursued, while the progress of the natural and social sciences and in particular of psychology has made it possible to attempt a radical analysis of their nature, functions and effects. Theology was once called the Queen of the Sciences; but that was in an age when the word *science* was equated (as it still is on the continent of Europe) with the whole of organised learning. In the restricted modern English sense of the term, theology has been, as my grandfather T. H. Huxley said, only a pseudo-science. But if the scientific method were applied to its subject-matter, it could become a true science. As sub-sciences of such a truly scientific theology, we might envisage Comparative Theomorphology, Divine in addition to Animal and Plant Physiology, Psychodivinity, and Evolutionary Theobiology.

There are, it seems to me, three possible ways of envisaging and defining the nature of gods. In briefest terms, the first is that gods have real independent existence as personal but supernatural beings able to control or influence the natural world. The second is that gods are personalised representations, created by human minds, of the forces affecting human destiny. And the third, which is in a sense a compromise between the other two, is that they are more or less adequate attempts by man to describe or denote a single eternal suprapersonal and supernatural Being with a real existence behind or above nature.

Before going further, I had better amplify these statements a little. By *personal beings,* I mean beings endowed with the higher attributes of human personalities —knowing, feeling, and willing—integrated in an organised and enduring unity of consciousness: by *suprapersonal,* I intend a being with a nature akin to human personality, but beyond our limited

From Julian Huxley, *Religion Without Revelation* (1957), Ch. III. Reprinted by permission of A. D. Peters and Harper & Row, Publishers.

human understanding: and by *personalised representation* I mean an attempt to describe or interpret natural phenomena with an objective existence, in terms of action by hypothetical personal beings in or behind phenomena—in psychological terms, the projection of the idea of supernatural personality into our experience of nature and our ideas about destiny.

There are of course other types of attempted definition of gods. For the consistent materialist and the fanatical rationalist, gods are pure fictions, not only without any real existence, but without any basis or background in fact, invented by priests and rulers to keep ordinary people in intellectual and moral subjection. This is, to me, itself a fiction as gross as the one it pretends to demolish, an error as childish as the semantic error of taking the existence of the word God as evidence of His real existence.

Then there are the attempts of theologians to evade the dilemmas in which they are landed by the acceptance of an all-wise, all-good and all-powerful God as ruler of a world in which chaos and ignorance, suffering, strife and evil are such regrettably prominent features. Some take refuge in the thesis that God is beyond human comprehension, and that we must therefore accept the apparent contradiction resignedly without attempting to understand. This is a counsel of despair and an abrogation of man's intelligence and mental powers. If the universe is ruled by a god, it must be our business to try to understand his policy: if there is a divine design for the world, a prime task of religion must be to discover and interpret it. If such understanding and discovery are intrinsically impossible, then belief in god is a poor basis for religion or for conduct.

Then there are the attempts to redefine god so as to fit in with historical and scientific knowledge. We are told that god is the Absolute, whatever that may mean; or 'a power, not ourselves, that makes for righteousness'; without specifying the nature of that power; or a general spiritual force behind phenomena; or the everlasting ground of being; etcetera. However, to assert, like some idealist philosophers, that the ground of all reality is wholly spiritual, and then, after christening this hypothetical ground the Absolute, to pretend that it is a new and better version of the god built up by religion out of quite other aspects of reality, is intellectually unjustified. Such a god is only a dummy divinity, a theatrical *deus ex machina* dropped on to the religious stage through the trap door of metaphysics.

And for theologians to claim that god is 'in reality' some abstract entity or depersonalised spiritual principle, while in practice their churches inculcate belief in a personal divinity who rules and judges, who demands worship and submission, who is capable of anger and forgiveness —that is plain intellectual dishonesty.

Let me return to the three possible ways of envisaging the nature of gods. In the light of our present knowledge I maintain that only the second is tenable—that gods are creations of man, personalised representations of the forces of destiny, with their unity projected into them by human thought and imagination.

In parentheses I should say that I do *not* mean only our present knowledge in the field of natural science, but also our knowledge in the fields of history, prehistory, and cultural anthropology, of human psychology and of comparative religion.

This general statement on the nature of gods can be profitably reformulated and spelled out somewhat as follows. History shows an increasingly successful extension of the naturalistic approach to more and more fields of experience, coupled with a progressive failure and restriction of supernaturalist interpretation. The time has now come for a naturalistic approach to theology. In the light of this approach, gods appear as interpretative concepts or hypotheses. They are hypotheses aiming at fuller comprehension of the facts of human destiny, in the same way that scientific hypotheses aim at fuller comprehension of the facts of nature.[1] They are theoretical constructions of the human mind, in the same way as are scientific theories and concepts: and, like scientific theories and laws, they are based on experience and observable facts.

God hypotheses are part of a more general theory, the daimonic theory as it is usefully called, according to which supernatural spiritual beings, good, bad, or indifferent, and of very different degrees of importance, play a part in the affairs of the cosmos.[2]

The analogy between theology and natural science deserves a little further exploration. In the history of natural science the absolutist approach, involving *a priori,* dogmatic or purely rationalistic methods, has been gradually given up in favour of scientific naturalism—the progressive method of observation and hypothesis, followed by the checking of hypothesis by fresh observation.

As every schoolboy knows, many hypotheses and theories and so-called laws of nature have been abandoned or superseded in the light of new factual knowledge. Thus for centuries astronomical theory was subordinated to the *a priori* principle that perfection reigned in celestial affairs and that accordingly, since the circle was the perfect form, the heavenly bodies must move in circles. This led to the impossible complications of Ptolemaic astronomy, which fell like a house of cards when Kepler showed that elliptical orbits provided a simpler and more adequate explanation of the observed facts.

Again, the classical theory (which might better be described as a scientific myth) of the Four Elements—Earth, Air, Fire and Water—held the field for centuries, and it was possible by ingenious manipulation to fit a great many facts into its theoretical framework. But eventually this became impossible—the framework proved to be not merely inadequate but downright wrong; and the atomic theory, which is still in process of development, took its place. Similarly in biology, Darwin's work necessitated the immediate abandonment of the theory of creation in favour of evolution; and the Lamarckian theory of evolution by the inheritance of acquired characters has been dropped because it no longer fits the facts.

Gods, like scientific hypotheses, are attempts to understand the cosmos and explain or at least interpret the facts of experience. But they differ from modern scientific hypotheses in various ways. For one thing, they are still largely dogmatic or *a priori,* deriving from authority or feeling or intuition instead of from constant checking and rechecking against fact. As a consequence, they no longer fit the facts; but in so far as they are formulated in absolutist terms, they cannot afford to die and be reborn in new guise. Authoritarian dogmas and revelations resemble the Struldbrugs of *Gulliver's Travels* in being condemned to an uncomfortable survival long after their original vigour and significance have been exhausted. Luckily, however, they differ from Struldbrugs in not being immortal. They *can* die—though usually their death is belated, so that they have kept their youthful competitors in the world of ideas

[1] For an interesting philosophical discussion of the problem see Professor John Wisdom's essay on Gods in his *Philosophy and Psychoanalysis.* He rightly points out that statements about God are often statements about real phenomena, in the shape of experiences, but he does not come to grips with the view that the term *God* itself involves a hypothesis or assumption.

[2] See Professor Ralph Turner's discussion of 'the Daimonic Universe' in his *The Great Cultural Traditions,* vols. 1 and 2 (McGraw-Hill, New York, 1941).

out of their rightful place for far too long.

Gods differ even more radically from the hypotheses of science in being created by primitive and prescientific methods of thinking. They are thus unscientific in essence, and in the long run antiscientific in their effects. Gods are among the products of what Ernst Cassirer in his notable three-volume study, *The Philosophy of Symbolic Forms*,[3] calls mythical thought, which is basically non-rational: it fails to exclude feeling and fantasy from its judgments, and does not operate according to the laws of logic or by utilising scientific method.

Mythical thought in Cassirer's sense includes three rather different modes of thinking and of framing its ideas and symbols. The most primitive, and the one which appears to operate inevitably in the earliest stages of individual life, I would call the magic mode. For magic thinking, the world is basically a reservoir of magic power. It works as a system of interacting magic influences, some diffused, some concentrated in particular external objects or processes, some intrinsic in man and operating through verbal symbols and ritual actions. Magic thinking apparently grows out of the infantile phase that Freud has characterised as that of the omnipotence of thought. The early infantile world is a world of feeling and emotion, of the satisfaction and frustration of desires. The infant speedily discovers that he can often obtain satisfactions by expressing his emotions; such expression is of necessity to some extent symbolic, an external symbol to others of the internal reality. That reality is a reality of emotion, intense and without compromise. Emotional thinking operates by the primitive all-or-nothing methods of animal instinct: the personality is wholly possessed by one emotion—and then of

---
[3] Yale University Press, New Haven.

a sudden it is not possessed at all. The expression of his emotions is the infant's only method of communication with the world outside himself. Only after learning to speak does he acquire the capacity for rational thought and the communication of non-emotional experience.

It seems clear that the idea of magic influence originates from this pre-rational phase of individual mental life, but is later enlarged by primitive society to cover the workings of nature as a whole.

Whatever its actual origin, it is clear that the magic mode of thinking operates by extending the idea of immanent power, emotionally and morally charged, from man's primal experience of it within himself to the universe around him. Magic is an interpretation of destiny in terms of pervading spiritual—or rather, non-material—influences or forces, making for enjoyment or misery, good or evil, fruition or frustration, and capable of being humanly controlled by appropriate methods.

Magic thought is a coherent and self-consistent system. It is also delightfully elastic. Whenever magic methods fail to secure the desired control of events, an excuse is always ready to hand—the ritual was not properly executed, the spells not quite right, the occasion not propitious, another magician was making more powerful magic. . . .

The second mode of organising mythical thought may be called the projective, in which personality is projected into the external world.

After the primary infantile phase in which the baby lives in a world of his own emotions, the next step in experience is the awareness of personality—first other people's, beginning with the mother's, and later his own. Personal beings are recognised, and are found to influence the world of desires and emotions by their control of events. The natural and apparently inevitable consequence is for the child to personalise events and objects which arouse emotion and favour or frustrate his desires.

Lewis Mumford, in his admirable book *The Conduct of Life*,[4] has stressed the fact, too often neglected by the intellectualism of logicians and philosophers and the materialist 'scienticism' of empirical scientists and practical technicians, that the infant's early world is a world of feelings and people, in which objects are not separately distinguished, but are apprehended only as part of an emotional experience. This being so, it is inevitable that primitive thinking should operate in terms of emotional powers and personal agents.

Only later, with the aid of words as mental tools, can the child categorise experience in terms of things and ideas, and start thinking objectively and intellectually. And even then, objects and events often remain charged with the emotional forces and projected personalities of earlier modes of thought. Indeed language itself is primitively charged with such emotional and personal significance: the progress of human science and learning has been bound up with the development of appropriate language, more objective and more rational. Mathematics, of course, represents the fullest expression of such emotionally uncommitted language, while the arts have concentrated on emotionally charged and often non-verbal symbolism.

In any case, the projection of personality into external things and events provides the basis on which the daimonic phase of early human thinking was organised. Projective thought peopled the universe with demons, spirits, devils, ghosts and gods. And under the outer pressure of accumulated experience and the inner pressure of man's exercise of

4 Harcourt, Brace & World, New York, 1951.

logical reasoning, these cultural entities proceeded to evolve in fantastic multiplicity.

The third mode of mythical thought may be specifically called the mythological, which sets out to give theoretical explanations of phenomena, especially explanations of their origins, whenever factual knowledge is insufficient. To do this, it requires language and must wait on reason applied to experience; and so, like the later creation of gods by projective thinking, it can only operate when, with the aid of speech, the infant has become a child.

Just as magic becomes intertwined with daimonic thinking, so gods are frequently involved in mythology: the three modes of mythical thought, though apparently successive in origin, remain entangled for much of history. Sometimes, indeed, as with culture-heroes, mythology makes a novel use of the god-hypothesis as part of its explanation. All mythical thought is purposely interpretative, and attempts to confer significance on reality. The trouble is that, since it always starts from incomplete knowledge and almost always from false premises, its significances are usually wrong, distorted or misleading.

In passing, it should be noted that elements of the mythical modes of thinking may survive in naturalistic and scientific thought. Hypostasised 'forces' and 'principles' are de-emotionalised refinements of personalised thinking; and cosmological speculations like that of continuous creation are myths dressed up in scientific guise and expressed in the naturalistic mode.

I have spoken of the origin of gods: it remains now to consider the fascinating subject of their subsequent evolution.

In biological evolution, we find many different types, characterised by different plans of organisation (for instance insect *versus* vertebrate, or mammal *versus* reptile). Every successful type evolves into a large group, characterised by a rapid increase in numbers and in variety of sub-types. During its evolution, it shows gradual trends towards improvement—sometimes improvement in general organisation, sometimes in this or that specialised efficiency. In the great majority of cases, these trends eventually become stabilised. In plain language, they come to an end, and the type (if it does not die out) continues indefinitely on the same level of organisation or specialisation: it has exhausted its inherent possibilities of major improvement.

Further, every type of course finds itself in competition with other evolving types: and such competition may modify the course of its evolution, restrict its improvement, reduce its numbers and variety, and sometimes even lead to its virtual or total extinction. And large-scale biological progress occurs through the replacement of one successful or dominant type by another, as in the classical example of the replacement of the cold-blooded reptiles by the warm-blooded mammals and birds as the dominant type of land animals at the close of the Mesozoic about sixty million years ago.

Gods are not organisms, but they are organised cultural entities: like other cultural entities, they can and do evolve, and in a way which shows many points of resemblance (though also of difference) to the biological evolution of organisms. Substantially, they are organisations of human thought which seek to represent, canalise, and give a comprehensible interpretation of the forces affecting human destiny: formally, they are organised in the guise of personal beings.

The forces affecting human destiny that underlie the construction of gods are immensely various. They include the elemental forces of nature and its catastrophes, from earthquake to pestilence; the phenomena of growth and reproduction, plant, animal and human; the emotional forces aroused by the terrifying and the mysterious, and by the sense of sacredness experienced at the crises of human life, like birth and death, puberty and marriage; authority, of father and family, of priest and king, of law and church, of city, tribe and society at large; the power of conscience, of ideals, of the forces of light struggling with the forces of darkness; the power of all compulsions, whether external or internal.

In his religions, man starts with variety and gradually organises it into some sort of a unity. In certain stages, every society has multiform gods, often of different degrees of importance, representing different special bits of destiny and its forces. Particular objects or places may be deified; or separate aspects of nature like sea, sun, or storm; or different aspects of human natures as in the later Greek pantheon; the city may be represented by a god as in ancient Mesopotamia, or the tribes as in early Judaism, or the household as in ancient Rome; human individuals may be deified or divinised, whether for their mythical exploits like hero-gods, or by traditional virtue of their office like the Egyptian Pharaohs, or deliberately like Roman Emperors, or in their rôle as saviours like Jesus or the Buddha. There is, in fact, as in biological evolution, a proliferation of specialised variety.[5]

Improvement of the type also takes place. In the first place, gods are transferred from the natural to the supernatural world, from the material to the non-material or spiritual. It is no longer the tree or the rock, the animal or the image which is worshipped, but the spiritual being behind the object or above the phenomena. At the same time, gods are spiritualised: in their make-up, less emphasis is laid on the crude forces of

---

[5] Homer Smith's *Man and His Gods* (Little, Brown, Boston, 1952) gives a vivid picture of the evolution of gods during human history.

physical nature and life, more on the human ideals of justice and truth, benevolence and wise but firm authority, compassion and love. The conflict between the unimproved and the improved type of god is familiarly exemplified by the struggle of the Hebrew prophets against 'idolatry.'

This also illustrates another kind of improvement—the trend from variety towards unity or at least some degree of unification. A first approach may be made by erecting one god in a pantheon to the position of chief ruler, as occurred with Zeus in Greek religion; or by divinising a human ruler as symbolising the unity of a vast empire over and above the variety of other gods and cults which it contains, as with the Roman Emperors.

A further radical step may take place by the conversion of a tribal god into a universal deity, as in Judaism. Or the universality and singularity of the deity may be proclaimed from the outset, as with Islam. Or finally the difficulty of embodying all attributes of divinity in a single person may be met by that brilliant device of Christian theology, triunity— the tripartite unity of the Trinity.

During cultural as during biological evolution, there is a struggle for existence between ideas and beliefs. There is not only a struggle between gods, but gods in general come into competition with other cultural entities which are seeking to interpret a similar range of phenomena, and so compete for the same area of ideological territory. The most important of these competitors are scientific concepts concerning various aspects of man's destiny, beginning with the world of physical nature in which that destiny is cast, and gradually invading the field of human nature.

The so-called 'conflict between religion and science' results from, or indeed is constituted by, this competition. In broadest terms, the competition is between two dominant types of cultural entity—the god hypothesis organised on the basis of mythical thinking, and the naturalistic hypothesis, organised on the basis of scientific method.

As a matter of historical fact, the results of this competition have been to expel gods from positions of effective control, from direct operative contact with more and more aspects of nature, to push them into an ever further remoteness behind or beyond phenomena. Newton showed that gods did not control the movements of the planets: Laplace in a famous aphorism affirmed that astronomy had no need of the god hypothesis: Darwin and Pasteur between them did the same for biology: and in our own century the rise of scientific psychology and the extension of historical knowledge have removed gods to a position where they are no longer of value in interpreting human behaviour and cannot be supposed to control human history or interfere with human affairs. Today, God can no longer be considered as the controller of the universe in any but a Pickwickian sense. The god hypothesis is no longer of any pragmatic value for the interpretation or comprehension of nature, and indeed often stands in the way of better and truer interpretation. Operationally, God is beginning to resemble not a ruler, but the last fading smile of a cosmic Cheshire Cat.

There has been other competition too —from the progressive secularisation of the sacred. Many areas of life once unquestioningly recognised as God's domain, many activities originally regarded as pertaining solely to the service or worship of gods, have now been secularised. In ancient Mesopotamia, economic affairs were a province of the god of the city, and astronomy was practised only by his ministers. Government was originally a divine prerogative: the Pharaohs of Egypt ruled as gods, and the Divine Right of Kings survived into modern times. Drama was first liberated from religion in classical Greece, and Sunday still belongs almost entirely to God in parts of Scotland. For the Jews, morals were the edict of Jehovah. Only in high civilisations does art become emancipated from religious or pseudo-religious domination. The Bible was for long regarded as the Word of God: we all know how this notion of divine revelation has impeded the growth of knowledge.[6]

This secular competition has also modified the evolution of gods during history. The relations with social activities have become progressively restricted. Today, gods are no longer spearheads of history, as they were in early Islam or in the Spanish conquest of the New World; they no longer operate in international politics as the Christian god did in the medieval days of the Holy Roman Empire; they no longer enforce opinion and doctrine by war or punishment, torture or death as in the Albigensian Crusade or the early days of the Inquisition or in Calvin's theocracy, nor are they effective in inciting large-scale persecutions, as against witches; they no longer have much say in laying down the curriculum of universities, or in dictating how citizens shall spend their time on Sundays; they no longer dictate economic behaviour, as for instance by prohibiting the lending of money at interest in medieval Christendom.

---

[6] The grave results of authoritarianism based on the arrogant assumption of possessing the sole and absolute religious truth are well documented by Paul Blanshard in his trilogy, *American Freedom and Catholic Power; Communism, Democracy and Catholic Power;* and *The Irish and Catholic Power;* while the alarming effects of idolising a sacred book are shown in Marley Cole's study of *Jehovah's Witnesses* (1956).

Eric Fromm, in his brilliant book *Escape from Freedom,* has pointed out how human timidity and the desire for reassurance at all costs have inhibited the rational approach and encouraged the growth of authoritarian systems of belief which claim to have all the answers.

There are of course local exceptions, such as the Scottish sabbath I have already mentioned, or the invoking of God to justify *apartheid* in South Africa; and sex has not yet been secularised, at least in respect of marriage, divorce, and birth-control, for Roman Catholics. But by and large, in the Western world and in various other countries too, they have been forced out of public affairs and everyday activities, and their dominions have been in large measure taken over by the secular arm: their functions are now largely confined to providing individual salvation and assurance and—what is clearly of the greatest importance—awareness of a reality transcending customary limitations of time and space, more embracing than the nation, more enduring than any present organisation, larger than humanity.

But though their direct social and political functions have been diminished, they still continue to exert a powerful indirect influence on affairs. If men think about their destiny in terms of the god hypothesis it is impossible to avoid certain conclusions and practical consequences: belief in gods inevitably influences human conduct and the course of history. Among innumerable examples I may point to the rise of the Egyptian priesthood to powerful land-ownership; the weakness of the Aztec empire; the discouragement of many branches of science by the Church; and in our own day the effect of the Roman Catholic view of God on divorce, education, and population, or the attempts to impose a Koranic constitution on Islamic countries. T. D. Kendrick's admirable little book *The Lisbon Earthquake* gives a particular example of the practical effects of a theological as opposed to a scientific hypothesis of the causation of natural disasters.

The last major feature of biological evolution is progress by replacement of old by new dominant types of organism. This too is paralleled in cultural evolution. In the ideological field, as we have seen, cultural entities and systems concerned with destiny are of three main types—the magic, the divine, theistic or daimonic, and the naturalistic, the first organised on the magic hypothesis of pervading non-material power and magic influence, the second on the god hypothesis of supernatural beings, the third on the scientific hypothesis of comprehensible natural forces.

Some time in prehistory gods replaced magic as the dominant type of belief-system, though magical concepts continued to play a considerable but increasingly subordinate rôle. The naturalistic type of belief-system made a premature appearance in the classical Greek world: but its organisation was then inadequate to compete with the god-system, and after a limited and primitive flowering, it went through a long period of repression and subordination. Only when it achieved an adequate plan of organisation, with the conscious formulation of scientific method in the seventeenth century, did it begin to play any significant rôle on the stage of cultural evolution. But from that time on, its rise was assured.

There is a striking parallel with the biological evolution of a new dominant group such as the mammals. The earliest mammals appeared in the Triassic. But they were only proto-mammals, which had not achieved fully mammalian organisation. As a result they remained small and unimportant for the best part of a hundred million years. It was not until the reptiles had become stabilised and perhaps over-specialised, and the mammalian organisation at the same time radically improved, and after a worldwide climatic revolution had removed many competitors, that the mammals began their rapid rise to dominance.

Cultural evolution, however, is never identical with biological. Evolving biological entities are separate organic types.

A single original organic type can produce a group by branching into a number of distinct sub-types, the ramifications remaining separate down to the level of species. A dominant group is one in which this process of diversification has produced a large variety of sub-types and a very large number of species: it is a biological entity defined on the one hand by the common ancestry of all its separate members, and on the other by its evolutionary success.

In cultural evolution, however, convergence and fusion are increasingly superposed on divergence and separation. Originally separate cultural elements may diffuse from one culture to another, ideas and practices arising in one segment of cultural life may invade other segments. Accordingly any cultural entity or system dealing with a major social function, like law or religion or education, is bound to be in some sort of a synthesis, containing elements from other systems and other cultures.

For the materialistic and scientific approach, there is no such thing as religion in the abstract, only a number of actual religions. And all actual religions are organs of man in society for dealing with the problem of destiny on the one hand and the sense of the sacred on the other. If you like to combine the two, you can say that religion attempts to deal with the problem of destiny considered in the light of our sense of its essential sacredness and inevitable mystery.

Destiny confronts us in particular events of our individual lives—sickness, falling in love, bereavement, death, good or ill fortune. It is involved in the ordering of our personal existence on earth and the great question-mark of our continuance after death. In national guise, it confronts us through war, or hardship, or social evil that makes us ashamed. Finally, destiny extends beyond the nation to humanity at large; and beyond humanity to all of nature. Destiny confronts us in our ideals and our short-comings, our aspirations and our sins, in our questioning thoughts about what is most comprehensive and most enduring, and about all that remains unknown. Perhaps most embracingly, destiny is apprehended in the confrontation of actuality with unrealised possibility, of our sense of guilt with our sense of sacredness, of our imperfections with our possible perfectibility.

The time is ripe for the dethronement of gods from their dominant position in our interpretation of destiny, in favour of a naturalistic type of belief-system. The supernatural is being swept out of the universe in the flood of new knowledge of what is natural. It will soon be as impossible for an intelligent, educated man or woman to believe in a god as it is now to believe that the earth is flat, that flies can be spontaneously generated, that disease is a divine punishment, or that death is always due to witchcraft. Gods will doubtless survive, sometimes under the protection of vested interests, or in the shelter of lazy minds, or as puppets used by politicians, or as refuges for unhappy and ignorant souls: but the god type will have ceased to be dominant in man's ideological evolution.

However, this will not happen unless the emerging naturalistic type of belief is fully adequate to its task: and that task is the formidable one of interpreting and canalising human destiny. Thus the short-lived Goddess of Reason of the French Revolution was a non-viable hybrid between the naturalistic and the god type of belief.

Already some non-theistic belief-systems have emerged to dominate large sections of humanity. The two most obvious are Nazism in Germany and Marxist Communism in Russia. Nazism was inherently self-destructive because of its claim to world domination by a small group. It was also grotesquely incorrect and limited as an interpretation of destiny, analogous to some of the primitive products of the theistic type, such as deified beasts, bloodthirsty tribal deities, or revengeful divine tyrants.

Marxist Communism is much better organised and more competent, but its purely materialist basis has limited its efficacy. It has tried to deny the reality of spiritual values. But they exist, and the Communists have had to accept the consequences of their ideological error, and grudgingly throw the churches open to the multitudes seeking the spiritual values which had been excluded from the system.

Before an adequate naturalistic belief-system can develop, scientific method must have been applied in all the fields contributing to human destiny: otherwise the system will be incomplete and will merely provide one of the premature syntheses that Gardner Murphy [7] rightly stigmatises as standing in the way of fuller comprehension. To be adequate, it must include scientific knowledge about cultural as well as cosmic and biological evolution, about human nature and social nature as well as about physical and organic nature, about values and gods, rituals and techniques, practical moralities and religious ideals as well as about atoms and cells, moons and suns, weather and disease-germs.

Only when scientific knowledge is organised in a way relevant to our ideas about destiny can we speak of a naturalistic belief-system; and only when the scientific knowledge concerns all aspects of destiny will the belief-system begin to be adequate.

---

[7] *Proceedings of the Columbia Bicentennial*, 1954.

J. ARTHUR THOMSON
ARTHUR S. EDDINGTON

Science and Religion

Sir J. Arthur Thomson (1861–1933), a distinguished biologist, was
Regius Professor of Natural History at Aberdeen University
from 1899 to 1930.
Sir Arthur S. Eddington (1882–1944), Plumian Professor of Astronomy
at Cambridge University from 1913 to 1944, was not only a major
figure in physical science but an indefatigable worker at the task
of relating science to everyday thought and to religion.

CHAPTER II

J. ARTHUR THOMSON

What should we rank as Man's greatest achievements? Some would place first his making of societies—often chequered with imperfections, yet always far above not only herd but hive. Others would emphasise his conquest of many of the forces of Nature, notably electricity, which he has harnessed in his service in scores of ways. But others would think more of the arts—poetry and painting, music and architecture, with their unique power of expressing the inexpressible. So we might continue, but, whatever the order, the list must include *Science,* which makes the world translucent, and *Religion,* which hitches our wagon to a star.

From *Science and Religion* (1931), ed. by
M. Pupin, Ch. II, by Sir J. Arthur Thomson,
and Ch. IX, by Sir Arthur S. Eddington. Re-
printed by permission of Sir Landsborough
Thomson and Trinity College, Cambridge
University.

Now while it is more profitable to have a fierce controversy over great questions than to be for ever amiable over trivialities, it seems in some measure wasteful that two of man's greatest achievements—Science and Religion—should be so often pitted against one another. Would it not be better to spend the time and energy in gaining more science and more religion, for none of us has too much of either? Suppose it be allowed that religion, like science, is a natural and necessary activity of the evolving spirit of man; that both Religion and Science in pure form are inherently noble; that both, apart from perversions, make for the enrichment of life: then it seems a pity that they should be so often opposed as antithetic. Our first point is that, as regards essentials, the conflict between Science and Religion is very largely a false antithesis. It is due to a failure to understand the different aims and methods and ideas of the two great activities. This raises the questions: *What is Science?* and *What is Religion?*

Science is a system of criticised knowledge, giving empirical descriptions of things and changes, expressed in the simplest and tersest terms; it is based on experiment and observation, and verifiable by all normally constituted minds who can use the methods. Science aims at descriptive formulation in terms of the lowest common denominators available at the time, such as Electrons, Radiations, Protoplasm, and Mind—the measure of all. It seeks to answer the questions: *What is this? Whence is it? How does it come to be as it is, and how does it continue in being?* and sometimes *Whither away?* as when we contemplate an evolving species or a dying star. But Science as science never asks the question *Why?* That is to say, it never inquires into the meaning, or significance, or purpose of this manifold Being, Becoming, and Having Been. That is not its métier.

For many years now it has been recognised by all the great makers of new knowledge, that the aim of Science is *descriptive*. Science sums up in so-called 'Laws,' which are intellectual shorthand formulæ describing uniformities of sequence—'If this, then that,' in short. It is rather pedantic to say that science never *explains* anything, but it is true to say that its explanations are never in terms of purpose, or deep-down meaning. They simply amount to saying something like this: These puzzling occurrences are instances of Laws 3, 7, and 10; or, This state of affairs is the natural and necessary outcome of a long process of evolution, in which the following stages and factors can be recognised. Thus science does not pretend to be a bedrock of truth. It is an indispensable, yet partial and abstract, kind of knowledge—partial and abstract because it must restrict itself, if it is true to itself, to certain methods. To change the metaphor, science fishes in the sea of reality with particular kinds of net—called scientific methods—and there may be much in the unfathomed sea which

the meshes of the scientific net cannot catch. Thus the geologist as geologist does not consider the beauty of the countryside, though that is as real to us as its mineralogy. The astronomer, as astronomer, aims at a chemico-physical account of the nebular mass that gave rise to our Solar System, but he does not raise the point that from out of it there somehow emerged on our earth a complex world of life, including the astronomer himself. He abstracts the nebula from its remote results.

Science has not always been so modest, but we must deal with the science of today, and all its leaders are agreed that as scientific investigators they deal only with descriptions of what meets the eye—the scientific eye, of course, which can see the invisible. They are not concerned with anything ultimate, or with any question of the beginning or the ending, or with the purpose or meaning of it all. Science makes the world increasingly intelligible; but it does not even ask whether it is or is not rationalisable.

What then is Religion? In the course of the ages man has often become religious when he struggled poignantly to the limit of his reach—in doing, feeling, or thinking. In his struggle with a callous environment—storms, wild beasts, drought, floods, fire, famine—man has often found himself baulked and helpless. At the limit of his practical effort he became religious, stretching out his hands towards a supposed super-sensuous dynasty, towards unseen Powers, towards an unknown God. Whether he offered propitiatory gifts, or burnt incense, or prayed, matters not for our purpose here; the religious note is the appeal to some spiritual power. Nowadays, when man's mastery of Nature is so far-reaching, this practical pathway to religion is not much trodden, except by those who take very seriously their failures to live a good life. Modern man rarely prays for rain or for its cessation.

In the second place, man has often found himself overwhelmed by emotional stress—high joys, deep sorrows, the æsthetic thrill, a sense of mystery, the feeling of awesomeness or, as Professor Julian Huxley calls it, sacredness. An overwhelming surge of emotion has led many to religion in the past, and this emotional pathway remains wide open to-day, all the more since science in dissolving minor mysteries leaves the wonder of the world confessed. When the half-gods go, the God may arrive.

The third pathway to religious activity is found by some of those who strain hard at the limit of their intellectual reach. Science discloses a very impressive world —immense, intricate, orderly, progressive: it is difficult not to try to make sense of it as a whole. Has evolution some meaning? Is there any spiritual reality behind it all? Are we part of a great purpose? And so the perennial questions have arisen century after century, and are arising still. Some philosophies seek to answer; and religion, on its intellectual side, is often the layman's naïve philosophy.

In past ages man's religious activity has naturally found practical, emotional, and intellectual expression. Practical, for instance, when he offered propitiatory sacrifice or a life's devotion; emotional, for instance, when he worshipped; and intellectual, for instance, when he clutched at some interpretative idea or theory or 'over-belief.' All three expressions remain today.

Robert Bridges wrote a famous essay on 'The Necessity of Poetry'; so one may speak, if one believes in it, of 'The Necessity of Religion'—the necessity of beliefs to which men are led when they strain at the limits of their practical, emotional, or intellectual reach. To my thinking, the religious 'over-beliefs,' except in the low grade or degraded form that we call magic, always imply something beyond ordinary experience, some-thing spiritual or mystical. We hitch our wagon to a star; we send tendrils towards the absolute; we believe in God. Thus, there is little that is specifically religious in the idea of a god who is but the sum-total of the physical energies in the Universe. For such a god is still no more than a physical quantity. The God we would worship is spiritual. In the words of the Shorter Catechism, 'God is a Spirit, Infinite, Eternal, and Unchangeable in His Being, Wisdom, Power, Holiness, Justice, Goodness, and Truth.'

Here then we come back to our thesis, that if science is descriptive formulation and if religion (on its intellectual side) is a transcendental or mystical interpre-tation, there should not be any *radical* antithesis between them. Such a sorry cry as 'The Bible *or* Darwin' illustrates the false antithesis, sounding like 'Food *or* Fresh Air'; the plain answer in both cases being 'More of both.'

Our point is that Science describes in terms of the lowest common denomina-tors available; Religion interprets in terms of the greatest common measure. In essence they are incommensurables. There is no contradiction in saying in one sentence that Man evolved by natural processes from a Simian stock, and say-ing in another sentence that man is the child of God. But we must not try to speak two languages at once.

Our thesis is open to three obvious ob-jections. The first is on the part of those who declare that they feel no necessity for religion. They are satisfied with the knowledge that science affords; they do not strain at the limit of their intellectual reach; they are content not to try to ex-plain or interpret things; they distrust as an anachronism the feeling of mystery that remains after the scientific concepts have formulated all they can; they have no sense of the mystical, just as others have no ear for music. What can we reply to these stern spirits, save that most men, above the preoccupiedly grazing herd, will insist on putting the question Why? and on getting some answer; and furthermore that there is a hint of arrogance in dogmatically declaring that the only kind of trustworthy knowledge is that which is reached by scientific methods. Surely, science is not the only pathway to reality or to truth.

The second objection to our thesis—that science and religion speak different languages—is that it involves a relapse to the device of trying to have idea-tight compartments in the mind. We are asked: Is not your thesis too much like saying: Hold to your scientific formulæ and hold to your religious over-beliefs, but don't let them mix. Render unto Science the things that are Science's and unto Religion the things that are Religion's, but try to keep the rendering for different days of the week. But this is a caricature of our view. While we maintain that science and religion are two quite different ways of looking at things, and to be kept apart, we cannot contemplate giving houseroom to any religious conviction, or expression of a religious conviction, that is obviously contradicted by some securely established scientific conclusion. There must be consistency. Nor do we think of two domains, preserves for science and preserves for religion: all things are for religion and all things for science, save that by hypothesis science cannot apply its methods to the mystical or spiritual. We must apply science to everything that its methods will grip. Thus there is a science of æsthetics, of dreams, of ideals, even of religions. Similarly to the whole universe, broad and deep and high—including science itself—there is applicable the religious interpretation that it expresses part of a Divine idea, imagination, or purpose. The whole ocean is open to scientific and to religious inquiry; but the aims of the two inquiries are different.

To our view—that there should be no radical antithesis between science and religion—a third objection is that this is like asking the combatants in a protracted war to recognise that it has all been a misunderstanding. But our thesis is not that there is no conflict, but that it should not be radical. The religious doctrine of creation implies the belief that the institution of the Order of Nature expressed a Divine Purpose or Idea; it is not inconsistent with this to hold also to the scientific view that the mode of the Becoming has been evolutionary. The two views are complementary, not antithetic: the one is interpretative, the other descriptive.

But some measure of struggle and controversy must and should arise when the expression of the religious conviction jars with the expression of the scientific conclusion. For in the inexact sciences especially, the expression of the scientific conclusion—say the biological view of man—is often shot through with implications which are not scientifically warranted. Fundamentalism was in part a justifiable recoil from crudely expressed evolutionism, and similarly many scientific inquirers have justifiably recoiled from hopeless anachronisms in religious interpretation.

The history of intellectual development shows that science has repeatedly made certain a new view of the world and of man, and that after a period of struggle this has been followed by some adaptive change in the concept of God. Thus the scientific demonstration of what we may continue to call the 'Reign of Law' made it impossible for thoughtful men to think of a God who was always interfering with his Cosmos. Pope finished with that view in the irony of his familiar line: 'Shall gravitation cease when *you* go by?' Similarly, when Darwin made it quite clear that the origin of adaptations could be scientifically accounted for, it became impossible for thoughtful men to speak any longer of God as the Divine Artificer. But in both these cases, the result of controversy was refinement of the idea of God.

In most cases controversy arises and should arise when there is *trespass,* when the religious mind insists on being descriptive, or when the scientific mind insists on being interpretative. Thus, if science, unconsciously or ignorantly, incorporates some piece of bad metaphysics, and insists on an exclusively materialistic or even an exclusively behaviourist description of man, religion must rebel —not to speak of common sense. On the other hand when a certain Bishop Lightfoot (not the other one), writing in 1618, declared that man was created by the Trinity about 4004 B.C. and about nine o'clock in the morning, he was gratuitously asking for trouble, trespassing on the descriptive province of the anthropologist. Similarly, from the pulpit to-day we have heard statements made in regard to the resurrection of the body, which could not but be outrageous in the ears of any student of chemistry and physics. Yet we are quite prepared to hear that there is an esoteric religious truth within the out-of-date expression-husk in which the doctrine in question is enclosed.

Much controversy is due to trespass and might be avoided; but the subtler controversies are due to the difficulty of reconciling somewhat out-of-date religious expressions with somewhat premature scientific pronouncements, or vice versa.

In thinking of science and religion, two of the noblest expressions of the evolving spirit of man, we must not allow ourselves to be too much preoccupied with their conflicts, we should think also of their mutual stimulus. How has science helped religion and how may it continue to be of service? Science is continually giving man a new world, and every great discoverer—Copernicus, Newton, Darwin, Einstein—is a Columbus. To each successive new world it is for philosophy and religion to adjust man's outlook, and though the transitions are often painful, the result in the long run is bound to be progressive; for Evolution as a whole is integrative, and so it must be with the development of our world-outlook.

Our new world excels that of our forefathers in its grandeur, its orderliness, its beauty, its revelation of advance or progress, its disclosure of the growing emancipation of mind in animal evolution, in its strange organic anticipations of human ideals, in its deep awesomeness, and in its *suggestions* that Nature is Nature for a purpose. Here we partly mean that, just as we have become accustomed scientifically to see Man in the light of evolution, so philosophically we must try to see evolution in the light of Man—the whole process in the light of its present climax. We say climax since the evolutionist does not like to speak of ending, there being no warrant for supposing that the age-long advance is about to stop.

The religious mind must not be disappointed because the naturalist no longer argues from Nature to Nature's God; for that is not his aim, and it would in any case be a conclusion much too big for the premises—the fallacy of transcendent inference. But what we should be grateful for is that the naturalist has made it easier for the religious mood to breathe in the scientific world to-day than in that of our forefathers. Caprice has disappeared from the world; the fortuitous has shrivelled; it is an ascent not a descent that man has behind him; the momentum of Nature, embodied in flesh and blood, is much more on the side of the angels than was previously supposed, and it is with us at our best. Highest of all, the creationist's concept of the Supreme Reality has given place to the evolutionist's finer, though vaguer, vision. Jehovah's name has been changed from 'I am that I am' to 'I will be what I will be.' While it is not the business of science to search after God, as Mr Langdon-

Davies has mistakenly maintained in his brilliant book, *Man and His Universe,* we deliberately say that one of the great services of science to Man has been to lead him to a nobler view of God. In a very literal sense science has given man a new heaven and a new earth, and in this he continues to strain at the limit of his intellectual effort and often finds no peace except that which literally passeth understanding—a belief in God.

And not only has science given us a new world, it has given us a new man—a venerable antiquity and yet a newcomer; a repository of an inconceivably long past and yet a mutant still; a more intelligible being than he was to our grandparents and yet, in other ways, as the Greek poet said, the crowning wonder of the world. Sound science has done something to save us from an easygoing view of ourselves; but we must continue to see to it that our picture portrays man whole, omitting neither his pedigree and Primary Unconscious on the one hand, nor his high achievements and still higher aspirations on the other. Science warrants us in thinking nobly of Man, and many feel the need of a correspondingly noble religious interpretation. And we must not slur over the fact that among the data that lead us to religious feelings and beliefs when scientific formulæ stop short, is just Science itself—this eerie measurement of creation by one of its creatures. To some of us it is impossible to make sense of the fact of science save as a distant echo of the Divine Creator. In any case, if we are aiming at some resoluteness in our thinking, we must not simply take science for granted. Science has gradually grown from humble beginnings; it has become an august system of knowledge, and a light on man's path; it is in many ways astounding (what Aristotle called 'thaumaston'), and it seems to many to demand some interpretation, especially if we accept the Aristotelian doctrine that there is nothing in the end which was not also in kind in the beginning.

At the present climax of Science there is Reason triumphant; what then in the beginning? Here our straining at the limit of our intellectual endeavour brings us back perhaps to the wisdom of the old words:

In the beginning was Mind,
and that Mind was with God,
and the Mind was God.
All things were made by it;
and without it was not anything made
    that was made.
In it was life
and the life was the light of men.

Instead, then, of always thinking of the conflict between science and religion, with faults on both sides, we should also consider how science may be of service to religion, that is if we believe in the legitimacy of religion at all. Many men and women become religious traditionally, but if the initiative is their own, it is usually because they have reached some strain-limit—whether that be along practical, emotional, or intellectual lines. But we must not think of religious activities as mere attempts to eke out the normal by appeals to the mystical; they are that, but they are more, else too pathetically like tendrils clinging to tendrils. They have their reward, we believe, by bringing the religious supplicant, or worshipper, or faith-adventurer, into closer touch with the Supreme Reality. Religion would not have survived so long if the religious had not received *some* reward, which, at various times, they have called 'life,' 'salvation,' 'grace' or 'truth.' The evolving idea of God is man's largest thought, and what may it not mean for a man? But behind the idea there is the Supreme Reality itself, never far from any one of us. Even a glimpse of the Vision of God may be an enrichment of life.

Finally, I wish simply to raise the very unorthodox question: May science be helped by religion? Most of my scientific colleagues would answer with a thunderingly emphatic negative. For science follows the arduous path of accurate experiment and precise formulation; it analyses, measures, registers, and sums up, and all without being influenced in statement or methods by any hope or any fear. When at work, science keeps emotion at a spear's length; its emblem might be the light of the glow-worm, all light without any heat-rays. It will be an evil day when science at work stops to dance to any piping of poetry, philosophy, or religion. But let us beware of compartmental minds! Do not let us be too sure that science has nothing to learn from religion. That seems very unlikely on the face of it, for both are concerned with the enlightenment or enrichment of life in evolution. No doubt science aims primarily at understanding, being, as Bacon said, 'luminiferous' rather than "fructiferous.' Yet science is for life, not life for science, and it is continually being applied by man to practical problems— more so than ever to-day. But until recently, poetry, art and religion have always been far ahead of science in their intuition of ideals, with which, indeed, science as science is not directly concerned. Hence some possible value to science. Though science is impersonal and unemotional in its method of working, it sets itself to tackle practical problems in the light of sure knowledge. As Bacon said, it is not solely for the glory of the Creator, it is also for the relief of man's estate. It seeks primarily for understanding, but it also seeks, less directly no doubt, to remove evils and increase good. Now it is plain that religion must have to most of the evils of life, though not to ignorance, a more sensitive conscience than is possible to science. In this way, as spur and as reins, religion may help science towards the amelioration of life.

Take another instance: It is part of the ambition of the socialised biologist to understand human life, so as to help man to make the most of each stage in its trajectory from childhood to senescence. Now, as Professor Patrick Geddes has pointed out in scholarly detail, there is in Greek mythology—in Olympus and Parnassus alike—a great wealth of suggestion for psycho-biological and bio-psychological research and endeavour, sometimes along lines which are full of promise for eugenist and hygienist, educationist, moralist and more. Thus it seems vastly improbable that biology will not be illumined by a study of the Greek gods and goddesses, who were so largely idealisations of the various phases of human life, and by a study not of Olympus only, but of the muses and the furies too. Religion to the aid of biology!

To sum up our view. Much of the conflict between science and religion is the outcome of misunderstanding, of failing to distinguish empirical description and transcendental interpretation—the lowest common denominator from the greatest common measure. But much of the controversy is necessary and to the good of both sides; for it tends to the sublimation of religious ideas, and it tends to keep science conscious of its limitations. What we are surest about is that we need *more* science and *more* religion—ever so much more.

CHAPTER IX

ARTHUR S. EDDINGTON

If you will look up at the sky in the direction of the constellation Andromeda and spend a few moments scrutinising the faintest stars you see, you will notice one that is not a sharp point of light like the rest but has a hazy appearance. That star is unique among all that are visible to the naked eye. It is not properly a star; we might rather describe it as a universe. It teaches us that when we have taken together the Sun and all the other naked-eye stars and many hundreds of millions of telescopic stars we have not yet reached the end of things. We have explored only one island—one oasis in the desert of space; in the far distance we discern another island which is that faint patch of light in Andromeda. With the help of a telescope we can make out a great many more, in fact a whole archipelago of island universes stretching away one behind another till our sight fails. That speck of light which anyone may see is a sample of one of these islands; it is a world not only remote in space but remote in time. Long before the dawn of history the light now entering our eyes started on its journey across the great gulf between the islands. When you look at it you are looking back 900,000 years into the past.

Amid this profusion of worlds and space and time, where do we come in? Our home, the Earth, is the fifth or sixth largest planet belonging to an inconspicuous middle-grade star in one of the numerous islands of the archipelago. Doubtless there are other globes which are or have been tenanted by beings of similar nature to ourselves; but we have some reason to think that such globes are uncommon. It seems that normally matter collects in big lumps with terrifically high temperature; the formation of small cool globes fit for habitation is no part of the normal scheme, though it has happened occasionally by a rare accident. Nature seems to have been intent on a vast scheme of evolution of fiery globes, an epic of milliards of years. As for Man —that was an unfortunate incident which it seems rather ungenerous to refer to. It was only a trifling hitch in the machinery—not of very serious consequence to the universe. No need to be always raking up against Nature her one little inadvertence.

Is that how you and I come in? To realise the insignificance of our race amid the majesty of the universe is prob-

ably healthful. But it brings to us a more alarming thought. For Man is the typical custodian of certain qualities or illusions which make a great difference to the significance of things. He displays purpose in an inorganic world of chance. He *can* represent truth, righteousness, sacrifice. In him there flickers for a few brief years a spark from the divine spirit. Are these as insignificant as he is?

It may possibly be going too far to say that our bodies are pieces of stellar matter which by a contingency not sufficiently guarded against have taken advantage of the low temperature to assume unusual complication and perform the series of strange antics we call 'life.' But I do not combat this view; even if I doubt its tenability, I keep an open mind, and am unwilling to base philosophy or religion on the assumption that it must necessarily break down. But alongside this there is another outlook. Science is an attempt to set in order the facts of experience. Everyone will agree that it has met with wonderful success; and the picture which it draws of the physical universe is its answer to the problem. But it does not start quite at the beginning of the Problem of Experience. The first question asked about facts or theories such as I have been describing is 'Are they true?' I want to emphasise that even more significant than the astronomical results themselves is the fact that this question about them so urgently arises. The question 'Is it true?' changes the complexion of the world of experience—not because it is asked *about* the world but because it is asked *in* the world. If we go right back to the beginning the first thing we must recognise in the world is something intent on truth —something to which it matters intensely that belief should be true. We settle that as the first ingredient of the world of experience, before we invite science to take the problem in hand and put in order other facts of experience. If in its survey of the universe science rediscovers the presence of such an ingredient, well and good; if not the ingredient remains none the less essential, for otherwise the whole quest is stultified.

What is the truth about ourselves? We may incline to various answers. We are a bit of a star gone wrong. We are complicated physical machinery—puppets that strut and talk and laugh and die as the hand of time turns the handle beneath. But let us remember that there is one elementary inescapable answer. We are *that which asks the question*. Responsibility towards truth is an attribute of our nature. It is through our spiritual nature, of which responsibility for truth is a typical manifestation, that we first come into the world of experience; our entry via the physical universe is a re-entry. The strange association of soul and body—of responsibility for truth with a bit of stellar matter that got cold by accident—is a problem in which we cannot but feel intense interest, but not an anxious interest as though the existence and significance of a spiritual side of experience were hanging in the balance. The solution must fit the data; we cannot alter the data to fit the alleged solution.

I do not regard the phenomenon of living matter (in so far as it can be treated apart from the phenomenon of consciousness) as necessarily outside the scope of physics and chemistry. Arguments that, because a living creature is an organism, it *ipso facto* possesses something which can never be understood in terms of physical science, do not impress me. I think it is insufficiently recognised that modern theoretical physics is very much concerned with the study of organisation; and from organisation to organism does not seem an impossible stride. It may happen that some day science will be able to show how from the entities of physics creatures might have been formed which are counterparts of ourselves even to the point of being endowed with life. The scientist will perhaps point out the

nervous mechanism of this creature, its powers of motion, of growth, of reproduction, and end by saying 'That's you.' But remember the inescapable test. 'Is it concerned with truth as I am; then I will acknowledge that it is indeed myself.' We demand something more even than consciousness. The scientist might point to motions in the brain and say that these really mean sensations, emotions, thoughts; and perhaps supply a code to translate the motions into corresponding thoughts. Even if we accept this rather inadequate substitute for consciousness as we intimately know it, we must still protest: 'You have shown us a creature which thinks and believes; you have not shown us a creature to whom it *matters* (in any non-utilitarian sense) what it thinks and believes.' The inmost ego, possessing what I have called the inescapable attribute, can never be part of the physical world unless we alter the meaning of the word 'physical' to 'spiritual'—a change hardly to the advantage of clear thinking. But having disowned our supposed double, we can say to the scientist: 'If you will hand over this Robot who pretends to be me, and let it be filled with the attribute at present lacking and perhaps other spiritual attributes which I claim on similar though less indisputable grounds, we may arrive at something that is indeed myself.'

An interesting point is that the recent revolutionary changes of science have made this kind of co-operative solution of the Problem of Experience more practicable than it used to be. A few years ago the suggestion of taking the physically constructed man and adapting him to a spiritual nature by casually adding something, would have been a mere figure of speech—a verbal gliding over of insuperable difficulties. In much the same way we talk loosely of building a Robot and then breathing life into him. A Robot is presumably not constructed to bear such last-minute changes of design; he is a delicate piece of mechanism designed to work mechanically, and to adapt him for anything else would involve wholesale reconstruction. To put it crudely, if you want to fill a vessel with anything you must make it hollow, and the old-fashioned material body was not hollow enough to be a receptacle of spiritual nature. I know that the change in our conception of the material universe and of the aims of physics must be very puzzling to most people; but I have not time to explain or defend it. I will only say that any of the young theoretical physicists of to-day will tell you that what he is dragging to light as the basis of all the phenomena that come within his province is a scheme of symbols connected by mathematical equations. That is what the physical universe boils down into, when probed by the methods which a physicist can apply. Now a skeleton scheme of symbols is hollow enough to hold anything. It can be—nay it cries out to be —filled with something to transform it from skeleton into being, from shadow into actuality, from symbols into the interpretation of the symbols. And if ever the scientist solves the problem of the living body, he should no longer be tempted to point to his result and say 'That's you.' He will say rather: 'That is how I symbolise you in my description and explanation of those of your properties which I can observe and measure. If you claim any deeper insight into your own nature—any knowledge of what it really is that these symbols symbolise— you can rest assured that I have no rival interpretation of the symbols to propose.' The skeleton is the whole contribution of physics to the solution of the Problem of Experience; from the clothing of the skeleton it stands aloof.

I think we may say that, although the physicist has carried his work to greater perfection than formerly, he now puts it in a form which does not hide its incompleteness. Implicitly, if not explicitly, he advertises for someone to complete it. And we who are interested in the non-material aspects of experience are not butting in; we are answering his advertisement. But, of course, it does not follow that general opinion among physicists regards us as suitable applicants for the job; I admit that there are many who would say that it is better to let sound work remain uncompleted than to let it be embellished by incompetent workmen as they deem us to be.

The scientific conception of the world has come to differ more and more from the commonplace conception, until we have been forced to ask ourselves what really is the aim of this scientific transformation. The doctrine that 'things are not what they seem' is all very well in moderation; but it has proceeded so far that we have to remind ourselves that the world of appearances is the one we have actually to adjust our lives to. That was not always so. At first the progress of scientific thought consisted in correcting gross errors in the commonplace outlook. We learned that the earth was spherical, not flat. That does not refer to some abstract scientific earth, but to the earth we know so well with all its colour, beauty and homeliness. I confess that when I think of a Test Match in Australia I cannot help picturing it as played upside down—so much has the roundness of the earth become part of a familiar outlook. We learned that the earth was rotating. For the most part we give an intellectual assent to this without attempting to weave it into our familiar conception, but we can picture it if we try. In Rossetti's poem the Blessed Damosel looked down from the golden balcony of Heaven through

The void as low as where this earth
Spins like a fretful midge.

Looking from the abode of truth, perfect truth alone can enter her mind. She must see the earth as it really is—like a whirling insect. But now let us try something fairly modern. In Einstein's theory the earth, like other matter, is a curvature of space-time, and what we commonly call the spin of the earth is a ratio of two of the components of curvature. What is the Blessed Damosel going to make of that? I am afraid she will have to be a bit of a blue-stocking. Perhaps there is no great harm in that. I am not sure that I would think it derogatory to an angel to accuse him of understanding Einstein's theory. My objection is more serious. If the Blessed Damosel sees the earth in the Einsteinian way she will be seeing truly—I can feel little doubt as to that—but she will be *missing the point*. It is as though we took her to a picture gallery, and she (with that painful truthfulness which cannot recognise anything that is not really there) saw ten square yards of yellow paint, five of crimson, and so on.

So long as physics in tinkering with the familiar world was able to retain those aspects which appeal to the æsthetic side of our nature, it might with some show of reason claim to cover the whole of experience; and those who claimed that there was another, religious aspect of experience had to fight for their claim. But now that its picture omits so much that is obviously essential, there is no suggestion that it is the whole truth about experience. To make such a claim would bring protest not only from those religiously inclined but from all who recognise that man is not merely a scientific measuring machine. If it were necessary I would at this point turn aside to defend the scientist for pursuing the development of a highly specialised solution of one side of the Problem of Experience and ignoring the rest; but I will content myself with reminding you that it is through his efforts in this direction that my voice is now being heard by you. At any rate there is method in his madness.

Another striking change of scientific views is in regard to determinism—the view that the future is predestined, and that Time merely turns over the leaves of a story that is already written—

Yea the first Morning of Creation wrote
What the last Dawn of Reckoning shall read.

Until recently this was almost universally accepted as the teaching of science—at least in regard to the material universe. It is the distinctive principle of the mechanistic outlook which superseded the crude materialistic outlook. But to-day physical theory is not mechanistic, and it is built on a foundation which knows nothing of this supposed determinism. So far as we have yet gone in our probing of the material universe, we find no evidence in favour of determinism. The new theory recognises a wide domain of phenomena in which the future is for all practical purposes definitely predictable, and explains why this is possible; but it does not assume the same predictability for all physical phenomena. According to the type of phenomenon studied, forecasts of the future have different degrees of probability ranging from overwhelming odds to even chances. The denial of determinism is not merely qualitative but quantitative; we have actually a mathematical formula indicating just how far the course of events deviates from complete predictability.

I do not think there is any serious division of opinion as to the decease of determinism. If there is a division among scientists it is between the mourners and the jubilants. The mourners naturally hope that determinism will one day be re-established in its old position in physics; that is possible, but personally I see no reason to expect that it will return in any shape or form. In any case, our concern is not with prophetic anticipations of what science may be like in future, but with the relations between present-day science and religion. To discuss the extent and consequences of this change would lead to questions too technical to be dealt with here. (To avoid possible misunderstanding I had better say that I do not think it makes any important difference to special theological questions such as miracle, or 'direct answer' to prayer.) But I think there is no longer any need to doubt our intuition of free will. Our minds are not merely registering a predetermined sequence of thoughts and decisions. Our purposes, our volitions are genuine; and ours is the responsibility for what ensues from them. It seems necessary to admit this, for we are scarcely likely to accept a theory which would make the human spirit *more* mechanistic than the physical universe.

I now turn to the question, what must be put into the skeleton scheme of symbols. I have said that physical science stands aloof from this transmutation, and if I say anything positive on this side of the question it is not as a scientist that I claim to speak.

It was by looking into our own nature that we revealed the first failure of the physical universe to be co-extensive with our experience of reality. The 'something to which truth matters' must surely have a place in reality, if we are to use the term reality at all. In our own nature, or through the contact of our consciousness with a nature transcending ours, there are other things that claim the same kind of recognition—a sense of beauty, of morality, and finally at the root of all spiritual religion an experience which we describe as the presence of God. In suggesting that these things constitute a spiritual world I am not trying to substantialise them or objectivise them—to make them out other than we find them to be in our experience of them. But I would say that when from the human heart, perplexed with the mystery of existence, the cry goes up, 'What is it all about?', it is no true answer to look only at that part of experience which comes to us through certain sensory organs and reply: 'It is about atoms and chaos; it is

about a universe of fiery globes rolling on to impending doom; it is about tensors and non-commutative algebra.' Rather it is about a spirit within which truth has its shrine, with potentialities of self-fulfilment in its response to beauty and right. Shall I not also add that even as light and colour and sound come into our minds from a world beyond, so these other stirrings of consciousness come from something which, whether we describe it as beyond or deep within ourselves, is wider than our own individual personality?

It is the essence of religion that it presents this side of experience as a matter of everyday life. To live in it, we have to grasp it in the form of familiar recognition and not as a series of abstract scientific statements. Its counterpart in our outward life is the familiar world and not the symbolic scientific universe. The man who commonly spoke of his ordinary surroundings in scientific language would be insufferable; and if God really has a part in our everyday life, I do not think we need mind if the critic trips us up for speaking and thinking of him unscientifically.

But perhaps the earnest Christian will say: 'I am a plain man and I think of God unscientifically, as you allow. It means a great deal to me to conceive God as the Father, from whom comes power and guidance and to whom I may turn with devotion and trust. But just because it means so much, I have no use for it if it is only a convenient fiction which will not stand close examination. Can you not give some assurance that there is such a God in reality, and that belief in him is not merely a sop to my limited understanding?' The fear is that when we come to analyse that which we call religious experience, we shall find that the God apparently revealed in it is merely a personification of certain abstract principles. Now I frankly admit that the application of any method which we should call scientific to the examination of our religious experience is likely to work this kind of havoc. But what else could we expect? Although the method of physical science is inapplicable, the methods of the less exact sciences which are to some extent modelled on it may perhaps be applied. They involve the same kind of abstraction and codifying. If our treatment consists in codifying, what can we possibly get but a code? The fact that scientific method seems to reduce God to something like an ethical code may throw some light on the nature of scientific method; I doubt if it throws much light on the nature of God. If the consideration of religious experience in the light of psychology seems to remove from the conception of God every attribute that calls forth our worship or love, it is pertinent to consider whether something of the same sort has not happened to our human friends after psychology has systematised and scheduled them. It does not fall within my scope to give the questioner the assurance he desires; I doubt whether there is any assurance to be obtained except through the power of the religious experience itself; but I bid him hold fast to his own intimate knowledge of the nature of that experience. I think that that will take him closer to the ultimate truth than codifying and symbolising can reach.

I know that my writings have disappointed many because I set aside the question, Is God an objective reality? Before attempting to answer it it would be necessary to catechise the questioner as to what meaning—if any—he associates with the word objective. I do not think that it is possible to make the same hard and fast distinction between subjective and objective that we used to make. The theory of relativity has taught us that the subjective element in our experience of the physical universe is far stronger than we had previously suspected. It is true that in relativity theory we continue our attempt to reach purely objective truth. But what results? A world so abstract that only a mathematical symbol could inhabit it. In the other great modern development of physics—the quantum theory—we have, if I am not mistaken, abandoned the aim, and become content to analyse the physical universe into ultimate elements which are frankly subjective. If it is difficult to separate out the subjective element in our knowledge of the external world, it must be much more difficult to distinguish it when we come to the problem of a self-knowing consciousness, where subject and object—that which knows and that which is known—are one and the same.

I have been laying great stress on *experience;* in this I am following the dictates of modern physics. But I do not wish to imply that every experience is to be taken at face value. There is such a thing as illusion, and we must try not to be deceived. In any attempt to go deeply into the meaning of religious experience we are confronted by the difficult problem of how to detect and eliminate illusion and self-deception. I recognise that the problem exists, but I must excuse myself from attempting a solution. The operation of cutting out illusion in the spiritual domain requires a delicate surgical knife; and the only instrument that I, a physicist, can manipulate is a bludgeon which, it is true, crushes illusion, but at the same time crushes everything of non-material significance and even reduces the material world to a state of uncreatedness. For I am convinced that if in physics we pursued to the bitter end our attempt to reach purely objective reality, we should simply undo the work of creation and present the world as we might conceive it to have been before the Spirit moved upon the face of the waters. The spiritual element in our experience is the creative element, and if we remove it as we have tried to do in physics on the ground that it also creates illusion, we must ultimately reach the nothingness which was in the Beginning.

Reasoning is our great ally in the quest for truth. But reasoning can only start from premises; and at the beginning of the argument we must always come back to innate convictions. There are such convictions at the base even of physical science. We are helpless unless we admit also (as perhaps the strongest conviction of all) that we have within us some power of self-criticism to test the validity of our own convictions. The power is not infallible, that is to say it is not infallible when associated with human frailty; but neither is reasoning infallible when practised by our blundering intelligence. I think that this power can be nothing less than a ray proceeding from the light of absolute Truth, a thought proceeding from the absolute Mind. With this guidance we may embark on the adventure of spiritual life uncharted though it be. It is sufficient that we carry a compass.

C. D. BROAD

The Present Relations of Science and Religion

Fifty or sixty years ago anyone fluttering the pages of one of the many magazines which then catered for the cultivated and intelligent English reader would have been fairly certain to come upon an article bearing somewhat the same title as that ·of the present paper. The author would probably be an eminent scientist, such as Huxley or Clifford; a distinguished scholar, such as Frederic Harrison or Edmund Gurney; or a politician of cabinet rank, such as Gladstone or Morley. Whichever side he might take, he would write with the moral fervour of which Englishmen at that time had an inexhaustible supply. Nowadays the so-called 'conflict between Religion and Science,' which was then appetizingly hot from

From C. D. Broad, *Religion, Philosophy and Psychical Research* (1953). Reprinted by permission of Routledge & Kegan Paul Ltd., and Humanities Press Inc.

the oven, has acquired something of the repulsiveness of half-cold mutton in half-congealed gravy. There seems to be a widespread opinion that Sir Arthur Eddington and Sir James Jeans, with some highly technical and not readily intelligible assistance from Professor Whitehead, have enabled the lion to lie down with the lamb. Well, I have no wish to pipe a discordant note in this scene of Messianic harmony. But I cannot help reflecting that psychology, anthropology, and psychical research have made considerable advances as well as mathematical physics; and that they seem *prima facie* much more likely to be relevant to religion. Even the ordinary common sense of the lawyer and the historian may still have something useful to say on such topics. So, at the risk of being thought a profane disturber of the peace, I propose to raise once more the old questions, and to ask what bearing, if any, recent scientific developments have on the validity of religious beliefs.

In considering such beliefs I shall devote my attention mainly to Christianity, since this is the religion in which most of us were brought up, and is the only one with which most of us have any first-hand acquaintance. I fear that there may be some degree of unfairness in this. For there are certain peculiarities about Christianity which make it vulnerable to attacks that might be harmless to some of the other great religions, such as Buddhism, or to religion in general. I will therefore begin by mentioning the most striking of these peculiarities.

(1) The first and most important peculiarity of Christianity is that it is, to an unique degree, a doctrine about its own Founder. Some religions, e.g. Brahminism, do not claim to have any definite historical founder. Others, such as Buddhism in its original form and Confucianism, which trace their origin to a certain ostensibly historical person, claim no more for their founder than that he was an an exceptionally wise and good man who first discovered and promulgated certain important moral and philosophical truths, and illustrated his doctrine by the special sanctity of his life. Others, again, such as Judaism and Mahometanism, would claim more than this for their founders. Moses and Mahomet are supposed to have been the recipients of special revelations from God. This, it is alleged, enabled them to know facts about God's nature and His commands to humanity which no amount of reflexion on the data of ordinary experience would have disclosed to even the wisest and the best of men. But Judaism and Mahometanism would claim no more than this for Moses and for Mahomet respectively. These prophets are regarded as ordinary men who were extraordinarily favoured by God, not as supernatural beings occupying a uniquely important position in the universe. Now it is an essential part of Christian doctrine that, whilst it claims for the man Jesus all that Judaism claims for Moses or Mahometanism for Mahomet, it also claims something else which is different in kind and not in degree.

I have not been so fortunate as to meet with any account of the details of this doctrine about Jesus which I could fully understand. But, for the present purpose, a rough outline will be enough; and it may be given in the following propositions. (i) There is a single eternal and supernatural existent on which everything else that exists depends one-sidedly both for its origin and its continuance. This may be called 'the Godhead.' (ii) Within the unity of the Godhead there are three and only three most intimately interrelated 'factors' or 'moments,' each of which can properly be called God. (iii) A certain two of these factors in the Godhead stand in a peculiar kind of asymmetrical dyadic relationship, which is least imperfectly adumbrated by the analogy of fatherhood and sonship. In respect of this, one of them is called 'God the Father' and the other is called 'God the Son.' The third factor in the Godhead is related to *both* the others by another kind of asymmetrical dyadic relation. This is denoted by the phrase 'proceeding from,' and the factor in question is called 'God the Holy Ghost.' (iv) There is some uniquely intimate relation between that eternal factor in the Godhead called 'God the Son' and a certain man Jesus who was born at the village of Bethlehem during the reign of Augustus. This relation is such that it is appropriate to say of Jesus (and of no other man) that He was divine as well as human, and to say of God the Son (and of no other factor in the Godhead) that He is eternally human as well as divine. (I must confess that I can think of no interpretation of these statements which would enable me to attach a meaning to them.) (v) The birth of Jesus was miraculous, in so far as He had no human father. His mother was caused to conceive Him through the direct agency of the third factor in the Godhead, viz. the Holy Ghost. (vi) After preaching, and collecting a body of disciples, Jesus was eventually crucified at the instigation of the Jewish ecclesiastical authorities at Jerusalem. He died on the cross and was buried, but His body never suffered decay. On the contrary, at some period during His burial it underwent a miraculous change in consequence of which it ceased to be subject to the physical and physiological limitations of the ordinary human organism. He emerged from His tomb, which was found empty and open, although it had been carefully guarded; and for a period of forty days He appeared from time to time, visibly, tangibly, and audibly, to certain groups of His disciples. The circumstances of some of these manifestations were such that no ordinary living man could have appeared and disappeared in the way in which Jesus is alleged to have done. (vii) After the expiry of a certain time these manifestations ceased, and Jesus is said to have ascended to His Father in heaven. Since this statement can hardly be admitted to be intelligible if taken in a literal spatial sense, it may perhaps be interpreted as follows. At the end of this period God the Son resumed a relationship with God the Father which had been suspended during the earthly life of Jesus, and He suspended or modified a relationship to the material world which He had entered into at the conception of Jesus. (I do not pretend to understand what could be meant by changes in the relationship of an eternal being either to another eternal being or to the temporal order of nature.) (viii) Henceforth Jesus guides and influences individual Christians and Christian communities by insensible means. He will continue to do this until the Day of Judgment, when He will reappear physically and sensibly, will allot fitting rewards and punishments to the whole human race, and bring the present order of nature for ever to an end.

(2) The second peculiarity of Christianity is that it took over without question the Jewish sacred scriptures; that Jesus Himself appears to have accepted them; and that apostles, such as St. Paul, whose writings are held to be inspired by the Holy Ghost, used certain statements in them as premises for the exposition and development of Christian doctrines. Now these scriptures contain an elaborate cosmogonical scheme purporting to describe the creation of the world, of animals, and of man. They profess to account for the origin and propagation of moral and physical evil by the disobedience of our first parents to God's commands at the instigation of an evil supernatural created being. It is an essential part of the Christian doctrine that mankind was thus alienated from God, rendered incapable of amending themselves *proprio motu,* and justly liable to be eternally punished. It is also an essential part of that religion that the incarnation of the Son of God in the man Jesus, and the life, death, and resurrection of the latter, rendered it possible (though not inevitable) for men to reconcile themselves with God, to amend their lives, and to attain eternal happiness. I think it is fair to say that there is no general agreement among Christians as to the precise way in which this cause renders this effect possible; and that there are profound differences of opinion about the part played by the voluntary co-operation of men, which is admitted to be, in some sense, a necessary condition of their salvation.

(3) There is a third peculiarity of Christianity which is closely connected with the first. The Christian scriptures and traditions, like those of most religions, contain accounts of ostensibly super-normal events. Now these reported miracles fall into two very different classes,

viz. those which are part of the *content* of Christianity, and those which are, at most, part of the *evidence for* Christianity. It is an essential part of Christian doctrine that Jesus survived the crucifixion, and in some sense emerged from the tomb with a transformed body. Any ground for doubting or denying this is *ipso facto* a ground for doubting or denying a part of Christian doctrine. But it is no part of Christian doctrine that Jesus raised Lazarus from the dead or walked on the water without sinking. If every one of the latter miracles were rejected, this would not directly involve the rejection of a single Christian doctrine; though it might weaken the force of one line of argument for accepting Christian doctrines. Now the miracles of most religions fall entirely into the second class; i.e. they are, at most, evidential and not constitutive.

I hope that I have now indicated adequately and fairly the main peculiarities of Christianity. We can now ask ourselves how far, if at all, the various sciences are relevant to the truth of that religion. I must begin by mentioning an elementary logical distinction which is often overlooked. It is one thing to say of a fact that it conflicts with a certain theory. It is quite another thing to say of the same fact that it undermines the grounds on which people hold that theory. It is quite possible that the former statement should be false and the latter true. If that were so, the theory would not have been refuted and would not even have been shown to be intrinsically improbable; but we should have shown that those who accept it have no valid reason for doing so. Thus our question divides into two. (1) Do the generally accepted methods and results of the various sciences conflict with Christian doctrines, i.e. are they either logically incompatible with those doctrines or such as to render them extremely unlikely to be true? (2) Do they undermine the only grounds which people have ever had for believing Christian doctrines? We will now take these two questions in turn.

(1) The doctrines peculiar to Christianity may be divided into two classes, viz. those which are *about* Christ, and those which, though taught by Him or inferrible from His teachings, are not about Himself. I have already enumerated the former doctrines. As examples of the latter we may take the ethical doctrines enunciated in the Sermon on the Mount.

Now it is quite clear that none of the empirical sciences has or could have any logical bearing on a great deal of the Christian doctrine about Jesus. It is absurd to suppose that empirical science could prove or disprove, make probable or improbable, the doctrine of the existence and triune structure of the Godhead and of the uniquely intimate connexion between one of its differentiations and the man Jesus. The fundamental question is whether any part of this doctrine is intelligible, or whether it is nothing but meaningless verbiage masquerading in the grammatical form of intelligible sentences. Obviously that question cannot be answered by appealing to the methods or results of natural science. If any part of the doctrine be intelligible, the second question is whether it is true or false, antecedently probable or improbable. Now natural science is concerned with the interconnexions between things or events in space and time; and it is specially concerned to discover *uniformities* of co-existence and sequence among *classes* of phenomena, and to collect these, so far as may be, into a deductive system with a minimum of first principles. Therefore the question whether nature *as a whole system* depends on a timeless non-natural existent, and whether a certain *one* man once in the whole course of history was related in an absolutely *unique* way to the latter, evidently falls altogether outside the sphere of natural science. Either these questions are meaningless or they are not; and it is for philosophers, not scientists, to settle this preliminary question. If they are meaningless, conflict between science and Christian theology is impossible for the reason which prevents a lion from fighting with a hippogriff. If they are significant, such conflict is impossible for the reason which prevents a lion from fighting with a whale. And similar remarks apply to co-operation.

It would seem, however, that natural science might have a considerable bearing on the miraculous element which forms, as we have seen, an essential part of the content of Christian doctrine. This includes, undoubtedly, the resurrection of Jesus and His subsequent supernormal physical manifestations to His disciples. Whether it also includes the story of His supernormal conception is a doubtful matter which we may leave to experts. I think that here we are at once faced with the general question: 'Do the results of science make the occurrence of supernormal events impossible or highly improbable?' This question concerns other religions as well as Christianity, and it concerns alleged Christian miracles which are cited only as evidence for Christianity as well as those which are part of the content of Christian doctrine. Unless science has something to say against the possibility or probability of miracles as such, it can have nothing special to say against the possibility of those miracles whose occurrence is part of the content of Christianity. So it will be best to defer this question.

The sciences of geology, biology, archaeology, and anthropology have collected evidence which, in the opinion of everyone competent to judge, conclusively refutes the cosmogonical, biological, and anthropological doctrines of the Jewish scriptures. Though these doctrines are not in themselves essential parts of Christian theology, they are almost inextricably intertwined with others which are, e.g. with the doctrine that mankind is tainted and alienated from God, and that the incarnation, death, and resurrection of Jesus were necessary conditions without which no man could be saved. Moreover, the fact that these false propositions were, to all appearance, accepted literally by Jesus and made the basis of certain parts of His teaching would seem *prima facie* to throw some doubt on the Christian doctrine of His divine nature.

The only other point to be noticed under the present heading is that Christianity plainly presupposes that human beings survive the death of their present bodies and are, in fact, immortal. Since this doctrine is common to many religions, and is perhaps a necessary condition of any religion, we will defer the fundamental question whether science has anything relevant to say for or against it. For the present it will suffice to remark that, unless science renders the doctrine of an after-life as such, impossible or highly improbable, it will hardly affect the probability or improbability of the specifically Christian form of that doctrine. It is true that there are no empirical facts or scientific theories which would suggest that the present order of nature will be suddenly, radically, and permanently transformed at some date in the future. But it is no part of the Christian doctrine to assert that such a transformation will be due to the automatic development of natural processes. On the contrary, the Christian alleges that it will be due to the miraculous intervention of the Godhead. Therefore, unless science invalidates the other parts of Christian theology or renders survival and miraculous interventions unlikely or impossible, it has no relevant objection to make against specifically Christian eschatology.

It remains to consider whether science could render those parts of Christian doctrine which are not about Jesus and the Godhead improbable or impossible. For this purpose we may confine our attention to the ethical teachings of Jesus. Some people would hold that science makes complete determinism certain or extremely probable; and that, if men's actions be completely determined, the notions of moral good and evil and moral obligation can have no application. Some people would hold that anthropological and psychological investigations show that sentences in which ethical words and phrases occur merely express non-moral desires and emotions, repressed in the infancy of the individual or inherited from the pre-history of the race. We might describe either of these views as a form of 'ethical nihilism' based on science. Now the question whether science proves or strongly supports ethical nihilism is absolutely fundamental, and goes far beyond the relation of science to Christianity. We will therefore defer it for the present and content ourselves with the following conditional statement. *If* we have any moral obligations, then natural science can throw no light whatever on those of them which are *fundamental*. At most it might support or refute certain derivative and secondary moral rules which profess to tell us how to carry out our fundamental obligations in certain specified kinds of situation. No conceivable development of any of the natural sciences could be relevant to the question whether a person ought or ought not to love his neighbour as himself. At most it might show that some secondary rule, such as 'You ought to pour oil and wine into the wounds of persons whom you find lying injured by the wayside,' should be rejected because it is not an efficient means of doing good to your neighbour in the circumstances supposed. Now most of the ethical teachings of Jesus express primary or fundamental obligations. Either science shows that *all* talk of moral obligation is meaningless or inapplicable to men; or, if not, it is completely irrelevant to this part of Christian doctrine.

It should now be fairly clear that there are not many points at which the results of science and the doctrines peculiar to Christianity come into close enough contact for either conflict or co-operation between them to be possible. I think that similar reasoning would lead to a similar conclusion about the doctrines peculiar to any of the other great religions. If there is conflict, it will be over doctrines like the occurrence of miracles, the immortality of the soul, the freedom of the will, and the question whether moral predicates are significant and applicable to men and their actions. These doctrines are common to all, or nearly all, religions, and they are peculiar to none.

(2) We can now pass to our second question. Do the methods or results of the natural or the historical sciences undermine the grounds on which men have believed the doctrines of Christianity?

It seems to me that there is a fundamental logical difficulty, which is prior to any special objections that might be made to the evidences for Christianity on the score of literary and historical criticism or the comparative study of religions. It is this. I think it would be admitted by most Christians that an essential part of their reason for believing specifically Christian doctrines is that these were directly taught by Jesus or are necessary or probable consequences of other statements which He made. But this at once raises the question: 'On what grounds do you accept Jesus as an authority on these matters?' I suppose that the answer would be: 'Because He was a being of superhuman wisdom and goodness, who was in a position to know the facts and whose mission on earth was to reveal them to men.' But this is itself the most central and fundamental of Christian doctrines; and, if Christians accept *it* on the ground that Jesus asserted it or other things which imply it, their whole position is logically circular.

Are there any independent grounds

for accepting it? So far as I am aware, the only grounds that have been suggested are the following. Jesus wrought miracles in His lifetime, and was Himself the subject of the stupendous miracle of the resurrection after His death. He produced on those who knew Him so strong an impression of His divine nature and mission that many of them were ready to devote their lives and to meet a painful death in preaching His doctrines. St. Paul, who had never met Jesus and was bitterly and actively hostile to Christianity, underwent an experience which he took to be a manifestation of the risen Christ; he was converted thereby and confirmed in his new beliefs by subsequent supernormal experiences; and he spent the rest of his life in developing Christian doctrine and disseminating it throughout the Roman empire. Lastly, throughout history many people have found that certain Christian doctrines harmonize with their own deepest convictions, they have been willing to live and die for them, and they have had experiences which seemed to themselves to be evidence for the continued existence of Jesus and for His personal intercourse with them.

Let us begin by giving the fullest weight to this evidence and raising no questions as to whether there is adequate ground for believing that the alleged miracles really happened. At the very utmost it would show only that Jesus was an extremely remarkable and impressive personality; that a whole cluster of noteworthy supernormal phenomena, both psychical and physical, were initiated by His death and continued for some time afterwards in the regions in which He had preached; that certain parts of His teaching harmonized with certain deep-seated feelings and aspirations which the existing philosophies and religions of the Roman Empire failed to stir or to satisfy; and that subsequently,

when Christian institutions had been established and children were brought up in Christian tradition and doctrine, these teachings (developed, interpreted, supplemented, and modified almost out of recognition) continued to express the aspirations and to evoke the devoted loyalty of many good men.

I can see nothing in all this to justify the doctrine that Jesus occupied that uniquely exalted position in the universe which Christians assign to Him. Therefore it seems to me (as it has seemed to almost everyone *not* brought up in the Christian tradition) unreasonable to allege the mere *ipse dixit* of Jesus as an adequate ground for accepting otherwise unverifiable propositions about the Godhead, about His own relations to it, and about the supernatural origin and postmundane continuance of the human race. I should hold, then, that the only reasons which have been alleged for accepting the doctrines peculiar to Christianity are invalidated by these general objections, prior to all appeal to the methods and results of natural or historical science. Similar remarks would apply, *mutatis mutandis,* to any other religion which grounds its specific doctrines on the authority of its founder or its prophets. No doubt it is true to say that the development of Christianity was a unique phenomenon; but, in the only sense in which this is true, it is also true of any other great historical process, taken as a whole. No *single* historical event, such as the growth of communism or of national socialism since 1918, is *precisely* analogous to the growth of the Christian Church. But we can find a number of different *partial* analogies which, taken together, suffice to bring it into line with the rest of history. Again, it is true that the survival of Christianity in its infancy and its subsequent immense development depended on certain unpredictable and antecedently most improbable events, such as the conversion of St. Paul. It is natural for Christians, afterwards, to point to these events as 'providential.' But a moment's reflexion shows that there have been, and indeed must be, such events in the early stages of *any* historical movement which starts from very small beginnings, is faced with strong opposition and has to compete with many rivals, and does nevertheless survive and become dominant. The innumerable germs of possible religions and polities which have perished and left no trace in history were just those in connexion with which no such unlikely event happened. That is why such an event is called 'providential' when it does happen and is viewed in retrospect.

Before leaving this part of the subject, I must very briefly consider the following contention, which is sometimes made by Christians. 'If and only if,' it is said, 'you will consent to act *as if* Christianity were true and will take part uncritically in the corporate life of a Christian church, you will eventually have certain experiences which are in fact evidence for the truth of Christianity, and you will be in the right state of mind to appreciate their cogency.' Now it is just conceivable that this contention might be true. But it is evident that there would be other, and considerably more plausible, psychological explanations of the apparent facts. Moreover, a precisely similar claim might be made by the adherents of any other religion, and it is in fact made by the practitioners of the Indian systems of Yoga. Lastly, it is obviously impracticable to carry out this recommendation in connexion with all the important rival religions, and it is unreasonable to pick out one of them and to perform the experiment with that one only.

So far we have supposed, for the sake of argument, that there is good evidence for the miracles recorded in the Christian scriptures. We must now examine this supposition. Here again we can go a long way with the help of ordinary logic and common sense without needing to appeal to the special methods and results of the sciences. Let us grant for the present that miracles are not impossible, and that it is not inconceivable that there should be evidence available of such strength that it would be unreasonable to doubt that a certain alleged event did happen and was miraculous. Then I assert, without the slightest fear of contradiction from anyone who has studied the records, that there is no *direct* evidence for any of the New Testament miracles which is comparable in weight to the evidence for some of the alleged miracles of modern mediumship. For the levitation and other supernormal physical phenomena of D. D. Home we have the contemporary autographic testimony of Sir William Crookes, one of the ablest experimental scientists of the nineteenth century, who was deliberately investigating the phenomena in his own laboratory under controlled conditions. It would be merely impudent to suggest that the *direct* evidence for the resurrection or the ascension, available to us here and now, is comparable with this.

Now either a Christian apologist accepts these alleged mediumistic miracles or he rejects them. If he accepts them, he acts consistently, and moreover he can use them to show that the New Testament miracles are not altogether without parallel, and therefore not antecedently so improbable as sceptics allege. But, if he does so, he must give up the contention that the New Testament miracles testify by their uniqueness to the unique status of Christ and the complete reliability of His metaphysical and ethical teachings. If he rejects them, he can continue to hold that the New Testament miracles are unique. But now he must justify himself in accepting, on very weak direct evidence, antecedently improbable stories similar to those which he rejects where the direct evidence is extremely strong. So far as I can see, there are two and only two moves open to him at this point. The first is to allege that it is antecedently very improbable that miracles should happen in connexion with a decidedly second-rate human being, like D. D. Home, whilst it is antecedently quite likely that they should happen in connexion with a divine being such as Jesus was. So weaker evidence will prove in the latter case what even the strongest evidence cannot prove in the former. To this contention the simple and sufficient answer is that anyone who uses it cannot, without logical circularity, adduce the New Testament miracles as evidence for the divine nature and mission of Jesus; since he assumes the latter as part of his ground for accepting the former on the evidence available.

The other possible move is as follows. It might be said that, although the *direct* evidence available to us for the resurrection and the subsequent appearances of Jesus is incomparably weaker than the direct evidence for certain mediumistic miracles, yet the *indirect* evidence is overwhelming. The indirect evidence would be such facts as the change in the attitude of the apostles from despair to an active and lifelong conviction of Christ's survival, the conversion of St. Paul, and so on. I am certainly not inclined to underrate the force of this contention, for these changes seem well attested and very remarkable, and they do demand some kind of explanation. But the utmost that can be inferred is that *something* very queer must have happened soon after the crucifixion, which led certain of the disciples and St. Paul to believe that Jesus had survived in some supernatural way; and that they were able to transfer this conviction to many others. The following remarks may be made about this.

(i) I hold that the careful work of the Society for Psychical Research has made it almost certain that there is a residuum of truth in the many accounts of phantasms of the living at crises in their lives, of the dying, and of the recently dead, being 'seen' by educated Englishmen who were awake and in normal bodily and mental health at the time. I assume that such experiences are initiated by some kind of telepathic 'impact' received from the person whose phantasm is 'seen'; that this sets up a subconscious process in the mind of the recipient, analogous perhaps to that which takes place in post-hypnotic suggestion; and that eventually this ends by producing a sensory hallucination relevant in its details to the circumstances of the person from whom the telepathic impulse originated. Now I should think it quite likely that Jesus, who was plainly a very remarkable personality, might be strongly gifted with the power to send out such telepathic impulses at the great crises of his life and perhaps at other times too. But this would not be any good ground for attaching implicit belief to all His ethical and metaphysical teachings. I should not be at all surprised, e.g., to find that Herr Hitler had this power. But, if he had, I should not *ipso facto* accept without question all those racial and political theories which he preached with such intense conviction and applied for a time with such conspicuous success.

(ii) However this may be, it is plain that a telepathic impact, once received, would be much more likely to develop into a fullblown sensory hallucination in the minds of men like the disciples than in a contemporary educated Englishman. With the latter any such development has to overcome extremely strong inhibitions, since the final product would be utterly alien to the whole 'climate' of scientific materialism in which he has always lived and thought. Therefore I should expect that telepathically initiated sensory hallucinations, such as the S.P.R. have studied, would be far commoner and far more detailed and impressive among persons like the disciples than among contemporary educated Europeans.

(iii) A 'tough-minded' scientist, who rejects without question all the alleged evidence for contemporary supernormal phenomena, might find it difficult to deal with the indirect evidence for the resurrection and the subsequent appearances of Jesus, if he ever fairly faced it. Actually, of course, he adopts the attitude of the ostrich and faces *neither* problem. But even he could claim with justice that there might well have been some quite simple and honest mistake, or some deliberate malpractice or deception on the part of some interested person or group, in connexion with the body of Jesus; and that no direct evidence for it remains. Any particular theory of this kind will, no doubt, seem highly gratuitous and unlikely. But, after all, none of them can be so improbable antecedently as the theory that Jesus really rose from the dead, unless we assume what we have to prove, viz. that He was a divine being. And we must remember that, whilst *each one* of a number of alternative theories may be antecedently very improbable, it may be highly probable that *one or other* of them is true in view of the facts to be explained.

I should claim now to have disposed of all the alleged grounds for accepting specifically Christian doctrines, by the use of quite simple arguments without needing to appeal to modern science at all. I think we can safely assume that no appeal to science will *reverse* our decision, though it might reinforce it. It is also safe to say that we could have used similar arguments to show that there are no grounds for accepting the specific doctrines of any rival religion which relies on the authority of its founder or its prophets as the evidence for its teachings. I shall therefore devote the rest of my paper to certain wider questions, which we have hitherto set aside as being relevant to all or most religions, and not only or specially to Christianity. I will now take them in order.

(1) Has science anything to say for or against the possibility or the probability of miracles? Before we can answer this we must try to explain the term 'miracle' or 'supernormal event.' This is not easy to do, but I think that the following method of treatment is fairly satisfactory. There are certain very general principles, mostly of a negative or restrictive kind, about mind and matter and their mutual relations, which we all commonly assume without question. These form the rigid framework within which all our everyday practice, our scientific theories, and even our ordinary fictions and speculations are confined. The following are some of the most important of these principles. (i) A body cannot enter or leave a closed vessel so long as the walls are intact. (ii) The weight of an object at the earth's surface cannot be altered except by immersing it in fluids of various densities. (iii) A human mind cannot *directly* initiate or modify the motion of any material thing except certain parts of its own organism, such as its arms and legs. (iv) It is impossible for a person to perceive any thing or event at a given moment unless this object has set up a physical process which affects the percipient's organism at that moment and produces characteristic sensations in his mind. (v) It is impossible for a person to have knowledge of a past event, except by inference or report, unless one or other of the following conditions is fulfilled. (*a*) The past event initiated a physical process which was transmitted with a finite velocity through space and has now reached the observer's organism and produced a characteristic sensation in his mind. Or (*b*) the past event was either an experience had by this person, or was the object of such an experience. The first condition is fulfilled in the case of a man perceiving an event which happened long ago in a remote star. The second condition is

fulfilled in ordinary memory of past events. (vi) It is impossible for a person to have non-inferential knowledge of an event which has not yet happened. If he knows beforehand that such and such an event will happen, he must do so either by inferring this himself from his knowledge of general laws and particular facts about the past and the present, or by accepting the results of such an inference made and recorded by another person. Examples are provided by the two cases of an astronomer, and a student of the Nautical Almanac, knowing that a total eclipse of the sun will happen at a certain future date. (vii) It is impossible for one man A to know what experiences another man B is having, or what propositions B knows or believes unless one or other of the following conditions is fulfilled. (*a*) B makes a statement in speech or writing or some other form of conventional symbolism, and A perceives the record and is able to understand and interpret it. Or (*b*) A perceives B's gestures, facial expressions, interjections, etc., and draws inferences from them and from his knowledge of the general laws of human behaviour as to what is happening in B's mind. (viii) After a person has died, his mind either ceases to exist or, at any rate, ceases to be capable of affecting inanimate matter or the bodies or minds of living men and animals.

I would not claim that this list of eight restrictive principles is exhaustive, or that they are all independent of each other. But I think it is good enough for our present purpose, which, it will be remembered, is to explain what is meant by 'supernormal' or 'miraculous.' By an ostensible miracle' I mean any event which *seems* to conflict with one or more of these principles, whether it does so in fact or not. By a 'miracle' I mean an event which *really does* conflict with one or more of them. Phenomena which appear to conflict with well-established laws of nature, or which cannot be explained in terms of them, but which do not apparently conflict with any of these restrictive principles, may be called '*ab*normal'; but they will not be even ostensibly *super*normal or miraculous.

Evidently there are always two questions to be asked about any account of an ostensible miracle. (i) Did such an event as is reported really happen, and is the description of it which the witnesses give completely accurate so far as it goes? (ii) If so, is it really miraculous? Does it really conflict with any of the restrictive principles which mark off the realm of normal and abnormal phenomena from that of supernormal phenomena? Could it not be accounted for without going outside these limits?

About the first question, two of the sciences, both of fairly recent origin, have something very important to say. These are Abnormal Psychology and Psychical Research. It had always been known that human testimony is somewhat unreliable, and that human observation is somewhat defective as regards the details of perceived things and events. But no one had suspected how extremely unreliable they are, even under quite favourable conditions, until the S.P.R. investigated the matter experimentally. The classical paper on this subject is by Mr. S. J. Davey in Vol. IV of the Society's *Proceedings*. The extent to which intelligent and educated persons, who were under no emotional stress, erred, both by omission and by supplementation, in their reports of what they had seen, is almost incredible; but Mr. Davey's results have been fully confirmed by later experiments. The contribution of abnormal psychology and psycho-analysis is to show that the real causes of much human action are hidden from the agent's introspection, and are concealed rather than revealed by his overt speech and action. We know that these causes often produce an inability to perceive or to remember or to report certain facts which were physically and physiologically well within the witness's field of observation.

In regard to the second question the most important points to be made are the following. (i) We may dismiss at once, with the contempt which it deserves, the statement that 'Science proves miracles to be impossible.' This is just ignorant bluff and bluster, which a moment's reflexion on our definition of 'miracle' and the nature of inductive evidence suffices to deflate. (ii) The development of physical science has shown that many events which were ostensibly miraculous are capable of a normal explanation. The growth of our knowledge of hypnotism, of multiple and alternating personality, and of the extreme sensory hyperaesthesia which characterizes certain hypnotic and hysterical states, tends in the same direction. (iii) The facts and theories of psycho-analysis, already mentioned above, very much weaken the force of such familiar arguments as the following. 'This act must have been miraculous unless the agent was deliberately cheating. But it is incredible that a man of his high character, with absolutely nothing to gain by cheating, and much to lose if detected in fraud, should have practised deliberate deception. Therefore it must be miraculous.' (iv) In spite of all this, I must express my conviction that psychical research has made it far more probable than not that certain kinds of phenomena which are miraculous, in the sense defined above, do in fact occur. I include under this heading telepathy (both experimental and sporadic), certain of the *mental* phenomena of mediumship, and precognition. I should not, as at present advised, include with confidence any of the ostensibly supernormal *physical* phenomena of mediumship. It remains to note that, if these supernormal phenomena should ever become familiar and be found to fall under general laws, we should eventually reject the restrictive principles with which they conflict and should then cease to call them 'miraculous' or 'supernormal.'

(2) This naturally leads to our next question. Has science anything to say for or against the possibility or the probability of a person's mind in some sense surviving the death of his body? I will begin by remarking that, in my opinion, it is almost a *sine qua non* of any religious view of the world that some men at least should survive bodily death. I take it that one minimal demand of religion is that what we count to be the highest spiritual values shall not be merely ephemeral by-products of complicated material conditions which are fulfilled only occasionally in odd holes and corners of the universe, and are unstable and transitory when fulfilled. Another minimal demand is that there shall be at least rough justice, e.g. that evil deeds shall in the long run bring evil consequences on the doer of them, and not wholly or mainly on others. I do not see how either of these demands could be even approximately met if no man survives the death of his body. For, if this be so, not only does all the value which depends on the character and dispositions and the personal relationships of an individual vanish at his death; but also human society must eventually come to an end, and with it must perish all the values stored up in social institutions, works of art, and scientific treatises. Moreover, it is a commonplace that wicked men often die before they have brought on themselves either bodily suffering or remorse, or the disintegration of their characters or intellects, whilst wise and good men are often stricken down at the height of their powers, or survive into an old age of disease and dotage. Therefore, if science does make human survival impossible or very improbable, it does, in my opinion, deliver a fatal blow to *all* religion.

Now, with the doubtful exception of psychical research, none of the sciences tells us anything which lends the least probability to human survival. On the contrary, all that biology teaches of the detailed affinity of ourselves with the other animals, and all that physiology and anatomy tell us of the intimate connexion between lesions of the brain and nervous system and aberrations or obliterations of consciousness, produce an overwhelming impression of the one-sided dependence of mental life on certain very specialized and delicate material structures and processes.

As a professional philosopher, I am, of course, perfectly well aware that these scientific facts do not constitute a 'knockdown' disproof of survival. If there were any positive grounds *for* believing in survival, it would be easy enough to devise hypotheses to reconcile it with the biological and physiological facts which seem to make it so unlikely. I am also well aware that there are philosophical arguments against accepting the one-sided dependence of mind on body as an ultimate truth. (I have dealt with these in various parts of my published writings, and I do not find them very impressive.) In my opinion there is literally nothing but a few pinches of philosophical fluff to be put in the opposite scale to this vast coherent mass of ascertained facts, unless empirical evidence from psychical research should be available.

Do the findings of psychical research up to date do anything serious to redress the balance? Here we must distinguish between direct evidence for survival, and evidence which tends in the first instance only to throw doubt on the epiphenomenalist view of the relation of mind and body. As regards the direct evidence, there certainly exists a considerable amount of mediumistic communication which undoubtedly involves supernormal knowledge, and is in some respects strongly suggestive of the posthumous intelligent action of certain definite human beings, such as Edmund Gurney, Dr. Verrall, and others. Yet even this is so incoherent and repetitive, and so full of surprising ignorance and error, that one feels driven to seek some other supernormal explanation of it. Moreover, the contents of the communications give us no help in the frightfully difficult task of forming any plausible positive conception of life after the death of the present body.

This brings us to the second kind of evidence. If the occurrence of telepathy, clairvoyance, and precognition were established, this would have no *direct* bearing on the question of human survival. But it would have the following indirect relevance. It would tend to throw doubt on the adequacy of the theory (which all other known facts seem to support so strongly) that the human mind is one-sidedly and completely dependent on the brain and nervous system both for its existence and for every detail of its actions. Now it is this apparently well-established fact which makes the hypothesis of human survival antecedently so incredible. On the other hand, the establishment of telepathy, etc., would also work, for a different reason, in the opposite direction. For, if we grant these powers to ordinary men during their lifetime, we may be able to explain by means of them the mediumistic communications which constitute the only direct evidence for survival.

My conclusion is that, for this essential doctrine of religion, psychical research is the *only* possible gift-horse in the field of the sciences, and that even it is quite likely to prove to be a Trojan horse. In spite of the ambiguous character of the animal, I should hesitate, if I were a religious man, to look it quite so superciliously in the mouth as the leaders of religion commonly do.

Before leaving the subject of human survival I must touch very briefly on the following point. Christians often allege that the resurrection of Jesus constitutes evidence for human survival; that, without this evidence, the doctrine would be a mere pious aspiration; but that, with it, human survival becomes an established fact. This is a favourite theme of Easter Day sermons. Now, if I may say so without offence, this seems to me to be one of the world's worst arguments. Let us grant, what is at best questionable, that the resurrection really happened as described. Even so, the case of Jesus would differ from that of any ordinary man in at least two quite fundamental respects. In the first place, if Christianity be true, though Jesus was human, He was *also* divine. No other human being resembles Him in this respect. Secondly, the body of Jesus did not decay in the tomb, but was transformed; whilst the body of every ordinary man rots and disintegrates soon after his death. Therefore, if men do survive the death of their bodies, the process must be utterly unlike that which took place when Jesus survived His death on the cross. Thus the analogy breaks down in every relevant respect, and so an argument from the resurrection of Jesus to the survival of bodily death by ordinary men is utterly worthless.

(3) I have now taken in turn two general doctrines, viz. the possibility of miracles and human survival, one of which is vital to Christianity, and the other perhaps to all religions; and I have considered the bearing of science on each of them. In this, the concluding section of my paper, I find it convenient to proceed as follows. I propose to take certain of the sciences; to state how they have been relevant to religion in the past; and to consider whether (and, if so, how) their effect has been modified recently or is likely to be modified in future. Before doing so I will make two remarks. (i) The influence of a scientific discovery or theory on a religion can hardly ever be put in the form of a definite argument which can be tested by the criteria of formal logic or probability-theory. (It may not refute the religion, but it may make one's whole intellectual and emotional background so utterly different from that in which the religion originated and flourished that it becomes psychologically impossible for one to take the religion seriously. The religious beliefs of the ancient Greeks have never been refuted, and I do not see how they possibly could be. But no one would think it worth while nowadays even to raise the question whether there are beings answering to the description of Zeus or of Hera given in classical writings. (ii) In the case of any religion which is still alive, such as Christianity in contemporary England, the effect of such influences as I have been describing varies enormously from person to person even among those of much the same level of intelligence and culture. Moreover, those who are differently influenced *now* will, for that reason, be liable to make very different estimates as to the influence which the sciences are likely to exercise on religion in the future. Where this element of subjectivity is greatest I intend to make it quite explicit by talking in the first person and stating how *I* am affected and what *I* should anticipate. Such statements need not be of merely biographical interest, for they might happen to make explicit what many of my contemporaries are vaguely feeling. If and only if this is so, they are not wholly impertinent.

For our present purpose we may divide the sciences into three groups, viz. (i) the sciences of ostensibly non-living matter, (ii) the biological sciences, and (iii) the sciences which deal with specifically human topics. This classification is hierarchical, in the sense that the second group presupposes the first, and that the third presupposes the second. In the first group the most important for our purposes are astronomy and physics. In the third group the most important are history and archaeology and anthropology; psychology, normal and abnormal; and psychical research.

I will begin with astronomy. Any religion which can be taken seriously by intelligent men must be cosmic and not merely parochial. As men we shall necessarily be most concerned with that part of the divine system which immediately affects our race and our planet; and, if we believe that a religion has been revealed to men, we may reasonably expect that the revelation will be most explicit about that part of the system which most concerns ourselves, and which we could not have discovered by our own unaided efforts. Nevertheless, it is essential to any religion on the grand scale that what immediately concerns us should not be something isolated and self-contained, but should be an integral part of a wider system which covers the whole universe. Now Christianity, like all the great religions, claims to be cosmic in range. But it is also to a very marked extend geocentric and anthropocentric. Christ came to *earth,* He became a *man,* and eventually He went back and *ascended* to His Father in heaven. Now, as it seems to me, Christianity contrived to be at once geocentric and cosmic only because it originated and evolved against a background of astronomical theory in which the earth was the centre of the universe. This would naturally be assumed without question as a popular belief by the apostles and all the early Christians; and, in the detailed scientific form of the Ptolemanic system, it is explicitly taken by the great medieval theologians as the material setting of the divine drama. It seems to me to be assumed by Christ Himself; and some of His statements, which are perfectly sensible on that assumption, seem to be pointless on any other hypothesis.

Now, since the eighteenth century we have known that the earth is one of a number of planets at various stages of development circulating about one of a number of suns. Naturally I am not so silly as to suppose that this constitutes a *refutation* of Christianity. All I can do is to record the fact that for me personally the Christian story and the Christian theology in a Copernican universe wither like a plant taken from a hothouse and bedded out in the Siberian desert. I know well that many of the greatest astronomers have found no difficulty in remaining simple and earnest Christians. I have no comment to make except that the human mind has a wonderful power of keeping different parts of its knowledge and belief in water-tight compartments. If there is anything at all in the difficulty that I feel at this point, no progress in astronomy which has been made since Galileo and Newton and no progress that may conceivably be made in the future can make any difference.

I do not think that the revolution in astronomy need have that detrimental effect on religion in general, or on most of the other great religions which, in my opinion, it has on Christianity. It has been said that an atheistic astronomer must be mad. I am not at present concerned to dispute this. What I do wish to suggest is that a *Christian* astronomer must have a more than Nelsonian capacity for applying his blind eye to his telescope on occasion.

We may now leave astronomy and pass to physics. In my opinion the *logical* bearing of mathematical physics, whether of the classical or the relativistic and quantic kind, on any form of religion is quite trivial. I am inclined to think that the only real logical connexion is the following. The fact that all the immense variety of inorganic natural phenomena fall under a few very general laws, and that these laws are of a comparatively simple mathematical form, seems not to be logically necessary. It looks like a kind of uncovenanted mercy, and it constitutes a certain resemblance between inorganic nature and certain products of intelligent human action, such as games of skill, puzzles, musical compositions, etc. Again, the fact that human beings have been able to discover these fundamental laws of inorganic matter, and to acquire thereby a considerable degree of practical control over it, exalts our estimate of the human mind and enlarges the gap between it and any animal mind. These two facts and their interrelation do, so far as they go, lend some support to a view of man and nature which may fairly be called 'religious.'

I must next mention a supposed connexion between mathematical physics and religious belief which I suspect to be unreal. A distinction has been drawn between two kinds of physical law, viz. 'deterministic' and 'statistical.' Until quite recently the fundamental laws of physics were held to be of the deterministic kind, and the statistical laws were held to be derivative. Nowadays, in the opinion of many eminent physicists, the situation has been reversed, and henceforth we must hold that the fundamental laws of physics are of the statistical kind. Now it has been alleged that, if the fundamental laws of physics are deterministic, all human volitions must be completely ineffective, i.e. that nothing in the material world would have been different if there had been no volitions, or if human beings had made different decisions. It is also alleged that, if the fundamental laws of physics are statistical, it is at least possible that some human volitions do make a difference to the course of events in the material world. Now it is plain that the ethical content of religion is closely bound up with the common-sense opinion that some human volitions are effective. Therefore, if the allegation which I have stated were correct, it would be true to say that the classical physics was incompatible with an essential presupposition of religion. And it would be true to say that recent developments of mathematical physics had eased, if they had not completely removed, this conflict.

I believe that this argument is full of fallacies and confusions. I have gone very fully into the question in my contribution to the symposium on *Indeterminacy and Indeterminism* in the Aristotelian Society's Supplementary Volume x. I will therefore confine myself here to the following obvious remark. If the principles of classical physics do entail that all human volitions are ineffective, they conflict with the presuppositions of natural science just as much as with those of religion. For every scientist who ever devises and carries out an experiment assumes that his thoughts and volitions are making a characteristic modification in the course of events in the material world.

It remains for me to mention a certain psychological connexion which probably does exist in the minds of many people between their religious beliefs and what they have heard about recent developments in theoretical physics. The conceptions of classical physics were perfectly straightforward and easy for anyone to grasp and to picture. Mathematical knowledge was needed only for working out their detailed consequences. The concepts of relativistic and quantum physics cannot be grasped except by a person of considerable mathematical training who sees them as factors in a whole complicated context of theory. And they cannot be pictured at all. When attempts are made to express these concepts and laws in familiar language to uninstructed persons who interpret it literally, a mass of paradoxical and apparently self-contradictory verbiage results. Now in the good old days those who attacked Christianity from the standpoint of science could make great play by contrasting the plain common sense of physics with the mind-destroying hocus-pocus of theology. It can now be retorted that the principles of modern physics look as nonsensical as the Athanasian Creed, and yet are vouched for by eminent scientists and validated by practical applications which we can all use and abuse. In consequence some people are inclined to think that there may be something in the mysterious and apparently nonsensical verbiage of Christian theology after all.

Well, it is not for me to say that there may not be. But I do say, without the slightest hesitation, that the psychological cause which I have just described is no rational ground for thinking that there is. There is nothing mysterious or paradoxical or self-contradictory in the physical concepts and laws so long as they are formulated in the symbolism which is appropriate to them and are viewed in their own proper context. The mystery and the paradox arise only when this symbolism is translated into ordinary words which have certain familiar associations, and when those words are heard or read by persons who lack the knowledge which would enable them to reject or correct the images and ideas which they naturally evoke. I do not think that any theologian would pretend that the paradoxes and apparent contradictions of Christian theology arise simply from this kind of distortion of something which can be quite clearly and intelligibly stated in an appropriate symbolism to experts who have mastered it. Be this as it may, the following reflexion is surely obvious. The fact that contemporary physics has to enunciate its principles in the form of apparent paradox and nonsense may be a good reason for hesitating to reject off-hand *any* doctrine *merely* because it looks paradoxical and nonsensical when stated. But it cannot be a good reason for accepting any *one* form of apparent nonsense, e.g. the Athanasian Creed, in preference to any *other* form, e.g. the Kabbala or the Hegelian Dialectic.

We can now leave the science of inorganic matter and pass to the biological sciences. I said that Christianity was essentially geocentric and anthropocentric. We have considered its geocentric aspect in connexion with astronomy; it is the anthropocentric aspect of it to which biology is relevant. Christianity arose, and Christian theology developed, in a certain context of beliefs about the relation of man to other living beings on earth. Man was created 'a little lower than the angels,' and he occupies a unique status in a hierarchy of living beings at the dividing point between the angels, who are purely rational beings without material organisms, and the brutes, who are perceptive and sensitive but wholly non-rational animals. I must confess that this seems to me to be still the best available description of the peculiarities of man as he now is and as he has been throughout the whole of his written history. But contemporary biology makes it practically certain that, if we go back far enough into the pre-history of the human race, we find it developing by insensible steps from ancestors who were purely animal.

Now I do not think that there need be any great difficulty in fitting religion in general, or certain of the great historical religions, such as Buddhism, into this changed biological framework. But, for my own part, I find it difficult to see how Christianity can be fitted into it without being so radically transformed as to be unrecognizable. Certainly I know of no satisfactory attempt at such a reconstruction of Christian belief; and, unless it can be accomplished, I suspect that Christianity will become less and less credible with each succeeding generation. It may survive for a long time as a kind of religiously toned 'ethical uplift'; but I cannot believe that this will persist indefinitely when cut off from its cosmological and biological roots.

I have already said all that seems necessary about the bearing of abnormal psychology and psychical research on religious belief in general and on Christianity in particular. It only remains for me to add a few words about the influence of the other specifically human sciences. I think there is no doubt that, for many people, the results of the comparative study of religion, and the data supplied by anthropologists and archaeologists, make religious belief impossible. It seems to them to be a pathetic survival of certain beliefs, emotions, and practices, which were natural enough in the childhood and ignorance and impotence of the human race, but have now lost all meaning and relevance. This is not quite the impression which these facts produce on myself. It seems to me that science has equally humble and disreputable origins, that there has been a development in depth and insight in religion as well as in science, and that both must be judged ultimately by their fruits rather than by their roots. On the other hand, I find that the facts of anthropology and comparative religion make any claim by any particular religion to an exclusive possession of the truth too utterly ridiculous to be worth a moment's consideration.

I have one more remark to make before ending my paper. To me the occurrence of mystical experience at all times and places, and the similarities between the statements of so many mystics all the world over, seems to be a significant fact. *Prima facie* it suggests that there is an aspect of reality with which these persons come in contact in their mystical experiences, and which they afterwards strive and largely fail to describe in the language of daily life. I should say that this *prima facie* appearance of objectivity ought to be accepted at its face value unless and until some reasonably satisfactory alternative explanation of the agreement can be given. Now I am well aware that certain psycho-analysts would give one explanation of it, and that certain Marxian theorists would give another. Such explanations do satisfy some people who have studied them, and they form the staple diet of a great many more who

have not done so, but have swallowed them whole in order to be in the vanguard of culture.

Now I think that each of these two types of theory contains some interesting speculations which may turn out to be true, and may cover some of the facts. But each of them seems to me to suffer very obviously from two defects. The first is that they are plainly constructed by persons who have very little first-hand or even second-hand experience of religion, and are strongly antipathetic to it from one cause or another. I should feel some hesitation in accepting theories about the nature of music and its function in human life, excogitated by a tone-deaf psychologist whose wife had recently eloped with a musician. The psycho-analytic and the Marxian theories of religion seem to me to wear too jaundiced a complexion to inspire complete confidence. The second defect is this. Although the exponents of these theories make a tremendous parade of being 'scientific,' it is perfectly plain to anyone who has studied any genuine science that they have no idea of the *general* difficulty of proving any far-reaching explanatory hypothesis, or of the *special* difficulties which exist in a field where experiment is impossible, and even the 'observations' consist largely of hearsay and tradition. The degree of their confidence is a measure of their scientific incompetence. They seem to have no notion of the importance of confronting their theories with negative instances, or of considering whether half a dozen rival hypotheses would not explain the facts equally well.

I have been obliged to paint the scene as I see it; and the prospects of Christianity, as I see them, are somewhat gloomy unless applied science (that blind Samson) should uproot the pillars of the house and bury pure science with it in the ruins. Though I am not a Christian, and never have been one since I began to think for myself, I take no pleasure in this prospect. Whether Christianity be—true or false, Christ's parable about the subsequent fate of the man who was left 'swept and garnished,' after the expulsion of a demon that possessed him, seems to me to be profoundly true of humanity as a whole. Ordinary human nature abhors a vacuum, and it will not for long rest content without some system of emotionally toned and unverifiable apocalyptic beliefs for which it can live and die and persecute and endure. When I contemplate communism and fascism, the two new religions which have entered into the clean-swept place and possessed it, and when I consider the probable consequences of their sisterly bickerings, I appreciate the concluding lines of Mr. Belloc's *Cautionary Tale* about the boy who ran away from his nurse in the Zoo and was eaten by a lion. 'Always keep hold of Nurse, for fear of finding Something Worse.'

SUGGESTIONS FOR FURTHER READING

Joseph Needham, ed., *Science, Religion, and Reality* (New York: Macmillan, 1925), is an interesting collection of essays by various writers. Most contemporary writers on the subject proclaim the essential harmony of science and religion. See, for example, A. N. Whitehead, Ch. XII of *Science and the Modern World* (New York: New American Library, 1948); W. E. Hocking, *Science and the Idea of God* (Chapel Hill: Univ. of North Carolina Press, 1944); and W. A. Whitehouse, *Christian Faith and the Scientific Attitude* (New York: Philosophical Library, 1952). This unanimity is rudely shattered by Bertrand Russell, *Religion and Science* (London: Oxford Univ. Press, 1935), in which the conflict between the two is stressed.

In E. W. Barnes, *Scientific Theory and Religion* (New York: Macmillan, 1933), and E. L. Mascall, *Christian Theology and Natural Science* (New York: Ronald Press, 1956), we have works by theologians who are well versed in science and who examine various scientific theories in some detail. Some scientists have claimed that recent developments in science support something like theism. See James Jeans, *The Mysterious Universe* (New York: Macmillan, 1930); and A. S. Eddington, *The Nature of the Physical World* (New York: Macmillan, 1928), and *Science and the Unseen World* (New York: Macmillan, 1929). These views are criticized in Bertrand Russell, *The Scientific Outlook* (Glencoe, Ill.: Free Press, 1948); L. S. Stebbing, *Philosophy and the Physicists* (London: Methuen, 1937); and W. R. Inge, *God and the Astronomers* (London: Longmans, Green, 1933).

8.

RELIGIOUS ALTERNATIVES TO THEISM

Although it is, of course, possible to adopt a supernaturalistic world view other than theism—for example, the view favored by many mystics that the physical universe is an illusory appearance of an ineffable absolute One—the main alternative to theism in our society at the present time is naturalism. (See the introduction to Section 7.) Therefore in this section we shall be largely concerned with attempts to sketch a kind of religion which would be consistent with naturalism.

Having rejected theism, a naturalist may take any one of several tacks with respect to religion. For one thing he may reject religion altogether. He may take the position that it was all a horrible mistake and the less said about it the better. This attitude was more popular in the eighteenth and nineteenth centuries than it is today. The contemporary naturalist is usually convinced that religion plays a key role in human life, and so he is likely to try to find some substitute for traditional religion which will avoid any commitments to the supernatural. There are at least two major ways of making this attempt: He may retain all the trappings of traditional religion, including the doctrines, but reinterpret them so as to make them compatible with naturalism; or he may attempt to take a fresh start and draw a blueprint for a new kind of religion on a naturalistic basis. In our selections George Santayana represents the first sort of enterprise and Auguste Comte and H. N. Wieman represent the second.

Santayana's interpretation belongs to a large group of interpretations which regard religious doctrines as *symbolic* in character. Of course, symbolical (allegorical, figurative, metaphorical) interpretations have been common in religion for a long time; they are by no means confined to naturalistic reinterpretations. For example, many Christians have considered the Garden of Eden story not as what it appears to be—a report of an occurrence which happened at a certain point in time—but as an allegorical way of making a point about the condition of man at all times, namely, that man has an almost irresistible tendency to rebel against the authority of God and put himself in the center of his universe, and that the results are always catastrophic. Again, Biblical references to God's anger and wrath are usually not taken literally (for a perfect and immutable deity would not become angry), but as metaphors for His overwhelming power, or perhaps His strict justice. And attributions of various bodily parts to God are likewise understood metaphorically. To say "the hand of the Lord is upon me" is to say metaphorically that I have been chosen by God for something or other; to say "He hath showed strength with His arms" is simply to say in a poetic way that He is very powerful. And so on. But, of course, these interpretations would not satisfy a naturalist. For here the reality which is said to be symbolized by the story, statement, or word in question is as supernatural as the literal meaning. Even when the Garden of Eden story is interpreted allegorically (as this is usually done), it is still concerned with God and His relation to man. And to speak of God as being just or choosing someone is not less supernatural than to speak of Him as being angry or as laying His hand on someone. Of course, in these cases not all religious doctrines are taken to be symbolic. We are reserving some doctrines (God is powerful) to be used in specifying what the others are symbolizing. But a view which regards all religious doctrines as symbolic is not necessarily naturalistic. Paul Tillich holds that all religious doctrines are symbolic of being itself. (See the selection from Tillich in Section 6.) And Tillich's "being-itself" is almost as repugnant to a naturalist as a theistic God.

To de-supernaturalize religion we need an interpretation in which the doctrines are taken to symbolize some components of the natural world. And there are various ways of doing this. It has been held that religious doctrines should be regarded as symbolic of the feelings typically aroused in religious activities. Thus "God made the heavens and the earth" might be taken to symbolize a sense of awe evoked by the contemplation of the universe; "God watches over the affairs of men" might be taken to symbolize a sense of peace or a feeling of "at-homeness" in the universe. But on Santayana's view, religious doctrines are to be regarded as primarily symbolic of value commitments and attitudes of various sorts. Santayana says that there are two aspects or components to a religious doctrine (or "myth," as he calls it). There is (a) an evaluation of some sort, which is (b) expressed in the form of a picture or story. For example, the Christian myth of God's Incarnation in Jesus Christ and His sacrificial and unmerited death on the Cross to atone for the sins of men can be regarded as a symbol of the moral value of self-sacrifice. That is, instead of merely expressing their high evaluation of self-sacrifice by saying "self-sacrifice is a noble thing," the Christian community expresses it vividly and poetically in a story of the doings of a supernatural personal being. Likewise the ancient Hebrews expressed their conviction that the Israelite nation was of supreme value by telling stories of a supreme supernatural person Who had chosen Israel to be the recipient of special favors and the bearer of a special mission. In the course of telling this story the prophets and scribes would express their sense of the importance and great worth of certain acts—the deliverance out of bondage in Egypt and the conquest of Canaan—as due to the providence of God; and they would express their sense of guilt for the sins of their people by interpreting such events as the Assyrian conquest and the Babylonian exile as God's punishments for their sins.

Terms like *symbol* and *symbolize* are used in a great variety of senses, sometimes, I fear, without any clear meaning. Hence it is especially important to make explicit what is meant by these terms here. Stated briefly, Santayana takes religious doctrines to symbolize valuations in the sense that in affirming these doctrines one is expressing his attachment to certain values and is expressing his sense of their importance by depicting some embodiment of them (the Incarnation for example), or by depicting some situation which would naturally give rise to them. (Being guided by a supernatural deity would give the exodus of the Jews from Egypt the great significance it was felt to have.) Thus, on this account religious doctrines express valuational commitments not in the way disgust would be expressed by saying, "Ugh!" but in the way disgust would be expressed by saying that the world "is an unweeded garden . . . things rank and gross in nature possess it merely."

In this interpretation Christian doctrines will be acceptable to a naturalist, provided that a naturalistic theory of valuation can be carried through. But how much of their religious force is left? Santayana sometimes suggests that, except for a few theological pedants, religious doctrines have generally been understood in this way. But this cannot be so. Take two religious doctrines which Santayana would interpret as expressing the same moral conviction: the doctrine of the Incarnation in Christianity and the Buddhist doctrine that there are certain men (Bodhisattvas) who have satisfied all the prerequisites for entrance into Nirvana but who voluntarily postpone their entrance in order to stay in the world and help other men to reach that position. In Santayana's interpretation there could be no problem of choosing between these; one could not accept one and reject the other, for they are strictly equivalent. At most, one could regard one as a more apt expression than the other. But as these doctrines are ordinarily understood they are strictly incompatible. One cannot be both a Christian and a Buddhist. Thus if we are to make anything of Santayana's interpretation we shall have to take it to be a proposal for a reinterpretation.

With respect to this proposal one might raise the following question. Why should one symbolize his moral convictions by rehearsing these farfetched stories about the strange doings of a transcendent being when one does not believe in its real existence? What would be the point of it? I suppose that Santayana would give two answers to this question. First, there is a poetic, or more broadly an aesthetic, value in doing so—the same sort of value there is in expressing one's world-weariness by reciting Swinburne's "The Garden of Prosperine." Second, by embodying the moral attitudes in concrete narratives we consolidate them, extend their influence, promote their ability to be shared, render people more likely to adopt them. About these answers the following points can be made.

If the Bible and Christian theology are to be recommended on poetic grounds, they are clearly inferior to Shakespeare, Milton, Donne, and so on. If we wish to express feelings or attitudes, then surely we could do much better than the doctrine of the Trinity or Saint Paul's Epistle to the Romans.

It is true that religious doctrines often have profound influences on the feelings and moral attitudes of those who accept them. But that does not show that they have this influence as expressions of feelings or moral attitudes. Perhaps people's moral attitudes are influenced by the story of the Incarnation and Atonement to the extent that they take this to be a true account of the acts of a supernatural being. And if this is so, we may well suspect that if the assertive element were removed, the moral influence would greatly diminish or even entirely disappear. At least I see no reason to believe that religious doctrines would continue to have these effects if they were not regarded as giving us truths about an objectively existing supernatural being.

Let us now turn to the second kind of naturalistic philosophy of religion—the attempt to outline a new religion which would not involve any reference to the supernatural. We can, I think, best compare various forms of naturalistic religion in terms of what they put in place of God, what they set up as an object of worship. The possibility of such a substitution can be understood if we recall that the basic attributes of God fall under two main headings: goodness and power. This is not accidental. The reason God is worshipped, the reason characteristically religious responses like feelings of awe and adoration, prayer, and sacrifice are focused on him, is that He is thought of as the zenith of both goodness and power. Putting these together we might say that it is essential to religion to conceive God as a cosmic source of value. He is that being Who has control over the course of events, and Who can be depended on to exercise His power in the interests of the realization of the good. It is because He is thought of as occupying such a status that men are preoccupied with Him in the ways they typically are in religion.

This would suggest that to find a focus for religious responses within the natural world we need to find something which occupies a like position, which has an important role in determining the course of events, and which can be depended on to favor the good. In other words, we must look for a basic source or sources of values in the natural world. We can distinguish various naturalistic forms of religion in terms of where they find this source.

Speaking very broadly, we can say that achievements of value on the part of men are due to these factors: (1) man's own efforts and his natural endowments, together with the deposit of his past achievements in the cultural heritage of a society; we may call this the human side; (2) things and processes in non-human nature, on which he depends for the possibility of his successes, and indeed his very life; this includes the atmosphere, sources of food, the natural embodiments of beauty which serve as his first aesthetic stimuli, etc. Naturalists locate their religious object on one or the other side, or else in some combination of the two.

The human side is emphasized most strongly in what has been perhaps the most influential of all naturalistic philosophies of religion, that of the nineteenth-century French philosopher Auguste Comte, who is famous as the father of positivism and as the founder of sociology. In Comte's view it is to Humanity that the individual man owes everything that he is. It is because he shares in the general biological and psychological capacities of human nature that the individual is able to live a fully human life. And in the historical perspective, the men of one generation are able to enjoy the cultural advantages they do enjoy—artistic, technological, educational, social—because of the labors of their predecessors in building up this incomparable heritage. Moreover, according to Comte, the service of Humanity, in the many forms this can take, is the noblest ideal which could be proposed to an individual. And Humanity, unlike an omnipotent God, actually needs this service.

Unlike many naturalists, Comte was not at all vague as to the details of his Religion of Humanity. He was impressed with the ritual structure of Roman Catholicism, and took it as his model. He proposed a system of sacraments modeled after the Catholic sacraments, except that he went them two better, raising the seven to nine. In the analogue of Baptism, the Sacrament of Presentation, the parents in an impressive public ceremony would dedicate their child to the service of Humanity. At the age of fourteen, at the beginning of a new and crucial stage in his life, the child would dedicate himself anew to the service of Humanity in the Sacrament of Initiation, the analogue of Confirmation. These public observances were to be reinforced by the regular practice of private prayer on which Comte laid the greatest stress. Four periods in each day were to be devoted to prayer. Each prayer would be partly commemorative and partly purificatory. In its first part the prayer would invoke some great benefactor of humanity. By reflecting gratefully on the benefactor's deeds, the prayer would be inspired to follow his example and his love of humanity would be quickened. The purificatory part would give solemn expression to the noble desires thereby evoked; in it the individual would dedicate himself to the service of Humanity. Furthermore, Comte organized a Calendar of Saints of Humanity after the model of the Christian Calendar of Saints. Each month was devoted to a certain sphere of human activity—science, politics, literature, and so on. The month was named after a hero of the first class in the relevant category. Within the month each week was named after a hero of the second class, and each day after a hero of the third class. The hero of the month, week, and day were to be mentioned in the prayers on a given day.

Comte had some religious influence at the time, and a few actually functioning parishes of his Religion of Humanity grew up, but these have almost entirely died out since. And a revival in our time hardly seems feasible. We of the twentieth century, reeling under the impact of two catastrophic world wars, and almost hourly expecting the death knell of civilization, are not much inclined to grow misty-eyed over Humanity as a source of value and object of worship. In the nineteenth century when a faith in inevitable progress held sway, a religious worship of Man seemed appropriate to some, but since the advent of Freud and fascism, man no longer seems as worthy of worship. We are more likely to embrace a doctrine of original sin. Hence even recent humanists have tended to be more critical in their reverence for humanity. The latest fashion is to single out the more ideal aspects of man—his aspirations for truth, beauty, goodness, and so on—and the actual attainments he has to his credit—for religious worship. Or the emphasis shifts away from man as he actually exists, and what is proposed for an object of worship is the ideals themselves, which man in his better moments is pursuing. We find both these tendencies exemplified in John Dewey. In his book *A Common Faith,*[1] he defines God as "the unity of all ideal ends arousing us to desire and actions."

If we want to find a stress on the nonhuman side to counterbalance Comte, we will have to consider a litterateur like Richard Jeffries, who felt a kind of religious intoxication with inanimate nature but did not conceive of it as suffused with a spiritual being or beings. This is a naturalistic counterpart of the old nature worship of ancient Greece, just as Comte's Religion of Humanity is a naturalistic counterpart of Christianity or, more broadly, of ethical monotheism. But we would be hard-pressed to find this kind of emphasis in any carefully thought out philosophical naturalism. However, there is a marked tendency among contemporary naturalists to give much more stress to the nonhuman side than Comte did, or even than Dewey usually does. Many naturalists feel that Comte's approach is too anthropocentric, that in his zeal to do honor to man he is insensitive to the fact that man's achievements always depend on conditions in the nonhuman environment. Contemporary naturalistic philosophers of religion seem to be moving toward some sort of synthesis in which both the nonhuman conditions of value and the human realizers of value will be included in the object of worship. Thus in *Religion Without Revelation* (but not in the chapter included in this volume) Huxley sets forth a naturalistic version of the Christian doctrine of the Trinity, according to which God the Father is interpreted as the forces of nonhuman nature, God the Holy Spirit as the ideals for which men are striving (at their best), and God the Son as human life itself which is, more or less, utilizing the forces of nature in the pursuit of those ideals. The

---

[1] New Haven: Yale Univ. Press (1934), p. 42.

unity of these three Persons in one God is interpreted as the essential unity of all these aspects of nature.

H. N. Wieman belongs to this latter group. In the selection below he emphasizes what he calls the "creative event" (better termed "creative events," since Wieman does not really want to suggest that all the examples of the sort of thing he is talking about go together to form a tight unity). A creative event occurs whenever things are transformed so that new possibilities of value are revealed. In the selection below, Wieman sets out in some detail what he takes to be the main features of such events. But it is not very clear from this selection exactly what we are to regard as an object of religious worship. Is it "the creative event" itself or the totality of conditions which bring it about? In other places Wieman clearly chooses the former. In the cooperative volume *Is There a God?* [2] he defines God as "that interaction between individuals, groups, and ages which generates and promotes the greatest possible mutuality of good." As a naturalist, Wieman says that we should leave it to science to tell us in detail what is included in this pattern, and just how the various components are interrelated. In the meanwhile, we can make the typical religious responses of prayer, adoration, reverence, and so on, to this interaction, however scanty our present knowledge of it. To one who doubts the possibility of our making these responses to something which has not been more narrowly specified, and which we are denying to be a person, Wieman says: [3]

> Can men pray to an interaction? Yes, that is what they always pray to, under any concept of God. Can men love an interaction? Yes, that is what they always love. When I love Mr. Jones, it is not Mr. Jones in the abstract, but the fellowship of Mr. Jones. Fellowship is a kind of interaction. The reason I love human persons more than sticks and stones, is because they can enter more fully into such fellowship, or interaction. It is the interaction which generates love and is the real object of love, although we do not frequently stop to analyze the situation sufficiently to recognize that fact. I love humans and hills and trees and houses and landscapes only because they are caught up by this interaction which generates and promotes the rich body of shareable experience.

Thus far I have been considering attempts to replace supernaturalistic religious doctrines with naturalistic doctrines. But there is another way in which a naturalist might try to make religion acceptable to naturalism: by doing away with doctrines altogether. If a religion does not contain any beliefs at all in matters of fact, then *a fortiori* it cannot contain any beliefs which would contradict naturalism. But could there be a religion without any beliefs? What would it be like? It would consist in a systematic cultivation of the other aspects of religion— feeling, mystical experience, morality, ritual—but without linking all these to any object, supernatural or otherwise. Our contemporary naturalists do not seem to be interested in this sort of transformation of religion, and so for an example I have turned to Zen Buddhism, a form of oriental religion which has recently attracted widespread interest in the West. In the selection from Suzuki we have a

---

[2] With D. C. Macintosh and M. C. Otto, Chicago: Willett, Clark & Co. (1932), p. 13.
[3] *Is There a God?*, pp. 17–18.

good presentation of Zen's hostility to any sort of speculation or theorizing, of its emphasis on the cultivation of a certain kind of mystical experience, and of the special attitude toward life which results. By introducing Zen at this place I do not mean to suggest that it was developed out of a concern to make religion naturalistic, or that its avoidance of commitments to the supernatural is one of its main attractions to its adherents. Neither of these suggestions would be correct. Nevertheless, this religious position does constitute a live alternative for those who want to avoid the sort of supernaturalism we find in theism.

AUGUSTE COMTE

The Religion of Humanity

Auguste Comte (1798–1857) was the founder of the philosophical movement known as Positivism, an extreme form of empiricism which discourages attempts to go beyond what is directly perceived. He is also considered to be the founder of sociology.

. . .

All essential phases in the evolution of society answer to corresponding phases in the growth of the individual, whether it has proceeded spontaneously or under systematic guidance, supposing always that his development be complete. But it is not enough to prove the close connexion which exists between all modes and degrees of human regeneration. We have yet to find a central point round which all will naturally meet. In this point consists the unity of Positivism as a system of life. Unless it can be thus condensed, round one single principle, it will never wholly supersede the synthesis of Theology, notwithstanding its superiority in the reality and stability of its com-

From Auguste Comte, *A General View of Positivism,* tr. by J. H. Bridges (1880), Ch. VI. Reprinted by permission of Routledge & Kegan Paul Ltd.

ponent parts, and in their homogeneity and coherence as a whole. There should be a central point in the system towards which Feeling, Reason, and Activity alike converge. The proof that Positivism possesses such a central point will remove the last obstacles to its complete acceptance, as the guide of private or of public life.

Such a centre we find in the great conception of Humanity towards which every aspect of Positivism naturally converges. By it the conception of God will be entirely superseded, and a synthesis be formed, more complete and permanent than that provisionally established by the old religions. Through it the new doctrine becomes at once accessible to men's hearts in its full extent and application. From their heart it will penetrate their minds, and thus the immediate necessity of beginning with a long and difficult course of study is avoided, though this must of course be always indispensable to its systematic teachers.

This central point of Positivism is even more moral than intellectual in character: it represents the principle of Love upon which the whole system rests. It is the peculiar characteristic of the Great Being who is here set forth, to be compounded of separable elements. Its existence depends therefore entirely upon mutual Love knitting together its various parts. The calculations of self-interest can never be substituted as a combining influence for the sympathetic instincts.

Yet the belief in Humanity, while stimulating Sympathy, at the same time enlarges the scope and vigour of the Intellect. For it requires high powers of generalization to conceive clearly of this vast organism, as the result of spontaneous co-operation, abstraction made of all partial antagonisms. Reason, then, has its part in this central dogma as well as Love. It enlarges and completes our conception of the Supreme Being by revealing to us the external and internal conditions of its existence.

Lastly, our active powers are stimulated by it no less than our feelings and our reason. For since Humanity is so far more complex than any other organism, it will react more strongly and more continuously on its environment, submitting to its influence and so modifying it. Hence results Progress which is simply the development of Order, under the influence of Love.

Thus, in the conception of Humanity, the three essential aspects of Positivism, its subjective principle, its objective dogma, and its practical object, are united. Towards Humanity, who is for us the only true Great Being, we, the conscious elements of whom she is composed, shall henceforth direct every aspect of our life, individual or collective. Our thoughts will be devoted to the knowledge of Humanity, our affections to her love, our actions to her service.

Positivists then may, more truly than theological believers of whatever creed, regard life as a continuous and earnest act of worship; worship which will elevate and purify our feelings, enlarge and enlighten our thoughts, ennoble and invigorate our actions. It supplies a direct solution, so far as a solution is possible, of the great problem of the Middle Ages, the subordination of Politics to Morals. For this follows at once from the consecration now given to the principle that social sympathy should preponderate over self-love.

Thus Positivism becomes, in the true sense of the word, a Religion; the only religion which is real and complete; destined therefore to replace all imperfect and provisional systems resting on the primitive basis of theology.

For even the synthesis established by the old theocracies of Egypt and India was insufficient, because, being based on purely subjective principles it could never embrace practical life, which must always be subordinated to the objective realities of the external world. Theocracy was thus limited at the outset to the sphere of thought and of feeling; and part even of this field was soon lost when Art became emancipated from theocratical control, showing a spontaneous tendency to its natural vocation of idealizing real life. Of science and of morality the priests were still left sole arbiters; but here, too, their influence materially diminished so soon as the discovery of the simpler abstract truths of Positive science gave birth to Greek Philosophy. Philosophy, though as yet necessarily restricted to the metaphysical stage, yet already stood forward as the rival of the sacerdotal system. Its attempts to construct were in themselves fruitless; but they overthrew Polytheism, and ultimately transformed it into Monotheism. In this the last phase of theology, the intellectual authority of the priests was undermined no less deeply than the principle of their doctrine. They lost their hold upon Science, as long ago they had lost their hold upon Art. All that remained to them was the moral guidance of society; and even this was soon compromised by the progress of free thought; progress really due to the Positive spirit, although its systematic exponents still belong to the metaphysical school.

When Science had expanded sufficiently to exist apart from Philosophy, it showed a rapid tendency towards a synthesis of its own, alike incompatible with metaphysics and with theology. It was late in appearing, because it required a long series of preliminary efforts: but as it approached completion, it gradually brought the Positive spirit to bear upon the organization of practical life, from which that spirit had originally emanated. But thoroughly to effect this result was impossible until the science of Sociology had been formed; and this was done by my discovery of the law of historical development. Henceforth all true men of science will rise to the higher dignity of philosophers, and by so doing will necessarily assume something of the sacerdotal character, because the final result to which their researches tend is the subordination of every subject of thought to the moral principle; a result which leads us at once to the acceptance of a complete and homogenous synthesis. Thus the philosophers of the future become priests of Humanity, and their moral and intellectual influence will be far wider and more deeply rooted than that of any former priesthood. The primary condition of their spiritual authority is exclusion from political power, as a guarantee that theory and practice shall be systematically kept apart. A system in which the organs of counsel and those of command are never identical cannot possibly degenerate into any of the evils of theocracy.

By entirely renouncing wealth and worldly position, and that not as individuals merely, but as a body, the priests of Humanity will occupy a position of unparalleled dignity. For with their moral influence they will combine what since the downfall of the old theocracies has always been separated from it, the influence of superiority in art and science. Reason, Imagination, and Feeling will be brought into unison: and so united will react strongly on the imperious conditions of practical life; bringing it into closer accordance with the laws of universal morality, from which it is so prone to deviate. And the influence of this new modifying power will be the greater that the synthesis on which it rests will have preceded and prepared the way for the social system of the future; whereas theology could not arrive at its central principle, until the time of its decline was approaching. All functions, then, that co-operate in the elevation of man will be regenerated by the Positive priesthood. Science, Poetry, Morality, will be devoted to the study, the praise, and the love of Humanity, in order that under their combined influence, our political action may be more unremittingly given to her service.

With such a mission, Science acquires a position of unparalleled importance, as the sole means through which we come to know the nature and conditions of this Great Being, the worship of whom should be the distinctive feature of our whole life. For this all-important knowledge, the study of Sociology would seem to suffice: but Sociology itself depends upon preliminary study, first of the outer world, in which the actions of Humanity take place; and secondly, of Man, the individual agent.

The object of Positivist worship is not like that of theological believers an absolute, isolated, incomprehensible Being, whose existence admits of no demonstration, or comparison with anything real. The evidence of the Being here set forward is spontaneous, and is shrouded in no mystery. Before we can praise, love, and serve Humanity as we ought, we must know something of the laws which govern her existence, an existence more complicated than any other of which we are cognizant.

And by virtue of this complexity, Humanity possesses the attributes of vitality in a higher degree than any other organization; that is to say, there is at once more intimate harmony of the component elements, and more complete subordination to the external world. Immense as is the magnitude of this organism measured both in Time and Space, yet each of its parts carefully examined will show the general consensus of the whole. At the same time it is more dependent than any other upon the conditions of the outer world; in other words, upon the sum of the laws that regulate inferior phenomena. Like other vital organisms, it submits to mathematical, astronomical, physical, chemical, and biological conditions; and, in addition to these, is subject to special laws of Sociology with which lower organisms are not concerned. But as a further result of its higher complexity it reacts upon the world more powerfully; and is indeed in a true sense its chief. Scientifically defined, then, it is truly the Supreme Being: the Being who manifests to the fullest extent all the highest attributes of life.

But there is yet another feature peculiar to Humanity, and one of primary importance. That feature is, that the elements of which she is composed must always have an independent existence. In other organisms the parts have no existence when severed from the whole; but this, the greatest of all organisms, is made up of lives which can really be separated. There is, as we have seen, harmony of parts as well as independence, but the last of these conditions is as indispensable as the first. Humanity would cease to be superior to other beings were it possible for her elements to become inseparable. The two conditions are equally necessary:

but the difficulty of reconciling them is so great as to account at once for the slowness with which this highest of all organisms has been developed. It must not, however, be supposed that the new Supreme Being is, like the old, merely a subjective result of our powers of abstraction. Its existence is revealed to us, on the contrary, by close investigation of objective fact. Man indeed, as an individual, cannot properly be said to exist, except in the exaggerated abstractions of modern metaphysicians. Existence in the true sense can only be predicted of Humanity; although the complexity of her nature prevented men from forming a systematic conception of it, until the necessary stages of scientific initiation had been passed. Bearing this conclusion in mind, we shall be able now to distinguish in Humanity two distinct orders of functions: those by which she acts upon the world, and those which bind together her component parts. Humanity cannot herself act otherwise than by her separable members; but the efficiency of these members depends upon their working in cooperation, whether instinctively or with design. We find, then, external functions relating principally to the material existence of this organism; and internal functions by which its movable elements are combined. This distinction is but an application of the great theory, due to Bichat's genius, of the distinction between the life of nutrition and the life of relation which we find in the individual organism. Philosophically it is the source from which we derive the great social principle of separation of spiritual from temporal power. The temporal power governs: it originates in the personal instincts, and it stimulates activity. On it depends social Order. The spiritual power can only moderate: it is the exponent of our social instincts, and it promotes cooperation, which is the guarantee of Progress. Of these functions of Humanity the first corresponds to the function of nutrition, the second to that of innervation in the individual organism.

Having now viewed our subject statically, we may come to its dynamical aspect; reserving more detailed discussion for the third volume of this treatise, which deals with my fundamental theory of human development. The Great Being whom we worship is not immutable any more than it is absolute. Its nature is relative; and, as such, is eminently capable of growth. In a word it is the most vital of all living beings known to us. It extends and becomes more complex by the continuous successions of generations. But in its progressive changes as well as in its permanent functions, it is subject to invariable laws. And these laws considered, as we may now consider them, as a whole, form a more sublime object of contemplation than the solemn inaction of the old Supreme Being, whose existence was passive except when interrupted by acts of arbitrary and unintelligible volition. Thus it is only by Positive science that we can appreciate this highest of all destinies to which all the fatalities of individual life are subordinate. It is with this as with subjects of minor importance: systematic study of the Past is necessary in order to determine the Future, and so explain the tendencies of the Present. Let us then pass from the conception of Humanity as fully developed, to the history of its rise and progress; a history in which all other modes of progress are included. In ancient times the conception was incompatible with the theological spirit and also with the military character of society, which involved the slavery of the productive classes. The feeling of Patriotism, restricted as it was at first, was the only prelude then possible to the recognition of Humanity. From this narrow nationality there arose in the Middle Ages the feeling of universal brotherhood, as soon as military life had entered on its defensive phase, and all supernatural creeds had spontaneously

merged into a monotheistic form common to the whole West. The growth of Chivalry, and the attempt made to effect a permanent separation of the two social powers, announced already the subordination of Politics to Morals, and thus showed that the conception of Humanity was in direct course of preparation. But the unreal and anti-social nature of the mediaeval creed, and the military and aristocratic character of feudal society, made it impossible to go very far in this direction. The abolition of personal slavery was the most essential result of this important period. Society could now assume its industrial character; and feelings of fraternity were encouraged by modes of life in which all classes alike participated. Meanwhile, the growth of the Positive spirit was proceeding, and preparing the way for the establishment of Social Science, by which alone all other Positive studies should be systematized. This being done, the conception of the Great Being became possible. It was with reference to subjects of a speculative and scientific nature that the conception first arose in a distinct shape. As early as two centuries ago, Pascal spoke of the human race as one Man.[1] Amidst the inevitable decline of the theological and military system, men became conscious of the movement of society, which had now advanced through so many phases; and the notion of Progress as a distinctive feature of Humanity became admitted. Still the conception of Humanity as the basis for a new synthesis was impossible until the crisis of the French Revolution. That crisis on the one hand proved the urgent necessity for social regeneration, and on the other gave birth

[1] Toute la suite des hommes, pendant le cours de tant de siècles, doit être considérée comme un même homme qui subsiste toujours et qui apprend continuellement.—Pascal, Pensées, Part I, Art. I. [The whole succession of men during the course of so many centuries should be considered as one Man ever living and constantly learning.]

o the only philosophy capable of effecting it. Thus our consciousness of the new Great Being has advanced co-extensively with its growth. Our present conception of it is as much the measure of our social progress as it is the summary of Positive knowledge.

In speaking of the dignity of Science when regenerated by this lofty application of it, I do not refer solely to the special science of Social phenomena, but also to the preliminary studies of Life and of the Inorganic World, both of which form an essential portion of Positive doctrine. A social mission of high importance will be recognized in the most elementary sciences, whether it be for the sake of their method or for the value of their scientific results. True, the religion of Humanity will lead to the entire abolition of scientific Academies, because their tendency, especially in France, is equally hurtful to science and morality. They encourage mathematicians to confine their attention exclusively to the first step in the scientific scale; and biologists to pursue their studies without any solid basis or definite purpose. Special studies carried on without regard for the encyclopædic principles which determine the relative value of knowledge, and its bearing on human life, will be condemned by all men of right feeling and good sense. Such men will feel the necessity of resisting the morbid narrowness of mind and heart to which the anarchy of our times inevitably leads. But the abolition of the Academic system will only ensure a larger measure of respect for all scientific researches of real value, on whatever subject. The study of Mathematics, the value of which is at present negatived by its hardening tendency, will now manifest its latent moral efficacy, as the only sure basis for firm conviction; a state of mind that can never be perfectly attained in more complex subjects of thought, except by those who have experienced it in the simpler subjects. When the close connexion of all scientific knowledge becomes more generally admitted, Humanity will reject political teachers who are ignorant of Geometry, as well as geometricians who neglect Sociology. Biology meanwhile will lose its dangerous materialism, and will receive all the respect due to its close connexion with social science and its important bearing on the essential doctrines of Positivism. To attempt to explain the life of Humanity without first examining the lower forms of life, would be as serious an error as to study Biology without regard to the social purpose which Biology is intended to serve. Science has now become indispensable to the establishment of moral truth, and at the same time its subordination to the inspirations of the heart is fully recognized; thus it takes its place henceforward among the most essential functions of the priesthood of Humanity. The supremacy of true Feeling will strengthen Reason, and will receive in turn from Reason a systematic sanction. Natural philosophy, besides its evident value in regulating the spontaneous action of Humanity, has a direct tendency to elevate human nature; it draws from the outer world that basis of fixed truth which is so necessary to control our various desires.

The study of Humanity therefore, directly or indirectly, is for the future the permanent aim of Science; and Science is now in a true sense consecrated, as the source from which the universal religion receives its principles. It reveals to us not merely the nature and conditions of the Great Being, but also its destiny and the successive phases of its growth. The aim is high and arduous; it requires continuous and combined exertion of all our faculties; but it ennobles the simplest processes of scientific investigation by connecting them permanently with subjects of the deepest interest. The scrupulous exactness and rigorous caution of the Positive method, which when applied to unimportant subjects seem almost puerile, will be valued and insisted on when seen to be necessary for the efficacy of efforts relating to our most essential wants. Rationalism, in the true sense of the word, so far from being incompatible with right feeling, strengthens and develops it, by placing all the facts of the case, in social questions especially, in their true light.

But, however honourable the rank which Science when regenerated will hold in the new religion, the sanction given to Poetry will be even more direct and unqualified, because the function assigned to it is one which is more practical and which touches us more nearly. Its function will be the praise of Humanity. All previous efforts of Art have been but the prelude to this, its natural mission; a prelude often impatiently performed since Art threw off the yoke of theocracy at an earlier period than Science. Polytheism was the only religion under which it had free scope: there it could idealize all the passions of our nature, no attempt being made to conceal the similarity of the gods to the human type. The change from Polytheism to Monotheism was unacceptable to Art, because it narrowed its field; but towards the close of the Middle Ages it began to shake off the influence of obscure and chimerical beliefs, and take possession of its proper sphere. The field that now lies before it in the religion of Humanity is inexhaustible. It is called upon to idealize the social life of Man, which, in the time of the nations of antiquity, had not been sufficiently developed to inspire the highest order of poetry.

In the first place it will be of the greatest service in enabling men to realize the conception of Humanity, subject only to the condition of not overstepping the fundamental truths of Science. Science unassisted cannot define the nature and destinies of this Great Being with sufficient clearness. In our religion the ob-

ject of worship must be conceived distinctly, in order to be ardently loved and zealously served. Science, especially in subjects of this nature, is confined within narrow limits; it leaves inevitable deficiencies which esthetic genius must supply. And there are certain qualities in Art as opposed to Science, which specially qualify it for the representation of Humanity. For Humanity is distinguished from other forms of life by the combination of independence with co-operation attributes which also are natural to Poetry. For while Poetry is more sympathetic than Science, its productions have far more individuality; the genius of their author is more strongly marked in them, and the debt to his predecessors and contemporaries is less apparent. Thus the synthesis on which the inauguration of the final religion depends, is one in which Art will participate more than Science, Science furnishing merely the necessary basis. Its influence will be even greater than in the times of Polytheism; for powerful as Art appeared to be in those times, it could in reality do nothing but embellish the fables to which the confused ideas of theocracy had given rise. By its aid we shall for the first time rise at last to a really human point of view, and be enabled distinctly to understand the essential attributes of the Great Being of whom we are members. The material power of Humanity and the successive phases of her physical, her intellectual, and, above all, her moral progress, will each in turn be depicted. Without the difficulties of analytical study, we shall gain a clear knowledge of her nature and her conditions, by the poet's description of her future destiny, of her constant struggle against painful fatalities, which have at last become a source of happiness and greatness, of the slow growth of her infancy, of her lofty hopes now so near fulfilment. The history of universal Love, the soul by which this Great Being is animated; the history, that is, of the marellous advance of man, individually or socially, from brutish appetite to pure unselfish sympathy, is of itself an endless theme for the poetry of the future.

Comparisons, too, may be instituted, in which the poet, without specially attacking the old religion, will indicate the superiority of the new. The attributes of the new Great Being may be forcibly illustrated, especially during the time of transition, by contrast with the inferiority of her various predecessors. All theological types are absolute, indefinite, and immutable; consequently in none of them has it been possible to combine to a satisfactory extent the attributes of goodness, wisdom, and power. Nor can we conceive of their combination, except in a Being whose existence is a matter of certainty, and who is subject to invariable laws. The gods of Polytheism were endowed with energy and sympathy, but possessed neither dignity nor morality. They were superseded by the sublime deity of Monotheism, who was sometimes represented as inert and passionless, sometimes as impenetrable and inflexible. But the new Supreme Being, having a real existence, an existence relative and modifiable, admits of being more distinctly conceived than the old; and the influence of the conception will be equally strong and far more elevating. Each one of us will recognize in it a power superior to his own, a power on which the whole destiny of his life depends, since the life of the individual is in every respect subordinate to the evolution of the race. But the knowledge of this power has not the crushing effect of the old conception of omnipotence. For every great or good man will feel that his own life is an indispensable element in the great organism. The supremacy of Humanity is but the result of individual co-operation; her power is not supreme, it is only superior to that of all beings whom we know. Our love for her is tainted by no degrading fears, yet it is always coupled with the most sincere reverence. Perfection is in no wise claimed for her; we study her natural defects with care in order to remedy them as far as possible. The love we bear to her is a feeling as noble as it is strong; it calls for no degrading expressions of adulation, but it inspires us with unremitting zeal for moral improvement. But these and other advantages of the new religion, though they can be indicated by the philosopher, need the poet to display them in their full light. The moral grandeur of man when freed from the chimeras that oppress him, was foreseen by Goethe, and still more clearly by Byron. But the work of these men was one of destruction; and their types could only embody the spirit of revolt. Poetry must rise above the negative stage in which, owing to the circumstances of the time, their genius was arrested, and must embrace in the Positive spirit the system of sociological and other laws to which human development is subject, before it can adequately portray the new Man in his relation to the new God.

There is yet another way in which Art may serve the cause of religion; that is, in organizing the festivals, whether private or public, of which, to a great extent, the worship of Humanity will consist. For this purpose esthetic talent is far more required than scientific, the object in view being to reveal the nature of the great Organism more clearly, by presenting all aspects of its existence, static or dynamic, in idealized forms.

These festivals, then, should be of two kinds, corresponding to the two essential aspects of Humanity; the first illustrating her existence, the second her action. Thus we shall stimulate both the elements of true social feeling; the love of Order, namely, and the love of Progress. In our static festivals social Order and the feeling of Solidarity, will be illustrated; the dynamic festivals will explain social Progress, and inspire the sense of historical Continuity. Taken together, their periodic recurrence will form a continuation of Positive education. They will develop and confirm the principles instilled in youth. But there will be nothing didactic in their form; since it is of the essence of Art not to instruct otherwise than by giving pleasure. Of course the regular recurrence of these festivals will not prevent any modifications which may be judged necessary to adapt them to special incidents that may from time to time arise.

The festivals representing Order will necessarily take more abstract and austere forms than those of Progress. It will be their object to represent the statical relations by which the great Organism preserves its unity, and the various aspects of its animating principle, Love. The most universal and the most solemn of these festivals will be the feast of Humanity, which will be held throughout the West at the beginning of the new year, thus consecrating the only custom which still remains in general use to relieve the prosaic dullness of modern life. In this feast, which celebrates the most comprehensiveness of all unions, every branch of the human race will at some future time participate. In the same month there might be three festivals of a secondary order, representing the minor degrees of association, the Nation, the Province, and the Town. Giving this first month to the direct celebration of the social tie, we might devote the first days of the four succeeding months to the four principal domestic relations, Connubial, Parental, Filial, and Fraternal. In the sixth month, the honourable position of domestic service would receive its due measure of respect.

These would be the static festivals; taken together they would form a representation of the true theory of our individual and social nature, together with the principles of moral duty to which that theory gives rise. No direct mention is made of the personal instincts, notwithstanding their preponderance, because it

is the main object of Positive worship to bring them under the control of the social instincts. Personal virtues are by no means neglected in Positive education, but to make them the objects of any special celebration, would only stimulate egotistic feeling. Indirectly their value is recognized in every part of our religious system, in the reaction which they exercise upon our generous sympathies. Their omission, therefore, implies no real deficiency in this ideal portraiture of human faculties and duties. Again, no special announcement of the subordination of Humanity to the laws of the External World is needed. The consciousness of this external power pervades every part of the Positive system; it controls our desires, directs our speculations, stimulates our actions. The simple fact of the recurrence of our ceremonies at fixed periods, determined by the Earth's motion, is enough to remind us of our inevitable subjection to the fatalities of the External World.

As the static festivals represent Morality, so the dynamic festivals, those of Progress, will represent History. In these the worship of Humanity assumes a more concrete and animated form; as it will consist principally in rendering honour to the noblest types of each phase of human development. It is desirable, however, that each of the more important phases should be represented in itself, independently of the greatness of any individual belonging to it. Of the months unoccupied by static festivals, three might be given to the principal phases of the Past, Fetichism, Polytheism, and Monotheism; and a fourth to the celebration of the Future, the normal state to which all these phases have been tending.

Forming thus the chain of historical succession, we may consecrate each month to some one of the types who best represent the various stages. I omit, however, some explanations of detail given in the first edition of this General View,

ritten at the time when I had not made
ne distinction between the abstract and
concrete worship sufficiently clear. A few
months after its publication, in 1848, the
circumstances of the time induced me to
came a complete system of commemoration applicable to Western Europe,
under the title of *Positivist Calendar*.[2]
Of this I shall speak more at length in
the fourth volume of the present treatise.
Its success has fully justified me in anticipating this part of my subject. To it
now refer the reader, recommending
him to familiarize himself with the provisional arrangement of the new Western
year then put forward and already
adopted by most Positivists.

But the practice need not be restricted
to names of European importance. It is
applicable in its degree to each separate
province, and even to private life. Catholicism offers two institutions in which
the religion of the family connects itself
with public worship in its most comprehensive sense. There is a day appointed
in Catholic countries in which all are in
the habit of visiting the tombs of those
dear to them; finding consolation for their
grief by sharing it with others. To this
custom Positivists devote the last day of
the year. The working classes of Paris
give every year a noble proof that complete freedom of thought is in no respect
compatible with worship of the dead,
which in their case is unconnected with
any system. Again there is the institution
of baptismal names, which though little
thought of at present, will be maintained
and improved by Positivism. It is an admirable mode of impressing on men the
connexion of private with public life, by
furnishing every one with a type for his
own personal imitation. Here the superiority of the new religion is very apparent;
since the choice of a name will not be
limited to any time or country. In this,

---

[2] [See *The Positivist Calendar*, edited by
H. G. Jones (W. Reeves, 1905).]

as in other cases, the absolute spirit of
Catholicism proved fatal to its prospects
of becoming universal.

These brief remarks will be enough to
illustrate the two classes of festivals instituted by Positivism. In every week of
the year some new aspect of Order or of
Progress will be held up to public veneration; and in each the link connecting
public and private worship will be found
in the adoration of Woman. In this esthetic side of Positive religion everything
tends to strengthen its fundamental principle of Love. All the resources of Poetry, and of the other arts of sound and
form, will be invoked to give full and
regular expression to it. The dominant
feeling is always that of deep reverence
proceeding from sincere acknowledgment of benefits received. Our worship
will be alike free from mysticism and
from affectation. While striving to surpass our ancestors, we shall yet render
due honour to all their services, and look
with respect upon their systems of life.
Influenced no longer by chimeras which
though comforting to former times are
now degrading, we have now no obstacle
to becoming as far as possible incorporate
with the Great Being whom we worship.
By commemoration of past services we
strengthen the desire inherent in all of
us to prolong our existence in the only
way which is really in our power. The fact
that all human affairs are subject to one
fundamental law, as soon as it becomes
familiarly known, enables and encourages each one of us to live in a true sense
in the Past and even in the Future; as
those cannot do who attribute the events
of life to the agency of an arbitrary and
impenetrable Will. The praise given to
our predecessors will stimulate a noble
rivalry; inspiring all with the desire to
become themselves incorporate into this
mighty Being whose life endures through
all time, and who is formed of the dead
far more than the living. When the system of commemoration is fully developed,

no worthy co-operator will be excluded, however humble his sphere; whether limited to his family or town, or extending to his country or to the whole West. The education of Positivists will soon convince them that such recompense for honourable conduct is ample compensation for the imaginary hopes which inspired their predecessors.

To live in others is, in the truest sense of the word, life. Indeed the best part of our own life is passed thus. As yet this truth has not been grasped firmly, because the social point of view has never yet been brought systematically before us. But the religion of Humanity, by giving an esthetic form to the Positivist synthesis, will make it intelligible to minds of every class: and will enable us to enjoy the untold charm springing from the sympathies of union and of continuity when allowed free play. To prolong our life indefinitely in the Past and Future, so as to make it more perfect in the Present, is abundant compensation for the illusions of our youth which have now passed away for ever. Science which deprived us of these imaginary comforts, itself in its maturity supplies the solid basis for consolation of a kind unknown before; the hope of becoming incorporate into the Great Being whose static and dynamic laws it has revealed. On this firm foundation Poetry raises the structure of public and private worship; and thus all are made active partakers of this universal life, which minds still fettered by theology cannot understand. Thus imagination, while accepting the guidance of reason, will exercise a far more efficient and extensive influence than in the days of Polytheism. For the priests of Humanity the sole purpose of Science is to prepare the field for Art, whether esthetic or industrial. This object once attained, poetic study or composition will form the chief occupation of our speculative faculties. The poet is now called to his true mission, which is to give

beauty and grandeur to human life, b inspiring a deeper sense of our relatio to Humanity. Poetry will form the basi of the ceremonies in which the new priest hood will solemnise more efficiently tha the old, the most important events o private life: especially Birth, Marriage and Death; so as to impress the famil" as well as the state with the sense of thi relation. Forced as we are henceforth tc concentrate all our hopes and efforts upon the real life around us, we shall feel more strongly than ever that all the powers of Imagination as well as those of Reason, Feeling, and Activity, are required in its service.

Poetry once raised to its proper place, the arts of sound and form, which render in a more vivid way the subjects which Poetry has suggested, will soon follow. Their sphere, like that of Poetry, will be the celebration of Humanity; an exhaustless field, leaving no cause to regret the chimeras which, in the present empirical condition of these arts, are still considered indispensable. Music in modern times has been limited almost entirely to the expression of individual emotions. Its full power has never been felt in public life, except in the solitary instance of the *Marseillaise,* in which the whole spirit of our great Revolution stands recorded. But in the worship of Humanity, based as it is on Positive education, and animated by the spirit of Poetry, Music, as the most social of the special arts, will aid in the representation of the attributes and destinies of Humanity, and in the glorification of great historical types. Painting and Sculpture will have the same object; they will enable us to realize the conception of Humanity with greater clearness and precision than would be possible for Poetry, even with the aid of Music. The beautiful attempts of the artists of the sixteenth century, men who had very little theological belief, to embody the Christian ideal of Woman, may be regarded as an nconscious prelude to the representa-on of Humanity, in the form which of ll others is most suitable. Under the im-ulse of these feelings, the sculptor will vercome the technical difficulties of rep-esenting figures in groups, and will adopt uch subjects by preference. Hitherto this as only been effected in bas-reliefs, vorks which stand midway between paint-ng and sculpture. There are, however, ome splendid exceptions from which we an imagine the scope and grandeur of he latter art, when raised to its true po-ition. Statuesque groups, whether the igures are joined or, as is preferable, eparate, will enable the sculptor to un-dertake many great subjects from which he has been hitherto debarred.

In Architecture the influence of Posi-tivism will be felt less rapidly; but ul-timately this art like the rest will be made available for the new religion. The build-ings erected for the service of God may for a time suffice for the worship of Hu-manity, in the same way that Christian worship was carried on at first in Pagan temples as they were gradually vacated. But ultimately buildings will be required more specially adapted to a religion in which all the functions connected with education and worship are so entirely dif-ferent. What these buildings will be it would be useless at present to inquire. It is less easy to foresee the Positivist ideal in Architecture than in any other arts. And it must remain uncertain until the new principles of education have been generally spread, and until the Pos-itivist religion, having received all the aid that Poetry, Music, and the arts of Form can give, has become the accepted faith of Western Europe. When the more advanced nations are heartily engaged in the cause, the true temples of Humanity will soon arise. By that time mental and moral regeneration will have advanced far enough to commence the reconstruc-tion of all political institutions. Until then the new religion will avail itself of Chris-tian churches as these gradually become vacant.

Art then, as well as Science, partakes in the regenerating influence which Pos-itivism derives from its synthetic princi-ple of Love. Both are called to their proper functions, the one to contemplate, the other to glorify Humanity, in order that we may love and serve her more per-fectly. Yet while the intellect is thus made the servant of the heart, far from being weakened by this subordinate position, it finds in it an exhaustless field, in which the value of its labours is amply recog-nized. Each of its faculties is called di-rectly into play, and is supplied with its appropriate employment. Poetry institutes the forms of the worship of Humanity; Science supplies the principles on which those forms are framed, by connecting them with the laws of the external world. Imagination, while ceasing to usurp the place of Reason, yet enhances rather than diminishes its original influence, which the new philosophy shows to be as beneficial as it is natural. And thus human life at last attains that state of perfect harmony which has been so long sought for in vain, and which consists in the direction of all our faculties to one common purpose under the supremacy of Affection. At the same time all former efforts of Imagination and Reason, even when they clashed with each other, are fully appreciated; because we see that they developed our powers, that they taught us the conditions of their equilib-rium, and made it manifest that nothing but that equilibrium was wanting to al-low them to work together for our wel-fare. Above all do we recognize the im-mense value of the medieval attempt to form a complete synthesis, although, notwithstanding all the results of Greek and Roman civilization, the time was not yet ripe for it. To renew that attempt upon a sounder basis, and with surer prospects of success, is the object of those who found the religion of Humanity.

Widely different as are their circumstances and the means they employ, they desire to regard themselves as the successors of the great men who conducted the progressive movement of Catholicism. For those alone are worthy to be called successors, who continue or carry into effect the undertakings which former times have left unfinished; the title is utterly unmerited by blind followers of obsolete dogmas, which have long ceased to bear any relation to their original purpose, and which their very authors, if now living, would disavow.

But while bearing in mind our debt to Catholicism, we need not omit to recognize how largely Positivism gains by comparison with it. Full justice will be done to the aims of Catholicism, and to the excellence of its results. But the whole effect of Positivist worship will be to make men feel clearly how far superior in every respect is the synthesis founded on the Love of Humanity to that founded on the Love of God.

Christianity satisfied no part of our nature fully, except the affections. It rejected Imagination, it shrank from Reason; and therefore its power was always contested, and could not last. Even in its own sphere of affection, its principles never lent themselves to that social direction which the Catholic priesthood, with such remarkable persistency, endeavoured to give to them. The aim which it set before men, being unreal and personal, was ill-suited to a life of reality and of social sympathy. It is true that the universality of this supreme affection was indirectly a bond of union; but only when it was not at variance with true social feeling. And from the nature of the system, opposition between these two principles was the rule, and harmony the exception; since the Love of God, even as viewed by the best Catholic types, required in almost all cases the abandonment of every other passion. The moral value of such a synthesis consisted solely in the discipline

which it established; discipline of whatever kind being preferable to anarchy which would have given free scope to all the lowest propensities. But notwithstanding all the tender feeling of the best mystics, the affection which to them was supreme admitted of no real reciprocity. Moreover, the stupendous nature of the rewards and penalties by which every precept in this arbitrary system was enforced, tended to weaken the character and to taint our noblest impulses. The essential merit of the system was that it was the first attempt to exercise systematic control over our moral nature. The discipline of Polytheism was usually confined to actions: sometimes it extended to habits; but it never touched the affections from which both habits and action spring. Christianity took the best means of effecting its purpose that were then available; but it was not successful, except so far as it gave indirect encouragement to our higher feelings. And so vague and absolute were its principles, that even this would have been impossible, but for the wisdom of the priesthood, who for a long time saved society from the dangers incident to so arbitrary a system. But at the close of the Middle Ages, when the priesthood became retrograde, and lost at once their morality and their freedom, the doctrine was left to its own impotence, and rapidly degenerated till it became a chronic source of degradation and of discord.

But the synthesis based upon Love of Humanity has too deep a foundation in Positive truth to be liable to similar decline; and its influence cannot but increase so long as the progress of our race endures. The Great Being, who is its object, tolerates the most searching inquiry, and yet does not restrict the scope of Imagination. The laws which regulate her existence are now known to us; and the more deeply her nature is investigated, the stronger is our consciousness of her reality and of the greatness of her benefits. The thought of her stimulates all the powers of Imagination, and thus enables us to participate in a measure in the universality of her life, throughout the whole extent of Time and Space of which we have any real knowledge. All our real intellectual results, whether in art or science, are alike co-ordinated by the religion of Humanity; for its furnishes the sole bond of connexion by which permanent harmony can be established between our thoughts and our feelings. It is the only system which without artifice and without arbitrary restriction, can establish the preponderance of Affection over Thought and Action. It sets forth social feeling as the first principle of morality; without ignoring the natural superiority in strength of the personal instincts. To live for others it holds to be the highest happiness. To become incorporate with Humanity, to sympathize with all her former phases, to foresee her destinies in the future, and to do what lies in us to forward them; this is what it puts before us as the constant aim of life. Self-love in the Positive system is regarded as the great infirmity of our nature: an infirmity which unremitting discipline on the part of each individual and of society may materially palliate, but will never radically cure. The degree to which this mastery over our own nature is attained is the truest standard of individual or social progress, since it has the closest relation to the existence of the Great Being, and to the happiness of the elements that compose it.

Inspired as it is by sincere gratitude, which increases the more carefully the grounds for it are examined, the worship of Humanity raises Prayer for the first time above the degrading influence of self-interest. We pray to the Supreme Being; but only to express our deep thankfulness for her present and past benefits, which are an earnest of still greater blessings in the future. Doubtless it is a fact of human nature, that habitual expression of such feelings reacts beneficially on our moral nature; and so far we, too, find in Prayer a noble recompense. But it is one that can suggest to us no selfish thoughts, since it cannot come at all unless it come spontaneously. Our highest happiness consists in Love; and we know that more than any other feeling love may be strengthened by exercise; that alone of all feelings it admits of, and increases with, simultaneous expansion in all. Humanity will become more familiar to us than the old gods were to the Polytheists, yet without the loss of dignity which, in their case, resulted from familiarity. Her nature has in it nothing arbitrary, yet she co-operates with us in the worship that we render, since in honouring her we receive back 'grace for grace.' Homage accepted by the Deity of former times laid him open to the charge of puerile vanity. But the new Deity will accept praise only where it is deserved, and will derive from it equal benefit with ourselves. This perfect reciprocity of affection and of influence is peculiar to Positive religion, because in it alone the object of worship is a Being whose nature is relative, modifiable, and perfectible; a Being of whom her own worshippers form a part, and the laws of whose existence, being more clearly known than theirs, allow her desires and her tendencies to be more distinctly foreseen.

The morality of Positive religion combines all the advantages of spontaneousness with those of demonstration. It is so thoroughly human in all its parts, as to preclude all the subterfuges by which repentance for transgression is so often stifled or evaded. By pointing out distinctly the way in which each individual action reacts upon society, it forces us to judge our own conduct without lowering our standard. Some might think it too gentle, and not sufficiently vigorous; yet the love by which it is inspired is no passive feeling, but a principle which strongly stimulates our energies to the full extent compatible with the attainment of that highest good to which it is ever tending. Accepting the truths of science, it teaches that we must look to our own unremitting activity for the only providence by which the rigour of our destiny can be alleviated. We know well that the great Organism, superior though it be to all beings known to us, is yet under the dominion of inscrutable laws, and is in no respect either absolutely perfect or absolutely secure from danger. Every condition of our existence, whether those of the external world or those of our own nature, might at some time be compromised. Even our moral and intellectual faculties, on which our highest interests depend, are no exception to this truth. Such contingencies are always possible, and yet they are not to prevent us from living nobly; they must not lessen our love, our thought, or our efforts for Humanity; they must not overwhelm us with anxiety, nor urge us to useless complaint. But the very principles which demand this high standard of courage and resignation, are themselves well calculated to maintain it. For by making us fully conscious of the greatness of man, and by setting us free from the degrading influences of fear, they inspire us with keen interest in our efforts, inadequate though they be, against the pressure of fatalities which are not always beyond our power to modify. And thus the reaction of these fatalities upon our character is turned at last to a most beneficial use. It prevents alike overweening anxiety for our own interests and dull indifference to them; whereas, in theological and metaphysical systems, even when inculcating self-denial, there is always a dangerous tendency to concentrate thought on personal considerations. Dignified reaction where modification of them is possible; such is the moral standard which Positivism puts forward for individuals and for society.

. . .

The features of the system stand out already with sufficient clearness to enable us to begin at once the work of mental and social renovation for which our revolutionary predecessors so energetically prepared the way. They however were blinded to the Future by their hatred of the Past. With us, on the contrary, social sympathy rests upon the historical spirit, and at the same time strengthens it. Solidarity with our contemporaries is not enough for us, unless we combine it with the sense of Continuity with former times; and while we press on toward the Future, we lean upon the Past, every phase of which our religion holds in honour. So far from the energy of our progressive movement being hampered by such feelings, it is only by doing full justice to the Past, as no system but ours can do consistently, that we can obtain perfect emancipation of thought; because we are thus saved from the necessity of making the slightest actual concession to systems which we regard as obsolete. Understanding their nature and their purpose better than the sectaries who still empirically adhere to them, we can see that each was in its time necessary as a preparatory step towards the final system, in which all their partial and imperfect services will be combined.

Comparing it especially with the last synthesis by which the Western family of nations has been directed, it is clear even from the indications given in this prefatory work, that the new synthesis is more real, more comprehensive, and more stable. All that we find to admire in the mediaeval system is developed and matured in Positivism. It is the only system which can induce the intellect to accept its due position of subordination to the heart. We recognize the piety and chivalry of our ancestors, who made a noble application of the best doctrine that was possible in their time. We believe that were they living now, they would be found in our ranks. They would acknowledge the decay of their provisional phase of thought, and would see that in its present degenerate state it is only a symbol of reaction, and a source of discord.

And now that the doctrine has been shown to rest on a central principle, a principle which appeals alike to instinct and to reason, we may carry our comparison a step further, and convince all clear-seeing and honest minds that it is as superior to former systems in its influence over the emotions and the imagination, as it is from the practical and intellectual aspect. Under it, Life, whether private or public, becomes in a still higher sense than under Polytheism, a continuous act of worship performed under the inspiration of universal Love. All our thoughts, feelings, and actions flow spontaneously to a common centre in Humanity, our Supreme Being; a Being who is real, accessible, and sympathetic, because she is of the same nature as her worshippers, though far superior to any one of them. The very conception of Humanity is a condensation of the whole mental and social history of man. For it implies the irrevocable extinction of theology and of war; both of which are incompatible with uniformity of belief and with co-operation of all the energies of the race. The spontaneous morality of the emotions is restored to its due place; and Philosophy, Poetry, and Polity are thereby regenerated. Each is placed in its due relation to the others, and is consecrated to the study, the praise, and the service of Humanity, the most relative and the most perfectible of all beings. Science passes from the analytic to the synthetic state, being entrusted with the high mission of founding an objective basis for man's action on the laws of the external world and of man's nature; a basis which is indispensable to control the oscillation of our opinions, the versatility of our feelings, and the instability of our purposes. Poetry assumes at last its true social function, and will henceforth be preferred to all other studies. By idealizing Humanity under every aspect, it enables us to give fit expression to the gratitude we owe to her, both publicly and as individuals; and thus it becomes a source of the highest spiritual benefit.

But amidst the pleasures that spring from the study and the praise of Humanity, it must be remembered that Positivism is characterized always by reality and utility, and admits of no degeneration into asceticism or quietism. The Love by which it is inspired is no passive principle; while stimulating Reason and Imagination, it does so only to give a higher direction to our practical activity. It was in practical life that the Positive spirit first arose, extended thence to the sphere of thought, and ultimately to the moral sphere. The grand object of human existence is the constant improvement of the natural Order that surrounds us: of our material condition first; subsequently of our physical, intellectual, and moral nature. And the highest of these objects is moral progress, whether in the individual, in the family, or in society. It is on this that human happiness, whether in private or public life, principally depends. Political art, then, when subordinated to morality, becomes the most essential of all arts. It consists in concentration of all human effort upon the service of Humanity in accordance with the natural laws which regulate her existence.

. . .

GEORGE SANTAYANA

Religion as Moral Symbolism

George Santayana (1863–1952), born in Spain, and educated in the United States, taught at Harvard from 1889 to 1912. From 1912 until his death he lived in Europe, devoting himself to writing. Santayana's literary style is outstanding, and he has written poems, essays, and a novel, as well as philosophical works.

CHAPTER I

HOW RELIGION MAY BE AN EMBODIMENT OF REASON

Experience has repeatedly confirmed that well-known maxim of Bacon's, that "a little philosophy inclineth man's mind to atheism, but depth in philosophy bringeth men's minds about to religion." In every age the most comprehensive thinkers have found in the religion of their time and country something they could accept, interpreting and illustrating that religion so as to give it depth and universal application. Even the heretics and atheists, if they have had profundity, turn out after a while to be forerunners of some new orthodoxy. What they rebel against is a religion alien to their nature; they are atheists only by accident, and relatively to a convention which inwardly offends them, but they yearn mightily in their own souls after the religious acceptance of a world interpreted in their own fashion. So it appears in the end that their

From George Santayana, *Reason in Religion* (1905), Chs. I, III, IV, X, and XIV. Reprinted by permission of Constable & Co., Ltd., and Charles Scribner's Sons.

atheism and loud protestation were in fact the hastier part of their thought, since what emboldened them to deny the poor world's faith was that they were too impatient to understand it. Indeed, the enlightenment common to young wits and worm-eaten old satirists, who plume themselves on detecting the scientific ineptitude of religion—something which the blindest half see—is not nearly enlightened enough: it points to notorious facts incompatible with religious tenets literally taken, but it leaves unexplored the habits of thought from which those tenets sprang, their original meaning, and their true function. Such studies would bring the sceptic face to face with the mystery and pathos of mortal existence. They would make him understand why religion is so profoundly moving and in a sense so profoundly just. There must needs be something humane and necessary in an influence that has become the most general sanction of virtue, the chief occasion for art and philosophy, and the source, perhaps, of the best human happiness. If nothing, as Hooker said, is "so malapert as a splenetic religion," a sour irreligion is almost as perverse.

At the same time, when Bacon penned

the sage epigram we have quoted he forgot to add that the God to whom depth in philosophy brings back men's minds is far from being the same from whom a little philosophy estranges them. It would be pitiful indeed if mature reflection bred no better conceptions than those which have drifted down the muddy stream of time, where tradition and passion have jumbled everything together. Traditional conceptions, when they are felicitous, may be adopted by the poet, but they must be purified by the moralist and disintegrated by the philosopher. Each religion, so dear to those whose life it sanctifies, and fulfilling so necessary a function in the society that has adopted it, necessarily contradicts every other religion, and probably contradicts itself. What religion a man shall have is a historical accident, quite as much as what language he shall speak. In the rare circumstances where a choice is possible, he may, with some difficulty, make an exchange; but even then he is only adopting a new convention which may be more agreeable to his personal temper but which is essentially as arbitrary as the old.

The attempt to speak without speaking any particular language is not more hopeless than the attempt to have a religion that shall be no religion in particular. A courier's or a dragoman's speech may indeed be often unusual and drawn from disparate sources, not without some mixture of personal originality; but that private jargon will have a meaning only because of its analogy to one or more conventional languages and its obvious derivation from them. So travellers from one religion to another, people who have lost their spiritual nationality, may often retain a neutral and confused residuum of belief, which they may egregiously regard as the essence of all religion, so little may they remember the graciousness and naturalness of that ancestral accent which a perfect religion should have. Yet a mo-

ment's probing of the conceptions surviving in such minds will show them to be nothing but vestiges of old beliefs, creases which thought, even if emptied of all dogmatic tenets, has not been able to smooth away at its first unfolding. Later generations, if they have any religion at all, will be found either to revert to ancient authority, or to attach themselves spontaneously to something wholly novel and immensely positive, to some faith promulgated by a fresh genius and passionately embraced by a converted people. Thus every living and healthy religion has a marked idiosyncrasy. Its power consists in its special and surprising message and in the bias which that revelation gives to life. The vistas it opens and the mysteries it propounds are another world to live in; and another world to live in— whether we expect ever to pass wholly into it or no—is what we mean by having a religion.

What relation, then, does this great business of the soul, which we call religion, bear to the Life of Reason? That the relation between the two is close seems clear from several circumstances. The Life of Reason is the seat of all ultimate values. Now the history of mankind will show us that whenever spirits at once lofty and intense have seemed to attain the highest joys, they have envisaged and attained them in religion. Religion would therefore seem to be a vehicle or a factor in rational life, since the ends of rational life are attained by it. Moreover, the Life of Reason is an ideal to which everything in the world should be subordinated; it establishes lines of moral cleavage everywhere and makes right eternally different from wrong. Religion does the same thing. It makes absolute moral decisions. It sanctions, unifies, and transforms ethics. Religion thus exercises a function of the Life of Reason. And a further function which is common to both is that of emancipating man from his personal limitations. In different ways religions promise to transfer the soul to better conditions. A supernaturally favoured kingdom is to be established for posterity upon earth, or for all the faithful in heaven, or the soul is to be freed by repeated purgations from all taint and sorrow, or it is to be lost in the absolute, or it is to become an influence and an object of adoration in the places it once haunted or wherever the activities it once loved may be carried on by future generations of its kindred. Now reason in its way lays before us all these possibilities: it points to common objects, political and intellectual, in which an individual may lose what is mortal and accidental in himself and immortalise what is rational and human; it teaches us how sweet and fortunate death may be to those whose spirit can still live in their country and in their ideas; it reveals the radiating effects of action and the eternal objects of thought.

Yet the difference in tone and language must strike us, so soon as it is philosophy that speaks. That change should remind us that even if the function of religion and that of reason coincide, this function is performed in the two cases by very different organs. Religions are many, reason one. Religion consists of conscious ideas, hopes, enthusiasms, and objects of worship; it operates by grace and flourishes by prayer. Reason, on the other hand, is a mere principle or potential order, on which, indeed, we may come to reflect, but which exists in us ideally only, without variation or stress of any kind. We conform or do not conform to it; it does not urge or chide us, nor call for any emotions on our part other than those naturally aroused by the various objects which it unfolds in their true nature and proportion. Religion brings some order into life by weighting it with new materials. Reason adds to the natural materials only the perfect order which it introduces into them. Rationality is nothing but a form,

an ideal constitution which experience may more or less embody. Religion is a part of experience itself, a mass of sentiments and ideas. The one is an inviolate principle, the other a changing and struggling force. And yet this struggling and changing force of religion seems to direct man toward something eternal. It seems to make for an ultimate harmony within the soul and for an ultimate harmony between the soul and all the soul depends upon. So that religion, in its intent, is a more conscious and direct pursuit of the Life of Reason than is society, science, or art. For these approach and fill out the ideal life tentatively and piecemeal, hardly regarding the goal or caring for the ultimate justification of their instinctive aims. Religion also has an instinctive and blind side, and bubbles up in all manner of chance practices and intuitions; soon, however, it feels its way toward the heart of things, and, from whatever quarter it may come, veers in the direction of the ultimate.

Nevertheless, we must confess that this religious pursuit of the Life of Reason has been singularly abortive. Those within the pale of each religion may prevail upon themselves to express satisfaction with its results, thanks to a fond partiality in reading the past and generous draughts of hope for the future; but any one regarding the various religions at once and comparing their achievements with what reason requires, must feel how terrible is the disappointment which they have one and all prepared for mankind. Their chief anxiety has been to offer imaginary remedies for mortal ills, some of which are incurable essentially, while others might have been really cured by well-directed effort. The Greek oracles, for instance, pretended to heal our natural ignorance, which has its appropriate though difficult cure, while the Christian vision of heaven pretended to be an antidote to our natural death, the inevitable correlate of birth and of a changing and conditioned existence. By methods of this sort little can be done for the real betterment of life. To confuse intelligence and dislocate sentiment by gratuitous fictions is a short-sighted way of pursuing happiness. Nature is soon avenged. An unhealthy exaltation and a one-sided morality have to be followed by regretable reactions. When these come, the real rewards of life may seem vain to a relaxed vitality, and the very name of virtue may irritate young spirits untrained in any natural excellence. Thus religion too often debauches the morality it comes to sanction, and impedes the science it ought to fulfil.

What is the secret of this ineptitude? Why does religion, so near to rationality in its purpose, fall so far short of it in its texture and in its results? The answer is easy: Religion pursues rationality through the imagination. When it explains events or assigns causes, it is an imaginative substitute for science. When it gives precepts, insinuates ideals, or remoulds aspiration, it is an imaginative substitute for wisdom —I mean for the deliberate and impartial pursuit of all good. The conditions and the aims of life are both represented in religion poetically, but this poetry tends to arrogate to itself literal truth and moral authority, neither of which it possesses. Hence the depth and importance of religion become intelligible no less than its contradictions and practical disasters. Its object is the same as that of reason, but its method is to proceed by intuition and by unchecked poetical conceits. These are repeated and vulgarised in proportion to their original fineness and significance, till they pass for reports of objective truth and come to constitute a world of faith, superposed upon the world of experience and regarded as materially enveloping it, if not in space at least in time and in existence. The only truth of religion comes from its interpretation of life, from its symbolic rendering of that moral experience which it springs out of and which it seeks to elucidate. Its false-

hood comes from the insidious misunderstanding which clings to it, to the effect that these poetic conceptions are not merely representations of experience as it is or should be, but are rather information about experience or reality elsewhere —an experience and reality which, strangely enough, supply just the defects betrayed by reality and experience here.

Thus religion has the same original relation to life that poetry has; only poetry, which never pretends to literal validity, adds a pure value to existence, the value of a liberal imaginative exercise. The poetic value of religion would initially be greater than that of poetry itself, because religion deals with higher and more practical themes, with sides of life which are in greater need of some imaginative touch and ideal interpretation than are those pleasant or pompous things which ordinary poetry dwells upon. But this initial advantage is neutralised in part by the abuse to which religion is subject, whenever its symbolic rightness is taken for scientific truth. Like poetry, it improves the world only by imagining it improved, but not content with making this addition to the mind's furniture—an addition which might be useful and ennobling—it thinks to confer a more radical benefit by persuading mankind that, in spite of appearances, the world is really such as that rather arbitrary idealisation has painted it. This spurious satisfaction is naturally the prelude to many a disappointment, and the soul has infinite trouble to emerge again from the artificial problems and sentiments into which it is thus plunged. The value of religion becomes equivocal. Religion remains an imaginative achievement, a symbolic representation of moral reality which may have a most important function in vitalising the mind and in transmitting, by way of parables, the lessons of experience. But it becomes at the same time a continuous incidental deception; and this deception, in proportion as it is strenuously denied to be such, can work indefinite harm in the world and in the conscience.

On the whole, however, religion should not be conceived as having taken the place of anything better, but rather as having come to relieve situations which, but for its presence, would have been infinitely worse. In the thick of active life, or in the monotony of practical slavery, there is more need to stimulate fancy than to control it. Natural instinct is not much disturbed in the human brain by what may happen in that thin superstratum of ideas which commonly overlays it. We must not blame religion for preventing the development of a moral and natural science which at any rate would seldom have appeared; we must rather thank it for the sensibility, the reverence, the speculative insight which it has introduced into the world.

We may therefore proceed to analyse the significance and the function which religion has had at its different stages, and, without disguising or in the least condoning its confusion with literal truth, we may allow ourselves to enter as sympathetically as possible into its various conceptions and emotions. They have made up the inner life of many sages, and of all those who without great genius or learning have lived steadfastly in the spirit. The feeling of reverence should itself be treated with reverence, although not at a sacrifice of truth, with which alone, in the end, reverence is compatible. Nor have we any reason to be intolerant of the partialities and contradictions which religions display. Were we dealing with a science, such contradictions would have to be instantly solved and removed; but when we are concerned with the poetic interpretation of experience, contradiction means only variety, and variety means spontaneity, wealth of resource, and a nearer approach to total adequacy.

If we hope to gain any understanding of these matters we must begin by taking them out of that heated and fanatical atmosphere in which the Hebrew tradition has enveloped them. The Jews had no philosophy, and when their national traditions came to be theoretically explicated and justified, they were made to issue in a puerile scholasticism and a rabid intolerance. The question of monotheism, for instance, was a terrible question to the Jews. Idolatry did not consist in worshipping a god who, not being ideal, might be unworthy of worship, but rather in recognising other gods than the one worshipped in Jerusalem. To the Greeks, on the contrary, whose philosophy was enlightened and ingenuous, monotheism and polytheism seemed perfectly innocent and compatible. To say God or the gods was only to use different expressions for the same influence, now viewed in its abstract unity and correlation with all existence, now viewed in its various manifestations in moral life, in nature, or in history. So that what in Plato, Aristotle, and the Stoics meets us at every step— the combination of monotheism with polytheism—is no contradiction, but merely an intelligent variation of phrase to indicate various aspects or functions in physical and moral things. When religion appears to us in this light its contradictions and controversies lose all their bitterness. Each doctrine will simply represent the moral plane on which they live who have devised or adopted it. Religions will thus be better or worse, never true or false. We shall be able to lend ourselves to each in turn, and seek to draw from it the secret of its inspiration.

CHAPTER III

MAGIC, SACRIFICE, AND PRAYER

. . .

As sacrifice expresses fear, prayer expresses need. Common-sense thinks of language as something meant to be understood by another and to produce changes in his disposition and behaviour, but language has pre-rational uses, of which poetry and prayer are perhaps the chief. A man overcome by passion assumes dramatic attitudes surely not intended to be watched and interpreted; like tears, gestures may touch an observer's heart, but they do not come for that purpose. So the fund of words and phrases latent in the mind flow out under stress of emotion; they flow because they belong to the situation, because they fill out and complete a perception absorbing the mind; they do not flow primarily to be listened to. The instinct to pray is one of the chief avenues to the deity, and the form prayer takes helps immensely to define the power it is addressed to; indeed, it is in the act of praying that men formulate to themselves what God must be, and tell him at great length what they believe and what they expect of him. The initial forms of prayer are not so absurd as the somewhat rationalised forms of it. Unlike sacrifice, prayer seems to be justified by its essence and to be degraded by the transformations it suffers in reflection, when men try to find a place for it in their cosmic economy; for its essence is poetical, expressive, contemplative, and it grows more and more nonsensical the more people insist on making it a prosaic, commercial exchange of views between two interlocutors.

Prayer is a soliloquy; but being a soliloquy expressing need, and being furthermore, like sacrifice, a desperate expedient which men fly to in their impotence, it looks for an effect: to cry aloud, to make vows, to contrast eloquently the given with the ideal situation, is certainly as likely a way of bringing about a change for the better as it would be to chastise one's self severely, or to destroy what one loves best, or to perform acts altogether trivial and arbitrary. Prayer also is magic, and as such it is expected to do work. The answer looked for, or one which may be accepted instead, very often ensues; and it is then that mythology begins to enter in and seeks to explain by what machinery of divine passions and purposes that answering effect was produced.

Magic is in a certain sense the mother of art, art being the magic that succeeds and can establish itself. For this very reason mere magic is never appealed to when art has been found, and no unsophisticated man prays to have that done for him which he knows how to do for himself. When his art fails, if his necessity still presses, he appeals to magic, and he prays when he no longer can control the event, provided this event is momentous to him. Prayer is not a substitute for work; it is a desperate effort to work further and to be efficient beyond the range of one's powers. It is not the lazy who are most inclined to prayer; those pray most who care most, and who, having worked hard, find it intolerable to be defeated.

No chapter in theology is more unhappy than that in which a material efficacy is assigned to prayer. In the first place the facts contradict the notion that curses can bring evil or blessings can cure; and it is not observed that the most orthodox and hard-praying army wins the most battles. The facts, however, are often against theology, which has to rely on dialectical refinements to explain them away; but unfortunately in this instance dialectic is no less hostile than experience. God must know our necessities before we ask and, if he is good, must already have decided what he would do for us. Prayer, like every other act, becomes in a providential world altogether perfunctory and histrionic; we are compelled to go through it, it is set down for us in the play, but it lacks altogether that moral value which we assign to it. When our prayers fail, it must be better than if they had succeeded, so that prayer, with all free preference whatsoever, becomes an absurdity. The trouble is much deeper than that which so many people find in determinism. A physical predetermination, in making all things necessary, leaves all values entire, and my preferences, though they cannot be efficacious unless they express preformed natural forces, are not invalidated ideally. It is still true that the world would have been better to all eternity if my will also could have been fulfilled. A providential optimism, on the contrary, not merely predetermines events but discounts values; and it reduces every mortal aspiration, every pang of conscience, every wish that things should be better than they are, to a blind impertinence, nay, to a sacrilege. Thus, you may not pray that God's kingdom may come, but only—what is not a prayer but a dogma—that it has come already. The mythology that pretends to justify prayer by giving it a material efficacy misunderstands prayer completely and makes it ridiculous, for it turns away from the heart, which prayer expresses pathetically, to a fabulous cosmos where aspirations have been turned into things and have thereby stifled their own voices.

The situation would not be improved if we surrendered that mystical optimism, and maintained that prayer might really attract superhuman forces to our aid by giving them a signal without which they would not have been able to reach us. If experience lent itself to such a theory there would be nothing in it more impossible than in ordinary telepathy; prayer would then be an art like conversation, and the exact personages and interests would be discoverable to which we might appeal. A celestial diplomacy might then be established not very unlike primitive religions. Religion would have reverted to industry and science, to which the grosser spirits that take refuge under it have always wished to assimilate it. But is it really the office of religion to work upon external powers and extract from them certain calculable effects? Is it an art, like empiric medicine, and merely a dubious and mystic industry? If so, it exists only by imperfection; were it better developed it would coincide with those material and social arts with which it is identical in essence. Successful religion, like successful magic, would have passed into the art of exploiting the world.

What successful religion really should pass into is contemplation, ideality, poetry, in the sense in which poetry includes all imaginative moral life. That this is what religion looks to is very clear in prayer and in the' efficacy which prayer consistently can have. In rational prayer the soul may be said to accomplish three things important to its welfare: it withdraws within itself and defines its good, it accommodates itself to destiny, and it grows like the ideal which it conceives.

If prayer springs from need it will naturally dwell on what would satisfy that necessity; sometimes, indeed, it does nothing else but articulate and eulogise what is most wanted and prized. This object will often be particular, and so it should be, since Socrates' prayer "for the best" would be perfunctory and vapid indeed in a man whose life had not been spent, like Socrates', in defining what the best was. Yet any particular good lies in a field of relations; it has associates and implications, so that the mind dwelling on it and invoking its presence will naturally be enticed also into its background, and will wander there, perhaps to come upon greater goods, or upon evils which the coveted good would make inevitable. An earnest consideration, therefore, of anything desired is apt to enlarge and generalise aspiration till it embraces an ideal life; for from almost any starting-point the limits and contours of mortal happiness are soon descried. Prayer, inspired by a pressing need, already relieves its importunity by merging it in the general need of the spirit and of mankind. It therefore calms the passions in expressing them, like all idealisation, and tends to make the will conformable with reason and justice.

A comprehensive ideal, however, is harder to realise than a particular one: the rain wished for may fall, the death feared may be averted, but the kingdom of heaven does not come. It is in the very essence of prayer to regard a denial as possible. There would be no sense in defining and begging for the better thing if that better thing had at any rate to be. The possibility of defeat is one of the circumstances with which meditation must square the ideal; seeing that my prayer may not be granted, what in that case should I pray for next? Now the order of nature is in many respects well known, and it is clear that all realisable ideals must not trangress certain bounds. The practical ideal, that which under the circumstances it is best to aim at and pray for, will not rebel against destiny. Conformity is an element in all religion and submission in all prayer; not because what must be is best, but because the best that may be pursued rationally lies with the possible, and can be hatched only in the general womb of being. The prayer, "Thy will be done," if it is to remain a prayer, must not be degraded from its original meaning, which was that an unfulfilled ideal should be fulfilled; it expressed aspiration after the best, not willingness to be satisfied with anything. Yet the inevitable must be accepted, and it is easier to change the human will than the laws of nature. To wean the mind from extravagant desires and teach it to find excellence in what life affords, when life is made as worthy as possible, is a part of wisdom and religion. Prayer, by confronting the ideal with experience and fate, tends to render that ideal humble, practical, and efficacious.

A sense for human limitations, however, has its foil in the ideal of deity, which is nothing but the ideal of man freed from those limitations which a humble and wise man accepts for himself, but which a spiritual man never ceases to feel as limitations. Man, for instance, is mortal, and his whole animal and social economy is built on that fact, so that his practical ideal must start on that basis, and make the best of it; but immortality is essentially better, and the eternal is in many ways constantly present to a noble mind; the gods therefore are immortal, and to speak their language in prayer is to learn to see all things as they do and as reason must, under the form of eternity. The gods are furthermore no respecters of persons; they are just, for it is man's ideal to be so. Prayer, since it addresses deity, will in the end blush to be selfish and partial; the majesty of the divine mind envisaged and consulted will tend to pass into the human mind.

This use of prayer has not been conspicuous in Christian times, because, instead of assimilating the temporal to the eternal, men have assimilated the eternal to the temporal, being perturbed fanatics in religion rather than poets and idealists. Pagan devotion, on the other hand, was full of this calmer spirit. The gods, being frankly natural, could be truly ideal. They embodied what was fairest in life and loved men who resembled them, so that it was delightful and ennobling to see their images everywhere, and to keep their names and story perpetually in mind. They did not by their influence alienate man from his appropriate happiness, but they perfected it by their presence. Peopling all places, changing their forms as all living things must according to place and circumstance, they showed how all kinds of being, if perfect in their kind, might be perfectly good. They asked for a reverence consistent with reason, and exercised prerogatives that left man free. Their worship was a perpetual lesson in humanity, moderation, and beauty. Something pre-rational and monstrous often peeped out behind their serenity, as it does beneath the human soul, and there was certainly no lack of wildness and mystic horror in their apparitions. The ideal must needs betray those elemental forces on which, after all, it rests; but reason exists to exorcise their madness and win them over to a steady expression of themselves and of the good.

Prayer, in fine, though it accomplishes nothing material, constitutes something spiritual. It will not bring rain, but until rain comes it may cultivate hope and resignation and may prepare the heart for any issue, opening up a vista in which human prosperity will appear in its conditioned existence and conditional value. A candle wasting itself before an image will prevent no misfortune, but it may bear witness to some silent hope or relieve some sorrow by expressing it; it may soften a little the bitter sense of impotence which would consume a mind aware of physical dependence but not of spiritual dominion. Worship, supplication, reliance on the gods, express both these things in an appropriate parable. Physical impotence is expressed by man's appeal for help; moral dominion by belief in God's omnipotence. This belief may afterwards seem to be contradicted by events. It would be so in truth if God's omnipotence stood for a material magical control of events by the values they were to generate. But the believer knows in his heart, in spite of the confused explanations he may give of his feelings, that a material efficacy is not the test of his faith. His faith will survive any outward disappointment. In fact, it will grow by that discipline and not become truly religious until it ceases to be a foolish expectation of improbable things and rises on stepping-stones of its material disappointments into a spiritual peace. What would sacrifice be but a risky investment if it did not redeem us from the love of those things which it asks us to surrender? What would be the mis-erable fruit of an appeal to God which after bringing us face to face with him, left us still immersed in what we could have enjoyed without him? The real use and excuse for magic is this, that by enticing us, in the service of natural lusts, into a region above natural instrumentalities, it accustoms us to that rarer atmosphere, so that we may learn to breathe it for its own sake. By the time we discover the mechanical futility of religion we may have begun to blush at the thought of using religion mechanically; for what should be the end of life if friendship with the gods is a means only? When thaumaturgy is discredited, the childish desire to work miracles may itself have passed away. Before we weary of the attempt to hide and piece out our mortality, our concomitant immortality may have dawned upon us. While we are waiting for the command to take up our bed and walk we may hear a voice saying: Thy sins are forgiven thee.

CHAPTER IV

MYTHOLOGY

Primitive thought has the form of poetry and the function of prose. Being thought, it distinguishes objects from the experience that reveals them and it aspires to know things as they are; but being poetical, it attributes to those objects all the qualities which the experience of them contains, and builds them out imaginatively in all directions, without distinguishing what is constant and efficacious in them. This primitive habit of thought survives in mythology, which is an observation of things encumbered with all they can suggest to a dramatic fancy. It is neither conscious poetry nor valid science, but the common root and raw material of both. Free poetry is a thing which early man is too poor to indulge in; his wide-open eyes are too intently watching this ominous and treacherous world. For pure science he has not enough experience, no adequate power to analyse, remember, and abstract; his soul is too hurried and confused, too thick with phantoms, to follow abstemiously the practical threads through the labyrinth. His view of things is immensely overloaded; what he gives out for description is more than half soliloquy; but his expression of experience is for that very reason adequate and quite sincere. Belief, which we have come to associate with religion, belongs really to science; myths are not believed in, they are conceived and understood. To demand belief for an idea is already to contrast interpretation with knowledge; it is to assert that that idea has scientific truth. Mythology cannot flourish in that dialectical air; it belongs to a deeper and more ingenuous level of thought, when men pored on the world with intense indiscriminate interest, accepting and recording the mind's vegetation no less than that observable in things, and mixing the two developments together in one wayward drama.

A good mythology cannot be produced without much culture and intelligence. Stupidity is not poetical. Nor is mythology essentially a half-way house between animal vagueness in the soul and scientific knowledge. It is conceivable that some race, not so dreamful as ours, should never have been tempted to use psychic and passionate categories in reading nature, but from the first should have kept its observations sensuous and pure, elaborating them only on their own plane, mathematically and dialectically. Such a race, however, could hardly have had lyric or dramatic genius, and even in natural science, which requires imagination, they might never have accomplished anything. The Hebrews, denying themselves a rich mythology, remained without science and plastic art; the Chinese, who seem to have attained legality and domestic arts and a tutored sentiment

without passing through such imaginative tempests as have harassed us, remain at the same time without a serious science or philosophy. The Greeks, on the contrary, precisely the people with the richest and most irresponsible myths, first conceived the cosmos scientifically, and first wrote rational history and philosophy. So true it is that vitality in any mental function is favourable to vitality in the whole mind. Illusions incident to mythology are not dangerous in the end, because illusion finds in experience a natural though painful cure. Extravagant error is unstable, unless it be harmless and confined to a limbo remote from all applications; if it touches experience it is stimulating and brief, while the equipoise of dulness may easily render dulness eternal. A developed mythology shows that man has taken a deep and active interest both in the world and in himself, and has tried to link the two, and interpret the one by the other. Myth is therefore a natural prologue to philosophy, since the love of ideas is the root of both. Both are made up of things admirable to consider.

Nor is the illusion involved in fabulous thinking always so complete and opaque as convention would represent it. In taking fable for fact, good sense and practice seldom keep pace with dogma. There is always a race of pedants whose function it is to materialise everything ideal, but the great world, half shrewdly, half doggedly, manages to escape their contagion. Language may be entirely permeated with myth, since the affinities of language have much to do with men gliding into such thoughts; yet the difference between language itself and what it expresses is not so easily obliterated. In spite of verbal traditions, people seldom take a myth in the same sense in which they would take an empirical truth. All the doctrines that have flourished in the world about immortality have hardly affected men's natural sentiment in the face of death, a sentiment which those doctrines, if taken seriously, ought wholly to reverse. Men almost universally have acknowledged a Providence, but that fact has had no force to destroy natural aversions and fears in the presence of events; and yet, if Providence had ever been really trusted, those preferences would all have lapsed, being seen to be blind, rebellious, and blasphemous. Prayer, among sane people, has never superseded practical efforts to secure the desired end; a proof that the sphere of expression was never really confused with that of reality. Indeed, such a confusion, if it had passed from theory to practice, would have changed mythology into madness. With rare exceptions this declension has not occurred and myths have been taken with a grain of salt which not only made them digestible, but heightened their savour.

It is always by its applicability to things known, not by its revelation of things unknown and irrelevant, that a myth at its birth appeals to mankind. When it has lost its symbolic value and sunk to the level of merely false information, only an inert and stupid tradition can keep it above water. Parables justify themselves but dogmas call for an apologist. The genial offspring of prophets and poets then has to be kept alive artificially by professional doctors. A thing born of fancy, moulded to express universal experience and its veritable issues, has to be hedged about by misrepresentation, sophistry, and party spirit. The very apologies and unintelligent proofs offered in its defence in a way confess its unreality, since they all strain to paint in more plausible colours what is felt to be in itself extravagant and incredible.

Yet if the myth was originally accepted it could not be for this falsity plainly written on its face; it was accepted because it was understood, because it was seen to express reality in an eloquent metaphor. Its function was to show up some phase of experience in its totality and moral issue, as in a map we reduce everything geographically in order to overlook it better in its true relations. Had those symbols for a moment descended to the plane of reality they would have lost their meaning and dignity; they would tell us merely that they themselves existed bodily, which would be false, while about the real configuration of life they would no longer tell us anything. Such an error, if carried through to the end, would nullify all experience and arrest all life. Men would be reacting on expressions and meeting with nothing to express. They would all be like word-eating philosophers or children learning the catechism.

The true function of mythical ideas is to present and interpret events in terms relative to spirit. Things have uses in respect to the will which are direct and obvious, while the inner machinery of these same things is intricate and obscure. We therefore conceive things roughly and superficially by their eventual practical functions and assign to them, in our game, some counterpart of the interest they affect in us. This counterpart, to our thinking, constitutes their inward character and soul. So conceived, soul and character are purely mythical, being arrived at by dramatising events according to our own fancy and interest. Such ideas may be adequate in their way if they cover all the uses we may eventually find in the objects they transcribe for us dramatically. But the most adequate mythology is mythology still; it does not, like science, set things before us in the very terms they will wear when they are gradually revealed to experience. Myth is expression, it is not prophecy. For this reason myth is something on which the mind rests; it is an ideal interpretation in which the phenomena are digested and transmuted into human energy, into imaginative tissue. Scientific formulas, on the contrary, cry aloud for retranslation into perceptual terms; they are like tight-ropes, on which a man may walk but on which he cannot stand still. These unstable symbols lead, however, to real facts and define their experimental relations; while the mind reposing contentedly in a myth needs to have all observation and experience behind it, for it will not be driven to gather more. The perfect and stable myth would rest on a complete survey and steady focussing of all interests really affecting the one from whose point of view the myth was framed. Then each physical or political unit would be endowed with a character really corresponding to all its influence on the thinker. This symbol would render the diffuse natural existences which it represented in an eloquent figure; and since this figure would not mislead practically it might be called true. But truth, in a myth, means a sterling quality and standard excellence, not a literal or logical truth. It will not, save by a singular accident, represent their proper internal being, as a forthright unselfish intellect would wish to know it. It will translate into the language of a private passion the smiles and frowns which that passion meets with in the world.

There are accordingly two factors in mythology, a moral consciousness and a corresponding poetic conception of things. Both factors are variable, and variations in the first, if more hidden, are no less important than variations in the second. Had fable started with a clear perception of human values, it would have gained immensely in significance, because its pictures, however wrong the external notions they built upon, would have shown what, in the world so conceived, would have been the ideals and prizes of life. Thus Dante's bad cosmography and worse history do not detract from the spiritual penetration of his thought, though they detract from its direct applicability. Had nature and destiny been what Dante imagined, his conception of the values involved would have been perfect, for the moral philosophy he brought into play was Aristotelian and rational. So his poem contains a false instance or imaginary rehearsal of true wisdom. It describes the Life of Reason in a fantastic world. We need only change man's situation to that in which he actually finds himself, and let the soul, fathomed and chastened as Dante left it, ask questions and draw answers from this steadier dream.

Myth travels among the people, and in their hands its poetic factor tends to predominate. It is easier to carry on the dialectic or drama proper to a fable than to confront it again with the facts and give them a fresh and more genial interpretation. The poet makes the fable; the sophist carries it on. Therefore historians and theologians discuss chiefly the various forms which mythical beings have received, and the internal logical or moral implications of those hypostases. They would do better to attend instead to the moral factor. However interesting a fable may be in itself, its religious value lies wholly in its revealing some function which nature has in human life. Not the beauty of the god makes him adorable, but his dispensing benefits and graces. Side by side with Apollo (a god having moral functions and consequently inspiring a fervent cult and tending himself to assume a moral character) there may be a Helios or a Phaëthon, poetic figures expressing just as well the sun's physical operation, and no less capable, if the theologian took hold of them, of suggesting psychological problems. The moral factor, however, was not found in these minor deities. Only a verbal and sensuous poetry had been employed in defining them; the needs and hopes of mankind had been ignored. Apollo, on the contrary, in personifying the sun, had embodied also the sun's relations to human welfare. The vitality, the healing, the enlightenment, the lyric joy flowing into man's heart from that highest source of his physical being are all beautifully represented in the god's figure and fable. The religion of Apollo is therefore a true religion, as religions may be true: the mythology which created the god rested on a deep, observant sense for moral values, and drew a vivid, if partial, picture of the ideal, attaching it significantly to its natural ground.

The first function of mythology is to justify magic. The weak hope on which superstition hangs, the gambler's instinct which divines in phenomena a magic solicitude for human fortunes, can scarcely be articulated without seeking to cover and justify itself by some fable. A magic function is most readily conceived and defined by attributing to the object intentions hostile or favourable to men, together with human habits of passion and discourse. For lack of resources and observations, reason is seldom able to discredit magic altogether. Reasonable men are forced, therefore, in order to find some satisfaction, to make magic as intelligible as possible by assimilating it to such laws of human action as may be already mastered and familiar. Magic is thus reduced to a sort of system, regulated by principles of its own and naturalised, as it were, in the commonwealth of science.

Such an avowed and defended magic usually takes one of two forms. When the miracle is interpreted dramatically, by analogy to human life, we have mythology; when it is interpreted rationalistically, by analogy to current logic or natural science, we have metaphysics or theosophy. The metaphysical sort of superstition has never taken deep root in the western world. Pythagorean mysteries and hypnotisations, although periodically fashionable, have soon shrivelled in our too salubrious and biting air. Even such charming exotics as Plato's myths have not been able to flourish without changing their nature and passing into ordinary dramatic mythology—into a magic system in which all the forces,

once terms in moral experience, became personal angels and demons. Similarly with the Christian sacraments: these magic rites, had they been established in India among a people theosophically minded, might have furnished cues to high transcendental mysteries. Baptism might have been interpreted as a symbol for the purged and abolished will, and Communion as a symbol for the escape from personality. But European races, though credulous enough, are naturally positivistic, so that, when they were called upon to elucidate their ceremonial mysteries, what they lit upon was no metaphysical symbolism but a material and historical drama. Communion became a sentimental interview between the devout soul and the person of Christ; baptism became the legal execution of a mythical contract once entered into between the first and second persons of the Trinity. Thus, instead of a metaphysical interpretation, the extant magic received its needful justification through myths.

When mythology first appears in western literature it already possesses a highly articulate form. The gods are distinct personalities, with attributes and histories which it is hard to divine the source of and which suggest no obvious rational interpretation. The historian is therefore in the same position as a child who inherits a great religion. The gods and their doings are *prima facie* facts in his world like any other facts, objective beings that convention puts him in the presence of and with which he begins by having social relations. He envisages them with respect and obedience, or with careless defiance, long before he thinks of questioning or proving their existence. The attitude he assumes towards them makes them in the first instance factors in his moral world. Much subsequent scepticism and rationalising philosophy will not avail to efface the vestiges of that early communion with familiar gods. It is hard to reduce to objects of science what are essentially factors in moral intercourse. All thoughts on religion remain accordingly coloured with passion, and are felt to be, above all, a test of loyalty and an index to virtue. The more derivative, unfathomable, and opaque is the prevalent idea of the gods, the harder it is for a rational feeling to establish itself in their regard. Sometimes the most complete historical enlightenment will not suffice to dispel the shadow which their moral externality casts over the mind. In vain do we discard their fable and the thin proofs of their existence when, in spite of ourselves, we still live in their presence.

This pathetic phenomenon is characteristic of religious minds that have outgrown their traditional faith without being able to restate the natural grounds and moral values of that somehow precious system in which they no longer believe. The dead gods, in such cases, leave ghosts behind them, because the moral forces which the gods once expressed, and which, of course, remain, remain inarticulate; and therefore, in their dumbness, these moral forces persistently suggest their only known but now discredited symbols. To regain moral freedom—without which knowledge cannot be put to its rational use in the government of life—we must rediscover the origin of the gods, reduce them analytically to their natural and moral constituents, and then proceed to rearrange those materials, without any quantitative loss, in forms appropriate to a maturer reflection.

• • •

CHAPTER X

PIETY

Hebraism is a striking example of a religion tending to discard mythology and magic. It was a Hebraising apostle who said that true religion and undefiled was to visit the fatherless and the widow, and do other works of mercy. Although a complete religion can hardly remain without theoretic and ritual expression, we must remember that after all religion has other aspects less conspicuous, perhaps, than its mythology, but often more worthy of respect. If religion be, as we have assumed, an imaginative symbol for the Life of Reason, it should contain not only symbolic ideas and rites, but also symbolic sentiments and duties. And so it everywhere does in a notable fashion. Piety and spirituality are phases of religion no less important than mythology, or than those metaphysical spectres with which mythology terminates. It is therefore time we should quite explicitly turn from religious ideas to religious emotions, from imaginative history and science to imaginative morals.

Piety, in its nobler and Roman sense, may be said to mean man's reverent attachment to the sources of his being and the steadying of his life by that attachment. A soul is but the last bubble of a long fermentation in the world. If we wish to live associated with permanent racial interests we must plant ourselves on a broad historic and human foundation, we must absorb and interpret the past which has made us, so that we may hand down its heritage reinforced, if possible, and in no way undermined or denaturalised. This consciousness that the human spirit is derived and responsible, that all its functions are heritages and trusts, involves a sentiment of gratitude and duty which we may call piety.

The true objects of piety are, of course, those on which life and its interests really depend: parents first, then family, ancestors, and country; finally, humanity at large and the whole natural cosmos. But had a lay sentiment toward these forces been fostered by clear knowledge of their nature and relation to ourselves, the dutifulness or cosmic emotion thereby aroused would have remained purely moral and historical. As science would not in the end admit any myth which was not avowed poetry, so it would not admit any piety which was not plain reason and duty. But man, in his perplexities and pressing needs, has plunged, once for all, into imaginative courses through which it is our business to follow him, to see if he may not eventually reach his goal even by those by-paths and dark circumlocutions.

What makes piety an integral part of traditional religions is the fact that moral realities are represented in the popular mind by poetic symbols. The awe inspired by principles so abstract and consequences so remote and general is arrested at their conventional name. We have all read in boyhood, perhaps with derision, about the pious Æneas. His piety may have seemed to us nothing but a feminine sensibility, a faculty of shedding tears on slight provocation. But in truth Æneas's piety, as Virgil or any Roman would have conceived it, lay less in his feelings than in his function and vocation. He was bearing the Palladium of his country to a new land, to found another Troy, so that the blood and traditions of his ancestors might not perish. His emotions were only the appropriate expression of his priestly office. The hero might have been stern and stolid enough on his own martial ground, but since he bore the old Anchises from the ruins of Ilium he had assumed a sacred mission. Henceforth a sacerdotal unction and lyric pathos belonged rightfully to his person. If those embers, so religiously guarded, should by chance have been extinguished, there could never have been a Vestal fire nor any Rome. So that all that Virgil and his readers, if they had any piety, revered in the world had been hazarded in those legendary adventures. It was not Æneas's own life or private ambition that was at stake to justify his emotion. His tenderness, like Virgil's own, was ennobled and made heroic by its magnificent and impersonal object. It was truly an epic destiny that inspired both poet and hero.

If we look closer, however, we shall see that mythical and magic elements were requisite to lend this loftiness to the argument. Had Æneas not been Venus's son, had no prophetic instinct animated him, had no Juno been planning the rise of Carthage, how could the future destinies of this expedition have been imported into it, to lift it above some piratical or desperate venture? Colonists passing in our day to America or Australia might conceivably carry with them the seeds of empires as considerable as Rome's. But they would go out thinking of their private livelihood and convenience, breaking or loosening whatever pious bonds might unite them to the past, and quite irresponsibly laying the foundations for an unknown future. A poet, to raise them to the height of their unwitting function, would have to endow them with second sight and a corresponding breadth of soul and purpose. He would need, in a word, heroic figures and supernatural machinery.

Now, what supernatural machinery and heroic figures do for an epic poet piety does for a race. It endows it, through mythical and magic symbols, with something like a vision or representation of its past and future. Religion is normally the most traditional and national of things. It embodies and localises the racial heritage. Commandments of the law, feasts and fasts, temples and the tombs associated with them, are so many foci of communal life, so many points for the dissemination of custom. The Sabbath, which a critical age might justify on hygienic grounds, is inconceivable without a religious sanction. The craving for rest and emotion expressed itself spontaneously in a practice which, as it established itself, had to be sanctioned by fables till the recurrent holiday, with all its humane and chastening influences, came to be established on supernatural authority. It was now piety to observe it and to commemorate in it the sacred duties and traditions of the race. In this function, of course, lay its true justification, but the mythical one had to be assigned, since the diffused prosaic advantages of such a practice would never avail to impose it on irrational wills. Indeed, to revert to our illustration, had Æneas foreseen in detail the whole history of Rome, would not his faith in his divine mission have been considerably dashed? The reality, precious and inestimable as on the whole it was to humanity, might well have shocked him by its cruelties, shames, and disasters. He would have wished to found only a perfect nation and a city eternal indeed. A want of rationality and measure in the human will, that has not learned to prize small betterments and finite but real goods, compels it to deceive itself about the rewards of life in order to secure them. That celestial mission, those heavenly apparitions, those incalculable treasures carried through many a storm, abused Æneas's mind in order to nerve him to his real duty. Yet his illusion was merely intellectual. The mission undertaken was truly worth carrying out. Piety thus came to bear the fruits of philanthropy in an age when the love of man was inconceivable. A dull and visionary intellect could hit on no other way of justifying a good instinct.

Philosophers who harbour illusions about the status of intellect in nature may feel that this leadership of instinct in moral life is a sort of indignity, and that to dwell on it so insistently is to prolong satire without wit. But the leadership of instinct, the conscious expression of mechanism, is not merely a necessity in the Life of Reason, it is a safeguard. Piety, in spite of its allegories, contains a much greater wisdom than a half-enlightened and pert intellect can attain.

Natural beings have natural obligations, and the value of things for them is qualified by distance and by accidental material connections. Intellect would tend to gauge things impersonally by their intrinsic values, since intellect is itself a sort of disembodied and universal function; it would tend to disregard material conditions and that irrational substratum of reason without which reason would have no organs and no points of application. Piety, on the contrary, esteems things apart from their intrinsic worth, on account of their relation to the agent's person and fortune. Yet such esteem is perfectly rational, partiality in man's affections and allegiance being justified by the partial nature and local status of his life. Piety is the spirit's acknowledgment of its incarnation. So, in filial and parental affection, which is piety in an elementary form, there is a moulding of will and emotion, a check to irresponsible initiative, in obedience to the facts of animal reproduction. Every living creature has an intrinsic and ideal worth; he is the centre of actual and yet more of potential interests. But this moral value, which even the remotest observer must recognise in both parent and child, is not the ground of their specific affection for each other, which no other mortal is called to feel in their regard. This affection is based on the incidental and irrational fact that the one has this particular man for a father, and the other that particular man for a son. Yet, considering the animal basis of human life, an attachment resting on that circumstance is a necessary and rational attachment.

This physical bond should not, indeed, disturb the intellect in its proper function or warp its judgments; you should not, under guise of tenderness, become foolish and attribute to your father or child greater stature or cleverness or goodness than he actually possesses. To do so is a natural foible but no part of piety or true loyalty. It is one thing to lack a heart and another to possess eyes and a just imagination. Indeed, piety is never so beautiful and touching, never so thoroughly humane and invincible, as when it is joined to an impartial intellect, conscious of the relativity involved in existence and able to elude, through imaginative sympathy, the limits set to personal life by circumstance and private duty. As a man dies nobly when, awaiting his own extinction, he is interested to the last in what will continue to be the interests and joys of others, so he is most profoundly pious who loves unreservedly a country, friends, and associations which he knows very well to be not the most beautiful on earth, and who, being wholly content in his personal capacity with his natural conditions, does not need to begrudge other things whatever speculative admiration they may truly deserve. The ideal in this polyglot world, where reason can receive only local and temporal expression, is to understand all languages and to speak but one, so as to unite, in a manly fashion, comprehension with propriety.

Piety is in a sense pathetic because it involves subordination to physical accident and acceptance of finitude. But it is also noble and eminently fruitful because, in subsuming a life under the general laws of relativity, it meets fate with simple sincerity and labours in accordance with the conditions imposed. Since man, though capable of abstraction and impartiality, is rooted like a vegetable to one point in space and time, and exists by limitation, piety belongs to the equilibrium of his being. It resides, so to speak, at his centre of gravity, at the heart and magnetic focus of his complex endowment. It exercises there the eminently sane function of calling thought home. It saves speculative and emotional life from hurtful extravagance by keeping it traditional and social. Conventional absurdities have at least this advantage, that they may be taken conventionally and may come to be, in practice, mere symbols for their uses. Piety is more closely linked with custom than with thought. It exercises an irrational suasion, moralises by contagion, and brings an emotional peace.

Patriotism is another form of piety in which its natural basis and rational function may be clearly seen. It is right to prefer our own country to all others, because we are children and citizens before we can be travellers or philosophers. Specific character is a necessary point of origin for universal relations: a pure nothing can have no radiation or scope. It is no accident for the soul to be embodied; her very essence is to express and bring to fruition the body's functions and resources. Its instincts make her ideals and its relations her world. A native country is a sort of second body, another enveloping organism to give the will definition. A specific inheritance strengthens the soul. Cosmopolitanism has doubtless its place, because a man may well cultivate in himself, and represent in his nation, affinities to other peoples, and such assimilation to them as is compatible with personal integrity and clearness of purpose. Plasticity to things foreign need not be inconsistent with happiness and utility at home. But happiness and utility are possible nowhere to a man who represents nothing and who looks out on the world without a plot of his own to stand on, either on earth or in heaven. He wanders from place to place, a voluntary exile, always querulous, always uneasy, always alone. His very criticisms express no ideal. His experience is without sweetness, without cumulative fruits, and his children, if he has them, are without morality. For reason and happiness are like other flowers—they wither when plucked.

The object most commonly associated with piety is the gods. Popular philosophy, inverting the natural order of ideas, thinks piety to the gods the source of morality. But piety, when genuine, is rather an incidental expression of morality. Its sources are perfectly natural. A volitional life that reaches the level of reflection is necessarily moral in proportion to the concreteness and harmony of its instincts. The fruits which such harmonious instincts, expressed in consciousness, may eventually bear, fruits which would be the aim of virtue, are not readily imaginable, and the description of them has long ago been intrusted to poets and mythologists. Thus the love of God, for example, is said to be the root of Christian charity, but is in reality only its symbol. For no man not having a superabundant need and faculty of loving real things could have given a meaning to the phrase, "love of God," or been moved by it to any action. History shows in unequivocal fashion that the God loved shifts his character with the shift in his worshippers' real affections. What the psalmist loves is the beauty of God's house and the place where his glory dwelleth. A priestly quietude and pride, a grateful, meditative leisure after the storms of sedition and war, some retired unity of mind after the contradictions of the world—this is what the love of God might signify for the levites. Saint John tells us that he who says he loves God and loves not his neighbour is a liar. Here the love of God is an anti-worldly estimation of things and persons, a heart set on that kingdom of heaven in which the humble and the meek should be exalted. Again, for modern Catholicism the phrase has changed its meaning remarkably and signifies in effect love for Christ's person, because piety has taken a sentimental turn and centred on maintaining imaginary personal relations with the Saviour. How should we conceive that a single supernatural influence was actually responsible for moral effects themselves so various, and producing, in spite of a consecutive tradition, such various notions concerning their object and supposed source?

Mankind at large is also, to some minds, an object of piety. But this religion of humanity is rather a desideratum than a fact: humanity does not actually appear to anybody in a religious light. The *nihil homine homini utilius* remains a signal truth, but the collective influence of men and their average nature are far too mixed and ambiguous to fill the soul with veneration. Piety to mankind must be three-fourths pity. There are indeed specific human virtues, but they are those necessary to existence, like patience and courage. Supported on these indispensable habits, mankind always carries an indefinite load of misery and vice. Life spreads rankly in every wrong and impracticable direction as well as in profitable paths, and the slow and groping struggle with its own ignorance, inertia, and folly, leaves it covered in every age of history with filth and blood. It would hardly be possible to exaggerate man's wretchedness if it were not so easy to overestimate his sensibility. There is a *fond* of unhappiness in every bosom, but the depths are seldom probed; and there is no doubt that sometimes frivolity and sometimes sturdy habit helps to keep attention on the surface and to cover up the inner void. Certain moralists, without meaning to be satirical, often say that the sovereign cure for unhappiness is work. Unhappily, the work they recommend is better fitted to dull pain than to remove its cause. It occupies the faculties without rationalising the life. Before mankind could inspire even moderate satisfaction, not to speak of worship, its whole economy would have to be reformed, its reproduction regulated, its thoughts cleared up, its affections equalised and refined.

To worship mankind as it is would be to deprive it of what alone makes it akin to the divine—its aspiration. For this human dust lives; this misery and crime are dark in contrast to an imagined excellence; they are lighted up by a prospect of good. Man is not adorable, but he adores, and the object of his adoration may be discovered within him and elicited from his own soul. In this sense the religion of humanity is the only religion, all others being sparks and abstracts of the same. The indwelling ideal lends all the gods their divinity. No power, either physical or psychical, has the least moral prerogative nor any just place in religion at all unless it supports and advances the ideal native to the worshipper's soul. Without moral society between the votary and his god religion is pure idolatry; and even idolatry would be impossible but for the suspicion that somehow the brute force exorcised in prayer might help or mar some human undertaking.

There is, finally, a philosophic piety which has the universe for its object. This feeling, common to ancient and modern Stoics, has an obvious justification in man's dependence upon the natural world and in its service to many sides of the mind. Such justification of cosmic piety is rather obscured than supported by the euphemisms and ambiguities in which these philosophers usually indulge in their attempt to preserve the customary religious unction. For the more they personify the universe and give it the name of God the more they turn it into a devil. The universe, so far as we can observe it, is a wonderful and immense engine; its extent, its order, its beauty, its cruelty, makes it alike impressive. If we dramatise its life and conceive its spirit, we are filled with wonder, terror, and amusement, so magnificent is that spirit, so prolific, inexorable, grammatical, and dull. Like all animals and plants, the cosmos has its own way of doing things, not wholly rational nor ideally best, but patient, fatal, and fruitful. Great is this organism of mud and fire, terrible this vast, painful, glorious experiment. Why should we not look on

the universe with piety? Is it not our substance? Are we made of other clay? All our possibilities lie from eternity hidden in its bosom. It is the dispenser of all our joys. We may address it without superstitious terrors; it is not wicked. It follows its own habits abstractedly; it can be trusted to be true to its word. Society is not impossible between it and us, and since it is the source of all our energies, the home of all our happiness, shall we not cling to it and praise it, seeing that it vegetates so grandly and so sadly, and that it is not for us to blame it for what, doubtless, it never knew that it did? Where there is such infinite and laborious potency there is room for every hope. If we should abstain from judging a father's errors or a mother's foibles, why should we pronounce sentence on the ignorant crimes of the universe, which have passed into our own blood? The universe is the true Adam, the creation the true fall; and as we have never blamed our mythical first parent very much, in spite of the disproportionate consequences of his sin, because we felt that he was but human and that we, in his place, might have sinned too, so we may easily forgive our real ancestor, whose connatural sin we are from moment to moment committing, since it is only the necessary rashness of venturing to be without foreknowing the price or the fruits of existence.

CHAPTER XIV

IDEAL IMMORTALITY

. . .

As the pathos and herosim of life consists in accepting as an opportunity the fate that makes our own death, partial or total, serviceable to others, so the glory of life consists in accepting the knowledge of natural death as an opportunity to live in the spirit. The sacrifice, the self-surrender, remains real; for, though the compensation is real, too, and at moments, perhaps, apparently overwhelming it is always incomplete and leaves beneath an incurable sorrow. Yet life can never contradict its basis or reach satisfactions essentially excluded by its own conditions. Progress lies in moving forward from the given situation, and satisfying as well as may be the interests that exist. And if some initial demand has proved hopeless, there is the greater reason for cultivating other sources of satisfaction, possibly more abundant and lasting. Now, reflection is a vital function; memory and imagination have to the full the rhythm and force of life. But these faculties, in envisaging the past or the ideal, envisage the eternal, and the man in whose mind they predominate is to that extent detached in his affections from the world of flux, from himself, and from his personal destiny. This detachment will not make him infinitely long-lived, nor absolutely happy, but it may render him intelligent and just, and may open to him all intellectual pleasures and all human sympathies.

There is accordingly an escape from death open to man; one not found by circumventing nature, but by making use of her own expedients in circumventing her imperfections. Memory, nay, perception itself, is a first stage in this escape, which coincides with the acquisition and possession of reason. When the meaning of successive perceptions is recovered with the last of them, when a survey is made of objects whose constitutive sensations first arose independently, this synthetic moment contains an object raised above time on a pedestal of reflection, a thought indefeasibly true in its ideal deliverance, though of course fleeting in its psychic existence. Existence is essentially temporal and life foredoomed to be mortal, since its basis is a process and an opposition; it floats in the stream of time, never to return, never to be recovered or repossessed. But ever since substance be-

came at some sensitive point intelligent and reflective, ever since time made room and pause for memory, for history, for the consciousness of time, a god, as it were, became incarnate in mortality and some vision of truth, some self-forgetful satisfaction, became a heritage that moment could transmit to moment and man to man. This heritage is humanity itself, the presence of immortal reason in creatures that perish. Apprehension, which makes man so like a god, makes him in one respect immortal; it quickens his numbered moments with a vision of what never dies, the truth of those moments and their inalienable values.

To participate in this vision is to participate at once in humanity and in divinity, since all other bonds are material and perishable, but the bond between two thoughts that have grasped the same truth, of two instants that have caught the same beauty, is a spiritual and imperishable bond. It is imperishable simply because it is ideal and resident merely in import and intent. The two thoughts, the two instants, remain existentially different; were they not two they could not come from different quarters to unite in one meaning and to behold one object in distinct and conspiring acts of apprehension. Being independent in existence, they can be united by the identity of their burden, by the common worship, so to speak, of the same god. Were this ideal goal itself an existence, it would be incapable of uniting anything; for the same gulf which separated the two original minds would open between them and their common object. But being, as it is, purely ideal, it can become the meeting-ground of intelligences and render their union ideally eternal. Among the physical instruments of thought there may be rivalry and impact—the two thinkers may compete and clash—but this is because each seeks his own physical survival and does not love the truth stripped of its accidental associations and provincial accent. Doctors disagree in so far as they are not truly doctors, but, as Plato would say, seek, like sophists and wage-earners, to circumvent and defeat one another. The conflict is physical and can extend to the subject-matter only in so far as this is tainted by individual prejudice and not wholly lifted from the sensuous to the intellectual plane. In the ether there are no winds of doctrine. The intellect, being the organ and source of the divine, is divine and single; if there were many sorts of intellect, many principles of perspective, they would fix and create incomparable and irrelevant worlds. Reason is one in that it gravitates toward an object, called truth, which could not have the function it has, of being a focus for mental activities, if it were not one in reference to the operations which converge upon it.

This unity in truth, as in reason, is of course functional only, not physical or existential. The beats of thought and the thinkers are innumerable; indefinite, too, the variations to which their endowment and habits may be subjected. But the condition of spiritual communion or ideal relevance in these intelligences is their possession of a method and grammar essentially identical. Language, for example, is significant in proportion to the constancy in meaning which words and locutions preserve in a speaker's mind at various times, or in the minds of various persons. This constancy is never absolute. Therefore language is never wholly significant, never exhaustively intelligible. There is always mud in the well, if we have drawn up enough water. Yet in peaceful rivers, though they flow, there is an appreciable degree of translucency. So, from moment to moment, and from man to man, there is an appreciable element of unanimity, of constancy and congruity of intent. On this abstract and perfectly identical function science rests together with every rational formation.

The same function is the seat of human immortality. Reason lifts a larger or smaller element in each man to the plane of ideality according as reason more or less thoroughly leavens and permeates the lump. No man is wholly immortal, as no philosophy is wholly true and no language wholly intelligible; but only in so far as intelligible is a language a language rather than a noise, only in so far as true is a philosophy more than a vent for cerebral humours, and only in so far as a man is rational and immortal is he a man and not a sensorium.

It is hard to convince people that they have such a gift as intelligence. If they perceive its animal basis they cannot conceive its ideal affinities or understand what is meant by calling it divine; if they perceive its ideality and see the immortal essences that swim into its ken, they hotly deny that it is an animal faculty, and invent ultramundane places and bodiless persons in which it is to reside; as if those celestial substances could be, in respect to thought, any less material than matter or, in respect to vision and life, any less instrumental than bodily organs. It never occurs to them that if nature has added intelligence to animal life it is because they belong together. Intelligence is a natural emanation of vitality. If eternity could exist otherwise than as a vision in time, eternity would have no meaning for men in the world, while the world, men, and time would have no vocation or status in eternity. The travail of existence would be without excuse, without issue or consummation, while the conceptions of truth and of perfection would be without application to experience, pure dreams about things preternatural and unreal, vacantly conceived, and illogically supposed to have something to do with living issues. But truth and perfection, for the very reason that they are not problematic existences but inherent ideals, cannot be banished from discourse. Experience may lose any of its data; it cannot lose, while it endures, the terms with which it operates in becoming experience. Now, truth is relevant to every opinion which looks to truth for its standard, and perfection is envisaged in every cry for relief, in every effort at betterment. Opinions, volitions, and passionate refusals fill human life. So that when the existence of truth is denied, truth is given the only status which it ever required—it is conceived.

Nor can any better defense be found for the denial that nature and her life have a status in eternity. This statement may not be understood, but if grasped at all it will not be questioned. By having a status in eternity is not meant being parts of an eternal existence, petrified or congealed into something real but motionless. What is meant is only that whatever exists in time, when bathed in the light of reflection, acquires an indelible character and discloses irreversible relations; every fact, in being recognised, takes its place in the universe of discourse, in that ideal sphere of truth which is the common and unchanging standard for all assertions. Language, science, art, religion, and all ambitious dreams are compacted of ideas. Life is as much a mosaic of notions as the firmament is of stars; and these ideal and transpersonal objects, bridging time, fixing standards, establishing values, constituting the natural rewards of all living, are the very furniture of eternity, the goals and playthings of that reason which is an instinct in the heart as vital and spontaneous as any other. Or rather, perhaps, reason is a supervening instinct by which all other instincts are interpreted, just as the *sensus communis* or transcendental unity of psychology is a faculty by which all perceptions are brought face to face and compared. So that immortality is not a privilege reserved for a part only of experience, but rather a relation pervading every part in varying measure. We may, in leaving the subject, mark the degrees and phases of this idealisation.

Animal sensation is related to eternity only by the truth that it has taken place. The fact, fleeting as it is, is registered in ideal history, and no inventory of the world's riches, no true confession of its crimes, would ever be complete that ignored that incident. This indefeasible character in experience makes a first sort of ideal immortality, one on which those rational philosophers like to dwell who have not speculation enough to feel quite certain of any other. It was a consolation to the Epicurean to remember that, however brief and uncertain might be his tenure of delight, the past was safe and the present sure. "He lives happy," says Horace, "and master over himself, who can say daily, I have lived. To-morrow let Jove cover the sky with black clouds or flood it with sunshine; he shall not thereby render vain what lies behind, he shall not delete and make never to have existed what once the hour has brought in its flight." Such self-concentration and hugging of the facts has no power to improve them; it gives to pleasure and pain an impartial eternity, and rather tends to intrench in sensuous and selfish satisfactions a mind that has lost faith in reason and that deliberately ignores the difference in scope and dignity which exists among various pursuits. Yet the reflection is staunch and in its way heroic; it meets a vague and feeble aspiration, that looks to the infinite, with a just rebuke; it points to real satisfactions, experienced successes, and asks us to be content with the fulfilment of our own wills. If you have seen the world, if you have played your game and won it, what more would you ask for? If you have tasted the sweets of existence, you should be satisfied; if the experience has been bitter, you should be glad that it comes to an end.

Of course, as we have seen, there is

a primary demand in man which death and mutation contradict flatly, so that no summons to cease can ever be obeyed with complete willingness. Even the suicide trembles and the ascetic feels the stings of the flesh. It is the part of philosophy, however, to pass over those natural repugnances and overlay them with as much countervailing rationality as can find lodgment in a particular mind. The Epicurean, having abandoned politics and religion and being afraid of any far-reaching ambition, applied philosophy honestly enough to what remained. Simple and healthy pleasures are the reward of simple and healthy pursuits; to chafe against them because they are limited is to import a foreign and disruptive element into the case; a healthy hunger has its limit, and its satisfaction reaches a natural term. Philosophy, far from alienating us from those values, should teach us to see their perfection and to maintain them in our ideal. In other words, the happy filling of a single hour is so much gained for the universe at large, and to find joy and sufficiency in the flying moment is perhaps the only means open to us for increasing the glory of eternity.

Moving events, while remaining enshrined in this fashion in their permanent setting, may contain other and less external relations to the immutable. They may represent it. If the pleasures of sense are not cancelled when they cease, but continue to satisfy reason in that they once satisfied natural desires, much more will the pleasures of reflection retain their worth, when we consider that what they aspired to and reached was no momentary physical equilibrium but a permanent truth. As Archimedes, measuring the hypothenuse, was lost to events, being engaged in an event of much greater transcendence, so art and science interrupt the sense for change by engrossing attention in its issues and its laws. Old age often turns pious to look away from ruins to some world where youth endures and where what ought to have been is not overtaken by decay before it has quite come to maturity. Lost in such abstract contemplations, the mind is weaned from mortal concerns. It forgets for a few moments a world in which it has so little more to do and so much, perhaps, still to suffer. As a sensation of pure light would not be distinguishable from light itself, so a contemplation of things not implicating time in their structure becomes, so far as its own deliverance goes, a timeless existence. Unconsciousness of temporal conditions and of the very flight of time makes the thinker sink for a moment into identity with timeless objects. And so immortality, in a second ideal sense, touches the mind.

The transitive phases of consciousness, however, have themselves a reference to eternal things. They yield a generous enthusiasm and love of good which is richer in consolation than either Epicurean self-concentration or mathematical ecstasy. Events are more interesting than the terms we abstract from them, and the forward movement of the will is something more intimately real than is the catalogue of our past experiences. Now the forward movement of the will is an avenue to the eternal. What would you have? What is the goal of your endeavour? It must be some success, the establishment of some order, the expression of some experience. These points once reached, we are not left merely with the satisfaction of abstract success or the consciousness of ideal immortality. Being natural goals, these ideals are related to natural functions. Their attainment does not exhaust but merely liberates, in this instance, the function concerned, and so marks the perpetual point of reference common to that function in all its fluctuations. Every attainment of perfection in an art—as for instance in government—makes a return to perfection easier for posterity, since there remains an enlightening example, together with faculties predisposed by discipline to recover their ancient virtue. The better a man evokes and realises the ideal the more he leads the life that all others, in proportion to their worth, will seek to live after him, and the more he helps them to live in that nobler fashion. His presence in the society of immortals thus becomes, so to speak, more pervasive. He not only vanquishes time by his own rationality, living now in the eternal, but he continually lives again in all rational beings.

Since the ideal has this perpetual pertinence to mortal struggles, he who lives in the ideal and leaves it expressed in society or in art enjoys a double immortality. The eternal has absorbed him while he lived, and when he is dead his influence brings others to the same absorption, making them, through that ideal identity with the best in him, reincarnations and perennial seats of all in him which he could rationally hope to rescue from destruction. He can say, without any subterfuge or desire to delude himself, that he shall not wholly die; for he will have a better notion than the vulgar of what constitutes his being. By becoming the spectator and confessor of his own death and of universal mutation, he will have identified himself with what is spiritual in all spirits and masterful in all apprehension; and so conceiving himself, he may truly feel and know that he is eternal.

H. N. WIEMAN

The Creative Event

Henry Nelson Wieman (1884–   ) is one of the leaders of liberal Protestant thought. He taught for many years at the University of Chicago Divinity School.

CHAPTER I

THE WAY GOOD INCREASES

. . .

Naturalism

This reply to the question "What is value?" is the answer of the newer naturalism, a movement or development in contemporary thought akin to, but to

From H. N. Wieman, *The Source of Human Good* (1946), Chs. I–III. Reprinted by permission of H. N. Wieman.

be sharply distinguished from, the older naturalisms, which tended toward reductive materialism. It asserts that there is nothing in reality accessible to the human mind more basic than events and their qualities and relations. ("Relations" is another word for "structure.") No knowable cause or explanation for anything that happens can reach deeper than events and their structure and qualities. This view claims to be able to take account of all the intricacies and subtleties—all the height, breadth, and depth of human existence—omitting, explaining away, flattening out, or truncating nothing. We shall have no recourse to any "transcendental grounds, orders, causes or purposes" [1] beyond events, their qualities, and relations. Naturalism bases this claim on thorough analysis of the method by which any knowledge whatsoever can be obtained. We shall interpret value, in the following pages, entirely in terms of events, their qualities and relations (structure). The richest and highest values sought and found by religion and morals are interpreted as structured events and their possibilities.

In selecting this naturalistic version of reality, we have had to choose between two great traditions which Western civilization has inherited. Each presents its own interpretation of what is supremely important for all human living. One is Jewish Christian, the other Greek Christian. The Jewish tradition declares that the sovereign good works creatively in history. While this ruling creativity is said to have form, the importance of it lies in its creative potentialities and not in its form. The Greek tradition, on the other hand, declares that the sovereign good is essentially a system of Forms or a Supreme Form. The one tradition gives supreme authority to the creative event, the other to the Form. Our interpretation follows the Jewish tradition in giving priority to the creative event.

But there is one respect, being naturalists, in which we depart from both traditions: we ignore the transcendental affirmation in the Jewish Christian tradition of a creative God who not only works in history but resides beyond history. The only creative God we recognize is the creative event itself. So also we ignore the transcendental affirmation in

the Greek Christian tradition of the reality of Forms of value, uncreated and eternal, having causal efficacy to constrain the shape of things without themselves being events at all. The only forms of value we recognize are produced by the creative event. Even possibilities, so far as relevant to actual events, are created. The form of the creative event itself at our higher levels of existence is determined by the creative process at more elementary levels. In our view the higher levels of existence spring from, rest upon, and are undergirded by the lower.

Thus the active God derived from the Jewish tradition and the Forms derived from the Greek tradition are both brought down into the world of time, space, and matter and are there identified as events displaying a definite structure with possibilities. When we insist that nothing has causal efficacy except material events, by "material" we mean not merely pellets of inanimate matter but also events that include the biological, social, and historical forms of existence. These, however, never cease to be material. Nothing has value except material events, thus understood, and their possibilities.

These claims rest upon an analysis of our experience, revealing that no transcendental reality could ever *do* anything. It could not make the slightest difference in our lives except in the form of some happening, some event. In other words, nothing can happen if it does not happen. But when the transcendental becomes an event, it is no longer transcendental. We cannot know anything, and nothing can make the slightest difference in our lives unless it be an event or some possibility carried by an event. Transcendental realities literally have nothing to do after we have discovered that all value, all meaning, and all causal efficacy are to be found in the world of events and their possibilities. Therefore, the

---

[1] See *Naturalism and the Human Spirit,* ed. Yervant Krikorian, especially the chapter on "Categories of Naturalism," by William Dennes; see also D. C. Williams, "Naturalism and the Nature of Things," *Philosophical Review,* LIII (1944), 417–43.

transcendental must be ignored, except as an imaginative construction of the human mind. Since we never shall know everything, the transcendental might be retained as a mythical way of representing what is yet to be discovered. But that device has proved so confusing and misleading that we think it is better dropped. Since this is our position, an alternative title for this book might read: "What Is Value? Naturalism Answers."

. . .

CHAPTER II

THE HUMAN PREDICAMENT

Three features intrinsic to man's way of apprehending value render life perilous, with the rising power of technology. This peril can be escaped by redirecting human endeavor from service of good already created to service of the generating source of all good. To accomplish this reversal in the direction of human devotion, we must have a reinterpretation of human good and how it originates. Catastrophe waits on exercise of the power of modern technology if this reversal is not accomplished, because our sense of values is wholly inadequate and unreliable to serve as a guide in use of such power. So long as power was weak, this unreliability of the human value-sense did not invite disaster. Now it does. To see the treachery inherent in man's appreciative consciousness when it directs the tremendous power of modern technology, we must examine the three characteristics which make his apprehension of value unreliable.

Faults of the Human Value-sense

The first of these characteristics is the limited range of human appreciation. The values which man can appreciate are microscopic compared to the depth and fulness of value involved in every important human undertaking. To label unappreciated values "potential" removes the danger and difficulty of this human predicament not at all.

There is a second crippling fault in the human sense for value. Whatever apprehension of good and evil man attains is always distorted, when not perverted, by the domination of self-concern. Even when my action seems not to be self-centered because it is directed to certain interests of other people, nevertheless it is self-centered in the sense that these interests of others have some special bearing upon my own fulfilment, and exclude from my consideration other interests not so apparently relevant to this prime concern of mine.

A third feature of man's way of discerning good and evil is equally dangerous to our existence when technology magnifies the power of human control over the course of events. It is resistance to change in the structure of appreciative consciousness. Man distinguishes good and evil according to certain forms which have been called the Gestalt of his conscious awareness. One might say they are the apertures through which the mind senses the good and evil of events and possibilities. They are slits variously structured for different minds. For each man they are shaped by his intimate group, by his ruling interest, and by his past experiences. These forms, structures, apertures, always become more or less fixated and will not undergo the transformations required to detect values peculiar to other groups, other cultures, and other interests and situations different from his own past experience.

Here again we have a characteristic of the human way of apprehending value not seriously dangerous throughout most of man's history except in rather unusual circumstances. Man did not and could not deal very potently with situations involving basic values for other intimate groups, cultures, and interests alien to his own. Above all, the world did not undergo radical and swift transformation as a rule. So the narrow slits of conscious awareness, determined by past experience and marking out the distinctions between good and evil for human discernment, were fairly reliable.

Today modern technology has changed all that. Newly generated distinctions of good and evil peculiar to the new situation often carry the issues of life and death, because the power we wield today involves us with groups and cultures alien to our own, accelerates change, and deepens the level at which it occurs. But it is not possible to transform the structure of consciousness so as to catch these newly emergent distinctions at the level and with the scope necessary to direct aright our power of control. The tender growth of emergent good derived from other groups and created anew as life goes on is the only ground of hope we have in a close-knit and changing world. But we kill the undetected growth of new values because the structure of our awareness excludes them from our apprehension.

How, then, can we be saved? Only, we repeat, by seeking another guide to direct our use of power very different from the human way of apprehending value. We cannot change the structure of the human value-sense in a way to make it fit to direct our power grown mighty with technology. The three limitations noted are intrinsic to the human consciousness. Scope of appreciation can be widened, to be sure; distortion and perversion by self-concern can be mitigated; established forms of appreciation can be rendered somewhat more transformable. But these improvements are negligible for the problem under consideration, namely, finding a directive which will so guide our use of power that it will not destroy the good we have and cut off hope of any increase but will rather serve to order the world so that good will grow and previously undetected

values will break into consciousness. When we continue to use our power in service of the good we discern with the faulty sense of value peculiar to our minds, darkness swiftly gathers. The more strenuously we act and the more earnestly we serve under such guidance, the more swiftly comes the night. This is the fate of man when technology gives him power.

Religious Obstruction

This fate can be escaped. But when we turn to follow the way of salvation, we find a barrier set up by the great redemptive religions—and pre-eminently by Christianity. Here is the most tragic irony of all: The great religions, seeking to save, have developed an ideology peculiarly fitted to the need of man in the days of his weakness. But this very same ideology, now in the days of his power, blocks the way of salvation. If we look down the path of escape, we can see how one of the major teachings of Christianity bars the way.

The way of escape, we remember, is to use the power of technology not to serve the good as discerned through the structure of appreciative awareness but to serve the creative source of all good. The creative event magnifies the good of the world, both the good appreciated and the good beyond the reach of appreciation, called "potential" if you wish. It expands the range of appreciation to the limit of human capacity when conditions are provided to release its efficacy. It corrects self-concern to the bounds of our willingness to meet its demands, and it transforms the established structure of conscious appreciation so that we can apprehend newly emergent values in a changing world. Above all, by serving the creative source we serve the good of all, as we cannot do when we serve only the created good which is accessible to our appreciation through the narrow and distorted slits of conscious awareness.

This is the way we must go when the power of technology is put into our hand, but it is not the way men generally have gone. Doubtless, a few saints and sages and fellowships of faith have lived under dominant devotion to creative good rather than allow created good to direct their lives. But today science and technology at our command must be put to the service of creative good. No longer is it sufficient for individuals in personal commitment to do this. The powerful shapers of social structure and human history must be put to this service.

Here is our problem, perhaps the most pressing of our time. Science must be directed to searching out the conditions demanded by the source of human good so that this creative power may produce the values of life for all; and technology must be applied to setting up those conditions which science discovers to be required. If science and technology are not used in this way, they will destroy us because they will then be put into the service of those diverse and conflicting values which the restricted, self-centered, and group-centered consciousness of man can apprehend. But the creative source of human good is not now interpreted in such a way that science and technology can be applied to its service. The great religions portray it as being the shaper of events, or the overruler of them, or somehow generating them, but not itself a structure of events. Yet science cannot find the demands of an alleged reality which is not an order of events, nor can technology serve it, because these mighty instruments can work only in the world of events. Therefore, unless we can find the source of human good in the form of an order of events, we are doomed, if our analysis of the human predicament is correct.

This is not the problem of "reconciling science and religion" as ordinarily understood, namely, removing contradiction between their respective affirmations.

That problem is twaddle compared to this. We are here discussing, not logical inconsistency, but life and death.

. . .

CHAPTER III

CREATIVE GOOD

Creative good is distinguished from two kinds of created good, one of which is instrumental and the other intrinsic. Instrumental and intrinsic created good are alike in the sense that both are made up of events meaningfully connected; but in the instrumental kind the quality of the events is either negligible or irrelevant to their positive value. Eating tasteless or nauseating food might have the instrumental value of providing me with energy for participation later in events yielding intrinsic value. If the food is tasteless, the quality is negligible; if nauseating, there is quality, but the quality is irrelevant to the instrumental value. The eating of such food might, however, take on intrinsic value through other meaningful connections then and there experienced—the friendliness of associates, memories recalled, and happy anticipations. All these qualities flood in upon me from near and far and are experienced in the very act of eating with these people at this time and place. In such an event the eating ceases to be instrumental by taking on rich quality through meaningful connection with many other happenings. The same system of events may be in one reference an instrumental, and in another reference an intrinsic, good.

The shift from instrumental to intrinsic value, through acquisition of qualitative meaning, is a common occurrence in human life. For example, when I chop wood to sustain that other structure of happenings called "the life of my family in our home," the values of the activity may be purely instrumental if *the qualities pertaining to life in my home cannot freely enter conscious awareness as I chop*. However, if bonds of meaning are developed between my chopping of the wood and the life of my home, so that the lives of the children and the affection of the wife are vivified in conscious awareness by the very act itself, then the activity ceases to be merely instrumental. Then chopping the wood has taken on those qualities pertaining to the total structure of events called "the life of my home." It is an intrinsic good, no matter how fatiguing it may be.

Therefore, intrinsic value may be defined as a structure of events endowing each happening as it occurs with qualities derived from other events in the structure. On the other hand, instrumental value is a structure of events whereby each happening as it occurs does not acquire qualities from other events in the structure, or, if it does, these qualities are irrelevant to the value of the structure in the reference under consideration.

When there is a break between two or more systems of events such that the qualities of the one system cannot get across to the other, the only meaningful connection between the two must be nonqualitative and instrumental. It is nonqualitative either because the qualities of these connecting events are negligible or because they are irrelevant to the good that is served.

Life can break apart into separate systems of qualitative meaning, when each system is an intrinsic good and when the disjunctions between them are bridged by instrumental good. Any meaningful connection between events which does not carry the qualities from one part of life over to the other parts is, on that account, instrumental in respect to this connective function. It is possible that life might break up into smaller and smaller units of intrinsic good, each unit being separated further and further from the others by longer and longer stretches

of instrumental value, relatively barren of qualitative meaning. These instrumental stretches might include events that had intense quality in themselves as bare and isolated events. But value as here interpreted is not merely events having intense quality, even when the quality is pleasant; it is events having rich quality derived from other events through meaningful connection with them. Of course, the quality peculiar to the event now happening may make its own contribution; but it is qualitative meaning, not merely events having quality, which is the good distinctive of human existence. Such good is our concern here.

When good increases, a process of reorganization is going on, generating new meanings, integrating them with the old, endowing each event as it occurs with a wider range of reference, molding the life of a man into a more deeply unified totality of meaning. The wide diversities, varieties, and contrasts of all the parts of a man's life are being progressively transformed into a more richly inclusive whole. The several parts of life are connected in mutual support, vivifying and enhancing one another in the creation of a more inclusive unity of events and possibilities. This process of reorganization is what we shall call the "creative event." It is creative good, standing in contrast to both kinds of created good we have been considering. By means of this creative good, systems of meaning having intrinsic value, previously disconnected so that the qualities of the one could not get across to the other, are so unified that each is enriched by qualities derived from the other. Meaningfully connected events, once instrumental, now become component parts of a total meaning having intrinsic value.

In contrast to the disintegration of life previously sketched, the opposite occurs when creative good is dominant. Under the control of this creativity the life of an individual might, in theory at least, be progressively organized so that the qualities of each part could be experienced while the individual was engaged in some minor role, like walking to town. If this were the case, one's whole life could be qualitatively tasted by way of meaning when one was engaged in any part.

This creative good has kinship with instrumental value, but it is very different from the kind of instrumental value we have described as one kind of created good. It has kinship because it produces more intrinsic created good, and in many cases its own qualities are negligible or are not discriminated and appreciated. Yet it is not instrumental because it transforms the mind and purpose so radically that what it produces is never what the initiating mind intended. Therefore, the initiating mind cannot use it as a means for achieving any anticipated consequence of value that can be foreseen in its specific character. The creative event cannot be used to shape the world closer to the heart's desire because it transforms the heart's desire so that one wants something very different from what one desired in the beginning.

The creative event also has kinship with intrinsic value and yet is very different. It has kinship because in some instances the qualities of the creative event have maximum abundance. The creative event in the life of the artist is sometimes an ecstasy. So also the emergence of new transformative ideas in the mind of the creative thinker, the moment of vision for the prophet, the "rebirth" of the religious convert, or the communion of friends may stand forth as a peak of qualitative meaning. However, in the ordinary run of life, for the most part, the creative event reorganizes the mind and transforms its appreciable world without the qualities of the creative event being themselves discriminated and distinguished from the newly emergent meaning. Rather it is the newly created

good that is qualitatively appreciated and not the creative event producing it.

The creative event is so basic to all our further interpretation of value that we must examine it with care. It is made up of four subevents; and the four working together and not any one of them working apart from the other constitute the creative event. Each may occur without the others and often does, but in that case it is not creative. We have to describe them separately, but distinctions made for the purpose of analysis must not obscure the unitary, fourfold combination necessary to the creativity.

The four subevents are: emerging awareness of qualitative meaning derived from other persons through communication; integrating these new meanings with others previously acquired; expanding the richness of quality in the appreciable world by enlarging its meaning; deepening the community among those who participate in this total creative event of intercommunication. We shall examine each of these subevents in detail.

The First Subevent

Let us remember that qualitative meaning consists of actual events so related that each acquires qualities from the others. Every living organism so reacts as to break the passage of existence into units or intervals called "events" and to relate these to one another in the manner here called "qualitative meaning." So long as this is done by the organism without the aid of linguistic communication, the range and richness of qualitative meaning is very limited. Not until the single organism is able to acquire the qualitative meanings developed by other organisms and add them to its own can the world of meaning and quality expand to any great compass. Therefore the first subevent in the total creative event producing value distinctively human is this emerging awareness in the individual of qualitative meaning communicated to it from some other organism.

Interaction between the organism and its surroundings, by which new qualitative meaning is created without communication or prior to communication, is certainly creative. If we were studying the creative event as it occurs at all levels of existence, this creativity at the sub-communicative level would be included. But we have chosen to give attention to what creates value at the human level. What creates value at the biological level is basic to human existence, but it is not distinctively human. We shall give some attention to it, but only for the purpose of seeing more clearly the character of the creative event as it works through intercommunication in human society and history. It is here, where one organism can acquire the meanings gathered by a million others, that the miracle happens and creativity breaks free from obstacles which elsewhere imprison its power. Only at this level can the creative event rear a world of quality and meaning expanding beyond any known limit, sometimes by geometrical progression.

The Second Subevent

The individual becomes more of a personality when these meanings derived from others are integrated with what he already has. His thoughts and feelings are enriched and deepened. This integrating does not occur in every case of communicated meaning, since there is much noncreative communication in our modern world by way of radio, television, movies, newspapers, and casual interchange between individuals. The mere passage through the mind of innumerable meanings is not the creative event. These newly communicated meanings must be integrated with meanings previously acquired or natively developed if the creative event is to occur. This integrating is largely subconscious, unplanned

and uncontrolled by the individual, save only as he may provide conditions favorable to its occurrence. This integrating is, then, the second subevent in the four, which together make the total event creative of all human value.

It is in this second subevent that man seems most helpless to do what must be done. The supreme achievements of this internally creative integration seem to occur in solitude, sometimes quite prolonged. When many meanings have been acquired through communication and through much action on the material world, there must be time for these to be assimilated. If one does not for a time draw apart and cease to act on the material world and communicate with others, the constant stream of new meanings will prevent the deeper integration. A period of loneliness and quiet provides for incubation and creative transformation by novel unification. If new meanings are coming in all the time, the integration is hindered by the new ingressions. The creative integration may be greatly aided by worship when worship allows a supreme good to draw into a unity of commitment to itself all the diverse values that have been received from many sources.

Jesus in the wilderness of "temptation" and in Gethsemane, Buddha alone under the Bo tree, Paul in the desert on the way to Damascus, Augustine at the time of his conversion—all these exemplify creative integration in solitude. Many of the great innovating ideas in literature, philosophy, and science have come to men in their loneliness. Also it seems that the individuals through whom the creative event has done most to transform and enrich the world with meaning have been more lonely than other men and have spent more time in lonely struggles. Yet with equal emphasis it must be said that they have had profound communication with others, if not face to face, then through writing and meditation on written words.

But mere solitude is not enough. Nothing can be more deadening and dangerous to the human spirit than solitude. If the mind degenerates into a state of torpor, as it generally does when isolated from communication with others, solitude is not creative. If the mind wanders in vagrant fancy, one idea following another by accidental association, there is no creativity. Or if one engages in minute and intensive analysis of a particular problem or is harassed with many worries, fears, and hopes, solitude may yield nothing. What is required of one in solitude that it may be fruitful? We do not know. We only know that one who is continuously in association with others is not likely to be the medium through whom great creative transformations occur. They who struggle in loneliness to overcome conditions that seem to block the good of human existence are the ones through whom this second stage in the creative event can be fulfilled. Whitehead has said that religion is what a man does with his solitude, and this is profoundly true, even though it be but part of the truth, since much more than solitude is needed. But one of the major unsolved problems of our existence is to learn how to make solitude creative instead of degenerative, as it most commonly is.

The creative event, in all four of its stages, is going on all the time in human existence. When we speak of prolonged solitude, on the one hand, and intensive and profound communication, on the other, as being prerequisite to creative transformation, we refer only to the more striking examples of it. In obscure and lowly form it is occurring continuously in human life, even when decline and disintegration also occur. The latter might be more rapid than the creative process until human life itself disap-

peared. Nevertheless, the creative event must continue so long as human life goes on because it is necessary to the human level of existence.

The Third Subevent

The expanding and enriching of the appreciable world by a new structure of interrelatedness pertaining to events necessarily follow from the first two subevents. It is the consequence of both the first two, not of either one by itself. If there has been intercommunication of meanings and if they have been creatively integrated, the individual sees what he could not see before; he feels what he could not feel. Events as they happen to him are now so connected with other events that his appreciable world has an amplitude unimaginable before. There is a range and variety of events, a richness of quality, and a reach of ideal possibility which were not there prior to this transformation.

This creative increase in qualitative meaning may not be dramatic and sudden; it may be imperceptible, except as one compares the world accessible to the man of thirty with what he could see and feel and do when he was one year old. However, one must remember that mere expanse in range and complexity of events is not an increase in qualitative meaning. Mere expanse may be achieved by multiplying and lengthening instrumental connections so that life becomes a burden and a weariness. When this happens, it is due to conditions which prevent the creative event from producing increase in intrinsic value. These conditions may be physiological, psychological, social, or historical and most probably are a combination of all of them.

Also it should be noted that this expanded world of qualitative meaning does not continue as a steady vision. The appreciable world in which each man lives from day to day expands and contracts through great variations. Yet the expanded world, once acquired, is not entirely lost, unless some degeneration sets in. It is not always immediately accessible, certainly not in the torpor of sleep and under many other conditions; yet one can at times recover what has been achieved if he retains his vitality and conditions are not too unfavorable. It is at least a memory and a conceivable hope, as it was not prior to the creative transformation.

One important thing to note is that this expanding of the appreciable world may make a man more unhappy and more lonely than he was before; for now he knows that there is a greatness of good which might be the possession of man but is not actually achieved. One is reminded of the man who preached through all his life: "God is my Father and all you are my brothers," declaring continuously the blessedness of all-encompassing love and yet living in a world so barren of love that he must have been heart-breakingly lonely through all the days of his life. This loneliness comes to agonized expression in the story of the temptation, Gethsemane, and the cry on the Cross.

Such a profound sense of loneliness is difficult for any man to bear, and yet it is the hope of the world because the man who feels it is aware of a greatness of love that might be but is not. Such loneliness indicates a vast emptiness which love between men might fill. This loneliness might become so deep and so intense that a man could not endure it unless he were permitted to die upon a cross for love; he might then fill an emptiness no actual love can fill by a sacrificial expression of love. This seeking for a love that is never fulfilled might become so deep and so intense that a man would spend all his life preaching the principles of a kingom of love that would sound like the beatitudes of madness in a world

like this. They could be made intelligible only by attributing them to an illusion that the world was shortly to come to an end and would be transformed miraculously into such a kingdom. Perhaps such loneliness, born of such craving for love between men, would drive a man to that desperate madness in which he dreamed that by dying on a cross he could somehow bring this kingdom of love into existence.

This expanding of the appreciable world, accomplished by the third subevent, is not, then, in its entirety the actual achievement of an increase of value in this world, although it will include that. But it is also, perhaps even more, an expansion of the individual's capacity to appreciate and his apprehension of a good that might be, but is not, fulfilled. It is the awakening of a hunger and a longing which, in one aspect at least, is a craving for more love between men than ever can be in the compass of his life.

The Fourth Subevent

Widening and deepening community between those who participate in the total creative event is the final stage in creative good. The new structure of interrelatedness pertaining to events, resulting from communication and integration of meanings, transforms not only the mind of the individual and his appreciable world but also his relations with those who have participated with him in this occurrence. Since the meanings communicated to him from them have now become integrated into his own mentality, he feels something of what they feel, sees something of what they see, thinks some of their thought. He may disapprove, deny, and repudiate much that has been communicated to him from them, but this is a form of understanding and community. Perceptions and thoughts that are denied are as much a part of one's mentality as those affirmed. They may contribute as much to the scope and richness of one's mind, to one's appreciable world, and to the depth of one's community with others as perspectives which we affirm and with which we agree.

This community includes both intellectual understanding of one another and the feeling of one another's feelings, the ability to correct and criticize one another understandingly and constructively. It includes the ability and the will to cooperate in such manner as to conserve the good of life achieved to date and to provide conditions for its increase.

Paradoxical as it may sound, this increased community between persons may bring with it a sense of alienation and wistful hunger and even anguish, because one is now aware of misunderstandings in the other. He apprehends in the mind of the other, as he could not before, bitterness, fear, hate, scorn, pride, self-concern, indifference, and unresponsiveness when great need and great issues call. Likewise, the other may apprehend in him in somewhat different areas these ailments of the human spirit. Increase in genuine community, which is not mere increase in back-slapping geniality, will include all this discernment of illness and evil in one another. Increase in community is not necessarily pleasant; the good produced by the creative event brings increase in suffering as well as increase in joy; community brings a burden as well as a release. Those who cannot endure suffering cannot endure the increase of human good. Refusal to take suffering is perhaps the chief obstacle to increase in the good of human existence.

These are the four subevents which together compose the creative event. They are locked together in such an intimate manner as to make a single, total event continuously recurrent in human existence. The creative event is one that brings forth in the human mind, in society and history, and in the appreciable world a new structure of interrelatedness, whereby events are discriminated and related in a manner not before possible. It is a structure whereby some events derive from other events, through meaningful connection with them, an abundance of quality that events could not have had without this new creation.

. . .

It should be noted that the creative event, together with every one of the subevents, is an -*ing*. The subevents are emergings, integratings, expandings, deepenings, that is, they are not accomplished facts. After the event is accomplished, it is no longer creative. Hence the creative subevents (as well as the total creative event) are events in process. They are happenings in transit, not finished products, although they yield a finished product. The finished product of these four -*ings*, and hence the product of the total creative event, is always a new structure, whereby some events are more widely and richly related in meaningful connections.

This, then, is creative good. Created intrinsic good, on the other hand, is the appreciable world made richer with quality and meaning by this creative event. It is culture. Instrumental good, which is also created, is a structure pertaining to events wherein the qualities of the events are not relevant to the value of the structure. It is civilization or technology, in contrast to culture. This threefold distinction of values into creative, created intrinsic, and created instrumental has practical importance, we believe, because the three kinds of value require different kinds of action if human good is to be promoted.

The Human Problem

The human problem is to shape human conduct and all other conditions so that the creative event can be released to produce maximum good. While this event is continuously occurring in human life, more often despite the efforts of men than because of them, it is not always equally potent and effective. The richness and scope of meaning that it creates, moment by moment, may vary from a minimum to a maximum. What it creates may be small compared to what is destroyed by the impact of uncreative existence. Nevertheless, the whole struggle of human life, the basic problem of industry and government, of education and religion, of sex and personal conduct, of family and neighborhood organization, is to provide and to maintain those conditions wherein the creative event can produce the maximum of qualitative meaning with minimum destruction of previously developed structures which enrich the world.

Much in human life hampers the full release and creative power of this event. When men deceive or fear or distrust one another, when they inflict injustice or smart beneath it, they refuse to communicate meanings that are rich, deep, and precious to them. The worldly-wise wear a poker face, hide behind a mask of bravado or indifference lest others discover the absurd and despicable pretensions they know within themselves. They hold back, lest servants disobey master, lest heroes be dragged from their pedestals. Fear, hate, and suspicion; deceit, concealment, and exploitation; misunderstanding, indifference, and sloth; vindictive cruelty, lust, and sadistic desire; complacency, arrogance, and the insatiable need to feed the ego—all these block and frustrate the creative event. The list runs on without end. Thus the great problem is how to provide conditions more favorable for this creative event so that it can bring forth structures which will endow events with more richness of quality and scope of meaning.

· · ·

Creative Good Is Supra-human

Serving the creative event that renews itself is the work of man—the supreme vocation of human history. Innumerable things can be done by men to remove obstacles and provide sustaining conditions which release the power of creative good to produce value. Every serious practical and theoretical problem finds its solution in clearing the path for creative transformation, and there is nothing else to be done that is worthy of man. Meeting the demands of this source of human good calls for all the moral rigor, all the labor and sacrifice, all the religious commitment of faith which human capacity can afford. There is, therefore, plenty for man to do in helping to create a better world.

The emphasis just made is important because of a persistent misunderstanding that arises when it is said that man cannot do what the creative event does. All we mean to say is that the creative event produces a structure which could not be intended by the human mind before it emerges either in imagination or in the order of actual events.

Human effort cannot accomplish anything which the human mind cannot imagine. If something results from human effort which was not intended and which the human mind could not imagine prior to its occurrence, it is an accident relative to human effort. It is not, of course, an accident in the absolute sense of being without cause. But, even though the existence and the labors of men are part of the many causes issuing in this consequence, the consequence is not the work of man if the human intent sought a result different from this consequence.

The structure of value produced by the creative event cannot be caused by human intention and effort, because it can be produced only by a transformation of human intention and effort. We saw how the creative event transforms the human mind, the reactions of the human organism, the community of associated individuals, and the very structure of events as they occur in the appreciable world. Obviously, this cannot be the work of man in the sense that he can foresee the structure yet to be created. He cannot strive to achieve it before he has sufficient imagination to conceive it and the required hunger to seek it.

Many protest when we claim that man cannot be creative. Of course, man in many senses of the term is creative: he exercises his imagination to envision something that never was in existence and then proceeds to construct it. But man cannot exercise his imagination to envision what is inaccessible to imagination prior to the transformation which gives his mind the added reach. Man can do only what lies within the scope of the imagination that he has; he can seek only the good that he, to date, is able to appreciate. To do what lies beyond the reach of his imagination, a greater imagination must be created in him. To seek a good beyond what he can appreciate, a greater appreciation must be developed in him. The creative event, not man himself, creates this greater imagination and this more profound and discriminating appreciation.

What we have said demonstrates that man cannot be creative in the sense in which this term applies to the creative event we have been describing. Man's creative ability is something produced in him as a consequence of the prior working of the creative event. To fall into controversy over whether or not man is creative is to use the same word for different things. Such an argument is as futile as a merry-go-round.

The creative event is supra-human, not in the sense that it works outside of human life, but in the sense that it creates the good of the world in a way that man cannot do. Man cannot even approximate the work of the creative event. He would not come any closer to it if his powers were magnified to infinity, because the infinite increase of his ability would have to be the consequence of the prior working of the creative event.

The work of the creative event is different in kind from the work of man. Any attempt to measure the power of man against the power of the creative event is defeated at the start because one cannot compare the two. It is true that man can set up conditions that obstruct the work of the creative event so that the good it produces will be much less than it would have been if men had met its demands. Also, he can serve it by removing obstacles. Men can do this in their personal conduct, in the organization of society, in the physical and biological regime which they maintain. When men do meet its demands, the creative event faithfully produces a far greater abundance of human good. But the actual creative event is never the work of man and cannot be. In that sense it is supra-human and transcendent, but the transcendence pertains to its character as creative of the appreciable world created to date. This appreciable world contains the meanings and the things, the goods and the goals, which are subject to human control. It is the world in which man lives his conscious life for the most part. Since creativity is not readily accessible to awareness, we can speak of creativity as "transcendent." But it is not transcendent in the sense of being nontemporal, nonspatial, and immaterial. It can be discovered in this world by proper analysis.

Since this creativity has the character just stated, it was almost inevitable that man should think it supernatural. Nature, for the ordinary man, is his appreciable world. Therefore, what is not accessible to his appreciation must be supernatural, especially when it is creative of this world which he appreciates. Creativity is not beyond all human appreciation. It can be appreciated, and, when proper social conditions and required knowledge have been achieved, it can be known as a part of the temporal, spatial, material world. But, generally speaking, it has been mythically represented as supernatural; and, if the creative event be of the sort we have described, the human mind could hardly have approached it otherwise until certain cultural conditions and scientific knowledge had been achieved, especially knowledge in the fields of biology, psychology, and social psychology. Expert specialists in these several fields might not find it, but one who can draw from all of them and from other cultural conditions might well do so. Many have done so in recent years.

Like the ancient supernaturalism, and in opposition to almost all religions and philosophies that stand over against supernaturalism, the naturalism here defended repudiates the supremacy in value of all the goods and goals of the created appreciable world and turns to what creates them for the sovereign good of life.

Instrumental Value

"Instrumental" refers to what man can use and control as a means to an end. As we have seen, man cannot use and control the creative event because the structure of value it produces can never in its specific character be intended, desired, or sought by man. Man can, of course, know that the creative event will produce good and can welcome the need of his and the world's transformation; but he cannot know the kind and form of good it will produce, and if he could foresee, *per impossibile,* with his untransformed perception, what the creative event would produce, it would at times seem hateful and fearful and the opposite of good. The kind and form of good

actually produced by creativity inevitably transcends, and in some ways runs counter to, the present order of human desire; for one of the necessary subevents of the creative event is precisely this transformation of the previously existing order of human desire. The primary demand which the creative event makes upon man is that he give himself over to it to be transformed in any way that it may require. Obviously, man cannot use as a means or instrument the generative process which transforms him so as to create values which he cannot in their specific nature anticipate or see or desire.

Creative Good Is Absolute Good

The claim that creative good is the only absolute good can be defended only after we are clear on what is meant by "absolute" in this context. When we speak of "absolute good" we shall mean, first of all, what is good under all conditions and circumstances. It is a good that is not relative to time or place or person or race or class or need or hope or desire or belief. It is a good that remains changelessly and identically the same in character so far as concerns its goodness. It is a good that would continue to be so even if all human beings should cease to exist. It is a good that retains its character even when it runs counter to all human desire. It is a good that continues to be identically the same good even when it works with microscopic cells prior to the emergence of any higher organism.

Creative good meets all these requirements pertaining to absolute good. Its goodness is not relative to human desire, or even to human existence, although it is also good when desired and when working in the medium of human existence.

On the other hand, created good—the structure of meaning connecting past and future that we feel and appreciate—

is relative value in all the senses that stand in contrast to the absolute as just described. The particular chains of qualitative meaning having value for man do not necessarily have value for microbes. The structure of interrelatedness pertaining to events which increases quality and meaning relative to one organism or race or class or culture will not ordinarily be equally good for another. Thus created good does not retain the same character of goodness under all circumstances and conditions and in relation to every different sort of organism, human person, or social culture. The creative good which does retain its character of goodness under all these changing conditions is, then, the only absolute good.[1]

A second mark of absolute good is that its demands are unlimited. A good is absolute if it is always good to give myself, all that I am and all that I desire, all that I possess and all that is dear to me, into its control to be transformed in any way that it may require. If there is some point beyond which the cost is too great to justify the claim that a good makes upon me, then it is relative in that respect. Creative good is absolute in this sense for there is no amount of created good opposed to it which can diminish the claim that it makes upon me. The value of the creative source of all good is immeasurable compared to any particular instance of good derived from this source.

Thus in a third way, inseparable from the second, creative good is absolute. It is unlimited in its demands because it is infinite in value. Its worth is incommensurable by any finite quantity of created good. No additive sum of good produced in the past can be any compensation for the blockage of that creativity which is our only hope for the future. And the created good of the past sinks into oblivion when not continuously revitalized by the recurrent working of the creative event.

Fourth, absolute good is unqualified good. There must be no perspective from which its goodness can be modified in any way. Always, from every standpoint, its good must remain unchanged and self-identical, whether from the worm's view or the man's view, whether under the aspect of eternity or under the aspect of time, whether viewed from the standpoint of the beginning or the ending, whether judged by its origin or by its final outcome, whether viewed as means or as end. In respect to created good one can always find some standpoint from which its value disappears or changes; it must be qualified. But in this sense, too, creative good is absolute.

Finally, creative good is absolute in that it is entirely trustworthy. We can be sure that the outcome of its working will always be the best possible under the conditions, even when it may seem to us to be otherwise. Even when it so transforms us and our world that we come to love what now we hate, to serve what now we fight, to seek what now we shun, still we can be sure that what it does is good. Even when its working re-creates our minds and personalities, we can trust it.

We can also be sure that creative good will always be with us. When all other good is destroyed, it springs anew; it will keep going when all else fails. In this dual sense creative good is absolutely trustworthy: it always produces good; it never fails.

A further claim might be made for an absolute good, but this claim cannot apply to the creative event. Neither can

---

[1] "Absolute" in any intelligible sense cannot mean "out of relation." It is relative to conditions, circumstances, organisms, and the like; but its character of goodness does not change when these relations change. Instead of being out of all relations, it is rather the one kind of goodness that, without losing its identity, can enter into all relations. It is good always and everywhere, therefore relative to everything.

it be applied coherently to any other interpretation of the nature of absolute good. This claim is that absolute good means all-powerful good. It means a good that overrules all evil so that in the end everything will come out all right, no matter how long and how great the intervening evils may be. According to neo-orthodoxy, this blissful outcome is postponed to "the end of history," whatever that may mean. There is a transcendent realm, so it is asserted, where perfect and almighty good reigns supreme; but in our world of time and space and matter and history this almighty power of good is only partially regnant. Life may be a valley of frustration, but nothing can prevent ultimate, absolute, and complete regnancy of supreme value, somehow, sometime, somewhere, although the human mind cannot know how this may be.

The claim that any kind of good is almighty cannot be defended. Creative good is not absolute in that sense, but neither is anything else.

. . .

D. T. SUZUKI

The Nature of Zen

D. T. Suzuki (1870–   ) is Professor Emeritus of Buddhist Philosophy at Otani University in Kyoto, Japan. He is the leading interpreter of Zen Buddhism to the West.

INTRODUCTION

Zen in its essence is the art of seeing into the nature of one's own being, and it points the way from bondage to freedom. By making us drink right from the fountain of life, it liberates us from all the yokes under which we finite beings are usually suffering in this world. We can say that Zen liberates all the energies properly and naturally stored in each of us, which are in ordinary circumstances cramped and distorted so that they find no adequate channel for activity.

From D. T. Suzuki, *Essays in Zen Buddhism: First Series* (1927), "Introduction." Reprinted by permission of Grove Press, Inc., and Hutchinson & Co. (Publishers) Ltd.

This body of ours is something like an electric battery in which a mysterious power latently lies. When this power is not properly brought into operation, it either grows mouldy and withers away or is warped and expresses itself abnormally. It is the object of Zen, therefore, to save us from going crazy or being crippled. This is what I mean by freedom, giving free play to all the creative and benevolent impulses inherently lying in our hearts. Generally, we are blind to this fact, that we are in possession of all the necessary faculties that will make us happy and loving towards one another. All the struggles that we see around us come from this ignorance. Zen, therefore, wants us to open a "third eye," as Buddhists call it, to the hitherto undreamed-of region shut away from us through our own ignorance. When the cloud of ignorance disappears, the infinity of the heavens is manifested, where we see for the first time into the nature of our own being. We now know the significance of life, we know that it is not blind striving, nor is it a mere display of brutal forces, but that while we know not definitely what the ultimate purport of life is, there is something in it that makes us feel infinitely blessed in the living of it and remain quite contented with it in all its evolution, without raising questions or entertaining pessimistic doubts.

When we are full of vitality and not yet awakened to the knowledge of life, we cannot comprehend the seriousness of all the conflicts involved in it which are apparently for the moment in a state of quiescence. But sooner or later the time will come when we have to face life squarely and solve its most perplexing and most pressing riddles. Says Confucius, "At fifteen my mind was directed to study, and at thirty I knew where to stand." This is one of the wisest sayings of the Chinese sage. Psychologists will all agree to this statement of his; for, generally speaking, fifteen is about the age youth begins to look around seriously and inquire into the meaning of life. All the spiritual powers until now securely hidden in the subconscious part of the mind break out almost simultaneously. And when this breaking out is too precipitous and violent, the mind may lose its balance more or less permanently; in fact, so many cases of nervous prostration reported during adolescence are chiefly due to this loss of the mental equilibrium. In most cases the effect is not very grave and the crisis may pass without leaving deep marks. But in some characters, either through their inherent tendencies or on account of the influence of environment upon their plastic constitution, the spir-itual awakening stirs them up to the very depths of their personality. This is the time you will be asked to choose between the "Everlasting No" and the "Everlasting Yea." This choosing is what Confucius means by "study"; it is not studying the classics, but deeply delving into the mysteries of life.

Normally, the outcome of the struggle is the "Everlasting Yea," or "Let they will be done"; for life is after all a form of affirmation, however negatively it might be conceived by the pessimists. But we cannot deny the fact that there are many things in this world which will turn our too sensitive minds towards the other direction and make us exclaim with Andreyev in "The Life of Man": "I curse everything that you have given. I curse the day on which I was born. I curse the day on which I shall die. I curse the whole of my life. I fling everything back at your cruel face, senseless Fate! Be accursed, be forever accursed! With my curses I conquer you. What else can you do to me? . . . With my last thought I will shout into your asinine ears: Be accursed, be accursed!" This is a terrible indictment of life, it is a complete negation of life, it is a most dismal picture of the destiny of man on earth. "Leaving no trace" is quite true, for we know nothing of our future except that we all pass away, including the very earth from which we have come. There are certainly things justifying pessimism.

Life, as most of us live it, is suffering. There is no denying the fact. As long as life is a form of struggle, it cannot be anything but pain. Does not a struggle mean the impact of two conflicting forces, each trying to get the upper hand of the other? If the battle is lost, the outcome is death, and death is the fearsomest thing in the world. Even when death is conquered, one is left alone, and the loneliness is sometimes more unbearable than the struggle itself. One may not be conscious of all this, and may go on indulging in those momentary pleasures that are afforded by the senses. But this being unconscious does not in the least alter the facts of life. However insistently the blind may deny the existence of the sun, they cannot annihilate it. The tropical heat will mercilessly scorch them, and if they do not take proper care they will all be wiped away from the surface of the earth.

The Buddha was perfectly right when he propounded his "Fourfold Noble Truth," the first of which is that life is pain. Did not everyone of us come to this world screaming and in a way protesting? To come out into cold and prohibitive surroundings after a soft, warm motherly womb was surely a painful incident, to say the least. Growth is always attended with pain. Teething is more or less a painful process. Puberty is usually accompanied by a mental as well as a physical disturbance. The growth of the organism called society is also marked with painful cataclysms, and we are at present witnessing one of its birth-throes. We may calmly reason and say that this is all inevitable, that inasmuch as every reconstruction means the destruction of the old regime, we cannot help going through a painful operation. But this cold intellectual analysis does not alleviate whatever harrowing feelings we have to undergo. The pain heartlessly inflicted on our nerves is ineradicable. Life is, after all arguing, a painful struggle.

This, however, is providential. For the more you suffer the deeper grows your character, and with the deepening of your character you read the more penetratingly into the secrets of life. All great artists, all great religious leaders, and all great social reformers have come out of the intensest struggles which they fought bravely, quite frequently in tears and with bleeding hearts. Unless you eat your bread in sorrow, you cannot taste of real life. Mencius is right when he says that when Heaven wants to perfect a

great man it tries him in every possible way until he comes out triumphantly from all his painful experiences.

To me Oscar Wilde seems always posing or striving for an effect; he may be a great artist, but there is something in him that turns me away from him. Yet he exclaims in his *De Profundis:* "During the last few months I have, after terrible difficulties and struggles, been able to comprehend some of the lessons hidden in the heart of pain. Clergymen and people who use phrases without wisdom sometimes talk of suffering as a mystery. It is really a revelation. One discerns things one never discerned before. One approaches the whole of history from a different standpoint." You will observe here what sanctifying effects his prison life produced on his character. If he had had to go through a similar trial in the beginning of his career, he might have been able to produce far greater works than those we have of him at present.

We are too ego-centred. The ego-shell in which we live is the hardest thing to outgrow. We seem to carry it all the time from childhood up to the time we finally pass away. We are, however, given many chances to break through this shell, and the first and greatest of them is when we reach adolescence. This is the first time the ego really comes to recognize the "other." I mean the awakening of sexual love. An ego, entire and undivided, now begins to feel a sort of split in itself. Love hitherto dormant deep in his heart lifts its head and causes a great commotion in it. For the love now stirred demands at once the assertion of the ego and its annihilation. Love makes the ego lose itself in the object it loves, and yet at the same time it wants to have the object as its own. This is a contradiction, and a great tragedy of life. This elemental feeling must be one of the divine agencies whereby man is urged to advance in his upward walk. God gives tragedies to perfect man. The greatest bulk of literature ever produced in this world is but the harping on the same string of love, and we never seem to grow weary of it. But this is not the topic we are concerned with here. What I want to emphasize in this connection is this: that through the awakening of love we get a glimpse into the infinity of things, and that this glimpse urges youth to Romanticism or to Rationalism according to his temperament and environment and education.

When the ego-shell is broken and the "other" is taken into its own body, we can say that the ego has denied itself or that the ego has taken its first steps towards the infinite. Religiously, here ensues an intense struggle between the finite and the infinite, between the intellect and a higher power, or, more plainly, between the flesh and the spirit. This is the problem of problems that has driven many a youth into the hands of Satan. When a grown-up man looks back to these youthful days he cannot but feel a sort of shudder going through his entire frame. The struggle to be fought in sincerity may go on up to the age of thirty, when Confucius states that he knew where to stand. The religious consciousness is now fully awakened, and all the possible ways of escaping from the struggle or bringing it to an end are most earnestly sought in every direction. Books are read, lectures are attended, sermons are greedily taken in, and various religious exercises or disciplines are tried. And naturally Zen too comes to be inquired into.

How does Zen solve the problem of problems?

In the first place, Zen proposes its solution by directly appealing to facts of personal experience and not to book-knowledge. The nature of one's own being where apparently rages the struggle between the finite and the infinite is to be grasped by a higher faculty than the intellect. For Zen says it is the latter that first made us raise the question which it could not answer by itself, and that therefore it is to be put aside to make room for something higher and more enlightening. For the intellect has a peculiarly disquieting quality in it. Though it raises questions enough to disturb the serenity of the mind, it is too frequently unable to give satisfactory answers to them. It upsets the blissful peace of ignorance and yet it does not restore the former state of things by offering something else. Because it points out ignorance, it is often considered illuminating, whereas the fact is that it disturbs, not necessarily always bringing light on its path. It is not final, it waits for something higher than itself for the solution of all the questions it will raise regardless of consequences. If it were able to bring a new order into the disturbance and settle it once for all, there would have been no need for philosophy after it had been first systematized by a great thinker, by an Aristotle or by a Hegel. But the history of thought proves that each new structure raised by a man of extraordinary intellect is sure to be pulled down by the succeeding ones. This constant pulling down and building up is all right as far as philosophy itself is concerned; for the inherent nature of the intellect, as I take it, demands it and we cannot put a stop to the progress of philosophical inquiries any more than to our breathing. But when it comes to the question of life itself we cannot wait for the ultimate solution to be offered by the intellect, even if it could do so. We cannot suspend even for a moment our life-activity for philosophy to unravel its mysteries. Let the mysteries remain as they are, but live we must. The hungry cannot wait until a complete analysis of food is obtained and the nourishing value of each element is determined. For the dead the scientific knowledge of food will be of no use whatever. Zen therefore does not rely on the intellect for the solution of its deepest problems.

By personal experience it is meant to get at the fact at first hand and not through any intermediary, whatever this may be. Its favourite analogy is: to point at the moon a finger is needed, but woe to those who take the finger for the moon; a basket is welcome to carry our fish home, but when the fish are safely on the table why should we eternally bother ourselves with the basket? Here stands the fact, and let us grasp it with the naked hands lest it should slip away —this is what Zen proposes to do. As nature abhors a vacuum, Zen abhors anything coming between the fact and ourselves. According to Zen there is no struggle in the fact itself such as between the finite and the infinite, between the flesh and the spirit. These are idle distinctions fictitiously designed by the intellect for its own interest. Those who take them too seriously or those who try to read them into the very fact of life are those who take the finger for the moon. When we are hungry we eat; when we are sleepy we lay ourselves down; and where does the infinite or the finite come in here? Are not we complete in ourselves and each in himself? Life as it is lived suffices. It is only when the disquieting intellect steps in and tries to murder it that we stop to live and imagine ourselves to be short of or in something. Let the intellect alone, it has its usefulness in its proper sphere, but let it not interfere with the flowing of the life-stream. If you are at all tempted to look into it, do so while letting it flow. The fact of flowing must under no circumstances be arrested or meddled with; for the moment your hands are dipped into it, its transparency is disturbed, it ceases to reflect your image which you have had from the very beginning and will continue to have to the end of time.

Almost corresponding to the "Four Maxims" of the Nichiren Sect, Zen has its own four statements:

A special transmission outside the Scriptures;
No dependence upon words and letters;
Direct pointing to the soul of man;
Seeing into one's nature and the attainment of Buddhahood.

This sums up all that is claimed by Zen as religion. Of course we must not forget that there is a historical background to this bold pronunciamento. At the time of the introduction of Zen into China, most of the Buddhists were addicted to the discussion of highly metaphysical questions, or satisfied with the merely observing of the ethical precepts laid down by the Buddha or with the leading of a lethargic life entirely absorbed in the contemplation of the evanescence of things worldly. They all missed apprehending the great fact of live itself, which flows altogether outside of these vain exercises of the intellect or of the imagination. Bodhi-Dharma and his successors recognized this pitiful state of affairs. Hence their proclamation of "The Four Great Statements" of Zen as above cited. In a word, they mean that Zen has its own way of pointing to the nature of one's own being, and that when this is done one attains to Buddhahood, in which all the contradictions and disturbances caused by the intellect are entirely harmonized in a unity of higher order.

For this reason Zen never explains but indicates, it does not appeal to circumlocution, nor does it generalize. It always deals with facts, concrete and tangible. Logically considered, Zen may be full of contradictions and repetitions. But as it stands above all things, it goes serenely on its own way. As a Zen master aptly puts it, "carrying his home-made cane on the shoulder, he goes right on among the mountains one rising above another."

It does not challenge logic, it simply walks its path of facts, leaving all the rest to their own fates. It is only when logic neglecting its proper functions tries to step into the track of Zen that it loudly proclaims its principles and forcibly drives out the intruder. Zen is not an enemy of anything. There is no reason why it should antagonize the intellect which may sometimes be utilized for the cause of Zen itself. To show some examples of Zen's direct dealing with the fundamental facts of existence, the following are selected:

Rinzai [1] (Lin-chi) once delivered a sermon, saying: "Over a mass of reddish flesh there sits a true man who has no title; he is all the time coming in and out from your sense-organs. If you have not yet testified to the fact, Look! Look!" A monk came forward and asked, "Who is this true man of no title?" Rinzai came right down from his straw chair and taking hold of the monk exclaimed: "Speak! Speak!" The monk remained irresolute, not knowing what to say, whereupon the master, letting him go, remarked, "What worthless stuff is this true man of no title!" Rinzai then went straight back to his room.

Rinzai was noted for his "rough" and direct treatment of his disciples. He never liked those roundabout dealings which generally characterized the methods of a lukewarm master. He must have got this directness from his own teacher Obaku (Huang-nieh), by whom he was struck three times for asking what the fundamental principle of Buddhism was. It goes without saying that Zen has nothing to do with mere striking or roughly shaking the questioner. If you take this as constituting the essentials of Zen, you would commit the same gross error as one who took the finger for the moon.

As in everything else, but most particularly in Zen, all its outward manifestations or demonstrations must never be regarded as final. They just indicate the way where to look for the facts. Therefore these indicators are important, we cannot do well without them. But once caught in them, which are like entangling meshes, we are doomed; for Zen can never be comprehended. Some may think Zen is always trying to catch you in the net of logic or by the snare of words. If you once slip your steps, you are bound for eternal damnation, you will never get to freedom, for which your hearts are so burning. Therefore, Rinzai grasps with his naked hands what is directly presented to us all. If a third eye of ours is opened undimmed, we shall know in a most unmistakable manner where Rinzai is driving us. We have first of all to get into the very spirit of the master and interview the inner man right there. No amount of wordy explanations will ever lead us into the nature of our own selves. The more you explain, the further it runs away from you. It is like trying to get hold of your own shadow. You run after it and it runs with you at the identical rate of speed. When you realize it, you read deep into the spirit of Rinzai or Obaku, and their real kindheartedness will begin to be appreciated.

Ummon [2] (Yun-men) was another great master of Zen at the end of the T'ang dynasty. He had to lose one of his legs in order to get an insight into the life-principle from which the whole universe takes rise, including his own humble existence. He had to visit his teacher Bokuju (Mu-chou), who was a senior disciple of Rinzai under Obaku, three times before he was admitted to see him. The master asked, "Who are you?" "I am Bun-yen (Wen-yen)," answered the

---

[1] The founder of the Rinzai School of Zen Buddhism, died 867.

[2] The founder of the Ummon School of Zen Buddhism, died 996.

monk. (Bun-yen was his name, while Ummon was the name of the monastery where he was settled later.) When the truth-seeking monk was allowed to go inside the gate, the master took hold of him by the chest and demanded: "Speak! Speak!" Ummon hesitated, whereupon the master pushed him out of the gate, saying, "Oh, you good-for-nothing fellow!" While the gate was hastily shut, one of Ummon's legs was caught and broken. The intense pain resulting from this apparently awakened the poor fellow to the greatest fact of life. He was no more a solicitous, pity-begging monk; the realization now gained paid more than enough for the loss of his leg. He was not, however, a solitary instance in this respect, there were many such in the history of Zen who were willing to sacrifice a part of the body for the truth. Says Confucius, "If a man understands the Tao in the morning, it is well with him even when he dies in the evening." Some would feel indeed that truth is of more value than mere living, mere vegetative or animal living. But in the world, alas, there are so many living corpses wallowing in the mud of ignorance and sensuality.

This is where Zen is most difficult to understand. Why this sarcastic vituperation? Why this seeming heartlessness? What fault had Ummon to deserve the loss of his leg? He was a poor truth-seeking monk, earnestly anxious to get enlightenment from the master. Was it really necessary for the latter from his way of understanding Zen to shut him out three times, and when the gate was half opened to close it again so violently, so inhumanly? Was this the truth of Buddhism Ummon was so eager to get? But the outcome of all this singularly was what was desired by both of them. As to the master, he was satisfied to see the disciple attain an insight into the secrets of his being; and as regards the disciple he was most grateful for all that was done

to him. Evidently, Zen is the most irrational, inconceivable thing in the world. And this is why I said before that Zen was not subject to logical analysis or to intellectual treatment. It must be directly and personally experienced by each of us in his inner spirit. Just as two stainless mirrors reflect each other, the fact and our own spirits must stand facing each other with no intervening agents. When this is done we are able to seize upon the living, pulsating fact itself.

Freedom is an empty word until then. The first object was to escape the bondage in which all finite beings find themselves, but if we do not cut asunder the very chain of ignorance with which we are bound hands and feet, where shall we look for deliverance? And this chain of ignorance is wrought of nothing else but the intellect and sensuous infatuation, which cling tightly to every thought we may have, to every feeling we may entertain. They are hard to get rid of, they are like wet clothes as is aptly expressed by the Zen masters. "We are born free and equal." Whatever this may mean socially or politically, Zen maintains that it is absolutely true in the spiritual domain, and that all the fetters and manacles we seem to be carrying about ourselves are put on later through ignorance of the true condition of existence. All the treatments, sometimes literary and sometimes physical, which are most liberally and kindheartedly given by the masters to inquiring souls, are intended to get them back to the original state of freedom. And this is never really realized until we once personally experience it through our own efforts, independent of any ideational representation. The ultimate standpoint of Zen, therefore, is that we have been led astray through ignorance to find a split in our own being, that there was from the very beginning no need for a struggle between the finite and the infinite, that the peace we are seeking so eagerly after has been there all the time.

Sotoba (Su Tung-p'o), the noted Chinese poet and statesman, expresses the idea in the following verse:

Misty rain on Mount Lu,
And waves surging in Che-chiang;
When you have not yet been there,
Many a regret surely you have;
But once there and homeward you wend,
How matter-of-fact things look!
Misty rain on Mount Lu,
And waves surging in Che-chiang.

This is what is also asserted by Seigen Ishin (Ch'ing-yuan Wei-hsin), according to whom, "Before a man studies Zen, to him mountains are mountains and waters are waters; after he gets an insight into the truth of Zen through the instruction of a good master, mountains to him are not mountains and waters are not waters; but after this when he really attains to the abode of rest, mountains are once more mountains and waters are waters."

Bokuju (Mu-chou), who lived in the latter half of the ninth century, was once asked, "We have to dress and eat every day, and how can we escape from all that?" The master replied, "We dress, we eat." "I do not understand you," said the questioner. "If you don't understand put your dress on and eat your food."

Zen always deals in concrete facts and does not indulge in generalization. And I do not wish to add unnecessary legs to the painted snake, but if I try to waste my philosophical comments on Bokuju, I may say this. We are all finite, we cannot live out of time and space; inasmuch as we are earth-created, there is no way to grasp the infinite, how can we deliver ourselves from the limitations of existence? This is perhaps the idea put in the first question of the monk, to which the master replies: Salvation must be sought in the finite itself, there is nothing infinite apart from finite things; if you seek something transcendental, that will cut you off from this world of relativity, which is the same thing as the annihilation of yourself. You do not want salvation at the cost of your own existence. If so, drink and eat, and find your way of freedom in this drinking and eating. This was too much for the questioner, who, therefore, confessed himself as not understanding the meaning of the master. Therefore, the latter continued: Whether you understand or not, just the same go on living in the finite, with the finite; for you die if you stop eating and keeping yourself warm on account of your aspiration for the infinite. No matter how you struggle, Nirvana is to be sought in the midst of Samsara (birth-and-death). Whether an enlightened Zen master or an ignoramus of the first degree, neither can escape the so-called laws of nature. When the stomach is empty, both are hungry; when it snows, both have to put on an extra flannel. I do not, however, mean that they are both material existences, but they are what they are, regardless of their conditions of spiritual development. As the Buddhist scriptures have it, the darkness of the cave itself turns into enlightenment when a torch of spiritual insight burns. It is not that a thing called darkness is first taken out and another thing known by the name of enlightenment is carried in later, but that enlightenment and darkness are substantially one and the same thing from the very beginning; the change from the one to the other has taken place only inwardly or subjectively. Therefore the finite is the infinite, and *vice versa*. These are not two separate things, though we are compelled to conceive them so, intellectually. This is the idea, logically interpreted, perhaps contained in Bokuju's answer given to the monk. The mistake consists in our splitting into two what is really and absolutely one. Is not life one as we live it, which we cut to pieces by recklessly applying the murderous knife of intellectual surgery?

On being requested by the monks to deliver a sermon, Hyakujo Nehan (Pai-chang Nieh-p'an) told them to work on the farm, after which he would give them a talk on the great subject of Buddhism. They did as they were told, and came to the master for a sermon, when the latter, without saying a word, merely extended his open arms towards the monks. Perhaps there is after all nothing mysterious in Zen. Everything is open to your full view. If you eat your food and keep yourself cleanly dressed and work on the farm to raise your rice or vegetables, you are doing all that is required of you on this earth, and the infinite is realized in you. How realized? When Bokuju was asked what Zen was he recited a Sanskrit phrase from a Sutra, "Mahaprajnaparamita!" The inquirer acknowledged his inability to understand the purport of the strange phrase, and the master put a comment on it, saying:

My robe is all worn out after so many years' usage.
And parts of it in shreds loosely hanging have been blown away to the clouds.

Is the infinite after all such a poverty-stricken mendicant?

Whatever this is, there is one thing in this connection which we can never afford to lose sight of—that is, the peace of poverty (for peace is only possible in poverty) is obtained after a fierce battle fought with the entire strength of your personality. A contentment gleaned from idleness or from a *laissez-faire* attitude of mind is a thing most to be abhorred. There is no Zen in this, but sloth and mere vegetation. The battle must rage in its full vigour and masculinity. Without it, whatever peace that obtains is a simulacrum, and it has no deep foundation, the first storm it may encounter will crush it to the ground. Zen is quite emphatic in this. Certainly, the moral virility to be found in Zen, apart from its mystic flight, comes from the fighting of the battle of life courageously and undauntedly.

From the ethical point of view, therefore, Zen may be considered a discipline aiming at the reconstruction of character. Our ordinary life only touches the fringe of personality, it does not cause a commotion in the deepest parts of the soul. Even when the religious consciousness is awakened, most of us lightly pass over it so as to leave no marks of a bitter fighting on the soul. We are thus made to live on the superficiality of things. We may be clever, bright, and all that, but what we produce lacks depth, sincerity, and does not appeal to the inmost feelings. Some are utterly unable to create anything except makeshifts or imitations betraying their shallowness of character and want of spiritual experience. While Zen is primarily religious, it also moulds our moral character. It may be better to say that a deep spiritual experience is bound to effect a change in the moral structure of one's personality.

How is this so?

The truth of Zen is such that when we want to comprehend it penetratingly we have to go through with a great struggle, sometimes very long and exacting constant vigilance. To be disciplined in Zen is no easy task. A Zen master once remarked that the life of a monk can be attained only by a man of great moral strength, and that even a minister of the state cannot expect to become a successful monk. (Let us remark here that in China to be a minister of the state was considered to be the greatest achievement a man could ever hope for in this world.) Not that a monkish life requires the austere practice of asceticism, but that it implies the elevation of one's spiritual powers to their highest notch. All the utterances or activities of the great Zen masters have come from this elevation. They are not intended to be enigmatic or driving us to confusion.

They are the overflowing of a soul filled with deep experiences. Therefore, unless we are ourselves elevated to the same height as the masters, we cannot gain the same commanding views of life. Says Ruskin: "And be sure also, if the author is worth anything, that you will not get at his meaning all at once—nay, that at his whole meaning you will not for a long time arrive in any wise. Not that he does not say what he means, and in strong words, too; but he cannot say it all and what is more strange, will not, but in a hidden way and in parable, in order that he may be sure you want it. I cannot see quite the reason of this, nor analyse that cruel reticence in the breasts of wise men which makes them always hide their deeper thought. They do not give it you by way of help, but of reward, and will make themselves sure that you deserve it before they allow you to reach it." And this key to the royal treasury of wisdom is given us only after patient and painful moral struggle.

The mind is ordinarily chock full with all kinds of intellectual nonsense and passional rubbish. They are of course useful in their own ways in our daily life. There is no denying that. But it is chiefly because of these accumulations that we are made miserable and groan under the feeling of bondage. Each time we want to make a movement, they fetter us, they choke us, and cast a heavy veil over our spiritual horizon. We feel as if we are constantly living under restraint. We long for naturalness and freedom, yet we do not seem to attain them. The Zen masters know this, for they have gone through with the same experiences once. They want to have us get rid of all these wearisome burdens which we really do not have to carry in order to live a life of truth and enlightenment. Thus they utter a few words and demonstrate with action that, when rightly comprehended, will deliver us from the oppression and tyranny of these intel-lectual accumulations. But the comprehension does not come to us so easily. Being so long accustomed to the oppression, the mental inertia becomes hard to remove. In fact it has gone down deep into the roots of our own being, and the whole structure of personality is to be overturned. The process of reconstruction is stained with tears and blood. But the height the great masters have climbed cannot otherwise be reached; the truth of Zen can never be attained unless it is attacked with the full force of person-ality. The passage is strewn with thistles and brambles, and the climb is slippery in the extreme. It is no pastime but the most serious task in life; no idlers will ever dare attempt it. It is indeed a moral anvil on which your character is ham-mered and hammered. To the question, "What is Zen?" a master gave this answer, "Boiling oil over a blazing fire." This scorching experience we have to go through with before Zen smiles on us and says, "Here is your home."

One of these utterances by the Zen masters that will stir a revolution in our minds is this: Hokoji (P'ang-yun), form-erly a Confucian, asked Baso (Ma-tsu, −788), "What kind of man is he who does not keep company with any thing?" Replied the master, "I will tell you when you have swallowed up in one draught all the waters in the West River." What an irrelevant reply to the most serious question one can ever raise in the history of thought! It sounds almost sacrilegious when we know how many souls there are who go down under the weight of this question. But Baso's earnestness leaves no room for doubt, as is quite well known to all the students of Zen. In fact, the rise of Zen after the sixth patriarch, Hui-neng, was due to the brilliant career of Baso, under whom there arose more than eighty fully qualified masters, and Hokoji, who was one of the foremost lay dis-ciples of Zen, earned a well-deserved reputation as the Vimalakirti of Chinese

Buddhism. A talk between two such veteran Zen masters could not be an idle sport. However easy and even careless it may appear, there is hidden in it a most precious gem in the literature of Zen. We do not know how many students of Zen were made to sweat and cry in tears because of the inscrutability of this statement of Baso's.

To give another instance: a monk asked the master Shin of Chosa (Chang-sha Ching-ch'en), "Where has Nansen (Nan-ch'uan) gone after his death?" Replied the master, "When Sekito (Shih-tou) was still in the order of young novitiates, he saw the sixth patriarch." "I am not asking about the young novitiate. What I wish to know is, where is Nansen gone after his death?" "As to that," said the master, "it makes one think."

The immortality of the soul is another big question. The history of religion is built upon this one question, one may almost say. Everybody wants to know about life after death. Where do we go when we pass away from this earth? Is there really another life? or is the end of this the end of all? While there may be many who do not worry themselves as to the ultimate significance of the solitary, "companionless" One, there are none perhaps who have not once at least in their lives asked themselves concerning their destiny after death. Whether Sekito when young saw the sixth patriarch or not does not seem to have any inherent connection with the departure of Nansen. The latter was the teacher of Chosa, and naturally the monk asked him whither the teacher finally passed. Chosa's answer is no answer, judged by the ordinary rules of logic. Hence the second question, but still a sort of equivocation from the lips of the master. What does this "making one think" explain? From this it is apparent that Zen is one thing and logic another. When we fail to make this distinction and expect of Zen to give us something logically consistent and intellectually illuminating, we altogether misinterpret the signification of Zen. Did I not state in the beginning that Zen deals with facts and not with generalizations? And this is the very point where Zen goes straight down to the foundations of personality. The intellect ordinarily does not lead us there, for we do not live in the intellect, but in the will. Brother Lawrence speaks the truth when he says (*The Practice of the Presence of God*), "that we ought to make a great difference between the acts of the understanding and those of the will: that the first were comparatively of little value, and the others, all."

Zen literature is all brim full of such statements, which seem to have been uttered so casually, so innocently, but those who actually know what Zen is will testify to the fact that all these utterances dropped so naturally from the lips of the masters are like deadly poisons, that when they are once taken in they cause such a violent pain as to make one's intestines wriggle nine times and more, as the Chinese would express it. But it is only after such pain and turbulence that all the internal impurities are purged and one is born with quite a new outlook on life. It is strange that Zen grows intelligible when these mental struggles are gone through. But the fact is that Zen is an experience actual and personal, and not a knowledge to be gained by analysis or comparison. "Do not talk poetry except to a poet; only the sick know how to sympathize with the sick." This explains the whole situation. Our minds are to be so matured as to be in tune with those of the masters. Let this be accomplished, and when one string is struck, the other will inevitably respond. Harmonious notes always result from the sympathetic resonance of two or more chords. And what Zen does for us is to prepare our minds to be yielding and appreciative recipients of old masters. In other words, psychologically Zen releases whatever energies we may have in store, of which we are not conscious in ordinary circumstances.

Some say that Zen is self-suggestion. But this does not explain anything. When the word "Yamato-damashi" is mentioned it seems to awaken in most Japanese a fervent patriotic passion. The children are taught to respect the flag of the rising sun, and when the soldiers come in front of the regimental colours they involuntarily salute. When a boy is reproached for not acting like a little samurai, and with disgracing the name of his ancestor, he at once musters his courage and will resist temptations. All these ideas are energy-releasing ideas for the Japanese, and this release, according to some psychologists, is self-suggestion. Social conventions and imitative instincts may also be regarded as self-suggestions. So is moral discipline. An example is given to the students to follow or imitate it. The idea gradually takes root in them through suggestion, and they finally come to act as if it were their own. Self-suggestion is a barren theory, it does not explain anything. When they say that Zen is self-suggestion, do we get any clearer idea of Zen? Some think it scientific to call certain phenomena by a term newly come into fashion, and rest satisfied with it as if they disposed of them in an illuminating way. The study of Zen must be taken up by the profounder psychologists.

Some think that there is still an unknown region in our consciousness which has not yet been thoroughly and systematically explored. It is sometimes called the Unconscious or the Subconscious. This is a territory filled with dark images, and naturally most scientists are afraid of treading upon it. But this must not be taken as denying the fact of its existence. Just as our ordinary field of consciousness is filled with all possible kinds of images, beneficial and harmful,

systematic and confusing, clear and obscure, forcefully assertive and weakly fading; so is the Subconscious a storehouse of every form of occultism or mysticism, understanding by the term all that is known as latent or abnormal or psychic or spiritualistic. The power to see into the nature of one's own being may lie also hidden there, and what Zen awakens in our consciousness may be that. At any rate the master speak figuratively of the opening of a third eye. "Satori" is the popular name given to this opening or awakening.

How is this to be effected?

By meditating on those utterances or actions that are directly poured out from the inner region undimmed by the intellect or the imagination, and that are calculated successfully to exterminate all the turmoils arising from ignorance and confusion.[3]

It may be interesting to readers in this connection to get acquainted with some of the methods used by the masters in order to open the spiritual eye of the disciple. It is natural that they frequently make use of the various religious insignia which they carry when going out to the Hall of the Dharma. Such are generally the "hossu,"[4] "shippe,"[5] "nyoi,"[6] or "shujvo" (a staff). The last-mentioned seems to have been the most favourite instrument used in the demonstration of the truth of Zen. Let me cite some examples of its use.

According to Ye-ryo (Hui-leng), of Chokei (Chang-ch'ing), "when one knows what that staff is, one's life study of Zen comes to an end." This reminds us of Tennyson's flower in the crannied wall.

---

[3] Zen has its own way of practising meditation. Zen has nothing to do with mere quietism or losing oneself in trance.

[4] Originally a mosquito driver in India.

[5] A bamboo stick a few feet long.

[6] Also a stick or baton fancifully shaped and made of all kinds of material. It means literally "as one wishes or thinks" (cinta, in Sanskrit).

For when we understand the reason of the staff, we know "what God and man is"; that is to say, we get an insight into the nature of our own being, and this insight finally puts a stop to all the doubts and hankerings that have upset our mental tranquillity. The significance of the staff in Zen can thus readily be comprehended.

Ye-sei (Hui-ch'ing), of Basho (Pa-chiao), probably of the tenth century, once made the following declaration: "When you have a staff, I will give you one; when you have none, I will take it away from you." This is one of the most characteristic statements of Zen, but later Bokitsu (Mu-chi), of Daiyi (Ta-wei), was bold enough to challenge this by saying what directly contradicts it, viz.: "As to myself, I differ from him. When you have a staff, I will take it away from you; and when you have none, I will give you one. This is my statement. Can you make use of the staff? or can you not? If you can, Tokusan (Te-shan) will be your vanguard and Rinzai (Lin-chi) your rear-guard. But if you cannot, let it be restored to its original master."

A monk approached Bokuju and said, "What is the statement surpassing [the wisdom of] all Buddhas and Patriarchs?" The master instantly held forth his staff before the congregation, and said, "I call this a staff, and what do you call it?" The monk who asked the question uttered not a word. The master holding it out again said, "A statement surpassing [the wisdom of] all Buddhas and Patriarchs —was that not your question, O monk?"

Those who carelessly go over such remarks as Bokuju's may regard them as quite nonsensical. Whether the stick is called a staff or not it does not seem to matter very much, as far as the divine wisdom surpassing the limits of our knowledge is concerned. But the one made by Ummon, another great master of Zen, is perhaps more accessible. He also once lifted his staff before a congre-gation and remarked, "In the scriptures we read that the ignorant take this for a real thing, the Hinayanists resolve it into a nonentity, the Pratyekabuddhas regard it as a hallucination, while the Bod-hisattvas admit its apparent reality, which is, however, essentially empty." "But," continued the master, "monks, you simply call it a staff when you see one. Walk or sit as you will, but do not stand irreso-lute."

The same old insignificant staff and yet more mystical statements from Ummon. One day his announcement was, "My staff has turned into a dragon, and it has swallowed up the whole universe; where would the great earth with its mountains and rivers be?" On another occasion, Ummon, quoting an ancient Buddhist philosopher who said "Knock at the emptiness of space and you hear a voice; strike a piece of wood and there is no sound," took out his staff and, striking space, cried, "Oh, how it hurts!" Then tapping at the board, he asked, "Any noise?" A monk responded, "Yes, there is a noise." Thereupon the master exclaimed, "Oh you ignoramus!"

If I go on like this there will be no end. So I stop, but expect some of you to ask me the following questions: "Have these utterances anything to do with one's seeing into the nature of one's being? Is there any relationship possible between those apparently nonsensical talks about the staff and the all-important problem of the reality of life?"

In answer I append these two passages, one from Jimyo (Tz'u-ming) and the other from Yengo (Yuan-wu): In one of his sermons, Jimyo said: "As soon as one particle of dust is raised, the great earth manifests itself there in its entirety. In one lion are revealed millions of lions, and in millions of lions is revealed one lion. Thousands and thousands of them there are indeed, but know ye just one, one only." So saying he lifted up his staff, and continued, "Here is my own staff, and where is that one lion?" He set the staff down, and left the pulpit.

In the *Hekigan* (Pi-yen-lu), Yengo expresses the same idea in his introductory remark to the "one-finger Zen" of Gutei (*Chuh-chih i chih t'ou ch'an*):

"One particle of dust is raised and the great earth lies therein; one flower blooms and the universe rises with it. But where should our eye be fixed when the dust is not yet stirred and the flower has not yet bloomed? Therefore, it is said that, like cutting a bundle of thread, one cut cuts all asunder; again, like dyeing a bundle of thread, one dyeing dyes all in the same colour. Now yourself get out of all the entangling relations and rip them up to pieces, but do not lose track of your inner treasure; for it is through this that the high and the low universally responding and the advanced and the backward making no distinction, each manifests itself in full perfection."

SUGGESTIONS FOR FURTHER READING

Various symbolic interpretations of religious belief can be found in W. T. Stace, *Time and Eternity* (Princeton: Princeton Univ. Press, 1952); W. M. Urban, *Language and Reality* (New York: Macmillan, 1939); Philip Wheelwright, *The Burning Fountain* (Bloomington: Indiana Univ. Press, 1954); and Edwin Bevan, *Symbolism and Belief* (Boston: Beacon Press, 1957).

For attempts at a naturalistic reconstruction of religion see Ludwig Feuerbach, *The Essence of Christianity,* George Eliot, tr. (New York: Harper, 1957); E. S. Ames, *Religion* (New York: Holt, 1929); John Dewey, *A Common Faith* (New Haven: Yale Univ. Press, 1934); Erich Fromm, *Psychoanalysis and Religion* (London: Victor Gollancz, 1951); and Julian Huxley, *Religion Without Revelation* (New York: New American Library, 1958).

For Zen Buddhism, in addition to Suzuki's *Essays,* see A. W. Watts, *The Spirit of Zen* (London: John Murray, 1936).

INDEX

A

Absolutism, 326; and religious belief, 446-51

Adaptation, and teleological argument, 82-83. *See also* Evolutionary theory, Darwinian

Aesthetic value, and theism, 75-78

Agnosticism, 430; James's criticism of, 446-51; Kant on, 357

Alacoque, Margaret Mary, 143

Alexander the Great, 414

Al-Ghazzali, 137-38

Amiel, H. F., 133

Analogy, doctrine of, 223

Analytical philosophy, 209, 275; and proofs of God, 106-15. *See also* Logical positivism

Anselm, Saint, 18, 26, 108; definition of God, 323, 324; ontological argument of, 26-28

Apostle's Creed, 340

Aquinas, Saint Thomas, 18-21, 29, 73, 166, 170, 321, 322, 390, 429, 432; Copleston on, 31-38; and existence of soul, 345-47, 350-52; five arguments for God's existence, 29-30, 40-41, 106, 107; and im-

mortality, 340; on reason and revelation, 395-402. *See also* Thomism

Argument from design, 164. *See also* God, existence of: teleological argument

Aristotle, 47-48, 90, 347; and Aquinas' philosophy, 29-30, 31, 38; concept of "unmoved mover," 40; on truth and reason, 395, 396, 397, 399

Arnold, Matthew, 3, 10, 88

Art and religion, 508; Comte on, 552, 556, 560-61; similarity of, 569

Assertions, religious: as explanations, 279, 281, 281-82; logical nature of, 275-94; meaningfulness of, 276-77, 283. *See also* Beliefs, religious; Logical positivism; Theism

Athanasian Creed, 539, 540

Atheism, 321, 430; logical analysis of, 325, 326, 328, 329

Augustine, Saint, 321, 348, 352, 401; on evil, 242

Authoritativeness, of religious belief, 288, 291

Awefulness, 192-96

Ayer, A. J., 224

Empirical tests: for objective existence, 224-27; for religious experience, 119, 123-24. *See also* Verifiability

Empiricism: and Aquinas' proof of God's existence, 33-34; and contemporary theology, 68; and religious belief, 446-51; and teleological argument, 83. *See also* Logical positivism

Engels, Friedrich, 314, 314n, 315-19

Energy (or Urgency), 198

Epicurus, 41

Epistemological argument, 70-71

Ethics. *See* Morality

Euclid, 322, 404

Evans, T. S., 88

Evil, problem of, 221-22, 229-40, 241-59, 280, 331-32; and free will, 245-48; and general laws of nature, 237-38; and man's limitations, 238-39; moral, 245-52; and moral choice, 245-48; physical, 253-56; and pleasure-pain principle, 237; privation theory of, 242-43; and world order, 239, 244

Evolutionary theory, Darwinian, 87, 494-95, 503, 507, 514, 515; and teleological argument, 21-22, 71-74

Existence, concept of, 17, 18

Existentialism, 435

Experience, religious, 117-220; argument from widespread occurrence, 123, 145; causal conditions of, 165; and cognition, 175-77, 182-83, 209-19; delusive, 167, 183; as descriptions of objective reality, 185-88; emotions in, 189-208; and existence of God, 164-72, 174-82; and pathological states, 119, 121-22; psychology of, 125, 164-65; as subjective accounts, 173-85; and traditional beliefs, 166-67; and use of drugs, 122, 130-32; validity of, 165, 184; veridical, 165, 183; verifiability of, 119, 123-24. *See also* Delusion; Mysticism

Extrasensory perception, 377, 379-82. *See also* Psychic phenomena

F

Faith, 12-13, 15, 258-59, 392, 429-91; as alternative to logic, 280; Aquinas on, 402; Christian, 421-24; of empiricist vs. absolutist, 446-51; vs. logic, 282-83; and morality, 451-55; and reason, 403-08; and revelation, 258-59; sources of, 484-86; as subjective truth, 456-81; symbols of, 486-91; as "ultimate concern," 481-91. *See also* Miracle; Revelation

Faith-state, 149, 152, 160

Farmer, H. H., 173, 175, 176

Farrer, A. M., 283n, 286

Fascination, 202-08

Ferm, Vergilius, 362n

Fichte, Johann Gottlieb, 198

Flew, Antony, 275; on immortality, 343, 344; on immortality and psychic phenomena, 371-87; on theism, 224, 225, 275-77, 281-83

Frazer, J. G., 2

Free will, 2; and moral choice, 245-48

Freud, Sigmund, 296; on ego and superego, 483; on infantile omnipotence, 504-05; on mystical experience, 120; theory of religion, 227-29, 296-311

Fromm, Eric, 508n

G

Galileo, 53

Gasking, D. A. T., 106n

Gaunilon, 18

Geddes, Patrick, 517

Gersonides, 322

Gilson, Etienne, 398n

Glasgow, W. D., 182

God: alternative conceptions of, 320-37; apprehended in parables, 291; attributes of, 233, 235, 323-27; as cultural entity, 506-10; ethical nature of, 331-32, 337; and human purpose, 83-85; and immortality, 362-63; limitedness of, 223, 324-37; moral attributes of, 222-23, 232-36, 262-66; and moral consciousness, 86-93; natural attributes of, 261-62; perfection of, 322, 327-29, 337; as presupposition for morality, 25-26, 270-71; and problem of evil, 221-22, 229-40, 241-59, 282; traditional concepts of, 322, 323; unbound by laws of nature, 124-25. *See also* Experience, religious; Revelation

God, existence of, 17-115; aesthetic argument for, 75-78; Aquinas on, 29-30; argument from design, 164; argument from ethics, 164; and authority of Christ, 288, 291; contemporary critique of arguments for, 105-15; contemporary summary of arguments for, 39-48; cosmological argument for, 18-21, 39-44; epistemological argument for, 70-71; and immortality, 362-63; Kant's arguments against proofs of, 95-103; and mystical experience, 164-72, 174-82; ontological argument for, 17-18, 20, 26-28; teleological argument for, 21-24, 48-67, 68-86. *See also* Faith; Experience, religious

Goethe, Johann Wilhelm von, 198, 208, 557

Greeks: idea of immortality, 354; religious tradition of, 590

Gulshan-Râz, 147

Gurney, Edmund, 163, 373, 524, 536

H

Haldane, John, 87

Haldane, R. B., 87

Happiness, as goal of Christianity, 457-58
Hare, R. M., 226, 277-79
Harrison, Frederic, 524
Hartmann, Edouard von, 87
Hartshorne, Charles, 18, 223, 228, 229, 320; on alternative conceptions to God, 320-37
Hawkins, D. J. B., 110*n*
Hebrew tradition, 579, 590; idea of immortality, 354. *See also* Judaeo-Christian tradition; Judaism
Hedonism, 245
Hegel, G. W. F., 18, 131*n*, 145, 348
Heiberg, J. L., 462
Henderson, Alexander, 73
Herodotus, 416
Hesiod, 67
Hick, John, 125, 209-19, 226
Hilary, Saint, 402
Hinduism, 7, 321, 322; and mystical experience, 136-37, 147
Hinton, Charles H., 448
Hobbes, Thomas, 261*n*
Hodgson, Leonard, 162
Holbach, Baron P. H. D. d', 125, 222, 223, 229, 260; on theism, 260-75
Home, D. D., 531
Hooker, Thomas, 566
Human Predicament, 591-93, 599-602
Humanism, 9
Hume, David, 19, 21, 36, 42, 48, 366; on evil, 229-40, 254, 320, 329, 332; on miracles, 391-92, 408-19; and moral goodness, 47-48; teleological argument of, 48-67, 112-15
Huxley, Julian, 501; on conflict of science and religion, 494, 496, 499-500, 501-10; naturalistic version of Trinity, 548
Huxley, Thomas, 79-80
Huxley, T. H., 445, 446, 501, 524
Hyslop, James Hervey, 162

I

Identification, feelings of, 197-98
Ideology, 311-19; class interest of, 317-19; as conscious process, 314; of Medieval Church, 228, 313, 317; and morality, 312, 315; as process of inversion, 314-17; as reflection of socioeconomic relations, 311-13; spontaneous character of, 313-14. *See also* Illusion
Ignatius, Saint, 140, 142, 144
Illusion: and error, 303; ideological, 311-19; and science, 310-11
Immortality: arguments against, 360-70; empirical argument for, 357; ethical argument for, 357-59; and evil, 257; and existence of God, 362-63; general concepts of, 339-44; and human mind, 353-59; ideal, 341, 584-89; Kierkegaard on,

461-65; metaphysical arguments for, 343-52; and psychic phenomena, 371-87; psychological basis for belief in, 357, 360-62; psychophysical evidence against, 363-70; scientific view of, 357, 535-37
Incarnation, doctrine of, 328
Ineffability, 117, 127
Immutability, as attribute of God, 261, 322
Infinity, as attribute of God, 261, 261*n*, 322, 325; concept of, 19, 235
Interpretation, as related to consciousness, 210-19
Islam, 7, 8, 14, 390

J

James, William, 4, 12, 126, 321, 327, 339; on faith, 429; on religious experience, 118, 120, 123, 124, 126-63, 191*n*, 197, 206, 225; on "will to believe," 430-31, 442-55
Jeans, James, 524
Jeffries, Richard, 150, 548
Job, 396
John of the Cross, Saint, 140, 141*n*, 144
Johnston, T. A., 110*n*
Jones, H. G., 359*n*
Joshua, 391
Judaeo-Christian tradition, 11, 14
Judaism, 6, 8, 14, 390, 525
Jung, Carl, 228

K

Kabbala, 540
Kant, Immanuel, 18, 24-25, 75, 76, 82, 93, 94, 152, 160, 321, 429, 448; argument for immortality, 357-58; and destruction of soul, 343-44; on moral nature of man, 47-48; ontological argument, 109-11; on proof of God's existence, 94-104
Kardec, Allan, 379
Karma, 155, 161
Kendrick, T. D., 508
Kepler, Johannes, 503
Kierkegaard, Soren, 393, 456; on faith, 429, 431-36, 456-81; on immortality, 461-65
Kingsley, Charles, 129
Knowledge. *See* Cognition; Experience, religious; Mystical experience; Revelation
Koran, 390, 391
Krikorian, Yervant, 590*n*

L

Laird, John, 366
Lamarck, J. B. P., 83, 503
Lamont, Corliss, 363*n*
Langdon-Davies, John, 515-16
Laplace, Pierre Simon, Marquis de, 507
Lawrence, Brother, 614
Lecomte du Nouy, Pierre, 349-50
Leibniz, G. W., 18, 221, 321, 351

Lenin, V. I., 314*n*
Leonard, Mrs. Osborne, 371-72, 374
Leuba, J. H., 153
Lewis, H. D., 184, 185
Linguistic analysis. *See* Logic; Logical positivism
Locke, John, 403, 429; on faith and reason, 403-08; on immortality, 342
Logic: and analysis of God's attributes, 323-37; and conceptions of God, 322-37; and religious beliefs, 284-94. *See also* Logical positivism; Verifiability
Logical positivism, 224, 321; analysis of theism, 224-27, 275-77, 279-83, 336-37
Lotze, Rudolf Hermann, 241, 243
Love: and concept of God, 321; as perfection in God, 337; universal, 556, 558, 561, 565
Luther, Martin, 193, 198, 425

M
Macaulay, F. W., 372-73
Macaulay, Thomas, 88
Magic: Marxist account of, 316; and mythology, 578, 579; and prayer, 571-74; as pre-scientific thinking, 504
Magnus, Albert, 356
Mahometanism. *See* Mohammedism
Maimonides, 321, 398*n;* on the soul, 356
Malcolm, Norman, 18
Man: and evil, 238-39; moral nature of, 44-48, 79-80
Manicheans, 396
Marcus Aurelius, 414
Maritain, Jacques, 345; on immortality, 345-52
Martin, C. B., 119, 123, 172, 224; on religious experience, 172-88
Martineau, James, 2, 254, 255
Marx, Karl, on religion, 228-29, 313-19
Materialism, 260; and conflict of science and religion, 497-98; dialectical, 311; and evil, 241
Matthews, W. R., 321
Maysenbug, Malwida von, 134
Meyerson, M., 43
Mill, John Stuart, 43
Mind, physiological basis for, 353-59
Miracles, 389-95; definition of, 411*n;* rational basis for belief in, 408-19; scientific view of, 529-35. *See also* Experience, religious; Mystical experience; Revelation
Mitchell, Basil, 225, 279
Mohammedism, 400-01, 415, 525; and mystical experience, 136, 137-39
Monism, 145, 163
Monotheism, 3, 551, 557, 558; Freudian account of, 299
Montague, W. P., 325

Moore, G. E., 108
Morality, 8, 10; and cosmic process, 79-80; founded upon morality of God, 270-72; and free will, 245-48; as ideological illusion, 312, 315-16; and God, 86-93; and moral code, 5; and nature, 253-55; and proof of God's existence, 25-26; and reason, 88-89; and religion, 90-93
More, Henry, 113
Moses, 389-91, 394, 405
Mozart, W. A., 84
Mozley, J. B., 77*n*
Mukerjee, Radhakamal, 321
Mumford, Lewis, 505
Murphy, Gardner, 363*n*
Myers, Frederic, 156
Myers, F. W. H., 373-74, 376, 382, 386
Myths, religious, 489-91, 504-05, 545, 574-79
Mysterium tremendum, 191-202
Mystical experience, 126-63; and pathological conditions, 143; philosophical directions of, 145; and psychic phenomena, 127-51; as subjective states, 118. *See also* Experience, religious
Mysticism: authoritativeness of, 148-52; Christian, and God, 147, 159, 161, 162-63; intellectual content of, 154-63; and sensory images, 140; significance of, 126-63; traits of, 126-48; subjective utility of, 152-54

N
Naturalism: religions consistent with, 543-617; as replacement for theistic world view, 501-10; as rival to theistic world view, 496-99
Naturalism, mechanistic: and conflict of science and religion, 497-99; and evil, 241, 242
Nature: beauty of, 75-78; and cosmological argument, 39-44; and evil, 239; general laws of, 237-38; and knowledge, 70-71; and moral order, 253-55; plurality of, 43-44; regularity of, 253-54; and teleological argument, 69-83, 85
Nazism, as non-theistic belief system, 510
Neanderthal man, belief in immortality, 349
Neo-Platonism, 46, 147
Neurosis, as basis for religious belief, 307
Nicene Creed, 340
Nirvana, 137, 207
Noah, 404
Noetic quality, 118, 127
Numinous, 189-91

O
Object-significance, 211, 212
Occam, William of, 91, 376

Ontological argument, 17-18, 20, 26-28, 95-98, 107-11; criticism of, 107-09
Optimism, 145, 148, 151
Origen (Adamantius), 356
Orison, 140, 142; of union, 141
Orphism, 7, 8
Orwell, George, 282
Osty, Dr., 377
Otto, Rudolf, 125, 189-208
Overbelief, 120, 158, 159, 160
Overpoweringness, 196-98

P

Paley, William, 72, 76, 80, 91, 113, 252
Pantheism, 148, 150, 157; logical analysis of term, 325
Papal authority, 500
Paradoxes: as essential to Christianity, 465-81; logical, 107-08
Paranoia, 150
Paris, Abbé, 416
Pascal, Blaise, 444, 446, 451, 554n
Passivity, 118, 127
Pasteur, Louis, 507
Paul, Saint, 146, 390, 396, 400
Paulsen, F., 365
Pathological states, in religious experience, 119, 121-22, 130, 143
Paz, Alvarez de, 185, 186
Peirce, Charles, 327, 334, 362
Perfection: as attribute of God, 322, 323, 325; concept of, 17, 18; ethical, of God, 337; logical analysis of, 325, 327-29; love as, 337
Piety, 579-84
Pigou, A. C., 378
Philo, 322
Plato, 25, 38, 67, 289, 318; on immortality, 340, 341; on morality, 47-48; on souls, 385
Pleasure-pain principle, and evil, 237
Plotinus, 56, 147
Pluralism 43-44, 241, 242
Plutarch, 410, 415, 416
Polytheism, 3, 163, 326, 551, 556-58, 562, 565
Positivism, 321; of Comte, 550-53, 559. See also Logical positivism
Pratt, J. B., 361
Prayer, and magic, 570-74
Price, H. H., 385-86
Prince, Morton, 365, 374
Pringle-Pattison, A. Seth, 78-79
Protestantism, 8; and capitalism, 317; contemporary, 326; and departure from traditional theology, 321; and mystical experience, 140; and philosophy of religion, 420-24
Psychic phenomena: and immortality, 371-87, 536-37; and miracles, 530-35

Psychical research, 344
Psychoanalysis, 303, 306
Psychology and religion, 524-42; analysis of, 164-65, 296-311; criticism of theism, 227-29; and mystical experience, 126-63
Psychometry, 379n

Q

Quakers, 8

R

Rashdall, Hastings, 25-26, 86-93
Rationalism, 149
Reason: and belief in miracles, 408-19; as embodied in religion, 566-70; and faith, 403-08; and God's existence, 58-67, 70-71; and harmony with revelation, 395-402; and morality, 88-89
Récéjac, M. 197
Recognition, as related to consciousness, 212
Reid, L. A., on credulity, belief, faith, 429, 438-41, 448
Reik, Theodor, 307
Relativity, theory of, 523
Religion: Comte's "religion of Humanity," 547-48; definitions of, 2-5; features of, 5-13; as ideological illusion, 311-19; Kant's rational basis for, 103-04; and morality, 90-93; as obsessional neurosis, 307; prophetic, 390; significance of, for revelation, 420-47. See also Revelation; Science; Theism
Retz, Cardinal de, 415
Revelation, 389-408, 420-27; Bible as, 425-27; of God's will, 272-73; and harmony with reason, 395-402; through parable, 288, 291; and philosophy, 420-27; relation to faith and reason, 403-08; relation to rational and irrational, 421-24. See also Miracles
Rinzai (Lin-chi), 609
Ritschl, Albrecht, 195
Ritual, 5-6, 7-8, 10; and doctrine, 6-7. See also Magic; Prayer; Totemism
Roman Catholic Church, 7, 8, 29
Royce, Josiah, 322
Ruskin, John, 613
Russell, Bertrand, Lord, 18, 23-24, 121, 122

S

Sacred, and profane, 5-6
Samâdhi, 137
Sankhya, 150
Santayana, George, 437, 566; and ideal immortality, 341, 584-89; religion as moral symbolism, 544-46, 566-89
Sartre, Jean Paul, 435
Schleiermacher, F. D. E., 189-90, 195, 196, 205, 337
Schlick, Moritz, 224
Scholasticism, 337, 345-50

Schopenhauer, Arthur, 198
Science: and idea of immortality, 353-59; vs. illusion, 310-11; and teleological argument, 24, 74-75, 80-83
Science and religion: as complementary, 511-17; Comte on, 551-52; conflict between, 493-500; cultural evolutionary view of, 501-10; and modern physics, 517-24; objective vs. creative realities, 517-24; present relations between, 524-42; and psychological research, 524-42; and scientific method, 499-500, 529-35
Scriptures. *See* Bible
Secrétan, Charles, 453
Sellars, Roy Wood, 344, 353-59
Sense perception, 121; and mysticism, 140, 167, 168, 169
Shelley, P. B., 71
Sidgwick, Henry, 373, 382
Significance, as related to consciousness, 125, 210-19; divine, 217-19; moral, 216-17, 218; natural, 215, 218; object, 211, 212; situational, 211, 213-15
Silesius, Angelus, 146, 147
Singularism, 241, 242
Smart, J. J. C., 18, 20; on proof of God's existence, 105-15
Smith, N. Kemp, 114
Soal, S. G., 377-78, 382
Social group, 5, 8
Socinians, 322
Sociology and religion, 227, 311-19
Socrates, 467-69
Sophocles, 207, 208
Sotoba (Su Tung-p'o), 611
Soul, immortality of. *See* Immortality
Spencer, Herbert, 42, 451
Spinoza, Benedict, 8, 322
Spirit return, 126
Stalin, Joseph, 314n
Stephen, Fitz-James, 442, 455
Stephen, Leslie, 442
Subconscious, 120, 156. *See also* Freud, Sigmund; Psychology and religion
Sufism, 137-39; and mystical experience, 147
Supernaturalism, 148, 151, 160-62; and naturalism, 161; and supernatural beings, 5, 8, 9-10. *See also* Miracles
Survival. *See* Immortality
Suso (Seuse), Heinrich, 147
Suzuki, D. T., 549-50, 605-17
Symbolism, religious: meaning and significance of, 486-91; Santayana on, 544-46, 566-89
Symonds, J. A., 129, 130n, 131

T

Tacitus, 415
Taylor, A. E., 18-19, 39, 392; argument for

God's existence, 39-48; on immortality, 344
Teleological argument, 21-24, 48-67, 68-86, 71-75, 80-83, 112-15; criticism of, 112-15
Telepathy, 379-82, 536. *See also* Psychic phenomena
Tennant, F. R., 21-22, 24, 68, 221, 321; and cosmic theology, 68-86; on evil, 241-59
Tennyson, Alfred, Lord, 128, 128n
Teresa, Saint, 119, 141-44, 166, 187
Thackeray, W. M., 84
Theism: alternatives to, 510, 543-617; criticisms of, 221-337; internal inconsistencies of, 222; tenets of, 14-15; traditional and "new" doctrines of, 321-37. *See also* Assertions, religious; Beliefs, religious
Theology, cosmic, 68-86
Thomism, 19, 20, 326. *See also* Aquinas, Saint Thomas; Scholasticism
Thomson, J. Arthur, 496, 511-17
Thought-transference, 126
Tiele, C. P., 3
Tillich, Paul: on faith as "ultimate concern," 429, 436-38, 481-91; and symbolic interpretation of religion, 486-91, 544
Titus Livius, 415
Tolstoy, Leo, 149, 153
Totemism, 301-02
Transcendental idealism, 134, 150, 157, 159-60, 161n. *See also* Kant, Immanuel
Transiency, 118, 127
Transubstantiation, 6-7
Trevor, J., 134
Truth, divine, 395-402. *See also* Revelation
Tryde, Dean, 462
Turner, Ralph, 503n
Tylor, E. B., 9

U

Ummon (Yun-men), 609
Universe, as system and design, 48-67
Upanishads, 145, 157

V

Validity, and religious experience, 165. *See also* Verifiability
Veck, Toby, 76
Vedantism, 137, 147, 150, 157
Verifiability (empirical), 224, 229; legitimacy of, 292-93; of theistic assertions, 275-77, 278, 281, 292
Verrall, Mrs., 373-75
Verrall, A. W., 373-75, 378, 536
Virgil, 580-81

W

Ward, James, 321
Ward, Wilfrid, 451n
Weismann, August, 73, 451

B 5
C 6
D 7
E 8
F 9
G 0
H 1
I 2
J